The Encyclopedia of
Police Science

The Encyclopedia of
Police Science

THIRD EDITION

Volume 2
J–Z
INDEX

Jack R. Greene
Editor

Routledge
Taylor & Francis Group
New York   London

Routledge is an imprint of the
Taylor & Francis Group, an informa business

Routledge
Taylor & Francis Group
270 Madison Avenue
New York, NY 10016

Routledge
Taylor & Francis Group
2 Park Square
Milton Park, Abingdon
Oxon OX14 4RN

© 2007 by Taylor & Francis Group, LLC
Routledge is an imprint of Taylor & Francis Group, an Informa business

Printed in the United States of America on acid-free paper
10 9 8 7 6 5 4 3 2 1

International Standard Book Number-10: 0-415-97000-8 (Hardcover)
International Standard Book Number-13: 978-0-415-97000-6 (Hardcover)

Library of Congress Cataloging-in-Publication Data

The encyclopedia of police science / edited by Jack R. Greene. -- 3rd ed.
 p. cm.
 Previous ed. edited by William G. Bailey.
 Includes bibliographical references and index.
 ISBN 0-415-97000-8 (978-0-415-97000-6 : alk. paper)
 1. Police--United States--Encyclopedias. 2. Justice, Administration of--United States--Encyclopedias. I. Greene, Jack R.

HV7901.E53 2007
363.203--dc22   2006026827

Visit the Taylor & Francis Web site at
http://www.taylorandfrancis.com

and the Routledge Web site at
http://www.routledge-ny.com

CONTENTS

ASSOCIATE EDITORS

Gary W. Cordner
College of Justice and Safety
Eastern Kentucky University, Richmond, Kentucky

Edward R. Maguire
Administration of Justice Program
George Mason University, Manassas, Virginia

Peter K. Manning
College of Criminal Justice
Northeastern University, Boston, Massachusetts

CONTRIBUTORS

Julie C. Abril
University of California, Irvine

Geoffrey Alpert
University of South Carolina, Columbia

Karen L. Amendola
Police Foundation, Washington, DC

Malcolm Anderson
University of Edinburgh, Scotland

W. Carsten Andresen
Northeastern University

Edward J. Appel
Joint Council on Information Age Crime
Bethesda, Maryland

Richard M. Ayers
Fredericksburg, Virginia

Ryan Baggett
Eastern Kentucky University

William G. Bailey
Sam Houston State University

Thomas E. Baker
University of Scranton

Clifford Barcliff
Police Futurists International

Emmanuel P. Barthe
University of Nevada–Reno

Margaret E. Beare
Nathanson Centre for the Study of
Organized Crime and Corruption
York University, Toronto, Canada

Joanne Belknap
University of Cincinnati

Eric Bellone
University of Massachusetts–Lowell

Trevor Bennett
University of Glamorgan
Pontypridd, Wales

Julie Berg
Institute of Criminology, University of
Cape Town, South Africa

Elizabeth P. Biebel
Eastern Kentucky University

Pia Biswas
Rutgers University

William P. Bloss
The Citadel

John M. Boal
The University of Akron

Heidi S. Bonner
State University of New York at Albany

Jeb A. Booth
Northeastern University

Anthony V. Bouza
Minneapolis Police Department

Lorenzo M. Boyd
University of North Texas

Rebecca J. Boyd
Indiana University of Pennsylvania

CONTRIBUTORS

Anthony A. Braga
Harvard University

Jean-Paul Brodeur
Université de Montreal, Québec, Canada

Michael F. Brown
Southeast Missouri State University

Michael E. Buerger
Bowling Green State University

Richard Butler
New Jersey State Parole Board

Donald A. Cabana
University of Southern Mississippi

Dawn M. Caldwell
Isle of Palms Police Department

Jack E. Call
Radford University

Liqun Cao
Eastern Michigan University

Philip E. Carlan
University of Southern Mississippi

David L. Carter
Michigan State University

Derral Cheatwood
University of Texas at San Antonio

Steven Chermak
Indiana University, Bloomington

Alice H. Choi
California State University, Sacramento

Stephen E. Clark
University of California, Riverside

Janice E. Clifford
Auburn University

Peter A. Collins
Boise State University

John A. Conley
University of Wisconsin–Milwaukee

Ed Connors
Institute for Law and Justice
Alexandria, Virginia

Gary Cordner
Eastern Kentucky University

Elizabeth Corzine McMullan
University of Southern Mississippi

Tom Cowper
Police Futurists International

Stephen M. Cox
Central Connecticut State University

Charles Crawford
Western Michigan University

Shea W. Cronin
American University

G. David Curry
University of Missouri–St. Louis

Douglas Davenport
Truman State University

Phillip A. Davidson
Tennessee Law Enforcement
Training Academy

Andrew Davies
State University of New York at Albany

Michael Davis
Illinois Institute of Technology

Robert C. Davis
Police Foundation, Washington, DC

Scott H. Decker
University of Missouri–St. Louis

Mathieu Deflem
University of South Carolina, Columbia

Rolando V. del Carmen
Sam Houston State University

Ronald G. DeLord
Combined Law Enforcement Association
of Texas

Stephen Demuth
Bowling Green State University

Ramesh Deosaran
The University of the West Indies
St. Augustine, Trinidad

Sara Buck Doude
University of Southern Mississippi

Jerry L. Dowling
Sam Houston State University

Roger G. Dunham
University of Miami

Terence Dunworth
Justice Policy Center, The Urban
Institute, Washington, DC

Mary Ann Eastep
University of Central Florida

Max Edelbacher
Federal Police of Austria

Steven A. Egger
Sangamon State University

Katherine W. Ellison
Montclair State University

Preston Elrod
Eastern Kentucky University

Ayn Embar-Seddon
Capella University

Edna Erez
Kent State University

Richard V. Ericson
University of Toronto

Michael Erp
Washington State University

Finn-Aage Esbensen
University of Missouri–St. Louis

Stephanie Fahy
Northeastern University

David N. Falcone
Illinois State University

Amy Farrell
Northeastern University

Graham Farrell
Loughborough University
Leicestershire, United Kingdom

Gilles Favarel-Garrigues
Centre d'Etudes et de Recherches
Internationales, Paris, France

Mora L. Fiedler
Denver, Colorado Police Department

Nigel G. Fielding
University of Surrey, United Kingdom

Janet E. Fine
Massachusetts Office for Victim
Assistance, Boston, Massachusetts

Vern L. Folley
Independent Scholar

David R. Forde
University of Memphis

Brian Forst
American University

J. Price Foster
University of Louisville

James Alan Fox
Northeastern University

Lorie A. Fridell
Police Executive Research Forum
Washington, DC

CONTRIBUTORS

Larry K. Gaines
California State University,
San Bernardino

Catherine A. Gallagher
George Mason University

Venessa Garcia
Kean University

Jennifer F. Gardner
University of Alabama

Shirley Garick
Texas A&M University

Gilbert Geis
University of California, Irvine

Martin Gill
Perpetuity Research & Consultancy
International Ltd
Leicester, United Kingdom

Lauren Giordano
Northeastern University

Ronald W. Glensor
City of Reno, Nevada, Police Department

Barry Goetz
Western Michigan University

Zenta Gomez-Smith
University of Florida, Gainesville

Lindsey Green
University of Missouri–St. Louis

Jack R. Greene
Northeastern University

Roberta Griffith
Northeastern University

M. R. Haberfeld
City University of New York

Douglas R. Haegi
Georgia State University

Kevin D. Haggerty
University of Alberta, Edmonton,
Alberta, Canada

Bernard E. Harcourt
University of Chicago

Erin Harrell
Eastern Kentucky University

Craig Hemmens
Boise State University

Nicole J. Henderson
Vera Institute of Justice, New York

Vincent E. Henry
Homeland Security Management Institute
of Long Island University

Matthew J. Hickman
U.S. Department of Justice
Washington, DC

Dennis E. Hoffman
University of Nebraska–Omaha

Larry T. Hoover
Sam Houston State University

Frank Horvath
Michigan State University

Martin Innes
University of Surrey
Guildford, Surrey, United Kingdom

Silvina Ituarte
California State University, East Bay

Jenephyr James
Indiana University of Pennsylvania

John P. Jarvis
Federal Bureau of Investigation

Charles L. Johnson
Washington State University

Richard Johnson
University of Cincinnati

Greg Jones
Police Foundation
Washington, DC

Tom Jordan
Texas A&M University

Josephine A. Kahler
Texas A&M University

Robert J. Kane
Northeastern University

Victor E. Kappeler
Eastern Kentucky University

Sinead Keegan
City University of New York

Todd D. Keister
Bureau of Criminal Investigation
Binghamton, New York

Roger L. Kemp
City Manager
Vallejo, California

Michael Kempa
University of Ottawa, Ontario, Canada

Dennis Jay Kenney
City University of New York

Raymond G. Kessler
Sul Ross State University

Denise Kindschi Gosselin
Western New England College

William R. King
Bowling Green State University

Brian F. Kingshott
Grand Valley State University

Paul M. Klenowski
Indiana University of Pennsylvania

David Klinger
University of Missouri–St. Louis

Peter B. Kraska
Eastern Kentucky University

Tyler S. Krueger
University of Georgia

Kristen J. Kuehnle
Salem State College

Joseph B. Kuhns, III
University of North Carolina at Charlotte

Henry C. Lee
University of New Haven

Tina L. Lee
The University of Tennessee at Martin

David Lester
Stockton State College

John Liederbach
University of North Texas

Edith Linn
Kean University

Elizabeth Loftus
University of California, Irvine

Kamala London
University of Toledo

Vivian B. Lord
University of North Carolina, Charlotte

Roy Lotz
City University of New York

Nicholas P. Lovrich
Washington State University

Cynthia M. Lum
George Mason University

Arthur J. Lurigio
Loyola University Chicago

M. Kimberly MacLin
University of Northern Iowa

CONTRIBUTORS

Donal E. J. MacNamara
City University of New York

Sean Maddan
University of Nebraska at Omaha

Edward R. Maguire
George Mason University

Peter K. Manning
Northeastern University

Catherine M. D. Marcum
Indiana University of Pennsylvania

Otwin Marenin
Washington State University

Chris E. Marshall
University of Nebraska at Omaha

Ineke Haen Marshall
Northeastern University

Mark Marsolais
Northern Kentucky University

Gary T. Marx
Massachusetts Institute of Technology

Bill Maxwell
Royal Canadian Mounted Police

David C. May
Eastern Kentucky University

Linda Mayberry
Eastern Kentucky University

Lorraine Mazerolle
Griffith University
Brisbane, Queensland, Australia

Paul Mazerolle
University of Queensland, Brisbane,
Queensland, Australia

Kimberly A. McCabe
Lynchburg College

Timothy E. McClure
Eastern Kentucky University

Jack McDevitt
Northeastern University

David McDowall
State University of New York at Albany

J. Thomas McEwen
Institute for Law and Justice,
Alexandria, Virginia

Paul McKenna
University of Toronto

E. Roland Menzel
Texas Tech University

Greg Meyer
Los Angeles Police Academy

J. Mitchell Miller
University of South Carolina,
Columbia

Gilbert Moore
U.S. Department of Justice
Washington, DC

Andrew Morabito
International Association of Chiefs of
Police, Alexandria, Virginia

Stephen J. Morewitz
The Society for the Study of Social
Problems, San Francisco, California

Laura J. Moriarty
Virginia Commonwealth University

Frank Morn
Illinois State University

Nancy Morris
University of Maryland

Gregory B. Morrison
Ball State University

Melissa Motschall
Eastern Michigan University

Jerry Needle
International Association of Chiefs of
Police, Alexandria, Virginia

Elaine Niederhoffer
New York City Public School System

Robert S. Newsom
San Diego County Sheriff's Department

Lisa S. Nored
University of Southern Mississippi

Carla M. Noziglia
Las Vegas Metropolitan Police

Martin L. O'Connor
Long Island University

Timothy N. Oettmeier
Houston Police Department

Godpower O. Okereke
Texas A&M University

Lacey N. Ore
Lynchburg College

Timothy M. Palmbach
University of New Haven

George Parangimalil
Texas A&M University

Joseph E. Pascarella
University of Maryland

Nikos Passas
Northeastern University

Allan D. Pass
National Behavioral Science Consultants

Antony M. Pate
Development Services Group
Washington, DC

April Pattavina
University of Massachusetts–Lowell

Derek Paulsen
Eastern Kentucky University

Brian K. Payne
Old Dominion University

Kenneth J. Peak
University of Nevada–Reno

William V. Pelfrey, Jr.
University of Wisconsin–Milwaukee

Wendy Perkins
University of Cincinnati

Glenn L. Pierce
Northeastern University

Alex R. Piquero
University of Florida, Gainesville

Mark R. Pogrebin
University of Colorado, Denver

Eric D. Poole
University of Colorado, Denver

Gary W. Potter
Eastern Kentucky University

Tony G. Poveda
State University of New York at
Plattsburgh

Tim Prenzler
Griffith University
Brisbane, Queensland, Australia

Daniel Price
Providence College

Faiza Qureshi
Loughborough University
Leicestershire, United Kingdom

Michael L. Radelet
University of Colorado–Boulder

CONTRIBUTORS

R. K. Raghavan
Tata Consultancy Services Limited

Raymond R. Rainville
St. Peter's College

Melissa M. Reuland
Police Executive Research Forum
Washington, DC

Malcolm Richards
Gloucestershire Constabulary
United Kingdom

James F. Richardson
University of Akron

Albert R. Roberts
Rutgers University

Jennifer B. Robinson
Northeastern University

Marcus K. Rogers
Purdue University

Jeff Rojek
University of South Carolina

Kevin Roland
Urban Institute, Washington, DC

Michael R. Ronczkowski
Miami-Dade Police Department

Danielle Rousseau
Northeastern University

Lorie Rubenser
Sul Ross State University

Gregory Saville
University of New Haven

Kathryn E. Scarborough
Eastern Kentucky University

Joseph A. Schafer
Southern Illinois University,
Carbondale

Christopher J. Schmidt
Pennsylvania Supreme Court

Jennifer Schwartz
The Pennsylvania State University

Forrest R. Scogin
University of Alabama

Ellen Scrivner
Bureau of Administrative Services, City of
Chicago Police Department

Thomas M. Seamon
Hallcrest Systems, Inc.
North Wales, Pennsylvania

Thomas D. Shahady
Lynchburg College

Clifford Shearing
The Australian National University
Canberra, Australia

Lawrence W. Sherman
University of Pennsylvania

Stan Shernock
Norwich University

Wallace W. Sherwood
Northeastern University

Eli Silverman
City University of New York

David R. Simon
University of North Florida

Simon I. Singer
Northeastern University

Wesley G. Skogan
Northwestern University

John J. Sloan, III
University of Alabama–Birmingham

Beverly A. Smith
Illinois State University

Loretta J. Stalans
Loyola University, Chicago

Darrell Steffensmeier
The Pennsylvania State University

Dennis J. Stevens
University of Southern Mississippi

James K. Stewart
Center for Naval Analysis
Alexandria, Virginia

Victor G. Strecher
Sam Houston State University

Kathleen M. Sweet
Purdue University

Gary W. Sykes
Mercyhurst College

Morris A. Taylor
Southern Illinois University

Robert W. Taylor
University of North Texas

R. Alan Thompson
Old Dominion University

Jeremy Travis
City University of New York

Craig D. Uchida
Justice and Security Strategies
Silver Spring, Maryland

Jason S. Ulsperger
Arkansas Tech University

Sean P. Varano
Northeastern University

Tracy A. Varano
Criminal History Systems Board
Chelsea, Massachusetts

William J. Vizzard
California State University,
Sacramento

Robert B. Voas
Pacific Institute for Research and
Evaluation, Calverton, Maryland

Maria R. Volpe
City University of New York

Donald B. Walker
Kent State University

Jeffery T. Walker
University of Arkansas, Little Rock

Samuel Walker
University of Nebraska at Omaha

Harvey Wallace
California State University, Fresno

Patrick D. Walsh
Loyola University, New Orleans

John Wang
California State University, Long Beach

Richard H. Ward
Sam Houston State University

Vincent J. Webb
Southern Illinois University, Carbondale

Barbara Webster
Institute for Law and Justice
Alexandria, Virginia

Ralph A. Weisheit
Illinois State University

L. Edward Wells
Illinois State University

William Wells
Southern Illinois University, Carbondale

Chuck Wexler
Police Executive Research Forum
Washington, DC

Carrie Morgan Whitcomb
National Center for Forensic Science
Orlando, Florida

CONTRIBUTORS

Michael D. White
City University of New York

Brian N. Williams
University of Georgia

Frank Williams
University of Houston–Downtown

Donald C. Witham
FBI Academy

Russell Wolff
Northeastern University

Robert E. Worden
State University of New York at Albany

Shiho Yamamoto
California State University, Fresno

Olivia Yu
University of Texas–San Antonio

Jihong Zhao
University of Nebraska at Omaha

Israt T. Zohra
University of Arkansas, Little Rock

INTRODUCTION

The Encyclopedia of Police Science, Third Edition, elaborates and extends the discussion of its previous two volumes by deepening and broadening scientific knowledge about policing. The study of police science has undergone considerable change in the decade since the last publication of this *Encyclopedia* and the nearly two decades since the first edition. This advancement in knowledge about the police is linked to, yet separate from, the conceptual and methodological underpinnings of criminology and the administration of justice. These linkages and differences are important to highlight to better understand their contribution to "explaining" policing.

Criminology is focused on explanations of crime and society's reaction to crime. As a social science that attempts to explain criminal behavior first, and then how justice and other systems react to crime, criminology has often been separated from the study of the police. For many years criminology rarely informed policing, except perhaps in macro level discussions about deterrence.

Since the early 1980s and continuing to the present, however, the overlap in criminological study with that of the police has substantially increased, making criminology more relevant to the study of the police, and policing more acceptable as a target of criminological research. This is particularly the case when considering recent emphases in criminology and policing on communities as major places for crime and partners in crime prevention, deterrence, or mitigation.

Similarly, study of the administration of justice has often focused on the serial ordering of offenders as they pass through criminal justice institutions, as well as how these same institutions react to victims and the public at large. And, while policing was included within the general purview of the administration of justice, much of that literature was at best distant from the range of decisions and actions police undertook to make cities and towns safer.

In recent years, police science has incorporated the best from both the criminological and administration of justice perspectives. From criminology, police science adopted a broader array of theory—theory about individuals, groups, communities, and institutions—that better informs our understanding of the question "why policing," while also incorporating the advantage of a methodological revolution in criminology. From the administration of justice perspective police science has integrated a broader policy research viewpoint, as well as greater emphasis on evidence of what works through better and more systematic (and scientific) evaluation research.

By incorporating the best from the perspectives of criminology and the administration of justice, police science has greatly accelerated scientific knowledge about what constitutes policing, how it is made operational in a variety of social settings, how its institutions reflect or diverge from broader social and political values, what theoretical frameworks guide policing, and how police perform and their effect. So, today police science integrates the social theories of criminology with the institutional and systems perspectives of the administration of justice. In this respect police science has become more theory driven and evidence-led. *The Encyclopedia of Police Science, Third Edition*, reflects these important developments.

Even with the inclusion of criminological and administration of justice perspectives, police science still remains different in focus and in the use of other conceptual frameworks that inform our understanding about the police. Police science is concerned with policing in its broadest sense ranging from policing as an individual set of behaviors through the interconnections of policing across the world. It rests at the intersection of law, the physical sciences (in the case of forensics), psychology, social psychology, sociology, public policy, history, economics, and evaluation methods and statistical analysis, as well as criminology and the administration of justice. Variety is considerable in the domains of knowledge that informs our understanding of policing. The breadth of entries in this volume attests to the complexity of studying the police, and the multiplicity of perspectives used and indeed needed for such understanding.

The Evolution of Study on the Police

The social, formal, and institutional nature of policing and police science has changed profoundly in the last half of the twentieth century, continuing into the twenty-first century. While yesterday's police were largely concerned with fighting crime and maintaining order in public places, today's police are confronted by the globalization and internationalization of crime and terrorism, their manifest connection with new and complicated technologies, the newly emerging networked and organized varieties of criminal enterprise, the shift toward new forms of crime and deviance, and the confounding effects these changes have on effectively providing public safety and security. At the same time, modern-day police agencies must continue to address and cope with their historical functions, including social regulation and the prevention and response to "ordinary crime." In most respects the police remain the foremost organization people call when they are confronted by life's crimes as well as its annoyances.

Policing in this modern era has changed its language, symbols, technology, and analytics, while also broadening its range of interventions, clients, and outcomes. Yet in some ways the police remarkably resemble their nineteenth-century predecessors, presenting themselves in symbolic and substantive ways as singularly responsible for public safety in its broadest sense, while often replicating bygone service delivery patterns. As much as the police are thought to have changed, they continue to present themselves in very consistent ways over time. To the general public the police continue to represent a visible, uniformed force charged with responding to citizens' crime, order, and safety concerns.

Perhaps the most strident changes that have occurred in policing over the past half century are: (1) the broader role the police play in providing public safety and in the reassurance of safety to the public through programs focused on community quality-of-life, the coproduction of safety with community and other institutional partners, and community policing; (2) the change in data-driven and intelligence-led models of policing, including such issues as problem solving, crime analysis, crime mapping, COMPSTAT, and other more empirical and technological approaches to understanding and then addressing crime and social disorder problems; (3) the reemergence of concerns with police ethics and accountability, including the need for assuring police legality and judicial oversight of police actions, the legitimacy they derive from their communities, and the all-too-often revelations about police misconduct, abuse of authority, and public trust; (4) the internationalization of policing to include issues of addressing terrorism (domestic and international), police intelligence gathering and its legal consequences, and the cross-jurisdictional and trans-national interactions of police agencies throughout the world; (5) the changing nature of police work itself and those who undertake it, including shifts in the demographics of the police in terms of diversity, increased concerns with stress and its implications for those who do policing, and the professional expectations and outcomes that policing sets for itself; and, (6) the application of scientific methods, including the growth of the forensic sciences in police investigation and legal practice, and the emergence of a broad social science research literature on the police, their functioning, and impacts. These major trends are continuing to shape the structure and function of policing and they portend greater changes for law enforcement agencies and police officers in the coming years. Some brief consideration of these trends is warranted by way of introduction to *The Encyclopedia of Police Science, Third Edition.*

Broadening the Police Role

Beginning in the early twentieth century, policing has continued to evolve and change in light of broad and substantial social, economic, and political changes that have occurred in society. Entering the twentieth century the police in the U.S. were closely connected to local political sponsorship, but over the past century they have taken on more professional administrative practice and symbolism, have gotten closer to the communities they serve, have built extra-institutional alliances to prevent and respond to crime, have broadened their role from crime fighting to providing community quality of life and reducing fear of crime, and have taken on a more expansive public safety role through problem solving. Importantly, the police are now struggling with their appropriate role in matters of national security and terrorism.

Throughout these changes the police institution, albeit at times begrudgingly, has changed, opening itself more toward externals—particularly the community and other institutional partners. The movement in community policing, actually begun in the 1940s and 1950s over matters of race relations, and carried into the 1980s and 1990s as a means of improving police effectiveness particularly in disadvantaged communities, has helped to shape the police internally on matters of police training and socialization, and externally in matters of their interactions and cooperation with a wide array of others. All of these changes have import for how we see the role of the police in a democratic society. How the police will continue to evolve in light of their new challenges with terrorism is yet unknown. Nonetheless, it is anticipated that what the police have learned in their former transformations may help them grapple with an increasingly complex world.

Policing in an Information Age

In the nineteenth-century, police technology involved a good pair of shoes, a truncheon, and perhaps a firearm. Police collected and acted on information, but as individuals, not as a police system. Beginning in the early twentieth century with the advent of auto and radio technology, policing got greater mobility, but not much more information. While radios were a lifeline to the police headquarters, they were used more for "managing" police officers at a distance, rather than as conduits of information about crime and crime problems within neighborhoods or business districts. The widespread adoption of

911 computer-assisted dispatch systems has indeed altered the ways in which the police first understand and then manage their workload.

With the further development of information technology in the 1950s to the present, policing has often followed trends in government that emphasize greater information collection, storage, retrieval, and analysis. In the 1990s, information technology began to more clearly permeate the boundaries of police organizations, and practices and the language of "accountability" began to fuel the use of such technology as more sophisticated records management systems, calls for service technology, and crime analysis in its many varieties came on line. Whereas in the history of policing information was private and built on the knowledge of individuals, toward the end of the twentieth century information took on a more strategic posture and its character shifted from an individual perspective to that of the organization, or at least larger parts of the organization.

Managing patrol operations, detective caseloads, crime responses targeted to particular communities or crime types, and adopting the language and symbolism of efficient information use, captured the imagination and some of the practice of policing. And, while struggles remain in information sharing both within and outside police agencies, their characterization by Bittner paraphrased as "police agencies being bureaucracies or hierarchies built on the premise of systematic information denial," has indeed changed over the past fifty years. The police now collect, process, and use much more information than they have in the past, and in this sense, have truly joined the information age.

Police and Legitimacy: A Return to Roots

Progress in policing attributable to changes in their modes of operation (shifting from reactive to proactive), their problem focus, and the aggressive crime attack model of policing that has been part of the fabric of policing from its onset, more recently revived as zero-tolerance, has also resurfaced problems in public acceptance of police methods. Concerns with abuse of those in disadvantaged communities, or members of various racial and ethnic groups have fueled a discussion about how the police derive and sustain the legitimacy they need to work in community settings.

Here concerns with racial profiling, zero tolerance, and other aggressive police practices that appear to have differential application and impact have once again raised the specter of an equity divide between the police and those policed, most especially if those policed are from minority, multiethnic, or socially and economically disadvantaged communities. Revelations of police abuse of power found in several of America's largest cities continue to reinforce the idea of different forms of justice aimed at different types of people. Such practices and the beliefs that they sustain call into question the legitimacy given to the police by the body politic, or at least subsets of it.

While policing in the late nineteenth and early twentieth centuries was perhaps seen as more communal (although highly political and disproportionately adverse to minority communities), shifts in police focus and institutional arrangements seem to reinforce a drift of the police away from their roots—the community. At times it has been clear that the police have lost their community context. This loss of community context appears throughout the history of U.S. policing, and continues to be a problem, most particularly in large urban cities.

Recent research on how the legitimacy of the police either supports or deflects their efforts, particularly in marginalized communities, reminds us that the police derive their authority (not their power) from the larger community, and that their actions and behavior can reinforce or detract from the authority the community actually gives to the police. Linking police effectiveness to community acceptance of the police and their actions reinforces the notion that legitimate authority, not institutional power, is a fundamental requirement in democratic policing.

The Scope of Policing: From Street Corner to World Stage

Policing in the US and elsewhere began as a localized public place issue, providing some level of oversight to public places so that people could use them without fear of victimization. And, in earlier societies the police were also the "watch and ward" focused on sounding the alarm for fires, toppled buildings, wayward livestock or other public hazards that might occur.

The watching role of the police continues to this date, albeit in a more sophisticated way with the use of technologies of all sorts. But the premise, that crime and other forms of deviance will be dissuaded when there is someone watching (now called a capable guardian) remains fundamental in the crime prevention literature.

With the advent of modern terrorism, the local watching role of the police has been made more complicated. Now the police must watch for suspicious behaviors that may lead to crime or terrorism. Moreover, transposing a political idea that "all terrorism is local" in its effects and consequences, has raised the bar for the local police, coupled with state, federal, and international policing to assess risk and vulnerability, and design programs and actions that prevent, mitigate, or respond to the consequences of such acts.

Policing on the world stage includes concern for extra-jurisdictional crimes that have local consequences. This includes Internet child pornography and fraud, the trafficking of women and children for the sex industry, and any number of international criminal organizations focused on the sale of drugs, people, identities, or other fungible commodities that, while having a market, are illegal. Moreover, new cyber-crimes challenge old assumptions about the relationship between offenders and victims and the distances over which crime and victimization can occur. Indeed, whether such criminal organizations are local or not, their local impact is indisputable. So policing worldwide has been challenged to share information and participate in what might be called a "collective policing" effort. This, of course, is new territory for the police, as such arrangements are emergent, their practices and consequences remain uncertain, yet the need for their rapid evolution is equally compelling. This is indeed the new frontier for policing in the twenty-first century.

Policing as Practice

Just as policing institutions have been reshaped over the past century, and most especially in the second half of the twentieth century, so too have the practices, orientations, and behaviors of individual police officers. Moreover, those who "do policing" are different from their historical referents—they include more persons of color and women for example. The demographic changes within policing have been substantial, often reflecting greater diversity among the people who take up policing as an occupation. This has resulted in a rather subtle reshaping of policing, in that as new people come to this occupation, so too do their values, expectations, and ideas.

INTRODUCTION

In addition to the demographic changes in policing we have witnessed, policing as a set of occupational practices and cultures has changed as well. With the advent of information and dispatch technology, community and problem-oriented policing concepts and practices, and focuses such as preventing crime and improving quality-of-life, police officers have acquired a wide range of techniques and orientations their predecessors generally lacked.

Today's police are generally better educated, trained, equipped, supervised, and disciplined in comparison to police of the late nineteenth and early twentieth centuries. They are also tasked with a wider array of responses and interventions that require broad-based knowledge in topics like conflict resolution, consensus building, public speaking as well as understanding an ever more complex set of local ordinances, and state and federal laws. Whereas police at the mid-point of the twentieth century needed to be philosophers, friends, and guides, today's police need to add to that set of qualities such skills as first medical responder, community advocate and problem solver, and legal practitioner operating with a complex set of powers and responsibilities. Indeed, as we move into the twenty-first century, changes in police practice and those who "do policing" are likely to continue, perhaps more rapidly than over the past fifty years or so. Fast changing technologies, social problems, and world events seem to be accelerating change and are likely to continue to do so in the near and long-term.

Scientific Policing

At its onset policing was rather a-scientific, that is, not well connected to scientific knowledge. Rapid advancements in science throughout the twentieth century have altered the need for police scientific proficiency. This is not to mean that all police officers need to be scientists; rather, it suggests that the actions and practices of the police condition and influence the use of science in the detection and amplification of crime, and in the identification of offenders.

In the late twentieth century the forensic sciences finally took their rightful place in the crime detection business. Indeed the police early on quickly embraced finger printing and blood typing as investigative tools to address serious crime. But acceptance and adoption of other scientific practices has been uneven. While forensic sciences have been on the back stage of policing for many years, a few notorious trials involving the use of physical evidence moved forensics to the front stage of the criminal justice process, including policing. Moreover, the use of forensics investigation technologies and techniques, particularly DNA technology, has resulted in a number of offender convictions being overturned or reviewed, and, in at least one state, the mass commutation of death sentences was tied to concerns about the adequacy of physical evidence used to convict these people. Such scientific concerns now place greater burdens on the police in the identification, collection, preservation, and analysis of physical evidence.

As we crossed into the Millennium, the role of scientific investigation and inquiry expanded and is likely to continue to expand with advances in the forensic sciences. Moreover, from about the early 1970s to the present there has been a heightened level of research and scientific inquiry into what the police actually do, and the impacts and unintended consequences of police actions. Federal funding for these efforts, coupled with an expanded police research community, has resulted in better knowledge about policing. And, while the application of science to policing has many unresolved issues, it is clear that the body of research on the police continues to shape the research community's and the practitioners' understanding of the police, their role and function in society, and their interventions and public acceptance of those interventions. In many ways this edition of *The Encyclopedia of Police Science* benefits immensely from such advances in knowledge about the police.

On the Third Edition

The vast changes to policing occurring in the last two decades of the twentieth century are well reflected in this third edition of *The Encyclopedia of Police Science*. They include a revolution in thinking about the police and their clientele (community and business interactions), community and problem-oriented policing, crime prevention, placed-based theories of crime, police accountability, "quality of life" policing, zero-tolerance, and the like. Moreover, police interventions with youth, family violence, and other forms of interpersonal problem solving are included in this volume as well. And, the emerging role of the police in providing responses for terrorism and domestic security, which have emerged in the past five years, also broadens the role of policing in democratic society, and is considered here as is the growing emphasis on the internationalization of crime and hence, of policing.

This volume of *The Encyclopedia of Police Science* expands on the work of its predecessors (the first and second editions) by incorporating these changes and many others that confront modern-day police agencies. This edition is a robust collection of entries that review and expand our knowledge on topics that have shaped and continue to shape policing. Entries included in the third edition of *The Encyclopedia of Police Science* were written and selected emphasizing three important criteria:

First, we designed this collection and selected entries on their ability to inform readers about recent trends in policing. Of the 354 topics covered in this work, 196 are new to this edition and an additional 127 entries have been updated from the previous edition. Our editorial group sought to expand the range of topics previously presented, in part reflecting the changes that policing has confronted over about a decade since the last edition, but also to provide readers with a broad, contextual understanding of the police as they are imbedded in larger social, economic, and political changes that have occurred in rapid succession. Viewing the police in this context, we believe, helps readers make the connection between policing, government, and social change.

Second, we emphasize a connection in these trends to the underlying research on policing that addresses such trends. As previously indicated, the second half of the twentieth century witnessed an explosion in research on the police. Prior to the 1970s there were a handful of well-crafted, often observational studies, of the police. Since then the research community, fueled by federal research investments and a growing acceptance of police and criminal justice studies at major universities, has produced a voluminous body of research on policing, especially in the U.S., Canada, western Europe, and Australia.

Police studies have continued to migrate throughout the world and today the range of interest and scholarship on the police is remarkable. This edition of *The Encyclopedia of Police Science* sought to capture the state of research on policing over a myriad of topics. Our intent was to help codify extant policing research and literature into a usable volume as a premier source for information about policing. Research-led inquiry, then, was an important aspect of commissioning the entries contained in this volume.

Third, our focus spans all levels of discussion about police, from concerns for and with police officers, their subcultures, their organizations and institutions, and the web of interactions they have with the public and other institutional actors. The idea of taking on a project that had the ambition of accurately describing policing of necessity requires that the units of analysis vary. That is to say, policing can be variously understood as the behaviors, attitudes, and orientations of individual police officers; police work cultures and the informal or social organization of policing; police organizations themselves including their various structural and functional subdivisions; and, the larger "institution" of policing, spanning many police agencies and largely defining the occupational trends, practices, beliefs, and symbols that shape police organizations and the public's understanding of them. As the reader will see, all these levels of policing are discussed in this volume, and through the use of cross references contained within each entry, the connection of these units of analysis is made possible throughout the edition.

How to Use This Book

Just as important as the coverage itself, each entry provides a substantial reference base for the reader to further explore any particular topic under consideration. Authors have provided detailed **References and Further Readings** for this purpose within each entry. Moreover, the collective reference library that emerges from all of the entries contained in this edition, should be a substantial aid to the serious scholar as well. Cross references with other entries, noted in the **See also** section of each entry, suggest the close relationships among many topics covered herein; both beginning and more advanced students will benefit from using the **See alsos** to guide them from entry to entry. With 354 entries, each with its own references, and cross listings with other entries, *The Encyclopedia of Police Science, Third Edition*, represents one of the most up-to-date references libraries on policing. Two hundred and ninety-two serious scholars have provided materials contained in this volume; their collective effort represents a major contribution to the codification of scientific knowledge on the police.

Volumes like this third edition of *The Encyclopedia of Police Science* are indeed long-term projects. Like the epic movies of the past, editions like the current volume take years to stage and complete, while combining the orchestrated (and sometimes random) efforts of hundreds of people. And, like those epic movies, volumes such as these have a broad and detailed story to tell; they span large time frames, while capturing the moments in time of individuals and events. They draw attention to the macro, meso, and micro level interactions that shape events, and they arrive at destinations built on analysis of these interactions. I hope this edition of *The Encyclopedia of Police Science*, like an epic movie, provides a broad and sweeping context to the many individuals, organizations, and events that have shaped policing we have come to know. It is a deep and rich story, certainly one worth telling, and I hope the price of admission.

Throughout the development of this third edition of *The Encyclopedia of Police Science*, I have been mindful of the work that has gone before, most especially the work of William G. Bailey, editor of the first two editions. Professor Bailey's sharp eye on matters of policing shaped and filled in the contours of the first two editions, setting the stage for the present work. I hope that Professor Bailey would have approved this expansion of his original work, and I hope he would be pleased with the outcome—building on his legacy was an opportunity and burden, an opportunity to carry on an important line of work, and a burden to make sure this work advances on each and every level, just as the previous volumes under Bailey's direction. I leave it to the reader to determine whether the opportunity was maximized and the burden overcome.

I would also like to thank all of the contributors to this volume, 292 in all. In e-mails and telephone conversations with many of them, as well as reading their entries, I have come to know the vibrancy of this field and the passion of those who contribute to our understanding of police and policing. Reading the range of entries contained in this edition of *The Encyclopedia of Police Science* was to me an affirmation of scholarship on the police, and the ways in which that scholarship is defined and presented. There is no single method advocated here; just the consistent admonition to be clear and direct.

To my associate editors who served as the editorial board to this project, Drs. Gary W. Cordner of Eastern Kentucky University, Edward Maguire of George Mason University, and Peter K. Manning of Northeastern University, I offer my deepest appreciation, in helping to shape and recruit for the entries, and as the reader will see, making important contributions to the third edition. The collegiality, patience, and good humor of Cordner, Maguire, and Manning, as well as their scholarship and intellect are especially admired—I hope I have represented them well in this enterprise.

I am also indebted to Routledge, the publisher of this edition. Recommissioning a third edition some ten years after the last edition demonstrated to me a commitment to advancing scholarship on the police and a willingness to broaden that discussion with, perhaps a newer generation of scholars. Marie-Claire Antoine, acquisitions editor for Routledge, was a kind philosopher, friend, and guide throughout this process, supportive of innovation, yet clearly focused on the final product. She was instrumental in drawing my colleagues and me to this project, and then holding us accountable for the work that needed to be done.

Special appreciation is also extended to Susan Cronin, assistant development editor, at Routledge who was "task mistress" for this project. Susan praised, coaxed, cajoled, at times demanded adherence to time lines and work product. While we may have set the time, Susan ran the clock with precision, and while academics are want to drift off into some contemplation of future states, Susan kept me at least in the here and now. I thank her for her perseverance, tact and drive; conditions without which this edition may have faltered. And, to the editorial staff at Routledge I am also deeply appreciative of your focus on the detail and copyediting of this volume. This entire effort was greatly enhanced in the team spirit that shaped and completed this third edition of *The Encyclopedia of Police Science*.

Lastly, I would like to acknowledge the work of my departed mentor Robert S. Sheehan, the founding dean of the College of Criminal Justice at Northeastern University. Bob was a stickler for detail, and a visionary for police science; I sincerely hope he is pleased with the results of this work.

Jack R. Greene
Boston

LIST OF ENTRIES
A–Z

J

JAIL

Jails are the point of entry into the criminal justice system; they are correctional facilities operated by local authorities that confine people before or after conviction. Jail is also where arrested persons are booked and held pending court appearance if they cannot arrange bail. Jail is also generally the local detention facility for persons serving misdemeanor sentences, which in most states cannot exceed one year. Jail differs from prison in three important ways. Prisons are operated by state or federal governments, house only convicted offenders, and house offenders for more than one year. Jails are operated by city or county governments, house both offenders awaiting trial and convicted offenders, and generally house offenders sentenced to less than one year.

Jails also serve a variety of other purposes, including, but not limited to, detaining juveniles until their custody is transferred to juvenile authorities, detaining mentally ill persons until they are moved to appropriate mental health facilities, providing protective custody, and holding witnesses for court.

Most estimates suggest that there are approximately 3,365 jails in the United States, housing more than seven hundred thousand inmates. Of this number, about 2,700 are operated by county governments. Sheriffs are typically responsible for jail supervision and operations, although in some jurisdictions, a jailer is elected to operate the jail. Six states (Alaska, Connecticut, Delaware, Hawaii, Rhode Island, and Vermont) have state-operated jails. There are also more than thirteen thousand lockups (or "drunk tanks") and other short-term detention facilities. The largest jails are the Los Angeles County jail, the New York City jail, and the Cook County, Illinois, jail. All three jails house an average daily population of ten thousand residents or more. Most jails hold fewer than fifty people (Schmalleger and Smykla 2005).

The term *jail* is derived from the English word *gaol*. Gaols were locally administered and operated facilities that originated in

England in the twelfth century. Gaols held criminals, but also held a number of people who were not criminals, including beggars, drunkards, vagrants, and orphan children. This trend has continued until the twenty-first century; even today, jails often house alcohol and drug abusers, homeless people, and people with mental illnesses who do not pose enough danger to themselves or others to be housed in a mental health residence facility, but create enough problems that their neighbors complain about their behavior to local authorities. Jails remain the first stop on the "social services highway" for many disadvantaged groups. Many scholars agree with Irwin (1985) who suggests that the purpose of jails is to control society's undesired members. As Irwin suggests, these groups are often arrested more because they are offensive than because of their criminal behavior.

The first jail in the United States was the Walnut Street Jail in Philadelphia, Pennsylvania, built in 1776. The jail did not segregate by gender, age, or offense, and quickly became a facility where all kinds of scandalous behaviors took place. The Philadelphia Quakers attempted to reform the jail by making one wing of sixteen cells a penitentiary, or a place where convicted offenders could go to reflect on the error of their ways and reform themselves through penitence. That wing became the forerunner of the first prisons in the United States. By the close of the nineteenth century, most large cities had jails to hold persons awaiting trial and punish convicted felons.

Most people who are admitted to jail stay for a very short time, generally forty-eight hours or less. Whereas most inmates may take a day or two to make bail, many jail inmates serve months (or even years) prior to their court appearances and may also receive a year-long sentence afterwards. About half of those in jail who stay longer than forty-eight hours are being detained prior to trial (pretrial detainees). The average length of stay for pretrial detainees is about two months. The average

length of stay for sentenced prisoners is about five months and the average stay for all jail inmates is about three months. Moreover, jails hold increasingly large populations of inmates awaiting transfer to overcrowded state prisons. It has been estimated, for instance, that as many as 10% of all jail inmates are state prisoners awaiting transfer (Harrison and Beck 2005). In addition, many county jails now regularly house state inmates serving brief prison terms, and charge states a fee for doing so, ostensibly to alleviate crowding in state prison systems.

Almost nine in ten people in jail are male and almost all are over eighteen years of age. Three in five jail inmates are not convicted for their alleged offense. About equal proportions (two in five) of jail inmates are white, non-Hispanic or black, non-Hispanic, while about one in five jail residents are Hispanic. About equal proportions of people are in jail for violent, property, drug, and public order offenses (Harrison and Beck 2005). Most persons who are arrested, booked, and held in jail are not charged with serious crimes. Most are charged with petty crimes or with behavior that is noncriminal.

Jails in the United States were originally constructed using a linear design. In these eighteenth-century, first-generation jails, inmates lived in cells stacked horizontally down long corridors extending from a central "hub" area. This design made supervision both sporadic and difficult. Second-generation jails originated in the 1960s. These jails were designed so that staff was stationed in a secure control booth (typically circular with windows on all sides) in the middle of the cell house. Although this design increased surveillance capabilities, it did little to increase office/staff interaction. Direct supervision jails emerged in the 1970s to alleviate this problem. In direct supervision jails, inmates are housed in a pod that contains sleeping areas, necessary hygiene features, and sufficient tables and seats so that inmates can have a place to sit outside their sleeping area. Staff is stationed in the pod with inmates. This design encourages staff to interact with the inmates and allows them more direct control over the activities of the pod residents (Schmalleger and Smykla 2005).

DAVID C. MAY and ERIN HARRELL

See also **Crime Control Strategies: Selective Prosecution/Incarceration; Jail Assaults; Sheriffs**

References and Further Reading

Feeley, Malcolm. 1979. *The process is the punishment*. New York: Russell Sage.

Goldfarb, Ronald. 1975. *Jails: The ultimate ghetto of the criminal justice system*. New York: Doubleday.

Harrison, Paige M., and Allen J. Beck. 2005. *Prison and jail inmates at midyear 2004*. Washington, DC: Bureau of Justice Statistics.

Irwin, John. 1985. *The jail: Managing the underclass in American society*. Berkeley: University of California Press.

Moynahan, J. M., and Earle K. Stewart. 1980. *The American jail: Its development and growth*. Chicago: Nelson-Hall.

Mullen, Joan, et al. 1980. *American prisons and jails*. 5 vols. Washington, DC: U.S. Department of Justice, National Institute of Justice.

Rothman, David. 1971. *The discovery of the asylum*. Boston: Little, Brown.

Ruddell, Rick. 2005. Long-term jail populations: A national assessment. *American Jails*, March/April, 22–27.

Schmalleger, Frank, and John O. Smykla. 2005. *Corrections in the 21st Century*. 2nd ed. Boston: McGraw-Hill.

Thompson, Joel A., and G. Larry Mays, eds. 1990. *American jails: Public policy issues*. Chicago: Nelson-Hall.

JAIL ASSAULTS

The topic of jails in general, and jail assaults in particular, is one of the more underdeveloped research topics in the field of criminal justice. Even those studies that purport to examine assaults in correctional settings typically use samples of prisoners (not jail inmates) and typically focus on either inmate-to-staff assault or sexual assault among inmates. As such, the research surrounding jail assaults is quite limited. For example, a detailed examination of the literature on jail assaults provides neither a solid estimate of the prevalence, incidence, or types of assaults that occur in jails. In other words, despite the widely accepted belief that assaults are common in jails (particularly inmate-to-inmate assaults), the scholarly literature offers no suggestions regarding what percentage of jails have assaults each year, what types of assaults occur in those jails that do have assaults, and how many of those assaults occur.

Most studies of inmate assaults in correctional settings have been limited to the study of assaults in prisons housing male inmates. Because research on assaults in jails is quite limited, studies of prison assaults in relation to crowding, population density, demographic variables, and the theoretical models that might help explain assault in the correctional setting are often examined instead.

Although some have suggested that increased institutional violence in jails or prisons may be related to the effects of increased population density in these settings, the evidence supporting this claim is inconclusive. Increased density in prisons has been linked both to increased assaults and to fewer assaults (see Sechrest 1989 for a review). Additionally, in the most recent study focusing specifically on assaults in jails, neither the size nor the design of the jail had a significant impact on assaults in Texas (Kellar and Wang 2005).

Both Sechrest (1991) and Kellar and Wang (2005) suggest that inmate-to-inmate assault rates in jails are better explained in terms of the types of inmates housed within the facility. Both suggest that assaults on other inmates tended to occur in the jails or on the floors of the jail that held the most troublesome inmates. Sechrest (1991) found that the highest staff assault rate occurred in the areas of the jails that held the highest number of misdemeanants; Keller and Wang (2005) determined that jails holding maximum security inmates had higher inmate-to-staff assault rates than jails holding less troublesome inmates.

While research regarding the impact of demographic characteristics of inmates on the amount of assaults in a correctional facility is primarily limited to prisons, this research suggests that males, African Americans, and younger inmates are more likely to engage in assault than their counterparts (see Kellar and Wang 2005 for a review). Nevertheless, given the dearth of research regarding assaults in jails, translating these findings to jail settings should be done with caution.

One of the most controversial debates surrounding behavior in correctional settings concerns the theoretical models used to explain inmate behavior in both prisons and jails. Kellar and Wang (2005) suggest that there are three models that could be used to explain assaultive behavior in correctional settings. These theoretical models include the deprivation model, the importation model, and the managerial model.

The deprivation model is based on Clemmer's classic study (1958). According to this model, inmates adopt a wide variety of aspects of the prison culture over time and develop a set of unique norms to guide their behavior within the incarcerative setting. One of these norms includes a preference for violent behavior as a means of settling disputes. Being incarcerated produces a wide variety of negative emotions (anger, stress, frustration, and so on) and these negative emotions lead to assaultive behaviors.

The importation model was originated by Irwin and Cressey (1962). This model suggests that many inmate behaviors that occur inside a correctional facility are due to the environmental and cultural influences brought into the facility by the inmates themselves. According to this model, assaults are caused by factors external to the institution that trigger violence as a means of coping with the hostile environment of incarceration. The finding discussed earlier that an inmate's race, gender, and age predict inmate-to-inmate assault supports the thesis of the importation model.

The third theoretical model used to understand assaults in jail and prison is labeled the managerial model (DiIulio 1987). DiIulio suggests that jail and prison management can either increase or decrease levels of inmate assault by the decisions that they make. DiIulio suggests that assaults are due to poor management; in other words, inappropriate security procedures, improper classification strategies, and poor training and professionalism of correctional staff all increase the amount of inmate assaults in the correctional setting. A number of studies support this model (see Kellar and Wang 2005 for a review).

Since the 1970s, jail managers have been experimenting with different types of supervision practices in order to control assaults and other disruptive behaviors. One of these newer types of supervision is called *podular* or *direct* supervision. These terms refer to the architectural design that has developed with these innovative practices, in which inmates are placed in pods with individualized sleeping quarters and have access to a large open area where they spend the vast majority of their waking hours. Officers are typically no longer separated from the inmates but are stationed inside the pod with them, with the hope that more direct interaction will decrease violence and increase communication between the inmates and the officers. Anecdotally, practitioners suggest that this design is a more effective form of inmate supervision. Nevertheless, despite the popularity of these designs, scant research has compared assault rates among inmates in different types of housing units.

The topic of jail assaults is one that has been widely ignored in the scholarly research. Future research efforts should attempt to not only estimate the prevalence of jail assaults, but also provide a better understanding of the causes and correlates of these assaults. Until these research efforts occur, the scientific evidence regarding jail assaults is questionable at best.

DAVID C. MAY and ERIN HARRELL

See also **Jail; Sheriffs**

References and Further Reading

Clemmer, Donald. 1958. *The prison community*. New York: Holt, Rinehart, and Winston.

DiIulio, John, Jr. 1987. *Governing prisons: A comparative study of correctional management*. New York: The Free Press.

Irwin, John, and Donald Cressey. 1962. Thieves, convicts, and the inmate culture. *Social Problems* 19: 142–55.

Kellar, Mark, and Hsiao-Ming Wang. 2005. Inmate assaults in Texas county jails. *The Prison Journal* 85 (4): 515–34.

Sechrest, Dale K. Population density and assaults in jails for men and women. *American Journal of Criminal Justice* 14 (1): 87–103.

———. 1991. The effects of density on jails assaults. *Journal of Criminal Justice* 19: 211–23.

JUVENILE CRIME AND CRIMINALIZATION

The latter part of the twentieth century brought with it a rise in the rate of officially recorded juvenile crime and its subsequent criminalization through legal procedures in juvenile and criminal court. Perceived and real changes in juvenile crime have had implications for the way that the police and other officials confront troubled youth. More so today than in previous generations, police officials must make difficult decisions to arrest a juvenile as a status offender, delinquent, or criminal. In some states, the legal ways of defining troubled juveniles are quite complex, requiring consideration of such categories as "restrictive juvenile delinquent" or "youthful offender." An important question that needs to be repeatedly addressed is why these legal categories have emerged, and how they may relate to the current state of criminalization and to police decision making.

Juveniles who are charged as juvenile offenders, youthful offenders, or criminal offenders are today subject to a criminalized legal process. But this was not always the case. In the latter part of the nineteenth century, institutions devoted specifically to the education and treatment of juveniles began to emerge. The juvenile court was just one of those institutions. The juvenile court responded to society's emerging need to treat juveniles as different from adults. The reasons are many, but one important reason for criminal justice officials is that it became increasingly difficult for police officers and prosecutors to charge juveniles in criminal court. To many jurors and criminal court judges, juveniles late into adolescence looked more like children than adults. Criminal justice officials began to advocate for another legal setting that would take into account the fact that juveniles were different from adults.

Decriminalization

The social reformers who created the first juvenile courts advocated a nonadversarial process in which decision making was to be guided by pursuit of the "best interests" of the child. The purpose of this newly created civil court was not to punish, but to treat the determinants of the juvenile's offensive behavior. The juvenile court was accepted as a reform because it was not only viewed as being in the best interests of the juvenile, but also as in the best interests of the state. The less severe penalties of juvenile court and its informal legal procedures made it easier to implement government forms of control through status-offense categories, probation, and reformatories. Acts of crime committed by young people were subsequently considered acts of delinquency.

Criminalization

The informal, nonadversarial administrative procedures of the juvenile court came under attack in the United States and in other countries when juvenile crime commissions, state legislators, and academic commentators viewed its rehabilitative model as no longer appropriate for juveniles charged with serious offenses. The first major reform occurred when the U.S. Supreme Court for the first time in its history considered in 1966 the case of Morris Kent. The court did not question the appropriateness of Kent's punishment for rape and burglary. After all he was a chronic delinquent who the court viewed at the age of sixteen as an inappropriate candidate for treatment in juvenile court. Instead, the court focused on the administrative procedure for transferring Kent to criminal court without an adversarial hearing in juvenile court. The majority of Supreme Court justices agreed for the first time in U.S. history that the constitutional due process rights of a juvenile had been violated. The Court stated essentially that Kent should have been provided with a hearing in juvenile court where he was represented by legal counsel.

The next year the U.S. Supreme Court went a step further in expanding the possible list of constitutional rights for juveniles in its 1967 *Gault* decision. In the case of a juvenile who was incarcerated for an obscene call, the Court ruled that juveniles have the right to legal representation in all cases of delinquency. The *Gault* decision moved the juvenile court away from its creator's vision of a traditional nonadversarial, civil court to a court that more closely resembled a criminal court. Scholars such as Barry Feld (1999) referred to the *Kent* and *Gault* decisions as "criminalizing" the juvenile court.

Waiver Legislation

The criminalization of the juvenile court is just one part of the story. Legal procedures remained mainly confidential and the Supreme Court rejected mandating that juvenile courts look exactly like criminal courts. For example, the Court rejected for juveniles the right to a trial by jury. In other words, the Supreme Court wanted to maintain a juvenile court but it also wanted certain legal procedures that would provide delinquents with a fair trial within its rehabilitative mandate. But to many, the social welfare and justice models were like mixing water and oil. To some policy makers concerned about rising rates of juvenile crime, the juvenile court needed to act more like a criminal court not only in its legal procedures, but also in the kinds of penalties that it implemented to prevent and control juvenile crime.

A growing number of critics of the juvenile court and state legislators also argued that the juvenile court was inappropriate for those juveniles who committed serious offenses. They felt that such juveniles did not deserve the treatment-oriented procedures of a juvenile court, and should be sentenced directly in adult criminal court. In many states, this was always the case for older juveniles who were charged with homicide. But criminalization went a step further by requiring the police and other officials to consider younger juveniles for a wider range of offenses. The popularized adage "old enough to do the crime, old enough to do the time" reflected public and official sentiment to criminalize juvenile crime.

But the particular form of criminalization may have appeared especially harsh on juveniles and officials who were required to implement newly created juvenile justice reforms. This came a decade after the *Gault* decision in the form of automatic waiver or waiver by offense categories. Recall that *Kent* mandated a hearing in juvenile court. Automatic waiver legislation bypassed the juvenile court by requiring the police to arrest an eligible juvenile as if he or she were an adult and for prosecutors similarly to charge the arrested juvenile in criminal court. Certain conditions were required, such as that the offense be one for which the juvenile could be considered criminally responsible. These vary from state to state and depend on the particular legal statutes and the range of ages and offenses for which juveniles could be considered as if they were adults.

Offense-based forms of legislative waiver became increasingly popular so that every state in the United States soon found itself with new rules for bringing juveniles into criminal court. The particular form of legislation depends on the state's unique history of juvenile justice and its political and organizational concerns and interests. Political interests were satisfied by showing the public that officials were willing to address the problem of rising rates of violent juvenile crime. Organization interests were satisfied by providing officials with a new legal avenue in which to implement the threat of harsher forms of governmental control. New forms of waiver may have saved the juvenile court by eliminating from its population the more difficult, chronic delinquents. Juvenile courts were now able to treat less serious delinquents and consequently increase their levels of success.

Criminologically, there is no convincing evidence that criminalization in the form of adult court and harsher penalties reduced rates of violent juvenile crime. Moreover, it can be suggested that criminalization has increased the uncertainty of punishment for serious delinquents by subjecting them to a criminal court where they do not look as serious as older, adult offenders. Holistic processing theory would suggest that the likelihood of punishment is greater in a juvenile court where chronic delinquent behavior is viewed as particularly serious in relation to more trivial acts of delinquency. Indeed, the threat of criminalization can be viewed as more "bark" than "bite." The harsher

penalties of criminal court are viewed by officials as inappropriate for many less serious delinquents. Like those at the turn of the century, prosecutors may realize that they would have a hard time convincing a judge or jury that the juvenile is deserving of the same kind of penalties as an adult. Also police officers in arrest situations may reduce the severity of the charges knowing that the juvenile might be placed in the adult legal system. There is evidence that this is indeed the case based on research that Singer (1996) had conducted showing that only 25% of eligible juvenile offenders are convicted in criminal court. In contrast, the vast majority of similarly charged adult offenders are convicted in criminal court. Every state has "reverse" waiver procedures that allow criminal justice officials to indicate that it is more appropriate for the juvenile to be charged in juvenile court. This safety valve in the criminalization of juvenile justice can create opportunities for discrimination and disparities based on the characteristics of juveniles (Bishop 2000). Singer (1996) found this to be the case in New York where black juveniles were more likely to face conviction in criminal court for less serious offenses than white juveniles. Moreover, white juveniles were more likely to receive probation than black juveniles convicted in criminal court.

Consequences of Criminalization

Disparities in the administration of criminal justice for juveniles need to be examined more closely in a variety of legal settings and jurisdictional contexts. The proportion of juveniles who are subject to the harsh and stigmatizing effects of criminal punishment in the adult criminal justice system face lengthy periods of incarceration in maximum security juvenile and then adult prisons. They are deprived of normal adolescent experiences. Their attachments are now confined mainly to other inmates. Some of these juveniles will eventually leave as adults and desist from repeating their offenses, because they were too young to become committed to a life of crime or their families were there to support them. Others will never have the opportunity to have those normal adolescent social bonds, and will suffer the effects of long-term incarceration.

Of course, the debate is not over regarding how best to balance society's best interests in preventing and controlling juvenile crime. Criminalization has not reduced the rate of crime based on quasi-experimental studies of juvenile crime rates in states with and without offense-based waiver legislation. However, criminalization has given juveniles the right to legal representation in juvenile court, and has contributed to a fairer justice system in the determination of delinquency. Few policy makers are willing to return to a traditional, nonadversarial juvenile court. The part of criminalization that is most troubling is the appropriate response to serious delinquent behavior. Moreover, the juvenile court is still viewed as the most appropriate legal setting for the vast majority of youth. The criminal court is seen as inappropriate for most of the troubling behavior of juveniles. The juvenile court seems better equipped to experiment with different kinds of treatment, such as restorative forms of justice that advocate bringing victims and offenders together. Furthermore, the therapeutic model has expanded in ways that take into account a new rehabilitative model that is open to adolescent social and psychological disorders, such as depression, attention deficit disorder, and learning disabilities. These are taken into account in a juvenile court that is geared toward the treatment-oriented judgments of professionals. The best forum for doing so is not an adversarial criminal court, but a court that still is guided by the principle of pursuing the "best interests" of the child. In returning juvenile justice back to the juvenile court, McCord, Widom, and Crowell (2004) confirmed repeatedly what many police officers on the beat and parents have long noted: that kids are different, they behave differently, and that our response should take into account that they are not yet fully responsible adults.

SIMON I. SINGER

See also **Youth Gangs: Definitions; Youth Gangs: Dimensions; Youth Gangs: Interventions and Results**

References and Further Reading

Bishop, Donna. 2000. Juvenile offenders in the adult criminal justice system. In *Crime and justice: A review of research*, vol. 27, ed. M. Tonry, 81–167. Chicago: University of Chicago Press.

Feld, Barry. 1999. *Bad kids: Race and the transformation of juvenile court.* New York: Oxford University Press.

McCord, Joan, Cathy Spatz Widom, and Nancy A. Crowell. 2004. *Juvenile crime juvenile justice.* Washington, DC: National Academy Press.

Singer, Simon I. 1996. *Recriminalizing delinquency: Violent juvenile crime and juvenile justice reform.* Cambridge Criminology Series. New York: Cambridge University Press.

JUVENILE DELINQUENCY

From a legal perspective, delinquency consists of behaviors that are prohibited by the family or juvenile code of the state and that subjects minors (that is, persons not legally adults) to the jurisdiction of the juvenile court. These behaviors can be grouped into two general categories: (1) behaviors that would constitute criminal offenses if committed by adults (for example, murder, aggravated assault, larceny, robbery, motor vehicle theft) and (2) behaviors that are only prohibited for minors, which are called status offenses (for example, truancy, running away from home, incorrigibility).

Although the concept of delinquency is familiar to contemporary Americans, it is an historically recent term that did not gain widespread acceptance until the early

1800s. Prior to this time, most people viewed the young as miniature adults. Consequently, when youths were apprehended for violating local laws, they were subject to the same criminal justice process as other adults. This was possible because contemporary ideas about childhood and adolescence did not exist. By the early 1800s, however, more modern conceptions of childhood and adolescence as distinct periods in the individual's life had developed. Moreover, they were seen as times during which the individual needed to be nurtured, guided, and controlled in order to become a healthy and productive adult. These developing ideas of childhood and adolescence also made possible the development of the concept of delinquency, and the development of a separate juvenile justice process to deal with delinquent behavior (Bernard 1992).

A distinctive feature of the concept of delinquency is that it is committed by individuals who are *not* adults. Consequently, the juvenile justice process that has developed to deal with delinquent behavior contains a number of features that distinguish it from the adult criminal justice process. These features include a concern with treatment and rehabilitation rather than punishment, a higher degree of procedural informality than is found in adult courts, and a distinctive lexicon.

Contemporary Delinquency

Although the concept of delinquency seems straightforward, delinquency is, in reality, a complex phenomenon. For example, police only respond to some of the actions that are legally defined as delinquent, frequently ignoring some (typically minor) illegal behaviors that are prohibited by law while aggressively pursuing others. Furthermore, there is some variability across and within jurisdictions in the types of delinquent behaviors that are ignored or pursued. In addition, the delinquent activities of some youths (for example, poor and minority youths) tend to be more visible than the activities of others (those from affluent backgrounds), thus increasing the likelihood that certain youths will come to the attention of the police and be labeled delinquents. Being caught and processed by juvenile justice agencies may actually increase the likelihood of subsequent delinquency if juvenile justice processing leads to the development of a delinquent identity, encourages law-abiding persons to avoid those with delinquent labels, and/or leads to a loss of conventional opportunities (Garfinkel 1956; Lemert 1951).

Importantly, defining delinquency as behavior that violates the legal code ignores nuances in juvenile justice practice that lead to an increased likelihood that some youths and not others will comprise what is commonly—and incorrectly—seen as representative of the delinquent population. In reality, delinquency is a common adolescent activity because it comprises an extremely broad range of behaviors from incorrigibility (that is, not obeying one's parents) to serious criminal actions (for example, homicide). Consequently, almost all minors could be considered delinquents, because most engage in at least one illegal behavior at some time during their juvenile years. For example, a 2001 survey of high school seniors' drug and alcohol use revealed that 85% had used alcohol and 52% had used marijuana (Pastore and McGuire 2001). Furthermore, the percentage of youths who fail to obey their parents, also illegal in many jurisdictions, is likely to be even higher (Elrod and Ryder, forthcoming).

The Nature and Extent of Delinquent Behavior

To examine the extent of delinquent behavior, it is necessary to understand the primary ways in which delinquency is measured and the picture of delinquency that is presented by these measures. Although a number of measures of delinquency exist, three important sources of data that can be used to understand the nature and extent of delinquency are arrest data, self-report data, and data collected from cohort studies.

The most comprehensive source of arrest data is the FBI's *Uniform Crime Reports* (UCR), which separates crimes into Part I (or Crime Index) offenses and Part II crimes. These crimes are further separated into Crime Index violent offenses (murder and non-negligent manslaughter, forcible rape, robbery, and aggravated assault) and Crime Index property offenses (burglary, larceny theft, motor vehicle theft, and arson). According to the UCR, juvenile crime represents a significant problem in the United States. In 2002, there were more than 1.6 million arrests of persons under eighteen years of age. However, the great majority of those arrests (85%) were for nonviolent crimes. In 2002, persons under the age of eighteen accounted for 15% of all arrests for Crime Index violent offenses and 30% of all arrests for Crime Index property offenses (FBI 2003).

With the exception of a marked increase in arrests of persons under eighteen years of age for Crime Index violent offenses between 1988 and 1994, juvenile arrest trends have been quite stable since the early 1970s. Moreover, the upward trend in violent juvenile arrests seen between 1988 and 1994 has reversed and has been going down since that time. Altogether, data on juvenile arrests provide no evidence of a trend toward increased levels of juvenile crime, nor do they reveal a continuing escalation of juvenile violence.

In addition to information about numbers of arrests, the UCR also provides information on the race and gender of persons who are arrested. According to 2002 UCR data, whites accounted for approximately 72% of the arrests of persons under eighteen years of age. Whites accounted for the great majority of arrests for Crime Index property offenses and for

slightly more than half of those arrested for Crime Index violent crimes (FBI 2003). With respect to gender, in 2002 females accounted for approximately 29% of all arrests of persons under eighteen years of age. Females accounted for about 18% of persons under eighteen years of age arrested for Crime Index violent offenses and approximately 32% of those under age eighteen arrested for Crime Index property crimes (FBI 2003). Males are more likely to be arrested for Crime Index offenses, particularly violent offenses, than females.

Although an examination of juvenile arrests provides some insight into the extent of delinquency, arrest data are plagued by several significant shortcomings. First, police are more likely to focus attention on some youths and behaviors than others. Thus, arrest data reveal as much about police practices as they do about youths' behavior. Second, many delinquent acts do not come to the attention of the police (this is often referred to as the "dark figure" of crime). Third, arrest data tend to *overestimate* juveniles' involvement in criminal activity. This occurs because juvenile offending is more likely to involve other persons, often other juveniles, than crimes committed by adults. As a result, juvenile offenses are more likely than adult offenses to involve multiple arrests, even though some of those arrested are not knowing or willing participants in criminal activity (Snyder 2001).

Another important source of data on juvenile crime is self-report studies that ask people to report on their own behavior, such as the survey of high school seniors' drug and alcohol use noted earlier. A primary advantage of the self-report method is that it can elicit information on offenses not known to the police. Consequently, it allows researchers to better understand the *dark figure* of juvenile crime. Another advantage is that self-report studies are well suited for examining a variety of factors that are believed to be related to delinquency (for example, income, education, quality of life, work, family life, and peer group affiliations).

Not surprisingly, self-report studies indicate that youths engage in a considerable amount of delinquency that goes undetected by the police. Offenses such as school truancy, alcohol consumption, using a false ID, petty larceny, and vandalism appear to be rather normal adolescent behaviors. More serious forms of delinquency are far less common, although almost 12% of the respondents in a 2000 study indicated that they had hurt someone badly enough to require a doctor's attention and approximately 10% indicated that they had stolen something worth more than $50 (Pastore and Maguire 2004).

Self-report studies also reveal some important findings regarding the relationship between race, social class, and delinquency. These studies indicate that racial differences in levels of offending are quite similar, although African American youths report slightly more involvement in serious crimes (Elliott and Ageton 1980). Also, there is little difference in the proportion of middleclass and lowerclass youths who engage in delinquency. They do, however, vary in the types of offenses they tend to commit. Middleclass youths have the highest rates of involvement in such offenses as stealing from their family, cheating on tests, cutting classes, disorderly conduct, lying about their age, and drunkenness. Lowerclass youths have higher rates of involvement in more serious offenses such as felony assault and robbery (Elliott and Huizinga 1983).

Self-report studies also have examined the relationship between gender and delinquent behavior. Overall, these studies indicate that females engage in considerably more delinquency than is indicated by arrest data. However, females engage in less delinquency than males, and they tend to be involved in less serious types of delinquency, although differences in delinquent behavior between males and females are much smaller when minor offenses are examined (Chesney-Lind and Shelden 2004).

A very important point to note regarding recent self-report research is that it produces an overall picture of delinquency that is similar to that painted by official data. Although the extent of delinquency depicted in self-report research is considerably greater than is depicted in arrest data, and while racial differences in offending are not as great as that depicted by arrest data, the pattern of delinquency is similar. Moreover, neither arrest data nor self-report data indicate that juvenile crime has become significantly worse over time.

A third source of information on delinquency is data collected from cohort studies. Cohort studies are designed to examine specific groups of youths over a period of time. Several important cohort studies have been published since the 1970s, and these provide a valuable picture of delinquency within the juvenile population. Some of the most important cohort studies were published by Marvin Wolfgang and his colleagues at the University of Pennsylvania, who examined cohorts of youths born in Philadelphia in 1945 and 1958. They found that youths who had five or more contacts, whom they labeled "chronic recidivists," made up no more than 7% of the cohort but accounted for more than half of all the offenses attributed to the cohort. Even more striking was the fact that this 7% accounted for more than 60% of the homicides, rapes, robberies, and aggravated assaults attributed to the cohort. Despite these findings, there was no evidence that youths' delinquent behavior will necessarily become more serious over time, although when youth do repeat offenses, increases in severity are common (Tracy, Wolfgang, and Figlio 1990; Wolfgang et al. 1972).

Cohort studies that have focused on violent juvenile offenders have also provided some important insights on the size and characteristics of the violent juvenile offender population. Rather than discovering a large number of violent youth, this research indicates that only a small percentage of the juvenile population, usually less than 6%, engages in serious delinquency, and few youths are involved in repetitive acts of violence (Hamparian 1978; Office of Juvenile Justice and Delinquency Prevention 1989; Snyder 1988). Moreover, serious juvenile violence is not evenly distributed across communities across the country, but tends to be concentrated in relatively few communities within large urban areas (Snyder and Sickmund 1999).

Overall, the findings noted earlier indicate that small populations of youths engage in primarily status or serious violent offenses, but most youths engage in a variety of mostly minor delinquent behaviors during their adolescent years. Some delinquent behavior is serious, and there are violent and dangerous juvenile offenders, although this is the exception rather than the rule. Indeed, public concerns about an increasing wave of juvenile crime and violence appear to be unfounded. Although some areas have experienced and continue to experience significant problems with juvenile crime, there is no indication that it has, in general, become more serious over time.

Preston Elrod

See also **Juvenile Crime and Criminalization; Juvenile Delinquency: Status Crimes; Juvenile Diversion; Juvenile Justice System; Youth Gangs: Definitions; Youth Gangs: Dimensions; Youth Gangs: Interventions and Results**

References and Further Reading

Bernard, T. T. 1992. *The cycle of juvenile justice*. New York: Oxford University Press.

Chesney-Lind, M., and R. G. Shelden. 2004. *Girls, delinquency and juvenile justice*. 3rd ed. Belmont, CA: Wadsworth-Thomson Learning.

Elliott, D. S., and S. S. Ageton. 1980. Reconciling race and class differences in selfreported and official estimates of delinquency. *American Sociological Review* 45: 95–110.

Elliott, D. S., and D. Huizinga. 1983. Social class and delinquent behavior in a national youth panel. *Criminology* 21: 149–77.

Elrod, P., and R. S. Ryder. Forthcoming. *Juvenile justice: A social, historical, and legal perspective*. Sudbury, MA: Jones and Bartlett.

Federal Bureau of Investigation. 2003. *Crime in the United States 2002, Uniform crime reports*. Washington, DC: U.S. Government Printing Office.

Garfinkel, H. 1956. Conditions of successful degradation ceremonies. *American Journal of Sociology* 61: 420–24.

Hamparian, D. 1978. *The violent few*. Lexington, MA: Lexington.

Lemert, E. 1951. *Social pathology: A systematic approach to the study of sociopathic behavior*. New York: McGraw-Hill.

Office of Juvenile Justice and Delinquency Prevention. 1989. *The juvenile court's response to violent crime. Update on Statistics*. Washington, DC: U.S. Department of Justice.

Pastore, A. L., and K. Maguire, eds. 2001. *Sourcebook of criminal justice statistics*. October 17. http://www.albany.edu/sourcebook/1995/pdf/t368.

———, eds. 2004. *Sourcebook of criminal justice statistics*. February 24. http://www.albany.edu/sourcebook/1995/pdf/t346.pdf.

Snyder, H. 1988. *Court careers of juvenile offenders*. Washington, DC: Office of Juvenile Justice and Delinquency Prevention.

———. 2001. *Law enforcement and juvenile crime. Juvenile Offenders and Victims: National Report Series*. Washington, DC: Office of Juvenile Justice and Delinquency Prevention.

Snyder, H. N., and M. Sickmund. 1999. *Juvenile offenders and victims: A national report*. Washington, DC: Office of Juvenile Justice and Delinquency Prevention.

Tracy, P. E., M. E. Wolfgang, and R. Figlio. 1990. *Delinquency careers in two birth cohorts*. New York: Plenum Press.

Wolfgang, M., et al. 1972. *Delinquency in a birth cohort*. Chicago: University of Chicago Press.

JUVENILE DELINQUENCY: STATUS CRIMES

A status crime is defined as an action deemed illegal for a youth but not for an adult. A youth is usually defined as anyone between ten and seventeen years old. Status crimes include alcohol and tobacco use, curfew violations, habitual truancy, running away from home, and refusing to follow parents' rules. The intent of the definition is early intervention, before the youth starts to engage in serious delinquency. Specifically, the goal is to decriminalize specific behaviors and to reduce the stigma associated with being labeled delinquent while acknowledging and enforcing rules applicable only to juveniles.

Origins, Development, and Historical Evolution

In 1646, Massachusetts passed its Stubborn Child Law, which allowed children to be put to death for not obeying their parents. This was the first legislation identifying an act illegal only for minors (Hess and Drowns 2004). It was commonly accepted that children under eight were unable to act in a knowingly criminal manner, and that children between eight and fourteen could distinguish good from evil but might not be able to distinguish right from wrong (Hess and Drowns 2004). Youth under eight who committed minor acts would likely be returned home. Those eight and older who committed serious acts would enter the justice system more formally.

After the Industrial Revolution, the family declined as an agent of social control. A fear of "dangerous and wayward youth" began to grow (Platt 1977). Increasingly harsh treatment of juvenile offenders in houses of refuge, reform schools, and foster homes led to the Child Savers movement, the thrust of which was that wayward children were fundamentally good, suffered from poor environmental influences, and should not be subjected to the harsh criminal justice treatments of adults. By 1899, the first juvenile court was established in Illinois, solidifying the belief that children should be considered differently than adults. Within this court system, differences among offenses were established, distinguishing criminal from less serious offenses. The less serious offenses came to be known as status offenses.

In 1961, California became the first state to decriminalize status offenses. New York followed in 1962. States moved away from identifying youth as simply "incorrigible" and created terminology to identify those needing services for committing status offenses such as curfew violation, truancy, running away, and alcohol or tobacco use. These classifications carried with them a criminal justice or social services response. Included were PINS (Person in Need of Supervision), CINS or CHINS (Children in Need of Supervision), MINS (Minor in Need of Supervision), JINS (Juveniles in Need of Supervision), and FINS (Families in Need of Supervision). In 1967, the President's Commission on Law Enforcement criticized the institutional confinement of status offenders, saying that they were more likely in need of services than of criminal justice. In 1974, the Juvenile Justice and Delinquency Act was passed, with the explicit goal, among others, of reducing such confinements. In 2002, the act was reaffirmed. All states and territories must comply with the act to receive social services grants (U.S. Office of Juvenile Justice and Delinquency Prevention 2003).

Status Crimes and Trends

Tobacco and Alcohol

In 2004, 28% of eighth graders, 41% of tenth graders, and 53% of twelfth graders reported having smoked cigarettes. Survey results also show that in the thirty days before the 2004 survey, those figures were 9%, 16%, and 25%, respectively. This increase as youth age is true for both males and females. Use is lowest for blacks and highest for whites, with Hispanics falling between. Use declined by more than 35% among eighth graders, nearly 22% among tenth graders, and close to 15% among twelfth graders between 1991 and 2003 (Johnston et al. 2005).

Alcohol use also tends to increase as youth age. Survey results indicate that 14.5% of eighth graders, 35% of tenth, and almost 52% of twelfth graders reported having been drunk in the previous year. These percentages, however, also decreased between 1991 and 2003 (Johnston et al. 2005). Lifetime use declined as well, with the greatest reduction (35%) among eighth graders.

Arrests related to alcohol use among juveniles decreased between 1980 and 2003 (National Center for Juvenile Justice 2005). For liquor law violation, male arrests declined 22%, but female arrests rose almost 24%. White, black, American Indian, and Asian arrests for youth drunkenness all decreased between 1980 and 2003. Arrests for youth liquor law violations increased 4% among blacks, nearly 16% among American Indians, and almost 41% among Asians.

Running Away and Curfew Violations

Arrests for running away generally decreased between 1980 and 2003, whereas those for curfew violations increased. Arrest rates for running away dropped by 17% overall (National Center for Juvenile Justice 2005). Male and female rates were similar. Across racial groups, however, only white rates declined. Asian rates increased most dramatically, at 92%. It is important to note that these rates are adjusted for changing population sizes. According to the juvenile court statistics for 2000 (Puzzanchera et al. 2004), most runaways appearing in court were female. Most were also white.

Arrest rates for curfew and loitering violations are combined because enforcement is also often in tandem. Since 1980, curfew and loitering arrests have increased by 48%. Rates were higher for females (91%) than for males (34%). By race, arrest rates for whites and Asians increased nearly 50%, and for blacks and American

Indians by 39% and 15%, respectively (National Center for Juvenile Justice 2005). An increase in arrests for curfew violations may reflect an increase in police attention to the provision rather than a change in youth behavior.

Truancy and Incorrigibility

Juvenile court statistics for 2000 (Puzzanchera et al. 2004) show that most truants are between the ages of fourteen and fifteen, slightly more likely to be male, and predominantly white. Those brought into the court system for incorrigibility (also known as ungovernability) were also between fourteen and fifteen and tended to be male. Approximately 72% were white, 26% were black, and the remaining 2% all other groups.

Police Response

Police often have more options when addressing status offenses. Typically the response will be influenced by local community standards, the local justice system, and officer discretion. Other factors may include the youth's age, gender, race, demeanor, family situation, prior record or contact with police, and the availability of appropriate services. The response may be to take no action, to refer the juvenile to social services, or to take the youth into custody and petition the youth to the juvenile court. Those petitioned to court may be released to their parent or guardian or detained in a juvenile facility.

Academic and Theoretical Debates

One notable debate related to status offenses touches on the "net widening effect"—when youth who would otherwise have been sent home to parents are instead taken into custody and the juvenile justice system. One opinion suggests that formally processed juveniles gain status among delinquent peers, are labeled delinquent by others (including parents, teachers, and community members), and subsequently adopt delinquent behavior. Another perspective links status offending to future criminal behaviors and social problems—viewing truancy with dropping out, or alcohol use with criminal drug use, to take two examples. Last, violating curfews and running away—both of which put youth "at risk"—are thought by some to increase both criminal behavior and victimization. Advocates see status offenses as an opportunity for early intervention.

A second debate is that between proponents of get tough policies and those supporting treatment and rehabilitation. Although the juvenile justice system seems founded on the notion of a second chance and on rehabilitation, even the child savers were historically tough on youth and believed in combining punishment with training. This more conservative perspective views punishment as a deterrent and holds that youth will view the system as an empty threat if their crimes carry no serious consequences. Lowering of the age for treatment of juveniles as adults and the large proportion of youth taken into custody and then sent to juvenile court are examples of the conservative perspective. A more liberal view sees status offenses as symptomatic of a child in need and attempts to address the root causes of the behavior. Community-based sanctions, the deinstitutionalization and decriminalization of status offenses, and the use of formal terms such as CHINS (Children in Need of Services) or PINS (Persons in Need of Services) to identify youth "at risk" and in need of early intervention are examples of the liberal view.

JEB A. BOOTH

See also **Juvenile Crime and Criminalization; Juvenile Delinquency; Juvenile Diversion; Juvenile Justice System**

References and Further Reading

Allinson, Richard, ed. 1980. *Status offenders and the juvenile justice system: An anthology*. 2nd ed. Hackensack, NJ: National Council on Crime and Delinquency.

Baker, Myriam L., Jane Nady Sigmon, and M. Elaine Nugent. 2001. *Truancy reduction: Keeping students in school*. Washington, DC: Office of Juvenile Justice and Delinquency Prevention Bulletin.

Bloom, Barbara, Barbara Owen, and Jill Rosenbaum. 2003. Focusing on girls and young women: A gendered perspective on female delinquency. *Women and Criminal Justice* 14: 117–36.

Bozynski, Melanie, and Linda Szymanski. 2004. National overviews. In *State juvenile justice profiles*. Pittsburgh, PA: National Center for Juvenile Justice.

Elrod, Preston, and R. Scott Ryder. 2005 *Juvenile justice: A social, historical, and legal perspective*. 2nd ed. Sudbury, MA: Jones and Bartlett.

Federal Bureau of Investigation. 2004. *Crime in the United States 2003*. Washington, DC: U.S. Government Printing Office.

Hess, Karen M., and Robert W. Drowns. 2004. *Juvenile justice*. 4th ed. Belmont, CA: Wadsworth-Thomson.

Hoyt, Dan R., Kimberly D. Ryan, and Ana Mari Cauce. 1999. Personal victimization in a high-risk environment: Homeless and runaway adolescents. *Journal of Research in Crime and Delinquency* 36: 371–92.

Johnston, L. D., P. M. O'Malley, J. G. Bachman, and J. E. Schulenberg. 2005. *Monitoring the future national results on adolescent drug use: Overview of key findings, 2004*. NIH Publication No. 05-5726. Bethesda, MD: National Institute on Drug Abuse.

Kassebaum, Gene, Nancy L. Marker, and Patricia Glancey. 1997. *A plan for prevention, resolution and controls for the problem of youth on the run*. Honolulu: Center for Youth Research, Social Science Research Institute, University of Hawaii at Manoa.

Krisberg, Barry, Ira M. Schwartz, and Edmund F. McGarrell. 1993. Reinventing juvenile justice: Research directions. *Crime and Delinquency* 39: 3–124.

Maxson, Cheryl L., and Malcolm W. Klein. 1997. *Responding to troubled youth*. New York: Oxford University Press.

National Center for Juvenile Justice. 2005. *Juvenile arrest rates by offense, sex, and race*. Pittsburgh, PA: National Center for Juvenile Justice. http://ojjdp.ncjrs.org/ojstatbb/crime/excel/JAR_20050228.xls.

Platt, Anthony M. 1977. *The child savers: The invention of delinquency*. 2nd ed. Chicago: University of Chicago Press.

President's Commission on Law Enforcement and Administration of Justice Task Force. 1967. *Juvenile delinquency and youth crime: Report on juvenile justice and consultants papers*. Washington, DC: U.S. Government Printing Office.

Puzzanchera, Charles, Anne L. Stahl, Terrence A. Finnegan, Nancy Tierney, and Howard N. Snyder. 2004. *Juvenile court statistics 2000*. Pittsburgh, PA: National Center for Juvenile Justice.

Scott, Michael S. 2001. Disorderly youth in public places. Problem-Oriented Guides for Police Series No. 6. Washington, DC: U.S. Department of Justice.

U.S. Office of Juvenile Justice and Delinquency Prevention. 1995. *Unlocking the doors for status offenders: The state of the states*. Washington, DC: U.S. Government Printing Office.

———. 2003. *Guidance manual for monitoring facilities under the Juvenile Justice and Delinquency Prevention Act of 2002*. Washington, DC: U.S. Government Printing Office.

Whitbeck, Les B., and Dan R. Hoyt. 1999. *Nowhere to grow: Homeless and runaway adolescents and their families*. Hawthorne, NY: Aldine de Gruyter.

JUVENILE DIVERSION

Diversion involves efforts by juvenile justice decision makers (for example, police or juvenile court personnel) to respond to delinquent youths in ways that avoid formal court processing. Law enforcement officers, school officials, and others who commonly refer youths to juvenile courts exercise discretion. Rather than referring youths who are alleged to be engaged in delinquent behavior to juvenile court, they may decide to take no formal action by warning the youth, asking parents to take action, or referring the youth and possibly the family to a local program for assistance. In addition, when law enforcement officers, school personnel, or others make referrals to juvenile court, juvenile court personnel exercise similar discretion; they may decide to warn the youth and dismiss the case or refer the case to a local program for services.

Decisions to treat youths in ways that avoid formal juvenile court processing represent examples of juvenile diversion, and they are common responses to delinquent behavior. Indeed, many cases that could result in the arrest of a juvenile are handled in some other way by the police and juvenile courts. For example, in 2000, slightly more than 20% of youths taken into custody by the police were handled within the department and released, and almost 1% were referred to social service agencies (Maguire and Pastore 2005). Approximately 42% of the cases referred to juvenile courts in 2000 were handled informally (Stahl, Finnegan, and Kang 2005).

Diversion is based on the fact that formal responses to youths who violate the law, such as arrest, adjudication, and the creation of a formal juvenile court record, are not always in the best interests of children, nor do such responses necessarily protect community safety. Consequently, efforts to divert youths from the formal juvenile justice process (for example, by warning and releasing youths or by referring them to local agencies) have long been a part of juvenile justice practice. Even before the development of the first juvenile court in Cook County, Illinois, in 1899, youths were often spared the harshest punishments because many recognized that formal responses were often counterproductive. Indeed, the development of the juvenile court itself can be seen as a mechanism for diverting youths from the adult criminal justice process. More recently, diversion has also found support among those concerned with the problem of disproportionate minority confinement and overrepresentation in the juvenile justice system.

The Theoretical and Practical Rationale for Diversion

Historically, many law enforcement officials, judges, attorneys, child advocates, academics, and others have questioned the reformative potential of adult courts, jails, and prisons and have sought to spare youths from criminal processing. Even after the creation of juvenile courts, questions have been raised about the ability of juvenile courts and corrections programs to meet the needs of many youths and protect community safety. Concerns about the appropriateness of criminal or juvenile justice processing of juveniles were heightened during the political and social unrest that characterized much of the 1960s and 1970s—a time when increasing numbers of youths were coming to the attention of the police and courts. In addition, a well-developed theoretical rationale for diversion became popular during this time. This theoretical rationale, typically referred to as *societal reaction* or *labeling theory*, indicated that formal processing may actually lead to an *increase* in delinquent behavior.

Societal reaction or labeling theory focused on three interrelated topics: (1) the process by which deviant or criminal labels are developed; (2) the process by which deviant or criminal labels such as "delinquent" are applied; and (3) how being labeled influences an individual, as well as others' reaction to that individual (Pfohl 1994). Although diversion had long been a response to many youths involved in illegal behavior, labeling theory's focus on the application of labels to the individual and concern over the effects of labels served as the impetus for a renewed interest in diversion and the expansion of diversion programs for youths during and after the 1970s. Recommendations made by the 1967 President's Commission on Law Enforcement and the Administration of Justice that were intended to improve juvenile justice noted the following:

> The formal sanctioning system and pronouncement of delinquency should be used only as a last resort. In place of the formal system, dispositional alternatives to adjudication must be developed for dealing with juveniles, including agencies to provide and coordinate services and procedures to achieve necessary control without unnecessary stigma. . . . The range of conduct for which court intervention is authorized should be narrowed, with greater emphasis on consensual and informal means of meeting the problems of difficult children.

According to societal reaction or labeling theorists, labels such as *delinquent, chronic juvenile offender, thief, doper, problem youth,* and the like can have a variety of negative consequences for those who are given such labels. For example, labels can lead others to assume things about an individual that may not be true. A youth who has broken the law in the past and has been labeled a delinquent may be incorrectly treated as untrustworthy and undeserving and may be subjected to a variety of punitive responses as a result of being labeled. Indeed, the perceptions that adults, authority figures, and peers have of others appear to play an important role in how youths are treated. If, through being labeled, youths are believed to possess undesirable characteristics associated in the public mind with criminality or potential criminality, they are more likely to be formally processed by police and other control agents and to be avoided by law-abiding individuals.

In addition, youths saddled with a negative label often have fewer opportunities for involvement in normal law-abiding activities. Without such opportunities, they are more likely to associate with those in similar circumstances, thus increasing the likelihood of further deviance. Furthermore, responding to youths as if they were a lesser form of human being may lead them to see themselves in a more negative light.

One important issue raised by societal reaction theorists is whether responses to deviant behavior such as delinquency can increase the likelihood of subsequent offending. This possibility was spelled out by sociologist Edwin Lemert in 1951, when he distinguished between *primary* and *secondary deviance*. According to Lemert:

> Primary deviance is assumed to arise in a wide variety of social, cultural, and psychological contexts, and at best has only marginal implications for the psychic structure of the individual; it does not lead to symbolic reorganization at the level of self-regulating attitudes and social roles. Secondary deviation is deviant behavior, or social roles based upon it, which becomes a means of defense, attack, or adaptation to overt and covert problems created by the societal reaction to primary deviation. In effect, the original "causes" of the deviation recede and give way to the central importance of the disapproving, degradational, and isolating reactions of society.

Diversion Programs and Their Effectiveness

Essentially, two types of diversionary responses are used with juvenile offenders. One response consists of minimal or no intervention whenever possible in order to avoid the negative consequences of labeling. This approach is often called *true diversion* or what sociologist Edwin Schur (1973). calls *radical nonintervention* (that is, leaving children alone whenever possible).

A second response consists of referral to a diversion program. Often these programs are operated by local private or public social service agencies, although they are sometimes operated by law enforcement agencies or juvenile courts. Collectively, these programs offer a variety of services to children and in many cases families. Common types of programs use interventions such as family crisis intervention; individual, family, and group counseling; mentoring and child advocacy; individual and family counseling coupled with employment, educational, and recreational services; basic casework services; and "scared straight" programs that expose youths to the harsh realities of jails and prisons through tours and/or encounters with prisoners.

Supporters of diversion maintain that it decreases the number of youths involved in the formal juvenile justice process, frees up scarce resources for responding to more serious offenders, reduces offending among youths who receive diversionary treatment, minimizes the stigma associated with formal intervention, is more cost effective than formal processing, reduces the level of coercion employed in juvenile justice, and lessens minority overrepresentation in juvenile corrections. Moreover, there is evidence that diversion including radical nonintervention can be more effective than formal court processing in reducing recidivism and minority overrepresentation in some cases. Programs that employ mentoring and child advocacy, family crisis intervention, and offer multiple services such as individual treatment, family services, educational and job training, exposure to positive role models, peer discussion, and involvement in community projects are potentially viable diversion approaches (Lundman 2001). In addition, there is clear evidence that radical nonintervention can be as effective as referral to a diversion program or to juvenile court in some instances (Dunford, Osgood, and Weichselbaum 1981). However, other research indicates that some diversion programs, notably those designed to scare kids straight and those that encourage loosely structured relationships between youths and adult helpers, are associated with higher levels of subsequent offending (Davidson et al. 1990; Finckenauer and Gavin 1999).

In addition to increased recidivism, other problems have been found to plague some diversion programs. Although these programs are often touted as a way to reduce the number of youths involved in the juvenile justice process, some diversion programs may actually lead to *net widening*, which is the practice of processing youths who would otherwise be left alone if not for the program. Research on diversion programs has found that they sometimes lead to an increase in the number of youths involved in the juvenile justice process. Overuse of diversion programs may lead to increased costs and reduce the resources available for serious offenders. Moreover, involvement in diversion programs can lead to the stigmatization; youths and their parents are often coerced into these programs, which raises concerns about a lack of due process associated with some diversionary programs.

The research on diversion has produced mixed results. Clearly, there are problems associated with diversion that must be considered prior to its implementation, and existing programs should be carefully evaluated to assess the extent to which they meet their goals and objectives. Nevertheless, diversion holds promise as an effective mechanism for helping some youths avoid juvenile justice processing, protecting the scare resources of juvenile courts, and reducing recidivism among program participants.

PRESTON ELROD

See also **Juvenile Crime and Criminalization; Juvenile Delinquency; Juvenile Delinquency: Status Crimes; Youth Gangs: Definitions; Youth Gangs: Dimensions; Youth Gangs: Interventions and Results**

References and Further Reading

Davidson, W. S., R. Redner, R. L. Admur, and C. M. Mitchell. 1990. *Alternative treatments for troubled youth: The case of diversion from the juvenile justice system*. New York: Plenum Press.

Dunford, F. W., D. W. Osgood, and H. F. Weichselbaum. 1981. *National evaluation of diversion projects: Final report*. Washington, DC: Office of Juvenile Justice and Delinquency Prevention.

Lemert, E. M. 1951. *Social pathology*, 48. New York: McGraw-Hill.

———. 1967. The juvenile court: quest and realities. In *President's Commission on Law Enforcement and Administration of Justice Task Force report: Juvenile delinquency and youth crime*. Washington, DC: U.S. Government Printing Office.

Lundman, R. J. 2001. *Prevention and control of juvenile delinquency*. 3rd ed. New York: Oxford University Press.

Maguire, Kathleen, and Ann L. Pastore, eds. 2005. *Sourcebook of criminal justice statistics*. http://www.albany.edu/sourcebook/ (accessed February 11, 2005).

Pfohl, S. 1994. *Images of deviance and social control: A sociological history*, 2nd ed. New York: McGraw-Hill.

President's Commission on Law Enforcement and Administration of Justice. *Task force report: Juvenile delinquency and youth crime*, 2. Washington, DC: U. S. Government Printing Office.

Schur, E. M. 1973. *Radical nonintervention: Rethinking the delinquency problem*. Englewood Cliffs, NJ: Prentice-Hall.

Stahl, A., T. Finnegan, and W. Kang. 2005. *Easy access to juvenile court statistics: 1985–2000*. http://ojjdp.ncjrs.org/ojstatbb/ezajcs/ (accessed February 11, 2005).

JUVENILE JUSTICE SYSTEM

Juvenile justice consists of a series of stages found within police departments, juvenile courts, and juvenile corrections agencies where decisions are made about how to respond to youths who have engaged in, or who are alleged to have engaged in, illegal behavior. Although the decision-making stages that make up juvenile justice are often called the "juvenile justice system," the extent to which juvenile justice decision making represents a systematic response to juvenile offending is a matter of debate. Although there is some degree of coordination between police, juvenile courts, and juvenile corrections agencies, juvenile justice also involves considerable conflict between individual decision makers over differing ideas about why youths engage in delinquent behavior and what should be done about it (Elrod and Ryder 2005). Nevertheless, juvenile justice does have some distinct features that differentiate it from the adult justice process. These features consist of an historic concern with rehabilitation, serving the best interests of children, and procedural informality, and they continue to influence juvenile justice decision making today.

The Development of the Juvenile Court and Juvenile Justice

The development of a separate justice process for minors is an historically recent development. It was not until 1899 that the first juvenile court was established in Cook County, Illinois, although specialized correctional institutions for youths began to appear in the United States in the mid-1820s. Although children were often treated like adults when they broke the law and were placed in adult jails and prisons prior to the establishment of the juvenile court, in other cases youths were spared the harshest punishments because of their age. Indeed, a primary impetus for the development of the juvenile court was a desire on the part of those concerned with children's issues in the late 1800s (often called the "child savers") to reform and control the many wayward and criminal poor children who populated the country's growing urban areas. The perceived need to control and help youths who made up what was seen by many as an expanding "dangerous class" of persons posing a threat to domestic tranquility, changing ideas about childhood, the belief that it was possible to reform wayward children into productive members of society, and a concern that adult courts often failed to control problem children all contributed to the development of the first juvenile courts during the first quarter of the twentieth century.

It is worth noting that the new juvenile courts were civil or chancery courts and not criminal courts concerned with punishment. To reform and control problem youths, juvenile courts were given jurisdiction over a broad range of behaviors. These behaviors consisted of criminal or what in many jurisdictions are referred to as delinquent offenses. These included offenses that are also illegal for adults (for example, robbery, theft, arson) as well as *status offenses*, or offenses that are only illegal for minors (for example, running away from home, truancy, incorrigibility). Also,

juvenile court was presided over by a special judge in a closed courtroom and used probation officers to provide services and exercise control over youths.

The legal doctrine that served as the basis of the court was *parens patriae,* which essentially means the state acting as parent or protector of children. Because the juvenile court was seen as the protector of children, informality rather than due process was emphasized. This meant that in early courts youths often had no legal representation, children and their parents were not advised of rights, and records of hearings were not kept. In many instances children were helped by early juvenile courts; in other instances children and their families were harmed by courts that provided them few if any due process protections.

The informality that characterized the early juvenile courts began to receive the attention of the U.S. Supreme Court during the 1960s and 1970s. In a series of important cases beginning with *Kent v. United States* (1966), the Supreme Court scrutinized the informal nature of juvenile courts and mandated increased due process protections for youths, particularly those at risk of institutional placement. Perhaps the most important of these cases, *In re Gault* (1967), was illustrative of the potential harm that could be inflicted by juvenile courts that had broad discretionary power to punish children but afforded clients few due process protections. The case involved a fifteen-year-old male, Gerald Gault, who was taken into custody and detained on the verbal complaint of a neighbor who alleged that he and another boy had made an obscene phone call to her residence. After two court hearings that were not recorded, where there was little advance warning of the hearings and the charges were not specified (Gerald was charged simply with being a delinquent), where Gerald was not afforded legal representation and the complainant was not present so that Gerald could challenge her allegations, the juvenile court judge sentenced Gerald to the state industrial school for boys until he was twenty-one unless he was released earlier by the court. In effect, Gerald received a sentence of up to six years for an offense that could have resulted in a maximum sentence of two months in jail and a $50 fine had he been an adult. The majority opinion rendered by the Supreme Court chided the juvenile court for its lack of due process and required juvenile courts to provide youths with the following due process rights where juveniles were at risk of institutional placement: (1) the right to reasonable notice of charges, (2) the right to counsel, (3) the right to confront and cross-examine witnesses, and (4) the right against self-incrimination.

In a subsequent U.S. Supreme Court case, *In re Winship* (1970), the Court ruled that proof beyond a reasonable doubt was required in juvenile cases. However, in the following year an opinion in still another case involving juvenile court practice, *McKeiver v. Pennsylvania* (1971), the Court indicated that juveniles were not entitled to jury trials because juries were unnecessary in deciding the facts of a case and they might go too far in taking away from the unique aspects of the juvenile court. Collectively, these cases were important because they extended due process protections to juveniles and changed in important ways the operation of juvenile courts. However, while these cases have had a significant influence on juvenile court practice, the courts continue to employ an informality that is not found in criminal courts. The fact that juveniles have been given many, but not all, of the due process protections afforded adults does not mean that these due process protections are understood by youths and their parents or made available to youths. For example, research indicates that juveniles may not have a clear understanding of the meaning and significance of police interrogations and Miranda warnings (Robin 1982; Holtz 1987). Furthermore, there is other evidence that many youths lack counsel in juvenile court hearings or that available counsel is inadequate (Puritz et al. 1995).

Contemporary Juvenile Justice

Three types of agencies comprise the juvenile justice process: police, courts, and corrections. Although police are the gatekeepers of the formal juvenile justice process, juvenile justice processing typically begins with citizens who come into contact with youths who are believed to be involved in delinquent or problem behaviors. Citizens exercise discretion and make decisions to handle problems themselves, ignore them, ask parents to get involved, or contact the police. Once the police are involved, they also exercise considerable discretion, though police decisions about how to respond to youths are influenced by a variety of factors. The most important of these factors is the seriousness of the offense. As offense seriousness increases, so does the likelihood of arrest, but it is important to note that most police–juvenile encounters do not involve serious offenses. In these instances, a variety of other factors have been found to influence police decision making, including departmental policies and culture (more legalistic departments are more likely to formally process juvenile suspects), the wishes of complainants (police are sensitive to citizens' demands that they make arrests), demeanor (youths who are hostile to the police or unusually difficult are more likely to be taken into custody), race and social class (in some jurisdictions there is evidence that blacks or lower socioeconomic status individuals are more likely to be arrested), and gender (research indicates that females are more likely to be formally processed for status offenses than males) (Elrod and Ryder 2005).

Two things are clear regarding police interactions with juveniles. First, police arrest a large number of youths each year. In 2002, police arrested some 1.6 million persons under eighteen years of age. Second, when police take youths into custody, they are more likely to formally process juveniles today than in the past. For example, in 1972 only 52% of the juveniles taken into police custody were referred to juvenile court. However, by 2002, almost 73% were referred to juvenile court by the police (McGuire and Pastore 2005).

Contemporary law enforcement agencies employ a variety of strategies and programs in response to youths' delinquent behavior. As noted earlier, police exercise considerable discretion in their handling of juvenile cases. Options open to the police include warnings, requesting that parents or guardians take appropriate actions, referring cases to diversion programs (some of which are operated by police departments), or making referrals to juvenile court. Larger police departments often have specialized juvenile or gang units that deal with more serious types of delinquent behavior or deal with youths involved in gang activity.

Although law enforcement agencies have an important responsibility to deal with youths who engage in illegal behavior, many are also involved in a variety of activities designed to prevent or deter delinquency. Many departments assign school resource officers (SROs) to schools where they may engage in a variety of prevention activities within schools and the surrounding communities. Also, many law enforcement agencies staff programs such as Drug Abuse Resistance Education (D.A.R.E.) and Gang Resistance Education and Training (G.R.E.A.T.). These programs are led by police officers who facilitate activities intended to help students develop the necessary skills to avoid experimentation with tobacco and other drugs, including alcohol, or to lessen the likelihood that youths will become involved in gangs and delinquent behavior. Unfortunately, evaluations of these programs completed to date have not shown them to be completely effective (Esbensen and Osgood 1999;

Rosenbaum 1994). In addition, other police agencies have implemented youth-oriented community policing programs in their jurisdiction. These programs are designed to provide coordinated responses to youth and family problems that may involve the police, social service agencies, health departments, schools, and other agencies.

When police take formal action in delinquent cases, officers complete the necessary paperwork and forward it to the intake department. Juvenile court intake can be located in the prosecuting or district attorney's office, a juvenile probation department, or within the juvenile court itself depending on the state. Regardless of where it is located, the primary mission of intake is to make decisions about how cases should be handled. Intake personnel also exercise discretion. Like police officers, discretion on the part of intake personnel is bounded by court guidelines. In the case of intake, these guidelines typically specify the types of cases that must be formally processed. Nevertheless, court guidelines usually allow intake personnel considerable discretion in deciding how cases should be handled. Options available to intake staff may include a warning and dismissal of the case, referral to a diversion program, a request for the detention of the juvenile, or authorization of a petition for formal court action. A petition is a legal document that specifies the charges against the juvenile and requests that a formal court hearing take place. In 2000, approximately 58% of all cases handled by juvenile courts resulted in a formal hearing (Stahl, Finnegan, and Kang 2003).

In most cases, juveniles taken into custody (arrested) by the police are released to their parents pending further court action. However, in some instances police request that the juvenile be detained. Depending on the jurisdiction, juveniles may be detained in a juvenile detention facility or an adult jail. In recent years there has been an effort to remove youths from adult jails. The placement of juveniles in adult jails often creates significant problems for jail administrators who must ensure that there is sight and sound separation of adult and juvenile prisoners. Adult jails typically lack the staff and programming necessary to meet adolescents' needs, there have been many instances of abuse of juveniles in adult jails, and juveniles are at much greater risk of self-destructive behaviors in jail settings than in juvenile detention facilities (Memory 1989; Schwartz 1989).

Regardless of where juveniles are detained, state laws require juvenile courts to hold detention hearings within a specified time, usually twenty-four to seventy-two hours. The purpose of the detention hearing is to determine if there is probable cause to hold the youth, to decide the appropriateness of filing a petition requesting formal court action, and to consider the youth's placement pending formal court action if the petition is filed.

In addition to intake screening, typically several pretrial events occur prior to formal juvenile court action. In many courts preliminary hearings or arraignments are common. At these hearings the charges are reviewed, the parties are advised of their due process rights, a plea may be entered, and a date for the adjudication (trial stage of the juvenile justice process) may be set. Also, plea bargaining and preadjudication conferences are common in juvenile courts. In many instances the parties are encouraged to come to a mutually satisfactory solution to the matter before the court, and it is not uncommon for agreements to be reached that allow youths to avoid adjudication where they receive a formal delinquency record. In 2000, for example, only 38% of the youths processed in juvenile courts were actually adjudicated (Stahl, Finnegan, and Kang 2003).

One special type of case screening involves the transfer of juveniles to adult court for trial. Each state and the District of Columbia have some mechanism (commonly called waiver transfer, certification,

or remand) by which certain juveniles, sometimes as young as thirteen years of age, can be tried as adults. Although the options vary from state to state, there are three types of waiver mechanisms: (1) judicial waiver, where a hearing is held in juvenile court to consider waiver; (2) prosecutorial waiver, where the prosecuting attorney decides to file the case in adult or juvenile court; and (3) legislative waiver, or statutory exclusion, which requires certain cases to be tried in criminal court. In each of these three instances, before a juvenile can be waived, he or she must meet certain age and offense criteria. For example, state law may require that a youth be at least thirteen years of age and charged with a class A felony.

The adjudication is a critical hearing in the juvenile court because it represents the fact-finding or trial stage of the juvenile justice process. It is the point at which the youth comes under the continuing jurisdiction of the state and receives a formal delinquency record. In most instances, adjudications are not contested hearings. Those cases that are contested proceed much like trials in criminal court, and in some states juveniles have a right to a jury trial, though these are rare even in states that allow youths this right. If the juvenile is adjudicated, it is common for the hearing officer (for example, judge, referee, master, or commissioner) to enter temporary orders pending the disposition.

The disposition is the juvenile court equivalent to sentencing in criminal court. Prior to the disposition it is common for a presentence or predisposition investigation to be completed by a probation officer. This report will often contain a social history of the youth and may include information on the youth's family background, school performance and behavior, neighborhood conditions and peer associations, delinquency history, and the results of psychological tests, substance use assessments, and other information felt to be pertinent to the case. The predisposition report also contains recommendations regarding the appropriate disposition in the case—recommendations that are usually followed by the court. At this stage of the juvenile justice process, the court puts in place a plan for responding to the youth's illegal behavior that can include a variety of rules and expectations that both youths and parents are obligated to follow.

The most common disposition rendered by juvenile courts is probation, the disposition given in approximately 70% of all adjudications in 2000 (Stahl, Finnegan, and Kang 2003). Probation is a type of community-based corrections option that consists of the supervised release of a youth into the community under the supervision of the court. However, the actual practice of probation varies considerably across and within jurisdictions. As a result, probation may entail regular contacts with probation officers or infrequent contacts. It also may mean that youths and their families receive a number of services from probation staff or as a result of the efforts of probation officers, or that they receive little assistance. Many jurisdictions have developed intensive probation programs in recent years as well as house arrest programs, day treatment programs, and evening or day reporting centers that are designed, in part, to ensure more regular supervision of some juvenile offenders. In addition, probation is often combined with other community-based programs such as substance abuse treatment, restitution and community service, outdoor experiential programs, and group or foster home placement.

Another option that may be exercised by juvenile courts is institutional or residential placement. In 2000, almost 24% of youths who were adjudicated were placed in some type of out-of-home placement at disposition (Stahl, Finnegan, and Kang 2003). These placements can consist of a variety of residential settings (although the options available to courts will vary across jurisdictions), including detention centers, boot camps, substance abuse treatment programs, state training schools or youth development centers, farms, ranches, and mental health placements. Some of these placements are privately operated programs while others are publicly operated, and some are long-term programs while others are short term.

Although a wide variety of community and institutional corrections programs are available for youths across the country, juvenile corrections continues to face a number of serious problems such as disproportionate minority confinement (DMC), a lack of quality programming and resident abuse in some institutions, and a failure to adequately monitor and assess the extent to which programs are meeting their stated goals and objectives. Nevertheless, effective prevention, community-based, and institutional programs do exist, including programs for serious juvenile offenders. These programs prevent youths from engaging in initial acts of delinquency and prevent recidivism among youths who have already begun delinquent careers (Howell 2003).

PRESTON ELROD

See also **Juvenile Crime and Criminalization; Juvenile Delinquency; Juvenile Delinquency: Status Crimes; Juvenile Diversion; Youth Gangs: Definitions; Youth Gangs: Dimensions; Youth Gangs: Interventions and Results**

References and Further Reading

Elrod, P., and R. S. Ryder. 2005. *Juvenile justice: A social, historical, and legal perspective*. 2nd ed. Sudbury, MA: Jones and Bartlett.

Esbensen, F., and D. W. Osgood. 1999. How great is G.R.E.A.T.? Results from a longitudinal quasi-experimental design. *Criminology and Public Policy* 1: 87–118.

Holtz, L. E. 1987. *Miranda* in a juvenile setting: A child's right to silence. *Journal of Criminal Law and Criminology* 78: 534–56.

Howell, J. C. 2003. *Preventing and reducing juvenile delinquency. A comprehensive framework*. Thousand Oaks, CA: Sage.

In re Gault, 387 U.S. 1, 87 S. Ct. 1428, 18 L. Ed. 2d 527 (1967).

In re Winship, 397 U.S. 358, 90 S. Ct. 1068, 25 L. Ed. 2d 368 (1970).

Kent v. United States, 383 U.S. 541 86 S. Ct. 1045, 16 L. Ed. 2d 84 (1966).

Maguire, K., and A. L. Pastore, eds. 2005. *Sourcebook of criminal justice statistics*. http://www.albany.edu/sourcebook/ (accessed February 16, 2005).

McKeiver V. Pennsylvania, 403 U.S. 528, 91 S. Ct. 1976, 29 L. Ed. 2d 647 (1971).

Memory, J. M. 1989. Juvenile suicides in secure detention facilities: Correction of published rates. *Death Studies* 13: 455–63.

Platt, A. 1977. *The child savers: The invention of delinquency*. 2nd ed. Chicago: University of Chicago Press.

Puritz, P., S. Burrell, R. Schwartz, M. Soler, and L. Warboys. 1995. *A call for justice: An assessment of access to counsel and quality of representation in delinquency proceedings.* Washington, DC: American Bar Association, Juvenile Justice Center.

Robin, G. D. 1982. Juvenile interrogations and confessions. *Journal of Police Science and Administration* 10: 224–28.

Rosenbaum, D., R. Flewelling, S. Bailey, C. Ringwalt, and D. Wilkinson. 1994. Cops in the classroom: A longitudinal evaluation of Drug Abuse Resistance Education (D.A.R.E.). *Journal of Research in Crime and Delinquency* 31: 3–31.

Schwartz, I. M. 1989. *(In)justice for juveniles. Rethinking the best interests of the child.* Lexington, MA: Lexington Books.

Stahl, A., T. Finnegan, and W. Kang. 2003. *Easy access to juvenile court statistics: 1985–2000.* http://ojjdp.ncjrs.org/ojstatbb/ezajcs/ (accessed February 17, 2005).

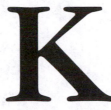

KANSAS CITY PREVENTIVE PATROL EXPERIMENT

The Kansas City Preventive Patrol Experiment was designed to test, empirically, the validity of one of the major strategies of modern policing: routine, visible, motorized, "random" patrol. In modern democratic societies, 60% to 65% of police personnel are assigned to such patrol activities (Bayley 1994). The most important, albeit sometimes implicit, objectives of this strategy are to deter crime, arrest offenders, and reduce the fear of crime. However entrenched this strategy might have been, by the early 1970s no systematic measurement or credible evidence had been presented to demonstrate the effectiveness of such an approach. In an effort to address this evidence gap, a task force, including researchers from the Police Foundation, and patrol officers and supervisors of the Kansas City Police Department's South Patrol Division, worked to develop and implement an experimental research design that would test the effectiveness of routine preventive patrol.

Experimental Design

Within the South Patrol Division's twenty-four-beat area, nine beats were eliminated from consideration as unrepresentative of the city's socioeconomic composition. The remaining fifteen-beat, thirty-two square mile experimental area encompassed a commercial-residential mixture, with a 1970 resident population of 148,395 persons, and a density of 4,542 persons per square mile. Median family income ranged from $7,320 to $15,964 (in 1970 dollars). The percentage of African American residents ranged from 1% to 78%. The fifteen beats were computer matched on the basis of recorded crime, number of calls for service, ethnic composition, median income, and transiency of population into five clusters of three comparable beats each. Within each cluster, one beat was assigned to one of three experimental conditions:

1. *Reactive,* in which routine preventive patrol was eliminated and officers

were instructed to respond only to calls for service.

2. *Proactive,* in which patrol visibility was increased by two to three times its usual level, both by the assignment of additional marked patrol vehicles and the presence of units from adjacent "reactive" beats.

3. *Control,* in which patrol was maintained at one marked car per shift.

Implementation

Implementation of the experiment began on July 19, 1972. By mid-August, both the Police Foundation and the Kansas City Police Department recognized that several problems had arisen that fundamentally threatened the integrity of the experiment. The first problem was that the South Patrol Division had fallen to a dangerously low level of manpower for experimental purposes. To correct this problem, the department assigned additional police officers. A second problem involved violations of the experimental guidelines. Specifically, it was determined that officers assigned to "reactive" beats were not adhering to the guideline that stipulated that they not enter their beats except in response to a call for service. Additional training was provided, and administrative measures were taken, to ensure adherence to the guidelines. A third problem was boredom among officers assigned to "reactive" beats. To counter this, the guidelines were modified to allow an increased level of activity by "reactive"-assigned officers in "proactive" beats. The revised guidelines stressed adherence to the spirit of the project, rather than to unalterable rules.

On October 1, 1972, the experiment resumed. It continued successfully for twelve months, ending on September 30, 1973. Findings were produced in terms of the effect of experimental conditions on a wide variety of outcome measures, as described later.

Data Sources

The task force decided to test the possible effects of routine preventive patrol by collecting a wide variety of data from as many diverse sources as possible. Sources used included departmental data, surveys of community residents, surveys of commercial managers, surveys of persons encountered by police, a response time survey, surveys of police officers, participant observer surveys, officer activity analyses, and others. A summary of the various data sources is provided next:

- *Community survey.* A survey of approximately twelve hundred, randomly selected residents was conducted before the experiment began; the sample was spread throughout all fifteen experimental beats. Respondents were asked about their fear of crime, attitudes about their neighborhood, satisfaction with police service, victimization experiences, and other matters. One year later, twelve hundred respondents were again interviewed, with six hundred chosen from the original groups (producing a repeated sample), and six hundred chosen randomly (for a nonrepeated sample.)

- *Commercial survey.* A survey of representatives of commercial enterprises in all of the experimental beats was conducted both before and one year after the experiment began. As with the community survey, respondents were asked about their fear of crime, attitudes about the neighborhood, satisfaction with police service, and victimization experiences.

- *Encounter survey.* Because household surveys tend to interview relatively few persons who have experienced actual contact with the police, an additional survey was conducted of those persons in the experimental area who experienced direct encounters with police officers. The survey was conducted during a four-month period (July–October 1973) and collected information from 331 citizens who were involved in either an officer-initiated incident (vehicle check, pedestrian check, or a traffic violation) or citizen-initiated incident (one in which the citizen called for police service). Respondents were asked questions about the nature of their encounter with the police and their evaluation of the service provided.

- *Participant observer transcriptions.* Participant observers were hired to make observations of police activity in all fifteen experimental beats. These observations served two purposes: (1) to monitor adherence to experimental guidelines and (2) to observe and describe interactions between officers and citizens.
- *Recorded crime data.* Monthly totals for recorded crime, by type, for each experimental beat over the October 1968 through September 1972 (pre-experimental) period and over the October 1972 through September 1973 (experimental) period were extracted from departmental records.
- *Traffic data.* Monthly totals concerning two categories of traffic accidents (noninjury and injury/fatality) were collected for each experimental beat for the October 1970 through September 1972 (pre-experimental) period and for the October 1972 through September 1973 (experimental) period.
- *Arrest data.* Monthly arrest data were collected, by crime type, for each experimental area for the three-year period prior to the experiment and during the experimental year.
- *Response time data.* Computerized records concerning the time required for police to respond to calls for service were not available, making comparisons between pre-experimental

and experimental periods impossible. To compensate, police response time in the experimental area was measured by a response time survey completed by the participant observers and citizens who had called the police for service. In measuring the time taken by the police in responding to calls, emphasis was placed on field response time (that is, the amount of time occurring between the time a police unit on the street received a call from the dispatcher and the time when that unit contacted the citizen involved). In measuring citizen satisfaction with response time, the entire range of time required for the police to respond to a call was considered, including time spent talking with the police operator, time taken by a police dispatcher, and field response time.

Findings

Overall, the experiment found that there were no significant differences among the three experimental conditions concerning recorded crime, reported victimization, citizen fear of crime, citizen satisfaction with police service, police response time, arrests, traffic accidents, or other major indicators. In particular:

- As revealed in the victimization surveys, there were no significant differences among or between the experimental conditions concerning recorded residence and nonresidence burglaries, auto thefts, larcenies, robberies, or vandalism, crimes traditionally considered to be deterrable through preventive patrol.
- In terms of rates of reporting crimes to the police, few differences and no consistent patterns of differences occurred across experimental conditions.

- In terms of recorded crime, only one set of differences across experimental conditions was found, and this was judged likely to have been a random occurrence.
- Few significant differences and no consistent pattern of differences occurred across experimental conditions in terms of citizen attitudes concerning police services.
- Citizen fear of crime, overall, was not affected by experimental conditions.
- There were few differences and no consistent pattern of differences across experimental conditions in the number and types of anticrime protective measures used by citizens.
- In general, the attitudes of businessmen toward crime and police services were not affected by experimental conditions.
- Experimental conditions did not appear to affect citizen satisfaction with the police as a result of their encounters with police officers.
- Experimental conditions had no significant effect on either police response time or citizen satisfaction with police response time.
- No significant differences in traffic accidents or injuries were found across experimental conditions.

Conclusion

Overall, the results of the Kansas City Preventive Patrol Experiment challenged the conventional wisdom that "random" patrol had a significant effect on crime and fear of crime. The study was not without its detractors. Some critics argued that Kansas City was not representative of the vast range urban environments in the nation. Others contended that the study did not contain enough beats, that the samples of citizens surveyed were too small, and that the statistical power of the tests was too limited. Nevertheless, the study, by calling into question basic assumptions of police strategy, led to a wave of empirical research that has caused a wide-ranging reappraisal of police strategy and tactics.

ANTONY M. PATE

See also **Accountability; Attitudes toward the Police: Measurement Issues; Patrol, Types and Effectiveness of; Performance Measurement**

References and Further Reading

Bayley, David H. 1994. *Police for the future.* New York: Oxford University Press.

Kelling, George, Tony Pate, Duane Dieckman, and Charles E. Brown. 1974a. *The Kansas City Preventive Patrol Experiment: A summary report.* Washington, DC: Police Foundation.

———. 1974b *The Kansas City Preventive Patrol Experiment: A technical report.* Washington, DC: Police Foundation.

KNAPP COMMISSION

The Knapp Commission was a committee of five citizens established and impanelled by then-New York City Mayor John Lindsay in 1972 that endeavored to investigate corrupt activities of police officers, detectives, and supervisors working in the New York Police Department (NYPD). Mayor Lindsay was pressured to investigate corruption in the NYPD after a series of articles that appeared in local newspapers detailed a wide breadth of corrupt activities of officers throughout the NYPD. The first article in the series was written by a reporter named David Burnham and the article appeared in the *New York Times*. The impetus and primary sources of information for Burnham's article were two NYPD police officers, Frank Serpico and David Durk.

Frank Serpico and David Durk were once both idealistic officers who became increasingly frustrated after attempting to report corrupt activities to their supervisors. From initial indoctrination into the NYPD, the officers noticed that other officers received free food and coffee and often were offered bribes in lieu of issuing summonses. When Frank Serpico was transferred into an undercover plain-clothes unit, he discovered that corruption there was even more systematic and sophisticated in that many officers and detectives were on "pads" (controlled payments to the police). Serpico and Durk eventually complained to the district attorney's office, an authority outside of the NYPD.

Dissatisfied with the resolution of the investigation, Serpico, Durk, and other officers who were also disgusted with the systematic corruption befriended a reporter named David Burnham who worked for the *New York Times* and on April 25, 1970, an article about the corrupt activities of the NYPD appeared on the front page. The article ushered in one of the biggest scandals in NYPD history and Mayor Lindsay created the Knapp Commission in 1971, named after a judge Mayor Lindsay chose, Whitman Knapp.

The enormity of New York City, the size of the NYPD, and New York City's preeminence as the media capital of the world intensified the scrutiny on the NYPD and the NYPD's police officers. The NYPD, as a formal police agency, was chartered and centralized in 1844. Early NYPD "patrolmen," as they were known then, were appointed at the bequest of local ward politicians and expected to protect the illegal rackets of the ward politician who appointed the patrolmen, particularly the vice rackets, which at that time in history consisted mainly of selling alcohol illegally and prostitution-related criminal activity. Thus began a cyclical pattern of corruption and reform. One of the earliest police reformers in New York City, future President of the United States Theodore Roosevelt, was the police commissioner of New York City. Roosevelt, along with a reform-minded clergy official, Charles Henry Parkhurst, initiated the Lexow Committee to investigate police corruption in New York City. According to the Lexow Committee's findings, police corruption in New York City was firmly enmeshed in local government politics. Other commissions that investigated police misconduct in the NYPD followed in 1913, 1930, and 1950.

The Knapp Commission was the next major commission to investigate police misconduct and corruption. The Knapp Commission found that the most serious police misconduct involved the enforcement of prostitution, gambling, and narcotics. New York City was enduring an increase in the illegal street narcotics trade (mainly of heroin) that led to new opportunities for corruption prior to the creation of the Knapp Commission investigation.

The Knapp Commission found that corrupt NYPD police officers were collecting "protection money" and were on the "pad," which meant that they took bribes from criminals to ensure the criminals that their illicit activities could continue without the threat of being investigated or arrested by the police. Many of the criminals involved in bribing police officers prior to the Knapp Commission were involved in vice crime rackets such as prostitution and gambling. However, the Knapp Commission and subsequent investigations found that the easy flow of currency involved in the illicit narcotics trade afforded new corruption opportunities. One of the commission's chief witnesses was a police officer named William Phillips who was caught receiving bribes during an investigation conducted by the commission.

The Knapp Commission findings prototyped two main types of corrupt officers, "grass eaters" and "meat eaters." Grass eaters would accept free meals and bribes that were offered to them. Meat eaters would openly solicit free meals and would proactively solicit bribes and would attempt to obtain assignments in enforcement units that were mandated to enforce gambling, prostitution, and narcotics laws. One of the principal recommendations of the Knapp Commission was to appoint a special prosecutor (outside of New York City) to investigate police corruption, reorganization of the NYPD's Internal Affairs Division, and command-level responsibility for corrupt officers.

Frank Serpico was shot in the face during an undercover narcotics operation on February 3, 1971, and was seriously wounded. He did ultimately testify before the Knapp Commission and recommendations of the Knapp Commission led to many anticorruption policies in the NYPD. A movie detailing Serpico's efforts was made in 1973 starring Al Pacino as Serpico. Serpico retired in 1972 on a disability pension and currently remains active in police reform efforts. David Durk also testified before the Knapp Commission and his career reportedly suffered as a result and he eventually retired in 1985.

Eventually, another commission named the Mollen Commission was established in 1992 to investigate alleged police corruption in the NYPD. A New York City police officer named Michael Dowd was arrested for trafficking illegal narcotics in New York City and outside New York City in a suburban area where Dowd lived. The advent of the street crack-cocaine trade in New York City in the 1980s, like the burgeoning heroin trade of the 1960s, afforded increased opportunities for corruption. The corrupt activities consisted of police officers stealing narcotics and cash from narcotics dealers and, in some cases, protecting the illegal narcotic activities. Unlike the Knapp Commission findings, the Mollen Commission found that these corrupt activities were limited only to a few precincts. The Mollen Commission did not find that corruption was systematic in the NYPD, as had previous NYPD corruption investigations. The Mollen Commission found that corrupt activities were the actions of a "crew" operation, a small group of police officers usually working in the same assignment and during the same work hours.

JOSEPH E. PASCARELLA

See also **Accountability; American Policing: Early Years; Corruption; Deviant Subcultures in Policing; Ethics and Values in the Context of Community Policing; Integrity in Policing; Mollen Commission; New York Police Department (NYPD); Occupational Culture**

References and Further Readings

Armstrong, Michael. 1995. Symposium speeches: Police corruption: An historical overview. *New York Law School Law Review* 40: 59–64.

Baer, Harold, and Joseph P. Armao. 1995. The Mollen Commission report: An overview. *New York Law School Law Review* 40: 73–94.

Chevigny, Paul. 1999. Book review: Review of New York City police corruption investigation commissions, 1894–1994. *Western New England Law Review* 21: 233–41.

City of New York. 1994. Commission report: The City of New York Commission to investigate allegations of police corruption and the anti-corruption procedures of the police department, Milton Mollen, chair. July 4.

Columbia Encyclopedia. 2003. *Parkhurst, Charles Henry*. http://encyclopedia.com/html/p/parkhurs.asp.

Herbert, Bob. 1997. In America, remaining blind to brutality. *New York Times*, September 25, A31.

Jeffers, H. Paul. 1994. *Commissioner Roosevelt: The story of Theodore Roosevelt and the New York City police, 1895–1897*. New York: John Wiley & Sons.

Knapp, Whitman. 1973. *Report of the New York City Commission to investigate allegations of police corruption and the city's anticorruption procedures*. New York: George Braziller.

Lardner, James. 1996. *The hell-raising career of Detective David Durk*. New York: Random House.

Lardner, James, and T. Repetto. 2000. *NYPD: A city and its police*. New York: Henry Holt and Company.

Maas, Peter. 1973. *Serpico*. New York City: Harper Collins.

Mayor's Office of New York City. 2003. *Commission to combat police corruption*. February 25. http://nyc.gov/html/ccpc/html/about.html.

McAlary, Michael. 1994. *Good cop, bad cop: Detective Joe Trimboli's heroic pursuit of NYPD Officer Michael Dowd*. New York: Pocket Books.

New York Legislature, Senate Committee on Police Department of the City of New York. 1895. *Report and proceedings of the senate committee appointed to investigate the police department of the city of New York*. Albany, NY: New York State Printer.

L

LAW ENFORCEMENT ASSISTANCE ADMINISTRATION

In 1965, the Office of Law Enforcement Assistance was created in the U.S. Department of Justice. This was the predecessor to the Law Enforcement Assistance Administration (LEAA), which was established as a result of the work of the President's Commission on Law Enforcement and Administration of Justice.

In 1967, the President's Commission on Law Enforcement and the Administration of Justice called for a revolution in the approach to crime. The commission developed seven specific goals that are relevant in the twenty-first century:

1. Prevent crime.
2. Adopt new ways of dealing with offenders.
3. Eliminate injustice and unfairness.
4. Upgrade personnel.
5. Conduct research to find new and effective ways to control crime.
6. Appropriate the necessary funds to accomplish the goals.
7. Involve all elements of society in planning and executing changes in the criminal justice system.

The commission further emphasized the need to consider law enforcement and criminal justice as a system and the need to improve its ability to prevent and reduce crime. The commission advocated maximizing the use of new technology, basing policy on proven facts, and maintaining American democratic values of fairness and respect for the individual (U.S. Department of Justice 1997, 3).

The commission attracted nationwide attention because of the status of its members, the growing public concern about crime, and the sharp division among commission members on some controversial topics. Congress responded to the report by enacting the landmark Omnibus Crime Control and Safe Streets Act of 1968. This act created the Law Enforcement Assistance Administration, which was the first comprehensive federal programmatic response to state and local crime control efforts, and provided extensive financial support. This support came in the form of block grants based on population and categorical grants. These funds were to be directed toward reducing crime by improving local criminal justice systems: police, courts, and corrections. One of the LEAA administrators, Donald Santarelli, observed that:

> The creation of LEAA was a direct response to the commission's report. Its creation signaled the makings of a significant change in the federal government's attitude towards crime, avoiding the federalization of state and local crime and assumption of operational responsibility, and with great respect for the dual federalism of government responsibility, it sought to strengthen the states rather than assume federal enforcement responsibility (U.S. Department of Justice 1997, 4).

To achieve this objective, the notion of criminal justice planning was introduced to the country. Heretofore, planning in criminal justice was virtually nonexistent. With the passage of the Omnibus Crime Control and Safe Streets Act, LEAA was authorized to provide funds to create a "state planning agency" in each state that would have as its primary function the responsibility to develop a comprehensive statewide plan for the improvement of law enforcement throughout the state. The act also authorized the states to make grants from a population-based block grant allocation to units of local government to carry out programs and projects in accordance with the planning effort to improve law enforcement (Hagerty 1978, 173).

Over time, it became clear that law enforcement had to be considered in the context of a larger criminal justice system consisting of police, the courts, and correctional systems. This was recognized in the 1973 and 1976 reauthorizations in which the role of LEAA was broadened to include assistance to all components of the criminal justice system (Hagerty 1978, 175).

The act also required the LEAA to develop a discretionary grant program and to establish a National Institute of Law Enforcement and Criminal Justice. This component of the LEAA had responsibility for encouraging research in criminal and juvenile justice.

In addition to the National Institute of Law Enforcement and Criminal Justice, the legislation created the Bureau of Justice Assistance to administer the block grant program and the Bureau of Justice Statistics to capture data about the system. In 1974, the Office of Juvenile Justice and Delinquency Prevention was created as a part of LEAA through separate legislation known as the Juvenile Justice and Delinquency Prevention Act.

One major office was created that was not congressionally mandated. The Office of Criminal Justice Education and Training was established in 1975 to administer the Law Enforcement Education Program (LEEP). This program was initially funded at $6.5 million and grew to $40 million per year throughout the 1970s. LEEP was the most popular LEAA program from a congressional perspective. At its height, the program supported more than one hundred thousand students through grants and loans in over a thousand colleges and universities. Other training and education programs developed and managed in the Office of Criminal Justice Education and Training included fellowships for graduate study, the Joint Commission on Criminology Education and Standards, the National Advisory Commission on Higher Education for Police Officers, and the National Consortium on Doctoral Programs in Criminology and Criminal Justice. The office also supported projects to develop and improve criminal justice manpower planning through such projects as the national manpower survey of the criminal justice system.

In 1982, federal funding for LEAA was withdrawn. However, it would be inaccurate to consider this the demise of LEAA. This agency can be credited with many accomplishments that still have a major influence on crime control policy today. Also, the Justice Assistance Act of 1984 created separate agencies to continue many of the same programs associated with

LEAA. With the Crime Bill of 1994, the Office of Justice Programs garnered more resources and influence than at any other time in history. Six presidential appointees administer the programs of the Office of Justice Programs, headed by an assistant attorney general. The Office of Justice Programs provides the umbrella agency for the following agencies: National Institute of Justice, Bureau of Justice Assistance, Office of Juvenile Justice and Delinquency Prevention, Bureau of Justice Statistics, and the Office of Victims of Crime (U.S. Department of Justice 1996, 2).

In a gathering of more than fifty current and former U.S. Department of Justice criminal justice administrators in July 1996, the group agreed that among its most significant accomplishments, LEAA:

- Encouraged for the first time state-level planning in criminal justice by spurring the formation of criminal justice state planning agencies (SPAs).
- Contributed to law enforcement professionalism by providing higher education opportunities. (A significant majority of current criminal justice leaders around the country are LEEP alumni.)
- Laid the foundation for the development of standards for police, courts, and correctional agencies.
- Encouraged the use of targeted strategies (for example, the establishment of career criminal units in prosecutors' offices).
- Launched the victim witness movement, encouraging prosecutors and other parts of the criminal justice system to undertake victim-witness initiatives.
- Enabled technological advances, including the development of bullet-proof vests and forensic applications of DNA technology (U.S. Department of Justice 1996, 3).

J. PRICE FOSTER

See also **Education and Training; Professionalism**

References and Further Reading

Bailey, William J., ed. 1995. *The encyclopedia of police science.* 2nd ed. New York: Garland.

Conley, John A., ed. 1994. *The 1967 President's Crime Commission Report: Its impact 25 years later.* Cincinnati, OH: Anderson Publishing Company.

Crank, John P. 2003. *Imagining justice.* Cincinnati, OH: Anderson Publishing Company.

Gest, Ted. 2001. *Crime and politics: Big government's erratic campaign for law and order.* New York: Oxford University Press.

Hagerty, James E. 1978. Criminal justice: Toward a new federal role. *Public Administration Review* 38: 173–76.

U.S. Department of Justice. 1967. *The challenge of crime in a free society.* Washington, DC: U.S. Government Printing Office.

———. 1996. *LEAA/OJP retrospective: 30 years of federal support to state and local criminal justice.* Washington, DC: U.S. Government Printing Office.

———. 1997. *The challenge of crime in a free society: Looking back, looking forward.* Washington, DC: U.S. Government Printing Office.

LIABILITY AND HIGH-SPEED CHASES

After observing a traffic violation or being alerted to a suspicious person or vehicle, a police officer can signal a driver to stop. Usually, the driver will pull over and the situation will end without further incident. However, on rare occasions, the driver will refuse to stop or take evasive action and flee. In such situations the police officer must decide whether or not to pursue, bearing in mind that if a driver refuses to stop the agency's pursuit policy attaches, and the officer must therefore take into account both policy and training before reaching a decision. Accordingly, the officer must balance both the risks and the potential benefits when deciding whether or not a pursuit is necessary.

A pursuit can be initiated when a suspect refuses to obey an officer's order to stop. The fleeing suspect is likely to become erratic and a danger to anyone in the vicinity. Under these conditions, when a police officer decides to chase the suspect, his or her driving is also fast, often dangerous, and presents an additional risk to the public. That is, the risks of a chase not only include the police officer and the suspect, but they also involve the public in an interactive triangle.

This interactive triangle is made up of (1) the officer, who is trying to apprehend a suspect; (2) the police vehicle; and (3) the environment, which includes the fleeing suspect, traffic, and pedestrians, all of which are forces brought into play in this interaction. The suspect's goal is to remain free and avoid arrest and, unless he has a death wish, he will often run until he believes he is safe, or crashes (Alpert 1997). The suspect, who has refused to heed the commands of the officer, has the primary responsibility to stop the chase by pulling over. The suspect is also directing the pursuit by selecting the course, speed, and recklessness of the driving. However, any increased recklessness on the part of the suspect may be affected by the officer's attempt to apprehend him. The officer's natural desire to apprehend the suspect must be tempered by concerns for public safety. Because of the nature of pursuits, the suspect is necessarily influenced psychologically by the officer's actions.

The goal of the officer is to apprehend the suspect and make the arrest. Accordingly, it is the officer who must become aware of personal capabilities and take into account environmental conditions that may affect his or her ability to accomplish the mission of police, which is to protect lives. The police officer must factor into the decision-making process the risk created by the suspect's driving; the potential actions of innocent bystanders, passengers, and others who may become involved; and how his or her actions influence the suspect's driving. In addition, the likelihood of apprehension must be factored into the decision to continue or not to continue a chase.

The officer must understand that when a suspect refuses to stop for the emergency lights and siren, a routine encounter turns quickly into a high-risk and dangerous event where a show of authority may affect the suspect's driving. If the suspect becomes more reckless than before or refuses to stop, it is the officer, based on policy and training, who must determine the value of continuing the pursuit and the risk of the pursuit. The officer and the supervisor must also understand the influence of the chase on the participants. The need to win and make that arrest is often influenced by the adrenaline rush felt by the officer. A pursuit is an exciting event and involves one person running to escape and another chasing to catch. If it continues, it resembles a drag race until one party terminates it or there is a crash.

Balancing Law Enforcement with Public Safety

The purpose of pursuit is to apprehend a suspect within the mission of police—to protect lives. Tactics and activities undertaken must consider apprehension secondary to public safety. One way to help officers understand this balance is to have them apply the same standards used in weighing the alternatives to firing a weapon in a situation where innocent bystanders may be endangered. Whenever an officer fires a weapon, he or she must be concerned that the bullet may accidentally hit an unintended target. By comparison, in pursuit, the officer has not only his or her vehicle to worry about, but also must consider the pursued vehicle, which is creating dangerous situations, and other vehicles, which may also be creating danger by attempting to get out of the way (Alpert and Fridell 1992).

Pursuit driving has historically been available to the police in the fight against crime. Unfortunately, the inherent nature of pursuit creates a significant danger to the officers, law violators, and the general public. Whether or not this danger and the resulting property damage, injuries, and deaths are worth the benefits is the question police administrators and courts have been examining for years. One appropriate response has been to limit pursuits to situations in which a fleeing suspect is suspected of a violent felony (Alpert 1997). By limiting pursuits to these serious felonies, the police are able to use their skills to attempt to apprehend the most serious criminals while protecting the public from risk created by chases for traffic and other minor offenses and limiting their exposure to lawsuits.

Pursuit Driving and Liability

As a general proposition, lawsuits involving pursuits are brought in either state court or federal court. Actions brought in a state court are commonly called "tort" actions. Actions brought under Title 42, Section 1983, of the U.S. Code will require a showing of violation of a federally protected constitutional or statutory right. Whether a cause of action is based on state tort or on Section 1983, the allegations of the plaintiff must establish responsibility on the part of the pursuit vehicle operator or the employing agency (see Alpert et al. 2000).

Responsibility of the operator is usually based on an allegation of some variety of negligence or on some greater degree of culpability. The responsibility of the employing agency may be based on a showing of failure to provide meaningful policy or adequate training. Because these federal claims are very difficult to prove and are relatively rare, we will focus on state claims.

Actions brought against an officer or the employing agency under state law are generally based on allegations of negligence, although some actions may be framed in terms of intentional acts of the officer. The legal formula for negligence can be summarized as follows:

1. A duty or obligation, recognized by the law, requiring the person to conform to a certain standard of conduct, for the protection of others against unreasonable risks
2. A failure on the person's part to conform to the standard required: a breach of the duty
3. A reasonably close causal connection between the conduct and the resulting injury; this is commonly known as *legal cause* or *proximate cause*, and includes the notion of cause in fact
4. Actual loss or damage resulting to the interests of another

From a practical standpoint, negligence in an emergency vehicle response may come about in any number of ways, including the three following representative situations:

1. An officer violates an applicable state statute that creates a duty to act or not act.
2. An officer violates pertinent department policy that creates a duty to act or not act.
3. An officer violates an established duty to use "due care" generally.

Regardless of whether the tort alleged involves an intentional or negligent act, a plaintiff may not recover for injury if there was no duty owed to the plaintiff by the officer who caused the injury. The term *duty*, as used here, means that there was some obligation recognized by the law to behave in a particular fashion toward the person who was ultimately injured. The law recognizes generally that if there was no duty to the injured on the part of a law enforcement officer, then there can be no responsibility on the part of the officer or the employer for payment of monetary compensation, known as "damages," or any other type of relief to the injured party.

Conclusion

Pursuit driving is one tactic that police have relied on for the apprehension of suspects. Until the 1980s, very little was known about the risks and benefits of pursuit. Today, the known risks and limited benefits have convinced many progressive police administrators to restrict their agencies' pursuit policies and provide decision-making training to officers. The trend that began in the 1990s and continues today includes an agency pursuit plan involving a policy, training, supervision, and accountability.

Research has demonstrated the need for a strong policy that takes most decisions away from officers who must make split-second decisions in the heat of a chase. Comparing pursuits to the use of firearms clearly demonstrates the potential deadly consequences of such actions. In fact, the more that is learned about pursuit, the more the tactic is controlled. Data from studies show that approximately 40% of pursuits result in crashes, 20% end in injuries, and 1% end in death. Although it is difficult to tell young police officers that they cannot chase a person who would not stop for them, it is more difficult to explain to a person that his family member was injured or killed in a pursuit for a traffic or property offense. The International Association of Chiefs of Police (IACP) Policy Center published a model policy and a policy concepts and issues paper evaluating pursuit driving. While they maintained a middle-of-the-road posture, they have summarized the indisputable need for reform (IACP Policy Center 1990, 1–2).

The policy issue confronting law enforcement and municipal administrators is a familiar one of balancing conflicting interests: on one side there is the need to apprehend known offenders. On the other side, there is the safety of law enforcement officers, of fleeing drivers and their passengers, and of innocent bystanders.

The model policy is relatively restrictive, particularly in prohibiting pursuit where the offense in question would not warrant an arrest. Most traffic violations, therefore, would not meet these pursuit requirements. It is recognized that many law enforcement officers and administrators may find this prohibition difficult to accept and implement, particularly where a more permissive policy has been traditionally accepted.

In this critical area of pursuit driving, law enforcement administrators must therefore be prepared to make difficult decisions based on the cost and benefits of these types of pursuits to the public they serve.

GEOFFREY ALPERT

See also **Accountability; Early Warning Systems; Fear of Litigation; Liability and the Police; Liability and Use of Force**

References

Alpert, Geoffrey. 1997. *Police pursuit: Policies and training.* Research in Brief, May. Washington, DC: National Institute of Justice.

Alpert, Geoffrey P., and Lorie Fridell. 1992. *Police vehicles and firearms: Instruments of deadly force.* Prospect Heights, IL: Waveland Press.

Alpert, Geoffrey, Dennis Kenney, Roger Dunham, and William Smith. 2000. *Police pursuits: What we know.* Washington, DC: Police Executive Research Forum.

International Association of Chiefs of Police Policy Center. 1990. *Pursuit model policy, and pursuit concepts and issues.* Gaithersburg, MD: International Association of Chiefs of Police Policy Center.

LIABILITY AND THE POLICE

Civil liability for officers and agencies may be imposed under either or both state or federal law. It is estimated that as many as thirty thousand civil lawsuits may be filed against the police each year. The estimates on the percentage of cases that plaintiffs win vary widely, from 8% to more than

50% (Kappeler 2001, 4–5). Damages are frequently awarded, especially in cases involving police violence (Bickel 2001), and damages assessed against police departments frequently run into millions of dollars (Kappeler 2001, 2). Further, the trend seems to be toward more lawsuits and more victories by plaintiffs (Kappeler 2001, 3).

Under both types of law, liability was not a significant issue until the 1960s. Before that time, neither the social nor legal climate was favorable to legal action against police or police agencies. The civil rights revolution of the 1960s changed both of these climates, especially at the federal level. Few legal avenues were available under federal law until the Warren Court reinvigorated federal civil rights statutes and expanded the rights of citizens and suspects (Collins 2001, chaps. 1 and 2).

Title 42 U.S. Code Section 1983

Today, most lawsuits against state and local police are brought under authority of Title 42 U.S. Code Section 1983. In relevant part, this statute provides:

> Every person who, under color of any statute, ordinance, regulation, custom, or usage, of any State or Territory or the District of Columbia, subjects, or causes to be subjected, any citizen of the United States or other person within the jurisdiction thereof to the deprivation of any rights, privileges, or immunities secured by the Constitution and laws, shall be liable to the party injured in an action at law, suit in equity, or other proper proceeding for redress, . . .

Lawsuits under this statute can be brought in either state or federal court. However, most such suits are brought in federal courts (Collins 2001, 247).

Although originally enacted in 1871, nearly one hundred years prior to the Warren Court, this statute was interpreted very narrowly and provided few avenues to impose liability. One of the key cases where the Supreme Court made this statute a broad source of liability was *Monroe v. Pape* (1961). The Court held that the "under color" language was not limited to acts that were legal under state law. Many lower courts had held that if the official action was illegal under state law, such action did not fall under color of state law as required by Section 1983. This was an extremely significant ruling because much, if not most, police misconduct is also a violation of state law. A ruling to the contrary by the Court would have meant that most police misconduct could not be the basis of a Section 1983 lawsuit. The Court also ruled that the Section 1983 plaintiffs did not have to exhaust state judicial remedies before bringing suit. A contrary ruling would have forced plaintiffs into generally unsympathetic state courts and state remedies first (Collins 2001, chaps. 1 and 2).

Although Section 1983 allows money damage actions against individual officers, and injunctions against government agencies, it was not until 1978, in *Monell v. Dept. of Social Services*, that the Court ruled that municipalities (and counties) can be liable in money damages for the acts of their employees. However, later in *Will v. Michigan Dept. of State Police* (1989), the more conservative Rehnquist Court held that states, while subject to injunctions, could not be sued for money damages because they were not included in the term "persons" in section 1983.

The federal government and federal officials cannot be sued under Section 1983 because they do not act under color of state law. Relief against federal officers for constitutional violations may be obtained under the Supreme Court's decision in *Bivens v. Six Unknown Named Agents* (1971). Lawsuits against the federal government and certain aspects of lawsuits against federal officers are governed by the Federal Tort Claims Act—28 U.S. Code Sec. 1346(b), 2671 et seq. (Avery, Rudovsky, and Blum 2001, chap. 5).

Remedies, Defenses, and Immunities

The two most commonly sought civil remedies are money damages and injunctions. When the law allows, damages can be obtained from both or either the officer and the government that employed the officer. Injunctions are obtained against the government (agency) and are court orders requiring that the agency do or stop doing specific acts, such as engaging in racial profiling (Collins 2001, chaps. 9 and 10).

The defendants will have defenses (for example, consent, good faith, legal justification), and immunities from money damage suits may also be available. In money damage suits against individual officers (personal capacity suits), the officer may have some form of official immunity that requires that the case be dismissed before trial if the immunity can be established. The type of official immunity most applicable to police officers is qualified immunity. Under federal law, and the law of many states, this requires that officers show that even though they violated the plaintiff's rights, they acted in an objectively reasonable fashion under the circumstances (Collins 2001, chap. 8).

The government (agency) may be able to have the suit dismissed if it can establish some form of sovereign immunity. Sovereign immunity protects a government from suit unless the government consents to suit. For the states, such consent is given in statutes, frequently called the "Tort Claims Act" (Collins 2001, chap. 7). The federal government has given limited consent to be sued in the Federal Tort Claims Act, 28 U.S. Code Sec. 1346(b), 2671 et seq.

If the plaintiff prevails in a Section 1983 lawsuit, whether brought in state or federal court, the court can award attorney's fees and related costs under Title 42 U.S.C. Section 1988(b). This statute has undoubtedly encouraged litigation against the police and other public officials (Collins 2001, 254–55).

Criminal Liability

Ordinary federal and state criminal statutes (for example, assault) apply against police officers just like ordinary citizens. However, every jurisdiction also has crimes (for example, official oppression) that can be committed only by public officials. Most federal prosecutions of law enforcement officers are brought under Title 18 U.S. Code Section 242, which is similar to the civil statute Section 1983. Section 242 provides:

> Whoever, under color of any law, statute, ordinance, regulation, or custom, willfully subjects any person in any State, Territory, Commonwealth, Possession, or District to the deprivation of any rights, privileges, or immunities secured or protected by the Constitution or laws of the United States, or to different punishments, pains, or penalties, on account of such person being an alien, or by reason of his color, or race, than are prescribed for the punishment of citizens, shall be fined under this title or imprisoned not more than one year, or both; and if bodily injury results from the acts committed in violation of this section or if such acts include the use, attempted use, or threatened use of a dangerous weapon, explosives, or fire, shall be fined under this title or imprisoned not more than ten years, or both; and if death results from the acts committed in violation of this section or if such acts include kidnapping or an attempt to kidnap, aggravated sexual abuse, or an attempt to commit aggravated sexual abuse, or an attempt to kill, shall be fined under this title, or imprisoned for any term of years or for life, or both, or may be sentenced to death.

This statute applies to all law enforcement officers, including federal officers. The U.S. Department of Justice is extremely selective in prosecuting law enforcement officers. The cases usually involve extreme forms of misconduct and/or cases where local prosecution is ineffective, such as the Rodney King case. State criminal prosecutions of police are also relatively rare (Cheh 1996, 251–60).

Future Trends

Most observers believe that police conduct grows out of organizational or systemic problems in policing and police agencies. Money damage awards and criminal prosecutions are probably going to have little impact on such problems. Broad, long-term injunctive relief may have resulted in major improvements in prisons (Feeley and Hanson 1990), but the U.S Supreme Court has not been willing to give federal courts such powers when dealing with police agencies in suits initiated by citizens against the police (Collins 2001, chap. 10).

However, as part of the Violent Crime Control and Law Enforcement Act of 1994 (18 U.S.C. Sec. 14141), the attorney general has the power to sue state and local governments over patterns and practices of policing that violate constitutional rights. These actions appear to be a mechanism for overcoming some of the prior limitations on equitable relief. In a number of cities, consent decrees involving major changes in police operations have been implemented. Independent monitors or auditors are appointed by the court to oversee implementation (Collins 2001, 186; Davis et al. 2001). Evaluation of the process in Pittsburgh, Pennsylvania, yielded encouraging results regarding positive change (Davis et al. 2001).

RAYMOND G. KESSLER

See also **Accountability; Fear of Litigation; Liability and High-Speed Chases; Liability and Use of Force; Police Legal Liabilities: Overview**

References and Further Readings

Avery, M., D. Rudovsky, and K. Blum. 2004. *Police misconduct: Law and litigation.* 3rd ed. New York: Clark Boardman Callaghan.

Bivens v. Six Unknown Named Agents, 403 U.S. 388, 91 S. Ct. 1999, 29 L. Ed. 2d 619 (1971).

Cheh, Mary H. 1996. Are lawsuits an answer to police brutality? In *Police violence*, ed. Geller and Toch, 247–71. New Haven, CT: Yale University Press.

Collins, Michael G. 2001. *Section 1983 litigation.* 2nd ed. St. Paul, MN: West Publishing.

Davis, R. C., C. W. Ortiz, N. J. Henderson, and J. Miller. 2004. Turning necessity into virtue: Pittsburgh's experience with a federal consent decree. In *Police integrity and ethics*, ed. M. Hickman, A. Piquero, and J. Green, 290–34. Belmont, CA: Wadsworth.

Feeley, M. M., and M. M. Hanson. 1990. The impact of judicial intervention on prisons and jails: A framework for analysis and a review of the literature. In *Courts, corrections and the Constitution*, ed. J. J. DiIulio, 12–46. New York: Oxford University Press.

Kappeler, Victor. 2001. *Critical issues in police civil liability.* 3rd ed. Prospect Heights, IL: Waveland Press.

Monnell v. Dept. of Social Services, 436 U.S. 658, 98 S. Ct. 2018; 56 L. Ed. 2d 11 (1978).

Monroe v. Pape 365 U.S. 167, 81 S. Ct. 473, 5 L. Ed. 2d 492 (1961).

Nahmood, S., M. Wells, and T. Eaton. 1995. *Constitutional torts.* Cincinnati, OH: Anderson Publishing Company.

Payne, Dennis M. 2002. *Police liability.* Durham, NC: Carolina Academic Press.

Ross, Darrell L. 2003. *Civil liability in criminal justice.* 3rd ed. Cincinnati, OH: Anderson Publishing Company.

Rudovsky, David H. 2001. Police abuse: Can the violence be contained? In *Police misconduct*, ed. M. Palmiotto, 452–81. Upper Saddle River, NJ: Prentice-Hall.

Silver, Isadore H. 2004. *Police civil liability.* Newark, NJ: LexisNexis/Matthew Bender.

Smolla, Rodney A. 1999. *Federal civil rights acts.* St. Paul, MN: West Publishing.

Vaughn, M., T. Cooper, and R. del Carmen. 2001. Assessing legal liabilities in law enforcement: Police chiefs' views. *Crime and Delinquency* 47: 3–27.

Will v. Michigan Dept. of State Police, 492 U.S. 58, 109 S. Ct. 2304, 105 L. Ed. 2d 45 (1989).

LIABILITY AND USE OF FORCE

Police work inevitably involves the use of force. There are two types of force: nondeadly and deadly. Nondeadly force is force that, when used, is not likely to result in serious bodily injury or death. Deadly force is force that, when used, would lead a reasonable police officer objectively to conclude that it poses a high risk of death or serious injury to its target. The amount of force a police officer may use depends on the facts of the situation. Generally speaking, an officer may use only so much force as is reasonable under the circumstances. Determining what is "reasonable" is where the law comes into play.

Inappropriate use of force by the police is actionable under state tort law, federal law (42 U.S.C. Sec. 1983), or both. Liability under state tort law is governed by state statute and court decisions; liability under Section 1983 is governed by federal law and federal court decisions. For Section 1983 to apply, the plaintiff must allege a violation of a constitutional right or of a right given by federal law.

Nondeadly Force

The general rule is that police may use nondeadly force as long as it is reasonable. Reasonable force is defined as only as much force as is necessary to achieve a legitimate result, such as an arrest or search. The term reasonable force is subjective, and thus what constitutes reasonable force depends on the circumstances of each case. Police may never use force to punish someone. Reasonable force is legal, whereas punitive force is illegal and exposes the officer and the department to civil liability.

Most lawsuits alleging police use of excessive nondeadly force take the form of tort claims of assault and battery. Although sometimes used as one term, assault and battery refer to two separate acts. Assault is defined as the intentional causing of an apprehension of unjustified, harmful, or offensive conduct. Battery is defined as the intentional infliction of unjustified, harmful, or offensive body contact. The police may use reasonable force when making an arrest, but unreasonable force constitutes battery. Additionally, if the arrest by the police is invalid, the handling and handcuffing of the arrestee constitutes a battery.

In *Graham v. Connor* (1989), the Supreme Court established the test to determine civil liability under federal law in excessive use-of-force cases. The Court held that allegations that police officers used excessive force in arrests, investigative stops, or other forms of seizure must be analyzed under the Fourth Amendment's "objective reasonableness" standard rather than under the "substantive due process" clause of the Fourteenth Amendment.

The facts of *Graham v. Connor* are as follows: Graham, a diabetic, asked a friend to drive him to a convenience store to buy orange juice to counteract the onset of an insulin reaction. Upon entering the store, Graham saw a number of people in line, so he asked his friend to drive him to another friend's house. Connor, a police officer, saw Graham enter and leave the store hastily. Suspicious, Connor ordered Graham and his friend to wait while he ascertained what happened in the store. Backup police arrived, handcuffed Graham, and ignored explanations about his diabetic condition. A scuffle ensued and Graham was injured. Graham was released when the officer learned that nothing happened in the store. Graham later sued, alleging excessive use of force by the police.

On appeal, the Supreme Court held that police officers may be held liable under the Constitution for using excessive force, but that such liability must be judged under the Fourth Amendment's "objective reasonableness" standard. There is no need to determine the motive of the police officer. Additionally, the reasonableness of a particular use of force by the police "must be judged from the perspective of a reasonable officer on the scene, rather than with the 20/20 vision of hindsight." This standard is considered more equitable by the police, whose main complaint in use-of-force cases is that they are second-guessed by judges or juries, deciding the case long after the fact. While the *Graham* test applies only to Section

1983 cases, a number of state courts have adopted the standard for tort claims.

Deadly Force

Deadly force is defined as force that, when used, would lead a reasonable police officer objectively to conclude that it poses a high risk of death or serious injury to its target. Firearms are obviously instruments of deadly force. A nightstick may be considered an instrument of deadly force, depending on how it is used.

The general rule is that a police officer may not use deadly force to make a misdemeanor arrest. The only exception is if deadly force is necessary for self-defense or defense of the life of a third person. The use of deadly force in misdemeanor cases raises questions of disproportionality because the designation of the offense as a misdemeanor means that society does not consider that offense serious in that state.

At common law, a police officer could use as much force as necessary, including deadly force, to make a felony arrest. This rule dates to a time when felonies were all punishable by death, police were not well trained, and they lacked sophisticated weapons. A police officer could also use deadly force to prevent a felony suspect from escaping; this was known as the "fleeing felon rule."

Until 1985 there were no guidelines from the U.S. Supreme Court regarding police use of deadly force. The limits for such use were set instead by state law or departmental rules. That changed in 1985 when the Court decided *Tennessee v. Garner*, a case that sets guidelines for the use of deadly force to prevent escape of fleeing felons. In *Garner*, two Memphis police officers one evening answered a "prowler inside call." Upon arriving at the scene, they encountered a woman standing on her porch and gesturing toward the adjacent house. The woman said she had heard glass shattering and was certain that someone was breaking in. One police officer radioed the dispatcher to say that they were on the scene, while the other officer went behind the neighboring house. The officer heard a door slam and saw someone run across the backyard. The fifteen-year-old suspect, Edward Garner, stopped at a six-foot-high, chain-link fence at the edge of the yard. With the aid of a flashlight, the officer saw Garner's face and hands. He saw no sign of a weapon and admitted later that he was fairly sure Garner was unarmed. While Garner was crouched at the base of the fence, the officer called out, "Police, halt!" and took several steps toward him. Garner then began to climb the fence. The officer shot him. Garner died; ten dollars and a purse taken from the house were found on his body.

In using deadly force to prevent the escape, the officer was acting under the authority of a Tennessee statute and pursuant to department policy, both of which followed the common law fleeing felon rule. The Supreme Court, however, concluded that the use of deadly force to prevent the escape of an apparently unarmed suspected felon was unconstitutional. The Court determined that apprehension by the use of deadly force is a seizure subject to the reasonableness requirement of the Fourth Amendment. (The Eighth Amendment prohibition on cruel and unusual punishment did not apply, as the use of force was not punishment, but a seizure.) The Court emphasized that "where the subject poses no immediate threat to the officer and no threat to others, the harm resulting from failing to apprehend him does not justify the use of deadly force," adding that "a police officer may not seize an unarmed nondangerous suspect by shooting him dead." Under Garner, it is constitutionally reasonable for an officer to use deadly force to prevent escape only when the officer has probable cause to believe that the suspect poses a threat of serious physical harm to the officer or others and if, where feasible, some warning is given.

759

Conclusion

Use of force is an inevitable part of policing that carries immense potential for liability. Use of force is an emotional issue and a flashpoint for potentially explosive police–community relations. It is imperative that officers know the limits of the use of both nondeadly and deadly force. The Supreme Court has provided some guidance. *Tennessee v. Garner* allows the use of deadly force to prevent escape only where the officer has probable cause to believe that the suspect poses a threat of serious physical harm either to the officer or to others. *Graham v. Connor* holds that the use of force in arrests, investigative stops, or other forms of seizure must be analyzed and judged under the "objective reasonableness" standard of the Fourth Amendment, as judged by a "reasonable officer on the scene," rather than with the "20/20 vision of hindsight." Police motivation for the use of force is irrelevant. Failure to adequately train and supervise police officers can lead to tragic events such as the Rodney King beating and the Abner Louima assault.

CRAIG HEMMENS

See also **Abuse of Authority by Police; Accountability; Arrest Powers of Police; Courts; Deadly Force; Excessive Force; Liability and the Police; Police Pursuits; Post-Shooting Review; Professionalism; Stress and Police Work**

References and Further Reading

Barrineau, H. E. *Civil liability in criminal justice.* 2nd ed. Cincinnati, OH: Anderson Publishing Company.
del Carmen, Rolando V. 1991. *Civil liberties in American policing: A text for law enforcement personnel.* Englewood Cliffs, NJ: Prentice-Hall.
———. 2006. *Criminal procedure: Law and practice.* 7th ed. Belmont, CA: Thomson.
Graham v. Connor, 490 U.S. 396 (1989).
Kappeler, Victor. 2001. Civil liability for police use of excessive force. In *Critical issues in police civil liability*, 3rd ed., 65–80. Prospect Heights, IL: Waveland Press.
Tennessee v. Garner, 471 U.S. 1 (1985).

LOS ANGELES COUNTY SHERIFF'S DEPARTMENT (LASD)

History

Originally a Spanish colony, California was ceded to the United States in 1848 after the Mexican–American War. In 1849, the great Gold Rush brought thousands of fortune hunters to California, many of them settling in Los Angeles County. Among the newcomers were fugitives, escaped criminals, and troublemakers. Murders, robberies, and lynchings were part of the routine. In April 1850, the Los Angeles County Sheriff's Department (LASD) was formed with Sheriff George T. Burrill and two deputies. As crime increased, a new type of posse, called the Los Angeles Rangers, was authorized by the sheriff. Mounted and uniformed, one hundred rangers made up the police force, patrolling the area and arresting criminal suspects.

During the next fifty years, the LASD experienced civil unrest, with two of its sheriffs killed in the line of duty. A civil riot occurred in 1871 after a massacre of local Chinese immigrants. During the first half of the twentieth century, LASD implemented policies and procedures of modern policing. The fee system of compensation was replaced by the civil service merit system in 1913. Starting in the 1920s, LASD began increasing the professional and technical divisions—Bureau of Identification, detention center, crime laboratory, the details of Homicide, Robbery, Narcotic, Auto Theft, and Liquor, and the Sheriff's Academy.

General Background

With a population exceeding ten million by 2004, Los Angeles County is the largest county in terms of its population in the United States. The Sheriff's Department covers approximately four thousand square miles and provides direct services to more than 2.2 million residents. The department contracts to provide services to forty cities. The Community College Bureau contracts with nine community colleges. The department currently employs around 8,200 sworn deputies and 5,800 professional staff. Among the sworn deputies, 85% are male and 15% are female. The racial breakdown includes 54% white, 30% Hispanic, 10% African American, and 5% Asian. Its total annual budget is $1.5 billion.

Patrol and Investigation

The LASD divides field operations (patrol and investigation) into three regions with twenty-four patrol stations: Region I (northern and western areas), Region II (central area), and Region III (eastern area). Each region has eight stations. The organizational hierarchy is as follows: region chief, region commander, station captain, bureau lieutenant, and team/unit sergeant. To illustrate station operations, consider the East Los Angeles Station. It has adopted service-oriented policing (SOP) strategies, permanently deploying line deputies in beat areas to meet residents and deal directly with community problems.

The Detective Bureau is composed of several investigative teams: Auto Theft/ Property Crimes (burglary and grand theft), Family Crimes (domestic violence, elder/child abuse, and sexual assault), and Robbery/Assault Crimes. Within the Safe Streets Bureaus, Operation Safe Streets and gang enforcement teams are responsible for gang prevention, intervention, and suppression. The Narcotics Bureau investigates the use, possession, sale, manufacture, and transportation of controlled substances. The Parole/Probation Task Force targets parolees and probationers, focusing on violent gang members. Task force members also act as a liaison between the California Department of Corrections, the California Youth Authority, the District Attorney's Office, the Los Angeles County Department of Probation, and the Los Angeles County Sheriff's Department. The station has implemented several prevention programs: Safety Through Our Perseverance Program (S.T.O.P.), Vital Intervention Directional Alternatives Program (V.I.D.A.), Community Prosecutor, and the Youth Athletic League (Y.A.L.).

The Detective Division

LASD utilizes a centralized model for major crime investigations. The Detective Division consists of five bureaus:

1. The Homicide Bureau conducts investigations of cases involving criminal homicide, missing persons, and questionable death (suicides, accidental drug overdoses, and infants), and a special unit handles unsolved cases.
2. The Major Crimes Bureau investigates specialized crimes: organized crime, vice, cargo theft, series and pattern robberies, crimes related to health care and illegal pharmaceuticals, and kidnapping. Extradition, surveillance operations, and apprehension of fugitives are also their jurisdiction.
3. The Narcotics Bureau is responsible for investigating drug-related cases. New initiatives include a team handling methamphetamine laboratories and the Marijuana Enforcement Team (MET), comprised of sheriff's narcotics investigators and members of the U.S. Forest Service.

4. The Commercial Crimes Bureau investigates white collar crime: forgery, fraud, and computer crimes. Los Angeles is known as the "fraud capital" of the country. The bureau's seven teams are divided into three teams targeting real estate, computer, and fraud by family members, and four teams conducting investigations into specifically assigned areas.

5. The Family Crimes Bureau handles cases of child sexual and physical abuse. Many investigators participate in a federal task force on child exploitation and multidisciplinary child abuse centers throughout Los Angeles County.

The County Jail System

The LA County Jail is the largest jail system in the world and is comprised of the Custody Operations Division and Correctional Services Division. On any given day, about twenty thousand inmates are housed in the system for one of four reasons: temporary custody awaiting trial; serving jail sentence after conviction; parole violator awaiting revocation hearing; and illegal immigrant detention. The system holds inmates in six facilities: the Men's Central Jail (the largest facility for high-risk offenders); Twin Towers (female and mentally ill detainees); Pitchess Detention Center–North (maximum security for presentenced and sentenced males); North County Correctional Facility (maximum security for presentenced and sentenced males); Pitchess Detention Center–East (parole violators); and Mira Loma Detention Center (illegal immigrant detainees). New technological measures are being developed. For example, closed-circuit TV and digital video recording at PDC–East have been implemented through a network video recording format to monitor inmates for jail automation or an event. The analog and digital images can be stored for transmission, analysis, and review.

The Correctional Services Division has a number of special units. The Inmate Reception Center provides physical/mental examinations. The Medical Services Bureau provides in-patient, nursing, and psychiatric services. The Transportation Bureau is responsible for transporting inmates to and from fifty-two court buildings with more than six hundred courtrooms and to state prisons. Finally, several programs provide goal-oriented inmates the opportunity to rehabilitate themselves through behavior modification, education, job training, and religious education. Currently, the division is implementing a jail information management system (JIMS), automating inmate information from booking to release with digital scanning.

The Court Services Division

The Court Services Division is the second largest division with more than eleven hundred sworn members and more than five hundred civilians. With the Central, East, and West Bureaus, and the Judicial Protection District, this division provides security and support services to fifty county superior courts. This includes staffing bailiffs, operating courthouse lock-ups, and serving and enforcing civil and criminal processes.

The Scientific Services Bureau

This bureau houses the crime lab, which is divided into three major groups. The Major Crime Group has four sections: Biology, Physical Evidence, Firearms, and Questioned Documents. The Chemical Abuse Group handles narcotics, clandestine laboratories, toxicology, and blood alcohol testing. The investigation group sections deal with identification, crime scenes, photographs, photo/digital imaging, and polygraphs. Currently, the bureau is capable of doing short tandem repeat (STR) for DNA testing and is compatible with the FBI's Combined DNA Indexing System (CODIS). Advanced techniques and database information have helped solve cold and serial rape cases.

Sheriff Leroy Baca

Born in East Los Angeles, Leroy Baca was sworn into the LASD as a deputy sheriff trainee in 1965. He worked custody, recruitment, and patrol, became an instructor at the academy, and advanced to captain, commander, and chief. As chief of the Court Services Division in 1994, he combined the Sheriff's and Marshal's Departments, saving the county $14 million a year. In 1993, he received his Ph.D. in public administration from the University of Southern California. In 1998, Leroy Baca was elected the thirtieth sheriff of the largest sheriff's department in the world. Sheriff Baca initiated a new regional High Tech Crime Task Force in 2002 and the Los Angeles Regional Gang Information Network (LARGIN) in 2003. The network collects intelligence information on street gang activities and coordinates anti-gang strategies using CalGang, a statewide database.

To improve officer education, Sheriff Baca started LASD University in 2001, a joint degree program (bachelor's and master's) with California State University–Long Beach and other local universities. Sheriff Baca emphasizes mentoring by providing leadership, management, and direction to thousands of deputy sheriffs and police officers. He also encourages international exchange programs through the International Liaison Office. Sheriff Baca serves on several community committees and organizations and is an adjunct professor of public administration at the University of La Verne. Sheriff Baca believes that the LASD is a leader in every aspect of law enforcement and ensures the trend will continue.

JOHN WANG

See also **Los Angeles Police Department (LAPD); Sheriffs**

References and Further Reading

Bennett, W., and K. Hess. 1988. *Management and supervision in law enforcement*. St. Paul, MN: West Publishing.

Berg, B., and J. Horgan. 1998. *Criminal investigation*. 3rd ed. New York: Glencoe/McGraw-Hill.

Birzer, B., and C. Roberson. 2006. *Policing today and tomorrow*. Englewood Cliffs, NJ: Prentice-Hall.

Brown, Lee P. 1991. Policing in the '90s: Responding to a changing environment. *The Police Chief*, March.

County of Los Angeles Sheriff's Department. 2004. *Year review of 2004*. Los Angeles.

Whisenand, P. 2005. *Managing of police organizations*. 6th ed. Englewood Cliffs, NJ: Prentice-Hall.

LOS ANGELES POLICE DEPARTMENT (LAPD)

The Los Angeles Police Department, the second largest police department in the United States, is responsible for providing police service to four million residents in an area encompassing some 467 square miles. The department is organized around eighteen broadly defined community areas in Los Angeles and is a full-service department providing marine, air, and terrorism responses as well as basic patrol and investigations services. A Board of Police Commissioners oversees all operations of the LAPD.

The department has had a complicated history and has been seen in the late nineteenth and early twentieth centuries as a corrupt agency, but it is emerging in the twenty-first century as a "model" of police professionalism. Rocked by a series of scandals including the Rodney King incident of 1991 and the Rampart Division corruption scandal of 1999, the LAPD continues to work to assure safety and security to Los Angelinos, while at the same time rebuilding public trust and confidence in the police.

History—The Early Years

California was admitted into the Union in 1850, the same year that Los Angeles was incorporated as a city. From its founding in 1850 until 1853, crime and order issues in the city of Los Angeles were the province of an elected sheriff, who "policed" Los Angeles and environs, generally with deputized assistants, whenever a show of force was necessary.

In its early years Los Angeles became a scene of considerable turbulence and bloodshed, a condition that lasted many years. This lawlessness developed as a major social problem in Los Angeles beginning in the "gold rush era" where a thirst for quick wealth brought many to California. Those seeking wealth from the mining of gold in California were often followed by an array of cheats, thieves, prostitutes, and others who worked to separate the miners from their newly found wealth. These conditions set the stage for a long era of corruption and violence in the "City of Angels."

In 1853 then-City Marshall Jack Whaling was assassinated in broad daylight, prompting in June of that year the creation of a "police force" comprised of one hundred volunteers, authorized by the common council. This first police force was called the Los Angeles Rangers; they were identified by a white ribbon that proclaimed "City Police—Authorized by the Council of Los Angeles."

In March 1855 the Los Angeles City Guards emerged as Los Angeles' police force. The guards were the first uniformed police in the city charged with preserving law and order, and they focused on patrolling the numerous saloons and gambling halls scattered throughout the city. This force, like the rangers, was composed of volunteers. In 1869 the police force shifted from being voluntary to being a paid force, and an ordinance created the Board of Police Commissioners to oversee the police.

Despite its paid police force, Los Angeles remained a "wide-open" city throughout the latter part of the nineteenth century and into the twentieth. Violence was rampant, vigilantism practiced with impunity, and racial discrimination commonplace. By the latter half of the nineteenth century, Los Angeles had become the intersection of several migrations—blacks from the South, Asians from China, and Native persons all migrated to California, with each group being systematically discriminated against, both in law and in its administration. The city and its police force condoned such behavior.

During the early 1900s the police in Los Angeles struggled to cover a sprawling land area, with continuing problems of lawlessness, corruption, and graft that took on more institutional forms in the 1920s and 1930s. Los Angeles in the early 1900s was a "machine politic" city. Political parties and "bossism" governed the city, and the appointment of police chiefs was at the whim of politicians. Political processes were in a constant state of turmoil resulting in the appointment of sixteen chiefs between 1900 and 1923. Despite such overt political interference, a civil service system was started in 1903, and the police force was increased to two hundred men. Gambling and vice prevailed in the latter half of the nineteenth century, and while periodically challenged by reformers of the time, rarely was affected in any meaningful way by such challenges.

Beginning in 1920 and for the two decades to follow, corruption of local government and the department continued unrestrained. This was the Prohibition Era and Los Angeles, known for its openness to vice and other forms of corruption, attracted all who would profit from such a wide-open city. Vice and other corrupt behavior flourished in large measure in the absence of legal action taken against such offenders.

Between 1919 and 1923, there were eight different police chiefs for the city of Los Angeles. Each of these chiefs faced a politically corrupt government and clear resistance to reform. After years of leadership turnover and a loosely knit organization August Vollmer, chief of the Berkeley (California) Police Department, agreed to serve for one year as the Los Angeles chief. Vollmer reorganized the department emphasizing efficient administration and scientific investigation. He required that professional officers be completely free of political influence, and he wanted to obtain the most intelligent, dedicated individuals available. Vollmer accomplished many things during his brief tenure as chief. Working conditions were improved, professional standards were established, and division of the city into major police areas was accomplished, thereby organizing police services under one command in several areas of the city. Unfortunately, when his year was up, politics again took over and remained a dominating influence until 1938 and a series of major reforms were instituted. Nonetheless, in one short year Vollmer had placed the LAPD on the road to professionalism.

James E. Davis followed Vollmer as chief of police in 1926, reinforcing the course of the department set by Vollmer, by emphasizing marksmanship, traffic enforcement, tracking down wanted criminals (known as the Dragnet system), emphasizing professionalism in police behavior, and, in his return to the role of chief of police in Los Angeles after a brief hiatus, focusing the department on the "Red Menace," communism. In this latter activity, Davis' LAPD returned to using highly questionable practices. Davis ultimately fell victim to corruption within and outside of the department, and was demoted to deputy chief in charge of traffic.

In the decade between the late 1930s and late 1940s, the LAPD continued to struggle with corruption and with the shifting social times characterized by World War II, labor strife, and the beginning of urban riots. Several chiefs came and went, but the department was being primed for a major reform, led by Chief William H. Parker.

The LAPD in Modern Times

William H. Parker took office during the city's centennial in 1950. He remained chief until his death sixteen years later, longer than any chief in the history of the LAPD. His tenure and leadership brought him and the LAPD international renown. Parker's innovations were many: He streamlined the LAPD to increase accountability and efficiency, rigidly enforced civil service procedures to ensure that ability and not political connections were the basis of promotions, insisted that the public be kept informed of department activities, demanded discipline, eliminated wasteful spending, and pioneered narcotics and civil rights enforcement. Governments throughout the world sought him out for his expertise and administrative acumen. For many, he remains the prototype of the quintessential professional police chief. His death in 1966 ended an era, perhaps the most productive and renowned in the history of American municipal law enforcement. Another tough-minded chief, Ed Davis, succeeded Chief Parker.

Chief Ed Davis was one of the department's more flamboyant and outspoken chiefs, frequently being quoted in the news media for various "outrageous" statements. A strong, no-nonsense leader, he once confided that to be a good chief in Los Angeles, "You had to be a tough son of a bitch." He implemented the basic car plan concept, bringing the police officer and the community closer together. An officer was no longer subject to a rapid succession of reassignments. Instead, he was assigned to the same area day in and out, creating a "territorial imperative," or officer ownership of the community policed. Chief Davis inaugurated the management principles, which continue to guide the department. These twenty principles stress the importance of public participation in crime prevention, of friendly enforcement, and the police–community partnership. Upon retiring from the police service, Chief Davis entered politics as a state senator.

Daryl F. Gates succeeded Chief Ed Davis in 1978. Gates inherited adversity—reduced resources due to the passage of Proposition 13 and increased demand for police services. He faced a court-ordered hiring injunction and a debilitated pension system. At that time massive tax cuts severely limited money for improvements. As a result, LAPD morale—which had increased during Parker and Davis eras—declined. Doing more with less became mandatory at a time when the city's population surpassed Chicago's to become the nation's second largest, and when Hispanics and Asians by the hundreds of thousands were relocating to Los Angeles.

Chief Gates was known for his Drug Abuse Resistance Education (D.A.R.E.) program, focused on educational interventions with youth to prevent their drug involvement. He was also instrumental in creating and elaborating on SWAT—the Special Weapons and Tactics (SWAT) teams. The SWAT model has been adopted throughout the world. Gates also continued in some of the work of his predecessors, implementing the Emergency Command Control Communications System (ECCCS), which placed computers in patrol vehicles.

The highly publicized Rodney King incident in 1991, in which LAPD officers beat a motorist who resisted arrest by taking the police on a dangerous high-speed pursuit, reflected badly on Chief Gates and almost obliterated any accomplishments he claimed. The King incident and the riots that followed the court decisions that involved officers who participated in King's beating sparked a national debate about police in Los Angeles and their relationships, particularly in minority communities. The Christopher Commission in investigating the LAPD portrayed the department as a "cowboy" organization that routinely violated citizen rights, and called for sweeping changes in oversight of the LAPD. The Christopher Commission called for Gates' resignation, and he retired in the summer of 1992.

With the retirement of Chief Gates, Chief Willie L. Williams became the fiftieth chief of police and the first African American and the first chief in more than forty years from outside the department to command the LAPD. Williams focused on changing the department by rebuilding the patrol force, rejuvenating the basic car plan, and restoring public confidence in the police department.

Williams' efforts produced some modest changes in the LAPD, but ultimately his leadership was challenged internally and he fell victim to the LAPD culture. Williams left the LAPD in 1997 and was replaced by Deputy Chief Bernard C. Parks, who was a long-standing LAPD insider.

Between 1997 and 2002 Chief Parks oversaw continued improvements in the LAPD, including a reorganization of the department and the creation of a command accountability philosophy that hearkened back to the Ed Davis management principles era, which by then had lost its internal appeal. Parks was ultimately undone by a scandal that emerged in the Rampart Division of the LAPD, where officers assigned to that division were found responsible for criminality, the planting of evidence, and intimidation of witnesses and those thought to be criminal. The Rampart incident resulted in a federal consent decree being entered into by the city of Los Angeles and the U.S. Department of Justice. The Rampart incident revealed a series of unfolding events and discoveries of police misconduct inside the LAPD. The scandal began with one LAPD officer, Rafael Perez, who charged that dozens of his fellow officers regularly were involved in making false arrests, giving perjured testimony, and framing innocent people. In the end Perez implicated about seventy LAPD officers, and the scandal then turned to LAPD leadership knowledge of actions of officers. This was a low ebb for the LAPD, emerging in the aftermath of the Rodney King incident.

Chief William H. Bratton was appointed as the fifty-fourth Los Angeles police chief on October 27, 2002. Bratton, a firebrand chief of police who had made an international reputation for reforming the New York City Police Department, was brought to Los Angeles to gain control over a department that was seen by many as "rogue."

Bratton's efforts have been aimed at accelerating recruitment into the LAPD, increasing force size, and implementing reforms outlined in the federal consent decree. An advocate of no-nonsense management and command accountability, Bratton is moving the department toward greater area decentralization while at the same time increasing accountability of the police to their local communities. Using programs such as COMPSTAT, which Bratton made famous in New York, he is trying to return the LAPD to its claim of a high level of police professionalism.

JACK R. GREENE

See also **Accountability; American Policing: Early Years; Civil Restraint in Policing; Community Attitudes toward the Police; Corruption; Drug Abuse Resistance Education (D.A.R.E.); Independent Commission on the Los Angeles Police Department (The Christopher Commission); Police in Urban America, 1860–1920; Vollmer, August**

References and Further Reading

The Los Angeles Police Department. http://www.lapdonline.org.

M

MANAGING CRIMINAL INVESTIGATIONS

One of the primary functions of a law enforcement agency is the investigation of crime. The study of criminal investigations is inherently multifaceted, by its very nature, in that there is a plethora of different types of crimes to be investigated. In small jurisdictions, where there is a limited number of criminal investigators, the investigators are forced to be generalists in that they have to have the knowledge to investigate various types of crimes, including crime scene processing. In larger agencies where there are a larger number of investigators, there are specialized units consisting of investigators or detectives who are assigned to their particular unit based on their expertise. In such cases, the criminal investigations division is separated into such units as persons (such as homicides, criminal sexual conduct, and assaults), property (such as grand theft auto, burglary, larceny, vandalism), narcotics and vice, crime scene, internal affairs, and juvenile.

Whether they are generalists or specialists, it is imperative that investigators utilize the same basic fundamentals, elements, and principles in order to achieve the same goals and objectives. Ideally, a systematic approach that is closely managed and monitored should ensure the successful resolution of an investigation.

This article is designed to provide the reader with a basic understanding of the role and intent of criminal investigations, how the criminal investigative function is assessed, and what measures have been put into place to determine effectiveness. The concept known as managing criminal investigations (MCI) will be explained, as well as how and why it came to be.

To fully understand the function of the criminal investigative process, its role in law enforcement, and the need for assessment, it is important to understand the history of law enforcement and the inception of the criminal investigations division.

American society has experienced significant changes in virtually every aspect of its existence. These changes did not occur overnight, but through the slow process of social evolution. Law enforcement, like many other social institutions, has evolved into what it is today as a result of societal changes. As society changed, law enforcement techniques and philosophies have adapted new strategies, leading to new policies, procedures, and methods of assessment (Caldwell 2001).

The foundations of modern law enforcement can be traced back to England as early as 900 C.E., with the emergence in American law enforcement dating to the country's beginnings in the seventeenth and eighteenth centuries. However, it was not until 1857 that the New York Police Department implemented the first nonuniformed detectives division (Lyman 2002). Thereafter, larger jurisdictions followed suit and the criminal investigations divisions (CIDs) were born across the United States.

The widespread inception of CID units was not without problems. Patrol officers were selected for CID units based upon friendships or clout and political considerations (Lyman 2002). The public was less than satisfied with the service provided by law enforcement agencies and did not feel that the investigators were capable of performing their duties. As a result, citizens would pay private companies, such as the Pinkerton National Detective Agency, to conduct criminal investigations (Maltz 1999). The Justice Department's Bureau of Investigations, developed in 1907, was also very ineffective. In 1924, the agency was renamed the Federal Bureau of Investigation and a new director, J. Edgar Hoover, took office and made it a goal to clean up the corruption.

In the late 1920s, the media began a public outcry by printing articles announcing crime waves. As a result, the International Associations of Chiefs of Police (IACP) created the Uniform Crime Reporting (UCR) program, in 1929, in an effort to collect data on national crime statistics to disprove media accounts of a crime wave (Maltz 1999). In the late 1960s, crime became even more of a public concern, and as a result, in 1967 crime control was the major campaign platform in the

Johnson–Goldwater presidential race (Osterburg and Ward 2004).

Following that, federal funds were made available to improve law enforcement, as a whole. The National Crime Victimization Survey (NVCS) was developed in 1973 and was linked to the UCR in an effort to determine the relationship between the effectiveness of arrest and the overall relationships between law enforcement agencies. Around the same time, criminal investigations divisions came under scrutiny for the first time. In the early 1970s, the National Institute of Law Enforcement and Criminal Justice awarded federal funds to corporations to conduct nationwide studies of criminal investigations divisions to determine how police investigations were organized and managed.

There were two significant studies that paved the way to what is now referred to as managing criminal investigations, or MCI. The RAND Corporation and the Police Executive Research Forum (PERF) conducted research to determine how criminal investigations could be more effective (Osterburg and Ward 2004). Information for the research was obtained from various agencies from across the United States, the UCR, and the NVCS. A collaboration of the two studies produced guidelines and suggestions aimed at improving the criminal investigative function (Champion and Hooper 2003). The guidelines produced consisted of five elements and four considerations.

The five proposed elements recommended addressing the following issues:

1. The initial or preliminary investigation
2. Case screening
3. Follow-up investigation and management of ongoing investigations
4. Police–prosecutor relations
5. Continuous monitoring of the investigative process

Further, four considerations were adopted that would assist law enforcement agencies in governing the assessment of the investigative function: Maintaining an account of

1. The number of arrests
2. The number of cases cleared
3. The number of convictions
4. The number of cases accepted for prosecution

The primary purpose of MCI is to improve the efficiency and effectiveness of criminal investigations by providing a framework by which cases are assigned, managed, audited, and closed. Law enforcement agencies began putting the concept of MCI to work by revamping departmental policies, procedures, and assessment methods to incorporate the aforementioned elements and considerations of MCI with basic criminal investigations functions. Before taking a more in-depth look at MCI strategies, a definition of criminal investigations will be provided, along with the intent or responsibilities of criminal investigations, which will provide a clearer understanding of how MCI strategies fit into the grand scheme of things.

Criminal investigations has been defined as "the collection of information and evidence for identifying, apprehending, and convicting suspected offenders" (Osterburg and Ward 2004). The primary responsibility of a criminal investigative unit is to determine if a crime has been committed. If so, the second step of the investigation would be to determine whether the crime was committed in their particular jurisdiction. Primary responsibilities of the criminal investigator also include collecting and preserving physical evidence, legally obtaining information pertaining to the crime, recovering stolen property, identifying suspects and witnesses, apprehending perpetrators, preparing cases for court, and serving as a witness in court.

After determining whether a crime has been committed and the matter of jurisdiction is cleared up, the case investigation begins with a preliminary investigation. One of the main goals of the preliminary investigation is to identify leads or clues as to the identity of the offender and to locate and preserve evidence. The preliminary investigation begins the moment the primary patrol officer is dispatched to a call for service. Patrol officers begin looking for suspects, victims, and/or witnesses while en route to the incident location, in case anyone has fled the scene. The primary patrol officer should obtain as much suspect, victim, and/or witness information from the dispatcher as possible while en route to the scene. Being well informed will assist the primary patrol officer with developing a plan of approach prior to his or her arrival on the scene.

The preliminary investigation may be sufficient to bring the case to a satisfactory conclusion, thus eliminating the need for a follow-up investigation. However, complicated investigations may require additional efforts beyond those listed above. In such instances, an investigator from the criminal investigations division (CID) may be notified and respond to the scene. Upon arrival of the investigator, the initial follow-up investigation begins.

The follow-up investigation should be conducted in a methodical manner, just as was the preliminary investigation, so as to not disturb the crime scene. The investigator should be briefed by the primary patrol officer before beginning the investigation. The investigator may also want to speak with the victim, witnesses, and perpetrator, if applicable, to clarify or expand upon information obtained by the primary patrol officer, before processing the crime scene or contacting the crime scene unit. Should the CID supervisor feel that there are potential solvability factors that were not seen by the primary patrol officer, he or she will assign the case to a criminal investigator for follow-up investigation.

The purpose of the follow-up investigation is to discover additional information in order to clear a case, identify and arrest an offender, recover stolen property, gather additional evidence, and present this evidence in court. The follow-up investigation may require that the assigned criminal investigator review and analyze all previous reports prepared in the preliminary stage, check department records for other reports of like nature or with the same subject, and review any laboratory examinations; conduct additional follow-up inquiries, interviews, and interrogations of victims, witnesses, responding officers, and/or suspects; seek additional information through interviews of uniformed officers, informants, or other groups; and/or plan, organize, and conduct searches and collect additional physical evidence.

Following these duties, the assigned criminal investigator is responsible for identifying and apprehending suspects, to include the use of physical and photo lineups; determining involvement of suspects in other crimes of a similar nature; checking all suspects' criminal histories at local, state, and national levels; preparing cases for court presentation by ensuring that case files are complete and accurate, that lab examination reports are on file, and that witnesses can be located. Finally, the case investigator should make a "second contact" with the victim in a case requiring follow-up investigation or when the case is closed.

As mentioned, the preliminary investigation begins immediately upon the arrival of patrol officers at the scene of an incident or upon taking a report and continues until such time as a postponement of the investigation or transfer of responsibility will not jeopardize the successful completion of the investigation. The officers assigned to the preliminary investigation will generally continue with the investigation as time and resources exist. In some instances, the preliminary investigation may produce enough evidence and perpetrator information to substantiate probable cause and result in an arrest at the scene, should the perpetrator still be present. If the perpetrator has fled the

scene, the same information may be used to obtain an arrest warrant, which may be entered into the National Crime Information Center (NCIC) computer system, until the perpetrator can be located. In other cases, the case information will be submitted in the form of an incident report, at which time the case is assigned to a criminal investigator for further follow-up investigation by a CID supervisor.

Each incident report is assigned a status by the primary patrol officer. The status assigned to an incident report was done as per the UCR until the inception of the National Incident Based Reporting System (NIBRS) in the early 1990s (Rantala 2000). The case status, assigned by the patrol officer, is based upon the findings during the preliminary investigation. The UCR provides three types of case clearances: cleared by arrest, closed by other, or unfounded. NIBRS, in effect, has provided additional or more specific case classification categories. Those categories are active, administratively closed, cleared by arrest, exceptionally cleared, or unfounded—shall be assigned to each case, as appropriate, to assist in case management and control. A description of each type of case status is as follows:

1. *Active* (open) indicates that the case is assigned to an officer and investigative efforts are active and ongoing.
2. *Administratively closed* (noncriminal incident or investigation suspended) indicates that all available leads have been exhausted, but the case has not been brought to a conclusion and investigative efforts may be resumed if new evidence or leads are discovered at a later date.
3. *Cleared by arrest* (closed) indicates that the case has been cleared by the arrest of the offender(s).
4. *Exceptionally cleared* (closed) indicates that the case has been cleared due to death of the offender, no prosecution, extradition denied, victim

declines cooperation, or juvenile—no custody.

5. *Unfounded* indicates that the alleged offense did not occur.

If the primary patrol officer is unable to apprehend the perpetrator during the preliminary investigation and there are no solvability factors apparent in the preliminary investigation of the case, the case may be immediately taken from an active status and placed in the administratively closed status. This may be done by the reporting officer, noting the lack of solvability factors clearly in the report and immediately advising the victim that the case will be suspended until investigative leads are developed or other information leading to a possible solution of the crime surfaces.

The initial report, taken by the primary patrol officer, is then reviewed by a CID supervisor for further case screening and a reassessment of solvability factors. A solvability factor is information about a crime, which can provide the basis for determining who committed the crime. Generally, departmental experience has shown that when a preliminary investigation or second contact fails to disclose one or more of these solvability factors, the case will have very little chance of being solved. CID supervisors may rely on certain solvability factors to determine whether to assign a case for follow-up investigation. Solvability factors may include whether a suspect can be named or otherwise identified or whether there is any physical evidence or witnesses from which a lead may be developed. If any of these factors exist, a follow-up investigation may be warranted. If no such solvability factors exist, the investigation may be suspended and the case may be considered administratively closed.

During the follow-up investigation, the investigator should maintain a case file for each assigned case. Some of the types of records that are maintained in the case file are copies of incident reports, investigator case log reports, copies of warrants, booking reports, statements, photos, lab reports, investigative notes, and so forth.

Upon completion of a follow-up investigation, the case file should be turned over to the CID supervisor, who will in turn document the final status of the case. A CID supervisor's log may consists of the following information:

1. Case number
2. Type of crime
3. Victims' names
4. Suspects' names (if applicable)
5. Investigator who was assigned to the case
6. Date that the case was assigned
7. Date the case was closed
8. Disposition
9. Amount of property recovered (if applicable)

The log serves as a tool in producing monthly reports that give department administrators feedback on the performance of the investigators by producing a closure rate or percentage. The report can be used to identify any possible inadequate or ineffective investigative techniques at either the preliminary or follow-up level, allowing law enforcement agencies to improve their overall solvability rate.

During the follow-up investigation, it is recommended that the case investigator maintain contact with the prosecutor. The development of positive relations between the police and the solicitor's or district attorney's office is essential in the successful prosecution of an offender. According to Osterburg and Ward (2004), there are five essential steps that should be followed to ensure cooperation and understanding between the police and the prosecutor:

1. Increased consultation between the police and the prosecutor
2. Increased cooperation between supervisors of both entities
3. Use of liaisons to communicate to police personnel the investigatory

techniques and evidence standards that the prosecutor requires to file a case

4. Improved case preparation procedures, including the use of forms and checklists

5. Development of a system of formal and informal feedback by keeping police personnel abreast or involved in court proceedings (Champion and Hooper 2003)

To measure and assess the effectiveness of MCI, law enforcement agencies have produced evaluations and case study reports of field tests. In 1979, many law enforcement agencies produced reports to the U.S. Department of Justice, via the Urban Institute, evaluating the MCI program. In an effort to show the effectiveness of MCI, reports from three different law enforcement agencies were provided.

The first agency is the Montgomery County (Maryland) Sheriff's Office (MCSO). The MCSO report covered the duration of the Law Enforcement Assistance Administration (LEAA) grant they received for assistance in implementing the MCI program, from December 1976 to August 1978. The primary focus of the MCSO was to decentralize investigative functions by involving patrol officers more in both the preliminary and follow-up investigations. Further, the MCSO replaced traditional ways of managing investigations with MCI case management procedures. The results concluded that the relationship between the patrol officers and investigators became more positive, while the relationship with the prosecutor changed very little. Finally, the MCSO reported that there was no change in the number of case clearances or the number of arrests (Nalley and Regan 1979).

The second case study is of the Birmingham (Alabama) Sheriff's Office (BCSO). The BCSO reported that they had set out to measure the effectiveness of MCI upon applying MCI strategies to the management of their criminal investigations unit.

The changes that the BCSO made were the decentralization of the criminal investigations function as well as implementation of MCI case screening techniques (Regan 1979). Their final evaluation report concluded that their two goals in implementing MCI, increasing arrests for serious crimes and increasing cases that prosecution accepted to pursue, had not been achieved. The final report provided statistics to the effect that at least 85% of the cases were cleared as needing no other follow-up or investigation. "The ratio of arrests to offenses maintained its previous pattern, fluctuating between 6% and 17% for burglary and continuing to decline for larceny" (Regan 1979). Although the BCSO reported that their goals were not met, they would continue applying the MCI strategies as a means of increasing the overall effectiveness of their investigative function.

The final report that will be examined here is from the Rochester (New York) Police Department (RPD). The RPD applied MCI techniques to four activities: managing continuing investigations, improving police–prosecutor relationships, conducting preliminary investigations, and case screenings. Police records and statistics revealed that little change had occurred, in the aforementioned areas, during or after the implementation of MCI techniques (Nalley 1979).

With the inception of the concept of MCI, criminal investigations divisions have in place a framework that will help them lead case investigations in a methodical manner. MCI considerations, in conjunction with basic investigative functions, have provided standards that will assist law enforcement agencies in becoming more effective. Further, MCI provides recommendations for governing the assessment of the investigative function from the preliminary investigation to case screening, the management and monitoring of an ongoing investigation, and the effect of police–prosecutor relations on the successful prosecution of an offender.

DAWN M. CALDWELL

See also **Criminal Investigation; Detective Work/Culture; Detectives; Investigation Outcomes**

References and Further Reading

Caldwell, D. M. 2001. *Investigating issues of law enforcement officer styles of policing and concerns when working off-duty assignments.* M.S. thesis, Arizona.

Champion, D. H., and M. K. Hooper. 2003. *Introduction to American policing.* Glencoe CA: McGraw-Hill.

Hess, K. M., and H. M. Wrobleski. 2003. *Police operations: Theory and practice.* Belmont, CA: Wadsworth.

Lyman, M. D. 2002. *Criminal investigation: The art and the science.* Upper Saddle River, NJ: Prentice-Hall.

Maltz, Michael D. 1999. *Bridging gaps in police crime data.* Bureau of Justice Statistics. Washington, DC: U.S. Government Printing Office.

Nalley, P. G. 1979. *Managing criminal investigations in Rochester, New York—A case study.* U.S. Department of Justice. Washington, DC: U.S. Government Printing Office.

Nalley, P. G., and K. J. Regan. 1979. *Managing criminal investigations in Montgomery County, Maryland—A case study.* U.S. Department of Justice. Washington, DC: U.S. Government Printing Office.

Osterburg, J. W., and R. H. Ward. 2004. *Criminal investigations: A method for reconstructing the past.* Cincinnati, OH: Anderson Publishing Company.

Rantala, Ramona R. 2000. *Effects of NIBRS on crime statistics.* U.S. Department of Justice. Washington, DC: U.S. Government Printing Office.

Regan, K. J. 1979. *Managing criminal investigations in Birmingham, Alabama—A case study.* U.S. Department of Justice. Washington, DC: U.S. Government Printing Office.

MEDIA IMAGES OF POLICING

Media images of policing abound in the news and entertainment media, television dramas and reality shows, film, news broadcasts, and other media formats. The representations of policing in these venues are frequently inaccurate, providing the public with misinformation about the nature of police work and police officers. The public opinion about police is based partly upon what it sees in the media, and these opinions are likely based on images that do not reflect reality.

Police in the Entertainment Media

Police officers are portrayed in a variety of ways in the entertainment media. Movies such as *Die Hard* and *S.W.A.T.* feature characters who are over-the-top heroes with unlimited firepower and unending bravery who eventually save people from a villainous adversary. The officers in TV's *NYPD Blue* and *Law and Order* are flawed but honest, hard-working heroes. The prime-time show *The Shield* portrays officers as rogues bent on administering street justice to criminals who never seem to get their due. Reality shows such as *COPS* largely feature patrol officers responding to the immediate needs of citizens. All of these films and shows ignore the realities of policing. In real life police resources are often limited, and officers who use illegal methods to mete out justice are the exception and not the norm. Finally, all of these venues portray police officers as crime fighters protecting the public, ignoring the service-oriented tasks police officers do as part of their job.

Analyses of prime-time police dramas demonstrate that the portrayal of policing is not accurate and paints a distorted picture of what the policing profession entails. Most of these dramas involve the officers investigating major crimes that are relatively rare occurrences in reality, ignoring the crimes that are committed the most. Rape and murder are two crimes unlikely to affect the general population, yet they tend to be the ones depicted most on police dramas (Dominick 1973, 246). This further perpetuates the crime fighting image of the police, ignoring the service functions of police officers. Real police officers frequently engage in service-oriented job tasks; very little time is actually spent as a crime fighter.

Police dramas also paint officers as being very successful in solving crimes. In reality, most crimes are not solved due to lack of evidence, unwillingness of witnesses to cooperate, or lack of a suspect. These shows also overrepresent the use of force and misrepresent the use of force against young non-Caucasian males. This can project the image that young, non-Caucasian males are dangerous and this is how the police respond to them (Mastro and Robinson 2000, 392).

One of the few accurate points in police dramas is the demographic makeup of fictional police departments. As in real life, most police-centered television dramas have primarily white male officers (Souilliere 2004, 220). Another accurate point in television dramas is the portrayal of officers as part of a team. While real patrol officers may be alone in their cars, there are usually other officers on duty at the same time. In addition, there are specialty officers that can be called in the event the patrol officer needs assistance. Frequent references to these specialty officers are made in television.

Reality-based policing shows such as *COPS* also provide the public with a look at the life of a police officer. Often these shows are not accurate portrayals, creating an image of policing that is more exciting and glamorous than it is in reality. Many of these shows focus on the patrol aspect of policing, misrepresenting the amount of teamwork that policing requires in solving crimes. These shows tend to depict officers as always being very busy while on duty. In reality, not all of an officer's duty time is spent in vehicle pursuits or investigating crimes; there are many other duties to fulfill. Some television reality shows, such as *The First 48*, focus on the detective work that must be invested in solving a major crime. While teamwork is represented, the emphasis is on major crimes and not on the minor crimes that are more common in society, further emphasizing the crime fighting image of police.

Other forms of entertainment media depict police officers and crime in a manner not true to life. True crime stories began hitting bookstores in earnest in the 1980s. Many of these portrayals brand officers as incompetent and dishonest and focus on serial murders, rapes, or other sensationalized crimes. This limits the image of the police role to the crime fighter, ignoring the service and order maintenance functions of the profession. True crime novels often inspire, and are inspired by, other forms of media. For instance, the true crime novel *Homicide* inspired a television depiction of policing in the form of *Homicide: Life on the Street*, and other novels are inspired by news headlines about major crimes (Wilson 1997, 718).

The Internet has also proved to be another source of policing images. An online search for policing nets millions of web pages for police departments, live police scanner feeds, and videos of police chases and shootings. While police department websites frequently feature mission statements emphasizing a dedication to service, other websites feature images of the crime fighting officer, with little space devoted to service and order maintenance tasks.

Police in the News Media

Similar to the entertainment media, police officers are often portrayed as crime fighters in the news media. Television newscasts frequently feature cases that officers are working on or have successfully solved (Maguire, Sandage, and Weatherby 1999, 185). This portrayal is sometimes the result of the police department working with the news media to control what information is released to reporters. Police departments tend to provide information to the media that reflects positively on the organization or that repairs a damaged reputation (Chermak 1995, 35). In effect, some police departments are partly responsible for the image projected in the news media.

Newscasts related to policing vary by venue. It appears that national broadcasts are less likely than local television agencies to carry stories related to the police. Police-related stories on national newscasts are frequently related to the FBI and not local departments. Local and regional news stations report more frequently on policing, but the type of images projected varies by location. Newscasts in smaller cities tend to report fewer crime-focused police activities than service-oriented activities, while those in larger cities focus more on crime. The latter also tend to report more on negative things the police have done. Overall, however, positive images of police officers are more common than negative images in news stories, and most police-related stories give information about a crime or event but are not focused on the actions of the police as positive or negative.

The Impact of Video Cameras on Media Images of Police

With the advent of video cameras, police practices can now be recorded and broadcast to the public as part of entertainment and news media. Often, the events that take place involve alleged police misconduct. There is some evidence that this type of behavior is reported more frequently in large cities than in smaller areas or on the national newscasts (Maguire, Sandage, and Weatherby 1999, 178). One issue with video tapings being released to the public is that the video camera seems to rarely catch an entire event. Often taping begins in the middle of a police–citizen confrontation and the public is not privy to the entire event. An example of this is taping of the beating and arrest of Robert Davis in New Orleans in the fall of 2005. Releasing videotapes of officers in these circumstances provides opportunity for

citizens to form opinions that may be negative based upon incomplete information (Jefferis et al. 1997, 391).

Effect of Media Portrayal on Public Opinion

The media portrayal of police officers likely has an effect on how the public views the police. The cultivation hypothesis states that repeated exposure to social issues on television influences a person's view of the world (Mastro and Robinson 2000, 386). Most people have likely been exposed to police dramas, reality shows, or news stories and have therefore been exposed to images of policing that are inaccurate. The apparent success of the police in solving crimes in both entertainment and news media may cause the public to have unrealistic expectations regarding what the police are able to accomplish. Further, the overrepresentation of violent and sensational crime in the media impacts the public's assessment of risk for that type of crime.

WENDY PERKINS

See also **Attitudes toward Police: Measurement Issues; Attitudes toward Police: Overview; Media Relations; Public Image of the Police**

References and Further Readings

Chermak, Steven. 1995. Image control: How police affect the presentation of crime news. *American Journal of Police* 14: 21–43.

Dominick, Joseph R. 1973. Crime and law enforcement on prime-time television. *The Public Opinion Quarterly* 37: 241–50.

Jefferis, Eric S., Robert J. Kaminski, Stephen Holmes, and Dena E. Hanley. 1997. The effect of a videotaped arrest on public perceptions of police use of force. *Journal of Criminal Justice* 25: 381–95.

Maguire, Brendan, Diane Sandage, and Georgie Weatherby. 1991. Television news coverage of the police: An exploratory study from a small town locale. *Journal of Contemporary Criminal Justice* 15: 171–90.

Mastro, Dana E., and Amanda L. Robinson. 2000. Cops and crooks: Images of minorities on primetime television. *Journal of Criminal Justice* 28: 385–96.

Souillere, Danielle M. 2004. Policing on primetime: A comparison of television and real-world policing. *American Journal of Criminal Justice* 28: 215–33.

Wilson, Christopher P. 1997. True and truer crime: Cop shops and crime scenes in the 1980s. *American Literary History* 9: 718–43.

MEDIA RELATIONS

For decades, law enforcement's relationship with the media was often described as antagonistic, adversarial, and strained. Police resisted dissemination of information that might threaten an investigation, create fear, or endanger the public, including the media. However, as police organizations moved from a paramilitary organizational structure toward a more open community service orientation, they began to understand the value of the media as an important resource. This organizational shift, led by national commissions on law enforcement standards and practices, has resulted in a greater emphasis on community interactions and partnerships (Sandler and Mintz 1974; Culbertson et al. 2000). One result of this shift was enhanced police–media relations.

For many contemporary police administrators, media relations is the most important aspect of a community outreach program. Today, the police see the many benefits of cooperating with the media. The media often are useful vehicles for making public appeals for information important to a case, they promote crime prevention efforts, and they can help to sell the value of agency services to local taxpayers who may be voting on a bond issue (Dwyer and Motschall 1996). Recognizing the ability of the media to reach specialized target publics and affect public opinion, large police departments are hiring public relations firms to design media campaigns that address image problems or recruitment efforts (Becton et al. 2005).

Commenting on the importance of police communication, one public relations executive asserted that "communication . . . is particularly important for a police agency. More than any other government agency, a police department needs the understanding and support of the general public and the municipal government to function to the best of its ability" (Stateman 1997, 18). Many law enforcement agencies today have instituted public information programs to inform the public about and involve community members in law enforcement activities. By educating and involving the public, police hope that citizens will put into perspective controversial events that typically involve just a few officers but that often reflect poorly on an entire department. Citizen police academies, which familiarize people with the roles, issues, and operations of police agencies, are one example of proactive communication efforts designed to "develop a relationship of trust and cooperation between the police and citizens" (Becton et al. 2005, 20).

An important factor in building positive, productive relationships with media is law enforcement's willingness to disseminate information. The media depend on timely, newsworthy information in order to inform the public. In response to the media's need for information, many medium- and large-sized municipal agencies, county departments, and federal law enforcement agencies have established public information officer (PIO) positions primarily to disseminate information to and build relationships with the media. The police PIO as media relations specialist is one important avenue for maintaining open communication.

Public Information Function

Public information is distinct from but related to other communication functions within a police organization. Community relations involves efforts to engage community groups through programs such as crime prevention, team policing, and school liaison (Miller and Hess 2002, 11). The public information function involves informing the media and the general public about these and other agency programs, operations, events, and activities. Further, the U.S. Department of Transportation's extensive *Reference Guide* for its *The Law Enforcement Public Information Workshop* states (pp. 2–3):

> In general, a PIO acts as a liaison between the agency and its administration, other government bodies, private organizations, and the media. This liaison function creates goodwill and positive publicity that enhances the agency's image and contributes to public support. The role of the PIO is to portray the agency as a professional organization whose mission is to protect life and property. Effective PIO performance will boost public support for the CEO as the agency strives to meet the needs of the community it serves. In general, the PIO should help the agency receive maximum positive media coverage.

Thus, the PIO acts as an information disseminator, primarily to the media. This often highly visible role as department spokesperson requires knowledge and skills that best represent the agency.

PIO Profile/Work Tasks

Recent studies (Motschall and Cao 2002; Surette 2001; Surette and Richard 1995) describe a profile of the PIO as older than forty, college educated (primarily criminal justice or journalism degrees), and a sworn officer who usually reports directly to the agency chief or director. PIO positions typically are considered management level, with few PIOs at a rank below the position of sergeant. PIO positions are mostly appointed, and the majority of individuals learn their duties on the job.

The U.S. Department of Transportation's *Law Enforcement Public Information Workshop Reference Guide* provides a comprehensive list of public information duties that are routinely performed by PIOs (pp. 3-4–3-6). They include:

- Reporting directly to the chief or director, representing him or her and the agency, and providing him or her with daily media information
- Handling daily media inquiries about routine investigations, traffic accidents, and other enforcement matters
- Coordinating all aspects of general public information and community relations programs that promote a positive departmental image
- Meeting all standards set by state statutes (for example, public records laws) and national organizations
- Organizing news conferences
- Responding to media requests for information (including Freedom of Information requests and supervising release of criminal information and photographs)
- Publishing the agency's newsletter
- Maintaining files (including media lists, story clippings, and photographs)

These duties illustrate the need for PIOs to have skills in or knowledge of written and oral communication, all forms of media (including print, broadcast, web based), basic research and data collection, publications management, special events coordination, media policy development, crisis management, and photography and videography.

Clearly, the primary activities that PIOs perform are media oriented. A study of the role and function of the PIO showed that of twenty-six different work tasks PIOs performed, the top six were media focused (Motschall and Cao 2002). More than 90% of PIOs write press releases, make contact with the media, and arrange for press conferences. Table 1 shows that there was little variation over time in the

Table 1   Type of PIO Techniques/Activities by Percentage of PIOs

Types of PIO Techniques/Activities	Percentage of PIOs	
	2000	1992
Write press releases	98.6	92.7
Make formal contact with media	94.4	95.1
Make informal contact with media	94.4	95.1
Hold press conferences	90.1	95.1
Advise in-house on media	78.9	[a]
Monitor, clip, and circulate stories	78.9	[a]
Make informal contact with public	74.6	73.1
Arrange for photos	69.0	82.9
Make presentations to community groups	69.0	60.9
Arrange for videos	61.9	75.6
Contact government officials	54.9	63.4
Prepare agency publications	50.7	78.0
Conduct interdepartmental training	50.7	68.3
Stage events	47.9	56.0
Write speeches	46.5	58.5
Make contact with thought leaders	40.8	43.9
Prepare departmental newsletter	39.4	*
Coordinate internal communication	39.4	[a]
Make presentations to city officials	38.0	41.4
Counsel management	32.4	63.4
Plan conventions	31.0	41.4
Prepare audio-visual materials	29.5	46.6
Conduct informal research before projects	23.9	31.7
Conduct informal research to evaluate projects	12.7	34.1
Conduct preproject surveys	12.7	24.4
Conduct postproject surveys	8.5	21.9

[a]Techniques were not on the 1992 pilot survey. They were added due to the number of write-ins.
Source: Motschall and Cao 2002, 167.
Note: N = 71.

high percentage of PIOs who perform media relations activities.

Work Techniques/Activities

A majority of PIOs also conduct in-house media advising and perform other communication or information activities, such as research, arranging for photography/videography, preparing agency publications, and conducting training. The wide range of activities suggests that PIOs need to be well trained in order to meet the information needs of the media and accurately and positively disseminate information on behalf of their organizations. The skill set may expand even more as police agencies embark on sophisticated media campaigns, which will require the PIO to know how to work with vendors, such as PR firms, media buyers, printers, graphic designers, and other specialists.

Training and Preparation

The growth in the public information function has created a demand for national and statewide professional associations that provide PIOs with training and professional development opportunities. The

National Information Officers Association (NIOA), which formed in 1989, is one such organization, whose six hundred members include law enforcement, fire, government, and emergency service PIOs from throughout North America. The association's organizers found that nearly three-quarters of PIOs affiliated with a state association had no media background or experience as a PIO. The NIOA began providing training and information on job techniques through association meetings and conferences. Today, more than half of PIOs have some media experience. The NIOA offers education, training, and networking opportunities through annual conferences and the bimonthly publication *NIOA News*. The organization plans to address future initiatives such as accreditation of PIOs and regional training (http://www.nioa.org).

Other professional associations, such as the International Association of Chiefs of Police (IACP), have established public information officer sections in response to this growing segment of law enforcement (http://www.theiacp.org). In addition, the essential skills of a PIO can be developed through programs offered at the Institute of Police Technology and Management at the University of North Florida and at the Federal Bureau of Investigation's National Academy Program, both of which emphasize media relations training. Participants learn such techniques as how to participate in media interviews, how to set up press conferences, and how to handle the media in emergency situations.

Local agencies also are encouraged to seek regional and local academy programs that provide media relations training. Often local media representatives are invited to deliver sessions, provide valuable tips, and conduct role playing on how to foster effective police–media relations. In addition, interdepartmental training programs and regular meetings with local media representatives are mechanisms for police and media to increase their level of understanding of one another's job expectations. They also are opportunities to provide feedback on important initiatives such as departmental media policies.

MELISSA MOTSCHALL

See also **Accountability; Attitudes toward the Police: Overview; Community Attitudes toward the Police; Crimestoppers; Fear of Crime; Media Images of Policing; Public Image of the Police; Television Images of Policing**

References and Further Reading

Becton, J. B., L. Meadows, R. Tears, M. Charles, and R. Ioimo. 2005. Can citizen police academies influence citizens' beliefs and perceptions? *Public Management*, May, 20–23.

———. 2005. Campaigns: LAPD uses films to spotlight benefits of joining the force. *PR Week*, January 31, 15.

Culbertson, H. M., D. W. Jeffers, D. B. Stone, and M. Terrell. 1993. Police in America: Catching bad guys and doing much, much more. In *Social, political, and economic contexts in public relations: Theory and cases*, ed. J. Bryant, 123–51. Hillsdale: Erlbaum Associates.

Dwyer, W. J., and M. Motschall. 1996. Making taxes less taxing: A public safety millage campaign. *FBI Law Enforcement Bulletin*, December, 15–18.

Miller, L. S., and K. M. Hess. 2002. *The police in the community: Strategies for the 21st century*. Belmont, CA: Wadsworth.

Motschall, M., and L. Cao. 2002. An analysis of the public relations role of the police public information officer. *Police Quarterly* 5 (June): 152–80.

Sandler, G. B., and E. Mintz. 1974. Police organizations: Their changing internal and external relationships. *Journal of Police Science and Administration* 2: 458–63.

Stateman, A. 1997. LAPD blues: We're cops. We're not PR people. *Public Relations Tactics*, April, 18.

Surette, R. 2001. Public information officers: The civilianization of a criminal justice profession. *Journal of Criminal Justice* 29 (March–April): 107–17.

Surette, R., and A. Richard. 1995. Public information officers: A descriptive study of crime news gatekeepers. *Journal of Criminal Justice* 23: 325–36.

U.S. Department of Transportation. 1994. *The law enforcement public information workshop: Reference guide*. July. Washington, DC: National Highway Traffic Safety Administration, Traffic Safety Programs.

MENTAL ILLNESS: IMPROVED LAW ENFORCEMENT RESPONSE

The trend in reduced funding for mental health services in the community and in hospital settings has continued into the twenty-first century as many states struggle to reduce huge budget deficits (Health Policy Tracking Service 2003). The consequences of this trend are fewer treatment options for people with mental illness and increased challenges for law enforcement agencies, because these agencies alone are responsible for emergency response for this population in crisis twenty-four hours each day, seven days each week (Finn and Sullivan 1987).

Law enforcement officers encounter people with mental illness in many realms—responding to calls for service from concerned family members, friends, and neighbors, conducting routine patrol of city streets large and small, and serving warrants and eviction notices. Because of the paucity of mental health resources, officers frequently must choose between leaving a person in crisis with only a short-term resolution and taking that person to jail.

When the person with mental illness is a crime victim, law enforcement faces complex evidence collection scenarios, because these individuals may confuse their victimization history as a consequence of their illness and be considered unreliable witnesses (Council of State Governments 2002). When confronted with the fact that people with mental illness are victimized disproportionately (Teplin 1999; Hiday et al. 1999), this situation becomes particularly challenging for law enforcement investigators and those organizations that provide resources to crime victims.

Many law enforcement personnel consider situations involving a person with mental illness to entail significant challenges (Borum et al. 1998; Deane et al. 1998). These encounters can be time consuming (DeCuir and Lamb 1996; Pogrebin 1987), can escalate quickly, and may result in injuries—or, more rarely, even in deaths—to officers and citizens.

Several law enforcement agencies have tracked the number of calls related to people with mental illness. For example, in New York City, the police department responds to a call involving a person with mental illness once every 6.5 minutes (Fyfe 2002). And, in one year, law enforcement officers in Florida transported a person with mental illness for involuntary examination (Baker Acts) more than forty thousand times, which exceeds the number of arrests in the state for aggravated assault or burglary. And, in 1996, the Los Angeles Police Department reported spending approximately twenty-eight thousand hours a month on calls involving this population (DeCuir and Lamb 1996).

The number of people with mental illness in jails and prisons reflects how often encounters with people with mental illness result in arrest—often for minor, disturbance-related offenses. For example, the prevalence rate of current severe mental disorder is estimated at 6.4% for male detainees entering the Cook County, Illinois, jail (Teplin 1990) and 12.2% for female detainees (National GAINS Center for People with Co-Occurring Disorders in the Justice System 2001).

These circumstances have propelled concerned community members and law enforcement officials to change their response policies and practices—both to improve outcomes for people with mental illness and to reduce injuries to all involved. Deane and her colleagues (Deane et al. 1999) surveyed the law enforcement agencies serving populations greater than a hundred thousand in the United States and identified three distinct models, two of which involve substantial changes in law enforcement policies and practices. This article reviews these important enhancements and program goals and achievements and discusses critical issues agencies face when attempting to implement such programs.

Specialized Police Responses to People with Mental Illness

Attention has increasingly focused on the work of law enforcement agencies in improving responses to people with mental illness (Reuland 2004; Council of State Governments 2002), and two centers receive federal funds to provide technical assistance to these communities (http://www.Consensusproject.org; http://www.gainsctr.com). The Criminal Justice/ Mental Health Consensus Report offers a comprehensive series of policy recommendations for law enforcement, courts, corrections, and mental health. A multidisciplinary advisory board composed of experts in mental health, advocacy, and law enforcement developed the recommendations based on the pioneering work of several law enforcement agencies (including Memphis, Tennessee, and San Diego County, California) and their own expertise.

These agencies developed two police-based approach styles: the crisis intervention team (CIT) response, where a cadre of specially trained officers responds to calls involving people with mental illness (Memphis Police Department), and a co-response model, where certain law enforcement officers pair with mental health professionals to offer crisis intervention and referral services while at the scene. A critical component to these programs is that officers volunteer to be a part of the program and must go though a selection process before they are chosen.

The Consensus Project Report provides guidance for developing such programs, but the report does not specify a particular model or approach. Instead, policy recommendations are offered for more than twenty decision-making points—from an initial failure to receive adequate mental health treatment to a release from incarceration—where criminal justice and mental health professionals must choose how best to respond to this population. It is left up to individual jurisdictions to decide where to focus their efforts (most likely where they are experiencing a problem) and which model to implement.

Several additional publications document in greater detail how law enforcement agencies in the United States have built on the work of the earlier innovators to develop these specialized police responses to people with mental illness. The Police Executive Research Forum (PERF) interviewed almost thirty agencies on two occasions to learn how core program elements—such as specialized training and partnership with mental health professionals—affect the police response from the initial point of contact through disposition (Reuland 2004; Reuland and Cheney 2005).

Goals and Achievements

Research done to date on these specialized approaches (Deane 1999; Steadman 2000; Council of State Governments 2002; Reuland 2004) has identified several core program elements, including mental health collaboration and specialized training. Program goals typically reflect a desire to improve these elements. For example, many communities aim to develop training for officers to improve their understanding of mental illness and crisis response in this population, while others hope to better their relationships with mental health professionals, people with mental illnesses, and their families. Agencies also seek to reduce injuries and provide better services to people with mental illnesses (Reuland and Cheney 2005).

Although long-term program outcomes have not been fully evaluated (Steadman 2000), agencies report that programs have achieved a great deal in the short term; many report that officers now have greater information and understanding about mental illness and have built strong, effective relationships with the community. Other data demonstrate that specialized responses reduce the frequency of arrest of people with mental illness (Steadman 2000). In addition, some jurisdictions report fewer injuries and SWAT team callouts (Reuland and Cheney 2005). A vast majority of the agencies PERF surveyed noted that strong partnerships with mental health service providers and people with mental illness and improved awareness of mental illness are critical to fostering better long-term outcomes for people with mental illness.

Core Element: Training

Agency training is so critical because so many different law enforcement staff members—from dispatchers, who must assess the nature of the call and dispatch it appropriately, to patrol officers, who must deescalate crises and select appropriate responses—play a crucial part in successfully handling calls involving people with mental illness. Like this nation's population, however, some of these personnel lack information and skills critical to responding effectively to these encounters.

Existing academy training requirements on effective response to people with mental illnesses are typically limited—most states require only two- to four-hour training blocks for officer certification, with little or no follow-up training required. The specialized approaches provide extensive training blocks—often forty hours—about mental illness assessment, crisis de-escalation techniques, and ways to determine appropriate responses to calls for service involving mental illness.

Several challenges exist for agencies implementing specialized training. For example, there is a lack of qualified trainers locally, and smaller or rural areas may lack resources either to send officers to outside training or to pay outside experts. In addition, although some topics related to policing and people with mental illness are standard, many topics must be tailored to a locality's available resources and philosophy about their response. This takes time and expertise and can be costly for communities with limited resources.

The Consensus Project report recommends that law enforcement agencies develop curricula in collaboration with mental health professionals, advocates, and consumer groups to offset these challenges (Council of State Governments 2002). The training should consist of standardized sections that provide an issue overview and teach skills needed to identify behavior that may be caused by a mental illness, to deescalate a crisis situation, to select the most appropriate police response, and, if needed, to reduce use of force. Additional sections should reflect local circumstances, and the training must offer opportunities for experiential learning. These training techniques are not didactic and can include ride-alongs, both with police and crisis workers, and visits to local mental health centers. These training events share day-to-day experiences of people with mental illness with officers who serve them and enlighten mental health partners about the realities of law enforcement.

Core Element: Collaboration

Strong collaboration among local advocates, consumers, medical and mental health professionals, and law enforcement will directly impact the quality and continuity of services provided to people with mental illness. Such collaborations promote effective communication on policy development, including ways to effect timely transfer of people with mental illness to the mental health system and to access mental health specialists on scene. Working in partnership with various stakeholders also supports innovative solutions to intransigent problems.

Collaboration is particularly important for programs aimed at diverting people with mental illness from jail. Diversion requires patrol officers to make a decision that a person would be more appropriately served through mental health treatment. And, although police officers may know about the availability of mental health services, department policy or state legislation may create pressure to select the "safest" response to avoid liability. Officers may fear that responses other than arrest may result in injury to the person or others or that the person will not receive proper treatment and will be back "on the streets." Therefore, an officer's fear of civil and criminal liability may prohibit him or her from selecting an alternative, perhaps more appropriate, response to people with mental illnesses. Collaboration with mental health partners can shape policies to encourage well-trained officers to use their discretion to select the most appropriate response, not the "safest" response.

In the PERF interviews, the agencies agreed that the police executive is crucial to the collaboration, as are mental health professionals, advocates, and consumers. However, some stakeholders may be more motivated than others and may face challenges engaging needed partners. The key to overcoming this challenge in all types of partnerships is to make sure that partners have a stake in the problem. Law enforcement agency executives are not likely to partner with mental health providers if they do not see that there is a problem with the current response. Similarly, mental health providers may be reluctant to partner with police if they perceive that the enhanced response will overtax already strained community resources. Partnership success is often a function of strong interpersonal relationships at the executive level, but this foundation can falter from staff turnover. An antidote to this challenge is the involvement of all organizational levels in transformational learning experiences noted above and in crafting the program within the agency from the outset.

Critical Considerations for Law Enforcement

Program implementation of any kind in law enforcement agencies is challenging. For specialized approaches such as those described here, demanding close partnerships with several disciplines and focusing on mental illness (around which significant stigma exists), several considerations are paramount for success.

First, as law enforcement approaches to improving the response to people with mental illness proliferate and become adapted, agencies will have more choices about which program elements and features to implement. It is critical that communities spend time adapting the approach to make it fit within the jurisdictional confines. The factors that may affect which program is best for the jurisdiction include, among other things, the department philosophy and community mental health resources. For example, CIT programs are well suited to agencies that support specialized teams. For agencies that follow a more generalized approach to policing, variations on the CIT model will likely be more appropriate and encounter less resistance.

Second, these specialized approaches require police officers to fill a crisis management role that is quite distinct from crisis management in other situations. For example, officers are typically trained to display their authority to gain control of a situation. In situations involving people with mental illness, however, officers must downplay this authority—by standing back and speaking softly in a nonthreatening way—since authoritative displays can exacerbate the crisis situation. Officers who choose to become involved in the specialized response—and volunteering for this role is strongly suggested by agencies—they must be able and ready to switch their tactics, depending on the assessment they make of the situation. The recruitment and selection process for these officers therefore is critical.

Third, because evaluation is so important to securing state and federal funding, practitioners must build into their programs mechanisms for measuring their success. Evaluation requires that communities set measurable goals and objectives and be able to track their progress with objective data collection. When an agency or community decides that it is going to embark on such a program, evaluation must be considered at the outset of program development so that baseline data may be collected against which future processes and outcomes can be compared.

Law enforcement agencies typically face challenges in collecting data about patrol situations that do not involve a crime. Although patrol officers may complete forms for incidents, they predominantly collect information for those calls that result in arrest, and the information is tailored to other reporting requirements. As a way to collect information on specialized police responses to people with mental illness, many agencies have required officers to complete a tracking form designed specifically for their response protocol. These forms typically capture information related to the cause of the disturbance, the behavior of the person with mental illness (including violence and alcohol or drug use), and the disposition. Data collection also permits partners to communicate about problems that arise and develop solutions to manage them.

Future Directions

In recognition of the promise of these kinds of specialized approaches, the Mentally Ill Offender Treatment and Crime Reduction Act (Sec. 1194), was approved by Congress and signed into law by the president in October 2004. If appropriated at the recommended level, this law would authorize $50 million in federal grants to promote criminal justice and mental health agency collaboration at the state and local level to improve responses to people with mental illness who come to the attention of the criminal justice system. Grants can be used to develop pre- and postbooking interventions (including crisis intervention teams and law enforcement training), as well as other diversion programs in court and correctional settings (http://www.consensusproject.org).

This law will allow more communities to attempt these types of specialized approaches. As these communities innovate and explore these programs, continual adaptation will occur. This situation presents a unique opportunity to conduct more rigorous evaluation of these approaches to determine which elements have the most impact on the stated goals—perhaps most important, the goal of improving the health and well-being of people with mental illness.

MELISSA M. REULAND

See also **Community-Oriented Policing: Practices; Nonlethal Weapons: Empirical Evidence; Problem-Oriented Policing; Psychology and the Police**

References and Further Reading

Borum, Randy, Martha Deane, Hank Steadman, and Joseph Morrissey. 1998. Police perspectives on responding to mentally ill people in crisis: Perceptions of program effectiveness. *Behavioral Sciences and the Law* 16: 393–405.

Council of State Governments. 2002. *Criminal justice/mental health consensus project report*. New York: Council of State Governments.

Deane, Martha, Hank Steadman, Randy Borum, Bonita Veysey, and Joseph Morrissey. 1999. Emerging partnerships between mental health and law enforcement. *Psychiatric Services* 50 (1): 99–101.

DeCuir, Walter, Jr., and H. Richard Lamb. 1996. Police response to the dangerous mentally ill. *The Police Chief*, October, 99–106.

Finn, Peter, and Monica Sullivan. 1987. *Police response to special populations*. Washington, DC: U.S. Department of Justice.

Fyfe, James. 2002. Director of training, New York City Police Department. Personal communication.

Health Policy Tracking Service. 2003. Mental health services budget cuts. http://www.hpts.org (accessed October 2003).

Hiday, Virginia, Marvin Swartz, Jeffrey Swanson, Randy Borum, and H. Ryan Wagner. 1999. Criminal victimization of persons with severe mental illness. *Psychiatric Services* 50 (1): 1403–11.

Memphis Police Department. n.d. *Memphis police crisis intervention team*. Memphis, TN: Memphis Police Department.

National GAINS Center for People with Co-Occurring Disorders in the Justice System. 2001. *The prevalence of co-occurring mental illness and substance use disorders in jails*. Delmar, NY: National GAINS Center for People with Co-Occurring Disorders in the Justice System.

Pogrebin, Mark R. 1987. Police responses for mental health assistance. *Psychiatric Quarterly* 58: 66–73.

Reuland, Melissa. 2004. *Guide to implementing a police-based diversion program for people with mental illness*. Delmar, NY: Technical Assistance and Policy Analysis Center for Jail Diversion.

Reuland, Melissa, and Jason Cheney. 2005. *Enhancing success in police-based diversion programs for people with mental illness*. Delmar, NY: Technical Assistance and Policy Analysis Center for Jail Diversion.

Steadman, Henry J., Martha Williams Deane, Randy Borum, and Joseph P. Morrissey. 2000. Comparing outcomes of major models of police responses to mental health emergencies. *Psychiatric Services* 51: 645–49.

Teplin, Linda A. 1990. The prevalence of severe mental disorder among male urban jail detainees: Comparison with the Epidemiologic Catchment Area Program. *American Journal of Public Health* 80: 663–69.

———. 1999. *Criminal victimization of the mentally ill*. Workshop on Crime Victims with Developmental Disabilities, National Research Council's Committee on Law and Justice, National Academy of Sciences, Irvine, CA, October 28–30.

MIAMI-DADE POLICE DEPARTMENT

The Miami-Dade Police Department is recognized as a leader in many aspects of law enforcement. However, this agency and the county that it represents have not always been the size that they are today. What is currently known as Miami-Dade County was originally established as Dade County on February 4, 1836, on the southeast tip of the Florida peninsula. The county, named after Major Francis Langhome Dade, is presently known as the "gateway to the Americas." The current demographic makeup is multiethnic and multicultural and is richly diverse. According to the 2000 census of Florida's sixty-seven counties, Miami-Dade is the most populous. Comprising 2,431 square miles, the county receives its primary law enforcement services and protection from the Miami-Dade Police Department.

The Dade County established in 1836 covered an area that encompassed present-day Miami-Dade, Broward, Palm Beach, and Martin counties and was policed by as few as three deputies. The department was known as the Dade County Sheriff's Posse. The sheriffs in the early years of the county were appointed by the governor of the state. From the turn of the twentieth century through most of the 1950s, sheriff was an elected position. This form of governing was transformed into a metropolitan form of government, a two-tier federation, in 1957 when voters approved a merger of the county's two departments, the Dade County Police Department and the Dade County Sheriff's Office, into a single Public Safety Department. This was made possible when Florida voters approved a constitutional amendment in 1956 that allowed Dade County to enact a home rule charter.

Constitutional officers, sheriff, property appraiser, supervisor of elections, and tax collector departments, according to the Florida Constitution, were able to be reorganized and perform duties as subordinate county departments. Consequently, nonelected sheriffs were appointed by the county manager to serve as director of the Public Safety Department and as sheriff of Metropolitan Dade County, a practice that remains in place.

In 1960, this newly merged agency had 623 personnel and by 1966 the number had increased to 850. The Public Safety Department's organizational structure was determined by metropolitan charter and included at the time the jail, fire protection, civil defense, animal control, and motor vehicle inspections. By 1973, the department had been divested of ancillary responsibilities and focused solely on police services. The agency continued to grow and during 1973 had twelve hundred employees. Today it employs more than forty-five hundred sworn and nonsworn professionals.

As the sophistication of its challenges grew, the Public Safety Department reorganized in July 1981 and was renamed the Metro-Dade Police Department. The new name remained in place until a countywide vote in September 1997, when the citizens of the county voted to change the name from Dade County to Miami-Dade County. Subsequently, in December 1997, the Metro-Dade Police Department changed its name to the Miami-Dade Police Department.

The continual increase in the county's population, along with the departmental growth, has resulted in making the Miami-Dade Police Department the largest police department in the southeastern United States.

The Department provides an array of traditional local and specialized police services in addition to many of the services provided by a traditional sheriff's office for the county's nearly 2.5 million residents. There are more than 1.2 million residents in the unincorporated areas of the county who receive their primary and continuous police service through the Miami-Dade Police Department.

It should be noted that the county's correctional duties, often associated with a sheriff's office, are not performed by the Miami-Dade Police Department. Rather, they are conducted by a stand-alone county department. The focus of the police services rendered by the department is provided to an area of the county referred to as the unincorporated municipal statistical area (UMSA). Due largely to its duties as a sheriff's office, many services are provided or made available to approximately thirty-five municipalities located within the county. In addition, the department offers contractual local and specialized police services to newly incorporated or existing jurisdictions.

Since 1836, the department has witnessed thirty-six members of its force make the ultimate sacrifice in the line of duty. The first recognized law enforcement official to lose his life while performing police duties in the county was Deputy Sheriff Murretus "Rhett" McGregor, who was murdered on August 9, 1895 (Wilbanks 1997), at the hands of a Lemon City saloon keeper who was being sought for a double murder.

The Miami-Dade Police Department, as of 2005, provides its professional police services directly to the citizens via nine police districts and is supported by twenty-eight specialized bureaus. Bureaus include robbery, sexual crimes, homicide, economic crimes, narcotics, warrants, strategic and specialized investigations, crime laboratory, crime scene, central records, property and evidence, personnel management, court services, and intergovernmental. Overall, the department comprises four services: departmental, investigative, police, and support. The personnel structure starts with the rank of police officer (deputy sheriff) and rises through a variety of positional classifications. The primary positions, in order of promotional advancements, are sergeant, lieutenant, captain, major, division chief, assistant director, deputy director, and director.

The diversity of the department is evident: Its personnel makeup mirrors the county's demographics. In 1997, the department witnessed its first Hispanic director, Carlos Alvarez, who rose through the ranks, was appointed, and proudly led the agency for approximately seven years. Following his retirement, the department again witnessed a first when Robert Parker, an African American, was appointed as director of the agency after attaining and serving in nearly every rank the department has to offer.

The department has and continues to receive accolades for many of its innovative approaches to the variety of challenges it has faced over the decades. From the department's approach to airline crashes in the Everglades and to natural disasters to its community programs and crime reduction initiatives, all have been used as models for agencies throughout the world.

MICHAEL R. RONCZKOWSKI

References and Further Reading

Miami-Dade Police Department. 2005. *Embracing the future—Annual report. 2004–2005.* Miami, FL: Miami-Dade Police Department
Miami-Dade Police Department. 2005. *Police Chief Magazine.* http://policechiefmagazine.org (accessed October 10).
Wilbanks, William. 1997. *Forgotten heroes: Police officers killed in Dade County 1895–1995.* Nashville, TN: Turner Publishing Co.

MILITARIZATION OF THE POLICE

Introduction: Blurring Military and Police

The trends discussed in this article constitute nothing short of a momentous historical change: The traditional distinctions in law, policy, and culture—between military, police, and criminal justice—are blurring (Kraska 1993, 2001). A few examples include the following:

- The erosion of the 1878 Posse Comitatus act, which prior to 1981 strictly prohibited the military's involvement in internal security or police matters
- The advent of an unprecedented cooperative relationship between the U.S. military and civilian police at both the highest and lowest levels of organization, including technology transfer, weapons transfer, information sharing targeted at domestic security, a close working relationship in the war on drugs and terrorism, and cross training in the areas of SWAT and counter–civil disturbance and antiterrorist exercises
- A steep growth in special units within both corrections and police that are modeled after military special operations squads such as the Navy SEALs
- A growing tendency to rely on the military model for formulating crime control rationale and operations

In the past fifteen years, the clear delineation between civilian police handling internal security matters and the military focusing on external security—a longstanding feature of democratic governance around the world—has blurred significantly (Kraska 1993, 2001). These trends—the militarization of police, the militarization of the criminal justice system, and the U.S. military engaged in more law enforcement functions—have intensified significantly since the September 11, 2001, terrorist event.

Militarization: Demystifying a Controversial Organizing Concept

The concepts used to organize this analysis are "militarization" and "militarism." Despite their tone, they do not have to be used polemically. Doing so, in fact, diminishes their power to help us think clearly about the influence the military model has on different aspects of our society. To say that the civilian police, for example, are becoming "militarized" may seem to some an inflammatory claim. However, assessing whether police institutions are becoming either *more or less militarized* is a worthwhile academic pursuit, and it can be accomplished through empirical evidence and rigorous scholarship and by avoiding emotional value judgments. Of course, the integrity of this endeavor hinges on the clarity of our concepts.

Militarism, in the most basic terms, is an ideology geared toward solving problems. It is a set of beliefs, values, and assumptions that stresses the use of force and threat of violence as the most appropriate and efficacious means to solve problems. It emphasizes the use of military power, hardware, operations, and technology as its primary problem-solving tools. *Militarization* is the implementation of the ideology—militarism. It is the process of arming, organizing, planning, training for, and sometimes implementing violent conflict. To militarize means to adopt and apply the central elements of the military model to an organization or particular situation.

To say that the police are becoming more militarized, therefore, is simply referring to the process whereby civilian police increasingly draw from, and pattern themselves around, the military model. Four dimensions of the military model provide us with tangible indicators of militarization:

- Cultural—martial language, style (appearance), thinking
- Organizational—martial arrangements such as "command and control" centers (for example, COMPSTAT) or elite squads of officers patterned after military special operations
- Operational—patterns of activity modeled after the military such as

in the areas of intelligence, supervision, handling high-risk situations, or war-making/restoration (for example, "weed and seed")
- Material—martial weaponry, equipment, and advanced technology

Put in this way, it should be clear that since their inception, the civilian police have shared many of these features, at least to some extent, with the military. After all, the foundation of military and police power is the same—the state-sanctioned capacity to use physical force to accomplish their respective objectives (external and internal security) (Kraska 1994). The police were developed, in fact, as a civilian alternative to the military for the sake of maintaining domestic security.

The real concern when discerning police militarization is one of degree, or put differently, the extent to which a civilian police body is militarized. Militarization must be conceived of on a continuum: Any analysis of militarization among civilian police has to focus on where the police fall on the continuum and in what direction they are currently headed (Kraska 1999).

The Rise of Police "Paramilitarism"

Based on this conception, there is no doubt that the U.S. police have moved much farther down the militarization continuum in the past fifteen years. This trend is not necessarily at odds, at least operationally, with community policing reform efforts (Kraska 2001).

I began documenting this trend by conducting an intense, two-year ethnography on a multijurisdictional SWAT team (Kraska 1996). This ground-level research demonstrated that police paramilitary units (PPUs) derive their appearance, tactics, operations, weaponry, and culture to a significant extent from military special operations. It is important to note that PPUs are only closely modeled after these teams; clearly there are also key differences between a police paramilitary unit and a military special operations unit—this is why they are referred to as police *para*military and not military units.

With full battle dress uniforms (BDUs), heavy weaponry, training in hostage rescue, dynamic entries into fortified buildings, and some of the latest military technology, it became obvious that these squads of officers are significantly farther down the militarization continuum—culturally, operationally, and materially—than the traditional, lone cop on the beat or road patrol officer.

It also showed that the paramilitary culture associated with SWAT teams is highly appealing to a certain segment of civilian police. As with special operations soldiers in the military, they see themselves as the elite police, involved in real crime fighting and danger. A network of for-profit training, weapons, and equipment suppliers heavily promotes paramilitary culture at police shows, in police magazine advertisements, and in training programs sponsored by gun manufacturers such as Smith & Wesson and Heckler & Koch. The "military special operations" culture—characterized by a distinct technowarrior garb, heavy weaponry, sophisticated technology, hypermasculinity, and dangerous function—is nothing less than intoxicating for its participants (Kraska 1996).

Two independently funded national-level surveys of both large and small police agencies yielded data documenting the certain militarization of a significant component of the U.S. police (Kraska and Kappeler 1997; Kraska and Cubellis 1997). This militarization is evidenced by a precipitous rise and mainstreaming of PPUs. As of 1996, 89% of American police departments serving populations of fifty thousand people or more had a PPU, almost double what existed in the early 1980s. Their growth in smaller jurisdictions (agencies serving between twenty-five people and fifty-thousand people) has been even more pronounced. There was an increase in the number of units in these small locales of about 175% between 1985 and 1996. Currently, about 70% of those small town agencies have a PPU.

While formation of teams is an important indicator of growth, these trends would mean little if these teams were relatively inactive. This was not the case. There had been an increase in the total number of police paramilitary deployments, or call-outs, of more than 1000% between 1980 and 1996. In addition, nearly 20% of PPUs conduct proactive patrol work in high-crime areas and are used as the "spearhead" for "crime sweep" operations. Today there are an estimated forty thousand SWAT team deployments a year conducted among those departments surveyed; in the early 1980s, there was an average of about three thousand (Kraska 2001). The trend line demonstrated that this growth began and peaked during the drug war of the late 1980s and early 1990s.

The No-Knock/Quick-Knock Phenomenon

These figures would not be controversial if this increase in teams and deployments was due to an increase in the PPU's traditional and essential function—a reactive deployment of high-risk specialists for particularly dangerous events already in progress, such as hostage, sniper, or terrorist situations. Instead, more than 80% of these deployments were for proactive drug raids, specifically "no-knock" and "quick-knock" dynamic entries into private residences, searching for contraband. This pattern of SWAT teams primarily being engaged in surprise contraband raids held true for the largest as well as the smallest communities. PPUs had changed from being a periphery and strictly reactive component of police departments to a proactive force actively engaged in fighting the drug war.

What exactly are no-knock or quick-knock raids? In essence, they constitute proactive contraband raids. The purpose of these raids is generally to collect evidence (usually drugs, guns, and/or money) from inside a private residence. This means that they are essentially a crude form of drug investigation.

A surprise "dynamic entry" into a private residence creates conditions that place the citizens and police in an extremely volatile position, necessitating extraordinary measures. These include conducting searches often during the predawn hours, usually in black military BDUs, "ninja" style hoods, and military helmets; a rapid entry into the residence using specialized battering rams or entry explosives; the occasional use of flash-bang grenades designed to temporarily disorient the occupants; a frantic room-by-room search of the entire residence, with all occupants expected to immediately comply with officers' screamed demands to get into the prone position; and, handcuffing all occupants. If a citizen does not comply immediately, more extreme measures are taken—these situations may involve nonlethal and lethal weaponry. Finally, the police aggressively search the entire residence for contraband.

I have collected well more than two hundred instances of botched SWAT raids on private residences (Kraska 2001). These are situations where either civilians or SWAT officers were killed or shot under highly questionable circumstances. (Numerous cases involved occupants opening fire on police, wrongly assuming that they were home invaders.) Botched PPU raids often devastate the communities and police departments involved, sometimes resulting in disbanded SWAT teams, laws being passed prohibiting or curtailing no-knock deployments, and expensive litigation judgments. One particularly disturbing case occurred in Modesto, California.

On September 14, 2000, federal law enforcement officials were conducting a joint drug investigation with the Modesto PD. Federal police had requested that Modesto PD deploy their SWAT team on a private residence to serve a federal search warrant. During the predawn morning of September 13, Modesto's SWAT team conducted a quick-knock dynamic entry into the residence using flash-bang grenades. As SWAT officers stormed through the home securing each room, an eleven-year-old boy, Alberto, complied with the officer's screams to lie face down on the floor with arms outstretched next to his bed. Less than thirty seconds later he was struck in the back and killed by a shotgun blast from the SWAT officer who stood over him—from all indications, an unintentional discharge. After an extensive search of the residence, no guns or drugs were found; the father named in the warrant did not have an arrest record.

This tragedy, and the massive monetary judgment won in subsequent litigation, led to the attorney general of California forming a special commission to investigate SWAT debacles and make recommendations for reform. They constructed a series of guidelines that will make it more difficult for police departments to conduct these types of raids—unless they want to risk serious litigation.

Only fifteen years ago, forced investigative searches of private residences, using the military special operations model employed during hostage rescues, was almost unheard of and would have been considered an extreme and unacceptable police tactic. Today it defines the bulk of activity most, and I must emphasize not all, police paramilitary teams are engaged in—again, in both small and large jurisdictions. (About 15% of SWAT teams have remained true to their original reactive function.) What this means is that these are not forced reaction situations; instead, they are the result of police departments *choosing* to use an extreme and highly dangerous tactic, not for terrorists or hostage takers but for small-time drug possessors and dealers. The potential benefits gained from this widespread and relatively new police practice does not, in this analyst's opinion, outweigh the potential costs.

Conclusion: Post-9/11

Attempting to control the drug problem by conducting forty thousand police special operations raids on people's private residences is strong evidence that the police, and the war on drugs in general, have moved significantly down the militarization continuum. The rapidly evolving war on terrorism will no doubt intensify the blurring between internal security and external security and between war and law enforcement that began during the 1980s war on drugs. It is also plausible to assume that our country, and those members of the government responsible for keeping us secure from terrorism, will more readily gravitate toward the ideology of militarism—both for internal and external security threats—when problem solving. Processing crime and drug control thinking through the filter of militarism will undoubtedly render a militarized response more appealing and likely.

What impact will this have on the militarization of American police? It could be that the war on terrorism provides such strong justification for the existence of PPUs that they might get out of the business of contraband raids and proactive patrol work, returning to their original status: reactive units that primarily train for the rare terrorist or hostage incident. While perhaps a welcome development, we might still be left with the problem of the regular police—operating in the context of a society that places a high level of emphasis on militarism—being increasingly seduced by the trappings of paramilitary subculture. Paramilitarism could exert even a stronger influence on what the regular police decide on for uniforms (for example, military BDUs), how they think, the weaponry and technology they employ, and the crime control solutions they devise.

Consequently, the community policing reform movement's call for democratization may be increasingly drowned out by the drumbeats of high-tech militarization. Whatever trajectory the future takes, keeping track of the movement of civilian police on the militarization continuum, and the extent to which the military becomes more enmeshed in police functions, will be increasingly important for our field of study.

PETER B. KRASKA

See also **Community Attitudes toward the Police; Crackdowns by the Police; Excessive Force; Sting Tactics; SWAT Teams**

References and Further Reading

Kraska, Peter B. 1993. Militarizing the drug war: A sign of the times. In *Altered states of mind: Critical observations of the drug war*, ed. P. Kraska. New York: Garland Publishing.

———. 1996. Enjoying militarism: Political and personal dilemmas in studying police paramilitary units. *Justice Quarterly* 3.

———. 1999. Questioning the militarization of U.S. police: Critical versus advocacy scholarship. *Policing and Society* 9 (2): 141–55.

———, ed. 2001. *Militarizing the American criminal justice system: The changing roles of the armed forces and the police*. Boston: Northeastern University Press.

Kraska, P. B., and L. J. Cubellis. 1997. Militarizing Mayberry and beyond: Making sense of American paramilitary policing. *Justice Quarterly* 14 (4): 607–29.

Kraska, P. B., and V. E. Kappeler. 1997. Militarizing American police: The rise and normalization of paramilitary units. *Social Problems* 44 (1): 1–18.

MILITARY POLICE

Military police organizations include the Army Military Police Corps (MPC), Marine Corps Military Police (MCMP), Air

Force Security Forces (AFSF), and Navy Master-at-Arms (MA) and Shore Patrol (SP). All have wide responsibilities, some identical to those of civilian agency counterparts and others unique to the missions of particular armed forces branches. Further, each branch also maintains a dedicated law enforcement unit, specializing in criminal investigations, apart from its primary policing unit. These structural separations are unlike the lines that delineate civilian detective divisions from parent police agencies. The military investigative units are the Army's Criminal Investigation Division (CID), Navy and Marine Corps' Naval Criminal Investigative Service (NCIS), and the Air Force's Office of Special Investigations (OSI).

The Coast Guard Investigative Service (CGIS) is excluded from this discussion, since the Coast Guard is not generally considered one of the armed forces. Long a part of the Treasury Department, the Coast Guard was transferred to Homeland Security under the major federal reorganization following the September 11, 2001, attacks. It continues its general policing, border protection, and public safety/rescue functions.

Historical Overview

Military police date from at least the 1100s, when the German Hohenstaufen rulers placed *provost* (pronounced "provo") marshals in charge of army units called *Kreigs-Polizei* (war police). The Holy Roman Empire, circa 1300, had provost guards under a provost marshal, and in the 1600s the French had similar *prevosts*. During the Revolution, the American Continental Army modeled its provost marshal, who oversaw a provost guard after the French *Marechausse* (mounted light dragoon company). From the end of the Revolutionary War until World War II, the Army disbanded its provost marshal units during peacetime only to reestablish them, in one form or another, during wartime.

Even the term "military police" was not in formal usage until the end of the nineteenth century, when it was coined by Brigadier General Arthur MacArthur, provost marshal of Manila, captured in the Spanish American War. During World War I, General John Pershing requested that the War Department reconstitute a military police force under the Office of the Provost Marshal General (OPMG). Shortly afterward, at the Army's first military police school at Autun, France, those new military policemen received their formal training following the British MP model.

Despite their considerable service, the military police units were all decommissioned shortly after the war. Not until the eve of World War II (September 26, 1941) were provost marshals and their respective military police units given permanent status within the Army's organizational structure, as distinct offices and a distinct corps. The reactivated Office of the Provost Marshal General continued until 1974, when the winding down of the Vietnam War, among other factors, led to its elimination.

As the Army continued to evolve, first the Provost Marshal General School and then its successor, the U.S. Army Military Police School (USAMPS), not surprisingly, relocated a number of times. From four different sites during WWII to the immediate postwar period at Carlisle Barracks, Pennsylvania, military police training was moved to Fort Gordon, Georgia, then Fort McClellan, Alabama, and finally Fort Leonard Wood, Missouri. As with its civilian police academy counterparts, the USAMPS has expanded its training from eight to twelve weeks; that more diversified training now includes, among other aspects, intelligence gathering, antiterrorism tactics, and computer crime.

In addition to their military police training, career military police personnel, especially commissioned officers, frequently attend such noted police training facilities as Northwestern University's Traffic Institute and the FBI Training Academy at Quantico, Virginia. Notably, as the armed forces' first general-service police, the MPC remains the dominant, perhaps archetypal model for other service-based units. Nearly all police from the other services at some time in their careers attend the USAMPS. Marine Corps military police, for example, have historically attended USAMPS for their recruit police training, although they train in separate companies. And Army military police train dog handlers, traffic managers, and accident investigators from all service branches at Lackland Air Force Base.

In the Army military policing is a military occupational specialty (MOS), which those joining the Army have long been able to designate at recruitment. Relying for so long on shore patrols, the Navy did not create a permanent police force until 1973. Only since 2000 has the Navy begun to recruit specifically for master-at-arms (MA) positions, rather than converting personnel from existing ratings. Masters-at-arms organize shore patrols, operate short-term brigs (jails), handle dogs, and conduct investigations of military protocol violations and minor criminal offenses. Immediately following its formal separation from the Army, and obviously taking the Army's model, the Air Force in 1947 established the Air Force Security Police (designated the AFSF in 1997).

Correctional and Criminal Investigative Units

Military police, as corrections specialists, provide custodial services for both pretrial detention facilities and prisons or, in the case of the Navy, brigs. In 1875, as part of the overall reform movement in corrections, the United States built its first permanent military prison, the U.S. Military Prison at Fort Leavenworth, Kansas. In 1915, that facility became officially the United States Disciplinary Barracks (USDB). Only in 2002 did a new USDB replace that famous prison, known unofficially as "the castle" for its imposing architecture.

The USDB is the only level-three military prison, housing male prisoners with sentences longer than five years from all the armed forces branches. The MPC provides the bulk of the unformed staff, but the other branches have their own detachment commanders and are there as medical, treatment, educational, and clerical staff. The USDB has the military's death row, and any executions would be carried out by lethal injection, in keeping with Kansas statute.

The Army, Navy, and Marines each maintain at least one level-two facility, housing inmates sentenced to confinement for from six months to five years. The Air Force uses the Navy's level-two consolidated brigs at Charleston, South Carolina, and Miramar, California, the latter housing level-three females from all branches. And inmates are assigned to level-two facilities based on geography and treatment needs, rather than branch of service. Level-one facilities, including those run by the Air Force, are scattered across the country and on bases abroad to house pretrial detainees and short-term inmates. The American Correctional Association has accredited the USDB and at least four level-two facilities.

Even more structurally separate are the military investigative units. In 1944, the Army created the CID as its centralized unit to investigate all felonies under the Uniform Code of Military Justice (UCMJ) and other related federal offenses against Army interests or personnel worldwide. In 2003, the Army consolidated the MPC, including the USAMPS and the CID, under a single command, namely a reactivated OPMG.

Interestingly, the Navy established its criminal investigative unit before formalizing its police. As far back as 1882, the Office of Naval Intelligence (ONI) handled both intelligence and criminal investigative caseloads. The first independent criminal investigative unit came in 1966 with the creation of the Naval Investigative Service (NIS), renamed in 1992 the Naval Criminal Investigative Service (NCIS).

The MCMP became a permanent unit within the Marine Corps in 1970. In 1999, the Marine Corps' Criminal Investigative Division was transferred to the NCIS, since the Marine Corps is organizationally situated within the Department of the Navy. Marine Corps and Navy lawyers also serve jointly in the Judge Advocate General's Corps. The Air Force, only one year after creating the AFSP, established its investigative OSI.

Notably, these criminal investigative units within the various armed forces branches perform important law enforcement roles that are separate and distinct from the general-purpose policing services or combat roles undertaken by military police.

Conclusion

Military police are tasked with special combat responsibilities, including escort guard duty, prisoner of war supervision, and combat rearguard, or even frontline, action, to mention only a few. Combat duties, clearly more dangerous than even those experienced by civilian SWAT teams, and structurally separate investigative units may seem to exclude comparisons with civilian departments or agencies. However, military police units can indeed be compared with county sheriffs' offices. In fact, the only duty undertaken by county sheriffs' deputies not commonly performed by military police is the service of civil court writs. Both sheriffs and military police provide nonemergency/enforcement services, transport prisoners, serve as court bailiffs, and administer jails and, in the case of the military, prisons. It is ironic that the nation's most militarized police

organization—the MPC—is most closely aligned with the most nonmilitarized of civilian policing—sheriffs' offices.

DAVID N. FALCONE and BEVERLY A. SMITH

See also **Academies, Police; Drug Interdiction; Militarization of the Police; Posse Comitatus; Sheriffs**

References and Further Reading

Craig, Ronald. 2004. Evolution of the office of the provost marshal general. *Military Police*, April, 1–5.

Falcone, David N., and L. Edward Wells. 1995. The county sheriff as a distinctive policing modality. *American Journal of Police* 14: 123–49.

Falcone, David N., and Beverly A. Smith. 2000. The army military police: A neglected policing model. *Police Quarterly* 3: 247–61.

Haasenritter, David K. 2003. The military correctional system: An overview. *Corrections Today* 65: 58–61.

Lishchiner, Jacob B. 1947. Origins of the military police: Provost Marshal General's Department, AEF, World War I. *Military Affairs* 11: 67–79.

Peck, William E. 2003. U.S. Navy Corrections: Confining sailors both at sea and on land. *Corrections Today* 65: 66–70.

U.S. Army Military Police School. 2004. History of the United States Army Military Police Corps. http://www.dutch23mp.bravepages.com/graphics/mphistory.htm (accessed April 2004).

MINNEAPOLIS DOMESTIC VIOLENCE EXPERIMENT

The Minneapolis Domestic Violence Experiment (MDVE) tested the deterrent power of police actions upon future violence in domestic relationships. Its major finding was that persons who were arrested were violent again at a much lower rate than those who were dealt with in other ways.

The MDVE is noteworthy for three reasons. (1) It was the first controlled field experiment in which police officers' responses to a particular problem (misdemeanor-level assault of a spouse or cohabiting adult) were dictated by random assignment rather than officer discretion. (2) It contributed to a nationwide trend toward proarrest policies in major city police agencies. (3) Because the findings were counterintuitive to prevailing "common sense" on the issue, the National Institute of Justice (NIJ) funded its only major initiative to confirm research, the Spousal Abuse Replication Project (SARP).

The MDVE took place during a time of changing attitudes toward violence within families and between intimates. A strong push for the criminal justice system to treat "domestic" violence on an equal footing with "stranger" violence had already resulted in a number of changes in the law that made the experiment possible. Most important was a change in the procedural rules binding police arrest powers. Ordinarily, police are forbidden to make a "probable cause" arrest for misdemeanor crimes they do not witness; they may act on probable cause only for felony offenses. Unless violence was occurring when the police arrived (and in the vast majority of cases it was not), officers could only advise the victim to swear out a warrant before a magistrate, in order to give the police the legal power to arrest the batterer. Many other circumstances thwarted that option—economic and emotional dependence, the need to care for children, transportation difficulties, and hassles at the courthouse—and most victims failed to follow through after the police left.

New laws created a time-specific window during which the police could make an arrest on probable cause in domestic violence cases: in Minnesota, it was four hours after the assault. Effectively, "probable cause" meant the victim's complaint, with or without visible injuries or corroborative testimony. Removal of the assailant from the household was presumed to protect the victim from immediate violence once the police left, though long-term consequences were not as clear.

Changing the law was justified by the greater potential for continued violence in ongoing relationships. Victims' advocates asserted that lack of action by the police provided affirmation that violence against women was permissible. Police responded that many victims not only failed to follow through but actively sought dismissal of charges when the batterer was arrested. Advocates in turn pointed to the many cases when women tried to extricate themselves from abusive conditions but were actively discouraged from doing so by the police.

The Experiment

The MDVE is the most famous of a series of studies stemming from a collaborative relationship between Minneapolis Chief of Police Anthony Bouza and Lawrence W. Sherman, of the Police Foundation and later the Crime Control Institute. Funded by a grant from NIJ, the experiment consisted of a volunteer team of police officers who responded to eligible incidents of misdemeanor assault. Thirty-eight officers were trained at the outset, and another eighteen later joined the experiment. Upon confirming an incident's eligibility, officers would take action according to a randomized sequence communicated to them by a researcher. The assailant would be arrested, sent from the scene, or "advised" and left at the scene with the victim.

A number of circumstances might exempt a case. If the offender had an outstanding arrest, an arrest would have to be made regardless of what the experimental protocol directed. An offender who assaulted a police officer would be arrested for that offense, negating the protocol as well. Police-delivered treatment was different from the protocols in 18% of the cases, primarily by arrests of resistant suspects, made when protocols indicated another action. "Arrest" in Minneapolis meant spending a night in jail, which may have created additional deterrent effect.

A total of 330 cases were entered into the experiment, and 314 deemed eligible for analysis. Two hundred of the cases were entered by a small group of twelve officers; seven officers entered only one case each, and some contributed none. Only one suspect designated for arrest was not arrested, but the "advised" and "sent" categories achieved only 78% and 73% fulfillment, respectively.

Sixty percent of the victim and suspect cohorts were unemployed; more than 40% of each group were high school dropouts. Most were cohabitating, some apparently only for a short time. Only 40% had been married at any time. Sixteen percent were Native American, 35% African American, and the remainder European American. Only 5% of the suspects had prior arrests for domestic violence, though almost 60% had criminal records. Overall, both victims and suspects in the experiment represented the "have-nots" of the city.

Victims were asked about subsequent violence at two-week intervals after the initial incident. Only 62% could be located for the first follow-up, and fewer than one-third were still involved at the six-month mark. Their responses were compared to official police records of repeat incidents, which contained all reports involving victims and suspects during the twelve-month follow-up period.

Results

The results indicated that 10% of arrested suspects committed subsequent acts of violence against the same partner, compared to 19% of those advised and 24% of those sent from the scene. (Analysis of the results "as assigned" by the protocols rather than "as delivered" by police produced repeat violence rates of 7%, 14%, and 18% in those categories.) The more complete official data demonstrate a similar pattern of fewer assault cases, but victim interviews indicated more violent behaviors, including threats and destruction of property. Several reanalyses of the experiment's data have been conducted,

revealing a calling bias (a majority of calls came from third parties, not the victim) and a potential erosion of deterrence by the end of the six-month follow-up period.

Aftermath

When announced in the context of the larger social movement, the experiment's results were widely cited by advocates pushing for more serious police attention to domestic violence. Sherman and Berk (1984b) cautioned against assuming that arrest worked best in all situations until replication could explore additional issues, including the potential for a "backfire effect" of arrest to increase future violence among the unemployed.

The publicity and the policy response generated considerable debate among researchers but succeeded in highlighting the need for replication. Other questions were raised, including whether Minneapolis was truly representative of American urban demographics, whether violence might have been displaced to other victims, and whether the erosion of victim follow-up data masked tactical displacements in violence against the victims. Concerns about interviewer effects, ineffective police mediation skills, and the effects of jail time (rather than the arrest itself) have also been voiced as problematic areas.

Replication

The importance of the issue and unanswered concerns spurred the National Institute of Justice to fund additional experiments in different cities: Omaha, Nebraska, Miami, Florida, Charlotte, North Carolina, Colorado Springs, Colorado, and Milwaukee, Wisconsin, whose replication project was directed by Sherman. Despite slight variations based in local conditions at each site, all five SARP experiments followed the Minneapolis model closely enough to allow valid comparisons.

No official data from the other sites confirmed a deterrent effect at the six-month mark (though Miami did find deterrence in one of the two official measures employed). Three (including a "borderline" finding in Omaha) observed deterrence effects in victim interviews during that period. An "escalation effect"—increased incidence of violence—was found in the official records from six months to a year after the initial contact in three cities, but no city had that effect with victim interviews. Results were slightly more positive for a period of thirty to sixty days after the initial contact, with four sites finding significant or borderline reductions in violence in the short term.

In the three cities that examined the issue (Milwaukee, Omaha, and Colorado Springs), the suspect's employment status had a significant and important impact. Suspects who were employed were more likely to be deterred by arrest, but unemployed suspects were more likely to engage in escalating violence.

The Minneapolis Domestic Violence Experiment provided the first statistically significant evidence for the effectiveness of any police policy. During the following decade and a half, many more randomized, controlled field experiments were conducted, including the Drug Market Analysis Program (DMAP) and experiments in proactive gun law enforcement. The experiment was a tipping point in police research, helping to bring policing out of the realm of craft and into that of scientific inquiry.

The experiment also helped to raise public awareness of the issue of domestic violence and prompted the police to reconsider their long-held assumptions. While many of the larger issues still remain, most notably the tendency of victims to seek temporary relief but avoid longer-term measures, one of the legacies of Minneapolis has been a sustained effort to address the problem effectively. "Preferred arrest" policies have replaced mandatory arrest, providing more latitude to officers, but victimless prosecution, mandatory counseling programs for batterers, and a growing network of shelters and assistance programs for victims continue the work begun in Minneapolis.

MICHAEL E. BUERGER

See also **Arrest Powers of the Police; Conflict Management; Crime Prevention; Discretion; Domestic (or Intimate Partner) Violence and the Police; Presumptive Arrest Policing; Zero Tolerance Policing**

References and Further Reading.

Berk, Richard A., Alec Campbell, Ruth Klap, and Bruce Western. 1992. The deterrent effect of arrest in incidents of domestic violence: A Bayesian analysis of four field experiments. *American Sociological Review* 57 (5): 698–708.

Dunford, Franklyn, David Huizinga, and Delbert S. Elliott. 1989. The role of arrest in domestic assault: The Omaha police experiment. *Criminology* 28 (2): 183–206.

Hirschel, J. David, Ira W. Hutchinson III, Charles W. Dean, Joseph J. Kelley, and Carolyn E. Pesackis. 1990. *Charlotte spouse assault replication project.* Unpublished manuscript. Washington, DC: National Institute of Justice.

Lempert, Richard. 1984. From the editor. *Law and Society Review* 18: 505–10.

Meeker, James W., and Arnold Binder. 1990. Experiments as reforms: The impact of the "Minneapolis Experiment" on police policy. *Journal of Police Science and Administration.* 17 (2):147–53.

Pate, Tony, and Edwin E. Hamilton. 1992. Formal and informal deterrents to domestic violence: The Dade County Spouse Assault Experiment. *American Sociological Review* 57 (5): 691–97.

Sherman, Lawrence W. 1984. Experiments in police discretion: Scientific boon or dangerous knowledge? *Law and Contemporary Problems* 47 (4): 61.

———. 1992. *Policing domestic violence: Experiments and dilemmas.* With Janelle D. Schmidt and Dennis P. Rogan. New York: The Free Press.

Sherman, Lawrence W., and Richard A. Berk. 1984a. The specific deterrent effects of arrest for domestic assault. *American Sociological Review* 49: 261–72.

———. 1984b. *The Minneapolis Domestic Violence Experiment*. Washington, DC: Police Foundation Reports.

Sherman, Lawrence W., and Ellen G. Cohn. 1989. The impact of research on legal policy: The Minneapolis Domestic Violence Experiment. *Law and Society Review* 23 (1): 117–44.

Sherman, Lawrence W., and Douglas A. Smith. 1992. Crime, punishment, and stake in conformity: Legal and informal control of domestic violence. *American Sociological Review* 57 (5): 680–90.

MINORITIES AND THE POLICE

Introduction

Kelling and Moore (1988) highlighted the history of American policing by identifying three general eras associated with its professional development and strategic orientations: the political, the reform, and the community eras. However, Williams and Murphy (1990) provided a minority perspective of Kelling and Moore's analysis and reframed the eras to include their impacts on enslaved Africans in America and their descendants. As a result, the political era was recast to encompass the inherent nature of policing the powerless, the reform era was refocused to highlight how the benefits of the reform movement eluded blacks, and the community era was elaborated upon by acknowledging the potential benefits and challenges of empowering and partnering with historically marginalized communities (Williams and Murphy 1990).

Drawing upon the analysis of Williams and Murphy and others, this article provides a historical overview of a select number of events that affected and continue to affect the relationship between minority communities in general and the black community in particular and local law enforcement agencies. It concludes by highlighting policy and practical implications.

Historical Tension between Blacks and Those in Blue

Tension between the police and racial/ethnic minority communities has been and continues to be one of the most pressing issues facing American police organizations (Culver 2004; Barak, Flavin, and Leighton 2001; Websdale 2001; Williams 1998). The history of American policing has been tainted by legally sanctioned, disparate service delivery and tarnished by the enforcement of racially motivated laws and statutes. Consequently, the present-day relationship between minorities and the police in America is one that has been impacted by the historical legacies of slavery, segregation, and discrimination, all part and parcel of racism at the societal, institutional, and individual levels.

The Political and Reform Eras: From Slave Patrols to Jim Crow

Compelling evidence exists that links the advent of America's modern style of policing with slave patrols. Walker (1977, 1980) suggests that slave patrols were the forerunners or precursors to American police agencies. As such, slave patrols played an instrumental role in maintaining public order by limiting slave resistance and insurrection and enforcing the existing laws of Southern societies as embodied by the slave codes (Websdale 2001). In essence, these slave codes served to regulate slave life, reinforce social boundaries, and uphold chattel slavery (Russell 1998).

Coinciding with the conclusion of the Civil War, the emancipation of enslaved Africans, and the Reconstruction of the South, the first black codes were adopted in 1865. These codes were enforced by local law enforcement. Although the black codes provided some rights to newly freed blacks, overall they helped to create a new system of involuntary servitude by criminalizing black unemployment or idleness as vagrancy and the congregating of blacks as unlawful assembly.

In essence, "the slave codes and the black codes represent two mutations of state sanctioned double standards" (Russell 1998, 22) and helped birth Jim Crow–era public policy, symbolized by the 1896 Supreme Court ruling of *Plessy v. Ferguson*. Nonetheless, two constants remained: Blackness itself remained a crime (that is, African Americans were disproportionately targeted for specific crimes such as vagrancy) and local police agencies were used as the instrument to enforce the laws.

The Community Era: From Kerner Commission to Contemporary Issues

To prevent a repeat of the riots of the 1960s and to address the more aggressive measures, negative interactions, and related effects of "saturation policing" associated with minority and poor communities, as well as the festering racial tension between the police and the African American community, the Kerner Commission recommended the establishment of police–community relations programs (Fogelson 1968; Websdale 2001). These helped to foster and further facilitate the community era of American policing.

The community era's generic approach to improving police–community relations has morphed into the more modern-day practices of community- and problem-oriented policing (COP/POP). Both approaches share an overarching philosophy of partnering with all segments of the community to better identify and understand community issues and concerns and ultimately solve community problems. Nonetheless, problems remain in police–community relations. This is evident by recalling incidents ranging from the beatings of Rodney King and Abner Louima

to the alleged "depolicing" of minority neighborhoods and communities, bias-based policing efforts that target members of a particular race or religion (for example, pulling over a disproportionate number of black drivers or suspecting someone of terrorist activities simply for being Muslim or Arab), and the excessive use of force toward members of marginalized populations.

Where Do We Go From Here? Policy Implications for the Twenty-First Century

Austin and Dodge (1992, 594) propose that "it is the reality blacks perceive that influences their discontent [with the police]. They [blacks] may base their expectations on the past and present of racial inequality and discrimination." This quote offers important policy and practical implications for local law enforcement, especially considering the contemporary context of American society and taking a more inclusive perspective of America's minority communities.

Local law enforcement agencies must be more creative and aggressive in their attempts to repair the damage done by slavery, discrimination, and past and current police practices supporting systems of racially and/or ethnically based oppression and exploitation. Likewise, police agencies and individual officers must be sensitive to the biased perceptions that persist in America, including those that have become more evident since the attacks of 9/11.

Accompanying local police agencies' efforts to engage in their duties, especially their efforts in the war on drugs and the campaign against terrorism, are public concerns about biased police practices that include racial, ethnic, and religious profiling. To address these perceptions, police agencies must become (1) more community oriented and culturally competent by inviting citizens to become involved and active participants in all stages of the recruitment, selection, training, and promotion process and (2) more transparent by embracing civilian review boards. An aggressive approach would have more impact in adapting American police practices and services to the changing landscape of American society.

Conclusion

As elucidated more than sixty years ago in Gunnar Myrdal's *An American Dilemma: The Negro Problem and Modern Democracy*, a strained relationship continues to exist between the minority community and local law enforcement agencies. Indeed, "there are remarkable and disturbing historical homologies among the control of African slaves in the American colonies, the regulation of freedmen and freedwomen during nineteenth-century Reconstruction and Redemption, and the close surveillance and punitiveness directed at blacks [and other minorities] in postindustrial inner cities" (Websdale 2001, 8). This presents a challenge for the profession of policing.

Local law enforcement agencies and individual officers of today must recognize, acknowledge, and understand how the historical legacy and practices of the police profession still affect the perception and participation of minority communities in collaborative problem solving and the coproduction of public safety and order. Creative approaches that encourage the confidence and support of the minority community can repair the damage that has been done and foster a symbiotic relationship between the minority community and local law enforcement.

BRIAN N. WILLIAMS

See also **Accountability; Attitudes toward the Police: Overview; Civil Restraint in Policing; Civilian Review Boards; Community-Oriented Policing: History; Discrimination;**

Ethics and Values in the Context of Community Policing; Immigrant Communities and the Police; Policing Multiethnic Communities; Racial Profiling

References and Further Reading

Austin, R., and H. Dodge. 1992. Despair, distrust, and dissatisfaction among blacks and women, 1973–1987. *The Sociological Quarterly* 33 (4): 579–98.

Barak, G., J. M. Flavin, and P. S. Leighton. 2001. *Class, race, gender, and crime: Social realities of justice in America.* Los Angeles: Roxbury Publishing.

Culver, L. 2004. *Adapting police services to new immigration.* New York: LFB Scholarly Publishing.

Fogelson, R. 1968. From resentment to confrontation: The police, the negroes, and the outbreak of the nineteen-sixties riots. *Political Science Quarterly* 83 (2): 217–47.

Kelling, G. L., and M. H. Moore. 1988. The evolving strategy of policing. *Perspectives on policing.* Washington, DC: National Institute of Justice.

Myrdal, G. 1944. *An American dilemma: Vol. II: The negro problem and modern democracy.* New York: Harper and Brothers.

Russell, K. 1998. *The color of crime: Racial hoaxes, white fear, black protectionism, police harassment and other macroaggressions.* New York: New York University Press.

Walker, S. 1977. *A critical history of police reform: The emergence of professionalism.* Lexington, MA: Lexington Books.

———. 1980. *Popular justice: A history of American criminal justice.* New York: Oxford University Press.

Websdale, N. 2001. *Policing the poor: From slave plantation to public housing.* Boston: Northeastern University Press.

Williams, B. N. 1998. *Citizen perspectives on community policing: A case study in Athens, GA.* Albany, NY: State University of New York Press.

Williams, H., and P. V. Murphy. 1990. The evolving strategy of policing: A minority view. *Perspectives on policing.* Washington, DC: National Institute of Justice.

MOLLEN COMMISSION

The Mollen Commission, officially the Commission to Investigate Allegations of Police Corruption and the Anti-Corruption

Procedures of the Police Department, was established by New York City Mayor David Dinkins in July 1992 to investigate corruption within the New York Police Department (NYPD).

The Mollen Commission's proximate cause was the public uproar surrounding the May 1992 arrest of NYPD police officer Michael Dowd and five other NYPD officers on drug trafficking charges by the suburban Suffolk County (New York) Police Department. It was revealed that although Dowd had been the subject of numerous corruption allegations and the target of multiple investigations by NYPD internal affairs personnel during the course of his nine-year career, none of those investigations uncovered any criminal behavior. The scandal unfolded against a larger political and social context of widespread public dissatisfaction with escalating levels of crime and disorder: New York City experienced the highest rates of crime in its history under the Dinkins administration. Dinkins appointed his former deputy mayor for public safety, Judge Milton Mollen, to head the investigation.

The Mollen Commission was the sixth major investigation into police corruption in New York, preceded by the Knapp Commission (1970–1973), the Helfand Investigation (1949–1950), the Seabury Investigation (1932), the Curran Committee (1912), and the Lexow Commission (1895). Each of these investigative entities delved into contemporary patterns and practices of police corruption in the NYPD, and each resulted in organizational changes and policy reforms designed to curtail or eliminate the prevailing corrupt practices of the day. While these reforms were moderately successful, in each instance new patterns of corrupt activity ultimately evolved within a period of about twenty years.

The 1973 Knapp Commission Report, for example, described pervasive and well-organized corruption within the NYPD, much of it related to bribery and graft

monies collected in return for protecting criminals involved in gambling, prostitution, and other vice crimes from investigation and arrest. The department's internal affairs units were restructured, and in conjunction with new anticorruption practices and management policies, they proved highly successful in eliminating these organized forms of corruption.

As the Mollen Report described, however, those structures, policies, and practices did not evolve in response to newly emerging corruption hazards or the opportunities afforded by the proliferation of narcotics through the 1970s and 1980s. It did not find highly organized forms of corruption throughout the agency, but rather discerned there were small pockets or "crews" of corrupt cops operating in a few high-crime precincts. Rather than profiting from casual graft related to vice crimes, this much smaller number of more predatory cops routinely stole cash and drugs from dealers (typically reselling the drugs to other dealers) or provided protection for drug operations.

Michael Dowd's drug-dealing activities were emblematic of the new face of corruption, and the internal affairs function was characterized by anachronistic structures and policies as well as by a high level of secrecy and management apathy toward corruption. One internal investigator, Sgt. Joseph Trimboli, testified that his pursuit of Down was routinely obstructed by superiors and that he and other investigators were hampered by an overwhelming caseload devoted largely to the investigation of minor administrative infractions. The decentralized internal affairs units did not routinely share information, they lacked equipment and other resources, and in general their investigators were not highly regarded or highly skilled.

The Mollen Commission also attempted to establish a nexus between police corruption and brutality in the NYPD, calling former officer Bernard Cawley (known on the street as "the Mechanic" because he frequently "tuned up," or beat, people), who testified that he administered at least three hundred beatings to drug dealers in a three-year police career that ended with a 1990 arrest by NYPD for trafficking in guns and drugs.

The commission also addressed the problem of police perjury. Although Dowd, Cawley, and a number of other former officers testified before the Mollen Commission in return for reduced sentences, Dowd nevertheless continued his criminal activities while on bail as a Mollen witness, plotting the kidnap and murder for hire of a drug dealer's wife and an escape to Nicaragua to avoid prison. He received a fourteen-year prison sentence one week after the Mollen report's release.

Police Commissioner Raymond Kelly, appointed following the August 1992 resignation of Dinkins' first police commissioner, Lee P. Brown, instituted a number of immediate reforms to reconstitute and strengthen the agency's internal affairs function. These reforms were further expanded and enhanced when Police Commissioner William Bratton, appointed by Mayor Rudolph Giuliani, took office in January 1994. The highly decentralized Internal Affairs Division was reorganized and elevated to the status of a bureau, and within one year its staff was entirely replaced with a new cadre of highly experienced investigators and supervisors— many of them "drafted" from among the agency's best investigative personnel.

New personnel recruitment and rotation policies and greater transparency removed much of the secrecy and suspicion surrounding internal investigations, state-of-the-art equipment was acquired, and new training programs were instituted, and the new Internal Affairs Bureau took on a proactive focus. This proactive focus involves more aggressive investigative practices, the sharing of intelligence information between the Internal Affairs Bureau and commanders of operational units outside the bureau, as well as continual monitoring and analysis of corruption allegations to identify emerging patterns and trends and to ensure that effective preventive and investigative strategies evolve in synch with those trends.

The Mollen Commission ultimately prescribed about 139 recommendations to reduce corruption through more cogent personnel recruitment and selection policies, structural changes to the internal affairs function, and improved or revised training. One of the Mollen Commission's principal recommendations was the establishment of a permanent and independent external watchdog entity to continually monitor the NYPD's policies, practices, and overall effectiveness in controlling corruption. In line with this recommendation, in 1995 Mayor Rudolph Giuliani established the Commission to Combat Police Corruption.

VINCENT E. HENRY

See also **Accountability; Codes of Ethics; Corruption; Deviant Subcultures in Policing; Knapp Commission; New York Police Department (NYPD)**

References and Further Reading

Commission to Investigate Allegations of Police Corruption and the Anti-Corruption Procedures of the Police Department. 1993. *Interim report and principal recommendations.* December 27. New York: Commission to Investigate Allegations of Police Corruption and the Anti-Corruption Procedures of the New York City Police Department.

———. 1994. *Commission report.* July 7. New York: Commission to Investigate Allegations of Police Corruption and the Anti-Corruption Procedures of the New York City Police Department.

Curran Committee Report. 1913/1997. Official title *Report of the special committee of the board of aldermen of the city of New York Appointed August 5, 1912 to investigate the police department.* Vol. II in *New York City Police Corruption Investigation Commissions, 1894–1994,* ed. Gabriel J. Chin. Buffalo, NY: W. S. Hein.

Helfand Investigation Report. 1955/1997. Official title *Report of special investigation by the district attorney of Kings County, and the December 1949 grand jury.* Vol. IV in *New York City Police Corruption Investigation*

Commissions, 1894–1994, ed. Gabriel J. Chin. Buffalo, NY: W. S. Hein.

Henry, Vincent E. 2004. Police corruption in a megalopolis: New York City. In *Police corruption: Challenges for developed countries—Comparative issues and commissions of inquiry*. Vol. 4.2 in *The Uncertainty Series*, ed. Menachim Amir and Stanley Einstein. Huntsville, TX: Sam Houston State University, Office of International Criminal Justice.

Henry, Vincent E., and Charles V. Campisi. 2004. Managing police integrity: Applying COMPSTAT principles to control police corruption and misconduct. In *Visions for change: Crime and justice in the 21st century*, ed. Roslyn Muraskin and Albert R. Roberts, 4th ed. Upper Saddle River, NJ: Prentice-Hall.

Lexow Committee Report. 1895/1997. Official title *Report of the special committee appointed to investigate the police department of the city of New York*. Vol. I in *New York City Police Corruption Investigation Commissions, 1894–1994*, ed. Gabriel J. Chin. Buffalo, NY: W. S. Hein.

New York City Commission to Investigate Allegations of Police Corruption and the City's Anti-Corruption Procedures. 1973. *The Knapp Commission Report on Police Corruption.* New York: George Braziller.

New York City Police Department (William J. Bratton, Police Commissioner). 1994. *Responses to the Mollen Commission Report*, July. New York: NYPD Office of Management Analysis and Planning.

Seabury Investigation Report. 1932/1997. Official title *Final report of Samuel Seabury, referee, in the matter of the investigation of the magistrates' courts in the first judicial department and the magistrates thereof, and of attorneys-at-law practicing in said courts.* Vol. III in *New York City Police Corruption Investigation Commissions, 1894–1994*, ed. Gabriel J. Chin. Buffalo, NY: W. S. Hein.

MONEY LAUNDERING

Origins

Law enforcement strategies change over time. The popularity of any one strategy may relate to initial perceived successes, political advantages, or technological changes that either facilitate new forms of criminal conduct or enable advancements in enforcement techniques. Money laundering is obviously not new; however, what is new is the international preoccupation with the rhetoric of fighting laundering and terrorist financing.

Traditionally, law enforcement focused on the illegal activities of the criminal enterprises, with few resources targeting the illicit proceeds. However, beginning in the mid-1980s, this changed. As the chairman of the President's Commission on Organized Crime in the United States commented in 1984: "Money laundering is the lifeblood of organized crime . . . without the ability to freely utilize its ill-gotten gains, the underworld will have been dealt a crippling blow." At that time, the attempt to seize and freeze illicit proceeds appeared to be a well thought out strategy that followed on the heels of the realization that "kicking down doors" had no lasting impact on drug trafficking.

Likewise, the "targeting up" efforts against the so-called kingpins was dubious given both the difficulty of actually convicting these people *and* the realization that the criminal operations could succeed quite well, often continuing to be run by the big-shot from a jail cell. The argument then became the too easily tossed off line: "The heads of these criminal organizations may not dirty their hands with the drugs, but they do take possession of the cash." If profits motivate criminals, then taking away the profit should reduce crime. Hence, law enforcement should go after the proceeds of crime. However, the difficulty is that despite the illegality and underworld connotations of the proceeds of crime, the laundering process itself is not an economic aberration. Indeed, it thrives and survives on the very same commercial transactions that most people utilize to sustain their own economic well-being and that drive the economy.

During the 1990s, the pressure from the international community intensified—most specifically due to the momentum and influence of the Financial Action Task Force (FATF). The FATF outlined a series of "recommendations" (that were later enhanced) that specified what the member countries ought to put in place in order to illustrate their commitment to the "war" against money laundering. Countries that did not comply were criticized and/or blacklisted for failing to put in place provisions such as a mandatory reporting regime for suspicious transactions and for failing to have a central financial intelligence unit to which all such reports could be sent. All of these changes occurred within little more than a decade. After 9/11, additional requirements were introduced when the FATF included fighting terrorist financing as part of its anti–money laundering mandate.

What Is Money Laundering?

As first described in the 1988 United Nations *Convention Against Illicit Traffic in Narcotic Drugs and Psychotropic Substances*, a comprehensive money laundering operation satisfies three essential objectives:

- It *converts* the bulk cash proceeds of crime to another, less suspicious form.
- It *conceals* the criminal origins and ownership of the funds and/or assets.
- It *creates* a legitimate explanation or source for the funds and/or assets.

To realize the greatest benefit from money laundering, criminally derived cash should not simply be converted to other less suspicious assets. The illicit source of the assets must also be hidden. The third objective, while less frequently satisfied in most money laundering operations, is no less important than the former two. The effectiveness of a laundering scheme will ultimately be judged by how convincingly the scheme creates a legitimate front for illegally acquired cash and assets. In short, money is not truly laundered unless it is made to appear sufficiently legitimate that it can be used openly. This is the objective of the final stage of the cycle. One of the keys to satisfying the objectives of the laundering process is to conduct commercial and financial transactions that appear as legitimate as possible. The more successful a money laundering operation is in emulating the patterns of legitimate financial or commercial transactions, the less suspicion it will attract.

To satisfy the aforementioned objectives, the money laundering process generally entails four stages: placement, layering, integration, and repatriation. The initial *placement* stage is where the cash proceeds of crime physically enter the legitimate economy, which satisfies the first objective of the laundering process. Once the funds have been placed in the legitimate economy, a process of *layering* takes place. It is during this stage that much of the laundering activity takes place, with funds being circulated through various economic sectors, companies, and commercial or financial transactions in order to conceal the criminal source and ownership of the funds and obscure any audit trail.

The penultimate step of the money laundering process is termed *integration* because having been placed initially as cash and layered through a number of financial operations, the criminal proceeds are fully integrated into the financial system and can be used for any purpose. The final stage of the process involves *repatriating* the laundered funds back into the hands of the criminal entrepreneur, ideally with a legitimate explanation as to their source, so that they can be used without attracting suspicion.

The placement stage is the most perilous for the launderer since it involves the physical movement of bulk cash, usually in small denominations. It is at this stage that the offender is most vulnerable to suspicion and detection and where the funds can most easily be tied to criminal sources. Most often the money must enter a financial institution, and it is now mandatory for financial institutions, in countries that have complied with the recommendations of the FATF, to report all suspicious transactions to a central financial intelligence body within their jurisdiction. The financial institutions become "enforcement" bodies in this fight against money laundering in order to detect laundering. Once the funds are placed within the legitimate economy and converted from their original cash form, the opportunities for money laundering are increased exponentially: The funds can be transferred among and hidden within dozens of financial intermediaries and commercial investments, domestically and internationally.

The above description is what a "good" laundering scheme should be. Most of the money laundering literature continues to pay homage to this U.N. definition or a similar description of money laundering and then proceeds to ignore what is required in order for criminal proceeds to be actually "laundered." In reality, what has become accepted as money laundering is the mere use or deposit of proceeds of crime. In many of the cases that are called money laundering, the illegally derived revenue was merely deposited or spent on expensive commodities with little attempt to hide the original source of the proceeds. However, in other cases, millions of dollars of criminal funds were proficiently cleansed through elaborate operations that involved numerous economic sectors, dozens of professionals, a myriad of illusory guises and techniques, and hundreds, if not thousands, of obfuscating transactions. For both analytical and law enforcement purposes, attention should be paid to how the proceeds of crime are disposed of by the criminal element—with particular emphasis on how it enters and circulates within the legitimate economy—regardless of whether these transactions satisfy the definition of money laundering.

In a 1990 *Tracing of Illicit Funds* report completed for the Canadian government, an analysis was completed on all cases identified by the Royal Canadian Mounted Police as having a large financial component. The analysis of these police cases revealed that the sectors of the business or financial markets most often used by criminal enterprises in their laundering activities or to facilitate these schemes included the following:

- Deposit-taking institutions
- Currency exchange houses
- Securities markets
- Real estate
- Incorporation and operation of companies
- Miscellaneous laundering via big purchases (vehicles, boats, planes, travel agencies, gems, jewelry, and so forth)
- White collar professionals such as lawyers and accountants

The report concluded that money laundering in Canada was a thriving industry that had demonstrated that it could utilize any number of economic sectors and services. The Canadian findings were also shown to be true elsewhere. Australia replicated the study and produced similar results, detailed in a 1992 report titled *Taken to the Cleaners: Money Laundering in Australia.*

Laundering Schemes

Laundering schemes range from the extremely simple to the extremely sophisticated. The majority of the cases that the police identified were drug related, were located in the largest urban centers, and tended to make use of nominees to conceal ownership of the proceeds. We might consider the laundering schemes falling along a continuum. The basic distinctions reflect the degree of seriousness of the schemes—serious in terms of the amount of money involved and the ongoing nature of some of the schemes.

Some cases involved a *simple-limited* scheme. These cases involved a low amount of money being laundered on an ongoing basis. A typical scheme might involve a tavern, restaurant, vending machine company, or actual laundry—any business where the inventory is flexible and dirty money can be claimed as profit from the legitimate business. There is obviously a fairly restrictive ceiling on how much money can be pushed through these laundering operations. The business owner would have to pay taxes on these claimed profits, but this amount would be thought of as a business expense. The criminal proceeds gain the appearance of legitimate earnings that could be openly used.

Some fairly simple schemes are, however, less restrictive. This second category was referred to as *simple-unlimited.* There are businesses that have such large budgets and involve such a high level of technical expertise that it is typically very hard to refute the amounts of money required in the various operations. Dredging, waste, scrap metal, and construction industries are particularly suited for long-term, high-quantity laundering activity.

The next level of schemes becomes harder to trace, because in fact "tracing" is required. We might differentiate between *serial-simple* and *serial-complex cases.* A final category would be the *international* schemes. In reality, many of the serial cases, and certainly most of the truly complex schemes, involve an international component. The *serial-simple* schemes involve a large number of financial transactions and account manipulations. The movement of the money through these accounts is designed to deceive the police. However, in most of the cases involving these schemes, once the police begin to investigate, the schemes fail to protect the illicit proceeds. The ability to follow an audit trail will reveal the true source of these funds—or at least reveal that there is no legitimate source.

The *serial-complex* schemes are by definition more complex. These schemes usually require the assistance of professionals such as lawyers and accountants. Imaginative real estate flips, complex invoice manipulations, and penetration of the stock markets may be involved. In the 1990 Canadian study, 80% of the cases had an international component. The movement of dirty money across borders provides a powerful concealing advantage. Exporting the illicit funds offshore and then repatriating the profits back to the country where the proceeds originated allows the criminals to make use of the proceeds to perpetuate their criminal operation (that is, purchase more drugs) and then make use of legitimate business opportunities such as the provisions available in some jurisdictions that allow for tax incentives for foreign investment. "Loan-back" schemes, front companies, and double invoicing are all part of any of these schemes.

The Role of White Collar Professionals

As noted above, the more sophisticated a scheme is, the more likely a professional will have facilitated the process—either knowingly as an accomplice or unwittingly by merely operating in a professional capacity. Legitimate businesses may knowingly accept cash for expensive purchases while ignoring the likely source of the funds. Michael Levi refers to the "symbiotic relationship" between otherwise legitimate businesses and laundering. Professionals such as lawyers and accountants are seen as the gatekeepers, intermediaries, or facilitators of major laundering operations. They are able to offer not only their expertise but also their status, which serves to legitimate the various financial transactions that may be part of laundering schemes.

Lawyers, for example, may serve by providing a nominee function, conducting the various commercial and financial transactions, incorporating companies on behalf of clients, and managing the illicit cash, including coordination of international transactions. It is significant, therefore, that it is the lawyers in some jurisdictions that have resisted being included in some of the anti–money laundering enforcement requirements claiming solicitor–client confidentiality as the reason for their exclusion. While these professionals are often implicated in the criminal laundering, they are also valuable in working in a forensic capacity in partnership with law enforcement in fighting money laundering.

Impact on Policing

From a policing perspective, a focus on money laundering involves different types of skills, including training or recruiting special "proceeds of crime" investigators. "Traditional" policing seldom has the resources to successfully build complicated cases and follow the paper trails that often wind through numerous jurisdictions, making use of multiple corporations and nominees. Different policing structure, different policing expertise, and different working relationships with other police departments, other regulatory agencies, professional associations, and international contacts are all required. Investigators may require forensic accounting skills, computer intelligence systems, and sophisticated analytical work.

Increasingly, police are forming "integrated" units that include this expertise in the form of having forensic accountants working directly with the police in assisting to trace the illicit proceeds. Ironically, one now must expect more laundering rather than less. As long as enforcement targets illicit proceeds, there will be more of a need for money laundering. In other words, enforcement that targets the proceeds of crime actually promotes more sophisticated forms of money laundering.

An earlier preferred theory was that organized criminals would use their illicit proceeds in order to "buy into" the legitimate society and hence become legitimate (or at least allow their next generation to be legitimate). To the extent that enforcement has any impact on the criminal operations, enforcement activities may serve to ensure that criminals remain outside legitimate operations and only use legitimate businesses to further their criminal operations or to hide their proceeds before moving them elsewhere.

Unresolved Issues

The massive international antilaundering campaign is not a neutral activity but rather has been carried out at considerable expense in terms of resources, impact of the blacklisting sanctions imposed on certain of the more vulnerable nations, and possibly even on the way in which criminals conduct their business.

The results from all of the antilaundering strategies have been difficult to measure. As Levi states, "... there are few defensible positive findings about the direct, short-term impact of money laundering reporting on prosecutions and on confiscations." Assigning private sector institutions, such as financial institutions, enforcement responsibilities traditionally carried out by the state has numerous limitations. Different institutional cultures, different mandates, the profit-oriented and cost reduction goals of financial institutions, and hence different priorities will obstruct full compliance with the antilaundering requirements.

Given what remains a dearth of empirical information regarding the impact of laundering, the size of the laundering operations, or the impact of enforcement on the laundering operations, some critics question the international focus on anti–money laundering and challenge the notion that terrorism can be reduced via a focus on terrorist financing. The allure of seized dollars, the political sway over non-compliant states, the related focus on flee-ing tax dollars, and/or capital flight all make these antilaundering campaigns at-tractive, and critics argue that the object-ive behind the antilaundering campaigns may have little relationship to crime con-trol or even to terrorism.

Left as one policing tool among many, taking the profits of criminal activity away from convicted criminals makes sense. Using the intelligence gathered from the antilaundering strategies to advance police investigations is beneficial. However, the priority given to this approach and the international consequences of a "harmon-ized" global commitment to the anti–money laundering strategies are perhaps more questionable. While one would not refute that organized criminal activities, such as drug trafficking, have a serious impact on society, the evidence is less strong that the criminal proceeds derived from these activities pose a significant *ad-ditional* harm, nor that the limited abil-ity—regardless of the resources used in the effort—to deprive criminals of their profits will reduce the amount of these types of criminal operations.

Money laundering may, depending on the source of the funds, in fact have some positive benefits for some societies because it involves the transfer of funds from the underground economy (where it goes un-taxed and may be used to fund criminal activities) to the legitimate economy (where it may be invested or spent on legitimate goods and services and can be taxed). A more balanced focus on the criminals, their criminal activities, and the illicit pro-ceeds may be the next enforcement shift.

MARGARET E. BEARE

See also **Criminal Investigation; Federal Police and Investigative Agencies; Identity Theft; White Collar Crime**

References and Further Reading

Beare, Margaret. 2003. *Critical reflections on transnational organized crime, money laun-dering and corruption.* Toronto: University of Toronto Press.

Beare, Margaret, and Stephen Schneider. 1990. *Tracing of illicit funds: Money laundering in Canada.* Ottawa: Solicitor General Canada.

Egmont Group. 2005. Financial intelligence units of the world. http://www.egmontgroup.org/list_of_fius_062304.pdf (accessed August 2005).

Financial Action Task Force (FATF). 2005. *Annual report 2004–2005, June.* http://www.fatf-gafi.org/dataoecd/41/25/34988062.pdf (accessed August 2005).

Financial Crimes Enforcement Network. *2000–2005 strategic plan.* http://www.treas.gov/FinCEN/pub_FinCEN_reports.html.

Gilmore, William C. 1999. *Dirty money: The evolution of money laundering countermea-sures.* 2nd ed. Brussels, Belgium: Council of Europe Publishing.

Gold, M., and Michael Levi. 1994. *Money-laundering in the UK: An appraisal of suspi-cious-based reporting.* London: Police Foun-dation.

Levi, Michael. 2002. Money laundering and its regulation. *Annals of the American Academy of Political and Social Science* 582 (July).

National Crime Authority, Australia. 1992. *Taken to the cleaners: Money laundering in Australia.* Canberra: National Crime Au-thority.

Naylor, R. T. 1999. *Follow-the-money methods in crime control policy.* December. Study prepared for the Nathanson Centre for the Study of Organized Crime and Corruption, York University. http://www.yorku.ca/nathanson/Publications/washout.htm.

———. 2002. *Wages of crime: Black markets, illegal finance, and the underworld economy.* Ithaca, NY: Cornell University Press; Mon-treal: McGill-Queen's University Press.

Possamai, Mario. 1992. *Money on the run: Canada and how the world's dirty profits are laundered.* Toronto: Viking.

Reuter, Peter, and Edwin Truman. 2004. *Chas-ing dirty money: the fight against money laundering.* Washington, DC: Institute for International Economics.

Schneider, Stephen. *Money laundering in Canada: An analysis of RCMP cases.* http://www.yorku.ca/nathanson.

United Nations. 1988. *United Nations Conven-tion Against Illicit Traffic in Narcotic Drugs and Psychotropic Substances.* E/CONF 82/15, December 19, Vienna.

———. 2003. *The money laundering cycle*. Office on Drugs and Crime, http://www.unodc.org/unodc/money_laundering_cycle.html (accessed June 15, 2003).

U.S. Presidential Commission on Organized Crime. 1984. *The cash connection: Organized crime, financial institutions and money laundering*. October. Washington, DC: Presidential Commission on Organized Crime.

Van Dyne et al., eds. 2004. *Threats and phantoms of organized crime and terrorism: Critical European perspectives*. Nijmegen, The Netherlands: Wolf Legal Publishers.

MOUNTED PATROL

Definition

Mounted patrol may be defined and described as follows (Carfield 1995, 371):

> Horse-mounted police are special units within police departments or public safety organizations that use horses either for patrol activities or for special operations. Sometimes the horse is used primarily for transportation to facilitate and inspire personal interaction among officers and citizenry. During special operations, the height and bulk of the horse enhance the mounted officer's command presence and authority.

Significance

Although many departments now rely on vehicles (including cars, motorcycles, and bicycles) to patrol areas, some still use horse-mounted units to patrol certain areas or for special occasions. Police mounted units may also be used for special operations to supplement traditional patrol units, especially when dealing with crowd control. Horse-mounted units, traditionally based upon military discipline and command models, are special units that have a special history and unique position within policing.

Several departments within the United States either use horse-mounted patrols to supplement automobile, motorcycle, bicycle, or foot patrol for certain events or certain patrol activities or rely on them as regular patrol details during shifts. Paradoxically, mounted police units still thrive in urban and densely populated areas (Roth 1998, 707). Some departments that still either utilize horse-mounted patrol or have regular horse-mounted patrols are the New York Police Department, Los Angeles County Sheriff's Department, Pennsylvania State Police, Philadelphia Police Department, and the New Orleans Police Department. In addition, several departments outside the United States still rely on horse-mounted patrols as specialized units within departments.

History

According to Roth (1998, 707), "While it is unknown when the first horse was used in police action, most historians trace the utilization of mounted forces in peacekeeping activities to King Charles' *Articles of War*, published in 1629." London's Horse Patrol, created in 1805, was the earliest formal mounted police force, and by the 1820s both Australia and Texas had implemented horse-mounted patrol units.

The London Bow Street police established a mounted patrol unit in 1758, and by 1805, the horse patrols "consisted of fifty-two men and animals and were charged with patrolling main roads up to twenty miles distant of London" (Campbell 1968; also Roth 1998, 708). This unit mainly handled the threat of highwaymen on the roads leading into London and patrolled the main roads to prevent these threats. Originally, the London Bow Street Horse Patrol did not deal with crowds or riots as later horse-mounted patrols did and still do (Roth 1998). The numbers of the Bow Street Horse Patrol were increased in the 1820s because they had proved to be a success, and by the beginning of the 1840s they were an integral part of the London Metropolitan Police (Roth 1998).

The role of the mounted police changed more to crowd control during the nineteenth century due to an increase in social disorder and rioting (Roth 1998). Instead of just patrolling the roads leading into London to discourage highwaymen, the duties of the mounted police by 1910 included patrolling common lands, controlling strike-breaking violence and other horsemen, escorting members of the monarchy, and searching for lost children and escaped criminals. "In 1919 the mounted branch of the metropolitan branch was reorganized into a model resembling today's branch" (Roth 1998, 708). In addition to London, other towns and cities within England adopted this type of unit to supplement police patrols. Newcastle-upon-Tyne adopted a mounted patrol in 1836 and still uses a force of six mounted officers to patrol the woodlands and parks that surround the city (Roth 1998). Eighteen U.K. police forces had mounted patrol branches by the end of 1982.

Police departments in the United Kingdom were not the only ones to implement mounted patrols during this time. Police departments in Australia also created mounted patrol units in the 1800s. Mounted patrols were responsible for most law enforcement in the gold fields during the 1850 gold rush and for controlling rioting in Sydney and finding runaway convicts as well during this time. To the present day, mounted patrols have been maintained within Australia. "The New South Wales mounted force today assists the police on special operations such as traffic control at major celebrations and sporting events; searches for missing persons in wilderness areas; searches for escapees, drug plantations and retrieving stolen livestock" (Roth 1998, 709).

Horse-mounted patrols within the United States are often equated with the history of the Texas Rangers in the late 1800s. During the nineteenth century, the rangers had an on-and-off existence but were formally organized in 1835, forming an auxiliary military body to patrol the frontiers between the Colorado and Trinity rivers (Roth 1998). The other main responsibility of the rangers was to protect the Texas frontier from Indian attacks during this time. Following the Civil War, their duties shifted from border patrol to straight police work against outlaws.

Following the example of the Texas Rangers, other states, such as Arizona and New Mexico, also implemented horse patrols around the 1900s to improve law enforcement. The main mission of these units was to reduce predations by outlaws. Although many mounted patrols were reduced or disbanded by the introduction and proliferation of automobile and highway patrols, many departments within the United States and the world still have departments with horse patrols that are still used today, yet "there are no accurate statistics on the number of mounted forces in the world today. According to one source there were between seventy and eighty-two units in the USA alone in the early 1980s" (Carfield 1982; also Roth 1998, 718).

Advantages and Justifications of Horse Patrols

Often cited as the reasons for mounted patrols are riot and crowd control, visibility, community relations, and park patrol. Also, horse patrols are often used in parades, funerals, special operations, and traffic. The advantages of patrolling on horseback include having a clearer view of an area, greater public visibility, and the ability to operate in close places. However, there are disadvantages as well, which include exposure to inclement weather, limited carrying capacity, "litter" (that is, waste), vulnerability, and lack of speed over long distances (Carfield 1995; Doeren 1989; Roth 1998). "Nevertheless, mounted patrols persist for reasons which clearly exceed mere sentimentality. Many communities are willing to maintain mounted units, despite their limitations, in order to realize perceived benefits" (Roth 1998, 718).

Horse Selection

The physical attributes that are of primary significance in selecting a horse for law enforcement work are gender, weight, age, height, and breed. The majority of mounted patrol units rely on geldings (altered male horses), though some do use mares and/or stallions. Geldings are often preferred to mares or stallions because they tend to possess an overall quieter disposition and are usually safer and easier to handle (Doeren 1989, 10–11).

Often the preference is for larger horses, around 15.2 hands tall or taller and between a thousand and twelve hundred pounds. Departments choose larger horses for several reasons: They are better suited for carrying heavier officers, they provide greater visibility, and they are often more effective in crowd control situations (Doeren 1989). Most departments also prefer to select young or "green broke" (minimally trained) horses, between three and seven years old. While some training has already begun, such a horse is still susceptible to training and will be able to work for a maximum number of years. In addition, most programs utilize quarter horses, thoroughbreds, Morgans, or mixed-breed horses that are like the quarter horses or Morgans (Doeren 1989). Horses that have a good disposition (quiet, even tempered, and devoid of bad habits) are also preferred for police work.

Horses are acquired by departments in five different ways: (1) purchase, (2) donation, (3) loan, (4) trade, and (5) officer owned (compensation), though most programs rely on purchase and/or donation. "Most training of horse and rider is carried on by the local department, but there are prominent training centers that will lend a hand in Chicago, St. Louis, and Detroit, and under the auspices of the National Park Service" (Carfield 1995, 372). Specialized training is required for both horse and rider.

Although not as prominent as before the introduction and proliferation of the automobile, horse-mounted units are still used by police departments today. Essential functions of horse-mounted patrols still include crowd control, presence at special events, patrolling highly congested areas, and public relations. Even though horse-mounted patrols are sometimes difficult to implement and maintain by departments, most that use these special patrols believe the advantages of having them outweigh the few disadvantages.

JENEPHYR JAMES

See also **Crowd/Riot Control; Patrol, Types and Effectiveness of; Texas Rangers**

References and Further Reading

Campbell, J. 1968. *Police horses.* New York: A. S. Barnes and Company.

Carfield, William. 1995. Horse mounted police. In *Encyclopedia of police science,* ed. W. G. Bailey, 371–73. New York: Garland Press.

Coonradt, V. R. 1999. A history: Community service from the back of a horse. *Women Police* 33 (4): 3–4.

Doeren, S. E. 1989. Mounted patrol programs in law enforcement. *Police Studies* 12 (1): 10–17.

Fine, J. C. 2001. Police on horseback: A new concept for an old idea. *FBI Law Enforcement Bulletin* 70 (7): 6–8.

Roth, M. 1998. Mounted police forces: A comparative history. *Policing: An International Journal of Police Strategies & Management* 21 (4): 707–19.

MULTIETHNIC COMMUNITIES: INTERACTIVE MODEL

A major issue facing modern policing is how to operate effectively in light of the ever increasing ethnic diversity of our population. History has demonstrated that most police issues, ranging from personnel to excessive use of force, are linked closely to the challenges that result from the increasing ethnic diversity found in our cities and suburbs. The difficult challenge of policing in rapidly changing multiethnic communities has resulted in riots triggered by conflict between police officers and members of ethnic communities, including those in Los Angeles and Miami (Alpert and Dunham 1992; Porter and Dunn 1984).

Leaders of metropolitan areas with less ethnic diversity than Los Angeles and Miami may think that these types of problems do not concern them. However, these ethnically diverse cosmopolitan areas are prototypes of the American urban scene. In most communities, ethnicity seems to complicate police procedures and encounters between the police and the public. Progressive police administrators have been searching for solutions to the problems inherent in this type of potentially explosive interaction. Improved policies, training, enhanced supervision, and the decentralization of administrative duties are just some of the solutions that have been attempted.

However, it must be realized that information about potential clients, that is, members of the various ethnic groups, and their views toward police and policing is necessary to guide these solutions. Questions such as the following need to be answered by the police to help design an effective approach to policing: How do members of each ethnic community conceptualize the police? What are their cultural expectations? Which policing procedures will receive community support and the cooperation of the law-abiding residents and which will be rejected with noncooperation and perhaps violence?

The police, the other partner in the relationship, often come to view the ethnic community and its members as antagonistic to them and their role in the community. When the police feel that they have no citizen support in the area, they begin to focus more and more on the lack of citizen respect for the police, refusals to cooperate with the police, and antagonistic bystanders taunting police officers while an investigation or arrest is in process. This type of reciprocal mistrust can develop into a cycle that escalates into extreme conflict such as resulted in the Rodney King case in Los Angeles and the Diallo case in New York City.

Formal and Informal Social Control

To couch the multiethnic policing problem in sociological terms, it is one of disjuncture between formal and informal social control structures. Further, when all is said and done, it is the informal social control structure that revolves around intimate or primary relationships that has the greatest impact on social control. In fact, for the formal control structure (that is, the police and courts) to have any degree of effectiveness, it must be supported and given credibility by the informal structure.

When the intimate relationships of the primary groups are weakened, social control is gradually dissolved. The resulting indirect or secondary relationships have a much different effect on social control. As Park (1925, 26) noted almost eighty years ago:

> It is characteristic of city life [in the absence of neighborhood cohesion] that all sorts of people meet and mingle together who never fully comprehend one another. The anarchist and the club man, the priest and the Levite, the actor and the missionary who touch elbows on the street still live in totally different worlds. So complete is the segregation of vocational classes that it is possible

within the limits of the city to live in an isolation almost as complete as that of some remote rural community.

Park observed differences between social control based on mores and neighborhood cohesion and social control based on indirect and secondary relationships and positive law. The latter is much weaker and less capable of establishing order.

More recently, Greenberg and Rohe (1986, 79) have reviewed the empirical research on the relationship between informal control and crime. They concluded that emotional attachment to the neighborhood, perceived responsibility for the control over the neighborhood, and the expectation that oneself or one's neighbors would intervene in a criminal event are associated with low crime rates. This evidence suggests a relationship between the informal control of a cohesive neighborhood and crime.

Informal social control in the residential context refers to the development, observance, and enforcement of local norms for appropriate public behavior (Greenberg and Rohe 1986, 80). It is the process by which individual behavior is influenced by a group and usually functions to maintain a minimum level of predictability in the behavior of group members and to promote the well-being of the group as a whole. Sampson et al. (1997) refer to this as "collective efficacy," or the collective capacity of residents to effectively supervise children and maintain public order.

Formal social control is based on written rules or laws and prescribed punishments for violating these rules and laws. The police and the courts are the institutions most directly charged with maintaining order under formal social controls. The means of formal social control are not very effective without the direct support of the informal means of control. The combination and the interaction of the two are central to establishing effective social control.

The stigma of a police car in one's driveway, being handcuffed and placed in a police car in front of family members and long-time friends and neighbors, and the sting of gossip is feared much more in cohesive neighborhoods than the actual punishments of the formal system. Of course, maximum effectiveness of the control system requires that the norms and values of the informal system be consistent with those of the formal system. Wilson and Kelling (1982, 34) advocate this level of integration:

> The essence of the police role in maintaining order is to reinforce the informal control mechanisms of the community itself. The police cannot, without committing extraordinary resources, provide a substitute for that informal control. On the other hand, to reinforce those natural forces, the police must accommodate them.

If the local values and customs of a neighborhood dictate that the police are outsiders and arrest is the imposition of unfair and biased rules on fellow residents, then the stigma of arrest is absent and the informal control system works against the formal system.

Informal social control is not present in every neighborhood; rather it is a variable that differs both in form and degree among neighborhoods. Many lack any degree of fundamental integration and thereby the means for an effective informal social control system. More specifically, the results of research on neighborhoods indicate that shared norms are less likely to develop in low-income neighborhoods that are heterogeneous with regard to ethnic composition, family type, or lifestyle than they are in low-income, culturally homogeneous neighborhoods or in middle-class neighborhoods (Sampson and Wilson 1995; Greenberg and Rohe 1986; Merry 1981). Residents of low-income heterogeneous neighborhoods tend to be more suspicious of each other, to perceive less commonality with other residents, and to feel less control over their neighborhood than do the residents of more homogeneous areas.

For example, many inner-city black neighborhoods lack a dominant cultural group. Even though the residents are all black, housing discrimination and other factors result in neighborhoods that vary considerably in the social values, lifestyle, and family type characteristic of its residents (Erbe 1975). As a result of this diversity, residents have little consensus on conceptions of appropriate public behavior, and informal social control within the neighborhood tends to be weak. In extreme cases, the conceptions of appropriate public behavior are in conflict among neighborhood residents.

The situation in predominately white, middle-class neighborhoods is much different. These neighborhoods tend to be more homogeneous due to self-selection resulting from the greater freedom of choice in locating a residence. Residents tend to self-select their location based upon similarities of other residents to their family type, lifestyle, and values. This process tends to group residents according to their basic underlying assumptions of appropriate public behavior and values. Therefore, informal social control tends to be much more developed in these types of neighborhoods than in low-income neighborhoods.

An Interactive Model

The neighborhood unit still is a social unit as well as an ecological category, even though neighborhoods have undergone considerable change in the past fifty years. These changes have resulted in considerable variation among neighborhoods in their degree of cohesiveness and the strength of their informal social control systems. It is still true that neighborhood context can provide an important source of integration into the larger society for its residents. In fact, cohesive neighborhoods provide alternative means for residents to respond to and adapt to the larger, more complex society. In addition, cohesive neighborhoods incorporate an important system of informal social control that can be crucial to establishing order and controlling crime, if it is integrated into the formal social control system involving the police and the courts. The key is the interaction between the formal social control system of the larger community and the informal control systems operating in the various neighborhoods.

One of the early functions of developing urban police forces was to establish social regulation to supplement law enforcement duties. This need developed when police effectiveness declined, as urbanization increased, and as communities became more cosmopolitan (Black 1980; Kelling 1985). In the most disorderly parts of American cities, the traditional police officer became an "institution" who responded to a "moral mandate" for informal social control in situations where individuals violated community or neighborhood norms and impinged on the personal and property rights of others. "Street justice" was another name for this function (Sykes 1986). "Street justice," then, is a response to a community or neighborhood mandate that something be done about situations where formal institutions cannot or will not act for a variety of reasons. When this function became linked to ethnic and racial prejudice in the 1950s and 1960s, however, it ushered in decades of reform.

Skogan (1990) has analyzed indicators of neighborhood decline that lead to disorder. These include public drinking, corner gangs, street harassment, drugs, noisy neighbors, commercial sex, vandalism, dilapidation/abandonment, and rubbish. Other research has also revealed that neighborhoods are declining but that the community policing philosophy is still appropriate for many areas. Further, it is possible to create community spirit in those areas that never had any or that have lost it (Alpert and Dunham 1988).

The traditional model of policing, whether it is labeled "street justice" or "order maintenance," represents a model of policing that integrates the informal control system of the local community with the formal control system of the police. The more recent model of policing, whether it is called "law enforcement" or "professional," attempts policing with minimal integration between the formal control system of the police and the informal control system of the local neighborhood.

The interactive model calls for policing strategies that integrate formal procedures and practices with the informal social control system operating within the various neighborhoods. To reach maximum effectiveness, police discretion and strategies must be organized within the established norms of public behavior in the neighborhood. Policies must be developed with an understanding that the neighborhood has established alternative ways that residents adapt to and cope within the larger social system, including the police and the laws they enforce.

Community-Oriented Policing

There has been a resurgence of interest in this policing strategy and a recent increase in the number of programs that have been initiated in agencies around the country. This interest may be more a function of the failure of the "law-enforcement" or "professional" models discussed earlier than an increase in support for this type of policing. Regardless of the reasons, significant attention and resources are being allocated to community-oriented policing.

The purpose of the model is to place a greater emphasis on nonadversarial problem solving in lieu of traditional strategies that conflict with normative structures in the neighborhood. Nonadversarial policing is achieved through the development of specific tasks and policing strategies, which are based upon a combination of law enforcement requirements, community needs, and techniques of problem solving. The question still remains: How can the police gain a greater understanding of the unique characteristics of specific communities so that a bond will form?

Geographic Focus of Police Responsibility

Most departments stress the need for police officers to return to the old meaning of "beat officer." That is, to emphasize "the geographic basis of officer assignment and responsibility by shifting the fundamental unit of patrol accountability from time of day to place" (Cordner 2005, 406). Officers need to learn about the residents and business people in their neighborhoods and to see them and be seen in situations that are not always defined as negative or at best neutral.

To reduce isolation, officers must first be assigned to community beats for an extended period, supervised by command staff. This move toward stability will increase the identification of an officer with the residents, geography, politics, and other issues of a given neighborhood. Second, there must be the traditional police–community relations meetings or citizens' advisory groups. Even when these two elements are operating, successful community policing requires proper training, feedback mechanisms, and an institutionalized reward system.

Neighborhood Training

Neighborhood training can effectively inform the officers as to what they can expect from the residents, physical surroundings, or other influences. This in-service training introduces officers to community characteristics while working the streets under supervision (in a way similar to a field training officer). Clear differences divide officers and citizens concerning preferred styles of policing. To match style of policing with community needs, knowledge of community values and beliefs as well as the attitudes and priorities of police officers must be part of the training mix.

The needs of the community can be determined by periodic social surveys that, if linked to census data and local planning information, can inform officials of the changing nature of a given neighborhood. While it is relatively easy to identify what constitutes negative behavior, it is difficult to ascertain exemplary behavior. A blue-ribbon committee studying the Miami Police Department came to a similar conclusion. In its final report (Overtown Blue Ribbon Committee 1983, 199), it noted

> It is our conclusion that a minor organizational change can have a major impact on community relations and on the interrelationships between citizens and police. We believe that confidence in the police will be enhanced if the police measure and make more visible the activities they perform. Moreover, police work is usually rewarded by the gratitude an officer receives from those who he or she helps. Status in the department, promotions, raises, commendations, etc., rest largely on his or her crime-fighting activities, the number of arrests, crimes he or she solves, etc. As a result, the patrol officer may regard service calls as a necessary evil.

Both the crime fighting and the service function of the police need to be evaluated on the institutional and individual levels. First, an ongoing study of victimization can provide police with data on how well their agency provides services. Second, a random survey of consumers of police services can provide administrators and planners with feedback on their services and the officers who provide them.

Rewarding the Police Officer

Most police departments provide incentives for their officers. These include traditional promotions, merit increases, and "officer-of-the-month" recognition. Traditionally, these rewards have been based on aggressive actions that have led to an arrest(s), the capture of a dangerous felon, or some other heroic activity. These criteria for rewarding police officers are important and serve to encourage similar actions from others. Yet other types of police behavior deserve recognition, such as exemplary service to the community and the diffusion and reduction of violence. The actions of an officer who avoids a shooting or talks a suspect into custody may not be known to his or her superiors, and when they are, the officer may be labeled a "chicken" or one who cannot provide needed backup to fellow officers. This type of nonaggressive behavior—consistent with neighborhood norms—deserves attention and reinforcement.

Toward an Interactive Model

The model will work most effectively in homogeneous neighborhoods and in areas where police administrators have strong control of their officers. It is important that police officers work for the community, not merely to impress their supervisors. Some cities will find it quite reasonable to divide police jurisdictions to facilitate the proposed model, as many geographic locations attract or limit certain groups of people. Other cities may find their demographic mix too complex for this type of policing. Regardless of the administrative level of commitment, patrol officers are in the best position to understand the varied and changing needs of the community.

ROGER DUNHAM and GEOFFREY P. ALPERT

See also **Boston Police Department; Community Attitudes toward the Police; Community-Oriented Policing: Effects and Impacts; Community-Oriented Policing: History; Community-Oriented Policing: International;**

Community-Oriented Policing: Practices; Community-Oriented Policing: Rationale

References and Further Reading

Alpert, Geoffrey, and Roger Dunham. 1988. *Policing multi-ethnic neighborhoods.* Westport, CT: Greenwood Press.

———. 1992. *Policing urban America.* Prospect Heights, IL: Waveland Press.

Black, Donald. 1980. *The manners and customs of the police.* New York: Academic Press.

Cordner, Gary W. 2005. Community policing: Elements and effects. In *Critical issues in policing,* ed. R. Dunham and G. Alpert, 5th ed. Long Grove, IL: Waveland Press.

Dukes, Richard, and Geoffrey Alpert. 1980. Criminal victimization from a police perspective. *Journal of Police Science and Administration* 8: 21–30.

Erbe, Brigette. 1975. Race and socioeconomic segregation. *American Sociological Review* 40: 801–12.

Furstenberg, Frank, and Charles Wellford. 1973. Calling the police: The evaluation of police service. *Law and Society Review* 7: 393–406.

Greenberg, Stephanie, and William Rohe. 1986. Informal social control and crime prevention in modern neighborhoods. In *Urban neighborhoods: Research and policy,* ed. R. Taylor. New York: Praeger.

Greene, Jack. 1987. Foot patrol and community policing: Past practices and future prospects. *American Journal of Police* 6: 1–18.

Kelling, George. 1985. Order maintenance, the quality of urban life, and police: A different line of argument. In *Police leadership in America: Crisis and opportunity,* ed. William Geller. New York: Praeger.

Mastrofski, Stephan. 1983. Police knowledge on the patrol beat: A performance measure. In *Police at work: Issues and analysis,* ed. R. Bennett. Beverly Hills, CA: Sage.

Merry, Sally E. 1981. *Urban danger: Life in a neighborhood of strangers.* Philadelphia, PA: Temple University Press.

Moore, Mark. 1992. Problem-solving and community policing. In *Modern policing,* ed. Michael Tonry and Norval Morris. Chicago: University of Chicago Press.

Moore, Mark, and George Kelling. 1983. To serve and protect: Learning from police history. *The Public Interest* 70: 49–65.

Overtown Blue Ribbon Committee. 1983. *Final report.* Miami: City of Miami.

Park, Robert, et al. 1925. *The city.* Chicago: University of Chicago Press.

Porter, Bruce, and Marvin Dunn. 1984. *The Miami riot of 1980.* Lexington, MA: Lexington Books.

Sampson, Robert J., Stephen W. Raudenbush, and Felton Earls. 1997. Neighborhood and violent crime: A multilevel study of collective efficacy. *Science* 277 (Aug. 15): 918–24.

Sampson, Robert J., and William J. Wilson. 1995. Toward a theory of race, crime and urban inequality. In *Crime and inequality,* ed. J. Hagan and R. D. Peterson. Stanford, CA: Stanford University Press.

Skogan, Wesley. 1990. *Disorder and decline: Crime and the spiral of decay in American neighborhoods.* New York: Free Press.

Steinman, Michael. 1986. Officer orientations toward the community. *Urban Affairs Quarterly* 21: 598–606.

Sykes, Gary. 1986. Street justice: A moral defense of order maintenance policing. *Justice Quarterly* 3: 497–512.

Walker, Samuel. 1984. Broken windows and fractured history: The use and misuse of history in recent police patrol analysis. *Justice Quarterly* 1: 75–90.

Wilson, James Q., and George Kelling. 1982. The police and neighborhood safety. *Atlantic Monthly,* March, 29–38.

N

NASSAU COUNTY (NEW YORK) POLICE DEPARTMENT

Nassau County was created in 1899. It occupies a 287-square-mile portion of Long Island, located in the southeast portion of New York State. The county is bounded on the south by the Atlantic Ocean, on the north by the Long Island Sound, on the east by Suffolk County, and on the west by New York City. Nassau County is divided into two cities, three towns, and more than eighty villages.

When Nassau County was created, it was a rural area with a population of approximately thirty thousand. The county was composed of large farms and some prominent estates on its north shore, known as the "Gold Coast." In the 1920s, residents began commuting to Nassau County via the Long Island Railroad, and many of the local farms were sold, subdivided, and developed into various communities. The population of the county increased to almost two hundred thousand. This significant growth prompted government officials to consider the creation of a countywide police agency.

The Nassau County Police Department (hereinafter NCPD) was created April 16, 1925. Fifty-five men who were special deputy sheriffs became the first sworn officers. The new commissioner of police, Abraham Skidmore, designated one of the officers as a captain, two as sergeants, one as a fingerprint expert, eleven as motorcycle patrol officers, and thirty-nine as foot patrol officers. The first precinct was created in the unincorporated areas of the southern half of the county.

At its inception, a unique organizational and taxing structure was established to fund the Nassau County Police Department. The department was divided into two components: headquarters and the police district. The headquarters unit would provide support services such as a countywide crime laboratory, a police academy, and homicide squad detectives to serve all areas of Nassau County whether the area was patrolled by the county police or by a local police department. Thus, all residents of the county would pay for the cost of the police services provided by the components of the head-quarters unit. The police district unit provided routine patrol and other po-lice services to those towns and villages that requested basic patrol services. The district taxing structure would de-rive revenue only from those areas that were actually patrolled by county police officers.

From 1925 to 1945, hundreds of sworn officers were hired, and several police pre-cincts were created to subdivide police ser-vices in the county. Several incorporated villages and unincorporated areas abol-ished their local police departments and opted for patrol service to be provided by the Nassau County Police Department. In 1930, a police headquarters building was erected in Mineola, and it remains at this location today.

By 1946, the population of Nassau County increased to almost four hun-dred thousand, and the police department grew to 587 sworn members. Various po-lice subdivisions were created, and a ma-rine bureau was established to provide police patrol on the waterways adjacent to the north and south shores of the county.

The end of WWII created an unprece-dented demand for housing for returning veterans and others seeking to own a home. Many remaining farms in Nassau County were converted into huge com-munities such as Levittown. Nassau County experienced explosive growth. The number of sworn officers in the de-partment more than doubled by the early 1960s. In 1968, the population of the coun-ty grew to more than one million, and the county police department had almost thir-ty-two hundred sworn officers. The NCPD became the second largest police depart-ment in New York State and the eighth largest municipal police agency in the nation.

In 1966, a new police commissioner, Francis B. Looney, began to emphasize the importance of college education for police officers seeking higher ranks. Com-missioner Looney established a liaison with local colleges and universities and officers were encouraged to seek college degrees. With the cooperation of the civil service commission, Commissioner Loo-ney instituted a college education incentive system that favored college educated offi-cers in the promotion process.

Also in 1966, the first sworn female officer, Kathleen Reilly, joined the ranks of the department. Tragically, less than two years later she was killed in an acci-dent while assisting a disabled motorist. Today, there are 296 female officers in the department, and male and female offi-cers work side by side in every aspect of policing. Several female officers have been promoted to precinct commanders or have achieved administrative positions, and at least one of the top-ranking admin-istrative officers in the department is a female.

In 1967, the New York legislature fully recognized municipal labor unions. Since the enactment of this legislation, NCPD police unions have become a very power-ful labor and political force in Nassau County, and these unions have dramati-cally changed the wages, hours, and work-ing conditions of the sworn officers in the department.

In June 1974, the police department employed 3,900 sworn officers. In the late 1970s, the population of Nassau County leveled to approximately 1.3 million. The number of officers employed by the police department began a steady decline in the 1980s and 1990s. In June 2000, a state financial control board was estab-lished to oversee the county budget pro-cess because of the extraordinary deficit spending that occurred between 1990 and 2000. Significant fiscal restraints have resulted in a reduction in the number of sworn officers in the department. In 2005, the NCPD was staffed by 2,722 sworn officers and 1,282 civilians, and the de-partment provided police service to almost

1.1 million residents. The department has more than nine hundred vehicles, and the 2005 NCPD budget was $619,220,662. Many sworn officers in the department have college degrees, and these officers are among the highest paid in the nation. When county officials develop plans to hire new police recruits, it is not uncommon for twenty-five thousand applicants to seek these sworn positions.

The NCPD is divided into a patrol division, support division, and detective division. The NCPD police academy trains police recruits in a nine-month training program, and it provides supervisory, in-service, and administrative training programs. The department has successfully operated its own ambulance service for more than fifty years. It has a marine/aviation unit, an emergency services bureau, a mounted unit, and specialized detective services.

Promotion in the police department is governed by written civil service examinations for police officer, sergeant, lieutenant, and captain. Thereafter, all administrative officers are appointed to higher rank by the commissioner of police. The department has a Commissioner, two deputy commissioners, one four star chief and three division chiefs. NCPD officials frequently profess that their police department is a service-oriented police agency and that community satisfaction is a major organizational goal. The police department's service orientation has been observed and confirmed by James Q. Wilson in his much quoted work *Varieties of Police Behavior*.

MARTIN L. O'CONNOR

References and Further Reading

Krieg, Joann P., and Natalie A. Naylor. 2000. *Nassau County from rural hinterland to suburban metropolis*. New York: Empire State Books.

Nassau County Police Department. 1985. *Behind the shield: 60 years of service, 1925–1985*. New York: Nassau County Police Department.

Smits, Edward J. 1974. *Nassau suburbia, USA: The first seventy-five years of Nassau County, New York, 1899–1974*. New York: Doubleday and Company, Inc.

Wilson, J. Q. 1968. *Varieties of police behavior*. New York: Harvard University Press.

NATIONAL ADVISORY COMMISSION ON CIVIL DISORDER

The first nine months of 1967 gave rise to 164 civil disorders around the country, largely in minority communities. These ranged from small-scale disorders to full-out riots. The United States appeared to be out of control. On July 27, 1967, President Lyndon Johnson signed Executive Order 11365, thus creating the National Advisory Commission on Civil Disorder.

The Kerner Commission, as it came to be known (chaired by Otto Kerner, then governor of Illinois), was charged with discovering the root causes for the disturbances and making suggestions for remedying these problems. During the course of its investigation, the commission studied twenty-four of the major disorders in twenty-three cities across the country. The study was accomplished through testimony before the commission, site visits, and interviews. As common grievances emerged, the commission created a three-tiered ranking system for these grievances and ranked the twelve most common grievances accordingly. At the top of the most serious tier was police behavior.

Not only was police behavior listed at or near the top of the grievance list in every city under study, police behavior was often cited as the immediate precursor to the riots. In many instances the police behavior in question was routine, such as a traffic stop. In one case it was a raid on an illegal drinking establishment in a black neighborhood.

The problem with the police was not just about the police officer. In many ways it was found to be about what the officer represented to the ghetto resident. The police represented the entire criminal justice system and all of its faults. Police were caught between those who demanded more enforcement to deal with increasing levels of crime and those who saw the police as a repressive invading force.

Major areas of concern in the realm of policing included the conduct of officers and patrol practices in the minority neighborhoods. Issues over police protection and use of force also emerged. In each area the issue was the difference in treatment afforded to blacks as compared to whites.

Beginning with police conduct and patrol practices, the commission found that blacks believed brutality and harassment were rampant. Police were accused of treating citizens with disrespect, targeting interracial couples for harassment, and spending an excess amount of time ordering groups of teens to move on or disperse. These actions were seen as degrading to the community members and unnecessary for crime prevention. Early warning–type systems were recommended to ensure that officers who developed a pattern of misbehavior could be disciplined effectively.

Further aggravating this problem were issues surrounding patrol practices. Increases in crime in the ghetto areas were often responded to with intensive patrol levels. This increased dramatically the number of police–citizen contacts and thus the chances that contact would be unsatisfactory. The commission also found that motorized patrol had contributed to these problems by isolating the officer from the members of the community. The officers in the patrol car went rapidly from one call to the next, giving the impression that they had little concern for the community beyond the one they would arrest next. Contacts with the police became formal, occurring only when there was a complaint or when the officers found something to intervene in. Stationing officers in the same area for lengthy periods of time and removing them from patrol cars would remedy this problem by allowing the officer and the community residents to get to know each other.

In the midst of this increase in patrol, ghetto residents also lodged complaints about a perceived lack of police protection. Police were seen as tolerating many crimes including drugs and prostitution in ghetto areas but not in white areas. They were also seen as placing a much lower priority on calls for service in the ghetto areas. Response times were slower and police were more interested in crimes that involved white victims. Much of this perception related to the need for the police to prioritize the calls they received in these areas. There were simply not enough officers available to handle the volume of calls received. Redistribution of the patrol force, and increased communication with the public about priorities, were recommended to address this problem.

Use of force was a particularly acute issue in the ghetto communities during the riots. The commission discovered that police were frequently involved in massive firefights with unseen snipers. These snipers turned out to be nonexistent. In one case the police opened fire in a massive display, only to discover the sniper they thought they were facing was a member of the National Guard who had fired a warning shot at a fleeing suspect. Police use of force during the riots was found to contribute to the ongoing outbreak of violence rather than to contain it.

The commission spent some time discussing how use of force issues were related to the technology available to the police; generally, a revolver or a nightstick were the only options. Chemical agents and other less-than-lethal weapons were more available to the army, but tensions between communities and the police were found to inhibit police exploration of these options. The commission recommended increasing police use of these alternative weapons and development of new options.

Another significant recommendation repairing the relationship between the police and the public was the creation of an easily accessible grievance procedure. Police departments needed clear written policies and enforcement mechanisms to ensure compliance. If the grievance procedure was handled with less secrecy, public trust in the police department would be increased.

In the years since the Kerner Commission report, some of the recommendations have become a reality. Many departments have citizen review boards and other forms of open grievance procedures. Community-oriented policing practices have been developed to create a better relationship in the community. Tasers, pepper spray, and many other less-than-lethal weapons have been developed. Even though evidence may exist that shows that police still have some of the same problems in the minority community, progress has emerged from the commission's work.

LORIE RUBENSER

See also **Conflict Management; Crowd/Riot Control; Excessive Force; Federal Commissions and Enactments; Minorities and the Police; Nonlethal (or Less-than-Lethal) Weapons: History**

References and Further Reading

Marx, Gary T. 1970. Two cheers for the National Riot (Kerner) Commission Report. In *Black Americans: A second look*, ed. J. F. Szwed. New York: Basic Books.

National Advisory Commission on Civil Disorders. 1968. *Report of the National Advisory Commission on Civil Disorders*. New York: Bantam Books.

Urban America Inc. and the Urban Coalition. 1969. *One year later: An assessment of the nation's response to the crisis described by the National Advisory Commission on Civil Disorders*. New York: Praeger.

Walker, Samuel, and Charles M. Katz. 2002. *The police in America: An introduction*. 4th ed. New York: McGraw-Hill.

NATIONAL ASSOCIATION OF WOMEN LAW ENFORCEMENT EXECUTIVES (NAWLEE)

History

Professional organizations for women in law enforcement have existed since 1915, with the International Association of Policewomen (IAP) being the only one exclusively for women at that time. While that organization struggled to maintain membership, in the 1950s, its name was changed to the International Association of Women Police (IAWP), and it saw increases in membership with its international status.

Today, there are many organizations dedicated to women in law enforcement, including the International Association of Women Police, the National Center for Women in Policing (NCWP), the European Network of Policewomen (ENP), the British Association of Police Women (BAP), and the Australasian Council of Women and Policing (ACWAP). There is only one organization, however, focused primarily on advancing women executives in law enforcement organizations, the National Association of Women Law Enforcement Executives (NAWLEE).

Now in its tenth year, NAWLEE provides opportunities for women of rank in a variety of local, state, and federal organizations who aspire to move up the ranks in their organizations. A nonprofit organization, it was established in 1995 under the guidance of a steering committee of five or six women chiefs at an annual

International Association of Chiefs of Police (IACP) meeting. The organization has grown from one of less than ten members to one with more than 350 members (Kyzer 2005).

Purpose and Scope

The general purpose and mission of NAWLEE is to promote the ideals and principles of women executives in law enforcement; to conduct training seminars to train and educate women executives in law enforcement, including but not limited to the areas of leadership, management, and administration; to provide a forum for the exchange of information concerning law enforcement; and to foster effective law enforcement in general.

Membership status includes executive, associate, and supporting members. Executive members are those who hold the rank of lieutenant (a person whose rank is above first-line supervision for the organization, or its equivalent) or above, in a federal, state, county, municipal, campus, or railroad law enforcement agency. Associate members must be a supervisory staff employee of a federal, state, county, municipal, campus, or railroad law enforcement agency below the rank of lieutenant (or equivalent). Supporting members must by reason of their vocation, profession, or business interest share concerns and objectives of the association and desire to demonstrate such support by membership.

Mentoring

One of the most useful features that NAWLEE has to offer are mentoring opportunities for women in midlevel management positions and those new to senior management positions and senior management roles, through a formal mentoring program. NAWLEE provides opportunities for men and women in senior management positions to better understand how to retain and mentor women in their organizations.

The following are the Mentoring Program goals (NAWLEE 2005):

- To provide a formal mentor program that will benefit NAWLEE members and will serve as a model for other police agencies and organizations
- To facilitate and oversee the pairing of NAWLEE members to enhance and develop professional growth
- To support and further advance women in law enforcement and to provide a medium for productive exchange of ideas, experience, and learning

The Mentoring Program is available online and provides for mentors to be matched with potential protégés who have similar backgrounds and common goals. Through this program, mentors provide support and guidance, information, knowledge, experience, insight, and mutual rewards to participants. Additionally, prior to the conference every year, mentoring workshops are conducted on how to be a successful mentor (Kyzer 2005). Research indicates that other organizations are also establishing formal mentor programs to ensure leadership development through requisite training and experiences to make the women ready for advancement within their organizations (Catalyst 1998).

Research

In a collaborative partnership with the International Association of Chiefs of Police (IACP), NAWLEE surveyed eight hundred law enforcement executives by phone, asking their perceptions of women in policing. The goal of the study was to determine the current status of women in law enforcement and to identify challenging issues that, if addressed, might help to increase the numbers of women in law enforcement. The respondents indicated that while the numbers of women in policing were increasing, there were still pressing issues for women that needed to be addressed (IACP 1998). Issues that were examined in the survey included the status and roles of women in policing, recruitment and selection, supporting and mentoring women officers, training and supervision as related to tenure, success and promotion of women officers, attrition and resignation of women officers, gender discrimination and sexual harassment, whether a "glass ceiling" exists as a barrier to promotion, and future directions for women in policing (IACP 1998).

While numerous pertinent findings were revealed, perhaps one of the most relevant is that there were very few mentoring programs for woman in law enforcement. Additionally, results indicated that many departments did not have recruitment strategies specifically for women and that women still face a glass ceiling that oftentimes precludes them from promotion. The current president of the IACP, Chief May Ann Viverette of Gaithersburg, Maryland, stated that, "As a successful woman police executive, it's my goal ... to ensure that more women become police officers and that more of these women become leaders" (IACP 1998). She continued that the results of the survey provided leaders with action items that could be undertaken to advance women in the organization. Furthermore, by virtue of her being the first woman president of the IACP, Chief Viverette is in an ideal place to ensure that some of these recommendations are undertaken.

Personal Context

Her personal experience with the organization provides additional insight into the value and benefits of the organization. Chief Viverette stated, "When I first joined NAWLEE, I was unsure of what the organization could do for me. After attending just the first NAWLEE conference, it became evident to me that NAWLEE is an important personal resource as well as a powerful organization. NAWLEE is often a source of information to those seeking advice from successful women in police leadership roles. It is also an organization where women can feel comfortable sharing common experiences that may differ in many ways to what men have experienced in similar jobs or duties. In IACP, we view NAWLEE as a credible organization that can provide valuable feedback to many of our programs. As president of IACP, I view NAWLEE as an organization that will provide much of the necessary input that we will need to make positive changes in law enforcement over the next decade, not only for women, but for *all* sworn and nonsworn personnel" (Viverette 2005).

Historically, it has been thought that it was unwise for a woman executive to speak out on gender issues. Now, however, one of the most important trends for women executives is to start and/or participate in women's networks (Catalyst 1999). In order for women to take advantage of networking and mentoring opportunities, it is imperative that they have the support of their supervisors, who, most of the time, are men. Research consistently shows that supervisor support is critical for women in the workplace (Thompson, Kirk, and Brown 2005). Additionally, the recognition of formal networks in a supportive organization can facilitate the identification of qualified women to higher ranking, managerial positions (Catalyst 1999).

Additional research indicates that the single most problematic issue for women in law enforcement is the negative attitudes of their coworkers, and consequently their exclusion from activities associated with the "brotherhood" of police (Price and Sokoloff 2004, 501). With networking and mentoring opportunities available through NAWLEE, some of the women's feelings of isolation may be decreased, in turn making them feel like a more valued part of the organization while giving them the desire to advance in organizations perceived as more friendly to women. Formal mentoring programs, some of which may begin even prior to a recruit entering the academy, have been known to increase the retention rate of women officers (Peak 2006).

One author states that, "Change will come about as women create bonds with one another, as we are provided with more role models . . ." (Hunter College Women's Studies Collective 1995, 558). With organizations such as NAWLEE, women may be able to realize their full potential and gain their rightful places in today's law enforcement organizations.

KATHRYN E. SCARBOROUGH and
LINDA MAYBERRY

See also **Women in Law Enforcement**

References and Further Reading

Catalyst. 1999. *Creating women's networks: A how-to guide for women and companies.* San Francisco: Jossey-Bass Publishers.

Hunter College Women's Studies Collective. 1995. *Women's realities, women's choices: An introduction to women's studies.* New York: Oxford University Press.

International Association of Chiefs of Police. 1998. The future of women in policing: Mandates for action. http://www.iacp.org/documents/pdfs/Publications/ACF830%2Epdf.

Kyzer, Susan. 2005. Personal e-mail communication (December 2, 2005).

National Association of Women Law Enforcement Executives. 2006. Mentoring in police organizations for recruitment, retention, and advancement of women and minorities. http://www.nawlee.com/mentoring.html.

Peak, K. J. 2006. *Policing America: Methods, issues, and challenges.* 5th ed. Upper Saddle River, NJ: Pearson/Prentice Hall.

Price, B. R., and N. J. Sokoloff. 2004. *The criminal justice system and women: Offenders,* *prisoners, victims and workers.* 3rd ed. Boston: McGraw Hill.

Scarborough, K. E., and P. A. Collins. 2002. *Women in public and private law enforcement.* Boston: Butterworth Heinemann.

Thompson, B. M., A. Kirk, and D. F. Brown. 2005. Work-based support, emotional exhaustion, and spillover of work stress to the family environment: A study of policewomen. *Stress and Health* 21: 199–207.

Viverette, Mary Ann. 2005. Personal e-mail communication. (November 29, 2005).

NATIONAL CRIME VICTIMIZATION SURVEY (NCVS)

For many years, the primary means available for describing crime in the United States was the *Uniform Crime Reports* (UCR). Compiled from data submitted by participating police agencies, the UCR continues to provide national and local figures on crimes known to the police. Recognizing that reliance upon police reporting created systematic gaps in the statistical description of crime, the National Crime Victimization Survey (NCVS) was developed in the 1960s and early 1970s and implemented in 1973. The NCVS remains an integral part of the national statistical program on crime.

The NCVS is an ongoing survey of nonfatal personal and property victimization in the United States of individuals ages twelve and older. It gathers detailed information on households, individuals, and crime incidents from respondents in a nationally representative sample of residential addresses. It is sponsored by the Bureau of Justice Statistics (BJS), a division of the U.S. Department of Justice, and implemented by the U.S. Bureau of the Census. According to BJS, the NCVS was designed with four specific goals in mind: "(1) to develop detailed information about the victims and consequences of crime, (2) to estimate the numbers and types of crimes not reported to the police, (3) to provide uniform measures of selected types of crimes, and (4) to permit comparisons over time and types of areas" (Bureau of Justice Statistics 2004, 9).

The methodology of the NCVS is rigorous. The selection of households into the sample is done through a multistage cluster sampling design. The process begins by stratifying all geographic areas (such as metropolitan areas, counties, and groups of smaller counties) by population size and randomly selecting one geographic area per stratum. Areas with exceptionally large populations are automatically entered into the sample. The next step is to randomly select what is called "census-identified enumeration districts." These are essentially smaller geographic areas, such as city blocks, that house approximately 750 to 1,500 residents. Finally, clusters of housing units are randomly selected from within the enumeration districts. The selected housing units remain in the sample for a period of three and one-half years.

The occupants of the selected housing units are interviewed once every six months for the three and one-half year period. The Census Bureau relies on in-person face-to-face, telephone, and computer-assisted telephone interviewing (CATI) to administer the NCVS questionnaire. The first and fifth interviews are typically in-person interviews. The first interview is considered the "bounding" interview for all subsequent interviews. Bounding is a technique that is used to limit respondent reference period recall error. Respondents often include events that happened prior to the survey reference period. This phenomenon is referred to as "telescoping." Bounding reduces the extent of this problem by anchoring respondents' reports with an initial interview. This first face-to-face bounding interview is not included in the public use files of the NCVS but is used by interviewers to make sure duplicate events are not reported. All of the subsequent six interviews should be bounded by the preceding interview.

There are two questionnaire instruments. The first begins by gathering information on household characteristics, such as the number of occupants, the household income, and the type of living quarters (for example, apartment, mobile home, or condo). Details on each household occupant age twelve or older are also collected in this section, including their age, sex, race, occupation, and education. Finally, household and individual "screener" questions are asked to determine whether any property or nonfatal personal crime victimization occurred in the six months prior to the interview.

If there is any indication during the screening that there was a victimization, the interviewer proceeds to the second instrument, the incident questionnaire. The incident questionnaire consists of about 160 questions that follow intricate skip patterns on the characteristics of the situation, the victims' actions, the offender, and responses to the incident. For example, a victim of violence would be asked (among other things) when and where the incident took place, the number of attacker(s) and age, sex, and race of each, whether weapons were used, the progression of events, including threats and victim resistance, whether the victim was injured and received medical care, and finally whether and how the police were involved.

The data derived from the NCVS are used in many ways. First, the data are used to develop national estimates of nonfatal crime and to track crime over time. Second, the data are compared with UCR figures to provide an overall portrait of crime in the United States from both official and self-reported data. And third, the data are used by researchers to test theories of victimization and crime events and to describe the risk and protective factors related to crime. It is possible, but labor intensive, to create longitudinal files that follow individual respondents through each wave of interviewing. Such files are used to examine victimization over time for individuals.

It should be noted that the instruments do not gather information about the offending and related behaviors of the individuals in the sample. This is a limitation in that the bulk of victimization research demonstrates a strong overlap between the risk of victimization and offending behaviors.

Every year, approximately 42,000 households, and 76,000 individuals participate in the NCVS. Since respondents are interviewed every six months, each year nearly 84,000 household records and 152,000 individual person-level records are gathered. During the period between 1992 and 2003, the household and person-level interviews produced 154,543 crime incident records. These figures are weighted to reflect the sampling methodology for public reports on crime rates. For example, if there were 10,272 incidents reported in the 1992 NCVS records, the weighted count of incidents would be 44,240,000.

The data are available to the public through the Inter-University Consortium of Political and Social Research (ICPSR) at the University of Michigan. There are four levels of files: address ID record, household record, person record, and incident record. These public use files do not contain geographic identifiers, though special requests may be made to the sponsor for those files. The files contain household, person, and incident weights.

CATHERINE A. GALLAGHER

See also **Crime Analysis;** *Uniform Crime Reports;* **Victims' Attitudes toward the Police**

References and Further Reading

U.S. Department of Justice, Bureau of Justice Statistics. 2004. *National Crime Victimization Survey, 1992–2003*. Computer file. Conducted by the U.S. Dept. of Commerce, Bureau of the Census, ICPSR ed. Ann Arbor, MI: Inter-university Consortium for Political and Social Research.

NATIONAL ORGANIZATIONS OF BLACKS IN LAW ENFORCEMENT

Introduction

There are local, state, regional, and national organizations that represent blacks in law enforcement. This article will focus on two national organizations that represent African Americans in law enforcement: the National Black Police Association (NBPA) and the National Organization of Black Law Enforcement Executives (NOBLE). [Attempts to interview the current president of the National Organization of Black Women in Law Enforcement (NOBWLE) in hopes of getting in-depth information were unsuccessful. That organization was founded in 1985 with a primary objective to further the hiring, training, retention, and promotion of black females in law enforcement.] Both organizations are post–Kerner Commission entities and represent a network of minority officers and/or law enforcement executives who share a commitment and dedication to promote justice, equity, and effectiveness in law enforcement and the administration of justice. A description and overview of each organization follows.

National Black Police Association

History, Mission, and Purpose

The National Black Police Association was chartered as a not-for-profit organization in November 1972. As the oldest nationwide organization representing blacks in law enforcement, the NBPA is a collection of local, state, and regional black police associations that was established to create a national voice to speak on issues of race and racism within police agencies and in regards to police practices within the African American community. The NBPA's mission is to increase the awareness of the community, to be the conscience of the criminal justice system, and to enhance the quality of life of the African American community. Toward this end, the NBPA serves as an organizational network to train all police officers and to educate the community at large on issues of race and policing.

The NBPA operates from an action orientation. In particular, it seeks to address those issues that affect the personal and professional lives of African American police officers and the quality of life for the African American community. These objectives include the following:

- To strengthen the relationship between local police departments as institutions and the minority community
- To analyze and assess the effects of the policies, practices, and programs within the criminal justice system upon the minority community
- To serve as a pipeline or conduit to recruit minority police officers on a national scale
- To expedite police reform in order to eradicate police corruption, police brutality, bias-based policing, and racial discrimination
- To educate and thereby better foster and facilitate a more professional, compassionate, and effective approach to policing

Organizational and Leadership Structure

The NBPA is divided into five regions (Northeast, Eastern, Southern, Midwest, and Western), consists of more than 140 chapters in thirty-four states and the District of Columbia, and represents more than thirty-five thousand African American police officers. In recent years, the NBPA has begun to cultivate and mentor future black officers by establishing student chapters on the campuses of historically black colleges and universities for those students who are interested in careers in law enforcement and criminal justice. Similarly, the NBPA was instrumental in the establishment of three international associations of blacks in law enforcement: the Association of Black Law Enforcers in Canada in 1992, the Metro London Black Police Association in 1994, and the National Black Police Association of the United Kingdom.

The organization is governed by its National Board of Directors, which consists of four members from each region, inclusive of an elected chairman, vice chairman, and other officers. Even though the board is responsible for the formulation of policy and the operation of the national organization, the National Office is the NBPA's administrative arm, which is under the direction of the executive director and is responsible for coordinating and monitoring all funded projects and program activities.

National Organization of Black Law Enforcement Executives

History, Mission, and Purpose

The National Organization of Black Law Enforcement Executives (NOBLE) was founded in September 1976 during a symposium to address issues associated with crime in the black community. This event was cosponsored by the Law Enforcement Assistance Administration, the Police Foundation, and the Joint Center for Political Studies (now the Joint Center for Political and Economic Studies) and resulted in the publication *Black Crime: A Police View* (Bryce 1977). The symposium brought together sixty top-ranking black law enforcement executives who represented twenty-four states and fifty-five major cities.

This gathering was conceived through the networking of Peggy Triplett, who began compiling the names and departmental affiliations of black executives in law enforcement agencies during her professional travels as a special assistant to the director of the National Institute of Law Enforcement and Criminal Justice, the precursor of today's National Institute of Justice. After realizing their potential for efficacy on the criminal justice system as a unified, collective voice of black law enforcement executives and recognizing that there was a greater agenda, the sixty attendees agreed to deviate from the program and form an organization, NOBLE.

NOBLE's mission is to ensure equity in the administration of justice in the provision of public service to all communities and to serve as the conscience of law enforcement by being committed to justice by action. NOBLE seeks to accomplish this mission by valuing diversity, encouraging law enforcement as an institution to respect the rights of all persons, being proactive in addressing those issues that are controversial in nature and that decrease the effective coproduction (that is, the partnership between law enforcement and community) of public safety and public order. In essence, NOBLE seeks to address and provide solutions to the issues that impact and affect effective law enforcement policies and practices, as well as those issues that impact community safety, health, and wellness.

Organizational and Leadership Structure

NOBLE is divided into six regions and consists of fifty-six chapters throughout the United States, in addition to one international chapter. The regions and chapters encompass thirty-one states, the District of Columbia, and the West Indies. Its current membership is approximately 3,500 past and present law enforcement executives of local, state, and federal law enforcement agencies, inclusive of college and university police and public safety agencies.

NOBLE is governed by its National Executive Board, which is made up of elected and appointed officers. The national president, who serves as the chief executive officer of the organization, presides over the board. Officers of the board also include the immediate past president, the national vice president, the national recording secretary, the treasurer, the financial secretary, the parliamentarian, the sergeant-at-arms, the federal assistant to the president, the special assistant for international affairs, two additional special assistants to the president, the regional vice president from each of the six regions, and a representative for associate members.

Conclusion

The National Black Police Association and the National Organization of Black Law Enforcement Executives are two of the more established national organizations that represent blacks in law enforcement, as well as the interests of the African American and other historically marginalized communities and populations. Both organizations have taken an active as well as proactive approach to address those issues impacting law enforcement and the American community, in general, and blacks in law enforcement and the African American community in particular. From writing papers on racial profiling and bias-based policing to publishing pamphlets and brochures on "What to do if you are stopped by the police," both organizations are committed to correcting the past and present mistakes made by law enforcement. In conclusion, both organizations hope to build a more equitable criminal justice system and facilitate a more symbiotic working relationship between the institution of law enforcement, African American officers and executives, and the various facets of the American community.

BRIAN N. WILLIAMS

See also **Accountability; Attitudes toward the Police: Overview; Community Attitudes toward the Police; Minorities and the Police; Professionalism**

References and Further Reading

Akers, Joseph. 2005. Deputy Director of the National Organization of Black Law Enforcement Executives. Personal communication.

Bryce, H. J., ed. 1977. *Black crime: A police view*. Washington, DC: National Institute of Law Enforcement and Criminal Justice.

Edwards, Clarence. 2005. National president of the National Organization of Black Law Enforcement Executives. Personal communication.

Hampton, Ronald. 2005. Executive director of the National Black Police Association. Personal communication.

National Black Police Association (NBPA). 2005. http://www.blackpolice.org/gen_info.html.

National Organization of Black Law Enforcement Executives (NOBLE). 2005. http://www.noblenational.org/displaycommon.cfm?an=1&subarticlenbr=16.

Triplett, Peggy. Personal communication.

NEIGHBORHOOD EFFECTS ON CRIME AND SOCIAL ORGANIZATION

A beginning point for examining neighborhood effects on crime and social organization is to define what is meant by "neighborhood." The concept is defined variously in the relevant research and has changed over time. Burgess and Park, for example, who are credited with beginning this area of research on crime in the United States during the early 1900s, originally divided Chicago into what they called "natural areas" (Park 1916, 147). These were areas of the city deemed to be similar enough based on the characteristics of the

people and institutions located within the respective boundaries and different enough from the surrounding area(s) so as to constitute a unique place.

As research on neighborhoods and crime has progressed, generally it is acknowledged that the definition of a neighborhood is often based on a combination of ecological characteristics and political forces. Currently, a neighborhood is defined as "... ecological unit(s) nested within successively larger communities" (Sampson 2002, 445). Most recent research on neighborhoods and crime relies, however, on boundaries as defined by the U.S. Census Bureau. The reliance on block groups and census tracks as defined by the U.S. census poses theoretical and methodological problems for neighborhood-based research and will be discussed below in more detail.

In general, neighborhood effects on crime and social organization can be divided into two areas: ecological effects and geographic characteristics. Ecological effects can be described by the demographic characteristics of places. Geographic characteristics may be described by characteristics of the built environment.

Neighborhood Ecological Effects

Following the lead of Park and Burgess, the work on neighborhood social organization and crime was followed by the work of Shaw and McKay in Chicago in the early 1900s. They explained higher rates of delinquency through the structural characteristics of "neighborhoods," including low economic status, residential instability, and ethnic heterogeneity. According to Shaw and McKay (1969), a neighborhood with high rates of delinquency was characterized by the conflicting values of residents that prevented the community from effectively controlling itself; such a neighborhood, they claimed, was "socially disorganized." Since its origins within the work of Shaw and McKay, the theory of social disorganization has evolved, and today there are a number of related perspectives that explain crime or describe processes by which crime can be reduced or prevented in neighborhoods.

Overall, areas in a city with higher rates of crime are likely to be characterized by lower income, higher rates of unemployment, higher percentages of minority populations, higher population heterogeneity, higher rates of households headed by a single female with children, and lower median property values. These types of areas also tend to be characterized by a population that has fewer ties to the formal economy and subsequently is more likely to be or have been engaged in criminal activity (Greenberg, Rohe, and Williams 1983). Many of these factors affect residents' ability to supervise and control the areas where they live. They may also affect residents' willingness and ability to intervene in problematic situations. Resident participation in supervision of youth and willingness to intervene are two key factors that are shown in the research to be related to the amount of crime in a place. These two key factors are explained in more detail below.

Where social cohesion between residents is high, they are more likely to have control over what happens on their block and in their neighborhood and are more likely to intervene in problematic events (Taylor, Gottfredson, and Brower 1984). Sampson and Raudenbush (1999) measured social cohesion and levels of social control among residents in Chicago neighborhoods and combined these indicators to develop a measure of what they refer to as "collective efficacy." Specifically, collective efficacy includes three elements: informal social control, organizational participation of residents, and the willingness of neighbors to intervene in problematic situations. In neighborhoods where collective efficacy was strong, signs of disorder and crime were lower, regardless of sociodemographic characteristics of the residents.

Within an ethnically heterogeneous neighborhood, or with a transient population, collective efficacy is likely to be lower, and aggressive space management is less likely to develop (Taylor and Covington 1988). A higher proportion of residents who are less involved reduces the likelihood that strong or united resistance will be offered against criminals moving to their area. These population and neighborhood factors, in other words, can produce more offenders or victims and fewer guardians against crime (Felson 1986). It also is more likely that in communities containing a more transient population, the friendship and kin networks that have been shown to reduce opportunities for crime in communities simply do not exist (Sampson and Raudenbush 1999; Taylor, Gottfredson, and Brower 1984). These "background factors" affect mediating processes to crime like criminal opportunity and community vigilance (Felson 1986).

These "background factors" may produce what Reiss (1986) describes as a "neighborhood effect on crime." Neighborhood structure and organization can disproportionately select households and unrelated individuals who form networks creating and supporting delinquency and adult crime—the opposite, in fact, of collective efficacy. Reiss says that the density of residence of adolescent or younger males mediates this effect. A higher residential density of a high-crime-committing group such as this results in an extensive peer network that is often located in neighborhoods where there are also a large proportion of single parent households, who may be less available to enforce controls on their children. In other words, in neighborhoods like this, there is a ready availability of co-offenders and, therefore, a higher density of offenders living close to their victims, thus also creating a high density of victims (Reiss 1986).

The perceptions and behaviors of residents of a residential setting, however, can influence spatial patterns of crime in that area in both positive and negative ways. In opposition to the crime-enabling effects on communities of "background factors" and "neighborhood crime effects" described by Felson (1986) and Reiss (1986) are the controlling or preventive influences of friendship and kin networks in communities. These types of local social ties contribute to a more cohesive social culture on a street block that appears to mitigate both crime and fear of crime among residents (Sampson and Raudenbush 1999; Taylor, Gottfredson, and Brower 1984).

In their research on community structure and crime, Sampson and Groves (1989) examined the relationships between (1) ability of a community to supervise and control teenage peer groups, (2) local friendship networks, and (3) local participation in formal and voluntary organizations and levels of crime. Their research showed the importance of the supervision of youths as a key component of effective neighborhood crime control. They also found that residential stability was a more powerful determinant of rates of crime in places than either socioeconomic or family status. Residential stability is important, they surmise, since it is directly related to the formation of important friendship networks, which in turn are important to effective social control.

Social control in a neighborhood generally comprises three forms: the private, parochial, and public levels of social control (Bursik and Grasmick 1993; Hunter 1974). Protecting one's street block against property crime assumes a "private" level of control, which requires familiarity with one's neighbors, or at least a strong acquaintance with one another. A private level of control is social control exercised by friends and family living proximate (in the same neighborhood) to each other (Bursik and Grasmick 1993; Hunter 1974). The parochial level of social control entails the level of involvement in broader local interpersonal networks in stores, schools, and churches among neighbors who do not

have the same sentimental attachment. The public level of social control describes a neighborhood's ability to lobby for and obtain public services including, for example, emergency services and funds for crime prevention efforts.

A higher level of private control is likely to facilitate the supervision of youth. It is unlikely that youth who are left unsupervised by single parents or double-earner households are going to be much controlled in their behaviors by people they do not know (and who subsequently do not know their parents) (Felson 2001). Both a private level of control and supervision of youth are more likely to occur (according to Bursik and Grasmick 1993 and Felson 2001) in stable places—places that are more likely to be populated by married home owners who have lived in the same home for at least five years.

Overall, there is disagreement in the literature as to what is the most significant explanation of crime in neighborhoods or places. Some research has pointed to the importance of socioeconomic status (SES) in predicting crime rates (as argued by Land, McCall, and Cohen 1990); others have argued for the importance of family structure (as argued by Sampson and Lauritson 1994); others have argued that residential stability is key (Sampson and Groves 1989). Perhaps the confusion regarding the relative contributions of SES versus family structure and other factors is the result of the influence of underlying, systemic processes, and other differences between groups, that are masked by higher levels of spatial aggregation such as the neighborhood. The processes that govern small-scale social units, such as the street block, are likely different, for example, from those that govern whole neighborhoods or even cities (Taylor, Gottfredson, and Brower 1984). Further discussion of methodological concerns relevant to the explanation of neighborhood effects on crime and social organization is included here, after the discussion of neighborhood geography effects.

Neighborhood Geography Effects

Although ecological characteristics of places are important to the explanation of crime in neighborhoods, as discussed, research on crime and place suggests that geographic characteristics of the built environment can also help to explain crime occurrence. Identifiable characteristics of the built and urban environment, including specific land uses (schools, retail establishments, shopping malls), land zoning (commercial, mixed, high-density residential), design of residential neighborhoods, design of the street network (accessibility), and modes of transportation (highways and public transit), are influential upon and are potentially powerful explanatory factors of spatial patterns of crime.

A neighborhood's permeability, for example, is related to the volume of crimes located within it. The permeability of a neighborhood is defined as the degree of openness of the neighborhood to traffic originating outside the neighborhood. Research that has measured the permeability of neighborhoods has found that opportunities for action or activity, both legal and illicit, have a greater likelihood of being exploited if they are located on comparatively accessible and frequently traveled streets (Brantingham and Brantingham 1994; White 1990).

Locations with a higher number of criminal opportunities are usually nested in areas of mixed land use [for example, residential areas with bars or shopping malls (Roncek, Bell, and Francik 1981; Roncek and Maier 1991; Roncek and Pravatiner 1989)]. Neighborhoods with high levels of mixed land use are found to have higher levels of both physical and social disorder (Kurtz, Koons, and Taylor 1998; Perkins et al. 1993; Sampson and Raudenbush 1999). Perkins et al. (1993) used land use composition (that is, "built and transient" space) to predict levels of street crime and delinquency at the street block. They noted that "stores, schools, and certain other common nonresidential buildings" were associated with higher reported crime rates. Perkins et al. also found that other types of open, publicly controlled space (for example, parks, public gardens, and playgrounds) are associated with lower levels of residential victimization. They concluded that instead of representing interruptions in territorial control, some open spaces might symbolize "secondary territories" that facilitate resident cohesion and interaction.

Areas with mixed land uses also provide higher levels of anonymity through reduced ability of residents to identify strangers and provide guardianship, usually because of higher population density in these areas and higher volumes of commercial traffic. According to Kurtz, Koons, and Taylor (1998) land use mix may be related to resident levels of fear of crime as well and may be even more important than the level of incivilities in that area in influencing fear. Where fear is higher, resident cohesion is likely to be lower (Taylor, Gottfredson, and Brower 1981).

Overall, therefore, this category of research suggests that identifiable characteristics of the built environment are strongly associated with levels of crime. Highly permeable neighborhoods, neighborhoods with mixed land uses, and areas with less desirable housing are all likely to have higher rates of crime and resident fear of crime.

Methodological Concerns Regarding the Unit of Analysis in Neighborhood Research

Existing research on neighborhoods and crime suggests that a relatively small level of aggregation is more appropriate than using data aggregated at higher levels such as the neighborhood. The relationship between size of place and ecological characteristics changes as the size of the "place" becomes either smaller or larger. Performing ecological analyses at lower levels of aggregation (a smaller area), for example, reduces the amount of within-unit heterogeneity (Brantingham, Dyreson, and Brantingham 1976).

There is no reason why the examination of smaller units of spatial aggregation should reveal relationships between community characteristics and crime that are different from those found at the neighborhood level, if those relationships are, indeed, valid. It could be, however, that the more precise definition of space would yield a more clear-cut understanding of the structural processes and ecological characteristics that govern what are known as "street crimes."

Each of these processes, if they exist, are more likely to be stronger at the block group level, because one is likely to be more familiar with neighbors closer in distance than a few streets away in the same neighborhood. Miethe and Meier (1994), for example, examined a number of criminologically traditional predictors of crime rates in places at three different levels of spatial aggregation: the Standard Metropolitan Statistical Area (SMSA), the city, and the census tract across a meta-analysis of criminological research. In general, they found that significant predictors of crime rates (predatory and property) at the census tract level were not necessarily significant at the two larger levels of aggregation. A key predictor of crime rate that was significant at the tract level, although not at the SMSA or city level, was residential stability.

Conclusion

Neighborhood effects on crime and social organization can be grouped into ecological effects and geographic characteristics of the built environment. There is disagreement in the literature as to what are the most significant explanations of crime

in place at the neighborhood level. Two common elements appear, however, as being central to the explanation of crime in neighborhoods, collective efficacy and social control. The literature also disagrees as to what is the most meaningful unit of analysis to explain crime in a spatial context. Current research uses smaller units of aggregation than the neighborhood more often since it is believed that these smaller units more accurately reflect structural processes of social organization that control and drive crime.

JENNIFER B. ROBINSON

See also **Broken-Windows Policing; Community-Oriented Policing: Practices; Crime Analysis; Crime Mapping; Criminology; Hot Spots; Intelligence Gathering and Analysis: Impacts on Terrorism; Problem-Oriented Policing; Social Disorganization, Theory of**

References and Further Reading

Brantingham, Patricia, and Paul Brantingham. 1994. Crime analysis using location quotients. In *Proceedings of the International Seminar on Environmental Criminology and Crime Analysis*, 83–94. Florida Statistical Analysis Center.

Brantingham, Paul, D. A. Dyreson, and Patricia Brantingham. 1976. Crime seen through a cone of resolution. *American Behavioral Scientist* 20: 261–74.

Bursik, Robert, and Harold Grasmick. 1993. *Neighborhoods and crime: Dimensions of effective community control.* New York: Lexington Books.

Felson, Marcus. 1986. Linking criminal choices, routine activities, informal control and criminal outcomes. In *The reasoning criminal, rational choice perspectives on offending*, ed. Derek Cornish and Ronald Clarke. New York: Springer-Verlag.

———. 2001. *Crime and everyday life: Insight and implications for society*. 2nd ed. Thousand Oaks, CA: Pine Forge Press.

Greenberg, S., E. Rohe, and J. Williams. 1982. Safety in urban neighborhoods: A comparison of physical characteristics and informal territorial control in high and low crime neighborhoods. *Population and Environment* 5:141–65.

Hunter, Albert. 1974. *Symbolic communities*. Chicago: University of Chicago Press.

Kurtz, Ellen, Barbara Koons, and Ralph Taylor. 1998. Land use, physical deterioration, resident-based control and calls for service on urban streetblocks. *Justice Quarterly* 15: 121–49.

Land, Kenneth, Patricia McCall, and Lawrence Cohen. 1990. Structural covariates of homicide rates: Are there invariances across time and social space? *American Journal of Sociology* 95: 922–63.

Miethe, Terence and Robert Meier. 1994. *Crime and its social context*. Albany, NY: State University of New York Press.

Park, Robert. 1916. Suggestions for the investigations of human behavior in the urban environment. *American Journal of Sociology* 20: 577–612.

Perkins, Douglas, Alan Wandersman, R. Rich, and Ralph Taylor. 1993. The physical environment of street crime: Defensible space, territoriality and incivilities. *Journal of Environmental Psychology* 13: 29–49.

Reiss, Albert, Jr. 1986. Why are communities important in understanding crime? In *Communities and Crime*, 8, ed. Albert J. Reiss, Jr. and Michael Tonry, 1–34. Chicago: University of Chicago Press.

Roncek, Dennis, and P. Maier. 1991. Bars, blocks and crimes revisited: Linking the theory of routine activities to the empiricism of hot spots. *Criminology* 29: 725–53.

Roncek, Dennis, and M. Pravatiner. 1989. Additional evidence that taverns enhance nearby crime. *Sociology and Social Research* 73:185–88.

Roncek, Dennis, R. Bell, and J. Francik. 1981. Housing projects and crime: Testing a proximity hypothesis. *Social Problems* 29: 151–66.

Sampson, Robert. 2002. Transcending tradition: New directions in community research, Chicago style. *Criminology* 40:213–30.

Sampson, Robert, and W. Byron Groves. 1989. Community structure and crime: Testing social disorganization theory. *American Journal of Sociology* 94: 774–802.

Sampson, Robert, and Janet Lauritson. 1994. Violent victimization and offending: Individual, situational, and community-level risk factors. In *Understanding and preventing violence, vol. 3: Social influences*, ed. Albert Reiss and J. Roth, 1–114. Washington, DC: National Academy Press.

Sampson, Robert, and Steve Raudenbush. 1999. Systematic social observations of public spaces: A new look at disorder in urban neighborhoods. *American Journal of Sociology* 105: 603–51.

Shaw, Clifford, and Henry McKay. 1969. *Juvenile delinquency and urban areas: A study of rates of delinquency in relation to differential characteristics of local communities in American cities*. Chicago: University of Chicago Press.

Taylor, Ralph, Steve Gottfredson, and Sidney Brower. 1984. Understanding block crime and fear. *Journal of Research in Crime and Delinquency* 21: 303–31.

Taylor, R. B., and J. Covington. 1988. Neighborhood changes in ecology and violence. *Criminology* 26: 553–89.

Taylor, Ralph, Steve Gottfredson, and Sidney Brower. 1981. Territorial cognition and social climate in urban neighborhoods. *Basic and Applied Psychology*, 238–51.

White, Garland. 1990. Neighborhood permeability and burglary rates. *Justice Quarterly* 7: 57–68.

NEIGHBORHOOD WATCH

Defining Neighborhood Watch

Neighborhood Watch (or Block Watch, Town Watch, Crime Watch) are programs whereby local residents commit to look out for suspicious activities in their locale and to report them either directly to the police or indirectly via a neighborhood watch "coordinator." Similar programs operate in respect of commercial premises, for example, Business Watch. The schemes aim to prevent crime, reduce fear of crime, and improve quality of life. Following the attacks on the World Trade Center and the Pentagon of September 11, 2001, they have also taken on a substantial terrorism awareness role in the United States.

In practice, most schemes are police dominated and rely for their public input on a few enthusiasts (for example, the coordinator). In the United States the programs are coordinated by the National Sheriffs' Association, in the United Kingdom by the Home Office and police forces. The programs emerged in the 1970s in the

United States and early 1980s in the United Kingdom. They have spread to other common-law jurisdictions in the English-speaking world but have a limited presence elsewhere. About 27% of U.K. households belonged to a scheme in 2000 and only 1% of people had never heard of Neighborhood Watch, compared to 6% in 1992 (Home Office 2001). Variation in the area covered is substantial, conveyed by the fact that in the United States there are a total of 15,000 schemes while in the United Kingdom there are 155,000.

Despite its relatively recent emergence, Neighborhood Watch has deep historical roots traceable to the British system of local constables and watchmen that preceded the formation of London's Metropolitan Police. Constables were originally householders elected or appointed to patrol and protect their communities as an unpaid duty on an annual rota basis, initially under a Statute of Winchester but later by the Watch Act 1705 (Rawlings 2002). The duty was unpopular and constables hired men to perform the watchman role in their stead, a fact with some irony in that contemporary Neighborhood Watch formally involves police "servicing" schemes that are ostensibly run by the citizenry, but the evidence is that without police input, most schemes would collapse. To evidence on the functioning and effects of Neighborhood Watch we now turn.

Empirical Research Evaluations

Neighborhood Watch schemes developed in the context of public policy concerned with risk management and alleviating fear of crime with a view to community cohesion. The relationship between perceived and actual risk is not straightforward and, paradoxically, those least at risk, such as the affluent and the elderly, may feel the most fearful. Those who are well off may have low actual risk but can best afford preventive measures such as burglar alarms and can muster the social resources to ameliorate perceived risk.

Neighborhood Watch schemes tend to emerge, reach the participation threshold set by the police, and maintain public commitment in residential areas associated with high status and income (Mayhew et al. 1989), areas having low relative crime vulnerability. Membership correlates with income more than with risk. Owner-occupied households and those with above-average annual income are most likely to belong, and areas with low burglary rates have a higher membership (32% in the United Kingdom) than high-rate areas (13%; Home Office 2001). Where respondents said that in their area "people try to help each other and do things together," membership stood at 37%, but it was only 19% where respondents said that in their area "people go their own way" (Home Office 2001). Evaluating Neighborhood Watch simply by residential crime rates is unsatisfactory because of problems in comparing like with like, differential take-up and interpretation, and low victimization levels (about 4% of U.K. households are burgled in an average year; Home Office 2001). As a result, evaluations focus on impact on crime fear.

While the avowed orientation is to the public "acting as the eyes and ears of the police," an underlying purpose is to reduce fear of crime by giving citizens a sense of control. This should be part of the equation when evaluating efficacy but complicates the matter because those who join tend to have above-average levels of concern, particularly when having previously been burgled is a motivator. There is modest evidence that participation gives rise to feeling better protected as a result of efforts such as installing security equipment but little evidence of an overall, clear-cut and marked impact on levels of fear (Bennett 1987, 1990). Findings on fear and participation from crime surveys in the late 1980s continue to hold. For example, the 1988 British Crime Survey found that 60% of Neighborhood

Watch participants were "very or fairly worried about being the victim of burglary" against 55% of nonparticipants (Mayhew 1985, 59), and the fact that this is not explicable by age, sex, and individual fear thresholds leads some to argue that the schemes may reinforce fear by raising awareness of crime risk (Hough 1994).

When logistic regression techniques are used to control other variables affecting fear, membership is found to have no significant effect on fear levels (Home Office 2001). More influential is level of perceived disorder; where this is high, so is fear of burglary (Budd and Sims 2001). There is some evidence that members are more likely to call police if witnessing vandalism but no significant difference in members and nonmembers' likelihood of calling police if witnessing an assault or theft from a vehicle.

Bennett's rigorous evaluations demonstrated that after initial enthusiasm, most schemes struggle to maintain committed participation, the information-gathering function is of limited value to police, and the schemes do little to raise established levels of notification of suspicious circumstances (Bennett 1987, 1990). Indeed, there is evidence that even among enthusiasts who set about raising the required number of participants for the police to install Neighborhood Watch signage (60% participation is often required), the perceived need may be met simply by the signs, and that information in Neighborhood Watch newsletters—often prepared and distributed by police themselves rather than local people—is seldom sufficiently current or local to be of crime preventive value (Fielding 1995). While signage may have deterrent value, its most tangible effect may be on property insurance premiums.

As well as evaluations based on before-and-after measures of burglary, a number of field studies have documented the workings of Neighborhood Watch. Among the significant issues arising is the problem of property alarms. The problem is effectively that of "crying wolf." Property alarms are mostly ignored, particularly in urban areas, and are regarded as an irritant both by city dwellers and police, the latter reporting that around 90% of activations are false alarms. Officers are sometimes informally advised to ignore them. Another notable finding relates to Neighborhood Watch's aim to have residents looking out for the security of each other's property. Such surveillance activity is extremely geo-local, extending to the property either side of the typical resident's own property and the property opposite (Shapland and Vagg 1987; Evans et al. 1991). Even this level of cooperative surveillance applies only to single-tenanted properties. In urban areas it also competes with norms of civil inattention that deter people from raising their own risk by getting involved.

Efforts at systematic evaluation are hampered by failure to accommodate variations in approach (Husain and Bright 1990) and the political agenda that may develop where proponents, detractors, and commentators all have interests that color the account given of effectiveness. Bennett's studies (1987, 1990, 1991) intentionally evaluated the most highly regarded schemes. The broad conclusion was that it was necessary to more closely examine the dynamics of how Neighborhood Watch was meant to work, since evidence was lacking of successful impact on crime levels, most likely as a result of implementation failure. As Pease (1997) observed, this was not to dismiss the concept—the schemes may simply have deviated from the principles on which Neighborhood Watch is based, or not achieved a practice in accord with them. When viewed in the round (rather than focusing on the best schemes, in the pursuit of best practice), Neighborhood Watch does appear to be marked by "low take-up rates, weak community penetration and limping, dormant or stillborn schemes" (McConville and Shepherd 1992).

The Effectiveness of Neighborhood Watch

The clearest picture from empirical evaluations of Neighborhood Watch, whether the analysis of crime statistics in areas with and without programs or the descriptive studies of Neighborhood Watch in action, is that effectiveness is elusive in statistical terms and that identifying the elements that make for best practice run up against confusions of purpose and variations in approach. Neighborhood Watch is seldom the only initiative operating in a given locale, especially where risk of residential crime is high, so there is difficulty in disentangling the effects of different programs. Neighborhood Watch and analogous programs suffer substantial ambiguity as to whether their aim is crime reduction or fear reduction, and they may attract the already exceptionally fearful and exacerbate concerns already felt.

Against this, Neighborhood Watch has embedded itself in public and police awareness (reinforced by the insurance industry), and despite difficulty in establishing that it has substantial impact, it is a relatively inexpensive program. Its manifest function may be less significant than its latent if modest effects on social cohesion, such as where Neighborhood Watch newsletters serve to reinforce a sense of community among citizens and provide basic information on crime prevention.

NIGEL G. FIELDING

See also **Alarms as Crime Prevention; Closed-Circuit Television Applications for Policing; Community Watch Programs; Crimestoppers; Neighborhood Effects on Crime and Social Organization**

References and Further Reading

Bennett, Trevor. 1987. *An evaluation of two Neighbourhood Watch schemes in London.* Cambridge: Cambridge Institute of Criminology.
———. 1990. *Evaluating Neighbourhood Watch.* Aldershot: Gower.
———. 1991. Themes and variations in Neighbourhood Watch. In *Crime, policing and place: Essays in environmental criminology*, ed. Evans, Fyfe, and Herbert. London: Routledge.
Budd, Tracy, and Lawrence Sims. 2001. *Antisocial behaviour and disorder.* Home Office Research Findings No. 145. London: Home Office.
Fielding, Nigel. 1995. *Community policing.* Oxford: Clarendon.
Home Office. 2001. *Neighbourhood Watch: Findings from the 2000 British Crime Survey.* London: Home Office Research, Development and Statistics Directorate.
Hough, Michael. 1994. *Anxiety about crime.* Home Office Research Findings No. 147. London: Home Office.
Husain, S., and Jon Bright. 1990. *Neighbourhood Watch and the police.* Swindon: Crime Concern.
Mayhew, Patricia, D. Elliot, and L. Dowds. 1989. *The 1988 British Crime Survey.* London: HMSO.
McConville, Sean, and D. Shepherd. 1992. *Watching police, watching communities.* London: Routledge.
Pease, Kenneth. 1997. Crime prevention. In *The Oxford handbook of criminology*, ed. Maguire, Morgan, and Reiner. Oxford: Oxford University Press.
Rawlings, Philip. 2002. *Policing: A short history.* Cullompton, Devon: Willan Publishing.
Shapland, Joanna, and Jonathan Vagg. 1987. Using the police. *British Journal of Criminology* 27 (1): 54–63.

NEW YORK POLICE DEPARTMENT (NYPD)

The New York Police Department (NYPD) traces its historical roots to 1845, when Mayor William Havemayer replaced the existing constabulary with a department numbering about nine hundred men. With a population of about four hundred thousand in 1845, New York City struggled with a host of crime and disorder problems associated with increased urbanization, poverty, gangs, and slums. The agency was then called the New York Municipal Police and, in terms of its structure and purpose, was modeled after the London Metropolitan Police.

Particularly during its early days, the competing political parties and factions active in New York City recognized the agency as a potential source of political power and patronage, and they actively sought to extend their influence and control over the department. The extent of political influence, like the corruption and patronage that accompanied it, was by no means unique to the New York police, but rather was characteristic of many or most urban police agencies during the period, often referred to as the Political Era of American policing. Among the department's responsibilities, for example, was the supervision of elections, and because officers were political appointees, many had a vested interest in the outcomes. This period predated the introduction of civil service protections, and police officers of all ranks typically purchased their position from the local political figures, to whom they were beholden. In many respects the police were adjuncts of the political machines that ran major American cities in that era, to the extent that police often used their powers to serve politicians as collectors of political graft and enforcers of political whim.

In 1857, political conflicts between the city's ruling Democrats and the Albany Republicans who controlled the state government caused the state legislature to create a rival police agency, the New York Metropolitan Police. Mayor Fernando Wood, however, refused to disband his Municipals and the chief of the Metropolitans ordered him arrested. In May 1857, about fifty members of the Metropolitans attempting to arrest Wood squared off against three hundred Municipals outside City Hall in a brawl that would lead to a three-day police riot. The National Guard was eventually called out to quell the riot, in which fifty-two officers were injured, and Wood was charged with inciting the riot and briefly arrested before being returned to office on bail.

Clashes continued throughout the summer of 1857, with officers from one department often refusing to take action when criminal gangs engaged in pitched battles with police from the other agency. It became common for members of one department to summarily release criminals arrested by members of the other department. The Metropolitans ultimately prevailed in the dispute, and the Municipals were disbanded. It was not until 1870 that control of the police was returned to local authorities.

Political influence and the corruption that attended it continued in various forms through the remainder of the nineteenth century despite various attempts to introduce reforms. Since 1895, the NYPD has faced no less than six major corruption scandals, with these scandals occurring at approximate twenty-year intervals. These take the form of a cycle in which corruption is followed by attempts to introduce reforms, which are in turn followed by political and organizational apathy and the reemergence of corruption in a modified form. Each scandal has been investigated by a commission of inquiry, the most recent being the Mollen Commission (1992–1994).

New York's first major police corruption scandal was the product of a campaign launched by the crusading Reverend Charles Parkhurst, who in 1892 took on the police and the local Tammany Hall political machine for their deep involvement in vice, gambling, and other criminal activities. The New York State legislature responded by appointing the Lexow Commission, and its report detailed systematic payoffs to police by brothels, gambling operations, and organized confidence rings, as well as police extortion of businesses over whom they had some regulatory authority. The report also described systemic corruption, the sale of police jobs, widespread police brutality, and police compliance in the fixing of elections for Tammany candidates.

The scandal led to the election of a progressive Fusion Party administration in 1895, as well as the appointment of reformer Theodore Roosevelt as president of the agency's board of commissioners from 1895 to 1897. He modernized management practices, introducing the department's first objective hiring standards as well as police training programs. Roosevelt also hired the NYPD's first woman employee.

A 1901 reorganization abolished the bipartisan board of commissioners and put the agency under the control of a single police commissioner, a mayoral appointee. Many of the appointees during the first decades of the new century had little or no background in law enforcement, but rather were prominent and politically connected citizens. One exception was Richard Enright, who served from 1918 to 1925. He was, previously, the president of the NYPD's lieutenant's union that had supported Mayor John Hylan's candidacy.

While some of Roosevelt's reforms were later undone by other administrations, his actions reflected a much larger reform movement in American urban politics. That modernizing movement made significant strides toward reducing patronage and improper political influence on police in New York City through the first few decades of the twentieth century. These strides included the introduction of a civil service system, the creation of a police academy providing entry-level and in-service training, more streamlined bureaucratic structures, procedures to impose stricter accountability and reduce police discretion, education and literacy standards, and the use of objective examination processes to determine promotions. Ultimately, the reform movement was subsumed by the philosophy and practices of the "professional" model championed by August Vollmer, O. W. Wilson, and others.

The professional model, which also emphasized administrative efficiency, better training, the use of technology, tighter lines of accountability, stricter supervision, and more highly centralized bureaucratic structures that limited police discretion by concentrating authority at the top of the organizational pyramid began to take hold

in the NYPD in the 1920s and continued to expand its influence through the 1960s and 1970s. These decades saw a trend toward increased specialization and the emergence of units and squads to deal with specific crime problems as well as greater use of patrol cars, radios, and other communications technology.

While the patrol function has always been the backbone of the department and still accounts for the greatest share of personnel and resources, the increasing complexity of urban life, technological developments, and a growing recognition that specific skills and approaches are required to effectively address difficult crime and disorder problems led to the creation of many specialized units. These included units focusing on narcotics, vice, robbery, juvenile aid, community affairs, and other police responsibilities. The NYPD also took on civil defense responsibilities during World War II and established a civilian air warden system to prepare for the possibility of enemy air raids on the city. The NYPD's administrative structures, regulations, and tables of organization changed frequently over these decades in response to newly emerging problems and issues.

The 1960s were a particularly turbulent decade for the NYPD, as it was for American policing in general. Rapid increases in crime occurred, with crime rates in New York City doubling during the decade, and like many other cities, New York faced urban riots in 1964 and 1968. The NYPD also achieved much greater diversity as increasing numbers of African Americans, Latinos, Asians, and women joined the department.

Until 1967, virtually all of the department's female officers had the civil service title of policewoman (entry-level male officers had the patrolman title) and were members of the separate Policewomen's Bureau. Their duties consisted primarily of searching and guarding female prisoners, serving as matrons, caring for lost children, juvenile aid, and clerical functions. Women were first assigned to patrol precincts, albeit in administrative assignments, in 1967, and it was not until 1972 that a small number of women were first assigned to patrol duties. The policewoman and patrolman ranks were abolished and merged into the police officer title in 1972. By the end of the decade, women were fully integrated into operational patrol, investigative, and enforcement assignments.

The decade of the 1970s began with yet another corruption scandal when allegations of pervasive graft raised by Sergeant David Durk and Patrolman Frank Serpico led to the creation of the Knapp Commission. The reforms and organizational changes that ensued were significant and led to substantial and largely effective changes in the agency's structure and cultural ethos. Police Commissioner Patrick V. Murphy brought the philosophy and practices of the professional model to their highest level in the NYPD's history, dramatically restructuring the agency and creating specialized bureaus and units to deal with organized crime, vice, narcotics, and internal affairs. Murphy also dramatically curtailed police discretion and expanded supervisory powers. The 1970s also saw continued rising rates of crime and violence, as well as an increase in domestic terrorist bombings and the targeting of NYPD officers for assassination by radical groups. In 1975, the city's fiscal crisis led to layoffs of police and civilian employees of the department, and the agency's head count of sworn personnel declined by almost seven thousand between 1975 and 1982.

Rising rates of crime and public disorder continued unabated through the 1980s and into the 1990s. The 1980s saw the emergence of the "crack epidemic" and the violent crime it entailed, and such signs of public disorder as graffiti and litter proliferated. Quality of life in the city continued in a declining spiral, and violent crime reached its pinnacle in the city in 1990, when 2,245 murders were reported. The NYPD made a substantial effort to introduce principles of community policing in the late 1980s and early 1990s, and although a slight dip in reported crime was achieved in 1993, the new philosophy's overall impact on crime and public disorder was negligible.

The first major inroads against crime and disorder were achieved in 1994, when Police Commissioner William J. Bratton revitalized the department in a process of organizational reengineering that dramatically realigned the bureaucratic structure and introduced a new philosophy of policing. Bratton streamlined the agency in 1994 and 1995, changing the management culture by reaching deep into the agency's ranks to promote its best and brightest managers to executive positions and charging them with the responsibility to aggressively fight crime and disorder. A series of crime control and quality of life strategies were developed and implemented, to great effect. Bratton also achieved a merger with both the Transit Police Department and the Housing Police Department, which had been separate and autonomous agencies since their creation in the 1950s and early 1960s, and he introduced a radically new management style known as COMPSTAT.

Using computer technology, crime mapping, the analysis of timely and accurate crime statistics, and highly effective crime-fighting strategies and tactics, the COMPSTAT process introduced in 1994 revolutionized the NYPD and resulted in immediate and dramatic crime reductions, to the extent that New York City is now the safest large city in the nation. Homicides, for example, declined more than 72% between 1993 and 2005, and more than 76% from their high point in 1990. Overall, the crime rate in New York City now stands at its lowest point since 1963. These precipitous declines are widely attributed to the NYPD's COMPSTAT management process, which has been broadly emulated by other police agencies.

The NYPD's most recent restructuring began in early 2002, in response to the new demands placed on the department and upon American policing in general by the devastating terrorist attacks of September 11, 2001. Twenty-three NYPD officers were among the rescuers who lost their lives in the World Trade Center attacks. Newly appointed Police Commissioner Raymond Kelly responded to these emerging demands by shifting personnel and resources to counterterrorism, intelligence, and emergency preparedness functions. He created a new Counterterrorism Bureau and dramatically enhanced the Intelligence Bureau, assigning several thousand officers to specialized antiterrorism duties in units throughout the agency. The department's innovative counterterrorism stance includes assigning NYPD liaison officers to law enforcement and intelligence agencies in cities around the world to facilitate the rapid collection, analysis, and sharing of terrorism-related intelligence.

The NYPD, with a current complement of about 35,000 sworn officers (down from a high of nearly 39,000 sworn officers in 2002) and approximately 14,500 civilian employees, is by far the nation's largest and arguably its most complex police agency. Like virtually every other American police agency, it is organized in the hierarchical paramilitary structure often referred to as the military model. Given the fact that both police and military organizations are characterized by similar operational demands involving issues of chain of command, unity of command, internal discipline, strict accountability, training, the use of force, and the need for effective supervision and leadership, the military model is generally considered an appropriate and generally viable organizational structure for police agencies. In policing, this tiered system interposes a layer of civilian control between the agency's uniformed members (that is, those with arrest and enforcement powers) and the political structure through which they are accountable to the public.

Entry-level NYPD officers, who are hired following a process involving a written civil service examination as well as medical, psychological, and background evaluations, hold the rank of police officer. They are supervised by sergeants. Lieutenants supersede sergeants, and lieutenants are supervised by captains. Each of these supervisory ranks are attained through an objective written civil service examination based on knowledge of law and department procedures. Detectives are not chosen through an examination process but rather are selected from among police officers and, as their designation implies, they perform investigative duties. Detectives do not have supervisory authority over police officers or any other rank.

The ranks above captain include deputy inspector, inspector, deputy chief, assistant chief, and bureau chief, filled by appointment at the discretion of the police commissioner from among those who have achieved the civil service rank of captain. There is also one chief of department, appointed by the commissioner, and this individual holds the agency's top uniformed position. The ranks from police officer through chief of department are collectively referred to as "uniformed ranks," and all are sworn officers with enforcement powers.

The agency is headed by a civilian police commissioner who is a mayoral appointee and who serves at the pleasure of the city's mayor. The police commissioner appoints a number of civilian deputy commissioners and civilian assistant commissioners. As civilians, these commissioners have responsibility for managing various administrative functions but do not have arrest or enforcement powers.

The NYPD's current organizational structure provides for fourteen deputy commissioners responsible for such functions as community affairs, legal matters, training, technology development, equal employment opportunity, public information, and strategic initiatives. They have little or no line authority over enforcement functions, which are generally under the command of a bureau chief. Among the NYPD's bureaus are the detective, internal affairs, patrol services, organized crime control, special operations, personnel, transportation, and housing bureaus.

By far the largest of these is the Patrol Services Bureau, which is the overhead command for the eight patrol boroughs that have geographic responsibility for large areas of the city. These are Patrol Boroughs Manhattan North, Manhattan South, Queens North, Queens South, Brooklyn North, Brooklyn South, Bronx, and Staten Island. The NYPD's seventy-six precinct commands provide police services in smaller geographic areas dispersed among these patrol boroughs—on average, there are ten precincts in each patrol borough.

Within the Transportation Bureau, which is responsible for the city's subways and rapid transit system, the equivalent of a patrol precinct is the Transit District, and nine Housing Police Service Areas (PSAs) also serve the city's public housing developments under the aegis of the Housing Bureau. These commands, it should be noted, are in addition to various investigative commands and specialized units. The NYPD's command structure and table of organization are fairly complex.

As the NYPD moves into the future, it continues to adapt and evolve in response to changing social, economic, political, and crime conditions, as it has over the course of its 160-year existence. Perhaps the greatest challenge the NYPD currently faces is the need to continue evolving to address the new threats posed by terrorism, all the while upholding and extending the civil rights of those who live, work in, or visit the city. New York City, with a population of about eight million, is home to the United Nations as well as the world's diplomatic and business communities, and it is both the corporate center and the continual focus of the national and international media. New York City, which bills itself as "The Capital of the World," is concurrently an exceptionally attractive high-value terrorist target, and the threat of terrorism is not likely to subside in the near future. In addition to combating traditional forms of crime and disorder, it is the NYPD's role and responsibility to assume new duties and functions and to evolve new methods that will prevent, detect, and investigate terrorist activities and the threats to public safety they pose.

VINCENT E. HENRY

See also **Accountability; American Policing: Early Years; British Policing; COMPSTAT; History of American Policing; Knapp Commission; Mollen Commission; Police in Urban America, 1860–1920**

References and Further Reading

Henry, Vincent E. 2002. *The COMPSTAT paradigm: Management accountability in policing, business and the public sector*. Flushing, NY: Looseleaf Law Publications.

Jeffers, H. Paul 1996. *Commissioner Roosevelt: The story of Theodore Roosevelt and the New York City Police, 1895–1897*. New York: John Wiley and Sons.

Lardner, James, and Thomas Reppetto. 2000. *NYPD: A city and its police*. New York: Henry Holt.

Pooley, Eric, with Elaine Rivera. 1996. One good apple: Police Commissioner William Bratton set out to prove that cops really can cut crime. The experts scoffed—but felony rates have dropped so far, so fast, that no other explanation makes sense. *Time* 147 (Jan. 15): 3.

Reppetto, Thomas A. 1978. *The blue parade*. New York: Free Press.

Wheatley, Richard. 1887. The New York City Police Department. *Harper's New Monthly Magazine* 74 (March): 7–30.

NIEDERHOFFER, ARTHUR

Arthur Niederhoffer (1917–1981), a street cop turned sociologist, was revered as a charismatic role model by thousands of police officers and students he taught, advised, and inspired. His multifaceted career in law enforcement as police officer, attorney, professor, author, and researcher broadened and sharpened his in-depth perspectives on the police.

Born in New York City, Niederhoffer, interestingly, as a child loved walking past the neighborhood police station. Educated in the city's public schools, Niederhoffer was encouraged in academics and athletics by his parents. His father, Martin, a court interpreter, graduated from City College in New York City. A brilliant student, Niederhoffer entered Brooklyn College at the age of fifteen and competed on the football and handball teams. After his graduation in 1937, he went on to Brooklyn Law School, where he earned his LL.B. cum laude (later converted to J.D. cum laude). In 1940, the same year he was admitted to the New York State Bar as an attorney, he joined the New York City Police Department. As a result of the depressed economy, there were fewer opportunities for lawyers, and he thought that as a policeman he would be able to put his legal background to use

"I learned about police work by pounding a beat," Niederhoffer often candidly admitted. He rose through the ranks—appointed sergeant in 1951, promoted to lieutenant in 1956. He achieved four departmental recognition awards for meritorious performance. In two separate incidents he rescued suicidal women—each 250 pounds—from drowning in the East River. After both acts of heroism he had to be hospitalized briefly due to the effects of submersion. In addition, he won a tuition grant for outstanding educational attainment in police-related studies.

During the final period of his twenty-one-year police career, Niederhoffer instructed, supervised, and trained recruits at the New York City Police Academy. As curriculum development officer in charge, he raised the educational level and requirements of the training program. He also lectured to community groups and did psychological testing, personnel evaluation, and research into the quality and performance of police at the academy.

In 1960 he served as executive aide to the police liaison officer of the American Institute for Research (AIR), a nationally known research group cosponsored by the Russell Sage and Rockefeller foundations. AIR conducted a long-range research program in the New York City Police Department aimed at improving selection and training procedures.

While still on the force, Niederhoffer returned to Brooklyn College and in 1956 earned a master's degree in sociology, conferred summa cum laude, an honor rarely bestowed by the department. His first book, *The Gang: A Study of Adolescent Behavior* (1958), written with sociologist Herbert A. Bloch, is based on Niederhoffer's masters thesis. From their extensive study of adolescent behavior in a variety of cultures, the researchers theorized that when a society does not make adequate provisions for the passage of adolescents into adult status, youths create equivalent groups to fill the void. Sometimes these groups become subverted into delinquent gangs. Bloch and Niederhoffer's theory is recognized in the field as an important explanation for juvenile delinquency.

Inspired by his successful return to academia, Niederhoffer continued his studies at New York University's Graduate School of Arts and Science. He was granted his Ph.D. in 1963, two years after his retirement from the police department.

"The job controls a police officer's life when he is on the force, and it haunts him when he leaves. Once a cop, always a cop," he asserted. Underscoring this credo, he drew upon his police career as a frame of reference for his doctoral dissertation, "The Mobile Force: A Study of Police Cynicism." He devised a questionnaire consisting of twenty open-ended statements about significant areas of police work to test eleven hypotheses concerning cynicism in an urban police department and administered it to a sample of 220 police officers.

From the analysis of his data, Niederhoffer concluded that cynicism becomes part of the occupational ideology learned by socialization into the police force. It is in the police academy that recruits initially acquire the stereotyped patterns of cynical attitudes, which are reinforced in the course of their police careers. He pointed out, however, that a police officer's attitude toward his role can change over time and can vary with his experience and background. For example, the brand new recruit will be less cynical than the more seasoned recruit. The recruit will be less cynical than the more experienced police officer. Superior officers will be less cynical than patrolmen. Patrolmen with a college education will be more cynical than their counterparts without education.

From this research study, Niederhoffer devised a cynicism scale, a linear causal model, which has been widely replicated to gauge cynicism in other urban police departments as well as in other occupations and professions.

Niederhoffer had always wanted to teach upon his retirement from the department. "I always had the vision of the scholar. To me the greatest honor is to be a man of learning and have people come to you and learn from you," he said. Consequently, the former police officer launched his professorial career with teaching stints at Queens, Brooklyn, and Baruch colleges of the City University of New York (CUNY); Hofstra University; Long Island University; and New York University. To his subject matter—courses in police administration, delinquency, police science, human relations, criminal justice, and sociology/anthropology—he contributed original thinking, historical and sociological perspectives, and an insider's down-to-earth overview, undergirded by his more than twenty-one years of police experience, with the added perk: a storehouse of colorful police anecdotes to enhance his teaching. He understood the problems of law enforcement, its stresses, and pressures. He had not been just a participant/observer

riding along for several months in a radio patrol car.

In 1967, he moved permanently to John Jay College of Criminal Justice (CUNY) as a professor of sociology, where he taught for fourteen productive years—stimulating, enriching, and inspiring his students and colleagues. Significantly, he was much appreciated as a conciliator, able to link police science and more traditional academic branches of the college.

On the fifteenth anniversary of the founding of John Jay College, Niederhoffer was awarded the college's presidential medal; not only was he the first and only member of the faculty to receive this honor, but he was also unanimously chosen. President Gerald W. Lynch, when presenting the award, described Niederhoffer as an "individual who exemplifies the genius of our faculty, who personifies the best tradition of the great scholar, teacher, and counselor to student and colleagues alike. He is a wonderful human being and one of the loveliest people I know." The citation reads:

> For your extraordinary and continuing career as a scholar, teacher, researcher, and author, for your outstanding contributions to the intellectual development of the field of criminal justice; for your seminal scholarship and numerous publications in sociology and criminology, and for your example to us all in the great tradition of the scholar professor.

With his students and colleagues he discussed topical and perplexing police questions such as, How does an idealistic rookie become cynical? Why are police vulnerable to corruption? Does police authoritarianism come into the force along with the recruits? Exploring these issues and probing some of the internal problems of police work motivated Niederhoffer to write his next book, *Behind the Shield: The Police in Urban Society* (1967). Grounded in his police experience and insights and supplemented by intensive interviews with police officers in other cities, the retired police officer/professor lifted the "blue curtain" of secrecy that had screened police work until then. Although it is an insider's view of an urban police department, it is not a critique or an exposé. Rather, it is a thoughtful, meticulously researched and documented study of the sociology of the police, written by a practicing sociologist, but without the sociological jargon.

In *Behind the Shield* Niederhoffer delineates a psychological and sociological profile of the urban police officer and the social forces that mold his personality. He examines a variety of police activities and describes in a series of vignettes the making of and molding of police officers—the rookie, the detective, the college man, the supervisor, and the old-timer. Niederhoffer analyzes and evaluates why they choose a police career, how they are trained, and what pressures they encounter. And he concludes that "it is the police system, not the personality of the candidate, that is the more powerful determinant of behavior and ideology." For example, on authoritarianism he comments:

> ... Police authoritarianism does not come into the force along with the recruits, but rather is inculcated through strenuous socialization and experience in the police social system.
> ... The police occupational system is geared to manufacture the "take-charge guy," and it succeeds in doing so with outstanding efficiency. ... The hostility and fear that press almost palpably against a policeman in lower-class areas aggravates his impulse to get tough.
> ... Since the policeman feels justified and righteous in using power and toughness to perform his duties, he feels like a martyr when he is charged with brutality and abuse of power.

Behind the Shield had been published shortly after racial riots—which many were convinced were triggered by police action—in Rochester, New York; Philadelphia; New York's Harlem; the Watts section of Los Angeles; and Newark, New Jersey. Consequently, the spotlight of the nation focused on the police. As a former police lieutenant, Niederhoffer had been able to put into words, with empathy and respect for the police image, what police officers actually live through. And as a professor of sociology he had the clout and credibility to clarify controversial police issues, tempered by his sociological insights. His national reputation escalated to the point where he was recognized as one of the foremost experts on police problems. A dynamic, down-to-earth, and provocative speaker, he was invited to lecture, participate in conferences on the police, and evaluate law enforcement programs all over the United States and in Canada.

Moreover, he was never afraid to step over the official "blue" line to express his convictions that targeted controversial police issues. Consider, for instance, his comments on crime:

> ... [C]rime is a community problem, not a police problem. A larger police force is not the answer.

On the legal system:

> ... [P]olice are solidly aligned against the U.S. Supreme Court, which they suspect is slowly but surely dismantling the hallowed foundation of law enforcement. I do not feel that Supreme Court decisions shackle police. Police will develop new techniques of investigation that will make them more effective.

On professionalism in police work:

> ... [T]he great stumbling block is in police work's traditionally low status in our culture. The public holds fast to the derogatory stereotypes of the grafting cop, the sadistic cop, the dumb cop, the chiseling cop, and the thick-brogued cop. There can be no profession where the public refuses to grant high status and prestige.
> ... [T]he rookie police officer is faced with the dilemma of choosing between the professional ideals acquired during his academy training and the pragmatic approach of the precinct—the requirements of the job.

On college education:

> ... We can't assume that education makes "A" a better police officer than "B," but education can improve a person. College can increase knowledge and give one a more open mind—perhaps more tolerant and sophisticated in what to look for—with more insights and alternatives for action.
>
> ... I feel that there is a danger in having an elite police force. I believe that the police force should be more representative of the population at large and permit a great number of persons without college degrees to enter. Although I would encourage every department to encourage as much as possible the study and improvement of the force by education at every rank.

And finally, with prophetic vision on the future of policing in America:

> ... There are three things that are very important: first, unionization. There is a split in the ranks over professionalism and unionism. (My prediction is that unionism will win because it appeals more and gives more protection to the officer at the lower echelon.) Next is the introduction of women into police work. And the third is the spread of college training for police.

Additionally, Niederhoffer applied his perceptions concerning law enforcement in a concrete way to the escalating problems of crime and violence in inner cities. He participated in several hands-on projects with the same objective—to build a bridge between the police and the community. Under the aegis of New York City's then–Mayor John V. Lindsay, Niederhoffer in 1968 helped to organize and supervise a community police corps to combat crime in Harlem. This innovative plan established a youth patrol using local residents to assist the police by performing certain street patrol functions to prevent crime. In the same year he was recruited, along with Alexander B. Smith, by the U.S. Department of Health, Education, and Welfare to submit a report entitled "The Development and Impact of the Police–Community Relations Project of the Office of Juvenile Delinquency." To assess the project, Smith and Niederhoffer visited eight police–community relations programs, conducted extensive interviews, and observed the plan in action.

In his most ambitious research to date, Niederhoffer functioned as director of research in a two-year-long major study during 1970–1971, sponsored by the U.S. Department of Justice's Law Enforcement Assistance Administration (LEAA), National Institute of Law Enforcement and Criminal Justice, Technical Assistance in Criminal Justice, Washington, D.C. Niederhoffer critiqued, evaluated, and commented on more than three hundred proposals on police, courts, criminal justice, crime prevention, and other subjects, already submitted to the institute for funding by LEAA and on ongoing and/or completed activities of institute grantees and contractors.

This in-depth project for LEAA underscored for him how strands of police action are inextricably intertwined with law enforcement and the fate of society. In his view:

> ... [P]olice will be at the storm center of each episode of crisis or catastrophe that is bound to occur in the ghetto, on the campus, at demonstrations, or wherever social protest is most threatening .... . Society is asking the police not only to protect it, but also to preserve it. The people of America turn to them as saviors and demand an end to lawlessness and violence.

Responding to this mandate in his own way, the retired police lieutenant published three more books and numerous articles in professional journals related to police and law enforcement (see References and Further Reading). Long Island University honored Niederhoffer with its Distinguished Service Award in recognition of his achievements in criminal justice.

In *The Ambivalent Force: Perspectives on the Police* (1970), a book of readings edited by Niederhoffer and Abraham S. Blumberg, the coeditors examine the harsh ambiguities and ambivalences of the police role. As a result of the tensions and conflicts of the occupation, police officers need more than technical and legalistic training. To broaden police perspectives, Niederhoffer and Blumberg present police in their anthology in a social, historical, and comparative setting, assembling articles by experts in their fields—the academic behavioral scientist, the journalist, the lawyer, the psychologist, the police officer, and the historian.

Building on their mounting interest in police–community relations, Niederhoffer and Smith wrote *New Directions in Police–Community Relations* (1974). Previously, the researchers had jointly paid on-site visits to police–community relations projects for their evaluation report to the Office of Juvenile Delinquency, U.S. Department of Health, Education, and Welfare. And, as research director for the LEAA study, Niederhoffer had reviewed numerous police–community programs. Smith, too, had been involved with community relations units of the police department when he headed a study of law enforcement efforts to prevent and control the illegal distribution and sale of pornography. *New Directions in Police–Community Relations* offers a practical guide to police–community relations, utilizing case studies, questionnaires, and interviews. To observe programs in action, the coauthors visited sites in New Orleans; Wilmington, Delaware; Houston, Texas; Enfield, Connecticut; Philadelphia; and New York City.

Niederhoffer subsequently explored the personal side of life on the force by contemplating such varied questions as, How does police work affect family relationships? Does the occupation precipitate suicide, marital instability, or divorce? Niederhoffer and his wife, Elaine, investigated these complex and pressing problems in *The Police Family: From Station House to Ranch House* (1978). In their well-documented book, the coauthors employed questionnaires, interviews, surveys, and rap sessions with officers in major police departments, their spouses, and their children and with police chaplains, revealing a behind-the-scenes view of the pressures on the families of police officers. Moreover, because the Niederhoffers lived for more than twenty years within the "blue circle," they were able to enliven their empirical study with personal anecdotes.

Admittedly, the couple wrote, "the shadow of the job darkens family relationships"; the omnipresent sense of danger arouses fear for the safety of loved ones; the oppressive revolving duty chart disrupts family routines; the high visibility of the police family's activities promotes surveillance by the community and media. But the Niederhoffers found that, by and large, police families made peace with the occupation; they coped with the distressing problems endemic to police work. The job "may be a jealous mistress," but "if the marriage is O.K., the job is O.K." Of course, marital dissatisfaction and unhappiness can affect working satisfaction, and occupational demands can cause marital dissatisfaction. "The rate of divorce for the occupation as a whole rises no higher than the average level of divorce in the United States. Divorce police style equates with divorce American style." And similarly, ". . . the rate of police suicide is about the same as that for the national adult male population."

Niederhoffer read what was to be his last paper, "Myths and Realities in Criminal Justice," at a meeting of the American Society of Criminology (ASC) in November 1980, feeling as vigorous as ever. He was elected a fellow of the ASC by his colleagues. Shortly after his return he was hospitalized, losing his heroic eight-year battle with lymphoma, and died on January 14, 1981. (In his typical courageous and dedicated way, he managed to grade papers and write to his students during the January intersession.)

At his memorial service, John Jay College President Gerald W. Lynch said:

... Arthur is the prototype of what John Jay College is; the practitioner who stood on the front line of police work; the thinker and explainer to us all of the reasons for social deviance and the proper responsibilities and limits of social control; the man of strong compassion for his fellow human beings who strove to help us understand police work and its stress, as well as the criminals the police must deal with.

In loving tribute, his colleagues, friends, and relatives established the Arthur Niederhoffer Memorial Fellowship, awarded annually to students in the doctoral program in criminal justice at John Jay College who "best epitomize in academic achievement and in the promise of future fulfillment the professional accomplishments of Arthur Niederhoffer."

ELAINE NIEDERHOFFER

See also **Cynicism, Police**

References and Further Reading

Niederhoffer, Arthur. 1967. *Behind the shield: The police in urban society.* Garden City, NY: Doubleday.

———. 1971. Police. *Encyclopedia Americana.* Danbury, CT: Grolier.

———. 1972. Prisons. *Encyclopedia Americana annual.* Danbury, CT: Grolier.

———. 1974. Modern prisons. *Encyclopedia Americana.* Danbury, CT: Grolier.

———. 1976. *Criminal justice higher education.* New York: Advanced Institutional Development Program (AIDP), John Jay College of Criminal Justice.

———. 1977. Police. *World book encyclopedia.* Chicago: World Book.

Niederhoffer, Arthur, and Herbert A. Bloch. 1958. *The gang: A study of adolescent behavior.* New York: Philosophical Library.

Niederhoffer, Arthur, and Abraham S. Blumberg, eds. 1970. *The ambivalent force: Perspectives on the police.* Waltham, MA: Ginn and Company, 1970; Corte Madera, CA: Rinehart Press, 1973; New York: Dryden Press, 1976.

Niederhoffer, Arthur, and Elaine Niederhoffer. 1978. *The police family: From station house to ranch house.* Lexington, MA: Lexington Books.

Niederhoffer, Arthur, and Alexander B. Smith. 1971. *Police–community relations: A study in depth.* Washington, DC: Office of Juvenile Delinquency, Department of Health, Education, and Welfare.

———. 1974. *New directions in police–community relations.* Corte Madera, CA: Rinehart Press.

NONLETHAL (OR LESS-THAN-LETHAL) WEAPONS: HISTORY

Nonlethal Weapons Unveiled, 1829

When London's new bobbies began patrolling the streets in September 1829, they were armed with a baton ("truncheon") that still today is a standard-issue weapon; it was made of hardwood, two to four centimeters in diameter, and thirty to sixty-five centimeters in length. Swords, although not a standard issue to the bobbies in the nineteenth century, were also kept in most police armories for possible use during riots or large demonstrations (Peak 1990).

Social turmoil in America between 1840 and 1870 brought increased use of force by the police. The New York City police and other departments were armed with thirty-three-inch clubs, which officers were not reluctant to use (Peak 1990).

Police and Less-Lethal Force, 1860–1959

International policing from 1860 to 1959 witnessed only one major addition to the small array of nonlethal police tools: chemical weapons. "CN" gas was synthesized in 1869 and was the first "tear gas," producing a burning sensation in the throat, eyes, and nose. (CN became available for use in aerosol cans in 1965, with Chemical Mace the most well-known variety.) By 1912, there was increased use of chemical weapons for riot situations and subduing criminals (Peak 1990).

"CS" gas was first synthesized in 1928 as a white powder, which stored well. It was adopted by many police forces because it had a greater effect than CN, causing a very strong burning sensation in the eyes that often caused them to close involuntarily. Severe pain in the nose, throat, and chest and vomiting and nausea are also associated with its use (Crockett 1968).

After the turn of the century, the baton remained a staple tool among American police. As late as 1900, when the Chicago Police Department numbered 3,225 officers, the only tools given the new patrolman were "a brief speech from a high-ranking officer, a hickory stick, whistle, and a key to the call box" (Haller 1976).

A Technological Explosion: The 1960s

The 1960s witnessed major technological advances in nonlethal weaponry. This was the age of rioting, both on domestic and foreign soil. Aerosol chemical agents, developed to provide alternatives to police batons and firearms, became the most widely used nonlethal weapons to emerge for police use. Mace was developed (Coon 1968), and thousands of law enforcement agencies later adopted Mace in some form.

A chemical wand was also developed, touted as "burning for five full minutes . . . giving off a steady stream of CS" (Peak 1990). "CR" gas appeared in 1962; six times more potent than CS and twenty times more potent than CN, it caused extreme eye pressure and occasional hysteria. CS gas cartridges, fired by shotguns at a range of 125 meters, were used in the United States and Great Britain as early as 1968.

In 1967, alternatives to lethal lead bullets were first attempted in Hong Kong. Wooden rounds, fired from a signal pistol with a range of twenty to thirty meters, were designed to be ricocheted off the ground, striking the victim in the legs. The wooden rounds proved to be fatal, however, and direct fire broke legs at forty-six meters. Rubber bullets were developed and issued to British troops and police officers in 1967, only a few months after the wooden rounds appeared. Intended to deliver at twenty-five meters a force equivalent to a hard punch, the rubber bullets caused severe bruising and shock. Also intended to be ricocheted off the ground, the rubber bullet was designed so that riot police could outrange stone throwers (Manwaring-White 1983).

British riot police also employed water cannons, designed to fire large jets of water at demonstrators on the streets of Derry in 1968, and later in Northern Ireland. Resembling armored fire engines, water cannons were also used in Germany, France, Belgium, and the United States. Nontoxic blue dye was added to the water for marking the offenders; for a time, the firing of a CR solution was contemplated (Manwaring-White 1983).

In 1968, another unique riot-oriented weapon was unveiled in America: the Sound Curdler, consisting of amplified speakers that produced loud, shrieking noises at irregular intervals. Attached to vehicles or helicopters, the device was first used at campus disturbances.

Beanbag Guns, Strobe Lights, and "New Age" Batons: The 1970s

Another unique nonlethal weapon was literally unfurled in 1970: a gun that shot beanbags rather than bullets. The apparatus resembled a large billy club with spiral grooves in the barrel; it fired a pellet-loaded bag that unfurled into a spinning pancake, capable of knocking down a two-hundred-pound person at a range of three hundred feet. Although it had potentially lethal capabilities, it quickly became popular in several countries, including South Africa, Saudi Arabia, and Malaysia (Peak 1990).

Several other inventions were added to the nonlethal arsenal of the police in the 1970s. The Photic Driver produced a strobe effect, its light causing giddiness, fainting, and nausea. A British firm developed a strobe gun, which operated at five "flickers" per second. Some of these devices also had a high-pitched screamer device attached. Another apparatus known as the Squawk Box had two high-energy ultrasound generators operating at slightly different frequencies, which produced sounds that also caused nausea and giddiness (Peak 1990).

Another invention of the early 1970s was injector dart guns, adapted from veterinarians' tranquilizer guns, which, when fired, injected the drug they carried. Other developments included an electrified water jet and a baton that carried a six-thousand-volt shock; shotgun shells filled with plastic pellets; plastic bubbles that immobilized rioters; a chemical that created slippery street surfaces for combating rioters; and an instant "cocoon," which was an adhesive substance that, when sprayed over crowds, made people stick together (Manwaring-White 1983).

A substantive change occurred with the police baton in 1972. A new baton had a handle about six inches from its grip end, which allowed (according to its manufacturers) its versatility to be virtually unlimited (Folley 1972). This "side-handle" baton did indeed become popular and remains popular among police officers today.

Two new tools were developed in 1974: the plastic bullet and the Taser. Research in England resulted in a seemingly "softer" plastic bullet. Made from hard white PVC, four inches in length, one and a quarter inches in diameter, the bullets resembled a blunt candle and could be fired from a variety of riot weapons. Their speed of 160 miles per hour and range of thirty to seventy meters made them attractive to riot police. However, the plastic bullet could be fatal as well, and a number of people died after being struck in the head with these bullets (Manwaring-White 1983).

The Taser resembled a flashlight and shot two tiny darts into its victim. Attached to the darts were fine wires through which a transformer delivered a fifty-thousand-volt electrical shock, which would knock a person down at a distance of fifteen feet. Police officers in every state except Alaska had used the device by 1985, but its use has not been widespread because of limitations of range and limited effectiveness on persons under the influence of drugs. Heavy clothing can also render it ineffective (Sweetman 1987).

The stun gun, also introduced in the mid-1970s, was slightly larger than an electric razor and delivered a fifty-thousand-volt shock when its two electrodes were pressed directly against the body. Like the Taser, its amperage was so small that it did not provide a lethal electrical jolt. Its target, rendered rubbery legged and falling to the ground, was unable to control physical movement for several minutes (Serrill 1985).

The Continuing Quest: The 1980s

During the 1980s, flashlights were marketed that had stun capacity or contained chemical agents (Cox et al. 1985). Also marketed were an expandable baton (from six to sixteen inches "with a flick of the wrist") and a six-inch steel whip, which when opened to its thirteen-inch length projected three steel coils and was transformed into something resembling the medieval cat-o'-nine-tails (Peak 1990).

Summary

Over the course of 175 years, attempts have been made to arm the police with effective alternatives to lethal force. Research and development continues, however, for effective alternatives to lethal force.

Kenneth J. Peak

See also **Crowd/Riot Control; Deadly Force; Liability and the Police; Nonlethal Weapons: Empirical Evidence; Police Legal Liabilities: Overview**

References and Further Reading

Coon, T. F. 1968. A maze of confusion over amazing Mace. *Police*, November–December, 45–47.

Cox, T., J. S. Faughn, and W. M. Nixon. 1985. Police use of metal flashlights as weapons: An analysis of relevant problems. *Journal of Police Science and Administration* 13(3): 244–50.

Crockett, T. S. 1968. Riot control agents. *The Police Chief*, November, 8–18.

Folley, V. L. 1972. The prosecutor: The new concept police baton. *Law and Order*, September, 46–50.

Haller, M. H. 1976. Historical roots of police behavior: Chicago, 1890–1925. *Law and Society Review* 10 (2): 303–23.

Manwaring-White, S. 1983. *The policing revolution: Police technology, democracy, and liberty in Britain*. Brighton, Sussex: The Harvester Press.

Peak, K. 1990. The quest for alternatives to lethal force: A heuristic view. *Journal of Contemporary Criminal Justice* 6 (1): 8–22.

Serrill, M. S. 1985. ZAP! Stun guns: Hot but getting heat. *Time*, May, 59.

Sweetman, S. 1987. *Report on the Attorney General's Conference on Less Than Lethal Weapons*. Washington, DC: Department of Justice, National Institute of Justice.

NONLETHAL WEAPONS: EMPIRICAL EVIDENCE

Compared to the number of arrests made by police officers, violent altercations are relatively few in number. Many police use-of-force situations are sudden close-contact situations, requiring immediate, instinctive response. Other situations begin as stand-off situations (with time for planning and maneuvering) but change to immediate-response situations if officers do not take aggressive actions to control the suspect before the stand-off situation deteriorates.

The term "nonlethal weapons" is used generically to identify devices that may be used to aggressively take control of a deteriorating tactical situation prior to the time when control holds, batons, or deadly force may become necessary, when it is unsafe for an officer to move to within contact range of the suspect, and when attempts by officers to control the suspect by conventional means will likely result in serious injury to officers, suspects, or both (Meyer et al. 1981).

Research and Testing

In 1979 and 1980, the Los Angeles Police Department (LAPD) researched more than a dozen innovative devices that attempt to control violent people (especially those under the influence of PCP) in a way that reduces injuries to suspects and officers. In 1981, the LAPD adopted Taser and chemical irritant sprays of the CS and CN types. The Taser and chemical irritant sprays had the advantage of being handheld, one-officer operations that allowed the officer to stay six to fifteen feet away from the suspect. The other devices required setup and application by trained teams to operate.

Practical Scenarios

During the 1970s, many officers around the country received major incapacitating injuries while attempting to take into custody persons under the influence of PCP, an animal tranquilizer known for giving human users "superhuman" strength. It was not unusual for the most aggressive efforts of five or six officers to be inadequate to control a single PCP suspect without serious injury to several of the involved parties.

It was in this context that the LAPD believed that any weapon was worth looking into if it could stop incidents from escalating to a point where deadly force may have to be used. Time (sudden attack versus a standoff situation) and distance between the officer and the suspect are the crucial factors in determining whether nonlethal weapons are appropriate for a situation. During the past twelve years, the Taser and chemical irritant sprays have been used in thousands of standoff situations. Such situations frequently deteriorate into immediate-response, deadly force situations if the suspect attacks with a knife or a club (or other dangerous implement amounting to less than a firearm) and if the suspect is not quickly controlled.

The vast majority of nonlethal weapon incidents involve unarmed suspects who exhibit resistive, violent, or bizarre behavior, thus presenting a significant safety threat to themselves, others, and the officers whose job it is to intervene.

Critique of the Literature

In 1980, the supervising physician of the Medical Services Division, Los Angeles City Personnel Department, wrote that the Taser was "reasonable and feasible and presents no undue risk to the recipient." In 1985, after the LAPD had used the Taser hundreds of times, a medical journal article concluded that "major injuries, either primary to the [electrical] current or secondary to [falling down], have not been reported" (Koscove 1985). The need for effective nonlethal weapons is also demonstrated by expensive litigation, which results from injuries produced by conventional tactics. Americans for Effective Law Enforcement, a Chicago-based legal and law enforcement educational association, has documented a number of

out-of-court settlements and jury awards in amounts ranging from tens of thousands of dollars to millions of dollars to compensate people for injuries they received from conventional tactics such as batons and flashlights.

In a landmark nonlethal weapons case in 1988 (*Michenfelder v. Sumner*, 860 F.2nd 328), a federal appellate court found the following:

> ... authorities believe the Taser is the preferred method for controlling prisoners because it is the "least confrontational" when compared to the use of physical restraint, billy clubs, mace, or [beanbag] guns .... When contrasted to alternative methods for physically controlling inmates, some of which can have serious after-effects, the Taser compared favorably.

The Meyer Study

LAPD records show that 1,160 of the reports for the first half of 1989 documented incidents in which officers attempted to control suspects by causing them to fall to the ground. A stratified sampling procedure yielded 395 reports in which any of six conventional force types (baton, kick, punch, flashlight, swarm technique, or miscellaneous bodily force) was documented as the effective force that controlled the situation; eighty-eight reports where Taser was the effective force; and nineteen reports where chemical irritant spray was the effective force. Thus, a total of 502 reports were subjected to analysis. Sixty-six of these documented more than one force type that fit the research scenario (that is, listed at least one force type that was ineffective in addition to the force type that succeeded), and care was taken to avoid double counting.

Variables from each of the 502 reports in the sample were coded and the data were entered into Stata, a statistical computer program, and subjected to analysis. Selected pairs of variables were cross-tabulated and subjected to chi-square testing to determine if statistically significant relationships existed. The purpose of such testing was to rule out as much as possible the hypothesis that the relationships that appeared to exist between tested variables were due to chance, that is, that there was no actual relationship. All of the relationships were of such significance that there was not one chance in two thousand that the relationships were due to chance.

Meyer created the injury classification scheme depicted in Table 1.

Findings

Table 2 reports injuries to suspects from the effective force types (that is, the force type that brought the incident to a conclusion).

Table 3 reports the number of injuries to officers that resulted from each effective force type.

Table 4 shows the varying success rates (that is, the percentage of incidents for which a given weapon or tactic was the effective force type) achieved by different force types, along with corresponding injury rates to officers and suspects.

The data clearly demonstrate that the Taser electronic weapon and chemical irritant spray caused fewer and less severe injuries than conventional force types. The data did not suggest any other rival hypotheses that might account for the results.

In police confrontations that cannot be controlled by verbalization, nonlethal weapons should be used early and aggressively to bring the situation to a conclusion as quickly as possible before it deteriorates into a confrontation requiring a greater level of force. This concept is the key to significantly reducing injuries to officers and suspects. Moral and legal constraints require officers to use the minimum amount of reasonable and necessary force

Table 1   Injury reporting designators used in this study

Injury Designator	Definition
None	No injury
Taser/gas	Effects from Taser or chemical irritant spray only
Minor	Complained of pain, minor scratches, skin redness
Moderate	Small lacerations, welts, contusions, bruises
Major[a]	Breaks, concussions, large lacerations or contusions, sprains, strains

[a]Officer placed off duty or on light (nonfield) duty; suspect usually hospitalized.

Table 2   Injuries to suspects by effective force type

Effective Force Type	None	Taser/Gas[a]	Minor[b]	Moderate[b]	Major[b]	Total
Baton	24	0	24	66	7	121
Kick	20	0	9	12	0	41
Punch	6	0	5	15	1	27
Miscellaneous force	51	0	20	58	6	135
Flashlight	4	0	0	14	6	24
Swarm	33	0	3	10	1	47
Chemical spray	0	18	1	0	0	19
Taser	0	88	0	0	0	88
Total	138	106	62	175	21	502

[a]Taser/gas means effects of Taser or chemical irritant spray only.
[b]Defined in Table 1.

Table 3   Injuries to officers by effective force type

Effective Force Type	None	Taser/Gas[a]	Minor[b]	Moderate[b]	Major[b]	Total
Baton	99	0	4	10	8	121
Kick	36	0	0	3	2	41
Punch	19	0	0	5	3	27
Miscellaneous force	109	0	5	13	8	135
Flashlight	20	0	3	1	0	24
Swarm	39	0	1	6	1	47
Chemical spray	14	5	0	0	0	19
Taser	88	0	0	0	0	88
Total	424	5	13	38	22	502

[a] Taser/gas means effects of Taser or chemical irritant spray only.
[b] Defined in Table 1.

Table 4   Success rates of force types, with corresponding injury rates

Force Type	Study Cases[a]	Success Cases	Success Rate	Major/Moderate Injuries[b]	
				Officers	Suspects
Baton	143	121	85%	16%	61%
Kick	47	41	87%	11%	26%
Punch	36	27	75%	36%	64%
Miscellaneous force	143	135	94%	15%	46%
Flashlight	25	24	96%	4%	80%
Swarm	51	47	92%	16%	24%
Chemical spray	21	19	90%	0%	0%
Taser	102	88	86%	0%	0%
Total	568	502	88%	13%	39%

[a] Includes effective and ineffective force types.
[b] Percentage of injuries, regardless of whether force was effective.

to control a confrontation. It hardly needs to be noted that those force types that are effective and result in the least severe injuries to officers and suspects are more reasonable than those that result in greater injuries.

GREG MEYER

See also **Arrest Powers of the Police; Conflict Management; Danger and Police Work; Excessive Force; Liability and Use of Force; Nonlethal (or Less-than-Lethal) Weapons: History**

References and Further Reading

Casey, Joe D. 1988. Research and development needed for less-than-lethal weapons. *Police Chief* 55 (Feb.): 7.

Geis, Gilbert, and Arnold Binder. 1990. Nonlethal weapons: The potential and the pitfalls. *Journal of Contemporary Criminal Justice* 6: 1–7.

Geller, William A., and Michael S. Scott. 1992. *Deadly force: What we know*. Washington, DC: Police Executive Research Forum.

Kornblum, Ronald N., and Sara K. Reddy. 1991. Effects of the Taser in fatalities involving police confrontation. *Journal of Forensic Sciences* 36: 434–48.

Koscove, Eric M. 1985. The Taser weapon: A new emergency medicine problem. *Annals of Emergency Medicine* 14 (Dec.): 112.

Meyer, C. Kenneth, et al. 1981. A comparative assessment of assault incidents: Robbery related, ambush, and general police assaults. *Journal of Police Science and Administration* 9: 1–18.

Meyer, Greg. 1981. Your nonlethal weapons alternatives. *Journal of California Law Enforcement* 15: 125–36.

———. 1991. *Nonlethal weapons vs. conventional police tactics: The Los Angeles Police Department experience*. Los Angeles: California State University.

Peak, Ken. 1990. The quest for alternatives to lethal force: A heuristic view. *Journal of Contemporary Criminal Justice* 6: 8–22.

Reddin, Thomas J. 1967. Non-lethal weapons—Curse or cure? *The Police Chief* 34 (Dec.): 60–63.

Scharf, Peter, and Arnold Binder. 1983. *The badge and the bullet*. New York: Praeger.

Sweetman, Sherri. 1987. *Report on the Attorney General's Conference on Less than Lethal Weapons*. Washington, DC: U.S. Department of Justice, National Institute of Justice.

O

OAKLAND POLICE DEPARTMENT

The Oakland Police Department is remarkable for its impact on police science and for changing the way professionals, scientists, academics, and communities view effective policing. In the 1960s, America was struggling with social, political, and economic forces that surprised most institutions. Unemployment, declining urban tax revenues, limited educational opportunities, gender roles, and discrimination were being challenged and the government authority to implement policy was being questioned. Traditional manufacturing jobs were moving offshore, fair housing issues and Supreme Court decisions were altering traditional communities, and people, especially ethnic minorities and students, were questioning the practical reality of "equal" justice in America.

Oakland, during the 1960s, had more diversity of social change than most other venues. The city was exposed to radical challenges that changed the landscape—social activism, political action committees, and new types of crime and disorder,

such as mass antiwar demonstrations. Oakland was the birthplace for the Black Panther Party ("Political Power Comes from the Barrel of a Gun"), the world headquarters of the Hell's Angels motorcycle gang, and home to Asian gangs, the Symbionese Liberation Army (which was responsible for the assassination of Oakland's Superintendent of Schools Dr. Marcus Foster), the Weather Underground, the American Communist Party, the John Birch Society, and many others. Many of these interest groups were in direct conflict with each other. Many police practices—laws of arrest and search and seizure—were ruled unconstitutional by the U.S. Supreme Court; rulings on the exclusionary rule significantly impacted police. (Earl Warren, Chief Justice of the Supreme Court during this turbulent era, had previously been a tough legalistic prosecutor from Oakland.)

Crime and protests were seen, by many, as instruments of social change and justice, subjecting police operations, policies, and demographics to intense controversy. Traditional police strategies and tactics came to be viewed as unfairly impacting specific ethnic groups. Justice institutions were not prepared to respond to social and political criticism. Criminal law and police tactics tend to lag behind rapid social progress, while activists tend to make radical demands for change. Many metropolitan centers, such as Los Angeles, Detroit, Newark, and Chicago, and university campuses such as Kent State in Ohio, experienced unprecedented social and moral conflicts and new forms of massive civil disorder and disobedience.

It was in this context that Oakland policy makers, police, business owners, and community leaders explored options to prevent an Oakland "meltdown into disorder, riots, loss of life and economic disaster." The context, viewed in retrospect, created an unusual opportunity for a natural experiment. A confluence of unique circumstances and actions made possible a chance for some important lessons to be learned. The following briefly outlines a few of the historic pivotal actions.

In 1955, the City of Oakland recruited a young, innovative city manager who immediately appointed a reform-minded, college-educated chief to modernize and reorganize the police department using the best information available from police science research, management theory, and community participation. The city manager and the new chief used an upcoming municipal election to advocate a series of charter amendments intended to authorize major changes in the department—reorganizing the Criminal Investigations Division, closing decentralized stations, establishing standards of accountability by centralizing departmental operations in one headquarters, and forming new bureaus headed by three appointed (exempt rank) deputy chiefs. Under this chief, professionalism was introduced (upgrading academic requirements, introducing new in-service training, implementing a professional code of ethics—modeled on the Hippocratic oath—requiring the rule of law and exemplary professional and private conduct). The members of the department began to internalize the ideal of professionalism.

The professional style of policing needed a new organizational structure and a new kind of candidate for police officer—one who was able to apply legalistic principles to enforcement; the lack of residency requirement and reduced age of entry allowed for targeting college graduates in a nationwide recruitment effort. As the hallmark of professionalism is using research and analysis to inform policies, the chief enlisted the assistance of O. W. Wilson, dean of criminology at the University of California, Berkeley, who proposed creating special police units to research the root causes of problems in policing, apply modern technology to solutions,and undertake systematic planning for the future challenges. Oakland's reforms launched the nation's first police unit dedicated solely to planning, research, and problem solving. Wilson's criminology students were recruited to staff and support this research capability and Dr. Kirk's crime lab.

The four years of new leadership (1955–1959) brought profound changes to the Oakland Police Department, and a new group of leaders was subsequently appointed to accelerate the policing innovations. The new chief organized special duty units to suppress crime and develop the nationwide recruitment. Innovations in technologies were introduced including the "alco-test" (which led to a 22% increase in drunk driving arrests) and the 1965 adoption of the computer-driven Police Information Network System (PIN). This electronic retrieval system brought instant information to officers on patrol—the status of license numbers reported stolen from anywhere in California and whether a driver had active criminal warrants, was a dangerous fugitive, or had a criminal record. The computer age reduced the backlog of warrants and helped police recover stolen vehicles, arrest auto theft suspects, and warn of dangerous subjects.

Antiwar Demonstrations (1963–1973)

In 1964, when antiwar militants reached beyond the UC Berkeley campus, targeting the Oakland Army Base and Naval Supply Center—the embarkation point for 220,000 soldiers over four years—the Oakland Police Department was directed to prevent unauthorized demonstrations, property damage, and injuries. The larger demonstrations (eight to twelve thousand militants) were a public safety risk that could result in large-scale property damage and violence to surrounding Oakland communities and businesses. Innovation and expert crowd control became a departmental trademark, recognized in policing circles as the best practice.

Civil Rights/Community Relations (1960–1966)

The chief decided to involve the department more extensively in improving the quality of life in Oakland's communities. This initiative went beyond speeches to participation in civic and service groups. There were increasing complaints from the black communities that legalistic policing had a disproportionately negative impact on its members, including its youths. The chief moved to create a meaningful dialog with the groups who were most affected by such problems. Top officials and commanders were required to personally attend community meetings and report comments, complaints, recommendations, and problems raised at these meetings. In 1964, the chief created a Community Relations Section to systematically document these efforts. There is significant testimony validating the department's progress with minority groups; the department was not viewed as oppressive or engaging in systematic or institutional abuse. Complaints and reports of misconduct were investigated by internal affairs and reported back to community groups.

The police leaders were confronted with an activist call for an independent civilian review board. The succeeding chief worked to instill a sense of mission for law enforcement in terms of service to the whole community. The chief believed (as research suggested) that problems of racial tension and citizen distrust could be resolved through in-person contacts. The chief personally led a series of behind-the-scenes meetings between police and juvenile gang leaders to prevent looting and vandalism in downtown Oakland. In 1966, the chief was praised by the mayor for dealing with the youth disturbances in East Oakland "with patience and calm restraint" while making clear that "the laws would be enforced justly."

Professional Credibility and Openness to Senior Academic Studies (1962–1969)

In the midst of dynamic police reorganization and social conflicts, the department leaders and chief granted permission to UC Berkeley professor Jerome Skolnick to perform a sociological analysis of law enforcement processes and decision making in Oakland. The chief set a single restriction—"that the analysis be objective and truthful." Dr. Skolnick spent more than two years observing the judgments, decisions, actions, and consequences of officers in daily enforcement situations. The subsequent analysis was published in a popular book *Justice Without Trial*. He observed the inherent tension between "law" and "order." Accordingly, "due process" and "enforcing the law" require discretionary judgments rather than universal application of a single standard of perfect procedures.

Dr. James Q. Wilson studied officers in eight different police agencies, focusing on departmental differences in applying police discretion to balance the needs for maintaining order and enforcing the law. Wilson distinguished police styles grouped in three typologies: watchman, legalistic, and service styles. Wilson interpreted the changes in Oakland's new policing style to be legalistic (single standard of community conduct). His analysis revealed some fundamental reasons for friction between the department and different elements of the community. He pointed out that the department's reforms (except for civil rights and community relations) really did not address the question of how to provide policing services to increasingly diverse communities with different needs and expectations for justice.

An analysis of the Oakland Police Department is presented in the text *Police: The Street Corner Politicians* by William Muir, a UC professor of political science. This study examines the range of moral, social, and political issues through "the moral development of young officers as they try to come to terms with the problem of how to achieve just ends with coercive means."

These studies produced debate and resulted in new programs aimed at family crisis intervention, violence prevention, and landlord–tenant dispute resolutions. These initiatives led the department into the "progressive era" of training and partnering with referral agencies to provide effective resolutions not requiring criminal court actions. Professor Muir attributes Chief Gain (1967–1973) as transforming the department from a legalistic style to a service-oriented style of policing. Since the community reacted negatively to police shootings of fleeing persons, Chief Gain changed the department's firearms discharge policies. The new policy prohibited using a firearm other than to protect the officer's life or that of a citizen. Police were no longer authorized to shoot fleeing burglary or auto theft suspects or persons under age eighteen. This policy was extremely controversial but became institutionalized. Chief Gain significantly

expanded the training of new and in-service officers to teach officers the reasoning employed in Supreme Court decisions and to get officers to work in harmony with evolving interpretation of the laws affecting police powers. The chief was explicit and adamant in his call for stopping all harassment of minorities; officers were under the threat of termination if they did not abide by antiharassment policies.

The Evolution of Policing Strategy: Beyond the 1960s

Chief Hart (a UC graduate who achieved the fastest career promotion of any chief), created an entirely radical policing strategy referred to as the "beat health concept." This concept, founded on operations analysis and personal identification with the beat conditions by the patrol officer, is potentially the most striking innovation and is considered the initiative that changed Oakland—and the field of police science—enormously for the better.

Since patrol officers spend more time on their patrol beats than they do in their own homes, they ought to treat the beat as their own neighborhood. The concept encourages frequent interactions with the community residents and participation in the life of the community, rather than focusing only on enforcing the law. The beat health concept anticipates the insights of James Q. Wilson's influential article on "broken windows" by almost seven years. The beat health approach has a legitimate claim to leading the strategic emergence of community policing and problem-oriented policing.

The success of the Oakland Police Department's transformation and its influence on policing across America are based on both police science and human organization. The chiefs and leaders of this department tried new and highly innovative operations and procedures. These models, informed by research, planning, and analysis, empowered the institution to change. Chiefs used a range of levers to redirect the department and guide its path in the uncharted waters of new social crises and conflicts.

The results of this era are well documented. The legacy is a better, more dedicated police department focused on bringing the Constitution to the streets and a better quality of life to the city's communities. The graduates of the Oakland Police Department's progressive era are now leaders of federal agencies and chiefs of progressive departments and are dedicated to using research and analysis to enhance law enforcement operations and policies.

JAMES K. STEWART

See also **Accountability; Attitudes toward the Police: Overview; Minorities and the Police; Police Reform in an Era of Community and Problem-Oriented Policing; Wilson, O. W.**

Reference and Further Reading

Skolnick, Jerome H. 1966. *Justice without trial: Law enforcement in democratic society.* New York: Wiley.

Wilson, James Q. 1968. *Varieties of police behavior: The management of law and order in eight communities.* Cambridge, MA: Harvard University Press.

OCCUPATIONAL CULTURE

Introduction

An occupational culture is a means for coping with the vicissitudes or uncertainties arising routinely in the course of doing a job. An occupational culture is a reduced, selective, and task-based version of culture that includes history and traditions, etiquette and routines, rules, principles, and practices that serve to buffer practitioners from contacts with the public. A kind of lens on the world, it highlights some aspects of the social and physical environment and omits or minimizes others. It generates stories, lore, and legends.

The sources of the occupational culture are the repeated, routinized tasks incumbent on the members, a technology that is variously direct or indirect in its effects (mediated by the organizational structure within which the occupation is done), and the reflexive aspects of talking about these doings. In this sense, an occupational culture reflects not only what is done and how it should (and should not) be done but also idealizations of the work.

An occupational culture is a context within which emotions are regulated and attuned to work routines. As Waddington (1998, 292–93) writes perceptively, the police culture is "... an expression of common values, attitudes, and beliefs within a police context." A political economy of emotions, or a distribution of emotions consistent with power, stratification, and control, complements characteristic value configurations and interactional patterns. These, in turn, are a reflection of the fit between the differential exposure of practitioners to work-based contingencies. This creates segments within the occupation.

Clearly, uniformed officers face different contingencies than do detectives, and supervisors differ in their experience from top management. Career success is based in part on skills, in part on politics and networks, as well as on reorganizing and reassembling one's emotional equipment. The emotional tone of an officer on the street may not suit for the demands of top command. Conversely, failure and status deficits may create a shadow world of invalidated role performers, those who are seen to have achieved their positions by political means. In this drama of work, of course, patterns of rise and fall, of failure, redemption, and renewal are seen. In recent years, these minidramas often surround key figures in sexual miscues, harassment, and discrimination by age, gender, or ethnicity. Such minitragedies, as in any occupation, mark its outer boundaries and provide warning signs and cautionary tales.

Policing is politics by other means. Ironically, as Hughes (1958) points out, an occupational mandate consists of setting aside functions others may not do as well as designating those that the occupation may or must do. As the guardians of order, they are "dirty workers," who must do what others may not: enabled to violate the law, they must act violently and intrusively, shoot, maim, and kill. They are also required to rationalize or justify the necessary. Perhaps because it is inherently political in function and origins, policing manifests a turgid and resilient occupational culture.

This culture resides within a police organization constituted by several occupations and specialties. Police officers and others police, while police organizations are the accountable means by which this is accomplished. The occupational culture in the literature often is depicted as that of one segment, the uniformed patrol, while the police organization includes and employs civilians (about 25% of the employees of local police organizations), janitors, cooks, consultants, lawyers and researchers, and other short-term employees. It is also entangled in intraorganizational relations as well as local politics. However, the uniformed police occupational culture shadows and dominates the several occupational groups within the organization, and its values are variously subscribed to by the several occupational groups working within the organization.

Structural Features of American Police Organizations That Divide and Unify the Occupation

The police occupational culture is shaped by five structural features of police organizations. The first is the inspectorial strategy of policing, which deploys a large number of low-ranking officers who are ecologically dispersed to monitor and track citizens in the environment and make complex, difficult decisions, usually alone, with minimal supervision and/or review. The second is the localistic, common-level entry and apprenticeship training pattern of police. In the United States, most officers serve their entire careers in one organization, and only top command officers join as a result of lateral mobility. Officers above superintendent are mobile in the United Kingdom.

The third feature is that the police organization is both fact rich and information poor. The police mission, to penetrate and control problematic environments, leads them to overemphasize secrecy and deception as means of achieving organizational ends. Police information consists of collections of scraps of unintegrated data, quasi-secret and secret intelligence files, an amalgam of outdated context-specific information, and a layered archaeology of knowledge. Although secrecy is not the highest value among officers, it is safe to say that the conditions under which information is shared (rarely) are carefully observed.

The fourth structural feature is that risk (positive and negative consequences of high uncertainty) is associated with policing. These features turn officers inward, away from the public, and laterally to their colleagues for support. The features vary empirically from force to force, and the salience of one or the other may vary by local political context.

The task-role complex of the job differentiates the police and serves to highlight variations within the occupational culture. The core tasks and routines are uncertain and unpredictable. Officers share assumptions about the nature of the work (risky, exciting, worthwhile, "clinical" in nature) and operate in an environment perceived or created by such work routines and codified definitions of relevant tasks. In urban policing, the cynosure of "the job" is "working the streets," patrol response to radio calls. Boredom, risk, and excitement oscillate unpredictably.

The technology, unrefined people-processing recipes, that is, judgments of officers working with little direct guidance, pattern work, and a rigid rank structure officially organizes authority. Policing is realized within a bureaucratic, rule-oriented, hierarchical structure of command and control on the one hand and a loose confederation of colleagues on the other. The interaction of these factors, tasks, environment, technology, and structure produces characteristic attitudes and an ideology, a set of explanatory beliefs rationalizing the work and its contingencies. The operation of these factors stratifies and differentiates the organization and partitions officers' experience.

Other structural factors unify police. These include the ideal of shared fate or of occupational unity, an experiential base (all served as officers initially), task dependency (officers rely on each other to accomplish joint tasks), and shared, mutually discrediting secrets. There is also an abiding ideology or mythology about policing that concerns the mandate, the legal and societal obligations, and the role as it is represented in public rhetoric, or "presentational strategies" (Manning 1997). These unifying factors stand in some tension with the differentiating factors. It should be further emphasized that the values produced are also points of ambivalence and counterpoint and do not form a single integrated whole. Unfortunately, detective work, specialized squads such as SWAT teams, and staff functions such as internal affairs are omitted in the descriptive catalogs of the police occupational culture (Reiner 2000; Crank 1998).

An Overview of Studies of the Occupational Culture

The academic view of the police occupational subculture is disproportionately influenced by a handful of studies of American or English uniformed patrol officers serving in large urban areas, and it has been reified by textbook treatments. Although rich ethnographic treatments of policing exist (Banton 1964; Holdaway 1983; Bittner 1990; Rubinstein 1972; Van Maanen 1974; and Simon 1991), the police are often flattened, desiccated, and displayed like insects pinned on a display board. Acute observers have noted the differentiation and segmentalization of policing using role types (Terrill, Paoline, and Manning 2003; Reiner 1992, 130–33), the conceptions of external publics (Reiner 1992, 117–21), the distinctive misleading binary subcultures such as a "street cop culture" and a "management culture" (Punch 1983), and the conflicts within forces based on ethnicity and gender (Foster 2004). Value variations based in part on task differentiation also exist within departments (Jermeir et al. 1991). Other social forces, especially technology, management training, the law, and pressures to produce such as traffic ticket quotas and case clearances in detective work, also impact policing.

Some recent work has worked toward a generalized model of the occupational culture (Klinger 2002; Paoline 2003). Janet Chan's work (1997) is the most theoretically informed of present work. She takes a complex Bourdieu-influenced perspective, arguing that policing is organized around various forms of knowledge and practice shaped continuously by a habitus or way of being and doing. Waddington (1998) has made the most important distinction in the study of the occupational culture in recent years, noting that the oral culture (see also Shearing and Ericson 1992) and the behavior of officers differs. His review points out the fallacy of generalizations based on talk rather than observation.

New Horizons

Three important changes have taken place in the past twenty years in policing. They suggest both the strength of the occupational culture and its roots. The first is the impact of new information technologies. Technology, especially information technology (IT), has eroded authority and altered police workloads. Although technology has absorbed and transformed some work tasks (such as immediate supervision), "middle managers" have grown in number and importance in policing. (Due in part to the effects of massive hiring between 1968 and 1975, these officers are now nearing retirement.) Ironically, spawned by paperwork and supervisory duties, these positions, sergeant, inspector, lieutenant, and superintendent, are threatened by the introduction of computer-based formal record-keeping systems. These developments suggest the existence of a management cadre or segment within the occupational culture. It has emerged between the lower participants and senior command officers. It also suggests that in the future a division across ranks will be between those who are computer facile and those who are not.

The second is the impact of female and minority officers. While their attitudes seem to fit closely with their colleagues on survey, closer studies (Morash and Haar 1991) suggest that modes of relating and coping and the stresses faced by female officers differ from males and that this may emerge as a cross-cutting segment unified not by rank but by shared sentiments. It already tightly shapes who interacts with whom and why (Haar 1990).

Finally, the rising educational levels within policing and the growth of suburban departments means that tensions arise between the educated officers and the others, that bias and prejudice exist, and that opportunities for promotion may be compromised not only by union rules but by prejudice against educated officers. The most powerful and systematic research, based on observation, interviews, and surveys done in England in the wake of the McPherson report on the investigation of the murder of Stephen Lawrence, shows that racial/ethnic bias remains very strong and virulent, that it affects promotion and rewards at every level of the force, and that the traditional themes of masculinity, violence, crime fighting, and danger remain thematic and not attributed to people of color and women.

Segmentation of the Nondetective Occupational Culture

A segment is a group of people loosely bound by interaction patterns. In policing, the limits on interaction are tightly drawn around rank, although some interaction occurs laterally via sponsorship of protégés and political ties based on religion, union membership, past links in the academy, and so on. The dominant values of the occupational culture, taken as a whole, are espoused throughout but are most salient in the lower segment, where they find a functional, task-relevant home. The occupational values cohere around the most sacred notion of the occupation: one must display, enact, and maintain them before authority. This is often connected to other general beliefs such as loyalty, honor, patriotism, and duty.

Independence, autonomy, authority, and uncertainty are key values of the police occupational culture. Each of these four values has its opposite: dependence, collective obligations, powerlessness, and certainty. They are in effect paired and dynamic oppositions that take meaning from each other. Kai Erikson (1976, 83) argues that "... people *think* or *feel* different things in the service of an overall pattern of coordination. In the same sense that people contribute different skills and abilities to the organization of *work*, so they contribute different temperaments and outlooks to the organization of *sensibility*." The occupational culture in some ways is a configuration of sentiments and values, core and counterpoint, that are more or less salient from time to time (Shearing and Ericson 1992).

The values are also linked to the structural factors noted above that sustain their reality. The dependence pair is linked to the control mission or mandate of policing, the autonomy pair is linked to the fixed character of the organization's normal functioning, the authority pair is linked to adversarial encounters, and the final pair, certainty, is animated by the appearance of risk.

Their dynamic relationship surfaces primarily in crises in which the veneer of authority is shattered, the public performance is threatened or collapses, or the officer is embarrassed or fails to fill role requirements. In these situations, the officer reflects, and draws on the occupational perspective for support and clarification. The residual of these encounters and their ambiguous outcomes is the basis for the narrative or storytelling that reinforces and renews the culture. The culture rises and falls in salience and does not remain a lens through which the world is always viewed.

Lower Participants

The "lower participant" segment is composed of officers and sergeants. Sergeants, like foremen in factories, interact in both segments and are occasionally caught between them. Organized in narrative form, the values connect in the following way. The uniformed officer works in an uncertain environment in which choice, action, and decision are emphasized, in which the veneer of objectively guided decision making is essential, and in which an often tenuous authority frequently must be asserted with strangers in public. The officer is routinely dependent on fellow officers and the public to maintain a credible performance of authoritative assertions and action, yet the occupation emphasizes autonomy. While dependent, the officer must

act authoritatively and without full knowledge of the facts or the consequences of potential actions. An underlying premise is that a neutral emotional tone is to be maintained, and the body, its posture, gestures, shape, and performance, are to be ready.

Working class culture, from which most police are recruited, supplies the most frequently noted emblems, or symbols, that collapse attitudes and practices into valuations of action characterizing policing. Thus, emphases upon individual control of situations, toughness, machismo, hedonism, deprecation of paperwork and abstraction, concrete language, and description are working class values. Officers "at the coal face" or "in the trenches" appear to exchange a degree of organizational autonomy to maintain a working class style. There are other visible signs of membership in this segment. Patrol officers, for example, unlike ranks above sergeants and including sergeants in some departments, may acquire overtime for court appearances, work rotating shifts, and wear a uniform and receive a uniform allowance, unless assigned to staff or detective work temporarily.

Lower participants generally emphasize dependence, autonomy, authority, and uncertainty. The latent function of these emphases is to suppress the equally powerful potential, evidence that suggests that police officers are often dependent upon and obligated to others, powerless, or are least relatively powerless, and quite clear and certain about the contours of their work.

The four value themes for the lower participants can be clustered into two metathemes: (1) "the job," an index of the interrelated themes of (job) dependency and autonomy, and (2) "real police work," an index combining authority and uncertainty in relationships with the public.

The Middle Management Segment

This segment is composed of officers in the ranks sergeant, lieutenant, inspector, chief inspector, and superintendent, or their equivalents. Stereotypically, their style portends an authoritative presence. They are in effect bureaucrats with guns. They walk, talk, and react as managers and persons whose authority rests on their verbosity, good humor, and ability to communicate in writing and verbally. Bodily skill is rarely required of managers. Officers in this segment perform their roles variously, depending on their orientation toward promotion, economic gain, or organizational change. They have achieved a desired rank, and some hope for promotion or transfer (into a detective or specialized unit, for example). Technological developments make management skill a likely consideration for promotion, for example, attending night school for an MBA rather than seeking a law degree.

Like other "white collar" workers, they are a middle mass with shared tenuous mutual identification, although they may have a separate union. This segment is likely to be riven with cliques (upwardly oriented groups) and cabals (groups resistant to change) and linked by interaction networks with other officers. Organizational politics, both of careers and of the top command, is a keen interest and concern of middle managers. Computer-assisted dispatch, management information systems, computer-based records, and crime analysis applications have altered their workloads (although not necessarily increased them). Symbolically located between command and other officers, they must adapt to organizational realities. They rarely earn overtime and work shifts if not assigned to staff positions. They generally wear uniforms, usually without the jacket since they work "inside," and are provided with a uniform allowance. Their claims for occupational prestige are aligned either up or down: toward administrative officers or those on the street.

Middle management officers emphasize independence and collective obligations to form the metatheme (3) "politics" (of the job or the occupation, oriented partially to internal and partially to external audiences), while the twin themes of authority and certainty (the need to control contingencies through supervision) are clustered as a metatheme (4) "management."

The Top Command Segment

The top command segment is composed of officers above the rank of superintendent (or commander), including chief and deputy chief(s). Their style is less obviously working class, and their speech and manner often emulates those they admire in the business world. They have options in dress—full or partial uniform, business suit, or casual wear—and some have adopted the term "CEO," mimicking business practice, and talk about "... changing the way we do business." They are oriented in a somewhat dualistic fashion, since they must seek the loyalty of the lower participants as well as city "fathers." They curry favor with officers on the street as well as external audiences, including political elites, elected officials, and worthy citizens' groups (Reiner 1991).

Much of their work is "fire fighting," managing various kinds of crises. In theory, they make "policy" decisions, or at least consider issues enduring beyond the end of a shift or day's work. The administrative cadre is dependent on the goodwill and discretion of officers, because "working the streets" produces most of the scandals and political incidents. The values of the lower participants remain surprisingly salient: They function as a ground against which the figure of commitment to the perks, rewards, and intrinsic satisfactions of command are seen. Some think of themselves as "good police officers," and emphasize their "street smarts," "toughness," or past crime fighting successes, rather than their administrative skills, wisdom as "people managers," or educational achievements. Command officers' views of policing are reflexive, because they are obligated to manage the consequences of decisions made by others. They must "read off" these value themes and metathemes to understand and interpret police work.

Command officers emphasize that they manage the dependence and autonomy issues that lower participants label "the job" and middle managers call "office politics." Top administrative officers also emphasize the "politics" and "management" themes of middle management. The refracted value tensions of lower participants and managers are an element of the command segment's work. One metatheme (5) is called "managing the job." They see their work bearing external responsibility, being accountable, while being dependent on lower participants. The second metatheme, (6) "policing as politics," glosses command responsibility. Command officers emphasize "management" rather than "the job" and view police management as paperwork and coping with and managing the lower participants' subculture. Uncertainty reappears, although administrators' uncertainty focuses on their authority in the context of dependence upon the discretion (in both senses of the word) and competence of the lower participants.

Finally, it appears that they combine two metathemes of other segments into a single megatheme, combining the metathemes "management" and "politics" into one that might be called "policing as democratic politics." This formulation glosses their interest in sustaining and amplifying the political power and independence of the police in the criminal justice system and dramatizes and displays the role of police in both the local and occasionally the national political system. Policing as democratic politics implies sensitivity to the encumbrances and political implications of policing.

The three segments within policing are indicated by values and value emphases that connote potential division within and across segments. The culture both divides and integrates the occupation, depending on the situation and the issue. These segments and value emphases signal a structural potential for conflict in the police organization. Conflict may arise not only from intrasegment variations in value emphases but from intersegment differences in the meaning of the work and modes of resolving differences.

The police occupational culture is not unique. It reflects the social values of Anglo American societies such as individualism, material success, bias against various others (minorities, people of color, women), and preference for the company of others like themselves. It is particularly shaped by local politics, situational pressures, and media dramatizations. On the other hand, police respond day by day to the untoward, the dirty, ugly, and violent and in general come when they are called. The emotional tone of policing as a practice, the laconic, somewhat distant view, when combined with the humor and stories, are sentiments that reveal basic humanity.

PETER K. MANNING

See also **Accountability; Autonomy and the Police; Codes of Ethics; Detective Work/ Culture; Deviant Subcultures in Policing; Ethics and Values in the Context of Community Policing; Information within Police Agencies; Police Solidarity; Unionization, Police**

References and Further Readings

Banton, Michael. 1964. *The policeman in the community*. New York: Basic Books.

Bittner, E. 1990. *Aspects of police work*. Boston: Northeastern University Press.

Chan, Janet. 1997. *Changing police culture*. Melbourne: Cambridge University Press.

Crank, John. 1998. *Occupational culture*. Cincinnati, OH: Anderson.

Erikson, Kai. 1976. *Everything in its path*. New York: Simon and Schuster.

Foster, J. 2004. Police cultures. In *Handbook of policing*, ed. T. Newburn, 196–227. Cullompton, Devon: Willan.

Haar, R. 1990. Interaction among police officers. *Justice Quarterly*.

Holdaway, S. 1983. *Inside the British police*. Oxford: Blackwell.

Hughes, E. C. 1958. *Men and their work*. New York: The Free Press.

Jermier, J., et al. 1991. Organizational subcultures in a soft bureaucracy. *Organization Science* 2: 170–94.

Klinger, D. 2000. *An ecological approach to the OC criminology*.

Manning, Peter K. 1997. *Police work*. 2nd ed. Prospect Heights, IL: Waveland Press.

Morash, M., and R. Haar. 1991. Stress and the officer. *Justice Quarterly*.

Paoline, E. A. 2003. Taking stock: Toward a richer understanding of police culture. *Journal of Criminal Justice* 31: 199–214.

Punch, M. 1983. *Officers and men in control in the police organization*. Cambridge, MA: The MIT Press.

Reiner, Robert. 1992. *The politics of police*. Oxford: Oxford University Press.

Rubinstein, J. 1972. *City police*. New York: Farrar, Straus and Giroux.

Shearing, C., and R. Ericson. 1992. Culture as figurative action. *British Journal of Sociology* 42: 481–506.

Simon, D. 1991. *Homicide*. New York: Simon and Schuster.

Terrill, W. E., E. Paoline, and P. Manning. 2003. Police culture and coercion. *Criminology* 41: 1003–34.

Van Maanen, J. 1974. Working the street. In *Prospects for reform in the criminal justice system*, ed. H. Jacob. Beverley Hills, CA: Sage.

Waddington, P. A. J. 1998. Police (canteen) culture. *British Journal of Criminology* 39: 287–309.

OFFENDER PROFILING

Offender profiling is a method of identifying the perpetrator of a crime based on an analysis of the nature of the offense, the victim, and the manner in which the crime was committed. The origins of offender profiling are unclear. Jacob F. Fries, an obscure author who wrote a handbook on criminal anthropology in 1820, related the nature of the crime to the personality of the individual. The writings of Arthur Conan Doyle may have been one of the more important springboards in bringing psychological profiling into existence. It is well known that the Sherlock Holmes series served as the seminal base for many of the modern scientific methods used in criminal investigations.

The first practitioner in modern times was James Brussel, a New York psychiatrist. Brussel assisted the New York City police and other law enforcement agencies on numerous occasions between 1957 and 1972, including creating the profile of the "Mad Bomber of New York" and the "Boston Strangler."

Depending on the amount of information that can be derived from the crime scene, a psychological profile can often provide an investigator with the probable sex and age of the perpetrator as well as his or her ethnic background, relative social status, marital situation, level of education, occupational category, possible criminal background, and potential for continued criminal activities. The profile can also provide information concerning the probable characteristics of any future attacks and the most productive investigative strategies for locating, apprehending, interviewing, and interrogating the offender.

A major advantage of this procedure is that it can be utilized after all other investigative methods have been tried to jump-start the investigation. (This is the case whether it is one crime that remains unsolved or a series of similar crimes.) Utilized in this manner, psychological profiling not only provides additional leads and direction but forces the investigator to re-examine all existing data on the case. The comprehensive review necessary for preparing the profile will in itself sometimes result in the discovery of previously overlooked evidence and investigative leads.

Unfortunately, this advantage can be completely nullified by a poor or incomplete crime scene investigation. The lack of complete crime scene descriptions, sketches, and photographs as well as accurate autopsy results and thorough background investigations of the victim(s) will severely limit the ability of the profiler to construct a usable description of the perpetrator. As with all forensic disciplines, the crime scene and its competent analysis are crucial.

Although a highly skilled profiler can create an offender profile for any type of offense, offender profiling is typically used when there is little physical evidence that can be used to identify a suspect, when the crime is over the top in unusual methods of commission and appears to be serial in nature, and of course when murder with sexual overtones is involved.

Offender profiling was initially thought to be a panacea, yet significant problems have come to light over the years. Three problems specifically detract from offender profiling being more useful to law enforcement: There has been significant definitional confusion surrounding the term "profiling"; most profiles that are created are too general and do not assist in the isolation of a particular suspect; there are few benchmarks for the creation of profiles.

The definitional confusion arises from the use of the term "profiling" to mean "racial profiling." Offender profiling is not racial profiling. Racial profiling is based on the biased association of race with certain types of criminal offenses. Confusion has also resulted from a variety of terms being used to refer to offender profiling, including "criminal personality profiling" and "psychological criminal profiling."

Many offender profiles that are created are not based on enough data points to give anything but a very general picture of the offender. The resulting offender profile is so general that it is unnecessary. It does not add anything to what the average police investigator already knows through on-the-job experience; therefore it is unhelpful and wastes both time and money.

Another limiting factor associated with offender profiling is the amount of training and preparation necessary to develop the skills to accurately profile a crime. The profiler must possess an excellent knowledge of abnormal psychology, human nature, crime scene investigative procedures, and forensic medicine. Further, the profiler must review countless cases before awareness of the underlying relationships between the perpetrator's psychological status and the details of the criminal act begin to emerge.

Profiles generated in the 1970s were generally more successful, assisting about 75% to 80% of the time, than profiles created as the technique became more popular and less qualified profilers began working in the field. Although the FBI has expended considerable money and effort on profiling, its success has been somewhat disappointing. In the 1990s, it has been estimated that only about 50% of profiles are particularly useful to law enforcement.

Some offender profiles suffer from the drawback of having not utilized benchmarks. A good profile should serve several purposes. First, it should narrow the suspect pool. Second, it should assist in the creation of an interview/interrogation schedule. Third, it should facilitate the arrest of the perpetrator.

To increase the usefulness and success of the offender profile, it is suggested that the following nine specific analytic elements be included: an analysis of the crime scene, a demographic analysis of the community, an autopsy review (when the crime is homicide), development of victimology, cross-referencing of how the murder (or crime) was committed, projective needs analysis, cross-referencing the projective needs analysis with known convicted felons, and a specific factor analysis. The end result of the process is the design of a suspect interview and interrogation form.

1. *Analysis of the crime scene.* The usual crime scene investigation concentrates on the collection and preservation of physical evidence. Offender profiling simply carries the process one step further. Using the same evidence found at the scene plus additional data about the particular type of crime and the victim, the profiler attempts to collect information relating to personality and motives. Both techniques have the same goal and both are dependent upon the ability and thoroughness of the crime scene investigator. The

crime scene must be analyzed prior to moving anything. The profiler's analysis utilizes the standard photographs of where the victim was found, along with photographs of the area surrounding the victims in concentric circles. The profiler also coordinates the analysis of the crime scene with the time of day, the date, and the environmental conditions of when the crime was committed. While the typical crime scene investigation simply seeks to gather physical evidence that will link a suspect to the crime scene, the profiler's analysis seeks to answer questions such as, Why this crime? Why this community? Why this victim?

2. *Demographic analysis of the community.* This takes into consideration what the community is like and who lives there. This portion of the profile will take into account how the crime and the victim fit into the wider community.

3. *Autopsy review.* In a homicide investigation, the autopsy provides critical information. It establishes the time and method of death. It will contain details of specific body conditions and outlines how the victim was destroyed. In the traditional investigation process, this is important to link, for example, the weapon to the crime scene or to the offender. The profiler uses this information to determine what sort of an offender would carry out this sort of destruction of a victim.

4. *Development of victimology.* In traditional crime scene investigation, the victim is considered as a witness (in the case of a living victim) and/or as a source of forensic evidence. In offender profiling, much more attention is given to who the victim is and what the victim represents. Victimology is developed through interviews with people in significant relationships with the victim. This victimology should strive to understand the victim's life and understand what the victim was doing up until the point of death (victimization) because the offender chose this particular victim for very specific reasons.

5. *Cross-referencing of how the murder was committed.* The profiler considers the weapon that was used in the offense, the damage that was inflicted on the body, and the physical and sexual positioning of the body. All of this is coordinated with the demographics of the community. This cross-referencing highlights the fact that the various factors involved in creation of the profile must be considered together and not just individually.

6. *Projective needs analysis (PNA).* This determines how the psychological needs of the perpetrator were satisfied during the commission of the crime. This is accomplished by looking at who the victim was, how the victim was destroyed, what was done during the offense, and who the victim was within the community.

7. *Cross-referencing the PNA with known convicted felons.* This is done in concentric circles from the point of the homicide (crime). This should be coordinated with police departments regarding offenders on parole/probation in the area. Offenders who have committed similar actions, of course, are of particular interest.

8. *Specific factor analysis.* This is done to cross-reference all of the seven factors previously obtained. This correlates victimology, cause of death, and suspect pool. All factors of the profile are brought together.

9. *Design suspect interview and interrogation form.* The desired end result of the profiling process is the

creation of an interview and interrogation form that will be used by law enforcement to obtain a confession through either a direct or an indirect admission.

AYN EMBAR-SEDDON and ALLAN D. PASS

See also **Criminal Investigation; Psychology and the Police**

References and Further Reading

Cleckley, Hervey. 1964. *The mask of sanity.* St. Louis, MO: C. V. Mosby.

Hazelwood, Robert R. 1983. The behavior-oriented interview of rape victims: The key to profiling. *FBI Law Enforcement Bulletin* 52 (9): 8–15.

Jackson, J. L., J. C. M. Herbrink, P. van Koppen. 1997. An empirical approach to offender profiling. In *Advances in psychology and law (international contributions)*, ed. S. Redondo, V. Garrido, J. Pérez, and R. Barberet. New York: Walter de Gruyter.

Pinizzotto, Anthony J. 1984. Forensic psychology: Criminal personality profiling. *Journal of Police Science and Administration* 12 (1): 32–40.

Pinizzotto, A. J., and N. J. Finkel. 1990. Criminal personality profiling: An outcome and process study. *Law and Human Behavior* 14: 215–34.

Reese, James T. 1979. Obsessive-compulsive behavior. *FBI Law Enforcement Bulletin* 48 (8): 6–12.

OFFICE OF COMMUNITY-ORIENTED POLICE SERVICES, U.S. DEPARTMENT OF JUSTICE

The Office of Community-Oriented Police Services (COPS) was created as a result of the Violent Crime Control and Law Enforcement Act of 1994. As a component of the U.S. Department of Justice, the mission of the COPS office is to advance the practice of community policing by state, local, and tribal law enforcement agencies throughout the country.

Community policing represents a shift from traditional law enforcement practices. Instead of emphasizing timely responses to calls for service and reactive patrol methods, community policing focuses on proactive problem-solving methods intended to address the factors that cause crime and social disorder within communities. This strategy also calls for law enforcement and citizens to work collaboratively in the course of both identifying and effectively addressing crime and disorder issues.

Moreover, community policing encourages law enforcement agencies to undergo fundamental changes that enable the agency to function effectively and efficiently in an organizational structure that provides as much decision-making authority as practical to patrol-level officers and units, who are closest to the community and likely to have the clearest understanding of problems that impact the community. This increased authority, coupled with increased mutual trust and respect between the community and patrol-level officers, can ultimately lead to relationships that help deter crime, bring needed services and resources, and engage community members in their own safety.

Since 1994, supporting the development of this type of strategic approach to policing has been the primary mission of the COPS office. From 1994 to 2005, COPS invested more than $11.8 billion to add community policing officers to the nation's streets and schools, enhance crime fighting technology, support crime prevention initiatives, and provide community policing training and technical assistance resources. During this period, COPS awarded more than 36,000 grants to more than 13,000 law enforcement agencies to fund the hiring of more than 118,000 community policing officers and deputies and to procure and deploy much needed crime fighting technology systems.

The COPS office has also provided training and technical assistance to law enforcement agencies through its national network of Regional Community Policing Institutes. These institutes train law enforcement officials, government executives, and community members side by side. To date, the institutes have trained more than five hundred thousand individuals on topics ranging from an introduction to community policing principles to terrorism prevention and response, all within the context of community policing.

COPS' other training and technical assistance resources include an annual community policing conference that attracts law enforcement officials and criminal justice experts from across the United States; training conferences and leadership symposiums on topics such as school safety, methamphetamine eradication, homeland security, intelligence gathering, and other emerging law enforcement issues; and a series of more than three hundred user-friendly publications that address a variety of crime and disorder topics.

In addition, COPS has distributed approximately four hundred thousand copies of publications from their *Problem-Oriented Guides for Police* (POP) series. These guides summarize knowledge about how police can reduce harm caused by specific crime and disorder problems. *Robbery at ATMs, Disorderly Youth in Public Places, Drug Dealing in Privately Owned Apartment Complexes*, and *Speeding in Residential Areas* are examples of the many topics covered in COPS' POP Guide series.

An October 2005 U.S. Government Accounting Office (GAO) report found that COPS funds significantly increased nationally reported levels of community policing practices. The GAO also concluded that COPS-funded increases in sworn officers per capita were associated with declines in the rates of total index crimes, violent crimes, and property crimes in their sample of agencies serving populations of ten thousand or more. Specifically, they estimate that for the years 1998 to 2000, COPS grant expenditures were associated with reductions in index crimes from their 1993 levels that ranged from about 200,000 to 225,000 index crimes. For 1998, they estimated that the crimes

reduced due to COPS grant expenditures amounted to about 8% of the total decline in index crimes and about 13% of the total decline in violent crimes from their 1993 levels. They calculated that during the years 1999 and 2000, the COPS-funded reductions in crime accounted for about 5% of the total reduction in index crimes and about 10% of the total reduction in violent crimes from their 1993 levels. These effects held after they controlled for other factors that could also affect crime, such as federal law enforcement grant program expenditures by agencies, local socioeconomic and demographic changes, and state-level factors such as increases in incarceration, changes in sentencing practices, and changes in other programs such as welfare.

The GAO analysis also found that COPS grant funds were associated with significant increases in average reported levels of policing practices (problem solving, place-oriented practices, crime analysis, and community collaboration). For example, among agencies that received COPS grant funds in this period, the average level of reported use of problem-solving practices increased by about 35%, as compared to about a 20% increase among nongrantee agencies. The increase in place-oriented practices among COPS grantee agencies was about 32%, as compared to about 13% among the non–COPS grantee agencies.

Finally, the GAO analysis concluded that COPS hiring grant expenditures were associated with increases in the net number of sworn police officers. They obtained these results after controlling for a large number of relevant factors, including other federal law enforcement grant expenditures, annual changes in local economic and demographic conditions in the county in which an agency was located, and changes in state-level factors that could affect the level of sworn officers. The GAO estimates that COPS expenditures were responsible for an increase in the number of sworn officers per capita of about 3%

above the levels that would have been expected without COPS funds.

COPS has made significant strides in helping law enforcement overcome numerous challenges through community policing and will continue working to provide timely, efficient, and strategically advanced support to police and sheriff's departments and the communities that they serve. Today's law enforcement officers, executives, and practices must be capable of responding to various challenges, and community policing is a dynamic strategy that can be adapted to meet a broad range of emerging public safety needs.

GILBERT MOORE

See also **Community-Oriented Policing: Practices; Problem-Oriented Policing**

References and Further Reading

U.S. Government Accounting Office. 2005. *Community policing grants: COPS grants were modest contributor to declines in crime in the 1990s.* Report to the Chairman, Committee on the Judiciary, U.S. House of Representatives. Washington, DC: U.S. Government Accounting Office.

OPERATIONAL COSTS

Effective law enforcement management is vastly different in today's difficult economic times. Gone are the days when the traditional response to meeting crime control problems and community service needs was to hire more officers and purchase more equipment. Now there is a critical need for managers to promote efficiency and effectiveness. Because this almost impossible responsibility of providing more service with less funding falls on the chief of police or sheriff, the easy way out is to tighten administrative screws and allow the burden to fall on the employees. However, this shortsightedness may well lead to resentment, labor–management conflicts, or serious morale and job satisfaction problems.

Administrators must be sensitive to the feelings and sentiments of the work force in order to implement the types of changes necessary to streamline law enforcement services. To achieve cooperation, managers should ask employees for cost-cutting ideas and maintain high visibility to facilitate formal and informal discussions. Furthermore, management should seek advice from other law enforcement agencies concerning their successes and failures in cost cutting.

National Executive Institute Survey

The FBI National Executive Institute (NEI) queried more than a hundred law enforcement executives in the United States and Canada on how to increase productivity while curtailing costs. Due to decreasing tax revenues, rising costs, and a down-turned economy, the executives were eager to share their experiences. Upon reviewing the survey results, the NEI found that the areas that provided the greatest opportunity for cost reduction involve overtime, vehicles, volunteers, civilian participation, automation, reducing false alarms, increased use of federal forfeiture funds, service fees, and subcontracting for services.

The following list illustrates specific measures suggested for cost reduction.

Automation

- Decentralize entry of police incident reports to reduce lag time and the number of mail runs to headquarters.
- Install phone mail on department telephone systems to automatically direct outside callers to the proper extension.
- Implement automation of tasks where feasible.

Administration

- Eliminate unnecessary business and training expenses.
- Delay promotions for forty-five days.
- Streamline administrative positions.
- Consolidate various job responsibilities.

- Increase use of civilian volunteers, auxiliary police officers, and cadets.
- Reduce overtime.
- Use flexed work schedules for some units, where possible.

Maintenance
- Use jail maintenance personnel and/or inmate labor to maintain grounds and buildings, to build K-9 pens for dogs, or to build a tactical recovery vehicle from an old patrol car and old bulletproof vests.
- Delay or cut back renovation projects not necessary to the department's mission.
- Repair radios in house.
- Subcontract for services.

Training
- Use video technology for roll call training.

Automobiles
- Implement an accident reduction program consisting of pursuit policy training and high performance driving techniques and sanction against negligent drivers.
- Remove roof-mounted emergency lights from a significant number of marked vehicles.
- Switch from premium to regular-grade gasoline.
- Install sophisticated radio equipment in operational vehicles only.
- Reduce the number of take-home cars.
- Defer replacing vehicles for one more fiscal year.
- Change marked vehicles from traditional two colors to less expensive and more visible single white color.
- Downsize investigative and administrative (unmarked and nonpursuit) vehicles to smaller, less expensive models.

Other
- Institute service fees for special events and extraordinary nonemergency services.

- Minimize police response to false alarms.
- Implement bicycle patrol in congested areas.
- Prohibit use of alcohol in park and beach areas to reduce calls for service.
- Use federal forfeiture funds to purchase computers, office equipment, and protection- and enforcement-related equipment.

Case Studies

Colorado State Patrol Photo Lab Cash Funding

Situation: The Colorado State Patrol has historically charged citizens and attorneys for copies of photographs of accidents and other incidents in which the private sector has a vested interest. All fees collected from the sale of photographs were deposited in the patrol's budget to be distributed as needed. Although fees collected exceeded the annual operating budget allocation, new expenditures were limited to essential needs only.

Solution: Proposals were submitted to the Office of State Planning and Budgeting to allow the photo lab to become fully cash funded. The process was complex, requiring justification and a guarantee that the arrangement would work. Few state agencies have cash-funded operations, but such arrangements are advantageous to both the agency and the state. The proposals were granted. So far, revenue generated has resulted in covering operating expenses, the upgrade of photographic equipment, and expansion into areas such as video. Moreover, the budget previously shared by the photo lab and the Education and Safety Unit now has one less user, leaving more money for improving safety and education programs.

Knoxville Police Department Work Scheduling

Situation: In 1982, Knoxville, Tennessee, hosted the World's Fair, creating a demand for greater police service. To meet the demand, the Knoxville Police Department changed its shift rotations. Since that time, the department has continued to maximize use of patrol personnel while reducing overtime and call-in costs.

Solution: The Uniform Division works a six-day-on, four-day-off schedule with five detachments. The morning and night shifts are nine hours and ten minutes and the evening shift is ten hours and ten minutes. The advantages of such an arrangement are two overlapping periods—one in the afternoon between 1400 and 1540, and one in the evening between 2145 and 0010. The afternoon overlap helps with court duty and allows two detachments to be on the street at once. The night overlap takes care of peak time hot calls for service. The overlap also adds flexibility to bring a shift in early or later by several hours to handle special events (football games, parades, and the like) without having to pay overtime. A power shift works from 1600 to 0200 (four days on, three off) to supplement the patrol detachments during the busiest hours of the evening.

Utah Law Enforcement Intelligence Network

Situation: No centralized coordination of narcotics and criminal intelligence existed in Utah. Its Department of Public Safety, Division of Investigation, and Department of Corrections joined for such a purpose to form the Utah Law Enforcement Intelligence Network. Federal funding assisted the formation of the network but did not pay all costs. Essential to the network, data entry personnel to feed network computers with information were one of those extra costs.

Solution: To remedy the shortfall of funds, the Division of Investigation contacted the Utah National Guard and proposed a pilot program. The program called for the National Guard to provide select individuals to perform data entry. After background checks and clearance, the individuals were placed on active duty under the direct supervision of a criminal information technician and the section sergeant. Between 1990 and 1995, the computer database of approximately twenty-five hundred names and intelligence data grew to near ten thousand—due to National Guard assistance.

Nassau County Police Department Automatic Alarm Permit System

Situation: Within the jurisdiction of Nassau County, New York, are more than 120,000 individual alarm subscribers. In excess of a hundred thousand alarm transmissions are received annually from either central stations or through automated dialing mechanisms. Each incident results in the dispatch of two police officers to investigate. Records show fewer than 1% of the alarms to be actual emergencies, with the major cause of the problem attributable to human error and to a much lesser degree the forces of nature, power disruptions, and mechanical failures. Some forty thousand premises a year are judged to be "alarm abusers," each having transmitted at least three false alarms within a ninety-day period.

Solution: As proposed, all alarm users register with the police department and after paying the prescribed fee are issued a permit that is subject to suspension and/or revocation contingent on the number of false alarms. Following a revocation, the alarm owner is required to reapply for a permit, which will be issued only upon the satisfaction of all outstanding penalties, submission of proof that the alarm system has been inspected and found to be in proper order, and the payment of an additionally prescribed alarm permit fee. Those not complying will no longer receive police response when their alarm is activated. A revenue enhancer, the new system should produce for Nassau County $1 million in its first year and nearly $400,000 in subsequent years.

Cooperative Agreement for Shared Law Enforcement Services

Situation: In Minnesota, the Hennepin County Sheriff's Department and the Minneapolis Police Department each needed special expertise and better equipment to strengthen their operations. Hennepin County wanted to add a bomb squad, and Minneapolis—which had a decent water rescue unit—sought superior equipment.

Solution: Hennepin County and Minneapolis entered into a formal agreement to provide services to each other. The Minneapolis Police Bomb Squad, because of a higher frequency of response, offered exactly what the Sheriff's Department needed. The Sheriff's Department, because of a statutory responsibility for water rescue, had developed a state-of-the-art underwater recovery unit. Capital expenditure estimates were as high as $75,000 for basic bomb squad equipment plus maintenance costs of $5,000 per year. Equipment and maintenance costs for an improved underwater recovery unit approached $10,000. Factoring in training and overtime expenses inflated the figures more. Both total amounts were saved.

Conclusion

Law enforcement leaders who tackle the problem of managing with less will be truly successful only when they recognize that the issue, much like violent crime, illegal drugs, and community unrest, requires long-term commitment and planned action.

For specific examples on how various law enforcement agencies have cut costs, contact the chief of the Education and Communication Arts Unit at the FBI Training Academy in Quantico, Virginia. This article is an abridgment of a report on cost reduction, which is an ongoing interest of the FBI Academy.

RICHARD M. AYERS

ORDER MAINTENANCE

A primary function of government is to provide for the security of its citizens. Related to this function is the perception of orderliness, constancy, and predictability. Without stable relationships among people and institutions, other values are jeopardized. For example, property rights are only protected if government can maintain a court system based on preserving these processes and rights. How governments perform this function is of critical importance. In both enforcing laws and maintaining order, governments employ non-negotiable coercive force inherent in the nature of *sovereignty* (Bittner 1970).

In many societies, order is maintained by an institutionalized police force that is separate from the military. Even in liberal democratic societies, however, the military is often called on if police authorities cannot control disorder. In democratic societies, the primary role for maintaining order is vested in the police function. Although most people associate police with their law enforcement or felony-chasing role, actual studies of police behavior reveal that they spend an overwhelming amount of their resources on order maintenance problems (Goldstein 1990). In other words, police officers spend most of their time dealing with incidents involving disturbances, political demonstrations, labor–management confrontations, neighborhood disputes, intoxicated persons, barking dogs, homeless persons, and a host of activities that involve "keeping the peace." In fact, the word "peacekeeping" is often used to describe the order maintenance function (Goldstein 1977).

A more formal definition of order maintenance policing is the intervention and suppression of behavior that threatens to be offensive, that threatens to disturb the public peace, or that emanates from conflicts among individuals that are public in nature. Order maintenance situations tend to be ambiguous, and the police have broad discretion in what their response should be (Kelling 1996).

In maintaining order, the police engage in an activity that is both necessary and controversial at the same time. It is necessary because citizens demand protection from disorder as a governmental function. It is controversial because it involves the use of authorized coercive force in a discretionary manner. There are no clear guidelines for what police should do and how they should do it in "keeping the peace" (Brown 1981). When the police enter a situation, they are empowered by their role to impose a solution to a problem, incident, or disturbance if, in their judgment, they deem it necessary. Using their authority in such situations is sometimes divisive in the community since they are acting against someone in using their powers to intervene in many disturbance or conflict situations (Bittner 1970).

In performing this role, the police engage in what some have called "social regulation" (Muir 1977). Complaints about homeless people sleeping in doorways or teenagers congregating in a restaurant often bring a police response that prompts criticism of the police. On the community level, the use of police discretion to control disorder sometimes can be perceived as racially motivated and lead to political controversies such as racial profiling (Skolnick and Fyfe 1993). How the police perform this role, what groups are the objects of their attention, and the legal basis for their actions are inherently divisive and subject to public criticism.

Scientific studies of police discretion support the viewpoint that police decision making in order maintenance situations involves such issues as whether to intervene, whether to make an arrest or issue a citation, and whether or not to use force and how much force should be employed (National Research Council of the Academies 2004). Police decision making is influenced by both legal and extralegal factors (Sykes 1986). Extralegal factors can include the preferences of the complainant who called the police, the attitude of the suspect, the social status of the offender, the kind of neighborhood, the perceived seriousness of the offense, or the perceived threat to the officer. In short, policing on the street tends be a very human activity that calls for making judgments and acting in a discretionary manner (Klockars 1985a).

Holding police accountable for discretionary decisions has been difficult and is often a source of community praise and criticism. In a liberal democratic society the exercise of power by the government is subject to review through oversight, rules, checks and balances, courts, and limitations imposed through law. The difficulty with discretionary activities in order maintenance policing is that they often occur in individual incidents where there are no credible independent witnesses. As a matter of necessity, the police version of events is presumed unless there is clear contrary evidence. Police are given the benefit of the doubt (Skolnick 1966). In sum, the order maintenance police function is an anomaly in a political culture based on the "rule of law" and the idea that power should be held accountable through administrative, procedural, or civil due process. Several police theorists suggest that order maintenance policing is "beyond the law" and the practical reach of the institutionalized systems of accountability (Bittner 1970; Klockars 1983; Sykes 1986).

Since the primary function of government is to provide for security, including the maintenance of order, the police contribute by helping to create that sense of order. They help to define the boundaries of community norms by what kinds of behavior they sanction. For example, if minor disturbances such as loitering, vagrancy, or juvenile harassment of passers-by are tolerated by the police, the quality of life is diminished and the fear of crime increases (Wilson and Kelling 1982). On the other hand, if police confront many kinds of behavior that are simply annoying but not necessarily criminal, they can be accused of harassment, racism, or running a "police state." Where the line should be drawn is often defined by the community norms, and police tend to reflect these norms (Sykes 1986).

Historically, the police always were a community-based institution primarily focused on disorder. Alleged abuses of their power, problems of misconduct, and corruption scandals led to reforms as part of the Progressive movement in the early part of the twentieth century (Toch and Grant 2005). Consequently, police departments became more insulated from politics and became more organizationally structured to control officer misconduct. In addition, police organizations became more bureaucratic and focused on the enforcement model under the later reforms advocated by O. W. Wilson and his followers during the period of the 1930s to the 1960s. Leading police administrators during this era of reform proposed what was called the "full enforcement paradigm" based on a paramilitary model of professionalism. This movement diminished the idea of order maintenance and peacekeeping policing in favor of an enforcement-oriented crime fighting model of policing (Goldstein 1990).

The turbulence of the 1960s with the civil rights movement, the anti-Vietnam War demonstrations, and the explosion of violent street crime created a new challenge to police reformers. The paramilitary professional departments failed to deal effectively with these issues, and new research emerged to challenge the enforcement-oriented strategies of random preventive patrol, rapid response, and follow-up investigation. Some observers argued that the police lost effectiveness because they failed to focus on neighborhood problem solving and order maintenance activities (Sykes 1986).

In response to pressures for change, there emerged the community policing movement that emphasized police problem solving, neighborhood-based strategies, and order maintenance programs. This reform effort suggested that disorder and crime were linked and that effective reductions in the fear of crime and actual crime were the result of order maintenance activities (Wilson and Kelling 1982). This seminal article propounded a viewpoint that came to be known as the "broken-window theory." This theory, based on studies of police foot patrol, argued that if broken windows, graffiti, or abandoned cars are allowed to go unattended, their existence sends out a message that "nobody seems to care," or "nobody is in charge," and/or "you can get away with anything." In this kind of disordered environment, the researchers concluded, crime is likely to escalate from minor to more serious offenses. The obvious police response is to expand their role in addressing the problems of disorder and move away from the model of policing committed to a "war on crime" enforcement approach with its strategies of rapid response, random preventive patrol, and criminal investigation (Goldstein 1979).

Critics of order maintenance policing pointed out that the paramilitary professional approach was never fully implemented, was effective in combating police corruption, and held police accountable through enhanced supervision, administrative policies, and regulations (Klockars 1985b). Others suggested that this approach would require a radical reorganization of police departments and the culture of their organizations. Further, critics pointed out that this expansion of the police role carries with it the potential for abuse of civil liberties, for racial and social regulation based on prejudice, and for actually creating the antecedents of disorder by singling out communities for widespread police surveillance (Manning 1978).

Despite the reservations of critics, order maintenance policing became a widespread movement in the 1990s and into the new millennium under various names— problem-oriented policing, zero-tolerance policing, neighborhood-oriented policing, and, broadly, community policing. Based on a comprehensive review of research related to this approach by the National Research Council of the National Academies (2004), recent studies do not provide strong support for the proposition that focusing on minor offenses results in major reductions of serious crime. In fact, many strategies based on this approach alienated some communities, especially minority communities. However, the research remains limited and incomplete, and they conclude (p. 243) that there is a "... growing body of evidence that problem-oriented policing is an effective approach."

Order maintenance is an essential function the police perform and will continue to be an enigma. How the police play this role depends on many individual, organizational, and political decisions that in a practical sense are difficult to hold accountable. Ultimately, officers and their agencies must be committed to the values of a democratic polity and, to some extent, police themselves in a trustworthy manner. Such an answer will not satisfy those who insist that the exercise of power be held strictly accountable to policies, rules, and laws. When it comes to police playing this role, it will always generate controversy.

GARY W. SYKES

See also **Accountability; Attitudes toward the Police: Overview; Broken-Windows Policing; Community-Oriented Policing: Practices; Discretion; Problem-Oriented Policing; Zero Tolerance Policing**

References and Further Reading

Bittner, Egon. 1970. *The functions of police in modern society: A review of background factors, current practices and possible role models*. Rockville, MD: National Institute of Mental Health.

Brown, Michael. 1981. *Working the street: Police, discretion and the dilemmas of reform*. New York: Russell Sage Foundation.

Goldstein, Herman. 1977. *Policing a free society*. Cambridge, MA: Ballinger.

———. 1979. Improving policing: A problem-oriented approach. *Crime and Delinquency* 25: 236–58.

———. 1990. *Problem-oriented policing*. New York: McGraw-Hill.

Kelling, George, and Catherine Coles. 1996. *Fixing broken windows: Restoring order and reducing crime in our communities*. New York: Free Press.

Klockars, Carl. 1985a. *The idea of police*. Beverly Hills, CA: Sage.

———. 1985b. Order maintenance, the quality of urban life, and police. In *Police leadership in America*, ed. William Geller, 309–21. New York: Praeger.

Manning, Peter. 1978. The police: Mandate, strategies and appearances. In *Policing: A view from the street*, ed. Peter Manning and John Van Maanen. Santa Monica, CA: Goodyear Publishing.

Muir, W. K., Jr. 1993. *Police: Streetcorner politicians*. Chicago: Chicago University Press.

National Research Council of the National Academies. 2004. *Fairness and effectiveness in policing: The evidence*. Washington, DC: The National Academies Press.

Skolnick, Jerome. 1966. *Justice without trial: Law enforcement in a democratic society*. New York: Wiley.

Skolnick, Jerome, and James Fyfe. 1993. *Above the law: Police and the excessive use of force*. New York: The Free Press.

Sykes, Gary. 1986. Street justice: A moral defense of order maintenance policing. *Justice Quarterly* 3: 497–512.

Toch, Hans, and J. Douglas Grant. 2004. *Police as problem solvers: How frontline workers can promote organizational and community change*. 2nd ed. Washington, DC: American Psychological Association.

Wilson, James Q., and George L. Kelling. 1982. The police and neighborhood safety: Broken windows. *Atlantic Monthly* 127: 29–38.

ORGANIZATIONAL STRUCTURE: THEORY AND PRACTICE

Organizational Structure Defined and Described

Police organizations, from the smallest to the largest, all have a social structure, composed of the social relationships among their members. These social relationships accomplish a number of tasks, from socializing new members to accomplishing the goals of the organization. Most importantly, organizational structure serves as the "apparatus through which organizations accomplish . . . the division of labor and the coordination of work" (Maguire 2003, 11). These structures allow police agencies to accomplish a range of goals, first by dividing workers into different work groups and specialties (called complexity), and second by facilitating the management and control of these workers (called control) (Maguire 2003; Wilson 2003).

Organizational complexity has three dimensions: vertical, functional, and geographic (Maguire 2003). Vertically, police agencies differ in the height of their hierarchy (chain of command) and the nature and shape of that hierarchy. For example, it is possible for an agency with a tall chain of command to still grant decision-making discretion to its line-level officers (King 2005). Furthermore, some agencies may have a large number of midlevel supervisors, which in effect causes the pyramid of their hierarchy to bulge in the middle.

Functionally, police agencies may divide their tasks among specialized units (such as a community policing unit or a traffic enforcement unit). Some agencies are very specialized, while others are not. Less specialized agencies will rely upon an undifferentiated group of generalist officers to accomplish organizational goals.

Finally, some police agencies are more spread out in terms of geography and territory. For example, some police organizations have many precinct stations, substations, and patrol beats, while other agencies rely upon one or a handful of precinct stations, and a limited number of patrol beats.

Increasing organizational complexity allows police agencies to better tailor their response to specific goals. For instance, an agency may opt to create a police substation in a depressed neighborhood and staff that substation with community police officers. Such a response permits this agency to address a specific problem in one community with a geographically targeted and functionally specialized response. It should be obvious, however, that this response also increases the complexity of that organization. To be effective, more complex organizations must also exert greater control over their workers.

Organizational control involves "the formal administrative apparatuses that an organization institutes in order to achieve coordination and control among its workers and its work" (Maguire 2003,16). Control consists of three dimensions; administration, formalization, and centralization of decision making. Administration refers to the resources and personnel an agency devotes to organizational maintenance and the day-to-day operation of the organization. Administration includes workers assigned to upper management and support functions (such as clerical workers, maintenance workers, and trainers). These workers and resources assist the organization in better coordinating and controlling its employees. Formalization refers to formal, codified, organizational rules and guidelines. Examples of formalization are standard operations procedures books (SOPs), employee manuals, and other written rules. Formalization assists in the control of workers by communicating the appropriate methods for achieving organizational goals. Centralization of decision making refers to the degree to which the authority to make decisions is concentrated in a relatively small number of workers (usually upper management) or is spread throughout the organization. Some police agencies are centralized, and thus important decisions are made by upper managers or supervisors; other agencies are decentralized, empowering line officers to make important decisions on their own.

Explaining the Structure of Police Organizations

Scholars have long sought to explain why different police organizations adopt different organizational structures (that is, different degrees of complexity and control). Generally, these police scholars have turned to two organizational theories: structural contingency theory and institutional theory.

Structural contingency theory posits that organizations alter their structures to best adapt to their rational/technical environments and thus improve organizational efficiency and effectiveness (Donaldson 1996). The rational/technical environment for police agencies differs from one agency to the next. Environments are usually composed of the population the agency serves (including the specific demands that population might put on the agency, such as an upper class suburb as compared to a less affluent inner-city neighborhood), the political system that oversees that police agency (such as city government or county government), and the degree and type of crime. Contingency theory posits that organizations must adapt their structures in order to appropriately respond to their specific environments (Zhao 1996). If a police agency adapts properly, it will be effective and efficient. If an agency fails to respond appropriately, however, it will be ineffective and inefficient. Since an agency's environment may be constantly changing, police organizations must be capable of change as well. Of course, some agencies enjoy the predictability of a relatively stable environment and thus need not change much or often.

Organizational institutional theory (often called institutional theory) contends that organizations change in response to their institutional (or symbolic) environment, but not due to their rational/technical environment (Meyer and Rowan 1977). This institutional environment is composed of powerful external constituents (called sovereigns), such as politicians, the media, community groups, and other police agencies. These powerful sovereigns create expectations about how "good" police agencies are structured and how they behave, and organizations in turn attempt to meet these expectations in order to receive legitimacy from their institutional environment.

Appropriate organizational structure (that is, the form of a "good" police agency) is not related to efficiency or effectiveness, but rather due to what the institutional environment deems to be appropriate, correct, or acceptable (Crank and Langworthy 1992; Mastrofski, Ritti, and Hoffmaster 1987). Police agencies that adapt and emulate the appropriate organizational forms dictated by their institutional environments are rewarded with greater legitimacy (and are often viewed as being better organizations). Police agencies that do not change risk being labeled as nonconforming and are sometimes labeled as bad organizations. Simply, institutional theory contends the police agencies change their structure in order to receive legitimacy from sovereigns, not to increase their efficiency or effectiveness.

Evidence Supporting These Theories of Police Organizations

Recent years have seen an increasing interest in empirically testing contingency and institutional theory with police agencies. To summarize this body of literature briefly, the results have been mixed, with neither theory gaining a supremacy on the landscape of theoretical explanation. It appears that contingency theory explains well some structural attributes, while institutional theory explains well other elements of police organizational structure.

Briefly, there is some evidence that police agencies alter their structures in order to cope with changes in their environments. Zhao's (1996) research indicated that police agencies located in more diverse communities were more likely to adopt community policing in response. Other researchers (Langworthy 1986; Maguire 2003) have also found significant relationships between an agency's environment and its structure.

Researchers exploring the relationship between police agencies and institutional environments have also discovered intriguing relationships. Katz's (2001) examination of the creation of a specialized antigang unit in one police agency (an example of increased agency complexity) supported institutional theory. Katz (2001) concluded that the gang unit was formed due to external pressure from powerful groups (but not due to a specific gang problem). Further, once formed, the gang unit mostly engaged in activities designed to grant it organizational legitimacy. Similarly, Mastrofski, Ritti, and Hoffmaster (1987) found that officers in smaller police agencies were more likely than officers in larger agencies to predict that they would behave in accord with perceived norms of proper police behavior. This finding also supports the contention made by institutional theorists that smaller agencies strive to bolster their legitimacy by emulating the structures and behaviors of larger and more legitimate agencies.

In sum, then, there is evidence that each of these theories applies to certain aspects of police agencies. In part, this finding indicates that police executives and their overseers (such as local politicians) can exercise some degree of control over the structures of their police agencies. However, some elements of structure are more amenable to change than are others (for example, see Maguire 2003, 225–27) and reformers should be careful about what reforms they undertake.

WILLIAM R. KING

See also **Accountability; Administration of Police Agencies, Theories of**

References and Further Reading

Crank, John P., and Robert H. Langworthy. 1992. An institutional perspective on policing. *The Journal of Criminal Law and Criminology* 83 (2): 338–63.

Donaldson, Lex. 1996. The normal science of structural contingency theory. In *Handbook of organization studies*, ed. Stewert R. Clegg, Cynthia Hardy, and Walter R. Nord, 57–76. Thousand Oaks, CA: Sage Publications.

Katz, Charles M. 2001. The establishment of a police gang unit: An examination of organizational and environmental factors. *Criminology* 39 (1): 301–38.

King, William R. 2005. Toward a better understanding of the hierarchical nature of police organizations: Conception and measurement. *Journal of Criminal Justice* 33 (1): 97–109.

Langworthy, Robert H. 1986. *The structure of police organizations*. New York: Praeger.

Maguire, Edward R. 2003. *Organizational structure in American police agencies: Context, complexity, and control*. Albany, NY: State University of New York Press.

Mastrofski, Stephen D., R. Richard Ritti, and Debra Hoffmaster. 1987. Organizational determinants of police discretion: The case of drinking–driving. *Journal of Criminal Justice* 15: 387–402.

Meyer, John W., and Brian Rowan. 1977. Institutionalized organizations: Formal structure as myth and ceremony. *American Journal of Sociology* 83 (2): 340–63.

Wilson, Jeremy M. 2003. Measurement and association in the structure of municipal police organizations. *Policing: An International Journal of Police Strategies and Management* 26 (2): 276–97.

Zhao, Jihong. 1996. *Why police organizations change: A study of community oriented policing*. Washington, DC: Police Executive Research Forum.

ORGANIZED CRIME

Organized crime is a topic of immense social, political, cultural, and economic interest. Hundreds of movies and television programs and thousands of novels have focused on organized crime; it has become an icon of popular culture. Journalists cover it with great regularity. National and international commissions have grappled with the complexities of this phenomenon. It consumes enormous law enforcement and criminal justice resources and effort. Yet, organized crime remains one of the most difficult crime-related terms to define with any degree of precision.

Definitions and descriptions of organized crime take many forms. There are legal definitions designed to facilitate prosecutions. There are criminological definitions designed to both operationalize and measure organized crime. There are descriptions of its attributes, its activities, and its forms or organization. But nowhere is there an accepted, agreed upon, comprehensive definition of one of the most prevalent criminal activities in the world.

Legal or juridical definitions are designed to define the parameters for investigations and subsequent prosecutions. The accepted federal definition is found in the Omnibus Crime Control and Safe Streets Act of 1968 (Pub. L. 90–381, Title I, Part F b):

> "Organized crime" means the unlawful activities of the members of a highly organized, disciplined association, engaged in supplying illegal goods and services, including but not limited to gambling, prostitution, loan sharking, narcotics, labor racketeering, and other unlawful activities of member of such organizations.

Similarly, California defines organized crime as follows (California Control of Profits of Organized Crime Act 1982, Penal Code Part 1, Title 7, 21: 186):

> "Organized crime" means crime which of a conspiratorial nature and that is either of an organized nature and which seeks to supply illegal goods and services, such as narcotics, prostitution, loan sharking, gambling, and pornography, or that, through planning and coordination of individual efforts, seeks to conduct the illegal activities of arson for

profit, hijacking, insurance fraud, smuggling, operating vehicle theft rings, or systematically encumbering the assets of a business for the purpose of defrauding creditors.

Two things need to noted about these definitions. First, they are tautologies, a not terribly useful definitional device. They define organized crime as "organized." Second, they define organized crime by the activities in which it might be engaged, not as an entity unto itself. In addition, they suggest some type of bureaucratic hierarchy that is engaged in conspiratorial activity but fail to specify either the nature of that bureaucratic organization or the conspiracy in which it engages. In other words, the legal definitions are of little use in understanding organized crime as either a social or criminological concept.

Investigating bodies have also attempted to define organized crime. Historically, the Chicago Crime Commission (1915), the Wickersham Commission (1929), the President's Commission on Law Enforcement and the Administration of Justice (1967), and the President's Commission on Organized Crime (1983) have all attempted descriptions or definitions. In its final report issued in 1986, the President's Commission on Organized Crime developed a contingency model as a way of defining the activities and organizational form of organized crime. That model specifies five levels of organization and six characteristics of organized crime groups.

The five levels of organization are (1) the criminal group, (2) the protectors, (3) specialized support, (4) user support, and (5) social support. The criminal group represents the criminal core of organized crime. Protectors include corrupt public officials, business people, judges, attorneys, financial advisers, and others who protect the interests of the criminal group. Specialized support includes persons who provide contract services that facilitate organized crime activities, such as pilots, chemists, arsonists, and smugglers. User support provides the criminal group with their consumer market: persons who purchase organized crime's illegal goods and services, such as drug users, patrons of bookmakers and prostitution rings, and people who knowingly purchase stolen goods. Finally, social support involves persons and organizations who create a perception of legitimacy for organized crime. Examples include politicians who solicit the support of organized crime figures, business leaders who do business with organized crime, social and community leaders who invite organized crime figures to social gatherings, and those who portray organized crime or its members in a favorable light.

The six characteristics used by the President's Commission to delineate the operation of organized crime groups include the following:

- *Continuity.* The organization continues operation beyond the lifetime of any member or any change in leadership.
- *Structure.* The criminal group is hierarchically structured, although the form of that structure varies from tight hierarchies to extremely loose associations.
- *Membership.* The criminal group has identifiable members selected on the basis of ethnicity, criminal background, or common interest in an enterprise.
- *Criminality.* Like any business, organized crime is directed by the pursuit of profit along well-defined lines. In the case of organized crime, the criminal group relies on continuing criminal activity to generate income.
- *Violence.* Violence or the threat of violence is employed as a means of control and protection.
- *Power and profit.* The purpose of the criminal group is the pursuit of profit. Power is achieved through corruption and the threat of violence.

The definition supplied by the President's Commission on Organized Crime

is important because it includes individuals in the environment of organized crime who are not directly members of the criminal group but who are vital to the success of any organized crime enterprise and because it specifies the general characteristics of an organized crime group.

Scholars studying organized crime have also made considerable use of its attributes in their definitions. Jay Albanese reviewed working definitions of organized crime and selected the most commonly mentioned attributes in developing his working definition (1989, 4–5):

> Organized crime is a continuing criminal enterprise that rationally works to profit from illicit activities that are in great public demand. Its continuing existence is maintained through the use of force, threats, and/ or the corruption of public officials.

Similarly, Kenney and Finckenauer (1995, 285) offer a definition making use of descriptive attributes:

> Our working definition of organized crime includes the following characteristics: a self-perpetuating, organized hierarchy that exists to profit from providing illicit goods and services, uses violence in carrying out its criminal activities, and corrupts public officials to immunize itself from law enforcement.

Donald Liddick (1999, 50) also makes reference to criminality but specifies more clearly the types of organizations found in organized crime and the importance of environmental forces in his definition:

> Organized crime [is] the provision of illegal goods and service, various forms of theft and fraud, and the restraint of trade in both licit and illicit market sectors, perpetuated by informal and changing networks of upper-world and under-world societal participants, who are bound together in complex webs of patron–client relationships.

Liddick's definition adds to the others by attempting to specify the type and style of organization found in organized crime. This builds on seminal research conducted by Joseph Albini on the organization of organized crime. Albini (1971, 35) suggests that the key term in organized crime is "organized" and that specifying the nature of that organization or association is the key to understanding the phenomenon:

It appears the most primary distinguishing component of organized crime is found within the term itself, mainly, organization . . . .

In a very broad sense, then, we can define organized crime as any criminal activity involving two or more individuals, specialized or nonspecialized, encompassing some form of social structure, with some form of leadership, utilizing certain modes of operation, in which the ultimate purpose of the organization is found in the enterprises of the particular group (Albini 1971, 37–38).

These scholarly definitions, and many others not discussed here, share several characteristics. First, there is recognition of some kind of social interaction between individuals composing a core criminal group. Second, there is a recognition of the pursuit of profit, primarily through criminality. Third, there is a recognition that organized crime conducts its business in a supportive environment, which entails corruption, market demand, and social support. Fourth, there is a recognition of continuity and persistence in the organized crime group. And finally, there is some consensus on the use of threats of violence and political corruption as means of doing business and protecting the enterprise.

It would seem that using the scholarly definitions and the observations of the President's Commission on Organized Crime, we can at least arrive at a description of organized crime as it existed in the United States in the twentieth century. However, changes in world markets and politics fundamentally impacted economies, governments, societies, and organized crime as we entered the twenty-first century. Massive increases in international travel and trade, the weakening of political states,

advances in technology, and the internationalization of finance all came together to offer organized crime new opportunities to pursue profits in new markets on an international scale. And as Letizia Paoli (2002) has observed, these forces have strongly mitigated against the development of large-scale, complex organizations. In fact, she concludes that in the global economy of the twenty-first century, there is an inexorable tendency in organized crime to develop as small groups of entrepreneurs who have only tenuous connections, or as she suggests, "network crime."

The concept of network crime is very compatible with the organizational descriptions provided by Liddick (1999) and Albini (1971). This tendency adds yet another complexity to attempts to define organized crime. Taking globalization and its impacts into account, the National Criminal Intelligence Service of the United Kingdom argued in 1998 that organized crime at the new millennium had four basic characteristics:

- Groups contain at least three people.
- Criminal activity is prolonged or indefinite.
- Criminals are motivated by profit or power.
- Serious criminal offenses are being committed.

Organized crime is a social phenomenon, and like all social phenomena, it is constantly changing and adjusting to new exigencies and conditions. As world economies and politics globalize, so does organized crime, and with that change its characteristics, attributes, structure, and definition change as well. Debate will continue on a twenty-first century definition of organized crime. But, as we entered the new millennium, a newer, more dynamic definition was already being proposed. It is, quite frankly, the best "new" working definition we have and an appropriate way to conclude this discussion (Schulte-Bockholt 2001, 238–39):

Organized crime is identified as a group generally operating under some form of concealment with a structure reflective of the cultural and social stipulations of the societies that generate it; and which has the primary objective to obtain access to wealth and power through the participation in economic activities prohibited by state law. Organized crime is a form of crude accumulation based on the use of threat of physical violence, which emerges—and has emerged—in different socioeconomic formations across time and place, and is generated by the specific conditions of that time and place.

GARY W. POTTER

See also **Federal Police and Investigative Agencies; Intelligence Gathering and Analysis: Impacts on Terrorism; International Policing; Racketeer Influenced and Corrupt Organizations Act (RICO); Transnational Organized Crime**

References and Further Reading

Albanese, J. 1989. *Organized crime in America.* 2nd ed. Cincinnati, OH: Anderson.

Albini, J. 1971. *The American mafia: Genesis of a legend.* New York: Appleton-Century-Croft.

Kenney, D., and J. Finckenauer. 1995. *Organized crime in America.* Belmont, CA: Wadsworth.

Liddick, D. 1999. *An empirical, theoretical and historical overview of organized crime.* Lewiston, NY: Edward Mellon Press.

Paoli, L. 2002. The paradoxes of organized crime. *Crime, Law and Social Change* 37 (1): 51–97.

Schulte-Bockholt, A. 2001. A neo-Marxist explanation of organized crime. *Critical Criminology* 10: 225–42.

P

PATRIOT ACTS I AND II

PATRIOT Act I

The Uniting and Strengthening America by Providing Appropriate Tools Required to Intercept and Obstruct Terrorism Act of 2001 (P.L. 107-56), known by the acronym USA PATRIOT Act, became effective on October 26, 2001. The formal title by Congress describes it as "an Act to deter and punish terrorist acts in the United States and around the world, to enhance law enforcement investigatory tools, and for other purposes."

The U.S. Department of Justice and Congress looked for ways to strengthen law enforcement powers in response to the terrorist attacks on the United States on September 11, 2001. The result was the PATRIOT Act, passed 98 to 1 in the Senate and 357 to 66 in the House of Representatives. The act amended a number of existing statutes and created new statutes to cover a wide variety of law enforcement initiatives. Government power was expanded, and some previously unregulated federal law enforcement practices were formalized and regulated.

The act covered a diverse range of issues, including new criminal statutes, government surveillance, investigations and information sharing, immigration law, money laundering and counterfeiting, increased funds for certain law enforcement activities, funds for training, funds for the study of critical infrastructure, the transportation of hazardous materials, financial assistance to victims of terrorist attacks, increased benefits for public safety workers, and other provisions. In addition, the act required the Department of Justice inspector general to receive complaints about civil liberties and civil rights abuses by the Department of Justice and report on those abuses to Congress. Other reports to Congress were also required, including the need for additional legislation, studies on how certain provisions of the act are working, and studies on new antiterrorism technology.

The PATRIOT Act has been controversial from inception because privacy advocates and civil libertarians were concerned that it infringes on fundamental liberties and gives too much unsupervised power to law enforcement agencies. Hundreds of communities, several major cities, and a few states have passed resolutions denouncing the act. A number of lawsuits have been filed against provisions of the act, with little effect. The Department of Justice responded with a series of initiatives to reassure concerned constituencies and the general public that the act was necessary to combat terrorism and did not violate civil liberties. This controversy was reflected in the fact that another act designed to further increase government powers, dubbed PATRIOT II, was not able to move through the legislative process. A number of provisions of the PATRIOT Act contained sunset clauses due to take effect in 2005. These sunset clauses would cause the subject provisions to expire. It is likely that efforts will continue to repeal the sunset provisions and broaden government antiterrorism powers.

The federal government's rationale for the PATRIOT Act was that, in light of the terrorist attacks on the United States and the unique challenges of terrorism, many existing laws and legal restraints on law enforcement needed to be updated. In addition, new law and criminal penalties needed to be created where none existed. Existing law impaired law enforcement's ability to gather, analyze, and share intelligence. In addition, the existing laws and law enforcement authority did not reflect the realities of new technologies such as computers, high-technology communication systems, and the Internet.

The act authorized law enforcement agencies to share terrorism-related intelligence with each other and with intelligence agencies. Previously prohibitions to share information or a "wall" existed between law enforcement officers and intelligence officers. FBI agents conducting intelligence investigations could not share information with FBI agents conducting criminal investigations, and vice versa. The FBI and CIA could not share certain terrorism-related information.

A number of criminal laws designed to thwart terrorists were part of the act. Laws were enacted or strengthened in the area of money laundering and against individuals who financed or aided terrorists. New laws against biological weapons and cyberterrorism were enacted and laws prohibiting attacks on mass transportation were added.

The advent of computers and advanced communications technology and the mobility of terrorists presented obstacles to government investigators. The PATRIOT Act was designed to overcome some of those obstacles. The act permitted investigators to gather some e-mail and Internet communications with subpoenas and search warrants, rather than the more difficult to obtain wiretap orders. Search warrants issued by a federal judge in one jurisdiction could be served anywhere in the country. Previously, a judge's warrant was valid only in that court's jurisdiction.

Cell phones and digital telephones presented law enforcement investigators with a number of problems that could not be addressed by existing statutes. Previously, wiretaps had been authorized only for a particular telephone number. The act enabled investigators to obtain a roving wiretap on any phone or computer the suspected terrorist used. In addition, these roving wiretaps were national, rather than restricted to the limited jurisdiction of a federal district judge.

The act increased the power and coverage of the Foreign Intelligence Surveillance Act (FISA). Enacted in 1978, FISA created a secret court with an exception to usual law enforcement searches. The Fourth Amendment's probable cause requirement that probable cause to believe a criminal act had occurred to grant search warrants and wiretaps need not be adhered to in foreign intelligence cases. The act amended FISA to significantly broaden the scope of the circumstances under which these warrants and wiretaps could be authorized.

The act codified the use of delayed notification search warrants by law enforcement and expanded the circumstances of their use. Usually law enforcement officers notify the subject of an investigation that their property is being searched. Delayed notification search warrants are used when the investigators do not want the subject to know that they are being investigated. The subject of the search still must be notified of the search at a later date.

The act attempted to prepare federal, state, and local law enforcement to deal with the rapid escalation of computer crime and the terrorist use of high technology. Funds were authorized to train law enforcement investigators in computer crime and to establish a network of regional computer forensic laboratories (RCFLs) around the country. These RCFLs were joint federal, state, and local law enforcement task forces that recovered evidence from seized electronic devices.

All of the provisions of the act were an attempt to provide increased power to federal law enforcement agencies, and in some cases all of law enforcement, to prevent terrorism and to investigate and apprehend terrorists. It was recognition that the country was involved in a far-reaching struggle against a number of terrorist groups intent on doing significant destruction.

Provisions of the PATRIOT Act

The following overview highlights some of the major provisions of the PATRIOT Act.

It sought to enhance domestic security by allowing the U.S. attorney general to request military assistance to deal with weapons of mass destruction. It established a counterterrorism fund for the Department of Justice. It increased funding for the FBI technical center and provided funds for the U.S. Secret Service to develop a network of electronic crime task forces. The president was empowered to confiscate the property of an enemy involved in hostile action against the United States.

Surveillance authority for federal law enforcement agencies was significantly increased. Stored voice communications could be obtained through a search warrant rather than a wiretap order. Subpoena power for electronic evidence was widened. Communications providers were permitted to disclose customer records to law enforcement in an emergency. A uniform statutory standard for the courts to authorize the delayed notice of searches by law enforcement was created. The act clarified law enforcement authority to trace communications on computer networks and the Internet and gave trace orders by the federal courts nationwide scope. Victims of a computer attack could authorize law enforcement to monitor trespassers on their computer systems. A search warrant issued by a federal judge in a terrorism case, or for e-mail, could now be served anywhere in the country.

The act expanded money laundering laws. It increased certain powers of the secretary of the treasury and increased the regulation and reporting requirements of financial institutions. Securities brokers and dealers were required to submit suspicious activity reports. Civil and criminal penalties for money laundering were increased, and the crime of bulk cash smuggling was created. Criminal penalties for counterfeiting were increased and counterfeiting U.S. obligations or securities outside the United States was made a crime.

The act allowed the U.S. attorney general to detain aliens for up to seven days if there were reasonable grounds to believe that they were involved in terrorism or posed a threat to national security. The grounds were broadened for denying an alien admission to the United States based on terrorism. The definitions of terrorist activity and terrorist organization were broadened.

The act strengthened investigative authority and information sharing between law enforcement authorities. It mandated information sharing between the

U.S. attorney general, the FBI, the State Department, and immigration authorities. Individuals convicted of terrorism crimes, violent crimes, and attempts or conspiracies to commit them were required to submit DNA samples. Federal officers investigating foreign intelligence cases could coordinate information with other federal law enforcement officers. The CIA and the FBI were required to improve information sharing between their agencies. They were also required to provide training regarding foreign intelligence information to federal, state, and local government officials. The U.S. attorney general could apply to the courts to obtain educational records to assist terrorism investigations. The attorney general and secretary of state were given increased authority to pay rewards for assistance in combating terrorism. The regional information sharing system to facilitate federal, state, and law enforcement responses to terrorist acts was expanded.

The act increased funding for the Border Patrol, Customs personnel, and Immigration and Naturalization Service inspectors along the northern border and provided funds for increased security technology. The federal benefit payment to public safety officers killed in the line of duty was increased. Also increased was funding for victim compensation and victim assistance programs.

The act established law prohibiting attacks against mass transportation systems. This included conventional attacks and weapons of mass destruction attacks against mass transportation systems and personnel. Mass transportation systems were defined as public transportation systems and school buses, charter, and sightseeing transportation.

The act created the new crime of harboring or concealing a terrorist. Material support for terrorism was also prohibited. The definition of material support or resources to aid terrorism was expanded to include funding and expert advice and assistance. The number of crimes covered by this section was also expanded. The act

also removed the statute of limitations on prosecuting federal terrorism crimes if the crime resulted in or created a risk of death or serious bodily injury.

The act established penalties for damaging federal computer systems. The U.S. attorney general was required to establish regional computer forensic laboratories and support existing ones.

The act made subject to civil forfeiture all foreign and domestic assets of persons or organizations involved in terrorism. It increase criminal penalties for a variety of crimes involving terrorism and made penalties for conspiracy to commit a variety of crimes the same as for committing the crimes. Domestic terrorism was defined, and several new crimes were added to the definition of the federal crime of terrorism.

The act extended the special and maritime criminal jurisdiction of the United States for crimes committed against Americans abroad. Federal terrorism crimes were brought under the provisions of the Racketeer Influenced and Corrupt Organizations (RICO) law.

The act required background checks for drivers transporting hazardous materials. The U.S. attorney general was required to assist the states in performing the background checks, and the states were required to report information on each license issued to the U.S. secretary of transportation.

The act prohibited the development, production, acquisition, or possession of biological agents, toxins, or delivery systems for use as a weapon. Certain people were prohibited from shipping, transporting, or receiving biological agents or toxins.

The act required the U.S. attorney general to provide grants to state and local governments to prevent terrorism and train public safety personnel to prevent and respond to terrorism. Funding was expanded and extended to improve federal, state, and local criminal history record systems and identification systems. Finally, the act required the federal government to provide a number of feasibility reports to Congress. These included providing airlines with computer access to suspected terrorists lists, fingerprint scanning systems for entrants to the United States, and enhancement to the FBI's computer fingerprint system.

Objections to the PATRIOT Act

The PATRIOT Act provoked great controversy from privacy advocates, civil libertarians, politicians, and others. They saw the act as threatening some Constitutional protections and giving too much power to the government. As time passed after 9/11 without another significant terrorist attack on U.S. soil, the voices calling for a rollback of many of the provisions of the act multiplied. Most Americans did not read the long and legally complicated PATRIOT Act; however, many rumors and exaggerations grew up surrounding its provisions. Many Americans first learned about the FISA court, delayed notification search warrants, government subpoena powers, and other law enforcement powers through publicity surrounding the act. A significant number erroneously believed that the act created these powers. Citizen exposure to knowledge about the law enforcement power of the federal government, provided by the public debate over the PATRIOT Act, resulted in a backlash to the efforts to increase law enforcement power to deal with terrorism.

A number of antiterrorism initiatives that were not connected to the act were linked to it in popular misconception. Civil rights abuses by federal law enforcement agents, military tribunals, closed immigration hearings, and the designation and treatment of enemy combatants all were incorrectly linked to the act.

The American Civil Liberties Union and other organizations and individuals sought to rally opposition against the PATRIOT Act and roll back its provisions through court challenges or legislative action. At the same time, the Justice Department waged a public relations campaign to reassure the public that the act was necessary, seeking not only to retain the act but to increase its scope and powers.

The section of the act that made it easier for law enforcement to search and obtain financial and administrative records without warrants and without the knowledge or consent of the people listed in the records created significant protest. The controversy was symbolized by the examination of library records by federal agents. Privacy advocates suggested that the government would monitor all American's library records to determine what they were reading. The Justice Department during testimony before Congress countered that requests for library records had been made a relatively small number of times since the inception of the act.

The change in the FISA act has elicited concern and opposition from privacy advocates. They worried that secret searches could be authorized by a secret court without law enforcement accountability as long as the government could allege a foreign intelligence connection. The Justice Department countered that requests for searches still required approval by the FISA court. The court, in its history, however, had rejected only a very small percentage of search requests. Before the PATRIOT Act the government needed to prove to the court that the primary purpose of the search was to gather foreign intelligence. Any intelligence gathered could not be shared with agents conducting criminal investigations. The act required the government only to show that a significant purpose of the search was to gather foreign intelligence. In addition, the results of the search could be shared with criminal investigators. This was a significant broadening of government power.

The expansion of the use of delayed notification search warrants was also controversial. Law enforcement advocates argued that law enforcement officers had been allowed in the past to delay notification of a warrant for a legitimate reason such as protection of an individual or an active investigation. This practice was upheld by the U.S. Supreme Court. However, the act greatly expanded the use of these warrants by criminal investigators. Privacy advocates worried that these secret searches would become commonplace, eroding constitutional protections against unreasonable search and seizure. A number of federal legislators introduced legislation to roll back this section of the act and limit these searches. They have not been successful.

The act lowered the standards for federal law enforcement to obtain court orders to use electronic monitoring devices that record the numbers dialed to and from a suspect's telephone. The requirement to obtain a warrant was removed, if the government certified that the investigation was linked to terrorism. Some federal legislators also attempted, without success, to rescind this provision.

The authority to monitor telephone conversations was also applied to the Internet. The act clarified that rules for Internet surveillance were the same as for telephone taps. There was concern that the act authorized the use of a controversial federal Internet surveillance tool known as Carnivore. The act did not authorize Carnivore. It did lay down rules for Internet surveillance when none existed before.

The act authorized roving wiretaps. This means that federal investigators could tap every telephone or computer the subject might use. This was a broad expansion of law enforcement power. When used with the act's national wiretap authorization, it limited a judge's ability to oversee the use of the surveillance court order by law enforcement investigators.

The act expanded the authority of the U.S. Justice Department to use National Security Letters. These letters require repositories of a person's personal records to turn over those records to the government.

The letters are similar to administrative subpoenas and are not reviewed by a court. Previously, these letters had been used only in espionage cases. The act allowed them to be used against anyone in a terrorism investigation. Some federal legislators have introduced bills to exempt libraries and booksellers from these letters.

Other sections of the PATRIOT Act have also raised concerns from various interest groups within the country. The act's creation of the new crime of domestic terrorism had some right-to-life advocates and environmental activists worried that it would be used against their lawful protest activities. The increased power of the government to detain and hold aliens for investigation was also of concern to civil rights advocates in that it would promote the abuse of aliens.

A number of the provisions of the PATRIOT Act were subject to sunset provisions in 2005, whereby they will be deleted from the law unless they are expressly reauthorized by Congress. Advocates for and against the act were engaged in efforts to support or oppose these sunset provisions.

PATRIOT II

Some federal legislators envisioned a second act to further enhance the powers of the government to battle terrorism. This Domestic Security Enhancement Act of 2003, dubbed PATRIOT II, was leaked to the media in draft form and provoked great controversy. Because of the expected political opposition, it was never introduced in Congress.

The PATRIOT II act would have permanently enacted many provisions of the PATRIOT Act that expired in 2005 and made technical corrections to fix deficiencies in the original act.

The act would have further increased the electronic surveillance authority of federal investigators. It would have authorized an increase of the scope of use of administrative subpoenas. The exemption from the Freedom of Information Act inquiries for terrorism investigation information would have been broadened. Further regulations to suppress money laundering and the financial support of terrorist organizations would have been enacted.

The act would have discontinued most consent decrees on federal, state, and local law enforcement that could impede their ability to perform terrorism investigations. It would have amended current extradition law and increased the number of and type of crimes for which the federal government could request and be granted pretrial detention. The government's authority to remove criminal aliens would have been expanded. Americans serving in a hostile terrorist organization would have automatically lost their U.S. citizenship.

While PATRIOT II was not introduced as legislation, efforts continue to strengthen the powers of government agencies to prevent and investigate terrorism. New legislation and regulations will continue to be introduced to further this end. The concern by civil libertarians and privacy advocates about potential abuses of power and the loss of constitutional rights will also continue.

THOMAS M. SEAMON

See also **Computer Crimes; Computer Forensics; Constitutional Rights: Privacy; Constitutional Rights: Search and Seizure; Department of Homeland Security; Federal Bureau of Investigation; Federal Commissions and Enactments; Federal Police and Investigative Agencies; Future of International Policing; Homeland Security and Law Enforcement; Identity Theft; Immigrant Communities and the Police; Information within Police Agencies; Intelligence Gathering and Analysis: Impacts on Terrorism; International Police Cooperation; INTERPOL and International Police Intelligence; Money Laundering; Surveillance; Terrorism: Domestic; Terrorism:** International; Terrorism: Police Functions Associated with; Transnational Organized Crime

References and Further Reading

Bulzomi, Michael J. 2003. Foreign Intelligence Surveillance Act. *FBI Law Enforcement Bulletin* 72 (6): 25–31.

———. 2002. Investigating international terrorism overseas. *FBI Law Enforcement Bulletin* 71 (7): 25–31.

Clifford, Michael P. 2002. Communications Assistance for Law Enforcement Act (CALEA). *FBI Law Enforcement Bulletin* 71 (7): 11–13.

Cogar, Stephen W. 2003. Obtaining admissible evidence from computers. *FBI Law Enforcement Bulletin* 72 (7): 11–15.

Collins, Jeffrey G., U.S. Attorney, Eastern District of Michigan. n.d *Questions and answers about the USA PATRIOT Act.* http://www.usdoj.gov/usao/mie/ctu/FAQ_PATRIOT.htm.

Kean, Thomas H. 2004. *The 911 Commission Report.* New York: W.W. Norton and Company.

Lithwick, Dahlia, and Julia Turner. n.d. *A guide to the PATRIOT Act.* http://slate. msn.com/toolbar.aspx?action=print& id=2087984.

OLR Research Report. n.d. *Summary of federal USA PATRIOT Act.* 2001-R-0851. http://www.cga.state.ct.us/2001/rpt/olr/htm/2001-r-0851.htm.

Schott, Richard G. 2003. Warrantless interceptions of communications. *FBI Law Enforcement Journal* 72 (1): 25–31.

U.S. Department of Justice. 2001. *Field guidance on new authorities* (Redacted). Enacted in the 2001 anti-terrorism legislation. http://www.cdt.org/security/011030doj.pdf.

———. 2003. Domestic Security Enhancement Act of 2003. http://www.publicintegrity.com/docs/patriotact/story_01_020703_doc_1.pdf.

———. 2004. *Report from the field: The USA PATRIOT Act at work.* http://www.lifeandliberty.gov/docs/071304_report_from_the_field.pdf

———. n.d. *Dispelling the myths.* http://www.lifeandliberty.gov/subs/u_myths.htm.

U.S. Senate. 2001. *An Act to Deter and Punish Terrorist Acts in the United States and Around the World, to Enhance Law Enforcement Investigatory Tools, and for Other Purposes.* H.R. 3162. http://www.epic.org/privacy/terrorism/hr3162.html.

PATROL, TYPES AND EFFECTIVENESS OF

Patrol accounts for the biggest portion of police work in most police agencies. The terms "patrolling" and "on patrol" generally refer to what officers do while not handling calls for service—officers do this mostly in patrol cars, but sometimes on foot, on bicycles, on horseback, or the like. While on patrol, officers may look for traffic violations, suspicious behavior, disorder, and unsafe conditions. They may also look for opportunities to interact with the public in casual or more formal situations. This is all considered patrolling.

The time that police officers spend handling calls for service is also considered part of patrol work. Officers on patrol respond to calls, take reports, quell disturbances, and so forth. The combination of these two sets of activities—patrolling and handling calls—occupy most of the time of patrol officers, who in turn represent most of the personnel in the typical police department. Thus, patrol is the main business of policing.

We closely associate the term "patrol" with the police today. New police officers are usually assigned to patrol duties and are often called patrol officers. The largest unit in most police departments is the patrol division; in small police departments, everyone patrols. When we call for police assistance, whether for an emergency, to report a crime, to quiet a disturbance, or to request some type of routine service, a patrol officer is typically dispatched. When we encounter the police in that most ubiquitous of all enforcement situations, a traffic stop, it is usually an officer on patrol who has stopped us.

Patrol as Watching

Before the advent of two-way radios, police on patrol had one primary purpose—*watching*. It was (and is) expected that police on patrol will prevent some crime and disorder by their watchfulness. Also, they should effectively intervene when they discover law breaking in progress. In the middle ages, the military and quasi-military precursors of modern police patrolled Europe, watching for highway robbers. In England, the sheriff and his men patrolled on the lookout for those who poached game on lands owned by the king and other nobles. In the American South in the 1700s, slave patrols watched for runaway slaves. As urbanization took hold in the early 1800s and 1900s, night watchmen and later uniformed foot patrol officers watched for all kinds of crime and disorder in cities and towns.

Patrol as Waiting

Automobiles and two-way radios dramatically affected police patrol in the twentieth century. As more and more of the public got into cars, so did the police. Motorized police patrol was deemed necessary to pursue motorized criminals and to enforce traffic laws. Motorized patrol also came to be seen as more efficient than foot patrol, since a larger area could be watched by police in cars. Then, the addition of the two-way radio made it possible for personnel at police headquarters to contact patrol officers in the field and dispatch them to respond to citizen requests for assistance. The impact of these two basic technologies should not be underestimated. Before cars and radios, police response to emergencies and other crises was more like the fire department model—from the station. Officers on patrol were out on the streets watching, but they were not in continuous communication with headquarters.

As the twentieth century progressed, police patrol became more and more dependent on the car and the radio. The public learned to call the police whenever crime or disorder was suspected, and calls for police assistance increased steadily. Over time, that portion of the workload of patrol officers represented by call handling increased. By the 1970s, a second fundamental purpose of patrol had taken root—*waiting*. Many patrol officers came to see their jobs primarily as handling calls, and when they were not "on a call" they were waiting for one. As waiting joined watching as a purpose of patrol, and in some cases largely replaced it, patrol became a more reactive and passive activity.

Research on Patrol

Careful research on the practice and effectiveness of police patrol started slowly in the 1950s and began to flourish in the 1970s. Early findings focused primarily on the discovery that patrol officers exercised wide discretion when enforcing the law and maintaining order. It was found that police invoke the law much less often than they could, often preferring to handle situations informally. Police officer discretionary decisions about whether to enforce the law are affected by such factors as department policy, victim/complainant preferences, suspect demeanor, and the seriousness of the offense.

Research on the makeup of patrol officer workload indicates about a fifty-fifty split between time spent handling calls and time spent patrolling, although, of course, this varies widely between jurisdictions and across different shifts. Officers on the day shift handle relatively more routine crime reporting and public service duties, evening shift officers handle more disorders and disputes and crimes in progress, and night shift officers have less human interaction and focus more of their attention on the few businesses open during those hours and the security of the many businesses closed for the night.

Patrol workload is neither all crime fighting, as media portrayals might suggest, nor all mundane public service, as some early studies seemed to indicate.

The best studies have shown that patrol work combines a variety of crime control, order maintenance, traffic enforcement, and service duties and requests. Of these four commonly used categories, crime control seems to account for the largest portion of calls handled by the police as well as police encounters with citizens, and pure service accounts for the smallest portion. However, it must quickly be emphasized that most crime-related calls and encounters involve minor offenses, routine report taking, and no arrests (often because a suspect is never identified). Patrol officers are more likely to take enforcement actions, in the form or arrests or citations, in order maintenance and traffic situations than in crime-related situations.

A major issue in the 1970s was one-officer versus two-officer patrol cars. The conventional wisdom at the time was that two patrol officers per car were more effective because of the value of two sets of eyes watching and two sets of hands if something happened. Also, it was assumed that two officers in a patrol car were safer than one officer alone. Research found, though, that one-officer cars were as safe and as productive as two-officer cars. To this day, many officers still prefer two-officer patrol cars for the companionship and perceived safety advantages that they offer, but modern practice relies mainly on one-officer cars in the vast majority of agencies.

Patrol Effectiveness

The seminal study of patrol effectiveness was the Kansas City Preventive Patrol Experiment, conducted by the Police Foundation and published in 1974. This experiment tested the impact of three levels of patrolling strength, ranging from no patrol to twice the normal level, in fifteen patrol beats during the course of a year. The results were surprising—there were no differences in victimization, reported crime, fear of crime, public perception of police presence, arrests, traffic accidents, or anything else that was measured. Police patrols (not all police presence, just regular patrols) were virtually eliminated from five beats for an entire year and nobody noticed. Similarly, patrols were doubled in five other beats and nobody noticed.

The internal and external validity of the Kansas City study have been debated for years by researchers, and its implications have been hotly debated by police practitioners. Regardless of the outcome of these debates, though, the theory and practice of police patrol have been changed forever. Few are willing to assume any longer that mere "visibility" and "omnipresence" are sufficient patrol strategies for reducing crime or fear of crime. Many are willing to take a more strategic approach to patrol deployment and tactics, since it no longer seems absolutely necessary to assign a patrol car to every beat on every shift just to provide police visibility.

Two other significant research contributions affecting police patrol came along in the 1970s and early 1980s. First, studies of police response time revealed, much to everyone's surprise, that immediate police response to reported crimes rarely leads to an arrest, nor is it the crucial factor in victim satisfaction. Immediate response rarely leads to arrests because the vast majority of crimes are property crimes reported after they have occurred—the suspect is long gone and the victim has no idea who did it. Moreover, victim satisfaction depends more on how empathetic and competent the officer is than merely on the rapidity of response. These findings had substantial practical implications precisely because, by the early 1980s, the primary purpose of police patrol had become one of waiting for calls and then responding rapidly.

The second major research contribution in the early 1980s was the rediscovery of foot patrol. Studies in Newark, New Jersey, and Flint, Michigan, each indicated that foot patrols might have some

of the positive effects that had been found wanting in Kansas City when motorized patrol was tested. Both studies suggested that foot patrols make residents feel safer and enhance the public's regard for the police. The Flint study also claimed that foot patrols reduced crime, but the Newark study did not. Still, in the aftermath of the Kansas City experiment, just finding that foot patrols had beneficial effects on fear of crime and attitudes toward police was enough to renew police interest in them.

Broken Windows and Community Policing

The rediscovery of foot patrol contributed to the development of the broken-windows thesis. In a nutshell, this thesis holds as follows: Foot patrol officers, as contrasted with motor patrol officers, are more likely to address minor crime and disorder problems on their beats, such as drunks, panhandlers, prostitutes, loud youths, and small-time drug dealers; when officers address these kinds of problems, residents notice, they feel safer, and they appreciate it; residents who feel safer and who have more confidence in the police are then more likely to assert informal social control, which makes the neighborhood even safer; reduced fear and enhanced safety encourages residents to remain in the neighborhood, spurs them to improve their properties, and attracts other residents and investors to the area; and a positive cycle of improvement continues. It should be emphasized that this broken-windows thesis is far from proven, but it has had a powerful impact on police strategies, crime prevention programming, and urban renewal over the past fifteen to twenty years.

The rediscovery of foot patrol also contributed directly to the rise of community policing. As a metaphor, foot patrol symbolized a police officer well known to neighborhood residents and working closely with them to address neighborhood problems, in contrast to the motorized patrol metaphor of an officer wearing reflector sunglasses darting into a neighborhood to enforce a law and then either disappearing or driving around staring at residents. This contrast had long been recognized and debated, of course, but prior to the several studies noted above, the police had been able to argue that motorized patrol and rapid response, though perhaps not warm and fuzzy, were effective and necessary. Research made these claims untenable and opened the door to a variety of strategic innovations, most notably community policing.

The practical impact of community policing on police patrol can be described in terms of purpose and workload. Instead of driving around in patrol cars watching and/or waiting, community policing officers are supposed to be working in partnership with neighborhood residents and other agencies to identify and solve specific local problems. This approach to patrol is more collaborative and more proactive than previous models. Naturally, these patrol officers still must handle reported crimes and other calls for assistance, but when not handling calls, they emphasize problem solving more than watching or waiting.

Strategic Patrol

Another strategic direction that patrol has taken in the past twenty years is toward a more focused or directed approach. One might think of traditional motorized patrol as the mayonnaise approach—spread evenly over the entire jurisdiction. Directed patrol, by contrast, tries to apply patrol in a more focused manner to particular locations where crimes or other problems are occurring. Enhancements in crime analysis and crime mapping in recent years have made this approach more feasible.

Technology continues to affect police patrol. Officers now commonly have computers in their cars, through which they can check vehicle registrations, driving records, criminal records, warrant files, and a host of other databases in seconds. Technology has also affected police weaponry, police protective gear, audio and video taping of police–citizen encounters, night vision, evidence location and collection, handling of high-speed pursuits, and many other conditions and aspects of the patrol officer's job.

Despite significant changes during the past century or two, the work of patrol officers remains very challenging and controversial. Most use-of-force incidents, including deadly force, involve patrol officers responding to calls or investigating suspicious situations. Most high-speed chases involve patrol officers. The current controversy in the United States surrounding so-called racial profiling or "driving-while-black" centers primarily on the practices of patrol officers in stopping and searching vehicles and pedestrians.

Police patrol officers are among the most powerful and visible point persons of our governmental apparatus. Police work, including patrol work, inherently entails the use of government authority to regulate and restrict peoples' behavior. Most of us resent such restrictions when they are applied to us, and errors are bound to be made when using such authority. More seriously, perhaps, the institutions that exercise such authority are unlikely to avoid the prejudices that permeate the societies in which they operate. New technologies, and new strategies such as community policing, have some potential for reducing abuses of authority and preventing use-of-force tragedies, but it is unlikely that the necessity for split-second life-or-death decision making can ever be completely eliminated from police patrol work.

GARY CORDNER

See also **Attitudes toward the Police: Overview; Community-Oriented Policing:**

Effects and Impacts; Community-Oriented Policing: Practices; Costs of Police Services; Crackdowns by the Police; Crime Analysis; Crime Control Strategies; Crime Prevention; Discretion; Dispatch and Communications Centers; Foot Patrol; Mounted Patrol

References and Further Reading

Boydstun, John E., Michael E. Sherry, and Nicholas P. Moelter. 1977. *Patrol staffing in San Diego: One- or two-officer units.* Washington, DC: Police Foundation.

Cordner, Gary W. 1989. The police on patrol. In *Police & policing: Contemporary issues,* ed. Dennis Jay Kenney. New York: Praeger.

Kelling, George L., Tony Pate, Duane Dieckman, and Charles E. Brown. 1974. *The Kansas City Preventive Patrol Experiment: A summary report.* Washington, DC: Police Foundation.

McGarrell, Edmund F., Steven Chermak, and Alexander Weiss. 1999. *Targeting firearm violence through directed police patrol.* Indianapolis, IN: Hudson Institute.

Police Foundation. 1981. *The Newark foot patrol experiment.* Washington, DC: Author.

Reichel, Philip. 1988. Southern slave patrols as a transitional police style. *American Journal of Police* 7.

Sherman, Lawrence W., and David Weisburd. 1995. General deterrent effects of police patrol in crime hot spots: A randomized, controlled trial. *Justice Quarterly* 12.

Spelman, William, and Dale K. Brown. 1981. *Calling the police: Citizen reporting of serious crime.* Washington, DC: Police Executive Research Forum.

Trojanowicz, Robert. 1982. *An evaluation of the Neighborhood Foot Patrol Program in Flint, Michigan.* East Lansing, MI: National Center for Community Policing, Michigan State University.

Wilson, James Q., and George L. Kelling, 1982. Police and neighborhood safety: Broken windows. *The Atlantic Monthly* 211 (March): 29–38.

PENNSYLVANIA STATE POLICE

Generally recognized as the first state police agency in the nation, the Pennsylvania State Police (PSP) patrols the highways and also serves a general policing function in the state. PSP officers are called "troopers." Duties of troopers include traffic enforcement as well as general law enforcement. Troopers patrol state and interstate roadways in Pennsylvania, enforcing the Pennsylvania Motor Vehicle Code. In addition, PSP troopers provide exclusive police coverage in 1,282 municipalities in Pennsylvania on a full-time basis and enforce laws on a part-time basis in another 2,565 municipalities in the commonwealth.

Additional duties include administering a forensic services bureau, which provides crime lab services for criminal investigations; the provision of protective services for the governor of Pennsylvania and certain other state officials; the administration of the PATCH (Pennsylvania Access to Criminal History) background check database; and oversight and administration of the Pennsylvania Uniform Crime Reporting system. PSP is accredited by CALEA (Commission for the Accreditation of Law Enforcement Agencies). PSP states that it is the largest internationally accredited law enforcement agency in the world.

At the turn of the twentieth century, Pennsylvania was changing rapidly from a state that was primarily agricultural to one that was experiencing new communities growing up around textiles, mills, and mining. Local law enforcement officers, who were able to keep the peace among the rural population, struggled to quell violence that occasionally came with the tougher labor issues of a rapidly industrializing society.

In 1865, the Pennsylvania Legislature passed State Act 228, authorizing railroads to organize private police to protect their property. A year later, the act was extended to anyone owning "any colliery, furnace or rolling mill within the Commonwealth" (Meyerhuber 1987, 152). Known as "Coal and Iron Police," these private police officers were paid by the companies that hired them, though they were commissioned by the state. They were used by business owners who paid them to protect their interests and performed such tasks and heavy-handed functions as evicting miners from company-owned properties, intimidating family members, and breaking up strikes. There were also serious allegations against the Coal and Iron Police of assault, kidnapping, rape, and even murder. In 1931, the governor revoked all Coal and Iron Police commissions.

Even as the Coal and Iron Police operated in the commonwealth, other serious problems associated with growth and urbanization began to emerge. These came to a head with the Great Anthracite Strike of 1902, which lasted for five months and created a nationwide coal shortage. In its aftermath, there was recognition of the need for a publicly employed statewide police force. In 1905, the Pennsylvania State Police was created. For the first twenty years of its existence, the complement of the PSP was limited to 228 men. Currently, the PSP has a complement of more than 4,545 sworn officers and employs more than sixteen hundred civilians, who serve in a range of support functions.

Over the years, the size, demographic composition, and specific tasks and operational functions of the PSP has grown and changed with the needs of the commonwealth. In 1923, the State Highway Patrol was created under the Department of Highways. Separate substations, or troops, developed to train and implement the Highway Patrol. In 1937, the State Highway Patrol merged with the State Police to form the Pennsylvania Motor Police. More responsibilities were added to the duties of the Motor Police, such as school bus inspections and the return of escaped convicts and parole violators. In 1941, the name of the organization was changed to the Pennsylvania State Police.

The PSP was established in a fashion similar to a military organization. Organizational divisions are called troops; officers are called troopers; and training headquarters are called barracks. From 1907 until 1961, troopers enlisted for two-year periods, after which they could honorably discharge and reenlist. Per order of the state police superintendent in 1907, enlistments were open only to single men. This order remained effective until 1961 as well. In 1927, a regulation was implemented that prohibited troopers from marrying without the approval of the superintendent. It was not until 1963 that married men were permitted to enlist. In 1972, the first female troopers graduated from an academy class of the PSP.

In contrast to many of its counterparts in other states and municipalities, there are several practices in which the PSP do not engage. Consistent with practices of early constables, PSP do not wear badges on their uniforms. They display patches, which are designed to reflect symbols specifically representing the history and traditions of the organization. Additionally, the PSP do not have a citizen ride-along program. Rationale for this decision focuses on liability concerns, safety issues, and privacy considerations related to the parties who may be crime victims or callers for police services.

The Pennsylvania State Police marked a century of service in 2005. A nonprofit organization dedicated to preserving the history and memorabilia of the PSP has acquired land and constructed a PSP Historical, Educational, and Memorial Center in Hershey, Pennsylvania. In addition to a collection of antiques, weapons, and photographs, the center houses a library, educational space, and a memorial and wall of honor. A recent project the group has undertaken has been the complete restoration of a 1972 Plymouth Fury to an authentic State Police Patrol vehicle. The project was completed in 2000.

The PSP has had several scandals within the past several years. In fall 2003, a state inspector general released a report making a number of recommendations related to the PSP practicing, condoning, and covering up "sexcapades," including sexual misdeeds involving more than seventy-five troopers. According to the report, "The

State Police must acknowledge the existence and extent of its problem. Sexual harassment and sexual misconduct at the State Police is not just an isolated incident. Changing procedures, attitudes, and cultures can go a long way in eliminating the problem" (*Philadelphia Daily News*, September 23, 2003).

Controversy also developed surrounding the reliability of the Genesis radar guns used by the PSP for speed detection. Phantom readings of seventy miles per hour were shown when the units were plugged into Ford Crown Victoria power sources, even when the radar guns were aimed at nonmoving objects. PSP claimed the guns had an override feature that kept the readings true, but the issue has advanced to federal court.

The first female to attain the rank of deputy commissioner was fired in June 2005 (also representing the first female of high rank to be fired). There were accusations that the firing was retaliatory, based on her filing of an internal affairs complaint related to perjury on the part of the commissioner. Because of the suspicious circumstances surrounding the firing, concern was expressed by other female officers, including the National Center for Women and Policing. A settlement was reached later in the year that provided for her rehiring and for generous retirement benefits, in exchange for her January 2006 retirement.

PSP maintains a comprehensive web presence at http://www.psp.state.pa.us. At this website, there is information related to the many programs and enforcement activities the organization directs, administers, and interfaces with.

MARY ANN EASTEP

See also **American Policing: Early Years; State Law Enforcement**

References and Further Reading

Baer, J. 2005. State Police ought to be ashamed. *Philadelphia Daily News*, March 15.

Conti, P. 1977. *The Pennsylvania State Police: A history of service to the Commonwealth, 1905 to the present*. Harrisburg, PA: Stackpole Books.

Egan, N. 2005a. State cops accused of deceit in radar-gun tests. *Philadelphia Daily News*, September 14.

———. 2005b. State cops explain rehire. *Philadelphia Daily News*, August 20.

Meyerhuber, C. 1987. *Less than forever: The rise and decline of union solidarity in Western Pennsylvania, 1914–1948*. Selinsgrove, PA: Susquehanna University Press.

Pennsylvania State Archives. n.d. *Records of the State Police*. Record Group 30. http://www.phmc.state.pa.us/bah/dam/rg/rg30.htm.

Pennsylvania State Police. n.d. http://www.psp.state.pa.us/.

———. n.d. Historical, Educational, and Memorial Center. http://www.psp-hemc.org/.

PERFORMANCE MEASUREMENT

Introduction

Gauging performance on tasks provides valuable information that individuals and groups can use to excel. It is difficult to improve performance and functioning if accurate and relevant information about performance is not available. Imagine young athletes trying to succeed in a chosen sport without an idea about how they are doing, or students trying to determine their comprehension of subject matter without getting a report card or feedback from teachers. In both cases the individuals require information about their performance on selected tasks in order to improve. The same idea holds true for organizations, including police departments. Unfortunately, the potential of effective performance measurement systems has not been realized in police departments.

Measuring the performance of the police extends back to 1930, when the Federal Bureau of Investigation's Uniform Crime Reporting (UCR) Program was launched and the crime clearance rate was proposed as an indicator of police effectiveness. Despite relatively early beginnings and well-known limitations of commonly used performance indicators, performance measurement has not evolved a great deal in police departments. The end of the twentieth century saw performance measurement play a significant role in many organizational development and management innovations that were taking place in the public and private sectors. Interest in making police performance measurement more effective also blossomed during this time.

Measuring police performance at the organizational level can serve two important purposes: ensuring accountability and promoting organizational learning. In a democracy, the police are accountable to the public through the political process. In this way a local community has a voice in what police do and how they do it. The process of holding police departments accountable is believed to promote effective and fair operations because evidence of shortcomings is expected to increase demands for improvement and evidence of success is expected to be rewarded. The public and individuals in positions of authority who make decisions about the police, including the allocation of resources and personnel decisions, must have accurate and relevant information that can be used to assess police performance. Without this information informed decisions cannot be made, undermining the potential for accountability to ensure quality performance.

A second purpose of performance measurement is to provide information that can ultimately improve police operations through organizational learning. A learning organization has been described as one that takes advantage of experiences, including those of other organizations, to improve its functioning. The assumption is that organizations can process information, learn, and then change. Without accurate and relevant information about performance or the ability to process it, organizational learning suffers. By measuring what is important about performance and building the means of using that information effectively, a police department is in a better position to take advantage of experience and make appropriate adjustments. Reformers advocated for police departments to become learning organizations in the late 1990s; improved performance measurement is a necessary part of this process because measurement provides the necessary raw material.

In addition to accountability and organizational learning, the performance measurement process itself holds the potential to affect police behavior. A performance measurement system sends subtle messages to employees and external audiences about what the organization values. By measuring certain aspects of police work a department sends messages about what it values most. This can motivate personnel to concentrate their efforts on what is being measured and possibly overlook other aspects of their work. This idea is reflected in the phrase "what gets measured gets done."

Problems the Police Face Today

In the general sense, measuring abstract phenomena, such as the quality of a service that has been provided and whether services have been provided in a fair manner, is challenging. This is no different for police departments; designing and utilizing an effective performance measurement system is a complicated process. First, police performance is multidimensional. In other words, police departments perform a wide range of tasks, and they may do some things better than others. In addition, police are responsible for employing just and fair procedures, meaning the way police do their jobs is an important dimension of performance.

A second complicating factor is that police have a complex mission. For indicators of performance to be useful they must be grounded in a clear understanding of what a police department does, what it is expected to do, and what it seeks to accomplish. It is critical that performance measures conform to what organizations do and what they intend to accomplish. A mismatch means the department is limited in how it can use feedback. Several problems can result from a disjunction: A police department may not learn about important dimensions of its behavior if those dimensions are not measured; when a department does not know how well it is performing important tasks or whether it is achieving intended outcomes, it is not in a position to evaluate, learn, and make appropriate changes; it is difficult to make sense of performance feedback that is only marginally related to what a department is attempting to accomplish; and a department might be judged unfairly if performance indicators focus on outcomes over which a department has little influence.

For these reasons it is difficult to identify a "bottom line" of policing. To treat crime as the "bottom line" of policing overlooks the fact that crime reduction is not an acceptable outcome if police employ unjust methods, and it ignores the fact that police provide many services not directly related to serious crime. Useful performance measurement schemes must include multiple indicators of what police do (that is, outputs), how it is done (that is, processes), and what is accomplished (that is, outcomes).

Police departments have traditionally relied on a limited set of indicators to monitor their performance, thus limiting their ability to learn and improve. These indicators include crime rates, crime clearances, arrests, and response times. While these measures are easily collected and inherently appealing, they are also limited in important ways. In their commonly used forms these indicators do not facilitate police accountability or organizational learning.

Crime rates are often measured with arrests, victimization surveys, and crimes reported to the police. A number of significant criticisms have been levied against the use of crime rates for the purposes of accountability and departmental learning. Crime control and prevention are only one part of what the police are expected to accomplish. A near-exclusive focus on measuring crime is problematic because other dimensions of police performance that are also centrally important, such as the use of fair and legal procedures and police responses to nonserious crime problems, are overlooked. In this case a department cannot understand how well it is meeting other responsibilities and how it can improve in these other domains.

Police have only a limited ability to affect some types of crimes. Recognizing that a host of societal factors combine to change levels of some crimes means it makes little sense to hold police accountable for any observed changes. For this reason crime rates do not offer the ideal and "bottom line" performance indicator they might seem to represent. In addition, police departments can influence crime data through a host of means that are independent of actual levels of crime in the community. Police agencies can inadvertently discourage crime reporting by community members and more overtly manipulate crime statistics to make it appear a department is keeping crime at an acceptable level. Thus, indicators of crime may not provide an accurate sense of police performance at keeping communities safe.

The crime clearance rate is also an inherently appealing indicator of police success because it measures how often police solve crimes that come to their attention. More specifically, clearance rates are used as indicators of investigative success. The clearance rate is calculated by dividing the number of crimes that are defined as "cleared" by the number of crimes that are officially recorded by the police. Despite their inherent appeal, crime clearance rates are also limited for monitoring police performance.

Clearance rates are not measured consistently across agencies, and their calculations can be manipulated. Thus, it is problematic to compare the performance of different departments. One department may appear to perform better than another simply because of the way clearance rates are calculated. For example, one police department may define crimes as cleared when a suspect is identified but not actually taken into custody, while another may employ strict criteria and define a crime as cleared only when a suspect is arrested. Similarly, the arrest of a single suspect can lead to several clearances if police personnel report that the suspect is responsible for other crimes.

Defining an event as a crime is easily manipulated, making clearance rates unreliable. Rather than officially define an event as a crime, personnel can categorize the event as "unfounded," which means the incident is not officially counted as a crime. This reduces the value of the denominator in calculations of clearance rates, thus increasing the clearance rate and making it appear that a department is more effective at solving crimes. That the information used to calculate clearance rates is easily manipulated has led experts to conclude that the clearance rate is a poor indicator of how police are performing.

A third commonly used measure of police performance is the number of arrests and citations issued. These are often considered indicators of police output because they measure work that seeks to accomplish the goal of keeping communities safe. As with the use of clearance rates, comparing police departments in terms of arrest rates is inappropriate because of inconsistent definitions and localized pressures that can affect how often officers make arrests. Departments that record arrests early in the process of detaining

individuals would appear to be more active than departments that record arrests later in the process, such as when an individual is booked. In this case both departments might be taking people into custody at the same rate, but one would appear to perform better only because of the definition used.

On a more abstract level, it is hard to judge whether relatively high arrest rates represent desirable or undesirable outputs. In some cases creative, nonarrest solutions may hold greater potential to achieve desired outcomes, such as increased community safety. For instance, in the 1990s many police departments were experimenting with creative partnership-based responses to the mentally ill that sought to reduce the chances of arrest. Furthermore, a near exclusive reliance on counting arrests means that the way police perform their duties takes a backseat.

Historically, police departments have dispatched officers to respond quickly when the public calls for service. Since it has become expected in many cases that police will be rapidly dispatched, it seems reasonable, on its face, to measure response time and use this information to gauge police performance. Rapid response is predicated on the belief that if police can get to the scene of a crime quickly, then the chances of arresting a suspect will increase. Research has shown that rapid police response is not responsible for appreciably increasing the chances of arresting a suspect. As with arrests, it is not clear that rapid response represents high levels of police performance. Not all calls for service, even about serious crime, demand a rapid response, and in some cases citizens are satisfied even if an officer will not be dispatched to the scene. Thus, agencies that work hard to reduce the time between call receipt and officer arrival on the scene are not necessarily making effective use of resources. Nevertheless, rapid police response is associated with citizens' positive assessments of police services.

Perspectives at the Turn of the Century

At the turn of the century, an innovative spirit was afoot in policing, and performance measurement systems were considered important mechanisms for improving policing and advancing reforms. Police practitioners and researchers were concerned with the state of police performance measurement, with generating new methods that would reflect accurately and comprehensively on police performance, and with ways of making better use of available performance indicators to improve the quality of policing. This heightened awareness about performance measurement was partially the result of community policing and problem-oriented policing reforms. These reforms forced a reexamination of the police mission, police organization, and how police do their jobs. In 2004, the National Academy of Sciences' Committee to Review Research on Police Policy and Practices concluded that measures of police performance commonly utilized were not useful for assessing how well police were filling contemporary conceptions of their mission.

Effective performance measurement has the potential to advance the practice of both community policing and problem-oriented policing because a police agency has the chance to learn about what it is doing well and how it may be failing in terms of reform efforts. For example, problem solving is promoted under both major reforms—community policing and problem-oriented policing—and represents a systematic method for officers to address significant community problems.

A performance measurement scheme must tap into the major components of problem solving for a police department to gauge how well specific elements of the practice are being implemented and whether it is achieving intended results. When a performance measurement system excludes indicators of problem solving, a police agency misses the chance to obtain feedback about how it might improve. These same ideas apply to many aspects of community policing, including police departments' efforts to engage and collaborate with communities, to reduce citizens' fear of crime, and to improve citizen satisfaction with police services.

A reconsideration of performance measurement systems means police departments must carefully and openly consider new sources of data that reflect on their performance and facilitate organizational learning rather than limit themselves to readily available administrative sources of data. New sources of data include employee surveys, direct observations of police–community encounters and community conditions, and information from other public and private organizations.

It is not reasonable to assume that police will abandon crime rates as an indicator of performance, but an improved measure of crime is available. Research has demonstrated the value of using crime rates that are adjusted for factors over which police have little control, such as shifting demographics and economic conditions. An adjusted measure of crime can indicate how much influence the police can have on crime. When combined with additional measures of police performance, adjusted crime rates have the chance to become an important part of a comprehensive performance measurement scheme.

Citizen surveys also represent an important source of information on performance that many police departments have been collecting. Citizen perceptions have long been recognized as an important and useful indicator of police performance. Public perceptions of the police are important because police effectiveness depends heavily on support from citizens, police are accountable to the public, and police services are frequently delivered at the point of contacts with citizens. Police can obtain valuable information from citizen surveys that is not easily obtained from other sources of data, including information about crime and community problems, citizen willingness to cooperate with police, and assessments of officer performance during specific encounters.

General community surveys seek to include individuals that represent a broad cross section of a particular area. One problem with general surveys is that a large portion of the community has not had recent contact with the police. This means that citizen perceptions of the police can be formed through mechanisms not directly related to police performance. Contact surveys help to overcome this problem by including individuals who have had some recent contact with the police, including arrestees, crime victims, and drivers. Police must pay careful attention to the way citizen surveys are constructed and implemented because important problems can result from surveys that are poorly designed and implemented.

It is important to include a representative sample in general and contact surveys. A sample of citizens that is disposed toward holding favorable (or unfavorable) perceptions of the police reduces the chances that police will learn about how the entire community and important subsections truly perceive performance. The inclusion of only certain citizens in a sample can distort results. While it may be tempting to exclude individuals who are presumed to hold generally unfavorable views of the police, these individuals can provide valuable insights a department can use.

The way survey items are worded can also affect results. Questions that are worded in vague and general terms will likely yield mostly positive results. This creates the opportunity for police departments to present themselves in a positive light rather than for purposes of gauging performance and organizational learning. These potential problems have led experts to recommend that police departments become more sophisticated in the way they collect survey data from citizens and in the ways they use this information. Very little is known about the way police departments use information gathered through citizen surveys.

Prior to selecting sources of data and collecting information, it is necessary for police departments to identify the performance dimensions they value. Police departments have traditionally lacked theoretical guidance about the dimensions they should assess. As interest in police performance measurement grew in the late 1990s, experts recommended sets of performance dimensions for departments to consider measuring. These included, for instance, the extent to which police hold offenders accountable, ensure the safety of public places, and limit fear of crime. Departments were also encouraged to measure the process dimension of police performance. The process aspect is unique because it focuses attention on measuring the manner in which police perform their duties rather than emphasizing measures of what police do and traditional outcomes. The process dimension of police work is illustrated by Stephen Mastrofski's (1999) six aspects of police service that he terms "policing for people": attentiveness, reliability, responsiveness, competence, manners, and fairness.

Including the manner in which police perform their duties in performance measurement systems is critical because scholars and practitioners recognize that the process of policing has important implications for the outcomes of policing. Research and theoretical work in the 1990s demonstrated that the way police treat citizens during encounters can affect citizen cooperation with the police and compliance with the law, two important outcomes for the police. In addition, fair and just treatment by the police is an important police product, independent of how such treatment affects crime and community order.

A Comparative Approach to Performance Measurement

One broad framework for rating the performance of organizations is with a comparative performance measurement system. This approach has been used across a range of service providers, including hospitals, local governments, and schools. Experts have recommended that this approach be used to evaluate police performance. Comparative performance measurement in policing would consist of measuring the performances of police departments and then comparing them over time and place. This allows the performance of a police department to be judged against the performance of others or against itself in a previous time period so that the department can learn how it is doing. Without some reference of comparison, it is difficult for individuals and organizations to understand and interpret their current level of performance.

Comparative performance measurement has typically come in the form of an organizational report card. The school report card, well known to teachers, children, and guardians, illustrates the value. A school report card communicates information about student performance to several people and can motivate students to excel through several mechanisms. This same logic can be applied to organizations; a performance grade is shared with a broad audience, and poor performance can motivate a department to search for ways to improve.

Organizational report cards differ from traditional forms of performance measurement because those traditional forms are largely self-assessments; the report card represents externally focused performance measurement. The grade an organization receives is communicated to a broad external audience, facilitating accountability. When performance indicators are not shared with external audiences, the chances for accountability are reduced, along with opportunities to improve performance.

The police would seem to be well-suited for organizational report cards because reports cards offer a unique mechanism for enhancing public accountability. The challenge for comparative performance systems is to yield appropriate comparison groups because police departments operate in distinct environments and face unique problems.

Policing scholars have advocated for national monitoring systems that would be akin to report cards. For instance, Tom Tyler (2002) recommends that police agencies conduct ongoing surveys of the citizens they serve to monitor public perceptions of police fairness and legitimacy. In 2004, the National Academy of Sciences' Committee to Review Research on Police Policy and Practices recommended a national effort to collect data on several aspects of police work. Finally, more than half of the states in the first decade of the twenty-first century mandated that police agencies collect and report data on traffic stops. The purpose was to monitor potential racial disparities in patterns of traffic enforcement and report individual agency performance to the public.

Unresolved Issues

Despite the innovative spirit that dominated policing from the 1980s into the twenty-first century and the belief that performance measurement systems have the power to facilitate improved service delivery, police organizations have not advanced their performance measurement systems. Advancing performance measurement schemes and promoting organizational learning represent processes that will persist into the twenty-first century as long as police departments are serious about implementing community policing and realizing the reform's full potential. The challenge lies not only in accurately measuring several important aspects of police performance with appropriate sources of data but also in determining how the information will be used to promote more effective, efficient, and fair police work.

WILLIAM WELLS

See also **Accountability; Attitudes toward the Police: Measurement Issues; Clearance Rates and Criminal Investigations; Police Reform in an Era of Community and Problem-Oriented Policing;** *Uniform Crime Reports*

References and Further Reading

Geller, William A. 1997. Suppose we were really serious about police departments becoming "learning organizations"? *National Institute of Justice Journal* 234: 2–8.

Gormley, William T., Jr., and D. L. Weiner. 1999. *Organizational report cards.* Cambridge, MA: Harvard University Press.

Langworthy, Robert H., ed. 1999. *Measuring what matters: Proceedings from the Policing Research Institute Meetings.* Washington, DC: U.S. Department of Justice.

Maguire, Edward R. 2003. *Measuring the performance of law enforcement agencies, Part 1.* CALEA Update 83. http://www.calea. org/newpub.newsletter/No83/measurement. htm.

———. 2004. *Measuring the performance of law enforcement agencies, Part 2.* CALEA Update 84. http://www.calea.org/newpub. newsletter/No84/maguirepart2.htm.

Maguire, Edward R., and Craig D. Uchida. 2000. Measurement and explanation in the comparative study of American police organizations. In *Criminal justice 2000*, Vol. 4, ed. Duffee, 491–557. Washington, DC: National Institute of Justice.

Mastrofski, Stephen D. 1999. *Policing for people. Ideas in American policing.* Washington, DC: Police Foundation.

Moore, Mark H. 2002. *Recognizing value in policing: The challenge of measuring police performance.* Washington, DC: Police Executive Research Forum.

———. 2003. *The "bottom line" of policing: What citizens should value (and measure!) in police performance.* Washington, DC: Police Executive Research Forum.

Skogan, Wesley, and K. Frydl, eds. 2004. *Fairness and effectiveness in policing: The evidence.* Washington, DC: National Academies Press.

Tyler, Tom R. 2002. A national survey for monitoring police legitimacy. *Journal of Research and Policy* 4:72–86.

PERSONNEL ALLOCATION

The allocation of personnel is the assignment of personnel to meet the operational needs of each organizational unit within an organization, to most effectively provide service and accomplish the stated mission of the agency. In the law enforcement profession, the demand for service and the increasing diversity of services provided by police departments must be balanced against personnel limitations created by fiscal constraints and continuously evaluated and adjusted to reallocate finite resources to meet existing and emerging needs.

Police administrators may encounter environmental factors such as changing demographic conditions or emergency situations that could impact the numbers and types of calls for service, and personnel issues such as collective bargaining agreements that must be adhered to when developing a personnel allocation strategy. Administrators may also have to contend with external political considerations that could dictate a change in the philosophical and operational directions of their agencies at any time and have an analogous impact on the deployment of personnel.

Any or all of these factors could have a significant influence on the implementation of an allocation plan, which is why the effective allocation of personnel continues to be one of the most critical challenges facing police managers.

Allocation Models in Law Enforcement

Much of the early research on personnel allocation in law enforcement agencies analyzed the deployment of the patrol and traffic components in larger municipal police departments. The advancement in the study of patrol allocation methods has been fueled greatly by two key developments, technological advancements in radio communications and the computerization of the patrol dispatch process.

The most widely known program utilizing radio dispatch and computerization is computer-aided dispatching (CAD), which greatly enhanced a police department's ability to more efficiently deploy patrol and traffic units and for the first time allowed police managers to implement allocation plans based on computer-generated data. The CAD system is a centralized dispatch station communicating directly with remote terminals, utilizing radio and computer technologies to relay all pertinent information to responding units. The computerization of the emergency call system also allowed for more efficient data storage capabilities and statistical analysis. As newer digital communication technologies such as the mobile data terminal (MDT) are developed to augment and enhance the CAD system, the speed of dispatch will continue to improve, and data storage capabilities will increase exponentially.

One of the most significant benefits to field personnel of digital upgrades such as MDT is real-time access, which allows the responding unit to access all available information from its remote location almost instantaneously. The availability of real-time information access can reduce time spent on each call for service, and this may have an appreciable impact on personnel deployment.

Other technological advances such as geographic information systems (GISs), created in the 1970s, which can produce maps for dispatchers to utilize in providing responding units with the most efficient travel route, and the global positioning system (GPS), which is utilized to track field units and also to cut response time by providing responding units the most direct route right on their remote terminals, may also be factored into any allocation plan since these advancements can impact response time, a critical component of any police department's allocation model.

The scientific study of personnel allocation in the United States began in the early 1900s with the work of August Vollmer. Vollmer listed the various police functions such as patrol, investigation, and crime prevention and set early standards for police patrol allocations. Vollmer was also one of the first advocates of utilizing communication technology to enhance patrol assignments (Swanson, Territo, and Taylor 1997). Fosdick expanded on Vollmer's concepts by incorporating changing demographic conditions into personnel allocation plans. In the 1940s, Wilson introduced the "hazard model," which called for the prioritization of the allocation of resources based on the type and severity of criminal activity. The "St. Louis model," introduced in the mid-1960s, was one of the first models to utilize a computer-assisted dispatch system to track the distribution of calls for service by prioritizing them by perceived seriousness, and responding based on need and not just time of call (Swanson, Territo, and Taylor 1997).

More recent allocation models include Larson's Law Enforcement Manpower Resource Allocation System (LEMRAS), which coded calls for service into one of three categories and assigned response priority based on severity of event, and the Patrol Car Allocation Method (PCAM), which was designed to optimize response times through improved dispatch and deployment. In 1983, the Commission of Accredited Law Enforcement Agencies (CALEA) set professional standards for personnel allocation in investigative services, and in 1993, the Police Allocation Model (PAM) was revised as part of a study conducted by the National Highway Traffic Safety Administration (NHTSA) and the Northwestern University Center for Public Safety.

The PAM was originally designed primarily for utilization in the deployment of patrol and traffic units, but its scope was expanded as a result of the NHTSA study. The model employs a "what works" methodology by incorporating components from various law enforcement agencies into a generic allocation formula that police administrators can utilize as a template when formulating their own personnel deployment plan or when drafting proposals to hire additional personnel to meet projected future staffing requirements.

In 1997, the Washington, D.C., police department implemented the Patrol Service Area (PSA) model, in which the District of Columbia was divided into eighty-three patrol service areas, with specific patrol units assigned to each area. The PSA model was introduced as part of that department's community policing initiative and was designed to strengthen bonds between police and the community by reducing the response area for each unit, thereby increasing the familiarity of the patrol units with the neighborhood and its residents. It was felt that this move away from traditional response-driven policing would better serve the community. An allocation formula was developed for Washington, D.C.'s PSA model, prioritizing each call for service based on its perceived seriousness (DC Watch 1999).

Workload Assessments

Police administrators recognize that the design and implementation of an allocation model for their agencies is only the initial step in an effective personnel deployment strategy. To maintain efficiency, any allocation plan must be followed by an ongoing workload assessment plan. Workload assessments are designed to improve efficiency by ensuring the equitable division of work assignments and allow for the most efficient allocation of personnel to meet the operational demands and service goals of the department.

The utilization of workload assessments as part of a personnel allocation plan can have a significant impact on the organizational structure and overall operational efficiency of a police department, can assist in determining future staffing requirements, and can serve as a justification for requesting increases in fiscal appropriations to meet future staffing needs. Since it is to be expected that workloads may fluctuate due to any number of factors, such as changes in the demographics of a particular district, it is essential that workload assessments be conducted on a regular basis to maintain effective deployment of manpower and to maximize the utilization of resources.

Factors to be considered in any workload assessment include the number of employees needed to complete each particular assignment, the type, complexity, and volume of tasks to be performed, and the time needed to complete the assignment. Another variable that must be addressed in any workload assessment is the relative importance of each task to the mission of the agency. The ability to effectively prioritize workload assignments, with a greater proportion of resources dedicated to tasks deemed to be of critical importance, is an essential element of any viable personnel allocation plan.

A critical aspect of workload assessment is choosing the correct method of evaluation. A faulty workload analysis can have detrimental long-term repercussions for a law enforcement agency, such as understaffing or inefficient deployment. Another potential problem could occur if an agency attempts to utilize one standard allocation format to assess all organizational units within the department. The assessment process to determine staffing needs may vary greatly in some organizational units within a police department. These may include but are not limited to the traffic safety, patrol, investigative, homeland security, or special operations and administration functions. It is essential that each organizational unit be evaluated based on its own needs, and those requirements must be prioritized as part of an overall assessment strategy.

Conclusion

The development and implementation of an effective personnel allocation model is one of the most critical challenges facing administrators of law enforcement agencies. Although most of the early studies on the allocation of personnel in law enforcement dealt primarily with the patrol and traffic functions, it is essential that all organizational units within the department be incorporated into the allocation model. The ability to prioritize work assignments and an ongoing workload assessment process are two key elements of allocation. A well-developed progressive allocation plan must ensure the continued deployment of sufficient personnel to accomplish most critical tasks while also anticipating trends such as political intervention or fiscal constraints, which could significantly impact allocation and future staffing capabilities.

RICHARD BUTLER

See also **Budgeting, Police; Calls for Service; COMPSTAT; Computer-Aided Dispatching (CAD) Systems; Computer Technology; Costs of Police Services; Crime Analysis; Crime Control Strategies; Operational Costs**

References and Further Reading

DC Watch. 1999. *Report to the Committee on the Judiciary—Manpower allocation.* Washington, DC. http://www.dcwatch.com/police/990713.htm.

Gill, Martin, Jerry Hart, Ken Livingstone, and Jane Stevens. 1996. *The Crime Allocation System: Police investigations into burglary and auto crime.* London: Home Office Police Research Group.

Gribble, Elliot. 1995. *Allocation of personnel: Methodology for required staffing of detectives.* http://www.fdle.state.fl.us/fcjei/SLP%20papers/Gribble.pdf.

Swanson, Charles R., Leonard Territo, and Robert W. Taylor. 1997. *Police administration: Structures, processes and behavior.* Upper Saddle River, NJ: Prentice-Hall.

Traffic Institute, Northwestern University. 1993. *Police allocation manual: Determination of the number and allocation of personnel for patrol services for state police departments.* http://ntl.bts.gov/lib/000/800/812/00333.pdf.

PERSONNEL SELECTION

The police officer should have the wisdom of Solomon, the courage of David, the strength of Samson, the patience of Job, the leadership of Moses, the kindness of the Good Samaritans, the strategy of Alexander, the faith of Daniel, the diplomacy of Lincoln, the tolerance of the carpenter of Nazareth, and finally an intimate knowledge of every branch of the natural, biological, and social sciences. If one has all these attributes, they might be a good officer. (Vollmer 1936, 222)

Police services are determined primarily by the quality of personnel, and police agencies' operating costs reflect the importance. Between 80% and 90% of an agency's budget is for police salaries, with the annual operating cost per officer at $85,786 (Reaves and Hickman 2002).

Local governments spend $50.7 billion, the federal government spends approximately $15 billion, and state governments spend approximately $10.5 billion annually for police services. In the past 20 years, the per capita expenditure at all governmental levels increased 202% for police protection (Bauer and Owens 2004).

The ratio of sworn officers to citizens varies. For large police agencies there are between twenty-three and thirty-one sworn personnel per ten thousand citizens, with Washington, D.C., having the highest ratio at sixty-three per ten thousand citizens

(Reeves and Hickman 2002). County and sheriff agencies average fourteen officers per ten thousand, and state agencies approximately two officers per ten thousand citizens (Reeves and Hart 2000).

Entrance Requirements

The level of performance of each officer is determined in advance by agencies' recruiting and training standards. On the average, for each individual hired, ten applicants are screened out (Leonard and Moore 1993). Criteria for entrance will vary across jurisdictions, but there are a number of qualifications that are fairly typical. Others are more controversial.

Residency requirement. Some departments require residency before an individual can apply, for example, having lived in the city for one year or more at the time of applying. Other agencies require officers to live within the jurisdiction or city limits once they are hired.

Level of education. The percentage of departments requiring new officers to have at least some college has risen to 37%, and those agencies requiring two-year or four-year college educations have grown to 14% (Reaves and Hickman 2002).

Physical requirements. Height and weight requirements have been discarded. Now the physical requirements must be job related and are usually measured with agility testing and weight proportional to height (*Smith v. Troyan* 1975). Eyesight is usually measured on correctable vision.

Age. The minimum age usually is twenty, with often no restriction of maximum age, although some agencies want to be able to get twenty years of service before retirement.

Court Decisions

There are several court decisions surrounding the process of selecting and the selection itself. In general, the selection process must be job related and nondiscriminating. The selection measures must be valid in that they test the type of knowledge, skills, and abilities needed for the job and do not place unequal impact on protected groups. In other words, the measures cannot have adverse impact or a different rate of selection (less than 80%) of individuals who are minorities based on race, sex, or ethnic group. Under the authority of Title VII of the Civil Rights Act of 1964 that was expanded in 1972 and then 1991, the Equal Employment Opportunity Commission (EEOC), which was established as the regulatory agency, issued guidelines on employment selection procedures. A number of cases subsequently arose from personnel practices involving police agencies regarding discrimination as interpreted by the courts.

The 1990 Americans with Disabilities Act (ADA) makes it unlawful to discriminate against people with disabilities in employment practices, including selection. Disabilities are defined as physical or mental impairments that substantially limit major life activities. ADA required law enforcement agencies to make substantial revisions, particularly in their selection process. Because no medical inquiries can be made of an applicant before a job offer is made, police agencies have to ensure that no questions are included in any of the processes used until they are ready to give a conditional job offer that is contingent upon the applicant's ability to pass the medical test. Police agencies had to detail the critical job functions of policing because it is allowable to question applicants about their ability to perform job-related functions as long as the questions are not phrased in terms related to a disability.

ADA also requires the consideration of applicants who can perform the essential functions of a position if reasonable accommodations can be made without undue hardship. Reasonable accommodations can include such things as job restructuring, modifying equipment and devices, and adjusting or modifying examination. Undue hardship is interpreted to mean unduly expensive, extensive, or substantially disruptive.

Mechanics for Selection

Depending on the area, personnel selection is the authority of a central personnel office that serves all departments of the local government, a civil service commission, or the police agency itself. Usually civil service commissions are involved in making final decisions or have control of the examinations for entry and hear appeals. The police agencies themselves usually are responsible for conducting many of the selection procedures.

Coordinated recruiting is especially helpful for smaller and medium-sized departments. It allows a more widespread recruiting effort and sophisticated advertising of opening. The applicant has the opportunity to take a single examination for openings in several jurisdictions. There are uniform procedures in applying for positions in all departments. Potential applicants then are informed of all vacancies in the participating police agencies.

Application

Most applications include the listing of all places and dates of residency, places of employment, educational institutions, financial history, criminal history (this includes arrests as well as convictions), and drug use. All of this information will be verified during the background investigation, and the applicant is likely to be asked about it during a polygraph examination if such is required. Other requirements might include a notarized signature, proof of residency, a copy of a Social Security card, a valid driver's license, educational transcripts, and military discharge papers.

Written Examination

Written examinations that are often used are cognitive tests measuring reading comprehension, mathematics skills, reasoning, and interests. The reading comprehension examination will usually include narratives consisting of a set of events with different characters and details. Spatial perception questions may be included in the initial written area or later in the psychological/intelligence testing. These questions are usually formatted into a series of three-dimensional figures, oriented in space and/or folded in different ways. The ability to select the matching figure helps test one's ability to visualize and orient objects spatially.

Physical Fitness/Agility Testing

The physical abilities tests must be job related and measure one's abilities to perform those activities required for the job. Physical fitness is the ability to carry out daily tasks with vigor and alertness, without undue fatigue, and with ample energy to engage in leisure time pursuits and to tolerate the above average stresses encountered in emergency situations. To determine the physical challenges that are posed for the police, most states and many local agencies have conducted job task analyses to determine the essential tasks for their law enforcement positions.

Although federal, state, and local agencies will vary in their physical requirements, they are primarily based on aerobic capacity, or cardiorespiratory endurance; strength, both lower and upper body; flexibility; and body fat composition.

Oral Interview

Agencies will vary in their use of interviews. All applicants will be interviewed at least by one human resource officer or police agency recruiting officer to gather some initial information and to explain the application process. Although the recruiting officer may screen for minimum standards, that officer may make no other employment decisions. Some agencies use oral boards consisting of supervisors of different ranks to interview applicants in the final phase of the hiring process. The primary purpose of the oral interview is for the agency administrators to get to know the applicant as a person as well as for the applicant to get a feel for the organization and decide whether it would be comfortable to work in.

The Conditional Offer

ADA protects individuals with disabilities from discrimination. In general, individuals cannot be asked questions about disabilities but rather whether they can perform the critical functions of the job. Because information about a disability might come out during the selection process, the process is divided into two steps, before and after a conditional job offer.

Before a conditional job offer is made, the agency's recruiting staff must restrict its assessment of a candidate to areas that will not disclose a disability but do help to ascertain the candidate's ability to perform the job. Qualified candidates may then be offered a position on the condition that they can successfully complete the rest of the selection process, such as the psychological exam, background investigation, medical exam, and polygraph—all of which are areas that might disclose a disability. A disability still cannot disqualify the applicant, as long as the person is capable of performing the job. When the applicant is conditionally offered a job, the condition might be documented during the medical exam; however, because the person passed earlier tests that allowed the conditional offer, this discovery should not affect the offer of a job.

The Background Investigation

Done properly, the background investigation is probably the most expensive and time-consuming portion of the law enforcement agency's recruitment and hiring process. It involves conversations with people who are familiar with the applicant professionally, academically, or personally. The background investigator will then verify all information that the applicant provided on the application form, such as dates and places of employment and reasons for leaving, graduation dates and degrees completed, and financial health. The investigator will interview not only the references that the applicant included but also people with whom the applicant worked, neighbors, and recent classmates.

Law enforcement agencies normally want to know about offenses for which the applicant was arrested, at any age (not just convictions as an adult). The agency will take into account the applicant's age at the time of committing the offense, but all arrests must be accounted for; omissions will be considered lying. Even offenses that have been expunged should be revealed. Most law enforcement agencies will not hire an individual who has been arrested for a felony as an adult. Certain felonies, however, under certain circumstances might not be enough to eliminate an applicant if the crimes were committed while the applicant was a juvenile.

Psychological Evaluation

The battery of psychological instruments will include at least one measure that identifies mental illness and one or more measures that assess traits important to police work. Such important traits include compatibility, self-confidence, diplomacy, independence, dependability, decisiveness, and integrity. Traits considered important for community-oriented policing and problem solving such as taking the initiative to analyze and solve neighborhood problems and communicate with different types of people without bias might be included.

If the psychological evaluation is conducted before the conditional job offer, the evaluation cannot include measures of mental illness. Some agencies will conduct a preliminary psychological evaluation that measures traits important to law enforcement, such as anger and stress-coping skills. Once a conditional job offer is given, then the applicant returns for a follow-up evaluation of mental illness.

The results of the evaluation are not ranked or graded but rather assessed as acceptable or not acceptable. Some psychologists will also have a "marginal" category. If the applicant is asked to see a second psychologist, more than likely the applicant has received a marginal rating. Applicants will also be told in the introduction to the test that the information belongs to the agency, not the applicant. The evaluation will be sent to the agency. The information will be kept confidential in the applicant's file; the applicant will not receive a copy of the results (Lord and Peak 2004).

Polygraph Examination

Although the polygraph examination, more commonly called a "lie-detector test," is not admissible in court for criminal cases, it is legal for law enforcement hiring purposes. The courts have ruled that it is in the public's interest to be able to ascertain the integrity and other characteristics of its future police officers, who will be carrying firearms and possess the authority to use lethal force. Most polygraph operators have been trained and certified by the American Polygraph Association.

The polygraph exam is based on the fact that when humans experience anxiety, their respiration, perspiration (galvanic skin resistance), and blood pressure rates increase. Its primary use is to substantiate the information collected during the selection process, particularly the background investigation (Frerkes 1998).

Drug Testing

Law enforcement agencies differ with regard to their requirements concerning experimental drug use. Preemployment drug testing is considered legal for any position in which public safety is a concern. Applicants for law enforcement positions may be tested for every form of controlled substance, including opiates, cocaine, marijuana, amphetamines, methamphetamines, barbiturates, and hallucinogenic drugs. If an applicant tests positive for any of these drugs, that person will be rejected for a law enforcement position.

Medical Examination

As with all of the other areas of the selection process, the medical decision is based on the applicant's ability to perform the duties of an officer. As with the psychological examination, findings are not rated on a scale but rather as being acceptable or not acceptable for hire.

Issues of Diversity in Selection

In recruiting minorities, the standards should remain the same for all candidates. If recruitment procedures fail to attract minority candidates from whom qualified applicants can be selected, there may be a need for new recruitment techniques. All procedures and practices in the area of selection, hiring, and promotions should be assessed for any discrimination.

Civilian Careers

Many tasks that are performed by sworn officers can be carried out effectively and for lower cost by nonsworn personnel. Activities such as administration, crime analysis, evidence collection, telecommunicating, provision of information related to nonemergency situations, and public relations do not require the exercise of police authority but are functions that require specialized training that can be acquired by civilians. Currently, 62% of technical support, 10% of administration, and 8% of field operations are provided by civilians (Reaves and Hart 2000).

VIVIAN B. LORD

See also **Accountability; Community-Oriented Policing: Practices; Early Warning Systems; Ethics and Values in the Context of Community Policing; Liability and the Police; Problem-Oriented Policing; Stress and Police Work**

References and Further Reading

Bauer, Lynn, and Steven Owens. 2004. *Justice expenditure and employment in the United States, 2001*. Washington, DC: U.S. Department of Justice.

Frerkes, Larry. 1998. *Becoming a police officer: A guide to successful entry level testing*. Incline Village, NV: Copperhouse Publishing Co.

Leonard, V. A., and Harry More. 1993. *Police organization and management*. 8th ed. Westbury, NY: The Foundation Press, Inc.

Lord, Vivian, and Ken Peak. 2004. *Women in law enforcement careers: A guide for preparing and succeeding*. Upper Saddle River, NJ: Pearson/Prentice-Hall.

Peak, Ken. 2004. *Justice administration: Police, courts, corrections management*. 4th ed. Upper Saddle River, NJ: Pearson/Prentice-Hall.

Reaves, Brian, and Timothy Hart. 2000. *Law enforcement management and administrative statistics, 1999: Data for individual state and local agencies with 100 or more officers*. Washington, DC: U.S. Department of Justice.

Reaves, Brian, and Matthew Hickman. 2002. *Police departments in large cities, 1990–2000.*
Washington, DC: U.S. Department of Justice.

Smith v. Troyan, 520 F.2nd 492, 6th Cir. (1975).

Swanson, Charles, Leonard Territo, and Robert Taylor. 1993. *Police administration: Structures, processes and behavior*. New York: Macmillan Publishing Co.

Title 42. The Public Health and Welfare Act, Chapter 126, 42 U.S.C. 12112. Equal Opportunity for Individuals with Disabilities (1990).

Vollmer, August. 1936. *The police and modern society*. Berkeley, CA: University of California Press.

PHILADELPHIA POLICE DEPARTMENT

The City

In 1680, William Penn purchased a large tract of land from the British Crown, on which a colony of Quakers settled. This area later became the Commonwealth of Pennsylvania. Penn's charter covered most of the lands that were then occupied by Dutch and Swedish settlements, but in acquiring this charter Penn assured those already living in the area that their personal, social, and religious habits would not be disturbed. Penn's legacy was to imbue this new "Pennsylvania" with the Quaker idea of tolerance (see Weigley 1982).

Philadelphia's location was strategic in that its settlement was at the convergence of two rivers (Delaware and Schuylkill), only about a hundred miles from the Atlantic and with good navigation, and on land as a connecting point between New York and the then-emerging South. Philadelphia was also situated in an area with considerable building materials (wood, stone, and the like), making the city an excellent location for shipping and commerce. Given that the Swedes had peacefully seceded the lands to Penn and given the underlying Quaker ideals embracing the city, the area took on its association with "Brotherly Love."

Penn's conception of Philadelphia can be seen as an attempt at utopian city planning, the city being conspicuously located on north–south and east–west axes, with considerable open or "green" space. The model was seen to replicate the ideas of gentlemen's estates borrowed from England, and the attention to open social spaces remains to this day. As a modern city, a large amount of Philadelphia's land area remains open parkland.

Penn's Philadelphia grew rapidly, so much that by 1743, only twenty-five years after Penn's death, Philadelphia had ten thousand inhabitants. Penn's legacy is not connected only with the City of Philadelphia; the governance system Penn initiated for Pennsylvania eventually became the model for Congress, and much of the Pennsylvania and Philadelphia experience set the stage for the founding of the U.S. Constitution and the Bill of Rights. In fact, between 1783 and 1800, Philadelphia was the capital city for the then-emerging United States of America.

The Police Department

Policing in Philadelphia stemmed from the patrol systems originated by the early Swedish settlers, and by the early 1700s a "town watch" system had emerged; these early colonial systems emphasized voluntary, unpaid citizen participation as the basis of patrol. Philadelphia's first paid police emerged in 1751 when the General Assembly created two "police" roles—wardens and constables—who patrolled the city on a limited and often sporadic basis. In 1850, a "police marshal" was appointed, taking jurisdiction of the city, and in 1854, the City of Philadelphia incorporated through annexation many outlying sections into the city and in doing so reorganized government, including the police. The modern-day city of

Philadelphia then emerged, comprising some 129 square miles. The city continued to revise its government, but the underlying structure of the area and police function remains largely in tact to this date.

Like many emerging urban cities, Philadelphia had its share of corruption throughout the late nineteenth and early twentieth centuries. In August 1928, for example, a grand jury presentment revealed that Philadelphia police officers at all ranks were involved in corruption and graft amounting to millions of dollars (Pennsylvania Crime Commission 1974). In 1928, 1937, 1951, and 1953, grand jury investigations involving allegations of police corruption were conducted. Each revealed an intimate connection between vice operators—gamblers, pimps, and prostitutes—and police officers, police officials, and political leaders within the city (Pennsylvania Crime Commission 1974). The consistency of the city's "scandals and reforms" followed much of that seen in other large cities, large-scale immigration from Europe and the South and ensuing struggles between political machines and urban reformers.

Philadelphia was and in some degree remains an interesting large, urban city. During the middle years of the twentieth century, national attention was largely focused on New York or Washington, D.C., as the economic and political capitals of the United States. Philadelphia's changes, politically, socially, and economically, were less visible nationally. From the 1940s and through the 1960s, that visibility changed, often portraying the city and its police in a less positive light.

During the 1920s, the Philadelphia Police Department was immortalized in the silent movies as the "Keystone Cops"—Pennsylvania being the Keystone State and Philadelphia its largest city. While the Philadelphia police lay dormant in the public view during the 1930s through the early 1950s, the city was racially divided, and the mode of policing in Philadelphia was tough.

Perhaps emblematic of the "tough policing style" that emerged in the Philadelphia Police Department was its very public police commissioner during the late 1960s and early 1970s, when Philadelphia, like other cities, experienced considerable social turmoil (see Rubenstein 1979). Rising through the ranks of the Phildelphia Polcie Department, which he joined in the 1940s, Frank Rizzo became police commissioner in 1967 and remained in this position until 1971. Rizzo had come up through the ranks of the department, garnering a reputation for rough-and-tumble policing in the city.

Known as the "Cisco Kid" on the street, a name modeled after a 1950s "shoot-em-up" cowboy western on television, Rizzo had been instrumental in cracking down on after hours nightclubs and coffee houses in West Philadelphia, an area largely populated by blacks and the then-emerging "beatnick" culture. His tactics and language were often aggressive, and his persona ultimately became that of the Philadelphia Police Department. Rizzo demanded personal loyalty, defended his police officers in the face of almost any complaint, was himself accused of abuse of authority and brutality, and ultimately ran the police department intermittently from the position of mayor of the city from 1972 through 1980. Throughout this period, the Philadelphia police continually distanced themselves from the public and embraced a strict policing style, especially in minority communities.

Rizzo was followed by Joseph F. O'Neill (1971–1980) and Morton Solomon (1980–1984). O'Neill differed stylistically from Rizzo, but not substantively, having himself come "up through the ranks" of the Phildelphia Police Department, while Solomon, another long-term veteran of the department, is credited with reigning in police use of force within the city, most particularly use of lethal force. While Solomon did indeed vastly improve some of the policies and procedures within the department, continuing internal problems beginning within his administration and revealed by the FBI in 1982 reinforced the idea that the depariment had not lost its taste for corruption.

In 1984, Gregore Sambor, a career officer in the department, assumed the role of chief of police and presided over one of the most public and bizzare police scandals of modern policing—the MOVE incident. Sambor's career was short lived, and he was succeeded by a series of reform chiefs that continue in one way or another to the present. The MOVE incident, followed in 1995 by a far-reaching scandal in the 39th Police District, resurfaced public concerns with the accountability and honesty of the Philadelphia Police Department.

MOVE and the 39th Police District Scandals

May 13, 1985, was a day of infamy for the Phialdelphia Police Department. A rather radical urban group known as MOVE was well known to Philadelphia and a great source of neighborhood conflict. MOVE had had several confrontations with the city and with Frank Rizzo. In 1978, MOVE had an open confrontation with the police department during which one officer was killed and the MOVE home leveled. Seven years later, MOVE had relocated to West Philadelphia and continued to stir up neighborhood conflict by harassing residents and piling up trash and waste that rotted on the MOVE property. On May 13, the Philadelphia Police Department, under the command of Commissioner Sambor, attacked the MOVE house, and in the ensuing conflict the house caught fire, the fire spread to encompass approximately two city blocks (sixty-one residences), displacing hundreds of residents, and eleven MOVE members lost their lives.

The MOVE tradegy and its investigative aftermath portrayed the Philadelphia Police Department and its leadership as "out-of-control" relative to how they approached this event, and in the aftermath of this incident, Gregore Sambor resigned. The Philadelphia Police Department had again lost public credibility. This loss followed an earlier 1984 scandal involving Sambor's deputy chief, James J. Martin, who was indicted for corruption within months of his appointment.

Ten years later, in 1995, officers primarily from the 39th District, one of Philadelphia's "busy" police areas, were indicted for alleged abuse of police authority and corruption. This scandal rocked the city, most especially in terms of the number of people affected. As of mid-1997, five police officers had been convicted on charges of making false arrests, filing false reports, and robbing drug suspects. These officers were said to have raided drug houses, stolen money from dealers, and beaten anyone who got in their way. Due to the actions of these officers, literally thousands of drug convictions were subjected to review as of the end of 1997. At that time, a substantial number of cases (upwards of 300) had been overturned because of the illegal and corrupt actions of these officers.

The 39th District scandal, not unlike the Rampart scandal of the LAPD and the Dowd scandal of the NYPD, served to strengthen the view of those who believed the department was always corrupt while undermining any confidence in the Philadelphia police the remaining public may have had.

The department in 1996 did reach an agreement for a more detailed and systematic review of complaints against police and created an independent Integrity and Accountability Office to investigate complaints, which has led to more systematic oversight of the police in Philadelphia and to better police and community interactions.

The current Philadelphia Police Department employs more than 6,600 officers and patrols an area of some 142.6 miles with a population of almost 1.5 million.

The department is subdivided into twenty-three patrol districts, and like many other large municipal police forces, it includes many special units. The department has made many improvements during the years, including implementing community policing and a business improvement district in the center city of Philadelphia. The department has also been recognized for its improved crime analysis. Such improvements have restored some of the public confidence that the past scandals eroded.

JACK R. GREENE

See also **Accountability; American Policing: Early Years; Community Attitudes toward the Police; Corruption; History of American Policing; Integrity in Policing; Police in Urban America, 1860–1920**

References and Further Reading

Anderson, John, and Hilary Hevenor. 1990. *Burning down the house: MOVE and the tragedy of Philadelphia*. Philadelphia: W. W. Norton and Co.

Daughen, Joseph R. 1977. *The cop who would be king: Mayor Frank Rizzo*. Boston: Little, Brown and Company.

NAACP, Philadelphia Branch, and Police-Barrio Relations Project, on behalf of themselves and their members v. City of Philadelphia. Civil action 96-6045 (September 4, 1996).

Pennsylvania Crime Commission. 1974. *Report on police corruption and the quality of law enforcement in Philadelphia*. St. Davids, PA: Pennsylvania Crime Commission.

Philadelphia Police Study Task Force. 1986. *Philadelphia and its police*. Philadelphia: Police Study Task Force.

Rubenstein, Jonathan. 1979. *City police*. New York: Ballantine Books.

Weigley, Russell. 1982. *Philadelphia: A 300-year history*. Philadelphia: W. W. Norton and Company.

PHYSICAL FITNESS STANDARDS

Police departments, like all public and private employers, must hire employees who are physically fit to perform the job.

Employers establish physical fitness standards for jobs, especially those that are physically demanding, and these standards are often used in the selection process. Police officers are unique in that, for the most part, the job is rather sedentary, with a few random instances where officers are required to exert tremendous strength and endurance. For most of their shifts, police officers drive patrol cars, walk a beat, and observe what is occurring in their patrol areas. Occasionally they must chase or wrestle with a suspect. Officers must be physically prepared for these random encounters. About half of all police agencies have a physical fitness requirement upon entry (Reaves and Goldberg 2000). Generally, only the smaller departments do not have such a requirement.

Historically, police agencies equated physical fitness to size. Until the 1970s, many police departments had height and weight requirements. For example, departments required that new officers be at least 5'7" in height and of proportionate weight. In the 1970s, the courts ruled such standards to be discriminatory because they had an adverse impact on females. For example, in *Vanguard Justice Society v. Hughes* (1979), the court concluded that Baltimore's 5'7" height requirement was unconstitutional since 95% of females were excluded while only 32% of the male population was deemed unqualified. The requirement violated Title VII of the 1964 Civil Rights Act, which forbids discrimination based on gender. The act essentially required agencies to establish the validity of their selection procedures when discrimination occurred. Police agencies could not show that taller officers performed better, resulting in height standards being abolished.

Departments migrated from height requirements to some form of physical fitness testing. For example, the Toledo (Ohio) Police Department adopted a test that included (1) fifteen push-ups, (2) twenty-five sit-ups, (3) a six-foot standing broad jump, and (4) a twenty-five-second obstacle course. The court in *Harless v. Duck* (1980) ruled the examination to be in violation of the Civil Rights Act. The court noted that the test did not sample job tasks or was not related to the job. In other words, officers did not perform sit-ups and push-ups on the job. In striking down these types of tests, the courts required departments to develop tests that reflected actual job behaviors.

As the result of legal challenges and the need to hire female officers, departments began to seek procedures that screened out those who were physically unqualified but did not adversely affect female applicants. In the 1980s and early 1990s, departments began to adopt a health-based testing procedure. The procedure adopted by most departments included (1) cardiovascular capacity, usually measured by a 1.5 mile run, (2) upper-body strength, measured by push-ups or a bench press, (3) abdominal strength, measured by sit-ups, (4) body-fat composition, measured using body calipers, and (5) flexibility, measured by a bend and reach. To avoid legal challenges and to increase the passing rate for females, departments used gender and age norms based on the general population. For example, a twenty-five-year-old female's performance on the events was compared to all other females within her age range (Gaines, Falkenberg, and Gambino 1993). This resulted in identifying healthy candidates, male and female, without having adverse impact. In *United States v. Wichita Falls* (1988), the court ruled that the health-based procedure did not violate the Civil Rights Act even when females were adversely affected since females were screened using female-based norms or standards.

The direction of physical fitness screening changed with the passage of the 1991 Civil Rights Act. One of the purposes of the act was to prevent employers from using self-imposed affirmative action programs. For example, many departments were using separate hiring and promotion lists for minority and white candidates in order to avoid discrimination or adverse impact problems (Gaines, Costello, and Crabtree 1989). Congress, in passing the act, reasoned that this procedure was unfair and invalid. Consequently, departments abandoned the health-based fitness testing procedures since they were based on separate male and female norms. However, the court in *Peanick v. Morris* (1996) ruled that health-based testing based on separate male and female norms did not violate the 1991 Civil Rights Act. The court ruled that even though different standards were used for male and female applicants, the passing point essentially identified candidates who were equivalent in terms of health.

Even though one court approved the health-based standards, most departments returned to some form of event-based physical fitness testing. Most departments were not familiar with the case, and the U. S. Department of Justice maintained that the health-based testing violated the 1991 Civil Rights Act. The event-based tests were similar to the one struck down by the court in Toledo, but the new procedures attempted to incorporate job samples, thus establishing some measure of content validity. Activities such as push-ups, sit-ups, and bench presses were avoided. Instead, events such as dry firing a handgun, scaling a six-foot wall, pushing a vehicle for a distance, obstacle courses, and running up and down a flight of stairs were used; all of these events are physical activities that police officers may perform as a part of their job.

The dominant issue in physical fitness testing is the establishment of cut-off scores. That is, at what point does a candidate pass? Given that females do not possess the strength that males possess, this is a difficult chore. If the cut-off score is lowered to allow more females to pass, it will also allow larger numbers of males to pass. Thus, unlike the health-based tests, these tests almost always result in adverse

impact on female applicants. The tests have withstood challenge since they are based on job samples and have some level of content validity.

Cut-off scores have been set by testing a sample of job incumbents. Here, events are identified and a sample of officers who are currently performing the job are tested. Most agencies have used one standard deviation below the mean or average as the cut-off. This means that about 34% of candidates fail the test. Problems with this procedure have occurred when a representative sample of officers have not been used. Too often departments have requested volunteers to participate in the validation process, which generally results in physically superior officers being used to establish the cut-off scores. When this occurs, larger numbers of females are rejected.

An examination of these tests shows that females have difficulty with one event—the six-foot wall climb. This event is used by a number of departments even though it is questionable whether an officer will ever scale a six-foot wall. Recognizing this problem, the San Bernardino County Sheriff's Department initiated a one-day training program to help prepare applicants to successfully scale the wall. Sheriff's officials recognized that successful completion of the event required technique as well as some level of upper-body strength and reasoned that most females failed the event because they were unfamiliar with the technique or right way to approach the obstacle. The training program resulted in larger numbers of females passing the physical fitness test. Thus, departments can increase the number of females passing their fitness requirements by providing an orientation or training.

A number of departments now have some form of physical fitness programs for veteran officers. These programs have taken a variety of directions. Some have been voluntary, while others have attached incentives. A number of departments now provide officers with physical fitness training facilities. Some departments have built their own facilities, while others have paid officers' dues to health clubs. In the latter case, officers are expected to maintain some level of fitness and to show that they have used the club's facilities. Other departments have provided officers with time off, for example, four hours a week. These departments monitor the program by requiring officers who take the time off to meet departmentally established physical fitness standards. Other departments have developed standards and provide pay incentives to officers who meet the standards. This is similar to specialist pay, which is used by a number of departments.

The problem in implementing physical fitness standards for veteran or new officers is establishing cut-off scores. Standards for veteran officers are not difficult since they can be linked to health-based standards, and officers can be required to maintain a level that is compared to gender and age norms. The 1991 Civil Rights Act does not apply to physical fitness maintenance programs. As noted above, most agencies establish cut-off scores for entry by developing a set of events and testing veteran officers with the cut-off score set at one standard deviation from the mean. Realistically, this means that about 34% of the officers who were involved in establishing the norms failed, but in fact, they were successful police officers. The bottom line is there is no scientific method for determining cut-off scores, and they are arbitrary. The courts have accepted physical fitness tests for entry as long as they contain content validity or reflect actual job components. Departments should monitor their standards and be mindful of the numbers of male and female applicants who are rejected. They should scrutinize the pool of applicants who are rejected and ensure that they truly are not physically capable of performing the job. It must be remembered that the police selection process is a multitiered process, and as the number of applicants rejected at

each stage increases, it becomes more difficult to fill hiring quotas.

LARRY K. GAINES

See also **Diversity in Police Departments; Police Careers; Women in Law Enforcement**

References and Further Reading

Gaines, L., P. Costello, and A. Crabtree. 1989. Police selection testing: Balancing legal requirements and employer needs. *American Journal of Police*, 8: 137–52.

Gaines, L., S. Falkenberg, and J. Gambino. 1993. Police physical agility testing: A historical and legal analysis. *American Journal of Police* 11: 47–66.

Harless v. Duck, 619 F.2nd 611 (1980).

Peanick v. Morris, 96 F.3rd 316 (1996).

Reaves, B., and A. Goldberg. 2000. *Local police departments, 1997*. Washington, DC: U.S. Department of Justice.

United States v. Wichita Falls, 704 F. Supp. 709 (N.D. Tex. 1988).

Vanguard Justice Society v. Hughes, 471 F. Supp. 670 (N. Md. 1979).

PINKERTON, ALLAN

In February 1855, Allan Pinkerton established the Northwest Police Agency in Chicago, Illinois. It was to be a regional police system for the fledgling railroad industry, extending over an area consisting of Illinois, Indiana, Michigan, Ohio, and Wisconsin. Shortly it would grow to cover the entire nation, and eventually it became the present-day Pinkerton, Inc., the world's largest private security and detective firm. Since federal detection was scant and city police were inefficient or corrupt, Pinkerton became the nation's preeminent detective force in the nineteenth century. In many respects Allan Pinkerton was to his century what J. Edgar Hoover was to the twentieth.

Pinkerton was born in Glasgow, Scotland, on August 25, 1819. Although his father had been a police officer, Allan apprenticed as a cooper. Young Pinkerton soon became involved with the Chartists, a workers' movement in Great Britain that was increasingly interpreted by officials as radical. Local political and police pressure compelled Allan Pinkerton and his new bride to flee Scotland in 1842. After a short stay in Canada and in Chicago, he settled in a small Scottish settlement called Dundee, forty miles northeast of Chicago. He opened a cooperage and employed eight apprentices.

Throughout the 1840s, numerous counterfeiters passed spurious money and made business haphazard in much of the rural Midwest. Out on an expedition hunting wood to be used as barrel staves in 1847, Pinkerton stumbled upon a camp of counterfeiters. He returned with the local sheriff to make the arrest and was heralded as a hero. Itinerant rogues nevertheless continued to travel the area selling bundles of fake money to those rustics wanting to turn a fast profit. Constables seemed powerless and a delegation of Dundee merchants pressured Pinkerton into watching for counterfeiters as a part-time deputy sheriff. A number of arrests followed, and Pinkerton began to be weaned away from barrel making.

By 1850, Pinkerton had given up his Dundee business and moved to Chicago. He was an avid abolitionist, but most Dundee residents were conservative on slavery. In his only bid for elective office in Dundee, Pinkerton had come in last in a field of nine candidates. He was convinced that his poor showing was due to his abolitionism. Chicago had a sizable abolitionist population, and he felt his views would be more acceptable there.

More important, requests for his services had increased. For example, the national government became interested in the counterfeiting problem in the Midwest. Because the Treasury Department would not have Secret Service agents to combat counterfeiting until after the Civil War, the secretary of the treasury had Pinkerton investigate the problem in Illinois in 1851 and 1853. In 1852, Cook County sheriff William Church asked Pinkerton

to rescue two kidnapped Michigan girls who had been taken westward. By 1854, he was an official deputy to the Cook County sheriff in Chicago. At the same time, the U.S. postmaster appointed him to be a special agent in the Chicago postal system. He was to investigate mail theft. In several spectacular cases he discovered postal employees stealing mail, and local newspapers proclaimed that "as a detective police officer Mr. Pinkerton has no superiors and we doubt that he has any equals in the country."

By mid-decade, as an official in the Cook County sheriff's office, which did much unofficial detecting, Pinkerton hovered between public and private policing. Then in February 1855, Pinkerton opened his agency. He made a commitment to private policing, but in a country with little official law enforcement, his duties took him across geographic and jurisdictional boundaries.

There was an explosion of railroad building in the 1850s. Illinois had ninety-eight miles of railroad track in 1851. Five years later that figure jumped to 2,086 miles. The figure would more than double by decade's end. The railroads faced the dual problems of rapid growth and America's "home rule" conception of law enforcement. Much vandalism and crime occurred on railroad property in the rural areas. Buildings and bridges were burned and trains were derailed. In addition, there were problems with railroad employees far from direct supervisory control. Railroad conductors, in their capacity of selling tickets on board the train, could take money and admit passengers but not issue tickets. With no record of a transaction, conductors could pocket the fare.

Opportunities were great. For example, in 1857 Illinois Central conductors sold $147,856 worth of tickets—officially, at least. Railroad management wanted to control the workers who were far away from headquarters. Pinkerton was to provide that control. A spying system—Pinkerton called it a "testing program"—was devised to watch conductors. Either Pinkerton himself or one of his employees (there were three at first, but the number grew rapidly in the next five years) boarded the trains, posed as a passenger, and watched the conductors.

Immediately, Oscar Caldwell was spotted taking money. An arrest, trial, and conviction followed. Caldwell's trial aroused considerable interest in Chicago and divided employee and employer. Most railroad workers in 1855 took sides against their bosses and this newly invented spy system. Shortly, Allan Pinkerton devised a symbol for the agency, the all-seeing eye. The eye began to convey double meanings. For railroad workers it meant distrust and deception; for the owner it meant accountability and control. In the next five years Pinkerton's testing program uncovered numerous cases of conductor dishonesty. In the same period railroad workers began to form unions. It seemed that war between the workers and the capitalists might erupt, but then another war got in the way.

Tensions between the northern and southern states over slavery continued to increase in the late 1850s and peaked with the election of Abraham Lincoln. The threat of secession was ominous, and so was the possibility of presidential assassination. One such attempt had occurred earlier, during Andrew Jackson's presidency. Rumor reached Pinkerton that Lincoln would be murdered as he traveled from Illinois to Washington, D.C. Pinkerton intercepted the president-elect in Philadelphia with the news that a murder conspiracy was afoot in Baltimore. Only with great effort did Pinkerton persuade Lincoln to be disguised and secretly escorted through Maryland. It was never proved that a real plot existed, however, and Pinkerton was accused of manufacturing one for his own benefit.

War broke out shortly after Lincoln's arrival in the nation's capital, and Pinkerton returned to Chicago. One of Pinkerton's close friends, George McClellan, became a general in the Midwest and used the detective to gather enemy intelligence. When McClellan was given command of all the Union forces, Pinkerton headed the spy service. A cause célèbre occurred when one of his agents, Timothy Webster, was discovered and executed by the Confederate government. The agency continued to spy on conductors and uncover government corruption in the awarding of wartime contracts. When McClellan was dismissed in 1863, Pinkerton returned to his private practice.

After the war Pinkerton's agency expanded. Offices opened in New York City (1865) and Philadelphia (1866). Testing the honesty of railroad employees continued, but emphasis shifted to the pursuit of train robbers. Kinship gangs such as the Renos, the Youngers, and the Daltons plagued the railroads. Frank and Jesse James emerged as folk heroes, especially after Pinkerton agents botched an ambush and injured the bandits' mother. Pinkerton continued to chase the railroad robbers, but as happened with the testing programs, the desperadoes made many think that detectives were merely representatives of the moneyed classes who were against the common people.

Although much of the animosity between Pinkerton agents and organized labor would occur after Allan Pinkerton's death in 1884, there were harbingers. A secret Irish fraternity named the Molly Maguires terrorized the Pennsylvania coal mines between 1867 and 1877. A Pinkerton agent infiltrated and exposed the organization, and several miners were tried, convicted, and executed. Coal workers claimed that Pinkerton's men were agents provocateurs, while mine owners felt terrorism had been dealt a decisive blow.

In the twenty years following the Civil War, the Pinkerton agency grew and became more visible. Agents served as private police who traveled across many boundaries doing very public acts. For many people, especially as Pinkerton and other private detective firms became more established, the entire profession hovered on the border of respectability.

As business grew, so did the number of Pinkerton operatives. By 1870, there were twenty detectives and sixty watchmen. In spite of economic recession and depression, the number would almost double in the next decade. The number of other detective agencies increased rapidly as well. Besides combating criminality and radicalism, Pinkerton set out to forge a profession. First, in a series of in-house publications, he defined business philosophy and employee conduct. This was done to control his own operatives and provide guidelines of behavior for other detective agencies. Like any respectable business, the Pinkerton agency worked for fees instead of rewards. Pinkerton would not accept disreputable work like so many divorce detectives did. Employees had to subscribe to a puritanical lifestyle. In short, his business—and by implication all proper private detectives—was to be a carbon copy of other respectable businesses. Contradicting prevailing attitudes that it takes a thief to catch a thief, Pinkerton told his operatives that "the profession of the detective is a high and honorable calling."

Second, Pinkerton tapped into a growing popular literature coming out of Edgar Allan Poe's earlier detective puzzles and the sensationalist, cheap "yellow book" publications. Both genres distorted real detectives and detection. To exploit this popularity and correct misperceptions, Pinkerton published sixteen detective books between 1874 and 1884. Actually, the literary output was a corporate endeavor: Several different authors, under his editorial supervision, put Pinkerton's memoirs to paper. Two types of publication resulted. The detective stories were matter-of-fact retellings of past cases. They were marked by a lack of excitement and sensation. The second type were not stories; they were descriptions of various crimes and criminal menaces in America. This allowed Pinkerton to pose as an expert on crime in America. Such knowledge was based on his "rogues' gallery" and network of agents throughout the country.

When Allan Pinkerton died in 1884, the management of the agency passed to his two sons, William and Robert. Much stormy history remained to be written in the late nineteenth century. But at his funeral Pinkerton was eulogized as a reformer because "the profession in this country of which, in its true dignity, he was the honored founder, is no mean profession. It is a social protector." Of course, not everyone shared that view.

FRANK MORN

See also **Detectives; History of American Policing**

References and Further Reading

Horan, James. 1968. *The Pinkertons: The detective dynasty that made history.* New York: Crown.

Morn, Frank. 1982. *"The eye that never sleeps." A history of the Pinkerton National Detective Agency.* Bloomington: Indiana University Press.

Rowan, Richard. 1931. *The Pinkertons: A detective dynasty.* Boston: Little, Brown and Company.

POLICE CAREERS

The central concepts in social science, as Burns (1953, 654) writes, "suffer[s] from confusion and ambiguity ...." Career is a context-burdened concept that varies in referent by usage and tacit assumptions. Lexicographically, the word has something to do with a path or direction and with careening. A career, stripped to bare minimum features, is a series of positions, or stages, a life course held over time by a social actor—an organization, group, or a person. The central feature of the work career in modern industrialized society is that it is the active link between an individual's paid work life and the contours of the division of labor.

The term is often applied to the accomplishments of those in high-status jobs, such as professors, actors, and athletes, but analytically it serves as well to illuminate the work trajectory of a burglar as well as a baker, a caretaker as well as a curate, a diver as well as a diplomat. Movements occur within and across occupational careers. Occupational mobility has both a vertical dimension, as measured by individuals' movement between or within occupations, and horizontal movement within an organization, occupational category, or grouping of similar occupations. Occupations as entities also have careers and movements, as exemplified by the changed status of policing as a career in the past thirty-five years. Careers are not merely individual pursuits or choices, they are much shaped by gender, ethnicity, and the market in which the career is enacted (industry, service, the professions, pink, blue, or white collar). While the American ideal of freedom is occupational choice, this is rarely the case.

Let us consider policing as a career. Historically, it has been seen as a stable, blue collar manual job with good pay and benefits and early retirement potential. There are many ways to study police careers. It has been assumed in criminal justice and sociology arenas that biogenetic, attitude-based, and social psychological studies predicated on innate matters or personality have little use for studying the dynamics of police careers. Police do not differ in their measured attitudes and personalities from others of similar class origins. Social psychological studies are not very revealing of differences among officers in career achievements. Autobiographies and biographies, perhaps the most engaging of subjective career studies, while they are notoriously rich in elaborated fabrications and tessellations on opportunities won and lost, are of marginal utility. They present at best an imagined career. The perspective one adopts alters what is seen.

Certainly, the occupational life course may be felt or experienced quite differently, depending on the point of origin or other social features that shape the career of a person. This felt or experienced career, an idea that hinges on emotional gains and losses, feelings of empowerment or obloquy, may sharply contrast with the stark realities of an objective charting of positions held, salaries paid, and achievements registered. As Wilensky (1958) has shown dramatically, disorderly careers and downward mobility have profound social and psychological consequences. These social changes produce social psychological costs.

Another systematic approach is to see career as a diachronic matter, something that unfolds over time. This unfolding can be charted chronologically as a series of points on a figure showing positions held, or as a series of turning points. These points indicate the trajectory of groups of people by age, gender, ethnicity, or social origins. The Chicago school of sociology has emphasized the study of the natural history of occupations, including recruitment, socialization, identification and commitment, shifts in work place and role, firing, termination, and retirement (Becker 1979; Hughes 1958). An alternative and contrasting framework for studying careers sees them at one point in time, a synchronic view. In this case, the correlates of career achievements are contrasted for a given sample, or samples.

The study of police careers has not yielded a rich harvest of insights. It has in large part been ignored as a facet of the work and its politics. This is true for several interrelated reasons. Policing is a traditional occupation and the police organization is a quasi-military structure that places the vast majority of its practitioners at the front lines, on the streets, and at the same rank throughout their careers. This pattern is reinforced by powerful unions that defend seniority as a basis for advantage and suppress merit and competition as the basis for salaries and the conditions of work.

The organization is roiled from time to time by three forces that alter this bottom-heavy, single-rank stasis: (1) reciprocated loyalty to those above in the organization and sponsorship that increases chances of promotion or assignment to political niches that attract ambitious officers (the chief's office, internal affairs), and special squads in current favor in the organization (the gang squad, SWAT teams); (2) political career-shattering moves; (3) movement, permitted in some states, into specialized roles in other police organizations that allows "leap-frogging" over others regardless of seniority.

The politics that have sustained this local career pattern have never been challenged in the United States, but alternative schemes were adopted in India and tried for a time in the United Kingdom after World War II. The United Kingdom experimented for some years with a plan called the Trenchard scheme, after a British brigadier. This plan permitted officers to enter as inspectors (lieutenants) or "gazetted officers," thus by-passing the ranks of constable and sergeant. It was abandoned, although various efforts to create a "fast track" or accelerated plans for those aspiring to officer rank remain in place, facilitated by the National Police College at Bramshill.

These schemes have never affected more than a handful of officers. Only chiefs in very large American cities or British constabularies, typically very visible and active media figures, operate in a national or rarely in an international career system. While they may move from a top position in one city to another or from the second-in-command spot to the top command spot in another organization, there is no systematic scheme for developing and training police officers beyond the academy or the odd certification scheme. Police careers are profoundly local.

There is presently no full study of police careers using a large sample study, nor a full one of the subjective aspects of police careers. There are classic and important studies carried out on urban police recruits, following them through their training and

a year or so into the job (Van Maanen 1975; Fielding 1986; Chan 2004), but these works focus on changes in attitudes and practices, not on the sequences of positions or ranks held. There are no studies of the career lines of federal officers, even the most important and prestigious forces such as the Federal Bureau of Investigation, the Drug Enforcement Administration, and what is now called homeland security as a result of the consolidation of customs and immigration, Border Patrol, and the Coast Guard.

There are no full studies of state police careers (there are forty-nine state police forces). Chiefs' biographies have been very informative, albeit a bit self-aggrandizing, while only two studies have focused on the careers of chief constables (Wall 1998, Reiner 1991). These men have achieved very high rank in a small number of organizations (fifty-three in the United Kingdom since the late 1960s). The studies do suggest some basic facts about them. They are on the one hand exceptional and on the other, nonexceptional, when compared to other police officers of their era with respect to class origins, modest initial ambitions, sponsorship and protection by those "above" them, and their definition and understanding of what the job requires. In this respect, they are not unlike the physicians studied by Oswald Hall (1948, 1949) more than fifty years ago.

The published research on police careers is thus an unsatisfying mosaic that does not produce a definitive picture of the dynamics, diachronic matters, nor the correlates of achieving a given rank, role (a particular short-term task force or assignment), or organizational position (one not based on rank, but a niche such as a computer repair man or a driver for the chief's office). However, several generalizations can be offered abut police careers. Very few officers experience upward rank-based mobility. Most types of mobility are horizontal. These are moves into niches, favored positions within the organization that are dependent more on skill than upon rank or that maximize some sorts of rewards (overtime, time off, prestige). The rewards sought vary by the location. Transfers from one district or position to another are sought for any and all of the following: convenience; workload variation (either more or less work); action or finding a niche conforming to a person's special skills or interests (research, laboratories, property room, shooting range); political advantage because assignment to certain squads, for example, homicide or SWAT, are fast tracks or essential to achieving higher rank; a sinecure in which little or no police work is required. In some ways, running a policing career is a kind of bargain since it can facilitate another parallel career such as repair work, construction, security in hotels, or dealing in real estate or insurance or various forms of nonrank reward (perks such as overtime, comp time, or assignment to paying police work via private contracts from sports franchises and contractors).

For top command exit strategies, typically the postretirement job, this parallel career involves cultivating private security firms or local politics (a striking number of ex-chiefs have become big-city mayors). In general, however, it can be said that prestige in the job flows to those serving in specialized units, investigative work, especially homicide, and positions most associated with crime control and crime suppression. The learned skills of policing are not transferable to other occupations or occupational clusters.

PETER K. MANNING

See also **Autonomy and the Police; Occupational Culture; Unionization, Police**

References and Further Reading

Becker, Howard S. 1979. *Sociological work, methods, and substance*. Chicago: Aldine.

Fielding, Nigel. 1986. *Joining forces*. London: Routledge Kegan Paul.

Hall, Oswald. 1948. Stages of a medical career. *American Journal of Sociology* 53: 327–36.

———. 1949. Types of medical careers. *American Journal of Sociology* 55: 243–53.

Hughes, E. C. 1958. *Men and their work*. New York: The Free Press.

Reiner, Robert. 1991. *Chief constables*. Oxford, UK: Oxford University Press.

Van Maanen, John. 1974. Working the street. In *The potential for reform in the criminal justice system*, ed. H. Jacob. Beverly Hills, CA: Sage.

Wall, D. 1998. *Chief constables*. Dartmoor, U.K.: Ashgate.

Wilensky, H. 1958. Disorderly careers. *American Journal of Sociology*.

POLICE CHIEF EXECUTIVE

Police chiefs have one of the most complex jobs in the world. They also have one of the most important and rewarding jobs in the world. They are responsible for the safety and security of their communities. Failure to do so can create an atmosphere of danger and an environment of fear. Many people feel they know what a police chief does and that they understand all of the responsibilities that accompany the job, but the job is extremely complex, not only because of the human factors involved but also because of the diverse makeup of the different police jurisdictions. The size of the department and jurisdiction are contributing factors to the many types of skills and experiences needed by an effective police chief.

The police chief is the chief executive officer of the police department. Police departments vary not only in size but also in the means of appointment for the chief of police. In some departments the chief may have risen through the ranks and been with the police department since first becoming an officer. In other departments the chiefs are appointed after a search for qualified candidates. The qualifications for the chief of police position can vary and are usually determined by local jurisdictions. The hiring process usually includes a background investigation but can vary from an interview to a written examination to a partial or full evaluation at an assessment center.

Many factors can contribute to the success of a police chief. To improve the chances for success in a department, the chief of police should have experience and/ or training in managing the police operation in a similar size community. A couple of areas that can contribute to the knowledge and skills of the chief of police are education and training. Police chief candidates have several unique opportunities to improve their ability to effectively supervise the police department. The Federal Bureau of Investigation Training Academy and the Southern Police Institute at the University of Louisville are two prime examples of programs that provide some of the best police executive training in the country. Many universities offer very good courses in public administration, criminal justice management, and various other leadership and management courses.

Regardless of the size of the department, the chief of police is the director of community safety. The chief draws from education, training, and experience to develop a department mission statement and strategic plan for the police department. The mission statement should clearly state the goals and objectives of the department and needs to be communicated to the community as well as the department. This is the guiding principle of the department and influences every facet of the department.

The strategic plan of the police department must consider all aspects of present and future safety and security needs of the community. To effectively develop and implement a comprehensive strategic plan, the chief needs the input from all community stakeholders. Open dialogue across the entire spectrum of stakeholders allows the chief to develop a comprehensive plan that will lead to effective and coordinated implementation.

The chief, as a communicator, must build lines of communications not only within the police department but among the community and other government entities. Many chiefs have long recognized the need for effective communication within the police department. The progressive chief realizes that the diversity and complexity of safety problems today call for increased resources. When local government financial resources have fallen or remained static, the chief of police must be innovative in getting the most from available resources. Partnerships and coordination of resources with other agencies is critical and can be a force multiplier.

The nature of police work makes the department susceptible to criticism at times. The chief is responsible and accountable for the actions of the department, which may sometimes have conflicting responsibilities of protecting citizens and preserving individual rights.

As a result of public examination of police actions, the chief of police is often in a position of having to deal with the media. It is important that the chief be as open as possible with the media. As public servants, chiefs are answerable to the public. At the same time the chief should be schooled in techniques used by the media to portray the chief in a light that would be detrimental and reflect badly on a personal, professional level and on the department. Above all else the chief needs to be in control, fair, unbiased, open, and as available as possible to the media. The media can be a positive resource for the chief if the relationship is positive for both parties. The media can be a valuable resource for communicating community safety concerns, needs for information, and opportunities for citizen input into the police operation.

Communities establish the different management skills, education, and training they expect from their chiefs of police. They may also expect the chief to have certain personal character strengths. The effective operation of a police department is highly dependent on the personal abilities and character standards of the chief.

The chief of police must have strong leadership skills. Leadership is a term that is difficult to define, yet its presence determines the culture and perspectives of the department. The chief of police should be a leader who embodies all the community comes to expect from all the officers in the department. Effective leadership is mandatory and should foster the development of the core values of the department. A strong ethical and moral leader is critical to instilling the core values into the department culture. The chief of police should be the example and model of the department's core values through effective leadership.

Leadership is not an innate trait; it must be developed, learned, and practiced just as any other skill. The most important leadership skill the chief can provide is directing the vision of the department. A clear and articulate vision is critical to developing all the day-to-day operations of the department and can promote the development of long-term and short-term goals. It should be developed with input from all parties that have a stake in the operation of the department. Getting the officers of the department to believe in the vision and help shape it through participation is key to its achievement.

Leadership differs from management. Frequently, management is telling people what to do and handling day-to-day problems by close supervision. Leadership is much more empowering. Leadership is getting people to think on their own, to become problem solvers, to make sound ethical decisions without being supervised. It is getting people to be self-motivators. It is being able to see the big picture and make decisions that will impact the department in the future. The capable leadership of the chief can contribute to the success and efficiency of the department.

One of the most important core values of a police chief is integrity, the cornerstone of a person's character. Integrity is a core value that if lost or compromised may never be regained. A chief of police must take extreme care to protect and promote his or her own integrity as well as the department's. This is critical to maintaining the confidence of the department and the community.

Another core value that is critical to the success of a chief is respect for other human beings. This includes the officers in the department as well as the citizens in the community. Respect is a core value that if practiced honestly will be returned to the practitioner. It not only instills confidence in the chief but also in the department as a whole. It can increase the positive interactions between the department and the community. It is being trustworthy and promoting a positive workplace environment with a culture of teamwork through respect. It is doing the right thing when it might not be the most popular option.

Trustworthiness is an essential characteristic of a chief of police. It can set the tone for dealings with the community and the department and represents a base value for all negotiations and agreements. The perception that the chief of police does not follow through on promises and agreements can have a chilling effect on future negotiations and agreements. Community and departmental input into decision making is critical to making the best informed and comprehensive decisions. If the chief of police is not trustworthy, the opportunity for this input and effective contributions to decision making is not possible. Trustworthiness is a value that keeps the lines of communication open.

Other skills are necessary for the chief to deal with the direct management of the department. One important management skill is planning. Successful planning can influence everything the department does. These plans are developed with the vision, goals, and objectives of the department in mind. In formulating the department's plans, the chief of police must consider the plans of the community and other agencies. The chief of police must take extreme care in formulating department plans so that they work well with the plans of the community. Not only must the chief consider a strategic plan, but also various tactical plans must be developed to allow the department to operate efficiently in tactical situations that arise. The types of tactical plans that are necessary for the department are dependent on a thorough risk assessment of the community and the types of tactical situations that are the most likely to occur.

The chief should also develop the skill of delegation. No police chief can hope to accomplish all the tasks that are necessary to effectively run the department alone. Delegation can be one of the most difficult skills to master. The chief must provide the employee with the authority and opportunity to complete the job delegated but cannot delegate the responsibility for getting the job done. Delegation does not absolve the chief of any responsibility for the operation of the department; it does require that the chief develop members of the department to accept responsibility while granting them the authority to carry out their mission to successful completion. Delegation also leads to another important function of the police chief's job—the professional development of the people working in the department. This sometimes requires the chief to provide support and direction in guiding the employee through the job.

The chief needs the ability to develop and manage the departmental budget. The development of the vision, strategic plans, and goals and objectives are critical factors in the preparation of the budget. One must have a clear vision of the direction of the department and the ability to evaluate the department's progress toward its objectives to be able to estimate the amount of finances the department will need to accomplish its mission. By incorporating the budget process in the overall strategic planning, the chief can adequately predict the amount of the budget for the coming year and often times for a few years ahead.

No matter what the size of the department, the chief of police is responsible for coordinating all of the police activities within a particular jurisdiction. In larger communities the coordination may require a great deal of effort and input from a variety of sources. In smaller communities the coordinating is done on a much smaller scale. In traditional policing much of the coordinating of police activities takes place within the police department and revolves around the priorities of the department. In a community policing environment with a much more diverse population, the chief of police must work with the community to obtain input into the areas that the residents feel should be the law enforcement priorities. Another factor complicating the coordinating of police operations is the increased speed of transportation through, across, and around jurisdictions, so the chief of police must be very aware of and willing to cooperate with a variety of other law enforcement jurisdictions.

As stated above, the position of chief of police is very complex. It requires an individual who is not afraid to fail and plans to succeed. The chief should be a lifelong learner. Succeeding at this job does not require a certain number of years on the job or a certain level of formal education, nor does it require that one be a particular gender, race, or age. It does require knowledge and skills to maintain an efficient, safe environment for the community, the ability to work with a diverse department and community, and all the skills and values previously enumerated.

Values of integrity, honesty, courage, justice, fairness, respect, and a strong ethical code and leadership skills are the core ingredients that the chief should possess before ascending to the position. These values must be developed over time and are not learned as easily as the managerial or administrative skills needed for the chief of police position. They become ingrained in one's character and are on display throughout the career of any candidate for chief of police. If the chief makes a minor mistake in budgeting, the mistake may well be forgotten by the next time budget preparations begin. If the chief makes a mistake in the core values, it may never be forgiven or forgotten.

The selection of a chief of police will set the tone of the department for a long time. The incorrect decision can have disastrous results for the department and the community. The failure to provide leadership can lead to a department without direction and one that is strictly reactive to situations. A much better police force is proactive and in touch with the community. The police chief should be leading that philosophy.

JOHN M. BOAL

See also **Accountability; Administration of Police Agencies, Theories of; Codes of Ethics; Ethics and Values in the Context of Community Policing; Media Relations; Police Careers; Professionalism**

References and Further Reading

Iannone, Nathan F., and M. D. Iannone. 2000. *Supervision of police personnel.* 6th ed. Upper Saddle River, NJ: Pearson/Prentice-Hall.

Meese, Edwin, III, and P. J. Ortmeier. 2004. *Leadership, ethics, and policing: Challenges of the 21st century.* Upper Saddle River, NJ: Pearson/Prentice-Hall,

Potts, Lee W. 1982. Police professionalism: Elusive or illusory? *Criminal Justice Review* 7 (2): 51–57.

Swanson, Charles, Leonard Territo, and Robert W. Taylor. 2004. *Police administration.* 6th ed. Upper Saddle River, NJ: Pearson/Prentice-Hall.

Thebault, Edward A., Lawrence M. Lynch, and Bruce R. McBride. 2004. *Proactive police management.* 6th ed. Upper Saddle River, NJ: Pearson/Prentice-Hall.

Whisenand, Paul M. 2004. *Supervising police personnel: The fifteen responsibilities.* 5th ed. Upper Saddle River, NJ: Pearson/Prentice-Hall.

POLICE EXECUTIVE RESEARCH FORUM

Introduction

Early in 1975, former New York Police Commissioner Patrick V. Murphy, then-president of the Police Foundation, invited ten police chiefs from communities across the country—from Peoria to Portland (Oregon) and from Boston to Berkeley—to an informal meeting in Washington, D.C. After discussing common concerns and exchanging ideas on emerging policing issues, they decided to continue to meet periodically. Eventually, they decided to create a network of colleagues for support and counsel. They envisioned an organization that would not be afraid to question and debate conventional thinking.

Today, that network numbers more than 1,100 police leaders and criminal justice practitioners, researchers, and academics and is known as the Police Executive Research Forum (PERF). The police executives who belong to PERF collectively serve more than half of the nation's population. But while PERF may have grown substantially in numbers, it has remained true to its original purpose—to take on tough issues and break down barriers to meaningful police reform.

In founding PERF, the original members who signed the incorporation documents in 1977 dedicated themselves to the following goals:

To professionalize police administration and policing at all levels

To encourage mobility of police chiefs and top administrators from city to city

To sponsor and promote research and the consideration and use of solidly grounded research findings

To develop national police leadership that takes public stands on critical issues affecting policing

PERF has met those goals and more in the many activities its members and staff have undertaken for the better part of thirty years.

Improving the Delivery of Police Services

PERF takes a proactive approach to solving public safety problems. It advocates problem-oriented policing and community policing, which have changed the face of policing in this country. PERF has worked on problem-oriented policing projects since 1983, when the concept was still novel. Chief Cornelius Behan allowed PERF to work in Baltimore County with that department's Citizen-Oriented Police Enforcement (COPE) unit. By involving PERF and Professor Herman Goldstein of the University of Wisconsin, Behan helped spearhead a movement that was to take PERF to the forefront of policing reform. Soon after, PERF was asked to conduct the first federally funded problem-oriented policing experiment in the nation that focused on a fully operational, department-wide effort. That experiment took place under Chief Darrel Stephens's leadership in Newport News, Virginia, and landmark advances were soon made in other cities across the nation.

For fourteen years, PERF sponsored an international problem-oriented policing (POP) conference in partnership with the San Diego Police Department, where successful POP programs were shared, and it published guides to help police practitioners implement the POP philosophy. It also created the award that recognizes exceptional police problem-solving projects—the Herman Goldstein Award for Excellence in Problem-Oriented Policing. The Goldstein Award encourages problem-solving initiatives in law enforcement and ensures that the very best of these efforts are replicated by other agencies in the United States and abroad.

PERF's contributions to advancing professionalism in the field are numerous. In the area of police use of deadly force, PERF has published several publications that are based on comprehensive research. *Deadly Force: What We Know* has been heralded by police, researchers, and city managers as the most comprehensive book ever written about such shootings. Other related titles include *The Force Factor: Measuring Police Use of Force Relative to Suspect Resistance* and *And Justice for All: Understanding and Controlling Police Abuse of Force* (Geller and Toch 1995). In 2005, PERF added to the available literature with the publication of *Chief Concerns: Exploring the Challenges of Police Use of Force* (Ederheimer and Fridell 2005), which details useful strategies being employed nationwide to deal with this complex issue. As of this writing, PERF is conducting groundbreaking research on the use of emerging less-lethal technologies.

But PERF does more than simply provide departments with the information they need to create sound policies; it often sets the national agenda on controversial, seemingly intractable problems. In 2000, PERF convened a group of police chiefs and community leaders from large cities for a closed-door, no-holds-barred meeting on how to address the issue of racial profiling. Similarly, PERF, together with the Boston-based Ten Point Coalition and the Boston Police Department, brought police chiefs from major cities and their faith-based partners to Catholic University of America in Washington, D.C., to explore innovative means for addressing violence and police–minority community tensions. For the past five years, PERF has worked with the Chicago Police Department to conduct regular citywide forums with the community and the police department. In Kansas City, PERF's efforts focused on race relations within the department itself in an innovative program called Kansas City Together.

PERF often takes on major issues at the local level. In November 1980, PERF undertook an unprecedented venture, bringing together the first team of expert homicide investigators from different police agencies nationwide to act as consultants on a serial murders case. During a sixteen-month period, eleven children in Atlanta had been murdered and another four were missing. PERF's action in forming the team marked a new level of information sharing and collegial support for the profession. More recently, PERF, with funding from the U.S. Department of Justice, published *Managing a Multijuristictional Case: Identifying the Lessons Learned from the Sniper Investigation* (Murphy and Wexler 2004), the result of a year-long study of the police work during the twenty-three-day shooting spree by a pair of snipers in the D.C. metropolitan area. This comprehensive report will help other law enforcement executives who may one day find themselves in the midst of a high-profile crime that crosses jurisdictional boundaries and involves multiple law enforcement agencies.

In the late 1990s, PERF worked with the Minneapolis Business Partnership, led by Honeywell Corporation, to assist in developing violence reduction strategies for their city. During the first year, a comprehensive study of all homicides was completed and a two-pronged strategy was implemented involving both law enforcement and community leaders. The result was a 40% reduction in homicides in Minneapolis. After a number of years of reduced violence in Minneapolis, there has recently been a spike in homicides there, so PERF was asked to return to the city, with the support of the General Mills Foundation, to revitalize its homicide-reduction program.

Such efforts to assist departments with local problems are not limited to the states. PERF has done considerable work internationally. It is currently implementing a three-year effort to bring community policing to, and reduce violence in, Kingston, Jamaica. In the Middle East, PERF has worked with Israeli and Palestinian police and has facilitated joint executive development initiatives. And, finally, PERF did an assessment of technology for the Hong Kong Police Department.

Finally, like the rest of the country—indeed, the world—the law enforcement profession and PERF have been impacted by the attacks on the World Trade Center and the Pentagon of September 11, 2001. PERF has undertaken a major initiative to provide law enforcement executives and government policymakers with practical recommendations for addressing key policing issues in the fight against terrorism. With funding from the Justice Department, PERF convened five executive sessions, with a resulting white paper to help police executives protect their communities from terrorism. Topics ranged from preparing for and responding to bioterrorism to working with diverse communities and sharing intelligence. A sixth session funded by the National Institute of Justice focused on preparing for and responding to critical incidents. PERF is currently conducting a major project on the security of our nation's busiest seaports and continues to research emerging issues in counterterrorism.

Cooperation and Debate of Police Issues

PERF's record of promoting cooperation and meaningful debate within the law enforcement community is reflected in its willingness to take on sensitive issues. The organization has been instrumental in raising the attention of the media, policymakers, and police practitioners to racial profiling, domestic violence, and the police response to special populations. PERF was one of the first organizations to advocate arrest for specific types of spousal abuse, and it led the way in providing detailed information and training materials to police on how to respond to elder abuse. Similarly, PERF's training and resource materials on addressing the needs of people with mental disabilities were on the forefront of the movement to respond effectively to special populations.

PERF has brought pro-life and pro-choice advocates together to find common ground on how police can address violence against abortion clinics. Other issues such as police oversight, school violence, and race relations have been the fodder for PERF debates and the sharing of innovative approaches.

Application of Research to Real Problems

PERF is a leader in research on policing issues that directly benefit police officers on the beat. The organization is committed to taking research off the shelves and putting it into the hands of practitioners by making research efforts responsive to the needs of members and ensuring that all study findings are easily understood and applied.

PERF has set the standard for how police services should be evaluated. In 2002, it published *Recognizing Value in Policing: The Challenge of Measuring Police Performance* (Moore 2002). Several other PERF publications have provided citizens and police practitioners objective means for evaluating the effectiveness of a police agency, dispelling many myths about crime rates and other traditional measures. More recently, PERF has published two important works on racially biased policing. *Racially Biased Policing: A Principled Response* (Fridell et al. 2001) outlines ways law enforcement agencies can address this volatile issue and includes a policy departments can adopt. *By the Numbers: A Guide for Analyzing Race Data from Vehicle Stops* (Fridell 2004) shows departments and other stakeholders how to analyze and interpret data from

vehicle stops to determine whether bias actually exists.

PERF Services and Leadership

Finally, PERF has met its goal of providing critical services and leadership to police professionals. PERF advances professionalism through its police chief selection and management services divisions. PERF partnered with the International City/County Managers Association to produce *Selecting a Police Chief: A Handbook for Local Government,* and PERF helps cities and other government agencies recruit police leaders. Most recently, PERF assisted Los Angeles, Nashville, Montgomery County, Maryland, and the U.S. capital with the process of finding a new police chief.

Through its Management Services Division, PERF staff and consultants provide critical technical assistance, reorganization studies, and other management assessments to police departments across the country. Its 2001 study of police services in Jamaica resulted in eighty-three recommendations and led to significant reform in the Jamaican Constabulary Force. Also, PERF, with the support of Motorola, Inc., worked with twenty-one police agencies around the world to help them adopt "process mapping" strategies that identified and eliminated inefficiencies in operations.

In addition, PERF publications focus on how police can advance their careers, increase professionalism, and overcome obstacles to managerial change. *Command Performance: Career Guide for Police Executives* (Kirchoff, Lansinger, and Burack 1999) is the definitive guide for those wishing to compete successfully for executive-level positions in law enforcement.

Another example of its service to police agencies is its dedication to executive development. PERF staff have trained officers and prosecutors on homicide investigations, gun tracing, community policing, and problem-solving techniques. Most important, PERF has sponsored an intensive three-week seminar for senior police executives—the Senior Management Institute for Policing (SMIP)—each summer in Boston. SMIP has already provided some seventeen hundred future police leaders with insight into the most progressive approaches to policing. The course draws on professors from Harvard University's Kennedy School of Government, Boston University, and other academic institutions to teach police executives how to apply business management principles and case studies to the policing context. The unprecedented demand for this program is reflected in the quadrupling of the class since its inception in 1980.

CHUCK WEXLER

See also **Accountability; Community-Oriented Policing: Practices; Police Chief Executive; Problem-Oriented Policing; Research and Development; SARA, the Model**

References and Further Reading

Ederheimer, Joshua A., and Lorie A. Fridell, eds. 2005. *Chief concerns: Exploring the challenges of police use of force.* Washington, DC: Police Executive Research Forum.
Fraser, Craig P., Michael Scott, John Heisey, and Robert Wasserman. 1998. *Challenge to change: The 21st Century Policing Project.* Washington, DC: Police Executive Research Forum.
Fridell, Lorie. 2004. *By the numbers: A guide for analyzing race data from vehicle stops.* Washington, DC: Police Executive Research Forum.
Fridell, Lorie, and Mary Ann Wycoff, eds. 2004. *Community policing: The past, present and future.* Washington, DC: Police Executive Research Forum.
Fridell, Lorie, Robert Lunney, Drew Diamond, and Bruce Kubu. 2001. *Racially biased policing: A principled response.* Washington, DC: Police Executive Research Forum.
Geller, William, and Hans Toch, eds. 1995. *And justice for all: Understanding and controlling police abuse of force.* Washington, DC: Police Executive Research Forum.
Glensor, Ronald W., and Gerard R. Murphy, eds. 2005. *Issues in IT: A reader for the busy police chief executive.* Washington, DC: Police Executive Research Forum.
Kenney, Dennis J., and T. Stuart Watson. 1998. *Crime in schools: Reducing fear and disorder with student problem solving.* Washington, DC: Police Executive Research Forum.
Kirchoff, William, Charlotte Lansinger, and James Burack. 1999. *Command performance: Career guide for police executives.* Washington, DC: Police Executive Research Forum.
LaVigne, Nancy, and Julie Wartell. 2001. *Mapping across boundaries: Regional crime analysis.* Washington, DC: Police Executive Research Forum.
Moore, Mark. 2002. *Recognizing value in policing: The challenge of measuring police performance.* Washington, DC: Police Executive Research Forum.
Murphy, Gerald R., and Chuck Wexler. 2004. *Managing a multijurisdictional case: Identifying the lessons learned from the sniper investigation.* Washington, DC: Police Executive Research Forum.
Plotkin, Martha R., and Tony Narr. 1993. *The police response to the homeless: A status report.* Washington, DC: Police Executive Research Forum.
Vila, Bryan. 2000. *Tired cops.* Washington, DC: Police Executive Research Forum.

POLICE FOUNDATION

The Police Foundation is a private, non-partisan, nonprofit organization dedicated to supporting innovation and improvement in policing through its research, technical assistance, training, and communications programs. Established in 1970 through a grant from the Ford Foundation, the Police Foundation has conducted seminal research in police behavior, policy, and procedure and works to transfer to local agencies the best new information about practices for dealing effectively with a range of important police operational and administrative concerns.

One of the guiding principles of the Police Foundation is that thorough, unbiased, empirical research is necessary to objectively advance and improve the field of policing. Furthermore, the connection to the law enforcement and academic/scientific communities will provide the impetus for new ideas that will help stimulate the field and provide solutions to the complex problems facing policing entities.

Unconstrained by partisan imperatives, the Police Foundation speaks with a unique and objective voice. Its focus and perspective represent the *whole* of American policing, rather than any single facet. Motivating all of the foundation's efforts is the goal of efficient, effective, humane policing that operates within the framework of democratic principles and standards, such as openness, impartiality, freedom, responsibility, and accountability.

The Police Foundation has established and refined the capacity to define, design, conduct, and evaluate controlled experiments that examine ways to improve the delivery of police services. Sometimes, foundation research findings have challenged police traditions and beliefs. Although police agencies employed routine preventive patrol as a principal anticrime strategy, a foundation experiment in Kansas City showed that routine patrol in marked patrol cars did not significantly affect crime rates. And although police officials expressed reservations about using women on patrol, foundation research in Washington, D.C., showed that gender was not a barrier to performing patrol work. Foundation research on the use of deadly force was cited at length in a landmark 1985 U.S. Supreme Court decision, *Tennessee v. Garner*. The Court ruled that the police may use deadly force only against persons whose actions constitute a threat to life.

The Police Foundation has done much of the research that led to a questioning of the traditional model of professional law enforcement and toward a new view of policing—one emphasizing a *community* orientation—that is widely embraced today. For example, research on foot patrol and on fear of crime demonstrated the importance to crime control efforts of frequent police–citizen contacts made in a positive, nonthreatening way.

As a partner in the Community Policing Consortium, the Police Foundation, along with four other leading national law enforcement organizations, plays a principal role in the development of community policing research, training, and technical assistance.

The Police Foundation's Crime Mapping and Problem Analysis Laboratory works to advance the application and understanding of geographic information systems (GISs) in conjunction with crime mapping and analysis techniques and principles; to support problem analysis in policing; to promote innovative projects and practical examples through a national newsletter; and to conduct pivotal research that involves examining the geographic dimensions of crime.

Since its inception in 1997, the laboratory has provided introductory and advanced training in crime mapping and analysis and problem analysis to a host of analysts from across the country and relevant resources including publications and documents created to assist analysts in their daily work. The following are some of the publications that have been developed:

Introductory Guide to Crime Analysis and Mapping
Guidelines to Implement and Evaluate Crime Analysis and Mapping
Manual of Crime Analysis Map Production
Users' Guide to Mapping Software for Police Agencies
Problem Analysis in Policing.

In addition, the Laboratory's *Crime Mapping News,* a quarterly newsletter, allows analysts to showcase and inform other analysts, academics, and criminal justice practitioners throughout the United States and abroad about innovative applications of crime mapping and analysis used to address crime and disorder problems. Topics in the newsletter have ranged from serial crime detection and privacy issues in the presentation of geocoded data to mapping prisoner reentry and gang mapping.

The Police Foundation has completed significant work in the areas of accountability and ethics, performance, abuse of authority, use of force, domestic violence, community-oriented policing, organizational culture, racial profiling, civil disorders, problem analysis, and risk management. Seminal research includes the following (chronologically):

- *Kansas City Preventive Patrol Experiment* (Kelling et al. 1975)
- *Minneapolis Domestic Violence Experiment* (Sherman and Berk 1984)
- Newark and Houston fear reduction studies (1985)
- Shoplifting experiment (Williams, Forst, and Hamilton 1987)
- Women in policing status report (Martin 1990)
- *Big Six Report,* on Chicago, Detroit, Houston, Los Angeles, New York, and Philadelphia (Pate and Hamilton 1991)
- Los Angeles civil disorder report (Webster and Williams 1992)
- *Metro-Dade Spouse Abuse Replication Project* (Pate, Hamilton, and Annan 1992)
- National study of *Police Use of Force* (Pate, Fridell, and Hamilton 1993)
- National *Community Policing Strategies* survey (Wycoff 1994)
- Oregon State Police ethics assessment project (Amendola 1996)
- National survey on gun ownership (Cook and Ludwig 1997)
- *National Survey of Abuse of Authority* (Weisburd et al. 2001)
- *Ideas in American Policing* series (Bayley 1998; Sherman 1998; Mastrofski 1999; Skolnick 1999; Foster 2001; Maguire 2004; and Klinger 2005)
- *Problem Analysis in Policing* project (Boba 2003)
- *Growth of COMPSTAT in American Policing* (Weisburd et al. 2004)

- *Richmond's Second Responders: Partnering with Police Against Domestic Violence* (2005)

The foundation has also developed two state-of-the-art technologies to enable police agencies to systematically collect and analyze performance-related data. The RAMS II (Risk Analysis Management software) is an early warning device that helps manage and minimize risk. The QSI (Quality Service Indicator) collects and analyzes officer–citizen contacts, including traffic stop data. Together, these two technologies allow police departments to enhance accountability, maintain quality service, ensure public confidence, and safeguard the careers of their officers. The Police Foundation is headed by a board of directors made up of highly distinguished leaders and scholars from public service, education, and private industry and is directed by its appointed president.

GREG JONES

See also **Abuse of Authority by Police; Crime Analysis; Crime Mapping; Domestic (or Intimate Partner) Violence and the Police; Early Warning Systems; Fear of Crime; Kansas City Preventive Patrol Experiment; Minneapolis Domestic Violence Experiment; Quality-of-Life Policing; Risk Management; Women in Law Enforcement**

References and Further Reading

Amendola, K. L. 1996. *Assessing law enforcement ethics: Summary report based on the study conducted with the Oregon Department of State Police.* Washington, DC: Police Foundation.
Bayley, D. H. 1998. *Policing in America: Assessment and prospects.* Washington, DC: Police Foundation.
Boba, R. 2003. *Problem analysis in policing.* Washington, DC: Police Foundation.
Cook, P. J., and Jens Ludwig. 1997. *Guns in America: Results of a comprehensive national survey on firearms ownership and use.* Washington, DC: Police Foundation.

Foster, D. W. 2001. *Policing anonymity*. Washington, DC: Police Foundation.

Kelling, G. L., A. Pate, D. Dieckman, and C. E. Brown. 1975. *Kansas City Preventive Patrol Experiment*. Washington, DC: Police Foundation.

Klinger, D. 2005. *Social theory and the street cop: The case of deadly force*. Washington, DC: Police Foundation.

Maguire, E. R. 2004. *Police departments as learning laboratories*. Washington, DC: Police Foundation.

Martin, S. 1990. *Women on the move? A report on the status of women in policing*. Washington, DC: Police Foundation.

Mastrofski, S. 1999. *Policing for people*. Washington, DC: Police Foundation.

Pate, A., and E. Hamilton. 1991. *The Big Six: Policing America's largest cities*. Washington, DC: Police Foundation.

Pate, A., E. Hamilton, and S. Annan. 1992. *Metro-Dade Spouse Abuse Replication Project: Technical report*. Washington, DC: Police Foundation.

Pate, A., L. Fridell, and E. Hamilton. 1993. *Police use of force: Official reports, citizen complaints, and legal consequences*. Washington, DC: Police Foundation.

Police Foundation. 1985. *Fear reduction reports*. Washington, DC: Police Foundation.

———. 2005. *Richmond's second responders: Partnering with police against domestic violence*. Washington, DC: Police Foundation.

Sherman, L. 1998. *Evidence-based policing*. Washington, DC: Police Foundation.

Sherman, L., and R. Berk. 1984. *Minneapolis Domestic Violence Experiment*. Washington, DC: Police Foundation.

Skolnick, J. H. 1999. *On democratic policing*. Washington, DC: Police Foundation.

Webster, W., and H. Williams. 1992. *The city in crisis: A report by the special advisor to the Board of Police Commissioners on the civil disorder in Los Angeles*. Washington, DC: Police Foundation.

Weisburd, D., R. Greenspan, E. Hamilton, K. Bryant, and H. Williams. 2001. *National Survey of Abuse of Authority*. Washington, DC: Police Foundation.

Weisburd, D., S. Mastrofski, R. Greenspan, and J. Willis. 2004. *Growth of COMPSTAT in American policing*. Washington, DC: Police Foundation.

Williams, H., B. Forst, and E. Hamilton. 1987. *Stop. Should you arrest that person?* Washington, DC: Police Foundation.

Wycoff, M. A. 1994. *Community policing strategies*. Washington, DC: Police Foundation.

POLICE IN URBAN AMERICA, 1860–1920

During the period following the Civil War, American policing developed the form and character that was to carry it into the 1980s. Uniformed police departments in the fifty-seven largest cities had been established between 1850 and 1880 (Monkkonen 1982, 54–57). Most cities had their own municipal police departments by the end of the nineteenth century. The social, political, and economic forces of the period between 1860 and 1920 defined the nature and scope of the police institution. By the 1920s, an outline of the parameters of police authority, a blueprint of the administrative structure of the police organization, and a rough approximation of the police function had emerged.

Although these characteristics developed more as a result of historical trial and error than careful planning, they collectively represented a foundation of policing that is recognizable to most people today. It is not an overstatement to say that in order to understand the strengths and weaknesses of American policing in the 1980s, one must be knowledgeable about the complex history of the police institution.

The purpose of this article is to present a historical analysis and overview of the significant themes surrounding the history of the police between 1860 and 1920. Details of that history will not be presented here, since they are available in the sources cited. Although much work remains to be done, available historical research provides a rich source of information about specific departments (Conley 1977; Monkkonen 1982).

Urban Conditions

Cities created police departments during a period of American history characterized by massive social change brought about by industrialization, immigration, and urbanization. Between 1860 and 1910, the modern American city emerged as the total population of the United States tripled to 92 million. The number of people living in cities grew from a low of 5% in the early nineteenth century to more than 45% by 1910. The largest cities—Boston, New York, and Philadelphia—had fewer than a hundred thousand people in the early nineteenth century but more than a million by 1890 (Johnson 1979, 4; Lane 1975, 161). This growth did not occur just on the eastern seaboard. Midwestern cities such as St. Louis, Cleveland, and Detroit ranked fourth, sixth, and ninth, respectively, by 1910. Chicago, which was eighth in 1860 with a population of a hundred thousand, moved to second place by 1910 with a population of more than two million.

Population shifts and immigration rates increased during prosperity and decreased during economic recessions. The resultant strains produced by these economic and population shifts created new challenges for the cities that had been organized and operated on a model more appropriate to the preurban period of the eighteenth century.

One of the new challenges was the need to address the problem of maintaining order in the cities. Cities such as New York, Boston, and Philadelphia created their uniformed police organizations during a period of great social and political turmoil. Some cities experienced riots, others saw rising property crimes, still others had social problems with immigrants and a mobile population. These problems varied in intensity and importance from city to city, but all cities experienced the effects of industrialization and urbanization in some form. Population growth mushroomed, and the demands on urban government for services increased dramatically.

There was a need for an effective order maintenance institution. The constable and watch systems of the eighteenth century did not contribute to a sense of security for the community and were not designed to address a preventive role. The constable was attached to the courts and did not serve as an official of city government. The constable–watch system did not act to prevent crime but operated on a reactive basis. For a fee, constables would investigate a crime after the fact and report to the victim who was paying the reward. This form of entrepreneurial policing, although beneficial to some, simply could not address the changing levels of disorder and crime (Lane 1975, 8–10; Richardson 1978, 17–19).

Theories on the Creation of Police

Historical research on the police has increased in quantity and quality in the past decade. Prior to the 1970s, histories of the police fell into the category of anecdotal or organizational descriptions with little analytical content or generalization (Conley 1977). Recent research has attempted to place police development in a larger context of the times, but more work on synthesizing and generalization is needed (Monkkonen 1982, 575).

There are three standard conceptual frameworks for examining the history of the police (Monkkonen 1981b, 49–61). One explanation for the rise of the urban police is that crime rose to such unprecedented levels that the constable–watch system was incapable of adjusting to the pressures of industrialization and urbanization and collapsed (Johnson 1979). There is no historical evidence that crime was rising, and if the evidence existed, it would have been verified by arrest data, which in turn would argue for the effectiveness of the traditional constable–watch system.

A second explanation argues that the riots of the early nineteenth century created such fears among the populace that alternative means of riot suppression were sought. Not willing to establish a standing army because of its potential threat to liberty, Americans created a paramilitary organization. This new police force contributed a visibility and continuity lacking in the traditional constable–watch system, presenting an organized show of force when required during civil disorders, but also allowed for civil control over the organization. The difficulty with this appealing interpretation is that only a few cities had riots before they established the new police, and even in these cities there was no connection between the riots and the creation of the police. The causal connection between riots and the establishment of the American police has yet to be proved.

Another explanation is that the elites feared the rising number of and threat from poor immigrants (Lane 1975, 23–25; Richardson 1970, 23–50). Whether it was a fear of the destruction of their societal values, a fear for their property, or a fear of the loss of control of the urban social order, the argument is that the elites established the police to control the "dangerous classes." This interpretation claims that the police served a social control function, while others claim a class control function (Harring 1983). The social control interpretation lacks evidence that connects this goal to the intent of the nineteenth-century proponents of the police.

The newest explanation for the creation of a uniformed police argues that the police represented just one of many urban government agencies created to provide services to meet the changing demands on city governments—just one example of the growth of "urban service bureaucracies" (Monkkonen 1981b, 55), such as those concerned with health, fire, and sewage. As city governments began to absorb a variety of these services once provided by entrepreneurs, they established bureaucracies to deliver them. Once larger cities adopted these models, other cities followed. Smaller cities learned of the innovation and established uniformed police organizations as part of the national movement of expanding city government.

Urban uniformed police emerged as part of the movement that increased governmental responsibility for a variety of direct services to the public.

Although public concern with order, riots, and crime—as well as a growing fear of the "dangerous classes"—played a role in shaping the new police, these issues did not dominate the debate around the establishment of the police. These specifically threatening social problems contributed to the debate and subsequent development of the police, but they served as precipitating events in most cases and not as preconditions to the establishment of the police.

Finally, there is no historical evidence to support the theory that any one or any combination of these social problems caused cities to create a uniformed police. In fact, most cities did not experience these social problems, yet they also created uniformed police organizations during the late nineteenth century. We have been too quick to seek out some catastrophic event as a causal factor for the origin of a uniformed police when the historical evidence suggests that its development was an innovation that followed a process of expanding urban government.

Decentralization and Authority

The police in America are unique in the Western democracies in that they are organized at the level of local government, with no formal connection to a central government. The nature of federalism in the United States and the inherent deep distrust of a central government dictated that governments be as close to the people as possible. For this reason police departments across the country are organized along the jurisdictional lines of the municipal government, not those of the county, the region, or the state. The decentralized nature of the American police, to a degree unheard of in Western Europe, dates back to the late nineteenth century (Fogelson 1977, 14–15).

Another characteristic of the American police system was deep partisan ties. Unlike their counterparts in England, the American police fulfilled the society's expectation that the police be organically involved in the local community. This expectation was a local extension of the American commitment to democratic government. In order to control the potentially awesome power of the police, Americans placed administrative responsibility in locally elected officials, aldermen, rather than in mayors or police chiefs. As a result, police officers not only actively participated in local politics, they also gave their allegiance to locally elected officials. Local ward bosses appointed police officers, controlled promotions, and held police accountable. There was no bureaucratic buffer between the public and the police and, as a result, the police reflected and acted out community tensions.

They also reflected the political conflicts of the day. Political power and the control of the cities shifted back and forth between the coalition of white Anglo-Saxon Protestants and rural legislators, and the urban political machines dominated by ethnic immigrants. The political struggle between these power groups directly shaped the police in modern America. Unlike their counterparts in England, who attempted to remain neutral, the American police sided with the majority during political conflicts. First, American police lacked any identification with a national symbol of law and thus had no formally defined authority upon which to base a position of neutrality. Political disorders were local in nature, and the threat was to local institutions and values. Second, conflicts in urban America were ethnicity based, not class based, so the visibility and identity of the majority was clear. Workers joined the upper class in their fear of and willingness to control the foreign elements, with their strange cultures and different religions.

As a result of these conditions, the police represented the majority and upheld the existing political institution of representative democracy. They felt little pressure to remain neutral to transcend social conflicts. This historical context had long-term implications because these conditions shaped the definition of authority of the police that is still applicable today.

The distinguishing characteristic of American policing is that police authority is personal and guided by popular control rather than the formal standards of the rule of law. Police authority emanates from the political majority of the citizens, not from abstract notions of law. Authority rested on a local and partisan base within limited legal and symbolic standards and was legitimized by informal public expectations (Haller 1976, 303–24). Because the police rested their authority on the basic principles of democratic government, closeness to the citizens, and informal power rather than bureaucratic rules and legal standards, they did not represent an impartial legal system, and they had wide discretionary powers (Johnson 1979, 184–85; Richardson 1978, 285).

This combination of the need to rely on personal authority and their wide discretionary powers led the police to develop an "arrogant insistence on a respectful acknowledgment of their authority" (Johnson 1979, 136). Failure to give prompt attention to police commands could result in an arrest or physical harm to a citizen. Police had only vague notions of how to do their job, and thus "personalized decision became the fundamental tool of policing" (Johnson 1979, 141–85). Yet the police also relied on cooperation from the public, partly because of their close social and political ties to the people on their beats and partly because of their need to maintain a level of order defined by the local neighborhood. As a result of these structural influences on the definition of police authority and the use of discretion, the application of police power resulted in a growing "dependence on the police to regulate the tensions of urban society" (Johnson 1979, 143).

The combination of decentralization, local political ties, and a reliance on popular authority shaped how the police performed, or did not perform, their functions. Brutality was widespread and was either generally accepted or ignored by the larger community. Although corruption contradicted official morality, it existed on such a large scale that it was not difficult for a reformer to raise a hue and cry. Inside police departments, promotions were bought and sold, retirements with full pensions could be had for a fee, and even assignments that had the potential for graft carried a price in the corrupt market. Outside the departments, employers and factory owners bought the services of the public police to break labor picket lines by dispersing or arresting picketers. In some situations the police actually worked for the employer or company owner as anti-labor enforcers.

The police also used their official role in counting ballots, selecting polling sites, and verifying voter registration lists to guarantee that their alderman won the election. There is no question that the historical record is peppered with examples of brutality and corruption and that many people suffered at the hands of the police. What we don't know is how functional this corruption may have been. One author suggests that it was a functional and also a logical extension of the informal political process of the time. Corruption provided a way of benefiting politicians for public service to their constituency and a degree of flexibility that allowed a wide variety of cultures and lifestyles to coexist in the urban environment, and it helped to modify official behavior (Richardson 1978, 186–287).

In spite of the contemporary charges and countercharges of corruption in the urban policing of the last half of the nineteenth century, which have to be viewed in the context of the intense political atmosphere of the era, there is evidence that support for the police institution did exist. The record, of course, is not clear. Competent and compassionate policing, heroic acts, and trustworthy officers who had good relationships with the citizens are not the stuff that ends up in official records, newspaper editorials, or reports of investigating committees. Yet from about 1860 until 1900, police departments had hundreds more applicants than positions available, and the earlier high turnover of officers subsided and stabilized by the last decade of the century.

Although politicians viewed urban police departments as agencies for the distribution of patronage, the competency and intelligence level of officers appeared to be average. The taxpayers approved attractive retirement pensions and paid salaries that competed well with contemporary wage rates. For example, the average police officer earned an annual salary of about $1,200 in the 1870s, which was $400–$600 more than that earned by skilled tradesmen and workers in manufacturing. These wages and the attractiveness of the job deteriorated around the turn of the century. Much of that change was probably due to the constantly changing economic conditions and the difficulty of performing the police function.

Role

If the police role originally was to prevent crime, there is little evidence that it became their primary function between 1860 and 1900. Indeed, created in the midst of social upheaval from rising immigrant populations and from the effects of the industrial revolution, the police absorbed tasks related more to social services than crime control. "Demands of the populace and by representatives of local government" shaped the duties of the police (Lane 1975, 119).

The police responded to the demands of the urban poor in a variety of ways. They provided free overnight lodging to the homeless immigrants, managed soup kitchens, responded to inquiries from mothers about their lost children, participated in controlling local elections, controlled the distribution of vice through their arrest patterns, and otherwise absorbed a variety of functions that tended to serve the lower classes. By performing these tasks, the police of the late nineteenth century contributed to urban order by mediating class conflicts and managing tensions in the urban community. Crime control was not a primary function of the police, nor was it a primary contributing factor to urban order.

This is not to say that nineteenth-century American police did not address criminal behavior in urban America. The data on the exact level of criminal activity for this period are either not available or very unreliable, but they acknowledge that crime peaked in the 1860s and 1870s (Lane 1975, 144). As is true today, crime patterns varied spatially and changed over time. Most of the criminal activity occurred in the heart of a city, which created some problems for the police. If they concentrated their forces in that area, citizens in outlying areas complained of not being sufficiently protected. On the other hand, commercial leaders obviously demanded more police in the center of the city. The police constantly had to balance their response to these contrasting political pressures.

Criminal activity was lively, and the police did respond. In the early nineteenth century, the primary crimes were burglary and arson. The later period saw increased activity in pickpocketing, theft, burglary, and vice. Criminals plied their trades, but there was no attempt to eradicate crime. The police regulated crime, which seemed to satisfy the community and to serve police objectives. The police worked closely with the criminal element to keep crime at an acceptable and nonthreatening level to avoid a public outcry or pressure from community elites. Vice was not suppressed; it was licensed by the police. Some of these conditions included payoffs to officers, keeping undesirable establishments out of middle- and upper-class neighborhoods, and maintaining an orderly place of business. The criminal was not totally secure, however, for there was a political need to make arrests, not all cops were crooked, and periodic enforcement crackdowns did occur. The overall evidence, however, does not portray the urban police as a crime fighting or primarily law enforcement institution.

From 1900 to 1920 and beyond, reformers attempted to change the police from a catch-all service agency of urban government to a specialized crime control bureaucracy. This transformation occurred in reaction to larger changes in urban America. The constituency of the police—the sick, poor, migrants, unemployed, mentally ill—began to have their own agencies of assistance because of the development of specialized organizations in the broad social services area. The change resulted, in part, from a national reform movement led by the Progressives, who argued for clean government, professional government employees, and rationalized and specialized governmental structure. The result was a reversal of the precinct-based, decentralized structure of the police organization, an upgrading of personnel through civil service requirements, and a change in function from maintaining urban order to crime control (Fogelson 1977, 92–116).

By the early twentieth century, this impetus for police reform came from within its ranks. The coalition of civic, religious, and commercial groups that led the reforms of the late nineteenth century gave way to leaders from the police field after the turn of the century. This period of reform has been labeled the second wave of reform (Fogelson 1977, 166–82) or the second transformation of the police (Monkkonen 1981b, 148–50). These leaders concluded that the police function was spread too thin and that the organization was a catch-all agency that absorbed too many social service responsibilities. They argued that these responsibilities detracted from what they saw as the primary goal of the police, crime control.

Relying on a model of professionalism, police leaders pushed for more centralization in the administration of the departments by lengthening the chief's tenure, developed a model that organized the departments along functional rather than geographic lines in order to close precincts and lessen the political influence of ward aldermen, and hoped to insulate the administration from politics by demanding more autonomy in controlling the police. These reformers hoped to remove police decision making from the ordinary citizen and place it in a rule-bound bureaucracy. They also proposed tougher entry requirements, increased salaries, and expanded promotional opportunities. These changes established a new image of the police based on a vocational, not a political, model and demanded a commitment from the officers in the organization.

The result of these reforms carried the police into the 1980s. They narrowed their functional responsibility to crime control and they changed their image from a social service agency to that of a crime fighting organization. The cost of that success was high, however, and for the past two decades those reforms have been questioned. The police succeeded in insulating themselves from the public, but they have also become isolated. The image of a crime control agency has had to be manipulated because of the impossibility of achieving that self-imposed mandate. The professional model they advocated has developed only at the top of police organizations; rank-and-file unions have filled the gap at the lower levels. The challenge of the next generation of police leaders will be to address the legacy of the reforms implemented between 1860 and 1920.

Conclusion

The formation of the urban police in America in the nineteenth century and the reforms attempted through 1920 represented a societal acknowledgment that the police function is vital to the well-being of the cities. This vitality emanated from the role played by the police in contributing to an orderly environment within which cities expanded, populations grew, and political processes developed.

That role, although cloudy, is still vital today. The lessons and legacy of the period from 1860 to 1920 are crucial to an understanding of the current pressures on the police. The reliance on personal authority rather than formal standards of the legal culture combined with the American citizen's unwillingness to accept governmental power without question places the police in the position of having to justify their actions in each police–citizen encounter. This climate contributes to an increase in community tensions and confrontations. The historical record shows that over time the police have learned to use their wise discretionary powers to ameliorate that tension.

The close linkage between the police and local politics, a linkage that relies on a process of informal political influence, allows the various publics to influence police policy and actions, but it also places the police in the position of choosing between groups. History informs us that the American urban police emerged as representatives of the political majority and have always sided with that majority. Again, the historical record suggests strongly that the police used their wide discretion and their capacity to provide immediate service to minority groups to forestall and ameliorate the potentially harsh effect of unchecked majority political rule.

The failure of the professionalism movement to become institutionalized and to permeate the organization, let alone the whole field, created a natural tension between administrators and the rank-and-file. In addition, the historical record makes it clear that at best, the professionalism movement masked many of the inherent characteristics of urban policing, such as its parochialism, its basis in local politics, and its inability to prevent crime. Current reformers who ignore that historical record are doomed to limited success or, quite possibly, failure.

JOHN A. CONLEY

See also **Boston Police Department; History of American Policing; Immigrant Communities and the Police; New York Police Department (NYPD); Philadelphia Police Department; Politics and the Police**

References and Further Reading

Carte, Gene, and Elaine H. Carte. 1975. *Police reform in the United States: The era of August Vollmer*. Berkeley: University of California Press.

Conley, John A. 1977. Criminal justice history as a field of research: A review of the literature, 1960–1975. *Journal of Criminal Justice* 5 (1): 13–28.

Fogelson, Robert M. 1977. *Big-city police*. Cambridge, MA: Harvard University Press.

Haller, Mark. 1976. Historical roots of police behavior: Chicago, 1890–1925. *Law and Society Review* 10 (Winter): 303–24.

Harring, Sidney L. 1983. *Policing a class society: The experience of American cities, 1865–1915*. New Brunswick, NJ: Rutgers University Press.

Johnson, David R. 1979. *Policing the urban underworld: The impact of crime on the development of the American police, 1800–1887*. Philadelphia: Temple University Press.

———. 1982. The origins and structure of intercity criminal activity 1840–1920: An interpretation. *Journal of Social History* 15 (4): 593–605.

Lane, Roger. 1975. *Policing the city: Boston, 1822–1885*. New York: Atheneum Press.

Monkkonen, Eric H. 1981a. A disorderly people: Urban order in the nineteenth and twentieth centuries. *Journal of American History* 68 (3): 539–59.

———. 1981b. *Police in urban America, 1860–1920*. Cambridge, MA: Harvard University Press.

———. 1982. From cop history to social history: The significance of the police in American history. *Journal of Social History* 15 (4): 575–91.

Richardson, James F. 1970. *The New York police: Colonial times to 1901*. New York: Oxford University Press.

Schneider, John C. 1980. *Detroit and the problem of order, 1830–1880: A geography of crime, riots, and policing*. Lincoln: University of Nebraska Press.

Walker, Samuel. 1977. *A critical history of policy reform*. Lexington, MA: Lexington.

POLICE LEGAL LIABILITIES: OVERVIEW

Police legal liabilities emanate from a variety of sources ranging from state to federal laws and carrying civil, criminal, and administrative sanctions. For the purpose of an overview, legal liabilities may be classified as in Table 1.

These liabilities apply to all public officers, not just to law enforcement personnel. Probation and parole officers, jailers, prison officials, and other personnel in the criminal justice system are likewise liable. An officer may be liable under any or all of the categories, based on what may essentially be a single act, if the act is serious and all elements that trigger liability are present. The double jeopardy prohibition of the Fifth Amendment does not apply because double jeopardy arises only in criminal prosecutions for the same offense by the same jurisdiction.

Although various legal remedies are available to the public, as the categories in the table indicate, plaintiffs are inclined to use two remedies against police officers. This discussion will therefore focus on those two liability sources to the exclusion of others. These sources are (1) civil liability under state tort law and (2) civil liability under federal law (42 U.S.C. Sec. 1983—also known as Civil Rights Cases).

Table 1   Classification of Police Legal Liabilities

	I. Under State Law	II. Under Federal Law
A. Civil Liabilities	1. State tort law	1. Title 42 of U.S.C. Sec. 1983—Civil Action for Deprivation of Civil Rights
	2. State civil rights law	2. Title 42 of U.S.C. Sec. 1985—Conspiracy to Interfere with Civil Rights
		3. Title 42 of U.S.C. Sec. 1981—Equal Rights Under the Law
B. Criminal Liabilities	1. State penal code provisions specifically aimed at public officers for such crimes as (a) official oppression (b) official misconduct (c) violation of the civil rights of prisoners	1. Title 18 of U.S.C. Sec. 242—Criminal Liability for Deprivation of Civil Rights
	2. Regular penal code provisions punishing criminal acts such as assault, battery, false arrest, serious bodily injury, homicide, and so forth	2. Title 18 of U.S.C. Sec. 241—Criminal Liability for Conspiracy to Deprive a Person of Rights.
		3. Title 18 of U.S.C. Sec. 245—Violation of Federally Protected Activities.
C. Administrative Liabilities	1. Agency rules or guidelines on the state or local level (vary from one agency to another)	1. Federal agency rules or guidelines (vary from one agency to another)

Civil Liability under State Tort Law

Tort is defined as a civil wrong in which the action of one person causes injury to the person or property of another, in violation of a legal duty imposed by law. Three general categories of state tort based on a police officer's conduct are (1) intentional tort, (2) negligence tort, and (3) strict liability tort. Of these, only intentional and negligence torts are used in police cases. Strict liability torts are applicable in activities that are abnormally dangerous, such that they cannot be carried out safely even with reasonable care. Police work does not fall under strict liability tort; hence that category will not be discussed.

Intentional Tort

This occurs when an officer intends to bring some physical harm or mental effect upon another person. Intent is mental and difficult to establish; however, courts and juries are generally allowed to infer the existence of intent from the facts of the case. In police work, the kinds of intentional tort often brought against police officers are as follows:

- False arrest and false imprisonment. In a tort case for false arrest, the plaintiff alleges that the officer made an illegal arrest, usually an arrest without probable cause. False arrest also arises if the officer fails to arrest the "right" person named in the warrant.

An officer who makes a warrantless arrest bears the burden of proving that the arrest was in fact based on probable cause and that an arrest warrant was not necessary because the arrest came under one of the exceptions to the warrant rule. If the arrest is made with a warrant, the presumption is that probable cause exists, except if the officer obtained the warrant with malice, knowing that there was no probable cause [*Malley v. Briggs*, 106 S. Ct. 1092 (1986)]. Civil liability for false arrest in an arrest with a warrant is unlikely unless the officer serves a warrant that he or she knows to be illegal or unconstitutional.

False arrest is a separate tort from a false imprisonment, but in police tort cases the two are virtually identical in that arrest necessarily means confinement, which is in itself an element of imprisonment. In both cases, the individual is restrained or deprived of freedom without legal justification. They do differ, however, in that while false arrest leads to false imprisonment, false imprisonment is not necessarily the result of a false arrest.

The best defense in false arrest and false imprisonment cases is that the arrest or detention was justified and valid. An officer who makes an arrest with probable cause is not liable for false arrest simply because the suspect is later proved innocent, nor does liability exist if the arrest is made by virtue of a law that is later declared unconstitutional. In the words of the U.S. Supreme Court: "We agree that a police officer is not charged with predicting the future course of constitutional law" [*Pierson v. Ray*, 386 U.S. 555 (1967)]. In these cases, however, the officer must believe in good faith that the law was constitutional. Also, the fact that the arrested person is not prosecuted or is prosecuted for a different crime does not make the arrest illegal. What is important is that there be a valid justification for arrest and detention at the time those took place.

- *Assault and battery*. Although sometimes used as one term, assault and battery represent two separate acts. Assault is usually defined as the intentional causing of an apprehension of harmful or offensive conduct; it is the attempt or threat, accompanied by the ability to inflict bodily harm on another person. An assault is committed if the officer causes another person to think that he or she will be subjected to harmful or offensive contact. In contrast, battery is the intentional infliction of a harmful or offensive body contact. Given this broad definition, the potential for battery exists every time an officer applies force on a suspect or arrestee. The main difference between assault and battery is that assault is generally menacing conduct that results in a person's fear of imminently receiving a battery, while battery involves unlawful, unwarranted, or hostile touching—however slight. In some jurisdictions, assault is attempted battery.

The police are often charged with "brutality" or using "excessive force." In police work, the improper use of force usually constitutes battery. The general rule is that nondeadly force may be used by the police in various situations as long as such force is reasonable. Reasonable force, in turn, is that force that a prudent and cautious person would use if exposed to similar circumstances and is limited to the amount of force that is necessary to achieve valid and proper results. Any force beyond that necessary to achieve valid and proper results is punitive, meaning it punishes rather than controls.

The defense in assault and battery cases is that the use or threat of the use of force by the police was reasonable under the circumstances; however, what may be reasonable force to one judge or jury may not be reasonable to another. The use of reasonable force includes self-defense or defense of others by the police. The defense is available not only when an officer is actually attacked but also when the officer reasonably thinks he or she is in imminent danger of an attack.

- *Wrongful death.* This tort, usually established by law, arises whenever death occurs as a result of an officer's action or inaction. It is brought by the surviving family, relatives, or legal guardian of the estate of the deceased for pain, suffering, and actual expenses (such as expenses for the funeral) and for the loss of life to the family or relatives. In some states, the death of a person resulting from the police's use of deadly force comes under the tort of misuse of weapons. An officer has a duty to use not merely ordinary care but a high degree of care in handling a weapon, otherwise he or she becomes liable for wrongful death.

    The use of deadly force is governed by departmental policy or, in the absence thereof, by state law that must be strictly followed. The safest rule for any agency to prescribe is that deadly force should be used only in cases of self-defense or when the life of another person is in danger and the use of deadly force is immediately necessary to protect that life. Agency rules or state law, however, may give the officer more leeway in the use of deadly force. These rules are to be followed unless declared unconstitutional.

    The use of deadly force to apprehend fleeing felons has been severely limited by the U.S. Supreme Court in *Tennessee v. Garner* [471 U.S. 1 (1985)]. In that case the Court said that deadly force is justified only when the officer has probable cause

to believe that the suspect poses a threat of serious physical harm, either to the officer or to others. Thus, if the suspect threatens the officer with a weapon or there is probable cause to believe that the suspect has committed a crime involving the infliction or threatened infliction of serious physical harm, the officer may use deadly force if necessary to prevent escape and if, when feasible, some warning has been given. Therefore, "fleeing felon" statutes in many states are valid only if their application comports with the requirements of *Tennessee v. Garner*. The use of deadly force to prevent the escape of a misdemeanant should not be resorted to except in cases of self-defense or in defense of the life of another person.

- *Intentional infliction of emotional distress.* This takes place when an officer inflicts severe emotional distress on a person through extreme and outrageous conduct that is intentional or reckless. Physical harm need not follow. What is "extreme and outrageous" is difficult to determine; moreover, the effect of an act may vary according to the plaintiff's disposition or state of mind. Most state appellate courts that have addressed the issue have held, however, that more than rudeness or isolated incidents is required. There is need for the plaintiff to allege and prove some kind of pattern or practice over time rather than just isolated incidents. The case law on this tort is still developing, but it has already found acceptance in almost every state.

Negligence Tort

For tort purposes, negligence may be defined as the breach of a common law or statutory duty to act reasonably toward those who may foreseeably be harmed by one's conduct. This general definition may be modified or superseded by specific state law that provides for a different type of conduct, usually more restrictive than this definition, in particular acts.

Some of the negligence torts to which police officers may be exposed are as follows:

- *Negligent operation of motor vehicle.* Police department manuals usually provide guidelines on the proper use of motor vehicles. These guidelines, if valid, constitute the standard by which the actions of police officers are likely to be judged. In some states departmental policies are admitted in court merely as evidence, while in other states the departmental policy is controlling.
- *Negligent failure to protect.* Police officers in general are not liable for injury to someone whom the police failed to protect; neither is any duty owed by the police to specific individuals to prevent crime. The police, however, have a general duty to protect the public as a whole and to prevent crime. What this means is that the police generally cannot be held liable if a member of society becomes a victim of crime. The exceptions, based on developing case law, are as follows:

1. If a "special relationship" has been created. Example: The police told a mother that there was nothing they could do when she asked them to protect her daughter from her father. A court order for protection had been issued by a family court; hence, a "special relationship" had been created because of such judicial order [*Sorichetti v. City of New York*, 482 N.E. 2d 70 (1985)]. Some states, however, are doing away with the requirement of "special relationship" and are following a trend toward liability based mainly on the general duty

of police to protect the public at large. Should this trend continue, possible liability based on negligent failure to protect will be an even bigger concern for officers in the future than it is now.

2. Where the police affirmatively undertake to protect an individual but negligently fail to perform. Example: The police assure a victim, who calls on a 911 emergency line, that assistance will be forthcoming; the victim relies on the promised assistance, but the assistance never comes and damage is suffered.

Whether the police are liable for injuries to third parties caused by drunken drivers who are allowed by the police to drive has caused a split in court decisions; some courts impose liability while others do not. This area of law is fast developing and changes may be forthcoming in the immediate future.

Civil Liability under Federal Law (Civil Rights or Section 1983 Cases)

The Law

Liability under federal law is based primarily on Title 42 of the U.S. Code, Section 1983, entitled Civil Action for Deprivation of Rights. This law provides as follows:

Every person who, under color of any statute, ordinance, regulation, custom, or usage, of any State or Territory, subjects, or causes to be subjected, any citizen of the United States or other persons within the jurisdiction thereof to the deprivation of any rights, privileges, or immunities secured by the Constitution and laws, shall be liable to the party injured in an action at law, suit in equity, or other proper proceeding for redress.

This law, usually referred to as the Civil Rights Law or Section 1983, is the most

953

frequently used remedy in the arsenal of legal liability statutes available to plaintiffs. The law, originally passed by Congress in 1871, was then known as the Ku Klux Klan law because it sought to control the activities of state officials who were also members of that organization. For a long time, however, the law was given a limited interpretation by the courts and was seldom used. In 1961, the Court adopted a much broader interpretation, thus opening wide the door for liability action in federal courts. Among the reasons for the popularity of this statute are that Section 1983 cases are usually filed in federal court, where discovery procedures are more liberal and attorney's fees are recoverable by the "prevailing" plaintiff in accordance with the Attorney's Fees Act of 1976.

Basic Elements of a Section 1983 Lawsuit

The two basic elements of a Section 1983 lawsuit are as follows:

1. *The defendant must be acting under color of law.* This means that the misuse of power possessed by virtue of the law and made possible only because the wrongdoer is clothed with the authority of the state cannot be tolerated. The difficulty is that while it is usually easy to identify acts that are wholly within the term "color of law" (as when an officer makes a search or an arrest while on duty), there are some acts that are not as easy to categorize. Examples: P, a police officer, works during off hours as a private security agent in a shopping center. While in that capacity, P shoots and kills a fleeing shoplifter. Was P acting under color of law? Or suppose an officer arrests a felon during off hours and when not in uniform. Is the officer acting under color of law?

   The answer usually depends upon job expectation. Many police depart-

ments (by state law, judicial decision, or agency regulation) expect officers to respond as officers twenty-four hours a day. In these jurisdictions any arrest made on or off duty comes under the requirement of color of law. In the case of police officers who "moonlight," courts have held that their being in police uniform while acting as private security agents, their use of a gun issued by the department, and the knowledge by department authorities that the officer has a second job all indicate that the officer is acting under color of law. On the other hand, acts by an officer that are of a purely private nature are outside the color of state law even if done while on duty.

   The courts have interpreted the term "color of law" broadly to include local laws, ordinances, or agency regulations; moreover, the phrase does not mean that the act was authorized by law. It suffices that the act appeared to be lawful even if it was not in fact authorized; hence, an officer acts under color of law even if the officer exceeds lawful authority. Moreover, it includes clearly illegal acts committed by the officer by reason of position or opportunity.

2. *There must be a violation of a constitutional or of a federally protected right.* Under this requirement, the right violated must be given by the U.S. Constitution or by federal law. Rights given only by state law are not protected under Section 1983. Example: The right to a lawyer during a police lineup prior to being charged with an offense is not given by the Constitution or by federal law; therefore, if an officer forces a suspect to appear in a lineup without a lawyer, the officer is not liable under Section 1983. If such right is given by state law, its violation may be actionable under state law or agency regulation, not under Section 1983.

Defenses in Civil Liability Cases

Various legal defenses are available in state tort and Section 1983 cases. Three of the most often used defenses are (1) probable cause, (2) official immunity, and (3) good faith.

The Probable Cause Defense

This is a limited defense in that it applies only in cases of false arrest, false imprisonment, and illegal searches and seizures, either under state tort law or Section 1983. For the purpose of a legal defense in Section 1983 cases, probable cause simply means "a reasonable good faith belief in the legality of the action taken" [*Rodriguez v. Jones*, 473 F.2nd 599 (5th Cir. 1973)]. That expectation is lower than the Fourth Amendment definition of probable cause, which is that probable cause exists "when the facts and circumstances within the officers' knowledge and of which they have reasonably trustworthy information are sufficient in themselves to warrant a man of reasonable caution in the belief that an offense has been or is being committed" [*Brienigar v. United States*, 338 U.S. 160 (1949)].

The Official Immunity Defense

Official immunity is composed of three categories: absolute, quasi-judicial, and qualified.

- *Absolute immunity*. This means that a civil liability suit, if brought, is dismissed by the court without going into the merits of the plaintiff's claim. Absolute immunity does not apply to police officers. It applies only to judges, prosecutors, and legislators. There is one instance, however, when police officers enjoy absolute immunity from civil liability. In *Briscoe v. LaHue* [460 U.S. 325 (1983)], the Supreme Court held that police officers could not be sued under Section 1983 for giving perjured testimony against a defendant in a state criminal trial. The Court said that under common law, trial participants—including judges, prosecutors, and witnesses—were given absolute immunity for actions connected with the trial process. Therefore, police officers also enjoy absolute immunity when testifying, even if such testimony is perjured. The officer may be criminally prosecuted for perjury, but that seldom happens.

- *Quasi-judicial immunity*. This means that certain officers are immune if performing judicial-type functions, but not when performing other functions connected with their office. An example is a probation officer when preparing a presentence investigation report upon order of the judge. Quasi-judicial immunity does not apply to police officers because the functions officers perform are executive and not judicial in nature.

- *Qualified immunity*. The qualified immunity doctrine has two related meanings. One is that the immunity defense applies to an official's discretionary (or optional) acts, meaning acts that require personal deliberation and judgment. The second and less complex meaning relates qualified immunity to the "good faith" defense. Under this concept, a public officer is exempt from liability if he or she can demonstrate that the actions taken were reasonable and performed in good faith within the scope of employment.

In *Malley v. Briggs* [106 S. Ct. 1092 (1986)], the Supreme Court said that a police officer is entitled only to qualified immunity in Section 1983 cases. The *Malley* case is significant in that the Court refused to be swayed by the officer's argument that policy considerations require absolute immunity when a police officer applies for and obtains a warrant, saying that qualified immunity provides sufficient protection for police officers because under current decisions the officer is not liable anyway if he or she acted in an "objectively reasonable manner." The Court has therefore made clear that in the immediate future, absolute immunity will not be available to police officers but only to judges, prosecutors, and legislators.

The Good Faith Defense

This is perhaps the defense used most often in Section 1983 cases, although it is not available in some state tort lawsuits. Good faith means that the officer acted with honest intentions under the law (meaning lawfully) and in the absence of fraud, deceit, collusion, or gross negligence. The definition of good faith, however, may vary from one state to another—either by judicial decision or legislation. In some cases, state law may provide that officials acting under certain circumstances enjoy good faith immunity.

Courts and juries vary in their perception of what is ultimately meant by good faith, but chances are that the good faith defense will likely be upheld in the following instances:

1. If the officer acted in accordance with agency rules and regulations.
2. If the officer acted pursuant to a statute that is believed to be reasonably valid but is later declared unconstitutional.
3. If the officer acted in accordance with orders from a superior that are believed to be reasonably valid.
4. If the officer acted in accordance with advice from legal counsel, as long as the advice is believed to be reasonably valid

Defendants in Civil Liability Cases—Legal Representation and Indemnification

Plaintiffs generally use the "shotgun approach" in liability lawsuits. This means that plaintiffs will include as parties-defendant everyone who may have any possible connection with the case. Example: A police officer, while on patrol, shoots and kills a suspect. The victim's family will probably sue under Section 1983 or state tort law and include as defendants the officer, his or her immediate supervisor, the police chief, and the city or county. The allegation may be that the officer is liable because he or she pulled the trigger; the supervisor, police chief, and the city are also liable because of failure to properly train, direct, supervise, or assign or because of an unconstitutional policy or practice. The legal theory is that some or all of the defendants had something to do with the killing; hence, liability attaches. It is for the court during the trial to sort out culpability and assign fault.

Individual Officer as Defendant

The officer is an obvious liability target because he or she allegedly committed the violation. The officer will be a defendant whether he or she acted within or outside the scope of authority. Most state agencies, by law or official policy, provide representation to state law enforcement officers in civil actions. Such representation is usually undertaken by the state attorney general, who is the legal counsel of the state.

The situation is different in local law enforcement agencies. In most counties, cities, towns, or villages, there is no policy that requires the agency to defend public officials in liability lawsuits. Legal representation by the agency is usually decided on a case-by-case basis. This means that the local agency is under no obligation to provide a lawyer should an officer be sued. If the agency provides a lawyer, it will probably be the district attorney, the county attorney, or another lawyer working in some capacity with the government. In some cases, the officer is allowed to choose a lawyer, and the lawyer's fees are paid by the agency. This is an ideal arrangement but is unpopular with agencies because of the cost factor.

Supervisors as Defendant

Although lawsuits against law enforcement officers are usually brought against field officers, a recent trend among plaintiffs is to include supervisory officials as defendants. The theory is that field officers act for the department and therefore what they do reflects departmental policy and practice.

There are definite advantages to the plaintiff in including supervisors in a liability lawsuit. First, lower-level officers may not have the financial resources to satisfy a judgment, nor are they in a position to prevent similar future violations by other officers. Second, chances of financial recovery are enhanced if supervisory personnel are included in the lawsuit. The higher the position of the employee, the closer the plaintiff gets to the "deep pockets" of the county or state agency. Third, inclusion of the supervisor may create inconsistencies in the legal strategy of the defense, hence strengthening the plaintiff's claim against one or more of the defendants.

If the supervisor does not want to defend the officer, a conflict of interest ensues. In these cases, the agency makes a choice, and that choice will probably be to defend the supervisor. There is nothing the officer can do about that choice, unless formal policy requires the agency to undertake the officer's defense even in these cases.

Governmental Agencies as Defendant

Most courts have decided that where supervisory liability extends to the highest ranking individual in the department, municipality or agency liability follows. The inclusion of the governmental agency (specifically the city or county) as defendant is anchored in the "deep pockets" theory, meaning that while officers and supervisors may have a "shallow pocket," agencies have a deep pocket because they can always raise revenue through taxation.

States and state agencies generally cannot be sued under Section 1983, because they enjoy sovereign immunity under the Eleventh Amendment to the Constitution. This does not mean that state officials are immune from liability. Sovereign immunity extends only to the state and state agencies; state officials may be sued and held liable just like local officials. While states are generally immune from liability in Section 1983 cases because of the Eleventh Amendment, such protection has largely been terminated for liability purposes in state courts. This means that states may generally be sued under state tort for what their officers do.

Local agencies (referring to agencies below the state level) enjoyed sovereign immunity in Section 1983 cases until 1978. That year the Court decided that local agencies could be held liable under Section 1983 for what their employees do, thus depriving local governments of the sovereign immunity defense [*Monnell v. Department of Social Services*, 436 U.S. 658 (1978)]. The Court held in *Monnell* that the municipality will be liable if the unconstitutional action taken by the employee was caused by a municipal policy or custom. The Fifth Circuit Court of Appeals [*Webster v. City of Houston*, 735 F.2nd 838 (1984)] defines "policy or custom" as follows:

1. A policy statement, ordinance, regulation, or decision that is officially

adopted and promulgated by the municipality's law-making officers or by an official to whom the lawmakers have delegated policy-making authority; or

2. A persistent widespread practice of city officials or employees that, although not authorized by officially adopted and promulgated policy, is so common and well settled as to constitute a custom that fairly represents municipal policy.

There are instances when an officer or a supervisor cannot be held liable for damages but the agency or municipality may be. In *Owen v. City of Independence* [445 U.S. 622 (1980)], the Court said that a municipality sued under Section 1983 cannot invoke the good faith defense that is available to its officers and employees if its policies violate constitutional rights. In *Owen*, a police chief was dismissed by the city manager and city council for certain misdoings while in office. The police chief was not given any type of hearing or due process rights because the city charter under which the city manager and city council acted did not give him any rights prior to dismissal. The Court held that the city manager and members of the city council acted in good faith because they were authorized by the provisions of the city charter but that the city itself could not invoke the good faith defense.

In a 1985 decision, the Supreme Court ruled that a money judgment against a public officer "in his official capacity" imposes liability upon the employing agency, regardless of whether or not the agency was named as a defendant in the suit [*Brandon v. Holt*, 105 S. Ct. 873 (1985)]. In *Brandon*, the plaintiff alleged that although the director of the police department had no actual notice of the police officer's violent behavior, administrative policies were such that he should have known. The Court added that although

the director could be shielded by qualified immunity, the city could be held liable.

In a 1986 case, the Court decided that municipalities could be held liable in a civil rights case for violating constitutional rights on the basis of a single decision (as opposed to a "pattern of decisions") made by an authorized municipal policy maker [*Pembaur v. City of Cincinnati*, 475 U.S. 469 (1986)]. In this case the county prosecutor in effect made official policy and thereby exposed his municipal employer to liability by instructing law enforcement officers to make a forcible entry, without search warrant, of an office in order to serve capiases (a form of warrant issued by the judge) on persons thought to be there. The case was brought by a Cincinnati, Ohio, physician, based on an incident where law enforcement officers, under advice from the county prosecutor, broke down the door in his office with an ax. The officers were trying to arrest two of the doctor's employees who failed to appear before a grand jury. The Court decided that this violated the Fourth Amendment rights of the office owners and concluded that the City of Cincinnati could be held liable.

Can the Police Sue Back?

Can the police strike back by suing those who sue them? The answer is yes, and some departments are in fact striking back. The number of civil cases actually brought by the police against the public, however, has remained comparatively small. The reality is that although police officers may file tort lawsuits against arrestees or suspects, there are difficulties in doing that.

One is that in a tort case, the officer will have to hire his or her own lawyer. This necessitates financial expense that the officer cannot recover from the defendant. Should the officer file a tort case for damages, the chances of meaningful success may not be good because most of those who run afoul of the law and have encounters with the police are too poor to pay damages. Moreover, officers oftentimes refrain from filing civil cases for damages because it is less expensive and more convenient to get back at the suspect in a criminal case. Almost every state has provisions penalizing such offenses as deadly assault of a peace officer, false report to a police officer, resisting arrest or search, hindering apprehension or prosecution, and aggravated assault. These can be added to the regular criminal offense against the arrested person, thereby increasing the penalty or facilitating prosecution.

Finally, many officers feel that the harsh treatment they sometimes get from the public is part of police work and is therefore to be accepted without retaliation. Whatever the attitude, the police do have legal remedies available should they wish to exercise them.

Conclusion

Liability lawsuits have become an occupational hazard in policing. The days are gone when the courts refused to entertain cases filed by the public against police officers and agencies. The traditional "hands-off" policy by the courts is out; conversely, "hands-on" is in and will be with us in the foreseeable future.

The effects of liability litigations on policing are significant and controversial. Advocates maintain that liability lawsuits afford the public a needed avenue for redress against police excesses and that this, in turn, has led to accelerated police professionalization. Opponents argue, however, that liability lawsuits hamper police work and curtail police effectiveness and efficiency. Whatever the real or imagined effects, liability lawsuits are here to stay. It is a reality that has become part

of the price we pay for policing a free society.

ROLANDO V. DEL CARMEN

See also **Accountability; Complaints against Police; Deadly Force; Discretion; Excessive Force; Fear of Litigation**

References and Further Reading

Butler, E. 1983. Liability of municipalities for police brutality. *Tennessee Bar Journal* 19 (May): 21–29.

del Carmen, Rolando V. 1987. *Criminal procedure for law enforcement personnel.* Monterey, CA: Brooks/Cole.

Elliott, C. J. 1985/1986. Police misconduct: Municipal liability under Section 1983. *Kentucky Law Journal* 74 (3): 651–66.

Fordham Urban Law Journal. 1982/1983. Municipal liability for requiring unfit police officers to carry guns. 11: 1001–38.

Higginbotham, J. 1985. Defending law enforcement officers against personal liability in constitutional tort litigation. Parts I and II. *FBI Law Enforcement Bulletin* 54 (4): 24–31, and 54 (5): 25–31.

Littlejohn, E. J. 1982. Civil liability and the police officer: The need for new deterrents to police misconduct. *University of Detroit Journal of Urban Law* 58 (Spring): 365–431.

McCoy, C. 1984. Lawsuits against police— What impact do they really have? *Criminal Law Bulletin* 20 (1): 49–56.

Ohio Northern University Law Review. 1983. When police lie: Federal civil rights liability for wrongful arrest. 10 (Summer): 493–518.

Rittenmeyer, S. D. 1984. Vicarious liability in suits pursuant to 42 U.S.C. 1983: Legal myth and reality. *Journal of Police Science and Administration* 12 (3): 260–66.

Silver, I. 1986. *Police civil liability.* New York: Matthew Bender.

POLICE MEDIATION

Significant aspects of police intervention have always included intermediary work in response to requests for assistance in handling conflict situations. While these police interventions are actually similar to those undertaken by mediators, the term "mediation" has not typically been used to describe these police actions. For the most part, this is due to the fact that when officers have managed differences between disputing parties as a go-between, they have done so intuitively, informally, and inadvertently.

Since the 1970s, two developments have begun to transform the police use of mediation. First, police officers have been receiving a variety of more formal and deliberate training in mediation skills and techniques. As a result, they can more intentionally utilize mediation expertise in their intervention work. Second, police have increasing access to community-based mediation and dispute resolution resources. As a result, police are able to refer cases that are in need of more protracted intervention to mediation experts.

Mediation

Generally speaking, mediation refers to the intervention by a third party who assists disputing parties to work through their differences and to reach mutually agreed upon understandings (Moore 2003). Within this general framework, there are many variations of how mediation is conducted. Mediation is sensitive to mediator personality, styles, training, and philosophy as well as parties' issues and relationships and the context within which the intervention occurs. Some of these variations are subtle, others more conspicuous. For example, some mediators are very elicitive and ask the parties a variety of questions, while others are quite directive in guiding the parties throughout the session, some separate the parties, others do not, some set ground rules, others rely on the parties to decide how they would like to structure their interaction, some meet with parties before bringing them together, others do not.

As mediation has evolved, several schools of thought have emerged. Best known is the facilitative style, where mediators ask the parties questions as a way of moving the process along. Over the years, the facilitative style has been the most popular mediation style. With the increasing acceptance of mediation in court-connected programs, evaluative mediation has grown in popularity. Parallels have been made between evaluative mediators and arbitrators since evaluative mediators are more likely to provide recommendations, suggestions, or opinions. A third style that has gained traction is the transformative style. Transformative mediation builds on facilitative mediation but relies even more heavily on the parties to participate in the process and create the context for any transformation of their behavior. Finally, some mediators use narrative mediation by drawing stories out of the parties and helping them to change the stories so that the new story enables the parties to move on.

Central to mediation, regardless of style, are standards established to help guide mediators' conduct (see Association for Conflict Resolution 2005). To understand how police use of mediation challenges conventional mediation practice, it is important to identify a few of the core standards that are of particular interest to mediation practitioners. The first is self-determination, that is, the need for parties to make free and informed choices. Unlike judges who make decisions, mediators must leave the decision making up to the parties themselves. What mediators do is provide the structure for the parties to share their perspectives, generate options, assess the pros and cons of each option, and craft understandings about the future.

The second key standard noted here is confidentiality. In order to provide parties with an opportunity to share candidly, mediators generally ensure parties that they will not discuss with others information that parties share during the mediation session, unless the parties agree that the information should be revealed. For the most part, the only communication provided to those who are not a part of the mediation is any written understanding reached by the parties.

Finally, a third key standard is impartiality. Mediators must conduct their sessions free of favoritism, bias, or prejudice. They cannot take sides; otherwise, they will lose their credibility and ability to intervene effectively.

Police Work and Mediation

With the proliferation of interest in mediation worldwide, many innovative uses of mediation have emerged, especially with the widespread growth of community dispute resolution centers. According to the National Association for Community Mediation (NAFCM), there are more than 550 community dispute resolution programs in operation in the United States (NAFCM 2005). Since community dispute resolution programs aim to work closely with citizens to solve problems, reaching out to local police departments to discuss their services has been a common extension of their work. Depending on the jurisdiction, the community dispute resolution centers have provided officers with mediation awareness sessions as well as mediation skills training. They have also developed relationships with their local police departments so that police cases could be referred to their centers.

Police Officers as Mediators

As an intervention approach, mediation affords police officers an opportunity to empower members of the community. This is particularly useful for community- and problem-oriented policing, where officers are expected to work more closely and resourcefully with the community. Mediation provides them with useful tools and techniques.

When serving as mediators, police help the parties to communicate directly with each other, to think creatively about ways to manage their differences, and to sort through their options. As such, police do not assume their more traditional role of taking some action. Mediation, in fact, slows down their intervention approach since they must listen to each side and if appropriate to actually convene the parties face to face. In some instances, the police will have to shuttle repeatedly to assess the suitability of bringing the parties together. All of this is often occurring while the parties are in the midst of their emotionally charged exchanges.

Active listening is a core skill for police mediation. Police need to listen to each of the parties and let them know that they have been heard. This may mean paraphrasing, reframing, or summarizing what was said in language that helps the parties to understand the other side and to move on. It is crucial for police to remain patient, impartial, and resourceful while in the role of mediator. They need to do this while on the scene with the parties, bystanders, the media, and others looking on. In this context, the officers have little if any time to establish any trust with the parties, a core concept often referred to by mediators.

Police Officers as Referrers of Cases to Mediation

In those instances where police decide that they are not the appropriate interveners or the situation requires more protracted intervention, they can refer the matter to a variety of mediation experts. Best known of the mediation resources are the community dispute resolution programs. Here, mediators, usually volunteers from the community who have been trained, can provide assistance.

For police, having mediation resources available gives them access to additional places for referrals in the community. Instead of arresting or perhaps doing nothing, they can steer citizens to a forum where the underlying concerns triggering the episode can be discussed and explored. For the most part, the cases referred to the centers consist of the less serious criminal matters where individuals have an ongoing relationship and have agreed to work through their differences voluntarily. Community dispute resolution programs also handle felony case matters, but serious criminal matters are less likely to be referred by the police. If needed, the community dispute resolution programs can hold multiple sessions, follow up with the parties, and check on compliance regarding any agreements reached.

Research

While efforts to increase the police use of mediation and police referrals to community dispute resolution centers have proliferated, there continues to be a dearth of empirical data. Research on the use of mediation by police continues to be largely anecdotal and impressionistic. Among the better known police efforts in using mediation are the Hillsboro, Oregon, and Harrisburg, Pennsylvania, police departments.

In 1996, the Hillsboro Police Department created the Hillsboro Mediation Program as part of its community policing efforts with the assistance of a start-up grant from the Oregon Dispute Resolution Commission. The program has provided mediation skills training to members of the Hillsboro Police Department and local community members who volunteer as mediators. With the exception of selected cases such as mental illness, the influence of chemical substance, or criminal, violent, or abusive behavior, police officers have referred a wide range of situations to the program involving differences among neighbors, consumers and merchants, family members, and employees and employers. As a result of the program, police are able to utilize their resources more efficiently (Williams 1997).

The Harrisburg Police Department has referred nonviolent, neighborhood problems to the Neighborhood Dispute Settlement Center of Dauphin County, Pennsylvania. The program has resulted in a reduction of cost per call for the department as well as in more time for police to spend on "proactive policing" since the program releases the officers from managing time-consuming interpersonal conflicts (Shepherd 1995, 2).

A variety of other research related to police mediation is beginning to emerge. In their research on police use of mediation in New York State, Volpe and Phillips (2003) found that the vast majority of police training consists of brief mediation awareness sessions rather than protracted skills training. They also found that, in fact, 83% of the local dispute resolution centers report receiving referrals from the police. In a recent study in Baltimore, Charkoudian (2005) found that when police refer cases to mediation, there is a reduction in repeat police calls to conflict situations. In his research on the influence of referral source on mediation participation and outcomes, Hedeen (2002) found that disputants referred by more coercive sources such as the police and courts are more likely to participate in mediation. However, he also found that the pressure to try mediation did not influence the parties to try to reach agreements any more than those referred from noncoercive sources.

Challenges

Despite the increase in police use of mediation, a wide range of challenges continue to exist. For mediation to be valued as a core policing approach, a major paradigm shift would have to occur to implement an approach that departs from many of the conventional police practices. Mediation is a complex process. To learn all aspects of mediation, police would have to receive additional intensive training. The limited exposure to mediation provided at roll call or in isolated modules is insufficient to conduct mediation.

New reward structures that recognize and give credit to police who use mediation would have to be considered. Unlike traditional police work, where officers respond quickly and move on, mediation requires more protracted intervention that can be time consuming. In those instances where differences between parties are long standing, the challenges can be even more noteworthy since the police officers' contact with the parties occurs at the conflict site when the parties are absorbed in their differences and often surrounded by bystanders, allies, adversaries, and the media, all of whom are interested in the unfolding events.

Quantifying police use of mediation is more difficult to do than measuring arrests and summons. For example, how would an attempted mediation be counted, namely, one where a considerable amount of time was spent but no progress made toward agreements?

The nature of police work is such that the cornerstones of good mediation practice can be readily challenged. For instance, self-determination as subscribed to by mediation practitioners may not be possible. Unlike mediation in other contexts, the bottom line is that police officers can take action if necessary by using force or arresting individuals against their will.

Similarly, impartiality may be difficult for police officers. While they can attempt to remain impartial, depending on the nature of the matter they have been asked to respond to, they may have to take sides, particularly when they have to take an action such as arresting someone.

Confidentiality is not something that officers can readily provide. Police are accountable to the public. At a minimum, they need to file reports and maintain records of their interventions. Moreover, their interventions occur on the parties' turf with a variety of observers present.

Depending on the situation, it is almost impossible for officers to convene parties behind closed doors or out of hearing distance of others as practiced by mediation experts. Finally, confidentiality as provided by mediators may impair the ability of police to have access to pertinent information for any follow-up calls.

In those instances when police may want to refer some of their cases to mediation, there may not be any mediation resources available to police departments. While community dispute resolution centers have become widely available, they are still not present in every community.

The Future

The potential use of mediation by the police has not been fully tapped. Not only do the police have to address a variety of pertinent mediation-related issues regarding skills, training, and intervention styles, the public has to come to understand and accept police intervention that is markedly different from their traditional response. Of particular importance, additional research is needed to help identify what police can do as mediators to assist people in conflict, what works and what does not.

MARIA R. VOLPE

See also **Community-Oriented Policing: Practices; Conflict Management; Discretion; Dispute Resolution, Community; Role of the Police**

References and Further Reading

Association for Conflict Resolution. 2005. *Model standards of conduct for mediators.* http://www.acrnet.org.

Charkoudian, L. 2005. A quantitative analysis of the effectiveness of community mediation in decreasing repeat police calls for service. *Conflict Resolution Quarterly* 23: 87–98.

Hedeen, Timothy. 2002. Does the journey change the destination? The Influence of referral source on mediation participation and outcomes. *New York Mediator* (Winter).

Moore, C. 2003. *The mediation process: Practical strategies for resolving conflict.* 3rd ed. San Francisco: Jossey-Bass.

National Association for Community Mediation (NAFCM). 2005. http://www.nafcm.org.

Shepard, R. 1995. *Neighborhood dispute settlement center's program with City of Harrisburg Bureau of Police.* Executive Summary for Board of Directors, Neighborhood Dispute Settlement of Dauphin County.

Volpe, M. 1989. The police role. In *Mediation and criminal justice: Victims, offenders, and community,* ed. M. Wright and B. A. Galaway. Newbury Park, CA: Sage.

Volpe, M., and N. Phillips. 2003. Police use of mediation. *Conflict Resolution Quarterly* 21 (2): 263–67.

Walker, S., C. Archbold, and L. Herbst. 2002. *Mediating citizen complaints against police officers: A guide for police and community leaders.* Washington, DC: U.S. Government Printing Office.

Williams, P. 1997. Police and mediation: Win–win partnership. *Oregon Police Chief* (Fall): 24–26.

POLICE MISCONDUCT: AFTER THE RODNEY KING INCIDENT

In the aftermath of the infamous 1991 videotaped beating of Rodney King in Los Angeles, questions about the prevalence and type of police misconduct persist. Subsequent acts of police wrongdoing have contributed to increased citizen distrust of the police, civil liability for police agencies, and claims of a pattern of systemic corruption among American police organizations.

Police misconduct involves a wide variety of malpractice. These variations are influenced by many factors dependent upon the local police culture, organizational framework, and personal ethics of the officer involved (Klockars, Ivkovic, and Haberfeld 2004). Estimates of the type and prevalence of police misconduct vary considerably based upon the definitions and methods used to measure its occurrence (Adams 1996). Though many police deviance typologies exist, they commonly include improper police behavior involving use of force, misconduct, corruption, and abuse of authority (Barker and Carter 1994).

Police officers are able to wield considerable official power in areas such as arrest, search, and seizure. Broad discretion is an inherent element in police officers' decision making that contributes to the circumstances under which they choose to take enforcement actions. Often, these actions involve the use of different degrees of force and methods of handling evidence.

Several highly publicized incidences of police brutality and misconduct have occurred since 1991. Among these are the Amadou Diallo shooting and Abner Louima brutalization in New York, Chicago Police Area Two interrogation abuses, Los Angeles Police Rampart Division scandal, Inglewood excessive force case, and others. The continuation of acts of brutality, excessive force, and corruption suggest that the problem may stem from systemic elements within the police culture rather than the isolated misbehavior of a few "rogue cops" (Bandes 2001).

The Rodney King Incident Revisited

The 1991 King incident involved four Los Angeles Police Department (LAPD) officers who were videotaped beating Rodney King after a high-speed traffic chase. After an acquittal in California state court on charges of assault under color of authority, the four officers were tried in federal court for depriving King of his constitutional rights. Two of the officers, Sergeant Stacey Koon and Officer Lawrence Powell, were found guilty on some of the allegations. In the immediate aftermath of the King incident, several events occurred that defined the episode for years. Civil unrest erupted in Los Angeles once the state verdict became known; at the same time, area police departments launched separate internal investigations into allegations of extensive officer misconduct.

Authored by Warren Christopher, the famed Christopher Commission internal report found that a culture existed within the LAPD that tolerated or supported officer excessive use of force (Christopher 1991). Its conclusions validated accusations from members of the Los Angeles ethnic community that had charged officers with abuse for years. Data collected by the Christopher Commission revealed that a core group of forty-four officers had generated repeated citizen complaints but had failed to be effectively disciplined by the department.

In its recommendation the commission cites deficiencies in recruit selection, academy training, field training, implementation of community policing, and misconduct discipline. Their findings suggested that each of these factors contributed to police prejudice, misconduct, and excessive force (Christopher 1991). Though the King case has become synonymous with police customary misconduct, other episodes of wrongdoing have occurred.

High-Profile Police Misconduct Cases after Rodney King

Chicago's Area Two Interrogation Probe

After more than twenty years of complaints of torture by interrogated suspects, the Chicago Police Department investigated the methods used by its Area Two Violent Crimes Unit. Their investigation concluded that the unit, under the command of Jon Burge, used beating, burning, mock execution, and electric shocks to obtain confessions from mostly African American suspects. In 1993, Burge was fired and labeled as a "bad apple" responsible for the abuses. Numerous wrongful criminal convictions, from as far back as the 1980s, continue to be dismissed, and

former inmates are being awarded millions of dollars in civil judgments against individual officers and the Chicago Police Department stemming from the brutality.

New York Police Department's Louima and Diallo Cases

Two New York Police Department (NYPD) force incidents in the 1990s gained widespread publicity. In 1997, two NYPD officers brutalized Haitian immigrant Abner Louima following an arrest at a nightclub brawl. Louima was taken to Brooklyn's 70th Precinct station, where in retaliation for a mistaken belief that he had assaulted both officers during the arrest, Officer Charles Schwarz held him on the station bathroom floor while Officer Justin Volpe viciously sodomized Louima with a broomstick. Louima suffered severe injuries to his bowel and bladder. Several NYPD officers were charged in federal court with violating Louima's civil rights and perjury. Volpe received a fifteen-year sentence and Schwarz pled guilty to perjury and got a five-year term. The other officers were acquitted and Louima was awarded an $8.7 million civil settlement stemming from the attack.

The following year, four officers from the NYPD Street Crimes Unit, in a hail of forty-one bullets, killed an unarmed West African immigrant Amadou Diallo while he stood in the doorway of his apartment. The officers were acquitted of criminal conduct based upon their testimony that Diallo made a threatening motion that caused them to shoot. Though the officers were exonerated of criminal wrongdoing, the episode has often been cited by critics as an illustration of excessive police force.

Los Angeles Police Department Rampart Division Scandal

Members of the Los Angeles Police Department's Rampart Division antigang unit were implicated in one of the largest corruption scandals in U.S. history. The allegations against seventy Rampart officers involve acts of evidence planting, evidence tampering, theft, perjury, false prosecution, civil rights violation, and unjustified use of deadly force. In exchange for immunity on some charges, former officer Rafael Perez provided investigators information leading to the uncovering of widespread misconduct by Rampart officers.

During the investigations, it was discovered that Perez and partner Nino Durden unjustifiably shot, and then framed with a planted gun, Javier Ovando for assaulting them. Both Perez and Durden entered into plea bargains and received two and seven years in prison, respectively. The Rampart scandal has led to the reversal of more than one hundred wrongful convictions and is projected to cost in excess of $125 million in lawsuit settlements.

Inglewood, California, Police Excessive Force Case

Inglewood Police Department Officer Jeremy Morse was videotaped by a bystander slamming sixteen-year-old Donovan Jackson onto the trunk of a police car then punching the handcuffed suspect in the face. Officer Morse stated that the suspect grabbed his genitals while draped over the trunk, thus provoking the facial blow. The officers alleged that the videotape only showed the culmination of a series of events in which Jackson had resisted arrest. Misconduct investigations were immediately launched by local and federal officials. Officer Morse was charged with assault and his partner Bijan Darvish with filing a false police report. After several deadlocked jury mistrials, prosecutors decided not to continue prosecution of the officers. Morse was terminated by the department and the Jackson teen filed lawsuits for civil rights violations. Community leaders voiced outrage citing circumstances reminiscent of the Rodney King incident in nearby Los Angeles.

There have been other incidences of alleged local police misconduct, excessive force, or corruption. When these receive media coverage, they evoke a discourse among the police, media, community, and scholars regarding solutions to the problem of police misbehavior that affects the fragile balance between community order and constitutional protection.

Explanations for Police Misconduct

Police Subculture Explanations

Scholars have proffered both individual and organizational explanations for police deviance (Worden 1995; Kappeler, Sluder, and Alpert 1997). At the individual level, researchers claim that the police occupation creates a perspective and working personality that explains many of the aspects of police behavior and may contribute to misconduct (Kappeler, Sluder, and Alpert 1997). Part of the ethos of the police occupational personality is an abiding suspicion of citizens. In his seminal work Skolnick (1966) posited that danger, authority, and isolation are all factors in molding the police personality. Officers can develop an "us versus them" perspective whereby they feel surrounded by critics and potential dangers, causing them to become defensive. And some officers rationalize their misconduct or abuse as being justified since they believe they represent a "thin blue line" as the last defense against criminals who prey on the law-abiding public (Van Maanen 1978).

Organizational Explanations

American police organizations have both a historical legacy and an institutional framework of autonomy, fraternalism, and secrecy that directly or indirectly produce conditions that support misconduct (Skolnick and Fyfe 1993). Some have argued that a pattern of misconduct has emerged that is sustained by the values and organizational structure of police agencies across the nation (Armacost 2004). Hence, the "blue code of silence," tolerance of "street justice" methods, and traditional procedures used to investigate citizen complaints may all contribute to a dysfunctional police disciplinary response that allows the corruption to continue.

The police organization contains many institutional features that create an environment that either provides conditions or produces attitudes that can lead to brutality, excessive force, and corruption. In fact, Fyfe (1999) found that among other factors, organizational philosophies and policies influenced the frequency of police use of deadly force. Whether individual or organizational, misconduct has a profound effect on the police community.

Consequences of Police Misconduct

Several remedies are available to citizens whose constitutional rights have been violated by the police. These include both criminal and civil actions in state and federal courts. Though police officers can be criminally prosecuted, one of the most common actions is the filing of a civil rights claim in federal court under 42 U.S.C. § 1983 (Ku Klux Klan Act of 1871). This federal law provides citizens lawsuit redress for constitutional violations committed by police officers acting under "color of law."

In addition to the liability attached to the individual officer, courts interpreting the provisions of this statute found that a police department can be held liable for both official policies and customary practices of officers if they lead to constitutional violations (*Monell v. Department of Social Services of the City of New York* 1978). Thus, police departments can be

held accountable for police officer practices that become commonplace. Common knowledge of officer conduct can be a means of establishing customary practice. However, the U.S. Supreme Court held in *Oklahoma v. Tuttle* (1985) that police agencies become liable for patterns of misconduct rather than a single incident.

Patterns of customary behavior can be interpreted by the courts using several factors. Repeated misconduct, such as excessive force, can be viewed as customary practice if police departments fail to take corrective measures against miscreant officers (Rudosky 1982). Departmental negligence can be established through "deliberate indifference" or failure to proactively correct patterns of deviant behavior. The U.S. Supreme Court ruled in *City of Canton, Ohio v. Harris* (1989) that police agencies are liable if they are aware of constitutional violations, either through defective policy or chronic conduct, and demonstrate a "deliberate indifference" toward the wrongdoing. This can be manifested by a failure to properly train, discipline, supervise, or assign personnel in a manner designed to control or correct police misconduct (del Carmen 1991).

Prospects for Change

Officer misconduct negatively affects the police department's reputation, operation, and relationship with the community. More than a decade ago the Christopher Commission recommended changes in the way the LAPD selected, trained, and disciplined officers in an effort to curb police misconduct. Their suggestions were consistent with those of others in terms of identifying and controlling patterns of police malpractice that stemmed predominantly from systemic organizational failures.

As witnessed by several episodes of police misconduct after the Rodney King abuse, the problem continues to plague the American police. As some have suggested, a fundamental change is needed in the structure, ideology, and values of police organizations to disrupt a pattern of police deviance (Armacost 2004; Bandes 2001). Chronic wrongdoing is perpetuated by an inability or unwillingness of the police professionals to initiate essential change in their response to police misbehavior.

WILLIAM P. BLOSS

See also **Abuse of Authority by Police; Arrest Powers of the Police; Autonomy and the Police; Citizen Complaints in the New Police Order; Complaints against Police; Constitutional Rights: In-Custody Interrogation; Constitutional Rights: Search and Seizure; Corruption; Deviant Subcultures in Policing; Discretion; Early Warning Systems; Excessive Force; Independent Commission on the Los Angeles Police Department (The Christopher Commission); Integrity in Policing; Liability and the Police; Liability and Use of Force; Occupational Culture; Police Legal Liabilities: Overview**

References and Further Reading

Adams, K. 1996. Measuring the prevalence of police abuse of force. In *Police violence*, ed. Geller and Toch, 52–93. New Haven, CT: Yale University Press.

Armacost, Barbara. 2004. Organizational culture and police misconduct. *George Washington Law Review* 72: 453–75.

Bandes, Susan. 2001. Tracing the pattern of no pattern: Stories of police brutality. *Loyola of Los Angeles Law Review* 34: 665–80.

Barker, Thomas, and David Carter. 1994. *Police deviance*. Cincinnati, OH: Anderson.

Christopher Commission. 1991. *Report of the Independent Commission on the Los Angeles Police Department*. Los Angeles, CA: The Commission.

City of Canton, Ohio v. Harris, 109 S. Ct. 1197 (1989).

del Carmen, Rolando. 1991. *Civil liabilities in American policing: A text for law enforcement personnel*. Englewood Cliffs, NJ: Brady.

Fyfe, J. 1999. Police use of deadly force: Research and reform. In *Police perspectives: An anthology*, ed. Gaines and Cordner, 408–34. Los Angeles, CA: Roxbury Publishing.

Kappeler, V., R. Sluder, and G. Alpert. 1997. Breeding deviant conformity: Police ideology and culture. In *Critical issues in policing: Contemporary readings*, ed. Dunham and Alpert, 284–301. Prospect Heights, IL: Waveland Press.

Klockars, Carl, Sanja Ivkovic, and M. Haberfeld. 2004. *The contours of police integrity*. Thousand Oaks, CA: Sage Publications.

Monell v. Department of Social Services of the City of New York, 436 U.S. 658 (1978).

Oklahoma v. Tuttle, 471 U.S. 808 (1985).

Rudosky, Leonard. 1982. *The politics of law*. New York: Pantheon Books.

Skolnick, Jerome. 1966. *Justice without trial: Law enforcement in democratic society*. New York: Wiley.

Skolnick, Jerome, and James Fyfe. 1993. *Above the law: Police and the excessive use of force*. New York: The Free Press.

Van Maanen, J. The asshole. 1978. In *Policing: A view from the street*, ed. Manning and Van Maanen, 221–38. Santa Monica, CA: Goodyear Publishing.

Worden, Robert. 1995. The causes of police brutality: Theory and evidence on police use of force. In *And justice for all: Understanding and controlling police abuse of force*, ed. Geller and Toch, 31–60. Washington, DC: Police Executive Research Forum.

POLICE PURSUITS

A police pursuit is an action in which a police officer driving an authorized police vehicle attempts to stop a suspect or violator who is operating a motor vehicle and evades, eludes, or flees from the officer. There are two general types of police pursuits. The first is the slow-speed pursuit, where a suspect-driver does not exceed the posted speed limit and commits few if any traffic violations. In this pursuit, the suspect-driver fails to immediately stop the vehicle at the direction of an officer; it typically ends when the suspect-driver arrives at a destination or has an accident or the vehicle runs out of fuel. Elderly citizens with dementia and people suffering from mental illness may commit these types of pursuits.

The second type of pursuit is the high-speed pursuit. In a high-speed pursuit, a suspect-driver persistently and aggressively exceeds the speed limit, disregards or violates numerous traffic and criminal laws, and generally threatens his or her own welfare and that of the public and the police. Additionally, a high-speed pursuit represents a significant threat to property (for example, other vehicles, buildings, residences).

Regardless of the type, a pursuit is a unique phenomenon that has far-reaching consequences for the police, the public, lawmakers, and governments.

Anatomy of a Police Pursuit

Although unique, each police pursuit can be understood as a four-stage continuum in which three sets of variables continuously interact. The four stages are as follows [National Law Enforcement and Corrections Technology Center (NLECTC) 1998]:

Prepursuit. The period when an officer attempts to stop a vehicle and when the officer realizes the suspect-driver is attempting to flee

Communication. The period when an officer notifies other officers and the dispatcher of the particulars of the pursuit and the officer's need for backup and other resources

Arrival of resources: The period when backup officers and resources arrive and attempt to terminate the pursuit

Postpursuit: The period when the pursuit is terminated because the suspect-driver has stopped or has eluded the police.

One set of variables in this continuum belongs to the pursuit officer. These variables include driving skills as determined by training and experience, physical and mental conditioning, familiarity with a pursuit area, knowledge of and willingness to abide by the department's pursuit policy, access to pursuit-stopping technology and tactics, and the condition of the officer's vehicle.

Significant environmental variables include the time of day, type of area (for example, rural or urban), types and conditions of roadways (for example, highway or street), traffic density, and weather.

The final set of variables is the suspect-driver's. It includes a suspect's infraction or crime, age, criminal history, mental state, physical state (for example, intoxicated or high), physical abilities, maturity, and the condition of the suspect's vehicle.

These variables interacting across the stages serve to produce a distinct pursuit.

Background of Pursuits

The study of police pursuits is a relatively new phenomenon, with the bulk of research occurring since 1990. Nonetheless, limited research provides a distinct picture of pursuits. Pursuits usually occur on local roads at night and are perpetrated by young males (Rivara and Mack 2004). There are a variety of reasons for pursuit initiation, such as traffic infractions, stolen vehicle, driving while impaired (DWI), wanted person, and crime-in-progress.

A traffic infraction is the most common event leading to a pursuit, followed by a suspect driving a stolen vehicle (Alpert 1997; Minnesota Department of Public Safety 2001; Nichols 2005). The most common reason for a pursuit termination is a suspect stopping voluntarily. A suspect crashing is the second most common cause of a pursuit termination, and this generally occurs before the sixth minute of a pursuit (NLECTC 1998).

Pursuits terminating in accidents pose serious and significant problems for the police and the public. An examination of fatalities related to police pursuits for a nine-year period (1994–2002) reveals the following (Rivara and Mack 2004, 93):

There were 260–325 police pursuits ending in a fatality annually in the United States for a total of 2,654 crashes involving 3,965 vehicles and 3,146 fatalities during the nine-year study period. Of the 3,146 fatalities, 1,088 deaths were of people not in the fleeing vehicle and 2,055 to people in the fleeing vehicle. Altogether 102 (3.2%) of the fatalities were non-motorists, 40 were police officers, 946 (30.1%) were occupants of vehicles uninvolved in the police pursuit, and three were unknown. Most of the innocent deaths were not vehicle occupants, with 102 being either pedestrians or bicyclists.

It is primarily the injurious and deadly nature of pursuit accidents that has driven pursuit-related research, legislative reviews, policy makeovers, public debate, liability lawsuits, and technological innovations (Alpert 1997; Jopson 2005; Rivara and Mack 2004).

Police Pursuit Policies

One of the unique characteristics of policing is the broad decision-making ability accorded police officers, especially those working in patrol. This decision-making ability is known as discretion, and as the gatekeepers to the criminal justice system, police officers hold a significant amount of discretionary authority. For example, a police officer has the authority to stop, search, interview, and arrest a citizen for hundreds of reasons. Conversely, a patrol officer exercises tremendous discretion when he chooses to ignore violations that he considers to be insignificant or bothersome (for example, littering, disorderly conduct, traffic violation, DWI).

As policing has evolved, however, there has been a concerted effort by many government entities to control the discretionary power of police. For example, legislatures have enacted laws that mandate the arrest of assaulters in domestic violence incidents. Prior to the enactment of domestic violence laws, police chose from a number of options when determining the fate of an abusive spouse (for example, arrest or physical separation or transporting the victim to a shelter). The Supreme Court severely curtailed the police's discretionary use of deadly force when confronting an unarmed fleeing felon (*Tennessee v. Garner* 1985). Although the Supreme Court and state legislatures delineated police discretion in these circumstances, it became the police departments' responsibility to ensure that their police officers understood these changes. These changes became written policies through administrative rule-making (Walker and Katz 2005).

Administrative rulemaking extends to police department pursuit policies. Monetary losses from wrongful death and injury lawsuits, a drive to professionalize policing, concern for citizens and community safety, passage of restrictive legislation, need for improved police–community relations, and advances in criminal identification and apprehension all serve to push police officials toward implementing pursuit policies. However, there are wide variations in the amount of discretion given to officers in pursuit policies. These policies fall into one of four categories: no pursuit, permissive, restrictive, and discretionary.

Generally, an agency establishes a no-pursuit policy when it is not set up to engage in high-speed pursuits. An agency with a small number of personnel, limited jurisdiction (for example, campus police), and/or lack of emergency-equipped vehicles may not permit its officers to take part in high-speed pursuits. An agency patrolling an area with rigid geographic boundaries (for example, an island municipality) may not have a need to conduct high-speed pursuits. Very few police agencies have a no-pursuit policy (NLECTC 1998).

A permissive pursuit policy generally encourages police officers to conduct pursuits in a safe and efficient manner. However, a permissive pursuit policy offers little or vague guidance to an agency's officers. For years, this policy was a standard for many of the nation's police departments. With courts, communities, and departments recognizing that unregulated and unchecked pursuits are injurious and dangerous, a majority of departments are discarding permissive policies and adopting either a restrictive or a discretionary pursuit policy.

A restrictive policy severely limits police officers' discretion in pursuits. It typically calls for the police to initiate or continue a pursuit only in felony circumstances or when a suspect presents a significant and immediate danger to the public (for example, Baltimore Police Department 1990). Under this type of policy, a police officer would be expected to pursue a murderer, rapist, robber, or other wanted felon who chose to flee. Additionally, police could pursue people suspected of injurious misdemeanors such as domestic violence and assault if their identities are unknown. Under a restrictive policy, police typically would not pursue a traffic violator, someone in possession of illicit drugs, or someone involved in a nonviolent crime unless that person represented a tremendous danger to the general public and the person's identification was unknown (for example, a DWI suspect who bolts an auto–pedestrian accident).

A discretionary pursuit policy provides specific guidelines to officers in departments that grant them authority to initiate and continue pursuits. The overriding goal of this type of policy seeks to balance the needs for the police to apprehend law violators with the requirement that police not unduly jeopardize public safety. In this vein, discretionary policies usually stipulate that police halt pursuits when the danger to the public is extreme. Also, a discretionary policy may limit the types of incidents where officers may initiate a chase but is not so restraining as a restrictive policy (Louisville Metro Police Department 2003; Streisand 2003). Typically, a discretionary policy provides a number of criteria that a department mandates its police officers abide by in pursuit decision making. Although each police department is free to tailor its discretionary policy to its prevailing legal, political, and community environments, the International Association of Chiefs of Police (IACP), recommends a number of elements that a policy should address (2004).

First, the IACP specifies that the initial decision to pursue a suspect-driver belongs to a pursuing officer, provided that the officer critically weighs the dangers of pursuing versus not pursuing. The IACP also calls for an officer to closely examine factors that are related to a pursuit, to include: (1) road and environmental conditions, (2) population density, (3) vehicular and pedestrian traffic, (4) performance ability of police vehicle and its driver, (5) suspect-driver's ability and vehicle, and (6) violation(s) leading up to the pursuit. The IACP policy provides operational guidelines for an officer in a pursuit. The policy stresses that once a pursuit operation commences, it should conform to established laws and regulations, that an officer will operate emergency equipment and communicate with other officers, that an officer shall have a backup unit or air surveillance, and that a supervisor will be involved throughout the pursuit. With regard to pursuit-stopping tactics such as roadblocks and spike strips, the IACP emphasizes that they must be governed by an agency's policy and deployed in a safe manner.

The IACP stresses that a pursuing officer or a supervisor may terminate a pursuit when the risks of the pursuit outweigh the benefits of its continuance or the suspect can be apprehended at a later date. The IACP recommends that an officer complete a written report of a pursuit and that the department immediately review it. Finally, the IACP suggests that all department pursuit activities be periodically analyzed and that adjustments to a department's policy and procedures be completed.

Legislative Response to Pursuits

In an attempt to deter people from fleeing the police and decrease incidents of high-speed pursuits, state legislatures make the act a crime or increase the criminal penalty for the act. For example, in recognition of the substantial risk that high-speed pursuits represent to persons and property, the Kentucky legislature enacted into law a felony charge for fleeing or evading police in a motor vehicle (Kentucky Revised Statutes 2005). Texas's customary penalty for evading a police officer is a misdemeanor (Texas Penal Code 2005). However, a suspect who uses a vehicle in flight is charged with a felony. If the person charged has a previous conviction for fleeing from the police, the penalty jumps to the next felony level.

California's Senate Bill 719 (2005) is comprehensive legislation addressing police pursuits. It amends a number of pursuit-related codes (for example, government, penal, and vehicle) and deals with victim compensation, criminal penalties, pursuit policy, public awareness, and pursuit reporting. Some of the provisions of the bill are the following:

- An innocent victim suffering injury or death as a result of a suspect fleeing from the police is entitled to compensation from the state's crime victim restitution fund.
- All police agencies must require their officers to undergo regular and periodic pursuit training.
- The state's driver's license examination will include a question on the risks and punishments associated with pursuits.
- All imprisonment terms for convictions for fleeing from the police are increased.
- State traffic safety programs will conduct police pursuit public awareness campaigns.

- All police agencies will provide comprehensive pursuit data to the California Highway Patrol within thirty days of any pursuits.

The federal government recognizes that police pursuits are a threat to the public and the police. In 1997, Congress introduced legislation to create a national program addressing police pursuits. The bill, entitled "National Police Pursuit Policy Act of 1998," calls for a mandatory minimum prison sentence of not less than three months for a motorist convicted of fleeing the police. Additionally, the bill recommends that a state seize an offender's vehicle. Finally, the bill directs each police agency across the nation to develop a comprehensive pursuit policy, track and document all pursuits, complete an annual pursuit report, and provide training for officers expected to engage in pursuits.

Pursuit Training

Throughout their careers, police officers must respond to a variety of situations and incidents. How a police officer responds to these incidents is largely dictated by an officer's training. Most police departments provide training to their officers through a basic academy program and an in-service training program. Two broad types of training offered in both of these programs are skills training and knowledge training. Skills training typically involves learning how to effectively apply one or more of the five senses in a police situation. How to safely search a building, how to accurately shoot a gun, and how to quickly put handcuffs on a suspect are some of the skills an officer learns. Additionally, an officer must be knowledgeable about laws and municipal ordinances, agency policies, and cultural diversity.

Much of an officer's training requires the blending of skills and knowledge. For example, in addition to an officer learning how to accurately fire a handgun, he must know when the law and policy permit him to do so. Putting handcuffs on a suspect requires that an officer understand the legal justifications for detaining or arresting a citizen. The same holds for pursuit training. Pursuit driving requires a high level of skills training. Additionally, pursuit driving requires that an officer know when to initiate and continue a pursuit according to state law and department policy (Hill 2002).

Initial pursuit driving and policy training typically occurs at a police academy. However, agencies have significant variation in how much training they offer to their officers. Indianapolis police undergo forty hours of initial vehicle and pursuit training (Trotter, Spalding, and Nichols 2005). Minnesota requires at least a seven-hour course in an officer's initial training (Minnesota Statutes 2005). In a national survey, Alpert (1997) notes that the average amount of time dedicated to initial pursuit training is less than fourteen hours. The Pursuit Measurement Task Force (NLECTC 1998) recognizes that it is most likely that smaller agencies skimp on pursuit training due to staffing and budget limitations.

As previously noted, pursuit driving tactics and policies continue to evolve. The dynamic nature of pursuit response requires that police officers be kept abreast of these changes. Police in-service training—training that police departments mandate for their veteran officers—is the best venue for introducing new skill sets and policy updates. However, as with initial training, there is variation from department to department. For example, California requires that its officers participate in regular and periodic training in pursuit practices, policies, and tactics (California Assembly 2005). Minnesota (2005) mandates at least eight hours of training every three years for every full- and part-time police officer employed by an agency. Although the Indianapolis Police Department has an updated pursuit policy, its officers have not been educated as to its contents or given refresher skills training (Trotter, Spalding, and Nichols 2005). The IACP (2004) maintains that all officers in a department assigned a police vehicle should undergo recurrent pursuit policy and tactics training.

Pursuit-Stopping Strategies and Tactics

Police depend on strategies and tactics to control or stop pursuits. One strategy that meets with success is the use of a helicopter. Alpert's (1998) examination of two metropolitan police departments shows that a helicopter unit provides a number of valuable roles in pursuits. First, a helicopter unit provides immediate assessments of traffic congestion and hazards and environmental conditions. Second, a helicopter can surreptitiously follow a fleeing vehicle, enabling patrol to back off and relieve the pressure of "pushing" a suspect. A helicopter unit increases the likelihood of apprehension should a suspect abandon the vehicle and flee on foot. A helicopter unit also brings powerful observation equipment to a pursuit, including a high-power spotlight and forward-looking infrared radar (FLIR) to assist with locating suspects and vehicles in low-light situations. A helicopter unit equipped with a video camera can record pursuits. Video records can provide evidence for criminal and civil lawsuits that invariably result from pursuits. Finally, a helicopter provides a significant psychological advantage in a pursuit in that a fleeing suspect ceases fleeing once he realizes he cannot escape the "eye in the sky."

There are several pursuit-stopping tactics that utilize mobile patrol vehicles. Police use their patrol vehicles to either corral or strike a fleeing vehicle (Eisenberg and Fitzpatrick 1996; Eric 2004; NLECTC 1998). Channelizing, boxing-in, and vehicle intercept are three common mobile corralling techniques, where several police vehicles strategically surround a target vehicle, blockade it from all sides, and either stop it from fleeing or bring its movement to a halt. Corralling techniques can be safely implemented at low speeds but are difficult to execute at high speeds.

> Ramming and the pursuit intervention technique also use mobile patrol vehicles. In ramming, police strike a fleeing vehicle with a police vehicle. The goal of ramming is to disable the vehicle to the point that it can no longer operate and/or to knock it from its fleeing path. Ramming can be dangerous and injurious; it may constitute an unreasonable seizure should a suspect-driver be injured or killed. Rammed and ramming vehicles can become uncontrollable projectiles that can strike innocent third parties. The pursuit intervention technique (PIT) is a controlled contact technique (Eric 2004; Yates 2005). In the PIT, a police officer aligns his or her vehicle's front bumper next to the suspect vehicle's rear wheel, then steers into it. Upon contact, the rear wheels lose their grip on the roadway and the vehicle goes into a spin, which leads to the vehicle's engine shutting down and the vehicle stopping. The PIT is used at low speeds, and damage to a police vehicle and suspect vehicle are minimal.

A roadblock is a static technique in which the police preposition police vehicles (or other vehicles) across the pursuit roadway in an attempt to get the suspect-driver to cease fleeing. Roadblocks not clearly visible or without an escape route may violate the Fourth Amendment's unreasonable seizure clause.

Pursuit-Stopping Technology

Pursuit-stopping technology refers to equipment and devices designed to halt the movement of a fleeing vehicle either by disabling the vehicle or interfering with the suspect's ability to operate the vehicle. The NLECTC groups these technologies into five categories: electrical, chemical, sensory, cooperative, and mechanical.

Electrical technology targets the fleeing vehicle's electronic operating systems (for example, charging, ignition, or computers) by interfering with their operation. This experimental technology is subdivided into three approaches: direct injection, radiative, and plasma beam. In the direct injection application, the police fire an electrical charge into a fleeing vehicle. Once activated, the resulting electrical charge damages the fleeing vehicle's electronics and the vehicle stops. A radiative system uses microwaves to interfere with or destroy a fleeing vehicle's electronics. Unlike direct injection, this system does not require direct contact with the fleeing vehicle. The plasma beam system focuses high-voltage radio frequency waves on the target vehicle, with the directed energy interfering with or destroying the fleeing vehicle's electrical components.

The chemical stopping system is another experimental system. In this system, the police shoot a compound at the fleeing vehicle. The substance enters the vehicle's air intake and alters the fuel/air mixture to the point that the engine quits.

Pursuit management using sensory technology comes from two approaches. In the first, police use light and sound technology to provide innocent citizens with advance warning of an approaching pursuit so that they can take evasive action (for example, pull over, clear an intersection). Technology that disrupts the fleeing suspect's senses is the second sensory approach. Use of bright lights and sonic waves to disorient and bring discomfort to a fleeing suspect are examples of this technology. Operation of these should cause a suspect to stop in an effort to cancel the uncomfortable stimulus.

A cooperative stopping system is vehicle-installed technology that permits the police to track or remotely shut down a vehicle. Tracking systems such as LoJack and OnStar permit the police equipped with tracking devices to locate stolen vehicles.

With these devices, police can track a stolen or wanted vehicle from a distance without initiating a pursuit. Another cooperative system uses a laser to shut off the target vehicle's engine or fuel supply. A cooperative system must be preinstalled, and the police must know it is present.

Currently, the police are using several mechanical stopping devices. Two of the devices are the Stinger Spike Strip and the Stop Stick. These devices are portable platforms that are armed with numerous hollow metal spikes. An officer positioned a safe distance ahead of the pursuit deploys the device across the roadway in front of the pursued vehicle. Upon hitting the strip, one or more of the spikes punctures and deflates the vehicle's tires. The officer deploying the strip withdraws it before the pursuing vehicles cross it. The expectation is that a suspect will stop the disabled vehicle. Spike strips are limited to the width of two lanes of traffic; if the roadway is wider (for example, an interstate highway), additional strips are needed or a driver-suspect will be able to drive around targeted lanes. Additionally, since an officer has to deploy the strip in front of a pursuit, it leaves an officer exposed to fleeing and pursuing vehicles. Despite their drawbacks, police have enjoyed success in stopping pursued vehicles with their use.

Another proposed mechanical device under consideration for pursuit termination is a net system. This device uses a rapidly deployed and anchored net housed in a specially designed "speed bump" to capture a fleeing vehicle. The net, while effective, requires a setup time of between one and two hours and is more appropriate for fixed traffic positions (for example, border checkpoints).

Pursuit Liability

Each state is expected to reasonably govern how its police officers conduct pursuits. Typically, states grant emergency driving exemptions and limited immunity to officers involved in pursuits. However, since a police pursuit may lead to significant property damage and/or death or injury to a person, a citizen may file a civil lawsuit against police officers, departments, and municipalities under state tort law. Generally, in a lawsuit, a state court considers the police's need to immediately apprehend criminals for the protection of the public against their duty to protect the safety of all citizens during a police operation. However, a citizen's success in a lawsuit hinges on the standard a state court applies to the pursuit actions of the police. Generally, if there is a "reckless disregard" or "gross negligence" on the part of the police, a state court will rule in the plaintiff's favor.

For example, in *City of Jackson v. Brister* (2003), the Mississippi Supreme Court held police liable when officers recklessly disregarded the safety of the public when they entered into a fatal pursuit with a nonviolent forgery suspect in violation of their department's policy. Additionally, the court found fault with the officers because they failed to take basic precautions to prevent the pursuit. Rhode Island police also must not "recklessly disregard" the public safety in a pursuit. In *Seide v. State of Rhode Island* (2005), the state's supreme court cited the police for failing to adhere to established policy during a pursuit of a stolen truck that concluded with a crash and an innocent citizen receiving serious disfiguring and crippling injuries.

The South Carolina standard for pursuit liability is "gross negligence" (*Clark v. South Carolina Department of Public Safety* 2005), as is North Carolina's (*Bullins v. Schmidt* 1988). In *Clark*, the state's supreme court agreed with the trial court's finding that a police officer was "grossly negligent" when he initiated and continued a pursuit of a traffic violator. The violator crashed and killed an innocent motorist. In *Bullins*, North Carolina's Supreme Court held that officers who engaged in an eighteen-mile pursuit with an intoxicated driver were not guilty of gross negligence when the suspect-driver struck an innocent person's vehicle head-on, killing its driver.

Some states use a "proximate cause" standard, where an officer's pursuit actions may lead to a citizen being killed or injured. For example, in *Meyer v. State of Nebraska* (2002), a trooper's thirty-seven-mile, high-speed pursuit of a suspect-driver suffering from a psychotic episode set off a series of events leading to the death of a female bystander. The Nebraska Supreme Court held that the trooper's actions in the pursuit were a proximate cause of the accident.

Both federal law and the U.S. Constitution govern police pursuits. Police cannot violate a citizen's rights as delineated in these two; otherwise, they can be sued. In order for an individual to sue the police for a pursuit-related injury or death, there must be an allegation of a civil rights violation under Title 42 of the U.S. Code, Section 1983 (Pipes and Pape 2001). In a Section 1983 lawsuit, a person typically alleges that the police action leading to an injury or death constituted an unreasonable seizure under the Fourth Amendment or that it was violative of substantive due process under the Fourteenth Amendment. To succeed with a Fourth Amendment lawsuit, a plaintiff must clearly demonstrate that the police's actions to stop a fleeing vehicle were unreasonable. For example, in *Brower v. County of Inyo* (1989), the Supreme Court ruled that the police's decision to stop a fleeing auto thief (Brower) by placing a tractor-trailer rig across a curved roadway constituted a seizure when he crashed into it and died. The Court held that a lower court was responsible for determining whether the seizure was unreasonable and whether the officers were liable.

Under the Fourteenth Amendment's guarantee of substantive due process, a state and its agents cannot "... deprive any person of life, liberty, or property,

without due process of law ...." Thus, a person injured or killed during a police pursuit may claim that a due process right was violated. However, in order to succeed in such a lawsuit, a person must show that the police's actions meet the current "shocks the conscience" standard. This standard supersedes the previous federal courts' "gross negligence" and "deliberate or reckless indifference" standards (Finarelli 1999). The Supreme Court established the "shocks the conscience" standard for federal Fourteenth Amendment lawsuits in 1998 in *County of Sacramento v. Lewis*. The facts of *Lewis* follow.

In 1990, a deputy and a police officer were at a fight scene when they observed a motorcycle approaching at a high rate of speed. An eighteen-year-old and his sixteen-year-old passenger (Lewis) were on the motorcycle. The police officer directed the operator to stop. However, the operator did not and fled from the two officers. The officers pursued the fleeing motorcycle in their patrol vehicles. The suspect-driver committed numerous traffic violations (for example, speeding, running red lights) as he fled through a residential area. Approximately two minutes into the pursuit, the motorcycle skidded to a stop. The deputy's patrol vehicle also skidded but did not come to a stop until after it had struck and killed the sixteen-year-old passenger.

Lewis's parents sued the deputy, the sheriff's department, and the county under the Fourteenth Amendment. The Supreme Court noted that the suspect-driver's lawless behavior led to an instinctive response from the deputy. Accordingly, it determined that the deputy did not enter into the pursuit with malice and with the intent to physically harm Lewis. His behavior, therefore, did not reach the "shocks the conscience" standard required to succeed in a Section 1983 lawsuit. The "shocks the conscience" standard is a high standard that may make Fourteenth Amendment lawsuits impossible (Urbonya 1998).

Conclusion

Police pursuits continue to be a significant source of concern for police, law enforcement agencies, lawmakers, and the general public. For the police, the dilemma is balancing the need to bring a lawbreaker into custody with the need to conduct the apprehension operation as safely as possible. There is no universal solution; it requires a conscientious and concerted effort on the part of the police, their departments, governments, courts, and researchers from the public and private sectors to develop and implement safe and reliable responses to fleeing vehicles.

MARK MARSOLAIS

See also **Academies, Police; Discretion; International Association of Chiefs of Police (IACP); Liability and High-Speed Chases; Police Legal Liabilities: Overview**

References and Further Reading

Alpert, Geoffrey P. 1997. *Police pursuit: Policies and training.* National Institute of Justice Research in Brief. Washington, DC: National Institute of Justice.

————. 1998. *Helicopters in pursuit operations.* National Institute of Justice Research in Brief. Washington, DC: National Institute of Justice.

Alpert, Geoffrey P., and Roger G. Dunham. 1990. *Police pursuit driving: Controlling responses to emergency situations.* Westport, CT: Greenwood Press.

Baltimore (Maryland) Police Department. General Order 11–90: Departmental Emergency Vehicle Operation (1990). http://www2.indystar.com/images/graphics/2005/05/0521_chasepolicy.html (November 2005).

Brower v. County of Inyo, 489 U.S. 593 (1989).

California Assembly. Police Pursuits. Senate Bill No. 719, Reg. Sess. (2005). http:// web.lexis-nexis.com/universe/document?_m=77726d98af26df007a.html (November 2005).

City of Jackson v. Brister, 838 So. 2d 274 (Miss. 2003).

Clark v. South Carolina Department of Public Safety, 608 S.E. 2d 573 (S.C. 2005).

County of Sacramento v. Lewis, 523 U.S. 833 (1998).

Eisenberg, Clyde, and Cynthia Fitzpatrick. 1996. Police practice: An alternative to police pursuits. *FBI Law Enforcement Bulletin* 65 (Aug.): 16–19.

Eric, J. S. 2005. Police end car chases with a spin. http://www.policedriving.com/article57.htm (November 2005).

Finarelli, Joseph. 1999. High-speed police chases and Section 1983: Why a definitive liability standard may not matter. *Defense Counsel Journal* 66 (April): 238–48.

Hill, John. 2002. High-speed police pursuits: Dangers, dynamics, and risk reduction. *FBI Law Enforcement Bulletin* 71 (July): 14–18.

International Association of Chiefs of Police. 2004. *Vehicular pursuit: Model policy.* Alexandria, VA: IACP.

Jopson, Debra. 2005. *Police pursuit death toll rises: 61 killed in 10 years.* http://www.smh.com.au/news/National/Police-pursuit-death-toll-rises-61-killed-in-10-years.html (October).

Kentucky Revised Statutes. Title L: Crimes and Punishments. Chapter 520: Escape and Other Offenses Relating to Custody. § 520.095: Fleeing or Evading Police in the First Degree (2005).

Louisville (Kentucky) Metro Police Department. Standard Operating Procedures: Pursuits (2003). http://www2.indystar.com/images/graphics/2005/05/0521_chasepolicy.html (November 2005).

Meyer v. State of Nebraska, 650 N.W. 2d 459 (Neb. 2002).

Minnesota Department of Public Safety. 2001. *Police pursuits.* CJIS-2001, http://www.dps.state.mn.us/bca/CJIS/Documents/Crime2001/Page-20–13.html (November 2005).

Minnesota Statutes. § 626.8458: Vehicle Pursuits: Policies and Instruction Required (2005). http://www.revisor.leg.state.mn.us/stats/626/8458.html (November 2005).

National Law Enforcement and Corrections Technology Center. 1998. *Pursuit Management Task Force report.* Washington, DC: National Institute of Justice.

Nichols, Mark. 2005. *What we found.* http://www2.indystar.com/images/graphics/2005/05/0522_chasewhatwefound.html (November 2005).

Pennsylvania State Police. 2005. *Pennsylvania police pursuits: 2004 annual report.* http://ucr.psp.state.pa.us/ucr/reporting/pursuit/annualpursuitUI.asp (November 2005).

Pipes, Chris, and Dominick Pape. 2001. Police pursuits and civil liability. *FBI Law Enforcement Bulletin* 20 (Jul.): 16–21.

Rivara, F. P., and C. D. Mack. 2004. Motor vehicle crash deaths related to police pursuits in the United States. *Injury Prevention* 20: 93–95.

Streisand, Betsy. 2003. And the chase is off. *U.S. News and World Report* 134: 31.

Tennessee v. Garner, 471 U.S. 1 (1985).

Texas Penal Code. Title 8: Offenses Against Public Administration. Chapter 38: Obstructing Governmental Operation. § 38.04 Evading Arrest or Detention (2005).

Trotter, Eunice, Tom Spalding, and Mark Nichols. 2005. *Are police chases worth dying for?* http://www.indystar.com/apps/pbcs.dll/article?Date=20050522&Category=SPECIAL01/505220468 (November 2005).

Urbonya, Kathryn R. 1998. Pleading the Fourth. *ABA Journal* 84 (Sept.): 36–37.

U.S. Senate. National Police Pursuit Policy Act of 1998. S.1236, 105th Cong., 1st Sess. http://www.aele.org/pursuit.html (November 2005).

Walker, Samuel, and Charles M. Katz. 2005. *The police in America: An introduction.* 5th ed. New York: McGraw-Hill.

Yates, Travis. 2005. Pursuit intervention technique: Myth vs. fact. http://www.policedriving.com/article59.htm (November 2005).

POLICE REFORM IN AN ERA OF COMMUNITY AND PROBLEM-ORIENTED POLICING

The era of community and problem-oriented policing arose from what had become a consistently negative critique of traditional policing. Traditional policing was seen as flawed; preventive patrol didn't work, follow-up criminal investigations lacked impact, crime, especially violent crime, was rising, and the police were estranged from their social communities. Policing was in crisis—it lacked efficiency, effectiveness, and context.

Community policing arose from the perceived need to balance the role of the police in pursuit of a broader range of community-based outcomes. Common "core" elements of community policing programs include a redefinition of the police role to increase crime prevention activities, greater reciprocity in police and community relations, area decentralization of police services and command, and some form of civilianization (Skolnick and Bayley 1986).

In adopting community policing the police have increasingly focused on a broad array of outcomes, including issues such as public safety, crime, fear of crime, and community quality of life. Moreover, whereas under traditional norms of policing the police were singularly responsible for crime control, under community and later problem-oriented policing (POP), communities and other public and private organizations came to be viewed as significant participants in shaping police objectives and interventions.

Ideas such as building and sustaining community partnerships to work with the police on matters of neighborhood crime and disorder underlie much of the community policing agenda. Building community-based capacities for crime prevention and victim assistance while reconnecting the police with their communities, particularly minority communities, required that the police become "invested" in neighborhoods (Mastrofski, Worden, and Snipes 1995). Partnerships between the police and external others were also a dominant value in the community-oriented policing (COP) movement (see Skolnick and Bayley 1986). To be effective, the police and the community must coproduce safety in neighborhoods, according to this view.

Community policing philosophies and programs also emphasized an "environmental openness," linking informal (community-based) and formal (police-based) social control. To do all of this, of course, requires a very different set of police officer skills, most especially communication, conflict resolution, and interaction skills.

From the perspective of the police organization and service delivery system, community policing was seen as a way of making police agencies less bureaucratic, specialized, and hierarchical, and police officers are seen as generalists, not specialists. Decentralized management and service delivery were cornerstones of the community policing movement, suggesting that the structure of traditional policing greatly inhibited the capacity of the police to deliver effective and efficient services to the public.

Allied to community policing, problem-oriented policing first and foremost sought to provide the police with better methodologies for addressing crime and disorder problems (Goldstein 1990). Applying a version of the scientific method—scanning the environment for problems, analyzing the nature and source of the problem, developing and implementing policy and community interventions to address the problem, and then evaluating the impact of the programs implemented—formed the basis of problem solving. Under the norms of problem-oriented policing, the police were to shift from their reactive mode of responding to calls for service to once emphasizing a proactive, analytic approach. Whereas community-oriented policing provided a broader vision of the police role in society, problem solving provided a set of "tools" to work with in that broader context.

Community and Problem-Oriented Policing Interventions

To understand what was intended of community and problem-oriented policing, it is important to see these efforts as a series of interventions that affect different things. In theory, these interventions occur at several levels. They impact communities, police organizations, and the nature of police work, including police officer attachment to community and crime prevention values and to a broader set of community service ideals.

At the environmental level, community and problem-oriented policing interventions sought to engage the police and the community in the coproduction of public safety. The police were to create linkages with external groups and organizations, and they were expected to focus on community capacity building and crime prevention. By mobilizing communities and focusing on discrete and identifiable crime, disorder, and fear problems, it was anticipated that communities could become more crime resistant. The police efforts were aimed at stabilizing neighborhoods, increasing neighborhood bonds and communication, increasing the capacity of the neighborhood to mediate in conflict situations, and ultimately strengthening neighborhood cohesion. Under problem solving, the police, with community partners, were to address visible and persistent crime and disorder problems occurring in neighborhoods.

At the organizational level, community and problem-oriented policing interventions were seen as affecting several police department issues. First, these interventions were to change the way in which the department converts inputs to outputs. This includes how (or if) the department currently defines and solves problems and how it values what it produces. Community policing interventions are also associated with affecting the department's structure, culture, and human resource systems including the mechanisms for selecting, training, rewarding, and socializing police officers. At the work group level, community and problem-oriented policing were meant to improve interpersonal communications and information sharing within and outside the agency while at the same time clarifying new and more analytic tasks for police officers and investigators.

At the individual level, changes implied by community and problem-oriented policing were often focused on police officer effectiveness, primarily through the mechanism of problem solving. Police officer performance, job satisfaction, and job attachment were thought to increase, given that officers were given more to do and more control over what they did. Lastly, the role of the police officer was to broaden under community and problem-oriented policing. Such changes anticipated in the police role included greater officer autonomy in decision making, job enrichment and job enlargement, increased feedback to officers regarding their community and problem-focused activities, and increases in the depth and range of skills officers are trained for and employ as part of their community and problem-oriented policing methodology.

The Impacts of Change

Environmental or Community Effects

Community policing has sought from its beginning to engage the community in matters of public safety while building and strengthening the capacity of communities to resist crime. For example, the Department of Justice's Weed and Seed Program focused on creating a visible and active police presence to impact distressed neighborhoods (weeding), as well as capacity building (seeding) in these same neighborhoods to sustain gains once they were achieved (see Roehl et al. 1995). More limited or focused crime interventions, such as the Boston Gun Project (see Kennedy 1998), also pursued dual strategies. In the case of the Boston project, the first strategy sought to identify youth who were likely to use guns to resolve disputes while also mobilizing government and community social institutions to address this serious and lethal community problem on several different fronts and in a coordinated and systematic manner. Programs such as Town Watch are also seen as community capacity building efforts, often linked to increasing surveillance over public places (Rosenbaum 1986, 1988; Rosenbaum, Lurigio, and Davis 1998).

In an assessment of the community impacts of community and problem-oriented policing, Cordner (1998) suggests

that the evidence is generally mixed. Some studies suggest declines in crime, fear, disorder, and calls for service. However, given design and research limitations identified more than a decade ago by Greene and Taylor (1988), much of the research remains difficult to interpret and generalize. There are, however, some promising findings upon which more rigorous assessments can be made in the future.

The cumulative findings of the fear reduction and foot patrol programs of the early 1980s suggested that changes in police strategy might have had different effects on communities. In the Houston and Newark studies, for example, there were indeed modest crime effects, although these programs appeared to influence community perceptions and fear of crime more than they did crime itself.

Neighborhood impacts associated with community and problem-oriented policing are varied and complex. They included resident perceptions of safety, fear of crime, use of public places, actual victimization, calls for service to the police, reported crime, self-protection measures, and community cohesion, to name a few. Given the range and complexity of outcome measures associated with community policing, it is often difficult to make comparisons across sites.

Skogan (1994), in an assessment of community policing impacts on neighborhood residents, examined six programs, conducted in Oakland, California; Birmingham, Alabama; Baltimore, Maryland; Madison, Wisconsin; Houston, Texas; and Newark, New Jersey. In assessing these programs Skogan (1994) assessed their effects on fear of crime, disorder, victimization, the quality of police services, and drug availability. His findings suggest that fear of crime was most affected by these interventions, and that it generally went down in five of the six sites. Disorder, by contrast, declined in three of the six sites, while victimization went down in half of the sites as well.

In 1993, the Chicago Police Department launched a community policing program called CAPS—Chicago's Alternative Policing Strategy. The program has been assessed by Skogan and his colleagues for several years (see Skogan et al. 1995 and Skogan and Hartnett 1997). A recent assessment of community policing impacts on neighborhoods in Chicago conducted by Skogan and Hartnett (1997) suggested that these efforts indeed had a significant impact on community problems and the quality of community life.

Police Organization Effects

One of the promises of community policing is that it would make police agencies kinder and gentler, both to their constituents and to their employees. Criticisms of the police bureaucracy, particularly under the traditional model of policing, are that it has alienated both the producers and consumers of police services. Such alienation creates great tension between the police and those policed.

On the philosophical level it is clear that many police agencies have adopted the language and symbolism of community and problem-oriented policing. In a study of the broadening of the police domain Zhao, Thurman, and Lovrich (1995) found that police organizations across America have been broadening their role over several years. In addition, they found that police agencies implementing community policing had also broadened the technologies they used, the populations they served, and the range of services they provided.

Police agencies throughout the United States have been adopting models of organization and training that bode well for community and problem-oriented policing. Zhao and his colleagues (1995) identified three factors around which organizational reform in policing is occurring. The

first factor is focused on improving police officer performance skills. The second factor seeks to improve middle management within police agencies. And the third factor is associated with implementing COP programs in culturally diverse communities with the intent of improving police and citizen interaction and community relations.

The reform of police agencies along the lines of community and problem-oriented policing has not been obstacle free. Zhao and his colleagues (1995) identified several impediments to organizational change under the norms of community and problem-oriented policing. They include resistance from middle managers and line officers, internal confusion as to the operational definition of COP, concerns that COP might be "soft on crime," lack of police officer training, and resistance from police unions.

Similarly, problems exist in the external environment's adoption of COP as an operating strategy for the police. Impediments identified by Zhao and his colleagues (1995) include community concerns about "fighting" crime, pressure for immediate results, and lack of support from other government agencies. Finally, transition problems in moving from traditional to community policing are largely centered on the need to balance community policing patrol strategies (foot and bike patrols, community ministations, and "park and walk" programs) with rapid response, particularly to potentially violent crime. These tensions continue to plague the adoption of community and problem-oriented policing in American police departments, although they are not insurmountable.

Private Changing Police Work

At both the organizational and individual levels, problem solving is said to be reshaping the intelligence of the police. This occurs in a process that involves scanning the environment and then defining problems, analyzing the causes and consequences of these problems, designing and implementing appropriate responses, and assessing the impact of interventions (Eck and Spelman 1987; Goldstein 1990).

Unfortunately, in a critique of problem solving, Clarke (1998, 315–27) suggested that much of what occurs under the label of problem solving is shallow, unanalytic, and largely ineffective. As Clarke suggests, the police fail in most of the problem-solving steps. During scanning, the police often fail to clearly specify the problem they seek to address. This creates considerable variance in what the police think they are addressing. Analysis of problems, according to Clarke (1998, 318), is also quite rudimentary: "[D]uring an investigation of calls for service or crime reports, they rarely identify patterns about how often or when a crime is occurring, or about where the problem is concentrated. They also make few attempts to disaggregate statistics to determine the precise nature of the problem."

When it comes to responses, Clarke suggests that much of what falls under the guise of community and problem-oriented policing is really traditional police tactics such as crackdowns, streets sweeps, and the use of arrest, often masked as community and/or problem-solving interventions. These tactics may be being applied to poorly defined and analyzed problems. Finally, Clarke argues that the most unused aspect of problem solving is the assessment of results.

Currently, many police departments across America have adopted a "framework" for response that includes elements of problem solving, including COMPSTAT (Silverman 1995) and hot spot analysis (Sherman, Gartin, and Buerger 1989; Sherman and Weisburd 1995; Weisburd and Green 1995). This framework is yet evolving, and with support and cross communication among police agencies, the "new technology" of policing will continue to emerge.

Impacts on Work Groups and Officers

Intended outcomes of community and problem-oriented policing are that police officers will (1) do their jobs differently, (2) identify with role changes associated with these new styles of policing, and (3) improve their attachment to work, the police profession, their departments, and one another—in short, improve job satisfaction.

In a few of the projects where there is community-focused data, such as the one conducted in Miami (Alpert and Dunham 1988), it is clear that police sensitivity to community norms and conversance with community expectations is both a long-standing complaint in minority communities and an occupational prerequisite if the police are to become truly "community oriented." In San Diego, a program to actively involve police officers in "understanding" the communities they policed resulted in positive police officer attitudinal changes (Boydstun and Sherry 1975). In Baltimore County, a problem-oriented approach to policing resulted in improved police officer job satisfaction and strengthening of the officers' orientation toward resolving community problems (Hayslip and Cordner 1987). In Philadelphia, a community–police educational program focused on communications and police–community problem solving demonstrated positive attitudinal results among participating police officers (Greene 1989; Greene and Decker 1989).

In Houston and in Newark, research conducted through the Police Foundation (see Skogan 1990 and Skolnick and Bayley 1986) suggested that the community improved their evaluation of police performance, including the quality of interaction with the police, with the advent of programs that sought to bring the community and police closer together, after years of conflict and animosity. In Houston this was brought about by creating community stations where community response teams attempted to mobilize and engage the community on matters of crime and disorder. In Newark the police response was to employ more traditional police methods (saturation patrol and more aggressive street enforcement tactics), but to do so with the focus of improving community "quality of life" by reducing the "signs of crime" in neighborhoods—unruly behavior and abandoned property (typically automobiles).

In New York City a program called the Community Patrol Officer Program (CPOP) sought to introduce a form of community policing to that city. CPOP officers were given responsibility for a wide variety of community and problem-solving activities. They were to mobilize communities and to identify and solve community problems (see Farrell 1988 and Weisburd and McElroy 1988).

While the initial assessment of this program focused on field supervisors and the adjustments they had to make to oversee CPOP officers, subsequent analyses of the CPOP program (McElroy, Cosgrove, and Sadd 1993) suggested that there were significant changes in attitudes for CPOP officers participating in the program, particularly in those attitudes toward the community and toward being a police officer. Here, officers in the CPOP program expressed more favorable attitudes toward the community and toward their identity with their jobs following their participation in the program. Interestingly, these same officers grew more critical of their department during the same time period.

In an assessment of role adaptation and job satisfaction among police officers in Joliet, Illinois, Rosenbaum and his colleagues (1994, 331–42) compared officers in this department who were part of a neighborhood-oriented policing (NOP) program with officers from a neighboring community without such a program. NOP officers reported more favorable attitudes toward community policing, were more likely to report that their jobs had broadened, and perceived an increase in job autonomy. They also reported higher

job satisfaction and reported higher confidence in their ability to solve problems.

In a study of police officer adaptation to community and problem-oriented policing in Chicago, Skogan and Hartnett (1997) found "evidence of modest opinion shifts" in police officers who participated in the Chicago Alternative Policing Strategy (CAPS) program. These modest changes were reflected in CAPS officers becoming more optimistic about their interventions being thought effective in regard to traditional police concerns (for example, crime reduction), their ability to actually solve problems, the impact of the program on police autonomy, and their satisfaction with the Chicago Police Department. Interestingly, this study also found that the CAPS program had a wider association with general improvements in police attitudes toward beliefs that the program was impacting communities and that community policing concepts were indeed viable as a policing strategy in Chicago.

The National Institute of Justice funded a collaborative research project in 1997 to measure the impact of the COPS AHEAD program in Philadelphia (see Greene et al. 1999). The Philadelphia study revealed that rookie COPS AHEAD officers were better prepared to "do" community policing, as evidenced by their higher scores on academy training scales for problem solving and dealing with diversity and conflict. Both rookie and veteran COPS AHEAD officers and the comparison group of community policing officers reported having stronger orientations toward problem solving and community policing than their motorized counterparts. COPS AHEAD rookies were more satisfied with work on their present job, as compared to other officers, and COPS AHEAD and motorized rookies were more satisfied with their coworkers, as compared to veteran officers. COPS AHEAD rookies had higher scores, indicating greater overall job satisfaction, as compared to other officers.

Collectively, then, police officer affective attachments to, and understanding of, the community have been enhanced in certain cities, as have officer role definitions as a result of police and community programs. These findings are indeed encouraging in that they suggest that police attitudes can be shaped toward the values and practices envisioned in community and problem-oriented policing.

Conclusions

Community and problem-oriented policing have shaped American law enforcement in important ways during the past twenty years or so. Generally speaking, the police have broadened their interactions with the public, increased attention to neighborhood crime and disorder problems, and better prepared officers for the new roles anticipated of them. Such changes have not been without their problems, but from the perspective of changing institutions, COP and POP have made some inroads in shaping policing for the twenty-first century.

JACK R. GREENE

See also **Accountability; Attitudes toward the Police: Overview; Autonomy and the Police; Boston Community Policing; Community-Oriented Policing: Effects and Impacts; Community-Oriented Policing: History; Community-Oriented Policing: International; Community-Oriented Policing: Practices; Community-Oriented Policing: Rationale; COMPSTAT; Future of Policing in the United States; Hot Spots; Problem-Oriented Policing**

References and Further Reading

Alpert, G., and R. Dunham. 1988. *Policing multiethnic neighborhoods.* New York: Greenwood Press.

Boydstun, J. E., and M. E. Sherry. 1975. *San Diego community profile: Final report.* Washington, DC: Police Foundation.

Clarke, R. V. 1998. Defining police strategies: Problem solving, problem-oriented policing and community oriented policing. In *Problem oriented policing: Crime-specific patterns, critical issues and making POP work,* ed. T. O'Connor Shelly and A. C. Grant. Washington, DC: Police Executive Research Forum.

Cordner, G. W. 1985. *The Baltimore County Citizen-Oriented Police Enforcement (Cope) Project: Final report.* New York: Florence V. Burden Foundation.

———. 1998. Problem oriented policing vs. zero tolerance. In *Problem oriented policing: Crime-specific patterns, critical issues and making POP work,* ed. T. O'Connor Shelly and A. C. Grant. Washington, DC: Police Executive Research Forum.

Eck, J. E., and W. Spelman. 1987. *Problem solving: Problem oriented policing in Newport News.* Washington, DC: Police Executive Research Forum.

Farrell, M. J. 1988. The development of the Community Patrol Officer Program: Community-oriented policing in the New York City Police Department. In *Community policing: Rhetoric or reality,* ed. J. R. Greene and S. Mastrofski. New York: Praeger.

Goldstein, H. 1990. *Problem oriented policing.* New York: McGraw-Hill.

Greene, J. R. 1989. Police officer job satisfaction and community perceptions: Implications for community policing. *Journal of Research in Crime and Delinquency* 26 (2) (May): 168–83.

———. 2000. Community policing in America: Changing the nature, structure and functions of the police. In *Criminal Justice 2000*, Vol. 3: *Policies, processes and decisions of the criminal justice system,* ed. J. Horney. Washington, DC: U.S. Department of Justice.

Greene, J. R., and S. H. Decker. 1989. Police and community perceptions of the community role in policing: The Philadelphia experience. *Howard Journal of Criminal Justice* 22 (2) (May): 105–23.

Greene, J. R., and R. B. Taylor. 1988. Community policing and foot patrol: Issues of theory and evaluation. In *Community policing: Rhetoric or reality,* ed. J. R. Greene and S. Mastrofski. New York: Praeger.

Kennedy, D. 1998. Crime prevention as crime deterrence. In *What can the federal government do to decrease crime and revitalize communities?,* 55–58. Washington, DC: National Institute of Justice .

Mastrofski, S. D., R. E. Worden, and J. B. Snipes. 1995. Law enforcement in a time of community policing. *Criminology* 33 (4): 539–55.

McElroy, J., C. A. Cosgrove, and S. A. Sadd. 1993. *Community policing: The CPOP in New York*. Newbury Park, CA: Sage.

Police Foundation. 1981. *The Newark Foot Patrol Experiment*. Washington, DC: Police Foundation.

Roelh, J. A., R. Huitt, M. A. Wycoff, A. M. Pate, D. J. Rebovich, and K. R. Coyle. 1995. *National process evaluation of the Weed and Seed initiative: Cross-site summary report*. Pacific Grove, CA: Institute for Social Analysis.

Rosenbaum, D. P., ed. 1986. *Community crime prevention: Does it work?* Beverly Hills, CA: Sage Publications.

Rosenbaum, D. P. 1988. Community crime prevention: A review and synthesis of the literature. *Justice Quarterly* 5: 323–95.

Rosenbaum, D. P., A. J. Lurigio, and R. C. Davis. 1998. *The prevention of crime: Social and situational strategies*. Belmont, CA: West/Wadsworth.

Rosenbaum, D. P., S. Yen, and D. Wilkinson. 1994. Impact of community policing on police personnel: A quasi-experimental test. *Crime and Delinquency* 40: 331–53.

Sherman, L. W., and D. Weisburd. 1995. General deterrent effects of police or police patrol in crime "hot spots": A randomized, controlled trial. *Justice Quarterly* 12 (4): 625–48.

Sherman, L. W., P. R. Gartin, and M. E. Buerger. 1989. Hot spots of predatory crime: Routine activities and the criminology of place. *Criminology* 27: 27–55.

Silverman, E. B. 1999. *NYPD battles crime: Innovative strategies in policing*. Boston: Northeastern University Press.

Skogan, W. G. 1990. *Disorder and decline: Crime and the spiral of decay in American neighborhoods*. New York: The Free Press.

———. 1994. The impact of community policing on neighborhood residents: A cross-site analysis *The challenge of community policing: Testing the promises*. Thousand Oaks, CA: Sage.

Skogan, W. G., and S. M. Hartnett. 1997. *Community policing, Chicago style*. New York: Oxford University Press.

Skogan, W. G., S. Hartnett, J. H. Lovig, J. DuBois, S. Houmes, S. Davidsdottir, R. Van Stedum, M. Kaiser, D. Cole, N. Gonzales, et al. 1995. *Community policing in Chicago: Year two—An interim report*. Chicago: Illinois Criminal Justice Information Authority.

Skolnick, Jerome, and David Bayley. 1986. *The new Blue Line*. New York: The Free Press.

Weisburd, D., and L. Green. 1995. Policing drug hot spots: The Jersey City Drug Market Analysis Experiment. *Justice Quarterly* 12 (4): 711–35.

Weisburd, D., and J. McElory. 1988. Enacting the CPO role: Findings from the New York City Pilot Program in Community Policing. In *Community policing: Rhetoric or reality*, ed. J. R. Greene and S. Mastrofski. New York: Praeger.

Zhao, J. 1996. *Why police organizations change: A study of community-oriented policing*. Washington, DC: Police Executive Research Forum.

Zhao, J., Q. Thurman, and N. He. 1999. Sources of job satisfaction among police officers: A test of demographic and work environment models. *Justice Quarterly* 16 (1): 153–73.

Zhao, J., Q. Thurman, and N. Lovrich. 1995. Community-oriented policing across the U.S.: Facilitators and impediments to implementation. *American Journal of Police* 14:11–28.

POLICE REFORM: 1950–1970

There have been two major periods of reform through the history of modern American policing. The first period of reform was sparked by August Vollmer in an attempt to move beyond the patronage and corruption that characterized policing during the late nineteenth and early twentieth centuries. Vollmer advocated professionalism, careful selection of officers, and rigorous training as the means to reform. By the 1930s, most major police departments had adopted Vollmer's initiatives and moved from the political era into the reform era (Kelling and Moore 1988). The influence of Vollmer and his protégés, O. W. Wilson and William Parker, was evident as police departments across the nation adopted a professionalism approach that defined police functioning from the 1940s into the 1960s.

The second period of reform was based in the 1960s and came to fruition in the 1970s. After World War II, America experienced an unusual period of tranquility. Soldiers returned home, found jobs in the booming American industrial economy, and settled in the suburbs. By the mid-1960s, the "baby boomer" generation had matured into their criminogenic period (age sixteen through twenty-five) and the resulting crime increase, movement toward racial and gender equality, and clashes with the police indicated a need for reform. This article describes the rise of police professionalism during the 1950s, the ensuing problems of the 1960s, and the eventual need for reform.

1950s—The Rise of Professionalism

During the 1950s, "professionalism" was the watchword of the day. Officers were encouraged to function and behave in a strict, legalistic fashion. As police departments moved forward in the shift toward reform and away from the corruption of the political era, the personality of the individual beat officer was no longer emphasized, and officers became cogs in the larger police organization. Officer-level attitudes and values during the reform era were significantly influenced by the shift to professionalism. As police agencies implemented a quasi-military model of policing through the 1940s and 1950s, the individuals who were drawn to policing began to reflect these ideals. More and more police were ex-military men.

This was a change from early American police, who were likely first- or second-generation immigrants tied to ethnic and political groups as a function of their own ethnic background (MacNamara 1967). This shift toward ex-military personnel distanced the police from concepts such as patronage and old European ideas, where those with political ambition could purchase public offices through favors or bribes (Wilson 1968). The applicants who filled the ranks of police after returning from the military during the Second World War were more accustomed to a hierarchical model of authority, and the police shift to professionalism was well on its way.

A variety of factors shaped individual, officer-level functioning during this period. As the Federal Bureau of Investigation, led by J. Edgar Hoover, rose to prominence during the 1930s, local law enforcement agencies sought to emulate the FBI's professionalism. The FBI gained notoriety through the pursuit and apprehension of public personality criminals (such as Bonnie and Clyde and Babyface Nelson). Unfortunately, local law enforcement has always had to deal with a myriad of issues and can never possess the discretion over case selection of the FBI. Thus, seeking to resemble the scientific, professionalism model of the FBI was an unattainable goal.

Another set of factors that influenced officer-level values and behavior during the 1950s concerned the technological advances available to the police. August Vollmer and O. W. Wilson, the leaders in police innovation during the first half of the twentieth century, advocated placing police officers in brightly marked patrol cars to conduct preventive patrol. As described by Uchida (1997), August Vollmer and O. W. Wilson advised placing police officers in highly marked patrol cars for several reasons (Wilson 1963). First, officers would be readily available to respond to calls. Second, officers would fulfill a deterrence function by driving around and being highly visible. Third, officers would be removed from society, only coming into direct contact with their constituents when summoned.

This third objective was developed in response to the corruption of the political era. Officers who had limited contact with the public were unlikely to develop the corrupt relationships that had precipitated the shift to the reform era. The increasing availability of the telephone and the two-way radio served to allow the public, and subsequently dispatchers, to contact the police and send them where they were needed. This provided a more responsive police force but served as a second step distancing the police from the public.

1960s—Factors Precipitating the Fall of the Reform Era

By the 1960s, the professionalization movement was entrenched, and most American police departments had adopted the tenets of the reform era. However, many of these agencies were emphasizing the law enforcement mission of the police to the detriment of the social service role and community relations. A series of Supreme Court decisions restricted police actions and "handcuffed" the police, requiring them to pay more attention to an individual's rights and constitutional protections (Skolnick and Fyfe 1993). The civil rights movements culminated in a series of riots during the 1960s, spotlighting the poor relations between the police and the population, especially among minorities, young activists, and the poor (Pelfrey 1998).

While officer attitudes and values during the first portion of the reform era were characterized by the shift toward professionalism, the latter portion of the reform era saw officers become insulated from society and the focal point of controversy. The emphasis on law enforcement during the early portion of the reform era served to focus the police profession and decrease the scope of corruption. However, when social conflict emerged, this reliance on law enforcement left the police unprepared and created a community relations crisis.

A variety of factors precipitated the eventual shift away from the reform paradigm. The withdrawn nature of the police, originally designed to reform corruption problems, eventually produced negative byproducts. The shift toward vehicle-based patrol as opposed to foot patrol kept officers away from the temptations of corruption; however, this practice served as the first of several steps to insulate the police from the public. When officers are in cars, they are much less accessible to the general public. Officers gradually lost the close relationship with their constituents and grew out of touch with the changing times of the 1960s.

Unfortunately, this withdrawn nature produced a negative and ultimately destructive byproduct—a police force that was out of touch with society. Officers came into contact with the public in limited, often problematic instances. This social distance culminated in the discord of the 1960s, where the police response to demonstrations sparked a variety of riots and critical incidents (Fyfe 1988). Since few police of that time were trained to handle civil disobedience on a broad scale, police often initiated violent conflict, ultimately exacerbating tumultuous conditions.

Although the civil rights movement began in the 1950s, it peaked during the 1960s. Protests, led by civil rights figures such as Martin Luther King, forced public attention on the conflicts between minorities and local governments. As these protests grew in numbers and prominence, the police were required (by local officials) to intervene. Since the police of the 1940s, 1950s, and early 1960s had little experience handling unruly crowds, disaster often ensued. The injury or killing of a protester could spark a riot, necessitating an even greater use of force by the police.

This problem was magnified by television—incidents of police battering unarmed, minority protesters in Newark, Los Angeles, and Detroit during the mid-1960s were televised and brought into the homes of citizens across the nation. Many of these citizens then rose in angry protest, leading to localized riots. Frustrated police in previously peaceful cities saw protests and riots develop as a result of, for example, a shooting in New York or a beating in Alabama. These frustrations, on the part of both the police and the protesters, evidenced a serious disconnect between the police and many of their constituents.

On the final day of one of the bloodiest riots of the 1960s (in Detroit in 1967), President Johnson appointed the Kerner

Commission to review current police practices and develop recommendations to avoid such conflict in the future. The Kerner Commission and the 1967 President's Crime Commission advised the police to institute new selection and training procedures, especially relating to minorities. They recommended police departments alter hiring practices to make the departments more closely resemble the populations they policed. The traditional attitudes and values of the police were suddenly spotlighted and questioned. The Kerner Commission observed that many of the cities with the most significant problems had the most highly respected and professional police departments in America.

The President's Crime Commission made a number of influential suggestions regarding the development of police–community relations and encouraged the review and adoption of alternative police strategies, suggesting the traditional role of the police should be considered and revised. In his review of this report, twenty-five years after its release, Walker (1994) states that the seeds of community policing are evident in the report.

An outcome of President Johnson's efforts was the LEAA—the Law Enforcement Assistance Administration. This federal agency provided funds for police to go to school and earn collegiate or graduate degrees. Many of these officers moved into academics and became the first wave of criminal justice scholars. The LEAA also distributed funds to study the basic precepts of policing. These studies, including the Kansas City Preventive Patrol Study, the Response Time Study, and the Rand Detective Study, represent landmark research in criminal justice and sparked many other important investigations.

The Supreme Court made a dramatic impact on policing during the 1960s. With Earl Warren serving as chief justice, the Court addressed numerous aspects of police discretion and elected to limit the scope of police power in virtually every decision. In *Katz v. United States* (1967) and *Chimel v. California* (1969), the Court forced the police to exercise much greater care in acquiring warrants and conducting searches of residences and defined the limits of a legal search. The Fifth Amendment protection of access to counsel received notable attention first in *Massiah v. United States* (1964), then in *Escobedo v. Illinois* (1964). In both the *Massiah* and the *Escobedo* decisions, the police were precluded from obtaining confessions from those suspects who had retained counsel. This protection forced the police to rely on investigative procedures to produce convictions as opposed to coercing, or forcing, a confession. Finally, with the *Miranda v. Arizona* (1966) decision, police were required to inform arrested individuals (who the police wished to question) of the basic protections extended by the government.

These and other Supreme Court decisions (such as *Mapp v. Ohio* and *Terry v. Ohio*) did more than restrict the police in their dealings with suspects. The police were forced to change their style—instead of a heavy-handed approach to policing, involving coercive tactics and the threat of force, the police had to rely on evidence, investigative technique, and forensics. This approach was not well suited to the stereotypical police officer who relied on force, or the threat of force, to achieve order and justice. Instead, an intelligent and educated officer who knew the utility of science and the law began to emerge as the prototypical police officer. Agencies picked up the forgotten admonitions of August Vollmer and became more active in recruiting educated candidates for police positions.

Social upheaval, exemplified by riots and the civil rights movements, forced police into dangerous situations, where they fared poorly (Kelling and Moore 1988). A series of commission reports suggested that the police had become disconnected from society, and serious questions were raised about the current practices and philosophies of police (Walker 1994).

By the end of the 1960s, the Supreme Court, social scientists, and police administrators turned their attention to decreasing the level of discretion available to police officers and improving the relationship between the police and the community (Pelfrey 1998).

1970—The Need for a New Paradigm

As the practices and philosophies of policing during the reform era began to fall under question, police administrators and researchers began to question standard police practices and their outcomes. Part of the difficulty police experienced during the 1960s was founded in the lack of contact with the public and the changing set of expectations of the community. Although community values changed, the police failed to adapt. This produced conflict and strife between the community and the police, evident through deteriorating police–community relations. The new philosophy of community policing encouraged officers to foster relationships with the community and develop an exchange of values. Wilson and Kelling (1982, 34) note, "The essence of the police role in maintaining order is to reinforce the informal control mechanisms of the community itself." This can only be achieved through an understanding of these informal control mechanisms, which is best derived through a community policing strategy (Manning 1988).

By 1970, the field of policing was ripe for change. The factors described previously demonstrated that the need for change was present. However, for a shift in paradigms to occur, there must be a new set of ideas available (Kuhn 1962). These ideas emerged through the research of the Police Foundation (1981) and Boydstun and Sherry (1975) and through the ideas of Herman Goldstein, who developed the problem-oriented policing philosophy (1979), and Wilson and Kelling, who fostered the broken-windows notion (1982).

WILLIAM V. PELFREY, JR.

See also **Accountability; Community Attitudes toward the Police; Community-Oriented Policing: History; Constitutional Rights: In-Custody Interrogation; Constitutional Rights: Search and Seizure; Corruption; Crime Commissions; Federal Bureau of Investigation; History of American Policing; Law Enforcement Assistance Administration; National Advisory Commission on Civil Disorder; Professionalism**

References and Further Reading

Boydstun, J. E., and M. E. Sherry. 1975. *San Diego Community Profile: Final report.* Washington, DC: Police Foundation.

Chimel v. California, 395 U.S. 752 (1969).

Escobedo v. Illinois, 378 U.S. 478 (1964).

Fyfe, J. J. 1988. Police use of deadly force: Research and reform. *Justice Quarterly* 5: 166–205.

Goldstein, H. 1979. Improving policing: A problem-oriented approach. *Crime and Delinquency* 25: 236–58.

Katz v. United States, 389 U.S. 347 (1967).

Kelling, G. L., and M. H. Moore. 1988. *The evolving strategy of policing.* Perspectives on policing, No. 4. Washington, DC: U.S. Government Printing Office.

Kuhn, T. S. 1962. *The structure of scientific revolutions.* 2nd ed. Chicago: University of Chicago Press.

MacNamara, J. 1967. Uncertainties in police work: The relevance of police recruits' backgrounds and training. In *The police: Six sociological essays*, ed. D. J. Bordeau. New York: John Wiley.

Mapp v. Ohio, 37 U.S. 643 (1961).

Miranda v. Arizona, 384 U.S. 436 (1966).

Pelfrey, W. V., Jr. 1998. Precipitating factors of paradigmatic shift in policing: The origin of the community policing era. In *Community policing: Contemporary readings*, ed. G. P Alpert and A. Piquero. Prospect Heights, IL: Waveland Press.

Police Foundation. 1981. *The Newark Foot Patrol Experiment.* Washington, DC: Police Foundation.

Skolnick, J. H., and J. J. Fyfe. 1993. *Above the law: Police and the excessive use of force.* New York: The Free Press.

Terry v. Ohio, 392 U.S. 1 (1968).

Uchida, C. D. 1997. The development of the American police: An historical overview. In *Critical issues in policing: Contemporary readings*, ed. R. G. Dunham and G. P. Alpert. Prospect Heights, IL: Waveland Press.

Walker, S. 1994. Between two worlds: The President's Crime Commission and the police, 1967–1992. In *The 1967 President's Crime Commission report: Its impact 25 years later*, ed. J. A. Conley. Cincinnati, OH: Anderson Publishing Company.

Wilson, J. Q. 1968. *Varieties of police behavior*. Cambridge, MA: Harvard University Press.

Wilson, J. Q., and G. L. Kelling. 1982. Broken windows: The police and neighborhood safety. *The Atlantic Monthly* 249: 29–38.

Wilson, O. W. 1963. *Police administration*. 2nd ed. New York: McGraw-Hill.

POLICE SOCIAL WORK TEAMS AND VICTIM ADVOCATES

Introduction

During the past three decades, there has been a growing realization among law enforcement agencies that because of the critical community need for police social service teams (also known as police victim assistance and police domestic violence units), they are in an ideal position to implement this collaborative team approach in response to such problems as child abuse and neglect cases, school violence incidents, domestic violence occurrences, and mentally ill persons in crisis. Whether a person is victimized in Rochester, New York, or Boca Raton, Florida, Pasadena, California, or Arlington, Texas, police victim advocate or social work teams are on call and accessible. There are several hundred police victim advocate teams throughout the United States, and most are available twenty-four hours a day, seven days a week. Most victim advocates have a social work background and specialized training in crisis intervention, domestic violence policies and intervention approaches, and the delivery of social services.

Social problems such as domestic violence, child abuse and neglect, and violent crimes are pervasive throughout society. Because of the volatility and life-threatening nature of these problems, a large number of police chiefs and community leaders are committed to intervening early, with the goal of sharply reducing the incidence of these major social problems. Police-based social workers are usually full-time civilian employees assigned to special units operated by police departments. The most common types of units are victim assistance, crime prevention, domestic violence, child abuse and/or missing children, drug education, and juvenile crime. In general, these types of specialized units have grown between 1990 and 2000, with the number of police-based victim assistance units almost doubling, domestic violence units increasing by 60%, and child abuse, crime prevention, drug education, and juvenile crime units remaining about the same (Roberts 2003).

A police–social services collaboration usually provides a coordinated community response from a group of agencies to deal with serious personal and family problems evidenced by repeat calls for police service. Traditionally, police, social work, and mental health agencies share the most demanding parts of the others' client caseloads, but there is minimal interagency communication or cooperation. In order to avoid fragmented and ineffective intervention, police responses must be the starting point of interagency coordination. Coordination is critical since all community agencies are responsible for intervening with community-wide social problems.

Police Social Work Teams

Police social work focuses on working with victims of crime in a variety of areas, including child abuse, sexual assault, family violence, elder abuse, and other crimes against persons (Knox and Roberts 2002, 669):

> Since the 1980s, the growing awareness by the law enforcement and social work professions of the impact of violent crimes on victims, witnesses, and family survivors has resulted in a team approach to provide crisis intervention and victim assistance services. Crime victims are harmed physically, emotionally, and/or financially by perpetrators. In the aftermath, crime victims and family survivors often have to cope with physical pain, acute stress, psychological trauma, phobias, fear, grief, loss, medical problems and expenses, financial needs, and court proceedings. Many crime victims, witnesses, and family survivors have their first contact through the police department.

This is a critical time for intervention, and police social workers have a unique opportunity to provide crisis intervention services (Knox and Roberts 2002).

Evidence-based studies have documented the fact that the impact of an acute crisis reaction can be temporary and quickly stabilized, especially when there is timely assessment, intervention, and follow-up care from police social work teams. These specially trained police and clinical social workers know how to interact with people in the midst of a crisis reaction. They know how to establish rapport and rapidly conduct a biopsychosocial and lethality assessment. They know how to provide early support and ego bolstering, as well as how to help the person examine the most realistic possible options and alternative coping skills. They know how to get closure by helping crime victims to plan and implement a short-term action plan. Thus, recovery from psychological trauma and crisis resolution is optimized, and social functioning is enhanced (Roberts 2005).

The majority of police calls for service are typically crisis-inducing and trauma-inducing situations. The major components of crisis intervention include rapid response, lethality and dangerousness assessment,

establishing rapport and gathering information, identifying and prioritizing the problem areas, and finding alternative coping skills, a feasible action plan, crisis stabilization, and crisis resolution (Roberts 2005). Police typically fulfill their mission when they respond relatively quickly, restore safety and order, make an arrest when appropriate, obtain a temporary protective order from a magistrate, and then leave.

Social workers continue the crisis stabilization process by assessing psychosocial needs, implementing the crisis intervention protocol, providing concrete services, and making referrals. Social workers also accept walk-in cases at the police department and referrals from detectives and police officers. In general, police social workers stabilize crisis-oriented situations by providing crisis intervention and/or developing a social service plan, which includes food vouchers and temporary housing/shelter in addition to time-limited counseling and court advocacy. Police social workers also link clients to appropriate community agencies, including rape crisis centers, battered women shelters, alcohol detoxification programs, and mental health centers.

History of Police Social Work

The social work profession has a long history of working with police departments to provide victim services and prevent crimes against children and women. A crucial first step in the gradual evolvement of the police social workers movement was the establishment of "women's bureaus" within police departments during the first half of the 1900s (Roberts 1997a). Law enforcement has traditionally been involved with crimes involving women, children, and juveniles, and the focus of most police social work services during this early period was on protective and corrective programs for these client populations.

In 1920, at the National Conference on Social Work, Mina Van Winkle, director of the Women's Bureau of the Metropolitan Police Department in Washington, D.C., described the Women's Bureau as a separate unit of the police department that works all cases where children and women are involved, with four types of responsibilities, protective, preventive, corrective, and general police work (Roberts 1997a). Her goal was to have a women's bureau in every major city's police department, and by 1930, there were more than five hundred policewomen in two hundred police departments throughout the United States (Roberts 1997a). There was a steady increase in the police social work movement during the next two decades; however, this growth was found primarily in large urban areas such as Chicago, Los Angeles, and New York City.

Throughout this time period, obstacles such as sexism, discrimination, and stereotypes of women in law enforcement impacted negatively on this movement and led to a decline in police social work programs by the 1950s (Roberts, forthcoming). It was not until the mid-1970s, when the battered women's and rape crisis movements became active, that the social work presence was focused again on crime victims. A major boost in funding police social workers came about throughout the 1970s and early 1980s through state and county block grants allocated through the federal Law Enforcement Assistance Administration (LEAA). These police social workers primarily focused on crime prevention activities and interventions on behalf of predelinquents, status offenders, and juvenile delinquents.

The Violence Against Women Act (VAWA) of 1994 resulted in more than $1 billion being allocated from 1995 through 2000 to state and city police departments and shelters to develop crisis intervention and domestic violence intervention programs (Brownell and Roberts 1999). In 2000, the U.S. Congress designated an additional $7.4 million from the federal Crime Victims Fund to support creating 112 full-time positions for victim assistance specialists in the Federal Bureau of Investigation (FBI), and in 2001, a second earmark was established to support additional victim/witness efforts by the FBI and U.S. Attorneys' Offices. In 2004, the Office of Victims of Crime celebrated its twentieth anniversary in recognition of the passage of the landmark Victims of Crime Act (VOCA) in 1984 (Office of Victims of Crime 2004).

Results of National Survey of Police Social Work and Victim Assistance

Knox and Roberts (2002) conducted a national study of law enforcement agencies from California, Colorado, Indiana, New Jersey, New York, South Carolina, Tennessee, and Texas. There were 111 responding agencies, representative of large suburban towns, mid-sized cities, and large urban areas. Those respondents indicated that 74% of police departments provide twenty-four-hour crisis intervention services, with 55% responding to requests by patrol officers on the scene and 70% providing on-call services. The primary locations for these programs are in police stations (72%) or sheriff's offices (19%). This national study focused on three main areas:

- *Social work direct services and roles.* Respondents indicated that *direct services and counseling roles* begin with the crisis intervention and on-the-scene work. However, one-third of the police social work teams and victim advocates also provide short-term counseling services, with referral to other community and social service agencies for long-term treatment (Knox and Roberts 2002). The role of *broker* of services is essential, with 90% of these programs referring clients to appropriate community and social service agencies. Basic *concrete needs and social services* are provided through home visits (64%), transportation services (56%), and emergency assistance funds (52%), and *Crisis response* through death notification (80%), hostage negotiation (36%), and crisis debriefing (45%) (Knox and Roberts, forthcoming).

- *Staffing patterns.* Staffing patterns from this survey range from small, one- or two-person units/programs (48%) to larger programs with five to eight victim advocates or police social workers and support staff (Knox and Roberts, forthcoming). These findings reveal the expansion of staffing by 2001 when compared to Roberts' earlier national study (1990), which indicated that three-fourths of the victim assistance programs were staffed by five or fewer full-time employees. The majority of the police social work teams and victim assistance units employ civilian personnel with a bachelor's degree in criminal justice, social work, or sociology, or an M.S.W. degree (Knox and Roberts, forthcoming).

- *Theoretical models.* The primary theoretical model used by the responding victim services programs was crisis intervention (68%), with grief and bereavement therapy used by 23% of the programs surveyed; other identified approaches that are used include brief or time-limited treatment (20%), cognitive behavioral approaches (9%), and family therapy (9%) (Knox and Roberts 2002).

Conclusion

Police social workers may have only episodic contact with their clients, but this type of intervention is of an urgent and emergency nature (Roberts, forthcoming).

The role of police social workers is expanding and will likely continue to receive support from a variety of sources. Police social work teams are dealing with the most at-risk and vulnerable clients—battered women, child abuse and neglect victims, sexual assault victims, adolescent runaways, and survivors of community disasters. Therefore, it is imperative that all police social workers and victim advocates be well trained in forensic social work and criminal justice.

Social work researchers and program evaluators can assist local and state governmental agencies in planning and conducting studies to determine the effectiveness of police-based social work teams. Social workers should take advantage of training opportunities in the field of forensic social work and victim services that will enable them to provide leadership and direction for police-based social work in the future.

ALBERT R. ROBERTS

See also **Child Abuse and Its Investigation; Domestic (or Intimate Partner) Violence and the Police; Elderly and Crime; Juvenile Delinquency; Law Enforcement Assistance Administration; Mental Illness: Improved Law Enforcement Response; Minneapolis Domestic Violence Experiment; School Violence; Victim Rights Movement in the United States; Victims' Attitudes toward the Police**

References and Further Reading

Brownell, P., and A. R. Roberts. 1999. A century of forensic social work: Bridging the past to the present. *Social Work* 44 (4), 359–70.

Knox, K. S., and A. R. Roberts. 2002. Police social work. In *Social workers' desk reference,* ed. G. Greene and A. R. Roberts, 668–72. New York: Oxford University Press.

———. Forthcoming. National survey of police social work. In *Handbook of forensic social work,* ed. A. R. Roberts and D. W. Springer. Springfield, IL: Charles C Thomas.

Office for Victims of Crime, U.S. Department of Justice. 2004. *Crime victims' rights in America: An historical overview. National*

Crime Victims Rights Week Resource Guide. http://www.boc.ca.gov/40thAnniversary-HistoricalOverview.htm (accessed September 28, 2005).

Roberts, A. R. 1990. *Helping crime victims: Research, policy, and practice.* Newbury Park, CA: Sage Publications.

———. 1997a. The history and role of social work in law enforcement. In *Social work in juvenile and criminal justice settings,* ed. A. Roberts, 2nd ed., 105–15. Springfield, IL: Charles C Thomas.

———. 1997b. Police social work: Bridging the past to the present. In *Social work in juvenile and criminal justice settings,* ed. A. Roberts, 2nd ed., 126–32. Springfield, IL: Charles C Thomas.

———. 2003. Crime in America: Critical issues, trends, costs, and legal remedies. In *Critical issues in crime and justice,* ed. A. R. Roberts, 2nd ed., 3–22. Thousand Oaks, CA: Sage Publications.

———, ed. 2005. *Crisis intervention handbook: Assessment, treatment and research,* 3rd ed. New York: Oxford University Press.

———. Forthcoming. Police social work: Bridging the past to the present. In *Handbook of forensic social work,* ed. A. Roberts and D. W. Springer. Springfield, IL: Charles C Thomas.

POLICE SOLIDARITY

The sociological concept of solidarity refers to the unique sense of identity, belonging, and cohesion that one develops as part of a group of colleagues who share in common social roles, interests, problems, concerns, and even lifestyles. Since solidarity refers to loyalty to one's colleagues instead of loyalty to an organization, community, or set of principles, it involves emotional ties and commitments rather than formal or contractual relationships.

A sense of solidarity, or unity as it is alternatively called, is the pivotal feature that pervades the police subculture and sustains its integrity. It derives from both common experiences police officers encounter in their working environment and from the socialization or social learning process inherent to the police subculture, which involves the transmission of social norms, values, and beliefs. It is *both* a consequence of other basic features of police subculture, such as a sense of social isolation, *and* a cause of other basic features, such as secrecy.

Solidarity as Loyalty to Colleagues Rather Than Loyalty to the Police Organization

As officers move into higher ranks, solidarity tends to decline. Conversely, members of the police administration are frequently seen by line officers in much the same way they perceive members of the community and other outsiders—as threatening the police subculture. Michael Brown (1981, 82) and Peter Manning (1978, 85–86) remark on how police loyalty and social bonds provide police safety from the arbitrary authority and power of aggressive administrators and supervisors. The very fact that officers feel detached from their departmental administrators and supervisors, and consequently develop in-group bonds as a collective protective response, may indicate that police solidarity is inversely related to organizational loyalty and respect for administrative authority.

In his study of civilianization of the communications division of police departments, Shernock (1988b) found that interpretations of membership in the police department differed for sworn and civilian communications personnel. Sworn personnel tended to interpret their membership in terms of their group identification with fellow officers, whereas civilian personnel tended to interpret their membership in terms of their identification with the organization itself.

In her study of police in New York City precincts, Elizabeth Reuss-Ianni (1983) concluded that there are two distinct cultures in policing: a street cop culture and a management cop culture, which have conflicting perspectives on policy, procedure, and practice in policing. The particularistic values of the street cop culture—the "we–they" worldview, secrecy, and solidarity—are juxtaposed against the new bureaucratic values of police reform that the management cop culture has adopted, where the rule book presumably takes precedence. In contrast to street cops, management cops take community relations, public opinion, and politics seriously and are concerned with public accountability, productivity, and cost effectiveness. Consequently, they are seen by street cops as not having loyalty to people but instead to social and political networks.

Shearing (1981) and Ericson (1981) argue, on the other hand, that what first might appear to be a conflict between subcultural and formal organizational norms can actually involve a complementarity between these ostensibly different norms. These authors interpret subcultural norms as providing direction and guidance for the real work of policing, while formal departmental rules provide the framework used in legitimating this work. In turn, top administrators support and reward those who are successful in managing both the "backstage" work carried out according to subcultural norms and the "front-stage" appearances of abiding by departmental rules. Leonard (1980, 67) adds that although police officers frequently complain about their agencies to their peers, any external complaint against or adverse publicity about their departments often results in an increased sense of solidarity among all members of the department.

In his empirical study on police solidarity, Shernock (1988a) found that the organizational loyalty of his respondents was not related to solidarity measured by either an index of "toleration toward the misconduct of and unequivocal trust toward fellow officers" or by the comparative value placed on loyalty to fellow officers. On the other hand, he found two separate measures of subordination to authority inversely related to solidarity. Obedience to superiors was negatively correlated with both measures of solidarity, and opposition to greater supervision was positively correlated with both measures of solidarity.

Although there has been some disagreement regarding solidarity between line officers and police administrators, there is virtually no such disagreement regarding solidarity between sworn officers and civilians within the police department. In his study of civilianization, Shernock (1988b) concluded that patrol officers were disingenuous when they remarked that "civilians can't be trusted to the same degree as sworn officers because they lack street and police background." The underlying problem of trust would not seem to reflect civilians' response to the pressures of their work, given their significantly lower levels of reported stress in their work compared to that of sworn communications personnel. The problem of trust also would seem to be based only minimally on civilians' perspectives toward work values and police functions, inasmuch as sworn officers performing the same work as these civilians do not differ significantly from them on these values and functions. Instead, given the significant differences in expressions of solidarity and loyalty between civilians and sworn officers in both similar and complementary positions to these civilians, the underlying problem of trust appears to be the threat of civilianization to "the indescribable bond between police officers."

Solidarity as Loyalty to Colleagues Rather Than Loyalty to the Community

Police solidarity has been most commonly seen as the consequence of a need for insulation from perceived dangers and rejection of the community. Even though actual violence occurs in probably fewer than 2% to 3% of police–civilian encounters, the highly unpredictable but potentially dangerous scene is always a part of police patrol. In order to deal with this constant threat of being in a potentially dangerous situation involving persons who cannot be identified in advance, patrol officers come to view everyone with suspicion. This omnipresent suspicion, in turn, serves to isolate police from the rest of society.

This sense of isolation is reinforced by citizens' failure to help the police in fights. The police officer's lack of confidence in receiving help from the public in dangerous situations leads officers to believe that the only people who can be counted on in tight or problematic situations are other police officers and to equate the very essence of survival with the existence of an unquestioned support and loyalty among fellow officers. Since the successful officer needs the full support of his or her partners in order to act in dangerous situations, to violate the sanctity of solidarity by reporting a fellow officer leads one to be viewed as an unsafe officer.

Probably the factor in the external working environment most frequently cited as contributing to both police solidarity and a negative community orientation is the police perception of public hostility toward law enforcement and police officers. During the 1960s, Skolnick (1966, 225) reported that the Westville police he studied felt the most serious problem they had was not race relations but some form of public relations, lack of respect for police, lack of cooperation in enforcement of the law, and lack of understanding of the requirements of police work. In his interviews of police officers, Westley (1970, 107) found that 73% of the officers interviewed believed that the public liked and supported the police. Similarly, Skolnick found that 70% of the 282 officers in the Westville police believed that the public rated the prestige of police work as either poor or only fair, while only 2% felt that the public rated it as excellent.

If this perception of hostility by the public toward the police is realistic, public hostility becomes an environmental precondition for police isolation and solidarity. On the other hand, if the perception is mistaken, it may indicate that the dynamic characteristic of the occupational subculture itself, which includes a sense of minority group status and solidarity, leads to the projection of hostility and, in turn, contributes to a negative community orientation.

Van Maanen (1978, 119) states that "in general, there is little to link patrolmen to the private citizen in terms of establishing a socially satisfying relationship" and that "patrolmen recognize accurately that few civilians are likely to return favors." The long and often irregular working hours, particularly as a result of shift schedules, do not allow police to develop off-duty friendships with nonpolice and thereby contribute to police isolation. Ferdinand (1980) found that until the age of forty, much of a police officer's social life is spent within the confines of the police subculture.

Police suspicion itself is reinforced by officers' work experiences, their being so frequently in an adversarial relationship with the public and being confronted daily by people who are weak or corrupt, as well as dangerous. Lundman (1980, 85) notes further how the public stereotypes and depersonalizes the police, conferring on them a master status that leads them to feel a loss of identity and a sense of being stripped of their individuality.

In contrast, Walker (1992, 226–27) states that police officers do not have an accurate perception of citizen attitudes and that survey data indicate citizens are supportive of police. He cites the 1975 National Crime Survey, which found that 84% of whites and 74% of blacks rated the police as good or average. Although Lundman (1980, 83–84) recognizes some factual basis to the police perception of public hostility, he also finds that the police academy and the field training experience communicate a defensiveness theme to recruits, emphasizing distrust of persons and organizations outside the police department.

The defensiveness theme is communicated by seasoned officers in their war stories and in their interpretations of both the community relations unit as merely functioning to deflect public criticism and of the internal inspection squad as merely functioning to protect the department from attempts to create a civilian review board. Thus recruits are presumably cautioned that "the only people to be trusted are other police officers."

As an outsider group, the patrol officers' occupational identity and subculture crystallize, wherein isolationism, secrecy, strong in-group loyalties, sacred symbols, common language, and a profound estrangement from the larger society intensify. Like other minorities, police officers not only tend to distrust members outside their in-group, but, moreover, tend to fraternize, both on and off the job, with members of their own minority group in order to avoid unpleasant interactions with civilians who view them only in terms of their police identity.

Thus, isolated by the hostility and stereotyping they perceive, the police compensate by developing an intense solidarity for self-protection and moral support (Westley 1970, 111). The consequent unity enables them to tolerate isolation from, hostility of, and disapproval of citizens. Police loyalty then can be seen as assuaging real and imagined wrongs inflicted by a hostile public. As the police bonds to the public become weaker and their in-group activities and cohesiveness become greater, the police become more suspicious of and more polarized from the public, wherein the police–public relationship often turns from supportive to adversarial.

In his study on the relationship between police solidarity and community orientation, Shernock (1988a) found that solidarity as measured by an index of "toleration toward the misconduct of and unequivocal trust toward fellow officers" was weakly related to less support for the service function and to the comparative value placed on respect for citizens, but not related to the comparative importance of the community relations function. On the other hand, when solidarity was measured as the comparative ranking of the value "loyalty to other police officers," it was found strongly related to a lower comparative value placed on respect for citizens and moderately related to less importance placed on the community relations function, but not related to less support for the service function when controlling for age and police experience and not related to defensiveness toward the media.

Shernock also found that antagonism toward externally imposed control over police discretion was found to be highly correlated with the first measure of solidarity and weakly to moderately correlated with the second measure of solidarity. There appears to be a definite tendency for solidarity among police to increase as their level of antagonism toward externally imposed control over police discretion increases.

Solidarity as Loyalty to Colleagues Rather Than Loyalty to Ethical Principles

As a shield against the attacks of the outside world and against public criticism, the police place a high value on secrecy within their subculture. This code of secrecy among police officers, which is not confined to American policing alone, appears to be the strongest code adhered to within the police agency and, according to Goldstein (1977, 165), is stronger than similar tacit norms in the highly regarded professions of media and law.

The perceived hostility toward the police fosters an "us versus them" attitude and a feeling that officers must stick together even to the point of lying about the misconduct of other officers. Secrecy is thus seen by Westley (1970, 111) as solidarity insofar as it represents a common front against the outside world. Blumberg (1976, 15) concurs, stating that "secrecy provides the glue that binds police solidarity." It maintains group identity and supports solidarity since it gives something in common to those who belong to the police subculture and differentiates those who do not. The sense of unity and loyalty that results from the demand for conformity to the values of the police subculture can someday be invoked by any officer to cover a serious mistake or to help the officer out in serious trouble.

Yet, as Westley (1970, 112) significantly observes, secrecy does not apply to achievement but to mistakes, to plans, to illegal actions, to character defamation. Because the police subculture requires that its members be loyal and trustworthy, officers feel obligated to cover up a fellow officer's brutal acts, petty thefts, extortionate behavior, abuses of police power, and other illegalities. "Blowing the whistle," "finking," and "squealing" are breaches of the code of silence and secrecy that represent the most heinous offense in the police world. It is an unwritten law in police departments that police officers must never testify against their fellow officers. Every officer tacitly agrees to uphold the secrecy code in order to claim solidarity rights to the unit or agency to which the officer belongs.

It is still uncertain, however, whether those conforming to the "code of silence" disapprove of the misconduct of fellow officers and whether tolerance of that misconduct indicates how individual officers themselves can be expected to behave. The answer from a number of students of police misbehavior is that there is a connection between an officer's own values and behavior and the officer's tolerance of the misconduct of fellow officers. Noting the effects of police subcultural expectations on recruits, Savitz (1970), in a longitudinal study at three different time periods, found that recruits not only became more permissive toward corrupt police conduct but approximated the values of experienced officers over time.

More specifically, Barker (1978) has observed that those police officers who believe that certain forms of misconduct will not be reported are probably more likely to engage in such misconduct. Stoddard (1968) has gone even further, noting that "whether one can inform on his fellow officers is directly connected with the degree of his illegal involvement prior to the situation involving the unlawful act." Likewise, Muir (1977, 67, 72) believes that once a police officer has violated a standard or rule, that officer is bound to remain silent regarding others' violations, even if they are more serious. It would thus appear, according to these critics, that tolerance toward the misconduct of other officers is more likely to be based either on a more complete socialization to the subcultural value systems or on complicity that develops as a result of one's own misconduct than on mere conformity to the "code of silence."

Conclusion

Some degree of solidarity may be very positive. Loyalty to fellow officers may bolster officers' self-esteem and confidence and may call forth a courageous reaction to threats to the interests of a member of a group to which one belongs. Nevertheless, attention has been focused on the police subcultural attribute of solidarity because of its perceived negative consequences for organizational control and change, public accountability, and ethical conduct.

The particularistic value placed on loyalty to colleagues often comes into conflict with the bureaucratic values of police reform, and police solidarity itself often undermines supervisory control by police administrators. The isolation associated with police solidarity may undermine loyalty to the community insofar as it influences officers to develop attitudes that are essentially different from those of the wider society within which the police function and whom they are charged to protect, and may create and sustain negative perceptions toward and hostile encounters with members of the public. Excessive loyalty to colleagues also has been seen as inconsistent with loyalty to the high ideals of the ethical canons of the profession and, consequently, as militating against the obligation impelled by a regulatory code of ethics to identify and mete out professional sanctions against those fellow practitioners who have failed to perform their duties properly.

While police officers might continue to express solidarity with fellow officers by maintaining the "code of silence," there are some indications that there are changes in patterns of fraternization among police that have bolstered solidarity in the past. Blumberg states that regardless of what a number of dated studies may show, his experience in contact with a variety of police departments would lead him to believe that the new generation of police recruits has developed a more expanded friendship network than their predecessors and that the social isolation of police is somewhat exaggerated.

There are also some indications, despite the need for more research, that the recruitment of women and African Americans has modified police solidarity. Martin found that the entrance of women into policing has diminished the traditional solidarity of the group because expressions of friendship that are acceptable between two males are problematic between officers of different sexes, and also because women officers do not share the same off-duty interests as male officers. While it might be assumed that increased educational qualifications and professionalization of the police might lead to conflicts between old-line officers, and thus at least temporarily weaken solidarity among police officers, the effects of these changes, as well as

others, must be determined by future empirical research studies.

STAN SHERNOCK

References and Further Reading

Alpert, Geoffrey, and Roger Dunham. 1992. *Policing urban America*. 2nd ed. Prospect Heights, IL: Waveland Press.

Barker, Thomas. 1977. Peer group support for police occupational deviance. *Criminology* 15.

———. 1978. An empirical study on police deviance other than corruption. *Journal of Police Science and Administration* 6: 264–72.

Bedrosian, Albert. 1981. An occupational hazard—The subculture of police. *Journal of California Law Enforcement* 15: 95–101.

Blumberg, Abraham. 1976. The police and the social system: Reflections and prospects. In *The ambivalent force: Perspectives on the police*, ed. Abraham Blumberg and Arthur Niederhoffer. New York: Dryden Press.

Brown, Michael. 1981. *Working the street: Police discretion and the dilemmas of reform*. New York: Russell Sage.

Conser, James A. 1978. A literary review of the police subculture: Its characteristics, impact, and policy implications. *Police Studies* 2: 46–54.

Ericson, Richard. 1981. Rules for police deviance. In *Organizational police deviance: Its structure and control*, ed. Clifford Shearing. Toronto: Butterworth.

Ferdinand, T. H. 1980. Police attitudes and police organization: Some interdepartmental and cross-cultural comparison. *Police Studies* 3: 46–60.

Gaines, Larry K., Victor E. Kappeler, and Joseph B. Vaughn. 1994. *Policing in America*. Cincinnati, OH: Anderson Publishing Company.

Goldstein, Herman. 1977. *Policing in free society*. Cambridge, MA: Ballinger.

Leonard, V. A. 1980. *Fundamentals of law enforcement: Problems and issues*. St. Paul, MN: West.

Lester, David, and William Tom Brink. 1985. Police solidarity and tolerance for police misbehavior. *Psychological Reports* 57: 326.

Lundman, Richard. 1980. *Police and policing: An introduction*. New York: Holt, Rinehart and Winston.

Manning, Peter. 1978. Rules, colleagues, and situationally justified actions. In *Policing: A view from the street*, ed. Peter Manning and

John Van Maanen. New York: Random House.

Martin, Susan. 1980. *Breaking and entering: Police women on patrol*. Berkeley, CA: University of California Press.

Muir, William. 1977. *Police: Streetcorner politicians*. Chicago: University of Chicago Press.

Reuss-Ianni, Elizabeth. 1983. *Two cultures of policing: Street cops and management cops*. New Brunswick, NJ: Transaction Books.

Savitz, Leonard. 1970. The dimensions of police loyalty. *American Behavioral Scientist* (May–June, July–August): 693–704.

Shearing, Clifford. 1981. Deviance and conformity in the reproduction of order. In *Organizational police deviance: Its structure and control*, ed. Clifford Shearing. Toronto: Butterworth.

Shernock, Stan. 1988a. An empirical examination of the relationship between police solidarity and community orientation. *Journal of Police Science and Administration* 16: 182–94.

———. 1988b. The differential significance of sworn status and organizational position in the civilianization of the police communications division. *Journal of Police Science and Administration* 16: 288–302.

Skolnick, Jerome. 1966. *Justice without trial*. New York: John Wiley and Sons.

Stoddard, Ellwyn. 1968. "The informal code" of police deviancy: A group approach to blue collar crime. *Journal of Criminal Law, Criminology, and Police Science* 59: 201–13.

Van Maanen, John. 1978. Kinsmen in repose: Occupational perspectives of patrolmen. In *Policing: A view from the street*, ed. Peter Manning and John Van Maanen. New York: Random House.

Walker, Samuel. 1992. *The police in America: An introduction*. 2nd ed. New York: McGraw-Hill.

Watkins, C. Ken. 1975. *Social control*. London: Longman.

Westley, William. 1956. Secrecy and the police. *Social Forces* 34: 254–57.

———. 1970. *Violence and the police*. Cambridge, MA: MIT Press.

POLICE STANDARDS AND TRAINING COMMISSIONS

Notwithstanding well-documented police lineage, the roots of organized American policing can be traced to 1845. In that year, the city of New York created the first official municipal police department against the backdrop of much public distrust. It is reasonable, then, to mark that historical era as the most probable beginning of formal concern regarding the standards and training expected of those anointed to guard societal liberties. This article chronicles the contributions of many prominent organizations and commissions to police standards and training advancements and concludes with an overview of the organizational controls currently used in the selection and development of police recruits.

International Association of Chiefs of Police (IACP)

Organized in 1893 as the National Chiefs of Police Union, the IACP is the most recognizable and influential police organization. Its constitutional mission reveals a commitment, among other things, to professional recruitment and training efforts. In support of that mission and dating back to 1934, the association publishes a monthly journal, *Police Chief*, that is widely regarded as the professional voice of law enforcement and training. A comprehensive accounting in this article of all contributions made by this organization to the police profession is impractical. At a minimum, though, it is important to acknowledge its encouraging role in the creation of the National Association of Directors of Law Enforcement Standards and Training (NADLEST; now an international association known as IADLEST) as the official association for Peace Officer Standards and Training organizations.

Wickersham Commission

Concerned with civil unrest and a general absence of prohibition enforcement,

President Herbert Hoover, in 1929, appointed the National Commission on Law Observance and Enforcement to conduct the first national investigation of the administration of justice. Under the guidance of George W. Wickersham, a former U.S. attorney general, the Commission's fourteen published reports (1931) represent the first national effort to synchronize local, state, and federal enforcement resources in the efforts to control crime. Its *Report on Lawlessness in Law Enforcement* made unexpected references to spiraling police misconduct, resulting in bold recommendations aimed at promoting police accountability through effective recruitment, training, and ethics enforcement.

Even though immediate actions on most recommendations failed to materialize, it is universally recognized that the commission's views paved the way for future change and progress. Of particular significance, however, was its progressive recommendation to require a college degree for entry-level policing employment at a time when a high school education was perceived as a sufficient education.

President's Commission on Law Enforcement and Administration of Justice

The President's Commission on Law Enforcement and Administration of Justice, also called the Katzenbach Commission after the attorney general and commission chair, is widely regarded as the most influential of all historical commissions for its revolutionary approach to the crime epidemic of the 1960s. Assembled under the leadership of President Johnson and comprised of a diverse body of experts from state and local governments, the commission conducted an extensive investigation into all aspects of crime and justice administration. The commission made thirty-four specific recommendations to improve police operations and relations, but its greatest contributions may well be its emphasis on the value of education (that all police officers should possess a college degree) and additional funding for training and crime prevention efforts.

The influence of the commission's work is best evidenced from the modern writings of its many advocates. As is true of most initiatives, however, there are voices expressing pessimism that the recommendations have not become entrenched in the realities of modern justice enterprises. One undeniable accomplishment, though, was its visionary approach to crime and justice as a "system." Prior to that time, the components were uncoordinated and viewed as distinct and separate units. The commission's recognition of this disconnect revolutionized policing (and other justice professions) as it created and simultaneously legitimized a criminal justice system.

National Advisory Commission on Civil Disorder

With widespread rioting in urban ghettos and police–community relations on the decline, President Johnson appointed the National Advisory Commission on Civil Disorder, also called the Kerner Commission, to formulate a strategic plan. Because of the mounting pressures from community deterioration and an approaching presidential election, the commission hurried its recommendations; as a result, the 1968 report did little more than to echo the recommendations of the President's Commission one year earlier. Its recommendations for local police planning and training, however, did contribute to riot operations in several instrumental ways. Mainly, it criticized the use of overly militaristic tactics as a control mechanism, opting instead to promote the more humanistic and service-oriented values accomplished through community support and interaction.

National Advisory Commission on Criminal Justice Standards and Goals

The Law Enforcement Assistance Administration, in 1971, funded this commission to determine the basic course of action necessary to reduce crime and societal fear of crime. In its 1973 *Report on Police*, the commission made many specific recommendations designed to enhance police effectiveness through recruitment, selection, and training procedures. The progressive recommendations most notably focused on the recruitment of minorities, women, and the college educated. Of major importance, however, was the recommendation that every state should enact legislation empowering a state commission to develop and enforce minimum mandatory standards for the selection and training of police officers. At that time, thirty-five states had passed such legislation, yet not all states required compliance with those standards. The commission also designed a highly vocational template for the distribution of training within a 400-hour minimum, with the greatest concentration dedicated to patrol and investigative procedures, and called for a minimum of forty in-service training hours to be completed on an annual basis.

Accreditation

Created in 1979, the Commission on Accreditation for Law Enforcement Agencies (CALEA) offers a voluntary accreditation process to all police agencies concerned with operational efficiency and professional standards. The accreditation process is costly and rigorous, and although departments benefit from enhanced professional status, fewer than 5% of police agencies nationally are accredited.

The Beginnings of Peace Officer Standards and Training (POST) Programs

The first state to mandate minimum standards and training requirements for all police departments was New York in 1959. California followed suit with the unveiling of its voluntary version later in that same year. Compared with the complexity of modern requirements, these programs were quite humble, yet were of monumental importance as role models for the nation as a whole, because all states had formed POST organizations by 1981.

Model Minimum Standards for Recruitment and Selection

The International Association of Directors of Law Enforcement Standards and Training (IADLEST) has been proactive in the pursuit of police professionalism. Comprising the directors of the respective state POST organizations, IADLEST promotes a model of minimum standards designed to encourage states to enact standards most consistent with the building of a professional police force. States adhere to these standards in differing degrees, but the composition of the model has been instrumental as a change agent. The following sections do not represent a comprehensive account of all minimum standards, but rather focus on those most derived from the influences of past commissions.

Character Screening

Given the widespread authority allocated to the police, it is imperative that police recruits be equipped with a solid moral foundation. To achieve this objective, police organizations use a variety of screening mechanisms to enhance recruitment success.

One requirement limits police employment to American citizens. The method of citizenship, however, is irrelevant and, therefore, this practice is not one of prejudicial origin. Rather, it is merely believed that enforcement of the law is best entrusted to those committed to American ideals and possessing a fundamental knowledge of its laws.

Law enforcement agencies also conduct investigations into the moral fabric of prospective applicants. Two basic investigations are completed in furtherance of this mission. One, a criminal history examination, is conducted to exclude convicted felons from employment eligibility and any others demonstrating a propensity for continued lawbreaking. Second, people with the best perspective regarding a candidate's moral character are interviewed. The background investigation ordinarily includes family members, neighbors, teachers, employers, and credit histories. Police recruits are also required to pass a drug test to ensure that those responsible for the enforcement of illegal drug use are not using the banned substances themselves. Drug use not only would compromise the integrity of the police department, but also would jeopardize the safety of the public.

Mental Fitness

Because of the myriad of difficult and unconventional situations encountered on a daily basis, officers must exhibit the capacity to formulate mature judgments. Police organizations use two major requirements to limit employment access to the mentally unstable. First, all applicants are psychologically tested to screen out those incapable of performing assigned duties or of enduring the stressors inherent in police work. It is extremely important that people with mental illnesses or those who are emotionally unstable be precluded from these positions of power and authority. A second initiative that strives to restrict policing duties to those of mental fitness is an educational requirement. At present, the minimum requirement is a high school diploma, but IADLEST strongly encourages all police departments to phase in a baccalaureate degree requirement in an effort to achieve the status of profession at some time in the future.

PHILIP E. CARLAN

See also **Academies, Police; Accountability; Codes of Ethics; International Association of Chiefs of Police (IACP); National Advisory Commission on Civil Disorder; Personnel Selection; Police Reform: 1950–1970; Professionalism; Psychological Standards; Wickersham, George W.**

References and Further Reading

Buerger, Michael. 2004. Educating and training the future police officer. *FBI Law Enforcement Bulletin* 73: 26–32.

Deakin, Thomas J. 1988. *Police professionalism: The renaissance of American law enforcement.* Springfield, IL: Charles C Thomas.

International Association of Directors of Law Enforcement Standards and Training. 2005. *Model minimum standards.* http://www.iadlest.org (accessed November 2005).

National Advisory Commission on Civil Disorders. 1968. *Report of the National Advisory Commission on Civil Disorders.* Washington, DC: U.S. Government Printing Office.

National Advisory Commission on Criminal Justice Standards and Goals. 1973. *Report on police.* Washington, DC: U.S. Government Printing Office.

President's Commission on Law Enforcement and Administration of Justice. 1967. *The challenge of crime in a free society.* Washington, DC: U.S. Government Printing Office.

Skoler, Daniel. *Organizing the non-system.* Lexington, MA: Lexington Books.

POLICE STATES

A police state is a nation whose rulers maintain order and obedience by coercion, terror, torture, propagandizing, brainwashing, mass surveillance, or any combination of these methods. A police state is inherently repressive and undemocratic. In its repressive aspects, a police state suppresses political dissent, curtails or eliminates civil liberties, and sometimes even tries to wipe out disagreeable ideas, feelings, memories, or impulses from the conscious minds of individuals. In its legal aspects, a *police state* is similar to martial law or the law imposed on a country by a state when civil authority has broken down. The two most infamous police states in world history—Nazi Germany under Adolph Hitler (1933–1945) and the former Soviet Union under Joseph Stalin (1929–1953)—are considered to be the prototypical police states. The definitive fictional treatment of a police state, which has also influenced contemporary usage of the term, is George Orwell's novel *1984.* Orwell's novel describes a regime that uses the excuse of endless war to justify thought police and security cameras for purposes of mass surveillance.

The term *police state* can also be used as an adjective to describe a technique of ruling. Implicit in this second usage is the notion that designating a country as a police state does not necessarily have anything to do with the structure of a state or a state's dominant political ideology. Therefore, it is possible for a democracy to use police state methods in dealing with a perceived threat. After the enactment of the USA PATRIOT Act in 2001, for example, some critics of the war on terrorism raised concerns that the United States was using police state tactics to fight terrorism on the domestic front. Although it is true that democracies sometimes employ police state tactics, most scholars hold that democracies do not become full-fledged police states unless they transform into authoritarian or totalitarian states.

Dichotomies, Democracies, and Police States

The recognition that democratic states occasionally use police state tactics raises an important question: Should scholars engaged in comparative research on police states treat the distinction between police states and democracies as a dichotomy or in terms of gradations? This question has implications for how research is organized, for how data are collected and analyzed, and for inferences about the causes and consequences of police states.

Unresolved conceptual issues center around these additional questions: Should social scientists treat "police stateness" as a property that regimes display in varying degrees? Do nations vary in the extent to which their governments meet the criteria for being classified as police states? Should police states be considered systems, that is, bounded wholes characterized by attributes and mechanisms that are either present or absent? Do intermediate cases exist in which countries lack all the attributes of the perfect or ideal police state and instead exhibit a mixture of qualities or characteristics of both democracies and police states? If so, how should these intermediate cases be labeled? A couple of possibilities would be to use the label "emerging police states" in cases where some but not all of the attributes of police states are present and to call cases in which civil liberties have been attenuated in democratic states "illiberal democracies."

Putting Police States in Context

Drawing a simple dichotomy between democracies and police states obscures the distinctiveness of the police state as a political phenomenon. A dichotomy does not adequately capture the political reality of police states. It is possible to distinguish particular historical forms of police states.

The "traditional police state," which existed in various countries in Europe from the seventeenth through the nineteenth centuries, had the best of motives. It was a mixture of autocratic reform, paternalistic benevolence, suspicion, and compulsion. In its emphasis on national development, it was similar to many so-called Third World countries today. Unlike police states of the twentieth and twenty-first centuries, however, the traditional police state was not known for its arbitrary and repressive rule. Extensive police powers were concentrated in a civil service under a single political will, with a police institution having responsibility for watching over the safety of the state, the integrity of public officers, and the morale of the population. By the end of the nineteenth century, the institutional and theoretical bases of the traditional police state had been demolished and the stage was set for the rise of a new type of police state.

The "modern police state" presupposes an authoritarian regime. Some scholars point to Nazi Germany from 1933 to 1939 as an example of this type of police state. Authoritarian regimes usually grant wide powers to law enforcement agencies; when this tendency is pushed to the extreme, a modern police state can develop. In such a police state, the rule of law either does not exist or is routinely ignored. A modern police state is considered to be completely formed when the police institution becomes immune to control by the civil service, the judiciary, and the army, and it is an independent leading state institution in its own right. The main difference between a traditional and a modern police state centers around the emergence of the secret police as an offensive weapon in the modern police state, reversing the traditional role of the police as defenders of the existing order.

Different issues arise in a "totalitarian police state." Some well-known examples include Nazi Germany between 1939 and 1945, fascist Italy, the Soviet Union, Ba'athist Iraq, Ba'athist Syria, Libya, Communist China, and the Democratic People's Republic of Korea (North Korea). Prominent features of totalitarian police states include an ideology supported by propaganda campaigns, a single political party committed to this ideology and usually led by a dictator, a secret police force, monopolistic control by the party over the media and other institutions, and concentrated power in an individual or an elite that is not accountable to the public and cannot be checked or dislodged by institutional means. Totalitarian police states prohibit all activities contrary to the regime's goals of (1) a radical restructuring of society to create a new economic order (Communism), (2) instituting racism (Nazism), (3) reconstituting human nature through fundamentalist religion (Taliban rule in Afghanistan), or (4) some combination of these. Historically, some totalitarian police states have maintained power by resorting to terroristic methods including police brutality, concentration camps and torture, political show trials, purges of the "old guard" of the ruling party, imprisonment and executions without proof of guilt, and repressive measures against whole categories of people. However, some totalitarian police states have replaced the open terror of violence on the streets and in the cells brought against opponents of the regime with the silent terror of manipulating citizens to collaborate, to inform, and to denounce. In these police states subtler tools of persuasion are used to create the state's version of the model citizen: a compliant zombie who obeys the law, causes no trouble, asks no questions, and does not resist. In some respects, twenty-first century Communist China approaches this sort of totalitarian police state.

Criminal Justice in Police States

Typically, a separate criminal justice system develops within a police state to dispense political justice to "enemies of the state." This new or special criminal justice system often consists of secret police, military tribunals, and concentration camps or "gulags."

Secret police are a species of internal security agency used as instruments of political repression, mass surveillance, and murder. *Secret police* is a blanket term used to refer to various kinds of political police agencies that are known to exist but that operate in the shadows. Some of the best known early twentieth-century examples are Communist Russia's KGB, Fascist Italy's OVARA, and Nazi Germany's Gestapo. Notorious ones established in the second half of the twentieth century are the DINA of Chilean President Augusto Pinochet Ugarte, the Savak of the Shah of Iran, and the Mukhabarat of Iraq's former president Saddam Hussein. "Thought police," the secret police in *1984,* whose job it was to uncover and punish thought crime, used psychology and omnipresent surveillance to find and eliminate members of society who were capable of the mere thought of challenging the ruling authority. What is distinctive about both real and imaginary secret police is that they are, perhaps more than any other institution, a menace to human rights (especially the right to privacy). Examples of harmful repressive measures attributed to secret police include genocide, assassinations, disappearances of political opposition figures, torture and/or other types of mistreatment of political prisoners in concentration camps, harassment of dissidents, and the use of psychiatric confinement against political opponents of a regime.

Gulag is a Russian acronym meaning Glavnoe Upravlenie Lagerei or Main Camp Administration (for concentration camps). The word has also come to refer to either the system of Soviet slave labor or the Soviet repressive system itself. The West first learned about gulags from concentration camp survivor Alexander Solzhenitsyn's novel about life in Soviet labor camps, *One Day in the Life of Ivan Denisovich.* His oral history of the camps, *The Gulag Archipelago,* also stirred interest when it appeared in 1974. Police states in both Russia and Germany have featured gulags. Regimes in both countries legitimized themselves by establishing categories of "enemies of the state" and then herding people from these categories into concentration camps. Within the camps dehumanization was extreme, helping to both intimidate victims and reinforce the victimizers' belief in the legitimacy of what they were doing. Whereas the primary purpose of the Soviet Gulag was economic (that is, to exploit slave labor), the Nazi concentration camps were not really labor camps, but rather death factories.

Military tribunals or "people's courts" substitute for regular courts in police states. Judicial independence is lacking in police state courts and evidentiary standards are very low—tips by anonymous informers and information obtained through torture are often accepted as admissible evidence. Take, for example, Nazi Germany's Volksgerichtshof (VGH) or "People's Court." Dissatisfied with "not guilty" verdicts in some cases involving political crimes, Hitler established "People's Courts" throughout Germany to increase the political reliability of the courts in politically sensitive cases. These courts became part of the Nazi system of terror, condemning more than 12,000 civilians to death and sending thousands more to concentration camps between 1934 and 1945. Another example is the NKVD troika (a three-member commission of Stalin's main state security agency). It began as an institution of the Cheka (the first of many Soviet secret police organizations), then later became prominent in the NKVD, when the troika was used during Stalin's Great Purge. The Great Purge consisted of campaigns of political repression in the Soviet Union during the late 1930s and included purges of the Communist Party.

Policing in Police States

Policing systems used in the former Soviet Union and Communist China are prototypes of control systems found in many police states. In the former Soviet Union, the state recruited some portion of the citizens to act as KGB agents. In typical encounters with fellow citizens, a citizen of the former Soviet Union would not know whether or not the other citizen was a KGB agent. Consequently, under the Soviet supervision system, a recurring decision problem for the typical citizen revolved around the question "What is the probability that this individual with whom I'm about to interact is a KGB agent?"

Compared to the former Soviet Union's variant of "police patrol," the system in Communist China is a self-policing system. It calls on citizens to report not only their own behavior, but also the behavior of others. The self-policing system is a system whereby neighbors are held accountable for each other's crimes if they fail to report them. Political control in Communist China resembles that of some other totalitarian police states in that it relies not only on the coercive power of the state, but also on citizens monitoring each other. The Chinese police state applies the self-policing system by focusing on the units or small groups where its citizens live or work.

Assessing the Impact

Understanding the nature of police states offers only a partial perspective on repressive regimes of the past and present. By focusing on the various impacts of police states, the real significance of the problem of police states becomes apparent.

From the viewpoint of the victim and the potential victim, police states pose a very real threat. The scale in number of lives lost, man-years lost in concentration camps, and people arrested and subjected to limitations of freedoms of movement in police states is so large that it is difficult to fathom. In *Mao: The Unknown Story,* Jung Chang and British historian Jon Halliday argue that Mao's police state was responsible for more than 70 million deaths in peacetime, and they argue that Mao was more extreme than Hitler or Stalin in that he envisioned a brain-dead Chinese society whose members would automatically obey his orders. Historian Robert Conquest estimates that around 1 million persons were executed in the Russian police state in the late 1930s. Based on a 10% death rate per annum, other historians estimate that 12 million prisoners died in Russian concentration camps from 1936 to 1950. Adding to them the million executions of the period, the casualties of another era of Stalin's rule (1930–1936), those sent to concentration camps who died, and the 3.5 million victims of Stalin's collectivization, Conquest reaches the figure of 20 million dead in twenty-three years of Stalin's rule. The best estimate of the number of victims of the Nazi "final solution of the Jewish problem" ranges between 4.2 and 4.5 million, with the total loss of Jewish life estimated at 6 million.

Opposition and Resistance

One gap in the work on police states is the lack of study of unsuccessful, but heroic resistance against police states. Over the years, a considerable amount of scholarly historical literature on resistance against Hitler's rule has been published. The myriad of other examples of opposition and resistance drawn from the twenty-first century range from the American Civil Liberties Union's international campaign against mass surveillance, to the Free Tibet movement, to the refusal of some of the highest ranking officers in the Sudanese army to bomb civilians in Darfur. Conceptual distinctions have been drawn between passive withdrawal, the assertion of autonomy by institutions and individuals, refusal to obey orders, organizing rebellion, and conspiratorial activities directed toward overthrowing regimes. A question that needs to be addressed is "At what point, when, and how can the establishment of police states be prevented?"

DENNIS E. HOFFMAN

See also **Accountability; Constitutional Rights: In-Custody Interrogation; Constitutional Rights: Privacy; Federal Commissions and Enactments; Informants, Use of; PATRIOT Acts I and II; Surveillance**

References and Further Reading

Applebaum, Anne. 2003. *Gulag*. New York: Doubleday.
Brehm, John, and Emerson M. S. Nious. 1997. Police patrol versus self-policing: A comparative analysis of the control systems used in the former Soviet Union and communist China. *Journal of Theoretical Politics* 9: 107–30.
Chang, Jung, and Jon Halliday. 1970. *Mao: The unknown story*. New York: Knopf.
Chapman, Brian. 1970. *Police state*. New York: Praeger.
Conquest, Robert. 1968. *The great terror: Stalin's purge of the thirties*. New York: Macmillan.
———. 1990. *The great terror: A reassessment*. New York: Oxford University Press.
Evans, Richard. 2004. *The coming of the Third Reich*. New York: Penguin Press.
Gause, Gregory. 2005. Can democracy stop terrorism? *Foreign Affairs* (Sep./Oct.): 62–76.
Hagan, John, Weona Rymond-Richmond, and Patricia Parker. 2005. The criminology of genocide. *Criminology* 43: 524–61.
Hohne, Heinz. 2000. *The order of the death's head: The story of Hitler's SS*. New York: Penguin Books.
Koch, H. W. 1989. *In the name of the volk: Political justice in Hitler's Germany*. New York: Barnes and Noble Books.
Linz, Juan. 2000. *Totalitarian and authoritarian regimes*. Boulder, CO: Lynne Rienner Publishers.
Orwell, George. 1949. *1984*. New York: Harcourt.
Powers, John. 2000. The free Tibet movement: A selective narrative. *Journal of Buddhist Ethics* 7: 126–44.
Sebag-Montegiore, Simon. 2004. *Stalin: The court of the red tsar*. New York: Knopf.
Shelley, Louise I. 1996. *Policing Soviet society*. London: Routledge.
Solzhenitsyn, Alexander. 1973. *One day in the life of Ivan Denisovich*. Paris: YMCA-Press.
———. 1974. *The Gulag archipelago*. New York: Harper and Row.

POLICE SUICIDE

Suicide among officers has been the topic of much speculation (Ellison 2004). Unfortunately, much of this speculation has been based as much on "received wisdom" and myth as on evidence. Even the research evidence that is available tends to be methodologically flawed and frequently contradictory. For example, several studies have seemed to show that, compared with other occupations and with the general public, police officers are especially prone to kill themselves. Kroes (1976) believes that officers are much more likely to die by their own hands than to be killed by others. Violanti (1996) puts the risk as twice as high.

Studies vary in their contentions about the rate of police suicide relative to those in other occupations. Gurlanick (1963) found that police have the highest rates of all professions, whereas Kroes (1976) found that police were less likely to kill themselves than laborers and lumbermen but somewhat more likely to do so than physicians. In contrast, Ivanoff (1994) found that physicians, dentists, and entrepreneurs have higher rates of suicide than police. (Ivanoff noted that people in these other professions serve the public and none regularly carry guns.) Still other studies have found suicide rates among police to be surpassed by rates among self-employed manufacturing managers (Labovita and Hagedorn 1971) or by rates among laborers and pressmen (Richard and Fell 1975).

As with most studies of policing, much of the data come from large agencies. Here we find wide discrepancies. Rates range from 15.5 per 100,000 in the New York Police Department for the years from 1990 to 1998 to 35.7 per 100,000 in the San Diego Police department during the same years. In 1998–1999, the U.S. Customs Service recorded a rate of 45.6 per 100,000. The rate for the general public in the United States in the years 1995–1996 was 11.8 per 100,000; this included men and women of all ages. However, the rate for the Caucasian men age twenty to sixty during this time frame was 15 to 25 per 100,000 (Campion 2001). Because most of the officers are healthy, white (81%), working-aged men (89%) (Aamodt and Stalkner 2001; Bergen, Deusch, and Best 2001), this is the most appropriate comparison group. However, even this group (Caucasian men ages twenty to sixty) presents a problem for comparison: Most do not have the officer's easy access to firearms, which are more likely to be lethal than many other methods of attempting suicide. Several studies have suggested a connection between availability of guns and suicide (Lester 1987; Killias 1993).

Aamodt and Stalkner's (2001) statistical analysis of suicide data demonstrates that differences between law enforcement personnel and the general public have not only been reduced, but have changed direction. Stalkner found that law enforcement personnel are 26% less likely to commit suicide than their counterparts of the same sex, race, and age not working in law enforcement. Thus, according to this study, attempts to attribute suicides by law enforcement personnel to unique characteristics of the job cannot be supported (p. 386).

In discussing police suicide, Bergen and his colleagues (2001) argued that "accurate recording and reporting of police suicides is the most critical current research issue. Departments must provide accurate data if meaningful changes are to be implemented" (p. 411). Indeed, all suicide data in the United States suffer from serious methodological problems in a number of areas. In our culture, where suicide is stigmatized and often results in loss of life insurance for survivors, there is a tendency for medical personnel to list a suspicious death as accidental if at all possible. The suicidal person may seek to spare his or her family and make the death seem accidental, for example, by driving a car into a tree or turning a boat over in deep water. Most experts estimate conservatively that the number of actual suicides is at least twice as high as the number reported.

Police data may be particularly suspect because other officers often are the ones who discover the bodies of their dead colleagues. In an attempt to protect the families and, perhaps, the department, they may attempt to cover up the cause of death, including destroying suicide notes (Bergen et al. 2001).

Violanti and his colleagues (1996) demonstrated that official records in Buffalo, New York, underestimated police suicides. They discovered cases labeled "undetermined" that involved gunshot wounds to the head. (Newspaper accounts sometimes record that the officer was cleaning his gun when it fired accidentally. Officers of my acquaintance suggest that the officer had the cleaning kit out in a deliberate attempt to protect the family by making the death seem accidental.)

The reasons officers commit suicide vary and are often difficult to determine. One study found that the "typical" officer who committed suicide was a white, 36.9-year-old married male with 12.2 years of law enforcement experience. The act was usually committed off duty (86.3%), at home (54.8%), and with a gun (90.7%) (Aamodt and Stalkner 2001). In a study of officers who were referred for fitness-for-duty evaluations, Janik and Kravitz (1994) found that those who reported marital difficulties were significantly more likely to have made a suicide attempt than those who did not report such difficulties.

Work-related problems trailed far behind relationship problems (26.6% including murder-suicide) and legal problems (14.9%). Alcohol is also mentioned as a contributing factor (Aamodt and Stalkner 2001), but this may be correlated with the other problems, including depression. Campion (2001), in a study of small, Midwestern departments, found that chiefs, sheriffs, and union officials believed that personal stress, depression, emotional problems, traumatic job stress, and alcohol abuse were major contributors to police suicide. (It must be noted here that much of this was conjecture; most of these agencies had had no direct experience with police suicide.) Additionally, escape from seemingly intolerable psychological pain and also the desire for revenge (anger, retribution, and manipulation of others) figure prominently is suicidal motivation in the general public (Marris 1992), and probably play a large role in police suicide.

In one of the earliest works about cases of suicide, the French sociologist, Emil Durkheim (1897–1951) speculated about the importance of what he called *anomie*: a lack of group cohesiveness, of a shared set of social norms and values. This also may be at work in police suicide (Slater and Depue 1891). Thus, an important deterrence to suicide may be a sense of personal involvement and identity with others. However, many studies have revealed feelings of isolation in officers (Ellison 2004; Lewis 1973).

Any consideration of suicide must also take into account unsuccessful attempts. These figures are even more difficult to obtain, but Gottesfeld (1979) estimates that about ten times as many people attempt suicide as succeed. There have been no studies of attempted suicide among police.

Some people actively try to kill themselves. Others may try passive, indirect means. They take unnecessary risks, or allow themselves to die by failing to attend to health problems or by abusing drugs and alcohol. Such behavior, which Farberow (1980) has called *indirect self-destruction,*

is not included in suicide statistics, and there is no hard evidence to indicate how common it is. Allen (1986), however, believes that for police officers, the likelihood of developing indirect self-destructive behaviors is great. Risk taking in its positive qualities has played a prominent role in the development of their identity as police officers, especially in the form of mastering fear-provoking situations and in facilitating ambitious achievement. In short, risk taking for the individual police officer has established the predominant motives of excitement and mastery (p. 414).

Prevention

Because most of the evidence about incidence and causes of police suicide is circumstantial, it is not easy to devise strategies for prevention. This is especially so because the typical officer is reluctant to admit emotional problems. Even those who discuss problems with fellow officers ordinarily will avoid seeking professional help for fear of damaging her or his career.

Further, prevention is very difficult to measure. However, in hopes of decreasing stress-related disorders and suicide, an increasing number of police departments are providing psychological services (Sheehan and Warren 2001; Reese and Goldstein 1986). These services include monitoring officers' performance for warning signs of possible suicide and providing stress management training and crisis intervention counseling, including counseling after potentially traumatic incidents.

Although many claims have been made for these programs (see Sheehan and Warren 2001 and Reese and Goldstein 1986), there is little solid, unbiased evidence to substantiate these claims. Even the best tend to have serious flaws. Unfortunately, too, most of these programs focus on the individual officer; few address the organizational factors that have been considered the greatest contributors to stress-related occupational problems (Ellision 2004). There are also serious practical and ethical considerations when the person doing the counseling also has the power to deprive the officer of his job. Officers often are loathe to discuss problems with a person whom they see, quite rightly, as a representative of the department.

There is a bright side to this picture. Strategies that work to reduce stress-related problems have much wider applicability than for suicide prevention. They can increase morale and productivity as well as decrease work-related stress reactions (Ellison 2004).

Conclusion

Many questions remain about the nature and causes of police suicide as well as the best strategies for prevention. However, there is general agreement that it is a serious enough problem to warrant continued study and an increase in efforts of prevention. These efforts must be multifaceted. Of course, they must include procedures for selecting the most appropriate individuals for the job, and helping those later found to be in trouble. They must also work to provide optimal organizational conditions that help to ameliorate the impact of the intrinsic and extrinsic stressors of the occupation.

KATHERINE W. ELLISON

See also **Psychological Fitness for Duty; Psychological Standards; Psychology and the Police; Stress and Police Work**

References and Further Reading

Aamodt, M. G., and Stalkner, N. A. 2001. Police officer suicide: Frequency and officer profiles. In *Suicide and law enforcement*, ed. D. C. Sheehan and J. I. Warren. Washington, DC: U.S. Government Printing Office.

Allen, S. 1986. Suicide and indirect self-destructive behavior among police. In *Psychological services for law enforcement*, ed. J. Reese and H. Goldstein. Washington, DC: U.S. Government Printing Office.

Bergen, G. T., A. Deusch, and S. Best. 2001. Police suicide: Why are the rates in some places so low? In *Suicide and law enforcement*, ed. D. C. Sheehan and J. I. Warren. Washington, DC: U.S. Government Printing Office.

Durkheim, E. 1987/1951. *Suicide and law enforcement.*

Kroes, W. 1976. *Society's victim: The policeman.* Springfield, IL: Charles C Thomas.

Labovits, S., and S. Hagedorn. 1971. An analysis of suicide rates among occupational categories. *Sociological Inquiry* 41: 57–71.

Lester, D. 1987. *Suicide, a learned behavior.* Springfield, IL: Charles C Thomas.

Lewis, R. 1973. Toward an understanding of police anomie. *Journal of Police Science and Administration* 1: 484–90.

Marris, R. W. 1992. How are suicides different? In *Assessment and prediction of suicide*, ed. R. W. Marris, A. L. Breman, J. T Maltsberger, and R. I. Yufit. New York: Guilford.

Reese, J., and H. Goldstein, eds. 1986. *Psychological services of law enforcement.* Washington, DC: U.S. Government Printing Office.

Sheehan, D. C., and J. I. Warren, eds. 2001. *Suicide law enforcement.* Washington, DC: U.S. Government Printing Office.

Slater, J., and R. Depue. 1981. The contribution of environmental events and social support to serious suicide attempts in primary depressive disorder. *Journal of Abnormal Psychology* 90: 275–85.

Violante, J. M. 1996. *Police suicide: Epidemic in blue.* Springfield, IL: Charles C Thomas.

POLICING MULTIETHNIC COMMUNITIES

Law enforcement and public safety in the United States are primarily local government functions that are typically the most visible and touch the lives of citizens in a direct way. In municipalities with large multiethnic populations, this visibility and bureaucratic discretion interact with local demographic change to make for a potentially sensitive and challenging job for police. Some immigrant ethnic groups, in their home countries, dealt with law enforcement officials who were corrupt or who used force indiscriminately; others lived in fear of government authorities more generally. Moreover, cultural practices among ethnic populations are often distinctive and may make them "stand out" in some communities. With their uniforms and patrol cars, police officers are probably the most obvious, and frequently encountered, representatives of local government.

Police are also quintessential "street-level bureaucrats"; although operating under a complex set of legal rules, they have considerable discretion in applying those rules to particular incidents and situations that occur on their rounds. Thus, the organizational culture of police departments and their standard operating procedures can differ dramatically from community to community (Ibarra 2003; Smith 1986). This article highlights some of the most pressing problems in policing multiethnic communities.

Police–Community Relations

Because of the constantly shifting and sometimes contradictory expectations of and demands for police services in multiethnic communities, police actions help set the tone for civic relationships between residents and local government. When the racial and ethnic demographics begin to change with the influx of immigrants, tensions between police and nonwhite residents often are heightened (Alpert and Dunham 1988). Ethnic change in neighborhoods has long been associated with social conditions that can make the job of police officers more challenging. In the popular media accounts of big-city ethnic neighborhoods, images such as youth gangs, extortion of small businesses, and fear or avoidance of the police are common. Moreover, reluctance to seek help from the police or to inform the police of criminal activity continues to be a significant problem in some ethnic communities

(Davis and Erez 1998; Poole and Pogrebin 1990). Explanations proffered for such reluctance include lack of familiarity with and trust in law enforcement, perceived nonresponsiveness and ineffectiveness of police services, and views of law enforcement personnel as intimidating, coercive, and discriminatory.

One of the most controversial issues associated with the rapid growth of ethnic communities involves problems posed by undocumented immigrants. Of special concern is the question of whether foreign government identifications—particularly the *matricula consular* issued by the Mexican government for Mexicans abroad—may be used as a valid form of identification for a variety of official purposes in the United States. These identification cards have been issued since 1871 by the Mexican Consulate to Mexican citizens abroad. The card, which resembles a driver's license, includes a picture, birth date, address in the United States of the individual, a phone number of the issuing consular office, and (on cards issued since March 2002) several visible and invisible security features. Cards typically expire after five years. Proponents say that the acceptance of the cards gives Mexican citizens the opportunity to open bank accounts, use libraries, and document their identification for minor police infractions. Without identification, they say, individuals could be jailed for even reporting or witnessing a crime.

The role of police departments is fiercely debated. Some critics of the card believe that police officers should contact federal immigration officials on the presentation of a consular ID. However, many police and sheriff departments throughout California accept the card as a valid identification document. They note that the cards can help them to increase trust among immigrant groups in reporting crimes, and that, when "pulling someone over" or questioning them for a crime, it is better to have some form of ID than none at all. Despite pressure from the Mexican government, the *matricula consular* is not recognized as proof of identity at the federal level in the United States. Fourteen states, with varying acceptance in some municipalities across the states, recognize the *matricula consular* as a valid form of identification. Colorado was the first state to enact legislation to bar the acceptance of the cards by state and municipal agencies; New York followed suit by officially refusing to accept the cards as proof of identity, citing security concerns regarding terrorism. By contrast, Los Angeles city officials have announced plans to accept ID cards from other countries. Mayor James Hahn, reportedly seeing the *matricula consular* as a model, signed an ordinance calling on city officials to develop safeguards toward accepting identification cards issued from the other 87 consulates in Los Angeles (Nash 2004).

A related issue that has received some attention is whether local police departments should contact federal immigration authorities (now part of the Department of Homeland Security) after determining that a suspect is in the United States illegally. For instance, the U.S. House of Representatives in 2003 debated the Clear Law Enforcement for Criminal Alien Removal (CLEAR) Act, which would authorize local and state police departments to "investigate, apprehend, detain, or remove aliens" and would withhold federal incarceration assistance to those authorities who failed to do so within two years of the act's passage. [The bill was not reported out of committee in the 108th Congress (2003–2004) and, as of this writing (2005), has yet to be reintroduced in subsequent terms.]

Many municipal, county, and state law enforcement agencies have resisted such measures, arguing that they should not be in the business of immigration law enforcement. Rick Turboch, president of the California Police Chiefs Association, stated in a letter to Attorney General John Ashcroft in 2002, "It is the strong opinion of [CPCA] that in order for local and state law enforcement organizations to be effective partners with their communities, it is imperative that they not be placed in the role of detaining and arresting individuals based solely on a change in their immigration status" (Richardson 2002). Because of such strong sentiments and broad opposition, only a small fraction of local law enforcement agencies cooperate with their federal counterparts on immigration-related matters. Still, those police departments that accept Mexican consular IDs as valid forms of identification typically refrain from contacting federal authorities when a person in custody is an undocumented immigrant. Research indicates that the inclination of police departments to contact federal authorities decreases with the Latino share of nonwhite residents. This relationship may be due to increased political clout of Latinos in areas where they constitute a larger share of the population. It is also possible that police departments in these cities may have adopted more permissive approaches out of a concern for establishing trust among residents of Latino communities.

Although some departments are willing to accept consular IDs for identifying witnesses and processing minor offenders, they are less willing to do so for more serious offenses that require detention. Police are yet to be convinced of the merits of consular IDs because of the potential for forgery and the problem of insufficient history linked to an identification card. Some departments reluctantly use the card if it is the only form of photo identification available, but they still view it as an unreliable way to authenticate someone's identity.

Day Laborers

Some cities have encountered conflicts regarding day laborers—individuals who gather, often outdoors, to seek manual labor jobs or other employment for the day. Without formal employment, these individuals—who may or may not have legal residency status in the United States— seek work from budget-minded employers who have learned the locations for a reliable source of eager and cheap temporary workers. Certainly not all day laborers are ethnic minorities, but the issue is closely associated with ethnic immigration, both legal and illegal. Although day labor has a long history in the United States, this issue has risen to a level of community controversy in several Western states (for example, California, Arizona, New Mexico, and Texas), judging by numerous media reports. Concerns have been raised over a host of issues, ranging from traffic congestion, crime, and visual blight in day-labor areas, to shakedowns and unsafe working conditions on the part of employers. Local police are sometimes asked to respond to these concerns.

Some city governments have made policy decisions to try to reduce day-labor activity or regulate its location. Other cities have attempted to move the activity off the streets by supporting hiring calls, often in partnership with nonprofit groups. Finally, some cities have attempted to make it illegal for day laborers to solicit work. An antisolicitation ordinance in the city of Agoura Hills, California, was challenged in state appellate court in 1994 but upheld, clearing the way for similar measures in other cities. In 2000, however, a federal judge ruled that a similar ordinance in Los Angeles County was unconstitutional, violating the First and Fourteenth Amendments.

Clearly, the infrastructure capacity of a city and its political leanings shape local policy responses to immigrants. Some cities are simply pressed by circumstances into developing a policy. The city council of Thousand Oaks, California, which for more than fifteen years had fielded numerous residents' complaints about the gathering of day laborers, voted in 2002 to construct a day-labor hiring site on public greenbelt land, providing such simple facilities as picnic tables, bicycle racks, toilets, and driveways designated as pickup zones. The deputy city manager explained, "We can't make the problem go away. We can't arrest the day laborers and contractors and make them go away" ("New Hiring Site for Laborers Open" 2002). However, emotions often run high on such approaches. One resident of Thousand Oaks wrote in an editorial that because most of the laborers are illegal immigrants, "what we are truly hiding in the greenbelt area is the fact that we are publicly endorsing an illegal activity" (Fisher 2002). While many cities with large immigrant populations have "visible" day-labor markets, no policy response has gained clear popularity, except perhaps avoidance of the issue. The police often become de facto policy makers, trying to balance the competing demands for community policing that address both the specific needs of the multiethnic community and the broader concerns of the host community (McDonald 2003).

Informal Businesses

Many multiethnic communities serve as both magnets and zones of transition for foreign immigrants. Immigrants are a select group, by virtue of their decision to uproot themselves from familiar surroundings and move to the United States. For many, economic advancement is the major goal, and many immigrants historically have engaged in entrepreneurship—running grocery stores or markets, operating restaurants, providing personal care services (massages, manicures, hair styling, and so on), or managing motels, for example. However, some newcomers with few formal resources, little access to credit, and incomplete knowledge of business regulation in their new country may resort to running small businesses informally or "under the table" (Kusenbach and Ibarra 2001).

Undocumented immigrants may also engage in informal businesses in an attempt to avoid detection by authorities. Although many such businesses are fairly invisible to the outside community, in other cases—as with day laborers—conflicts have arisen with neighbors and local authorities. Home-based businesses, such as car repair shops or beauty salons, street peddlers selling food or flowers in public areas, personal service providers operating without a business license, and other gray market enterprises, are tolerated in some communities but considered nuisances in others. It is possible that the presence of more immigrants makes unlicensed businesses more prevalent and thus more of a target for municipal code enforcement, either by building or health inspectors or by the police. Cities with higher shares of immigrant residents tend to be more aggressive in citing informal businesses, which may foster economic hardships and cultural tensions within multiethnic communities.

Police Review Boards

Another potentially important issue in diverse communities, given the potential conflicts inherent in policing, is whether residents have any forum or feedback mechanism to discuss the performance or practices of the local police. One potential forum would be to contact elected officials regarding concerns about the police. However, immigrant destination cities tend to have disproportionately few elected officials from Hispanic or Asian backgrounds, compared to the overall population. This might reduce the likelihood that some immigrants will contact officials because of perceived cultural or language barriers.

Another forum in some communities is the police review board or citizen review commission, an officially constituted group that has the power to review complaints and allegations by residents against police officers and recommend remedies or punishments. Research shows that review boards are *less* common in cities with higher proportions of immigrants. Because there is no reason to suspect that immigrants have a distinctive preference against the formation of review boards, it may be the case that immigrants have fewer political skills or less political power to mobilize on behalf of the creation of such a board.

In many ways, police departments are more proactive in their outreach efforts in multiethnic communities than are other municipal agencies or even elected officials. Many officials (elected or appointed) know little about the day-to-day problems residents face in multiethnic communities. Government officials often bemoan the lack of involvement by immigrants in local politics and elections, yet face-to-face meetings between elected officials and ethnic business owners or advocates are rare. Moreover, few governmental documents are translated into the multiple languages typical of multiethnic communities.

By contrast, local police agencies have often succeeded in learning about various ethnic communities and have gained a modicum of trust in many neighborhoods. Still, police interest in outreach toward ethnic communities is limited. Some departments' enforcement activities may exacerbate the difficulties residents experience in some ethnic neighborhoods. A police agency may aggressively enforce some ordinances that are less tenable in areas of overcrowded housing, such as prohibitions on fixing cars on the street or on storing personal property that is visible from public sidewalks. A municipal prohibition on loitering may mean that day laborers who often congregate in specific locations for drive-by work opportunities are dispersed from the street by police;

moreover, some police departments are particularly vigilant in cracking down on informal businesses, such as street vendors and unlicensed home enterprises.

Some may argue that these measures are based solely on concerns with public health, quality of life, and safety, and the collective community ultimately benefits from the enforcement of such laws. Yet if informal businesses and overcrowding are inevitable aspects of living in multiethnic communities (especially given the present state of wages, rents, and profit margins on ethnic-run businesses), then the enforcement of such ordinances increases both the costs of doing business and the costs of simply living. Many local governments have simply failed to address the issue of whether ordinances should be altered to suit the changing dynamics of the population and the local economy. As a result, police outreach to multiethnic communities is limited and structured by the department's overall concern with "quality-of-life" issues. The police role becomes one of conflict management with little hope for conflict resolution (Herbert 1995). And while the policing style may be described as problem oriented, there are few opportunities and even less resources available to law enforcement for actual problem solving. Such reactive approaches may simply reflect a benign neglect policy of local government, functionally restricting or preventing movement toward ethnic empowerment, where communities have a stake in the formulation of municipal policies.

Past studies have shown that although ethnic minorities are a sizable proportion of the resident population, they have remained relatively powerless in the political process for various reasons, including the lack of English proficiency, the relative marginality of organizations serving ethnic communities, and the sizable proportion of recent arrivals and undocumented immigrants among the foreign-born. Given these barriers to civic and political

participation, institutional policies and practices can go a long way toward ensuring that ethnic minority needs are considered in the decision-making processes of local governments. This is of critical importance with regard to the role of police in American society, because police are in close daily touch with city populations and depend on cooperation and information from the public to do their jobs. America's demographic dynamism seems to ensure that local police agencies will be under nearly continuous pressure to respond and adapt to the changing needs and demands of multiethnic communities.

ERIC D. POOLE and MARK R. POGREBIN

See also **Attitudes toward the Police: Overview; Civilian Review Boards; Community Attitudes toward the Police; Community-Oriented Policing: Practices; Immigrant Communities and the Police; Minorities and the Police; Multiethnic Communities: Interactive Model**

References and Further Reading

Alpert, Geoffrey P., and Roger G. Dunham. 1988. *Policing multi-ethnic neighborhoods.* New York: Greenwood Press.

Davis, Robert C., and Edna Erez. 1998. *Immigrant populations as victims: Toward a multicultural criminal justice system.* Washington, DC: U.S. Department of Justice, National Institute of Justice.

Fisher, Carl. 2002. Laborers' illegal activity. *Ventura County Star*, June 30.

Herbert, Steve. 1995. *Policing space: Territoriality and the Los Angeles Police Department.* Minneapolis: University of Minnesota Press.

Ibarra, Peter R. 2003. Contact with the police: Patterns and meanings in a multicultural realm. *Police & Society*, April, 133–64.

Kusenbach, Maggie, and Peter R. Ibarra. 2001. Patterns of neighborhood hustling: How residents 'work' with local resources. Paper presented to the Society for the Study of Symbolic Interaction, Anaheim, CA, August 19.

McDonald, William F. 2003. The emerging paradigm for policing multiethnic societies: Glimpses from the American experience. *Police & Society*, April, 231–53.

Nash, James. 2004. Other consular IDs welcome: City officials like Mexican plan results, want to add other countries. *Daily News of Los Angeles*, March 13.

New hiring site for laborers open. 2002. *Ventura County Star*, June 24.

Poole, Eric D., and Mark R. Pogrebin. 1990. Crime and law enforcement policy in the Korean American community. *Police Studies* 13: 57–66.

Richardson, Stella. 2002. California police chiefs stand up to feds. *ACLU News*, May.

Smith, Douglas. 1986. The neighborhood context of police behavior. In *Communities and crime*, ed. Albert J. Reiss and Michael Tonry, 314–41. Chicago: University of Chicago Press.

POLICING STRATEGIES

Policing strategies have evolved and experienced elaboration over time. During the political era of American policing, decentralized organizational structures were favored over centralized ones. In big-city police departments, the real power and authority belonged to precinct captains, not to chiefs or commissioners. Detectives usually reported to these precinct captains, rather than to a chief of detectives at headquarters. The reason for this decentralized approach was to protect local political influence over the police. Local political leaders ("ward bosses") picked their own precinct captains, who were in turn expected to be very responsive to the bosses' needs and demands. A strong central headquarters might have interfered with this politically based system.

Patrol officers operated on foot and without direct communication with the precinct house or police headquarters. Because of the difficulty of communicating with patrol officers in the field, special squads responding from the precincts were often used to conduct raids and react to major crimes. Police training was nearly nonexistent and personnel standards in general were minimal. Little supervision was provided. Police work was seen as nontechnical physical labor and as suitable reward for political loyalty, not as a profession or even a skilled craft.

From the Political Era to the Professional Model

Although complaints about police abuses and inefficiency were common in the 1800s, widespread criticism of the political model of policing, including its decentralization and acceptance of mediocre personnel, did not emerge until the beginning of the twentieth century. Since then, however, police practitioners, academics, and investigating commissions have decried the poor quality of police personnel; pointed out the need for intelligence, honesty, and sensitivity in police officers; called for stricter organizational controls; implemented preservice and in-service training; and significantly upgraded police technology.

Standard operational elements came into place in the professional model that remain relevant to this day. Most police officers are assigned to the patrol function. At the beginning of their workday, they are assigned to patrol areas, often called *beats*. Each officer patrols his or her beat, usually in a patrol car, until assigned a call by the police dispatcher. The officer responds promptly to the call; it could be a crime, a traffic accident, or a neighborhood dispute. The officer is expected to handle the call. This may involve writing a report, conducting a preliminary investigation, giving first aid, directing traffic, arresting or ticketing a citizen, breaking up an argument, giving advice, providing information, or even getting the proverbial cat out of a tree. As soon as the officer finishes handling the call, he or she returns to patrolling until the next call. If the call involves a crime or other serious matter, sometime later a detective may conduct a follow-up investigation to try to identify and arrest a perpetrator or recover stolen property. This brief description includes the three cornerstones of the professional police strategy for dealing with crime: preventive patrol, immediate response to calls, and follow-up investigation.

These three operational components were subjected to evaluative research in the 1970s and 1980s and were found to be less than effective. The Kansas City Preventive Patrol Experiment found that altering levels of routine patrolling between no patrol and two to three times the normal level of patrol had no effect on reported crime, victimization, fear of crime, citizen perceptions, or anything else that was measured. Studies of rapid response found that it rarely leads to on-scene arrests, mainly because most crimes are not discovered until after the fact, and even when citizens are aware of crimes while they are in progress, those citizens typically delay several minutes before calling the police. Studies of criminal investigation revealed that most crimes are never solved, most crime-solving success is more attributable to victims and witnesses than to detectives, and most detective work is mainly clerical.

The lack of effectiveness of its operational components was a tough blow to the professional model. In addition, reported crime rose throughout the 1970s during the very time period when the professional approach was in its heyday. Also, questions began to arise about whether the professional model might have a tendency to isolate the police from the community. In the 1950s and 1960s, many police departments established community relations units in response to perceived problems in police–community relations. Initially, these community relations units engaged mostly in public relations by presenting the police point of view to the community. This one-sided approach was soon recognized as inadequate and expanded to provide the community with a forum for expressing its views to the police. The two-way police–community relations philosophy emphasized the importance of communication and mutual understanding.

In the 1970s it became apparent that police–community relations officers and units were not effective in guaranteeing smooth relations between a community and its police department. A community experiences its police department through the actions of patrol officers and detectives more so than through the presentations of a few community relations specialists. Efforts were undertaken to train patrol officers in community relations and crime prevention techniques and to make them more knowledgeable about community characteristics and problems. Team policing programs were also implemented, in part, as a means of improving police responsiveness to community concerns.

From Professional to Community Policing

Many observers now believe that the abandonment of foot patrol by most American police departments by the mid-1900s changed the nature of police work and negatively affected police–citizen relations. Officers assigned to large patrol car beats do not develop the intimate understanding of and cordial relationship with the community that foot patrol officers assigned to small beats develop. Officers on foot are in a position to relate more intimately with citizens than officers driving by in cars.

The results of two research studies, together with the development of small police radios, gave a boost to the resurgence of foot patrol starting in the 1980s. Originally, the police car was needed to house the bulky two-way radio. Today, foot patrol officers carry tiny, lightweight radios that enable them to handle calls promptly and to request information or assistance whenever needed. They are never out of touch and they are always available.

An experimental study conducted in Newark, New Jersey, was unable to demonstrate that either adding or removing foot patrol affected crime in any way. This finding mirrored what had been found in Kansas City regarding motorized patrol. Citizens involved in the foot patrol study, however, were less fearful of crime and more satisfied with foot patrol service than with motor patrol. Also, citizens were aware of additions and deletions of foot patrol in their neighborhoods, a finding that stands in stark contrast to the results of the Kansas City study, in which citizens did not perceive changes in the levels of motorized patrol. A second major foot patrol research program in Flint, Michigan, reported findings that were similar to the Newark findings, except that crime decreased, too.

These studies were widely interpreted as demonstrating that, even if foot patrol did not decrease crime, at least it made citizens feel safer and led to improvements in police–community relations. Why the difference between motorized patrol and foot patrol? In what has come to be known as the broken-windows thesis, foot patrol officers pay more attention to disorderly behavior and to minor offenses than do motor patrol officers. Also, they are in a better position to manage their beats, to understand what constitutes threatening or inappropriate behavior, to observe it, and to correct it. Foot patrol officers are likely to pay more attention to derelicts, petty thieves, disorderly persons, vagrants, panhandlers, noisy juveniles, and street people who, although not committing serious crimes, cause concern and fear among many citizens. Failure to control even the most minor aberrant activities on the street contributes to neighborhood fears. Foot patrol officers have more opportunity than motor patrol officers to control street disorder and reassure ordinary citizens.

Geography plays a large role in determining the viability of foot patrol as a police strategy, of course. The more densely populated an area, the more the citizenry will travel on foot and the more street disorder there will be. The more densely populated an area, the more likely that foot patrol can be effectively used as a police strategy. Although foot patrol may never again become the dominant police strategy it once was, it can play a large role in contributing police services to many communities.

Starting in the 1980s an even broader approach than community relations and foot patrol began developing. More and more police departments began employing foot patrol as a central component of their operational strategy, rather than as a novelty or as an accommodation to downtown business interests. Crime prevention programs became more and more reliant on community involvement, as in neighborhood watch, community patrol, and crimestoppers programs. Police departments began making increased use of civilians and volunteers in various aspects of policing, and made permanent geographic assignment an important element of patrol deployment. This came to be called *community policing,* entailing a substantial change in police thinking involving increased citizen involvement, engagement, partnerships, and tailoring of policing to neighborhood needs and preferences.

Research on the effectiveness of community policing has yielded mixed results. Foot patrol seems to make citizens feel safer, but it may not have much of an effect on the amount of crime. A small study in Houston, Texas, which involved patrol officers visiting households to solicit viewpoints and information, did report both crime and fear decreases in the study area. A study of community constables in England, however, found that the constables actually spent very little of their time in direct contact with citizens, despite role expectations that emphasized community contact. An ongoing study of department-wide community policing in Chicago has similarly discovered some officer resistance to working closely with citizens, but nevertheless has yielded promising effects on public satisfaction, fear, disorder, and crime.

From Professional to Strategic Policing

Community policing has not been the only stream of development in the wake of dissatisfaction with the professional model. Another alternative that has developed is strategic policing, represented by operational refinements and increased technical sophistication. In the patrol arena, strategic policing incorporates directed patrol, saturation patrol, targeted patrol, crackdowns, hot-spot policing, and other techniques designed to apply patrol resources and energy in a more focused manner. Call-driven 911 policing has been replaced by differential responses, in which rapid response is reserved for in-progress situations, while other calls are handled through delayed response, telephone reporting, nonsworn personnel, and a variety of other methods. Traditional criminal investigations have been refined through the use of solvability factors, case screening, major crime teams and task forces, and a more managed approach to detective work.

One of the most celebrated manifestations of strategic policing has been COMPSTAT, a system developed by the New York Police Department primarily to establish command accountability. Headquarters staff utilize up-to-date crime data and crime maps in order to hold area commanders (precinct captains) accountable for having identified and responded to current crime problems. Commanders are encouraged to use their resources strategically to address immediate problems, instead of merely spreading their officers around the community and waiting for calls and crimes to happen.

The latest development in strategic policing is intelligence-led policing. This approach seems to have had several sources: (1) COMPSTAT; (2) the growing availability of crime analysis, crime mapping, data mining, and similar tools; (3) impressive national-level police initiatives in England and Australia; and (4) renewed police emphasis on intelligence collection and analysis in the aftermath of the terrorist attacks of September 11, 2001. *Intelligence-led policing,* perhaps better termed *information-led policing,* calls for all police resources to be deployed and directed on a continuous, real-time basis according to careful analysis of the latest intelligence and other data. It is a much more command-directed and demanding approach to police management than the traditional approach of assigning each officer to a beat and reminding him or her to "be careful out there."

The evidence in support of directed and focused policing is fairly strong. When police patrols and other resources are carefully targeted at hot spots and similar problems, crime is typically reduced. Some of the impact may be mere displacement, but some usually represents real reductions, and the bonus of diffusion of benefits is also frequently experienced. Targeted policing seems clearly superior to nontargeted policing, all other things being equal. COMPSTAT and intelligence-led policing, though, have not been adequately evaluated in their own rights to determine what additional benefits they provide, if any.

From Professional to Problem-Oriented Policing

The third major contemporary strategy to develop in the wake of the professional model is problem-oriented policing. Simply put, problem-oriented policing (POP) posits that police should focus more attention on *problems*, as opposed to *incidents*. Problems are defined either as collections of incidents related in some way (if they occur at the same location, for example) or as underlying conditions that give rise to incidents, crimes, disorder, and other substantive community issues that people expect the police to handle. By focusing more on problems than on incidents, police can address causes rather than mere symptoms, and consequently have a greater impact. The public health analogy is often used to illustrate this difference in conceptualizing the police role, with its emphasis on prevention and taking a proactive approach. This analogy is useful, too, because it reminds us that even with a strong public health approach, people still get sick and need medical attention— that is, police still need to respond to calls and make arrests, even as POP prevents some problems and reduces the demand for reactive policing.

One of the fundamental tenets of POP is that law enforcement, that is, using the criminal law, should be understood as one *means* of policing, rather than as the end or goal of policing. This is much more than a subtle shift in terminology. It emphasizes that police pursue large and critically important societal goals: controlling crime, protecting people, reducing fear, maintaining order. In every instance, police should choose those lawful and ethical means that yield the most efficient and effective achievement of these ends. Sometimes this may involve enforcement of the criminal law, and sometimes it may not. Thus, the words *policing* and *law enforcement* are not synonymous, and law enforcement is not the only, or even necessarily the principal, technique of policing.

In place of overreliance on the criminal law, POP recommends a rational and analytical approach to problem solving using a process best known in police circles as the *SARA model* (scanning, analysis, response, assessment). According to this approach, police should continually scan their areas of responsibility, drawing on a variety of sources of information, in order to identify apparent problems. Next, they should carefully analyze those problems, in order to verify, describe, and explain them. Only after this analysis stage should police turn their attention to responses, and when they do, they should identify and consider a wide range of responses before narrowing their focus down to the most promising alternatives. After implementing these responses, they should then carefully assess impact, in order to determine whether they need to try something else, and also to document lessons learned for the benefit of future problem-solving efforts.

Evaluations of the impact or effectiveness of POP have been generally positive, although most such evaluations have used rather weak research designs. Countless individual case studies have been completed with fairly convincing evidence that the problems that were targeted were substantially reduced. In some instances, it is clear that POP analysis led to a new understanding of the problem, and subsequently to innovative responses, which apparently "caused" the beneficial effect on the problem. In many other cases, however, the problem got better but it is not clear that it was careful analysis or innovative and tailor-made responses that made the difference. Often, in these cases, responses rely primarily on enforcement, and it seems that the POP terminology and process are merely used to "dress up" or legitimize a much more traditional approach to policing.

The most consistent criticism of POP-as-practiced is that analysis is often cursory or nonexistent. In the same vein, few documented POP projects reflect anything more than the most superficial assessment of impact. Even simple before-and-after comparisons are often omitted, and the utilization of any type of comparison or control group is rare. It is perhaps not surprising that POP-in-practice is not as analytical or scientifically rigorous as its proponents would like—most police officers are probably more prone to action than to research.

Even in the arena of action, though, there is some disagreement over whether the implementation stage of POP, that is, the identification and selection of responses, is as wide ranging and creative as it ought to be. Some observers have been disappointed that POP responses often emphasize enforcement and other conventional police practices. One careful study, though, found that most POP examples utilize multiple responses (five on average) and that enforcement is often employed to supplement more innovative responses, rather than as the main response.

One last major criticism of POP-in-practice is that it has lost focus and become trivialized under the umbrella of community policing. Under community policing, POP has drifted in two ways. First, in keeping with the broad mission of community policing, it has often been used to address the whole panoply of a neighborhood's problems—crime, fear, disorder, and so on—thus blunting the preferred sharp focus on a specific problem. Second, in keeping with the notion of empowering individual police officers to effectively serve their communities, POP has gradually migrated to "problem solving," something that individual police officers do, hopefully in conjunction with their constituents. Problem solving, in turn, has often come to be seen as what good police officers do when confronted with a particularly challenging complainant, call for service, or address. Thus, problem solving often amounts to creative handling of individual incidents, a far cry from taking a problem-oriented approach to a substantive problem of some significance. To be sure, this kind of problem solving probably represents improved police practice, but in scope of the problem, depth of analysis, or breadth of responses, it pales in comparison to ideal conceptions of POP.

The Contemporary Situation

Community policing, strategic policing, problem-oriented policing, and even the professional model all have their adherents and supporters today. Many police agencies would say that they implement all four of these strategies. In a situation of limited resources, however, agencies must inevitably emphasize one or two strategies over the others. In the current era of heightened concern about terrorism and weapons of mass destruction, strategic policing seems to have a certain advantage because of its connection to intelligence and its emphasis on enforcement and "no-nonsense" techniques. However, many police executives have asserted that community policing is the strategy most likely to produce the community-based intelligence that will identify hidden terrorists, as well as the strategy best suited to striking the difficult balance between civil liberties and safety from terrorism. Not to be overlooked is problem-oriented policing. Its analytical and preventive approach may be best suited to reducing the risks of both terrorism and ordinary crime.

The individual police agency may want to choose its primary strategy based on a careful analysis of the needs of its community. For the police field as a whole, it may be some years before experience and further research lead to additional elaboration or sorting out of the contemporary repertoire of policing strategies.

GARY CORDNER

See also **Accountability; Broken-Windows Policing; Calls for Service; Community-Oriented Policing: Practices; COMPSTAT; Crimestoppers; Homeland Security and Law Enforcement; Intelligence-Led Policing and Organizational Learning; Problem-Oriented Policing; SARA, the Model; Terrorism: Police Functions Associated with**

References and Further Reading

Goldstein, Herman. 1990. *Problem-oriented policing*. New York: McGraw-Hill.

Greenwood, Peter W., and Joan Petersilia. 1975. *The criminal investigation process volume I: Summary and policy implications*. Santa Monica, CA: RAND Corporation.

Kelling, George L., and Mark H. Moore. 1988. *The evolving strategy of policing*. Perspectives on Policing No. 4. Washington, DC: National Institute of Justice.

Kelling, George L., Tony Pate, Duane Dieckman, and Charles E. Brown. 1974. *The Kansas City Preventive Patrol Experiment: A summary report*. Washington, DC: Police Foundation.

Moore, Mark H., and Robert C. Trojanowicz. 1988. *Corporate strategies for policing*. Perspectives on Policing No. 6. Washington, DC: National Institute of Justice.

Police Foundation. 1981. *The Newark Foot Patrol Experiment*. Washington, DC: Police Foundation.

Scott, Michael S. 2000. *Problem-oriented policing: Reflections on the first 20 years*. Washington, DC: U.S. Department of Justice, Office of Community Oriented Policing Services.

Silverman, Eli B. 1999. *NYPD battles crime: Innovative strategies in policing*. Boston, MA: Northeastern University.

Skogan, Wesley, and Kathleen Frydl, eds. 2004. *Fairness and effectiveness in policing: The evidence*. Washington, DC: National Academies Press.

Spelman, William, and Dale K. Brown. 1981. *Calling the police: Citizen reporting of serious crime*. Washington, DC: Police Executive Research Forum.

Wilson, James Q., and George L. Kelling. 1982. Broken windows: The police and neighborhood safety. *The Atlantic Monthly*, March, 29–38.

POLICING THE OLYMPICS

The Olympics represent the preeminent venue for athletic competition. Hundreds of world-class athletes converge on the host city to display their athletic skills over a two- to four-week period, depending on whether it is the Winter or Summer Games. These events also draw thousands of spectators, including numerous high-profile dignitaries. This presence alone has important implications for the law enforcement community of the host city and country. The convergence of spectators and athletes swells the city's population and increases the potential calls for police service. Further, dignitaries and athletes require special security that draws officers away from routine patrol and investigative duties. This security concern is further complicated by the fact that the events are spread across large geographic areas. Security must be maintained around the clock at each of these locations, and must be provided for the dignitaries and athletes as they move to and from these locations. Thus, the Olympic Games can be taxing for the law enforcement agencies of the host city and country.

These service provision and security concerns are further complicated by the high media profile of the events. This attention makes the games a desirable target for social and political protest groups, as well as potential terrorist targets. The 1972 Munich Olympics illustrate that such protests can include violent acts of terrorism. With the initial hostage taking and eventual killing of Israeli athletes, the Black September organization was able to bring worldwide attention to the Palestinian cause. The 1996 Atlanta games were marred by the Centennial Park bombing that killed 1 and injured 112, which was allegedly committed by antigovernment and religious extremist Eric Rudolph. The terrorist attacks of September 11, 2001, have heightened the concern about the Olympics being a target for terrorism. This was illustrated with the 2002 Salt Lake City Winter Games that commenced five months after these attacks, where the security apparatus for preventing terrorism reached an unprecedented level.

Policing the Olympics in the context of protest and terrorism requires a massive effort, particularly in the United States given the balkanized nature of law enforcement in this country. The events are typically spread across a broad geographical area, as opposed to being within the boundaries of a single city. This means that many local law enforcement agencies within a host area may have an event within their jurisdiction. Each of these agencies will have to find a means for coordinating how many personnel it will devote to covering the added service and security demands in the region, and what type of collaboration is needed to handle these matters in a collective fashion. The necessity for interjurisdictional cooperation in providing security for such an event is another hurdle to be overcome in the provision of security for large events. Bill Clinton's 1998 Presidential Decision Directive 62 further mandates that these local agencies must also coordinate their efforts with federal law enforcement agencies. This directive articulates that the White House may designate specific high-profile events as National Special Security Events that require federal involvement. When this designation is invoked, the U.S. Secret Service becomes the lead agency for developing, implementing, and managing a security plan. In the case of the 2002 Salt Lake City games this meant that the Secret Service became the primary coordinator of local, state, and federal law enforcement agencies involved in Olympic security.

What ultimately results from different departments and agencies coming together to provide safety and security for the Olympics is the creation of a temporary law enforcement organization. For a time-limited period, these independent organizations are expected to function as if they are a single organization with a common purpose. This does not mean that there is a need for the formal merger of the organizations, but temporary protocols must be established. These protocols will have to address jurisdictional and task responsibilities, the creation of coordinating mechanisms for the overall and day-to-day security and safety response of the games, and the establishment of decision-making procedures for personnel with different task responsibilities. What also needs to be considered within this temporary organization are the other safety and criminal justice organizations that are impacted by the games. Any crisis situations in which citizens, spectators, and athletes are harmed will require this law enforcement apparatus to communicate and coordinate its activities with emergency response entities (fire, EMS, and hospitals). Further, any type of mass arrest situations, say, of protesters at a large demonstration, will require the assistance of the local prosecutor's office and jail facilities.

During the 2002 Salt Lake City games, a centralized organizational structure was developed to facilitate the functioning of the different law enforcement and emergency response agencies. In 1999 the Utah legislature passed a state bill that allowed for the formation of the Utah Olympic Public Safety Command (UOPSC). This entity, which included representatives from all levels of law enforcement and emergency response agencies, had the responsibility for developing the safety and security plan for the games. The various representatives of this committee negotiated the protocols discussed above. The organizational structure that was created by UOPSC to manage the day-to-day security and safety operations was a hierarchy of command centers. The Olympic Coordination Center (OCC) functioned as the superior command and control center for the games. Underneath the OCC were various regional command centers, referred to as area command centers (ACCs), and Olympic event command centers that were called venue command centers (VCCs).

The OCC had theater-wide responsibility for disseminating information and intelligence to the other command centers. It also coordinated the request for any additional assets that might have been needed to manage crisis situations. This included such assets as crowd control units, hostage rescue/SWAT teams, and federal antiterrorism units. The various ACCs were responsible for safety and security activities in defined geographical areas that fell outside the Olympic event locations, whether routine or otherwise. The VCCs were responsible for safety and security matters on the perimeter and within the

Olympic event locations. The result of this formalized structure was a temporary organization that was able to coordinate the actions of various independent agencies, which critics had argued was lacking at the 1996 Summer Olympics in Atlanta.

While the formal organization created by UOPSC provided a structure for maintaining safety and security, it could not account for all activities needed to carry out these tasks. What also facilitated the functioning of this temporary law enforcement organization was the development and maintenance of a dense web of communication networks among the various agency personnel. It is only through the ability of attentive personnel to accurately identify and communicate problems that the components of the formal structure (personnel, equipment, and so forth) can be put into place to prevent or effectively manage crisis situations. The sustainability of such organizational responsiveness through communication is a product of technical and cultural elements. In the case of the Salt Lake games this technical element included the use of handheld radios, secure Internet reporting systems, and Nextel phone systems. The cultural element of effective communication requires that the personnel in the various command centers envision themselves as being a component within a large organizational system, as opposed to an isolated entity. This was enhanced through training and table-top exercises.

When these temporary, large organizations come together, organizational members need to recognize that their observations may be relevant to others engaged in the safety and security effort, and thus need to be communicated. Further, each organizational member must also be attentive to the needs of others in the overall organization because their experience, knowledge, and resources may contribute the ability of these individuals to solve problems. The catch phrase used during to the Salt Lake games to capture this culture element was for members to maintain a "theater-wide orientation."

Finally, a risk management orientation is necessary for providing safety and security during the Olympics. All members must keep a preventive posture in which they are constantly scanning for potential hazards in order to head off disaster. Such an endeavor can become trying as the games progress past the first few days and tasks become mundane. It is in this lulled state that organizational members may ignore or fail to communicate hazards within their environment because their recent experience has led them to believe nothing will happen. Whereas security personnel may have treated an abandoned backpack at the beginning of the games as a possible explosive device that warranted the notification of others, the same situation may be seen as not worthy of attention given its routine nature by the second week of the games. While this latter assumption may often be correct, one such lapse in the risk management mind-set may render all the organizational elements for safety and security discussed above meaningless.

Jeffrey Rojek and Scott H. Decker

See also **Critical Incidents; Federal Police and Investigative Agencies; Homeland Security and Law Enforcement; Terrorism: Domestic; Terrorism: International**

References and Further Reading

Greene, Jack R., Scott H. Decker, Jack McDevitt, Vince Webb, Tim S. Bynum, Peter Manning, Jeff Rojek, Sean Verano, and William Terrill. 2002. *Safety and security at the Olympic Games in Salt Lake City.* Report produced for the Office of Domestic Preparedness, Department of Homeland Security.

Olympic Security Review Conference. 2002. Salt Lake City, UT: Governor's Office, State of Utah.

Weick, Karl, and Karlene Roberts. 1993. Collective mind in organizations: Heedful interrelating on flight decks. *Administrative Science Quarterly* 38: 357–81.

POLITICS AND THE POLICE

A police agency can be defined as a legitimate governmental body given the authority to maintain order, prevent crime, and enforce the laws of government. In other words, the police agency ensures that the government remains a stable and respectable entity within society. The job of the police does not exclude anyone from abiding by the law, in theory. In reality, political influence over the police has not allowed for the realization of this theory. Politics is the art of exerting one's power over the government or public affairs. Political action can result in imposing one's interests within the government, in leadership within the government, in control over resources, and in holding government office. Politics influences who will hold various criminal justice positions, such as sheriff, police chief, judge, prosecutor, and correctional executive.

County sheriffs are elected officials, whereas police chiefs are usually appointed by the highest political official, such as the mayor or city manager. As a result, the focus of these officials is to appease those who put them in office. As the preceding definitions imply, political control over the police necessarily leads to a redefinition of the police agency. That is, a police agency is a governmental body with the authority to maintain order over political enemies or other dangerous classes, to prevent the crimes of these people, and to enforce the laws of government over everyone, except those who politically influence the police. The by-product of political control over the police is corruption. This latter presentation of the police has been the focus of much reform effort throughout the history of the police organization.

History

The history of the police in the United States is the history of politics in this country and the attempts to remove political control over the police. Attempts to map out the history of policing reveal three commonly acknowledged eras of policing: (1) the political era; (2) the reform era, also known as the professional era; and (3) the community era. While the mapping of these eras has been debated, what has been acknowledged by scholars is the existence of a political era in the urban North. Between 1840 and the early 1900s, history has documented policing as being under tight control of political machines. In the urban North, police jobs were awarded to political patrons (party loyalists). Officers were hired, fired, and promoted based on their loyalty to the political bosses.

Those who remained loyal worked to increase the power of the political bosses through forcing votes or hindering votes; through enforcement of vice laws against political enemies, or at least, those who did not support the political bosses; and through lack of enforcement of vice laws against political bosses. The police did not hesitate to use brute force in furthering the interests of the political elite. It must be recognized that politicians saw the need not only to strong-arm the public but to please the voters as well. This resulted in an emphasis in social services for the community, under the charge of the police. Police often ran soup kitchens, aided in job location for the public, and worked with the homeless and wayward youth. Rooted in all of the good, however, was the vast corruption of the police that allowed them to enforce the laws in an arbitrary manner, at best, and to break the laws, at worst.

The controversy regarding the three eras of policing began with the criticism that the political era could only describe the urban North. In the South and West, for example, political machines were not a widespread social problem. In the South, however, the police organization was established as a slave patrol, whereas in the West county sheriff departments were the more common organization of law enforcement. The county sheriff's department is a level of government that expands beyond local concerns, but because the sheriff's position is an elected one, this form of law enforcement is highly influenced by politics just the same. Additionally, in the North and in the Reconstruction South it is well documented that free blacks as well as immigrants were defined as dangerous classes by capitalist elites, who also controlled government and politics. Often, the crimes of hate groups, such as the KKK, were ignored in order to keep these groups in place. Organized hate groups aside, much of the oppression experienced by these groups was allowed, if not perpetrated, by law enforcement. These tactics worked to control the labor power of these groups in order to further the economy within these regions. Therefore, while there has been debate over the so-called political era of policing, history reveals that politics have always determined police organization and policy.

Politicization of the Police

If a police agency operates within a corrupt political system, it is almost impossible to eliminate the corruption within the police agency. It has been recognized that since police departments are the enforcement arm of government, the relationship between the police department and the supervising executive branch of government must maintain a balance of political responsibility and operational independence. As a result, police reform has focused on eliminating, or at least minimizing the influence that politicians have over police agencies. However, the fragmented or decentralized model of policing in the United States emphasizes local concerns and local control of the police. While the reform era of policing replaced the political patronage system with the civil service and merit systems, the decentralized nature of

policing does not allow for complete elimination of political influence over the police. Furthermore, crime fighting and the current community policing model have been popular exploits by politicians.

Politics—both informal (community groups, ethnic minorities, and special interests of the community) and formal (elected public officials and representatives of political groups)—continues to pressure police chiefs and managers to answer to the community. Police leadership has fought to maintain independence of action from politics based on the premise that politicians and community groups do not understand the responsibilities of good practical policing. On the other hand, mayors are given the right and responsibility of hiring, firing, and supervising police chiefs. To protect police chiefs from political interference, many states have legislated civil service protection for police chiefs, while simultaneously requiring that police chiefs be held accountable for the actions of their departments by developing service contracts (usually a specific term of appointment) rather than by legislating tenure. Other large cities have established a director of public safety position, which is accountable to the mayor, to manage the police department rather than a police chief.

Police Involvement in Politics

Along with being highly influenced by politics, police have become successful participants in politics, influencing local elections and policy. Police have been influential in legislation on pay increase and benefits, as well as the death penalty and gambling laws. An increasingly popular method of police political involvement has been through the use of political action committees (PACs). PACs have mustered support for political candidates through financial contributions to campaigns. It is believed that in certain large cities, such as New

York City, a candidate running for mayor does not go far without the support of the New York Police Department. However, the concerns social scientists have posed regarding the involvement of police in politics is that the police have access to information that ordinary citizens and politicians do not have and that the police may discriminate in their enforcement of the law in their political battles.

Conclusion

The issue of politics and the police speaks to the integrity and legitimacy of the police as a law enforcement institution in society. The police institution possesses symbolic power that is taken for granted in a democratic society. This symbolic power gives the police institution a legitimacy that is often unquestioned. Furthermore, when there is a decrease of public trust and confidence in the police, during most eras in the history of the police in the United States this trust and confidence has remained relatively high. However, this symbolic power is not guaranteed to last when politics become too pronounced in the operations of the police organization. The police are required to appease the needs of the community while they engage in the powers legislated to them. In the wake of past political corruption, to ensure the civil rights of citizens and democratic government, police powers have been limited. The judiciary is the constitutional guardian and is often deferred to in order to provide guidance and direction when police action is questioned. The civilian review boards and the courts will continue to act as a venue for debating and establishing standards of police conduct and accountability. Interested parties on both sides of the argument will continue the debate on politics and the police.

VENESSA GARCIA and
RAYMOND R. RAINVILLE

See also **Accountability; American Policing: Early Years; Autonomy and the Police; Civilian Review Boards; Community Attitudes toward the Police; Corruption; Discrimination; Future of Policing in the United States; History of American Policing; Integrity in Policing; Professionalism; Role of the Police**

References and Further Reading

Barlow, David E., and Melissa Hickman Barlow. 2000. *Police in a multicultural society: An American story.* Prospect Heights, IL: Waveland Press.

Kelling, George L., and Mark H. Moore. 1988. The evolving strategy of policing. *Perspectives on Policing* 4: 1–15.

Purpura, Philip P. 2001. *Police and community: Concepts and cases.* Boston, MA: Allyn and Bacon.

Sewell, James D. 2002. *Controversial issues in policing.* Boston, MA: Allyn and Bacon.

Walker, Samuel, and Charles M. Katz. 2002. *Police in America.* New York: McGraw-Hill.

POLYGRAPHY

The polygraph has been used by the police in the investigation of serious crimes since at least the early 1900s. Historical development in the field can be traced along two lines, one involving instrumentation and the other testing techniques.

Polygraph Instrumentation

In 1895 Lombroso, an Italian criminologist, used a hydrosphygmograph and the "scientific cradle" to measure objectively the physiological changes associated with the detection of deception. Shortly after, an American psychologist, Munsterberg, noted the effect of lying on breathing, cardiovascular activity, and the galvanic skin response (GSR)—apparent changes in electrical resistance in the skin. In 1921 Larson devised an instrument for making continuous recordings of both blood pressure and breathing. In 1930, Keeler, generally credited with developing the prototype of the present-day polygraph, added a device for recording GSR.

Modern computerized polygraphs are technical improvements over earlier devices, although the physiological activities collected are essentially the same. The polygraph captures electrodermal activity (EDA) by means of two electrodes attached to the hand. A standard blood pressure cuff is used to record relative blood pressure and pulse rate. Finally, breathing activity is recorded by "pneumograph" tubes that expand and contract with chest cavity movement. Activity in each of these physiological systems is usually converted from analog to digital form for display on a computer monitor. The "chart" display can be stored permanently on standard media for on-line or off-line viewing and analysis.

Testing Techniques

There is no known physiological response that is unique to lying. Neither the polygraph nor any other device is capable of detecting a "lie." Lie detection is an inferential process in which "lying" is inferred from comparisons of physiological responses to questions that are asked during polygraph testing. There are three major families of testing procedures in use today: the relevant/irrelevant technique (R/I), the control question technique (CQT), and information recognition testing (IRT).

In its simplest form the R/I technique consists of asking a series of relevant questions, that is, those pertinent to the crime at hand (for example, "Did you shoot John Doe?"), along with irrelevant questions that are not crime related (for example, "Are you over eighteen years of age?"). The test questions are asked several times during the testing. An assumption implicit in the R/I technique is that truthful persons will not react differentially to a great

degree to relevant and irrelevant questions, whereas people who are lying will. This assumption has been seriously challenged and is the primary reason why CQT is preferred.

The control question technique was first developed by J. Reid in 1950. In the CQT the question list consists of irrelevant, relevant, and "control" questions, although other types of questions may also be included. The relevant and irrelevant questions are similar to those asked during R/I testing. Control questions deal with matters similar to, but of presumed lesser significance than, the offense under investigation. The examiner frames these questions so that they will be "probable lies."

In the CQT, more consistent and greater physiological responses to relevant questions than to control questions indicate lying on the relevant issues. Conversely, consistently greater physiological responses to control than to relevant questions indicate truthfulness in the matter under investigation.

The IRT is limited to situations in which specific details of a criminal offense are known only to the police and the actual perpetrator(s). A single "test" consists of the asking of a stem question and multiple options. The stem might be: "Do you know if John Doe was killed with a ____?" The options might be the names of various weapons, for example, gun, knife, club, including the actual weapon used. The guilty person, recognizing the correct option, would be expected to show a greater physiological response to that one than to the others, whereas an innocent person would not. Typically, a series of three or more such multiple-choice tests would be carried out, provided that sufficient detailed information about the offense is known.

Uses of Polygraph Testing

In police work specific issue testing is used to investigate whether a particular person was involved in the commission of a known offense. Polygraph testing has been shown to be extremely valuable in this regard and almost every large police agency employs one or more examiners. It is well established that polygraph testing identifies offenders and "clears" innocent suspects; the result is great savings of investigative time and effort.

Polygraph testing for preemployment screening of applicants for police work is widely used but controversial. Such testing substantiates information collected during traditional background investigations and it uncovers information not otherwise available.

Accuracy of Polygraph Testing

Field practitioners maintain that their overall accuracy is about 90%; errors tend to be "false negatives" rather than "false positives." (A false-positive error is made when a truthful person is found to be "deceptive" during polygraph testing. A false-negative error occurs when a person who lied is reported to be "truthful.") A great deal of controversy surrounds these claims because the scientific research is unclear. A recent review of that research by the National Research Council of the National Academy of Sciences concluded that a reasonable estimate of accuracy is between 85% and 90%, though there were caveats to be heeded.

Training and Regulation of Examiners

There are more than twenty private and governmental schools that serve as training facilities for polygraph examiners. The American Polygraph Association (APA), the major professional organization in the United States, accredits training facilities but only those choosing membership.

About forty states now regulate the activity of polygraph examiners. In some of these, mandatory licensure requirements are set out by statute. In others, the kinds of situations in which polygraph testing may be used are proscribed. The lack of uniform regulation is seen by many as a serious problem in the field.

Legal Status of Polygraph Examinations

The commonly held belief that polygraph examination results are not admitted into courtroom proceedings is not true. The initial judicial decision of *Frye v. U.S.* (293 F. 1013 [1923]) did exclude polygraph evidence. Today, however, polygraph results are admitted by stipulation. At the federal level there is no single standard governing admissibility; some courts have permitted polygraph evidence whereas others have not.

It is very common for prosecutors to use polygraph results to decide whether and which charges to file. It is also common for judges to use polygraph results in sentencing decisions. In addition, defense attorneys rely on polygraph testing to plan their defense and to negotiate pleas. Thus, polygraphy plays an important role in the justice system quite apart from its use by the police.

FRANK HORVATH

See also **Criminal Investigation; Forensic Investigations**

References and Further Reading

Ansley, N., and J. Pumphrey. 1985. *Justice and the polygraph: A collection of cases.* Severna Park, MD: American Polygraph Association.

Barland, G., and D. Raskin. 1976. *Validity and reliability of polygraph examinations of criminal suspects.* Contract No. 75-N1–99–0001. Washington, DC: National Institute of Justice, U.S. Department of Justice.

Horvath, F. 1972. The police candidate polygraph examination: Considerations for the police administrator. *Police* 16: 33–39.

———. 1980. Polygraphy: Some comments on the state of the art. *Polygraph* 9: 34–41.

———. 1984. Detecting deception in eyewitness cases: Problems and prospects in the use of the polygraph. In *Eyewitness testimony: Psychological perspectives*, ed. G. Wells and B. Loftus, 214–55. New York: Cambridge University Press.

———. Job screening. *Society* 22: 43–46.

Larson, J. 1932. *Lying and its detection*. Chicago: University of Chicago Press.

Lykken, D. 1981. *A tremor in the blood*. New York: McGraw-Hill.

National Research Council. 2003. *The polygraph and lie detection*. Committee to Review the Scientific Evidence on the Polygraph. Division of Behavioral and Social Sciences and Education. Washington, DC: National Academies Press.

Trovillo, P. 1939. A history of lie detection. *Journal of Criminal Law, Criminology, and Police Science* 29: 848–81.

Widacki, J., and F. Horvath. 1978. An experimental investigation of the relative validity and utility of the polygraph technique and three other common methods of criminal identification. *Journal of Forensic Sciences* 23: 596–601.

PORNOGRAPHY

The term *pornography* is derived from the Greek *porne*, meaning "to prostitute," and *graphein*, meaning "to draw or write" (Siegel 1998). Adult pornography is defined as pictures, literature, or other materials that are intended to stimulate sexual arousal rather than serve aesthetic or emotional purposes. These materials describe, suggest, or depict some form of sexual activity among adult participants. All fifty states prohibit (to some degree) the production, sale, and distribution of pornographic material. Child pornography is usually regulated under a separate legal category. Child pornography is defined to be images, literature, or other materials that depict a child (any individual under the age of eighteen) engaging in sexual activity or portray the child in a sexually explicit manner. Child pornography involves either the creation of materials depicting minors engaged in sexual activities or the production and distribution of materials harmful to minors.

Up until recently, the controversies surrounding pornography generally fell into two categories. The first consists of those that oppose restrictions on pornography based on free speech and other issues related to first amendment rights (West 2005). The first amendment prohibits law enforcement from limiting the right of free speech; however, in cases of victimization, especially the victimization of children, law enforcement's response often includes investigation of the case and arrest of the perpetrator(s).

The second category views pornography as a "gateway to violence" (West 2005). Two government commissions resulted from this controversy. The first, performed during the Lyndon Johnson administration in the 1960s, found little or no evidence supporting the belief that pornography is related to sexual violence. Further, the report recommended sexual education in schools, more research on pornography, and discouraged restrictions on adult pornography. The U.S. Congress eventually rejected this report on the basis of widespread criticism. A second report, funded by the Attorney General's Commission on Pornography and released in 1986, suggested that there is a possible relationship between pornography and sexual violence. In particular, the commission's report suggested that pornography may lead to a greater acceptance of violence toward women (Borda 2002).

To address the issue of pornography and computer technology, the 1977 Sexual Exploitation of Children Act prohibited the transportation of child pornography by mail or computer (McCabe 2000). In 1984, the Child Protection Act defined anyone younger than eighteen as a child. In 1988, the Child Protection Enforcement Act made it unlawful to use a computer to transport child pornography and provided a specific age definition of a child based on the child's physical characteristics. The

1996 Child Pornography Act amended this definition to include computer-generated children (McCabe 2003). Since 1996, the U.S. Congress has continued to pass various acts of legislation concerning child pornography and online child pornography. These include the Child Pornography Prevention Act of 1996, the Telecommunications Reform Act of 1996, the Child Online Protection Act of 1998, and the Children's Internet Protection Act of 2000.

The 1996 Child Pornography Prevention Act extended current child pornography legislation to include materials generated and disseminated using computer technology. This act defines child pornography in three parts. First, the production of the pornographic materials must involve the use of a minor in sexually explicit behaviors. Second, the visuals must appear to depict a minor engaging in sexually explicit behaviors. Last, the materials must be advertised, described, or presented in such a way that it implies that they suggest the depiction of a minor engaging in sexual explicit conduct.

The 1996 Telecommunication Reform Act, which included the Communications Decency Act as a rider, attempted to regulate information dispersed over the Internet, to including child pornography. However, in 2002, the U.S. Supreme Court decided to strike down a federal ban on "virtual" child pornography or the use of computer-generated child pornography. The content of the 1998 Child Online Protection Act (COPA), in contrast, concerns which websites children (under the age of seventeen) are permitted to access. More specifically, this legislation seeks to restrict children from accessing websites that may contain pornographic content. It also mandated a commission with the sole purpose of ascertaining methods by which children can be prevented from accessing websites deemed harmful. The 2000 Children's Internet Protection Act addressed similar concerns by mandating that schools and libraries receiving certain forms of federal funding must implement procedures to monitor Internet use by children including the use of filtration technology.

The Child Protection and Sexual Predator Punishment Act of 1998 was also intended to regulate the dissemination of child pornography on the Internet. This act has two parts. The first requires Internet service providers (ISPs) to report any possible or actual evidence of child pornography or abuse to the appropriate law enforcement personnel. ISPs are also required to report evidence of child abuse. The second portion of the act specifies that possession of child pornography is grounds for criminal prosecution.

One of the main difficulties with these acts of legislation is that they are repeatedly challenged in the courts, particularly for constitutionality issues. The 1995 Communications Decency Act (CDA), for example, prevented individuals from using the Internet to distribute materials deemed offensive to children. The U.S. Supreme Court ruled this act unconstitutional in 1997 on the grounds that its wording was too vague. To correct these errors, the 1998 COPA legislation was far more specific, perhaps too much so. However, on June 22, 2000, the U.S. Court of Appeals for the Third Circuit upheld an injunction against the act and held that the act may still be overbroad.

Unfortunately, technological advances in the last twenty years have created a plethora of difficulties for law enforcement. The first is that the legal system has yet to catch up to the latest Internet technology being used to create and distribute pornography, and there is much controversy over the rights of federal, state, and local governments to regulate material available on the Internet. A second problem is that although many law enforcement agencies have created specialized units to address the problem, some have neither the funds nor the resources to take such an initiative. This is problematic when combating online pornography.

Online child and adult pornography is distributed using a wide variety of techniques. These include e-mail and mailing lists, listservs, newsgroups, discussion boards, instant messaging, chat rooms, and personal websites. Pornography production, on the other hand, is aided by the use of web cameras and videophones. A new technique in the creation of child pornography, virtual child pornography, consists of images that are created using morphing techniques in which visual materials are combined to create a pornographic image. Due in part to the absence of a victim in its creation, this form of child pornography has only been banned in select jurisdictions.

During 1998, the U.S. Department of Justice and the Office of Juvenile Justice and Delinquency Prevention (OJJDP) awarded ten state and local law enforcement agencies the funds to design and implement a program to counter the emerging issue of child pornography and the sexual exploitation of children via the Internet. These law enforcement agencies became members of the Internet Crimes Against Children (ICAC) Task Force Program (McCabe 2003).

Under this program, the law enforcement agencies serve as regional resources in education and prevention of child sexual abuse via the Internet. In 2000, OJJDP funded twenty new awards across the nation to support similar efforts by other law enforcement agencies. Of these, one of the most recognized is Operation Blue Ridge Thunder in Bedford County, Virginia. Operation Blue Ridge Thunder (OBRT) is the code name for a task force of undercover law enforcement personnel who work to stop those who attempt to create or distribute child pornography on the Internet as well as those who use the Internet to lure children for illicit purposes. OBRT now includes a supervisor, two investigators, an analyst, and other law enforcement personnel dedicated to the prevention of the sexual exploitation of children. The Virginia State Police, U.S.

Customs, U.S. Postal Investigation Service, and the Federal Bureau of Investigation have also contributed to this endeavor. This coordinated effort has led OBRT to be the recipient of many national, state, and local awards. Due to the widespread media attention accorded the OBRT, several nonprofit organizations, celebrities, and other law enforcement agencies have instigated their own efforts. The Safe Surfin' Foundation (formed in 2000), for example, began its campaign as a support for the educational programs of the OBRT. Now, Safe Surfin' is dedicated to the education of the public about Internet crimes, specifically those involving children.

Pornography, particularly child pornography, is a prominent national issue that continues to surface within the political arena. In the last decade, a series of legislative acts have been passed in an effort to curb child pornography on the Internet and to prevent children from accessing pornographic materials. However, these acts are the subject of much debate in that they seek to regulate materials generally protected by the First Amendment. Regardless, law enforcement agencies (local, state, and federal) have combined resources to combat pornography, specifically child pornography. It is clear that pornography will continue to be a crucial issue facing law enforcement personnel in the years to come.

KIMBERLY A. MCCABE and
LACEY N. ORE

See also **Age and Crime; Computer Crimes; Gender and Crime**

References and Further Readings

Barkan, S. 2001. *Criminology. A sociological understanding.* 2nd ed. Upper Saddle River, NJ: Prentice-Hall.

Borda, D. 2002. An overview of recent federal laws regulating pornography on the Internet. *Law and the Internet.* November 21. http://gsulaw.gsu.edu/lawand/papers/fa01/caldwell/ (accessed December 5, 2005).

Crosson-Tower, C. 1999. *Understanding child abuse and neglect*. 4th ed. Boston, MA: Allyn and Bacon.

DeYoung, M. 1982. *The sexual victimization of children*. Jefferson, NC: McFarland.

McCabe, K. 2000. Child pornography and the Internet. *Social Science Computer Review* 18: 73–76.

———. 2003. *Child abuse and the criminal justice system*. New York: Peter Lang Publishing.

Siegel, L. 1998. Criminology. *Theories, patterns, and typologies*. 6th ed. Belmont, CA: West/Wadsworth.

West, C. 2005. Pornography and censorship. In *The Stanford encyclopedia of philosophy*, ed. Edward N. Zalta, Fall 2005 ed. http://plato.stanford.edu/archives/fall2005/entries/pornography-censorship (accessed December 4, 2005).

POSSE COMITATUS

Americans have a long-standing aversion to the use of the military in domestic affairs, one that antedates the founding of our republic. Concern about mistreatment by British soldiers was an animating force behind the American Revolution, and fears about the potential misuse of military power led the framers of the Constitution to, among other things, mandate civilian control of the armed forces, empower Congress to regulate the military, allow citizens to keep and bear arms and form citizen militias to quell uprisings, and place strict limits on when soldiers may be housed in citizens' homes. During the first several decades of U.S. history, soldiers infrequently became involved in domestic matters; when they did, they were subordinate to the civilian authorities who had called for their assistance. This changed in the 1850s when Attorney General Caleb Cushing ruled that federal troops under command of their officers could be used to assist federal marshals enforcing the Fugitive Slave Act of 1850.

The practice of using troops to enforce domestic law continued for the next two decades. Union soldiers served to keep the peace in the southern areas they occupied during the Civil War, and federal troops did the same during the Reconstruction Era as the national government averred that military power was needed to maintain order in the face of Southern hostility against the changes wrought by the Civil War. During Reconstruction, federal troops regularly took law enforcement action to keep the peace, prompting concerns regarding the legitimacy of using soldiers as a police force. These concerns became heightened in the wake of the exceptionally close 1876 presidential election (determined by a single vote in the electoral college), as President Ulysses Grant had sent troops to help federal marshals police the polls in several Southern states. Worried about the encroachment of the military in the critical democratic endeavor of electing civilian leaders, Congress soon took action to limit the capacity of the military to enforce civil law.

In 1878, Congress passed an appropriations bill that included a section forbidding Army troops from taking law enforcement action absent constitutional or statutory authorization. Section 15 of Chapter 263 of the appropriations bill read:

> From and after the passage of this act it shall not be lawful to employ any part of the Army of the United States, as a posse comitatus, or otherwise, for the purpose of executing the laws, except in such cases and under such circumstances as such employment of said force may be expressly authorized by the Constitution or by act of Congress; and no money appropriated by this act shall be used to pay any of the expenses incurred in the employment of any troops in violation of this section, and any person willfully violating the provisions of this section shall be deemed guilty of a misdemeanor and on conviction thereof shall be punished by fine not exceeding ten thousand dollars or imprisonment not exceeding two years or by both such fine and imprisonment.

Posse comitatus is a Latin term meaning "the power of the county," which refers to the capacity of a sheriff to enforce the criminal law within his or her county.

One of the powers sheriffs' posses is to authorize others to assist them in carrying out their duties. Those assisting a sheriff are acting as a "posse comitatus" (or just plain "posse," as in many movies about the Old West). Thus, the Army Appropriations Act of 1878 severely circumscribed both the power of local law enforcement authorities to call on members of the Army for assistance (that is, for soldiers to be employed as a posse comitatus) and for soldiers to otherwise take law enforcement action (that is, to otherwise execute the law). Given the prominent placing of the term *posse comitatus* in the section of the bill limiting the use of the military to enforce civilian law, the provision is commonly referred to as the "Posse Comitatus Act" (PCA).

In 1956, Congress amended the PCA to streamline its language and bring the Air Force (which came into being after World War II) into its statutory purview. The PCA took its current form in 1994, when Congress once again amended it. Section 1385 of Title 18 of the United States Code presently reads:

> Whoever, except in cases and under circumstances expressly authorized by the Constitution or Act of Congress, willfully uses any part of the Army or the Air Force as a posse comitatus or otherwise to execute the laws shall be fined under this title or imprisoned not more than two years, or both.

While the PCA mentions only the Army and the Air Force, in 1986, the Department of Defense issued regulations extending its provisions to the Navy and Marine Corps. Thus, the PCA effectively restricts the capacity of all branches of the U.S. armed forces to take law enforcement action to situations clearly authorized by the Constitution or federal statute.

This is not to say, however, that the U.S. military is universally forbidden to enforce domestic law. Among the notable exceptions to the restrictions set out in the PCA are that it applies to neither the Coast Guard nor the National Guard. The Coast Guard is excepted because during peacetime it falls under the authority of the Department of Transportation. The National Guard is not covered because guard units are state entities that operate under the authority of their governor (as per Title 32 of the U.S. Code), unless they are federalized by presidential authority (and then fall under Title 10 of the U.S. Code, which regulates the armed forces).

Another notable exception to the PCA is found in Chapter 15 of Title 10 of the U.S. Code, the so-called Insurrection Act. In short, the Insurrection Act permits the president to dispatch federal troops to enforce civil law on the request of state legislators or governors and when it is apparent that state authorities are either incapable of or unwilling to enforce federal law. This exception to the PCA was most recently used when California Governor Pete Wilson requested and received the assistance of federal troops during the 1992 Los Angeles riots. More recently, some commentators have asserted that the Insurrection Act should have likewise been invoked so that federal troops could help reestablish order in New Orleans in 2005, following Hurricane Katrina.

It is important to note that the PCA in no way proscribes the use of the military to carry out *non*-law enforcement activities on U.S. soil. Thus can the president, with no fear of running afoul of the PCA, order military units to assist local and state authorities in a variety of ways that bear no relation to enforcing the law when circumstances conspire to overwhelm them. In the wake of natural disasters or other sorts of crises, the military can deliver supplies, search for missing people, rescue stranded individuals, provide medical services, or supply any similar sort of assistance. While local, state, and federal civilian authorities can usually manage things following disasters, soldiers have occasionally been called on to help out, such as in San Francisco following the 1906 earthquake and in South Florida after Hurricane Hugo struck in 1992.

The notion that members of the military can assist civilian authorities as long as they do not enforce the law also applies to assisting police agencies in nonemergency situations. Soldiers can train local, state, and federal police officers; they can provide equipment and supplies to them; and they can offer technical assistance and do anything else that does not have them engaged directly in taking enforcement action. In recent decades, the military has been used to support a variety of law enforcement endeavors, most notably drug interdiction and policing our southern border.

That the military can, and does, legally work so closely with law enforcement agencies is a contentious topic. Some argue the status quo is sound, as military support is necessary for effective law enforcement; military assets are needed to effectively interdict drugs, for example. Others argue that allowing the military to so closely support the police is an invitation to disaster and the loss of the precious liberties the PCA is intended to protect. Those opposed to the close working relationship between the military and civilian law enforcement point to cases where the presence of the military has led to bad outcomes—the 1997 shooting death of a young man near the Mexican border by a Marine patrol that was helping out with immigration enforcement, for example—as evidence that it is not a good idea.

The controversy about the appropriateness of using the military to support law enforcement activities indicates that the long-standing American concern about military power is alive and well in the twenty-first century. The PCA—in its various manifestations—has played a central role in demonstrating this concern for the past century and a quarter even though no person has been prosecuted for violating it. As the new century unfolds and new law enforcement challenges arise in a post–September 11 world, the use of the military in American police work will continue to be a contentious topic. And, whether it retains its current form or is in some way altered, the Posse Comitatus Act will continue to play a crucial role in delimiting the bounds within which the military may be legally used in domestic law enforcement.

DAVID KLINGER and
CHRISTOPHER J. SCHMIDT

See also **Arrest Powers of the Police; Autonomy and the Police; Critical Incidents; Crowd/Riot Control; Homeland Security and Law Enforcement**

References and Further Reading

Brinkerhoff, John. 2002. The Posse Comitatus Act and homeland security. *Journal of Homeland Security* (Feb.).

Hammond, Matthew. 1997. The Posse Comitatus Act: A principle in need of renewal. *Washington University Law Quarterly* 75 (2).

Klinger, David, and Dave Grossman. 2002. Answering foreign terrorists on U.S. soil: Socio-legal consequences of September 11 and the ongoing threat of terrorist attacks in America. *Harvard Journal of Law and Public Policy* 25 (2).

POST-SHOOTING REVIEW

Instances where police officers shoot a citizen are the most traumatic to the police officer, the public, and to the potential image of the police agency. When a police officer is involved in a situation where deadly force is used, an investigation normally follows to avoid the impression of misconduct and issues concerning whether the shooting was justified, and to maintain the creditability of law enforcement actions. The investigation also seeks to identify potential errors in policies, supervision, or training. This investigation constitutes a post-shooting review of the officer's actions.

There are no standard procedures in post-shooting reviews. Although there are many common elements, most departments follow their own set of protocols and procedures. Agencies may also have different units within the department that are in charge of these types of investigations. Most investigations are conducted in a formal manner and are designed to be completed as early as possible to reach a decision on the validity of the officer's actions, to determine if any criminal or administrative actions need to be taken, and to bring closure for the community and those involved.

When a weapon is discharged, the officer involved must immediately contact and inform his or her supervisor. The officer is normally required to give up his or her weapon and file a written report explaining the circumstances of the shooting. The senior officer on scene will seize the weapon and take all precautions necessary to maintain the security of the scene. The supervising officer is usually responsible for conducting a preliminary investigation, which calls for collecting and securing physical evidence, recording activities such as people at the scene and procedures taken by police officers, and identifying people entering and leaving the crime scene. The senior officer will usually also conduct on-site interviews with the parties involved (including the officer in question), and inform the chief or sheriff, internal affairs, and the prosecuting attorney's office.

Depending on the size of the police agency, the preliminary investigation is followed by a more detailed investigation by officers of the internal affairs and/or detective unit. The first step in this type of investigation is to verify that all evidence is present, to advise officers not to discuss the matter to avoid rumors, and to respond to the officers' mental state. The officers involved in the shooting may be given leave time to recuperate and deal with any trauma or anguish they might face. Sometimes officers are ordered to take leave until the investigation is completed. Information gathered at this stage includes the time and date, weather, names of all officers involved, time of the dispatch call, type of call and whether officers were alerted to potential weapons or violence, detailed information of all people involved, and detailed information of all the witnesses.

Investigators will typically return to the scene of the shooting and visualize or re-create all or parts of the events that took place. This process enables the investigators to understand how the circumstances came about and if the use of deadly force was necessary. The investigators will also examine the backgrounds of all parties involved for previous actions that may be relevant. The investigators will also contact the coroner's office for its findings if the shooting resulted in death. The coroner's office will be helpful in understanding the wounds relevant to the position of the weapon and the position of both the officer and the person(s) involved. The coroner can also determine if other physical force was used.

The investigator will also maintain contact with the other investigators who may be examining other elements of the incident. Investigators will consider whether the situation could have been dealt with in another way and whether errors were made on the part of the officer. After understanding the circumstances and looking over all the evidence, the investigators will then interview all the officers, parties, and witnesses involved. This is a crucial point in the investigation because it enables investigators to get all sides of the story and attempt to determine what happened.

Officers involved in shooting incidents are typically questioned in one or both of two ways. The first way officers may be questioned is in relation to a potential criminal case as a result of their actions. This is somewhat rare, however. More often, officers are questioned pursuant to the case of *New Jersey v. Garrity*. The *Garrity* case held that information officers reveal during the course of an administrative investigation cannot be used against them in a criminal trial. This is an effort to make sure officers feel free to speak to investigators in these important matters.

Even under *Garrity*, officers have a right to refuse to answer questions, but their refusal can be grounds for disciplinary actions leading to dismissal, regardless of the outcome of the case. Again, this is in an effort to make sure officers tell investigators all they know and are completely truthful about the incident. After analyzing all the evidence and interviews, the investigator will report the findings to whomever will be responsible for making a final determination.

In larger law enforcement agencies, a special panel of individuals may be formed to investigate and/or reach a decision. This panel may be variously called a *shooting team*, *shooting review board*, or a *citizen review board*. The panel, although differing from agency to agency, usually consists of a senior person in the agency (assistant chief or chief deputy), supervisors, administrative officers, and sometimes citizens. In some circumstances, depending of the size of the police agency, the shooting review board might be the primary investigative body, replacing the use of an internal unit in the shooting investigation; or units within the department will conduct the investigation and the panel will decide the outcome. The role of the shooting review panel is to evaluate whether the shooting was justifiable, if procedures were followed, and if there is a need to change department policies and training methods.

Some agencies have several departments that work together to investigate a shooting incident. A typical example of the post-shooting process may be taken from the International Association of Chiefs of Police (IACP), which established a model policy as a guideline for police agencies. The policy states that the overall investigation should be led by the internal affairs, detective division, or the homicide unit. In larger agencies, a criminal investigation and an administrative investigation may be conducted to ensure that training and supervision was adequate and

department policies were followed. These investigations will also seek to determine whether criminal activity was involved on the part of the officer in question.

The supervising officer is in charge at the scene of the shooting until the investigating officers arrive, who then take responsibility for the criminal and administrative investigations. It is the responsibility of the investigators to take statements from the officers involved and update their supervisor(s), the chief of police, and the prosecuting attorney's office. After the investigations are finished, the investigators will send the report(s) to the chief of police for review.

Both the criminal investigation and the administrative investigation are often then sent to a board/panel (as discussed earlier), which then evaluates and reviews the use of deadly force. It attempts to determine whether the discharge of the weapon was necessary and/or justified. All shootings must be reviewed within a reasonable amount of time, which should be predetermined by the agency. The board may address the effectiveness of the training, the accuracy of the investigation, the adequacy of the supervision, and how to better handle similar situations in the future. After reviewing and discussing the reports, recommendations are sent to the chief of police for consideration of disciplinary actions or changes that needs to be made in training, supervision, or policy.

Regardless of whether a police agency follows this procedure or something simpler, it is vital that agencies have a strong post-shooting review process. Both the officers involved and the community must have confidence that police actions are justified and within the limits of law and policy. Further, research has shown that a strong use-of-force policy coupled with an understanding by officers that the chief or sheriff will back up the policy is the best method of controlling improper use of force. A post-shooting review is one element of the policy and process of ensuring officers' actions are properly evaluated and a decision made about whether the shooting was justified.

ISRAT T. ZOHRA and
JEFFERY T. WALKER

See also **Accountability; Civilian Review Boards; Critical Incidents; Deadly Force; Excessive Force**

References and Further Reading

Fyfe, James J., ed. 1982. *Readings on police use of deadly force*. Washington, DC: Police Foundation.

Fyfe, James J., and Jeffery T. Walker. 1991. Garner plus five years: An examination of Supreme Court intervention and legislative prerogatives. *American Journal of Criminal Justice* 14 (2): 167–88.

Garrity v. New Jersey, 385 U.S. 493 (1967).

Geller, William A., and Michael S. Scott. 1992. *Deadly force: What we know*. Washington, DC: Police Executive Research Forum.

International Association of Chiefs of Police. 1998. *Model policy: Investigation of officer-involved shootings*. Alexandria, VA: IACP National Law Enforcement Policy Center.

———. 1999. *Concepts and issues paper: Investigation of officer involved shootings*. Alexandria, VA: IACP National Law Enforcement Policy Center.

Little Rock Police Department. 2003. *General order 303: Use of force*. Little Rock, AR: Little Rock Police Department.

Pate, Anthony M., and Lorie A. Fridell. 1993. *Police use of force: Official reports, citizen complaints, and legal consequences*. Washington, DC: Police Foundation.

PRESUMPTIVE ARREST POLICING

The United States as a whole continues to grapple with finding the best solutions for coping with and ending the high incidence of domestic violence that currently exists today. Policy makers continue to struggle with identifying and implementing the most appropriate and effective response to this epidemic. The law enforcement community, in particular, has faced many challenges in responding to and developing new policies for coping

with the occurrence of domestic violence during the past two decades.

Law enforcement agencies have generally adopted three approaches over the years for responding to domestic violence calls for service. The first approach involves officers serving as mediators at the scene of domestic disputes, the second approach involves the use of presumptive arrest policies, and the third approach uses mandatory arrest policies. Mandatory and presumptive arrest policies are the latest approaches being implemented at the state level in an attempt to curb the prevalence of domestic violence. These types of policies have been the subject of recent research studies and have yielded inconsistent results. The progression of presumptive arrest policies will be outlined and explained in this article.

Social Changes

Traditionally domestic violence was viewed by society as a private family matter that did not warrant government intervention. This social view dates back to a time period when women and children were merely viewed as chattel. Common law allowed and even encouraged a man to use physical force against his family in order to maintain order or for disciplinary purposes under the belief that he would be held responsible for the actions of his family members. Society gradually became less tolerant of domestic violence, but the view that it was a private family matter remained until approximately twenty years ago. By the end of the nineteenth century, American appellate courts began to denounce the common law approach and refuse to recognize a spousal exemption in cases of assault and battery. During this same time, states began to amend divorce statutes to include cruelty as a ground for divorce.

Law enforcement officials were limited in their ability to respond to such calls for service due to the fact that domestic violence was not considered a crime. Probable cause is a requirement established by the Fourth Amendment of the Constitution. The Supreme Court held in *Gerstein v. Pugh*, 420 U.S. 103 (1975) and *Beck v. Ohio*, 379 U.S. 89 (1964) that "probable cause to arrest exists when the facts and circumstances known to the officer are sufficient to warrant a reasonably prudent person in believing that the suspect has committed or is committing a crime."

Two major motivators began to alter the way states responded to domestic violence cases. The federal and state courts began to establish the right to police protection from domestic violence in cases such as 1984's *Thurman v. City of Torrington*, 595 F. Supp. 1521. In the *Thurman* case a federal jury determined that the Torrington Police Department failed to adequately protect Mrs. Tracey Thurman and her son from domestic abuse. The case asserted that had Mrs. Thurman and her son been attacked by a stranger the police department would have reacted differently and this failure to act appropriately constituted a violation of Mrs. Thurman's Fourteenth Amendment rights under the Equal Protection Clause. The court awarded her $2.9 million dollars in damages. This case made it clear that inaction on the part of the law enforcement officials could have severe legal consequences.

Limitation of potential liability became one important motivator for the states to adopt a new policy toward domestic violence. The second major enticement occurred in 1994 when President Clinton signed into law a crucial federal crime bill that included the Violence Against Women Act. The significance of this act was that millions of grant funds were made available to those states that adopted pro-arrest or mandatory arrest legislation.

The three general approaches mentioned earlier that law enforcement agencies have adopted over the years for responding to domestic violence calls for service are explained in the following paragraphs. The first approach involves officers serving as peacekeepers at the scene of domestic disputes, the second approach involves the use of presumptive arrest policies, and the third approach uses mandatory arrest policies.

Law Enforcement Officers as Peacekeepers

Because domestic violence was not traditionally considered a crime and was viewed by most as a private family matter, law enforcement officers initially resorted to mediation techniques when responding to these calls for service. Law enforcement officers maintained a peacekeeping role on the scene and encouraged the couple to sort out their disagreement without the use of violence. Officers became makeshift counselors in this situation and often referred the victim and/or offender to counseling services that were available to them within their community. Sometimes an officer would involve social services after a visit. Many police agencies adopted a mediation policy that discouraged arrests and instead provided a cooling-off period for those involved with officer presence that would allow for a peaceful resolution to the dispute at hand.

In some cases, however, the mediation intervention was not enough, and the police presence may have served to further exacerbate the situation. Although the intentions behind this policy were good, it received its fair share of criticisms. One such criticism is that the adoption of a mediation policy approach enhances the perception that domestic violence is not a crime, but is instead a private family issue less worthy of legal intervention. Another criticism of mediation policy is that adoption of such a policy contributes to the offender's rationalization for the abuse, which leads to the belief that both the victim and offender are to blame for the abuse and almost ensures future abuse.

Critics of the mediation policy insist that a more punitive approach is needed for offenders of domestic violence in order to prevent it from happening on a regular basis.

Presumptive Arrest Policies

When the view of domestic violence began to shift and was no longer considered a private family matter, the response from the criminal justice system began to shift as well. Law enforcement agencies began implementing presumptive arrest policies due to the criminalization of domestic violence throughout the United States. A presumptive arrest policy is a type of pro-arrest policy that provides officers with discretionary abilities and allows them to make arrests when they deem them necessary.

There are two versions of pro-arrest policies. The first one typically encourages arrests through policy but leaves the decision to the officers who will be responding to the calls for service. This approach is often referred to as a *pro-arrest approach.* The second approach to domestic violence encourages officers to make an arrest but ultimately leaves this decision up to their discretion. This is what we call a *presumptive arrest policy.* This approach assumes that the officer will know best how to handle the situation based on his or her experience and expertise. It is presumed that an arrest will be made if the officer finds evidence that domestic violence has occurred.

The Progression of Presumptive Arrest Policies

In 1977, the state of Oregon experimented with mandatory arrest laws and concluded that the use of arrest and the threat of arrest were very powerful tools for deterring future acts of domestic abuse (Jolin 1983). In 1984, the Minneapolis Experiment was conducted to determine the most effective response to domestic violence calls for service. The researchers concluded that an arrest deterred future acts of domestic violence. Several studies replicated this experiment, but results varied (Berk and Newton 1985; Berk et al. 1992; Dunford 1992; Hirschel and Hutchinson 1992; Pate and Hamilton 1992; Sherman et al. 1992). Three subsequent studies, including ones conducted in Charlotte (Hirschel and Hutchinson 1992) and Omaha (Dunford 1992), concluded that an arrest actually increased future acts of domestic violence. Some researchers have argued that it is the inconsistency of the legal system that contributes to future acts of violence. When an offender is arrested but the case is dismissed in court, it defeats efforts made by the law enforcement community. The enactment and reenactment of the Violence Against Women Act has ensured that states take a serious approach to ending domestic violence through the enactment of appropriate legislation.

Mandatory Arrest Policies

The mandatory arrest approach does not allow officer discretion and requires by law that one or both parties involved in the dispute be arrested. There are two basic variations of the mandatory arrest policy. The first requires officers responding to a domestic violence call to arrest the primary aggressor. The criticism associated with this policy is that it is not always clear who the primary aggressor is, and the victim may actually end up going to jail simply because an arrest had to be made. The second variation generates the most criticism in that officers are required to arrest both parties involved and let the judge determine who is at fault later in a courtroom.

Many states have adopted mandatory arrest statutes that require law enforcement officers to arrest suspected batterers if there is probable cause that domestic violence has occurred. Furthermore, most mandatory arrest statutes are coupled with a warrantless arrest provision that allows law enforcement officers to make a misdemeanor arrest in cases where the officer has probable cause, but did not observe the battery. The probable cause element to this law helps prevent false arrests in cases where a person claims abuse to get revenge on the alleged offender. If probable cause cannot be established, law enforcement officials are not required to make an arrest. Victim advocates proclaim that dual arrest polices cause more harm than good and hinder the efforts of victims to seek help in the event of future victimization.

Conclusion

The debate over which policy is best continues today. Perhaps it is safe to conclude that a one-size-fits-all approach to domestic violence still does not exist. The mediation approach where the officer serves as a counselor has lost a lot of support over the years. Critics assert that this policy furthers the belief that domestic violence is not a crime and sends a message to offenders that physical abuse of family members is acceptable. The presumptive arrest policy encourages an arrest to be made but ultimately leaves this decision up to the officer's discretion. Critics of this policy assert that officers will not make an arrest when they are left with discretion and mandatory arrest is the best approach. Critics of the mandatory arrest policy claim it does more harm to the victim than it does good. There are drawbacks to each of the three types of polices. Perhaps researchers should examine the judicial response to domestic violence as well as the policies adopted by law enforcement officials.

ELIZABETH CORZINE MCMULLAN

See also **Arrest Powers of the Police**

References and Further Reading

Beck v. Ohio, 379 U.S. 89 (1964).
Berk, R. A., A. Campbell, R. Klap, and B. Western. 1992. A Bayesian analysis of the Colorado Springs spouse abuse experiment. *The Journal of Criminal Law and Criminology* 83: 170–200.
Berk, R. A., and P. Newton. 1985. Does arrest really deter wife battery? An effort to replicate the findings of the Minneapolis spouse abuse experiment. *American Sociological Review* 50: 253–62.
Dunford, F. W. 1992. The measurement of recidivism in cases of spouse assault. *The Journal of Criminal Law and Criminology* 83: 120–36.
Gerstein v. Pugh, 420 U.S. 103 (1975).
Hirschel, J. D., and I. W. Hutchinson III. 1992. Female spouse abuse and the police response: The Charlotte, North Carolina, experiment. *The Journal of Criminal Law and Criminology* 83: 73–119.
Jolin, Annette. 1983. Domestic violence legislation: An impact assessment. *Journal of Police Science and Administration* 11: 451–56.
Nored, L. S., and E. C. McMullan. 2006. Mandatory arrest. In *Encyclopedia of domestic violence*, ed. Nicky Ali Jackson. New York: Routledge.
Pate, A. M., and E. E. Hamilton. 1992. Formal and informal deterrents to domestic violence: The Dade County spouse assault experiment. *American Sociological Review* 57: 691–97.
Sherman, L. W., J. D. Schmidt, D. P. Rogan, D. A. Smith, P. R. Gartin, E. G. Cohn, D. J. Collins, and A. R. Bacich. 1992. The variable effects of arrest on criminal careers: The Milwaukee domestic violence experiment. *The Journal of Criminal Law and Criminology* 83: 137–69.
Thurman v. City of Torrington, 595 F. Supp. 1521 (1984).

PRISONER REENTRY, PUBLIC SAFETY, AND CRIME

In 2004, more than 630,000 individuals were released from state and federal prisons. Another ten to twelve million cycled in and out of local jails. Research has shown that as a group, this population has a significant effect on public safety; many return quickly to criminal behavior after their release, and a significant portion will be returned to prison for a new crime.

Clearly, the reentry of large numbers of individuals from prisons into communities presents a challenge to communities struggling to promote public safety. This challenge has grown over the years, as the cohort of prisoners released annually has more than quadrupled, tracking the growth in the nation's prison population (Travis 2005). Yet, viewed differently, the annual release of large numbers of high-risk prisoners also presents an opportunity to implement policy reforms and interventions that can, if successful, improve public safety. The phenomenon of prisoner reentry thus presents particular opportunities to police professionals to develop new crime reduction strategies.

There is a strong nexus between prisoner reentry and public safety, principally because the rates of recidivism among prisoners are so high. The Bureau of Justice Statistics (BJS) has published the most comprehensive studies of recidivism among prisoners (Langan and Levin 2002; Beck and Shipley 1989). The most recent study tracked the rearrests, reconvictions, and returns to prison of a sample of the 272,111 individuals leaving prison in fifteen states in 1994. According to this study, more than two-thirds (67.5%) of prisoners released in 1994 were rearrested for at least one new crime within three years. Nearly half (46.9%) were convicted of a new crime; more than half (51.8%) were returned to prison, either for a new crime or for technical violations of parole (Langan and Levin 2002). Findings from the earlier study of a 1983 release cohort were remarkably similar. Examining 108,580 state prisoners released in 1983 from eleven states, Beck and Shipley (1989) report that 62.5% were rearrested over a three-year period, very close to the 67.5% for the 1994 cohort. The reconviction rates varied little from the 1983 to the 1994 cohorts, with 46.8% of 1983 releases reconvicted. The return to prison rate was lower for the 1983 cohort, at 41.4%.

The released prisoners in the 1994 BJS sample were arrested for a wide range of crimes. Within three years, they were charged with violent offenses (21.6%), property offenses (31.9%), drug offenses (30.3%), and offenses against the public order (28.3%). (These percentages do not total 100% because some released prisoners were rearrested for more than one type of offense.) Many were arrested for crimes in more than one of these categories. In fact, they averaged four new crimes per person over the three years of the study. Over the three-year period, these 272,111 prisoners were charged with an estimated 2,900 homicides, 2,400 kidnappings, 2,400 rapes, 3,200 other sexual assaults, 21,200 robberies, 54,600 assaults, 13,900 other crimes of violence, 40,300 burglaries, 16,000 motor vehicle thefts, 79,400 drug possession violations, 46,200 drug trafficking charges, and 26,000 weapons offenses.

The BJS study underscores the magnitude of the public safety risk presented by returning prisoners. The public safety risk can be assessed in other ways, as well. Raphael and Stoll (2004), for example, have calculated that, compared with the general population, recently released prisoners are twenty to fifty times more likely to be arrested. From a community perspective, however, the public safety risk is best understood by determining what portion of all crimes can be attributed to recently released prisoners. If they are responsible for only a small portion, then successful crime control initiatives that focus on recently released prisoners will have only a small impact on overall crime rates. If, on the other hand, the reentry cohort is responsible for a substantial share of crimes in a community, then there is a more compelling policy argument for policing professionals and others to develop interventions that would reduce their rates of recidivism.

The BJS study sheds light on this view of the public safety risk of returning prisoners. The bureau calculated the crimes of the 1994 release cohort as a proportion of all criminal arrests in the selected states. Examining index crimes (murder, rape, robbery, aggravated assault, burglary, larceny, and motor vehicle theft; arson is not included in the study) in thirteen states, the researchers found that these released prisoners accounted for 140,534 arrests between 1994 and 1997. Dividing this number by the total number of adults arrested for these crimes during the same period (2,994,868), BJS found that the released prisoners in their study accounted for only 4.7% of all the arrests from 1994 to 1997 (Langan and Levin 2002).

This statistic provides only a partial insight into the public safety dimensions of prisoner reentry, however, because it reflects only those arrests attributed to the 1994 release cohort in the years 1994 through 1997. In each of those three years, more prisoners were released who committed crimes that contributed to the overall crime rates. Additionally, some prisoners who were released in the years before the 1994 cohort were still arrested for crimes committed in the years covered by the study. If we make the reasonable assumption that those released in years just prior to and after 1994 display recidivism rates similar to those of prisoners released in 1994, then we can make a more realistic estimate of the percentage of arrests for which recently released prisoners were responsible.

Following this logic, Rosenfeld, Wallman, and Fornango (2005) determined that, for the years 1994 to 1997 in the fifteen states in the BJS study, prisoners who had been released in the three preceding years accounted for between 13% and 16% of arrests. (This assumes the prisoners released between 1995 and 1997 were arrested at the same rates as those released in 1994, and does not include public order crimes.) Rosenfeld et al. (2005) also projected the 1994 cohort's recidivism rates for cohorts released between 1995 and 2001 and found that, by 2001, the arrests of prisoners released within the previous three years accounted for more than 20% of all arrests, up from 13% in 1994. This increase was not the result of increased

recidivism rates, but happened because this seven-year period witnessed two important trends in America: a rise in the number of prisoners being released and an increase in the number of arrests, reflecting the overall drop in crime rates. Because these two trends occurred simultaneously, the percentage of arrests attributable to recently released prisoners rose steadily.

Disaggregating the data by crime type also reveals distinct trends with important public safety implications. By 2001, prisoners released in the three preceding years accounted for approximately 30% of the arrests for violent crime, 18% of the arrests for property crime, and 20% of the arrests for drug offenses. Thus, police agencies interested in reducing violent crime in particular could reap significant reductions by paying close attention to individuals leaving prison, perhaps by coordinating with corrections departments and other government and social service agencies.

The BJS study provides yet another view of the public safety risks posed by returning prisoners, namely, the changing nature of the risk over the time following release. The arrests identified in the BJS study were not evenly distributed over the three-year period of the study. Nearly 30% of the released prisoners were arrested within the first six months after leaving prison. The cumulative total rose to about 44% within the first year, and almost 60% within the first two years following release (Langan and Levin 2002). Clearly the months and years right after the release from prison present the highest risk to public safety, and present the greatest opportunities for police agencies and others to reduce the recidivism rates of this population.

In addition to this temporal definition of public safety risk, a full analysis will include a spatial dimension. Returning prisoners cluster within major metropolitan counties and in a few major cities. For example, in Illinois, 53% of all prisoners are released to Chicago (La Vigne, et al. 2003b). In Maryland, 59% of all prisoners are released to Baltimore (La Vigne, et al. 2003a). Within these cities there is a further concentration of prisoners in a small number of neighborhoods. The communities receiving the highest proportion of prisoners are often the least well equipped to absorb them—these communities have higher proportions of families living below the federal poverty level, unemployed people, and female-headed households. The public safety risks posed by returning prisoners are absorbed by these underresourced communities.

The high recidivism rates of individuals released from prison are not surprising when their levels of preparation for success within the community are assessed. While employment often translates into lower recidivism rates, many are unemployed after release. In-prison job readiness and work release programs are helpful, but the availability of such programs has declined over recent years (Lynch and Sabol 2001). A significant number of individuals leaving prison have limited or negative employment experiences. In Maryland, for example, 45% of returning prisoners had been fired at least once (Visher et al. 2004). The BJS reports that only 46% of incarcerated individuals have a high school diploma or its equivalent (Harlow 2003). About two-thirds of people in prison and jail were employed—either full time or part time—during the month before they were arrested for their current offense, but individual earnings were low—the median income for those employed was less than $1,000 per month (BJS 2000; Harlow 1998).

This profile of limited employment skills and poor work histories is further complicated by the high portion of returning prisoners who have histories of substance abuse and mental illness. Another factor in the public safety equation is the high levels of prior criminal justice involvement among returning prisoners. Of those released in 1994, 81.4% had a prior conviction; 43.6% had a prior prison sentence (Langan and Levin 2002). The cohort of returning prisoners clearly presents many individual deficits that hamper their successful reintegration.

At the beginning of the twenty-first century, when crime rates are low and reentry rates are high, strategies that reduce recidivism rates of returning prisoners may have a more significant impact on public safety than at any time in recent history. The policy challenge is to fashion interventions that are likely to be successful. The traditional intervention is to provide postrelease supervision—or more intensive supervision—as a way to reduce recidivism. This strategy, standing alone, has serious limitations. First, not all returning prisoners are supervised. Nationally, about 20% of the individuals leaving prison—about 100,000 men and women—are released with no supervision. Supervision policies vary significantly among the states. In Massachusetts, for example, 58% of prisoners are released without any supervision. By contrast, in California, only 3% of prisoners are released unconditionally (Travis and Lawrence 2002). A more significant limitation is that traditional supervision has not been found to be effective at reducing crime. A study by the Urban Institute compared the recidivism rates of supervised and unsupervised returning prisoners in the BJS data and determined that the rearrest rates were virtually identical (Solomon, Kachnowski, and Bhati 2005). A study by the RAND Corporation, comparing recidivism rates of parolees and probationers under intensive supervision with rates of those under traditional supervision, found no difference (Petersilia and Turner 1993). Clearly, merely extending supervision practices to more returning prisoners—or merely increasing the intensity of supervision—is not likely to reduce crime rates.

The most promising strategy would start with a different premise, namely, to identify the times, places, and individuals presenting the highest risks and then to devote resources in ways that would reduce those risks. This strategy would begin with the goal of reducing the rates of failure following the release from prison, principally by developing transition plans for each returning prisoner. The focus would be on transition needs: housing, family reunification, continuity in drug treatment and health care, employment, and peer group support. This strategy would also be community based, deeply integrated into those neighborhoods with large numbers of individuals transitioning between prison and home. Finally, this strategy would develop a new approach to supervision, testing new models that will both promote public safety and enhance the legitimacy of this critical phase of the criminal justice system. Clearly, police agencies would play an important role in any successful strategy of this sort.

JEREMY TRAVIS and SINEAD KEEGAN

See also **Crime Control Strategies; Crime Prevention; Crime, Serious; Criminology**

References and Further Reading

Beck, Allen J., and Bernard E. Shipley. 1989. *Recidivism of prisoners released in 1983*. NCJ 116261. Washington, DC: U.S. Department of Justice, Bureau of Justice Statistics.

Bureau of Justice Statistics. 2000. *Correctional populations in the United States, 1997*. NCJ 177613. Washington, DC: U.S. Department of Justice.

Harlow, Caroline Wold. 1998. *Profile of jail inmates 1996*. NCJ 164620. Washington, DC: U.S. Department of Justice, Bureau of Justice Statistics.

———. 2003. *Education and correctional populations*. NCJ 195670. Washington, DC: U.S. Department of Justice, Bureau of Justice Statistics.

La Vigne, Nancy G., Vera Kachnowski, Jeremy Travis, Rebecca Naser, and Christy Visher. 2003a. *A portrait of prisoner reentry in Maryland*. Washington, DC: The Urban Institute.

La Vigne, Nancy G., Cynthia A. Mamalian, Jeremy Travis, and Christy Visher. 2003b. *A portrait of prisoner reentry in Illinois*. Washington, DC: The Urban Institute.

Langan, Patrick A., and David Levin. 2002. *Recidivism of prisoners released in 1994*. NCJ 193427. Washington, DC: U.S. Department of Justice, Bureau of Justice Statistics.

Lynch, James P., and William J. Sabol. 2001. *Prisoner reentry in perspective*. Crime Policy Report, vol. 3. Washington, DC: The Urban Institute.

Petersilia, Joan, and Susan Turner. 1993. *Evaluating intensive supervision probation/parole: Results from a nationwide experiment*. NIJ Research in Brief. Washington, DC: U.S. Department of Justice, National Institute of Justice.

Raphael, Steven, and Michael A. Stoll. 2004. The effect of prison releases on regional crime rates. In *The Brookings-Wharton papers on Urban Affairs 2004*, ed. William G. Gale and Janet Rothenberg Pack. Washington, DC: Brookings Institution Press.

Rosenfeld, Richard, Joel Wallman, and Robert J. Fornango. 2005. The contribution of ex-prisoners to crime rates. In *Prisoner reentry and public safety in America*, ed. Jeremy Travis and Christy Visher. New York: Cambridge University Press.

Solomon, Amy L., Vera Kachnowski, and Avinash Bhati. 2005. *Does parole work? Analyzing the impact of post-prison supervision and recidivism*. Washington, DC: The Urban Institute.

Travis, Jeremy. 2005. *But they all come back: Facing the challenges of prisoner reentry*. Washington, DC: The Urban Institute Press.

Travis, Jeremy, and Sarah Lawrence. 2002. California's parole experiment. *California Journal* 33 (8): 18–23.

Visher, Christy, Vera Kachnowski, Nancy La Vigne, and Jeremy Travis. 2004. *Baltimore prisoners' experiences returning home*. Washington, DC: The Urban Institute.

PRIVATE POLICING

Introduction

The past few decades have witnessed the exponential growth of private policing in developed and developing countries. Whereas at one time, the state police force was considered to be the sole provider of security, currently it is commonly accepted that the state police force is but one player in a range of security providers. Alongside the rise in crime rates and increased insecurity and fear of crime, new threats are constantly being identified. These have both local and global impacts. Responses to these challenges constantly reshape the security landscape. During the past half-century a significant feature of this landscape has been the growth and influence of private policing initiatives.

Defining Private Policing

There has been considerable debate over the terms *private police* and *private security*. Often the terms are used interchangeably. At other times the term *private police* is used to refer to a range of players (vigilante groups, gangs, neighborhood watches, and so forth) of which the private security industry is one player. For many authors the term *private police* is problematic because it suggests that the public police and other policing entities share characteristics when they believe they should be sharply distinguished. One resolution of this has been the adoption of the word private *policing*. This usage defines policing as a generic function that various bodies might undertake in ways that can be quite distinct (Jones and Newburn 1998). Another concept that has gained currency recently is the *governance of security*, a term used by the commissioner of the Metropolitan London Police, Ian Blair (1998). In developing this conception the governance of security has recently been conceived as involving various "nodes" and "networks" within a conception of "nodal governance" (Loader 2000; Johnston and Shearing 2003; Hermer et al. 2005). For the purposes of this overview, the terms *private security* and *private policing* will be used interchangeably to refer to the domestic and transnational private security firms and their diverse activities.

The Rise of Private Security

The rise of private security is not limited to the United States. Private security is a significant feature of the governance of security in many countries—for example, the United Kingdom, Canada, South Africa, Nigeria, Kenya, Brazil, and many countries in Asia. Private security in the United States, which is our focus in this article, has had a long history, starting with the first detective agency, the Pinkerton Agency—which coined the term *private eye* founded in 1850. The rapid development of other types of private policing soon emerged after that with the founding of the American Express Company in the same year. This later became the Adams Express Company, specializing in security transport. America's first central burglar alarm and cash-carrying private companies were founded in 1858 and 1859, respectively. These developments have been attributed to the geographic features of the United States, which required mechanisms for the secure transportation of goods that public police, with their primarily urban focus, were unable to provide (Draper 1978; Sklansky 1999).

The early twentieth century might be thought of as a golden age of private detective firms. The Pinkerton Agency, for example, is credited with influencing the development of investigation techniques used by the public police through its systems of surveillance and its development of a file system that was used by the Federal Bureau of Investigation until it developed its own case file system (Sklansky 1999; Draper 1978; O'Reilly and Ellison 2004). Indeed, it was not until the 1930s that private security stature and legitimacy came to be questioned. A significant event in this process was the establishment of the La Follette Committee to investigate threats to civil liberties (particularly labor-related threats) associated with the private security industry. A particular cause for concern was Pinkerton's use of espionage techniques and other methods to break strikes and monitor industrial activities.

The growth of both the size and stature of the public police began to surpass private security, and private policing remained largely unnoticed through the first half of the twentieth century (Sklansky 1999). In 1971 research conducted by the RAND Corporation revealed that the public police outnumbered private security agents and predicted that this trend would continue. By the early 1980s, however, a very different picture emerged. Private security was found to outnumber the public police and it was argued that this growth had begun in the 1960s and 1970s. One of the explanations offered for this trend was the inability of the public police to respond effectively to rising crime (Sklansky 1999; Joh 2004). This argument was confirmed in 1976 by a report commissioned by the Law Enforcement Assistance Administration that pointed to the inability of the criminal justice system to cope with crime on its own (Joh 2004). The possibility of partnership policing involving both public and private policing agencies has been a topic of debate since then. This debate has been accompanied by constant growth on the part of both the public police and private security.

During this period of sustained growth, private security firms undertook more and more of the tasks that had come to be regarded as the preserve of the public police. Indeed, today the private security industry in the United States performs many duties that were seen as core functions of public police—arrest, search and seizures, criminal investigation, public order policing, and patrolling public places. These are undertaken in addition to activities such as cash-in-transit operations, keyholding functions, security consultation, bodyguard and VIP protection services, and business intelligence services that are by and large the sole preserve of the private security industry (Draper 1978; O'Reilly et al. 2004).

Estimates of the size of private security in the United States draw primarily from two studies: "Hallcrest Report I: Private Security and Police in America" and "Hallcrest Report II: Private Security Trends 1970–2000," published in 1985 and 1990, respectively. These reports suggest that the private security industry is approximately three times the size of the public policing sector. More modest estimates suggest that there are three private security agents to every two public police officers (Joh 2004; Sklansky 1999). It has been estimated that there are some ten thousand security companies in the United States, employing between one and a half million to two million security personnel (Mandel 2001). While estimates vary there is consensus that the private policing sector is larger, more pervasive, and more adaptable than the public sector. It is estimated that this industry generates revenues of up to $10 billion per annum (Joh 2004).

Private policing is a transnational as well as a national phenomenon. The responses to the September 11, 2001, terrorist attacks have drawn attention to the existence of private military corporations (PMCs) that now operate in a variety of military capacities around the world. Many of these are based in the United States and the U.S. government is an important contractor for their services. It is estimated that this industry will be worth more than $202 billion by 2010. PMC services include tactical operations, logistical/intelligence support, technical military assistance and training, strategic advice/security consulting, and combat forces (Bharadwaj 2003; Singer 2005). Singer reports that the United States has signed more than three thousand contracts with PMCs during the past ten years.

Debates on Private Policing

With the rise in private policing there has been a concomitant rise in academic and policy debates about it. Since the early 1970s, research has been conducted on the size, scope, functioning, implications, and so forth of private policing. Described as a "quiet revolution" (Stenning and Shearing 1980), the rise of private policing has been attributed to a number of developments, including the rise in mass private property (Shearing and Stenning 1980), ideological shifts in governance, the rise of a market-driven agenda coupled with the increasing withdrawal of the state as a provider of public goods, increasing crime rates, and growing public fear of crime. This, it has been argued, has led to a search for alternatives to public policing that has challenged state claims to monopolize the provision of security. Much academic and policy debate has been centered on attempts to define private policing versus public policing and many legal, sociological, and operational definitions have been formulated over the years. Bayley and Shearing (2001), for instance, differentiate between *auspices* and *providers* to account for the various combinations of private and public role players controlling and providing policing.

Various global trends and ideologies have affected the way policing is understood in a consumer-oriented society, as police duties have become increasingly privatized and commercialized—policing it is argued has become a commodity that can be bought by those who can afford it. Debates have focused on the implications of private policing; for example, the claim that private security creates a dual system of police that creates inequalities between rich and poor. Concepts such as networks, pluralization, fragmentation, and multilateralization have been explored (Loader 2000; Reiner 1992; Newburn 2001; Bayley and Shearing 2001). Others have referred to plural policing as creating a "mixed economy" of policing (Crawford et al. 2005; Loader 1997). Yet other debates have focused on the changing nature of security governance with the state no longer necessarily controlling governance—the concept of "zones of private governance" or "nodes of governance" has been used to describe the predominance of nonstate agencies in the governance of "communal spaces" (for example, spaces associated with gated communities) and notions of "nodal-networked governance" used to describe the interaction of various nodes or loci of power (Hermer et al. 2005; Newburn 2001; Shearing and Wood 2003).

The changes in the nature of state provision of security have been described using the analogy of the state doing the "steering," while private corporations and organizations and the public are responsible for the "rowing" (Osborne and Gaebler 1992). Loader and Walker (2005) have argued that the state's engagement in steering has created a phenomenon of "state-anchored pluralism."

Debates have also surfaced on the utility of private–public partnerships and the ability of the private sector to not only serve as the "eyes and ears" of the public police but to formally supplement policing, thereby serving as a source of public goods. Opponents of this idea raise issues related to the nature of private policing as profit oriented, unaccountable to the general public, and relatively unregulated, as well as constitutional and practical concerns that have arisen as the further blurring of private and public policing duties has taken place.

The emergence of PMCs has also become a subject of contention. A variety of issues have been raised, for instance, the difficulties of regulating and holding

PMCs accountable, particularly in foreign contexts, and the ideological problems associated with using for-profit agencies in warfare. Another contentious issue has been the use of PMCs by governments as a means of conducting foreign policy by proxy (Smith 2002).

Regulating Private Security

Regulation of the private security industry in the United States has also been an issue of debate as policy makers and courts have attempted through the years to regulate the industry, without much success. Currently, the legal framework regulating private policing is a mix of state and local regulations, common law, case law, and state tort law, with very little regulation in terms of federal statutes (Joh 2004; Sklansky 1999). Criminal law doctrines of assault, trespass, and false imprisonment do apply to the private sector, but criminal procedural law has relatively little effect on the private sector (Sklansky 1999). According to the Hallcrest reports, a few states do not have regulatory legislation in place at all, whereas other states have only a few regulatory mechanisms in place.

Whereas the public police are regulated through the Fourth, Fifth, and Sixth Amendments, private security personnel are usually exempted from these restrictions due to their private nature. For instance, in *United States v. Lima,* a woman suspected of shoplifting in a department store was searched by a plainclothes store detective. Although the trial judge suppressed the stolen item, the District of Columbia Court of Appeals reversed the decision citing that the Fourth Amendment did not apply to "mere employees performing security duties" (Sklansky 1999). Private security personnel are also usually exempt from having to give the *Miranda* warning requiring that a suspect be informed of the right to remain silent and the right to legal counsel. For instance,

in *United States v. Antonelli* a dockworker was stopped in his car by a security guard who then requested that the trunk of the car be opened. Stolen items were found in the trunk and the dockworker made incriminating statements to the security guard. When he attempted to have these statements suppressed due to the guard not informing him of his *Miranda* rights, the motion was denied. This decision was based on the fact that the *Miranda* rules only apply to public law enforcement and that the security guard "had no pertinent official . . . connection with any public law enforcement agency" (Sklansky 1999). The exemption of private security personnel from constitutional restrictions has opened the door for the abuse of suspects' rights; evidence that would ordinarily be considered illegal if obtained by a state police official may be accepted in court if obtained by a private security official.

In terms of self-regulation, the private security industry does not have a national security industry such as the British Security Industry Association (BSIA), even though it was suggested in *Hallcrest Report II* that the American industry follow the U.K. example (Joh 2004). However, in 2003 the American Society for Industrial Security (ASIS), which is one of America's largest private security associations, produced a set of minimum guidelines for the selection of private security personnel for use by legislators (Joh 2004).

International debates have identified the difficulty—legally, practically, and otherwise—of regulating and holding accountable transnational private security corporations, especially PMCs (Singer 2005).

Future Prospects

The lack of regulation of private policing in the United States may be a factor preventing the systematic creation of partnerships between the two sectors.

However, in contrast the "new" global terrorist threat may be propelling the state to a redefinition of the role of state security in a global context. For instance, in October 2001 an executive order initiated by President George W. Bush established the Office of Homeland Security in response to the 9/11 terrorist attacks. The legislation contains provisions encouraging the cooperation of federal, state, local, and private entities to secure facilities from the terrorist threat (Pastor 2003). This may be a sign of things to come—the formalization of public–private partnerships—not only domestically but at a transnational level. Nations throughout the world are grappling with global threats to their internal securities with the private sector becoming a tangible option in the face of budget cuts, streamlining of public services, and the growing inability of the state to guarantee the provision of internal security.

CLIFFORD SHEARING and JULIE BERG

See also **American Policing: Early Years; Business Districts, Policing; Department of Homeland Security; Homeland Security and Law Enforcement; Terrorism: Police Functions Associated with; Vigilantism**

References and Further Reading

Bayley, D. H., and C. D. Shearing. 2001. *The new structure of policing: Description, conceptualization, and research agenda.* Washington DC: National Institute of Justice.

Bharadwaj, A. 2003. Privatization of security: The mercenary-market mix. *Defence Studies* 3: 64–82.

Blair, I. 1998. *The governance of security: Where do the police fit into policing?* Surrey Police Discussion Paper.

Crawford, A., S. Lister, S. Blackburn, and J. Burnett. 2005. *Plural policing: The mixed economy of visible security patrols.* Bristol: Policy Press.

Draper, H. 1978. *Private police.* Harmondsworth, UK: Penguin.

Hermer, J., M. Kempa, C. Shearing, P. Stenning, and J. Wood. 2005. Policing in Canada in the 21st century: Directions for law reform. In *Re-imagining policing in Canada*, ed. Cooley, 22–91. Toronto: University of Toronto Press.

Joh, E. E. 2004. The paradox of private policing. *Journal of Criminal Law and Criminology* 95: 49–131.

Johnston, L., and C. Shearing. 2003. *Governing security: Explorations in policing and justice.* London: Routledge.

Jones, T., and T. Newburn. 1998. *Private security and public policing.* Oxford: Clarendon Press.

Loader, I. 1997. Private security and the demand for protection in contemporary Britain. *Policing and Society* 7: 143–62.

———. 2000. Plural policing and democratic governance. *Social and Legal Studies* 9: 323–45.

Loader, I., and N. Walker. 2005. Necessary virtues: The legitimate place of the state in the production of security. In *Democracy, society and the governance of security*, ed. Wood and Dupont. Cambridge: Cambridge University Press.

Mandel, R. 2001. The privatization of security. *Armed Forces and Society* 28: 129–51.

Newburn, T. 2001. The commodification of policing: Security networks in the late modern city. *Urban Studies* 38: 829–48.

O'Reilly, C., and G. Ellison. 2004. The transnational ascendancy of private high policing. Paper presented to American Society of Criminology Conference, Nashville, TN.

Osborne, D., and T. Gaebler. 1992. *Rethinking government.* Harmondsworth, UK: Penguin.

Pastor, J. F. 2003. *The privatization of police in America.* Jefferson: McFarland.

Reiner, R. 1992. Policing a postmodern society. *Modern Law Review* 55: 761–81.

Shearing, C., and P. Stenning. 1983. Private security: Implications for social control. *Social Problems* 30: 493–506.

Shearing, C., and J. Wood. 2003. Nodal governance, democracy, and the new " denizens." *Journal of Law and Society* 30: 400–19.

Stenning, P., and C. Shearing. 1980. The quiet revolution: The nature, development and general legal implications of private policing in Canada. *Criminal Law Quarterly* 22: 220–48.

Singer, P. W. 2005. Outsourcing war. *Foreign Affairs* 84: 119–32.

Sklansky, D. A. 1999. The private police. *UCLA Law Review* 46: 1165–287.

Smith, E. B. 2002. The new condottieri and U.S. policy: The privatization of conflict and its implications. *Parameters* 32: 104–19.

United States v. Antonelli, 434 F.2d 335 (2d Cir. 1970).

United States v. Lima, 424 A. 2d 113 (D.C. 1980) (en banc).

PROBATION AND PAROLE

The majority of adults in the U.S. correctional system are not incarcerated in jail or prisons; in fact, 60% of adults under correctional supervision are on probation (Glaze and Palla 2005). *Probation* is the conditional release of a convicted offender into the community under the supervision of an officer of the court. Probation is a conditional sentence—in other words, an individual's probation can be revoked if he or she commits a new crime or if other conditions specified by the court are not met (Schmalleger and Smykla 2005). The goal of probation is to punish and deter offenders while reintegrating them into the community without exposing them to the negative environment of incarceration in prison. Supervision and conditions of probation help ensure crime control as well. *Parole* is the conditional release of a prisoner, prior to the completion of the sentence imposed by the sentencing authority, under the supervision of a parole officer (Schmalleger and Smykla 2005). Parole is usually granted from authorities within the correctional system after completion of some length of incarceration in prison. Probation is a sentence from a judicial officer that generally does not require incarceration in prison as part of that sanction.

Probation and parole provide alternatives to future incarceration for probationers and further incarceration for parolees. While probation serves those who have the potential of going to jail and parole serves those who are already in jail or prison, the overall function for both is to release offenders into the community, decrease incarceration, and still carry out the sanctions of the court.

Under both probation and parole, conditions are placed on the release of the offender into the community. These conditions generally fall into two categories. *Standard conditions* are those constraints imposed on all probationers and parolees in a given jurisdiction. Standard conditions typically require probationers and parolees to attend meetings with their supervising officers, seek permission from their supervising officer prior to leaving jurisdiction, and seek and/or maintain stable employment. *Punitive conditions* are those constraints imposed on some probationers or parolees to increase the restrictiveness of their sentence in an effort to make that probationer or parolee more likely to successfully complete their sentence. Examples include fines, community service, and restrictions associating with certain types of people. If these conditions are violated, probation or parole can be revoked and the offender can be sentenced to incarceration. Violation of these conditions is considered a technical violation. For both parole and probation, offenders are more likely to have their sentence revoked for a technical violation than for commission of a new criminal offense.

Probation in the United States dates back to the nineteenth century when John Augustus, a Boston shoemaker, began posting bail and paying fines for carefully selected offenders who were released to him for a term of approximately thirty days. In 1880, Massachusetts created the first statute authorizing statewide probation in the United States. Other states followed Massachusetts and by 1925, every state and every federal court district offered probation (Schmalleger and Smykla 2005).

The concept of parole is often attributed to British Navy Captain Alexander Maconochie, superintendent of a penal colony in Australia in the early 1840s. Maconochie implemented a "ticket of leave" system whereby inmates earned marks toward release by demonstrating improved behavior and good work habits. As such, inmates could earn early release from their penal duties by demonstrating that they were rehabilitating themselves. Sir Walter Crofton replicated Maconochie's ideas in Ireland in the 1850s; the Elmira Reformatory in New York was the first correctional institution in the United States to implement an extensive parole system in 1876. By 1889, twelve states had implemented parole programs, and by 1944, all forty-eight states had enacted parole legislation (Schmalleger and Smykla 2005).

On December 31, 2004, there were 4,151,125 people on probation and 765,355 people on parole in the United States. Of the 6,996,500 people under correctional supervision, almost 60% were on probation and slightly more than 10% were on parole. Half of all probationers were convicted of a misdemeanor and half were convicted of a felony. One in four probationers was on probation for a drug violation and 15% were on probation for driving while intoxicated. Three in four probationers were male and slightly more than half were white. About 60% of those eligible successfully completed their probation sentence in 2004 (Glaze and Palla 2005).

At the end of 2004, one in eight parolees (12%) was female; approximately equal percentages were white (40%) and black (41%). Approximately equal percentages of parolees (24% and 26%, respectively) were serving a sentence for violent and property offenses. One in three parolees (38%) was serving a sentence for a drug offense. Less than half (46%) of those eligible successfully completed their parole in 2004 (Glaze and Palla 2005).

Currently, offenders typically receive one of four types of probation. First, an offender can be sentenced to traditional probation in which he or she receives a suspended incarceration sentence and conditional release into the community. A second alternative is known as a split sentence, in which the court specifies a period of incarceration that will be followed by probation. An offender can also have his or her incarcerative sentence converted to a probation sentence. Through intermittent incarceration, it is also possible for an offender on probation to spend weekdays in the community and nights and/or weekends in jail. Finally, offenders can also receive shock incarceration. Under shock incarceration, offenders are sentenced to incarceration. After a short period of incarceration, they are then sentenced to probation. Because the offenders are unaware that they will be sentenced to probation instead of prison, the period of incarceration is used to "shock" them into complying with the rules of probation upon their release from incarceration.

Inmates are generally released to parole under one of two strategies. Discretionary release occurs when a *paroling authority*, generally known as a *parole board*, considers the case of an incarcerated offender and decides to release the offender to parole. The paroling authority's decision is based on some combination of the potential risk to the community, the inmate's institutional behavior and program participation, and the nature of the inmate's offense and prior criminal record. Historically, most states used this type of parole supervision until the 1980s when some states moved to mandatory supervised release. Mandatory release has become the most common method of release to parole today. Under mandatory release, inmates are given their conditional release from prison after serving a portion of their original sentence less the "good time" credits. These good time credits are reductions to an inmate's sentence given to the inmate for avoiding serious misconduct in prison or participating in various types of programs. These credits are generally given automatically. Thus, even with the move from discretionary parole, most inmates do not serve their entire prison sentence in an incarcerative setting and spend some time on parole in the community (Schmalleger and Smykla 2005).

Although there are numerous similarities between parole and probation, there are also two key differences. First, parolees are felons who are sentenced to confinement and are being granted early release from confinement; probationers may be felons or misdemeanants and are typically not sentenced to confinement as part of their probation. Second, parole supervision is generally more intensive than supervision for probationers.

Probation and parole offices vary in the jurisdiction and the branch of government that control them. With a centralized system, all of the probation offices in a state are administered by the state. In a decentralized system, the city or county has control over the probation office. The judicial branch still supervises probation in some jurisdictions but most jurisdictions are currently under the supervision of the executive branch. The executive branch is almost always responsible for supervision of parolees.

The shift of control to the executive branch has brought a shift in the focus of probation. While the original model of probation focused on humanitarianism and rehabilitation of offenders, today's model focuses on law enforcement and risk management. This has led the probation officer to become more of a law enforcement officer than a caseworker. Today, probation officers often have minimum contact with probationers. Probation officers often have role conflict because they are expected to exercise the power of the law but often do not have arrest powers, are not armed, and are powerless to revoke probation. As such, they often have to rely on authority rather than power.

The shift toward law enforcement is also reflected in the new role of the probation officer as a presentence investigator. Through a presentence investigation (PSI) report, probation officers provide detailed findings from an investigation of the convicted offender that includes such things as the offender's family and employment history, criminal record, and financial information. This information is collected through official records and interviews of the offender and the offender's family and acquaintances. The report also includes a statement from the victim and a sentence recommendation to the sentencing authority. The final report not only aids the court in determining the appropriate sentence,

but also aids probation officers in supervisory efforts during probation or parole, assists prison officials in classification, furnishes background information for parole decisions, and serves as a source of information for research.

TIMOTHY E. MCCLURE and DAVID C. MAY

See also **Prisoner Reentry, Public Safety, and Crime**

References and Further Reading

Champion, Dean J. 2005. *Probation, parole, and community corrections*. 5th ed. Upper Saddle River, NJ: Prentice-Hall.

Glaze, Lauren E., and Seri Palla. 2005. *Probation and parole in the United States, 2004*. NCJ 210676. Washington, DC: U.S. Department of Justice.

Morris, Norval, and Michael Tonry. 1990. *Between prison and probation: Intermediate punishments in a rational sentencing system*. New York: Oxford University Press.

Petersilia, Joan. 1997. Probation in the United States. In *Crime and justice: A review of the research*, vol. 22, ed. Michael Tonry, 149–200. Chicago: University of Chicago Press.

———. 2000. *When prisoners return to the community: Political, economic, and social consequences*. Washington DC: U.S. Department of Justice, National Institute of Justice.

Schmalleger, Frank A., and John O. Smykla. 2005. *Corrections in the 21st century*. Boston, MA: McGraw Hill.

PROBLEM-ORIENTED POLICING

Problem-oriented policing seeks to identify the underlying causes of crime problems and to frame appropriate responses using a wide variety of innovative approaches (Goldstein 1979). Using a basic iterative approach of problem identification, analysis, response, assessment, and adjustment of the response, this adaptable and dynamic analytic approach provides an appropriate framework to uncover the complex mechanisms at play in crime problems and to develop tailor-made interventions to address the underlying conditions that cause crime problems (Goldstein 1990; Eck and Spelman 1987). Researchers have found problem-oriented policing to be effective in controlling a wide range of specific crime and disorder problems, such as convenience store robberies (Hunter and Jeffrey 1992), prostitution (Matthews 1990), street-level drug markets (Hope 1994), and gang violence (Braga et al. 2001). Indeed, there is very promising evidence of the effectiveness of the approach (Skogan and Frydl 2004; Weisburd and Eck 2004; Braga 2002).

The Problem-Oriented Approach to Crime Prevention

Until recently, most police departments engaged in incident-driven crime prevention strategies. Such departments resolve individual incidents instead of solving recurring crime problems (Eck and Spelman 1987). Officers respond to repeated calls and never look for the underlying conditions that may be causing similar groups of incidents. Officers become frustrated because they answer similar calls and seemingly make no real progress. Citizens become dissatisfied because the problems that generate their repeated calls still exist (Eck and Spelman 1987). In 1979, Herman Goldstein proposed an alternative; he felt that police should go further than answering call after call and should instead search for solutions to recurring problems that generate the repeated calls. Goldstein described this strategy as the "problem-oriented approach" and envisioned it as a department-wide activity.

His proposition was simple and straightforward. Behind every recurring problem are underlying conditions that create it. Incident-driven policing never addresses these conditions; therefore, incidents are likely to recur. Answering calls for service is an important task and still must be done, but police officers should respond systematically to recurring calls

for the same problem. In order for the police to be more efficient and effective, they must gather information about incidents and design an appropriate response based on the nature of the underlying conditions that cause the problem(s) (Goldstein 1990). As summarized by Eck and Spelman (1987):

> Underlying conditions create problems. These conditions might include the characteristics of the people involved (offenders, potential victims, and others), the social setting in which these people interact, the physical environment, and the way the public deals with these conditions. A problem created by these conditions may generate one or more incidents. These incidents, while stemming from a common source, may appear to be different. For example, social and physical conditions in a deteriorated apartment complex may generate burglaries, acts of vandalism, intimidation of pedestrians by rowdy teenagers, and other incidents. These incidents, some of which come to police attention, are symptoms of the problem. The incidents will continue as long as the problem that creates them persists. (xvi)

And in Goldstein's (1979) words, the problem-solving process requires:

> Identifying these problems in more precise terms, researching each problem, documenting the nature of the current police response, assessing its adequacy and the adequacy of existing authority and resources, engaging in a broad exploration of alternatives to present responses, weighing the merits of these alternatives, and choosing among them. (p. 236)

The Practice of Problem-Oriented Policing

The problem-oriented policing approach was given an operational structure in Newport News, Virginia. Researchers from the Police Executive Research Forum (PERF) and a group of officers selected from the various ranks of the Newport News Police Department crystallized the philosophy into a set of steps known as the *SARA model* (Eck and Spelman 1987). The SARA model consists of these stages:

- *Scanning:* the identification of an issue and determining whether it is a problem
- *Analysis:* data collection on the problem to determine its scope, nature, and causes
- *Response:* use of information from the analysis to design an appropriate response, which can involve other agencies outside the normal police arena
- *Assessment:* evaluating the response and using the results to reexamine the problem and change responses or maintain positive conditions (Eck and Spelman 1987)

In practice, it is important to recognize that the development and implementation of problem-oriented responses do not always follow the linear, distinct steps of the SARA model (Capowich and Roehl 1994; Braga 2002). Rather, depending on the complexity of the problems to be addressed, the process can be characterized as a series of disjointed and often simultaneous activities. A wide variety of issues can cause deviations from the SARA model, including identified problems that need to be reanalyzed because initial responses were ineffective and implemented responses that sometimes reveal new problems (Braga 2002).

Scanning

Scanning involves the identification of problems that are worth looking at because they are important and amenable to solution. Herman Goldstein (1990) suggests that the definition of problems be at the street level of analysis and not be restricted by preconceived typologies. As he suggests,

It is not yet clear what significance, if any, there may be to the way in which problems are naturally defined. Nor is it clear if, for the purposes of analysis, one way of defining problems is preferable to another. It may be that none of this matters: that the primary concern ought to be to define the problem in terms that have meaning to both the community and the police. (Goldstein 1990, 68)

Goldstein (1990, 66) further clarifies what is meant by a problem by specifying the term as "a cluster of similar, related, or recurring incidents rather than a single incident; a substantive community concern; or a unit of police business."

There are many ways a problem might be nominated for police attention. A police officer may rely on his or her informal knowledge of a community to identify a problem that he or she thinks is important to the well-being of the community. Another possibility is to identify problems from the examination of citizen calls for service coming into a police department. This approach is implicitly recommended by those who advocate "repeat call analysis" or the identification of "hot spots" (Sherman, Gartin, and Buerger 1989). The notion is that citizens will let the police know what problems are concerning them by making calls as individuals. By analyzing these calls, and grouping them in ways that point to common causes or common solutions, the police may be able to develop a response that ameliorates the problem that is generating the calls. With the recent proliferation of computerized mapping technology in police departments, there has been a strong movement in police departments to use these techniques in the identification of crime problems (Weisburd and McEwen 1997).

Another approach to identifying problems is through consultation with community groups of different kinds, including other government agencies. This differs from analyzing individual calls for service because the demands come from groups, rather than individuals. If the police are interested in forging partnerships with groups as well as individuals, then it is important to open up channels through which groups can express their concerns such as community advisory councils or regular meetings held by the police to which all members of a community are invited (Skogan and Hartnett 1997). This approach has the advantage of allowing the community's views about what is important to shape police views about what is important rather than leaving the nomination of problems to police analysts. The best approach to identifying problems would be to combine these efforts.

Analysis

The analysis phase challenges police officers to analyze the causes of problems behind a string of crime incidents or substantive community concern. Once the underlying conditions that give rise to crime problems are known, police officers develop and implement appropriate responses. The challenge to police officers is to go beyond the analysis that naturally occurs to them; namely, to find the places and times where particular offenses are likely to occur, and to identify the offenders who are likely to be responsible for the crimes.

Although these approaches have had some operational success, this type of analysis usually produces directed patrol operations or a focus on repeat offenders. The idea of analysis for problem solving was intended to go beyond this. Goldstein (1990) describes this as the problem of "ensuring adequate depth" in the analysis and offers the following as an example of what he means:

A study of the problem of theft from merchants by shoppers illustrates the need. It is easy, accepting how we have commonly responded to shoplifting to become enmeshed in exploring new ways in which to increase the number of arrests—including more efficient processing by the police. If one digs deeper, however, it becomes apparent that shoplifting is heavily influenced by how the merchandise is displayed and the means used to safeguard it. The police often accept these merchandising decisions as givens and are resigned to processing as many shoplifters as a store chooses to apprehend and deliver into their hands. More in-depth probing raises questions about the effectiveness of arrests as the primary means to reduce shoplifting and the propriety of delegating to private interests the judgment of who is to be arrested. The police may then focus on ways to curtail theft and on use to be made of arrest, including criteria to be employed in deciding who to arrest. If the analysis of the shoplifting problem had been superficial, limited to exploring ways to increase the number of arrests, the whole purpose of the enterprise would have been lost. (pp. 98–99)

Response

After a problem has been clearly defined and analyzed, police officers confront the challenge of developing a plausibly effective response. The development of appropriate responses is closely linked with the analysis that is performed. The analysis reveals the potential targets for an intervention, and it is at least partly the idea about what form the intervention might take that suggests important lines of analysis. As such, the reason police often look at places and times where crimes are committed is that they are already imagining that an effective way to prevent the crimes would be to get officers on the scene through directed patrols. The reason they often look for the likely offender is that they think that the most effective and just response to a crime problem would be to arrest and incapacitate the offender. However, the concept of *problem-oriented policing* as envisioned by Herman Goldstein (1990) calls on the police to make a much more "uninhibited" search for possible responses and not to limit themselves to getting officers in the right places at the right times, or identifying and arresting the offender (although both may be valuable responses). Effective responses often depend on getting other people to take actions that reduce the opportunities for criminal offending, or to mobilize informal social control to drive offenders away from certain locations.

The responses that problem-oriented police officers develop may be close to current police practices or, in some instances, quite different. Goldstein (1990, 102–47) offers the following suggestive list of general alternatives police may consider in developing responses to neighborhood crime problems:

- Concentrating attention on those individuals who account for a disproportionate share of the problem
- Connecting with other government and private services through referral to another agency, coordinating police responses with other agencies, correcting inadequacies in municipal services, and pressing for new services
- Using mediation and negotiation skills to resolve disputes
- Conveying information to reduce anxiety and fear, to enable citizens to solve their own problems, to elicit conformity with laws and regulations that are not known or understood, to warn potential victims about their vulnerability and warn them of ways to protect themselves, to demonstrate to individuals how they unwittingly contribute to problems, to develop support for addressing a problem, and to acquaint the community with the limitations on the police and to define realistically what may be expected of the police
- Mobilizing the community and making use of existing forms of social control in addition to the community
- Altering the physical environment to reduce opportunities for problems to recur

- Increasing regulation, through statutes or ordinances, of conditions that contribute to problems
- Developing new forms of limited authority to intervene and detain
- Using civil law to control public nuisances, offensive behavior, and conditions contributing to crime

Assessment

The crucial last step in the practice of problem-oriented policing is to assess the impact the intervention has had on the problem it was supposed to solve. Assessment is important for at least two different reasons. The first is to ensure that police remain accountable for their performance and for their use of resources. Citizens and their representatives want to know how the money and freedom they surrendered to the police are being used, and whether important results in the form of less crime, enhanced security, or increased citizen satisfaction with the police have been achieved. A second reason assessment is important is to allow the police to learn about what methods are effective in dealing with particular problems. Unless the police check to see whether their efforts produced a result, it will be hard for them to improve their practices.

The assessment of responses is key in facilitating an active exchange of "what works" in crime prevention among police departments. As Clarke (1998, 319) suggests, "If law enforcement agencies do not have a mechanism to learn from others' mistakes and assist others to learn from their experiences, they will always be reinventing the wheel." The degree of rigor applied to the assessment of problem-oriented initiatives will necessarily vary across the size and overall importance of the problems addressed. Serious, large, and recurrent problems such as controlling gang violence or handling domestic disputes deserve highly rigorous examinations. Other problems that are less serious, or common, such as a lonely elderly person making repeated calls to the police for companionship, are obviously not worth such close examination. To meet the demands of measuring accountability and performance, problem-oriented police should, at a minimum, describe the scanning, response, and assessment phases by measuring inputs, activities, outputs, and whatever can be said about the outcomes of their initiatives.

In general, problem-oriented police should strive to conduct more rigorous assessments of their responses with due consideration to time and resource constraints. Depending on the availability of funds, police departments should consider partnering up with independent researchers to conduct systematic evaluations of their efforts. In the absence of such a partnership, Clarke (1998) suggests that police should take care to relate any observed results to specific actions taken, develop assessment plans while outlining the project, present control data when available and reasonably comparable to the subject(s) of the intervention, and, as will be discussed further, measure crime displacement. While the degree of rigor applied to the assessment of responses may vary, what must *not* be sacrificed is the goal of measuring results. This will keep the police focused on results rather than means, and that is one of the most important contributions of the idea of problem-oriented policing.

Current Issues in the Substance and Implementation of Problem-Oriented Policing

The U.S. National Academy of Sciences' Committee to Review Research on Police Policy and Practices concluded that problem-oriented policing is a promising approach to deal with crime, disorder, and fear and recommended that additional research was necessary to understand the

organizational arrangements that foster effective problem solving (Skogan and Frydl 2004). Several recently published volumes on problem-oriented case studies provide a good sense for the work being done as well as the strengths and weaknesses of some of the better problem-oriented efforts (see, for example, O'Connor Shelly and Grant 1998; Sole Brito and Allan 1999; Sole Brito and Gratto, 2000; Sampson and Scott 2000). The concept seems to have survived what Gary Cordner (1998, 305) has identified as first-generation issues:

- The view that problem-oriented policing was not "real" police work
- The view that problem-oriented policing was a fine idea but not practical because of limited resources (for example, time and personnel)
- The question of whether ordinary police officers had the analytic ability to conduct sophisticated problem-solving projects
- The question of whether other government agencies had the capacity to meet police halfway in solving chronic community problems
- The danger of falsely raising the community's expectations

Although these issues have not been completely resolved, the implementation of the concept went forward as more police officers grew more and more intrigued by the approach (Cordner 1998).

Although the problem-oriented approach has demonstrated much potential value in preventing crime and improving police practices, research has also documented that it is very difficult for police officers to implement problem-oriented policing strategies (Eck and Spelman 1987; Clarke 1998; Braga 2002). Cordner (1998) identifies a number of challenging second-generation issues in the substance and implementation of many problem-oriented policing projects. These issues include the tendency for officers to conduct only a superficial analysis of problems and rushing to implement a response, the tendency for officers to rely on traditional or faddish responses rather than conducting a wider search for creative responses, and the tendency to completely ignore the assessment of the effectiveness of implemented responses (Cordner 1998). Indeed, the research literature is filled with cases where problem-oriented policing programs tend to lean toward traditional methods and where problem analysis is weak (Eck and Spelman 1987; Buerger 1994; Capowich and Roehl 1994; Read and Tilley 2000). In his recent review of several hundred submissions for the Police Executive Research Forum's Herman Goldstein Award for Excellence in Problem-Oriented Policing, Clarke (1998) laments that many recent examples of problem-oriented policing projects bear little resemblance to Goldstein's original definition and suggests this misrepresentation puts the concept at risk of being pronounced a failure before it has been properly tested.

Deficiencies in current problem-oriented policing practices exist in all phases of the process. During the scanning phase, police officers risk undertaking a project that is too small (for example, the lonely old man who repeatedly calls the police for companionship) or too broad (for example, gang delinquency) and this destroys the discrete problem focus of the project and leads to a lack of direction at the beginning of analysis (Clarke 1998). Some officers skip the analysis phase or conduct an overly simple analysis that does not adequately dissect the problem or does not use relevant information from other agencies (such as hospitals, schools, and private businesses) (Clarke 1998). Based on his extensive experience with police departments implementing problem-oriented policing, Eck (2000) suggests that much problem analysis consists of a simple examination of police data coupled with the officer's working experience with the problem. In their analysis of

problem-oriented initiatives in forty-three police departments in England and Wales, Read and Tilley (2000) found that problem analysis was generally weak with many initiatives accepting the definition of a problem at face value, using only short-term data to unravel the nature of the problem, and failing to adequately examine the genesis of the crime problems. As noted earlier, the responses of many problem-oriented policing projects rely too much on traditional police tactics (such as arrests, surveillance, and crackdowns) and neglect the wider range of available alternative responses. Read and Tilley (2000) found that officers selected certain responses prior to, or in spite of, analysis; failed to think through the need for a sustained crime reduction; failed to think through the mechanisms by which the response could have a measurable impact; failed to fully involve partners; and narrowly focused responses, usually on offenders; as well as a number of other weaknesses in the response development process. Scott and Clarke (2000) observe that assessment of responses is rare and, when undertaken, is usually cursory and limited to anecdotal or impressionistic data.

Conclusion

Problem-oriented policing represents an important innovation in American policing. Unfortunately, the practice of problem-oriented policing sometimes falls short of the principles suggested by Herman Goldstein (1990). The substance and implementation of many problem-oriented policing projects are limited due to shortcomings in the links between analysis and response. The current state of knowledge among front-line police officers about the most effective and economical ways in which to address problems is limited, and often primitive (Scott 2000; Braga 2002).

Advocates such as Michael Scott, Rana Sampson, Ronald Clarke, John Eck, and Herman Goldstein have made a concerted effort to disseminate research methodologies, theoretical insights, and research findings to the police and the communities they serve. These scholars have been involved in the publication of many practical guides and volumes to further the practice of problem-oriented policing. Most recently, the *Problem-Oriented Guides for Police* series, published by the U.S. Department of Justice's Office of Community Oriented Policing Services (http://www.cops.usdoj.gov), represents a systematic effort to summarize research knowledge on how police can reduce the harm caused by specific crime and disorder problems. These guides present useful information on an impressive array of problems ranging from robberies at automated bank teller machines to rave parties to clandestine drug laboratories.

It is important to recognize that problem-oriented policing is still in its formative stages and its practice is still developing. Progress in policing is incremental and slow, and that does not make problem-oriented policing unrealistic. Indeed, the pioneers of this young and evolving approach have accomplished much since Herman Goldstein first presented the concept in 1979.

ANTHONY A. BRAGA

See also **Broken-Windows Policing; Community-Oriented Policing: Practices; COMPSTAT; Crime Analysis; Crime and Place, Theories of; Crime Control Strategies; Crime Mapping; Crime Prevention; Office of Community-Oriented Police Services, U.S. Department of Justice; SARA, the Model**

References and Further Reading

Braga, Anthony A. 2002. *Problem-oriented policing and crime prevention.* Monsey, NY: Criminal Justice Press.

Braga, Anthony A., David M. Kennedy, Elin J. Waring, and Anne M. Piehl. 2001. Problem-oriented policing, deterrence, and youth violence: An evaluation of Boston's Operation Ceasefire. *Journal of Research in Crime and Delinquency* 38: 195–225.

Buerger, Michael. 1994. The problems of problem-solving: Resistance, interdependencies, and conflicting interests. *American Journal of Police* 13: 1–36.

Capowich, George, and Jan Roehl. 1994. Problem-oriented policing: Actions and effectiveness in San Diego. In *The challenge of community policing: Testing the promises,* ed. Dennis Rosenbaum, 127–46. Thousand Oaks, CA: Sage.

Clarke, Ronald V. 1998. Defining police strategies: Problem solving, problem-oriented policing and community-oriented policing. In *Problem-oriented policing: Crime-specific problems, critical issues, and making POP work,* ed. Tara O'Connor Shelley and Anne C. Grant, 315–30. Washington, DC: Police Executive Research Forum.

Cordner, Gary. 1998. Problem-oriented policing vs. zero tolerance. In *Problem-oriented policing: Crime-specific problems, critical issues, and making POP work,* ed. Tara O'Connor Shelley and Anne C. Grant, 303–14. Washington, DC: Police Executive Research Forum.

Eck, John. 2000. Problem-oriented policing and it's problems: The means over ends syndrome strikes back and the return of the problem-solver. Unpublished manuscript, University of Cincinnati.

Eck, John, and William Spelman. 1987. *Problem-solving: Problem-oriented policing in Newport News.* Washington, DC: Police Executive Research Forum.

Goldstein, Herman. 1979. Improving policing: A problem-oriented approach. *Crime and Delinquency* 25: 236–58.

———. 1990. *Problem-oriented policing.* Philadelphia, PA: Temple University Press.

Hope, Timothy. 1994. Problem-oriented policing and drug market locations: Three case studies. *Crime Prevention Studies* 2: 5–32.

Hunter, Ronald, and C. Ray Jeffery. 1992. Preventing Convenience Store Robbery Through Environmental Design. In *Situational crime prevention: Successful case studies,* ed. Ronald V. Clarke, 194–204. Albany, NY: Harrow and Heston.

Matthews, Roger. 1990. Developing more effective strategies for curbing prostitution. *Security Journal* 1: 182–87.

O'Connor Shelly, Tara, and Anne Grant, eds. 1998. *Problem-oriented policing: Crime-specific problems, critical issues, and making POP work*. Washington, DC: Police Executive Research Forum.

Read, Tim, and Nick Tilley. 2000. *Not rocket science? Problem-solving and crime reduction*. Crime Reduction Series Paper 6. London: Policing and Crime Reduction Unit, Home Office.

Sampson, Rana, and Michael Scott. 2000. *Tackling crime and other public-safety problems: Case studies in problem solving*. Washington, DC: U.S. Department of Justice, Office of Community Oriented Policing Services.

Scott, Michael. 2000. *Problem-oriented policing: Reflections on the first 20 years*. Washington, DC: U.S. Department of Justice, Office of Community Oriented Policing Services.

Scott, Michael, and Ronald V. Clarke. 2000. A review of submission for the Herman Goldstein excellence in problem-oriented policing. In *Problem oriented policing: Crime-specific problems, critical issues, and making POP work*, vol. 3, ed. Corina Sole Brito and Eugenia E. Gratto, 213–30. Washington, DC: Police Executive Research Forum.

Sherman, Lawrence, Patrick Gartin, and Michael Buerger. 1989. Hot spots of predatory crime: Routine activities and the criminology of place. *Criminology* 27: 27–56.

Skogan, Wesley, and Kathleen Frydl, eds. 2004. *Fairness and effectiveness in policing: The evidence*. Committee to Review Research on Police Policy and Practices. Committee on Law and Justice, Division of Behavioral and Social Sciences and Education. Washington, DC: National Academies Press.

Skogan, Wesley, and Susan Hartnett. 1997. *Community policing, Chicago style*. New York: Oxford University Press.

Sole Brito, Corina, and Tracy Allan, eds. 1999. *Problem-oriented policing: Crime-specific problems, critical issues, and making POP Work*. Vol. 2. Washington, DC: Police Executive Research Forum.

Sole Brito, Corina, and Tracy Allan, eds. 2000. *Problem-oriented policing: Crime-specific problems, critical issues, and making POP work*. Vol. 3. Washington, DC: Police Executive Research Forum.

Weisburd, David, and John Eck. 2004. What can police do to reduce crime, disorder, and fear? *Annals of the American Academy of Political and Social Science* 593: 42–65.

Weisburd, David, and J. Thomas McEwen, eds. 1997. *Crime mapping and crime prevention*. Monsey, NY: Criminal Justice Press.

PROFESSIONALISM

The acquisition of professional standing is a universal theme permeating the fabric of all occupations. The tangible essence of professionalism continues to be elusive, though, as a multitude of characteristics are espoused to define its existence. From the more noble portraits as "men of wisdom" (Socrates) and "philosopher kings" (Plato) to the attributes of ethics, intelligence, and competence, adjectives abound when describing professionals. Further complicating the professionalism concept is the ambiguity associated with what actually constitutes a "profession," for it is a common proposition that one can be professional only within the context of a profession.

Professionalism Qualities and Challenges

Professionalism in policing is of extraordinary importance because of the authority vested in law enforcement officers. It reflects an implicit guarantee that the experience, education, and training of officers uniquely qualify them to meet the challenges present in a changing and dynamic society. Police officers are expected to successfully operate within many demanding and conflicting roles, and along these lines, are presumed to possess ethical qualities and competence far superior to those of the nonprofessional whose attitudes are misaligned with the goals of high standards. Oversight of standards has historically been within the exclusive jurisdiction of internal professional bodies; however, outside forces propelled by citizenry and governmental entities now exert considerable regulatory influence.

Although every profession suffers at some point from institutional indiscretions, most outside observers do not measure the total worthiness of the profession by the singular incidents of its members. Unprofessional acts of police officers, however, do not receive such equitable treatment. Since its inception in the mid-1800s, policing has operated under close political and societal scrutiny, quite often in the glare of media exposure that consistently indicts the whole of policing from the sum of a few renegade rogues. It is equally true that policing has not achieved the same degree of community respect as the traditional professions of law, medicine, education, and theology. Professional recognition is often contingent on being within a profession, and a profession requires commitment to educational attainment. Esteem for the police will surface only when specialized schools for police education are commonplace, and at this point, those kinds of facilities are still in the growth and development stage.

The Police Professionalism Movement

Appointed a magistrate in 1748 England, Fielding argued that the perpetual ineffectiveness of the police to curb crime was a by-product of inadequate selection criteria and substandard pay. Based on his philosophies, Fielding organized what came to be known as the Bow Street Runners, ultimately heralded as the first professional police force in England.

As the architect of the Metropolitan Police Act of 1829, Robert Peel set into motion the modern practice of community policing. His premise purports that successful policing depends on both public trust and the absence of crime and disorder, not the visible evidence of police action as the primary means of crime control. Dedicated to the selection and training of men with emotional balance, good appearance, and community admiration, his reforms are highly revered among the many contributions to American professional policing.

Having a limited education, the accomplishments of August Vollmer to the professionalism movement were unprecedented

and remain unparalleled. As Berkeley's town marshal and police chief, he was determined to transform the image of policing from illiterate cops to "truly exceptional men." In pursuit of that vision, Vollmer made numerous instrumental reforms. First, he instituted intelligence and psychological tests to screen new recruits. He then trained the recruits in scientific principles at his Berkeley Police School (created in 1908) and began offering police administration classes in 1916 at the University of California to ensure an ample pool of educated men from which to build a professional force. These contributions and many others as well have resulted in his being widely regarded as the father of modern police professionalism.

Two presidential commissions have made substantial contributions to the police professionalization movement. The Wickersham Commission, in 1931, and the 1967 President's Commission on Law Enforcement and Administration of Justice recommended a baccalaureate degree as an entry-level requirement for policing. Change has been slow at best, but continual progress remains as a remnant of their visionary spirit.

One criterion for receiving a professional designation is the presence of an organization or association charged with the representation of its membership. Unlike the traditional professions, no law enforcement group wholly functions in this capacity, but the International Association of Chiefs of Police (IACP) best fits the role. The most recognizable of all police organizations, the IACP is committed to professionalism and training. In furtherance of that mission, the IACP publishes a monthly journal, *Police Chief*, that has long been regarded as the professional voice of law enforcement and training.

Academics have also played a vital role in the police professionalization movement. In 1941, one of many educational contributions of August Vollmer surfaced with the formation of the American Society of Criminology (ASC). Then, in

1970, a number of academicians collaborated to create the International Association of Police Professors (now called the Academy of Criminal Justice Sciences, or ACJS). Collectively, these academic organizations continue to forge ahead with the educational advancement of the police profession.

Created in 1979, the Commission on Accreditation for Law Enforcement Agencies (CALEA) offers accreditation opportunities to all police agencies. Accreditation enhances professionalism efforts within organizations, while simultaneously communicating to the public a commitment to integrity and efficiency. Although not widely used to date (fewer than 5% of police agencies nationally), the accreditation opportunity is essential to the growth of professional policing.

Measuring Police Professionalism

Notwithstanding the complexity of meanings associated with the term *professionalism,* Richard Hall's (1968) construction of a professionalism scale to measure the ambiguous concept has been well accepted in research circles. The scale's ability to capture the true behavioral dimensions of professionalism is questionable, but its capacity to reflect identification with professionalism attributes is well established. The revised scale measures five theoretical dimensions.

Dimensions Consistent with Police Professionalism

Professionalism studies indicate that police rise to the level of three standards. First, most police officers exhibit a visible commitment to the mission of law enforcement and regard that mission as indispensable to society (referred to as a *belief in public service*). Second, the overwhelming majority

of officers seem to philosophically ascribe to the mentality that their occupational endeavors are so technical that only colleagues possess the competence to judge the work product (called a *belief in self-regulation*). The third and final component is a sense of calling that exudes total *devotion to the profession.* The fundamental tenet of this expectation is that the professional goes about his or her job for the satisfaction inherent in a job well done, not monetary incentives, as the primary objective. Police seem to embody this mental attitude as well.

Dimensions Inconsistent with Police Professionalism

One problematic component of police professionalism is the use of an organization as a major referent, meaning the degree to which occupational associations exert influence on the values and belief systems of law enforcement. To gain professional status, it is essential that the police be committed to and practice the standards of the profession. Many advocates claim that the numerous advancements in policing are implicit of the establishment of police professionalism. Meanwhile, the findings of Miller and Fry (1976) and Crank (1990) reflect little police commitment to the activities of professional organizations. Inasmuch as these findings cast doubt on the professionalism definition used across most disciplines, Crank contends that the basic orientation of the police still remains one of professionalism when compared to craftsmanship levels. Consistent with this optimistic bent is the finding that low levels of organizational commitment among police chiefs primarily exist in small departments. It appears, then, that commitment to police organizations as a major referent does exist in larger departments, and the concerns exist on just one level of policing.

A second professionalism component of questionable merit is autonomy, or the desire to make decisions free from administrative or outside constraints. Miller and Fry's findings (1976) uncovered a strong propensity against the perceived necessity for autonomy on two of five assessments. Using an altered version of autonomous measurement, however, Crank's autonomy results in 1990 were more favorable. Many suggest that the real issue is whether autonomy is an appropriate measure of police professionalism. Given that police authority was allocated with the understanding of accountability to the public first and foremost, one could argue that a strong commitment to autonomy may well reflect an unprofessional bent.

Conclusion

In light of its fluid definition, it seems that professionalism's multifaceted composition may well be its most prominent feature as it creates an all-encompassing receptacle for that which is good about mankind. To that end, many purport that absolute professionalism is unattainable, though the pursuit is admirable and essential to the construction and maintenance of a force of individuals faithful to public needs. Essentially, then, the quest for professionalism is best summarized from the perspective of August Vollmer—a search for the perfect man.

PHILIP E. CARLAN

See also **Academies, Police; Codes of Ethics; Education and Training; Ethics and Values in the Context of Community Policing; International Association of Chiefs of Police (IACP); National Association of Women Law Enforcement Executives (NAWLEE); National Organizations of Blacks in Law Enforcement; Personnel Selection; Police Careers; Police Chief Executive; Police Executive Research Forum; Police Foundation; Police Standards and Training Commissions; Vollmer, August; Wickersham, George W.**

References and Further Reading

Carte, Gene E., and Elaine H. Carte. 1975. *Police reform in the United States: The era of August Vollmer, 1905–1932*. Berkeley: University of California.

Crank, John P. 1990. Police: Professionals or craftsmen? An empirical assessment of professionalism and craftsmanship among eight municipal police agencies. *Journal of Criminal Justice* 18: 333–49.

Deakin, Thomas. 1988. *Police professionalism: The renaissance of American law enforcement*. Springfield, IL: Charles C Thomas.

Hall, Richard H. 1968. Professionalization and bureaucratization. *American Sociological Review* 33: 92–104.

Miller, Jon, and Lincoln Fry. 1976. Measuring professionalism in law enforcement. *Criminology* 14: 401–12.

Regoli, R. M., J. P. Crank, R. G. Culbertson, and E. D. Poole. 1988. Linkages between professionalization and professionalism among police chiefs. *Journal of Criminal Justice* 16: 89–98.

Snizek, William E. 1972. Hall's professionalism scale: An empirical reassessment. *American Sociological Review* 37: 109–14.

Souryal, Sam S. 2003. *Ethics in criminal justice*. 3rd ed. Cincinnati, OH: Anderson Publishing Company.

Trautman, N. E. 1988. *Law enforcement: The making of a profession*. Springfield, IL: Charles C Thomas.

Vogel, Ronald, and Reed Adams. 1983. Police professionalism: A longitudinal cohort study. *Journal of Police Science and Administration* 11: 474–84.

Vollmer, August. 1936. *The police and modern society*. Berkeley: University of California.

Vollmer, H. M., and D. L. Mills. 1966. *Professionalization*. Englewood Cliffs, NJ: Prentice-Hall.

PSYCHOLOGICAL FITNESS FOR DUTY

Increasingly, law enforcement agencies are faced with litigation based on officer performance, including abuse of authority and failure to perform (often referred to as *dereliction of duty*). The demands of law enforcement require police departments to ensure that their officers are emotionally and mentally stable or psychologically capable of performing their duties in a safe and effective manner. When an officer demonstrates that he or she may not be capable of doing so, a number of actions may be initiated by the agency including medical, supervisory, training, or disciplinary intervention, as well as the provision of psychological services. Psychological services in policing have greatly increased in recent decades and now include pre-employment testing, counseling, research, and fitness for duty (Scrivner and Kurke 1995).

Psychological fitness for duty is both an examination and assessment of risk and disability made by a qualified mental health professional (usually a licensed psychologist) when an incumbent officer demonstrates inability to perform his or her duties safely and effectively or when the officer's behavior presents a risk to himself or herself, to others, or to the agency, due to apparent psychological factors or impairment.

Such assessments, often called *fitness for duty evaluations* (FFDEs), are often made after critical incidents (for example, officer-involved shootings, hostage situations, witnessing crimes against children, brutal homicides, or death of fellow officers) or when an officer demonstrates that his or her emotional state may negatively affect the effective or safe performance of the job. Indicators of such a state may include signs of alcohol or drug dependence, excessive absence, numerous complaints from community members, emotional or physical outbursts, abuse of authority, or identification through an early warning system.

The decision to refer an officer for a psychological FFDE may be made by a supervisor, internal affairs investigator, training personnel, an employee assistance program counselor, personnel administrators, or other officials or agency representatives who may be privy to behavioral information on that officer. Thus the agency, not the officer, is the client of the evaluator.

Purpose

The purpose of the evaluation is not to provide a diagnosis but to determine whether the individual is currently capable of performing the essential functions of the job, and to "professionally notify" the department of mental illness, behavior, or personality issues that may affect performance of the officer's official role (Rostow and Davis 2002). As such, the evaluator examines the job description for the law enforcement position to determine how the person's psychological limitations may affect various job components and specific tasks, while examining the various risks associated with the officer continuing in his or her capacity.

Risks to the Officer

Police officers have a dangerous job, one in which lives and property are at stake. Police officers face a number of stressors, including major events (natural disasters, savage victimizations, crimes against children, and so on) over which officers may have little control, as well as those in which an officer must take control (officer-involved shootings, riot control, and so on). The negative outcomes from such events can have serious psychological consequences for even the most seasoned and experienced officers.

Part of the culture of policing is the image of police as strong, controlled, non-emotional, and tough. However, exposure to routine stressors or critical incidents can wear away at the coping mechanisms of many officers, leading them to feel isolated and unable to discuss their emotions with family or friends and creating a sense of embarrassment, failure, and even self-loathing. All of these issues may make an officer vulnerable to engaging in inappropriate, atypical, and/or threatening behavior or, in the worst case scenario, suicide.

Risks to Others

In situations where an officer may have experienced extreme stress, he or she could lash out at fellow officers, supervisors, or community members with little or no warning. These behaviors could be overtly aggressive, punitive, or hostile and could come across as insulting, unfair, defamatory, or even threatening and dangerous. Other mental or emotional issues could limit the officer's ability to render appropriate assistance or aid, restrain a violent offender, or protect the community from dangers.

Legal Considerations and Risks to the Agency

When an officer performs his or her duties inappropriately, the reputation of the agency can be tarnished. It is critical for police departments to maintain a professional and respectable reputation in the community in order to obtain the cooperation and support necessary to carry out its responsibilities effectively.

Because the outcomes of an FFDE could lead to a variety of negative employment consequences for the officer, legal quandaries for the agency may arise out of the evaluation or the failure to refer an employee for an FFDE. When an officer has behaved in a manner that is of sufficient concern to be referred for an FFDE, failure of departmental officials to make that referral can also present a risk of liability to the agency and perhaps even the individual who identified the initial problem, as well as supervisors and commanders responsible for overseeing the officer's performance. For example, *deliberate indifference,* a circumstance in which a plaintiff demonstrates that the agency had ignored signs of poor performance, and *negligent retention,* a situation in which an agency retains an employee

who has demonstrated that he or she is unfit for duty, can present legal difficulties for agencies.

Case law associated with psychological evaluations of law enforcement personnel has been established in a number of areas pertaining to FFDEs. Some of the issues raised in case law include an agency or agency official's right to mandate psychological testing (see, for example, *Conte v. Horcher,* 365 N.E.2d 567, 1977), an agency's responsibility to psychologically evaluate personnel (see, for example, *Bonsignore v. City of New York,* 683 F.2d 635, 1982), the presence of outside parties in psychological evaluations (see, for example, *Vinson v. The Superior Court of Almeda County,* 740 P.2d 404, 1987), and confidentiality (see, for example, *David v. Christian,* 520 N.Y.S.2d 827, 1987, and *Redmond v. City of Overland Park,* 672 F. Supp. 473, 1987). According to Super (1997), by June 1996 case law had established that (1) chiefs not only have the right to mandate FFDEs when an officer's mental health or emotional stability is called into question, they are "burdened with the responsibility to do so"; (2) officers referred for an FFDE do not have the privilege of having their attorneys present; and (3) psychological stability of law enforcement officers is a more compelling concern to the courts than the respective officer's privacy rights. Later in 1996, another court decision placed restrictions on psychologists from providing detailed case information unless authority is granted by the employee (see *Pettus v. Cole,* 49 Cal. App. 4th 402; 57 Cal. Rptr. 2d 46, 1996).

Professional Guidelines for the Conduct of FFDEs

In addition to legal requirements and issues, professional standards are also associated with FFDEs. The first initiative to establish guidelines for FFDEs was proposed by Inwald (1990). In 1998 the International Association of Chiefs of Police Psychological Services Section adopted a set of guidelines, which were later ratified in 2004. These guidelines were intended to standardize the process for FFDEs and to present commonly accepted practices.

Because the assessment of psychological capacity requires specialized training, knowledge, and experience, the IACP guidelines suggest that the evaluator "be a licensed psychologist or psychiatrist with education, training, and experience in the diagnostic evaluation of mental and emotional disorders." The guidelines further stipulate the need for experience in evaluating police personnel, familiarity with the research literature in police psychology, as well as knowledge of the functions of a law enforcement officer's job. Because numerous laws and professional practices govern or relate to FFDEs including those related to disability (for example, the Americans with Disabilities Act of 1990), privacy, and third-party liability associated with the outcomes of such evaluations, the IACP guidelines also stress the importance of evaluators having both knowledge of legal requirements and case law surrounding FFDEs.

When to Refer Someone for a Psychological FFDE

In many agencies, a variety of interventions may be provided to assist officers who are having difficulty. These could include remedial training, supervisory counseling, mentoring, critical incident stress debriefing (after events such as hostage situations, officer-involved shootings, or other types of tragedies or disasters), reassignment, or referrals to an employee assistance program counselor. When supervision, discipline, or other remedies are exhausted, an FFDE is warranted.

Components and Outcomes of a Psychological FFDE

The content of an FFDE typically consists of the reason for the referral, relevant background information, behavioral observations, psychological testing related to the referral reason, a face-to-face interview with the officer and other individuals who may have relevant information, and summary/conclusions (Super 1997; Blau 1994). On completion of an FFDE, the examiner supplies a report and recommendation regarding the officer's capacity to perform the job safely and effectively including his or her opinion as to the officer's fitness for unrestricted duty and sometimes suggestions for potentially corrective remedies. While an agency may ask the examiner to provide opinions regarding necessary work restrictions, accommodations, interventions, or causation, the IACP guidelines stipulate that the reasonableness of such recommendations must be made by the agency.

KAREN L. AMENDOLA

See also **Abuse of Authority by Police; Complaints against Police; Crime, Serious Violent; Critical Incidents; Cynicism, Police; Danger and Police Work; Deadly Force; Early Warning Systems; Liability and the Police; Liability and Use of Force; Occupational Culture; Performance Measurement; Police Legal Liabilities: Overview; Police Suicide; Stress and Police Work; Stress: Coping Mechanisms**

References and Further Reading

Americans with Disabilities Act of 1990. 42 U.S.C. 12101–12117. One Hundred First Congress, 2nd Sess. Washington, DC: U.S. Government Printing Office.
Blau, T. H. 1994. *Psychological services for law enforcement.* New York: John Wiley & Sons.
Bonsignore v. City of New York, 683 F.2d 635 (1982).
Caillouet, Beth A., Cary D. Rostow, and Robert D. Davis. 2004. Law enforcement officer seniority and PAI variables in psychological

fitness for duty examinations. *Journal of Police and Criminal Psychology* 19 (2): 49–52.

Conte v. Horcher, 365 N.E.2d 567 (1977).

David v. Christian, 520 N.Y.S.2d 827 (A.D. 2 Dept. 1987).

International Association of Chiefs of Police. 2004. *Psychological fitness-for-duty evaluation guidelines.* Los Angeles: IACP Police Psychological Services Section. http://www.theiacp.org/div_sec_com/sections/PsychologicalFitnessforDutyEvaluation.pdf.

Inwald, Robin. 1990. Proposed fitness for duty evaluation guidelines developed. *Criminal Justice Digest* 9 (8): 1–4.

Redmond v. City of Overland Park, 672 F. Supp. 473 (D. Kan. 1987).

Rostow, Cary D., and Robert D. Davis. 2002. Psychological fitness for duty evaluations in law enforcement. *Police Chief* 69 (9): 58–66.

Rybicki, Daniel J., and Randolph A. Nutter. 2002. Employment-related psychological evaluations: Risk management concerns and current practices. *Journal of Police and Criminal Psychology* 17 (2): 18–31.

Scrivner, Ellen M., and Martin I. Kurke. 1995. Police psychology at the dawn of the 21st century. In *Police psychology into the 21st century*, ed. Martin I. Kurke and Ellen M. Scrivner, 3–31. Hillsdale, NJ: Lawrence Erlbaum.

Stone, Anthony V. 1990. Psychological fitness-for-duty evaluation. *Police Chief* 57 (2): 39–42, 53.

Super, John T. 1997. Select legal and ethical aspects of fitness for duty evaluations. *Journal of Criminal Justice* 25 (3): 223–29.

Vinson v. The Superior Court of Almeda County, 740 P.2d 404 (Cal. 1987).

PSYCHOLOGICAL STANDARDS

Police officers must perform a wide variety of duties and interact with a variety of different individuals within a community. Officers have the ability to issue traffic tickets and other citations, to decide when to arrest or not arrest a person, and to make the decision on the degree of force necessary in order for them to subdue a resisting suspect or otherwise perform their job. Because of this, police departments must understand the psychological effects of the job and create standards that apply to the field. Law enforcement agencies must also have some method of determining who they should or should not hire for their agency. Some types of psychological problems that are of great concern to law enforcement and could adversely impact the field include police stress and police suicide, corruption, antisocial personalities, the inability to work with others, and drug and alcohol problems. Facing any of these issues can result in the financial and/or social ruin of a police department if it hires individuals who exhibit or might tend toward certain behaviors or anyone who is incapable of handling his or her job.

Many departments have set up psychological standards for those individuals applying for positions in law enforcement. Oftentimes, a recruit will have to take some type of psychological exam or personality test so that the departments can determine how well he or she will deal with the multifaceted duties of law enforcement personnel. While the best way to deal with those individuals who have the potential to cause problems is by not hiring them, police departments must also ensure that the psychological standards expected of applicants continue to be met after new recruits have become officers within their agency.

This article will discuss a variety of issues associated with the psychological toll of police work. The various problems facing police departments associated with the hiring of unqualified police officers will be addressed first. Understanding this issue is important in helping police departments identify what factors contribute to problems among police officers in order to develop solutions to such situations. One solution to dealing with the harm caused by unethical or unqualified officers is to conduct some type of preselection based on psychological standards or preemployment screenings used in recruiting individuals who want to become police officers. These preselection standards can help a department learn whether an individual possesses any preexisting characteristics that would impair his or her ability to perform the job. This article will conclude with a discussion of the issue of maintaining psychological standards that can be used to deal with the psychological effects of the job and decrease the number of problems a department faces from officers with psychological issues.

Impact of Unqualified Officers

Obviously the impact that stress and suicide have on the field of law enforcement is very important: "Ongoing stress reduces mental functioning, leading to slower, less accurate decision making; heightened unpleasant emotions such as anxiety and depression; and a loss of desirable personal dispositions such as self-esteem, confidence, and a sense of self-control in one's life" (Anshel 2000, 378). Stress affects more than just the individual police officer. Once a police officer exhibits symptoms of job-related stress, problems within the police department can develop. These problems may include (1) poor performance and a decrease in productivity by officers, (2) low morale among police officers, (3) lawsuits from police officers because of stress-related problems, (4) an increase in absenteeism and arriving to work late, (5) early retirement of officers, and (6) "[t]he added expense of training and hiring new recruits, as well as paying overtime, when the agency is left short-staffed as a result of turnover" (Finn 1997).

Because of the psychological effects of stress and the problems that arise for police departments as a result of stressed officers, police managers benefit from creating psychological standards that can weed out individuals who cannot perform the job or cannot handle the duties associated with the job. An officer who has psychological problems resulting from the inability to handle stress can harm the department and the community.

Once a police agency hires an officer, the agency is liable for the actions of that officer in the course of the job. If an officer who exhibits some type of psychological or personality problem—such as the inability to handle stress, antisocial personality, a tendency toward corruption, a record of prior deviant behavior or problems with the law, or substance or alcohol abuse—becomes involved in a conflict with a citizen, the consequences can be detrimental to the police department as a whole. This is especially true if the conflict results in physical harm to a citizen or if the officer engages in corrupt behavior. The community could lose faith in the police department and may see the whole department in a bad light. Hiring one unqualified police officer can cast a shadow on the whole agency that may take years for the department to recover from. Furthermore, the financial costs that can result from the failure of an officer to perform his or her duty properly can be devastating. Citizens can sue police departments if an officer violates their constitutional rights, causes physical harm to them, uses unlawful force or improperly uses deadly force, or falsely arrests a person.

Psychological Testing/Standards and Becoming an Officer

Many police departments have developed standards that individuals who want to become police officers must pass before the department will consider hiring them. "Police officer selection is vital not only for [organizational] effectiveness, but for the protection of other officers as well as the community that is served" (Coutts 1990 as cited in Simmers, Bowers, and Ruiz 2003, 277). Those individuals who are hired will be instrumental in maintaining or even improving the overall satisfaction and trust that the public has in the criminal justice process, particularly with regard to law enforcement. Police officers are given a lot of authority in terms of making arrests, issuing citations, enforcing laws, and using force in subduing suspects. If the department hires an individual who is violent, quick tempered, antisocial, or suffers from a psychological disorder that would interfere with job performance, this can have a tremendous impact on fellow officers, the department as a whole, and the citizens and community served by the department.

Police officers must be able to deal with all types of people. They must be able to deal with their fellow officers as well as various people within the community, from offenders to the elderly and children. Officers must be able to resist all types of unethical conduct, such as accepting bribes or gratuities, abusing drugs and alcohol, and discriminating against those different from them, in the performance of their duties. Police officers must have good communication skills and be able to come up with solutions to various problems that arise from day to day. In order for police departments to select candidates who are best for the job, standards and conditions figure into their hiring policies. There are education standards, physical standards, drug and alcohol use conditions, medical requirements, lie detector tests, and background checks that applicants must meet or submit to in order to get through the selection process.

Another type of standard that police departments apply to the hiring process is psychological standards. There are several reasons for the psychological screening of individuals before employment. This process helps weed out those individuals who are unable to perform the duties associated with the job due to a variety of factors. Another reason why preemployment psychological screening of individuals is important involves liability. Courts have taken the stance that police departments are to blame if they hire an individual who is psychologically unfit and problems arise (Simmers et al. 2003, 279). Different courts have also stated that the main job of police departments is the

protection of citizens in the community within their jurisdiction (Simmers et al. 2003, 279). This includes protecting citizens from officers who are psychologically unfit and can cause harm to the community; police departments can be sued for the actions of their employees.

Police departments use a variety of different psychological tests to screen applicants. Departments usually give applicants a personality test in order to obtain information about that person that is not readily available in the application paperwork. "Personality tests measure emotional, motivational, interpersonal, and attitudinal characteristics" (Coutts 1990 as cited in Simmers et al. 2003, 279). Having information about all of these variables can ensure that police departments only hire those who are qualified and who do not exhibit any severe psychological problems. The goal of screening potential employees by using a psychological or personality test is to evaluate the applicants for mental illness and other personality problems as well as to see who meets the necessary qualifications to perform the job (Varlea et al. 2004, 649–50). "Most frequent in the empirical literature are studies attempting to identify specific personality test scales or groups of scales that are predictive of objective performance criteria, such as termination, absenteeism, tardiness, citizen complaints, and commendations, or subjective performance criteria such as supervisor and peer ratings of performance" (Varlea et al. 2004, 650–51). All of these factors can impact the police department, not only because administrators have to put time, effort, and money into hiring new people, but also because they have to pay (financially, as well as in terms of time and departmental reputation) to investigate allegations of police misconduct. Furthermore, if police officers have to keep covering for ineffective, or even unethical, peers, they can feel negatively about the department.

One type of personality test used in preemployment screening is the Minnesota Multiphasic Personality Inventory

(MMPI), the latest version of which is known as the MMPI-II. Using this test to look at the characteristics of an applicant's personality, police departments can eliminate those individuals who have traits that will make them unsuccessful in police work such drug or alcohol dependency, lack of moral or ethical values, and antisocial problems. Police departments use the MMPI-II to screen out individuals with deviant, dangerous, and potentially problematic behavior that could affect the police department in the long run (Bannish and Ruiz 2003, 834). "The MMPI, a 566-item, true-false questionnaire, consisting of 10 clinical scales and four validity scales, was developed initially to screen patients for psychological problems related to medical symptoms" (Graham 1987 as cited in Simmers et al. 2003, 279). Based on the different scales and the answers of the applicant, screeners can get a feel for the person and predict the likelihood of his or her success in the profession. Studies have shown that personality tests are very useful in policing and have "reported significant relations between MMPI-II scales and such variables as automobile accidents, job tenure, academy performance and attrition, supervisors' ratings, promotions, and job problems" (Hargrave and Hiatt 1987 as cited in Simmers et al. 2003, 281). This means that such personality tests can be a good indicator of future behavior.

According to Arrigo and Claussen (2003, 278), the MMPI might not be the best instrument in terms of preemployment screening in the field of law enforcement. One reason given is that the MMPI was developed to measure psychological disorders, and some of the questions might sound awkward to applicants who are filling out the questionnaire in order to obtain a job in policing. According to some researchers, a better measure than the MMPI or MMPI-II at evaluating potential law enforcement personnel is the Inwald Personality Inventory (IPI). "The IPI is a structured measure of various personality characteristics and behavioral patterns specific to the psychological fitness of candidates applying for law enforcement positions" (Fekken as quoted in Arrigo and Claussen 2003, 279–80). This instrument was specifically designed for the psychological screening of potential law enforcement applicants. "Behavioral patterns and personality characteristics relevant to job performance can be identified, including substance abuse, trouble with the law, job difficulties, rigidity, suspiciousness, and interpersonal styles" (Arrigo and Claussen 2003, 280). This type of measure does a better job of predicting those people who are not qualified to become police officers or who will create problems for the department in the future in terms of liability, tardiness, and time loss.

The main reasons for having some form of psychological preemployment screening in the field of law enforcement is that the departments want to ensure that they hire the best people possible for performing the job. There have been too many high-profile instances in law enforcement involving excessive use of force, corruption, false arrests, and general misconduct among officers that have diminished the confidence and trust the people have in the criminal justice system as a whole and law enforcement in particular. Police officers are a highly visible presence in the community, and they come into contact with a variety of citizens, criminals and noncriminals alike. Police officers provide a variety of services to the community, and they need the cooperation and the trust of the community in order to perform their jobs. When police departments hire officers who are psychologically unstable in any manner, a multitude of problems could arise. Departments lose the money spent on training, paying, and, ultimately, investigating allegations brought against such officers when conflicts arise. Psychological standards and preemployment screening can provide tremendous benefits to the police department. The different testing instruments that are used in the recruiting phases of the process help police departments avoid the liability associated with hiring unqualified people.

Psychological Standards throughout the Law Enforcement Career

Law enforcement administrators can take many steps to ensure that continued psychological standards are met and evaluations of officers are performed. These include partnering with psychologists and psychiatrists who police officers can speak with about their concerns, fostering an environment that encourages communication by making sure that the administrator is available to officers, and creating programs within the department designed to alleviate the psychological tolls of the job. One of the main things that police departments can do is acknowledge the fact that they understand the stresses their employees face and send a message that they are willing to help officers. They have to ensure that "city leaders understand the negative effects of stress in order to garner support for stress management and stress reduction initiatives" (Standfest 1996).

Just knowing that an employer is concerned and willing to help officers can help to reduce stress within a department. By routinely evaluating the psychological well-being of their employees, police departments can also help ensure that citizens are receiving the best possible protection from their law enforcement personnel, and administrators can ensure that they have hired those individuals who are best qualified for the job and can detect problems before they get out of hand.

TINA L. LEE

See also **Personnel Selection; Police Suicide; Psychological Fitness for Duty; Stress and Police Work**

References and Further Reading

Anshel, Mark H. 2000. A conceptual model and implications for coping with stressful events in police work. *Criminal Justice and Behavior* 27: 375–400.

Arrigo, B. A., and N. Claussen. 2003. Police corruption and psychological testing: A strategy for preemployment screen. *International Journal of Offender Therapy and Comparative Criminology* 47 (3): 272–90.

Bannish, Holly, and J. Ruiz. 2003. The antisocial police personality: A view from the inside. *Internal Journal of Public Administration* 26: 831–81.

Finn, Peter. 1997. Reducing stress. *FBI Law Enforcement Bulletin* 66 (8).

Liberman, A. M., S. R. Best, T. J. Metzler, J. A. Fagan, D. S. Weiss, and C. R. Marmar. 2002. Routine occupational stress and psychological distress in police. *Policing: An International Journal of Police Strategies and Management* 25: 421–41.

Simmers, K. D., T. G. Bowers, and J. M. Ruiz. 2003. Pre-employment psychological testing of police officers: The MMPI and the IPI as predictors of performance. *Policing: An International Journal of Police Science and Management* 5: 277–94.

Standfest, S. R. 1996. The police supervisor and stress. *FBI Law Enforcement Bulletin* 65 (5).

Varlea, Jorge G., M. T. Boccaccini, F. Scogin, J. Stump, and A. Caputo. 2004. Personality testing in law enforcement employment settings: A meta-analytical review. *Criminal Justice and Behavior* 31 (6): 649–75.

PSYCHOLOGY AND THE POLICE

Psychologists working with law enforcement agencies deliver a range of direct psychological services to officers and the departments they serve. Until the 1960s, the disciplines of psychology and law enforcement seemed mutually exclusive. However, since that time the practice of providing psychological services to law enforcement agencies not only evolved, it has expanded. This expansion was due to forward-thinking law enforcement executives recognizing that repeated exposure to a difficult environment takes a toll on the human being. Further, they acknowledged that the unique culture of police work created its own set of stress factors and that few can help but be affected throughout the course of a career. Consequently, many of those responsible for public safety came to realize the need for proactive approaches to optimize the psychological functioning and personal adjustment of officers and deputies and to reduce occupational stress.

Historical Development

Historically, this development was initiated through the applicant screening venue when the Law Enforcement Assistance Administration (LEAA) provided federal funding that enabled the use of psychological tests to screen police officers and sheriff's deputies. As many departments took advantage of LEAA funds, the development of a psychological screening specialization was initiated. To a lesser extent, LEAA funds also were instrumental in psychologists becoming involved in operational areas such as assisting in criminal investigations and developing a hostage negotiation capacity in police departments. The success of those efforts eventually provided support for developing counseling programs for officers, particularly following line-of-duty critical incidents, and for training programs that addressed issues requiring psychological expertise.

Conversely, psychologists were also called on to perform fitness-for-duty evaluations (FFDEs). These mandatory evaluations involved ordering incumbent officers to be evaluated by a psychologist who would determine an officer's fitness to continue in his or her position. The latter activity was highly sensitive and posed a range of issues quite different from other psychological services that were designed to enhance performance both of the individual officer and their respective departments. Finally, psychologists also engaged

in organizational consulting and focused on strategies to enhance organizational performance. Throughout this evolution, the unique stressors experienced by law enforcement personnel were recognized and led psychologists to develop stress management programs to help law enforcement officers better manage their work and personal lives. Today, that emphasis has expanded into programs that focus on wellness and suicide prevention.

Gaining Credibility

Initially, tradition-clad law enforcement was not fully accepting of psychological services and psychologists had to work to gain credibility. In gaining credibility, however, psychologists also had to solve professional practice issues. Questions emerged as to *who was the client*: the job applicant or the organization; or, for counseling programs, the officer or the organization? The latter impacted confidentiality of communications, generally identified as the cornerstone of psychological services, but a concept that was not fully understood in non–health organizations that operated as closed systems. Although many of these issues were resolved by state laws that govern the practice and licensure of psychologists, the International Association of Chiefs of Police Psychological Services Section recently issued guidelines for police psychological services. Consequently, information on managing some of the more difficult issues is now in the public domain (*Police Chief* 2005).

The credibility of the police–psychology interface has been further confirmed by findings from three national surveys (Delprino and Bahn 1988; Scrivner 1994; VerHeist, Delprino, and O'Regan 2001). Survey results showed increases in law enforcement's use of psychologists and a wider availability of services provided for police and sheriffs. These findings, over time, demonstrate that psychology has made a strong impact on policing since it was first introduced in the 1960s. Accordingly, psychology also opened the door and created a level of acceptance for the involvement of other mental health service providers. A 1997 survey by Delprino, O'Quin, and Kennedy demonstrated that not all who provide mental health services to law enforcement are psychologists and that service providers from other disciplines, including police chaplains, now deliver services to law enforcement.

Framework of Psychological Services Provided to Law Enforcement

Psychologists clearly brought new sets of skills to law enforcement agencies. These skills are the core technologies of police psychology and constitute the basic framework of psychological services. They include evaluation, clinical interventions, training, and organizational work and are further detailed as follows:

- *Preemployment applicant screening:* Psychologists use psychological tests to identify successful candidates for law enforcement and evaluate them on a range of emotional stability criteria that are consistent with suitability for law enforcement work. Critical issues pertaining to this core technology include the need to use objective tests that can be justified in personnel decision making; communicating test results appropriately; engaging in ongoing validation of the assessment process; conforming to civil rights legislation, requirements of the Equal Employment Opportunity Commission (EEOC), and the Americans with Disabilities Act (ADA); and adhering to professional practices and psychological standards maintained by the testing industry and professional psychology.

- *Fitness for duty evaluation:* Once hired, do officers continue to be psychologically fit for duty? This question can arise in relationship to a work-related injury but also in response to questions about an officer's ability to safely and effectively perform his or her duty because of psychological factors. When behaviors of concern alert commanding officers that an individual officer may need attention, they have the option of making a referral for a fitness evaluation. The nature of FFDEs is different from other psychological services in that they involve a mandatory referral to the psychologist and fitness information is communicated to the department. Thus, confidentiality of communication is limited since the department, not the officer, is the client. The officer needs to be informed of this situation prior to any discussion with the psychologist.

- *Psychological counseling:* Psychologists assist officers by counseling them in response to an array of personal problems believed to be intensified by police work. Such problems include, but are not limited to, marital conflict and family problems, substance abuse, depression and anxiety, and suicidal tendencies. Recently, new emphasis has been placed on wellness programs.

- *Critical incident debriefing:* Psychologists provide a crisis response to officers involved in on-duty traumatic incidents, a situation that occurs in public safety occupations at frequencies that exceed those in the general population. This core technology involves short-term debriefing intervention(s) that are designed to help officers adjust to these incidents, and reduce the probability that longer term psychological problems will occur because of the incident.

- *Training:* Psychologists develop and conduct training sessions for officers ranging from topics as diverse as interview techniques and/or improving communication skills to managing stress to enhancing psychological resilience.

- *Forensic/operational*: This core technology involves the practical application of psychology to law enforcement operations. It can include assisting the department in criminal investigations, forensic hypnosis, developing a hostage negotiation capacity, and barricade call-out consultation. Recently, psychologists have been contributing their expertise to assisting departments with their antiterrorism strategies and responses.
- *Organizational*: Psychologists assist organizations, as well as the individual officers, to engage in strategic planning and organizational development to improve the agency's performance.

Building the Police–Psychology Interface

The widespread acceptance of psychologists by law enforcement was fueled by the Federal Bureau of Investigation Training Academy's initial willingness to take on a convener-facilitator role that helped jump start the capacity for police and psychologists to find common ground. By bringing them together in professional meetings, participants were able to identify, discuss, and write about the primary issues that needed to be addressed. These meetings helped to resolve unique professional issues faced by police psychology, built a network of psychologists working with law enforcement throughout the country, and generally enabled an enhanced understanding between police and law enforcement.

Equally important was the professional acceptance and peer recognition of this unique practice of psychology. Major professional organizations such as the American Psychological Association (APA) and the International Association of Chiefs of Police (IACP) developed sections devoted to this facet of psychology. Without that level of support, police psychology may not have become what it is today.

Key events that supported the development of professional police psychology (Scrivner 2005) include the following:

- Five police psychology conferences were hosted from 1984 to 2001 by the Behavioral Sciences Unit of the FBI academy that produced a set of published papers that identified critical issues for law enforcement.
- The formation of the Police Psychological Services Section of the IACP provided a forum for addressing critical issues. The section recently issued a series of guidelines to apply to pre-employment psychological evaluation services, psychological FFDEs, officer-involved shootings, and peer support.
- A Police and Public Safety Psychology Section was developed within the Division of Psychologists in Public Service (Division 18) of the APA. It, too, holds yearly meetings and presents professional papers at the APA's annual conference.
- Congressional testimony on police stress and family well-being, supported by APA, was the impetus for an amendment to the 1994 Omnibus Crime Act that provided funding for the Corrections and Law Enforcement Family Support Program (CLEF). The program was managed by the National Institute of Justice (NIJ), and responsible for funding approximately thirty innovative programs (1996–2003) to treat stress, deliver training, and conduct survey research on the needs of law enforcement and correction officers.

- An APA Police Chiefs Roundtable Series has been conducted. Fifteen years after affiliating with APA, police chiefs met with an APA governance committee and sought input on managing problems that affect the quality of American policing.

These developments have strengthened the professional dimensions of the field and facilitated a growing body of police psychology literature and scholarly research.

Delivering Psychological Services

Finn and Tomz (1997) provide a blueprint for how to establish a program of services for law enforcement. They show how models for delivery of services vary. Those that have become prevalent include the use of psychologist consultants, the most common model, or the use of employee assistance programs (EAPs). Some large departments provide a full range of psychological services to officers and the organization through in-house psychological service units, whereas in other departments the unions have assumed this responsibility. And, some confine services to building stress management skills.

Much of the CLEF work provided better definitions of law enforcement stress factors as applied to officers and their families and showed that although exposure to violence, suffering, and death is inherent to the profession, other sources of stress have a greater impact on officers and their families. These sources include light sentences for offenders, unfavorable public opinion of police performance, irregular work hours and shift work, dealing with abused children and child homicides, and ministering to survivors of vehicle crashes. Such is further complicated by organizational stress factors that include the nature of the organization, limited advancement potential, and excessive paperwork. Although officers now view stress as a normal part of their job, they also feel they are under more pressure today than what they experienced even ten years ago (Finn, Talucci, and Wood 2000).

Current Trends

As the police–psychology interface continues to expand, departments are finding new ways to use psychologists. Current trends include seeking assistance to address significant national policing issues such as acrimonious interactions between law enforcement officers and citizens, assistance in ending racial profiling, intervening in police brutality, strengthening police integrity, and developing greater understanding of police officer fear.

The APA roundtables mentioned earlier suggested that psychologists could also help in finding alternatives to arresting the homeless, intervening in the prevalence of hate crimes, developing officer skills in the areas of mediation and anger management, studying how observing violence affects police officers, particularly in relationship to domestic violence, or examining research on stereotypes to help develop interventions for ethnic profiling. Still others, such as the Los Angeles Police Department (LAPD), have moved their psychologists from the consulting rooms into the precincts in an effort to make them more accessible and less intimidating and to enhance their capacity for proactive outreach (Gelber 2003). These events demonstrate current trends in the activities of psychologists in law enforcement agencies and suggest a level of impact that would have been unbelievable forty years ago.

In the aftermath of the terrorist attacks of September 11, 2001, and the ongoing concerns about global terrorism, law enforcement organizations and their officers will confront new demands. With those demands will come new stressors as psychologists and officers begin to work in the threat-sensitive environment. However, law enforcement now has a much broader capacity to meet the changing needs of officers, their families, and their organizations because the police–psychology interface has now become institutionalized.

ELLEN SCRIVNER

See also **Danger and Police Work; Personnel Selection; Police Suicide; Psychological Fitness for Duty; Psychological Standards; Stress and Police Work; Stress: Coping Mechanisms**

References and Further Reading

Delprino, R. P., and C. Bahn. 1988. National survey of the extent and nature of psychological services in police departments. *Professional Psychology: Research and Practice* 19 (4): 421–25.

Delprino, R. P., K. O'Quin, and C. Kennedy. 1997. *Identification of work and family services for law enforcement personnel.* NIJ 171645. Washington, DC: National Institute of Justice, U.S. Department of Justice.

Finn, P., V. Talucci, and J. Wood. 2000. On-the-job stress in policing—Reducing it, preventing it. *National Institute of Justice Journal* (Jan.): 19–24.

Finn, P., and J. E. Tomz. 1997. *Developing a law enforcement stress program for officers and their families.* March. NCJ163175. Washington, DC: U.S. Department of Justice, National Institute of Justice.

Gelber, C. 2003. LAPD bureau psychologists to hit the streets. *Police Chief,* September, 29–31.

Kurke, M. I., and E. M. Scrivner. 1995. *Police psychology into the 21st century.* Hillsdale, NJ: Lawrence Erlbaum.

Police Chief. 2005. Guidelines for police psychological service. September. 68–86.

Scrivner, E. M. 1994. *The role of police psychology in controlling excessive force.* Washington, DC: National Institute of Justice, U.S. Department of Justice.

Scrivner, E. M. 2005. Psychology and law enforcement. In *Handbook of forensic psychology,* ed. I. B. Weiner and A. K. Hess, 3rd ed. Hoboken, NJ: Wiley & Sons.

VerHeist, R. A., R. P. Delprino, and J. O'Regan. 2001. *Law enforcement psychological services: A longitudinal study.* Paper presented at the annual convention of the American Psychological Association, San Francisco, CA.

PUBLIC HOUSING POLICE

The physical characteristics of public housing developments have often been considered conducive to crime. Living conditions are crowded, there are often few entrance and exit points, hallways are frequently unmonitored, and there is little visibility or exposure to the outside world. Within the boundaries of such communities, criminal activity is largely invisible to outsiders, including police. In addition, there are often high numbers of undocumented residents, many of whom are believed to have criminal records. Combined with the poverty and limited economic prospects of legal residents, these factors engender crime and criminal victimization. Establishing satisfactory levels of public safety and security has consequently proved to be a serious long-term challenge for housing authorities and police departments. The problem has been exacerbated by the fact that housing authorities—largely dependent on the federal government for their funding—often felt neglected by local authorities and local police agencies. Out of this came the idea for dedicated public housing police (PHP).

Federal Involvement in Public Housing Policing

In 1995, the U.S. Department of Housing and Urban Development (HUD), responding to political and public pressure concerning the severe problems of crime in public housing, analyzed public housing policing in seven major cities (Baltimore, Maryland; Boston, Massachusetts; Chicago, Illinois; Cleveland, Ohio; Oxnard, California; Memphis, Tennessee; and Seattle, Washington) and gathered information from more than three thousand people including public housing residents, police chiefs, public housing police chiefs, officers, housing authority representatives, and city officials. HUD's (1995) conclusions were as follows:

> The results of comprehensive analyses by HUD indicate that housing police departments begin without the proper infrastructure, such as establishing of a mission, goals, objectives, performance indicators, personnel management systems, formalized coordination with local law enforcement, encumbrance of funds to pay for the services, an integrated system of guards, police, physical security, resident input on a regular basis, timely feedback to residents about crime and safety issues, a clear connection between police and tenant patrols, lack of policy manuals for police and security personnel.

As a result of this analysis, HUD produced a document to provide technical assistance about why and how to set up a PHP department, including goals, problems to be addressed, and policy manuals. Operational elements specified in the plan include staffing criteria, beat design and descriptions, shift and tour schedules, community policing, surveillance procedures, report procedures, crime prevention plans, and patrol strategies. Different recommended patrol strategies include vertical patrol, foot patrol, bicycle patrol, and motorcycle patrol. Also included are elements for a technical services plan, administrative services plan (including accreditation), and formal resident participation (HUD 1995).

Several large cities had already established public housing police departments before HUD issued its guidelines. By and large, these cities did not make wholesale changes as a result of the guidelines, although marginal adjustments may have been made. In addition, because HUD did not mandate the adoption of PHP departments by other authorities and established few reporting requirements pertaining to public housing security, no unified approach to public housing police was developed. Housing authorities proceeded with individualized arrangements that had a variety of components. A synopsis of steps taken by some of the larger cities now follows.

Boston

The Boston Housing Authority (BHA) created its Department of Public Safety (DPS) in the late 1970s because city police forces were not considered adequate to meet the needs of tenants and managers. The department began with six professional staff members who investigated crime and disorder complaints in public housing facilities and interfaced with the Boston Police Department (BPD). By 1983, it had grown to forty-two investigators, who were trained at the Basic Police Recruit Academies of the Massachusetts Criminal Justice Training Council. DPS currently falls under the jurisdiction of the BPD.

Thus, the BPD serves as the primary police force for Boston's public housing, handling emergency calls, investigations, records management, and all other normal police functions. DPS personnel support BPD with investigative services, special programs, and community policing. The DPS divides the twenty-seven housing facilities in Boston into beats, tailoring its programs to crime in each. In addition, DPS runs several programs based on a community policing model: Senior Crime Watch, turkey dinner, holiday party, senior citizen activities, foot patrols of buildings and hallways, and community, resident, and manager meetings.

Chicago

The Chicago Housing Authority (CHA) had a 270-member police force that patrolled its facilities, beginning in the 1970s. However, under the city's 1999 Plan for Transformation, the force was disbanded, and its responsibilities were shifted to the Chicago Police Department. The crime response and control functions of the Chicago Police Department are supplemented by a number of CHA activities.

The CHA invests $2 million annually for tenant patrols in specific housing projects. A security guard service is funded at $5 million annually to provide a minimum of ten hours of coverage daily at each senior resident building. The CHA contracts with the Chicago Police Department to provide additional security at facilities including a $12 million annual contract for police and vertical patrol services at facilities including its senior locations, and a $3.5 million contract for additional police coverage at other facilities. Finally, CHA has spent more than $1 million to install security cameras at various developments.

Los Angeles

The Los Angeles Housing Authority had a small dedicated police force in the 1980s and 1990s, consisting of approximately fifty officers who were trained at the Los Angeles County Sheriff's Academy. This force never had responsibility for felony investigation, however, and was largely considered by the Los Angeles Police Department (LAPD) to be little more than a local security operation. In the mid-1990s the independent force was disbanded, and the housing authority entered into an interagency agreement with LAPD to address public safety and security, housing authority crime control policies, dispute/conflict resolution, and other issues.

Currently, police officers hold intermittent role-playing exercises with public housing residents to give residents perspective on police investigations. In 2001, for instance, an exercise was staged in which residents played the role of officers and vice versa. One element of this was a simulated murder investigation.

Jersey City, New Jersey

Jersey City's public housing authority and its police department cooperated to form

the public housing problem-oriented policing project to investigate serious crime problems across six public housing sites. Each site used a team consisting of public housing representatives, police officers, resident representatives, and social service representatives. These teams focused on violence and drug offenses. Responses varied from site to site. An evaluation of the project determined that the site team responses, rather than physical structure differences or site demographics, were responsible for reductions in calls for service.

New York

The New York City Housing Authority hired security guards to patrols its developments at its creation in 1934. In 1952, the Housing Authority Police (HAP) department was officially created and HAP officers received special training. However, the HAP was merged with the New York Police Department (NYPD) in 1995 and is now a formal division within the NYPD designated the Housing Bureau. Bureau officers coordinate with tenant patrols, community groups, and development managers to serve the 420,000 residents of public housing in New York City. The bureau is staffed by NYPD officers on assignment to the Housing Bureau, much as other officers are assigned to narcotics, organized crime, patrol, and so forth.

Washington, DC

The District of Columbia Housing Authority (DCHA) established its Office of Public Safety in 1995. It is a fully operational police force with three types of employees: resident monitors who screen visitors at DCHA developments, civilian administrative support, and dedicated but sworn DCHA police officers who have arrest powers in DCHA facilities that match those of at-large Metropolitan Police Department officers. This force is supplemented as needed by sworn police officers from the Metropolitan Police Department, who have general jurisdiction in housing developments as they do in the city generally.

The city is divided into three regions of public housing and caters its law enforcement programs to crime problems within each. Tactics include uniformed foot patrols, bike patrols, decoy operations, physical and electronic stakeouts, and surveillance operations, in addition to a variety of special operations. The Office of Public Safety has a community policing component, with officers attending resident council meetings on a regular basis to implement resident watch, youth basketball, and other programs.

Conclusions

As the preceding examples show, public housing policing has taken several forms. Some of the cities that had the largest public housing police (and the largest public housing crime problems—for example, New York and Chicago) have moved away from the dedicated housing police model, adopting instead an approach that created formal relationships between the housing authority and metropolitan police departments. Others have retained a dedicated security force that has public safety responsibilities that are under the guidance or control of police departments. Commonly found elements include collaborations with city police and housing authorities, elements of community policing, and some degree of training or certification of housing authority public safety personnel. Others have no staff dedicated to public safety.

In general, most efforts to establish distinct and independent housing authority police departments have been abandoned in favor of a model that assigns full jurisdictional responsibilities to a city police

department that works with local housing authorities and residents in varying degrees of cooperation. In fact, although there is no formal national documentation on this issue, it seems most likely that the vast majority of the several thousand housing authorities in the county have never had any dedicated police force at all, and have always been dependent on a local police department for public safety and the response to crime occurring in housing developments. There has been no national coordination, and little formal or informal coordination between cities. Each city, police department, or housing authority has therefore dealt with public safety in housing developments in unique ways, despite the fact that federal guidelines for this critical function have existed since the mid-1990s.

TERENCE DUNWORTH and
KEVIN ROLAND

See also **Autonomy and the Police; Community-Oriented Policing: Practices; Crime and Place, Theories of; Crime Control Strategies: More Police; Minorities and the Police; Policing Multiethnic Communities**

References and Further Reading

Boston Housing Authority. 2005. *Public safety*. http://www.bostonhousing.org/detpages/deptinfo31.html.

Chicago Housing Authority. 2000. *Plan for transformation*. http://www.thecha.org/transformplan/files/plan_for_transformation_year_1_english_final.pdf.

Chicago Housing Authority. 2003. *The CHA's plan for transformation*. http://www.thecha.org/transformplan/plan_summary.html.

District of Columbia Housing Authority. 2005. *Office of Public Safety*. http://www.dchousing.org/department/public_safety.html.

Los Angeles Police Department. 2004. *Announcement of funds for housing authority communities*. http://www.lapdonline.org/press_releases/2004/04/pr04214.htm.

Los Angeles Police Department. 2005. *Management Achievement Award for community/police partnership*. http://www.lapdonline.org/inside_lapd/ma_awards/comm_pol_part2.htm.

Mazerolle, Lorraine G., Justin Ready, Bill Terrill, and Frank Gajewski. 1999. *Problem-oriented policing in public housing: Final report of the Jersey City project*. Washington, DC: U.S. Department of Justice. http: //www. ncjrs.gov/pdffiles1/nij/grants/179985.pdf.

New York City Police Department. 2005. *Housing bureau*. http://www.ci.nyc.ny.us/html/nypd/html/hb/borohb.html.

New York City Police Museum. 2005. *About the history of the New York City Police Department*. http://www.nycpolicemuseum.org/html/faq.html#transit-housing.

Philadelphia Housing Authority. 2005. *Philadelphia Housing Authority Police Department*. http://www.pha.phila.gov/aboutpha/depart_police.aspx.

The View from the Ground. 2005. Kicking the pigeon #8: The CHA plan and public safety. http://www.viewfromtheground.com/archive/2005/07/ktp-8-the-cha-plan-and-public-safety.html.

U.S. Department of Housing and Urban Development. 1995. Guidelines for creating, implementing and managing public housing authority police departments in public housing authorities. http://www.hud.gov/offices/pih/publications/notices/95/pih95–58.html.

PUBLIC IMAGE OF THE POLICE

Public image is an import concept to consider when examining both the role and consequences of police in a democratic society. How the public views the police can determine the legitimacy of police authority and citizen compliance with the law (Tyler and Huo 2002). It also influences the extent and quality of citizen cooperation and interaction with the police. Members of the public who have relatively negative views of the police may be less likely to participate in investigations or community meetings and may be less compliant toward police during routine and otherwise benign police–citizen contacts (for example, vehicle stops). In addition, while public images of the police are formed both objectively and subjectively, the public's role in checking police authority depends on the formulation of a reasonably accurate image of the police and how they function (Skolnick and McCoy 1984).

There is no single coherent image of police in America. Mass media images of the police vary widely and are often inconsistent with the reality of policing (Surrette 1998). One can find, for example, images of the police ranging from the violent crime fighter (Dirty Harry, *Magnum Force*), to the good-natured incompetent buffoon (Chief Wigum, *The Simpsons*), to today's technically savvy detective (Gil Grissom, *CSI: Crime Scene Investigators*). Even news media reports about the police represent a filtered, perhaps sensationalized, view of police work to the public.

Further, the police present various images of themselves to the public that can impact their public image. The police have always employed powerful symbols to promote images of authority and capacity for control over crime to maintain their legitimacy as social control agents (Manning 1977). Yet the dominant presentation of their work has shifted from a "professional" image to more of a "community-oriented" image during the last three decades. While the former image highlights the police as neutrally competent law enforcement experts, the latter emphasizes the police as responsive partners with the public concerned with overall quality of life. Nevertheless, these dominant general images depart to some extent from the reality of the police role and function, and may influence the kinds of services the public expects from the police.

Factors Influencing the Public Image of the Police

Relative to other professional groups or institutions in society, the public image of the police is generally positive. The public ranks the police consistently high among other institutions in terms of confidence, according to periodic national polls (Gallup Organization 2005). As an occupation, being a police officer also receives high marks for occupational prestige from the public (Harris Interactive 2004). For example, the police rank among other public service occupations (nurses, military officers, teachers, fire fighters, doctors, and scientists) that tend to contribute to the community or society at large. Although this general public image of the police is positive, the image varies according to social group and along specific dimensions.

Because fairness is a fundamental value for democratic policing, the public image of the police held by various racial groups has been a central issue of study. Public opinion polls and research commonly show that whites have a more favorable general opinion of the police than do members of racial minority groups (Decker 1981; Gallup Organization 2005; Reisig and Parks 2000; Tuch and Weitzer 1997). Indeed, national polls conducted by the Gallup Organization show typically that while a clear majority of whites have a "great deal" or "quite a lot" of confidence in the police, usually a minority of black respondents hold these positive assessments. Minority group members are also more likely than whites to perceive the police, both in general and with respect to their particular community's department, as discriminatory or unfair in their treatment of nonwhite members of the public (see, for example, Tuch and Weitzer 2005; Rice and Piquero 2005).

In addition to observing racial differences, several studies have examined the role of gender, age, and social class in shaping public images of the police. Younger persons and males tend to be less satisfied with the police or view the police as discriminatory compared to other members of the public. While these negative evaluations may be the result of differential experience with the police, research has found these relationships to persist even after considering perceptions of specific encounters with the police (for example, Reisig and Parks 2000; Weitzer and Tuch 2005). The public image of the police does not appear to depend exclusively on an individual's socioeconomic status once other explanations are taken into account. The effect of social class position may be partly a function of—or confounded by—community norms and the expectations of social status.

Research shows that public perceptions of police often are linked to the neighborhood context in which people reside (Dunham and Alpert 1988; Reisig and Giacomazzi 1998; Reisig and Parks 2000; Sampson and Bartusch 1998). Neighborhoods characterized by high levels of concentrated disadvantage are less satisfied with the police independent of individual differences (Reisig and Parks 2000; Sampson and Bartusch 1998). For example, Sampson and Bartusch found that in Chicago, neighborhood social and economic characteristics explained away the racial differences that exist in the public image held by whites and black residents. Moreover, Weitzer (1999) found that respondents from a poor, black neighborhood felt that they were treated less fairly by the police compared to residents of affluent white neighborhoods and residents of a middle-class, black neighborhood. The differences according to neighborhood context may be attributable to actual differential treatment, perceptions of control over the police bureaucracy, or entrenched norms that develop in different areas as others have speculated (Weitzer 1999; Sampson and Bartusch 1998).

The quality of direct experiences with police agencies also shapes the way the public views the police. Citizens who come into contact with the police as suspects or have poor experiences with the police tend to have less favorable views of the police compared to people who report crimes or are otherwise assisted by the police (Reisig and Parks 2000; Reisig and Chandek 2001). It is important to note that citizens' preconceived image of the police and their appropriate role influences the assessment of specific contacts they have with the police (Brandl et al. 1994). If a preconceived image of the police influences how one evaluates police contacts, it may be a challenge for the police to improve the public assessment of their contacts by changing the way they interact with the public.

Such difficulties notwithstanding, people who perceive they have a voice in the mobilization of crime control bureaucracies, are familiar with their police, or believe the police distribute resources fairly to their neighborhood are more likely than others to hold positive impressions of both police efficiency and effectiveness (Sunshine and Tyler 2004). Each of these is an area in which police departments may be able to have a profound impact through changes in administrative practices.

Finally, the public image of the police can change in reaction to publicized events or highly scrutinized police actions. In Los Angeles as well as across the nation, public favorability toward the police declined substantially after the well-publicized Rodney King incident, according to polls (Tuch and Weitzer 1997). Although the police image held by the majority public often demonstrates some resiliency after such high-profile negative events by returning to pre-event levels within a few years, minority group members' attitudinal reactions to police brutality and discrimination are often more enduring. In contrast, highly public events that demonstrate police courage or heroism can often produce what some scholars call a "halo effect," in which the public's image of the police becomes abruptly and sharply positive. Perhaps the quintessential example occurred in the wake of September 11, 2001, where the entire police occupation— not just the New York Police Department and the other public services agencies directly involved in the World Trade Center and Pentagon attacks—enjoyed an almost simultaneous increase in positive public sentiment legitimacy. (Anecdotal evidence suggests that employment applications to police departments also rose dramatically after 9/11, providing further evidence of an elevated public image.)

Implications for the Public Image of the Police

Variability in the public's image of the police can have substantial consequences for policing in America. As the evidence suggests, when the image of the police is highly negative, legitimacy can suffer to the point where noncompliance becomes the norm rather than exception during police–citizen encounters. Similarly, when the police enjoy a halo effect, the public may fail to challenge police practices and strategies that may violate democratic principles. In the case of the former, police officers may become injured at high rates as suspect resistance increases concomitantly with declining respect for police authority. In the case of the latter, members of the public may become injured as the police distribute coercive force unequally across communities in the forms of aggressive arrest strategies, deployment of officers, and even excessive force. Thus, to ensure constructive and effective police functioning, a proper dose of "healthy skepticism" of practices and intentions should provide the balance between illegitimacy and unquestioned trust. Healthy skepticism allows the police to accomplish their public safety goals with the general consent of the public, while requiring them to periodically justify their policies and account for their strategies.

SHEA W. CRONIN and ROBERT J. KANE

See also **Attitudes toward the Police: Overview; Media Images of Policing**

References and Further Reading

Brandl, S. G., J. Frank, R. J. Worden, and T. S. Bynum. 1994. Global and specific attitudes toward the police: Disentangling the relationship. *Justice Quarterly* 11, 119–34.

Decker, S. 1981. Citizen attitudes toward the police: A review of past findings and suggestions for future policy. *Journal of Police Science and Administration* 9 (1): 80–87.

Dunham, R. G., and G. Alpert. 1988. Neighborhood differences in attitudes toward policing: Evidence for a mixed-strategy model of policing in a multi-ethnic setting. *Journal of Criminal Law and Criminology* 79: 504–23.

Gallup Organization. 2005 and earlier. *Gallup/CNN/USA Today poll.* http://www.poll.gallup.com.

Harris Interactive. 2004 and earlier. *The Harris poll.* http://www.harrisinteractive.com/harris_poll.

Manning, P. 1977. *Police work: The social organization of policing.* Prospect Heights, IL: Waveland Press.

Reisig, M. D., and M. S. Chandek. 2001. The effects of expectancy disconfirmation on outcome satisfaction in police–citizen encounters. *Policing* 24: 88–99.

Reisig, M. D., and A. L. Giacomazzi. 1998. Citizen perceptions of community policing: Are attitudes towards police important? *Policing* 21: 547–61.

Reisig, M. D., and R. B. Parks. 2000. Experience, quality of life, and neighborhood context: A hierarchical analysis of satisfaction with the police. *Justice Quarterly* 17 (3): 607–30.

Rice, S. K., and A. R. Piquero. 2005. Perceptions of discrimination and justice in New York City. *Policing* 28 (1): 98–117.

Sampson, R. J., and D. Bartusch. 1998. Legal cynicism and subculture? Tolerance of deviance: the neighborhood context of racial differences. *Law and Society Review* 32: 777–804.

Skolnick, J. H., and C. McCoy. 1984. Police accountability and the media. *American Bar Foundation Research Journal* 9 (3): 521–57.

Surrette, R. 1998. *Media, crime and criminal justice.* Belmont, CA: Wadsworth.

Tyler, T. R., and Y. J. Huo. 2002. *Trust in the law: Encouraging public cooperation with the police and courts.* New York: Russell Sage Foundation.

Tyler, T. R., and J. Sunshine. 2003. The role of procedural justice and legitimacy in shaping public support for policing. *Law and Society Review* 37 (3): 513–48.

Weitzer, R. 1999. Citizens' perceptions of police misconduct: Race and neighborhood context. *Justice Quarterly* 16: 819–46.

Weitzer, R. 2000. Racialized policing: Residents' perceptions in three neighborhood. *Law and Society Review* 34 (1): 129–55.

Weitzer, R., and S. A. Tuch. 1999. Race, class, and perceptions of discrimination by the police. *Crime and Delinquency* 45: 494–507.

Weitzer, R., and S. A. Tuch. 2005. Racially biased policing: A determinant of citizen perceptions. *Social Forces* 83 (3): 1009–30.

PUBLIC SAFETY, DEFINED

Safety, according to one dictionary, is "the condition of being safe from undergoing or causing hurt, injury, or loss" (*Merriam-Webster's Collegiate Dictionary,* eleventh edition). A more tendentious definition is provided by the *American Heritage Dictionary,* which claims that safety is "the state of being certain that adverse effects will not be caused by some agent under defined circumstances. . . ." Both of these definitions are reductive and individualistic. Safety in these definitions is a personal state of being, something like freedom from the impact of negative risks from whatever source. This "state" is a psychological matter, an internal condition. Factually, there is no such perfect safe state, given that risk can arise from any source and that risks (negative, unwanted dangers) are always present. Fear resides in every person from time to time, springing from a variety of imagined or real sources. While these are psychological in nature, safety has a public aspect.

The definition of public safety, like most concepts in social science, is either taken for granted, a concept that is rarely debated, or remains vague and subject to many conflicting and unclear definitions. It is often equated with and produced by law and law enforcement. This is false. It is defined elliptically as that which public safety agencies, usually meaning public police, fire, and emergency medical services, sustain or maintain. This is false because these groups are merely surrogates for the collective efficacy and attachment to their neighborhoods and communities that people feel together. It can be seen as a residual; that which is maintained by public agencies, once the order that is sustained by private agencies and informal social control is sorted out.

Law enforcement and the law are fantasy or imagined locations for safety in a conflicted democratic society. In fact, of course, they operate as reactive forces that, while sustaining the illusion of safety, are active only after the fact except in rare cases of known-in-advance collective occasions such as demonstrations, parades, and celebrations. The law serves primarily as a communicational code that enables conflicts to be resolved in the legal system. It is the vehicle of governmental social control (Black 1976). It cannot create or sustain safety because it is an abstraction that provides the *idealization* of order, not order itself.

The elliptical definition of public safety, what public safety agencies produce, has much to be said for it empirically. That is, the evidence of its works can be identified and measured, for example, via examination of crime rates, trust in police, cynicisms about criminal justice and policing, victimization studies, self-reported delicts, and civil suits. But these are failures in the safety net provided citizens, not evidence that the system works. Saying that these indicate the nature of public safety is like saying that a reduction in crime rates indicates crime prevention is at work. These are organizational definitions of what safety is not. A definition is weak that proceeds on the basis of what something is not, or a negation.

The definition "by residual functions" is also weak because it leaves the actual function or meaning of the concept of public safety unexplicated. The private industry called private policing in its many forms does not produce security nor safety; it manages the superficial aspects of that which is connected directly to generating, accumulating, accounting for, and otherwise enhancing capital. Private agencies are committed to sustaining the appearance of probity and handling deviance of various kinds privately and through negotiation. Their losses are accounted for internally except in the event of insurance claims, and they issue no public figures on crime committed on the premises. The question of the relationships between public order and private security remains quite controversial.

Public safety must also be distinguished from the agency focus as a consequence of what public safety agencies do. It cannot be built up from the ways, strategies, and tactics that such agencies use to affirm or deny safety through their practices. It cannot rest on a commodified, or industry-based, notion of a vague function. It does intrinsically have connection to the military, which has obligations for collective national security, the police, and other public safety agencies.

The concept of public safety must be defined positively and distinguished from individualistic notions of personal safety or even a sense of safety. As Rawls (2005, 89) writes, "The impossibility of explaining the origin of empirically valid general ideas in individual experience becomes the necessity for the group experience of enacted moral forces." Group experiences, such as the experience of public safety, must be explained collectively. Notions such as risk, fear, danger, and personal safety are in every way derivative.

Public safety obtains to the degree to which social integration among peoples is high. It is a surrogate term associated with social integration. It can be measured indirectly as in the case of suicide, murder, accidental death rates, or violent assaults, but these are not measures of social integration or the density of connection among people; they are indirect measures of a deeper and more complex matter, the collective conscience of a people. This integration is mobilized by joint emotional experience, sustained by celebration and dramatization, and symbolized imminently by the practices of security- and safety-based agencies. They are the representatives of trust in everyday life. On the other hand, collective efficacy, as a capacity or attitude toward others' willingness to be engaged in social control, to produce safety, must be distinguished from what people do, whether at the neighborhood, city, or national level. Public safety in this external sense glosses the nature of collective obligations one to the other, often now symbolized by the media, CNN, the various cable channels, and other shared screens. The social integration of cities, societies, and nation-states is now more likely to be linked to transnational trends and the military. The central trust-ensuring, violence-enacting institutions in public life, the police and army, are now working to increase their "market share" as notions of public safety change.

PETER K. MANNING

See also **Public Image of the Police; Public–Private Partnerships in Policing; Role of the Police; Social Disorganization, Theory of**

Reference and Further Reading

Black, Donald. 1976. *The Behavior Of Law.* New York and Orlando: Academic Press.
Rawls, Anne. 2005. *Durkheim's epistemology.* Cambridge: Cambridge University Press.

PUBLIC–PRIVATE PARTNERSHIPS IN POLICING

Policing has undergone profound changes in the United States and elsewhere since 1960, and the evolution of public–private partnerships is among the most significant of these changes. This article identifies and describes the sources of this development, its various manifestations, and implications for security in both the public and private sectors. Policies and programs designed to shape and manage partnerships between public law enforcement and private security agencies are then considered, along with their potential effects on public and private institutions and the general public. The essay concludes with a consideration of the prospects for the future of public–private policing partnerships.

Private security has been defined in various ways. For current purposes, it will mean services other than those provided by public law enforcement and regulatory agencies engaged primarily in the prevention and investigation of crime, loss, or harm to specific individuals, organizations, or facilities. It typically includes the work of security guards, corporate security and loss prevention personnel, private investigators, armored vehicle personnel, manufacturers of security equipment, locksmiths, alarm and surveillance specialists, security consultants and engineers, and people involved in a variety of related activities from private forensic laboratory scientists to guard dog trainers and drug testing specialists.

The Origins of Public–Private Partnerships in Policing

Public law enforcement officials have relied on private citizens for information in solving crimes and assisting the prosecutor in convicting offenders for centuries, long before the emergence of the first truly professional metropolitan police department in London in 1829. Bounty programs had been in effect for centuries prior to that, sometimes under the authority of the executive branch of government and sometimes under the jurisdiction of the courts, to encourage private citizens to bring information to law enforcement officials to assist them in solving crimes and bringing offenders to justice.

The professionalization of policing in the nineteenth century served to substantially legitimize and strengthen public safety and security as a more exclusively public sector responsibility, first in the United Kingdom and eventually in the United States and elsewhere. This began to change in the United States in the 1960s, as soaring crime rates exposed serious flaws in the professional model of policing. In 1960, police departments had been comfortably operating out of a set of notions about professionalism that had served the public well for decades, ideas that came to be substantially modified toward the end of the twentieth century: that the police were the primary authorities on crime and how to respond to it, that police supervisors and executives were the locus of authority within the police hierarchy, that it was too risky to allow patrol officers to exercise substantial discretion even in routine matters, that the basic pathways to reduced crime were through more rapid response to calls for service and more arrests, that more police could only help to increase arrest rates and shorten response times, that the public was not equipped to provide much help to police other than as witnesses, that building good community relations was useful primarily for damage control rather than as an end in itself, and that adherence to these precepts would give the police a better image and earn respect among the general public. This model of policing made sense in the first half of the twentieth century, when many police departments throughout the country had been struggling for years to overcome reputations for ineptness, corruption, and brutality.

Several factors emerged in the 1960s and 1970s that induced police practitioners and policing scholars to reassess the professional model. The fact that professionalism did little to stem the explosion in crime during this period was surely one factor: Homicide rates doubled and burglary and robbery rates tripled nationwide, and they increased even more in large urban centers. Research conducted in the 1970s found little support for notions that were core aspects of the professional model: that saturation random patrols would be effective in reducing the time to respond to calls for service, increasing crime clearance rates and reducing crime rates. In fact, rapid police response was found to contribute little to the solving of crimes. The most critical delays were private, between the time of the offense and the time of the call for service. After the first few minutes of the commission of the crime, it was learned that it makes little difference whether the police arrive afterward in a matter of seconds or minutes.

Adjustments to the crime explosion and information about the ineffectiveness of standard practices were eventually made, first in the private sector. Commercial establishments and citizens who could afford private protection chose not to wait for breakthroughs in public policing that would make them safer. Corporate complexes, shopping malls, sports arenas, and small businesses hired security guards, installed surveillance and alarm systems, and hardened targets with stronger locks, doors, and new architectural designs and layouts. Many private households employed such resources as well, with some of the more affluent citizens moving to gated communities that probably made them less vulnerable to crime and, in any case, helped make them feel safer.

The numbers associated with this shift to privatization are not precisely known, but they have been estimated to be substantial. Although the number of sworn officers exceeded the number of persons employed in the private security field in the 1960s, by 1990 the numbers had shifted to the point where an estimated three persons were employed in private security for every sworn officer in the United States (Forst and Manning 1999).

Few accounts of the history of policing give significant attention to this explosion in private policing in the 1970s and 1980s. It is widely asserted that the professional era of the mid-twentieth century gave way eventually to the era of community policing by the end of the century. A more compelling case can be made that the professional era gave way to the era of privatization throughout the 1970s and most of the 1980s, before community policing resurrected public policing. This unprecedented shift to the private market for security occurred initially with little coordination with public policing authorities.

In time, however, it became clear that lack of coordination between public and private policing frequently produced serious lapses, and that more thoughtfully developed public–private coordination was essential. Awareness of this need arose naturally as private security agents found themselves charging more and more suspects with crimes and turning them over to local police. The police found some of these cases too trivial to bring to the prosecutor, others worthy of formal arrest and prosecution but in need of additional evidence and information, and still others ready to take forward to prosecution without further work. Improved coordination became apparent especially in the first two categories. Even when private security agents fully expected the police to refuse to process a case for prosecution, it became a common practice for security guards to detain suspects, with aims of achieving at least modest levels of deterrence and retribution. This practice may deter impressionable young first offenders, but may have little effect on others, and could well induce still others to commit more crimes in the future, upon learning that the formal system of justice does not take their crimes seriously.

The Maturing of Public–Private Partnerships

Police departments became increasingly aware of the need for improved coordination in the late 1980s and 1990s, as community policing gained currency among municipal police departments throughout much of the United States and in developed nations throughout the world. Partnership with the public is, after all, the central principle of community policing—an expanded awareness of the needs of local individuals and improved coordination with private institutions serving local neighborhoods.

In moving from principle to action, a particularly valuable resource for improved coordination soon became evident to the police: Private security agents were often more familiar than sworn officers with certain crimes in the places in which they operated, including the sources of those crimes. The advantages of improved coordination became equally apparent to the more professional of the private security agents, who were keenly aware that their livelihoods and reputations depended on their ability to deal with crimes quickly and effectively, and working more effectively with the local police in those areas could enhance the prospects of bringing offenders to justice.

Perhaps the most pervasive form of these partnerships consists of government purchases of private security resources to protect the public, government facilities, personnel, and operations. Communities throughout the United States, burdened with the difficulties and expenses of maintaining conventional police services, have elected to bypass their police agencies and contract out substantial portions of public protective services to civilians and private agencies, especially functions on the periphery of front-line crime control and investigation: providing technical assistance at crime scenes, serving summonses, moving and monitoring suspects and prisoners, managing juveniles, providing court security, conducting traffic control, and so on. These activities have been found to be well within the capacities of private agents. Sworn officers are expensive to recruit and train, and more expensive still to maintain, given relatively high salaries and costly fringe benefits, indirect and support costs, and pension programs. Moreover, many private agents are former police officers with extensive experience in policing.

Lakewood, Colorado, a city in the Denver area with some 150,000 residents, hires trained citizen volunteers for police support services, including fingerprinting, issuing of parking tickets, enforcing graffiti violations, doing investigative follow-up work, and preparing affidavits. The Lakewood Police Department also contracts with a private security firm to guard hospitalized prisoners and provide assistance in protecting crime scenes. These officers provide twenty-four-hour assistance and often attend the department's roll calls for training. Many are certified police officers in the state of Colorado (Youngs 2004). Such arrangements are common in communities throughout the United States.

They are common elsewhere in the world as well. Much of Great Britain and Australia have developed public–private partnerships in policing, including both the police department's contracting out of policing functions to private agents and the development of collaborations between sworn police and private security agents operating independently in a particular jurisdiction (Sturgess 2002). The Vera Institute has reported a similar array of public–private policing partnerships in Brazil, India, Indonesia, Kenya, Nigeria, and South Africa (Bhanu and Stone 2004).

The privatization of services previously done by sworn officers, even when under contract with police departments, is a type of public–private partnership, but is fundamentally different from partnerships in which sworn officers collaborate with private security agents already working in the jurisdiction. In Great Britain, Prime Minister Tony Blair has strongly discouraged the former and encouraged the latter as a means of providing public services generally (Sturgess 2002). Of course, much of this is based on political considerations rather than economic, driven by Blair's Labor Party ties to government employment unions and concerns about the loss of jobs. In Britain, as in the United States, many policing functions previously done by sworn officers, both in the form of back-office technical support and front-line policing service, have in fact been turned over to civilian specialists and contracted out to private security agencies with a net gain in employment, and few take serious issue with the increases in efficiency that also result from these arrangements.

Circumventing public expenses through privatization and civilianization has not been costless. State and local government spending on private services escalated from $27 billion in 1975 to some $100 billion in 1987, with the federal sector contributing another $197 billion of public expenditures for private security services in 1987. Los Angeles County awarded dozens of contracts for guard services in the early 1980s at an estimated 74% of the cost of the county policing alternative. Other municipalities have gone still further, experimenting with all-private police forces, and have found them capable of delivering high-quality services at lower costs (Forst 2000).

More conventional public–private partnerships manifest through both formal and informal mechanisms. The informal arrangements are the most common and often the most effective. They arise naturally through situational needs that can occur daily; or occasionally in the form of breakfast and luncheon meetings between sworn officers and private agents, typically without a formal agenda; and sometimes as flexibly coupled teams and task forces. They sometimes arise in a more structured way through formal public–private alliances with periodic meetings: to deal with specific problems, often related to gangs, hot spots, or other chronic issues that interfere with both public and private interests; to draft legislation on the licensing of private security functions; to arrange training programs for sworn officers or private agents; or to share information of a more general nature, such as technology or new strategies for protecting property and enhancing security. An even more structured arrangement occurs in the form of partnership contracts, such as the creation of "business improvement districts" that work out specific divisions of responsibility between sworn officers and private security agents working in a common area (Connors, Cunningham, and Ohlhausen 1999).

These various forms of public–private partnership have not always been simple and riskless. As the partnerships have matured, specific problems have become readily apparent. Foremost among these have been occasional tensions between enhanced public security and police legitimacy. Closer public partnerships with private institutions can and often do serve special interests, through financial and nonfinancial inducements that attract police away from their larger responsibility to protect and serve the general public. This can and often does come at a steep cost to the integrity and reputation of police departments and individual officers.

The primary problem arises from the fact that private security personnel are agents accountable to the principal who hires them, while sworn officers are accountable to the much broader public at large. From the perspective of the private security agents, the partnership must serve the principal, and from the perspective of the police department the partnership must serve the general public. Individual officers frequently face conflicts between their sworn duty to serve the general public and the sometimes strong draw to serve some constituents disproportionately, often through seemingly benign favors or privileges. Officers working at night as security guards for commercial establishments face a conspicuous conflict of interests in their daytime beats. Many police departments have imposed clear restrictions against such moonlighting arrangements, but many have not. Public agencies should make clear to their officers that compromising the public interest is unacceptable, that they cannot accept such inducements and continue to receive full benefits as sworn officers.

Another problem is that private security personnel are not subject to the same standards of screening and eligibility as are sworn officers, hence they can be a less reliable resource for public safety. This can pose problems when the private agents represent the police department even in an auxiliary capacity. Police departments might have good reasons to limit the closeness of partnerships with people who can bring more troubles than benefits to the department. Clearly, the formation of specific partnerships with private agents must be sufficiently flexible to ensure that the benefits of the partnerships exceed the burdens to the greatest extent possible. No formula can be given in advance to determine the scope and nature of a particular partnership, other than that the arrangement should be fluid enough to accommodate changing circumstances and needs.

Trends and Implications for the Public and Private Policing Sectors

The rise of a substantial and multifaceted private security industry has imposed new demands on and problems for police departments, but it has simultaneously raised rich opportunities for law enforcement agencies to leverage their scarce resources toward a more effective and efficient capacity for serving the general public. As they exploit such opportunities, however, the police must be mindful of the need to develop partnerships with private agents with eyes wide open to the risks inherent in those pursuits. A fundamental objective should be to establish a coherent framework for assessing public–private partnerships, to ensure that arrangements that bolster public safety and security are strengthened while ones that harm society or offer costly, ineffective, or ethically dubious solutions to security are quickly revealed and aborted.

Are partnerships involving sworn officers, private security personnel, and civilians generally superior to the use of any of these components alone? Can future police partnerships with private businesses be structured more constructively, without eroding the legitimacy of police organizations? Should we expect these partnerships to be adversely affected in the new era of terrorism? One answer to all of these questions is clear: Sweeping generalizations are dangerous and cookie cutter solutions are likely to be unsuccessful. To be effective, public–private security partnerships must be developed situationally. This has been established cross-nationally (Bhanu and Stone 2004), and it is likely to be equally true from one jurisdiction to another within any large political entity.

The varieties of public policing, private security forces, and modes of civilianization are as vast as the needs of the public. Private security alternatives range from well-trained and well-paid agents, often current or former sworn officers who operate in coordination with municipal police departments, to plant guards whose job is simply to call the police when they observe suspicious activity, to vigilante groups and gang-like organizations that often compete with local police for the control of neighborhoods. Similarly, civilianization in a given department may be warranted for some positions but not others, depending on the needs of the community, the skills of the sworn officers, local labor market conditions, and other factors. Meaningful comparisons require a thorough assessment of the key particulars in the matter.

As local budgets for public safety continue to become constricted by taxpayers increasingly unwilling to tax themselves, municipal police and county sheriff's departments must find new ways to leverage their scarce resources by building even stronger alliances with private security agencies and personnel that satisfy conventional norms of legitimacy. When they fail to do so, they risk losing some of their most capable officers to lucrative positions as private investigators and executives of private security agencies.

The great challenge in forming effective public–private partnerships for the future is to do so with job enrichment inducements that maintain the loyalty of the most valuable personnel resources. Opportunities to prevent and solve potentially grave problems in the new era of terrorism certainly provide one such inducement. Officers so motivated are less likely to be interested in leaving the department and less likely to bend when faced with tensions between public responsibilities and private inducements. Partnerships are fine when they serve the general public, but they must be built on a foundation that ensures that the officer's overarching responsibility to serve public interests will not be compromised.

More enlightened policing, especially in the form of community policing and problem-oriented policing, has been credited with a substantial share of the decline in crime throughout the end of the twentieth and early part of the twenty-first centuries. One cannot discard the prospect that improved public–private partnerships in policing have contributed to these developments. As long as police departments maintain a healthy set of incentives and provide strong, ethical leadership, the public safety sector should be able to build on these gains for the foreseeable future.

BRIAN FORST

See also **Airport Safety and Security; Business Districts, Policing; Situational Crime Prevention**

Reference and Further Reading

Bhanu, Chitra, and Christopher Stone. 2004. *Public–private partnerships for police reform.* New York: Vera Institute. http://www.vera.org/publication_pdf/230_441.pdf.

Connors, Edward F., William C. Cunningham, and Peter E. Ohlhausen 1999. *Operation cooperation: A literature review of cooperation and partnerships between law enforcement and private security organizations.* Alexandria, VA: Institute for Law and Justice.

Forst, Brian. 2000. The privatization and civilianization of policing. In *Boundary changes in criminal justice organizations.* Vol. 2 of *Criminal justice 2000.* Washington, DC: National Institute of Justice.

Forst, Brian, and Peter Manning. 1999. *The privatization of policing: Two views.* Washington, DC: Georgetown University Press.

Sturgess, Gary L. 2002. Private risk, public service. *Policy,* Autumn. http://www.cis.org.au/Policy/aut2002/polaut02–1.htm.

Youngs, Al. 2004. The future of public/private partnerships. *FBI Law Enforcement Bulletin* (Jan.).

QUALITY-OF-LIFE POLICING

Quality-of-life policing is one of several varieties of police strategies that evolved under the more general framework of community-oriented policing. Although it is not possible to pinpoint the exact date or location of the origins of this form of policing, much of its development can be traced to the evolution of community-oriented policing in the 1980s and 1990s. Gary Cordner (1998) points out that quality-of-life policing is based on the premise that controlling crime requires the police to be attentive to social and physical disorder, minor crime, and appearances of crime.

Quality-of-life policing is not just one form of policing or one policing strategy; rather it encompasses a variety of community policing strategies that involve aggressive enforcement of social disorder offenses such as public drinking, panhandling, public urination, street-level drug dealing, loitering, vandalism, and prostitution. Enforcing municipal ordinances aimed at controlling physical disorder such as dilapidated housing, abandoned automobiles and refuse, and graffiti is often used as a quality-of-life policing strategy. *Order maintenance* and *zero tolerance policing* are other labels given to these aggressive policing strategies (Katz, Webb, and Schaefer 2001).

Eck and Maguire (2001) differentiate quality-of-life policing from other community-oriented policing strategies by pointing out that they emphasize the aggressive policing of disorder and place less emphasis on community cooperation. Quality-of-life policing differs from other aggressive policing strategies in that its aggressive focus is on social and physical disorder and not on serious crime per se. While a limited number of police agencies have made quality-of-life policing an agency-wide strategy (Bratton 1996), it is more typically applied to specific geographic areas or neighborhoods that have high rates of disorder and crime.

Factors Influencing the Development of Quality-of-Life Policing

Police scholars (Weisburd and Greene-Mazerolle 2000) have identified several influences leading to the development of quality-of-life policing. One such influence was an increased concern in the 1980s on the part of citizens about social and physical disorder in their neighborhoods. This awareness was partly due to the increased use of community surveys by police departments and researchers alike to ascertain citizen perceptions of crime and disorder problems as well as their preferences and priorities for police services. Related to this was an increased demand for the police to address neighborhood disorder problems.

Another important influence on the development of quality-of-life policing was a growing body of research that indicated that traditional methods of policing such as routine patrol and responding to calls for service were relatively ineffective. The recognition of the ineffectiveness of traditional policing methods led to the development of new approaches to policing, including community-oriented policing and related strategies such as problem-oriented policing and zero tolerance policing—all of which focused on the problem of disorder.

A growing awareness of the importance of focusing resources on the spatial distribution of crime also influenced the development of quality-of-life policing. The recognition that crime tended to cluster into "hot spots" led to the realization that scarce police resources could be used more effectively and efficiently if they were concentrated on hot spots or areas characterized by high levels of social and physical disorder and serious crime.

The Broken-Windows Hypothesis and Quality-of-Life Policing

Probably the greatest intellectual force leading to quality-of-life policing was the development of the "broken-windows" hypothesis proposed by Wilson and Kelling in 1982. They argued that crime and disorder were intimately linked in a spiral-like manner where increased disorder leads to increased crime, and increased crime leads to increased disorder. This process is complex, with initial signs of social and physical disorder (for example, "broken windows") in a neighborhood sending a message to would-be criminals that crime and delinquency are likely to be tolerated in the neighborhood.

If unchecked, visible social and physical disorder lead to increased fear of crime, and residents come to believe that their neighborhood is unsafe. This can lead to physical withdrawal as well as withdrawal from neighborhood social networks. This withdrawal weakens the informal social control mechanisms that help maintain order and law-abiding behavior in the neighborhood. The natural supervision of young people and watchful guardianship provided by residents in orderly neighborhoods starts to break down. Neighborhood residents no longer engage in the supervision of juveniles and others with tendencies to engage in minor forms of delinquency and crime. Less serious forms of crime in the neighborhood leads to more serious forms; social and physical disorder leads to serious crime indirectly by first making the neighborhood ripe for minor forms of criminal offending.

From a policy perspective, the logical response to the broken-windows hypothesis is to focus the police response on the root causes of serious crime, which are social and physical disorder. Weisburd and Greene-Mazerolle (2000) argue that according to many criminologists and crime prevention experts, concentrating police efforts on disorder will produce declines in serious crime. It would seem then, that quality-of-life policing is a logical policy response to the broken windows hypothesis. Katz, Webb, and Schaefer (2001) trace the origin of quality-of-life policing directly back to the broken-windows hypothesis. They conclude that based on this hypothesis, the police should refocus their efforts away from traditional crime fighting approaches and place greater emphasis on combating neighborhood disorder. According to Kelling and Bratton (1998), reacting to serious crime once a pattern of offense has occurred is too late. According to Skogan (1990), the police need to respond to the first signs of disorder before the disorder-to-serious crime spiral becomes operational.

Quality-of-Life Policing and Social Influence and Norm Theories

Closely related to the broken-windows explanation of the disorder–crime linkage are explanations that rely heavily on the concepts of social influence and social norms. In attempting to account for crime, these approaches, which borrow directly from the broken-windows explanation, focus on the development of social meaning that influences changes in the norms or rules that guide behavior. The idea is that in neighborhoods with significant disorder, conventional norms, beliefs, and values break down and are replaced by those that favor the commission of criminal acts. Visible social and physical disorder conveys social meaning that influences the definition of which behaviors are acceptable and valued. Disorder conveys the message that residents in the neighborhood do not care about the neighborhood and that it is okay to break the law and engage in uncivil behavior.

In this perspective, the spiral of disorder leading to serious crime is seen as resulting from changing definitions of acceptable behavior. Kahan (1997) has noted that social meaning has an independent effect on crime because it directs social influences on behavior quite independently of the law. Accordingly, criminal behavior is a function of social influences and meaning associated with visible disorder within the neighborhood, and ignoring these influences and meanings when trying to control crime is futile. Roberts (1999) describes the social influence explanation basis or crime as a process where neighborhood disorder raises fear levels to the point where law-abiding residents either flee the neighborhood or withdraw to their homes. In turn, the disorder that negatively impacts law-abiding citizens attracts law violators to the neighborhood, which results in increased levels of serious crime.

For social norm and social influence theories, it follows that policies that attempt to control crime by increasing penalties, or through other traditional deterrence strategies, are likely to be ineffective. From this perspective quality-of-life policing strategies and tactics are believed to be the most desirable crime control policy option. Aggressive policing that attacks the signs of disorder that convey to would-be law violators that criminal and delinquent behavior is acceptable in the neighborhood is the preferred policy option (Kahn 1997). One example of a quality-of-life strategy consistent with this perspective is the aggressive enforcement of gang-loitering laws, such as the one that was implemented in Chicago in 1992 that resulted in more than 40,000 arrests in a three-year period (Roberts 1999). Note that the Chicago ordinance was eventually held to be unconstitutional by the U.S. Supreme Court.

Empirical Evaluations of Quality-of-Life Policing

Evaluating whether or not quality-of-life policing accomplishes the goal of reducing serious crime by focusing on disorder requires an examination of the results of quality-of-life policing as well as its underlying foundation, including the broken-windows hypothesis itself and aggressive policing as effective policing strategies.

Skogan's (1990) research involving residents in forty neighborhoods in six cities, which looked at the links between perceptions of crime and fear of crime and related these to physical and social disorder, was one of the earliest assessments of the broken-windows hypothesis. Skogan concluded that perceptions of crime and fear of crime were causally related to disorder. He also concluded that disorder occurred before serious crime took place in the study neighborhoods. This finding is consistent with the causal sequence of disorder–fear–crime spiral, which is the essence of the broken-windows hypothesis. However, Skogan's findings have been reanalyzed by other researchers (Harcourt 1998) who concluded that there was no relationship between disorder and serious crime. These researchers argue that it was only a small number of "outlier" neighborhoods that were responsible for finding a relationship among disorder, fear, and crime.

Because most quality-of-life policing strategies are based on aggressive policing, it is logical to consider research and evaluations that have attempted to determine if aggressive policing per se achieves its intended outcomes. If aggressive approaches to policing do not work, there is little reason to expect quality-of-life policing to work since it requires the use of aggressive policing strategies. Several researchers have produced evidence that aggressive policing does control crime (Sherman 1997). Examination of the relationship between the issuance of traffic citations and serious crime has been one approach to evaluating aggressive policing. Using the rate of traffic ticket issuance per officer as a measure of aggressive policing, Wilson and Boland (1978) found that the higher the rate of traffic citations issued by patrol officers, the lower a city's robbery victimization rate. Other researchers (Sampson and Cohen 1988) have found a similar relationship between aggressive policing and decreased robbery rates.

Even though there is evidence that aggressive policing produces its intended outcome of a reduction in serious crime, other evidence suggests that, although it might produce an increase in arrests for disorder crimes, for example, driving under the influence and minor drug offenses, it might not produce increases in more serious crimes (Cordner 1998; Weiss and Freels 1996).

In addition to research examining the foundation of quality-of-life policing, there is a growing body of evidence bearing on whether or not quality-of-life policing strategies per se reduce serious crime. Sherman carried out some of the earliest research when he examined the impact of an order maintenance crackdown on drinking and parking violations in Washington, D.C. He found that although the crackdown produced an increase in public perception of safety, it did not reduce serious crime in the form of street robbery. A 1999 study by Novak et al. concluded that intensive enforcement of liquor laws did not affect the more serious crimes of robbery and burglary.

Katz, Webb, and Schaefer (2001) evaluated the impact of an aggressive quality-of-life policing strategy that focused on both social disorder crimes and physical disorder. The strategy was intended to reduce serious crime by focusing policing efforts on social disorder such as prostitution, drug-dealing, loitering, and impacting physical disorder through trash removal, graffiti abatement, and property inspections to ensure ordinance compliance. They found that quality-of-life policing had the greatest impact on social disorder, especially public morals crimes, and physical disorder, but not on more serious forms of crime.

Still other studies of quality-of-life policing strategies provide additional evidence that quality-of-life policing can reduce social disorder including a study conducted by Green (1996) that found that a combination of enforcing code violations and increased police presence reduced drug activity and physical disorder. However, this evaluation had little bearing on whether or not quality-of-life policing reduced more serious forms of crime.

Other evidence, however, suggests that quality-of-life policing can produce the intended outcomes of reducing serious crime. In a somewhat unique application of quality-of-life policing, Kelling and Coles (1996) worked with the New York City Transit Police Department to design a strategy that targeted minor crimes and disorder in the New York subway system. This strategy involved enforcing disorder laws and removing loitering youth and homeless persons from subway tunnels and stations. In addition, physical disorder was addressed by improving the physical appearance of substations. The research team concluded that law enforcement focus on disorder in the subway system resulted in a substantial drop in serious crime.

Concerns about Quality-of-Life Policing

Whether or not quality-of-life policing works as intended—by producing a decrease in serious crime by addressing social and physical disorder—is yet to be determined. There is only limited evidence that it impacts serious crime, but greater evidence that it can produce a decrease in disorder. Even if it works as intended, there are still concerns about its desirability as a policing strategy. For example, local ordinances that enable quality-of-life policing such as Chicago's 1992 gang-loitering ordinance can be so vague that they facilitate police abuse and the harassment of law-abiding citizens. Vague ordinances can make it necessary for police officers to exercise subjective judgments about who has a legitimate reason for being on a street

corner, which in part is why the Supreme Court struck down the Chicago ordinance.

Related to this is the concern that some quality-of-life policing strategies can disproportionately and unfairly target racial and ethnic minorities. As Roberts (1999) points out, for many Americans race is an indicator of the propensity for criminality. There is concern that in some quality-of-life policing strategies the police will use race or ethnicity as the basis for estimating criminal propensity and inadvertently arrest law-abiding citizens. In other words, quality-of-life policing can potentially exacerbate the problem of racial profiling.

Some quality-of-life strategies may defeat the purpose of community-oriented policing by weakening the links between the police and the community. Excessive police presence and disproportionately high arrest rates of neighborhood youths can build up neighborhood mistrust of the police, making public cooperation difficult while negating potential reductions in serious crimes due to quality-of-life policing efforts.

Somewhat related to the problem of police mistrust is the potential for some quality-of-life policing strategies to be at odds with minority cultures. Quality-of-life policing strategies typically reflect the values of the dominant culture. What appears to be *disorder* from the perspective of dominant culture can be *order* from the perspective of a minority culture. Quality-of-life policing strategies involving code enforcement; for example, prohibitions against loud music, may conflict with cultural practices involving the playing of such music and public drinking at the end of the workweek. The adage that "one person's junk is another person's gold" is a consideration for quality-of-life policing. Code enforcement efforts directed at removing what appears to be junked auto parts or abandoned cars could jeopardize the potential effectiveness of quality-of-life policing approaches if those items are commonplace and valued by neighborhood residents.

Whether or not quality-of-life policing works as intended remains to be seen, but in some form it will probably be part of the American policing landscape for the foreseeable future. Police researchers are most certainly going to continue to examine its effectiveness, and civil libertarians will continue to be watchful for its potential abuse. One recent proposal calls for the implementation of *situational policing*, a new strategy that calls for enhancing the capacity of neighborhood residents to control what goes on in their neighborhood while continuing to focus on social and physical disorder (Nolan, Conti, and McDevitt 2005). This form of policing is "situational" in that it is premised on the need to customize policing styles to meet the different needs of neighborhoods with different conditions. This approach holds promise for the continued development of quality-of-life policing.

VINCENT J. WEBB

See also **Broken-Windows Policing; Community-Oriented Policing: Practices; Problem-Oriented Policing; Social Disorganization, Theory of; Zero Tolerance Policing**

References and Further Reading

Bratton, W. 1996. Remark: New strategies for combating crime in New York City. *Fordham Urban Journal* 23: 781–85.

City of Chicago v. Morales, 119 S. Ct. 1849, 1856 (1999).

Cordner, G. 1998a. The effects of directed patrol: A natural quasi-experiment in Pontiac. In *Contemporary Issues in Law Enforcement*, ed. J. Fyfe. Beverly Hills, CA: Sage.

———. 1998b. Problem-oriented policing vs. zero tolerance. In *Problem oriented policing*, ed. T. Shelly and A. Grant. Washington, DC: Police Executive Research Forum, 1998.

Eck, J., and E. Maguire. 2000. Have changes in policing reduced crime? An assessment of the evidence. In *The crime drop in America*, ed. A. Blumstein and J. Wallman. Cambridge, UK: Cambridge University Press.

Harcourt, B. 1998. Reflecting on the subject: A critique of the social influence conception of deterrence, the broken-windows theory, and order maintenance policing New York Style. *Michigan Law Review* 95: 2477–88.

Kahan, D. 1997. Social Influence, social meaning, and deterrence. *Virginia Law Review* 83: 367–73.

Katz, C., V. Webb, and D. Schaefer. 2001. An assessment of the impact of quality-of-life policing on crime and disorder. *Justice Quarterly* 18 (4): 825–76.

Kelling, G., and W. Bratton. 1998. Declining crime rates: Insiders' views of the New York City story. *Journal of Criminal Law and Criminology* 88:1217–31.

Kelling, G., and C. Coles. 1996. *Fixing broken windows*. New York: The Free Press.

Novak, K., J. Hartment, A. Holsinger, and M. Turner. 1999. The effects of aggressive policing of disorder on serious crime. *Policing* 22:171–90.

Roberts, D. 1999. Forward: Race, vagueness, and the social meaning of order-maintenance policing. *Criminal Law and Criminology* 89: 775–836.

Sampson, R., and J. Cohen. 1988. Deterrent effects of the police on crime: A replication and theoretical extension. *Law and Society Review* 22:163–89.

Sherman, L. 1997. Policing for crime prevention. In *Preventing crime: What works, what doesn't, what's promising*, ed. L. Sherman, D. Gottfredson, D. MacKenzie, et al. Washington, DC: Office of Justice Programs.

Skogan, Wesley. 1990. *Disorder and decline*. New York: The Free Press.

Weisburd, D., and L. Green-Mazerolle. 2000. Crime and disorder in drug hot spots: Implications for theory and practice in policing. *Police Quarterly* 3 (3): 332–49.

Wilson, J., and B. Boland. (1978). The effect of police on crime. *Law and Society Review* 12: 367–90.

Wilson, J., and G. Kelling. Broken windows: The police and neighborhood safety. *Atlantic Monthly*, March, 29–38.

RACIAL PROFILING

History

Starting in the late 1990s, law enforcement in the United States faced allegations that they were "racially profiling." The charge was that police were targeting drivers who were black or Hispanic for vehicle stops based on beliefs about the propensities of these groups to commit crime.

There are two ways to conceptualize the history of racial profiling—the short-term view and the long-term view. The short-term view extends back to the 1990s and focuses on police bias manifested in stops and searches of drivers. Two lawsuits were key to these allegations. In *New Jersey v. Soto,* a case brought in 1990, public defenders representing Pedro Soto and others sought to suppress evidence obtained during searches conducted by New Jersey troopers, alleging the searches were the result of racial profiling practices. These public defenders had detected an alarming number of cases involving black people who were stopped by troopers on the New Jersey Turnpike. The defendants obtained data on New Jersey State Police traffic stops in various areas from 1988 through 1991 and hired a social scientist to analyze the data. The court relied heavily on the results of the analysis of those data—which indicated an overrepresentation of blacks among people stopped—in deciding to suppress the evidence. *Wilkins v. Maryland* was brought in 1992 by a Harvard-educated public defender who was detained with his family by the side of an interstate highway by the Maryland State Police. After refusing the troopers' request to search, the family was required to stand in the rain while a drug-sniffing dog checked the car, finding nothing. The American Civil Liberties Union filed a suit on behalf of Wilkins and his family, alleging that the police detention was the result of racial profiling. The case was eventually settled. The settlement included a mandate for the Maryland State Police to collect data on traffic stops. These cases sparked additional stories and lawsuits that police were engaging in racial profiling and the issue became one of the most critical facing law enforcement in the late 1990s.

In tracing the origin of racial profiling in the context of the short-term view, some law enforcement practitioners and other experts point to the use of drug courier profiles developed during the war on drugs and, in particular, training conducted by the Drug Enforcement Administration (DEA) during the 1980s. While DEA officials claim that race was never part of the training on profiles, other observers and some local/state law enforcement practitioners report that local and state police came to link blacks and Hispanics with criminal drug activity as a result of exposure to this training.

The long-term view goes far back into the history of this country and also conceptualizes racial profiling more broadly—that is, the broader view would encompass all law enforcement decisions by police, not just decisions to stop and search drivers. In this expanded, longer term view, *racial profiling* is just a new term for long-standing allegations that police (and other components of the criminal justice system) treat minorities differently because of their race and ethnicity. These charges were very much a part of the civil rights movement and, indeed, many of the riots occurring during the volatile years of this movement were precipitated by incidents in which officers were alleged to have misused force or other authority against minority subjects.

Terminology and Definitions

In addition to various histories, various terms and definitions are used to characterize this critical issue facing police and their communities (see Batton and Kadleck 2004). The most frequently used definition in the late 1990s included the word *solely*. Pursuant to this definition, police are prohibited from taking law enforcement actions (for example, stopping, questioning,

arresting, searching) based *solely* on a person's race or ethnicity.

The popularity of this definition has waned because stakeholders have recognized that it references a small (arguably *very* small) subgroup of incidents that might reflect bias on the part of police. Even a racially prejudiced officer likely uses more than the single factor of race when conducting biased law enforcement. For example, officers might make biased decisions based on the neighborhood and the race of the person, the age and the race of the person, or the gender and the race of the person. Activities based on these sample pairs of factors would fall outside this narrow definition of racial profiling. Moreover, one could interpret this common definition of racial profiling to exclude activities that are legally supportable in terms of reasonable suspicion or probable cause, but are nonetheless racially biased. Because the traditional definition only prohibits actions based *solely* on race, it does not encompass decisions based on reasonable suspicion or probable cause *plus* race. That is, this definition could be interpreted to exclude, for instance, officers' pulling over black traffic violators and not white *because* of race, or citing Hispanic, but not white, youth for noise violations *because* of race/ethnicity. Such disparate treatment would not necessarily be encompassed by a definition that referred to actions based "solely" on race, because the officers would have acted on the basis of reasonable suspicion or probable cause, as well as race.

Over time definitions have expanded and new terms have been introduced to reflect these expanded definitions. For instance, the Police Executive Research Forum (PERF; Fridell et al. 2001) introduced the term *racially biased policing* and defined it to encompass all incidents in which race/ethnicity is used inappropriately by officers in deciding with whom and how to intervene in a law enforcement capacity. Terms such as *bias-based policing* and *race-based policing* were also introduced, and definitions of the various terms included the following, which maintain that the negative behavior in question occurs when police use "race as a key factor in deciding whether to make a traffic stop" (Langan et al. 2001, 20). Another definition says ". . . police routinely use race as a negative signal that, along with an accumulation of other signals, causes an officer to react with suspicion" (Kennedy 1999, 11).

Police rely "on the race, ethnicity or national origin rather than the behavior of an individual or information that leads the police to a particular individual who has been identified as being, or having been, engaged in criminal activity" (Ramirez, McDevitt, and Farrell 2000, 3).

Agency Policies

When agencies formulate their policy on racial profiling, they adopt a definition so that they can tell officers when they can and cannot use race/ethnicity to make law enforcement decisions. There are significant differences of opinions regarding this issue and these views are reflected in the various policies that have been adopted around the nation to address racial profiling. While virtually no one believes officers should be allowed to use race/ethnicity as a *sole* basis to justify law enforcement action, beyond that consensus there are differences of opinion regarding the circumstances under which it is acceptable to use race and ethnicity as one factor among several to justify law enforcement action.

Many of the early policies (some still in effect) are based on the *solely* definition. These policies prohibit officers from using race/ethnicity as the sole basis for law enforcement actions (for example, make a stop, conduct a search, request for consent to search). For the reasons explained earlier, this policy does not place significant parameters on police use of race/ethnicity. The most restrictive policy model is commonly referred to as the "suspect-specific policy." Suspect-specific policies generally read as follows: *Officers may not consider the race or ethnicity of a person in the course of any law enforcement action unless the officer is seeking to detain, apprehend, or otherwise be on the lookout for a specific suspect sought in connection with a specific crime who has been identified or described in part by race or ethnicity.*

The key to this model is that the set of identifiers—which includes reference to race/ethnicity—must be linked to a particular suspect who is being sought for a particular crime. Thus, if reliable witnesses describe a convenience store robber as five feet, eight inches tall, lean, long haired, and Asian, *Asian* can be considered along with the other demographics and with other evidence in developing reasonable suspicion to detain or probable cause to arrest.

The law enforcement field has received very limited guidance from the U.S. Supreme Court regarding when race can and cannot be used to make law enforcement decisions. Constitutional parameters could emanate from either the Fourth or Fourteenth Amendments. The Fourth Amendment requires that detentions, arrests, and searches be "reasonable." The Fourteenth Amendment guarantees equal protection of the law. The U.S. Supreme Court has decided some isolated cases that pertain to the use of race to make law enforcement decisions (for example, *United States v. Brignoni-Ponce*) as have lower courts (for example, *U.S. v. Montero-Camargo*), but case law has not fully identified the circumstances when race/ethnicity can (and cannot) be used to support law enforcement actions.

Causes of Racial Profiling

Why might an officer misuse race/ethnicity information in deciding with whom and how to intervene in a law enforcement capacity? We referenced earlier the possibility that some officers have been trained to use race/ethnicity in a manner that some would argue is unjustified. Another answer is that the officer may be racist. That is, the officer may harbor animus toward minority groups and believe that these groups are a danger to society, in need of harsh treatment, unworthy of respect, and so forth. Some stakeholders alleging widespread racial profiling believe that the cause is widespread racism among the law enforcement profession. This narrow way of characterizing the potential causes has led to defensive reactions on the part of chiefs who deny widespread racism in policing.

With the help of social psychologists, the discussion of the potential "causes" of the misuse of race/ethnicity in law enforcement has broadened. Through lab experiments, social psychologists have determined that racial bias is still widespread in our society. Their research indicates that (1) people link minority status to criminal activity, and (2) this association affects perceptions and behavior (Eberhardt et al. 2004; Correll et al. 2002). This phenomenon has been referred to as *unconscious bias* because many subjects are not aware of the degree to which they link minorities to crime and many even test as "nonprejudiced." This science leads to another possible explanation for why an officer might misuse race/ethnicity. Some police (like people in any other profession) may not be fully cognizant of the extent to which race/ethnicity affects their perceptions and enters into their decision making.

Such a view has important ramifications for the potential of training to reduce the incidence of racial profiling. Some progressive training programs help police recognize the existence and power of unconscious bias and give them tools to ensure that those biases do not affect decisions.

Community and Police Perceptions of Racial Profiling

A December 1999 Gallup Poll showed that a majority of both whites and blacks surveyed believed that racial profiling on the part of police was prevalent. Fifty-six percent of the whites and 77% of the blacks believed the following practice was widespread: "police officers stopping motorists of certain racial and ethnic groups because the officers believe that these groups are more likely than others to commit certain types of crimes." (Data were not provided for other races/ethnicities.) A 2001 Gallup Poll indicated that 44% of blacks surveyed believed that "police have stopped them at some point in their life because of their race or ethnic background." Only 7% of the white respondents and 29% of the Hispanic respondents felt this way.

In 2001, more than a thousand executives from a stratified random sample of local and state law enforcement agencies completed surveys about this issue (Fridell et al. 2001). Items on the survey included the following:

- To what extent do you think "racial profiling/stereotyping" or racially biased policing is a problem in your jurisdiction?
- To what extent do the racial minority citizens in your jurisdiction think that "racial profiling/stereotyping" or biased policing is a problem in your jurisdiction?

The results indicated that—at least at the time the survey was completed—law enforcement administrators for the most part did not believe that "'racial profiling/stereotyping' or racially biased policing" was a serious problem in their jurisdictions, and they believed that the racial minority citizens in their areas would generally agree with them. While no subsequent survey has been conducted to empirically assess changes in agency executive views, there are indications that during the past few years, law enforcement leaders have increasingly perceived racial profiling and the perceptions of racial profiling to be a significant issue with which they must deal. This is indicated by the actions they have taken to address these issues as listed in the next section.

Police Response

Agencies have responded to the issue of racial profiling and the perception of its practice in the following ways:

- Adopting antibiased policing policy
- Training officers not to engage in racial profiling
- Modifying recruitment and hiring in an attempt to hire officers who can act in an unbiased fashion and officers who reflect the racial/ethnic makeup of the jurisdiction
- Enhancing supervision and accountability methods
- Reaching out to diverse communities to discuss racial bias and to improve police–minority relationships
- Collecting data on the stops made by police

Interestingly, data collection has been a particularly popular response as indicated by the number of state-level legislative enactments requiring data collection on the part of police and by the unknown number of agencies voluntarily collecting data. The agencies involved in data collection require officers to report information on each targeted stop. Most agencies are collecting data for just traffic-related stops or for all vehicle stops (the latter includes traffic-related stops and crime-related stops of vehicles). The information collected by officers includes the race/ethnicity of the driver and other information about the driver (for example, age, gender) and the stop (for example, reasons for the stop, disposition of the stop, whether a search was conducted, outcome of the search). A major debate centers on whether the data collected on police stops can indicate whether a police department is or is not engaged in racial profiling.

To draw definitive conclusions regarding police–citizen contact data that indicate disproportionate engagement of racial/ethnic minorities, a researcher needs to be able to identify and disentangle the impact of race from legitimate factors that might reasonably explain individual and aggregated decisions to stop, search, and otherwise engage people. In an attempt to rule out alternative factors, researchers strive to develop comparison groups against which to evaluate their police–citizen contact data. Agencies strive to develop comparison groups ("benchmark" groups) that most closely reflect the demographic makeup of groups at risk of being stopped by police *assuming no bias*. For example, a department collecting data on traffic stops would, ideally, want to compare the demographics of those stopped by police for a traffic violation with the demographics of those people legitimately at risk of a stop, taking into consideration numerous factors, including, but not limited to, driving quantity, driving quality, and driving location.

Many agencies that are collecting data are analyzing their data using relatively weak benchmarks. For instance, many agencies are conducting "census benchmarking" whereby the analyst compares the demographic profile of drivers stopped by police to the U.S. Census Bureau demographic profile of jurisdiction residents. This is a weak benchmark because the group of people who reside in a jurisdiction do not reflect the group of people who are at legitimate risk of being stopped by police. Not all people who are stopped by police live in the jurisdiction and not everyone who lives in the jurisdiction drives the same amount or violates traffic laws at the same rates.

Researchers and practitioners are struggling to identify methods for developing valid comparison groups. As yet, there is no consensus on what might be the most cost-effective and valid benchmark(s). Some jurisdiction teams are comparing the demographic profiles of persons stopped with the demographic profiles of licensed drivers, people involved in vehicle crashes, or persons observed to be driving in the jurisdiction. In jurisdictions with cameras that record the license plates of vehicles running red lights (a "color-blind" form of enforcement), the demographic profile of the owners (unfortunately, not the *drivers, necessarily*) of those vehicles can be compared with the profile of persons stopped by police. Similarly, radar stops can be a color-blind form of enforcement allowing agencies to compare the demographic profile of citizens stopped with radar to the demographic profile of citizens stopped without radar. Jurisdictions can also rely on internal comparisons—comparing the profiles of people stopped by individual officers or units to the corresponding data for other officers or units that are "matched" in terms of their assignments (for example, beat, shift). Resident surveys can be used to collect data, not only on the extent to which residents are stopped by police but also on the nature and extent of their driving. Corresponding to the data that police collect on their own activities, the survey could solicit information from the respondents regarding the frequency and nature of their encounters with the police. Corresponding to benchmarking efforts for department-collected stop data, such a survey could ask the residents about the nature (for example, speed, passing behavior, driving violations), location (for example, interstate highways, around their neighborhood), and amount of their driving.

The Impact of September 11, 2001

The terrorist attacks on September 11, 2001, had several impacts on how people in the United States conceived of racial profiling. Prior to the attacks the discussion about racial profiling focused primarily on the treatment of blacks and Hispanics. Following 9/11, the focus expanded to include people of Arab descent and Muslims. While many people in the United States recognized the potential to racially profile people of Arab descent and Muslims, they also reconsidered the extent to which racial profiling was bad and, accordingly, revised their views about when it was and was not

appropriate to use race/ethnicity to make law enforcement decisions. As one manifestation of this changed view—a change made in the context of a national crisis and citizens' associated fears—a Gallup Poll conducted soon after the terrorist attacks indicated that 71% of black respondents favored intense scrutiny of Arabs boarding airplanes.

LORIE A. FRIDELL

See also **Abuse of Authority by Police; Community Attitudes toward the Police; Discrimination; Minorities and the Police**

References and Further Reading

Batton, C., and C. Kadleck. 2004. Theoretical and methodological issues in racial profiling research. *Police Quarterly* 7 (1): 30–64.

Cleary, J. 2000. Racial profiling studies in law enforcement: Issues and methodology. St. Paul: Minnesota House of Representatives, Research Department.

Correll, J., B. Park, C. Judd, and B. Wittenbrink. 2002. The police officer's dilemma: Using ethnicity to disambiguate potentially threatening individuals. *Journal of Personality and Social Psychology* 83: 1314–29.

Eberhardt, J. L., P. A. Goff, V. J. Purdie, and P. G. Davies. 2004. Seeing black: Race, crime, and visual processing. *Journal of Personality and Social Psychology* 87 (6).

Fridell, L. 2004. *By the numbers: A guide for analyzing race data from vehicle stops.* Washington, DC: Police Executive Research Forum.

Fridell, L., R. Lunney, D. Diamond, and B. Kubu. 2001. *Racially biased policing: A principled response.* Washington, DC: Police Executive Research Forum.

Kennedy, R. 1999. Suspect policy. *The New Republic*, 13 (Sept. 30): 30.

Langan, P. A., L. A. Greenfeld, S. K. Smith, M. R. Durose, and D. J. Levin. 2001. *Contacts between the police and the public: Findings from the 1999 National Survey.* DOJ No. NCJ184957. Washington, DC: Bureau of Justice Statistics, U.S. Department of Justice.

Northwestern University Racial Profiling Data Collection Resource Center. http://www.racialprofilinganalysis.neu.edu.

Ramirez, D., J. McDevitt, and A. Farrell. 2000. *A resource guide on racial profiling data collection systems: Promising practices and lessons learned.* DOJ No. NCJ 184768.

Washington, DC: Bureau of Justice Statistics, U.S. Department of Justice.

United States v. Brignoni-Ponce, 422 U.S. 873, 1975.

United States v. Montero-Camargo, 208 F. 3d 1122, 9th Circuit Court of Appeals.

Walker, S., C. Spohn, and M. DeLone. 1996. *The color of justice: Race, ethnicity and crime in America.* New York: Wadsworth Publishing Company.

RACKETEER INFLUENCED AND CORRUPT ORGANIZATIONS ACT (RICO)

Introduction: Intent and Scope of RICO

The Racketeer Influenced and Corrupt Organizations Act (RICO), 18 U.S.C. §1962 et seq., was enacted by the U.S. Congress as part of Title IX of the Organized Crime Control Act of 1970 to eradicate organized crime and to combat the infiltration of legitimate businesses and labor unions by organized crime. Due to its liberal application, however, criminal RICO has been used not just against organized crime but against other illegal activities, including white collar crime, government corruption, and prostitution rings.

In addition to criminal prosecution, RICO permits the government to bring a civil action seeking equitable relief in a form of dissolution of an enterprise, restriction of future activities by the defendant, or divestiture of the defendant's interest in the enterprise. 18 U.S.C. §1963. Although the burden of proof in a criminal RICO action is high because the government must prove each element beyond a reasonable doubt, the burden of proof in a civil RICO action is lower at a preponderance of evidence. Thus, civil RICO actions can also be an effective way for the government to cripple organized crime. Additionally, a private person injured in his business or property by a RICO violation may file a civil action and seek treble damages, costs, and attorney's fees. 18 U.S.C. §1964(c).

States have also adopted their own anti-racketeering laws. However, state anti-racketeering laws vary from the federal version and from state to state. This chapter will focus mainly on federal criminal RICO actions.

RICO Violations and Elements of the Offense

There are four enumerated RICO violations in 18 U.S.C. §1962. Subsection (a) of §1962 prohibits a person or entity from using income derived from a pattern of racketeering activity or collection of an unlawful debt to acquire an interest in an enterprise engaged in or affecting interstate or foreign commerce. Subsection (b) prohibits a person or entity from acquiring an interest in an enterprise engaged in or affecting interstate or foreign commerce by way of a pattern of racketeering activity or collection of an unlawful debt. Subsection (c) prohibits a person or entity associated with an enterprise engaged in or affecting interstate or foreign commerce from conducting or participating "directly or indirectly, in the conduct of such enterprise's affairs through a pattern of racketeering activity or collection of an unlawful debt." Subsection (d) prohibits a person or entity from conspiring to commit any of the three prohibitions just listed.

The majority of the criminal RICO cases are charged under subsections (c) and (d) of §1962, and thus it is worthwhile reviewing the elements of those subsections in more detail. To establish the elements of a RICO violation under subsection (c), the government must prove that (1) an enterprise existed; (2) the enterprise affected interstate or foreign commerce; (3) the defendant associated with the enterprise; (4) the defendant participated, directly or indirectly, in the conduct of the affairs of the enterprise; and (5) the defendant participated in the enterprise through a pattern of racketeering activity by committing at least two racketeering (predicate) acts within a ten-year period. *U.S. v. Darden* 70 F. 3d 1507, 1518 (8th Cir. 1995).

To establish the charge of conspiracy under subsection (d) of §1962, the government must prove that (1) an enterprise existed; (2) the enterprise affected interstate or foreign commerce; (3) the defendant associated with the enterprise; and (4) the defendant "objectively manifested an agreement to participate in the affairs of the enterprise" through a pattern of racketeering activity. *Id.* It is not necessary for the government to prove that the defendant entered into an explicit agreement. The government can demonstrate merely that there was a tacit understanding between the parties. A tacit understanding may be shown entirely through the circumstantial evidence of defendant's actions. *Id.*

The government must obtain an indictment within five years of the last predicate act or racketeering activity under RICO. Thus, a criminal RICO prosecution would be barred if the last predicate act or racketeering activity was committed more than five years prior to the indictment.

What Constitutes a Pattern of Racketeering Activity?

A wide range of state and federal crimes constitutes a predicate act or racketeering activity under RICO as delineated in §1961 subsection (1). State crimes that can constitute racketeering activity under RICO are an act or threat involving murder, kidnapping, gambling, arson, robbery, bribery, extortion, dealing in obscene matter, or trafficking a controlled substance or chemical.

Federal offenses that can constitute racketeering activity include offenses indictable under Title 18 of the United States Code and specifically listed in §1961(1)(B), such as bribery, counterfeiting, theft from interstate shipment, embezzlement from pension and welfare funds, mail fraud, wire fraud, falsifying citizenship or naturalization, or obstruction of justice. Federal offenses under Title 29 relating to payments and loans to labor organizations or embezzlement from union funds may also constitute racketeering activity. Other offenses that can qualify as racketeering activity are (1) any offense involving fraud connected with a case under Title 11; (2) any act that is indictable under the Currency and Foreign Transactions Reporting Act; (3) a violation of the Immigration and Nationality Act for financial gain; and (4) any act indictable under any provision listed in 18 U.S.C. §2332b(g)(5)(B) relating to terrorism.

RICO does not apply to one predicate act or racketeering activity. A defendant in a RICO case must have committed a "pattern" of racketeering activity, which consists of at minimum two acts of racketeering activity committed within ten years of each other. However, under case law, the two acts of racketeering activity cannot be isolated acts but rather they must be both related and amount to a continuous criminal activity. This is referred to as the "continuity plus relationship" test. Thus, to prove a pattern of racketeering activity the government must show that (1) the predicate acts or racketeering activities are related and (2) they amount to or pose a threat of continued criminal activity.

Predicate acts or racketeering activities are related if they have "the same or similar purposes, results, participants, victims, or methods of commission, or otherwise are interrelated by distinguishing characteristics." *H.J. Inc. v. Northwestern Bell Telephone Co.* 492 U.S. 229, 240 (1989). A pattern under RICO cannot be established by sporadic activities such as two widely separated and isolated criminal offenses.

The government may show "continuity over a closed period by proving a series of related predicates extending over a substantial period of time. Predicate acts extending over a few weeks or months and threatening no future criminal conduct do not satisfy this requirement: Congress was concerned in RICO with long term criminal conduct." *Id.*, at 242. If continuity cannot be established by proving a series of related predicates over a substantial and closed period of time, the government must show that there is a threat of continuity. *Id.* A RICO pattern may be established if the related predicates themselves include a specific threat of repetition extending into the future; for example, extortion and threat of future extortion on a regular basis have a threat of continuity. The threat of continuity is also established by showing that the predicate acts are part of the entity's regular way of doing business. *Id.*, at 242–243.

What Is an Enterprise Engaged in or Affecting Interstate or Foreign Commerce?

Under RICO, an " 'enterprise' includes any individual, partnership, corporation, association, or other legal entity, and any union or group of individuals associated in fact although not a legal entity." 18 U.S.C. §1961(4). To prove the existence of an enterprise in the majority of the federal circuits, the government must prove that the enterprise had a common purpose, a formal or informal organization of the participants in which they functioned as a unit, and an ascertainable structure. *U.S. v. Darden* 70 F. 3d 1507, 1518 (8th Cir. 1995).

In addition to the entities statutorily identified under RICO, courts have held that an enterprise may also include government units such as a judicial office, police department, state legislature, fire department, office of the prosecuting attorney, and state department of transportation.

RICO also requires that the enterprise engages in or affects interstate or foreign commerce. This requires minimal interstate or foreign activity, and in the case of interstate commerce, it would be sufficient to show interstate travel, buying equipment made in another state, and making or receiving interstate telephone calls.

Criminal Penalties

RICO provides for drastic remedies in the form of severe criminal penalties and forfeiture of illegal proceeds. A defendant found guilty of violating RICO can be imprisoned for up to twenty years or "for life if the violation is based on a racketeering activity for which the maximum penalty includes life imprisonment." §1963(a). Additionally, the court can order the defendant to pay a fine in the amount of twice the gross profits made from a RICO violation and to forfeit to the United States any interest in an enterprise that was the subject of the RICO case. §1963(a).

ALICE H. CHOI

See also **White Collar Crime**

References and Further Reading

Floyd, John E. 1998. *RICO state by state: A guide to litigation under the state racketeering statutes*. American Bar Association: Section of Antitrust Law.

Higgins, Amy L. 2005. Pimpin' ain't easy under the Eleventh Circuit's broad RICO enterprise standard: *United States v. Pipkins. University of Cincinnati Law Review* 73:1648–64.

Marcus, Paul. 2005. *Prosecution and defense of criminal conspiracy cases*. Matthew Bender & Co.

Ragland, Steven P. 2001. Using the master's tools: Fighting persistent police misconduct with civil RICO. *American University Law Review* 51: 139–77.

Sacks, M., T. Coale, and L. Goldberg. 2005. Twentieth survey of white collar crime: Racketeer influenced and corrupt organizations. *American Criminal Law Review* 42: 825–75.

Welling, S., S. Beale, and P. Bucy. 1998. *Federal criminal law and related actions: Crimes, forfeitures, the false claims act and RICO.* St. Paul, MN: West Group.

Wentzel, Suzanne. 1995. *National Organization for Women v. Scheidler*: RICO a valuable tool for controlling violent protest. *Akron Law Review* 28: 391–408.

H. J. Inc. v. Northwestern Bell Telephone Co. 492 U.S. 229, 109 S. Ct. 2893, 106 L. Ed. 2d 195 (1989).

U.S. v. Darden 70 F. 3d 1507 (8th Cir. 1995).

RADELET, LOUIS A.

Louis A. Radelet was born in Green Bay, Wisconsin, on December 10, 1917. He attended the University of Notre Dame where he earned his undergraduate degree and an MSW. He taught there before moving to New York City to work with the National Conference of Christians and Jews. In the mid-1950s, he came to the Michigan State School of Police Administration, as it was then known. He established the infrastructure of colleagueship, thinking, and feeling that emerged as the major movement designed to transform American policing. He died in 1991 having only had a glimpse of the ramifying power of his influence.

His many contributions to the thinking of many of the major figures in the field of criminal justice are beyond easy elaboration. These include his publications, his tolerance of eccentricities, and his invitation to and hosting of speakers such as Michael Banton, Richard Myren, James Q. Wilson, and David Bordua. He also nurtured the hopes of marginalized officers throughout the Midwest, people of color, females—bright and innovative officers and other visionaries who rallied together yearly at his Police and Community Relations (PCR) conferences first held in East Lansing in 1955. Because he was both kind and generous, his good humor and gentility almost endless, his intense focus on doing the right thing and his burning sense of obligation to the collective good were sometimes overlooked. He saw through falseness and pretensions with uncanny wisdom. His ability to bring out the best in people was unrivaled.

Radelet fashioned his own view of policing and its obligations from the ground up, not from the then-scant literature. He relied on his acute and abiding commitment to democratic values. These, for him, were not the narrow pseudo-legalistic and positivistic standards that were emerging in the 1970s. He integrated conceptions of fairness, justice, and equal access to service into the standard views of "professional policing." He assembled in his own vision the vast chaotic, uneven, and proscriptive literature in what became, in part through his influence, the field of criminal justice. He was a *bricoleur,* picking up bits and pieces of ideas when others were still opting for the positivism of the social sciences, or the simple (still popular) idea that vicious attacks on minorities masquerading as "crime crackdowns" and attention to "hot spots" were the route to social order. He argued that there could be no social order under a crime-focused police. According to Radelet, the way to reduce crime was to increase justice.

The turning point of Radelet's career, and indeed of the field, was the rebellious outbursts in the late 1960s in Detroit, Los Angeles, and other cities, and the dramatic Kerner Report (1968) and the Report of the Presidents' Crime Commission (1968). At this time, Radelet seized the opportunity to carry out some sponsored research. He had the help of the Chief of Police in Toledo, Ohio, a young graduate student, Robert Wasserman, and funding from the Law Enforcement Assistance Administration (LEAA). Police and community relations (PCR) was dismissed in most police departments as code for "giving in to minorities." The Toledo project was intended to make PCR the deep commitment of every officer in practice, rather than an isolated and unrewarded concern of a few officers. This project was not realized, but it was the first serious attempt to implement what was later christened "community policing." This idea of police reform that addressed the divide between "two societies, black and white" and the conditions that produce violence and hatred began to be woven into the rhetoric of policing. It is far too early to say whether and to what degree they altered police practice.

Michigan State University created an undergraduate program in police administration and graduated its first class in 1938. In time, Radelet became its moral and intellectual leader. In part as a result of his quiet stewardship, it could grant a Ph.D. after 1969, and was renamed the School of Criminal Justice in 1970. In those days, the school was seen as a bit too applied even for a land-grant university. The Ph.D. program, with its associated research impetus, brought to the surface a long-running tension between "academics" and "professionals" within the school. In fact, some faculty were both, some were one and not the other, and some were neither. The transition from General Arthur Brandstatter to George Felkenes and later to Robert C. Trojanowicz was toward a research-based school. As the critical mass of Ph.D.-trained researchers grew, Radelet mediated between the lawyers, political scientists, and practice-oriented colleagues to produce a grounding for and clarify the mission of the school. It was grounded on shared values, not on publication, research, or even disciplinary pedigrees. The students and young Ph.D. faculty of the school in the late 1970s are among the present leaders in criminal justice.

Radelet (he pronounced it "Radlet" not "Radlay") wrote the first scholarly book intended to speak to the police as holding a convent of trust—to assess trust, to be trustworthy, to represent trust—*Police and the Community* (1973). This book was a very new kind of text—not a proscriptive laundry list; not a pleading assemblage of tasks and exhortations; not full of "war stories" passing as systematic knowledge. It was a creative and wholly original effort to imagine a field. The book remains a best–seller. He wrote it in his basement, mobilizing tidy piles of notes, reprints, typescripts, and mimeos for each chapter. His lust for detail was as extraordinary as was his assessment of people. The book was finished before the American Society of Criminology (ASC) became a major force, before the Academy of Criminal Justice Sciences (ACJS) was assembled, before there was a national stage for policing. This was a move to reshape "the job" from a craft to a kind of knowledge-based work.

Because Radelet was a deeply committed person, he made some academics uneasy. He radiated intensity. He knew his position, he knew why he took it, and he said so if necessary. Nevertheless, as might be expected, others who grew under his direct influence took credit awkwardly and incompletely for his ideas. Lacking his depth and insight, they bowdlerized them. Ironically, his originality became the cant of superficial followers in later years and the conventional rhetorical wisdom of the last fifteen. These ideas, principles of a kind, include the following:

- The social distance of police from their public(s) is problematic and not to be assumed or maintained exclusively by threat or violence.
- Fairness and justice must be done and seen to be done.
- Police organizations are neither just nor fair in their own internal operations.
- The criteria for success of police should be the absence of crime and the presence of orderliness.
- The police should be held accountable and responsible for their actions and words.
- The police and the community are essentially mirror images of each other.

A further irony of his gracious and lively career is that as those who followed his lead became seduced by the rhetoric of his vision as they imagined it, the conventional wisdom of the police elites and their admirers transmogrified the above principles. The present generation sees his ideas as a shadow, not in their elegant shape as principles.

In many ways, Radelet must be counted with those who shaped the field of criminal justice—he stands with practitioners Vollmer and O. W. Wilson, with scholars such as Banton, Wilson, Bittner, and Westley, and with other fine teachers.

PETER K. MANNING

See also **Accountability; Attitudes toward the Police: Overview; Community-Oriented Policing: Practices; Minorities and the Police**

References and Further Reading

Brandstatter, A. F. and Louis A. Radelet, eds. 1968. *Police and community relations: A sourcebook*. Beverly Hills, CA: Glencoe Press.

Radelet, Louis A., and Hoyt Coe Reed. 1973. *The police and the community*. Beverly Hills, CA: Glencoe Press.

REISS, ALBERT J., JR.

Best known for his concepts of "proactive" vs. "reactive" mobilization of police action, Albert John Reiss, Jr., was a criminologist who pioneered the use of systematic research methods to study the causes and consequences of police behavior.

Born in Cascade, Wisconsin, on December 9, 1922, Reiss received his Ph.D. in sociology from the University of Chicago in 1949, where he taught before moving successively to Vanderbilt, Wisconsin, and Michigan. He served Yale University as the William Graham Sumner Professor of Sociology for a quarter-century. After completing major contributions of widely cited research on juvenile delinquency, Reiss began field observations of police work with the Detroit and Chicago Police Departments in 1963 and 1964, respectively. It was during these patrols that he developed his conceptual framework on the mobilization of the police.

Reiss described police patrol as primarily "reactive" in the sense that it is directed to tasks generated by people, such as crime victims, who are located outside of the organization. Reiss contrasted the most common form of police work with police-initiated detection of crimes, or "proactive" law enforcement. These terms spread like wildfire after they were first published in the mid-1960s (Bordua and Reiss 1966; Reiss and Bordua 1967), first among academic social scientists, then among police officials themselves, and finally to business, military, and organizational strategy. (This concept was not only new to police work. It was also new to the English language. On that basis, the *American Sociological Review* refused to print the article later published by the *American Journal of Sociology* in 1966, saying that the authors could not use the word *proactive* because it did not exist in the English language. The Oxford English Dictionary [1989, Vol. XII, 533 now credits Reiss with the first printed usage of the word.)

The importance of these concepts for policing derived from Reiss's (1971a) crucial observation about the legitimacy of police work, as well as its potential for corruption. When citizens mobilize police, as Reiss showed, officers encounter less violent resistance than when they enter a social setting uninvited by any of the citizen-participants. Mobilization decisions against such "victimless" criminals as drug dealers and gamblers, usually made internally by the government, offer greater potential for corruption. Without a citizen complainant, Reiss said, it is difficult to detect the fact that enforcement operations have ceased upon payment of a bribe.

In 1965, President Lyndon Johnson's Commission on Law Enforcement and Administration of Justice asked Reiss to undertake a major study of patterns of police contact with citizens in major metropolitan areas. Using the systematic social observation approach previously used only in laboratory settings (Reiss, 1971b), Reiss led the first quantitative field study of police encounters with citizens. In the summer of 1966, his team of thirty-six observers working in Boston, Chicago, and Washington, D.C., filled out observation forms on 5,360 mobilizations of the police—of which 81% were reactive—compiling detailed data on how police interacted with 11,255 citizens.

These data led to the first precise estimates on such key questions as how often citizens assault police and in what kind of circumstances, how often police use illegal force against citizens, whether black officers are less likely to use excessive force against black citizens than white officers (they were not), and the correlates of arrest decisions (see Reiss 1968). This work also contributed to a broader understanding of the reciprocal nature of respect and legitimacy in police–citizen encounters (Reiss 1971a). The research method became the gold standard for describing police conduct, with other social scientists replicating it with National Science Foundation support in 1977 (see Smith 1986) and with National Institute of Justice funding in 1995–96 (see Mastrofski, Reisig, and Snipes 2002). Access to the database has allowed many other researchers to publish analyses of the data, notably including Donald Black (1980) and Robert Freidrich (1977, 1980).

Reiss also developed the conceptual framework for understanding police strategies for "soft" versus "hard" crime (Reiss 1985), which was later used in the development of computerized crime mapping and hot-spot patrol practices (Sherman and Weisburd 1995). His work explored the view of police from the perspective of crime victims such as small business owners, who depend heavily on police in order to stay in business (Reiss 1969).

Perhaps the most significant contribution Albert Reiss made to policing has yet to be fully appreciated. His National Academy of Sciences review of patterns of co-offending in criminal careers (Reiss 1988) posed a major challenge to police organizations. It suggested the great importance of mapping the social networks of co-arrestees, identifying a small number of criminals who recruit a high percentage of all offenders into committing their first crime. The incarceration of such "Typhoid Marys," if found, could reduce the spread of "infection" of criminal events, and reduce the crime rate. The implication of Reiss's work on this subject is that police could do much more to reduce crime by focusing on such recruiters.

In addition to his own research, Reiss trained and advised the largest generation of police researchers so far produced in the Western world, either as graduate students or as leaders of research projects on which Reiss served as an adviser. He played key roles in overseeing the design of police research at both the (U.S.) Police Foundation and the National Institute of Justice. That research included the multicity Spouse Assault Replication Project or SARP (Sherman 1992), the multicity Drug Market Analysis Program or DMAP (see, for example, Weisburd and Green 1995), and the research program on deadly force by police.

In his writing for the latter program, he critiqued the widely held view of police shootings as "split-second decisions" made "only at the last minute when the citizen failed to heed all warnings" (Reiss 1980, 127). He urged all research projects to focus on the fundamental starting point in the sequence of decisions leading to police use of deadly force: the broader context of all policies and practices governing police operations. If that context lacks policies for structured alternatives that can de-escalate confrontations, such as waiting out a hostage situation, then the "final frame" of the sequence may have been determined well in advance by that context.

Reiss was elected president of both the American Society of Criminology, which honored him with its Sutherland Award, and the International Society of Criminology, which honored him with its Prix Durkheim. A *festschrift* honored his career with assessments of his contributions by leading criminologists (Waring and Weisburd 2002), and a distinguished scholarship prize named after him was established in 1996 by the American Sociological Association.

LAWRENCE W. SHERMAN

See also **Theories of Policing**

References and Further Reading

Black, Donald. 1980. *Manners and customs of the police.* New York: Academic Press.

Bordua, David J., and Albert J. Reiss, Jr. 1966. Command, control and charisma: reflections on police bureaucracy. *American Journal of Sociology* 72: 68–76.

Freidrich, Robert J. 1977. The impact of organizational, individual and situational factors on police behavior. Ph.D. diss., University of Michigan.

Mastrofski, Stephen D., Michael Reisig, and J. B. Snipes. 2002. Police disrespect toward the public: An encounter-based analysis. *Criminology* 40: 519–51.

Reiss, Albert J., Jr. 1968. Police brutality: Answers to key questions. *Transaction* 5: 10–19.

———. 1969. Appendix A—field survey. In *Crime against small business: A report of the Small Business Administration transmitted to the Select Committee on Small Business, United States Senate,* 53–143.

———. 1971a. *The police and the public.* New Haven, CT: Yale University Press.

———. 1971b. Systematic observation of natural social phenomena. In *Sociological methodology,* ed. Herbert Costner, 3–33. San Francisco: Jossey-Bass.

———. 1980. Controlling police use of deadly force. *Annals of the American Academy of Political and Social Science* 452: 122–34.

———. 1985. *Policing a city's central district: The Oakland story.* Washington, DC: National Institute of Justice.

———. 1988. Co-offending and criminal careers. In *Crime and justice: A review of research,* vol. 10, ed. Michael Tonry and Norval Morris, 117–70. Chicago: University of Chicago Press.

Reiss, Albert J., Jr., and David J. Bordua. 1967. Environment and organization: A perspective on police. In *The police: Six sociological essays,* ed. David J. Bordua, 25–55. New York: Wiley.

Sherman, Lawrence. 1992. *Policing domestic violence: Experiments and dilemmas.* New York: The Free Press.

Sherman, Lawrence, and David Weisburd. 1995. General deterrent effects of police patrol in crime "hot spots": A randomized, controlled trial. *Justice Quarterly* 12: 625–48.

Smith, Douglas A. 1986. The neighborhood context of police behavior. In *Communities and crime,* 313–41. Vol. 8 of *Crime and justice: A review of research,* ed. Albert J. Reiss, Jr., and Michael Tonry. Chicago: University of Chicago Press.

Waring, Elin, and David Weisburd, eds. 2002. *Crime & social organization: Essay in honor of Albert J. Reiss, Jr., Advances in Criminological Theory,* 10. New Brunswick: Transaction.

Weisburd, David, and Lorraine Green. 1995. Policing drug hot spots: The Jersey City drug market analysis experiment. *Justice Quarterly* 12: 711–35.

REPEAT OFFENDER PROGRAMS

National trends of recidivism indicate that more than 60% of the 650,000 prisoners released each year will be rearrested within three years of their release (Bureau of Justice Statistics [BJS] 2002). Recidivism is generally defined as the commission of a new criminal act by individuals previously incarcerated for an earlier criminal act (Maxwell 2005). The Bureau of Justice Statistics measures recidivism in three ways: rearrest within three years of exiting a correctional facility, reconviction within three years of exiting a correctional facility, and reincarceration within three years of exiting a correctional facility. To recidivate, an individual must either commit a new crime or commit a technical violation of their parole (BJS 2002).

Recidivism is a very complex issue. Correctional programs are assumed to be working effectively if the recidivism rate is low, based on the principles of deterrence and, to some extent, rehabilitation (MacKenzie 2000). If a given correctional program is an effective deterrent to future criminal behavior, then its recidivism rate will be low. Moreover, correctional programs are frequently assessed for cost effectiveness based on their recidivism rate (Maxwell 2005). Thomas (2005), however, maintains that correctional facilities cannot be held fully responsible for recidivism rates because behavior of the offenders is influenced by other factors (that is, social, economic).

A myriad of explanations are given to explain high recidivism rates. Individual factors include types of offenses committed, demographics, and societal factors. Research has indicated that property offenders are the most likely to recidivate with a rearrest rate of 73.8%. Drug offenders are rearrested at a rate of 66.7%. Lastly, violent offenders are rearrested at a rate of 61.7% (BJS 2002). Interestingly, Wilson (2005) has found that length of sentence is inversely related to reincarceration. Attributes linked to low recidivism rates include inmates who are older (a maturation effect), female, high school graduates, and those not convicted of property crimes (BJS 2002). Research by Austin and Hardyman (2004) links community characteristics to recidivism rates. They maintain, "community attributes have at least an equal if not greater impact on prisoner recidivism and public safety than the characteristics of the individuals released from prison" (p. 18). They further cite social disorganization studies to support their stance, and argue that residential instability and unemployment are related to high crime rates and violence, thus leading to the obvious conclusion that higher crime rates are associated with higher incarceration rates (Austin and Hardyman 2004).

Wilson (2005) asserts that recidivism rates do not reflect the commission of new crimes, but rather they reflect technical violations of parole conditions. In an analysis of Tennessee Department of Corrections data covering a span of seven years, Wilson found that a fourth of offenders were reincarcerated on the basis of the commission of a new crime, while roughly 75% were reincarcerated on the basis of technical parole violations. He concludes that parole violations are randomly enforced and vague in definition. Austin and Hardyman (2004) analyzed data from the Texas Department of Corrections and found that parolees accounted for 2.2% of all arrests.

In their analysis of Pennsylvania Department of Corrections data, they found that prisoners who were released without parole conditions had lower recidivism rates.

Reductions in recidivism have been attributed to certain characteristics of correctional programs. MacKenzie (2000) analyzed a variety of correctional programs and policies on their effectiveness in the reduction of recidivism. Only programs that met scientific rigor were used to assess effectiveness in her analysis. She found that rehabilitation programs utilizing multiple treatment modalities (that is, cognitive, behavioral, developmental) that focus on changing the behavior of the offender have been associated with the reduction of recidivism. Cognitive-behavioral therapy has also been effective in the reduction of recidivism, more specifically therapies that focus on changing the offender's thoughts and attitudes. Common methods to achieve this goal include moral development and problem solving. MacKenzie asserts that vocational education programs have been shown to reduce recidivism as well (MacKenzie 2000). Other studies have shown that offenders who obtain a G.E.D. or the equivalency while in prison are less likely to return to prison than those who do not participate in G.E.D. programs. This appears to be particularly true of those offenders under the age of 21 (Nutall, Hollmen, and Staley 2003).

MacKenzie (2000) also examined correctional programs that are not effective in the reduction of recidivism. Her analysis reveals that shock probation and Scared Straight Programs, as well as correctional boot camps are not as effective in the reduction of recidivism rates as earlier supported. Programs with unstructured counseling or those that increase supervision within the community (that is, intensive probation, home confinement) have also been relatively ineffective in the reduction of recidivism (MacKenzie 2000).

Still other research suggests that intensive supervision programs can be effective if they embrace certain characteristics. Paparozzi and Gendreau (2005) note that "intensive supervision programs that provide more treatment to high-risk offenders, employ parole officers with balanced law enforcement/social casework orientations, and are implemented in supportive organizational environments may reduce recidivism from 10% to 30% depending on the comparison being made" (p. 445).

Lowenkamp, Latessa, and Holsinger (2006) assessed the risk principle used in certain programs and its effect on recidivism. The risk principle, which states that the level of supervision should be proportionate with the level of risk of the offender, requires that high-risk offenders receive high levels of supervision. Furthermore, programs that target high-risk offenders are thought to be more effective in the reduction of recidivism than those programs that do not. Their analysis revealed that residential programs are more effective in the reduction of recidivism than nonresidential programs. In addition, programs that utilize cognitive-behavioral or behavioral treatment modalities are more effective in recidivism reduction than those that employ other treatment modalities. Offenders who are at higher risk have lower recidivism rates if they are provided more services and are required to stay in programming longer. They concluded that the placement of low-risk offenders in highly structured and controlling supervision programs actually increases recidivism rates. Curiously, their findings suggest that very few correctional programs adhere to the risk principle when considering services to be provided. Those that do employ the risk principle, however, are more effective in the reduction of recidivism than those that do not utilize the risk principle (Lowenkamp et al. 2006).

Governmental actions to reduce recidivism rates include the Serious and Violent Offender Reentry Initiative and the Second Chance Act of 2005 (H. R. 1704). The U.S. Department of Justice and the Office of Justice Programs developed the Serious and Violent Offender Reentry Initiative (SVORI) in 2002. This initiative is an effort to coordinate federal partners to address recidivism among juvenile and adult populations of high-risk offenders. This initiative provides funding to develop and enhance reentry strategies. SVORI initially awarded $100 million in grants to sixty-nine state agencies. Initiative goals include the development of model reentry programs to aid offenders in their transition from correctional facilities to communities. This initiative encompasses three phases of reentry: institution-based programs, community-based transition programs, and long-term community-based programs. Services to be provided during the institution-based phase include education, mental health and substance abuse treatment, job training, mentoring, and risk assessment.

Services to be provided during the community-based transition phase include education, monitoring, mentoring, life skills training, assessment, job placement, and mental health and substance abuse treatment. During the long-term community-based phase, programs are expected to provide individuals with a network of social service agencies and community-based organizations in order to sustain services and mentoring (Office of Justice Programs, n.d.).

Winterfield and Lindquist (2005) reported characteristics of SVORI programming in 2005, with all eighty-nine of the SVORI programs surveyed. Eighty percent of programs focused on "serious and violent" offenders with roughly 11% focusing on a subset of offenders. Most programs reported that they attempted to provide all needed services as opposed to a specific or more narrowly defined set of services. Primary services included employment, community integration, and family support/unification.

Lindquist assessed sustainability efforts of SVORI programming in 2005. That assessment suggests that efforts to sustain programs developed through SVORI funding appear to be promising. Most (94%) program directors indicate that SVORI programming is worth continuing, and 98% indicated that SVORI programming is helpful to the targeted population. Nearly all (94%) program directors agree that communication and information gathering among partnering agencies has improved. Lastly, 89% of program directors indicated that they plan to continue programs developed through SVORI.

In an effort to continue efforts promoted by the Serious and Violent Offender Reentry Initiative, the Second Chance Act of 2005 (H. R. 1704) was introduced in the U.S. House of Representatives in April 2005. The Second Chance Act of 2005 has an increased focus on employment, housing, mental health and substance abuse treatment, and family support/unification (Weedon 2005). In addition, the Second Chance Act of 2005 mandates that states examine policies that thwart full civic participation. Civil restrictions impeding reintegration into society include lack of voting privileges, conditions or bans impeding the completion of job applications, and eligibility to obtain public housing and public assistance (Pogorzelski et al. 2005).

DONALD A. CABANA and
SARA BUCK DOUDE

See also **Crime, Serious; Criminology; Social Disorganization, Theory of**

References and Further Reading

Austin, J., and P. L. Hardyman. 2004. The risks and needs of the returning prisoner population. *Review of Policy Research* 21 (1): 13–29.

Bureau of Justice Statistics. 2002. *Recidivism of prisoners released in 1994*. Washington, DC: U.S. Department of Justice.

Lindquist, C. 2005. *The multi-site evaluation of the Serious and Violent Offender Reentry Initiative: Sustainability of SVORI programs*. http://www.svori-evaluation.org.

Lowenkamp, C. T., E. J. Latessa, and A. M. Holsinger. 2006. The risk principle in action: What have we learned from 13,676 offenders and 97 correctional programs? *Crime & Delinquency* 52 (1): 77–93.

MacKenzie, D. L. 2000. Evidence-based corrections: Identifying what works. *Crime & Delinquency* 46 (4): 457–71.

Maxwell, S. R. 2005. Rethinking the broad sweep of recidivism: A task for evaluators. *Criminology & Public Policy* 4 (3); 519–26.

Nuttall, J., L. Hollmen, and E. M. Staley. 2003. The effect of earning a GED on recidivism rates. *Journal of Correctional Education* 54 (3): 90–94.

Office of Justice Programs. n.d. *Learn about reentry*. http://www.ojp.usdoj.gov/reentry/learn.html.

Paparozzi, M. A., and P. Gendreau. 2005. An intensive supervision program that worked: Service delivery, professional orientation, and organizational supportiveness. *The Prison Journal* 85 (4): 445–66.

Pogorzelski, W., N. Wolff, K. Y. Pan, and C. L. Blitz. 2005. Behavioral health problems, ex-offender reentry policies, and the "Second Chance Act." *American Journal of Public Health* 95 (10): 1718–24.

Second Chance Act of 2005, H.R. 1704, 109th Cong. 1st Sess. (April 19, 2005).

Thomas, C. W. 2005. Recidivism of public and private state prison inmates in Florida: Issues and unanswered questions. *Criminology & Public Policy* 4 (1): 89–100.

Weedon, J. R. 2005. The Second Chance Act of 2005. *Corrections Today* 67 (5): 12.

Wilson, J. A. 2005. Bad behavior or bad policy? An examination of Tennessee release cohorts, 1993–2001. *Criminology & Public Policy* 4 (3): 485–518.

Winterfield, L., and C. Lindquist. 2005. *The multi-site evaluation of the Serious and Violent Offender Reentry Initiative: Characteristics of prisoner reentry programs*. http://www.svori-evaluation.org.

RESEARCH AND DEVELOPMENT

The purpose of research and development is to help guide management and organization-wide planning services in decision making at the executive, managerial, and line levels within the law enforcement agencies they serve. The goal is to promote efficient and effective police services through professional planning, problem solving, research, program development, and implementation of police department initiatives.

O. W. Wilson documented the first prescribed role of "planning and research" in 1950 as studying department needs, implementing policy, directing efforts within the operational areas, and guiding training and performance (Wilson 1950, 1963).

This original "planning and research" concept has evolved into a more dynamic function called "research and development." In police organizations today, the research and development function has expanded through advancements in technology and research methodology. In addition, local, state, and federal government entities have increased their role in supporting police services during the past several decades. These government agencies, such as the Police Executive Research Forum, the National Institute of Justice, the Community Oriented Policing Services Office, the Bureau of Justice Assistance, and state criminal justice departments have provided programs for grants, accreditation, and legislative advocacy.

Civilians perform most of the jobs in research and development. The work done in research and development often requires specialized knowledge and expertise. In addition, most agencies are hiring civilians for administrative positions because it is more cost effective. However, there is also value in rotating some sworn positions in research and development because police officers can bring the street experience to the creative process. It is an excellent site for developing future leaders and managers due to the nature of the work done and the organization-wide perspective gained.

The reporting structure of research and development varies across agencies depending on department size. For example, a small law enforcement agency may not have the capacity to staff an actual bureau (division, department, or unit). Consequently, the assignment of research and development work may be to one person or to several individuals performing multiple jobs throughout the organization. Larger agencies have a formal Research and Development Bureau. The chain of command for research and development typically reports to the deputy chief, division chief of administration, or division director.

An important task of research and development is to identify innovative and effective practices in police work. Overarching the entire research and development process is the role of communicating with and obtaining information from local, state, and federal agencies to identify innovative policing trends in areas such as management, technology, equipment, community programs, and operational tactics. Recommendations resulting from the findings of this department are then given to the chief for consideration. Research and development also supports the chief's initiatives through researching, planning, and implementing the programs. Again, the ultimate goal is to help develop the organization to improve police services.

The Different Functions of Research and Development

The functions of research and development can be broken into four distinct areas: strategic planning, operations support, production, and research (see Figure 1). The first area identified in the diagram is strategic planning, which involves identifying a short- and long-term plan for the organization. Strategic planning involves the following steps (Kuykendall and Unsinger 1975; Goodstein, Nolan, and Pfeiffer 1993; Mintzberg 1994; Senge 1994):

1. Identifying where the organization is going by identifying the mission, vision, goals, and objectives
2. Conducting a risk analysis that identifies the threats, opportunities, strengths, and weaknesses of achieving the plans
3. Developing a road map on how to achieve the plan by identifying the tasks, determining who will complete the tasks, and establishing a timeline

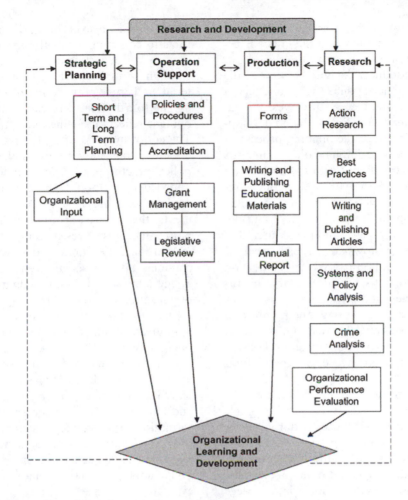

Figure 1   Research and Development Responsibilities.

Strategic planning is an inclusive process that involves people throughout the organization in its development. Research and development facilitates the planning process, monitors its implementation, and documents the results of the goals and objectives. The outcome of strategic planning is a general and flexible "road map" for the department. However, perhaps even more importantly, the ultimate goal is to develop strategic thinking and performance at all levels of the organization, particularly among management.

The second area of responsibility is operations support. These duties include developing and monitoring policies and procedures, overseeing the accreditation requirements, writing and managing grants, and conducting legislative review.

Consistent, contemporary, and relevant policies and procedures are critical to guiding the department and holding officers to a performance standard. In addition, the policies and procedures protect the department in litigation. In 1979, the establishment of a national accreditation commission for law enforcement occurred in order to establish policy and procedure standards to improve police services. The Commission on Accreditation for Law Enforcement Agencies, Inc. (CALEA) is the accrediting authority, and the International Association of Chiefs of Police, the National Organization of Black Law

Enforcement Executives, the National Sheriff's Association, and the Police Executive Research Forum developed it. CALEA conducts the initial review of the agency's policies and then conducts a compliance audit every three years to re-accredit an agency. Research and development can manage the ongoing process of updating and reviewing policy standards to ensure compliance with CALEA. If an agency chooses not to be accredited, research and development is still responsible for the ongoing review, revision, and development of policies and procedures. Accreditation bestows an official "seal of approval" and enhanced credibility on the department's operations, administration, policies, and procedures.

Grant seeking, writing, and monitoring occur throughout the year. Grant funds are invaluable to an organization because they augment an agency's general fund and provide extra capacity to develop and implement programs, technology, or equipment.

Legislative review occurs during local, state, and national congressional and legislative sessions to determine if any proposed bills will adversely affect police operations. Research and development reviews the legislative bills as they are proposed. They make recommendations to the chief regarding the pros and cons of endorsing the proposed bills. Additionally, newly enacted federal, state, and local legislation is analyzed and disseminated to ensure that the department and its officers are meeting and enforcing current statutory requirements. Production, the third area of responsibility, involves the writing, reviewing, revising, and ordering of forms and educational material developed and used by the department. This may not apply to all agencies, depending on their philosophy, size, and reporting structure. Police work involves a lot of documentation, such as offense reports, supplemental forms, citations, and specialized forms designed to address specific crime issues, such as domestic violence. Research and

development is also in charge of developing tools to communicate with citizens about the police department and their work through annual reports, educational material, and crime prevention information.

The fourth area of research and development reflects its namesake, "research." The contributions during the past several decades from universities, colleges, and police practitioners have broadened the knowledge, methodology, and utility of applied research. Due to these developments, the research arm has evolved into more than just "researching the latest innovation." Research and development conducts applied social science research, policy analysis, program evaluation, and organizational problem solving and performance evaluation. The bureau also collaborates with universities and colleges on police studies.

Action research is the study of policing in the field by developing and using research tools, such as surveys, focus groups, and interviews, that provide expedient information. Policy and systems analysis provides information to understand the effectiveness and efficiency of operations. Policy analysis is very similar to program evaluation, which assesses the process, outcome, cost/benefit, and cost effectiveness of implementing a program, but policy analysis also forecasts policy options (Guess and Farnham 2000). Systems analysis studies the processes and outcomes of each police function to determine how proficient and successful they work within their area and across functions in the department. The objective of these types of program analyses is to identify obstacles and develop strategies to achieve high performance (Wholey, Newcomer, and Associates 1989).

Measuring police accountability and organizational performance started with the initiative of "Measuring What Matters" by the National Institute of Justice in the 1990s. Accountability measures ensure the review of department performance and offer the organization information to assess its strengths and needs to improve service delivery.

Technology has transformed the world of crime analysis. Initially, police officers tracked crime patterns using pushpins to identify events on a city map. Nowadays, sophisticated software programs conduct spatial analyses of crime events and map predictive patterns of criminal predators. Tactical crime data informs officers of emerging risks, patterns, and suspects. Selected crime and call-for-service data shared with the public helps the community to better protect itself through target hardening, neighborhood watch groups, and cooperation with the police. Technology has also enhanced research and development's ability to communicate and identify what is termed "best practices" in policing through e-mail and the Internet. Publishing research findings also promotes information sharing.

Conclusion

The responsibilities of research and development have evolved during the past fifty years. This important administrative function supports police service delivery and practices to promote organizational learning and development. Research and development is the hub for assisting the chief, his or her staff, and all members in developing an efficient, effective, and progressive police department.

MORA L. FIEDLER

See also **Accountability; COMPSTAT; Computer Technology; Crime Analysis; Crime Mapping; Intelligence-Led Policing and Organizational Learning;** *Uniform Crime Reports*

References and Further Reading

Goodstein, Leonard, Timothy Nolan, and J. William Pfeiffer. 1993. *Applied strategic planning—How to develop a plan that really works*. New York: McGraw-Hill.

Guess, George M., and Paul G. Farnham. 2000. *Cases in public policy analysis*. Washington, DC: Washington Press.

Kuykendall, Jack L., and Peter C. Unsinger. 1975. *Community police administration*. Chicago: Nelson-Hall.

Mintzberg, Henry. 1994. *The rise and fall of strategic planning*. New York: The Free Press.

National Institute of Justice. 1999. *Measuring what matters: Proceedings from the Police Research Institute meetings*. July. Washington, DC: U.S. Government Printing Office.

Senge, Peter. 1994. *The fifth discipline fieldbook*. New York: Doubleday.

Vollmer, August. 1936. *The police in modern society*. Berkeley: University of California Press.

Wholey, Joseph S., Kathryn E. Newcomer, and Associates. 1989. *Improving government performance—Evaluation strategies for strengthening public agencies and programs*. San Francisco: Jossey-Bass.

Wilson, O. W., and Roy Maclaren. 1950. *Police administration*. 1st ed. New York: McGraw-Hill.

———. 1963. *Police administration*. 2nd ed. New York: McGraw-Hill.

RESPONDING TO SCHOOL VIOLENCE

Introduction

During the latter part of the 1990s, school violence received widespread attention nationwide and internationally as a result of a small number of traumatic and highly publicized school shootings. In these shootings, which occurred in rural or suburban settings, a student or pair of students carried firearms to school and opened fire, injuring and, in some cases, killing teachers and multiple students. The most infamous of these shootings occurred at Columbine High School in Littleton, Colorado, in 1999, where two students shot and killed fourteen students and one teacher, before turning their guns on themselves and committing suicide. Such events, while relatively rare, were so terrible—the murder of children at their school—that they attracted national and international media attention.

Many people found their perceptions of school violence to be affected by these shootings, which seemed to happen at least once a year from 1996 to 2000. The coverage of these events by the media also enhanced public belief that this type of extreme violence in a school setting was increasing and becoming commonplace. At the same time, various stakeholders—state and local policy makers, law enforcement, school officials—rushed to create and implement polices to predict, prevent, and respond to future incidents of this type of school violence.

The horrific nature of these shootings captured the public's attentions and stoked their fears, but also, unfortunately, obscured the reality of trends in school violence. Although misbehavior among a small percentage of students is relatively commonplace, major violence is relatively rare in a school setting and, contrary to public belief, decreased during the latter 1990s, and continues to decrease into the first years of the twenty-first century. Furthermore, the schools that dealt with the most widespread violence and disorder were often urban schools rather than suburban or rural schools, where the rare instances of mass violence largely took place. The degree of violence was so great in these shootings, however, that it overshadowed how rarely violence occurred.

During the latter 1990s, as a result of a growing awareness of the problem of school violence, there were also improvements in the recording of such events that revealed a few fundamental findings about school violence in general. First, the traumatic school shootings were rare, isolated events, and not at all reflective of typical school violence. Second, the majority of school violence incidents involve more traditional forms of adolescent violence such as fighting and bullying. Although these are serious events, their results are not even close to the damage and violence that occurred as a result of the school shootings. Moreover, some degree of violence, including bullying and fighting, has been a part of

the growing-up experience of adolescents, especially males, for decades. Finally, the majority of incidents of adolescent violence do not happen at school settings or even during school hours. Rather, juveniles most often tended to act violently or become the victims of violence after school, in the afternoon and evening, off school property. Schools, compared to other places that adolescents may go, have become safer and more stable environments in recent years (Devoe et al. 2005).

This article will examine some of the contemporary responses to school violence. First, it will examine the initial response to school shootings. Second, it will examine how violence is recorded. How do stakeholders get their information to measure levels of school violence? At the same time, this entry will report on recent trends in school violence, relying on several different measures, which show serious violence to be relatively rare, with additional decreases in recent years. Finally, this article will discuss the policies that different schools have utilized to prevent and respond to problems with violence. We will examine both responses to serious violence and more commonplace and milder violence, with a summing up of the effectiveness of each approach.

School Shootings during Mid-1990s

During the late 1980s and early 1990s, prior to the highly publicized mass shootings, policy makers created punitive school policies that addressed violence in inner-city schools (Burns and Crawford 1999). The penalties for school violence increased in 1994, when President Clinton signed into law the Gun Free School Safety Act. This law made it a zero tolerance offense to bring a gun or other weapon to school, with the penalty being that the offending student had to be expelled for a year. In response, every state in America created similar gun-free policies.

At the same time, schools also increased their partnerships with police and criminal justice agencies in a way that was for the most part new (Burns and Crawford 1999). While sometimes police had been involved in schools, it was usually in the capacity as an instructor, such as through the use of D.A.R.E., where officers provided education modules on illicit drug use to students. With the changes in policy making, however, police began to engage in more preventive and reactive patrol work in schools, dealing with instances of student behavior, treating such instances as law enforcement issues, and sorting out whether a student had violated a criminal law. While some school systems had experimented with having police in their schools as early as the 1960s, these officers had usually been put into position to foster police and citizen relations. Therefore, the use of criminal justice modalities in the school was largely a new approach for policy making in the schools.

The first high-profile school shootings occurred on February 2, 1996, in Moses Lake, Washington (*Washington Post* 2000). During the next few years, there were eleven additional high-profile school shootings in other American schools. Of the twelve shootings, three resulted in injuries (no fatalities), three resulted in a single fatality, and six resulted in multiple fatalities. These shootings took place in rural or suburban schools, and often involved Caucasian shooters from middle-class backgrounds, who might have a history of misbehavior in some cases, but nothing to suggest the capability for this level of violence (although some shooters had told other students of their plans).

Due to the media coverage attracted by these shootings, the public began to assume that such events were commonplace and increasing. Burns and Crawford (1999) suggest that the media sensationalized the shootings so that they seemed like commonplace events. The media's descriptions of the events included phrases such as "an all-too-familiar story" or "another in a recent trend" to refer to shootings, as if these were regular events (Donohue, Schiraldi, and Ziedenberg 1998). This was inaccurate. Furthermore, part of the media coverage may have been driven by the fact that this type of violence was so rare and exotic—there was nothing commonplace about it (Donohue et al. 1998).

After the school shootings, Burns and Crawford (1999) suggested that there emerged a moral panic about mass violence at schools. School administrators, teachers, students, and parents began to feel as if violence was inevitable and suddenly perceived certain behaviors or manners of dress as threats to their safety. Wary of future violence, they tried to identify potential shooters, creating profiles of those at risk of committing violence, despite having little information to inform these profiles. Because of the perceived risk of an episode of mass violence, the need to maintain public safety seemed to justify an extreme response.

While previous school violence prevention policies focused on inner-city schools, the reaction to the mass shootings expanded the focus on violence from inner-city schools to suburban schools (Burns and Crawford 1999). This led school administrators to seek ways of enhancing security by creating additional policies and increasing penalties for certain types of behavior. One consequence of the moral panic was the implementation of zero tolerance policies that swept up many students for nonillegal and/or low-level transgressions. According to Burns and Crawford (1999) some schools' responses included:

> hiring additional security officers in schools (Sanchez 1998); installing metal detectors in schools (Page 1998) . . . bullet drills in which school children drop and take cover (Tirrell-Wysocki 1998); [and] requiring at least a few school teachers to carry concealed weapons at school (Page 1998). (p. 152)

In the following years, these policies have met resistance as being ineffective and overly punitive. Yet, at the same time, many people believed this was the only response to school violence.

Several students who engaged in low-level offenses ran afoul of these new policies. There has been limited scholarly work that traces the way the moral panic identified such students. Some articles, however, sum up the media accounts from all over the country (Richart, Brooks, and Soler 2003; Skiba 2000). In certain areas, students were prohibited from bringing to school such nonthreatening items as asthma inhalers. Students were arrested and/or expelled for offenses that included bringing to school breath mints, over-the-counter medications, plastic knives in their sack lunches, and pockets knives (Richart et al. 2003; Skiba 2000). Schools have also punished students for pointing their finger at other students in a pretend gun fight and for making comments or jokes about gun violence (Newman 2000; Richart et al. 2003; Skiba 2000).

Many zero tolerance policies also took steps to buttress schools to repel potential attacks. For the zero tolerance polices, schools limited what students could bring to school, ways that students could behave, and words that they could say. Anything that could be perceived as indirectly related to school violence was enough to get a student in serious trouble. In 1999–2000, the target hardening of schools mostly involved limiting the access to school by locking doors, having security fences, school check-ins for visitors to the school, and metal detectors. Each of these policies has been unsuccessful or had limited results (Gottfredson et al. 2004).

Different reports from different states suggest that zero policy programs in schools are unsuccessful and cause harm to those who find themselves ensnared in them. Reports have found that zero tolerance programs are expelling students for drug violations (Potts and Njie 2003), as well as drug and minor violations (Richart et al. 2003). Also there are disparities in who is expelled/punished under programs, with students of color and special education students receiving the most discipline (Potts and Njie 2003; Richart et al. 2003; Michigan Nonprofit Association 2003).

Results are mixed in terms of whether metal detectors have reduced violence. At the end of the 1980s and early 1990s, some sources reported reductions in suspensions for carrying weapons to school and reductions of instances where weapons were brought to school (New York City Board of Education 1991; U.S. General Accounting Office 1995, as cited by Anderson 1998). Other research, however, suggests that metal detectors have little effect on incidents of violence as measured by numbers of victimizations (Schreck, Miller, and Gibson 2003). There have also been issues with how metal detectors are used. Gottfredson and Gottfredson (2001) found that some metal detectors were not plugged in. They also questioned the use of random searches with handheld metal detectors as dangerous: Do you really want to surprise an armed student?

Ways in Which Adolescent Violence Is Recorded

In the last fifteen years changes have occurred in how school violence is recorded. Under the Safe and Drug-Free Schools and Communities Act of 1994, the National Center for Education Statistics (NCES), a federal organization, is mandated to collect information about violence in elementary and secondary schools (OVC Legal Series 2002). The NCES "is the primary federal entity for collecting, analyzing, and reporting data related to education in the United States and other nations" (DeVoe et al. 2004).

One of the primary sources for getting information about violence in schools comes from the *Indicators of School Crime and Safety,* an annual report since 1998 that is prepared by the NCES and the Bureau of Justice Statistics. This report contains information about violent and nonviolent crime that happens to students at school or on their way to and from school. The information in the report comes from self-reports of experiences and behaviors from "students, teachers, principals, and the general population," and data compiled from several different national surveys.

According to the *Indicators of School Crime and Safety* (DeVoe et al. 2004), serious violence in schools is a relatively rare event. Between 1992 and 1999, the number of homicides hovered between twenty-eight and thirty-four nationally, and only one to seven suicides, with no increase or decrease (DeVoe et al. 2004, 6). There was a decrease in homicides among students at school for the academic years 1998–1999 and 1999–2000, with thirty-three and fourteen homicides, respectively (DeVoe et al. 2004). The most recent years for which data are available, 2000–2001 and 2001–2002, show homicides fluctuating between twelve and seventeen incidents at school per year. The more commonplace school violence, student fighting at school, has also declined from 1993 to 2003 (DeVoe et al. 2004, iv). Finally, between 1993 and 2003, there was a decline in the number of students who said they had brought weapons to school from 12% to 6% (DeVoe et al. 2005).

The *Indicators of School Crime and Safety* also reveals that the school is a safe environment, with more violence occurring off school grounds. During the academic year of 1999–2000, there were 2,124 homicides and 1,992 suicides outside of school property among minors ages five to nineteen; by comparison, there were only twenty-four homicides and eight suicides on school property during that time frame. During the year 2002, students ages twelve to eighteen became victims of serious violence only 88,000 times at school compared to 309,000 outside of school (DeVoe et al. 2004, iv).

There are also other indications that schools are relatively safe places for students. In 2003, 13% of students in grades 9 through 12 said they had been involved in a fight at school, compared to 33% who said they had been in a fight off school grounds (DeVoe et al. 2005). Also, 6% of students in grades 9 through 12 said they had carried a weapon with them at school, compared to 12% who said they had carried a weapon with them anywhere (DeVoe et al. 2005).

In addition to the *Indicators of School Crime and Safety* reports, many states have passed legislation requiring schools to collect more information about school violence (OVC Legal Series 2002). Many states require schools to maintain and report information on violence, but there are variations across states regarding what types of behavior must be recorded and how much information must be taken. Many states also require schools to report any criminal activity, including violence, to the appropriate police agency. In turn, police agencies in certain states are supposed to reciprocate school reporting by reporting any incidents of juvenile crime that come to their attention to school officials. The OVC Legal Series (2002) identifies the following as continuing issues for law enforcement: "improvements to statistical reporting," "school crime hotlines," and "enforcement of reporting laws."

Finally, it is worth noting that, in total, juvenile violence appears to have dropped according to arrest statistics (Snyder 2005). As of the end of 2003, violent crime arrests of juveniles are lower than they have been since 1987. Between 1994 and 2003, arrests among juveniles dropped 32% for all violent crimes, with drops of 68% for murder, 24% for forcible rape, 43% for robbery, and 26% for aggravated assault. Finally, as of 2003, fewer juveniles are dying as a result of murders, with the numbers at their lowest level since 1984.

Schools Have Different Approaches to Violence

Schools seek to reduce two types of violence: the first being major violent incidents and the second being general violence (bullying, fighting). Reddy et al. (2001) note that students who have engaged in extreme violence are different from those students who engage in lower levels of violence frequently. For extreme situations of violence involving mass shootings, Reddy et al. (2001) note that three types of interventions are commonly used, and describe each as insufficient. These three approaches are (1) "profiling," (2) "guided professional judgment/structured clinical assessment (including the use of warning signs and other checklists)," and (3) "automated decision making (including the use of actuarial formulas and expert systems)."

Profiling involves examining past offenders of mass violence to try to predict who will commit targeted violence (Reddy et al. 2001). There are several problems with using profiling to predict behavior that has yet to occur. First, it is difficult to identify who potentially might commit targeted violence. If the potential offender does not share a specific trait with a past offender, she or he will be wrongly excluded from selection. There is also a lot of room for false positives. There may be several traits that both offenders and nonoffenders may share, and therefore it is possible by this commonality to select people who pose no threat. In a report, the U.S. Secret Service described that "there is no accurate or useful profile of 'the school shooter'" (National Institute of Justice 2002, 12). Also, the report mentions that:

> Knowing that an individual shares characteristics, features, or traits with prior school shooters does not advance the appraisal of risk. The use of profiles carries a risk of overidentification, and the vast majority of students who fit any given profile will not actually pose a risk. The use of these stereotypes will fail to identify some students who do, in fact, pose a risk of violence, but who share few characteristics with prior attackers. (p. 13)

A second problem with profiling is the precision of the profile (Reddy et al. 2001). There have been so few events that it is difficult to develop an accurate profile of a potential offender. Also, different profiles include/exclude different events. Information in one profile might not be as inclusive as another profile. Third, it is also difficult to measure the accuracy of the profile, and to determine if the profile has identified the right variables. The profile could have identified the wrong variable (wearing black clothing), which just happens to correlate with the event, rather than to cause the event to occur (carrying a weapon and several rounds of ammunition to school) (Reddy et al. 2001). There are also problems in that the school official may only focus on variables that confirm their suspicions, rather than examining variables that should exclude the individual from the profile. Finally, the use of profiles is unpopular with everyone: school representatives, parents, and students.

Guided professional judgment/structured clinical assessments involve using a professional, such as a psychologist or counselor, to identify someone who could be a possible threat of committing targeted violence (Reddy et al. 2001). There are also flaws with using guided professional judgment/structured clinical assessment. The case rate, which is the number of prior offenders who have committed mass shootings, is too small to be able to use this to identify potentially violent people (Sewell and Mendelsohn 2000). Similar to the problem with creating a profile, there have been so few offenders that it is impossible to construct a theoretical model of a potential offender. Second, there is little preexisting research on this specific type of violence and, at the same time, the literature of general juvenile violence may not be acceptable. Also, the usual assessments and tests of psychologists may not capture a potential for violence of this magnitude.

Automated decision making involves making a database or management system that can identify someone at potential risk of committing targeted violence (Reddy et al. 2001). There are problems with automated decision making because there is little research and no agreement on risk factors. Similar to the public's growing awareness of serial killers in 1980s and terrorists since 2001, school shooters received a lot of media and pop culture attention, despite being a relatively rare phenomenon. Due to the heavy and protracted attention this rare phenomenon attracts, the public assumes that this is a commonplace event. There is a paucity of research literature about them because students rarely commit mass shootings. Because there are so few, it has been difficult to create databases or management systems, which rely on patterns of behavior from a large sample of subjects. Database and management systems also operate best when they monitor a multitude of different fields, with thresholds in each of these fields set by baselines of the sample they are monitoring. This, then, assumes two things. First, that there is a sufficiently large sample of students generally and, second, that there are enough prior shooters that thresholds can be set from a cross section of their behaviors that will provide a means to recognize and identify future potential shooters. Neither appears to be true in the area of school shootings.

The second set of programs attempts to deal with the problem of violence generally in schools. These programs are interested in preventing the more commonplace types of violence that a larger number of students engage in compared to the rare phenomenon of school shootings. Schools break programs into different groups. Wilson and Lipsey (2005), for example, divide the programs into the following groups:

- *Universal programs*: "these programs are delivered in classroom settings to the entire classroom; children are generally not selected individually for treatment but receive treatment simply because they are students in a program classroom. However, schools are frequently selected because they are in low-socioeconomic-status and/ or high-crime neighborhoods. The children in these universal programs may be considered at risk by virtue of their socioeconomic background or neighborhood risk."

- *Selected/indicated programs*: "these programs are delivered to students who are selected especially to receive treatment by virtue of the presence of some risk factor, including disruptiveness, aggressive behavior, activity level, etc. Most of these programs are delivered to the selected children outside of their regular classrooms but are targeted for the selected children."

- *Special schools or classes*: "these programs involve special schools or classrooms that (for the students involved) serve as a usual classroom or school. Children are placed in these special schools or classrooms because of some behavioral or school difficulty that is judged to warrant their placement outside of mainstream classrooms. The programs in this category include special education classrooms for behavior disordered children, alternative high schools, and schools within schools programs."

- *Comprehensive/multimodal programs*: "these programs generally involve multiple modalities and multiple formats, including both classroom-based and pull-out programs. They may also involve programs for parents and capacity building components for school administrators and teachers in addition to the programming provided for the students. The defining characteristic of these programs is that they include multiple treatment elements and formats." (pp. 10–11)

Schools have also devoted resources to trying to design crime out of schools through changes to the physical school buildings (Gottfredson et al. 2000). Schools have limited access, through locking some doors so that students and visitors have to enter through a specific entrance or entrances. Schools have also required visitors to sign in at the main office of the school. Finally, schools have relied on metal detectors, both stationary detectors that students have to walk through to enter the school, and portable metal detectors that faculty can check specific students with during the day.

Evaluations of Violence Reduction Programs

The programs that have worked for general school violence are universal programs, selected/indicated programs, and comprehensive/multimodal programs (Wilson and Lipsey 2005). Specifically, these programs reduced behaviors that included "fighting, name-calling, intimidation, and other negative interpersonal behaviors, especially among higher risk students" (Wilson and Lipsey 2005, 24). The special schools or classes were ineffective at reducing these behaviors.

The impact that these program had on youth violence was related to other variables outside the type of program itself (Wilson and Lipsey 2005). For the successful programs, treatment dose, implementation, and the comprehensiveness of the program were important. Gottfredson et al. (2004) findings also suggest that implementation is important to the success of a program. Further, programs had the greatest impact on higher risk students, because there were greater levels of violence, both in quantity and quality, which could be reduced.

Despite a few meta-analyses and evaluations of programs, there are few examinations of the effectiveness of violence reduction programs. Gottfredson et al. (2004) note that several of the violence strategy programs have not been evaluated, including "school security practices, architectural arrangements, counseling approaches to problem behavior" (Gottfredson and Gottfredson 2004, 11).

JACK MCDEVITT and
W. CARSTEN ANDRESEN

See also **Crime Prevention; Drug Abuse Resistance Education (D.A.R.E.); Gang Resistance Education and Training (G.R.E.A.T.); Juvenile Crime and Criminalization; School Resource Officers**

References and Further Reading

Anderson, David C. 1998. Curriculum, culture, and community: The challenge of school violence." *Crime and Justice* 24 (7).

Burns, Ronald, and C. Crawford. 1999. School shootings, the media, and public fear: Ingredients for a moral panic. *Crime, Law and Social Change* 32: 147–68.

DeVoe, Jill F., K. Peter, P. Kaufman, A. Miller, M. Noonan, T. D. Snyder, and K. Baum. 2004. *Indicators of school crime and safety: 2004.* NCES 2005–002/NCJ 205290. Washington, DC: U.S. Departments of Education and Justice.

DeVoe, Jill F., K. Peter, M. Noonan, T. D. Snyder, and K. Baum. 2005. *Indicators of school crime and safety: 2005.* NCES 2006-001/NCJ 210697. Washington, DC: U.S. Departments of Education and Justice.

Donohue, Elizabeth, V. Schiraldi, and J. Ziedenberg. 1998. *School house hype: School shootings and the real risks kids face in America.* Washington, DC: Justice Policy Institute.

Gottfredson, Gary D., and D. C. Gottfredson. 2001. *Gang problems and gang programs in a national sample of schools.* Grant No. 98-JN-FX-0004, awarded by the Office of Juvenile Justice and Delinquency Prevention, Office of Justice Programs, U.S. Department of Justice; and Grant No 96-MU-MU-0008, awarded by the National Institute of Justice, Office of Justice Programs, U.S. Department of Justice. October.

Gottfredson, Gary D., D. C. Gottfredson, E. R. Czeh, D. Cantor, S. B. Crosse, and I. Hantman. 2000. *National study of delinquency prevention in schools*. Grant No. 96-MU-MU-0008, awarded by the National Institute of Justice, Office of Justice Programs U.S. Department of Justice. November.

Gottfredson, Gary D., D. C. Gottfredson, E. R. Czch, D. Cantor, S. B. Crosse, and I. Hantman. 2004. *Toward safe and orderly schools—The national study of delinquency prevention in schools*. Research in Brief, November. Washington, DC: National Institute of Justice, Office of Justice Programs U.S. Department of Justice.

Michigan Nonprofit Association. 2003. Zero tolerance policies and their impact on Michigan students. Prepared by the Institute for Children, You, and Families at Michigan State University. http://www.mnaonline.org/pdf/spotlight%202002_12.pdf (accessed January 9, 2006).

National Threat Assessment Center. 2002. Preventing school shootings. *NIJ Journal* 248: 11–15.

New York City Board of Education. 1991. *Fernandez moves to bolster school safety*. Press Release. New York: New York City Board of Education, Division of Public Affairs.

Page, Clarence. 1998. Laws alone can't stop the killing. *Ft. Lauderdale Sun Sentinel,* May 28, 19A.

Potts, Kim, and B. Njie. 2003. Zero tolerance in Tennessee schools: An update. August. http://www.comptroller.state.tn.us/orea/reports/zerotoler2003.pdf (accessed January 9, 2006).

Reddy, Marisa, R. Borum, J. Berglund, B. Vossekuil, R. Fein, and W. Modzeleski. 2001. Evaluating risk for targeted violence in schools: Comparing risk assessment, threat assessment, and other approaches. *Psychology in the Schools* 38 (2): 157–72.

Richart, David, K. Brooks, and M. Soler. 2003. *Unintended consequences: The impact of zero tolerance and other exclusionary policies on Kentucky students*. Building Blocks for Youth Initiative. http://www.buildingblocksforyouth.org/kentucky/kentucky.html (accessed January 9, 2006).

Sanchez, Rene. 1998. Educators pursue solutions to violence crisis: As deadly sprees increase, schools struggle for ways to deal with student anger. *Washington Post,* May 23, A12.

Schreck, Christopher J., J. M. Miller, and C. L. Gibson. 2003. Trouble in the school yard: A study of the risk factors of victimization at school. *Crime and Delinquency,* 29 (3): 460–84.

Snyder, Howard N. 2005. Juvenile arrests 2003. *Juvenile Justice Bulletin*, August.

Tirrell-Wysocki, David. 1998. Bullet drills teach students to drop, seek cover. *Ft. Lauderdale Sun-Sentinel,* June 11, 5A.

U.S. Department of Justice. 2002. *Reporting school violence*. Legal Series Bulletin 2, January. Washington, DC: U.S. Department of Justice.

U.S. General Accounting Office. 1995. *School safety: Promising initiatives for addressing school violence*. Report to the Ranking Minority Member, Subcommittee on Children and Families, Committee on Labor and Human Resources, U.S. Senate. Washington DC: U.S. General Accounting Office.

Washington Post. 2000. Juvenile violence time line. http://www.washingtonpost.com/wp-srv/national/longterm/juvmurders/timeline.htm (accessed January 9, 2006).

Wilson, Sandra Jo, and M. W. Lipsey. 2005. The effectiveness of school-based violence and prevention programs for reducing disruptive and aggressive behavior. Commissioned Paper, September. Washington, DC: U.S. Department of Justice.

RISK MANAGEMENT

The concept of risk management is now familiar in various institutional contexts, including health, criminal justice, national security, and business. In the sphere of policing, risk management initiatives seek to address some long-standing inefficiencies in police practice. As such, it is an umbrella concept that subsumes both a new orientation to the job of policing as well as a number of specific policing projects.

The risk management framework is usefully contrasted with several attributes of the traditional crime fighting model. That approach is characterized by a reactive "call for service" orientation where officers spend most of their time being dispatched to an eclectic array of incidents that prompt calls to the emergency 911 system. Officers often arrive on the scene only long after a crime has occurred, making the entire approach subject to the criticism that it resembles closing the barn door after the horse has escaped. Moreover, over periods of weeks or months, officers can make several return visits to particularly troublesome locations without ever resolving the problem that is at the root of such repeat calls. While this reactive model still represents the type of service that citizens expect from their police, it is increasingly criticized for being a highly inefficient use of resources. Blame for this failure is often directed at the police tendency to prioritize the use of criminal law and criminal justice institutions, both of which are now recognized as being rather blunt and ineffective tools for modifying human behavior and reducing crime.

Risk management, in contrast, approaches crime in a manner that is reminiscent of an insurance model (Reichman 1986). It explicitly focuses on anticipating the likelihood of future untoward eventualities and developing prospective initiatives to manage those risks. In such an orientation most crimes are recognized as being rather mundane and resulting from the contextually specific actions of unremarkable individuals. Crimes, therefore, are not considered to be the acts of morally reprehensible criminals that violate deeply held sentiments. All but the most spectacular (and rare) crimes are increasingly approached as being amoral; that is, they are predominantly understood to be negative eventualities that can be prospectively guarded against or eliminated through a combination of expert advice, insurance, environmental design, and anticrime technologies (O'Malley 1992). In the process, anticrime initiatives start to resemble how most individuals mitigate the prospect of a car accident.

Risk management is consciously proactive in that it involves attempts to anticipate the statistical likelihood of untoward events and to prospectively mitigate or eliminate those risks. One of the most significant developments of this orientation is that it privileges the place of information work and data analysis in policing. While police still occasionally investigate spectacular crimes and capture notorious criminals, the reality of everyday police work is much more mundane. Officers spend much of their time simply collecting and processing data about assorted low-level incidents on myriad official forms and databases. While individual officers often resent such work, this police-initiated process of social enumeration generates knowledge that is vital to risk management initiatives. Because risks are typically understood to entail some form of statistical probability, it is necessary for officials to have accurate and timely data that would allow them to construct risk profiles and develop appropriate policies (Ericson and Haggerty 1997).

Only a fraction of the information that officers accumulate, however, is required to process offenders through the courts. Most is collected on behalf of a network of public and private agencies such as customs, immigration, alcohol and drug research centers, and insurance companies. These institutions use police-generated knowledge to fashion programs to manage the risks posed to different populations and client groups. Hence, a significant portion of the risk management work of the public police involves collecting a plethora of data on behalf of risk management institutions external to the police.

A quite different development characteristic of the risk management approach is that the mandate of the public police starts to expand beyond "law enforcement" to include "security provision." This change entails an important reconfiguration of the police role. It provides the police with a much wider ambit of expertise than is typical of their "law enforcement" mandate, as officers are now expected to offer advice on how to manage a host of additional eventualities that are only tangentially related to crime including urban disorder, fear, and quality-of-life issues. These initiatives assume many different forms, such as having officers sit on urban planning boards, give lectures to schoolchildren, and encourage community groups, corporations, and individual citizens to take steps to enhance their security. Much of this guidance involves persuading citizens to take responsibility for their own security by capitalizing on the security expertise of other private and public institutions and to use assorted security services and technologies.

In the process the traditional emphasis in police culture on using the criminal law to try to resolve any and all problems is displaced in three distinct ways. First, criminal law becomes simply one among many forms of risk management. Intelligence-led policing, for example, entails efforts to capitalize on statistical knowledge about the patterns and regularities of criminal events and to deploy officers prospectively to specific areas at particular times that are known to be problematic. In such an orientation law enforcement is not conceived of as an end in itself, but as a means to manage the crime risks characteristic of certain geographic locations. Second, the criminal law is also displaced as alternative legal regimes are recognized as providing potentially useful ways to manage risk. This is particularly apparent in efforts toward addressing urban disorder problems through administrative and regulatory law and in attempts to employ the considerable powers vested in contract law to manage public housing problems. Third, risk management approaches often forgo the criminal law entirely in order to mitigate security risks through advances in urban planning and design. This forges a tight connection between risk management efforts and the criminological focus on microengineering local environments to reduce the risk of crime and disorder (Felson 2002).

The emphasis on capitalizing on aggregate knowledge in developing risk management regimes also encourages the greater embrace of new information and surveillance technologies in policing. Such devices are not used simply to monitor individual offenders, but are also key in allowing officers to collect, manage, and exploit the information they collect, and to communicate risk knowledge to appropriate audiences.

Qualifications

There are also a series of questions about the assumptions and practices of the risk management model. One important issue relates to the degree to which risk management initiatives actually live up to their statistical, quantitative, and actuarial pretensions. Much of what passes for risk management can actually be developed in the absence of statistical knowledge of risks (O'Malley 2004). Part of the reason for this is that many events that police agencies try to manage are sufficiently rare or unique that there is no opportunity to collect the baseline data necessary to create statistical profiles. Even in those situations where the police do collect a great deal of information, however, another potential problem arises. In particular, the proliferation of statistical knowledge about various routine events creates an opportunity for police officials and politicians to selectively draw from such studies to legitimate programs and policies that have been developed because they cohere with local political priorities or institutional preferences. In such situations the police fail to live up to the type of objective model of policy development that the risk management paradigm suggests.

Concerns about the objective and actuarial basis of risk management initiatives also encourage a reconsideration of the claim that risk management programs are amoral. Rather than security risks being treated as amoral eventualities, it is more accurate to suggest that a re-moralization of crime and deviance is occurring. Moral considerations, for example, inform what risks are selected as warranting official response and the nature of that response. Risk management also prompts new forms of moral evaluation of citizens who might not live up to their responsibilities for managing their own risk profile.

The claim that risk management initiatives are proactive whereas crime control approaches are reactive also needs to be refined. In fact, both crime fighting and risk management efforts have forward- and backward-looking dynamics. The forward-looking dimension of risk management—which entails attempting to predict the future likelihood of untoward eventualities—is itself predicated on the analysis of historical data about prior events. Likewise, although crime fighting efforts clearly involve reacting to prior incidents, the entire justification for the crime-control response has always entailed a forward-looking desire to prospectively reduce crime through some combination of deterrence or incapacitation.

In conclusion, it is worth emphasizing that the risk management orientation exists alongside and often builds on other policing models and initiatives. Some longstanding police practices have been supplemented by the risk management focus, whereas others have been reconfigured as a form of risk management. Policing remains a multifaceted endeavor that cannot be neatly captured by any prevailing model of police practice.

KEVIN D. HAGGERTY

See also **COMPSTAT; Crime Control Strategies; Crime Control Strategies: Crime Prevention through Environmental Design; Crime Prevention; Hot Spots; Intelligence Gathering and Analysis: Impacts on Terrorism; Intelligence-Led Policing and Organizational Learning; Situational Crime Prevention; Technology and the Police**

References and Further Reading

Baker, Tom, and Jonathan Simon, eds. 2002. *Embracing risk: The changing culture of insurance and responsibility*. Chicago: University of Chicago Press.

Ericson, Richard V., and Kevin D. Haggerty. 1997. *Policing the risk society*. Toronto: University of Toronto Press, and Oxford: Oxford University Press.

Felson, Marcus. 2002. *Crime and everyday life*. 3rd ed. Thousand Oaks, CA: Sage.

Haggerty, Kevin D. 2001. *Making crime count*. Toronto: University of Toronto Press.

Hughes, Gordon. 1998. *Understanding crime prevention: Social control, risk and late modernity*. Buckingham: Open University Press.

O'Malley, Pat. 1992. Risk, power and crime prevention. *Economy and Society* 21: 252–75.

———. 2004. *Risk, uncertainty and government*. London: Glass House.

Reichman, Nancy. 1986. Managing crime risks: Toward an insurance based model of social control. *Research in Law, Deviance and Social Control* 8:151–72.

ROBBERY

Introduction and Definitions

Robbery is defined as "taking or attempting to take anything of value from the care, custody, or control of a person or persons by force or threat of force or violence and/ or by putting the victim in fear" (Federal Bureau of Investigations [FBI] 2004b, p. 21). It is an instrumental form of violence that is motivated primarily by anticipated economic rewards. Robbery can be distinguished from seemingly similar types of crimes such as larceny/theft and burglary in that it is committed *in the presence of a victim*. Robbery can be considered one of the most serious crime types because it involves close personal contact between offenders and victims, holds the potential for inflicting serious injury, and holds a high potential for economic loss. Approximately 60% of all robbery victims sustain injuries significant enough to require emergency room care and nearly 80% result in economic loss (FBI 2004a, Table 81). Close personal contact and potential for harm likely explain why many citizens fear becoming a victim of the crime of robbery (Sims and Johnston 2004).

Robbery Trends

Criminal incidents reported to the police are categorized into crime groups by police officers who file the reports that document incidents. Police officers who take reports about crime victims, for example, determine if an apparent break-in is a burglary or illegal trespassing or if an assault is aggravated or simple. This is important because robbery is often confused with other crimes such as assault, larceny/theft, or burglary yet is distinguished by the use or *threatened* use of force and direct contact between the victim and offender. One may typically hear a victim of a burglary exclaim "I was robbed," when in fact they were the victim of a burglary. This is a common mischaracterization. The responding officer considers the known circumstances of an incident when making the determination of whether a crime has actually occurred and proper classification of the event.

Approximately 458,000 robbery incidents were reported to state and local police in 2002. This amounts to approximately 512,000 robbery victimizations because robbery incidents are one of the most likely types of personal crimes to involve multiple victims (Bureau of Justice Statistics [BJS] 2003a, Table 26). Like other personal crime, robbery rose dramatically from the early 1960s to the early 1990s. After reaching a peak of approximately 600,000 incidents in 1981, robbery decreased for the next few years only to rise once again during the late 1980s and early 1990s. The total volume of robbery peaked at more than 680,000 incidents in 1991, and then decreased by nearly 40% where it has leveled off since 2000 at approximately 425,000 incidents.

It is also important to consider trends in robbery *rates* in addition to total volume because rates take into account changing population patterns. The highest robbery rate during the thirty-year period between the years 1973 and 2003 was in 1981 where it peaked at 7.4 per 1,000. The rate then fluctuated between 5 and 6 per 1,000 for much of the next decade only to peak again at 6.3 in 1993. Robbery rates subsequently decreased by nearly 80% between 1981 and 2002 from 7.4 to 2.5 per 1,000 (BJS 2003b).

Although these trends are similar in many ways, the post-1990s decrease in robbery rates appears more dramatic.

Characteristics of Robbery Incidents

Approximately one-half of all robbery incidents include some type of weapon. This compares to only a quarter of all assaults and 8% of rapes/sexual assaults. Hand guns represent the most common type of weapon used in robbery incidents (25%) followed by knives/cutting instruments (13%) and blunt objects (5%) (Perkins 2003, Table 2). The presence of a weapon is important in several ways including how successful offenders are in completing transactions. Incidents involving weapons are almost 20% more likely to be completed (79%). In contrast, only 57% of incidents involving knives/cutting instruments and 67% involving blunt objects are completed (Perkins 2003, 3).

Robbery is the quintessential street crime because it depends on generating fear in victims. Most robberies are directed against persons, as opposed to commercial institutions such as banks, and occur most often on streets or other public settings. The seemingly random nature of robbery along with the potential for harm generates fear. Offenders rely on this fear to expedite transactions successfully and quickly (Wright and Decker 1997). National data indicate that 43% of robberies occur on streets/highways, and 14% in both commercial houses and residences, respectively. There appears to be a noticeable regional effect where the percentage of incidents occurring on public streets was highest in the Northeast (57%) and lowest in the South (37%). The lower number of street/highway robberies in the South corresponds with a sizable increase in robberies occurring in residential locations (19%) (FBI 2004a, Table 2.19).

Understanding the victim–offender relationship (VOR) in robbery events is also important. Robbery typically involves victims and offenders who are strangers because it is an instrumental form of violence that is almost always motivated by financial gain. Compared to other forms of personal violence, robbery involves a greater percentage of victims and offenders who are strangers. For example, 63% of victim/offenders in robberies are strangers compared to 32% of rape/sexual assault cases and 51% of aggravated assaults (FBI 2004a, Table 43). This is generally expected because close personal relationships (for example, family and close friendships) are expected to insulate or protect individuals from instrumental forms of violence (see Decker 1993).

Victim and Offender Characteristics

Robbery is a younger person's game. Juveniles represent the largest percentage of arrest populations for robbery compared to other forms of personal violent crime such as murder, forcible rape, and aggravated assault. Snyder (2004, 2) reports that juveniles comprise approximately 23% of those arrested for robbery compared to only 10% for rape, 17% for forcible rape, and 13% for aggravated assault. Younger individuals are also disproportionately represented among robbery victims. Robbery victimization rates for individuals ages 16 to 24 are nearly 50% higher than among individuals ages 35 to 49 (FBI 2004a, Table 3).

Official statistics also reveal important features of offender and victim race as it relates to robbery. The National Crime Victimization Survey lets one determine the degree to which victim and offender demographic characteristics correspond through interviews with a sample of crime victims. Victims report on a series of issues relating to victimizations including perceptions of offender demographic characteristics.

Research consistently finds that crime is largely an intraracial phenomenon. For all personal crimes of violence, 73% of incidents involving white victims involve white offenders, and 75% of black victims were victimized by black offenders. The trend is stable for most violent personal crimes including rape/sexual assault and assault, yet it does not consistently hold for robbery victims. The intraracial nature of robbery is particularly strong for robberies involving black victims of whom 85% report being victimized by black offenders. White victims, however, stand in sharp contrast to this pattern. For example, 44% of white robbery victims reported being victimized by an offender of a different race. Thus, white robbery victims seem to have a greater chance of being victimized by an offender of a different race than other victims of robbery or any other type of personal crime (FBI 2004a). This form of interracial victimization along with any disproportionate attention given to such events by the news media holds the potential for increasing fear of crime.

Drugs–Robbery Nexus

Drug markets hold the potential for high levels of violence. The explosion in crack use in the 1980s is partly responsible for the increase in serious violent crime during that period. The most direct connection between drugs and robbery is through economically compulsive behavior that compels individuals to seek ways to generate income quickly and easily in the pursuit of the "next fix." Individuals involved in robbery are often involved in lifestyles of intense partying where drugs play a pivotal role. Robberies require very little skill, are often opportunistic in nature, and represent immediate access to the cash necessary for supporting such a lifestyle (Wright and Decker 1997).

A large percentage of offenders arrested for robbery are active drug users and often are motivated to commit crime to support drug habits. For example, a 1991 study of arrestees in twenty-four cities indicated that two-thirds of males arrested for robbery tested positive for some illegal substance as did three-quarters of females. The rate for males was second only to those arrested for burglary (68%) and drug sale/possession (79%) (BJS 1994, Table 2). As a class of offenders, those arrested for robbery are also *most likely* to report committing their offense to obtain money to buy drugs (BJS 1994, Table 3).

SEAN P. VARANO and
SCOTT H. DECKER

See also **Crime, Serious Violent; Drug Markets; Fear of Crime;** *Uniform Crime Reports*

References and Further Reading

Bureau of Justice Statistics. 1994. *Fact sheet: Drug-related crime*. NCJ149286. Washington, DC: U.S. Department of Justice.
———. 2003a. *Criminal victimization in the United States, 2002 statistical tables*. Washington, DC: U.S. Department of Justice.
———. 2003b. *Reported crime in United States—Total*. http://www.ojp.usdoj.gov/bjs (accessed April 14, 2005).
Decker, S. H. 1993. Exploring victim–offender relationships in homicide: The role of individual and event characteristics. *Justice Quarterly* 104: 585–612.
Federal Bureau of Investigation. 2004a. *Crime in the U.S.: 2003*. Washington, DC: United States Department of Justice.
———. 2004b. *Uniform crime reporting handbook*. Washington, DC: U.S. Department of Justice.
Perkins, C. 2003. Weapon use and violent crime. NCJ194820. Washington, DC: U.S. Department of Justice.
Sims, B., and E. Johnston. 2004. Examining public opinion about crime and justice: A statewide study. *Criminal Justice Policy Review* 15 (3): 270–93.
Snyder, H. N. 2004. *Juvenile arrests 2002*. NCJ204608. Washington, DC: U.S. Department of Justice.
Wright, R. T., and S. H. Decker. 1997. *Armed robbers in action: Stickups and street culture*. Boston, MA: Northeastern University Press.

ROLE OF THE POLICE

The enforcement of the law is one of the most influential mechanisms for social control. In fact, there exists no governmental function that controls or directs the activities of the public as much as law enforcement. Law enforcement is a government service with which the public has frequent contact. Such contact and control is constant and, if it is not experienced directly through personal contact, it is at least felt indirectly through the visible or implied presence of police personnel.

To most people the phrase *law enforcement* relates directly to the responsibility of uniformed police officers or to police activities in the community. This relationship is correct since the police are most surely involved in the enforcement of the law and, by definition, police officers are persons employed by municipal, county, or state governments and charged with the responsibility of enforcing the law and maintaining order. Typically, they are referred to as city police, county sheriffs and deputies, and state police or highway patrol officers.

Not valid, however, is the tendency to think of crime control and the maintenance of order as the exclusive responsibility of the police. This misconception is easily understood, however, when we consider the visible activities of the police. The police have the responsibility for dealing with crime and traffic on a twenty-four-hour basis, are usually conspicuously visible to the public, and are the agents that immediately respond when violations of the law occur. The police, however, are just one segment of the mechanism our society uses to maintain the standards of conduct necessary to protect individuals in the community. This system has four generalized and separately organized units: police, prosecution, courts, and corrections. Generally speaking, the police are charged with the detection, identification, and apprehension of law violators. The prosecutor's office will determine whether to charge or not charge the offender; if a charge is filed, what to charge; if appropriate, to plea bargain; and if a charge is filed, to prosecute. Courts hear cases, weigh evidence, interpret law, and determine guilt or innocence. When guilt is the finding, the sentence may be suspended or, if a sentence is imposed, it may be probation, a fine, incarceration, or some combination of these. Corrections is charged with detention and rehabilitation of the offender. This is obviously an oversimplification of the process, but it does place in perspective the special generalized role of the police in conjunction with the other segments of the system.

Types of Police

City police derive their authority from the state constitution, and their administrative operations are defined by each municipal government. Municipal police are granted full police powers.

In addition to municipal police, there are county sheriffs' departments, which in large parts of the United States constitute full-fledged police organizations. In some states, however, they are restricted to the administration of the county correctional facility, the serving of court orders and documents, and provision of security for courts.

State police units exist in all but a few of the states. They may be called state police, public safety departments, or highway patrols. In some states they practice full police activities, but typically they limit their function to highway traffic control, enforcement, and accident investigation.

Although the U.S. Constitution did not specifically establish federal police agencies, Congress created them for the enforcement of specific legislative acts. For example, the Constitution stipulates that Congress has the power to coin money and punish counterfeiters (Article I, Section 8). Concurrently, Congress has the authority to establish the Secret Service to detect and arrest counterfeiters. Other examples of federal police agencies include the Federal Bureau of Investigation, Internal Revenue Service, and the Drug Enforcement Administration.

The Police Responsibility

The municipal, county, and state police of the United States are charged with responsibilities that rank second to none in importance in our democratic society. The police service is that branch of government that is assigned the awesome task of securing compliance to the multitude of laws and regulations deemed beneficial to society. Because law is society's means of achieving conformance to desired norms, the police are society's agents for the maintenance of harmony within the community.

Within this broad context the police are charged with (1) safeguarding of lives and property, (2) preservation of the peace, (3) prevention of crime, (4) suppression of crime through detection and arrest of violators of the law, (5) enforcement of the law, (6) prevention of delinquency, (7) safeguarding the constitutional rights of individuals, (8) control of vehicular traffic, (9) suppression of vice, and (10) provision of public services.

The police have not always had these broad responsibilities. For years the police, and even the public, generally believed the police were fulfilling their responsibility by investigating crime and attempting to apprehend criminals. No thought was given to the concept of prevention, and most certainly citizens did not expect the police to intervene in domestic disputes or problems related to their youngsters. Police officers saw themselves as "crime fighters" and in fact many officers still hold to such provincial thinking. Role conflict is unavoidable as the police oscillate between competing traditions such as control of the public versus social service to the public. So strong is the influence of the past that typical police officers show deep resentment when an outsider attempts to confront them with evidence of the change.

Although the police function is old, it has begun, of necessity, to change in order to meet changing needs. The process of law enforcement has gone through a gradual development along with the country's urbanization, which has enlarged the police role significantly.

Even though the police of this country are changing, certain of society's expectations are beyond their capability. For example, even under the most favorable conditions the police cannot eliminate crime. The police do not create the social conditions conducive to crime nor can they resolve them. The police do not enact the legislation that they must enforce. They do not adjudicate the offenders they arrest, and they are only one of the agencies of criminal justice.

Most certainly the police role still involves their being "crime fighters," but in a much broader context. In addition to the suppression of crime and enforcement of the law, the police are becoming increasingly involved with crime prevention and public service. Theirs is an expanding role and now includes such activities as family crisis intervention, juvenile diversion, social agency referral services, youth programs, rape victim assistance, and other public service functions. Since *Miranda v. Arizona*, which required police officers to inform suspects of their constitutional rights before questioning, the police have come to recognize their role in safeguarding the constitutional rights of individuals.

It is even being suggested by some criminologists and a few police administrators that police organizations should become known as "departments of police services" rather than police departments or, worse yet, police forces. They suggest that law enforcement is a "police service" rather than a "police force." By definition, the word *force* denotes coercion, power, compulsion, brawn, might, and generally refers to troops of an army. Service on the other hand denotes help, duty, and aid, which is a more appropriate description of the police function. In support of this view, some police organizations have recognized law enforcement as a community responsibility, with the police assuming a leadership profile rather than an autocratic role.

Police Power/Authority

The concept of "police service" must not, however, infer erosion of the authority of the police officer in terms of the legal definition of his or her responsibility for enforcement. Unfortunately people have demonstrated their inability to live in harmony with their neighbors, thus the need for exercising police authority and the legal power of arrest. In conjunction with the "power to arrest," the police do have the authority to use force in securing compliance with the law and this authority is in fact basic to their role in maintaining public order. This awesome but essential authority carries with it the responsibility of using only that force absolutely necessary in any given situation in order to achieve a legal objective. The possible consequences of the use of force demand that it be exercised with the greatest degree of discretion. The police officer should always try for voluntary surrender in any arrest situation, but need not retreat or desist from his or her efforts by reason of the resistance or threatened resistance of the person being arrested.

To really understand the role of the police in achieving their objectives, it is necessary to review operational line functions. *Line functions* are police activities directly related to the achievement of objectives. They are, typically, patrol and criminal investigation.

Patrol

Patrol refers to moving on foot or by vehicle around and within an assigned area for the purpose of providing police services. Police officers are usually in uniform, and when a vehicle is used, it is usually conspicuously marked. The purpose of patrol is to distribute police officers in a manner that will eliminate or reduce the opportunity for citizen misconduct, increase the probability of apprehension if a criminal commits a crime, and provide a quick response when a citizen requests police assistance. The patrol unit is the backbone of police operations and operates twenty-four hours each day.

The patrol function is so basic to fulfilling the police responsibility that its goals are essentially synonymous with the total police objective. As such, the patrol officer is the most important position of the police organization. The patrol officer is responsible for all activities within his or her geographical assignment and will respond to all situations related to police service. He or she will institute constant surveillance techniques, arrest violators when he or she observes the commission of a crime, respond to radio-dispatched calls as requested by citizens, control vehicular and pedestrian traffic, direct traffic, enforce traffic regulations, investigate traffic accidents, conduct preliminary investigations following the commission of a crime, investigate public accidents involving personal injury, mediate family disputes, search for lost children, refer people to social agencies able to offer specialized assistance outside the realm of police services, give directions to motorists, and provide a wide variety of other public services.

Criminal Investigation

The investigation of crime becomes necessary when patrol has failed as a deterrent or has been unable to apprehend the criminal immediately after the commission of a crime. The initial purpose of investigation is to identify, locate, and arrest the perpetrator of the crime. The secondary but equally important purpose is to prepare the case for court and assist in the prosecution of the offender.

The police officer who investigates such crimes is usually referred to as a detective. Generally the detective goes to work after the fact and must rely on such things as physical evidence, witnesses, and information obtained from various sources. As a general rule, the detective works in civilian clothing so that he or she is inconspicuous when moving about the community in pursuance of the investigative task.

Unlike patrol officers, detectives are not usually involved in crime prevention but with the repression of crime through the subsequent arrest of offenders. Briefly stated, the detective becomes involved in such activities as searching the crime scenes, securing physical evidence, interviewing witnesses, interrogating suspects, obtaining warrants of arrest, taking suspects into custody, preparing written reports for prosecution, and testifying in court.

Crime Prevention

As stated previously, in recent years the police have become more involved with crime prevention. Crime prevention is primarily an additional responsibility of uniformed patrol officers and personnel assigned to a specialized crime prevention organizational unit.

The primary means by which patrol prevents crime is through being conspicuous and available. The obvious presence of the police discourages the criminal from committing a crime for fear of being caught. This indicates the importance of the conspicuously marked vehicle. Not only does this show their presence, but it also gives the impression of police saturation. Patrol officers also prevent crime by becoming familiar with juveniles within their patrol area or beat. A healthy relationship built on mutual respect between the patrol officers and juveniles will do more toward the prevention of delinquency than any other police activity. The patrol officer is the person the juveniles see and identify as the authority symbol. Respect for the officer promotes respect for the law, and such respect will discourage unlawful conduct.

A very important, but often overlooked, role of patrol in crime prevention is the securing of information that can be passed to other units of the police department. With such information the specialized units can work on a potential problem prior to its actually becoming a problem. The patrol officer is on the street and is in the best possible position to obtain information on such things as the formation of a juvenile gang, the underlying frustrations of the community, and the use of narcotics.

A specialized unit for crime prevention may become involved with such things as coordination of neighborhood watch programs, diversion programs for juveniles, public education, improving community relations, involvement with community organizations, youth programs, and working with other public agencies.

Support Services

Other police officers work within organizational units that exist to assist the line activities of the police organization. These men and women may be assigned to the crime laboratory, communications center, records, equipment maintenance, research and planning, inspections, jail, identification center, property management, personnel recruitment and selection, and training.

Police Role in the Protection of Individual Freedom

In effect, people of the community realize their civil rights through the interpretive actions of the police. In other words, police procedures and policies are in a sense telling the public what they can or cannot do. There are, of course, many controls from the federal level relative to civil rights, but implementation is the major responsibility of the local police departments, and they must be totally cognizant of the ramifications and importance of these rights.

In addition to interpretive actions defining civil rights, the police have the role of instructing citizens with regard to their duties, obligations, rights, and privileges in terms of the law. They should, for example, publish pamphlets that describe the citizens' rights under the Constitution of the United States, the state, and the municipality within which they live. The police might also stress the public's responsibility in relation to those protective privileges that they have under the law.

VERN L. FOLLEY

ROUTINE GUARDIANSHIP

The fear of crime and victimization is ever present. Recent statistical evidence from the Federal Bureau of Investigation's *Uniform Crime Reports* supports this contention with a violent crime (homicide, robbery, forcible rape, and aggravated assault) reported to occur every 23.1 seconds and a property crime (burglary, larceny-theft, and motor vehicle theft) every 3.1 seconds (Federal Bureau of Investigation [FBI] 2005, 7). This frequency of criminal victimization along with a myriad of other social, political, and economic factors contributes to an atmosphere of fear when it comes to crime in our communities.

In this kind of climate, the public continually looks to law enforcement to provide daily protection from such criminal offenders. A challenge to police functioning in this capacity occurs when the true nature and extent of crime in communities is unknown. This is substantiated by findings from the National Crime Victimization Survey, whereby only 40% of violent and property crimes nationwide combined were reported by citizens to the police (U.S. Department of Justice 2005, Table 91).

Defining Guardianship

Beyond these statistics, in many other respects, society relies on the police to serve their communities daily by routinely protecting both persons and property. As such, among the many roles that police assume is that of a guardian to the members of a community. In this respect, the police officer acts much like a parent in protecting a child. In the guardianship role, law enforcement officials often serve as the first line of third-party intervention in mediating everyday disputes between people or over property. This notion of guardianship is rooted in the criminological theory of *routine activities first* offered by Cohen and Felson (1979; see more recently Tark and Kleck 2004). According to routine activities theory, criminal behavior is a result of interactions between motivated offenders, available targets, and a lack of capable guardianship that converges in place and time.

If, as Cohen and Felson (1979) hypothesize, there are individuals in society who have the propensity or inclination to offend, crime prevention efforts aimed specifically at reducing the motive for offending may meet with only limited success. Therefore, more effective prevention strategies may need to center on elevating both the real and perceived level of risk for the potential offender when committing the crime. This notion is tied strongly to deterrence theories of criminality.

According to deterrence theory (Beccaria 1963; Bentham 1948), criminals are discouraged from committing criminal acts if the following conditions exist: the certainty of apprehension is known, a severe penalty is proscribed for the behavior, and the penalty is delivered swiftly. In particular, while severity of the penalty has been the emphasis in many crime control policies, the swiftness of the punishment for the crime and the certainty of apprehension have been much less examined as potential leverages in the control of criminal behavior. From a deterrence standpoint, it is believed that the potential offender will evaluate the benefit of committing the crime in relation to the relative risks. Here, the degree of certainty of apprehension is associated with the existing level of guardianship. Coupling this deterrence notion with routine activities theory yields the contention that the exercise of effective guardianship over people, places, and property contributes to the deterrence of criminal behavior of motivated offenders against available targets.

However, in practice, the routines of everyday life often expose victims to variable levels of exposure, or threat, to the intentions and effects of would-be offenders. These routine daily behaviors are not only carried out by victims and offenders, but also by the police, which typically are the most visible representatives of guardianship. Yet current FBI statistics report the national rate of full-time law enforcement employees to be just 3.5 per 1,000 U.S. inhabitants (FBI 2005, 370). These sheer numbers alone cast doubt on the ability of the police to provide active capable guardianship over the routine behavioral transactions of approximately 270 million people on a daily basis. These numbers suggest, according to some observers, that the challenges to effective police guardianship over people and property are unrealistic given the density of police to population (Goldstein 2003). Therefore, as a matter of practicality, routine guardianship cannot be limited to the particular dynamics of police practices. That is, communities, neighborhoods, families, and individuals, as well as technology, can and do provide for varying types and degrees of capable guardianship on a routine basis.

The Context of Guardianship

Capable guardianship is exercised in the many aspects of everyday life that seldom involve the direct presence or actions of the police. Individual efforts such as use of target hardening methods have been found to effectively increase guardianship over one's own personal property (Miethe and Meier 1990). Similarly, looking at community settings, higher levels of cohesion among residents has been associated with greater likelihood of intervention in public criminal and deviant activities (Sampson and Raudenbush 1997). Therefore, in well-integrated communities, the risk for victimization appears to be lower because these areas tend to display active social control (Lee 2000). The presence of "collective efficacy" within communities conveys within an informal context that guardianship exists within neighborhoods. Likewise, more formalized community efforts to reduce crime through existing neighborhood watch programs, which is one of the initiatives stemming from community-oriented policing strategies, assist law enforcement by empowering citizens to serve in some capacity as guardians of their own environmental space (see also Nolan, Conti, and McDevitt 2005).

The everyday activities of shopping in a mall, going out for a meal, commuting to work, or simply sitting on your front porch often constitute what may be viewed as forms of guardianship. Each of these activities suggests a higher likelihood that any criminal behavior in these arenas will be observed by someone. This observer, or witness, in turn introduces a number of potential consequences. First, the probability of behavior being witnessed probably increases the risk of the offender not only being identified, but getting caught.

Second, and perhaps more important, the presence of these individuals potentially provides some degree of protection or intervention against would-be offenders. Third, as a latent consequence, if offenders work within criminal networks, conveyance of information about the level of guardianship in a specific location may serve to deter other would-be offenders from victimizing that particular target (Whine 1999). This increase in the level of guardianship, therefore, contributes to reducing the availability of suitable targets and further may discourage motivated offenders from committing criminal acts.

Routine guardianship has other dimensions as well. Thus far, the discussion has focused on overt, or manifest, guardianship exercised by individuals over people, property, or places. Similarly, covert, or latent, guardianship also occurs through many mechanisms that are common to daily routine activities. That is, in today's world, manifest guardianship is typically associated with the actions of the police or interactions of individuals in public spaces. Advanced technologies, as well as developing innovations in the design and construction of both public and private spaces, have enhanced the opportunity for effective latent guardianship to be exercised throughout many facets of everyday life.

In terms of physical structures, significant advances in crime prevention have occurred by incorporating environmental design factors such as lighting, access, visibility, and security in the construction phases of community and economic development. This crime prevention approach uses architecture and urban planning as an environmental improvement process for solving crime problems better known as crime prevention through environmental design (CPTED). Such an approach has been shown to be successful as one crime prevention strategy (Brantingham, Brantingham, and Taylor 2005). Moreover, crime prevention efforts that have been tied to current technologies provide more abundant examples: Traffic cameras commonly used by news agencies, the availability and use of handheld video recorders, and closed-circuit TV in both public and private buildings, including commercial, residential, and retail enterprises, provide video surveillance and recording of behavior that may occur in those settings. These are just a few of the many technologies available today that afford forms of guardianship. Physical security systems in residences and the workplace are also common. Even in computing environments, electronic transactions such as e-mail traffic, voice retrieval, geographic positioning systems, and both wire and wireless transfers of financial information may provide opportunities for surveillance of behavior in a variety of settings.

Each of these technological developments has become increasingly present in everyday life and has improved the likelihood that guardianship can be exercised over varieties of human behavior that previously were nonexistent. Although such routine guardianship is likely to decrease opportunities for criminal victimization, some individuals are concerned about whether the availability of these sources of guardianship promotes an erosion of personal privacy and increases the potential for policing authorities of the state to abuse such information in the name of public safety. Although perhaps a legitimate concern, the balance between constitutional rights to privacy and prevailing needs for ensuring the public's security continue with the capacity and means of routine guardianship by the state at the heart of the debate. Nonetheless, routine guardianship persists in various forms and provides for enhanced security and protection of life and property when employed properly.

JANICE E. CLIFFORD and JOHN P. JARVIS

See also **Community-Oriented Policing: Practices; Crime Analysis; Role of the Police; Situational Crime Prevention**

References and Further Reading

Beccaria, Cessare. 1963. *On crimes and punishments.* Trans. H. Paolucci. Indianapolis, IN: Bobbs-Merrill. Original work published 1764.

Bentham, Jeremy. 1948. *An introduction to the principles of morals and legislation,* ed. W. Harrison. Oxford, England: Basil Blackwell. Original work published 1789.

Brantingham, Patricia L., Paul J. Brantingham, and Wendy Taylor. 2005. Situational crime prevention as a key component in embedded crime prevention. *Canadian Journal of Criminology and Criminal Justice* 47 (20): 271–93.

Cohen, Lawrence E., and Marcus Felson. 1979. Social change and crime rate trends: A routine activity approach. *American Sociological Review* 44 (1979): 588–608.

Cordner, Gary, and Elizabeth Perkins Biebel. 2005. Problem-oriented policing in practice. *Criminology & Public Policy* 4 (2): 155–80.

Federal Bureau of Investigation. 2005. *Crime in the United States 2004.* Washington, DC: U.S. Department of Justice.

Goldstein, Herman. 2003. On further developing problem-oriented policing: The most critical need, the major impediments, and a proposal. *Crime Prevention Studies* 15: 13–47.

Lee, Matthew. 2000. Community cohesion and violent predatory victimization: A theoretical extension and cross-national test of opportunity theory. *Social Forces* 79 (2): 683–88.

Levin, Bernard H., and Richard W. Meyers. 2005. A proposal for an enlarged range of policing: Neighborhood-driven policing. In *Neighborhood driven policing,* ed. Jensen and Levin, 3–9. Quantico, VA: U.S. Department of Justice, Federal Bureau of Investigation.

Mesko, Gorazd, and Branko Lobnikar. 2005. The contribution of local safety councils to local responsibility in crime prevention and provision of safety. *Policing: An International Journal of Police Strategies & Management* 28 (2): 353–73.

Miethe, Terance D., and Robert F. Meier. 1990. Opportunity, choice and criminal victimization: A test of a theoretical model. *Journal of Research in Crime and Delinquency* 27: 243–66.

Nolan, James J., Norman Conti, and Jack McDevitt. 2005. Situational policing. *Law Enforcement Bulletin* 74 (11): 1–9.

Sampson, Robert J., and Stephen W. Raudenbush. 1997. Neighborhoods and violent crime: A multilevel study of collective efficacy. *Science* 227 (5328): 918–24.

Tark, Jongyeon, and Gary Kleck. 2004. Resisting crime: The effects of victim action on the outcome of crimes. *Criminology* 42 (4): 861–909.

Tewksbury, Richard, and Elizabeth Ehrhardt Mustaine. 2003. College students' lifestyles and self-protective behaviors: Further consideration of the guardianship concept in routine activity theory. *Criminal Justice and Behavior* 30 (3): 302–27.

U.S. Department of Justice. 2005. *Criminal victimization in the United States: 2003 statistical tables from the National Criminal Victimization Survey*. NCJ207811. Washington, DC: Office of Justice Programs, Bureau of Justice Statistics.

Whine, Michael. 1999. Cyberspace—A new medium for communication, command, and control by extremists. *Studies in Conflict and Terrorism* 22: 231–45.

ROWAND AND MAYNE, FIRST POLICE COMMISSIONERS, UNITED KINGDOM

Rowan, Sir Charles, KCB (ca. 1782–1852), and Mayne, Sir Richard, KCB (1796–1868).

The two founding commissioners of the Metropolitan Police were deliberately chosen for their differences. Sir Charles Rowan was a military man born in Ulster who had been wounded at Waterloo in 1815, for which service he was created Companion of the Bath. Sir Richard Mayne, born in Dublin and fourteen years Rowan's junior, was a lawyer who had been called to the bar and was practicing on the Northern Circuit. Home Secretary Robert Peel's (1778–1850) design was to unite a military man "of great energy, great activity both of body and mind" with "a sensible lawyer" and give them the freedom to fashion a professionalized, permanent police force for the capital (Critchley 1977, 88). Others deliberated and refused before Rowan and Mayne accepted the appointments in 1829; Mayne, at thirty-three, becoming the force's youngest commissioner to this day. Both would make the Police of the Metropolis their life's work, and both would see elevation to the status of Knights Commander of the Bath for this service before their deaths.

Rowan and Mayne were first introduced by Peel on July 6, 1829, and were entrusted with making his vision a reality. The establishment of a permanent police force in London presented Peel and the commissioners with substantial political challenges, however. Widespread suspicion among political elites that the establishment of a professional police force would amount to the introduction of tyranny to England presented a serious ideological obstacle. The idea had been proposed and dismissed twice before as recently as 1818 and 1822. The spectacle of espionage and oppression under the auspices of police in France and Prussia were alarming enough to cause the House of Commons to accept in 1818 that such a proposal would "of necessity be odious and repulsive" (Tobias 1975, 98). As *The Standard* would protest shortly after the force's establishment, "The thing is not—never was English" (Elmsley 1983, 59).

Peel's great achievement was to describe a model of policing that did not appear incompatible with the unspoken principles of English liberty. At the same time, the establishment of the police formed an important component of a broader plan to overhaul the "bloody code." The Metropolitan Police were but one component of Peel's commitment to a preventive, rather than a harshly punitive, solution to crime. "I want to teach people," he would write, "that liberty does not consist in having your house robbed by organized gangs of thieves, and in leaving the principal streets of London in the nightly possession of drunken women and vagabonds" (Tobias 1975, 100).

The 1829 Police Act, which created the positions of the two commissioners, did not specify how the force was to be organized. That task fell directly on the shoulders of the two men. As Mayne himself would remark before a parliamentary committee in 1834, "[e]verything that has been done since the commencement has originated with the Commissioners; the whole of the organization has been made by them alone" (Critchley 1977, 89).

The operation was performed with astonishing speed. By the end of July, they had been allocated office space at 4 Whitehall Place, backing onto Great Scotland Yard, where they would form a headquarters. Men were recruited, equipment purchased, and a detailed *General Instruction Book* drafted that included a description of the intended organizational structure of the force and the legal status and responsibilities of the constable. On August 29 Rowan and Mayne were sworn in as magistrates, and on September 16 they personally swore in their fledgling force of 1,011 men.

Each man was required to be more than five feet seven inches tall, strong, in good health, and under age thirty-five, though it appears some were older. Strict rules of behavior, designed in part to distinguish this new force from the notoriously corrupt and patchy provision provided by nightwatchmen and others, applied to constables whether on or off duty. Swift and summary dismissals for drunkenness or absenteeism would help to ensure that by the time the force was two years old no fewer than half of its recruits had been discharged. A new uniform, carefully designed to appear civilian and nonmilitary in nature, was issued to each man every year, and wages were a guinea a week.

The organizational scheme for the new police was Rowan's creation. Applying his military experience to the task of establishing a highly visible patrol presence on the streets of the capital, he conceived a system of "beats" to which constables could be assigned and which they would patrol at regular intervals. Though military nomenclature was in the main avoided, the seven-square-mile area under the force's purview was parceled into "divisions," to each of which was allocated a "company" of men, headed by a "superintendent." Standard-issue wooden rattles ensured constables could call for help at a moment's notice.

The high standards of accountability and behavior to which constables were subject were stressed in Rowan and Mayne's instructions. A constable was "not to interfere idly or unnecessarily in order to make a display of his authority." Rather, he would act "with decision and boldness" only when required, and in doing so "may expect to receive the fullest support in the proper exercise of his authority" (Critchley 1977, 91).

If traditional English liberties and due process of law were not enough to govern the constables' discretion, Mayne's legal perspective added prudential reasons for circumspection. Unlike elsewhere in Europe, he stressed, English constables could be held personally liable for acts committed in their respective public capacities. If suspected of corruption, they did not have the luxury of immunity against being hauled before a court in either civil or criminal actions.

The new force, dubbed "Peel's private army" and "Bobbies" by detractors, evolved in an uncertain political atmosphere. Criticism continued well beyond the early days and was inevitably at its strongest when the police faced large-scale public order challenges. Mayne had his resignation refused at least twice late in his career following particularly visible blunders surrounding the 1866 Hyde Park riot and the Clerkenwell bombing the subsequent year.

The original emphasis on public visibility, with its appearance both of moral transparency and of effective deterrence, however, were never lost, and helped to ensure the Metropolitan Police's survival beyond its modest beginnings. Rowan retired in 1850 and died in 1852 at his home in Park Lane. By the time of Mayne's death in 1868 he was the sole commissioner at the head of a force of almost eight thousand men, whose geographical remit had increased tenfold. In addition, the capital had become a model for policing that had been adopted by counties across the entire country. Had it not been for Peel's decision to combine military know-how with legal continence, this vision of policing in a liberal democracy may never quite have been born.

ANDREW DAVIES

See also **Accountability; British Policing; Crime Prevention**

References and Further Reading

Critchley, T. A. 1977. Peel, Rowan and Mayne: The British model of urban police. In *Pioneers in policing,* ed. P. J. Stead. Montclair, NJ: Patterson Smith.

Emsley, C. 1983. *Policing and its context 1750–1870.* Hong Kong: Macmillan.

Fido, M., and K. Skinner. 1999. *The official encyclopedia of Scotland Yard.* London: Virgin Publishing.

Mason, G. 2004. *The official history of the Metropolitan Police.* London: Carlton.

Tobias, J. J. 1975. Policing and public in the United Kingdom. In. *Police forces in history,* ed. G. L. Misse. Beverly Hills, CA: Sage.

RURAL AND SMALL-TOWN LAW ENFORCEMENT

While it is common to think of America as an urban society, significant parts of the country remain outside major cities. About 70% of the land in America and about 20% of America's population is in nonmetropolitan counties—counties with fewer than fifty thousand people that are not adjacent to and economically dependent on large urban areas. In America, most *people* live in urban areas, but most *places* are rural. Further, the rural population of the United States is larger than the population of blacks or of Hispanics. It is greater than the population of Canada, Spain, Columbia, or Australia, and about the same as the population of France or Germany.

The image of rural life as crime free is largely a myth. While it is true that overall crime is lower in rural areas, the rates of drug use and domestic violence are about the same in rural and urban areas. Further, there are pockets of rural America with very high crime rates. For example, of the thirty counties in the United States with the highest homicide rates, nineteen are nonmetropolitan and eleven of these are so sparsely populated that they have no community of 2,500 or more. Thus, rural areas often have very real crime problems.

Before proceeding, a word of caution is in order. It is difficult to provide a simple description of rural police while also recognizing that rural areas and small towns vary tremendously from one part of the country to the next. Some rural communities have extreme levels of violent crime, whereas other rural areas have relatively little. Many nonmetropolitan counties are steeped in poverty, others are relatively wealthy. Some have very stable populations while others experience great population mobility. Parsimony demands that the current discussion focus on the typical or average rural agency, recognizing that not all rural areas are alike.

Public images of the police are largely shaped by media portrayals of large urban police agencies. Scholarly research on the police has also focused on these agencies, leaving the impression that police agencies and police work everywhere mirror that found in the largest central cities. However, real differences exist between police in rural and urban areas. First, let us consider urban–rural differences in the nature of the agencies themselves, and then turn our attention to differences in the nature of police work.

Rural and Small-Town Police Agencies

Although some police agencies operate within rural areas, they are not truly of those areas, and their impact is relatively small. These include the state police, state and federal conservation agents, park rangers, and numerous other state and federal agencies. These agencies may operate in rural areas and small towns, but they are accountable to their parent agency and not to local citizens. They typically have specialized police functions and do not act in a general law enforcement capacity. For these reasons, the focus here is on policing by county sheriffs and by municipal police, agencies that account for the overwhelming majority of rural police activity.

Municipal police generally limit their work to the borders of their towns. The municipal police chief is usually appointed by and accountable to the city council, and in many communities can be fired at will. In contrast, the sheriff is usually elected and is thus more directly accountable to local citizens. Sheriff's offices have countywide jurisdiction. In addition to traditional law enforcement, sheriff's offices are usually responsible for running the local jail, providing court security and prisoner transport, and serving civil papers.

There are more than 3,100 counties in the United States, each with a locally elected sheriff, and more than three-fourths of those counties are nonmetropolitan. Similarly, there are more than fifteen thousand municipal police departments in the United States and just under half of those are in nonmetropolitan counties. While large agencies fit common stereotypes of police, these stereotypes are wrong. Nationwide, 90% of all police agencies have fewer than fifty sworn officers, and half of all agencies have fewer than ten officers. Considering only nonmetropolitan areas, the typical municipal police department has three officers and the typical sheriff's office has eight officers.

Police Work in Small Towns and Rural Areas

Police work in small towns and rural areas often differs in style and substance from that in the largest cities. It would be a mistake to label the work of rural and small-town police as law enforcement, because their duties go far beyond enforcing the law. It would be more accurate to describe their work as policing. In many rural areas and small towns, the police are the only social service agency available around the clock 365 days a year, and they may be called on to deal with problems that in urban areas would be handled by other agencies. For example, some small town police chiefs' duties included putting up Christmas lights on city streets and checking on chemicals in the water treatment plant. They may be called on to respond to barking dogs or to take medicine to an elderly shut-in.

Because rural and small town departments often have a small number of officers, rural police are more likely to be generalists. Rural police chiefs and sheriffs routinely take patrol shifts and rural officers may be called on to handle a variety of tasks, including community relations, evidence gathering, escorting funeral processions, investigating accidents, seizing methamphetamine laboratories, and responding to a bank robbery. This array of tasks, some of which urban police would consider menial, combined with the public perception that rural areas are crime free, leads many to believe that rural policing is safe while urban policing is dangerous. In reality, rural police work is both demanding and dangerous. The rate at which rural officers are killed in the line of duty is about double that of the largest cities.

The typical rural and small town officer must work with a series of restrictions not experienced by most urban officers. First, rural and small-town agencies are often restricted by a small tax base for funding their operations. The average per-officer expenditure for rural police is about one-half that of urban police, and in some jurisdictions rural police work without benefits packages. Some rural police must pay for their own uniforms and weapons, and job applicants who have already paid for state-mandated training often have an edge in hiring. Rural police often lag behind urban police in their access to and familiarity with technology, such as in-car computers and less-than-lethal force devices. Rural police are less likely to be unionized, hampering efforts to demand more resources.

A second limitation of rural police is the small size of most agencies. In a three-officer department, for example, officers are likely to patrol alone and without back-up from their own agency. Small department sizes also make access to training difficult. In a small agency, sending one officer away for two weeks of training places a hardship on the remaining officers and may upset residents who expect their officers to be available at all times.

Finally, rural agencies must often deal with the problems posed by geography. Arizona, for example, has fifteen counties that are on average about the size of New Jersey. Long distances can mean a long response time and a long wait for back-up. In some parts of the country, remote terrain also means numerous "dead spots" where communication equipment, including personal cell phones, does not work.

Despite the obstacles, rural policing has some advantages over urban policing. For example, rural police work is highly public and visible. The citizen stopped for speeding may well ask, "Why am I getting a ticket when you didn't give one to Fred last week?" Familiarity and visibility may make rural police agencies more accountable to their public, a notion consistent with what urban police have tried to accomplish with community policing programs. Accountability is enhanced by the fact that sheriffs may be voted out of office and municipal chiefs can be dismissed by the city council, often at will with little notice.

Another advantage of rural policing is that the rural officer is likely to live among the people he or she polices. The officer will know citizens personally, seeing them while off duty as well as while on duty. In turn, local citizens will know a great deal about the officer and his or her family. Although communication skills are important in any police department, they are particularly necessary for rural police. In urban areas respect is often given to the uniform, but in rural areas respect is given to the officer as an individual. Thus, in rural areas donning a uniform is not enough. Respect must be earned. This, in turn, puts pressure on the police to be sensitive to citizen concerns.

An emphasis on accountability, combined with a personal familiarity, may help explain why rural citizens have a more positive view of their police than do urban residents. For example, urban citizens are three times more likely than rural citizens to believe their police engage in brutality and corruption.

Despite the handicaps they face, rural police do a better job of solving crime. For every major index offense, clearance rates (the percentage of crimes solved through an arrest) are higher in rural agencies than in urban agencies. For example, in rural areas about 78% of murders are solved through an arrest, whereas in the largest cities only about 57% are solved. Despite substantial advances in technology and in the science of criminal investigation, homicide clearance rates in the largest cities have dropped substantially during the past forty years, but have only dropped slightly in rural areas.

Rural and small-town police have been little studied and are poorly understood. This is unfortunate because in many ways rural police are models of how police agencies can do more with less. On the whole, when the obstacles and benefits are considered together, rural and small-town policing holds up well against what is done in urban areas. Rural and small-town police are more well liked and respected by the public than urban police, and they do a better job of solving crimes than do urban police. Rather than taking urban police as the model to be emulated, perhaps it is time to see what urban police can learn from their rural counterparts.

RALPH A. WEISHEIT, DAVID N. FALCONE and L. EDWARD WELLS

See also **Accountability; Community-Oriented Policing: Practices; Constables; Problem-Oriented Policing; Sheriffs**

References and Further Reading

Falcone, David N., and L. Edward Wells. 1995. The county sheriff as a distinctive policing modality. *American Journal of Police* 3: 123–48.
Falcone, David N., L. Edward Wells, and Ralph A. Weisheit. 2002. The small-town police department. *Policing: An International Journal of Police Strategies and Management* 25: 371–84.
Thurman, Quint C., and Edmund F. McGarrell. 2003. *Community policing in a rural setting.* 2nd ed. Cincinnati, OH: Anderson Publishing.
Weisheit, Ralph A., David N. Falcone, and L. Edward Wells. 1999. *Crime and policing in rural and small-town America.* 2nd ed. Prospect Heights, IL: Waveland Press.
Weisheit, Ralph A., L. Edward Wells, and David N. Falcone. 1994. Community policing in small-town and rural America. *Crime and Delinquency* 40 (4): 549–67.

RUSSIAN POLICING

Since the late 1980s, de-Sovietization of the political regime and liberalization of the economy have led to a restructuring of policing in Russia. The rapid and highly publicized development of violent crime, traditional illegal markets, and predatory economic crime in a context of economic crisis has prompted various security demands. Protection of private goods and property rights has become a service offered by various providers of policing: private protection companies, internal security departments in large firms, and state police agencies, which are also offered on a contractual basis by the latter.

The same holds true for maintaining public safety, which is ensured, to varying degrees depending on the local situation, by federal, regional, and municipal bodies, private sponsors, and communities of residents, which sometimes reactivate modes of social mobilization that had been in practice under the Soviet system.

Within this landscape, in the early 2000s, the Interior Ministry (MVD) managed a set of police agencies devoted to crime fighting, ensuring public safety, and maintaining public order and also the Interior Troops. This bureaucracy is still militarized and centralized, but public safety and, to a lesser extent, criminal investigation missions are often supported by regional political leaders and/or businessmen, which prevents such investigations from being uniformly implemented across the Russian state.

The missions and prerogatives of the MVD were considerably reduced during the 1990s. The fire brigade and penitentiary administration were placed under the authority of the Ministries of Emergency Situations and Justice, respectively. In fact, the country's leaders preferred to create new law enforcement agencies, such as the tax police, active from 1993 to 2003, rather than assign the MVD new missions. Nevertheless, the Interior Troops had become increasingly powerful during the 1990s through their active participation in the first Chechen war, waged from 1994 to 1996 on Russian Federation soil. Despite a reduction in numbers undertaken in 1998 and their lesser role in the second Chechen conflict, they remain a military force that some sources have put at 220,000 soldiers strong (Bennett 2000, 13). In the early 2000s, plans were announced numerous times to transform them into a national guard, further reduce their numbers, and redefine their missions.

The organization of Russian police agencies has undergone countless administrative reforms. In the judicial police, priority was given to departments fighting organized crime, which gained progressively more autonomy during the 1990s. Their regional structure in fact did not match that of other Interior Ministry departments, precisely in order to prevent collusion between local organized crime groups, law enforcement officers, and political staff. Since the early 2000s, the departments responsible for fighting drug trafficking and economic and fiscal crime, a reincarnation of the former tax police, have also risen in power within the ministry.

These reforms have not significantly transformed the repressive practices inherited from the Soviet era, even though the police as an institution adopted new statutes in 1991 that placed the defense of persons over that of state interests. The goal of bringing the police closer to the citizens conflicted with the government's need to resort to emergency measures to deal with criminal threats it believed might jeopardize the political and social order. In such a context, the police continue to exercise their activity according to a results-based rationale: Their superiors set goals and priorities and evaluate the local departments according to quantified activity indicators, related especially to incidents reported and crime solving rates, which they themselves are responsible for presenting. This bureaucratic mode of organizing police activity encourages police officers to fulfill and/or report the successful performance of their duties by all possible means, by falsifying activity indicators and selecting the easiest cases to handle.

Moreover, it allows them free time to utilize their position for their own interests. Given their very low income, police officers readily admit to seeking to improve their daily fare, on duty or off, by, for instance, taking on legal protection assignments or even accepting bribes. These activities can assume far more sophisticated criminal forms, such as when a group of officers specializes in selling stolen cars or racketeering.

The everyday visibility of these practices in departments such as the highway police causes distrust among the population. Sociological studies stress the extent to which the police force is a feared and dreaded institution. Police brutality, denounced by national and transnational nongovernmental organizations, is a mystery to no one. The reputation of the police is also related to the fact that many officers leave the force for private security firms, and this loss is compensated by a recruitment policy with lowered standards: All applicants are accepted as long as they have no police record and they have fulfilled their military obligations. Given the salaries offered, the possibilities of finding illicit sources of income are an incentive to become a police officer.

In such a context, control measures have taken the place of announced reforms. Since Vladimir Putin rose to the presidency in 2000, the policy conducted toward the Interior Ministry has been characterized by greater penetration of secret service agents (FSB, ex-KGB) in the administration. New control bodies have emerged, particularly within the federal districts created in 2001, to better coordinate the implementation of the fight against crime. This policy has led to staging spectacular dragnet operations conducted in the name of the fight against corruption, which have revealed to the general public the existence of violent criminal organizations within the MVD. All of these measures have prompted the renewal of regional ministerial cadres, but have not called into question the traditional modes of bureaucratic organization of police activity.

GILLES FAVAREL-GARRIGUES

See also **International Police Cooperation; International Police Missions**

References and Further Reading

Bennett, Gordon. 2000. *The Ministry of Internal Affairs of the Russian Federation*. Conflict Studies Research Centre. http://english. mn.ru/english/issue.php?2002-43-6.

Favarel-Garrigues, Gilles, and A. Le Huérou. 2004. State and the multilateralization of policing in post-Soviet Russia. *Policing and Society* 14 (1): 13–30.

Gilinskiy, Yakov. 2005. Police and the community in Russia. *Police Practice and Research* 6 (4): 331–46.

Gregory, Frank, and G. Brooke. 2000. Policing economic transition and increasing revenue: A case study of the Federal Tax Police Service of the Russian Federation, 1992–1998. *Europe-Asia Studies* 52 (3): 433–55.

Los, Maria. 2002. Post-communist fear of crime and the commercialization of security. *Theoretical Criminology* 6 (2): 165–87.

Petrov, Nikolay. 2005. Siloviki in Russian regions: New dogs, old tricks. *Power Institutions in Post-Soviet Societies* 2. http://www.pipss.org/document331.html.

Shelley, Louise. 1996. *Policing Soviet society: The evolution of state control.* London: Routledge.

Solomon, Peter H. 2005. The reform of policing in the Russian Federation. *Australian and New Zealand Journal of Criminology* 38 (2): 230–40.

Volkov, Vadim. 2002. *Violent entrepreneurs. The use of force in the making of Russian capitalism.* Ithaca, NY: Cornell University Press.

S

SAN ANTONIO POLICE DEPARTMENT

The Nineteenth Century

San Antonio was chartered in January 1837 as an incorporated city under a town council form of government. In 1846, the Town Council created the post of city marshal with a monthly salary of $50. City marshals changed frequently in the nineteenth century at the will of the mayor, a city official elected every two years. Between 1846 and 1900, the city had twenty-nine men in this position; their average term was less than twenty-three months. The first marshal, James Dunn, served less than a month.

In 1857, the so-called Cart War erupted between Texas and Mexican teamsters on the cargo routes connecting San Antonio and gulf ports. In response to violent turmoil, the city added an assistant marshal to the law enforcement staff. In 1861, the Civil War began and Texas seceded from the Union and joined the Confederate States. At the end of the war in 1865, all city officials including the city marshal were ousted from office; military occupation leaders replaced them with loyal officials. For the most part of the 1860s, federal and state officials controlled the city's law enforcement.

The post–Civil War reconstruction brought prosperity to San Antonio in the last three decades of the century. The city's population reached 53,321 in 1900, an increase of more than fourteen times from a population of 3,488 in 1850. San Antonio was the largest city in Texas between 1840 and 1910.

John Dobbin was appointed marshal in January 1873 and served six years. It was the longest term served up to that time. During this period, the San Antonio police transformed from a cowboy-type group into an organized police department. Officers were uniformed and required to wear a shield and conceal their firearms under the uniform coat.

An Age of Modernization and Professionalism

Though the San Antonio Police Department (SAPD) entered the twentieth century on horseback, it was greeted with an ever increasing presence of automobiles and the need for traffic enforcement. In 1910, the department purchased a new Franklin air-cooled automobile and motorcycles for patrol, marking the beginning of a motor fleet. In 1924, the department retired its last police horse. In the 1930s, SAPD had its first four high-speed emergency autos and equipped all patrol vehicles with two-way radios; a police radio broadcasting station was built at headquarters. By the end of the fifth decade, the department had an aerial surveillance unit and an urban expressway system.

SAPD started eight-hour shifts and created a "Manual of Directives" in 1917. Some of the rules included shaving every other day, no smoking between 6:00 A.M. and 11:00 P.M., and never sitting down while on duty. Beginning in 1929, all SAPD officers were required to be fingerprinted. In 1933, SAPD officers had a new badge featuring a shield and a fine image of the Alamo with the officer's number and the words "San Antonio Police Department." This has been the badge of SAPD officers to the current date. In 1939, a formal police academy began its operation and graduated the first class of twenty-four SAPD officers.

During the first half of the twentieth century, eighteen men served as the city's police chief; five of them stayed on the position for three years or longer. In 1951, the city council shifted to a council manager form of government. The new management model augmented the stability of the position of police chief. George W. Bichsel was appointed chief in 1953 and served nineteen years; only five other men served as chief for the rest of the century.

As the city's population and traffic grew rapidly, SAPD responded with expansion in both human resources and facilities, particularly in the 1950s. The number of sworn officers grew from 370 in 1954 to 516 in 1958, averaging almost a 10% increase annually.

In 1957, police consultant Donald S. Leonard conducted a survey study and presented the results and his 147 recommendations to the SAPD and city council in a 350-page report. As a result, a $6 million bond issue was approved in 1958 for a new jail and new police headquarters building. In the same year, SAPD relocated its communications to a spacious new communications center with modern equipment and separate dispatchers' booths. In addition, the department adopted a two-frequency radio operation, expanded crime laboratory, and increased support staff.

The modernization of SAPD continued in the 1960s and accelerated in the 1970s. The department started using polygraph for lie detection in 1966, breathalyzer for blood alcohol level analysis in 1967, radar for monitoring traffic in 1973, and computer-aided dispatch in 1974. The 911 service became operational in 1979. In the same year, its computer system became linked to the Texas Crime Information Center and the National Crime Information Center. The Regional Crime Lab was created as a unit of SAPD in 1973; a mobile crime lab was added in 1976. SAPD's Helicopter Unit was also established in the 1970s.

Embracing Community Policing

SAPD began to decentralize patrol functions to six substations in the mid-1980s. A series of community policing programs followed and continued into the 1990s. Downtown foot patrol began in 1986. Officers on bicycles joined foot patrol officers in 1990, forming the Downtown Foot and Bicycle Patrol Unit. The bike officers may wear special SAPD bicycle uniforms with shorts in summer and dark fatigue trousers in winter. Patrol bikes are equipped with headlamps and reflectors for the officer's safety and with a back rack and carry case. Like their counterparts riding automobiles, bike officers carry radios; many also take with them hand-held mobile data units. In 2005, the bicycle fleet had sixty bikes and a full-time civilian mechanic in charge of their maintenance.

Among other community policing programs were Family Assistance Crisis Teams (FACT, 1988), Drug Abuse Resistance Education (D.A.R.E., 1988), Alamo City Heat Band (1988), Cellular on Patrol (1993), Citizen Police Academy (1994), San Antonio Fear Free Environment (SAFFE, 1995), Victims Advocacy Section (1995), and Volunteers in Policing (VIP, 1997).

Partnership with citizens has interested not only individuals but the business community as well. Zachary Construction Company mandated, for example, that as a requirement of employment, all security employees of the company enroll in the SAPD's eleven-week Citizens Police Academy. In 1998, the National League of Cities presented an award of Excellence in Community Policing to SAPD for its web page, which was first published in 1996 and has since been expanded and updated. Through the increased utilization of volunteers, SAPD has been able to increase its visibility and better serve the community. The programs have been particularly valuable in the wake of the September 11, 2001, terrorist attacks, when budget constraints were felt by law enforcement agencies in large cities across the country.

Minorities and Women

San Antonio's population grew from 406,811 to more than 1.2 million between 1954 and 2004, when the city was ranked the second largest in Texas and the eighth largest in the United States. In these fifty years, SAPD expanded from 370 sworn officers and 67 civilians to 2,008 sworn officers and 480 full-time civilians; its salary budget grew from $1.5 million to $190 million. In 2000, 68% of the city's population was minority, including more than 58% with a Hispanic origin, while 48% of the city's sworn officers were minorities. SAPD's first female officer was hired in 1900 to monitor female prisoners. In 2000, 6% of the officers were women; it was the lowest female rate among the police departments of sixty-two large American cities (serving a population larger than 250,000). In 2005, 7% of SAPD officers were female—a 1% increase in five years.

OLIVIA YU

See also **American Policing: Early Years**

References and Further Reading

Handbook of Texas Online. 2005. Cart war. http://www.tsha.utexas.edu/handbook/online/articles/CC/jcc1.html (November 2005).
———. 2005. San Antonio, TX. http://www.tsha.utexas.edu/handbook/online/articles/SS/hds2.html (November 2005).
Pittman, J. 2005. *Private security organizations and SAPD*. ASSIST Online, Associated Security Services and Investigators. http://www.assisttexa.org/art97.shtml (November 2005).
San Antonio Police Department. 2005. *History of SAPD*. http://www.sanantonio.gov/sapd/history.asp?res=800&ver=true (November 2005).
U.S. Census Bureau. 2005. *San Antonio (city), Texas*. State and County Quick Fact. http://quickfacts.census.gov/qfd/states/48/4865000.html (November 2005).
U.S. Department of Justice, Bureau of Justice Statistics. *Police departments in large cities, 1990–2000*. Special Report NCJ 175703. Washington, DC: U.S. Department of Justice.

SAN DIEGO COMMUNITY POLICING

The San Diego Police Department was at the forefront of many new developments in policing between 1970 and 2000. In the 1970s, the department was the site of three early Police Foundation studies—*San Diego Field Interrogation* (1975), *San Diego Community Profile* (1975), and *Patrol Staffing in San Diego: One- or Two-Officer Units* (1977). In the late 1980s, the department was one of five cities selected to implement field experiments in problem-oriented policing (POP).

In the 1990s, the department was selected to host a Regional Community Policing Institute and to serve as a National Community Oriented Policing Demonstration Center. Also in the 1990s, the department began hosting the annual International Problem-Oriented Policing Conference and won several national awards for community policing and problem-oriented policing. In 2001, the department won an "Excellence in Equality" award for its integration of gays and lesbians throughout the agency. Most recently, the department was one of the first in the country to voluntarily agree to collect vehicle stop data in response to the racial profiling issue and has been widely recognized for engaging community groups in the early stages of that process.

San Diego's early adoption of community-oriented and problem-oriented strategies is interesting because California police departments did not generally embrace these developments before the 1990s. One exception, Santa Ana, was an early proponent of community policing, owing to the leadership of Chief Ray Davis, but otherwise California departments seemed to put more emphasis on the professional model and the legalistic style of policing, as epitomized by Los Angeles and Oakland. In the middle 1980s, the new strategy of community policing tended to be more associated with Houston, Newark, and Madison, while problem-oriented policing was identified with Newport News and Baltimore County. This early period of community policing and problem-oriented policing development represented an important shift in the epicenter of policing innovation from the West Coast to the Midwest and East Coast.

San Diego shares one important characteristic with many other California and Southwest police departments—low police staffing in relation to population. In 2004, for example, large cities in the West averaged 1.9 sworn officers per thousand population compared to 4.3 officers in the Northeast. San Diego has even fewer officers than the average for the West—1.6 officers per thousand. These low levels of police staffing have generally led California and other western departments to emphasize efficiency, out of necessity. Whereas Los Angeles and some other agencies developed a "lean and mean" culture as their adaptation to insufficient police personnel starting in the 1980s, San Diego looked to its community for volunteer assistance and to analytical methods for policing smarter, such as problem-oriented policing.

Much of the credit for San Diego's community-oriented path goes to a succession of police chiefs, particularly William Kolender (1976–1988), Robert Burgreen (1988–1993), and Jerry Sanders (1993–1999). Chief Kolender (who has subsequently served as sheriff of San Diego County since 1995) emphasized diversity and equal opportunity in the department and oversaw the initial implementation of problem-oriented policing in the department. Chief Burgreen instituted town hall meetings, initiated neighborhood policing, and started the annual POP conference in San Diego in conjunction with the Police Executive Research Forum (PERF). Chief Sanders (who was elected mayor of San Diego in 2005) implemented several internal organizational measures to put greater emphasis on problem-oriented policing, expanded problem-oriented policing department-wide, continued and expanded the POP conferences, promoted the widespread use of volunteers, and placed San Diego in the vanguard of departments working with the new Office of Community Oriented Policing Services (the COPS Office) in the U.S. Department of Justice during the 1990s.

In addition, beginning in 1988, PERF was instrumental in providing the police department with technical assistance to implement and enhance problem-oriented policing. PERF placed Nancy McPherson in the department to help with its POP demonstration project. She remained with the department after the grant expired, assisting with problem-oriented policing efforts, and later went on to serve in assistant chief–level positions in the Seattle and Portland police departments.

Community Profiling

This project, begun in 1973 with research assistance from the Police Foundation, required patrol officers to systematically profile their beats by gathering information about resident demographics, businesses, social service agencies, crime, and calls for service. The premise was that officers should become more knowledgeable about their beats and the people living in them in order to do a better job of policing, identifying problems, and tailoring solutions. Results indicated that officer attitudes became more community-oriented—officers came to believe that they should be more knowledgeable about their beats and residents, that stronger ties to community members were more important than they had thought, and that random patrol was less effective than previously believed.

This very early community profiling initiative presaged national developments in U.S. policing over the next two to three decades. For San Diego it laid the foundation for further expansion into community policing and problem-oriented policing.

Problem-Oriented Policing

For a decade or longer, San Diego was widely recognized as a leader in problem-oriented policing, particularly among large cities. POP training was started in the department in the late 1980s. The International Problem-Oriented Policing Conference was held annually in San Diego, cosponsored by the police department, from 1990 to 2003. Problem solving was formally incorporated into field training in 1996, as one of the anchors on recruits' daily performance evaluation forms. The department was one of the first in the country, in 1998, to integrate problem solving throughout its recruit-training academy. In the department's triannual performance review program for sworn officers, problem solving was one of fourteen specific criteria that were scored.

The department developed its own database, POP-Track, for storing and retrieving information on POP projects. San Diego police officers have delivered POP training around the country, and former police department employees have been hired by other agencies to help them implement POP. Former San Diego police commanders have been hired as police chiefs in other major cities, including Norm Stamper in Seattle and John Welter in Anaheim, in large measure due to their expertise in POP and community policing.

Prior to 1993, much of the problem-solving activity in the department was accomplished by Neighborhood Policing Teams (NPTs), which had been established as part of community policing implementation. Subsequently, the department's official policy was that all officers (and all other employees) should incorporate problem solving into their regular duties, leading to the elimination of the NPTs and department-wide implementation of POP. A number of organizational systems were implemented to support both POP and community policing, including (1) a crime analysis unit, based at headquarters, that was nationally recognized for its sophistication; (2) a Neighborhood Policing Support Team (NPST) that helped mentor officers and squads in the field (this team's mission was broadened in 2001 to include providing a range of administrative and field assistance related to problem solving, community policing, and crime prevention); (3) a Problem Analysis Advisory Committee (PAAC) that met monthly to help officers analyze problems and brainstorm responses (the committee and its meetings were renamed Problem Solving Meetings in February 2000); (4) a computerized record keeping system for problem-oriented policing projects (POP-Track); and (5) a departmental strategic plan that identified POP as a critical component for achieving department goals.

Research on POP in San Diego has demonstrated the difficulty of changing the way the average officer does his or her work in a big police department. Capowich and Roehl found in 1989 that the role played by citizens was limited and that problem analysis tended to be superficial. Cordner and Biebel found in 2000–2001 that San Diego's POP projects tended to focus on small-scale problems (one address, one intersection, one park, and so forth) and to employ relatively weak analysis and assessment methods. On the positive side, however, these studies found that officers accepted the importance of taking a problem-oriented approach; that most officers could point to recent POP projects in which they had been involved; and that officers typically employed a combination of traditional and nontraditional responses in their problem-solving efforts. While routine police activity in San Diego did not consistently measure up to award-winning POP standards, it was more systematic, analytical, and substantive than the incident-oriented style of policing practiced in most police agencies.

As of 2005, the department's commitment to POP seemed to have waned. Chief David Bejarano (1999–2003) emphasized community policing but relaxed specific expectations regarding problem-oriented policing. Chief William Lansdowne (2003–), who came to San Diego from the San Jose Police Department, has experienced significant financial challenges during his administration and seems to have emphasized more traditional approaches with

less support for department-wide problem-oriented policing than was evident in the 1990s.

Volunteers

An important aspect of San Diego's approach to community policing has been widespread use of volunteers. The police department initiated its volunteer program in 1986 when Crisis Intervention Teams were developed to assist victims and witnesses and relieve patrol officers of sometimes time-consuming duties. This program struggled initially, but by 1989, volunteers were responding to an average of twenty calls per month. By 1995, the workload handled by volunteers had grown to about fifty calls per month.

The department broadened its volunteer program in 1989 following a careful study and the establishment of policies, procedures, volunteer positions, selection requirements, and minimum expectations. Over the course of several years, the number of active volunteers grew to about a thousand. Presently, volunteers serve in one of four general capacities: (1) Volunteers in Policing (VIP), (2) Retired Senior Volunteer Patrol (RSVP), (3) crisis intervention, and (4) reserves. These volunteers are expected to donate a minimum of twenty to twenty-four hours per month. VIP assignments are in area stations, storefronts, the telephone reporting unit, and other department units. RSVP volunteers assist area stations with various crime prevention programs. Crisis intervention volunteers are on call to respond to critical incidents and assist victims and witnesses. Reserves perform police duties alongside full-time officers.

The San Diego Model

Over and above specific programs and initiatives, the San Diego model is often identified as a big city alternative to the archetypal LAPD and NYPD models. The LAPD model of the 1980s emphasized enforcement, specialization, and toughness. The NYPD model, beginning in 1994 with COMPSTAT, emphasized broken-windows theory, quality of life enforcement, and zero tolerance. In contrast to these approaches, the San Diego model emphasized community policing and problem-oriented policing.

Which approach worked most effectively? Evaluations on such a grand scale are difficult at best, but San Diego managed to avoid the police–community relations tensions and scandals of its Southern California neighbor the LAPD in the 1980s and 1990s. Less well known is that San Diego experienced almost exactly the same crime rate decreases as the "New York miracle" of the 1990s and early 2000s, with about a third the number of police officers per population. Arguably, New York achieved its noisy miracle with a heavy-handed enforcement approach and a very expensive level of police staffing, while San Diego quietly enjoyed the same level of success by analyzing repeat crime and traffic problems, applying both traditional and nontraditional responses, and engaging those affected by crime problems in their solution.

GARY CORDNER

See also **Community-Oriented Policing: Practices; Problem-Oriented Policing**

References and Further Reading

Boydstun, John E. 1975. *San Diego field interrogation: Final report*. Washington, DC: Police Foundation.

Boydstun, John E., and Michael E. Sherry. 1975. *San Diego community profile: Final report*. Washington, DC: Police Foundation.

Boydstun, John E., Michael E. Sherry, and Nicholas P. Moelter. 1977. *Patrol staffing in San Diego: One- or two-officer units*. Washington, DC: Police Foundation.

Burgreen, Robert, and Nancy McPherson. 1990. Implementing P.O.P.: The San Diego experience. *The Police Chief,* October.

Capowich, George E., and Janice A. Roehl. 1994. Problem-oriented policing: Actions and effectiveness in San Diego. In *The challenge of community policing: Testing the promises,* ed. Dennis P. Rosenbaum. Thousand Oaks, CA: Sage.

Cordner, Gary W. 1998. Problem-oriented policing vs. zero tolerance. In *Problem-oriented policing: Critical issues, crimespecific problems and the process of making POP work,* ed. Tara O'Connor Shelley and Anne C. Grant. Washington, DC: Police Executive Research Forum.

Cordner, Gary W., and Elizabeth Perkins Biebel. 2005. Problem-oriented policing in practice. *Criminology & Public Policy* 4 (2): 155–80.

Kessler, Kathy, and Julie Wartell. 1996. *Community law enforcement: The success of San Diego's volunteer policing program*. Reason Public Policy Institute. http://www.rppi.org/ps204.html.

San Diego Police Department. n.d. http://www.sandiego.gov/police/.

SARA, THE MODEL

The SARA model is the most familiar process for doing problem-oriented policing (POP). The acronym SARA stands for scanning, analysis, response, and assessment. The model was first published in the evaluation report on problem solving in the Newport News (Virginia) Police Department in 1987. It is usually attributed to John Eck, one of the authors of the Newport News report.

The four steps are straightforward. Scanning involves looking at data, talking to people, and observing the community in order to identify potential problems. Analysis involves studying potential problems to determine if they deserve concerted attention and, if so, trying to develop accurate descriptions and explanations of them. Response involves searching for a wide range of solutions and then choosing and implementing the ones with the most promise. Assessment involves collecting data after the response to determine if the problem has been eliminated or at least reduced. If success has not been achieved, then further analysis and a different set of responses may be needed.

The SARA model has attained celebrity status within policing for several reasons. Perhaps most important, it is an easily remembered acronym. Also, it entails just four steps—most people can remember them. Of course, it was important that POP became a popular, appealing, and effective police strategy beginning in the 1980s. Moreover, problem solving using the SARA model was incorporated into community policing in the early 1990s. From that point forward, training, publications, and even federal grant programs incorporating SARA became commonplace.

Two shortcomings of the SARA model have been noted. First, SARA implies that problem solving is, or should follow, a linear process. The model seems to suggest that first you do scanning, then you do analysis, then you do response, then you do assessment, and then you are done. In practice, though, problem solvers seem to engage in a lot more back-and-forth activity. For example, they may be responding to a problem when they learn something new about it, which makes them realize that it is really a different problem than they originally thought. Another common experience is that some problems require immediate response as soon as they are recognized. In this situation, officers may engage in response at the same time that they are trying to verify the real status of a perceived problem (scanning) and while they are also trying to figure out what is causing the problem (analysis).

Another complaint about SARA is that it does not formally incorporate the community. As outlined, the SARA model can be carried out entirely by the police. If so, however, the risk is that only problems considered important by the police will get attention, only police data will be used to analyze the problems, only police-led responses will be employed, and assessment will declare victory or defeat solely on the basis of police criteria. Because of these concerns, when problem solving is incorporated within community policing, it is usually termed collaborative problem solving, in order to emphasize the importance of community involvement in each step of the SARA process.

A concept that was developed to help enhance the SARA model is the problem analysis triangle. The three sides of the triangle are victims, offenders, and locations. When analyzing specific problems, officers are encouraged to focus on victims (who are they, what harms do they suffer, why are they victimized but others are not?), offenders (who are they, why do they choose to commit these offenses?), and locations (where do the problems occur, why do they occur in some places and not others?). Carefully focusing on these factors makes sense because crime and other police problems usually are not randomly distributed. Rather, crimes and many other problems are concentrated among a relatively small number of offenders, victims, and locations.

Another feature of the problem analysis triangle aids problem solvers at the response stage. Once problems have been analyzed and attention turns to responses, it is helpful to consider whether there are guardians of victims (for example, parents), handlers of offenders (for example, teachers or employers), or managers of locations (for example, landlords) who can be convinced to exercise authority and oversight in such a way that the problem might be reduced. Thinking about the roles that might be played by guardians, handlers, and managers helps problem solvers identify additional responses, especially ones that are not completely police dependent.

The SARA model is not the only process for carrying out problem-oriented policing or problem solving. Herman Goldstein, the inventor of POP, used the terms "identifying problems," "analyzing problems," "the search for alternatives," and "measuring the effectiveness of alternative responses"—clearly the same meaning as SARA, but slightly different terminology.

The Royal Canadian Mounted Police adopted the CAPRA acronym, which stands for clients, acquire/analyze information, partnerships, responses, and assessment of action taken. This model keeps most of the basic problem-solving process but incorporates a focus on clients (the citizens whose problems need to be addressed) and partnerships (working together with the community to solve problems).

Two problem-solving processes have been developed in the United Kingdom. One adopted by the Home Office, called the Five I's (or 5 I's), entails intelligence, interventions, implementation, involvement, and impact. The other, developed by the London Metropolitan Police and enhanced by the company Sixth Sense, uses a longer process that includes the following steps:

1. *Identify.* Where is the demand coming from?
2. *Demand.* What do they want?
3. *Problem.* Prepare an overview of the perceived problem.
4. *Aim.* What is the aim in general?
5. *Problem.* Define the problem.
6. *Aim.* What is your aim?
7. *Research.*
8. *Analysis.*
9. *Options.* Think creatively.
10. *Responses.* Negotiate and initiate action plan.
11. *Evaluation.* Was the aim met?
12. *Review.* What went well?
13. *Success.* Acknowledge and share good practice.

The value of this more detailed elaboration of the process is that it helps remind problem solvers of specific steps and considerations that can make problem solving more effective.

GARY CORDNER

See also **Community-Oriented Policing: Practices; Problem-Oriented Policing**

References and Further Reading

Center for Problem-Oriented Policing. 2005. *The problem analysis triangle.* http://www.popcenter.org/about-triangle.htm (accessed November 15, 2005).
————. 2005. *The SARA model.* http://www.popcenter.org/about-SARA.htm (accessed November 15, 2005).
Eck, John E., and William Spelman. 1987. *Problem solving: Problem-oriented policing in Newport News.* Washington, DC: Police Executive Research Forum.
Goldstein, Herman. 1990. *Problem-oriented policing.* New York: McGraw-Hill.
Royal Canadian Mounted Police. 2005. *Community policing problem solving model: CAPRA.* http://www.rcmp-grc.gc.ca/ccaps/capra_e.htm (accessed November 15, 2005).
Sixth Sense. 2005. *Problem solving process (PSP).* http://www.sixthsensetraining.co.uk (accessed November 15, 2005).

SCHOOL RESOURCE OFFICERS

History of School Resource Officers

Police have been involved in schools for a very long time (Morrison 2003; McNicholas n.d.). The origin of school resource officers (SRO) dates back to the 1950s, when Flint, Michigan, assigned an officer to a school in 1953. In the 1960s and 1970s, various towns in Florida also had local police that assigned officers to some schools—the term "school resource officer" is credited to a Miami police chief (Griffin 2000). SROs also began in Tucson, Arizona, in the early 1960s. During the late 1960s, the Fresno Police Department in California also stationed seven officers in elementary and junior high schools to try to better relations between the police and the community (West and Fries 1995).

During the 1980s and early 1990s, the development of SROs lapsed (McDaniel 1999/2001). Local police departments, however, began utilizing officers to provide an educational role in the school. In

1983, the Los Angeles Police Department established the Drug Abuse Resistance Education (D.A.R.E.) program for students. In D.A.R.E. programs, police officers originally presented a fifteen-hour curriculum to students in fifth and eighth grades. The program was intended to be presented during the final year of a student's time in a particular level of education, such as elementary school and middle school. This plan was modified by many school departments to meet local needs. As it developed, D.A.R.E. expanded its curriculum to all grades from kindergarten through the senior year in high school.

D.A.R.E. represented the first widespread formal and ongoing partnership between the police of a local community and the schools in that community. Much controversy exists as to the effectiveness of the D.A.R.E. curriculum in preventing future drug use and abuse by students. Interestingly, though, D.A.R.E. has a previously unrecognized benefit—the development of positive relationships between D.A.R.E. officers and both students and administrators who work in the schools. These relationships helped to dispel many myths about the negative consequences of having police officers on school grounds. At present, D.A.R.E. "is now being implemented in nearly 80%" of American school districts and "more than fifty-four countries around the world" (D.A.R.E. website).

Building off the D.A.R.E. curriculum, the Phoenix (Arizona) Police Department and the U.S. Bureau of Alcohol, Tobacco, Firearms and Explosives began the Gang Resistance Education and Training program (G.R.E.A.T. website). This began as an eight-lesson program curriculum for middle school in 1992. Now, G.R.E.A.T. is a thirteen-lesson, thirteen-week program that is offered to elementary and middle school students. It is also offered in summer programs.

While G.R.E.A.T. seems to have more success than D.A.R.E. (Peterson and Esbensen 2004; Esbensen et al. 2001),

both programs served as opportunities for police to interact with students in a school setting. These programs and many similar local programs that have developed during the past twenty years have brought police into schools in a crime prevention role. These programs used police to present a curriculum but not to play a broader role in school safety or student counseling. In these programs the police office would go into the school each week and present the next module of the curriculum and then leave. The officer would not have a formal role in the safety issues facing the school.

Development of SRO Program

In the mid-1990s, new communities developed SRO programs out of a national perception that school violence was increasing. A series of high-profile killings occurred between 1996 and 2000 in school settings. In at least twelve separate incidents throughout the United States, students who brought guns to school injured or killed other students and teachers (*Washington Post* 2000). These incidents occurred in elementary, junior high, and high schools. This led people to pay more attention to creating and further developing the function of the SRO.

While subsequent analyses have demonstrated that there was no increase in the level of school violence during this period, the public fear and concern increased dramatically. In response to the public concern, in 1999 the Office of Community Oriented Policing Services (COPS) initiated the Cops in Schools (CIS) Program to fund police officers in schools across the country. The CIS program provided support for police officers who worked in schools. The COPS office provides a three-year grant to local police agencies to support officers who would work with the schools.

As of 2004, the COPS office had awarded more than $748 million for the program. This funding has provided support for approximately 6,500 SROs across the country. The SRO program was the first national program to develop a model where officers became involved in a broad range of school safety initiatives and to include officers whose regular assignment was to be present at individual schools for all or most of their workday.

The Model of SRO Programs

There are a few different official definitions of what an SRO is exactly, and local communities have tailored the function of SROs to fit their needs. Most SROs, however, are officers who serve in schools full time. The initial model of school resource officers has been described as the "triad" concept, where the SRO's job is divided into the roles teacher, counselor, and law enforcement. It is important to note that this model is a model suggested by both the COPS office and the National Association of School Resource Officers (NASRO) but may not be the model that is implemented in individual schools across the country.

The model as suggested describes a police officer who is assigned full time to a school, or set of schools, who engages in a combination of activities. The officer will enforce the laws of the jurisdiction within the school setting. In this regard the officer will investigate drug distribution networks, gambling operations, and thefts that occur in or around school settings.

The second area of activity is teaching. In schools where the SROs teach, they may teach a legal issues course or a life skills course, but it appears to be much more common that SROs teach a day or a module of an existing course. These lectures or modules frequently include topics such as drug education, drunk-driving prevention, legal rights, and, in middle school, bullying prevention.

The final area of activity is counseling. In this capacity officers may work with individual students to deal with substance abuse problems and refer them to existing programs; officers may also work with students who are having difficulty at home and help them get in touch with programs that can support them. It is important to note that SROs are not trained counselors, so their role is to connect students experiencing difficulties in their lives with programs that can help them.

Officers do appear to do more than just law enforcement. In a NASRO survey in 2002, officers reported spending more than half their time in non–law enforcement tasks. It is worth noting that the amount of law enforcement tasks an officer engages in may differ depending on whether the officer serves a junior high or high school.

Recent work has also focused on developing principles and standards for SRO training. NASRO has developed the NASRO Practitioner Program. This program is a way to ensure that officers have an appropriate background, and the appropriate training, to become an SRO. To enter into the program, an officer has to have been an SRO for three years, must attend forty hours of training and a twenty-four-hour supervisor training course, and finally must complete 160 hours of additional in-service training (NASRO website).

Finally, the SROs have developed security plans for potential catastrophic events. An additional action taken by a large number of SROs has been to review or develop a school security plan in the event of an incident such as occurred at Columbine High School, in Colorado, in 1999, or even a terrorist attack. These plans spell out evacuation procedures and communication lines and also include an up-to-date functional layout of the building(s) so that emergency responders can quickly assess the situation and vulnerabilities.

Extent of the SRO Programs

As noted above, the COPS office estimates that it has funded more than 6,500 SROs since the inception of the COPS in Schools program. Since many SROs cover more than one school, it is likely that more than seven or eight thousand schools have an SRO assigned.

NASRO, which began in 1990, estimates that it has a total of fifteen thousand members from all fifty states, many of whom have attended their training programs. The primary reason for the discrepancy between the two figures may be that as officers get promoted or otherwise reassigned, multiple officers from a single agency may attend NASRO training.

SROs are most likely to be assigned to local high schools than to middle schools and less often assigned to elementary schools. This reflects the law enforcement orientation of SROs in that high schools are the most frequent school setting for illegal activity.

Officers generally volunteer for the SRO program. They are most frequently assigned full time to the local school or schools. Many SROs do not report to roll call at the police department but in fact spend their entire day within the school setting.

Many SROs receive training—frequently they attend programs presented by NASRO—but it is often the case that due to scheduling conflicts, this training comes after the officers have already begun their assignments as SROs.

Challenges of SRO Programs

The single largest challenge of the SRO programs involves continued funding. The COPS office originally provides three years of funding to communities to begin or expand their SRO programs. When communities reach the three-year sunset point, they are faced with the difficult decision of how to replace the federal funding with local funds. In some communities SRO programs have been eliminated since alterative funding could not be identified. However, due to the widespread popularity of these programs, in many communities the costs of such programs were either absorbed into the overall police budget or the community voted on a tax increase or additional levy to continue the program. In a large number of communities taxpayers have approved these requests.

A second set of challenges involves the administration of the program. In many communities a conflict has arisen around the ability of school administrators to set goals and provide direction to SROs about how they should function on a day-to-day basis.

A related challenge is the role the SRO plays in enforcing school discipline. Some conflicts have developed around the SRO's responsibility in enforcing school policies. Some school administrators believe that the SRO should support the mission of the school by enforcing school policies. Many SROs resist this role since they view it as being in conflict with the educator and counselor roles they are also expected to fulfill.

The SROs also have to decide on whether they are serving as an assistant to the school administrator or as a police officer in the school (Morrison 2003). The authority of these two positions differs. The SRO has to contend with various constitutional issues in deciding whether to issue the *Miranda* warning and in matters involving search and seizure. The criteria in deciding whether to search a student vary for school staff and officers. Also, this can cause problems when a principal asks an officer to search a student: Is the officer searching the student as an officer (who makes decision based on the request of the principal) or as a subordinate of the principal who must do what the boss asks (Morrison 2003).

Another issue facing SROs regarding their role is deciding whether to wear a uniform on duty in the school (Girouard 2001). Some argue that the police should wear uniforms to serve as an easily recognizable police deterrent. Others argue that SROs should wear either civilian clothes or a modified "soft uniform" (that is, dress pants and polo type shirt with an official monogram). This position argues that the official police uniform might intimidate students and thwart police and community relations. Finally, some argue that police should wear their regular uniforms part of the week and their soft uniform or civilian clothes the other part of the week, allowing the students to see both sides of the officer.

JACK MCDEVITT and W. CARSTEN ANDRESEN

See also **Crime Prevention; Drug Abuse Resistance Education (D.A.R.E.); Gang Resistance Education and Training (G.R.E.A.T.); Juvenile Crime and Criminalization; Responding to School Violence**

References and Further Reading

Drug Abuse Resistance Education. 2005. http://www.dare.com/home/default.asp.

Esbensen, Finn-Aage, O. D. Wayne, T. J. Taylor, D. Peterson, and A. Freng. 2001. How G.R.E.A.T. is G.R.E.A.T.? Results from a longitudinal quasi-experimental design. *Criminology and Public Policy* 1 (1): 87–118.

Gang Resistance Education and Training. 2005. http://www.great-online.org/.

Girouard, Cathy. 2001. *School resource officer training program.* Office of Juvenile Justice and Delinquency Prevention Fact Sheet, March. Washington, DC: U.S. Department of Justice.

Griffin, Patrick. 2000. Pennsylvania's school resource officers. *Pennsylvania progress: Juvenile justice achievements in Pennsylvania* 7 (1): 1–8. National Center for Juvenile Justice, Pittsburgh, PA.

McDaniel, Joanne. 1999/2001. *School resource officers: What we know, what we think we know, what we need to know.* Center for the Prevention of School Violence. Originally for School Safety Strategic Planning

Meeting. Washington, DC: U.S. Department of Justice.

McNicholas, Christopher F. (n.d.) *School resource officers: Public protection for public schools.* International Foundation for Protection Officers. 2002–2005. http://www.ifpo.org/articlebank/school_officers.htm (accessed November 1, 2005).

Morrison, Kevin. 2003. *School crime and school resource officers: A desk reference for prosecutors.* Special Topic Series, December. Alexandria, VA: American Prosecutors Research Institute, Office of Juvenile Justice and Delinquency Prevention, U.S. Department of Justice.

National Association of School Resource Officers (NASRO). 2002. *School resource officer survey: Final report on the 2nd Annual National Survey of School-Based Police Officers.* September 25.

———. 2005. http://www.nasro.org/practitioners.asp (accessed November 1, 2005).

Peterson, Dana, and F. Esbensen. 2004. The outlook is G.R.E.A.T.: What educators say about school-based prevention and the Gang Resistance Education and Training (G.R.E.A.T.) program. *Evaluation Review* 28 (3): 218–45.

Washington Post. 2006. Juvenile violence time line. http://www.washingtonpost.com/wp-srv/national/longterm/juvmurders/timeline.htm (accessed January 9, 2006).

West, Marty L., and J. M. Fries. 1995. Campus-based police/probation teams—Making school safer. *Corrections Today* 57 (5): 144–48.

SCHOOL VIOLENCE

Until 1997, most Americans considered the schools their children attended to be relatively secure environments where the children could focus on academics, free from distraction from the outside community. The spate of school shootings that began in October 1997 (when Luke Woodham opened fire in his high school in Pearl, Mississippi) and reached a terrifying peak on April 20, 1999, in Littleton, Colorado, with the "Columbine massacre" (where Eric Harris and Dylan Klebold killed thirteen before taking their own lives) led many parents, legislators, and educators to believe that violence has increased in schools and, indeed, that schools have become violent, dangerous environments.

In fact, polls conducted in the late 1990s determine that three in four Americans thought it was likely that a school shooting could happen in their community, and three in five reported that school violence was an issue that "worried them a great deal." The execution of 350 students, teachers, and parents in Beslan, Russia, in a school taken hostage by more than thirty gunmen in fall 2004 further suggests that schools, viewed as "soft targets" by terrorist groups, may become victims of terrorism in the near future. Thus, the issue of school violence remains at the forefront of concern for many American citizens.

When most people think of school violence, they think of school shootings such as those mentioned above. Even among researchers and school administrators, there is no consensus on how to define school violence, and it is difficult to provide a comprehensive overview of the idea of school violence. Nevertheless, school violence can be considered to exist ". . . along a lengthy continuum, at one end marked by minor incidents involving everyday fighting, name calling, bullying, and minor property destruction and at the other end marked by extortion, rape, homicide, and mass murder" (Gerler 2004, xxiii).

The primary sources of data regarding school violence are public records, newspaper reports, and national surveys of students, teachers, and administrators. These data suggest that while it may be true that isolated schools in isolated sections of the country are dangerous, violence-prone environments, this is certainly not the case in most schools in most areas of the country. In fact, schools are one of the safest places that children can spend their time (Small and Tetrick 2001).

Nevertheless, most data available suggest that most schools have some form of school violence and that regardless of the type of violence, school violence is more likely to occur in high schools than in middle schools and more likely in middle schools than in elementary schools. Additionally, the amount of school violence increases as the number of students in a school increases. Violent activities are also less likely at rural schools than urban schools. In 1999–2000, 7% of all public schools were responsible for half of the total violent incidents reported, and 2% of the schools accounted for half of the serious violent incidents. In general, schools with high levels of serious violent activity tend to have (1) larger enrollments, (2) higher percentages of students who score lower on standardized tests, (3) higher student-to-teacher ratios, (4) higher numbers of students transferring from the school, and (5) higher numbers of serious discipline problems and schoolwide disruptions (U.S. Department of Education 2003).

School-Associated Violent Deaths

School-associated violent deaths are rare events. Fewer than 1% of the children murdered annually are killed on school property or at school-related events (Small and Tetrick 2001), and the chance of suffering a school-associated violent death is less than one in a million (U.S. Departments of Education and Justice 1999). Most of the data available regarding school-associated violent death are derived from data collected by the National School Safety Center (NSSC), which, until early 2004, collected annual data regarding the number of school-associated violent deaths, using newspaper reports from throughout the United States.

The NSSC defined a school-associated violent death as any suicide, homicide, or weapons-related death in the United States that occurs on school property, on the way to or from school, or at a school-related event or that was a direct result of school incidents or activities, whether or not the death occurred on school grounds (see www.nssc1.org for definition and numbers). In 2002–2003, there were twenty-one school-associated violent deaths, a number that represents a dramatic decrease from the early 1990s (fifty-six in 1992–1993 and fifty-four in 1993–1994) and a slight decrease from the mid-1990s. Thus, contrary to popular rhetoric, if there is a trend in deaths on school properties, the trend is toward a reduced amount of death on school grounds, not an increased amount.

Nonfatal Crimes against Students and Teachers

Nonfatal serious school violence (for example, rapes, robbery, aggravated assault, simple assault) is also far less likely to occur at school than away from school. In fact, the rates of serious violent crime are between two and three times higher away from school than at school. Additionally, most injuries received at school are not the result of violent activity, as 90% of children admitted to hospitals for an injury sustained at school are injured unintentionally through falls, sports, and school equipment (for example, wood shop equipment) (U.S. Departments of Education and Justice 1999).

Nevertheless, most schools do experience some form of nonfatal violence. According to the U.S. Department of Education (2004), seven out of ten public schools experience some form of violence every year, and one in five report some form of serious violence (for example, rape, sexual battery other than rape, physical attack or fight with a weapon, threat of physical attack or physical attack, or fight with or without a weapon). On average each year, there are also slightly more than 130,000 violent crimes against teachers at schools; about four teachers per thousand are the victims of serious violent crime at school.

Weapons at School

Recently, the general public appears to have developed the perception that the prevalence of weapons in and around schools has increased dramatically. Incidents such as those referred to above have led many to believe that our schools are inundated with weapons and are no longer safe places for children to learn. This perception, however, directly contradicts empirical evidence to the contrary and perceptions of students, teachers, and law enforcement officials nationwide that violence and weapons in public schools have decreased.

Nationally, slightly more than one in five students have carried a weapon to school in the past thirty days, and approximately one in fifty twelfth graders have carried a gun to school in that same time period (U.S. Departments of Education and Justice 1999). Furthermore, slightly more than one in ten students are involved in a fight on school property each year, and almost one in ten are threatened or injured with a weapon on school property each year (Grunbaum et al. 2004). Contrary to popular opinion, however, both student weapon carrying and fighting at school have also declined steadily during the past few years.

Causes of School Violence

Gerler (2004) suggests that school violence is caused by a combination of factors from several different domains of human functioning and argues that a number of elements that are unique to the school environment interact to create school violence. These elements include the following:

- Students who engage in violent behavior often receive attention from their peers, teachers, school administrators, and (in extraordinary cases) the media that they do not receive for conformist behavior.

- The school environment, particularly in the large, urban settings referenced above where school violence is most problematic, is often characterized by large enrollments and unmanageable class sizes.
- Many students find school boring and unstimulating and act out in abusive and angry manners. They may become involved in drugs and alcohol, which increase the likelihood that they will engage in violent behavior.
- Youth who have peers that engage in violence at school and those who feel isolated or alienated in the school setting are more likely to engage in violence.
- Youth who are unattached to their parents, teachers, and other conformist aspects of the school setting are more likely to engage in violence as well.

Reducing School Violence

Gottfredson (1997), in a comprehensive evaluation review of school-based crime prevention program evaluations funded by the National Institute of Justice, determined that there were several types of school-based programs that worked to reduce school violence. These programs can be broadly grouped into three categories: (1) programs empowering youth, parents, and community members to play an active role in improving the school setting, (2) programs aimed at setting expectations and norms for student behavior, and (3) programs that provide comprehensive instruction focusing on a number of social competency skills (for example, social problem solving, responsible decision making, developing self-control).

One program that Gottfredson reviews is Promoting Alternative Thinking Strategies (PATHS). This program is delivered to students by teachers in kindergarten through fifth grades as part of the regular curriculum. In this program, students are taught lessons in relationship building, self-control, emotional understanding, problem-solving skills, and social competence. Several evaluations (including the one by Gottfredson) suggest that youth in the PATHS program are significantly more likely to recognize and understand emotions, understand social problems, develop effective alternative solutions, use nonviolent conflict resolution strategies, and decrease frequency of aggressive/violent behaviors. Thus, PATHS should help reduce school violence wherever it is applied.

Another program designed to reduce school violence is the Second Step program developed in 1989 by the Committee for Children as a program to reduce violence and build self-esteem among students in kindergarten to the eighth grade. Second Step consists of 20 forty-five- to fifty-minute lessons delivered to students by their classroom teachers. These lessons teach students empathy, problem-solving skills, and anger management techniques. The lessons consist of discussion, activity, and role playing, with older students also participating in discussions and watching videos that demonstrate good behavioral strategies. Evaluations of the program indicate that students who participated were significantly more likely than students who did not participate to decrease physical aggression and increase neutral and prosocial behavior and were less likely to choose aggressive behavior as an alternative to conflict. Thus, Second Step appears to be another option for reducing school violence.

Despite the effectiveness of the programs demonstrated above, many school administrators have chosen alternate programs whose effectiveness is either unknown or questionable. Interviews with school administrators from throughout the country demonstrate that almost all have incorporated automatic suspension as punishment for violations involving weapons and other serious violent acts, and most have designated their schools as a "gun-free zone" and have begun to use dress codes to reduce gang behavior (with the idea that dress codes will discourage gang colors). Some suggest that school violence is viewed by most school administrators, teachers, and parents as one of the most problematic aspects of the school setting.

Another popular program to reduce violence in school involves using law enforcement officers or other security personnel to deter school violence. The National School Safety Center suggests that use of security personnel and law enforcement officers can effectively reduce weapons possession at school if they meet the following criteria: (1) are trained in current law enforcement practices, (2) use the principles of community policing, and (3) communicate regularly with teachers, administrators, and students about their role in school safety to establish a positive reporting climate so that students feel comfortable reporting potentially violent situations before they actually occur. Despite this claim, limited research has examined the effectiveness of law enforcement officers in the school setting in reducing school violence. This research does suggest that police officers in school increase perceptions of safety among students, faculty, and administrators.

Summary

Despite the rhetoric in the media and commonly held beliefs among parents that schools are more violent than ever, empirical evidence does not support this claim. Most children are safer in school than in their own neighborhoods. Additionally, the causes of violent activity in school mirror those in the larger community: a need for acceptance among adolescents, weak bonds between parents and their children, and deviant peer networks. As such, any efforts that reduce violence in the community outside the school context will probably reduce violence in school as well.

DAVID C. MAY

See also **Criminology; Responding to School Violence; School Resource Officers**

References and Further Reading

Gerler, Edwin R. 2004. *Handbook of school violence*. New York: The Haworth Reference Press.

Gottfredson, Denise C. 1997. School-based crime prevention. In *Preventing crime: What works, what doesn't, and what's promising*, ed. Sherman, Gottfredson, MacKenzie, Eck, Reuter, and Bushway, 5-1–5-74. College Park: University of Maryland, Department of Criminology and Criminal Justice.

Grunbaum, Jo Anne, L. Kann, S. Kinchen, J. Ross, J. Hawkins, R. Lowry, W. A. Harris, T. McManus, D. Chyen, and J. Collins. 2004. *Youth risk behavior surveillance—United States, 2003*. Atlanta, GA: Centers for Disease Control and Prevention.

Shaffi, Mohammad, and S. L. Shaffi, eds. 2001. *School violence: Assessment, management, prevention*. Washington, DC: American Psychiatric Publishing.

Small, Margaret, and K. D. Tetrick. 2001. School violence: An overview. *Journal of the Office of Juvenile Justice and Delinquency Prevention* 8: 3–12.

U.S. Department of Education, National Center for Education Statistics. 2004. *Violence in U.S. public schools: 2000 School Survey on Crime and Safety*. Washington, DC: U.S. Government Printing Office.

U.S. Departments of Education and Justice. 1999. *1999 Annual report on school safety*. Washington, DC: U.S. Government Printing Office.

SERGEANTS/MIDDLE MANAGEMENT

The Sergeant

The role of the police sergeant is arguably one of the most important and perhaps least understood aspects of police management. Historically, sergeants have performed not only first-line supervisory practices in terms of oversight of uniformed patrol officers (Gocke and Stallings 1955) but have also been responsible for ensuring efficient street level implementation of departmental policies in an effort to interdict crime and control patrol officers' behaviors (Engel 2001).

Given the traditional quasi-military structure of most U.S. police departments, sergeants have historically been engaged in oversight and discipline, as advisers to new officers, leadership and morale builders, information processors, and policy change agents (Gocke and Stallings 1955), with other duties depending upon the structure and culture of the police organization and the community in which it is anchored and that it serves (Wilson 1968). These types of responsibilities require sergeants to possess myriad skills and abilities and a great deal of knowledge, some of which can be taught but much of which has accumulated after years of experience, training, and additional education.

Attaining the rank of sergeant in a medium- to large-sized police department in the United States will depend on the specific police organization's internal rules governing promotion. However, most sergeants have normally served as a uniformed patrol officer for a specified period of time prior to taking any qualifying promotional examinations.

Although many officers may be well qualified to become sergeants, it is quite common for some to not pursue this career path. Some of the reasons for avoiding the sergeant's position may be personal, professional, or organizational. The prevailing personal reason cited is loss of income, since some officers feel more comfortable remaining at a relatively stable pay grade. Other officers want more control of their duty assignments, but many have concerns about their organizations' sincerity and commitment to them; this is most notable among female and African American officers, who sometimes perceive the testing and selection process as disingenuous and unfair. Furthermore, many officers do not want the added burden of possibly supervising their former street-level colleagues; nor do they wish to be possibly characterized as part of administration (Whetstone 2001).

Nevertheless, there is still considerable fierce competition for the limited number of openings for sergeants' positions, and the promotional opportunities, requirements, and conditions for selection vary widely among police departments in the United States. Even the length-of-service requirements are in stark contrast. In some departments a patrol officer may be promoted to sergeant in less than three years, while in others it could take more than fifteen.

Street Sergeants versus Station Sergeants

Depending in part on the culture of upper and middle management and their philosophy of policing, patrol officers with extensive patrol experience may not be the most viable candidates for sergeant. There is often concern about them being too street oriented, thus making it difficult for them to support policing reform. However, these potential sergeants are often popular among rank-and-file street-level cops because of the vast knowledge they have accumulated, thereby earning them the right to be a sergeant.

Stationhouse or desk sergeants, however, may not have had significant street experience, or they may have been out of the uniformed division for an extended period. Thus, they are sometimes unfamiliar with current street-level activities and cultures of policing and often receive qualified respect from their subordinates.

Both street and station sergeants have strengths and weaknesses. The former are very good street-level arbiters and can more easily direct the activities of street officers; the latter are often administratively astute and able to understand budget concerns and administrative procedures necessary for planning and development; they are also, in many respects, more likely to be promoted to middle management because they have acquired more managerial skills because of their presence in the stationhouse. But they may not be as savvy as street-level sergeants. If there is an advantage to either, it would probably favor the stationhouse sergeant from the perspective of middle and upper management and the street-level sergeant from the beat officer's view (Van Maanen 1985).

As a practical matter it is very difficult to generalize because of the divergent types of police organizations and the nature of their embedded cultures, not only within departments as a whole but also within discreet street-level units among various platoons. It is quite possible, and in many cases the rule, to have sergeants that possess *both* stationhouse and street-level expertise. Variations in community social conditions of policing require well rounded, balanced sergeants who are capable of adapting to dynamic conditions wherein change is the norm and uncertainty is guaranteed.

As a result, the nature and scope of responsibilities of sergeants could range from supervising patrol officers in specialized SWAT units to proactive problem solving requiring prolonged community engagement and substantial commitment of time for training, direction, and supervision. But in some communities the role of the sergeant, and middle managers, is more public relations and community service oriented. Thus, in some regards, demographic socioeconomic conditions and sergeant socialization may affect both style of policing and style of supervisory practices.

Supervisory Style

Because of the large amount of discretion afforded police officers in general and management in particular, the range of activities performed by sergeants varies considerably across jurisdictions. In some smaller departments sergeants may perform patrol functions in addition to their supervisory responsibilities, while in others they may be far removed from street-level activities. Consequently, the notion of routine activities of police sergeants is a fiction, but the focal activity of most first-line supervisors concerns controlling patrol officers' behavior. Four supervisory styles have been identified as impacting behavior: (1) traditional, (2) innovative, (3) supportive, and (4) active supervisors (Engel 2001, 2003).

Traditional Supervision

Traditional supervisors tend to support aggressive enforcement techniques of their officers as opposed to focusing on problem solving inherent in community-oriented policing. These types of supervisors are more likely to employ a micromanagement style wherein they will "take over" an incident—addressing both the citizen's concerns and directing the officer on how to handle various situations. Accordingly, they are task oriented and focus on quantitative evaluative assessments such as number of arrests and citations issued. They also are comfortable with considerable paperwork detailing the nature of their subordinates' actions.

Additionally, these types of sergeants and lieutenants tend to be more directive and punitive toward their patrol officers and are less likely to reward them or to form personal relationships. Their primary goal is control over their officers' behavior, but they are likely to support new

1167

innovations such as community policing if it is anchored in and compatible with aggressive, proactive policing. In fact, a little more than 60% of these types of supervisors believe strict law enforcement is the primary objective of their patrol officers (Engel 2003).

Innovative Supervision

Innovative supervisors tend to develop relationships with their officers and are not merely task oriented. They generally embrace new innovations in policing such as problem solving and community-oriented policing. They are also more in tune with community norms and expectations and encourage and help their officers achieve success in these areas. Typically, these supervisors may assist their subordinates in implementing community policing using a variety of strategies ranging from mentoring to coaching. They also are more likely to delegate authority, not focus too heavily on rules or report writing, require their officers to come up with innovative strategies for problem solving, and spend considerably more time personally interacting with both citizens and patrol personnel (Engel 2003).

Supportive Supervision

Supportive supervisors are likely to support subordinate officers, and they often attempt to shield them from upper management scrutiny and discipline. As a result, they may not have strong ties with upper-level command staff managers. This type of supervisory gatekeeping is more in line with a process of protecting rather than supporting. Furthermore, these supervisors seem to care less about strict enforcement of departmental rules and more about bestowing frequent praise upon their officers (Engel 2003).

Active Supervisors

Sergeants who are active tend to "lead by example" and, thus, provide subordinates with a model of expected behavior. Under this style it is common for supervisors to be engaged in patrol activities including car stops and traffic enforcement. However, this type of supervisory style is very hands-on and borders on micromanaging. Under this style supervisors tend not to encourage team building and are generally not concerned with mentoring or coaching. In many regards, these types of supervisors are relics of the traditional quasi-military models of the professional era of policing retrofitted for community-oriented or problem-solving policing (Engel 2003).

Supervisory Styles and Impact

The four supervisory styles yielded differential impacts on arrests and issuing of citations, use of force, self-initiated activities, community policing and problem solving, administrative activities, and personal business. The likelihood of an officer making an arrest or issuing a citation was not affected by supervisory style. In non-traffic instances, a supervisor's presence had minimal influence on officer behavior, yet the longer a supervisor remained at the scene, the more likely an arrest would be made.

Use of force was twice as likely to occur when patrol officers are supervised by active supervisors as opposed to other supervisory styles, and active supervisors are more likely to employ force themselves, but their presence at the scene, standing alone, had no significant impact on the use of force by patrol officers.

Self-initiated proactive activities of patrol officers were more prevalent with active supervisors. The degree of proactivity excluded time spent for handling radio-dispatched assignments or activities directed by the supervisor, routine patrol, administrative functions and personal business, or traveling to specific locations.

In the area of community policing and problem solving, officers working for active supervisors spent more time per shift on problem solving and community-based initiatives than with other types of supervisors. However, in terms of administrative activities, patrol officers with active supervisors spent considerably less time per shift on administrative functions.

In the area of non–work related functions, supervisory style had minimal effect on patrol officers' time spent conducting personal business. The style that appears to have the most significant impact is that of active supervisor. Those supervisors that tend to lead by example may provide the best chance for implementing new innovations such as community and problem-solving policing on the one hand, but they may also impede effective and efficient supervision on the other.

Middle Managers

The role of police middle manager, just like that of the sergeant, varies among jurisdictions. Middle managers typically could include sergeants, lieutenants, and captains, depending on the jurisdiction, and their activities may range from actual patrol work to largely administrative review, rarely interacting with their subordinate sergeants, officers, and citizens. However, their traditional role has focused largely on supervisory control and efficiency, but they also carry a significant leadership role that is important for implementing policy.

It is well known that successful implementation of departmental policies requires considerable support from police middle managers, who are often uniquely attuned to the culture of their organization. Their understanding of the embedded mores of their departments helps them to accelerate or impede policy changes. Hence, police middle managers have been much maligned in that they have sometimes been characterized as obstructionists to organizational reform (Angell 1971). This was evident during many of the early team policing innovations of the 1970s. In fact, some commentators have advocated for the elimination of police middle managers due to their alleged obsession with control and their tendency to obfuscate new ideas, thereby frustrating meaningful change.

Middle managers have been accused of not providing real leadership by not inspiring subordinates, acting creatively, or leading innovative change. Yet in many police organizations, middle managers have varied responsibilities that are not always organizationally compatible. For example, most middle managers are lieutenants, captains, or civilian middle managers who are normally assigned to three functional areas: patrol management in the form of watch commanders, specialized units such as tactical operations or chief of detectives, and internal affairs, police academy training, or other strictly administrative roles in the form of research development (Reuss-Ianni 1983).

The uniformed street-level middle manager, for example, is responsible for a range of activities such as establishing operational priorities within the unit; supervising subordinates, coordinating with other departmental units such as patrol and detectives, scheduling assignments including shift and work days, preparing precinct budgets, managing complex crime scenes, responding to news media inquiries, and reviewing and evaluating data from early warning systems to address problematic officers.

Consequently, depending on the size and scope of police operations and the competing demands placed on middle managers, it is sometimes difficult to ensure harmonious and focused supervisory practices. In some very large police organizations anchored in communities that are steeped in crime and disorder and immersed in intractable socioeconomic issues such as lack of education, adequate housing, and health care—both physical and mental—the challenge for middle managers is daunting.

Nevertheless, the role of the police middle manager is now viewed as a source of strength and positive innovation—if utilized correctly (Sherman 1975; Geller and Swanger 1995). This is especially important for successful implementation of community-oriented and problem-solving policing wherein middle managers must focus on two dimensions of executive leadership—police culture and community cultures—and four related functions: (1) the socialization process of officers, (2) administrative techniques that directly affect efficient police operations, (3) positive and negative reinforcement of police officers, and (4) education of the community and the news media.

These types of responsibilities are considerably different from previous middle management responsibilities that focused largely on maintaining the status quo through strict command and control techniques (Gocke and Stallings 1955). The major emphasis for middle mangers is now participatory management and focuses on community-based problem solving in addition to their traditional responsibilities.

Scholarly studies on police management vary considerably. Large departments such as those in New York City, Los Angeles, Houston, Philadelphia, Detroit, and Chicago are considerably different from the 9,594 police departments with fewer than twenty-five officers (Bureau of Justice Statistics 2003). There are differences in demographics, organizational cultures, political and fiscal environments, law, and executive leadership—all of which make if difficult to generalize about the role of sergeants and middle management in a very precise manner.

This is particularly evident in today's modern police departments, wherein regardless of size, there is generally a commitment to community-oriented or problem-solving philosophies, focusing on officer behaviors and attitudes (Engel and Worden 2003). Yet, while the role of sergeants and middle managers may have commonalities across jurisdictions, their activities may be unique and customized to fit differing approaches to policing (Sparrow 1992).

Middle Management Implications

Police middle manager in the twenty-first century in the United States must be astute in dealing with complex issues involving race, class, ethnicity, gender, and sexual orientation, not only in the context of the public served but also within their own police organizations (Goldstein 1990). Sergeants and middle mangers must also be cognizant of increased intergovernmental interdependence. This is most evident following the attacks on the World Trade Center and the Pentagon on September 11, 2001, and the Hurricane Katrina disaster in New Orleans in August 2005.

Finally, a major factor that both sergeants and middle managers must now confront concerns supervising a changing workforce and the expectations of new generations of officers and the communities they serve. Those born since around 1970 are significantly different from preceding generations, and they are moving into the workforce, including policing, during a time of unprecedented demographic change. Sergeants' and middle managers' expectations for these individuals may require rethinking. These individuals may or may not have the same level of commitment as prior police recruit generations, thus requiring new strategies of supervision and management.

MORRIS A. TAYLOR

See also **Changing Demographics in Policing; Community Oriented-Policing: Practices; Police Careers; Supervision**

References and Further Reading

Angell, John E. 1971. Toward an alternative to the classic police organizational arrangement: A democratic model. *Criminology* 8: 185–206.

Bureau of Justice Statistics. 2003. *Local Police Departments, 2000*. Washington, DC: U.S. Government Printing Office.

Engel, Robin S. 2001. The effects of supervisory styles on patrol officer behavior. *Police Quarterly* 3: 262–93.

———. 2003. Supervisory styles of patrol sergeants and lieutenants. *Journal of Criminal Justice* 29: 341–55.

Engel, Robin S., and Robert E. Worden. 2003. Police officers' attitudes, behavior, and supervisory influences: An analysis of problem solving. *Criminology* 41: 131–66.

Geller, William A., and Guy Swanger. 1995. *Managing innovation in policing—The untapped potential of the middle manager.* Washington, DC: National Institute of Justice.

Gocke, B. W., and H. L. Stallings. 1955. *The police sergeants manual.* Los Angeles: O. W. Smith Publisher.

Goldstein, Herman. 1990. *Problem-oriented policing*. Philadelphia, PA: Temple University Press.

Reuss-Ianni, E. 1983. *Two cultures of policing: Street cops and management cops.* New Brunswick, NJ: Transition Books.

Sherman, Lawrence W. 1975. Middle management and police democratization: A reply to John E. Angell. *Criminology* 12 (4): 363–78.

Sparrow, Malcolm K. 1992. Integrating distinct managerial styles: The challenge for police leadership. *American Journal of Police* 12 (2).

Van Maanen, John. 1985. Making rank: Becoming an American police sergeant. *Urban Life* 13: 155–76.

Whetstone, Thomas. 2001. Copping out: Why police officers decline to participate in the sergeant's promotional process. *American Journal of Criminal Justice* 25:146–59.

Wilson, James Q. 1968. *Varieties of police behavior: The management of law and order in eight communities.* Cambridge, MA: Harvard University Press.

SERIAL MURDER

Working Definition

Only a few attempts have been made to define serial murder. Frequent references to serial murder are made using the term "mass" to depict a number of victims. This misuse of the term has resulted in general confusion as to what is meant by serial murder. The following working definition by Egger (1984) provides the most extensive definition available:

Serial murder occurs when one or more individuals (males in most known cases) commit a second murder and/or subsequent murder; is relationshipless (victim and attacker are strangers); is at a different time and has no apparent connection to the initial (and subsequent) murder; and is usually committed in a different geographical location. Further, the motive is not for material gain and is believed to be for the murderer's desire to have power over his victims. The series of murders which result may not appear to share common elements. Victims are perceived to be prestigeless and, in most instances, are unable to defend themselves, and are powerless given their situation in time, place, or status, within their immediate surrounding (such as vagrants, prostitutes, migrant workers, homosexuals, missing children, and single and often elderly women).

Some better known examples of serial murderers are Ted Bundy, John Wayne Gacy, Henry Lee Lucas, and Ken Bianchi and Angelo Buono, the Hillside Stranglers.

Extent and Prevalence

There have been numerous estimates regarding the incidence of serial murder and the number of serial murderers at large. However, these estimates are based on extrapolations from total reported homicides in a given year or from identified serial murderers. Most of the serial murders are believed to be encompassed within the total number of reported stranger-to-stranger homicides for which the relationship of victim to offender is unknown or that of a stranger, as presented in the *Uniform Crime Reports*. Estimates of the number of serial murder victims are based only upon the confessions of serial murderers or when a pattern of serial murders is identified.

Whether the phenomenon is on the increase in this country has not been empirically determined. Many references are made by the mass media to such an increase, but research is limited by the fact that the serial murder, per se, is not reported in official crime or mortality statistics. Media reports are currently the only source from which to determine increase as well as the actual incidence of the phenomenon. Such information lacks reliability and validity. Historical research by Eric Hickey and others reveals numerous reports of serial murder and refutes the notion that serial murder is a contemporary phenomenon. Cross-national comparisons, although limited, indicate that serial murder is not strictly an American phenomenon either.

People Who Kill Serially

Research on serial murder, although limited, shows it to be a stranger-to-stranger crime. Practically all of the psychological research attempting to explain the causes of the serial murderer's acts is conducted from a case-study-specific approach. There has been little or no effort to combine this research into an aggregate description so that etiological theories can be derived or to facilitate general observations on the serial murderer. Terms most frequently used to describe the serial murderer are "psychopath" or "sociopath"; however, the meaning of these terms is subject to a great deal of disagreement among psychologists and psychiatrists, and the terms are no longer used in the *Diagnostic and Statistical Manual for Mental Disorders*. General etiological theories of inadequate socialization are the most frequently cited explanations of the serial murderer's behavior (that is, child abuse and neglect, broken home, alcoholism, and the like).

Developing Taxonomies

Legal classifications of homicide are not useful in describing or categorizing serial murder or the serial murderer. The range of geographical and chronological patterns identified provide only a few typologies or categories that are limited in nature and scope. Many serial murderers are very mobile and roam across state lines, while others act within a relatively small geographic area. Motive typologies such as "lust," "sex," or "sadism" are not unique to serial murder. The "organized nonsocial" and the "disorganized social" dichotomy developed by Robert R. Hazelwood and John E. Douglas is currently being used by the Federal Bureau of Investigation (FBI) in its psychological profiling program.

The Victims

There is an even greater paucity of research on the serial murder victim. In almost all cases the victims have been strangers to the serial murderer. Victim selection would appear to be random in nature. Limited research indicates victim selection may be based on the murderer's perception of the victim as vulnerable or as a symbolic representation.

Current Investigative Strategies

There are currently six general responses by law enforcement to the serial murderer: conferences, information clearinghouses, task forces, investigative consultant teams, psychological profiling, and the centralized investigative networks. Conferences, information clearinghouses, and task forces require coordination and cooperation among law enforcement officers on an intraagency or interagency basis within a relatively limited geographical area. Conferences have, at times, been provided on a national as well as a regional basis. The investigative consultant team is a somewhat unique response, found only in response to the Atlanta, Georgia, child murders. Psychological profiling is a recent development to assist criminal investigators. The most active research and development of this investigative tool has been conducted by the FBI's Behavioral Science Unit. A centralized investigative network is the most recent response to serial murder.

On a national level, the Violent Criminal Apprehension Program (VICAP), a component of the FBI's National Center for the Analysis of Violent Crime, is collecting information on unsolved homicides, persons missing under suspicious circumstances, and unidentified dead bodies in order to search for patterns and alert the appropriate police agencies regarding these patterns. On a state level, New York State is currently developing the Homicide Assessment and Lead Tracking System, which will be compatible with VICAP and operate in a similar fashion on a state level. In each instance, state-of-the-art computer software is being developed for use by crime analysts.

The Problem of Serial Murder: Linkage Blindness

With the exception of psychological profiling, a specific investigative tool, the above law enforcement responses to serial murder have all been attempts to increase common linkages or networks among law enforcement agencies or officers regarding unsolved homicides or in instances when a serial murderer has been apprehended. For the latter, the focus is not on pattern similarity but on the identification, documentation, and verification of the serial murderer's trail of victims across numerous jurisdictions. By definition, all of the responses involve stranger-to-stranger homicides, which greatly increases the investigator's need for information not readily available. Thus, the lack of any prior relationship between the serial murderer and his victim and the high rate at which multiple jurisdictions are involved in a serial murder mean that the central problem of serial murder investigation in this country is the lack of information.

Information is necessary to establish that a single homicide event is part of a series of events. Second, information is necessary to establish modus operandi patterns. Information is also necessary to evaluate the physical evidence from identified series. To obtain access to this kind of information, an investigator or agency must expand and develop new sources of information beyond jurisdictional boundaries. The obvious sources of this information are law enforcement counterparts in other jurisdictions that encompass the series of common homicide events.

The lack of law enforcement efforts to expand sources of information to other jurisdictions has been characteristic of most of the incidents of serial murder in this country. The nation's law enforcement community very infrequently makes the necessary effort to seek sources of information outside their respective jurisdictional boundaries because of blindness, forced or intentional, to the information linkages necessary to respond effectively to the serial murderer. This does not mean that law enforcement agencies intentionally keep valuable information on unsolved homicides from other agencies.

However, this "linkage blindness" means that the police in this country do not seek such information beyond the structural purview of their work environments.

Simply stated, there is a lack of sharing or coordination of investigative information relating to unsolved murders and a lack of networking among law enforcement agencies in the United States. The greatest cause of this linkage blindness is the fact that American policing is very decentralized and fragmented. Other critics would attribute such blindness to a jealousy and competitiveness among law enforcement officers and agencies. The point is that no structure or formal network currently exists to allow officers in different agencies and in different states to share information on criminal investigations.

The Future: Expanded Research and Correcting Police "Vision"

There has been precious little money, talent, or time devoted to research of the serial murder phenomenon. In addition to increased communication, coordination, and cooperation to reduce linkage blindness and increase police "vision," research and systematic study of this phenomenon must occur so that we can better understand it and develop more effective tactics and strategies for reducing its prevalence and for increasing the identification and apprehension of serial murderers.

STEVEN A. EGGER

See also **Homicide and Its Investigation; Homicide: Unsolved**

References and Further Reading

Abrahamsen, D. 1973. *The murdering mind.* New York: Harper and Row.
Egger, Steven A. 1984. A working definition of serial murder and the reduction of linkage blindness. *Journal of Police Science and Administration* 12 (3): 348–57.
———. 1985. Serial murder and the law enforcement response. Ph.D. diss. College of Criminal Justice, Sam Houston State University, Huntsville, TX.
———. 1986a. Law enforcement's response to serial murder: A communication problem. *New York Law Enforcement Journal* 1 (2): 27–33.
———. 1986b. A challenge to academia: Preliminary research agenda for serial murder. *Journal of Ideology* 10 (1).
Fox, J. A., and J. Levin. 1985. *Mass murder: America's growing menace.* New York: Plenum.
Guttmacher, M. 1960. *The mind of the murderer.* New York: Grove Press.
Lunde, D. T. 1976. *Murder and madness.* Stanford, CA: Stanford Alumni Press.
Office of Juvenile Justice and Delinquency Prevention. 1983. *National Missing/Abducted Children and Serial Murder Tracking and Prevention Program.* Washington, DC: U.S. Department of Justice.

SHERIFFS

Introduction

The office of the county sheriff has now entered its second millennium, having originated in the late tenth century. But, despite its long history and the vital role it continues to play in the administration of justice, very little empirical research has been conducted regarding this unique general-service county-level policing organization in the United States or the numerous other common-law nations that have inherited it. It is primarily, however, in the United States where the county sheriff has shown the most staying power and ability to remain relevant in the twenty-first century.

Given that the county is the political level at which justice is most often administered in the United States, the county sheriff plays a complex and pivotal role, providing court security, process service (both civil and criminal), management of the county jail, general police services, reactive and proactive law enforcement, and numerous other services not generally provided by other police agencies.

Despite the prediction by some observers that this ancient policing agency would soon fall into dormancy, especially as the incorporated areas of most counties continue to increase in size, it remains a vibrant and vital part of modern policing in the majority of states across America. As an open and nonmilitarized model of policing, the county sheriff's office stands well situated, both organizationally and in terms of inherent service style, to embrace community-oriented policing.

Historical Overview

Because the office of the county sheriff has its origins in the shires of England, it is important to understand the etymology of the term, which sheds light on the formation and evolution of this important modern-day American police agency. The progenitor of the ancient English sheriff was first known as a "reeve," the locally elected conservator of the King's peace within a shire, the equivalent of an American county; the term "shire reeve" later evolved to become the word sheriff, the term we recognize today. Shortly after the Norman invasion of 1066, the office was removed from local elective control and placed under the centralized authority of the national government, as an appointive office, changing fundamentally the relationship between the sheriff and the citizens of the shire.

Researchers have argued that it was the removal of the sheriff from its local origins and control to a distant national office that eventually led to the demise of the English sheriff's office (now the ceremonial office of the high sheriff) as a functional policing entity; today it is little more than an ornamental historical artifact of

British government, serving no substantive policing function. By contrast, in the United States the sheriff's office, as a result of its local elective nature, remains a vitally active county-level component within the contemporary criminal justice system.

By the mid-1600s, the English sheriff's model and its inherent multiple policing functions had been imported to the burgeoning American colonies with little change, save the fact that it was eventually reconstituted in the colonies as an elective office. In the United States today, there exist approximately 3,100 sheriffs' agencies, generally at the county or parish level. There also exist a small number (approximately 1%) of all sheriffs' agencies at the municipal level in "independent" cities, for example, St. Louis, Missouri, and Baltimore, Maryland, where these municipalities are not physically located within a county. As a result, these independent municipalities must replicate all county services, including a sheriff's department; these "city" sheriffs serve in only a custodial and process serving capacity, with no legally recognized law enforcement powers.

Sheriffs are elected officials in all but two states (Hawaii and Rhode Island) and are mandated constitutional officers in thirty-five of the fifty states. The constitutional basis of the office is of no small importance, and differentiating between sheriffs' offices and departments is fundamental to understanding the legal authority of the two forms of this policing entity. First, the majority of sheriffs are of constitutional origins, being stipulated by the organic legal document of the sovereign. As an office, it cannot be placed under the direct control of the county board, nor can its powers be delimited by legislative enactments, nor can the sheriff be removed from office except for criminal conduct, where he generally may be arrested only by the county coroner. The sheriff is the county's chief law enforcement officer and possesses the power of *posse comitatus* (the power of the county), whereby all able-bodied citizens between stipulated ages, often eighteen and sixty-five, must assist the sheriff at his or her request under penalty for noncompliance.

States that have created sheriffs as a matter of legislative enactment, as opposed to a constitutional provision, have sheriffs' departments, rather than sheriffs' offices. These are departments, under the executive branch of government, whose duties and responsibilities are overseen by a county board of supervisors, to whom the sheriff is directly accountable. This sheriff's model is likened to that of an appointed chief of police at the municipal level of government, who may be easily removed from office, unlike the constitutionally based counterpart. Under a sheriff's department modality, the agenda of the sheriff may be largely determined by an oversight body, such as a county board.

Jurisdiction

The sheriff's jurisdiction is considerably greater than that of a chief of police, in terms of geography, bodies of law covering the jurisdiction, and the legal right to command and direct citizens as well as other police and law enforcement agencies within the county to assist in specific work. First, county sheriffs have full legal authority over an entire county, including incorporated areas, although as a matter of practice, sheriffs generally police only the unincorporated areas of their counties. Second, sheriffs, as officers of the court, have full legal authority over both criminal and civil matters, unlike their municipal and state counterparts. Last, because sheriffs hold *posse comitatus* powers, they may exercise their authority over other police or law enforcement agencies within the county, although this power is rarely employed, as a matter of legal *comity* (agreement), political realities, and budgetary constraints.

Organizational Structure and Service Style

Sheriffs' agencies fall roughly into a four-part typology, including (1) the full-service model, where the agency provides the full range of policing, law enforcement, process serving, custodial, and court security responsibilities; (2) the law enforcement model, where there exists a separate police department within the sheriffs' agency, or a separate countywide police department where the sheriff's office has been abolished, with other services carried out by separate process serving and correctional/custodial departments (this type of arrangement is commonly known as a "sheriff's police" department and is generally allowed only in counties with populations of more than a million); (3) the civil-judicial model, which involves only court-related responsibilities; and (4) the correctional/custodial-judicial type, wherein all functions except law enforcement are provided.

Sheriffs' agencies tend to be open institutions, sensitive to community needs and agendas, willing to work toward community betterment with their constituents. This organizational openness results partly from the sheriffs' dependence on a favorable public image, necessary for reelection. This organizational openness inclines sheriffs' agencies to be receptive to community needs and demands as well as newer modes of policing that are more community sensitive, that is, community-oriented policing.

Correspondingly, sheriffs' agencies are less militaristic than their municipal and state counterparts, with little affinity for military protocol and symbolism or modes of policing that pit the agency against the community in a metaphorical "war on crime." This stands in stark contrast against the common posture found among municipal police departments nationwide, which are committed to a "crime attack" approach under a "professional model" or zero tolerance model of policing.

The form and function of sheriff's agencies vary according to their size. As they increase in size (in terms of the number of sworn officers) and formality (bureaucratization), they tend to replicate more closely the traditional/professional model of policing (a closed system), where officers work as crime fighting specialists in discrete bureaus within the agency. On the other hand, as sheriffs' agencies become smaller and are less formalized, they tend to become more institutionally open and committed to community coproduction as generalist officers in a collateral approach to the crime problem, which is less invasive and less potentially damaging to the community fabric. Interestingly, it is these small informal sheriffs' agencies that have the highest crime clearance rates; they also experience less community tension than their big-city counterparts.

If the military metaphor is to be used, as it so often is in discussions regarding police agencies, formalized big-city police departments and large urban-based sheriffs' agencies with their high degrees of officer specialization, formality, bureaucratization, and war on crime mentality can be said to selectively replicate the military model or a "paramilitarized" model (one that selects recruits from outside the community, in a process based entirely on qualifications and credentials). Smaller sheriffs' agencies that are informal, rurally based, nonbureaucratized, with officers who function as generalists, replicate more closely a "militia model" of policing (a locally based unit instituted for mutual community betterment and protection, staffed by local residents).

DAVID N. FALCONE and L. EDWARD WELLS

See also **American Policing: Early Years; British Policing; Community-Oriented Policing: History; History of American Policing; Jail; Los Angeles County Sheriff's Department (LASD); Posse Comitatus**

References and Further Reading

Brown, Johnny M. 1993. Sheriff's Department versus Office of the Sheriff. *Sheriff,* March–April, 9.
Brown, Lee P. n.d. The role of the sheriff. In *The future of policing,* ed. A. W. Cohn, 227–28. Beverly Hills, CA: Sage.
Falcone, David N., and L. Edward Wells. 1995. The county sheriff as a distinctive policing modality. *American Journal of Police* 14 (3/4): 123–48.
Law Enforcement and Administrative Statistics (LEMAS). 2004. Data set. Washington, DC: Bureau of Justice Statistics, U.S. Department of Justice.
Mahon, John K. 1983. *History of the militia and the National Guard.* New York: Macmillan.
Reaves, Brian A. 2001. Sheriffs' offices 1999. Law Enforcement and Administrative Statistics (LEMAS), *Bureau of Justice Statistics Bulletin,* 1–13.
———. 2002. Census of state and local law enforcement agencies, 2000. *Bureau of Justice Statistics Bulletin.*
Sattler, Ted. 1992. The High Sheriff in England today: The invisible man? *Sheriff* 44 (4): 20–23, 48.
Struckhoff, David R. 1994. *The American sheriff.* Chicago: The Justice Research Institute.

SHIFT WORK AND FATIGUE

Shift Work

Shift work refers to a work schedule that is different from the traditional eight-hour, five-day-per-week daytime schedule. Examples of shift work include evening and night shifts, compressed schedules (fewer than five days, more hours per day), and shift schedules that rotate (working daytime for a period and then moving to evenings or nights or working the same shift but rotating days off). Shift work is common in a number of occupations that require round-the-clock operations such as public safety, medicine (doctors, nurses, technicians, and so on), and transportation (trucking, airlines, and so on) as well as mining and manufacturing, where full-time operations are necessary for profit making.

A significant amount of research has been conducted on the impact of shift work in the areas of medicine, transportation, and manufacturing, whereas there has been limited attention paid to shift work in public safety, even though the potential for harm may be equally or more pronounced. Much of the accumulated evidence on the impact of shift work has led to greater regulation of work hours and schedules in some fields in order to protect the public and improve worker safety. Needless to say, law enforcement schedules and hours are not regulated, although many agencies have adopted policies limiting work hours per day, pay period, or month.

What Is Fatigue?

Fatigue is the subjective experience of being persistently tired, weak, weary, or exhausted mentally and/or physically (Dittner, Wessely, and Brown 2004). Fatigue is often either a characteristic of, or contributor to, various diseases and conditions including chronic fatigue syndrome (CFS), cancer, multiple sclerosis, and depression (Dittner, Wessely, and Brown 2004). Fatigue is often the result of overexertion both mentally and/or physically, but interestingly can also be caused by boredom.

Rosekind and his colleagues (1994) asserted that sleep loss and circadian disruption are the two principal physiological sources of fatigue. Other nonprimary causes of fatigue include long and irregular work hours, moonlighting, shift work, stress, and poor sleep quality (Vila 2005). Fatigue is also a fundamental source of stress among police (see, for example, Brown and Campbell 1994; Burke 1994; Violanti and Aron 1993). Shift rotations or changeovers to new shift schedules can disrupt circadian rhythms and sleep

length, thereby resulting in fatigue. Shift changes and extended shifts lead to increased fatigue, and according to Worden (1995), it is common for police to work double shifts due to staffing needs of community policing demands. Additionally, agency demands and required court appearances may lead to the need for increased overtime on the part of officers, thereby lengthening their shifts.

The Effects of Fatigue

Across a broad array of occupations, it has been reported that chronic sleep restriction in which one gets fewer than seven hours of sleep per night for an extended period has been shown to be associated with on-the-job errors, injuries, traffic accidents, personal conflicts, health complaints, and drug use (Dinges, Rogers, and Baynard 2004). It has been well established that increased fatigue worsens mood, decreases alertness, impairs performance, adds to the likelihood of poor judgment, and can lead police to misuse of force (Vila 1996; Vila et al. 2000). Fatigue may also impact family relationships as well as officer stress and associated reactions. According to Vila (2005), fatigue in police undermines justice by reducing humanity (depriving them of health and ability to reason); reduces attentiveness, the ability to temper frustration, and the ability to regulate; increases fear, anxiety, and proneness to anger; and narrows perspective, thereby impacting decision making.

In a recent national study of work schedules and fatigue in major police agencies, researchers found that officers who routinely worked more consecutive hours than would be legal in other public service industries were six times more fatigued than those in industrial and mining jobs (see Vila et al. 2000). The study also revealed that 14% of officers reported being tired regularly and 16% had trouble staying awake at work.

There are two variables to consider when examining the effects of fatigue from shift work. The first has to do with the time of day of the shift. Studies have shown that the performance of those working the night shift is slower and less accurate (Smith, Totterdell, and Folkard 1995) and results in poor sleep (less sleep time and that of a lesser quality) primarily due to problems associated with circadian rhythms. However, a recent study showed that officers were more willing to shoot and less likely to take cover in a "difficult to justify" shooting simulation during the early day shift (beginning at 6:00 A.M.) as compared to the evening or midnight shift.

The other important variable to examine when evaluating the effects of fatigue is the length of the shift. In a review article, researchers concluded that the results across studies are equivocal, with few differences between eight- and twelve-hour shifts, although they noted that fatigue and safety are concerns with twelve-hour shifts (Smith et al. 1998). In a more recent report from the National Institute for Occupational Safety and Health (NIOSH), researchers indicated that "a pattern of deteriorating performance" is observed across studies, particularly when combining twelve-hour shifts with more than forty hours of work per week (Caruso et al. 2004). Evidence does suggest that fatigue is linked to long working hours, but there is not conclusive evidence on the number of hours it takes for an individual to become fatigued (White and Beswick 2003).

Effects of Fatigue on Cognitive Functioning

Fatigue can interfere with decision making by limiting the formation of sound decisions, encouraging overly constrained choices, and inducing poor responses due to increased irritability (Vila et al. 2000).

Research suggests that fatigue can narrow one's perspective, increase anxiety and fearfulness, and limit one's ability to handle complex, stressful situations. In fact, Dawson and Reid (1997) reported that twenty-four hours of sustained wakefulness decreases performance to a level equivalent to a blood alcohol concentration of .10%, which in all U.S. jurisdictions is considered legally drunk.

Effects of Fatigue on Performance

Fatigue has been linked to vehicle and on-the-job accidents in many occupations. However, there has been little research among law enforcement. Nevertheless, a greater proportion of police officers are killed in vehicle accidents, falls, and accidental shootings today since the 1970s, when soft body armor was widely adopted. Given that accidents are more dangerous to police than gunfights, domestic disturbances, arrests, and traffic stops, it is perhaps more important than ever that we examine the link between fatigue and accidents among police. One study found that those officers who reported being tired at the beginning of their work shifts were more likely to be involved in accidents (Vila et al. 2000).

Measurement of Fatigue

A large number of scales have been developed to assess the nature, severity, and impact of fatigue (Dittner, Wessely, and Brown 2004). However, the majority of the measures are designed for use with clinical populations rather than the general population. As such, numerous instruments exist for measuring fatigue in those patients with cancer, depression, chronic fatigue syndrome, multiple sclerosis, and other illnesses. Nevertheless, the measurement of fatigue generally focuses on both acute fatigue (often experienced at the end of a long day) and cumulative fatigue (experienced even after a good night's sleep).

Fatigue can be measured both subjectively and objectively. One such subjective measure of fatigue is the Pittsburgh sleep quality index (PSQI), a global index measuring sleep quality, sleep latency (time to fall asleep), sleep duration, habitual sleep efficiency, sleep disturbances, use of sleep medication, and daytime dysfunction (Buysse et al. 1989). This measure is often used as a measure of fatigue. An example of an objective measure of fatigue is the fitness-for-duty (FIT) workplace screener, a noninvasive eye reaction test that taps into the influence of fatigue on involuntary eye reactions to light, so the responses are not consciously controlled by the participant (see, for example, Krichmar et al. 1998).

In policing, early detection of fatigue is essential for preventing accidents, injuries, or other forms of behavior that could be detrimental. While coworkers and supervisors may be the most capable of observing fatigue among fellow officers, a properly designed and implemented early warning and intervention system may be useful in identifying those officers whose performance may indicate an underlying fatigue problem. Proper controls ought to be implemented to assess the amount of overtime that officers work, and systems should be in place to account for off-duty employment (that is, moonlighting). In combination with other routine officer stress factors, fatigue can be very detrimental to officers if they are unable to cope with the stress of the job or get enough sleep to ensure health and safety.

Controlling Fatigue

While the impact of fatigue on police officers can have dire consequences, Vila (2005) argues that much of fatigue is avoidable and that there are ways to control it. He notes that practitioners and administrators see fatigue as part and parcel of the police environment, making it easy to ignore. Our expectations of police both emotionally and physically are often unrealistic. Yet Vila asserts that by initiating organizational work hour policies and reduced demands for overtime or double shifts, much of police fatigue can be organizationally controlled.

KAREN L. AMENDOLA

See also **Danger and Police Work; Early Warning Systems; Stress and Police Work; Stress: Coping Mechanisms**

References and Further Reading

Brown, J., and E. Campbell. 1994. *Stress and policing: Sources and strategies.* Chichester, UK: Wiley and Sons.

Burke, R. 1994. Stressful events: Work-family conflict, coping, psychological burnout, and well-being among police officers. *Psychological Reports* 75: 787–800.

Caruso, C. C., E. M. Hitchcock, R. B. Dick, et al. 2004. *Overtime and extended work shifts: Recent findings on illnesses, injuries, and health behaviors.* Pub. No. 2004-143.

Dawson, D., and K. Reid. 1997. Fatigue, alcohol, and performance impairment. *Nature* 388 (July): 235.

Dinges, D. F., N. L. Rogers, and M. B. Baynard. 2004. Chronic sleep deprivation. In *Principles and practice of sleep medicine,* ed. Kryger, Roth, and Dement, 4th ed., 67–76. Philadelphia: W. B. Saunders Company.

Dittner, A. J., S. C. Wessely, and R. G. Brown. 2004. The assessment of fatigue: A practical guide for clinicians and researchers. *Journal of Psychosomatic Research* 56: 157–70.

Krichmar, J., J. Pollard, M. Russo, et al. 1998. Oculomotor indicators of fatigue and impairment. *Psychophysiology* 35 (Suppl. 1): S4.

Rosekind, M., P. Gander, D. Miller, et al. 1994. Fatigue in operational settings: Examples from the aviation environment. *Human Factors* 36: 327–38.

Smith, L., S. Folkard, P. Tucker, and I. Macdonald. 1998. Work shift duration: A review comparing eight hour and twelve hour shift systems. *Occupational Environmental Medicine* 55: 217–29.

Smith, L., P. Totterdell, and S. Folkard. 1995. Shiftwork effects in nuclear power workers: A field study using portable computers. *Work Stress* 9 (2–3): 235–44.

U.S. Department of Health and Human Services, Centers for Disease Control and Prevention, National Institute for Occupational Safety and Health.

Vila, B. J. 2005. Paper presented at the American Society of Criminology Annual Conference, Toronto, Ontario, Canada.

Vila, B. J., D. J. Kenney, G. B. Morrison, and M. Reuland. 2000. Evaluating the effects of fatigue on police patrol officers. Washington, DC: Police Executive Research Forum, under U.S. Department of Justice Grant #96-IJ-CX-0046.

Violanti, J., and F. Aron. 1993. Sources of police stressors: Job attitudes, and psychological distress. *Psychological Reports* 72: 899–904.

White, J., and J. Beswick. 2003. *Working long hours,* HSL/2003/02. Sheffield, UK: Health and Safety Laboratory. http://www.hse.gov.uk/research/hsl_pdf/2003/hsl03-02.pdf.

Worden, R. 1995. Personal communication with B. J. Vila, November 30.

SITUATIONAL CRIME PREVENTION

Introduction

A simple but profound shift in thinking has helped police organizations to realize new gains in crime control, crime reduction, victimization, and fear. Many police agencies have adopted prevention as the overarching goal of policing, rather than as a specialized function or set of activities. Understanding prevention as the strategic goal of the policing process puts into practice Sir Robert Peel's ninth principle of policing: "The test of police efficiency is the absence of crime and disorder, not the visible evidence of police action in dealing with them" (Lee 1901).

For police, prevention in the past has consisted primarily of exhorting people to "lock it or lose it" and dispensing advice on door locks and window bars for their homes and businesses. Crime prevention typically was (and often still is) an add-on program or appendage to the police agency, which normally included a few officers who were trained to go to citizens' homes and perform security surveys or engage in public speaking on prevention topics.

The introduction of situational crime prevention (SCP) in the 1980s by Ronald V. Clarke (1983) offered a new, proactive crime prevention and control strategy to law enforcement practitioners and academics alike. SCP departs from most criminological theories by focusing on the occurrence of crime rather than the detection of offenders. Simply put, SCP provides a means of reducing crime by reducing crime opportunities and increasing the risks to offenders.

The Evolution of Situational Crime Prevention

Crime prevention is not a new idea. Our earliest ancestors maximized lighting from the sun and moon and employed defensive placement of homes on the side of cliffs, with only one entrance and exit (Scanlon 1996). Cave dwellers established ownership of a space by surrounding it with large boulders. The Romans developed and enforced complex land laws. Walled cities and castles exist throughout the world. It is a natural human impulse to claim and secure an area to prevent problems (U.S. Department of Housing and Urban Development, n.d.).

In the early 1960s, environmental prevention strategies emerged in the works of Jane Jacobs (1961), author of *The Death and Life of Great American Cities*. She argued against urban renewal strategies that promoted the building of high-rise public housing complexes that invited crime through poor design. Jacobs' ideas about safe neighborhoods also incorporated the urban areas surrounding buildings themselves.

A decade later, C. Ray Jeffrey (1971), drawing on Jacobs' works, coined the phrase "crime prevention through environment design" in a book of that title. Jeffrey believed that the proper design and use of the environment can help reduce the incidence of crime and improve people's overall quality of life. Concurrent with Jeffrey's work, Oscar Newman (1972), an architect, argued that flaws in the physical environment were responsible for, or at least facilitators of, criminal behavior. Newman believed that the physical characteristics (building design) of an area could suggest to residents and potential offenders that the area is well cared for and protected, or that it is open to criminal activity.

The 1970s experienced a rise of community-based crime prevention programs, such as the neighborhood or block watch. These programs were based on Jacobs', Jeffrey's, and Newman's physical design approaches. The focus is on such strategies as citizen surveillance and action (for example, cutting back bushes, installing lighting, removing obstacles to enhance sight lines, organizing security surveys, and distributing news about crime and crime prevention) (Lab 1977).

Later, James Q. Wilson and George Kelling's (1982) broken-windows theory extended Newman's (1972) focus on housing projects to entire neighborhoods. "Broken windows" refers to physical signs that an area is unattended and purposely ignored and neglected. They found that abandoned vehicles and buildings, trash and litter, and broken windows and graffiti are physical indicators that no one cares, thus sending the message that neighborhood disorder is acceptable. In addition to these physical indicators are social manifestations of the same problems, such as loitering youths, public drunkenness, prostitution, and vagrancy.

Both the physical and social indicators are typically referred to as signs of incivility that attract offenders to the area.

The most recent, and perhaps most promising, movement in crime prevention focuses efforts and interventions on attacking specific problems, places, and times. Clarke (1983) proposed "situational prevention," measures directed at highly specific forms of crime that involve earlier environmental strategies in ways that reduce the opportunities for crime and increase its risk. Examples of situational prevention include the installation of surveillance equipment in parking lots experiencing vandalism, erecting security screens in banks to stop robberies, altering traffic patterns in a drug market neighborhood, using electronic tags for library materials, and using caller ID for obscene phone calls (Lab 1977, 8–9).

Situational Crime Prevention

While working at the Home Office, London England, Ronald Clarke introduced SCP as a method of improving our understanding of crime, crime reduction theory, and crime changes. SCP draws upon the following criminological theories:

- *Rational choice theory.* Crime is committed by rational individuals who weigh the benefits against the risks (Cornish and Clarke 1986).
- *Routine activity theory.* A crime is possible when a motivated offender and a suitable target (victim) come together in space and time, absent a capable guardian (a person whose mere presence would deter potential offenders including passersby, security guards, and street vendors) (Cohen and Felson 1979).
- *Lifestyle theory.* The risk of victimization is related to a person's lifestyle; such things as work environment and

leisure activities may expose people to potential offenders (Fattah 1993; Farrell and Pease 1993).

As indicated, SCP provides a change in focus from most crime prevention theories that are primarily concerned with the person committing the crime. SCP seeks to not eliminate criminal or delinquent tendencies through improvement of society or its institutions, but also making criminal action less attractive to offenders (Clarke 1997, 2). SCP is a practical "environmental criminology" approach that seeks to reduce crime opportunity by making settings less conducive to unwanted or illegal activities, focusing on the environment rather than the offender (Clarke 1997, 2).

SCP relies on the rational choice theory of crime, which asserts that criminals choose to commit crimes based on the costs and benefits involved with the crime. For example, a potential offender will commit a high-risk crime only if the rewards of the crime outweigh the risks (Clarke 1997, 8–9).

The Five Strategies and Twenty-Five Techniques of Situational Crime Prevention

Cornish and Clarke's (2003) five SCP strategies and twenty-five techniques (five for each strategy) are as follows:

1. *Increasing the effort needed to commit the crime.* Crimes are easy to commit, and the average person is susceptible to engage in criminal activity if the right opportunity arises. These casual criminals, as they are called, may be eliminated by increasing the effort needed to commit a crime:
   * *Hardening targets.* Install locks, bolts, protective screens, and other physical barriers to obstruct an offender's access to a potential target.
   * *Controlling access control.* Install barriers and design walkways, paths, and roads to keep unwanted users from entering vulnerable areas.
   * *Screening exits.* Require tickets at the door of a theater and use electronic devices at stores to detect the theft of music, DVDs, and clothing.
   * *Deflecting offenders.* Discourage crimes by giving people alternate, legal venues for their activities, such as decreasing littering by providing litter bins or separating fans of rival teams after athletic events.
   * *Controlling tools and weapons.* Implement universal measures such as firearm permit regulations and specific measures such as metal detectors in community centers.

2. *Increasing the risks associated with the crime.* Offenders who believe they are at risk of being apprehended are less likely to offend. For example, a simple "How's my driving?" sign with a toll-free phone number on the back of a delivery truck may deter the driver from speeding or committing other traffic violations. The five ways to increase the risk are as follows:
   * *Extending guardianship.* Going out at night in groups increases personal safety. Carrying a cell phone provides the opportunity to report suspicious incidents quickly. The police notification to neighbors about a burglary in the area extends the number of "eyes on the street" and enhances safety.
   * *Assisting natural surveillance.* This includes the surveillance provided

by people as they go about their daily activities; also included are removal of advertisements from storefront windows, removing hedges in front of businesses, and constructing glass-encased stairways on the outside of parking structures .

- *Reducing anonymity.* The display of taxi and limousine driver IDs for passengers, for example, increases people's familiarization with one another.
- *Utilizing site managers.* The presence of building attendants, concierges, maintenance workers, and attendants increases site surveillance and crime reporting.
- *Strengthening formal surveillance.* Using security personnel and hardware (such as closed-circuit TV and burglar alarms) is a deterrent to unwanted activities.

3. *Reducing the rewards.* Reducing the rewards from crime makes offending not worthwhile. Following are techniques for doing so:

- *Concealing targets.* Keeping valuables out of plain view of potential offenders can reduce temptation; also included are hiding jewelry while walking alone, keeping cell phones and other valuables out of plain sight in parked vehicles, and keeping one's name gender-neutral on any phone lists.
- *Removing targets.* Eliminate crime motivation from public areas by following such examples as a no-cash policy and keeping valuable property in a secure area overnight.
- *Identifying property.* Inscribe indelible ownership marks on property to prevent individuals from reselling it.
- *Disrupting markets.* Reducing the market for stolen goods may have significant impact on burglary

and theft. This may include the police monitoring pawn shops and crackdowns on flea markets and illegal street vendors. It may also involve the mandatory licensing of door-to-door solicitors.

- *Denying benefits.* Offenders may be deterred if they are denied the benefit of their efforts. Included are having PIN numbers on debit cards and photos on credit cards, engaging in rapid graffiti removal, and attaching ink tags on clothing.

4. *Reducing provocation.* The environmental situation or the manner in which places are managed may provoke crime and violence. Reducing provocations focuses on situations that precipitate or induce crime. For example, busy bars and unmonitored drinking will inherently combine to provoke physical violence. The following techniques assist in the reducing of provocations:

- *Reducing frustration and stress.* People are easily angered and frustrated in today's busy world. Studies show that improving lighting enhances people's mood and morale in the workplace. Additional seating and soothing music may reduce people's frustrations in crowded public places. Online drivers' licensing and motor vehicle registration eliminates the need to stand in long lines.
- *Avoiding disputes.* Wearing a San Francisco 49ers jersey at an Oakland Raiders football game is inviting a fight. Fixed cab fares in airports helps avoid fare disputes. Reducing the amount of time that public transportation is available from large concerts and sporting events reduces the chance of fights occurring that are related to drunkenness and crowded conditions.

- *Reducing emotional arousal.* Laws that restrict convicted pedophiles from living within a certain distance from schools help to reduce the temptation of being in contact with children. Many states require a ten-day "cooling off" period to purchase a gun.
- *Neutralizing peer pressure.* Peers evoke a strong influence in others in school, work, and play. "Friends don't let friends drink and drive" slogans are designed to positively influence drunk driving using peer pressure. There are several prevention programs for parents who struggle with a child negatively influenced by friends.
- *Discouraging imitation.* The rapid repair of vandalized property (carving park benches) and the prompt removal of graffiti reduce the likelihood of repeat incidents. This is the thesis of Wilson and Kelling's (1982) broken-windows theory mentioned earlier. Cable companies allow parents who are concerned about the influence of television violence on juveniles to easily block out violent and sexually explicit programs.

5. *Removing excuses.* Many offenders argue that they didn't know they were doing anything wrong. Informing people of the law and the rules eliminates any excuses for engaging in illegal activity. For example, "no parking" and "no trespassing" signs are enforceable if they are posted. The following techniques prevent offenders from excusing their crimes by claiming ignorance or misunderstanding.

   - *Set rules.* Rules govern behavior. Charging a person's credit card a fee helps to reduce restaurant no-shows. Signed agreements regulate the behavior of students living in dorms. Many companies establish strict telephone procedures to ensure that good customer service is delivered.
   - *Post instructions.* "No parking," "no smoking," "handicap parking," and "no trespassing" signs remove any claims of ignorance of the law.
   - *Alert people's conscience.* "Copying is a crime" warnings in bold letters on music CDs and DVDs are designed to get people's attention. Digital signs that display a vehicle's speed are commonly used by police to slow traffic in high-accident areas and school zones.
   - *Assist with people's compliance.* Programs that provide free taxi rides to bar patrons during the holidays and bars that offer free nonalcoholic drinks to designated drivers help patrons adhere to drunk driving laws. Adequate garbage receptacles and public lavatories on beaches and in parks reduce littering and public urination.
   - *Control drug and alcohol abuse.* Free breathalyzer tests in bars and bartender training reduce the risks of intoxication and drunk driving.

Conclusion

Clearly, the field of crime prevention has matured from its very early primitive forms, now involving more sophisticated methods for adapting the environment and for targeting homes and businesses. SCP has emerged as an essential crime prevention and control strategy by focusing on reducing opportunities that are provided to offenders motivated to commit crimes. The emphasis on proactive crime prevention is far preferred to the more traditional reactive approach, by which the police are primarily involved in taking crime reports and investigating but a small proportion of offenses.

RONALD W. GLENSOR

See also **Broken-Windows Policing; Closed-Circuit Television Applications for Policing; Crime Control Strategies: Crime Prevention Through Environmental Design; Crime Prevention; Problem-Oriented Policing; Routine Guardianship**

References and Further Reading

Clarke, Ronald V. 1983. Situational crime prevention: Its theoretical basis and practical scope. In *Crime and justice: An annual review of research,* vol. 4, ed. Michael Tonry and Norvel Morris, 225. Chicago: University of Chicago Press.

———, ed. 1997. *Situational crime prevention: Successful case studies.* 2nd ed. New York: Harrow and Hesston.

Cohen, L. E., and Marcus Felson. 1979. Social change and crime rate trends: A routine activity approach. *American Sociological Review* 44: 588–608.

Cornish, D. B., and Ronald V. Clarke. 1986. *The reasoning criminal.* New York: Springer-Verlag.

———. 2003. Opportunities, precipitators and criminal decisions: A reply to Wortley's critique of situational crime prevention. In *Theory for situational crime prevention studies,* vol. 16, ed. Smith and Cornish, 41–96. New York: Criminal Justice Press.

Farrell, Graham, and Ken Pease. 1993. *Once bitten, twice bitten: Repeat victimization and its implications for crime prevention.* Crime Prevention Unit Paper 46. London: Home Office.

Fattah, E. A. 1993. The rational choice. Opportunity perspectives as a vehicle for integrating criminological and victimological theories. In *Routine activity and rational choice. Advances in criminological theory,* vol. 5, ed. Ronald V. Clarke and Marcus Felson. New Brunswick, NJ: Transaction Publishers.

Felson, Marcus. 2002. *Crime and everyday life.* 3rd ed. Thousand Oaks, CA: Pine Forge.

Goldstein, Herman. 1990. *Problem oriented policing.* New York: McGraw-Hill.

Jacobs, Jane. 1961. *The death and life of great American cities.* New York: Random House.

Jeffrey, C. Ray. 1971. *Crime prevention through environmental design.* Beverly Hills, CA: Sage.

Lab, Steven P. 1977. Crime prevention: Where have we been and which way should we go? In *Community policing at a crossroads,* ed. Steven P. Lab, 1–13. Cincinnati: Anderson.

Lee, W. L. Melville. 1901. *A history of police in England,* Chap. 12. London: Methuen.

Mahew, P., R. V. Clarke, A. Sturman, and J. M. Hough. 1976. *Crime as opportunity.* London: Her Majesty's Stationery Office.

Newman, Oscar. 1972. *Defensible space: Crime prevention through urban design.* New York: Macmillan.

Scanlon, Cynthia. 1996. Crime prevention through environmental design. *Law and Order,* May, 50.

Tilley, N., and G. Laycock. 2002. *Working out what to do: Evidence-based crime reduction.* Crime Reduction Series Paper 11, Briefing Note. London: Home Office.

U.S. Department of Housing and Urban Development. n.d. *Crime prevention through environmental design: Crime prevention brief.* Washington, DC: U.S. Government Printing Office.

Wilson, James Q., and George Kelling. 1982. Broken windows. *The Atlantic Monthly* 211: 29–38.

Wortley, R. 2001. A classification of techniques for controlling situational precipitators of crime. *Security Journal* 14: 63–82.

SMITH, BRUCE

Bruce Smith (1892–1955), police consultant and criminologist, was born in Brooklyn, New York, the son of a banker and real estate operator. He was regarded as something of a rebel, even from his first collegiate experience at Wesleyan University. While there he delighted in rolling cannonballs down the main street and in firing a shotgun from his dormitory window. He was expelled in his senior year for publicly ridiculing the college chaplain because he had conducted a prayer that went on for more than seven minutes—Smith had clocked him with a stopwatch.

Moving on to Columbia University, presumably a more serious student, he earned his B.S. degree in 1914. One of his professors, Charles A. Beard, also director of the New York Bureau of Municipal Research, acted as his mentor and convinced him to remain at Columbia for graduate study. In 1916, Smith was granted both the LL.B. degree and the M.S. in political science. After graduation he worked with Beard at the Bureau of Municipal Research, later renamed the Institute of Public Administration.

That same year he was assigned to study the police department in Harrisburg, Pennsylvania. Unfamiliar with police operations, he wondered why he had been chosen. About the Harrisburg experience he reflected, "That's how I got into police work. I was dragged in squealing and protesting. I knew nothing about cops. Boy, how I hated to leave those actuarial tables."

Soon World War I intervened, and as a second lieutenant Smith served in the U.S. Air Force from 1917 to 1919. The war over, he returned to the Institute of Public Administration and quickly rose to the position of manager, which he held from 1921 to 1928. During those hectic years, he acquired invaluable knowledge collaborating with the Missouri Association for Criminal Justice, the National Crime Commission, and the Illinois Association for Criminal Justice. From 1941 to 1946 and from 1950 to 1952, he was acting director of the institute; in 1954, he became director until his death, thus fulfilling the promise Charles Beard had seen in him.

Throughout the second half of his life, Smith was associated with so many commissions on the administration of justice and on law revision that it would take a catalog to enumerate them, and a book to cite his many contributions. But the keystone of his career was his monumental work in surveying police departments in about fifty leading American cities and in eighteen states, in creating the *Uniform Crime Reports* (1930)—devised after an exhaustive study of Western European practices and adopted by the Federal Bureau of Investigation—and in writing several police treatises, most notably *Police Systems in the United States.*

Smith, who never wore a police uniform, nonetheless earned the respect of the cop on the beat. In such statements as this about protracted entrance exams, he championed the recruit: "I don't care if a rookie thinks the duke of Wellington is a man, a horse, or a smoking tobacco . . . . What counts is a man's character." His sympathy for the job of policing ran deep: "Rarely does a major piece of police work receive the accolade of general approval . . . . The environment in which police must do their work is therefore certain to be unfavorable." And he saw clearly the obstacles to improvement: "No police force . . . is ever quite free of the taint of corruption; none succeeds in wholly repressing or preventing criminal acts, or in effecting arrests and convictions in any large portion of the total offenses reported; many are deeply involved in political manipulations of various kinds." So he fought for better methods of selection and training of personnel, a different system of promotion, increased discipline, and severance from political control and the Civil Service Commission, to name a few of his reforms.

Furthermore, he encouraged police departments to give civilians the desk jobs, thereby returning police to the streets. Interestingly, as a consultant to the U.S. Army Air Force during World War II, he advocated the same tactic; because of him, 350 colonels were reassigned from offices to field duty.

But Smith did not always meet with success. Even though he was mostly welcomed by police departments, revered by the officers, and acknowledged as an authority, he became a Sisyphus-like figure. In 1923, he made sweeping recommendations for reform of the New Orleans Police Department; in 1946, upon his return, he found almost the same disgraceful situation in the department as had appeared earlier—a disheartening déjà vu. In another instance, fourteen years after analyzing the St. Louis Police Department, when asked for further guidance, he suggested reform measures nearly identical to the ones he had offered before since little had changed. Often, in the case of Smith, it seemed that his sound advice went too much against the grain for the entrenched police departments to carry out.

Smith contributed regularly to professional journals, both American and British. He wrote the standard articles on police for the *Encyclopedia Britannica, Encyclopedia Americana, Collier's Encyclopedia,* and the *Encyclopedia of Social Sciences.* In tribute, O. W. Wilson wrote, "Smith combined the best qualities of policeman, executive, statesman, and scholar." He was married in 1915 to Mary Rowell; they had two children. Late in life Smith purchased a yacht—the *Lucifer*—and indulged his passion for sailing. While aboard the *Lucifer* he was stricken by a lung ailment, later dying in Southampton Hospital in New York of a heart attack. At the time of his death he was writing a book about British police, whose organization he wanted to elucidate for American police. He died a young sixty-three.

WILLIAM G. BAILEY

References and Further Reading

Current Biography, 1953. 1954. Bruce Smith. Pp. 577–79. New York: H. W. Wilson.

Smith, Bruce. 1949. *Police systems in the United States.* 2nd ed. New York: Harper and Brothers.

Watts, Eugene J. 1977. Bruce Smith. *Dictionary of American Biography* 14 (5): 638–39. New York: Charles Scribner and Sons.

Wilson, O. W. 1956. Bruce Smith. *Journal of Criminal Law, Criminology and Police Science* 47 (2) (July–August): 235–37.

SOCIAL DISORGANIZATION, THEORY OF

Introduction

The spatial concentration of crime and victimization at geographic locations is a well known and robust empirical finding within criminology. Several studies have indicated that crime is concentrated at micro places such as street addresses, segments, and block groups (Sherman, Gartin, and Buerger 1989; Weisburd et al. 2004), and evaluations of place-based policing tactics at micro places indicate that geographically focused policing tactics are a promising crime reduction strategy (Braga 2001; Weisburd and Eck 2004). The implementation of such micro place policing strategies was guided, in part, by the empirical finding of crime concentration at places and theoretical insights from situational crime prevention theory, routine activities theory, and the ecology of crime literature (Skogan and Frydl 2004; Weisburd and Eck 2004).

As a result, many policing scholars have noted that the police are more likely to make observable impacts on crime when they target the criminal event itself and the environmental conditions that allow for it to occur, rather than targeting the development of the individual criminal offender (Weisburd 1997). Although criminal activity is concentrated at a larger level of geography as well, such as communities or neighborhoods (Shaw and McKay 1942/1969), the policing literature has not yet fully incorporated theoretical insights from the social disorganization literature in the research on policing of larger units of place.

This article discusses the relevance and implications of social disorganization theory for the policing of community-level areas characterized by structural and social disadvantage. Social disorganization theory and policing are linked through such concepts as procedural justice and legitimacy. Research from the social disorganization literature has shown that communities characterized by concentrated disadvantage (that is, extreme structural and social disadvantages such as poverty, public assistance, high percentage of female heads of household, unemployment, percentage of youth) influence the formation of individual perceptions regarding the legitimacy of the police and the extent of criminal activity within the area (Kubrin and Weitzer 2003a). In the sections that follow, I review social disorganization theory and several key insights and discuss the implications of those insights for policing areas of concentrated disadvantage, most notably the importance of perceptions of favorable police legitimacy and procedural justice.

Social Disorganization Theory

Social disorganization theory is among the oldest and most prominent of criminological theories. Originating in the 1930s from the influential Chicago School, Shaw and McKay (1942/1969) developed an ecological theory of delinquency based on the finding that high rates of delinquency remained stable over time in certain neighborhoods regardless of changes in the racial or ethnic composition of residents. Social disorganization refers to the inability of a community to regulate the activities that occur within its boundaries, the consequences of which are high rates of criminal activity and social disorder (Kornhauser 1978; Sampson and Raudenbush 1999; Markowitz et al. 2001).

Structural disadvantages such as population heterogeneity, residential instability, and poor economic conditions hinder the formation of community cohesion by limiting informal social networks and weakening a community's ability to exercise effective informal social control

over the activities that occur within its boundaries. The focus in social disorganization theory is on the dynamics of criminogenic places, and how such contexts influence and impact individual behavior as well as community-level cohesion and behavior.

There have been several revisions and extensions to the original social disorganization theory put forth by Shaw and McKay. In particular, scholars began to clearly articulate and measure the intervening mechanisms by which neighborhood structural disadvantages lead to increased criminal activity (Bursik 1988; Sampson and Groves 1989; Bursik and Grasmick 1993; Sampson, Raudenbush, and Earls 1997). In an influential test of the intervening mechanisms of social disorganization theory, Sampson and Groves (1989) found that a neighborhood's informal social control abilities (for example, ability to supervise and control teenage peer groups, strength of local friendship networks, and rate of participation in voluntary associations) substantially mediates the relationship between structural disadvantage and crime and victimization rates.

More recent studies have noted the distinction between the presence and type of informal social relationships within communities (Kubrin and Weitzer 2003a). For example, the presence of informal social networks within communities is beneficial for crime reduction in so much as they result in strong community cohesion and solidarity between residents that is prosocial in nature and results in both the desire and resources necessary to obtain collective valued goals. Several researchers have appropriately noted that we cannot assume that all informal social networks are created equally and that the nature of the network greatly dictates the nature of the potential resources and outcomes (Kubrin and Weitzer 2003a).

Further refinements to social disorganization theory include distinguishing between the presence of informal social networks and the potential resources or outcomes that are derived from involvement in such networks (Sampson, Raudenbush, and Earls 1997). Concepts such as social capital and collective efficacy reflect the valuable resources generated from involvement in social networks and refer to the degree of mutual trust and cohesion between community members and their ability to work cooperatively toward collective goals (Sampson, Raudenbush, and Earls 1997).

In one of the most statistically sophisticated tests, Sampson and colleagues (1997) found that after controlling for individual-level traits and neighborhood-level concentrated disadvantage, collective efficacy was negatively related to neighborhood-level violence. In addition, other studies have observed that there is a positive association between crime and social disorder, and the mediating effects of collective efficacy between structure and crime also applies to the relationship between structure and disorder. The former suggests that social disorder has a causal impact on crime, the latter suggests that disorder and crime reflect the same underlying process at different levels of severity (Skogan 1990; Sampson and Raudenbush 1999; Markowitz et al. 2001). Moreover, concentrated disadvantage was negatively associated with collective efficacy, indicating that areas with structural and social disadvantages are less able to form the informal social networks necessary to generate cohesion and a willingness to obtain collective goals.

It is important to note that exact causal paths and directions linking structural traits, informal social networks and community cohesion, fear of crime, and disorder and crime are debatable, as many of these variables can theoretically impact each other simultaneously, indicating joint causation. For example, few studies have adequately examined the possibility that not only do social disorder and decay lead to low social cohesion but that low social cohesion also impacts the presence of social disorder (Markowitz et al. 2001; Kubrin and Weitzer 2003).

Further improvements to social disorganization theory include focusing on social networks between the community and external local institutions, such as the police, as social networks important for shaping the nature of the dynamics as well as the strength of informal social control within communities (Bursik and Grasmick 1993; Sampson, Raudenbush, and Earls 1997; Kubrin and Weitzer 2003a). Social networks that link community residents to outside conventional institutions provide residents with both normative and tangible resources to regulate criminal activity, and recent research has indicated that public social networks may provide the greatest crime reducing benefits for disadvantaged communities (Velez 2001).

Using data from the Police Services Study, Velez (2001) found that structurally disadvantaged communities that had strong relationships with the police, as measured by the quality and frequency of interaction with the police, had lower victimization rates than did disadvantaged communities that had weak ties to the police. There is much evidence indicating that residents living in areas of concentrated disadvantage have weaker networks and perceptions of legitimacy toward the police (Kubrin and Weitzer 2003b; Anderson 1999).

Legitimacy, Procedural Justice, and Policing

Perceptions of legitimacy toward the police refers to the degree to which residents view the police as fair, just, and appropriate (Tyler 1990). Police legitimacy acts as a source of social control based on normative beliefs and represents the individual's belief in or bond to conventional society. Perceptions of procedural justice, the belief that the police use fair and just procedures in interaction with citizens, are closely related to and in fact influence perceptions of legitimacy (Tyler 1990; Skogan and Frydl 2004).

Several scholars have argued that macro social factors resulted in the economic segregation of minorities into structurally disadvantaged areas, resulting in a clustering of multiple social and structural disadvantages within communities and an intense feeling of social segregation and isolation among residents of disadvantaged communities (Wilson 1987; Sampson and Wilson 1995). According to Anderson's (1999) ethnographic study of violence in inner-city ghettoes of Philadelphia, violence results from the void left by the declining significance of social institutions and conventional norms for those living in poverty and economic deprivation and the alienation these individuals feel from mainstream society. The resulting pattern of norms that arise is what Anderson calls the "code of the street." Thus, the code of the street arises as a result of a profound lack of legitimacy in conventional institutions such as the police and "emerges where the influence of the police ends" (Anderson 1999, 34).

Sampson and Bartusch (1998) confirm this relationship between community structure and perceptions toward the police in their study of 8,782 residents of 343 Chicago area neighborhoods. They found that after accounting for individual sociodemographic traits (for example, race) and differences in crime rates, neighborhoods characterized by concentrated disadvantage, as compared to more affluent areas, had higher levels of dissatisfaction with the police and legal cynicism. Neighborhood structural traits shape the "cognitive landscape" in which normative orientations and perceptions about the law are formed (Sampson and Bartusch 1998). Harsh structural conditions that result in social isolation lead to a feeling in which violence is inevitable and the police mistrusted and avoided.

As a result of evidence such as this, many social disorganization researchers have argued for the theoretical inclusion of subcultural factors to help explain the relationship between concentrated disadvantage and crime (Kubrin and Weitzer 2003; Sampson and Bartusch 1998). Structural contexts of social and economic disadvantage can attenuate individual-level normative values and bonds to conventional society, which create a lack of legitimacy and subsequent void in which competing norms and modes of conduct can develop. This is especially relevant for policing since the police are viewed as the law enforcement agency of conventional society and as representative of the dominant conventional culture (Anderson 1999; Easton and Dennis 1969; Tyler and Huo 2002).

Kubrin and Weitzer (2003b) state that perceptions of police practices in poor communities largely revolve around two themes related to police discretion, underpolicing and overpolicing. Residents of poor communities largely perceive the police as providing insufficient protection from crime and victimization, noting that the police have little regard for the occurrences within their community (Kane 2005; Kubrin and Weitzer 2003b).

Conversely, perceptions of police services also tend to focus on the opposite end of the continuum, with several studies reporting that individuals from areas of disadvantage perceive high levels of police misconduct or overpolicing such as unwarranted traffic stops and searches, racial profiling, and verbal and physical abuse (Kubrin and Weitzer 2003b; Kane 2005). Overpolicing tactics such as racial profiling are also related to unfavorable perceptions of police legitimacy and procedural justice (Tyler and Wakslak 2005). Furthermore, since African Americans are overrepresented in communities of concentrated disadvantage, findings indicating that African Americans have unfavorable perceptions of police legitimacy are relevant for the policing of disadvantaged areas. Equally if not more important are emerging findings that suggest legitimacy and procedural justice perceptions are significantly associated with law breaking (Tyler 1990; Paternoster et al. 1997; Kane 2005).

Paternoster and colleagues (1997) reanalyzed data from the Milwaukee Domestic Violence Experiment to examine the impact of perceptions of procedural justice on the probability of future spouse assault. Their findings indicate that those offenders who felt as if they were treated fairly by the police had a lower number of rearrests, as compared to those offenders who reported low perceptions of procedural justice. In addition, after controlling for individual traits and prior offending, Paternoster and colleagues found that recidivism counts among those offenders that had been arrested but reported being treated fairly by the police were as low as those of offenders that had not been arrested but instead were released.

Additionally, findings from a study examining the relationship between variations in police legitimacy and violent crime at New York City police precincts from 1975 to 1996 (Kane 2005) found further support. Findings indicate that low police legitimacy, measured as police misconduct and underpolicing and overpolicing, is statistically related to violent crime rates, but only among those communities characterized by structural disadvantage.

This is not surprising, given prior research in the social disorganization literature linking concentrated disadvantage to both weak formal and informal social relationships within communities; more affluent communities likely have strong informal social networks, high levels of collective efficacy, and less need for formal social control mechanisms that result from relationships with the police. For communities with extreme structural and social disadvantages, the issue of police legitimacy is more salient, given the typical absence of strong prosocial intracommunity informal networks, and the crime

reducing impacts of favorable perceptions of police legitimacy are greater (Velez 2001).

Policing tactics can be better informed by an understanding of the relationship between disadvantaged communities and the mistrust of authorities it fosters. Given the literature concerning the relationship between concentrated disadvantage and crime rates as well as perceptions of legitimacy, it is likely that policing tactics may have differential impacts, in terms of outcome effectiveness and citizen reactions, across degrees of neighborhood-level structural disadvantage.

For example, community-oriented policing (COP) tactics rely heavily on the support and cooperation of community residents in implementing crime and disorder reducing programs. The community and the police are seen as coproducers in the creation of community safety, order, and well-being (Moore 1992). There are several elements and goals of community policing, one of which requires the police to increase social interactions with community members and develop relationships with the community that facilitate the reduction of disorder and crime. Community policing also encourages community involvement in the defining and solution of community problems, but if perceptions of police illegitimacy lead to decreased involvement and willingness to become involved among residents, the application of COP tactics may be problematic.

Although the COP approach is promising for increasing perceptions of police legitimacy, it is important to note that there may be some difficulties associated with the application at neighborhoods of concentrated disadvantage. There has been substantial literature on the difficulties of applying the COP model to police departments due to deeply rooted beliefs in the traditional model of policing (Weisburd and McElroy 1988); however, much less has been mentioned of the difficulties of applying the COP model to communities characterized by concentrated disadvantage.

Just as the normative, cultural, and organizational context of traditional policing made adoption of the seemingly equal role between police and community as crime fighters more difficult, it is likely that the normative, cultural, and structural context of extremely disadvantaged communities will result in reluctance to trust the police and resistance to increased interaction with the police. COP reflects an example of Bursik and Grasmick's public network and thus represents the intersection of formal and informal social control in communities. Findings from the social disorganization literature suggest that approaches such as COP may face resistance from residents of structurally disadvantaged communities and that pre-existing perceptions of low police legitimacy may be difficult to overcome in a short time and may in fact be exacerbated by increased police activity within the community.

The potential difficulties in implementing certain policing tactics in structurally disadvantaged communities is also applicable to policing tactics that are focused at micro places or reducing social disorder. Micro places such as street segments or addresses are situated within larger macro social contexts of the community and urban political economy; thus, it is likely that the environmental aspects, as well as situational aspects, of both the micro place and the community will matter for the commission or prevention of crime.

Additionally, "hot spots" policing is tightly focused and targeted on small units of place, and this type of policing may perpetuate or contribute to perceptions of overpolicing and subsequent low police legitimacy (Tyler and Wakslak 2005). Similarly, order maintenance policies that seek to reduce crime by reducing perceived and observed social disorder, thereby reducing fear of crime and crime

itself, are also susceptible to accusations of overpolicing, since zero tolerance policing tactics have the potential to be viewed as harassment and contribute to low levels of police legitimacy (Wilson and Kelling 1982; Skogan 1990; Skogan and Frdyl 2004).

In conclusion, findings from the social disorganization literature are relevant to the study of policing for several reasons. First, individuals living in areas of concentrated disadvantage are more likely to be dissatisfied with police services, have higher perceptions of legal cynicism, and hold less favorable perceptions about the procedural justice and legitimacy of the police (Sampson and Bartusch 1998; Anderson 1999; Sunshine and Tylor 2003; Kubrin and Weitzer 2003a, 2003b). Second, favorable perceptions of procedural justice and legitimacy toward the police are related to compliance with the law and lower crime rates (Tyler 1990; Paternoster et al. 1997; Kane 2005). Third, policing tactics such as community-oriented policing rely on garnering support from the community; thus, the effectiveness of these tactics is likely to vary by the degree of community disadvantage. Moreover, even policing tactics that are focused at the micro place level, and hence have less reliance on community support, are vulnerable to the ill effects of low police legitimacy, since these micro places are often embedded within larger macro social contexts that are characterized by concentrated disadvantage.

NANCY MORRIS

See also **Accountability; Attitudes toward the Police; Community-Oriented Policing: History; Crackdowns by the Police; Criminology; Minorities and the Police; Policing Multiethnic Communities; Quality-of-Life Policing; Zero Tolerance Policing**

References and Further Reading

Anderson, E. 1999. *Code of the streets*. New York: Norton.

Braga, A. A. 2001. The effects of hot spots policing on crime. *The Annals of American Political and Social Science* 578: 104–25.

Bursik, R. J. 1988. Social disorganization and theories of crime and delinquency: Problems and prospects. *Criminology* 26: 519–51.

Bursik, R. J., and H. G. Grasmick. 1993. *Neighborhoods and crime: The dimensions of effective community control.* New York: Lexington.

Kane, R. 2005. Compromised police legitimacy as a predictor of violent crime in structurally disadvantaged communities. *Criminology* 43: 469–98.

Kornhauser, R. 1978. *Social sources of delinquency.* Chicago: University of Chicago Press.

Kubrin, C. E., and R. Weitzer. 2003. New directions in social disorganization theory. *Journal of Research in Crime and Delinquency* 40 (4): 374–402.

Markowitz, F. E., P. E. Bellair, A. E. Liska, and J. Liu. 2001. Extending social disorganization theory: Modeling the relationships between cohesion, disorder, and fear. *Criminology* 39: 293–319.

Moore, M. n.d. Public health and criminal justice approaches to prevention. In *Crime and justice,* vol. 19, ed. Albert Reiss and Michael Tonry, 237–63. Chicago: University of Chicago Press.

Paternoster, R., R. Bachman, R. Brame, and L. W. Sherman. 1997. Do fair procedures matter? The effect of procedural justice on spousal assault. *Law and Society Review* 31: 163–204.

Sampson, R. J., and D. J. Bartusch. 1998. Legal cynicism and (sub-cultural?) tolerance for deviance: The neighborhood context of racial differences. *Law and Society Review* 32: 777–804.

Sampson, R. J., and W. B. Groves. 1989. Community structure and crime: Testing social disorganization theory. *American Journal of Sociology* 94: 774–802.

Sampson, R. J., and S. W. Raudenbush. 1999. Systemic social observation of public spaces: A new look at disorder in urban neighborhoods. *American Journal of Sociology* 105: 603–51.

Sampson, R. J., and W. J. Wilson. 1995. Toward a theory of race, crime and urban inequality. In *Crime and inequality,* ed. John Hagan and Ruth D. Peterson, 37–54. Stanford, CA: Stanford University Press.

Sampson, R. J., S. W. Raudenbush, and F. Earls. 1997. Neighborhoods and violent crime. *Science* 277: 918–24.

Shaw, C. R., and H. McKay. 1942/1969. *Juvenile delinquency and urban areas.* Chicago: University of Chicago Press.

Sherman, L. W., P. R. Gartin, and M. E. Buerger. 1989. Hot spots of predatory crime: Routine activities theory and the criminology of place. *Criminology* 27: 27–56.

Skogan, W. G. 1990. *Disorder and decline.* New York: The Free Press.

Skogan, W. G., and K. Frdyl. 2004. *Fairness and effectiveness in policing: The evidence,* ed. W. G. Skogan and Frdyl. Committee to Review the Research on Police Policy and Practice, National Research Council of the National Academies. Washington, DC: The National Academy Press.

Sunshine J., and T. Tyler. 2003. The role of procedural justice and legitimacy in shaping public support of policing. *Law and Society Review* 37: 513–47.

Tyler, T. R. 1990. *Why people obey the law.* New Haven, CT: Yale University Press.

Tyler, T. R., and Y. J. Huo. 2002. *Trust in the law: Encouraging public cooperation with the police and courts.* New York: Russell Sage Foundation.

Tyler, T. R., and C. J. Wakslak. 2004. Profiling and police legitimacy: Procedural justice, attribution of motive, and acceptance of police authority. *Criminology* 42: 253–82.

Velez, M. 2001. The role of public social control in urban neighborhoods. *Criminology* 39: 837–63.

Weisburd, D. 1997. *Reorienting crime prevention research and policy: From the causes of criminality to the context of crime.* Washington, DC: U.S. Government Printing Office.

Weisburd, D., and J. E. Eck. 2004. What can police do to reduce crime, disorder, and fear? *The Annals of American Political and Social Science* 593: 42–65.

Weisburd, D., and J. E. McElroy. 1988. Enacting the CPO (community patrol officer) role: Findings from the New York City Pilot Program in Community Policing. In *Community policing: Rhetoric or reality,* ed. J. R. Greene and S. Mastrofski, 89–102. New York: Praeger Press.

Weisburd, D., S. Bushway, C. Lum, and S. M. Yang. 2004. Trajectories of crime at places: A longitudinal study of the street segments in the city of Seattle. *Criminology* 42: 283–321.

Wilson, J. Q., and G. Kelling. 1982. Broken windows. *The Atlantic Monthly* 211: 29–38.

Wilson, W. J. 1987. *The truly disadvantaged: The inner city, the underclass, and public policy.* Chicago: University of Chicago.

STATE LAW ENFORCEMENT

As it has evolved since the 1835 formation of the Texas Rangers, state law enforcement has fallen primarily into three categories: state police forces, highway patrols, and other enforcement agencies. That last category represents a myriad of agencies, most with very specific, limited regulatory functions that may or may not include the power to arrest. Highway or state patrols, as their names imply, were created to patrol roadways in order to enforce driving regulations, licensing requirements, and weight limitations for commercial traffic. Not all agencies that bear that designation have remained so limited in function. State police forces traditionally have had the broadest arrest powers and, in some instances, the most diverse roles, including investigating crimes on their own initiative and/or in response to requests from sheriffs' offices or local police departments.

State governments, particularly in periods of budgetary restrictions, continue to reorganize, even eliminate, their law enforcement agencies. In addition, advancements in identification technologies, public pressure for protection of children, and most recently rising terrorist threats have led to realignments and additional functions for state agencies in all three categories. With certain exceptions, it would be fruitless here to count the number of agencies involved in any specific aspect of state policing/law enforcement; however, certain agencies do illustrate types of policing and state law enforcement.

State Regulatory Enforcement Agencies

These agencies largely fall into three loosely defined groupings: revenue collection, capitol protection, and conservation or environmental policing. But their functions are often blurred. State budgets rely heavily on taxes applied to tobacco, alcohol, gasoline, and most recently gambling. Indiana State Excise Police, for example, regulate the sale of tobacco and alcohol primarily to collect revenue but also to protect public safety by prohibiting after-hours or underage drinking. Besides checking the licenses of commercial vehicles, the South Carolina State Transport Police ticket for littering and arrest for unsafe transport of hazardous materials, among other duties. Nevada relies on its long-standing Gaming Control Board agents to police its very extensive gambling industry. In other states that more recently have been experiencing the rise of casino or riverboat gambling, such as Louisiana, Maine, Missouri, New Jersey, and Oregon, gaming law enforcement has been entrusted to the state police or highway patrol.

Protection for state capitol complexes ranges from small, nonsworn units, such as in Minnesota, to divisions or bureaus of the state police or highway patrol. Even smaller uniformed units, as in Alabama or Delaware, have statewide arrest powers and provide security for various official buildings and state executives. One of the oldest, the Pennsylvania Capitol Police, originated in 1895, a decade before the Pennsylvania State Police. Some capitol police, such as those in Kansas, Idaho, and Iowa, have been and remain part, respectively, of their states' highway patrol, state police, and state patrol. The trend may well be for capitol police to be absorbed into larger existing agencies. Citing 2001 terrorism, Florida's legislature moved its capitol police from the more mundane Department of Management Services to the Florida Department of Law Enforcement.

Conservation police are variously known as fish and game wardens, park rangers, conservation agents, natural resources police, and other designations. They represent what may well be the oldest type of state-level policing, originally relying on licenses and fines to pay officers. For example, Maryland saw its first state oyster police in 1868, more than six decades before its state police in 1935; Utah had fish and game wardens forty-five years before establishing a highway patrol in 1941. Typically these small, understaffed agencies have been under conservation departments or, more recently, departments of natural resources (DNRs), responsible for parks, waterways, forests, wetlands, and even private hunting preserves. Long engaged in public service through education, accident prevention, and rescue operations, these officers have enhanced policing roles, recognized in the shift to DNRs and necessitated by changing park usage.

Recreational land use continues to rise. And elusive armed poachers have been replaced by even more dangerous marijuana growers or methamphetamine lab operators. Additionally, the U.S. Department of the Interior's Fish and Wildlife Service (USFWS) can commission wardens (or comparable) as deputy agents with authority to enforce federal wildlife laws. In Illinois, for example, conservation police operate jointly with USFWS agents at O'Hare International Airport concerning exotic or even endangered species.

State Criminal Investigative Agencies

Statewide criminal investigative functions are organized primarily under two models—detective bureaus within state police or highway patrols or autonomous agencies, for example, the Kansas Bureau of Investigation or the Georgia Bureau of Investigation. Particular arrangements often are in a state of flux. For example, Illinois originally created what amounted to a detective bureau within its state police. During the 1960s, it elected to create an autonomous investigative agency, the Illinois Bureau of Investigation (IBI); only a couple of decades later, it disbanded the IBI in favor of the Division of Criminal

Investigation, once again as a bureau under the umbrella of the Illinois State Police.

History of State Police Forces and Highway Patrols

The earliest attempts to establish state police forces were really militias, vice units, or border guards; only the Texas Rangers, itself periodically disbanded, evolved into a modern statewide investigative force. Socioeconomic and political trends led to the first modern state police forces, initially in states with large-scale industries, transportation, and mining.

In 1905, Pennsylvania formed the first sworn, unformed state police force. Bloody strikes connected to rural coal mines and urban steel plants had led to demands for a police force to step between owners and labor unions. For decades, the latter would oppose state police forces as repressive, capitalist tools. Irish immigrants, strongly represented in labor unions, took little comfort in the fact that the first state police were modeled after the Royal Irish Constabulary, which had been used to quell nationalist dissent. Others feared that the state police forces, proudly adopting a military model, might prove to be virtually standing armies.

But the constabulary model would prevail. Wartime emergencies, municipal police strikes, pandemic influenza, "red scares," corruption and brutality among local police, rising rural crime, and illegal liquor manufacture and sales all argued for professional, supposedly less corrupt state law enforcement. Progressive reformers (1880–1920) linked those claims with their campaigns for "good roads." Built and maintained, in part, through licensing fees and traffic fines, those paved highways were to increase taxable commerce and diminish rural isolation. Statewide police forces, within a civil service framework, were to model efficient, honest law enforcement for municipal police and sheriffs' offices. The 1929 Wickersham Commission echoed the call for state police forces, and by 1941 every state except Hawaii had some form of state police or highway patrol. However, for decades Progressive aspirations for policing the commonwealth were diminished by political patronage, limited authority, piecemeal development, and shifting administrative oversight.

Highway or State Patrols and State Police

Today state policing services are predominantly provided by highway patrols, state patrols, and state police. In some of the nation's smallest states, such as Connecticut and Rhode Island, the state police have long carried out the patrol and investigative work customarily done by sheriffs' offices. Although the mission statements of state police customarily include the duty to assist, not supplant, all other police agencies, the trend has been for state-level policing agencies to expand their authority.

The past half century has seen the original highway patrols and virtually synonymous state patrols leave behind their limited patrol, traffic enforcement, and commercial trucking supervisory duties to become state police in fact, if not in name. That trend is clearest with the Mississippi Highway Patrol, Missouri State Highway Patrol, Nebraska State Patrol, and Ohio State Highway Patrol, which have both uniformed and plainclothes officers who can arrest and investigate statewide for nontraffic criminal offenses. Even the more limited highway patrols have become centers for crime data collection, fingerprint identification, missing children alerts, sexual offender/predator tracking, and most recently antiterrorism security measures.

Highway patrols and state police share certain other characteristics. Responding to societal pressure and legal precedents, agencies generally recruited their first African American officers in the 1960s and first female officers in the 1970s. Both consistently school their officers in their own training academies, open in some states to local police. Motorcycle units, featured in the 1920s and 1930s, have reappeared after a hiatus. And, more important, whether highway patrols or state police, these agencies are called in to supplement correctional personnel during prison riots and local police overwhelmed by urban riots.

Typical traditional patrols are the Utah Highway Patrol (begun in 1923) and the North Dakota State Patrol (created in 1935). Responding to increasing numbers of vehicles and accidents, highway commissions in both states singled out a handful of employees for part-time use on the state roadways outside municipalities. Those troopers or patrolmen, as they soon came to be known, searched the highways for speeders and other violators, administered driving exams once licenses became mandatory, and inspected vehicles, both private and commercial. Those early officers were neither appointed nor promoted under civil service regulations. During subsequent decades, both forces expanded in size, increased officers' training, implemented civil service testing, employed new technologies, and utilized canine units. Those changes reflected not only increased drug enforcement and anti-terrorism security but also continuing service on the highways and in response to natural disasters, inclement weather, and other emergencies.

Other state agencies with similar origins, for example, the Virginia State Police or the Illinois State Police (ISP), have evolved beyond a chief emphasis on traffic enforcement. Despite organized labor's long-standing opposition, between 1921 and 1923, Illinois established three state highway units: one directly under the governor that would become the ISP, another that still exists as the Illinois Secretary of

State Police (ISSP), and a third under the public works department, absorbed into the ISP in 1939. The ISSP investigates auto theft and licensing fraud, provides security for the state capitol complex, and houses the state's bomb unit. Much larger and more diverse in its responsibilities is the ISP, under a merit system by 1949. The ISP maintains a central repository for criminal statistics, histories, and fingerprints; has forensic laboratories around the state for its own and other jurisdictions' investigations; registers firearms; employs polygraph operators; and investigates medical insurance and other fraud, elder and child abuse, and terrorist threats. It also still patrols the highways, responds to disasters or accidents, and quells riots.

In the 1920s, Illinois State Police advocates wanted to establish a force much like the state police in New Jersey (1921), New York (1917), West Virginia (1919), and most notably Pennsylvania (1905). Initial efforts failed, but the ISP—much like the Maryland or Michigan State Police—grew into that model in a piecemeal fashion. State police, and some highway patrols, are diverse forces that investigate crimes far removed from roads they first patrolled.

BEVERLY A. SMITH and DAVID N. FALCONE

See also **History of American Policing; Militarization of the Police; Pennsylvania State Police; Texas Rangers; Traffic Services and Management; Weed and Seed; Wickersham, George W.**

References and Further Reading

Bechtel, H. Kenneth. 1995. *State police in the United States: A socio-historical analysis.* Westport, CT: Greenwood Press.

Blackburn, Bob L. 1978. Law enforcement in transition: From decentralized county sheriffs to the highway patrol. *Chronicles of Oklahoma* 56: 194–207.

Falcone, David N. 1998. The Illinois State Police as an archetypal model. *Police Quarterly* 1: 61–83.

———. 2001. The Missouri State Highway Patrol as a representative model. *Policing: An International Journal of Police Strategies and Management* 24: 585–94.

———. 2004. America's conservation police: Agencies in transition. *Policing: An International Journal of Police Strategies and Management* 27: 56–66.

Florida Department of Highway Safety and Motor Vehicles. 2005. *Florida Highway Patrol.* http://www.fhp.state.fl.us/html/story.html (April 2005).

Office of the New Jersey Attorney General, Department of Law and Public Safety. 2005. *New Jersey State Police.* http://www.state.nj.us/lps/njsp/index.html (April 2005).

Ray, Gerda W. 1995. From cossack to trooper: Manliness, police reform, and the state. *Journal of Social History* 28: 565–86.

Smith, Beverly A., David N. Falcone, and Jason E. Fuller. 2003. Establishing a statewide police force in Illinois:-Progressive reform in a political context. *Journal of Illinois History* 6: 82–104.

Tobias, Michael. 1998. *Nature's keepers: On the front lines of the fight to save wildlife in America.* New York: John Wiley and Sons.

Torres, Donald A. 1987. *Handbook of the police, highway patrols, and investigative agencies.* Westport, CT: Greenwood Press.

Utley, Robert M. 2002. *Lone Star justice: The first century of the Texas Rangers.* New York: Oxford University Press.

STING TACTICS

Police often apprehend criminals through deception or sting tactics. To hasten compliance to laws, police utilize their knowledge of crime to construct circumstances that invite criminals to commit more crime in a recordable way, enhancing the likelihood of apprehension of criminals who otherwise would be difficult to detect and prosecute (Crank 2004).

Stings typically employ enforcement officers, cooperative community members, and apprehended offenders to play a role as a criminal partner or potential victim in order to gather evidence of a suspect's wrongdoing. Stings are conducted by local, state, and federal enforcement agencies. Sometimes agencies operate stings independently, and other stings are mutual efforts consisting of many agencies, including agencies of other nations.

Stings vary in the scope of their operations and techniques, suggesting numerous variations, yet their objectives are similar: Attract and build a case toward identification, apprehension, and conviction of offenders who often go undetected through traditional police initiatives. One way to examine stings is to review federal and local police sting experiences, components of a legal sting, and the perspectives of sting critics.

Federal Stings

Federal enforcement agencies conduct local, national, and international stings. Federal stings are conducted by the Drug Enforcement Administration (DEA), Federal Bureau of Investigation (FBI), Department of Homeland Security (HS), Bureau of Alcohol, Tobacco, Firearms and Explosives (ATF), and U.S. Immigration and Customs Enforcement (ICE). Publicized stings often include terrorism and arms smuggling, child pornography and pedophile activities, bank laundering of illegal funds, and cigarette and drug trafficking.

Terrorism and arms smuggling stings are typified by a New Jersey case. A suspect was charged with the crimes of providing material support for terrorism and smuggling firearms (IGLA-2 surface-to-air missile) into the country (Federal Bureau of Investigation 2003). The buyers were FBI agents pretending to be a terrorist cell, the sellers were undercover Russian enforcement agents, and the apprehended broker was a British citizen (BBC News 2003).

National stings (that is, operations Artus, Avalanche, Candyman, Blue Orchid, Hamlet, and Rip Cord) and international stings (operations Ore, Snowball, and Twins) have detected and apprehended pornographers and pedophiles (Weiss 2003). For example, Operation Candyman uncovered an estimated seven thousand subscribers linked to a pornographer's website. Those arrested included day care workers, clergy members, law enforcement personnel, and military personnel. Operation Rip Cord identified more than fifteen hundred child pornographer suspects who also solicited child sex through websites in several countries (CNN 1997). An investigator was so disgusted by the materials he viewed that he ripped a computer plug from the wall, giving the sting its name. Operation Twins, the global Internet investigation into a pedophile ring known as "the Brotherhood," was led by the United Kingdom's National High Tech Crime Unit (NHTCU), the FBI, the Royal Canadian Mounted Police (RCMP), and the police forces of Norway and Germany.

Stings have been conducted by individual federal agencies in other nations, such as Operation Casablanca. Three large Mexican banks were charged by the DEA with laundering millions of dollars from Mexican and Colombian drug cartels (Zinser 1998). The successful sting was called a national insult by the Mexican government because they were never informed of its operation.

Smuggled cigarettes (both counterfeit and genuine) represent a federal tax revenue loss and potential health risk and many smugglers are linked to terrorists (Demetriou and Silke 2003). ICE, ATF, and U.S. Customs conduct stings to apprehend cigarette smugglers.

To control drug trafficking, FBI agents posed as cocaine traffickers in Arizona, resulting in the capture of sixteen American soldiers and law enforcement personnel (Sherman 2005). Those arrested had received an estimated $220,000 in bribes and were responsible for more than 1,230 pounds of cocaine smuggled into the country.

Finally, in this regard, two celebrated stings historically provided future sting experience: Abscam and DeLorean. Abscam was a political scandal in 1980 that led to the arrest of members of the U.S. Congress for accepting bribes for favors from Middle Eastern sheiks who were actually FBI personnel (Lescaze 1980). Some convictions were overturned resulting from entrapment. John Z. DeLorean, a man *People Weekly* described as "the Auto Prince," was arrested for buying a hundred kilos of cocaine in 1982 (Eighties Club 2000). DeLorean testified that his intention was to salvage his company.

Local Police Stings

Local police stings include but are not limited to fencing (purchase) of stolen goods, covert cameras designed to detect traffic speeders, prostitution and drug stings, and those targeted to detect alcohol, cigarette, and illegal firearm ammunition sales to youths.

Theft stings are typified by antifence operations, whereby police pretend to fence stolen property and transact business with criminals such as in Birmingham, Alabama (Langworthy 1989). A storefront operation was established to attract and detect auto thieves. However, auto thefts increased by 4.46 cars per day during its operation and decreased to previous levels after the sting.

The Texas commissioner of alcoholic beverages promoted youth stings (Garza 2005). Texas officials reported that stings were an excellent means of combating problems of the unlawful purchase and consumption of alcoholic beverages among minors. Youth stings gain credibility and community support among police departments. Another alcohol sting employed underage police cadets to purchase packaged beer at retail stores in Denver (Preusser, Williams, and Weinstein 1994). Cadets purchased beer 59% of the time, and subsequent stings resulted in beer purchases between 32% and 26% of the time.

Stings include covert cameras (speed cameras that are hidden from view) designed to detect speeders (Reinhardt-Rutland 2001). For instance, nine automated cameras designed to detect speeders traveling ten miles faster than the posted speed limit produced $12 million annually for Cincinnati (Sickmiller 2005).

Baltimore launched the Youth Ammunition Initiative in 2002 (Lewin et al. 2005). The initiative addressed gun violence by targeting illegal firearm ammunition sales. Businesses and public agencies supplied undercover investigators. By interrupting the flow of ammunition, youth violence was reduced.

Prostitution stings include female officers posing as prostitutes. Because of a lack of a complainant, prostitution is often seen as a "victimless" crime; therefore, police must initiate investigations on their own (Walker and Katz 2005, 245). An example is typified by the Waco (Texas) Police Department (Waco PD), which reported that prostitutes are carriers of sexually transmitted infections or the HIV virus (Waco PD 2004). A typical prostitution sting in Waco can produce twenty-five arrests among prostitution customers, or johns. After a customer is arrested, his picture graces a website. The Metropolitan Police (Metro PD) in Nashville, Tennessee, post the names of customers on their website (Metro PD 2004), and their stings typically result in forty to forty-five arrests.

Drug stings are common among enforcement agencies. Often several agencies combine resources and information. For instance, multicounty drug task units and state agency participation are characteristic of many efforts, especially in rural areas. For example, the Sheriff's Anti-Crime/Narcotics (SAC/Narc) unit includes deputies from Whiteside County and the Illinois State Police (Lewis 2005). One sting recovered ten pounds of marijuana, eighteen doses of heroin, and ten Endocet pills and resulted in four seized vehicles. SAC/NARC identified about 750 drug county outlets and see stings as the most productive strategy towards detection.

What Is a Legal Sting?

Law enforcement is allowed to engage in deceit, pretence, and trickery to determine whether an individual has a predisposition to commit a crime, and they can provide an opportunity for an individual to commit that crime, all without being guilty of entrapment. Guidelines for determining entrapment were established in *Sorrells v. United States* (1932), which set the precedent for taking a "subjective" view of entrapment. That is, police cannot provoke an act from an innocent person. Defendants have the right to challenge evidence and can invoke the defense that they would not have broken the law if not tricked into doing it, or entrapment, which can lead to dismissal of the charges (Clarke 2003). For example, a Nebraska farmer was indicted for receiving child pornography through the mail after agents spent twenty-six months offering him pornography.

In *Jacobson v. United States* (1992), prosecutors failed to show that a defendant had been "predisposed, independent of the government's acts and beyond a reasonable doubt, to violate the law," Justice Byron White wrote (see Supreme Court Decisions). That is, a suspect's tendency to commit a specific crime must have existed prior to enforcement attention.

The sting controversy mandated the Los Angeles Police Department to develop and initiate a plan for organizing and executing regular, targeted, and random integrity audit checks, or "sting" operations, to identify and investigate officers engaging in at-risk behavior, including unlawful stops, searches, seizures (including false arrests), uses of excessive force, or violations of the department's codes (U.S. District Court 2001).

Stings enhance police power despite *Jacobson*. For instance, in *United States v. Jimenez Recio* (2003), the court ruled that the contraband seizure of drugs does not end the probe into conspirators and that a sting can be launched to trip up criminals without breaking the law.

Sting Issues

In San Diego County, 138 tobacco retailers paid an annual licensing fee for police stings and the salary of a code enforcement officer who issued and renewed licenses. Those caught selling tobacco to minors faced penalties ranging from $100 to $500 and could lose their license. A licensee argued that because only one of eighteen merchants sold illegal products to minors, funds to enforce codes should be refunded and tobacco licenses should cost less.

Also, a reasonable expectation of privacy exists even in a sting sex case (that is, whether a particular place is isolated enough that a reasonable person would see no significant risk of being discovered) (Kiritsy 2005). The Massachusetts State Police settled a charge on behalf of a gay man who alleged that troopers harassed him at a highway rest stop. The settlement included state police guidelines preventing officers from deliberately trudging into wooded areas near rest stops.

Operation Lightning Strike, an FBI sting aimed at trapping NASA personnel and its contractors, included an agent who pretended to have developed a (phony) device. Millions were spent on luxury hotel suites, gourmet meals, deep-sea fishing trips, and strip clubs. Agents had few suspects but Strike was a scenario similar to dozens of alleged failed stings uncovered by the *Pittsburgh Post-Gazette* (Moushey 1999).

Sting Debate

Stings are often justified because of the detrimental effects certain violations have upon quality-of-life issues. This thought is consistent with the broken-windows precept: Eliminating minor disorder deters serious crime because of the social influence that order exerts on the disorderly and on law-abiding people (Kelling and Wilson 1982). Breaking any law, no matter how trivial, should end with an arrest in order to maintain order (Bratton and Knobler 1998).

Yet, both scholars and courts recognize that law on the books is not "what law is" (Gould and Mastrofski 2004). That is, policy and practice associated with sting tactics are distinctively different. For instance, high rates of unconstitutional police searches are documented in the literature (Gould and Mastrofski 2004). Researchers found that an estimated 30% of police searches (115 searches) conducted by officers in a department ranked in the top 20% nationwide had violated Fourth Amendment prohibitions on searches and seizures. The majority of the unconstitutional searches, thirty-one out of thirty-four, were invisible to the courts, having resulted in no arrest, charge, or citation. If general searches produce civil rights violations, then it is an easy throw to argue that since the centerpiece of sting tactics is deception, stings can produce similar, if not greater, civil rights violations. The thought paints a troubling picture of police practices and raises a number of difficult questions about discretionary police practices.

Based on this argument, sting tactics tend to increase criminal victimization and citizen dissatisfaction, while fear of crime and residents' perceptions of disorder remain unaffected (Harcourt 2004). This perspective reveals stings as counter to respectable behavior because they promote and reward liars, deception, concealment, and betrayal, Klockars (1991, 258) clarifies, by implying that "the more successful police are in appearing really bad, the more successful they must be in appearing good."

Also, since enforcement employs deception to detect and record criminal activities, when they testify against offenders in the courtroom, "where the stakes—their jobs, the case" are much higher, will officers deceive a jury (Crank 2004, 303)? Other critics argue that the price for more freedom is likely to be less order and the price for more order is likely to be less freedom (Langworthy and Travis 2003). However, two thoughts remain: (1) Stings tend to be covert tactics, and all of their working components tend to be less publicized, as are their failures, and (2) crime has been on the decline for some time, and stings are practiced by many police agencies. Thus, tentative inferences can be endorsed.

DENNIS J. STEVENS

See also **Accountability; Bureau of Alcohol, Tobacco, Firearms, and Explosives; Computer Crimes; Constitutional Rights: Privacy; Crackdowns by the Police; Criminal Informants; Drug Enforcement Administration (DEA); Entrapment; Federal Bureau of Investigation; Fencing Stolen Property; Terrorism: Overview; Undercover Investigations; White Collar Crime**

References and Further Reading

BBC News. 2003. *Russian press hails missile sting*. http://news.bbc.co.uk/go/pr/fr/-/1/hi/world/europe/3151195.stm (August 14, 2003).

Bratton, William, and Peter Knobler. 1998. *Turnaround: How America's top cop reversed the crime epidemic*. New York: Random House.

Bureau of Justice Statistics. 2004. *Violent crime and property crimes remained at thirty-year lows*. http://www.ojp.usdoj.gov/bjs/pub/press/cv04pr.htm.

Clarke, Rachel. 2003. *What is a legal sting?* Washington, DC: BBC News. http://news.bbc.co.uk/2/hi/americas/3148267.stm (September 23, 2003).

CNN. 1997. *Internet sting identifies 1,500 suspects of child pornography*. U.S. News: Story Page. http://www.cnn.com/US/9709/30/cybersting/.

Crank, John. 2004. *Understanding police culture*. 2nd ed. Cincinnati, OH: Anderson.

Demetriou, Christina, and Andrew Silke. 2003. A criminological Internet "sting." Experimental evidence of illegal and deviant visits to a website trap. *The British Journal of Criminology* 43 (1): 213–22.

Eighties Club. 2000. *The rise and fall of John DeLorean.* http://eightiesclub.tripod.com/id305.htm.

Federal Bureau of Investigation. 2003. *War on terrorism: International undercover operation stings deal for surface-to-air missiles.* http://www.fbi.gov/page2/aug03/miss081303.htm (August 2003).

Garza, Rolando. 2005. *Minor sting guidelines for law enforcement.* Texas Alcoholic Beverage Commission. Austin, TX: State of Texas.

Gould, Jon B., and Stephen D. Mastrofski. 2004. Suspect searches: Assessing police behavior under the U.S. Constitution. *Criminology and Public Policy* 3 (3): 315.

Harcourt, Bernard E. 2004. *Unconstitutional police searches and collective responsibility.* http://www.law.uchicago.edu/faculty/harcourt/resources/CPP312.pdf.

Jacobson v. United States, 503 U.S. 540 No. 90-1124 Decided (1992).

Kelling, George L., and James Q. Wilson. 1982. Broken windows: The police and neighborhood safety. *The Atlantic Monthly* 211: 29–38.

Kiritsy, Laura. 2005. *Police sting nets gays. Practice harks back to anti-gay raids of the 1950s.* Bay Window. http://www.baywindows.com/media/paper328/news/2005/01/20/LocalNews/Police.Sting.Nets.Gays-836768.shtml (October 29, 2005).

Klockars, Carl. 1991. The modern sting. In *Thinking about policing,* 2nd ed., ed. Klockars and Mastrofski, 258–67. New York: McGraw-Hill.

Langworthy, Robert. 1989. Do stings control crime? An evaluation of a police fencing operation. *Justice Quarterly* 6: 27–45.

Langworthy, Robert, and Lawrence Travis. 2003. *Policing in America. A balance of forces.* 3rd ed. Upper Saddle River, NJ: Prentice Hall.

Lescaze, Lee. 1980. Reporters find FBI eager to make improvements. *Washington Post.* February 4.

Lewin, N. L., J. S. Vernick, P. I. Beilenson, J. S. Mair, M. Lindamood, S. P. Teret, and D. W. Webster. 2005. The Baltimore Youth Ammunition Initiative: A model application of local public health authority in preventing gun violence. *American Journal of Public Health* 95 (5): 762–65.

Lewis, Raymond. 2005. *Major Whiteside County, Illinois, drug sting in progress.* Mount Morris, IL: Lewis Information Services. http://camerahacks.10.forumer.com/viewtopic.php?t=1641 (October 6, 2005).

Metropolitan Police, Nashville, Tennessee. 2004. http://www.police.nashville.org/news/media/2004/05/04c.htm.

Moushey, Bill. 1999. A sting gone awry: When a trap didn't net big game. *Post-Gazette* (Pittsburgh), November.

Neely, Liz. 2004. Tobacco law may be in line for review. *The San Diego Union-Tribune,* August 13.

Preusser, D. F., A. F. Williams, and H. B. Weinstein. 1994. Policing underage alcohol sales. *Journal of Safety Research* 25 (3): 127–33.

Reinhardt-Rutland, A. H. 2001. Roadside speed-cameras: Arguments for covert sting. *The Police Journal* 74 (4): 312–15.

Sherman, Mark. 2005. *Military, law enforcement caught in FBI drug sting.* Associated Press, May 12.

Sickmiller, Mark. 2005. *Speeder-catching cams to really pay off.* 9News. http://www.newsbackup.com/about337463 (January 16, 2005).

Sorrells v. United States, 287 U.S. 435, 442 (1932).

United States v. Jimenez Recio, (01-1184) 537 U.S. 270 (2003) 258 F. 3rd 1069.

U.S. District Court for the Central District of California v. City of Los Angeles, California, Board of Police Commissioners of the City of Los Angeles, and the Los Angeles Police Department. Consent decree. 2001. http://news.findlaw.com/hdocs/docs/lapd/usvla-consentdec.pdf (July 1, 2001).

Waco Police Department. 2004. *Prostitution sting.* http://www.waco-texas.com/city_-depts/police/.

Walker, Samuel, and Charles M. Katz. 2005. *The Police in America: An Introduction.* 5th ed. Boston: McGraw Hill.

Weiss, David L. 2003. *Major child pornography. Focus of social issues: Pornography Quick Facts.* http://www.family.org/cforum/fosi/pornography/facts/a0026237.cfm (May 2003).

Zinser, A. A. 1998. Operation Casablanca's sting. *World Press Review* 45 (8): 48.

STRATEGIC PLANNING

There is a growing and rather extensive literature on strategic planning. For example, the Learning Resource Center at the FBI Training Academy has compiled a ten-page bibliography on strategic planning. This bibliography lists items available at the FBI Academy Library. Melcher and

Kerzner (1988, 20), tracing the evolution of strategic planning theory, write that the first interest in the subject can be traced to the Harvard Business School in 1933, when top management's "point of view" was added to the business policy course. This perspective emphasized incorporating a firm's external environment with its internal operations.

George Steiner's classic work *Strategic Planning: What Every Manager Must Know* was published in 1979 and is generally considered to be the bible of strategic planning. Steiner asserts that strategic planning is inextricably interwoven into the entire fabric of management. Steiner lists fourteen basic and well-known management processes (for example, setting objectives and goals, developing a company philosophy by establishing beliefs, values, and so forth) that make up the components of a general management system and links them to a comprehensive strategic planning process (7–8).

There are many different models or approaches to strategic planning. Melcher and Kerzner's book *Strategic Planning: Development and Implementation* provides an excellent description and review of various models. In essence, strategic planning is a highly rational approach to the management process. It seeks to answer the following questions: Why does the organization exist? What is the organization doing today? What should the organization be doing in the future? What short-term objectives and longer-term goals must be accomplished to bridge the gap from the present to the future?

There is some debate among strategic planners as to whether this analysis can be meaningful without identifying the organizational culture, its values and norms, and the values of critical decision makers. Thus, a number of models of the strategic planning process include a values identification, audit, and analysis step. Many other models do not include this step. The writer's experience has been that many law enforcement officials are turned off by what they see as "mushy, touchy-feely, organizational psychology concepts" intruding into the planning process.

The writer believes that an understanding of the organizational culture is extremely important to the success of any attempt to change an organization. Strategic planning is such an effort—changing the organization from its present to its future. Nevertheless, many organizations and their members are not ready for this kind of self-examination. Strategic planning can assist law enforcement agencies in performing their mission without including the values analysis step.

Evolution of Management Thought

Up until the 1950s, organizations were governed by one set of rules. There were a variety of highly respected theories about organizations, including Henry Fayol's classical organization theory/administrative science, Max Weber's bureaucratic theory, and Frederick Taylor's scientific management, but all prescribed the same set of rules. First, simplify work as much as possible. Second, organize to accomplish routine activities. Third, set standards of control to monitor performance. Finally, take no notice of any changes in the world at large that might affect the organization. There was very little expectation of change and no effort made to anticipate it.

However, these theories with their "principles" of administration did result in dramatic gains in productivity. In fact, these ideas led to substantially enhanced profits and corresponding salary increases for workers. Why? Because they placed a premium on a rational approach to organizing work, and they stressed the importance of qualified and competent managers—a definite departure from earlier approaches that encouraged nepotism and amateurism.

Unfortunately for these ideas, the world changed. In the latter half of the twentieth century, change itself became the critical variable. Once we could safely wager that tomorrow would be like today in all important respects, today it is a fool's bet.

Beginning around 1950, we saw the development of administrative philosophies that recognized this new pervasiveness of change. Change was viewed as a certainty, not as an anomaly. It was not to be treated normatively (that is, as either good or bad) but was seen as inevitable. Thus, organizations had to be structured to accommodate and anticipate change. Also, the focus was shifted from the routine duties that employees perform each day to the results that were expected to flow from all of this effort. The new buzz phrase was "manage for results." The new paradigm called for flexible or ad hoc organizational structures that organized for desired results, developed goals to direct or focus effort, and anticipated changes.

Many readers are familiar with some of these new paradigm theories: management by objectives (MBO), planning, programming budget system (PPBS), zero-based budgeting (ZBB), contingency approaches, and situational theories. For a variety of reasons these administrative efforts met with varying levels of success—mostly disappointing—when implemented by organizations. For example, the federal government tried and abandoned PPBS, then MBO, and finally ZBB. Even so, management philosophies that emphasize end results have remained popular.

As a next step managers not only wanted to know the future direction of their organizations, they also wanted to identify their strengths and weaknesses. This approach is called long-range planning. In the United States, long-range planning became a popular management philosophy in the early to middle 1970s. Long-range planning, however, also has its shortcomings, primarily because it ignores external factors that affect an organization's performance. Some people felt that long-range planning focused too exclusively on internal factors and created an introspective mind-set. Strategic planning, by contrast, is conceived as a

management-for-results philosophy that uses both an internal assessment and an environmental assessment.

A major difficulty in understanding these different managerial philosophies is that writers use different names for these ideas and they also develop unique definitions for them. Nevertheless, almost all are in agreement that strategic planning is a results-oriented philosophy that employs both an internal organizational assessment and an external environmental analysis.

Models of Strategic Planning

As detailed earlier there are a number of different approaches to strategic planning, requiring varying levels of resource commitments, and each organization needs to adapt or modify these different ideas to fit its unique situation. There is no universal "best way."

In this section two models will be described. The first of these, applied strategic planning, is defined as "the process by which the guiding members of an organization envision its future and develop the procedures and operations necessary to achieve that future" (Pfeiffer et al. 1986, 1). The environmental scanning process should be continual and ongoing over the entire process because strategic planning demands that an organization keep a finger on the environmental pulse that can and will affect its future.

The performance audit step in the model includes a simultaneous study of internal strengths and weaknesses and an effort to identify significant external factors that might affect the organization. The organization may well be continually scanning its environment, but here is where the environmental information is actually analyzed in the context of internal assessment data and future goals.

A second model, developed by United Way of America, is called strategic management. United Way defines it as "a systematic, interactive process for thinking through and creating the organization's best possible future" (United Way of America 1985, 3). The purpose is to enhance an organization's ability to identify and achieve specific desired results by integrating information about its external environment, internal capabilities, and overall purpose and direction.

The Essential Elements of Strategic Planning

This section provides a number of ideas and suggestions to help readers understand how to conduct strategic planning efforts in their own departments. The first element—a manage-for-results orientation—requires people to distance themselves somewhat from their daily duties and think about the big picture. What are the major issues affecting my department? What's happening in the community? What do I want this department to look like and be doing in five to ten years?

Since this manage-for-results perspective is common to most current administrative approaches (such as MBO, PPBS, and ZBB), many individuals and departments are familiar with various methods to accomplish it. Frequently a management retreat is conducted at a nearby hotel or resort. Sometimes key managers are asked to prepare a list of those factors or results most critical to the success of the organization. A group facilitator can then lead a meeting in which a master list of these results is produced.

A couple of cautions are in order, however. First, when describing the desired future direction of the organization, people must be realistic and identify attainable results that are consistent with anticipated resources. Second, beware of a future that looks exactly like the past. It has been said that the largest impediments between humans and their future are human

themselves and what they are able to imagine and conceive.

The second element is environmental analysis. The primary activities here are data gathering and analysis of relevant trends. Where do you look for these data? At a national level, the U.S. Census Bureau's *Census of Population and Housing* is a valuable tool. The Department of Commerce's *City and County Data Book,* as well as reports of the Department of Labor and other national indicators, can also be helpful. With respect to criminal activity, *Crime in America,* compiled by the FBI, is an excellent source. Academic and professional journals and societies frequently focus on developments and events that will significantly affect law enforcement organizations.

At the local level, relevant and critical trend data can often be obtained at area universities—particularly business schools, economics departments, and sociology departments. The chamber of commerce, local trade associations, and municipal, county, and state governments generally are good sources of information. A survey of knowledgeable people in the community may also help identify relevant information.

A seldom-used form of environmental analysis, scenario development, is the most future-oriented approach. Scenarios attempt to integrate a number of separate trends and develop a consistent and coherent view of plausible, alternative futures. Generally, several scenarios will be developed and a few will be selected for planning purposes. This approach has special significance in university and "think tank" institutions.

Obviously, the goals of environmental analysis are to identify the most significant trends for the organization and describe their likely implications. Contingency plans can be prepared or special monitoring arrangements can be set up to track these trends.

The third element is organizational assessment, a step that determines an organization's capabilities (its strengths and weaknesses). Generally, a number of resource assessments (for example, human, facilities, financial) are conducted. For instance, does the organization have enough people with the appropriate education and skills to accomplish its purposes? Also, an examination can be made of an organization's structure and culture. Are they consistent and compatible with the mission and future direction of the agency?

It is important to review the previous performance of an organization and its major entities. Were previous objectives achieved? Are records and reports of a high quality? Employee or customer surveys and interviews can shed much light on perceptions of performance. In the FBI, for example, the inspection, evaluation, and audit processes tell a lot about the performance of various organizational components and programs.

The product of this step should be a precise listing of all the organization's competencies and shortcomings. Obviously, this knowledge, coupled with relevant environmental information, will help determine the future direction of the organization.

Strategic Planning in the FBI

Strategic planning in the FBI is the responsibility of the director. Early each fall the director and several top executives review, revise, and revalidate the FBI mission and the component missions. A strategic plan is prepared each year, projecting FBI activities five years into the future. The mission and components are carefully examined to ensure that they describe the major purposes toward which FBI efforts will and should be expended over the next several years.

This "mission review" step begins the development of the new plan. It is also the place where the director and senior executives articulate their vision regarding the future direction of the FBI, focusing on exactly what the bureau wants to achieve during the next five years. At this stage the vision is broad in scope.

Subsequently, other FBI executives and program managers develop precise objectives and action strategies that give practical shape to the director's vision. While the writer was chief of the Strategic Planning Unit (SPU) of the FBI Inspection Division, he authored a detailed reference, "A Guide to Strategic Planning in the FBI," to help FBI employees develop these precise objectives and action plans. Also, he prepared a pamphlet entitled "An Overview of FBI Strategic Planning Efforts." In an organization the size of the FBI, the planning document is quite voluminous. Still, it is critical that precise strategies and action plans be prepared that will lead to the accomplishment of the organization's broad purposes.

The strategic planning process itself, that is, scanning the environment, assessing performance, thinking about the future direction of the FBI, and developing action plans to achieve stated goals, is more important than the document that contains the strategic plan. Still, the plan is a tremendous vehicle for communication within the bureau. One of the most common reasons for organizations failing to achieve their purposes is that many people do not know what is expected of them. They don't understand what the organization is trying to achieve and how their work fits into the overall picture. The strategic plan assists all FBI employees in understanding their contributions to the work of the bureau.

The SPU is responsible for conducting the environmental analysis function for the FBI. This unit performs exactly the kinds of activities and analyses described earlier. With respect to the internal organizational assessment step, the SPU coordinates the activities of various FBI entities. As described previously, the inspection reports of FBI offices, program evaluation, and audits provide invaluable performance information.

The FBI has been involved in strategic planning since the spring of 1987. The process is evolving, and nobody would argue that it is perfect. Still, FBI leaders are convinced that it is the most appropriate managerial approach for the administration of the agency.

Conclusion

Strategic planning grows out of administrative philosophies that emphasize a management-for-results approach and recognize the pervasiveness of change throughout society. Although there is no standard or universally accepted definition of strategic planning, most administrators would agree that it has three primary elements:

1. Management-for-results orientation
2. External environmental analysis
3. Internal organizational assessment

While some writers distinguish between strategic planning and strategic management, the author believes that the primary difference is one of semantics.

Ideas and theories about how best to organize will continue to evolve in the years ahead. Still, it is reasonable to expect that future concepts will be built upon many of today's ideas. In this light, the essential elements of strategic planning—managing for results, environmental analysis, and organizational assessment—can be expected to remain important tenets of future philosophies.

This article has described the benefits of strategic planning for law enforcement agencies and outlined some of the steps necessary to perform the essential elements of strategic planning. Effective American law enforcement is a goal to which all Americans are entitled. Although there are no magic panaceas or guarantees of effectiveness, strategic planning is a straightforward administrative approach with a proven track record. All law enforcement officials are encouraged to consider this approach as they guide their organizations into the future.

DONALD C. WITHAM

References and Further Reading

Melcher, Bonita H., and Harold Kerzner. 1988. *Strategic planning: Development and implementation.* Blue Ridge Summit, PA: TAB Professional and Reference Books.

Pfeiffer, J. William, et al. 1986. *Applied strategic planning: A how to do it guide.* San Diego, CA: University Associates.

Steiner, George A. 1979. *Strategic planning: What every manager must know.* New York: The Free Press.

United Way of America. 1985. *Strategic management and United Way.* Alexandria, VA: United Way of America.

University Associates Consulting and Training Services, 8380 Miramar Mall, Suite 232, San Diego, CA 92121 (619 552-8901).

STRESS AND POLICE WORK

Defined

Research physician Hans Selye introduced the concept of stress to the life sciences and later defined stress as the organism's response to any demand placed on it (1946, 1976). Although there has been extensive research on the topic of stress, there is not necessarily a commonly accepted definition of the term. Stressors are physical or psychological stimuli that impact on one's state of arousal and are often seen as threatening, frustrating, or conflicting and therefore can lead to anxiety. Therefore, while hard to define, stress clearly involves both psychological and physiological processes.

Anxiety is a common reaction to stress and is marked by both physical and psychological components such as "fear, anger, apprehension, and muscular tension" (Bartol and Bartol 1994). Fear then often leads to increased engagement, avoidance, or incapacitation (the so-called fight, flight, or freeze phenomenon), speech difficulties, generalized irritability, or other relief behaviors like biting nails, smoking, or drinking. This form of anxiety, known as state anxiety, is to be differentiated from trait anxiety, an individual characteristic or personality attribute that is associated with a more chronic form of stress (Spielberger 1966).

Effects of Stress

There is no doubt that the effects of stress can be harmful. There are many illnesses thought to be brought on or exacerbated by the amount and experience of stress including heart disease, alcoholism, sleep disorders, and psychological disorders, to name a few. Research on stress has suggested that too little or too much stress can negatively impact performance, although this relationship has not been well established in the research on police (Sewell, Ellison, and Hurrell 1988).

How Stressful Is Policing?

Policing has been described as the most stressful job in America (see, for example, Kupelian 1991; Greaves 1987; Bartol 1983), yet recent research has refuted that claim with evidence suggesting it may be no more stressful than many other occupations (Anson and Bloom 1988; Malloy and Mays 1984). While an Australian police study showed police to have higher incidences of heart disease, hypertension, asthma, hay fever, skin illnesses, nervous breakdowns, and divorce rates than those of the general population, other research comparing police officers to other public workers found few differences in the level of stress experienced. There is some indication, however, that there are differences in the sources of stress associated with various jobs.

Sources of Stress in Policing

Many of the stresses police officers encounter are unique to their profession. While much of police work is routine, there is the possibility of great risk and danger at any moment. Additionally, police officers are often called to the scene of trouble and therefore are exposed to trauma, both physical and emotional. They frequently deal with individuals who are antisocial, antiauthority, angry, violent, emotionally disturbed, manipulative, or under the influence of alcohol and/or drugs.

Police also work in paramilitary organizations with rigid lines of authority, numerous rules and regulations, and the threat of disciplinary action when their behavior does not conform to laws, policies, procedures, or public expectations. In addition, many police find it difficult to build and sustain relationships outside the profession, since there is often a sense that no one else understands the pressures of the job. Most recently, newer sources of stress have emerged, including fear of contracting HIV/AIDS, having to become more "politically correct" in dealing with issues such as cultural diversity, and the transition to community policing (National Institute of Justice 2000).

There are two major theoretical approaches to stress. The first is based on the assertion that major life events trigger stress reactions, a so-called critical life events approach. Examples of these types of sources include dealing with homicide victims, child sexual assault or homicide victims, or deadly vehicle crashes or causing the death of someone through a shooting or vehicle accident. The other is based on a more chronic model of stress and focuses on daily routine activities that impact upon stress. These may include things such as administrative hassles, boredom, shift work, poor working conditions or pay, lack of public support, a bogged down and overburdened criminal justice system, and local politics.

These routine stressors may include stress from the organization, stress associated with the job or the criminal justice system as a whole, stress from external sources, and that which stems from one's personal situation. Organizational stressors may include things such as limited career advancement, little professional incentives or development, excessive paperwork, and lack of administrative support. Examples of job and criminal justice stressors are rotating shifts, excessive paperwork, the potential for citizen violence even when dealing with routine traffic investigations or domestic disturbances, and unfavorable court decisions. External stressors are things such as lack of community support and unrealistic public expectations, as well as pressure from politicians and the media.

Finally, there are a whole range of personal circumstances and stressors that could impact upon stress levels of police officers, both critical life events such as divorce, financial difficulties, or serious illness of a family member as well as routine stressors such as child care management, balancing family responsibilities, or commuting time. Therefore, both types of stress can burden a police officer on a temporary or chronic basis and pose a threat to health, safety, and well-being.

Approaches to Measuring Stress

There are a number of biological and psychological measures of stress. Among the biological measures useful for assessing stress are hormones and cortisol levels, arterial viscosity (thickness), heart rate (often taken on a treadmill, a so-called stress test), blood pressure, brain activation, and more. Psychological measures are typically self-reports of individual officers through questionnaires.

The approaches to the assessment of psychological stress clearly grow out of the theoretical models. The first, the critical life events model, is best represented by the Social Readjustment Rating Scale (Holmes and Rahe 1967), a self-report measure in which one identifies those critical life events experienced within the past year. The forty-three-item scale includes things such as death of a child (at the top of the list), bankruptcy, divorce, traffic accidents, and so on and are weighted based on their severity and duration of effects in order to determine the amount of stress being experienced. While still considered a tool for assessing stress, many argue that it is unreliable since the subjective, personal experience of stress varies across individuals, perhaps due to personality, health, and coping skills. A more recent adaptation of this scale developed by Sewell (1983) for law enforcement is the Law Enforcement Critical Life Events Scale, which includes police-specific events such as taking a life in the line of duty.

The other stress measurement approach is based on the model of everyday stressors and is perhaps best exemplified by the daily hassles model, recently adapted for policing by Hart, Wearing, and Headley (1993). This measure takes into account many of the external, internal, task-oriented, and organizational stressors mentioned above, often believed to be more influential in assessing one's overall stress level.

Effects of Stress on Police

Officers report high rates of divorce, emotional problems, health ailments, alcoholism, and performance problems including increased absenteeism, excessive aggressiveness, and reduced efficiency (see, for example, National Institute of Justice 2000; Delprino, O'Quin, and Kennedy 1997). Stress over prolonged periods can have negative consequences for the physical, psychological, and emotional well-being of police officers. The severity of these consequences depends in large part on an officer's personality, temperament, and adaptive coping skills as well as on the success of various management interventions such as counseling, training, and improved working conditions.

Physical Outcomes of Stress

Stress among police officers has been associated with numerous physical and psychological consequences including alcoholism, back pain, burnout, cardiovascular disorders, depression, early mortality, gastrointestinal disorders and ulcers, migraines, sleep loss and sleep disorders, and even suicide (see, for example, Bartol and Bartol 1994; Violanti 1983, 1985).

Psychological Outcomes of Stress

Stress also places undue influence on families of police officers and can adversely impact the stability of family relationships. Financial arguments, separation, and divorce are symptomatic of the tensions and strains of policing. Research has suggested dissatisfaction by spouses of police officers. For example, Maynard and Maynard (1982) found that wives of officers report high levels of conflict, particularly in the area of making personal sacrifices because of the job (52% had to give up job opportunities or other plans) and also being discouraged from making plans too far in advance (60%). Also, 57% of wives surveyed felt that officers generally don't feel family and marriage are important, and 55% felt that the department thinks it is better to be divorced or single. Indeed, in that police agency, 70% are divorced within the first five years on the job. Rotating shift work and times of shifts often interfere with long-term family planning and the spouse's career choices as well.

Acute stress can often trigger a condition known as post-traumatic stress disorder (PTSD), in which flashbacks, hypervigilance, and nightmares are common. PTSD can lead to withdrawal, and when untreated can be debilitating. At its worst, acute or chronic stress can lead to suicide. Indeed, suicide rates for law enforcement officers have been reported to be much higher than that of the general population. More recent data, however, suggest that rates of police suicide have sharply declined during the past few decades. Decreasing rates of suicide may be attributable to more sophisticated and scientifically based hiring practices, stress management seminars, greater numbers of police psychologists working in urban departments, and other management responses discussed below (Bartol and Bartol 1994; Bartol 1983).

Group Differences in Stress Levels among Police

The level of stress experienced and its duration may be impacted by tenure in the department and sex. Violanti (1983) noted that those in the earlier career years (up to almost fifteen) are under greater job stress due to concerns about their own competence, the need to handle large amounts of paperwork, and their perceived gap between formal academy training and the real-world skills necessary for effective performance. Female officers may experience higher levels of stress levels due to lack of social support, negative attitudes of male officers, lack of role models and mentors, overcoming perceived barriers that they are not as equipped to do the job, and sexual harassment on the job.

Managerial Approaches to Stress Management

Police managers have implemented various practices in responding to the problem of police officer stress. These involve detecting, assessing, and providing interventions designed to minimize the level of stress or increase coping skills in officers. Clearly, the past two decades have seen an increase in the psychological and counseling services available to police, as well as programs designed to reduce stress and enhance the coping capacity of officers (see, for example, Delprino and Bahn 1988).

Psychological Fitness for Duty Evaluations

When there is evidence of excessive stress, particularly that which may manifest in job performance, officers may be referred to or ordered to undergo a psychological fitness-for-duty evaluation (FFDE). A fitness-for-duty evaluation is a disability assessment to determine one's capacity to perform the functions required of a police officer. It often involves an assessment of the emotional and mental capacities of the officer, including judgment skills, cognitive impairments, and emotional disturbances that may disrupt one's ability to function in a safe and effective manner.

Early Warning and Intervention Systems

In recent years, a growing number of law enforcement agencies have been developing or purchasing automated human resource management systems that provide alerts to supervisors or commanders when officers are at risk or may pose a risk to the agency or community. Spurred mainly by liability concerns and increasing litigation against police departments, early warning and intervention systems (EWIS) track a number of performance factors and allow supervisors to compare officers to similarly situated officers to determine if aspects of performance may be indicators of problems such as stress, fatigue, or physical or psychological problems. An EWIS often captures information on complaints filed against the officer, vehicle accidents, sick leave, on-duty injuries, number of arrests, vehicle pursuits, traffic stops, and uses of force. The comparisons can be helpful in assisting supervisors in early detection and intervention when officers are at risk.

Stress Programs

During the 1990s, the National Institute of Justice (NIJ) supported evaluations of stress reduction programs in policing through its Corrections and Law Enforcement Family Support (CLEFS) program. One such program was the New York City program to train peer counselors so as to prevent suicide after a spike in suicides in 1994 and 1995. Other stress programs include services of private mental health professionals or psychological services in the agency including through the union, police chaplain, or employee assistance program. In total, the NIJ has sponsored research and program development in thirty agencies and organizations, including treatment and training programs.

Coping

Certain personality characteristics and personal habits can reduce the amount of stress experienced by police officers, as well as help them more effectively cope with and manage stress. Proper diet and eating habits can play a role in reducing the impact of stress. Because police are often called suddenly into action, it can be difficult to eat at a relaxed pace or to gain access to healthier quality of foods as opposed to high-fat, high-sugar, fast-food diets.

Physical exercise can reduce stress and increase an officer's ability to adapt to organizational stressors. The Dallas Police Department implemented a physical exercise program and studied the overall effects on officer job performance, finding that it led to a significant reduction in sick days and citizen complaints (Swanson and Territo 1984). Other techniques such as relaxation and meditation can also prove beneficial.

Unfortunately, too often police rely on unhealthy or counterproductive strategies for coping with stress. For example,

Maynard and Maynard found that 33% use alcohol as a coping mechanism, even though this strategy may cause an increase in stress over time and can be very dangerous.

Conclusion

There is no question that police officers experience unique stressors that ultimately result in a range of minor and serious physical and psychological symptoms. However, the belief that policing is the most stressful job is not accurate; indeed, those in other public safety occupations and unrelated careers also experience high levels of stress. Although the sources of stress for these occupations may be different, the consequences may put the public at greater risk. The good news is that there are a number of managerial prerogatives that are designed to reduce the negative impacts of stress, as well as personal behaviors that can improve one's ability to cope.

It is promising that some of these efforts are on the increase in American policing. However, it is important that additional research on the negative impacts of stress on police be conducted and that police leaders become increasingly more responsive to the findings of such research, including the negative impact of rotating shifts (especially backward-rotating schedules), and provide more support systems to minimize the negative impacts of stress.

KAREN L. AMENDOLA

See also **Complaints against Police; Critical Incidents; Cynicism, Police; Danger and Police Work; Early Warning Systems; Police Suicide; Psychological Fitness for Duty; Stress: Coping Mechanisms**

References and Further Reading

Anson, R. H., and M. E. Bloom. 1988. Police stress in an occupational context. *Police Science and Administration*, 229–35.

Bartol, C. R. 1983. *Psychology and American law*. Belmont, CA: Wadsworth.

Bartol, C. R., and A. M. Bartol. 1994. *Psychology and law: Research and application*. Belmont, CA: Brooks/Cole Publishing Company.

Delprino, R. P., and C. Bahn. 1988. National survey of the extent and nature of psychological services in police departments. *Professional Psychology: Research and Practice* 19 (4): 421–25.

Delprino, R. P., K. O'Quin, and C. Kennedy. 1997. *Identification of work and family services for law enforcement personnel*. Final Report (Grant #95-IJ-CX-0113). Washington, DC: National Institute of Justice.

Greaves, A. 1987. Managing with stress. *Police Review*: 2114–15.

Hart, P. M., A. J. Wearing, and B. Headley. 1993. Perceived quality of life, personality, and work experiences: Construct validation of the police daily hassles and uplifts scales. *Journal of Criminal Justice and Behavior* 21 (3): 283–311.

Holmes, T. H., and R. H. Rahe. 1967. The Social Readjustment Rating Scale. *Journal of Psychosomatic Research* 11: 213–18.

Kupelian, D. 1991. The most stressful job in America: Police work in the 1990s. *New Dimensions. The Psychology Behind the News,* August, 18–33.

Malloy, T. E., and G. L. Mays. 1984. The police stress hypothesis: A critical evaluation. *Criminal Justice and Behavior* 11: 197–223.

Maynard, P. E., and N. E. Maynard. 1982. Stress in police families: Some policy implications. *Journal of Police Science and Administration* 10: 309.

National Institute of Justice. 2000. On-the-job stress in policing—Reducing it, preventing it. *National Institute of Justice Journal,* January, 19–25.

Selye, H. 1946. The general adaptation syndrome and the diseases of adaptation. *Journal of Clinical Endocrinology* 6 (2): 117–230.
———. 1976. *The stress of life*. New York: McGraw-Hill.

Sewell, J. D. 1983. The development of a critical life events scale for law enforcement. *Journal of Police Science and Administration* 11: 109–16.

Sewell, J. D., K. W. Ellison, and J. J. Hurrell. 1988. Stress management in law enforcement: Where do we go from here? *Police Chief,* 94–99.

Spielberger, R. D. 1966. The effects of anxiety on complex learning and academic achievement. In *Anxiety and behavior,* ed. C. D. Spielberger. New York: Academic Press.

Swanson, C. R., and L. Territo. 1984. *Police administration: Structures, processes and behavior*. New York: Macmillan.

Violanti, J. M. 1983. Stress patterns in police work: A longitudinal study. *Journal of Police Science and Administration* 11: 213.

———. 1985. Stress coping and alcohol use: The police connection. *Journal of Police Science and Administration* 2: 108.

STRESS: COPING MECHANISMS

Police work is highly stressful since it is one of the few occupations where employees are asked to continually face physical dangers and to put their lives on the line at any time. The police officer is exposed to violence, cruelty, and aggression and is often required to make extremely critical decisions in high-pressured situations (Goolkasian et al. 1985; Territo and Vetter 1983). Officers are often called upon to maintain social order while working long hours, experiencing conflicts in their job demands, and having to face hostile feelings of an unusually nonsupportive community (Fell, Richard, and Wallace 1980).

Law enforcement officers can use both adaptive and maladaptive strategies to cope with stress. Whether a police officer uses adaptive or maladaptive approaches depends on the officer's understanding the stressful situation, making sense of it, and developing appropriate responses to it (Lazarus 1967).

Adaptive coping strategies are problem-solving approaches that help law enforcement professionals deal directly with the stressful situation by seeking and implementing solutions. The active-cognitive coping category includes trying to interpret the meaning of the event, logical analysis, and mental preparation. Problem-focused coping involves the practical aspects of seeking information and support, taking action, and identifying alternative rewards. These are adaptive strategies.

One of the functions of adaptive coping behaviors is to decrease the impact of the demands of stress (Marshall 1979; Pearlin and Schooler 1978). Therefore, the use of an appropriate coping strategy might function as a buffer against stress, both present and future, and limit the negative impact of the stress. A model offered by Zeitlin (1984) depicts adaptive coping as a process in which personal resources are used to manage stress. This model approaches adaptive coping from a cognitive and behavioral standpoint and emphasizes the importance of both external and internal resources for coping with stress.

In contrast, maladaptive approaches are emotion-focused coping strategies. These maladaptive strategies include affective regulation, emotional discharge, and resigned acceptance of the stress. These maladaptive coping approaches frequently do not deal directly with the problem and therefore are not likely to relieve the individual's anxiety. Indeed, maladaptive coping strategies are more likely to exacerbate stress and have a negative effect on job satisfaction (Parasuraman and Cleek 1984).

Research by Kirmeryer and Diamond (1985) indicates that the personality type of each police officer strongly dictates that officer's selection of a coping mechanism. Police officers who have a type A personality are more likely to make emotive-focused coping decisions, while type B personality types are more likely to react slowly to the stress and maintain their emotional distance. All of this research indicates that police personnel are experiencing high levels of stress without a clear understanding of how to alleviate that stress in acceptable ways.

Research by Violanti and Marshall (1983) has indicated that police officers utilize coping mechanisms that increase the stress rather than alleviate it (Violanti and Marshall 1983; Violanti, Marshal, and Howe 1985). This research showed that police officers used maladaptive coping mechanisms, such as alcohol, drugs, deviance, and cynicism. The use of these emotion-focused solutions has a tendency to change the law enforcement officer into a law violator, thus increasing not only personal stress but also that of the department and fellow officers.

Additional research has shown that law enforcement officers have no preference for adaptive coping mechanisms over maladaptive coping mechanisms, and in many instances could not identify coping mechanisms that were maladaptive (Fain and McCormick 1988).

The coping strategies of police officers can be enhanced by training programs that are designed to improve their use of adaptive coping skills rather than maladaptive skills (Anderson and Bauer 1987). Ellison and Genz (1983) offer techniques for individual stress management that include goal setting, time management, financial planning, and physical fitness. Norvell and Belles (1987) have designed a forty-hour training program for supervisory personnel. The purpose of this training program is to reduce the stress of the participating officers and at the same time provide them with information that will allow them to observe stressful behavior in fellow officers.

In addition to counseling by professionals, the use of police peer counseling has become increasingly popular. Klein (1989) describes the program that eligible police officers go through, under the guidance of a clinical psychologist, to be trained as a peer counselor. These peer counselors are trained to help officers with developing constructive ways of dealing with stress and with recognizing what they can change and what they cannot. Peer counselors also make recommendations for further counseling or other types of mental health assistance.

An example of a training program that has proved successful with other professionals in high-stress occupations is the stress management workshop. This four-hour workshop focuses on the individual and attempts to increase the participants' awareness of stresses both at work and at home. The majority of the training involves helping the professional learn techniques for healthy coping. The areas emphasized are personal management skills, relationship skills, outlook skills, and stamina skills.

This training helps law enforcement professionals create a supportive environment for others, improve contact skills to help form friendships, enhance listening skills to attend to others, as well strengthen assertiveness skills to address self needs. Outlook skills are taught to enable the participant to view life from different perspectives, to learn what situations must be surrendered to, and what situations must be taken on faith. However, it also includes learning how to use positive self-reaffirming statements, imagination, and humor effectively. Finally, stamina skills involve learning how exercise, relaxation, and nutrition will fortify the participant to resist stress and relieve tension when they arise.

Of equal importance are the external resources that a police officer can depend upon. Social supports play a "buffering" role in the potential impact of stressor events, contribute to overall improved physical health by placing the individuals in a better position to cope with the stress, and, finally, play a preventive role in reducing the number of stressful events that one experiences (Steinglass, Weisstub, and De-Nour 1988). Many times police officers hold their families and spouses at bay, not allowing them to experience the hardships that accompany being a police officer (Besner and Robinson 1982; James and Nelson 1975; Stratton 1984). This can be alleviated in part by providing the same training to family and spouses that is provided to police officers for stress management. In addition, social support systems should receive additional training in the recognition of the danger signs of burnout from occupational stress (Stratton 1984).

STEPHEN J. MOREWITZ

See also **Psychological Fitness for Duty; Role of the Police; Stress and Police Work**

References and Further Reading

Anderson, W., and B. Bauer. 1987. Law enforcement officers: The consequences of exposure to violence. *Journal of Counseling and Development* 3: 65, 381–84.

Besner, H. F., and S. J. Robinson. 1982. *Understanding and solving your police marriage problems,* 40–54. Springfield, IL: Charles C Thomas.

Ellison, K. W., and J. L. Genz. 1983. *Stress and the police officer,* 106–34. Springfield, IL: Charles C Thomas.

Fain, D. B., and G. M. McCormick. 1988. Use of coping mechanisms as a means of stress reduction in North Louisiana. *Journal of Police Science and Administration* 16: 121–28.

Fell, R. D., W. C. Richard, and W. L. Wallace. 1980. Psychological job stress and the police officer. *Journal of Police Science and Administration* 8: 139–44.

Goolkasian, Gail A., et al. 1985. *Coping with police stress.* J-LEAA-013–78. Washington, DC: National Institute of Justice, U.S. Department of Justice.

James, P., and M. Nelson. 1975. *Police wife: How to live with the law and like it,* 13–26. Springfield, IL: Charles C Thomas.

Kirmeryer, S. L., and A. Diamond. 1985. *Journal of Occupational Behavior* 6: 183–95.

Klein, R. 1989. Police peer counseling. *FBI Law Enforcement Bulletin* 10: 1–5.

Lazarus, R. S. 1967. Cognitive and personality factors underlying threat and coping. In *Psychological stress,* ed. Appley and Trumball, 151–81. New York: Appleton-Century Crofts.

Marshall, J. R. 1979. Stress, strain and coping. *Journal of Health and Social Behavior* 20: 200–01.

Norvell, N., and D. Belles. 1987. A stress management curriculum for law enforcement personnel supervisors. *Police Chief* 8: 57–59.

Parasuraman, S., and M. A. Cleek. 1984. Coping behaviors and managers' affective reactions to role stressors. *Journal of Vocational Behavior* 24: 179–93.

Pearlin, L. I., and C. Schooler. 1978. The structure of coping. *Journal of Health and Social Behavior* 19: 2–21.

Steinglass, P., E. Weisstub, and A. K. DeNour. 1988. Perceived personal networks as mediators of stress reactions. *American Journal of Psychiatry* 145: 1259–64.

Stratton, J. G. 1984. *Police passages,* 101–48, 287–318. Manhattan Beach, CA: Glennon Publishing.

Territo, L., and H. J. Vetter. 1983. Stress and police personnel. *Journal of Police Science and Administration* 11: 195–207.

Violanti, J. M., and J. R. Marshall. 1983. The Police Stress Process. *Journal of Police Science and Administration* 11: 389–94.

Violanti, J. M., J. R. Marshall, and B. Howe. 1985. *Journal of Police Science and Administration* 13 (2): 106–10.

Zeitlin, S. 1984. *The coping inventory.* Bensenville, IL: Scholastic Testing Service.

STRIKES AND JOB ACTIONS

Strikes and job actions are intentional alterations, disruptions, or suspensions of the work roles of a significant number of employees for the purpose of forcing employers to satisfy worker demands. Among public safety employees, these actions have included a number of *covert* job actions and *overt* strike tactics. The former category includes principally the "ticket blizzard," in which the issuing of traffic citations reaches epidemic proportions, and the "blue flu," or sick-ins, during which extraordinary numbers of officers report themselves ill and unable to work, as well as other speed-up and slow-down tactics. The latter category is reserved for the strike, in which significant numbers of officers overtly refuse to work in order to achieve their collective goals. Such activities have been widely and popularly perceived as disruptive of and an interference with, if not a grave threat to, commonwealth interests. This article focuses principally on the *overt* strike, and only incidentally addresses covert forms of job action.

Arguments: Pro and Con

At the outset, it is well to recognize that "unionization" and "strikes" are not coextensive phenomena. Nonetheless, in the public perspective on these matters, fear of strikes by police often appears to dominate the collective consciousness. Anticipation of the strike, then, necessarily influences attitudes toward unions. For that reason, arguments regarding the propriety of police unionization and the right of officers to strike are intimately related. Publicly accepted understandings of the purpose and role of unions, on the one hand, and the importance assigned to the role of police, on the other, have often led unions and police to be seen as incompatible. As a result, the unionization of and strikes by public sector employees have traditionally been regarded as inappropriate. Only since the 1960s and 1970s has this attitude tended to soften and become less rigid. The opposition has several facets.

When applied specifically to public safety workers such as police, the foregoing arguments have been refined and supplemented. Of particular importance is the issue of strikes among employees who provide allegedly essential services, that is, those regarded as indispensable for maintaining the health, safety, and well-being of the populace. There are several facets to this issue: First is the concern over the fear generated in the population by the suspension of such services. Second, there is concern that the supposedly essential nature of their duties affords these workers undue influence in the collective bargaining process. The third concern is that, taken together, these and other matters put government at a disadvantage in negotiations. However logical this may seem, evidence suggests that the foundations on which much of this concern rests, that is, the dire consequences of suspending essential services, including injury, loss of life, destruction of property, loss of property, loss of profits and revenue, and a decline in public order, are more anticipated than real.

Additionally, arguments developed in opposition to specific reforms sought by line officers have frequently been converted into arguments opposing unionization of police officers. For example, efforts to establish a dues check-off system, of great help in maintaining organizational stability and rank-and-file solidarity, were attacked on the grounds that government agencies cannot be used to collect private debts.

Line officers' quests for the establishment of formal grievance procedures were opposed by many police administrators, who labeled such advances as a threat to the civil service system and to the customary lines of authority in police departments. Furthermore, efforts to secure collective bargaining agreements have been beaten back as unconstitutional delegations of authority. Further granting police the right to unionize and engage in collective bargaining has been staunchly opposed by those who regard police in the military/soldier model. Given that perception, police are not entitled to the same rights granted other public sector employees. Finally, one alternative model of police, that of professional, has also been used to argue against police unionization, on the grounds that such an arrangement is contrary to professionalization.

Brief History

By the early 1900s, police were unionized in no fewer than thirty-seven American cities. One of the earliest and most indelible American experiences with a police strike was the 1919 walkout of Boston police due to dissatisfaction with wages and general working conditions (police in Cincinnati, Ohio, had struck in September 1918). For three days thereafter, Boston was the scene of an inordinate degree of robbery, vandalism, petty theft, looting, and general mob behavior. In all, eight persons were killed. Order was not restored before the mayor's request for the mobilization of the state guard was met by then-Governor Calvin Coolidge. Beyond the riotous actions of citizens, this strike ushered in several decades of strongly negative sentiment regarding unionization of public employees in general and police officers in particular. In some jurisdictions, even police benevolent and fraternal societies were outlawed.

In the years following the Boston police strike of 1919, the legitimacy and hence the organizational basis necessary for initiating successful job actions by police was largely extinguished in the United States. Thus, despite efforts to restore police unions prior to mid century, it was not until the 1950s and 1960s that police fraternal and benevolent associations and other labor organizations experienced significant official approval in the form of dues check-off systems, formal grievance procedures, and collective bargaining rights. To be sure, such recognition and concessions were not won without the threat and/or use of job actions, such as sick-ins, slowdowns, and ticket blizzards in places such as Atlanta, Boston, Detroit, New York, and Pittsburgh. However, it was not until the decade of the 1970s that police strikes occurred in any regular way.

Such antiunion sentiment did not survive, however, and during the post-World War II period, the unionization of police officers was again being pursued with growing vigor. By the late 1960s and the 1970s, the "ghost" of 1919 had been dispelled. To no small degree, the aggressiveness of the increasing number of police unions at this time was matched and likely encouraged by similar activity among other public employees. Indeed, the militancy of public workers during the 1970s was in keeping with the generally militant, antiestablishment attitude that prevailed during that and the preceding decade. Thus, relative to other categories of public employees, police job actions at that time were hardly unique.

Effects of Police Strikes

The outcomes of police strikes may be assessed in any of several ways. One is to examine the effects on working conditions for officers, including changes in wages or benefits and other work-related issues. A second area of assessment is the influence of these actions on law and public policy pertaining to such job action among public

sector employees. A third area is the analysis of the organizational structure of the union itself, including geographic location, size, membership, and perspectives on police–labor relationships. Finally, one may assess their outcomes vis-à-vis alteration in crime patterns and, related to that, the meaning of police strikes for the security of persons and property in our society.

There are two schools of thought concerning the effects of police strikes on criminal activity. First is the view that during the officer's absence, the criminal and lawless elements are free to indulge their perversities and pose a threat to social orderliness and that police stand as a "thin blue line" between civility and savagery. The disorderly conditions during and allegedly because of, for example, the Boston police strike are often cited to support this perspective. The second and competing perspective suggests that, in fact, police have less influence on fluctuations in the rates of crime than any of several other factors and that police have little or no way of preventing or controlling criminal behavior.

Conclusions

It is apparent that these few paragraphs stand as the briefest survey of a complex, highly emotional issue. We may nonetheless conclude that, characteristically, the politicization of police, including the resort to unionization and strikes, rests on the same general issues leading other workers to take similar action—wages, benefits, and general work conditions. Despite this common element, a resort to unionization and striking by police (and a few other categories of public workers) has been defined and evaluated in qualitatively different terms and almost exclusively on the basis of short-run, parochial interests. On that basis, job actions among police have been the topic of far more discussion and resistance, and the basis of more public anguish than their scope and consequences would necessitate.

PETER A. COLLINS

See also **Accountability; Administration of Police Agencies, Theories of; Boston Police Strike; Unionization, Police**

References and Further Reading

Bopp, William J., and Michael Wiatrowski. 1982. Police strike in New Orleans: A city abandoned by its police. *Police Journal* 55 (April): 125–35.

Burpo, John H. 1979. *Police unions in the civil service setting.* October. Washington, DC: Law Enforcement Assistance Administration, U.S. Department of Justice.

Gammage, Allen Z., and Stanley L. Sachs. 1972. *Police unions.* Springfield, IL: Charles C Thomas.

Gentel, William D., and Martha Handman. 1979. *Police strikes: Causes and prevention.* Gaithersburg, MD: International Association of Chiefs of Police.

Grimes, John A. 1970. *Work stoppages: A tale of three cities.* Washington, DC: Labor Management Relations Service.

Juris, Hervey A., and Peter Feuille. 1973. *Police unionism, power and impact in public sector bargaining.* Lexington, MA: Lexington.

Kadleck, Colleen. 2003. Police employee organizations. *Policing: An International Journal of Police Strategies and Management* 26: 341–51.

Larson, Richard E. 1978. *Police accountability, performance measures and unionism.* Lexington, MA: Lexington.

Magenau, John M., and Raymond G. Hunt. 1996. Police unions and the police role. *Human Relations* 49 (Oct.): 1315–44.

Pfuhl, Erdwin H., Jr. 1983. Police strikes and conventional crime: A look at the data. *Criminology* 21 (Nov.): 489–503.

Swank, Calvin J., and James A. Coner. 1983. *The police personnel system.* New York: John Wiley and Sons.

Wellington, Harry H., and Ralph K. Winter, Jr. 1972. *The unions and the cities.* Washington, DC: Brookings Institution.

STYLES OF POLICING

Police officers typically have a large amount of discretion when deciding what situations to become involved in and how to handle them. While a few situations demand specific and well-defined responses (for example, mandatory arrests in domestic violence cases), the vast majority allow for a variety of possible responses that are neither correct nor incorrect. As with any job that allows discretion, police departments and police officers develop "working personalities" or "styles" that guide their general decision making.

Police personalities and policing styles are informal approaches to police work and represent ways that police officers "do their jobs." They tend to be unique for each police department and police officer and can change from situation to situation. Departmental policing styles are influenced by the mission and goals of the department, the needs of the town or jurisdiction, and residents' views of the role of the police in their community. In addition, individual policing styles are influenced by an officer's personal belief system, moral character, and outlook on police work.

A department's policing style greatly influences individual policing styles through hiring decisions (hiring those officers whose personal belief system mirrors that of the department), recruit training (selecting trainers who best represent the mission and philosophy of the department), and rewards and disciplinary action (promoting officers whose performance is most in line with the departmental style while punishing officers whose behavior deviates from it).

Departmental Policing Styles

Police departments have their own styles that reflect the organizational culture of the department. The departmental style influences every aspect of police work in that jurisdiction, ranging from hiring and promotional decisions, everyday police–community interactions, and budget decisions and resource allocation to police strategies and identification of crime problems within the jurisdiction.

The most widely cited study on police departmental styles was conducted by James Q. Wilson (1968). He found three distinct departmental styles: watchman, legalistic, and service. The watchman style is based mostly on order maintenance. With this style, police officers judge the seriousness of violations by examining the immediate and personal consequences of the offense rather than the legal status of the offense. A watchman style department focuses its law enforcement activities on keeping the peace in the community. A police officer in a watchman department typically has the most discretion.

In contrast, legalistic style departments have one standard: strict enforcement of the law. This type of department produces large numbers of arrests and traffic citations. Most calls for service are resolved in a formal manner in which an arrest or a formal complaint is made. The third type, the service style department, prioritizes all requests for assistance without differentiating between order maintenance or law enforcement functions. Police officers in these departments are not likely to make an arrest unless the situation renders it absolutely necessary.

For example, in handling a situation where a group of youths is out past the town's curfew, police officers in a watchman style department may not intervene at all, speak with the group without taking any further action, or simply tell them to go home, whereas police officers in a legalistic department would more likely write them a citation or arrest them. If the community or department deems the juvenile curfew as important, police officers operating in a service style would not be as likely to make an arrest as officers from a legalistic department but would intervene in some way, perhaps by taking the youths home or calling their parents to pick them up.

State police and state highway patrol agencies more closely follow a paramilitary structure than other police departments and are most likely to have a legalistic style. These departments view themselves as law enforcers and require every officer to handle every situation in a similar manner. Suburban police departments usually follow service-oriented styles, since their role is defined by the community in which they serve. Suburban communities want the police to maintain public order and intervene whenever possible but tend to prefer informal outcomes to arrests. By their nature, rural and small-town police departments afford their officers the most discretion and are most likely to fit the watchman style. In these departments, police officers are asked to perform an array of nontraditional police functions and often have little outside assistance to complete them (Weisheit, Falcone, and Wells 1999).

Individual Styles of Policing

While departmental policing styles do influence individual performance and behavior, police officers have their own unique policing styles. These individual styles are based on predispositions that provide police officers with an array of responses to various situations. They reflect the officers' attitudes, personal beliefs, morals and values, professional aspirations, and views of police work.

William Muir (1977) believed that officers developed distinctive styles and that their selection of an operational style was premised on whether officers possessed two specific attitudes. The first attitude, which Muir termed passion, pertained to whether officers recognized the need to use coercion and were willing to employ it to attain job-related goals and objectives. The second attitude, perspective, involved the willingness of officers to empathize with the circumstances of citizens with whom officers interacted. Muir developed a typology based on these attitudes. The typology consists of four policing styles: professionals (officers possessing both passion and perspective), enforcers (officers possessing passion but not perspective), reciprocators (officers possessing perspective but lacking passion), and avoiders (officers who had neither passion nor perspective).

Some officers will be able to justify their use of force and will not feel guilt or remorse for their actions (an integrated morality of coercion), while other officers may hesitate to use force and will be unable to justify its use even when necessary (conflicted morality of coercion). Muir's professional policing style has both the tragic perspective and the integrated morality of coercion. Police officers with a professional style will carefully evaluate each situation before taking actions and will use force only when necessary, using only the amount of force appropriate to the situation. These police officers view their roles as being both difficult and complex. The professional understands and accepts the limits of the police. Professionals tend to have high levels of job satisfaction.

In contrast, enforcers have a more cynical perspective that results in "us versus them" and "good guy versus bad guy" attitudes. Enforcers see police work as strictly enforcing the law and can become too task oriented to understand or care about offenders' motivations or mitigating circumstances. These police officers have a higher likelihood of becoming frustrated with the limited amount of time they can be crime fighters.

The reciprocator is similar to the professional in that these officers have a more tragic perspective. They are oriented to helping people in ways that will have a lasting effect. Unlike the professional, reciprocators have a conflicted morality of coercion. They are uncomfortable with using force as part of their law enforcement responsibilities. Reciprocators tend to believe that every citizen has a good side and should be given second chances. These police officers are more likely to suffer from job dissatisfaction and burnout due to their frustration and disappointment.

The avoider style is the exact opposite of the professional style. Avoiders have a cynical perspective and a conflicted morality of coercion. Assuming that most social and crime-related problems are beyond their control, avoiders approach law enforcement as if they only want employment and minimally perform their duties. Since avoiders have little motivation to be police officers, they have a high level of job dissatisfaction.

John Broderick's "working personalities" (1977) consisted of four individual policing styles (realists, optimists, enforcers, and idealists) that were based on two dimensions (emphasis on due process of law and emphasis on the need for social order). The emphasis on due process of law calls for the protection of one's constitutional rights through strict enforcement of the law, while the emphasis on the need for social order reflects order maintenance duties. Broderick believed that while some officers viewed law enforcement as their most important function, other officers viewed themselves as public servants.

Like Muir's enforcers, Broderick's enforcers view policing as the means to protect society and place low value on individual rights. Enforcers see their role as strictly performing police work and tend to become frustrated when required to perform non–crime fighting activities. Idealists place a high value on both due process and the need for social order. Like Muir's reciprocators, idealists believe that every person has a good side, and they try to bring it out while enforcing the law. It is common for idealists to become frustrated and dissatisfied.

Broderick's optimist mirrors Muir's professional. Optimists are oriented toward helping people but realize the limits of trying to enforce the law and can avoid becoming frustrated when their goals are not met. Their emphasis on due process is high, while their emphasis on the need for social order is low. These police officers acknowledge that they will not be spending most of their time fighting crime. The fourth type of Broderick's styles is the realist. These police officers are low in both dimensions and, like Muir's avoiders, see many problems with no solutions. A typical response to any problem is that it is not police business and there is little the police can do to resolve the matter.

Michael Brown (1981) also created a theory of four individual policing styles using two different underlying dimensions: "selectivity of enforcement" and "aggressiveness on the street." His four styles were old style crime fighter, clean beat crime fighter, service style I and II, and professional style. The old style crime fighter and the clean beat crime fighter are similar to Muir's enforcers. They are very aggressive when enforcing the law but are also very selective. The old style crime fighter will solve problems using all available means, legal or illegal, while the clean beat crime fighter will only use legal means. These police officers are very selective, choosing to enforce all serious crime while not wasting time looking for minor violations. Like Muir's enforcers, they become frustrated when forced to perform duties other than enforcing the law.

The service style I is related to Muir's reciprocator. This type of officer is sensitive to community values and needs while not being overly concerned with the suppression of crime. These police officers are not aggressive and tend to be selective in enforcing those laws that are deemed important by community standards. The service style II type is very selective in enforcement and not very aggressive. As in the case of Muir's avoiders, this type of police officer does not want to be involved and may even have chosen police work

simply as an alternative to unemployment. The professional style is nonselective as well as nonaggressive. Enforcing the law is very important but should not be the sole aim of police work. The professional style is directly in line with Muir's professional and Broderick's idealist police officers. This type of police officer uses the greatest amount of discretion in choosing what will be enforced and how it will be enforced.

Table 1 compares the underlying dimensions of the three types of individual policing styles. Muir's passion, Broderick's due process of law, and Brown's selection of enforcement center on police officers' decisions to strictly enforce the law. In contrast, the other dimensions are based on the amount of compassion police officers undertake when carrying out their duties. The differences are that Brown concentrated on use of force, Muir on the lack of use of force, and Broderick on officers' emphasis on the need for social order.

One way to compare the actual individual policing styles of Muir, Broderick, and Brown is to place these types into Wilson's departmental styles. It is likely that Muir's and Broderick's enforcers and Brown's old style crime fighters would be found in legalistic police departments (with their heavy emphasis on a paramilitary structure). Professionals and optimists as well as reciprocators, idealists, and service style I police officers would more commonly be found in departments that emphasize the service aspects of police work. Finally, avoiders, realists, and service style II police officers would best fit into Wilson's watchman style department.

Table 1 Dimensions of Individual Policing Styles

	Decision to Enforce the Law	Level of Compassion
Muir (1977)	Passion	Perspective
Broderick (1977)	Due process of law	Emphasis on need for social order
Brown (1981)	Selection of enforcement	Aggressiveness on the street

Table 2. Types of Individual Policing Styles

Wilson's Department Styles	Individual Policing Styles		
	Muir (1977)	Broderick (1977)	Brown (1981)
Legalistic	Enforcer	Enforcer	Old style crime fighter
Service	Professional	Optimist	Professional
Service	Reciprocator	Idealist	Service style I
Watchman	Avoider	Realist	Service style II

Influences of Policing Styles

It is popular to stereotype police officers and compartmentalize their behavior, and it is commonly done so that future behaviors can be predicted based on prior typologies. However, police work entails a variety of activities that may call for behaviors that cannot be placed in a single category (Cox and Frank 1992). While research has supported the notion that police officers have general styles that influence their behavior, consensus on styles dissipates when other issues are examined. These factors can be personal (age, race/ethnicity, gender, education, experience), situational (reactive call for service or proactive police-initiated contacts, demeanor of involved parties, seriousness of the offense, mental state of the citizens involved), environmental (socioeconomic status of the neighborhood, amount of crime, presence of social disorganization, racial or ethnic composition, and racial or ethnic homogeneity), and organizational (departmental style, work shift, and supervisory support for certain police actions) (Roberg, Novak, Cordner 2005; Brooks 1997).

Two factors appear to have significant influences on policing styles. First, situational factors have been found to influence behavior to a far greater degree than other factors. One such situational factor is the manner in which the officer enters the situation (proactive versus reactive). In the proactive situation a police officer takes the initiative to get involved. As such, the police officer will first make a decision whether police intervention is even necessary. In contrast, reactive situations typically require some type of police response to a citizen complaint. The behavioral decision focuses on how to intervene, not whether to intervene.

Second, the contextual characteristics of the neighborhood in which the behavior occurs can have a large influence on the behavior of police officers. Several researchers have found that police in high-crime areas adopted a style that presumably differed from the style utilized in other types of communities (Roberg, Novak, Cordner 2005; Brooks 1997). For instance, police officers tend to be more aggressive in high-crime neighborhoods but rely more on informal dispositions in low-crime neighborhoods.

Policing styles, whether departmental or individual, play an important role in understanding police attitudes and behaviors. Many police departments make hiring and promotional decisions based on a police personality that is closely aligned with the goals and mission of the department. In addition, assignments to specialized units are made with policing styles in mind (for example, youth bureau, detective bureau, community police officers, school resource officers, SWAT teams, and so forth).

STEPHEN M. COX

See also **Order Maintenance; Role of the Police; Theories of Policing**

References and Further Reading

Broderick, John. 1977. *Police in a time of change*. Prospect Heights, IL: Waveland Press.

Brooks, L. W. 1997. Police discretionary behavior: A study of style. In *Critical Issues in Policing,* 3rd ed., ed. Dunham and Alpert, 149–66. Prospect Heights, IL: Waveland Press.

Brown, Michael. 1981. *Working the street: Police discretion and the dilemmas of reform*. New York: Russell Sage.

Cox, Stephen. M., and J. Frank. 1992. The influence of neighborhood context and method of entry on individual styles of policing. *American Journal of Police* 11:1–22.

Muir, William. 1977. *Police: Streetcorner politicians*. Chicago: University of Chicago Press.

Roberg, Roy, K. Novak, and G. Cordner. 2005. *Police & Society*. 3rd ed. Los Angeles: Roxbury Publishing.

Weisheit, Ralph A., D. N. Falcone, and L. E. Wells. 1995. *Crime and policing in rural and small-town America*. 2nd ed. Prospect Heights, IL: Waveland Press.

Wilson, James Q. 1968. *Varieties of police behavior*. Cambridge, MA: Harvard University Press.

SUPERVISION

Police supervision is the act of supervising, directing, or overseeing the day-to-day work activities of police officers. In most law enforcement agencies the majority of the policing services provided to the public are provided by uniformed patrol officers and detectives. These officers and detectives make up the lowest level of their departments' hierarchical structure and are supervised by a chain of command consisting of multiple layers of supervisory officers. The chain of command structure of most police agencies is similar to that found in military units, where each employee in the chain usually answers to only one immediate supervisor. Requests and other sorts of communication within the organization usually flow up and down through each level of the supervisory hierarchy, and rarely is a level of command bypassed.

Although rank designations for supervisory positions vary from agency to agency, the immediate supervisor of patrol officers or detectives is often a sergeant. (Some agencies also utilize a rank called corporal or officer in charge, which are basically officers who temporarily assume the role of the sergeant if a sergeant is unavailable at the time.) Sergeants in turn are usually supervised by a lieutenant, and lieutenants are supervised by a captain. The larger the police organization, the more ranks or levels of command that will exist, with some larger organizations having the ranks of major, lieutenant colonel, commander, or colonel. At the head of the police organization is a single police executive, often referred to as a chief or director in state and municipal police organizations or a sheriff in county law enforcement agencies.

Difficulties in Supervising Officers

Supervision of the activities of police officers is often very difficult for three primary reasons. First is the fact that uniformed officers usually patrol alone or in pairs, are mobile, and are dispersed across a wide geographic area. For example, in large-city police departments a sergeant may be responsible for simultaneously supervising up to twelve patrol officers, each patrolling independently, dispersed across an area of a dozen square miles. In sheriff departments or state police agencies sergeants may supervise fewer officers; however, these officers may be dispersed across even larger geographic areas, such as one or more counties. When not handling calls, uniformed officers are usually free to patrol randomly in an effort to detect criminal activity and be a visible deterrent to crime. Therefore, it can be difficult for a sergeant to locate subordinate officers and directly observe their behavior when they are not handling a call for service.

Likewise, detectives spend the majority of their time out of the office conducting follow-up interviews with victims and witnesses. Contacting these witnesses may require travel to a number of different areas within the jurisdiction within one workday or even require travel outside the agency's jurisdiction. Therefore, a detective sergeant supervises a unit of detectives who are constantly coming and going from the office at various times and traveling various distances. Rarely is the detective supervisor able to be present with subordinates while they follow up on investigative leads.

A second reason it is difficult to directly supervise police officers is that they are afforded a high degree of decision-making discretion. Although police officers are guided in their decisions by the law and a host of departmental rules, regulations, and procedures, these guides can never cover every situation that an officer may potentially encounter in the normal course of police duties. When encountering suspicious circumstances, police officers must decide whether they should investigate, whether a law has been broken, whether there is enough evidence to support a search or an arrest, and whether it is in the best interest of those involved to make an arrest.

Every individual situation encountered in policing is unique, and therefore police officers must be able to exercise some discretion in deciding what constitutes a violation of the law and how and when laws should be enforced. Therefore, not only is it difficult for police supervisors to be present in the field to directly observe and supervise their officers on the job, even the rules and regulations set forth by the supervisors must often be open to some degree of interpretation by the officers who are expected to obey them. Unless supervisors were present at the scene of a call and witnessed the circumstances encountered by the officer, it is sometimes difficult for them to determine if the officer's actions were appropriate.

The third reason that it is difficult to directly supervise the conduct of police officers is the amount of administrative

work police supervisors are often required to perform. Although specific duties vary across departments, it is not uncommon for police sergeants and lieutenants to be expected to schedule their officers' shift and beat assignments, review all of their officers' written reports for clarity and accuracy, attend meetings with upper management or other government agencies, attend meetings with community groups, approve officer use of overtime compensation, answer telephones at the police station, process citizen complaints about officer conduct, compile and monitor crime statistics for their districts, write personnel evaluations, and issue disciplinary reports.

These extensive and time-consuming administrative activities can severely limit the time a supervisor has available to go out into the field to directly monitor or supervise officers. Supervisors have even less time available to sculpt officer work behaviors and improve individual officer performance through training, coaching, or mentoring. Therefore, most police supervisors attempt to control officer behavior through indirect methods.

Methods of Supervising Officers

The most formal methods of officer behavior control used by police supervisors (especially high-ranking supervisors) are written rules, regulations, and directives. Most police organizations have extensive operations manuals containing regulations and directives to guide officer conduct in a number of situations. The reliance on written rules and regulations for supervising police officers has several weaknesses. First, it is impossible for rules and regulations to be created that would govern every situation that police officers will encounter, requiring officers to sometimes use entirely their own judgment or attempt to interpret and follow the spirit rather than the letter of the rules. Second, rules can be enforced only when rule violations are detected. Within the police subculture there usually exist two separate subcultures for officers and management. As part of the patrol officer subculture's code of silence, few officers will report rule violations by their fellow officers to management. Also, as noted above, direct supervision in the field that may catch rule violating behavior is difficult to achieve.

Nevertheless, social science research has demonstrated that the use of rules and regulations can be relatively effective at controlling some types of officer behaviors. For example, research has documented a consistent pattern of significant reductions in the number of police shootings of citizens experienced by police departments after these departments instituted written rules limiting the circumstances under which officers may fire their weapons (Fyfe 1979). The creation of stricter use-of-force regulations within the department usually resulted in officers exercising more restraint in their use of force. Similar results have also been found with the implementation of formal department rules governing nonlethal uses of force, involvement in vehicle pursuits, and arrest decisions in domestic violence situations.

However, most of the evidence suggesting the effectiveness of written rules and regulations deals with what are often termed "high-visibility" decisions by police officers. These are decisions that are unlikely to go undetected by management and are subject to review by the courts or a supervisor. For example, the discharge of a firearm at a citizen would be extremely difficult to keep from being detected by a supervisor due to the noise, danger, and community reaction involved. Because of the seriousness of the use of lethal force, these officer decisions are usually investigated and reviewed by police supervisors and the local prosecutor. Therefore, uses of deadly force proscribed as inappropriate by department regulations are highly likely to be uncovered and disciplined during the departmental investigation of the shooting. However, it is unlikely that department rules and regulations governing behaviors that are less likely to be subject to detection—such as sleeping on duty—are as effective at controlling officer behavior.

Another common method police supervisors use to control officer behavior is through a transactional leadership style, where the supervisors use a system of simple rewards to promote the behaviors they desire and punishments to discourage undesirable officer behaviors. Police sergeants and lieutenants often use their authority over officer beat assignments, transfer requests, day off requests, overtime compensation, partner assignments, and performance evaluations to manipulate officer behavior. Officers come to learn that when their behavior conforms to their supervisors' expectations, they are granted requests in these areas more frequently. When their behaviors fail to meet their supervisors' expectations, officers find it much harder to receive special assignments, extra days off, or assignments that provide overtime pay.

If the behavior of an officer consistently violates the supervisor's expectations over time or involves a serious breach of department rules and regulations, the officer may also receive more formalized discipline, such as a letter of reprimand, suspension without pay, or termination of employment. This type of behavioral control can be accomplished without direct supervision in the field, explaining why it is employed so often in modern policing.

As with formal rules and regulations, systems of rewards and punishments are usually most effective with activities that will be reviewed or outcomes that can be measured, such as the number of tickets issued, citizen complaints received, or arrests made. Research by Stephen Mastrofski and his associates has illustrated the effectiveness of rewards in controlling officer behavior (Mastrofski, Ritti, and Snipes 1994). Their research revealed that when officers are directed by their supervisors to aggressively arrest drunk drivers and the officers perceive that such arrests will result in various rewards from within the police organization, officers are more likely to comply with these requests and produce high levels of drunk driver arrests. It was also found that in situations where police supervisors discouraged officers from making drunk driver arrests and such arrests were not perceived to result in any special rewards, most officers refrained from making such arrests.

Similar results have been found in the study of officer involvement in problem-oriented policing, where officers who were directed by their supervisors to engage in community problem solving and perceived that they would be rewarded for this activity did so more frequently than other officers. Therefore, with activities that can be objectively measured, rewards and punishments can be an effective police management strategy.

As mentioned earlier, direct supervision of officers in the field is frequently difficult in policing, yet research has revealed that when it can be accomplished, it has a significant influence on officer behavior. Research has found that when supervisors are able to be in the field, responding to calls with their subordinates, observing their behavior on traffic stops, and attempting to locate officers while they go about their patrol duties, officers frequently respond by conforming most of their behaviors to the expectations made clear by their supervisors (Engel 2000).

When officers receive higher levels of direct supervision in the field, they tend to make more arrests, engage in more proactive investigative activity, engage in more community problem solving, and spend less time on personal activities not officially permitted by the department while they are on duty. Research also suggests that this occurs primarily because officers are aware they are more likely to be caught and disciplined for disobeying rules if the supervisor is frequently present in the field and that many patrol officers voluntarily conform their behavior to match the expectations of these supervisors out of respect for the

supervisor's willingness to engage in patrol officer work and assist them at calls (Van Maanen 1983). Nevertheless, the direct supervision of officers in the field is very difficult to achieve in most police departments due to the number of administrative duties sergeants and lieutenants have also been assigned.

Issues in Police Supervision

In spite of the fact that police officers have a great degree of autonomy and freedom to use discretion, police supervisors have traditionally been reluctant to delegate any additional authority to patrol officers. However, one of the key elements of community policing strategies involves empowering individual patrol officers to develop creative solutions to recurring problems of crime and disorder.

Nevertheless, due to concerns about civil liability issues, police supervisors are often reluctant to let officers implement new plans or operations on their own. As a result of the decisions in federal court cases such as *Monell v. New York City* and *City of Canton v. Harris,* police supervisors can often be held civilly liable for the negative consequences that can result from the actions of their subordinates. Therefore, police supervisors can become understandably nervous when their officers attempt to act proactively by implementing unique and untried tactics rather than simply maintaining the status quo of reactively responding to calls. This reluctance to delegate operational authority continues to be a frequent obstacle to the implementation of community policing programs.

Another problematic issue in police supervision is the lack of training police supervisors receive. In most police departments officers do not receive any leadership or supervisory training until they are promoted to the rank of sergeant. Even after being promoted, new sergeants usually do not receive formal training in how to be a supervisor for a number of months or even years. In some small departments with tight budgets, supervisors may never receive formal supervisory training.

This general lack of training is often the result of the cost of training and the fact that when a supervisor is away at training, the department is shorthanded. Some police executives also hold the opinion that officers selected for promotion already have the natural talents and abilities to be good leaders and therefore do not need training. This lack of training also poses problems for the implementation of community policing since many supervisors are unfamiliar with how to supervise officers effectively while also empowering them to develop unique responses to crime and disorder.

RICHARD JOHNSON

See also **Accountability; COMPSTAT; Inspection; Managing Criminal Investigations; Organizational Structure: Theory and Practice; Risk Management**

References and Further Reading

Allen, D. N. 1982. Police supervision on the street: An analysis of supervisor–officer interaction during the shift. *Journal of Criminal Justice* 10: 91–109.

Birzer, M. L. 1996. Police supervision in the 21st century. *FBI Law Enforcement Bulletin* 65: 6–10.

Bradstreet, R. 1997. Policing: The patrol sergeants' perspective. *Journal of Police and Criminal Psychology* 12: 1–6.

DeJong, C., S. D. Mastrofski, and R. B. Parks. 2001. Patrol officers and problem solving: An application of expectancy theory. *Justice Quarterly* 18: 31–61.

Del Carmen, R. V. 1989. Civil liabilities of police supervisors. *American Journal of Police* 8: 107–35.

Engel, R. S. 2000. Effects of supervisory styles on patrol officer behavior. *Police Quarterly* 3: 262–93.

Fyfe, J. J. 1979. Administrative interventions on police shooting discretion: An empirical examination. *Journal of Criminal Justice* 7: 309–23.

Mastrofski, S. D., R. R. Ritti, and J. B. Snipes. 1994. Expectancy theory and police productivity in DUI enforcement. *Law and Society Review* 28: 113–48.

Reuss-Ianni, E. 1983. *Two cultures of policing: Street cops and management cops.* New Brunswick, NJ: Transaction Publishers.

Van Maanen, J. 1983. Boss: First-line supervision in an American police agency. In *Control in the police organization,* ed. Punch, 275–317. Cambridge, MA: MIT Press.

———. 2001. Making rank: Becoming an American police sergeant. In *Critical issues in policing: Contemporary readings,* ed. Dunham and Alpert, 5th ed., 146–61. Prospect Heights, IL: Waveland Press.

Wilson, O. W. 1963. *Police administration.* New York: McGraw-Hill.

SUPREME COURT DECISIONS

While often characterized as enforcers of the law, police in America must also be upholders of the law. In carrying forth their law enforcement functions the police are sworn to uphold the Constitution. This oath demands that all arrests, searches, and the like be conducted in compliance with constitutional rules. Although all courts possess the power to declare a law to be in violation of the U.S. Constitution, the final judge of constitutionality is the Supreme Court. This article will highlight the primary Supreme Court decisions that have most affected the way police officers perform their law enforcement role.

Arrest and Detention of Suspects

Today, the circumstances under which an arrest may lawfully be made are normally specified by state statute, but certain minimum constitutional standards, such as the Fourth Amendment requirement of probable cause, must be met. The Supreme Court has indicated that the law of arrest has constitutional dimensions beyond the requirement of probable cause, however. In *United States v. Watson,* 423 U.S. 411, 96 S. Ct. 820, 46 L. Ed. 2d 598 (1976), the Court ruled that while the preferred practice is to obtain an arrest warrant prior to making an arrest, the Constitution does not require issuance of a warrant prior to arresting a suspect in a public place, even if officers had the time and opportunity to obtain a warrant. In *Payton v. New York,* 445 U.S. 573, 100 S. Ct. 1371, 63 L. Ed. 2d 639 (1980), the Court ruled that absent exigent circumstances or consent, police officers may not enter a private home to make a warrantless arrest. Issuance of an arrest warrant is a prerequisite to a valid entry in nonemergency circumstances. Further, the warrantless entry into a home to arrest an individual for a minor offense is rarely permissible, *Welsh v. Wisconsin,* 466 U.S. 740, 104 S. Ct. 2091, 80 L. Ed. 2d 732 (1984). Justices have also held that the Constitution permits full custody arrests even for minor traffic offenses punishable only with a fine, *Atwater v. City of Lago Vista,* 532 U.S. 318, 121 S. Ct. 1536, 149 L. Ed. 2d 549 (2001), and that the motive behind an officer's decision to arrest is irrelevant to its legality so long as constitutional minimum standards are complied with, *Whren v. United States,* 517 U.S. 806, 116 S. Ct. 1769, 135 L. Ed. 2d 89 (1996).

Recognizing the need to balance reasonable police procedures against the constitutional right of citizens to be free from unreasonable seizures, the Supreme Court has granted limited power to the police to conduct temporary detentions short of an arrest. In a case styled *Terry v. Ohio,* 392 U.S. 1, 88 S. Ct. 1868, 20 L. Ed. 2d 889 (1968), the Court ruled that when an officer has a reasonable suspicion to believe that criminal activity is afoot and offers identification as a police officer, the officer may lawfully stop an individual for questioning. If the results of the inquiry do not dispel fear that the suspect is armed, the officer may conduct a frisk for weapons for the purpose of self-protection.

Search and Seizure

A prime investigatory activity of law enforcement is the gathering of evidence to aid in case solution and prosecution. Such seizures of physical evidence may occur as an adjunct to an arrest for some viewed offense or may be the result of direct questioning for previously identified items, such as a murder weapon. Concurrently, due to the potentially violent circumstances in which the police become involved, safety of the officer from those the officer seeks to arrest is a major concern to the police and the courts. It is in this area of search and seizure of items for prosecutorial purposes and officer safety that the day-to-day work of police officers has been most affected by Supreme Court opinions.

Search Incident to Arrest

While the authority of a police officer to conduct a search at the time of an arrest has long been recognized, the case styled *Chimel v. California,* 395 U.S. 752, 89 S. Ct. 2034, 23 L. Ed. 2d 685 (1969), involving a search of a burglary suspect's home, presented the opportunity to clarify the rule. In *Chimel,* the court ruled that a peace officer may conduct a search of the person and the area within the person's immediate control contemporaneous with an arrest for the purpose of removing weapons, preventing possible escape, and locating evidence that might otherwise be destroyed. The scope of the search is limited to the body of the arrestee and the general armspan area. Since the search is protective in nature, absent a search warrant or an emergency, no constitutional justification exists for extending the search further.

In *United States v. Robinson,* 414 U.S. 218, 94 S. Ct. 467, 38 L. Ed. 2d 427 (1973), the Supreme Court ruled that the search incident to arrest doctrine applied to any "full custody" arrest, regardless of the severity of the offense. Thus, the arrest of a traffic offender who will be taken to jail justifies a search of the offender's person, but mere detention for issuance of a ticket, without more, does not warrant a search.

Additionally, in *New York v. Belton,* 453 U.S. 454, 101 S. Ct. 2860, 69 L. Ed. 2d 768 (1981), the Court held that following the lawful full custody arrest of the driver, the interior passenger compartment of an automobile may be searched.

Warrantless Searches for Evidence

Use of a magistrate as an intervening arbitrator between the police and the citizen is a matter of continuing emphasis by the Supreme Court. However, the Court recognizes circumstances do exist where obtaining judicial approval prior to questing for evidence would be impractical.

Searching a motor vehicle for evidence is likely the most frequent application of this exception to the warrant requirement. Police officers are permitted to conduct warrantless searches when probable cause exists to believe the automobile contains evidence, *United States v. Ross,* 456 U.S. 798, 102 S. Ct. 2157, 72 L. Ed. 2d 572 (1982). If officers have the requisite probable cause, they may search a vehicle, including its trunk, glove box, and any packages therein that could reasonably contain the evidence they seek.

Search under a Warrant

Courts have jealously protected privacy rights when a search of an individual's residence is involved. Barring an emergency, such as a crime in progress or the immediate destruction of evidence, the Court requires a search warrant to enter a residence without the resident's consent, *Mincey v. Arizona,* 437 U.S. 385, 98 S. Ct. 2408, 57 L. Ed. 2d 290 (1978).

Confessions

In the 1960s, the Supreme Court evidenced concern that the traditional "voluntary-involuntary" test for confession admissibility did not provide sufficient citizen protection in cases of psychological coercion by the police. Following a finding that the Fifth Amendment also encompassed an absolute right to silence, *Malloy v. Hogan,* 378 U.S. 1, 84 S. Ct. 1489, 12 L. Ed. 2d 653 (1964), the Court sought to develop a bright line rule to provide police officers guidance when interrogating criminal suspects.

The rule came in one of the most controversial court cases in American legal history: *Miranda v. Arizona,* 384 U.S. 436, 86 S. Ct. 1602, 16 L. Ed. 2d 694 (1966). A majority of the Court ruled that any questioning of a person who is under arrest is inherently coercive and jeopardizes the free exercise of the Fifth Amendment right to silence. A divided Court ruled that the prosecution may not use statements that are a product of custodial interrogation of a suspect unless it proves that the suspect's privilege against self-incrimination was protected and a knowing waiver of that privilege was made.

Protection of the privilege against self-incrimination was to be accomplished by advising in-custody suspects that they had the right to remain silent, anything said could be used against them in court, they had the right to talk to a lawyer prior to questioning, and if they could not afford a lawyer, one would be provided. If a suspect did confess, the burden fell upon the state to prove that the warning had been given and a knowing waiver of rights had occurred.

Later rulings have clarified the scope of the coverage of the *Miranda* holding, including a determination that the procedure "has become embedded in routine police practice to the point where the warnings have become part of our national culture," *Dickerson v. United States,* 530 U.S. 428, 120 S. Ct. 2326, 147 L. Ed. 2d 405 (2000).

Use of Force

In providing police officers with the authority and duty to enforce the criminal law, the government has granted them the privilege to use reasonable force, including deadly force, against persons to carry out that responsibility. Historically, the Court has deferred to the state legislatures to define the level of force that police officers were permitted to use, but in *Tennessee v. Garner,* 471 U.S. 1, 105 S.Ct. 1694, 85 L.Ed.2d 1 (1985), the Supreme Court ruled that a common law rule permitting use of deadly force against any fleeing felon was unreasonable under the Fourth Amendment and, therefore, unconstitutional. The court noted that it was not better that all persons die than that they escape. Deadly force may be constitutionally used only if the officer has probable cause to believe that the suspect poses a serious threat of harm to the officer or another person.

Conclusion

The legal authority of police officers is significantly influenced by judicial decisions. Foremost are the opinions of the Supreme Court that attempt to balance the constitutional protection of the citizenry against the needs of the government, through its police forces, to maintain law and order and bring criminal offenders to justice.

JERRY L. DOWLING

See also **Arrest Powers of the Police; Constitutional Rights: In-Custody Interrogation; Constitutional Rights: Privacy; Constitutional Rights: Search and Seizure; Exclusionary Rule; Interrogations, Criminal**

References and Further Reading

del Carmen, Rolando V. 2004. *Criminal procedure: Law and practice.* Belmont, CA: Wadsworth.

Saltzburg, Stephen A., and Daniel J. Capra. 2003. *Basic criminal procedure.* St. Paul, MN: West.

U.S. Supreme Court. n.d. Opinions. http://www.supremecourtus.gov/opinions/opinions.html.

Zalman, Marvin. 2002. *Criminal procedure: Constitution and society.* Upper Saddle River, NJ: Prentice Hall.

SURVEILLANCE

In the popular imagination, surveillance involves public police agents working undercover against foreign enemies, organized crime networks, corporate fraudsters, drug dealers, and ordinary crooks in hot spots of thieving. The police do undertake such work, although it has a minor role in their repertoire of investigative methods (Marx 1988; Ericson 1993; Sharpe 2002).

Surveillance of this type is more common among private security operatives, who have the advantage of greater legal and practical access to private spheres compared to their counterparts in public policing. Moreover, they can be paid at a fraction of the cost of public police officers for what is labor intensive and sometimes unproductive work. Some industries have developed substantial private investigation units based on this type of surveillance. For example, the insurance industry uses both internal special investigation units and private investigators on contract to conduct surveillance regarding fraud (Ericson, Doyle, and Barry 2003; Ericson and Doyle 2004).

The undercover police operative who observes and records is only one role in the division of labor for surveillance. Surveillance is best defined as the production, analysis, and distribution of information about populations in order to govern them (Giddens 1987; Dandeker 1990; Haggerty and Ericson 2005). As such, surveillance is integral to the activities of all major social institutions, for example, governments that administer police, military, taxation, and social security systems, banks that profile credit ratings of customers, health service providers that compile medical histories, insurance companies that form risk pools for efficient underwriting and claims management, and marketing agencies that use media audience consumption and ratings data to place their ads and target consumers.

Surveillance has been greatly enhanced by the development of electronic technologies—for example, computers, smart cards, video cameras, and satellites—that produce information about populations instantly and with worldwide transmission capabilities. Surveillance technologies not only monitor people as individuals but also through processes of disassembling and reassembling data about them. People are broken down into a series of discrete information flows that are stabilized and captured according to preestablished classifications. Their reconfigured identities are then transported to data systems to be reassembled and combined in ways that serve the specific purposes of the institutions involved. The accumulated information constitutes one's "data double," a virtual/informational profile that circulates in the electronic networks of various institutions and their specific contexts of practical application.

One result of this process is an enhanced capacity to govern populations across institutions through "datamatching" or "dataveillance" (Garfinkel 2000). Another result is "datamining," using applied mathematics and sophisticated computer systems to discover new data and patterns that are useful in strategic intelligence. Datamining has been used extensively in target marketing, but it also has a number of security applications, for example, to identify attacks on computer systems based on deviations from the normal flow of server traffic.

The new surveillance capacities of data systems are making information an increasingly valuable commodity. Indeed, the population database of an organization is often one of its most valuable assets, sold selectively to other organizations that can use the data for further surveillance and their own purposes of policing and governance. For example, insurers access data from government statistical agencies, credit agencies, and marketing firms to decide whether an applicant for insurance is suspect and to investigate fraudulent activities (Ericson, Barry, and Doyle 2000). At the same time, disclosure of information is highly selective and at times politically charged. In the commercial sector there are many trade secrets. In the public sector the state protects a wide range of information, especially that deemed in need of secrecy for national security purposes.

Public police agencies now operate in an assemblage of data systems (Chan 2003). Most of a police officer's time is spent in producing information about people and incidents encountered during routine patrol and investigation (Ericson and Haggerty 1997). This information is demanded not only for internal police purposes and those of the criminal justice system but also by a range of external institutions—for example, insurance companies, health service providers, safety inspectors, and schools—that require knowledge of incidents for their own practical purposes of case settlement, statistical profiling of risks, and security provision. In turn, the police access data from external institutions for their own law enforcement purposes.

The role of the police as information workers in surveillance networks developed long before the attacks on the World Trade Center and the Pentagon of September 11, 2001. However, it has accelerated with the PATRIOT Act and other enabling legislation that gives police access to a broader range of databases in both public and private institutions (Lyon 2003). The main justification for such enhancement is that aggregate data on populations improve the capacity for intelligence-led policing, especially that based on categorical suspicion. In the post-9/11 environment the police are moving from a system of resourceful intelligence for selective law enforcement purposes to one of universal suspicion where everyone is on a continuum of risk.

This post-9/11 environment has fostered a new politics of surveillance and visibility in which critical issues are contested. One key issue is privacy rights. Who has the right to information about the person, organization, community, or other entity? Who has the right to access information given up for one purpose but used for another purpose? What remedies are available for inaccuracies and misuses of information, where the concern is not so much "Big Brother" but "Big Bungler" (Brodeur and Leman-Langlois 2005)? The privacy concern is not only about the bits of information collected but also about the information systems involved and the program of policing with which they are associated. While it may be an exaggeration to claim that we are experiencing "the end of privacy" (Whitaker 2000), there is no doubt that we are in a new information age of surveillance and visibility with privacy problems that cannot be legislated away (Brin 1998).

Another critical issue is the transformation of legal principles and due process protections that is occurring in the new environment of surveillance and visibility. Surveillance is more pervasive and influential than criminal law or the criminal justice system in governing populations. Crime prevention and efficient forms of private justice can be accomplished through surveillance techniques beyond the law (Norris and Armstrong 1999). Furthermore, when the criminal law is invoked, surveillance mechanisms such as video evidence, financial transaction records, and DNA evidence are increasingly used to obtain confessions from suspects, guilty plea settlements, and other forms of expedient case resolution. In both prevention and enforcement contexts, the rise of surveillance is accompanied by a decline of innocence or presumption of guilt (Ericson and Haggerty 1997).

Surveillance is often seen negatively, especially among those concerned with privacy rights and the decline of innocence. This tendency is a legacy of two of the most influential writers on surveillance, George Orwell (1949) and Michel Foucault (1977).

Both Orwell and Foucault depict surveillance as a centralized, top-down capacity of Big Brother to know too much about populations to their detriment. But it should be kept in mind that surveillance has many benefits, for example, efficiency in the provision of goods and services, management of social security programs, detection of criminal activity, administration of taxation systems, and sharing of insurance risks.

Too much emphasis on privacy can inhibit the development of desirable social policies (Etzioni 1999). Some of the early developments in surveillance were a response to the problems of privacy and the need to develop more information about populations that would establish trustworthy identities for the collective good (Torpey 2000). Another consideration is that while people sometimes feel their privacy is "invaded," at other times they are happy to exchange personal data for perks, efficiencies, and other benefits offered by the institution concerned.

Surveillance is a necessary aspect of participation in the institutions that make modern life flow in efficient and rewarding ways. It is also clear that many people enjoy peering into the private lives of others. Reality television shows and other voyeuristic offerings on television and the Internet indicate a broader cultural acceptance of watching and being watched. The police also participate in this culture, whether it is through reality television shows or by encouraging citizens to use their own video and computer equipment to conduct surveillance as part of the law enforcement effort (Doyle 2003).

Contemporary surveillance differs from the Big Brother depiction in another respect. Far from being controlled by centralized institutions in a top-down manner, surveillance is now dispersed in myriad networks of knowledge and power. There is a "surveillant assemblage" (Haggerty and Ericson 2000) of criss-crossing, loosely connected information systems. These systems are composed of surveillance operatives observing and recording, smart cards reading the time and place of transactions, closed-circuit television cameras capturing the flows and foibles of populations, scanners penetrating material objects and human bodies, and data systems mining the products of all of the above for new patterns. These information systems are as likely to be owned by private entities and operated by their police as they are to be part of public policing. Moreover, these systems cut across the public–private divide. The border is now blurred, and it is increasingly difficult to make conventional distinctions such as public and private, inside and outside, inclusion and exclusion.

No one can escape surveillant assemblages and their capacity to make things visible, coordinate activities, exclude some, benefit others, and reconfigure social structure and organization. Everyone contributes to surveillant assemblages in some way, whether as sources of information, system operatives, system resistors, beneficiaries, subjects of control, or any combination thereof. The police are in the same position as other entities in this respect. Entwined in the surveillant assemblage, their methods and functions are being transformed. As information workers in a surveillance-based society, they participate in all of the productive gains as well as pitfalls of surveillance outlined here.

RICHARD V. ERICSON

See also **Closed-Circuit Television Applications for Policing; Community Watch Programs; Computer Forensics; Computer Technology; Crime Mapping; Crimestoppers; DNA Fingerprinting; Fingerprinting; Information within Police Agencies; Intelligence Gathering and Analysis: Impacts on Terrorism; Intelligence-Led Policing and Organizational Learning; INTERPOL and International Police Intelligence; Neighborhood Watch; Offender Profiling; PATRIOT Acts I and II; Private Policing; Technology and Police Decision Making; Technology and the Police; Technology, Records Management Systems, and Calls for Service; Undercover Investigations; Video Technology in Policing**

References and Further Reading

Brin, D. 1998. *The transparent society: Will technology force us to choose between privacy and freedom?* Reading, MA: Perseus Books.

Brodeur, J.-P., and S. Leman-Langlois. 2005. Surveillance: Fiction or higher policing? In *The new politics of surveillance and visibility,* ed. K. Haggerty and R. Ericson. Toronto: University of Toronto Press.

Chan, J. 2003. Police and new technologies. In *Handbook of policing,* ed. T. Newburn, 655–79. Cullompton, Devon, UK: Willan Publishing.

Dandeker, C. 1990. *Surveillance, power and modernity: Bureaucracy and discipline from 1700 to the present day.* New York: St. Martin's Press.

Doyle, A. 2003. *Arresting images: Crime and policing in front of the television camera.* Toronto: University of Toronto Press.

Ericson, R. 1993. *Making crime: A study of detective work.* 2nd ed. Toronto: University of Toronto Press.

Ericson, R. and A. Doyle. 2004. *Uncertain business: Risk, insurance and the limits of knowledge.* Toronto: University of Toronto Press.

Ericson, R., and K. Haggerty. 1997. *Policing the risk society.* Toronto: University of Toronto Press and Oxford: Clarendon Press.

Ericson, R., A. Doyle, and D. Barry. 2003. *Insurance as governance.* Toronto: University of Toronto Press.

Etzioni, A. 1999. *The limits of privacy.* New York: Basic Books.

Foucault, M. 1977. *Discipline and punish: The birth of the prison.* New York: Pantheon.

Garfinkel, S. 2000. *Database nation: The death of privacy in the 21st century.* Sebastopol, CA: O'Reilly.

Giddens, A. 1987. *The nation-state and violence.* Cambridge: Polity.

Haggerty, K., and R. Ericson. 2000. The surveillant assemblage. *British Journal of Sociology* 51: 605–22.

———, eds. 2005. *The new politics of surveillance and visibility.* Toronto: University of Toronto Press.

Lyon, D. 2003. *Surveillance after September 11.* Cambridge: Polity.

Marx, G. 1988. *Undercover: Police surveillance in America*. Berkeley: University of California Press.

Norris, C., and G. Armstrong. 1999. *The maximum surveillance society: The rise of CCTV*. Oxford: Berg.

Orwell, G. 1949. *Nineteen eighty-four*. New York: Penguin.

Sharpe, S. 2002. Covert surveillance and the use of informants. In *The handbook of criminal justice process,* ed. M. McConville and G. Wilson, 59–71. Oxford: Oxford University Press.

Torpey, J. 2000. *The invention of the passport: Surveillance, citizenship and the state*. Cambridge: Cambridge University Press.

Whitaker, R. 2000. *The end of privacy*. New York: New Press.

high-risk situations. But police executives were quick to recognize that the use of highly motivated, specially armed, specially trained, and exceptionally well-led reams of officers, when faced with heavily armed criminals or media happenings such as hostage incidents, usually reduced civil liability and complemented public relations when the incident was resolved successfully in favor of the police with little or no loss of life. By the end of the 1970s, all major departments across the United States had formed SWAT teams, and the rank-and-file police officers of America had accepted them as an integral part of police service.

SWAT TEAMS

In 1964, the Philadelphia Police Department, in response to an alarming increase in bank robberies, established a one-hundred-man Special Weapons and Tactics (SWAT) Squad. The purpose of this unit was to react quickly and decisively to bank robberies while they were in progress, by utilizing a large number of specially trained officers who had at their disposal a great amount of firepower. The tactic worked.

Shortly after the successes of the Philadelphia SWAT team were publicized, other departments formed similar special units, most notably the Los Angeles Police Department (SWAT). Many different names were given to these teams: Special Reaction Team (SRT) by the Los Angeles Sheriff's Department, Metro Unique Situation Team (MUST) by the Nashville Police Department, and hostage rescue team (HRT) by others, to name a few.

The formation of SWAT teams by major police departments marked a departure from traditional police service and the advent of a new method of crisis management by modern police executives. Many rank-and-file police officers were slow to see these teams as the most ideal element of a department to correctly handle certain

Staffing

SWAT teams are staffed by regular police officers selected for the teams after meeting certain stringent criteria. SWAT team members are required to have a normal psychological profile, with emphasis on the ability to work well as a member of a team. Without question, each member must be physically fit and not have any limiting physical characteristics, such as hearing loss or extreme myopia. Team members must be able to react well under stress and conditions of extreme fatigue. They must be capable of following orders without question and at the same time demonstrating the ability to lead others when called upon.

Equipment

Because SWAT teams are required to tackle situations that demand unorthodox entry into structures under extremely adverse conditions, they must be adept in the use of special equipment such as ropes and rappelling paraphernalia, which they can use to enter a structure from a rooftop or from a hovering helicopter. They must be able to use explosives to blast doors, walls, or roofs in order to make a quick and safe entry.

The SWAT team uniform must provide all-weather protection. It must be able to be worn at night without making the officer an easily identifiable target. It must be loose fitting in order to allow the officer freedom of movement. Many teams have opted for a ski mask type of wool cap, which can be rolled up during hot days and let down at night for concealment. Team members usually wear military-type boots. In recent years, the outfitting of SWAT teams has become a fast-rising business in America, with companies developing an exotic assortment of uniforms, SWAT weaponry, and even SWAT vehicles.

The weapons of a SWAT team are dictated by tactical necessity. In assaults on defended properties, teams use automatic rifles, usually stockless and short barreled and having a high rate of fire. A shotgun is usually brought along on every operation to provide long-range delivery for tear gas or smoke. Teams employ sharpshooters against snipers and to cover the movement of other team members. Sharpshooters use high-powered, long-range rifles, usually fitted with high-resolution scopes that can be used day or night. As a rule, teams issue automatic pistols to each member as personal, close-in weapons, because of their rapid fire and quick and easy reload capabilities.

Other equipment possessed by teams includes gas masks for each member, starlight scopes for night vision, flashlights attached to weaponry for nighttime target acquisition, bulletproof vests, SWAT vests that fit around the body and are capable of carrying everything from extra ammunition to water canteens, leg holsters for pistols to allow for quick draw, and high-band, voice-activated, silent listening radios for instant interteam communication that may be employed even while a team member is under fire. Last, teams have special SWAT vehicles, usually vans, that are brought to the scenes of incidents and

provide command post and logistic center functions.

Training

Because SWAT teams are required to perform the most hazardous of tasks, such as freeing hostages, it is of paramount importance that they be well trained. Each team should have a clearly defined yearly training program dictated by its potential missions. Types of training required for teams include the use of explosives for controlled entry into structures; live-fire target recognition and acquisition; day and night movement procedures in all types of terrain and in all types of weather; entry procedures for all types of structures; envelopment techniques; room- and building-clearing techniques; rappelling from buildings, cliffs, and helicopters; use of flash-bang and smoke grenades to cover movement and facilitate entries; physical conditioning; hand-to-hand combat; radio and nonverbal communication procedures in daylight and darkness; quick-kill techniques; antisniper and sniper techniques; small-unit organizational concepts; antiambush procedures; chemical agent use and recognition; cover, camouflage, and concealment use; movement under cover of fire; and small-unit leadership.

Team Characteristics

SWAT teams are characterized by several features that other police units do not possess. Regardless of their size (most teams average twelve members), teams are usually organized into two distinct groups: the assault group, whose function it is to enter and clear structures, and the cover group, whose function it is to cover the assault group and protect team perimeters. SWAT teams have clearly defined chains of command that flow from the team leader directly to the head of the department, thus eliminating intermediate commanding officers whose interference during critical calls could be disastrous. SWAT teams are on twenty-four-hour call and have a clearly defined call-up procedure that automatically goes into effect whenever a department dispatcher receives a potential SWAT call.

Uses

SWAT teams are used in any of five incidents: (1) In hostage-related incidents, although negotiation is the ideal method of resolution, negotiations sometimes break down and the crisis has to be resolved tactically. (2) Sniper situations pose a great threat to innocent civilians and must be resolved quickly and decisively. (3) Barricaded suspects often have to be overcome or arrested in order for public tranquility to return to a neighborhood or commercial area. (4) Sometimes other police units call upon SWAT teams to aid in the arrest of subjects who are heavily armed. Usually a team will have the upper hand in firepower. (5) Teams are usually called upon to provide antisniper protection for dignitaries.

Evolution

Since the advent of transnational terrorism with the massacre of Israeli athletes at the 1972 Olympic games in Munich, major countries have developed special units designed for counterterrorist duties. Great Britain utilizes the SAS (Strategic Air Service), West Germany its GSG-9 (Border Police Unit 9), France the Groupe D'Intervention Gendarmerie Nationale (National Police Intervention Group), and the United States formed its Delta Force.

All of these units are in the most fundamental sense large SWAT teams. They are direct descendants of the Philadelphia Police Department's one-hundred-man unit. They receive similar training, wear the same uniforms, use the same weapons, equipment, and organization, and have similar missions. The only real difference is that they operate on a much larger scale, with a wider jurisdiction.

Most jurisdictions throughout America have formed SWAT teams to handle hazardous situations. Teams with as few as five members function extremely well with adequate training. With the rising concern over domestic terrorism, specially trained units such as SWAT teams have become a vital part of U.S. law enforcement.

PHILLIP A. DAVIDSON

References and Further Reading

Beckwith, Charles A., and David Knox. 1983. *Delta force.* New York: Harcourt Brace Jovanovich.

Cappel, Robert P. 1979. *S.W.A.T. team manual.* Boulder, CO: Paladin Press.

Davidson, Phillip L. 1979. *S.W.A.T.* Springfield, IL: Charles C Thomas.

Jacobs, Jeffrie. 1983. *S.W.A.T. manual.* Boulder, CO: Paladin Press.

Kolman, John A. 1982. *A guide to the development of special weapons and tactics teams.* Springfield, IL: Charles C Thomas.

Miller, Abraham H. 1980. *Terrorism and hostage negotiation.* Boulder, CO: Westview Press.

T

TECHNOLOGY AND POLICE DECISION MAKING

"Technology," defined by *Webster's Collegiate Dictionary* (Ninth Edition) as "a particular means for achieving ends," is a denotative definition, that is, it is glossed as (extended in meaning to) the totality of means employed to provide objects necessary for human sustenance and comfort. Academic definitions range widely (for a daunting list, see Roberts and Grabowsky 1996, 411). The most sensitive of these suggests that technology includes what is seen and visible, as well as the material, logical, and social facets of technology.

In operation, technology requires the cognitive and imaginative work that is required to understand, fix, maintain, and use technology (Roberts and Grabowsky 1996). Organizational "technology," in general, is the means by which work is accomplished within a bounded authoritatively ordered social system defined in a narrow sense. It is a means of converting "raw materials" into "processed outputs." However, what is "raw" and what is "processed" remains complicated when both are the result of human interaction. A narrow definition, like *Webster's,* is inadequate when both raw materials and the means used are interacting persons.

Information technology (IT) is best seen as a means by which "raw data" or "facts" are converted or processed to become information, something that makes a difference in context. When applied to organizational analysis and when implemented with a clear intent and evaluated as to consequence, it is "knowledge." Framing technology as a means avoids the larger question of the values and purposes, the hopes and dreams of those who use it and the connotations of its working. Technology is not just used; it is imagined, and it is therefore always more than is seen.

Each technology competes for space, time, and legitimacy with other known means and is judged in policing by somewhat changing pragmatic, often nontechnical, values: its speed, its durability and weight, and its contribution to the uniformed officers' notion of the essential role and its routines. New equipment is generally introduced without experimentation, clear expectations or standards, or proper repair and maintenance contracts. There is little evidence that thirty years of funding technological innovations have produced much change in police practices or in their effectiveness. Recent developments suggest that informational technology is a new and useful management tool, rather than an effective deployment of resources for environmental impact.

Types of Technology

Six types of technology are seen in police organizations (Manning 2003, 129–33). They are of quite different significance operationally. The most important of these are the last three, the communicative, transformative, and analytic technologies.

The first type of technology is mobility technology, or ways of getting around— motorcycles, cars, trucks, SUVs, boats, bicycles, and horses. These are taken for granted as essential and are assumed to add speed, efficiency, and capacity to the force. The movement from foot patrol to mobile patrol increased the costs of patrolling beyond measure and when linked to computer-aided dispatch fueled the belief that reduced pass-through time increased the quality of policing. The consistent leader in expenditure and maintenance costs for technology is means of mobility. The purpose of mobility technology is to allocate officers to areas, and poise them to respond. The role of material technology in this connection has changed little since the 1930s, except for increases in the speed, number, and types of available vehicles. This cluster of technological advances grew in popularity with the recent emphases on satisfying citizen demand, active presence, and availability.

The second cluster of technologies includes those associated with training— lectures, demonstrations, simulations, and field training. Little is known about the content of police training curricula, and there are no national standards, but the core remains physical and symbolic (shaming, harassing, conditioning, rapid response to orders) and to a lesser degree "academic learning" about the law, diversity and cultures, interpersonal relations, and problem solving. There is some training in specialized weapons and tactics. There is little known about the impact of training. The general consensus of those who have studied training is that little is learned and most forgotten and that officers are systematically instructed to ". . . forget what you learned in the academy." Field training tends to be highly variable, a function of the skills and interests of a senior and respected officer, and produces variable skills in young officers (Fielding 1986).

A third type or cluster is transformative technology. These are devices used to extend human senses and to present evidence in scientific form. They have been vastly improved by the development of forensic sciences and their application in processing criminal evidence. Police cars are often equipped with video cameras, allowing police to capture, in video and audio, their interactions with suspects. Forensic scientists, once restricted to fingerprint evidence and blood typing, are now able to identify individuals by their DNA, or place them at the scenes of crimes using a variety of trace evidence (for example, hair or fiber). The Federal Bureau of Investigation and some states are also creating a DNA bank of known felons convicted of certain crimes. These have enormous potential to extend police power as well as to augment civil liberties of the accused and wrongly convicted. Increasingly, police departments have online data on mug shots, fingerprints, and criminal records.

A fourth type is analytic technology that allows police to aggregate, analyze, model, simulate, and otherwise shape data to facilitate crime mapping, crime analysis, and crime prevention. These are in effect anticipatory technologies, whereas all the others in this list are reactive and ex post facto, or ways to respond after crime has occurred. This growing function has been complemented by crime analysis meetings, visual presentations, hiring crime analysts, and current interest in more data-driven crime control efforts. Collection, storage, and retrieval of data by police, however, do not mean that the data are used for analytic purposes. Perhaps the technology of greatest interest to law enforcement currently is crime mapping, in large part due to its ability to facilitate problem solving and community policing via the identification of repeat calls for service or areas of concern.

Depending on the software used and the skill of the data analysts, crime mapping can be used to identify the locations of crime incidents and repeat calls-for-service, make resource allocation decisions, and evaluate interventions. Where crime mapping is used (typically larger, urban police departments with greater resources), one of the most important innovations has been the crime analysis meeting. In such meetings, data on problems including such things as crimes, gunshots, traffic problems, phone call traffic, arrests, drug problems, and problems of disorder are displayed. In Boston, for example, in monthly meetings, multimedia presentations are used to project maps, pictures, tables, graphs, and animated figures onto a screen while officers present a narrative to an audience of top command and others. A book is created and rehearsal used to polish the presentation. Questions are asked and officers are urged to use the problem-solving SARA model and present results. Districts rotate in their presentations, and sometimes a special presentation such as a recent successful drug raid and seizure is highlighted. In these meetings, a management approach is combined with data and feedback and evaluation to integrate the technological-derived data with practice and accountability.

The final type is communicative technology or information-processing technology used to link units within the department and the public.

Deciding

What is the relationship between these five types of technology and police decision making? An answer to this requires stating the organization's mandate. What does the organization presume its every day–any day activities are about? This cannot be answered by review of formal mission statements, value commitments, general orders, or rules and regulations. The fundamental police concern is to deal immediately with negative uncertain occasions, and to do so with dispatch. They define their overall aim as crime control, but their everyday practices are overwhelmingly responding to citizen-generated demand.

In this sense, the police in Anglo American societies are a democratic, demand-led service, not a form of political or high police concerned with national security. They do not much solve problems, control crime, or produce order: They process demand for service and, incidentally, selectively store, retrieve, and manage data. Ironically, given that the everyday world of policing is banal, policing operates in a crisis mode, that is, with concern for the current matter at hand. Even the top command is frequently overwhelmed with the present, the impending, or the possible crisis. This is often media driven and amplified. Police work is seen as being done on the ground, what can be considered the call-or-incident cynosure (the idea being, what it is I have to do now to clear this call?). Paperwork, abstraction, and long-term planning are anathema. The context of deciding varies in that the "on the ground" view is situational and short term, management and supervision take a retrospective-prospective view of deciding, and top command consider that planning has a role in the immediate deciding done.

Three kinds of deciding (making choices among options within the context of the law) take place in police. The first are "street decisions" made by officers in uniform. The second are detective or investigators' decisions. The third are management or top command decisions concerning policing, resource allocations, organization change and reorganization, as well as promotion to top positions.

Street decisions are the most studied and those most characterized in texts, and they constitute the public face of the organization. They usually are nonviolent, courteous, characterized by compliance on the part of citizens, and reflect citizens' preferences. They are shaped by the number of officers present and features of the situation and the people involved. The reasons for stops and inquiries seem intuitive and in that sense are not "decisions" (these involve weighing, comparing, and contrasting in reference to an imagined outcome). The role of technology, setting aside the technology required to make a mobile response (bicycle, SUV, van sedan), is to shape the options available on the menu if the decision is to be recorded once accepted.

Whether the officer queries the vehicle, record, of other details is typically dependent on whether the officer intends to act further concerning the stop or the answered call. Officers differentially query records and databases, and the more active they are in such enquiries, the more they are active to show results: arrests, stops, tickets (Meehan and Ponder 2004). In this sense, IT in the car, mobile data terminals, cell phones, radios, and even fax machines increase the speed of response, given a decision to intervene. In this sense, Pease argues that IT increases output and has increased impact on the environment.

Since there is no evaluation, little feedback on what is done, and no systematic scrutiny between ends and means, policing, and its shape as an organization, is almost entirely dependent upon the officers in uniform. This presupposition has serious consequence, as other observers

have noted (Goldstein 1960; Reiss 1971) because virtually all of the significant decisions outside investigative work are invisible, nonreviewed, and nonreviewable (see Manning 2003). That is, the decisions made on the ground, where no record is made, cannot be reviewed without a citizen complaint, and if there is a record made, it is a refined, edited, stylistic, and stylized rendition of what was done and why. The interaction between citizen and officer has been studied in several important research reports, but these decisions are shaped almost entirely by the verbal interaction, not other technology. The decision making that goes on between radio call, dispatch, and action is only vaguely known.

In detective work, there is some indication that computers have had an impact on confessions (Harper 1991), and certainly systems of accounting such as HOLMES and major incident formats used in Britain and Canada increase the likelihood of shared information on suspects and classifying and tracking work done, but there is no evidence that this increases clearances or "detection," only that it makes detectives more accountable for the decisions they report to have taken. The most systematic studies of detective deciding, primarily about what to investigate and at what length (Greenwood, Petersilia, and Chaiken 1977; Waegel 1981) suggest that these decisions are made on the basis of hunches, feelings, and the oral culture absent any significant impact of technologies. As Innes (2003) writes, the officers decide the outcome that appears reasonable and assemble evidence, legal scientific, interviews, and observations to support this presumption.

The study of management decisions in policing is restricted. An early study, the work of Hunt and Magenau (1993), describes how management took on three big questions and decided them. The sense of their case studies was the relatively dependent character of the chief's office, given the power of local political groups (both formal and informal), the police unions, and officers in the uniformed division. Chatterton and Hogard (1996) found that as authority to decide was devolved to basic units (subdivisions of the British police), it had negligible impact on operations. Their close study of superintendents in two forces revealed that little money was available for shifting from function to function, that superintendents tended to see their role as dealing with everyday problems directly by phone or in person, much as they did as patrol officers, and that they had no capacity or interest in long-term planning, setting objectives, or evaluating functions.

Thus, although it might be argued that as information passes up the organization, it becomes more abstract, transferable, and generalizable (what might be called knowledge), the mode of deciding remains focused on the incident and response to it. As a result, attempts to require higher degrees, management courses, or advanced education as a prerequisite to promotion has never been actively advocated within the occupation. The absence of a national police training system or a regional or national police college makes the United States unique in the Anglo American police world. The ideology of policing as a here-and-now service job for people trained primarily on the job remains strong, and thus technologies of various kinds are seen as ways to facilitate its practices rather than to alter them.

PETER K. MANNING

See also **COMPSTAT; Computer-Aided Dispatching (CAD) Systems; Computer Technology; Costs of Police Services; Crime Analysis; Crime Mapping; Forensic Investigations; Information within Police Agencies; Intelligence-Led Policing and Organizational Learning; Performance Measurement; SARA, the Model; Technology and Strategic Planning; Technology and the Police**

References and Further Reading

Chatterton, M., and P. Hogard. 1996. *Management at the subdivision (BCU) level*. Unpublished final report to the Home Office, Henry Fielding Center, Manchester University, Manchester, United Kingdom.
Fielding, N. 1986. *Joining forces*. London: Routledge.
Goldstein, J. 1960. Police discretion not to invoke the criminal process. *Yale Law Journal* 69: 543–94.
Greenwood, P., J. Petersilia, and J. Chaiken. 1977. *The criminal investigation process*. Lexington, KY: D. C. Heath.
Harper, R. R. 1991. The computer game. *British Journal of Criminology* 31: 292–307.
Hunt, R., and J. Magenau. 1993. *Power and the police chief*. Thousand Oaks, CA: Sage.
Innes, M. 2003. *Investigating murder*. Oxford: Oxford University Press.
Meehan, A. J., and M. Ponder. 2004. Race profiling. *Police Quarterly*.
Reiss, A. J., Jr. 1971. *The police and the public*. New Haven, CT: Yale University Press.
Roberts, K., and Grabowsky 1996. Organizational technologies. In *Handbook of organizations*, ed. S. Clegg. Thousand Oaks, CA: Sage.
Waegel, W. 1981. Case routinization in investigative police work. *Social Problems* 28: 263–75.

TECHNOLOGY AND STRATEGIC PLANNING

Introduction

Every criminal justice organization needs to occasionally examine its core values and evaluate the process by which it provides the advertised goods and services. Strategic planning provides the tools and steps required to examine the efficiency of an agency's product delivery systems. Both public and private agencies have an obligation to their service population, and without such planning, agencies risk failing to meet the needs of their customers. Therefore, strategic planning is an integral part of modern agencies concerned about fiscal responsibility and adequate service delivery (Haines 2000).

The push toward professionalism and public accountability has led police departments to adopt strategic planning measures and to apply concepts borrowed from the business world. The advent of information technology (IT) provides new opportunities and challenges for police strategic planning. Modern technologies have become indispensable parts of today's police planning process, whether to manage personnel or to anticipate how best to address the crime problems of tomorrow.

Basic Strategic Planning in Policing

Strategic planning holds many benefits for police leaders. It can help an agency to identify and anticipate key trends and issues facing the organization, both currently and in the future. The planning process also explores options, sets directions, and helps stakeholders make appropriate decisions. It facilitates communication among key stakeholders who are involved in the process and keeps organizations focused on outcomes while battling daily crises. Planning can be used to develop performance standards to measure an agency's efforts. Finally, and most important, it helps leaders to facilitate and manage change (Glensor and Peak 2005). Table 1 illustrates some strategic planning steps and the required actions.

The need for IT in strategic planning becomes even more acute where the organization has adopted and is practicing the community-oriented policing and problem solving (COPPS) strategy. For example, under COPPS, the organization necessarily needs to maximize communication with and obtain feedback from the citizenry. Some technology applications for these purposes can be quite simplistic, such as issuing cellular telephones to officers and publishing officers' telephone numbers. Or, on a higher plane, the agency might consider the development of a website. A web page can solicit input from the community concerning

Table 1 Strategic planning steps and required actions

Strategic Planning Step	Proposed Action/Questions
Identify concerned stakeholders	Invite city officials, police personnel, nonsworn staff, workers from other city agencies, and members of the public for their input and ask them to be part of the planning process.
Assess the current situation	How are things working? Are people satisfied with the agency? Are workers happy? Is the output satisfactory?
Define organizational needs	What are the short-term and long-term goals of the agency? Are there future goals that need to be anticipated?
Review procedures	How are things currently done? Are the systems in place efficient? Are there alternative methods?
Develop a plan	Incorporate needs analysis, available resources, and ideas from stakeholders into a viable and logical plan of action to help fulfill the agency's mission.
Implement the plan	Implement measures and ensure that they are carried out according to the proposed plan.
Evaluate outcomes	Were desired results achieved due to the new plan? Were the goals and objectives met? Is the agency prepared to meet future challenges?

- Criminal events or neighborhood problems
- Perceptions of the department over-all as well as of individual officer contacts
- Programs or activities that citizens would like to see implemented

Such information can be very helpful for strategically planning the agency's future. In addition, such areas as the agency's history, mission, vision, values, and philosophy/methods under COPPS can be presented and explained in this website.

IT thus can assist the organization in meeting its goals and objectives. The chief executive must ensure, however, that all personnel are aware of these technologies and are knowledgeable in terms of their use. To merge strategic planning and IT, then, law enforcement chief executives must do the following:

- Recognize that the agency should first prepare a strategic plan that articulates the organization's overall mission, goals, and objectives.
- Recognize the mission-critical role of technology in policing and de-velop a vision for IT and its role in the agency, keeping in mind that the strategic IT vision directly supports the mission, goals, and objectives of the agency.
- Create a systematic process for con-tinual planning, maintenance, and support of information systems. The use of IT for strategic planning is not a one-time effort and requires a cyclical process for planning, pro-curing, implementing, and managing IT.
- Develop a strategic IT vision docu-ment. This document will articulate how technology will assist the agency in meeting its core mission and estab-lish an ongoing process to evaluate, upgrade, and enhance those technol-ogies as agency goals and technology change.

Police Strategic Planning and Technology

The Office of Community Oriented Policing Services (COPS), created by the Crime Con-trol Act Of 1994, was largely responsible for bringing police departments up to date in terms of IT. "Under the MORE (Making Officer Redeployment Effective) program, the OCOPS delivered more than $1.3 bil-lion to nearly 4,500 police departments for the acquisition and implementation of IT systems" (Dunworth 2005, 7). This increase in IT has helped police organizations meet their objectives by integrating technolog-ical advances into the strategic planning process.

As noted above, it is extremely impor-tant for law enforcement organizations to engage in strategic planning. Just as im-portant, however, is the need for the chief executives to understand how IT can assist in strategic planning, as well as the kinds of technologies that are available for this undertaking. Technological improvements can now provide crucial information for strategic planning. As examples, com-puter-aided dispatching (CAD) now has the ability to supply real-time statistical in-formation, do screen mapping, prepare alarm bills and warnings, and issue and store various permits; records management systems (RMSs) now analyze crime statis-tics and maintain files related to people, vehicles, prisoners, and officer activities. Other technologies have been developed more recently and can provide a much bet-ter picture of the situation being examined and related long-term planning efforts.

Strategic Planning and Crime Reduction Applications

Strategic planning that involves preventive efforts or addressing specific, recurring problems can also benefit by employing IT. A few examples are as follows:

- *Crime prevention.* COPPS and IT can assist with strategic planning for crime prevention through its crime analysis function, by looking at means for denying offenders the opportunity to act in the first place. Using the SARA process, analysts can *scan* for crime problems, *analyze* the nature of criminal activity, *respond* by allocating the necessary police resources to thwart offenders, and *assess* by performing periodic evaluations to determine effectiveness (Helms 2002).

- *Mapping criminal events.* Computerized crime mapping combines geographic information from global positioning satellites with crime statistics gathered by the department's CAD system and demographic data. The result is a picture that combines disparate sets of data for a whole new perspective on crime. For example, a map of crimes can be overlaid with maps or layers of causative data: unemployment rates in the areas of high crime, locations of abandoned houses, population density, reports of drug activity, or geographic features (such as alleys, canals, or open fields) that might be contributing factors (Rogers 1997; Pilant 1997).

- *Accident investigation.* Some police agencies have begun using a global positioning system to determine such details as vehicle location and damage, elevation, grade, radii of curves, and critical speed. A transmitter takes a series of "shots" to gain the exact location and measurements of accident details such as skid marks, area of impact, and debris; that information is then downloaded into the system and the coordinates are plotted out onto an aerial shot of the intersection or roadway. Using computer technology, the details are then superimposed onto the aerial shot, thus re-creating the accident scene to scale. Finally, digital photos of the accident are incorporated into the final product, resulting in a highly accurate depiction of the accident (Bath 2003).

- *Gang intelligence systems.* Police now use their laptop computers and cellular phones to assist in solving gang-related crimes. Some states now have an intranet-linked software package that connects sites throughout the state. It is essentially a clearinghouse for information about individual gang members, the places they frequent or live, and the cars they drive. Within a few minutes, a police officer in the field can be linked to the net, type in information, and wait for matches (Dussault 1998).

- *Personnel and deployment applications.* Police departments need to deploy personnel efficiently. This can be achieved using different technological tools. For example, computerized personnel databases can identify officers with unusual sick time, or those who accumulate numerous public complaints. The biggest application of IT in terms of strategic planning involves patrol allocation. Using geographic mapping software, police officials can now calculate the crime problem at the beat level and allocate resources based on need within very small boundaries. This differs greatly from the traditional division of a city into four geographic quadrants or from the static beat allocation that often remains identical for many years, regardless of the changing crime problems.

EMMANUEL P. BARTHE and
KENNETH J. PEAK

See also **Administration of Police Agencies, Theories of; Attitudes toward the Police: Measurement Issues; Changing Demographics in Policing; Community-Oriented Policing: Effects and Impacts; Police**

Standards and Training Commissions; SARA, the Model

References and Further Reading

Bath, Alison. 2003. Accident scene investigation is high tech. *Reno Gazette Journal,* November 18, 4.

Dunworth, T. 2005. Information technology and the criminal justice system: An historical overview. In *Information technology and the criminal justice system,* ed. A. Pattavina, 3–28. Thousand Oaks, CA: Sage.

Dussault, R. 1998. GangNet: A new tool in the war on gangs. *Government Technology* (January): 34–35.

Glensor, R. W., and K. J. Peak. 2005. *Strategic IT planning. Issues in IT: A reader for the busy police chief executive.* Washington, DC: Police Executive Research Forum.

Haines, Stephen G. 2000. *The systems thinking approach to strategic planning and management.* Boca Raton, FL: CRC Press.

Helms, D. 2002. Closing the barn door: Police counterterrorism after 9/11 from the analyst's perspective. *Crime Mapping News (Police Foundation Newsletter)* 4: 1–5.

Pilant, L. 1997. Computerized crime mapping. *The Police Chief* (Dec.): 58.

Rogers, D. 1999. Getting crime analysis on the map. *Law Enforcement Technology* (Nov.): 76–79.

TECHNOLOGY AND THE POLICE

Security and Civil Liberties in the Twenty-First Century

We live in a time of rapid social change, being driven by technology. Consequently, policing is becoming increasingly difficult as the technologies driving change become more sophisticated and society becomes more dependent upon them. Criminals, too, are relying more on technology, increasing criminal opportunities and threatening civil liberties. Many scientists and technology observers suggest that the rate of technologically induced change is accelerating, compounding the problems facing law enforcement at a time when global terrorism and criminal networks are expanding. At the same time, surveillance cameras, radio frequency identification (RFID) devices, and computers are getting smaller, cheaper, and more powerful, while enormous commercial databases containing information on millions of citizens are proliferating. All of this is reducing personal privacy and fueling a growing anxiety among civil libertarians that we are moving closer to Orwell's *1984.*

Indeed, as the curve of technological advancement climbs exponentially and technology becomes cheaper, smaller, and more capable, it also becomes more usable and widely available to the average person and the average police department. As we move farther along the curve of advancement, new technology will give an increasing number of people the ability to do things that were once confined to large corporations and the military. There are, of course, tremendous benefits to society and the world as a result of this advancement. Technology drives economic prosperity, increases standards of living, and provides us with new and more powerful tools to mitigate or eliminate the death and destruction attributable to human-made and natural disasters.

Technology can also be used in a variety of ways that range from annoying to genocidal. From inexpensive microsurveillance cameras to Internet-accessible satellite imagery, citizens within our communities will have increasing capabilities to spy on their neighbors, take advantage of the weak, or in many other ways cause harm to others. Of even more concern are those individuals and groups bent on destruction and illegal gain, whose power to harm not just individuals but whole communities and nations accelerates along with the technological tools that aid them in their pursuits.

The first decade of the twenty-first century has shown there are many potential criminal and terrorist uses of technology.

Discussion of chemical and biological hazards, backpack nuclear devices and dirty bombs, and airline and border security are an everyday part of public discussion in the years since the attacks on the World Trade Center and the Pentagon of September 11, 2001. New books and movies depicting humanoid robots and genetically engineered dinosaurs running amok fuel growing public concern about technology getting into the wrong hands, increasing demands for government regulation and control of technology. But while the public lives in fear of another terror attack, with the Department of Homeland Security's terror alert system periodically changing between yellow, orange, and red, there appears to be even more concern with police misuse of surveillance technology and the growing body of private data on citizens available to law enforcement from open and private sources.

Programs to improve the ability of law enforcement to track criminals and terrorists through the sharing of information and the mining of large databases, such as the ill-fated Defense Advanced Research Projects Agency (DARPA) Total Information Awareness (TIA) project and Florida's Multistate Anti-Terrorism Information Exchange (MATRIX) program, have suffered tremendous criticism from civil liberties groups and subsequent cutbacks, or outright cancellation, at the hands of policy makers. If these trends continue, law enforcement will be forced to fight the information age wars on crime and terror armed with industrial age tools.

The public's trepidation regarding police use of technology to address law enforcement and homeland security challenges, now and in the future, is not completely without merit, and the issue remains highly controversial. For example, the use of facial recognition technology to search the faces of stadium-goers at the 2001 Super Bowl in Tampa, Florida, in an effort to identify and apprehend criminals and terrorists faced strong public criticism to this emerging technology, notwithstanding significant homeland security concerns. A similar problem was faced by the Transportation Safety Administration (TSA) in developing and deploying new technology for airline safety that attempts to positively identify air travelers. Even after the 9/11 attacks, the enhanced Computer-Assisted Passenger Prescreening System (CAPPS II) ran up against enormous hostility from a wide range of civil liberties groups and media outlets, eventually forcing the Department of Homeland Security to shelve the project.

As with technological advancement itself, however, police use of new technology is likely inevitable despite the concerns of privacy advocates. Billions of dollars continue to be invested in everything from digital statewide communication systems, computer networks, helicopters, and crime labs at the local, state, and federal levels to weapons of mass destruction (WMD) protective equipment and individual lethal and less-than-lethal weapons for officers on the street. New technologies, particularly those derived from military programs that have applicability to homeland security, are being marketed and sold to police agencies for their role in the war on terror.

But exactly how the wide range of existing and constantly emerging technologies will be used by the police, to what extent, and how efficient and effective their applications will be at stopping crime and terrorism remains to be seen. Clearly, there are important considerations regarding citizen privacy and the erosion of civil liberties. Just as clear, however, is the need to improve law enforcement operations to prevent the seriously destabilizing events such as 9/11 that create social turmoil and increase conflict within our world. Advanced and powerful technology will play a large role in achieving that improvement.

Crimes such as identity theft have severe impacts on the economy and erode faith in a nation's financial institutions. Terrorist events such as 9/11 create fear and paranoia that leads to demands for increased security and more restrictive government policies. Small acts of terror, such as a pair of snipers randomly shooting innocent people, paralyzing an entire region of the country, can be socially and economically destabilizing. The mere perception of terror is terror, and it can have devastating and widespread effects on citizens, their nations, and the global economy. Powerful new technologies in the hands of those willing to prey on the weak and helpless for profit or whose principal desire in life is to destroy others of different faiths and cultures makes police use of similarly powerful technology to identify, apprehend, prosecute, and incarcerate these social predators a necessity.

Effective use of technology that simultaneously improves police operations and upholds constitutional liberties may be one of the biggest challenges confronting police departments in the twenty-first century. History shows us that police use of new technology is often fraught with missteps and oversteps, but despite the abuses there are few alternatives to choose from that will better provide both security and protection of civil liberties for all people. Military and corporate security involvement in domestic law enforcement operations has been growing for several decades, precisely due to their technological resources and expertise, but their organizational missions and individual training do not necessarily involve protecting the rights of citizens in the performance of their duties. Soldiers are trained and equipped to win battles in combat, and private security guards are accountable to those who pay them. Police officers within the public sector are the only group with the clear mandate and comprehensive training to protect life and property within the bounds of the Constitution. While the public police will always have some need for military and corporate assistance, it remains the essential role of public police officers to protect all people, regardless of social or economic status, while preserving their freedoms.

To achieve both of these goals—effective law enforcement and the preservation of liberty—in a rapidly changing world, it is essential that the public police take the necessary steps to thoroughly understand technology and all of its implications. The public police need to be able to efficiently procure components, integrate them into comprehensive systems, and then maintain and constantly upgrade those systems while developing the operational policies, procedures, and protocols for effective and appropriate utilization by its members. This will require that police have a completely new appreciation of technology—how it affects society, their organization, and their mission.

First, the common practice within policing is to buy and implement new technology to accomplish traditional duties better or faster or more efficiently than in the past. This has been evident during the past ten years as police departments implement modern IT networks, transitioning their manual paper files directly to a digital facsimile. The power of modern IT systems is not found in their ability to store and retrieve the digital representations of paper reports. In fact, there is little benefit in terms of administrative efficiency and cost effectiveness in replicating paper processes in a digital format. The benefit of today's IT systems is that they allow organizations to do things that have never before been possible. Computer networks and relational databases allow agencies to gather, store, and instantaneously link what was once disparate data locked in metal file cabinets on paper reports and available only through intensive and time-consuming manual inspection. Similarly, shared wireless networks today allow both voice and data communication between multiple agencies and across jurisdictional boundaries. More than a simple patch between two adjoining radio networks or a few officers talking on interoperability channels at a crisis, shared digital networks give all officers the ability to communicate with the right people to acquire the right information to accomplish their mission and solve problems whenever and wherever they need it.

Second, modern technology and technological systems that are effective and easy to use in the real world are extremely complex and difficult to implement. And the complexity will continue to grow in the coming years. Technology is more than computers, radios, software, and hardware that are installed, turned on, and applied to solve a problem. Technologies are being interwoven into very sophisticated and intricate networks, systems of systems specifically tailored to meet a wide variety of requirements within the highly unique circumstances of individual organizations. Slight variations in the way a technology, or a component of the technology, is implemented or used can have a profound impact on the overall result.

It is therefore important that the education and training of everyone involved with technology for law enforcement purposes, from procurement, installation, and maintenance to its utilization on the street, have the necessary knowledge to do so effectively. As technologies and systems proliferate within and between agencies, the training time required to maintain proficiency and ensure effective utilization must also increase. Police chiefs and senior administrators will have to be able to articulate the importance of new technology and the need for additional training to budget offices and policy makers.

Complex technology and an increasingly technical society require police who are capable of using that technology safely, effectively, and wisely. Less-than-lethal weapons are only such when the officers using those weapons are fully trained in their use and have the judgment and restraint to use them safely. This has implications for the entry-level educational requirements, hiring practices, basic training, and continuing professional education programs of police agencies. A high school education will not be adequate preparation for the intellectual challenges facing twenty-first century police officers, and police departments should be placing a strong emphasis on locating, attracting, and hiring college graduates. To retain those educated officers and accomplish the goals necessary for information age success, the traditional recruit training academy that focuses on the obedience, conformance, and military-style discipline still popular with many agencies today must be transitioned to an educational atmosphere that develops creative, analytical thinkers who can readily adapt to rapidly changing circumstances and who are committed to life-long learning.

Lastly, police leaders need to re-create the culture of their organizations for the networked digital world within which they will operate. Accelerating changes driven by exponentially advancing technologies will directly impact crime, terrorism, and homeland security as well as the law enforcement tools and methodologies to deal with them. Emerging technologies such as augmented and virtual reality, unmanned aerial vehicles, artificial intelligence, robots, RFID chips, and "smart dust" will be commonplace and ubiquitous, turning our communities into intelligent environments where everything and everyone is connected. To be effective in the future networked world, police departments need to consider new methods of organization and operation.

Net-centric operations are becoming the focus of many corporations, the military services, and today's global terrorist organizations. These "edge organizations" are characterized by the empowerment of those individuals near the edges of the organization who perform the services and actions necessary to fulfill its mission. Empowerment comes from a streamlined hierarchical structure, decentralized decision making, and dramatic increases in available information made possible by information technology. Empowerment at the edge fosters a bottom-up self-synchronization created by enhanced peer-to-peer interactions that improve situational and organizational awareness. The real-time flow of information to whoever needs it, whenever they need it means that the actions of all individuals serve the same goals, even as those goals are constantly changing. To be effective against tomorrow's fluid and rapidly evolving criminal and terrorist networks, police agencies cannot continue to rely on the structures, policies, and methodologies developed for industries and bureaucracies of decades past.

Creating police organizations that are capable of operating effectively across the spectrum of present and emerging circumstances and situations, against the information age thugs of the twenty-first century, will take visionary leaders who can transform their organizations and build trust and confidence between police officers and the citizens they serve. Those leaders will have to develop strong police–community bonds in order to overcome the growing suspicions the public has concerning police use of technology. Lacking that public trust, it will be impossible for tomorrow's police agencies to acquire and utilize the advanced technologies that will be necessary to provide public safety and security. That same strong leadership will also be essential to ensuring that new technologies are implemented and used correctly by administrators and officers on the street, in ways that protect civil liberties while improving police effectiveness.

Today's and tomorrow's police officers should understand that technology is not a silver bullet and that it is not the most important aspect of policing in the future. On the contrary, it is the police officers, police administrators, and police chiefs who are the most important component of twenty-first-century policing. Our ability to anticipate, manage, and adapt to the increasing presence and impact of technology within society will be a critical determiner of policing success in the future. Police officers who can anticipate and plan for potential social impacts of technology and then create positive applications that mitigate the negative outcomes of those impacts could have a significant effect in reducing conflict and unrest within our communities.

The new capabilities offered by continuously emerging technology can be tailored in any number of ways to accomplish police objectives, some good and some bad. Every technology can be used by people for good or for bad purposes, depending on their levels of knowledge and their levels of ethics. Every technology can be used by police in ways that either enhance safety and freedom or detract from them. Every technology has problems and shortcomings that must be carefully considered and planned for. Strengths can be maximized and weaknesses minimized with careful planning and thorough systems integration, keeping the protection of civil liberties at the top of the list of law enforcement criteria for success. Success in the future will depend on how well the police understand technology, especially the implications of using it within a free society, and how hard they strive to use it within the context of freedom and liberty.

Tom Cowper

See also **Accountability; Airport Safety and Security; Computer Crimes; Computer Forensics; Computer Technology; Constitutional Rights: Privacy; Crime Analysis; Future of Policing in the United States; Homeland Security and Law Enforcement; Identity Theft; Information Security; Information within Police Agencies; Intelligence-Led Policing and Organizational Learning; Militarization of the Police; Research and Development; Strategic Planning; Surveillance; Technology and Police Decision Making; Technology and Strategic Planning; Terrorism: Police Functions Associated with; Video Technology in Policing**

References and Further Reading

Alberts, David S., and Richard E. Hayes. 2003. *Power to the edge: Command and control in the information age.* Washington, DC: CCRP.

Brin, David. 1998. *The transparent society: Will technology force us to choose between privacy and freedom?* New York: Perseus.

Buerger, Michael. 2000. Reenvisioning police, reinvigorating policing: A response to Thomas Cowper. *Police Quarterly* 3 (4) (Dec.): 451–64.

———. 2004. Educating and training the future police officer. *FBI Law Enforcement Bulletin* (January): 26–32.

Cato Institute. 2002. *Security and freedom in a free society.* Cato Policy Report XXIV (5) (Sep./Oct.): Washington, DC: Cato Institute.

Garfinkel, Simson. 2000. *Database nation: The death of privacy in the twenty-first century.* Sebastopol, CA: O'Reilly.

Kurzweil, Raymond. 1999. *The age of spiritual machines: When computers exceed human intelligence.* New York: Viking.

National Research Council, Computer Science and Telecommunications Board. 2002. *Cybersecurity today and tomorrow.* Washington, DC: National Academy Press.

National Science and Technology Council, Subcommittee on Disaster Reduction. 2003. *Reducing disaster vulnerability through science and technology.* http://sdr.gov/SDR_Report_ReducingDisasterVulnerability2003.pdf (July 2003).

TECHNOLOGY, RECORDS MANAGEMENT SYSTEMS, AND CALLS FOR SERVICE

Technology in Law Enforcement

Technology can generally be described as a tool with a purpose. In the twenty-first century, when we use the term, we generally mean an automated or mechanically driven tool. There are many technologies used in law enforcement, including information technology such as records management systems, communication systems such as radios and computer-aided dispatch systems, evidence-based technologies such as DNA, digital photography, closed-circuit television, less-than-lethal force devices, and geographic technologies such as mapping software, global positioning systems, and automated vehicle locator systems.

Information Technology in Law Enforcement

While there are numerous technologies used in law enforcement, perhaps the most readily used are the technologies that transmit, store, sort, compile, and maintain information. While communications technology is used for receiving calls for service, gathering descriptive information from the caller, dispatching police units to the scene, and gathering detailed information about the incidents from the officers themselves, information technology (IT) in policing allows police to recall stored information and use information for daily operations and responsibilities as well as for problem solving, protecting community and officer safety, and providing detailed information to supervisors.

Records Management Systems

A records management system (RMS), the primary IT system in law enforcement, is an automated system that provides the framework for entering, storing, retrieving, viewing, and analyzing all records, including incident reports, calls-for-service data, personnel data, criminal investigations, and related information. According to Harris and Romesburg (2001), twenty-first-century RMSs go beyond the collection and storage of information by offering robust analytical tools, seamless sharing of information, and complex linkages between different data sources. As such, RMS technology serves as a key component of effective decision making.

Data Inputs and Outputs

Information contained within an RMS is input from officers, call takers, investigators, the personnel office, supervisors, and others connected to daily law enforcement functions in the agency. Once stored, the information can be retrieved, analyzed, and archived (see, for example, Boyd 2001; Dunworth 2000). In turn, various types of information can be made available to agency users, other justice agencies, and the public, where appropriate. Information can be provided to users via various reports and downloads of automated data to other software programs.

Components and Uses of RMSs

The goal of an RMS is to provide a single source for integration of all key law enforcement data in order to improve efficiency and effectiveness of operations. There are numerous components and/or modules in an RMS. These include arrest, booking, case management, citations, collisions and related diagrams, complainant demographics, dispatch records, equipment records, evidence, field interviews, field reporting, global positioning system (GPS) integration, investigations, name indexes, National Incident-Based Reporting System (NIBRS), offender information, pawn, personnel, photos, property lists, sex offender information, training, Uniform Crime Reports (UCR), use of force, victim information, warrants, and more. Often this information is integrated with other existing systems such as computer-aided dispatch (CAD) records, mapping software, case management software, an early warning system, a report writing software package, and more.

A recent national survey supported by the U.S. Department of Justice, Office of Community Oriented Policing Services (COPS), was conducted by Amendola (forthcoming). The survey was conducted with all agencies having a hundred or more sworn personnel and a sample of all smaller agencies. The vast majority reported having an RMS (more than 87%), and 66% had purchased the RMS as part of an integrated CAD and RMS system. This likely represents the need for fully integrated communication, record keeping, and analysis systems in order to minimize the need for multiple interfaces. Still, many RMSs can interface with other criminal justice system databases at the local, state, and national levels. For example, many can link to the National Crime Information Center (NCIC), Automated Fingerprint Identification System (AFIS), and other sources.

Use of RMSs in U.S. Law Enforcement Agencies

Law enforcement agencies vary significantly in the types, amounts, and sources of their information, and therefore the functions and uses of RMSs also vary widely. Some use the RMS for simple data storage, retrieval, and reporting (for example, to assist with the COMPSTAT process), while others use it to aid in complex analysis and decision making, such as in crime analysis, strategic planning, personnel management and supervision, and community policing strategies.

Among the uses reported in the COPS survey, the majority of agencies use the RMS for crime/incident analysis (68%) as well as crime prevention (56%). A number of agencies were also using the RMS for strategic planning (48%), community policing (46%), and mapping (45%), but they reported using it to a much lesser extent for COMPSTAT (29%), personnel/human resources management (26%), and as an early warning system (less than 7%) (Amendola, forthcoming).

Challenges of IT Acquisition and Implementation

The successful design, acquisition, and implementation of complex IT such as an RMS can be very costly and take many months or years to achieve. Indeed, the COPS survey revealed that more than 30% of the chiefs/sheriffs responding said that the total cost of the RMS was more than the originally contracted price. Furthermore, while 22% of agencies implemented their RMSs in less than six months, 35% took up to a year, 28% took between one and two years, and 15% took two to three years or more.

Because the acquisition and implementation of an RMS is so complex, it is essential that such a project be carefully planned. Indeed, chiefs, sheriffs, and IT managers surveyed felt that project management was the most important factor to successful implementation of an RMS and that lack of planning was the thing that most hindered implementation (Amendola, forthcoming). Without proper planning and project management, agencies run the risk of acquiring a system that does not meet its needs and may need to be modified at least or completely redesigned or discarded altogether at worst. All of these prospects are extremely costly in budget dollars and human resources.

The challenge of rapid changes in IT can lead to a number of problems for organizations. In 1994, the Standish Group conducted a survey of 365 IT managers from small, medium, and large organizations across multiple industries (banking, manufacturing, retail, health care, insurance, and government). They also conducted focus groups and numerous personal interviews to provide a qualitative context for the survey results. A successful project was defined as one that was completed on time, on budget, and with the features and functions originally specified. A challenged project was defined as one that was completed and operational but over budget, over original time estimates, and offering fewer features and functions than originally specified. Finally, an impaired project was one that was canceled in the development cycle. Surprisingly, just 16% of projects were successful, 53% were impaired, and fully 31% were canceled due to impairment (Standish Group 1995). Of the challenged or impaired projects, the average cost overrun was 189% of the original cost!

A nationwide survey of a thousand IT managers from various types of organizations (manufacturing, government, education, computer services, insurance, health care, and so forth) provided evidence for nine distinct categories of problems emerging from rapid technological changes. These problems included IT vendor issues, acquisition and support difficulties, technological problems, and organizational problems. The researchers Benamanti and Lederer (2000) defined these as follows:

1. *Vendor neglect.* Vendors lack knowledge and experience with the products being sold, as well as having limited ability to assist in the integration of their products with those of other vendors.
2. *Vendor oversell.* Vendors release products that are unstable and show excessive enthusiasm for the products being sold.
3. *Acquisition dilemma.* Agencies have difficulty keeping up with the various products available and the differences between them and thus making the right choice for their departments.
4. *Support burden.* Agencies lack the structure or expertise to adequately support the system or enforce standards.
5. *Resistance.* Agencies are unable to use IT to its full extent due to lack of a unified understanding of the new IT product.

6. *Cascading needs.* There is an unexpected need for additional IT to fully meet requirements not met in the acquired technology.

7. *New integration.* Agencies have difficulty in maintaining the interfaces across various technologies, especially when vendor support and expertise are insufficient.

8. *Error.* There are explainable and unexplainable failures of the new IT to perform as expected, often arising out of early release of unstable products or lack of sufficient documentation.

9. *Training demands.* Agencies have a need for a wider variety of knowledge and extensive training, especially problematic when turnover of staff is frequent.

Other IT challenges include incompatible hardware and software, widely dispersed data and information throughout an agency, unreliable data sources, poor security systems, and inconsistent interfaces between divergent systems. As a result, it is extremely important that an agency focuses on the planning and project management stages of acquisition and implementation in order to avoid significant problems and challenges after acquisition or implementation.

There are a number of information sources available to guide agencies in acquiring appropriate technology, including the International Association of Chiefs of Police best practices guide entitled "Acquisition of New Technology" (Deck 2000), *A Guide for Applying Information Technology in Law Enforcement* (Boyd 2001), and the Office of Community Oriented Policing Services' *Law Enforcement Tech Guide* (Harris and Romesburg 2001).

KAREN L. AMENDOLA

See also **Calls for Service; COMPSTAT; Computer-Aided Dispatching (CAD) Systems; Computer Technology; Crime Mapping; Dispatch and Communications Centers; Early Warning Systems; Office of Community-Oriented Police Services, U.S. Department of Justice; Technology and Police Decision Making; Technology and Strategic Planning; Technology and the Police**

References and Further Reading

Amendola, K. L. Forthcoming. *Supporting acquisition and implementation of records management systems for community policing: Results of the national survey.* Washington, DC: U.S. Department of Justice, Office of Community Oriented Policing Services.

Boyd, D. G. 2001. *A guide for applying information technology in law enforcement.* NCJ 185934. Washington, DC: U.S. Department of Justice, National Institute of Justice, Office of Science and Technology.

Deck, E. F. 2000. Acquisition of new technology: A best practices guide. In *Big ideas for smaller police departments* 1 (1) (Spring), 1–14. International Association of Chiefs of Police.

Dunworth, T. 2000. Criminal justice and the IT revolution. In *Policies, processes, and decisions of the criminal justice system: Criminal justice 2000,* Vol. 3, 371–426. NCJ 182410. Washington, DC: U.S. Department of Justice, National Institute of Justice.

Foster, R. E. 2005. *Police technology.* Upper Saddle River, NJ: Pearson/Prentice-Hall.

Harris, K. J., and W. H. Romesburg. 2001. *Law enforcement tech guide: How to plan, purchase and manage technology (successfully!).* Sacramento, CA: SEARCH Group, Inc. Supported by U.S. Department of Justice, Office of Community Oriented Policing Services (#2001-CK-WX-K064).

Standish Group, International. 1995. *The chaos report (1994).* http://www.standishgroup.com/sample_research/chaos_1994_1.php.

TELEVISION IMAGES OF POLICING

From the very beginning, the oxygen that has given life to the Rodney King story is television. (Alter 1992, 43)

Nearly fifteen years have passed since the now-infamous "Holliday videotape" was aired across the country, but the images captured on that sixty-eight second video clip still resonate in the public's mind. California highway troopers attempted to stop Rodney King's vehicle for excessive speed, and when he failed to stop, the troopers requested assistance. By the time King stopped his vehicle, at least twenty-three officers had responded. The situation escalated quickly as the officers struggled to subdue him. George Holliday began videotaping when the situation had peaked: Despite being hit twice with Taser darts, King continued to resist. The videotape then captures several of the officers beating King with their batons, pausing, and then beating him again. Estimates of the number of times King was hit and kicked vary, ranging from twenty-three to fifty-six (see Schlief 2005), but the impact of the video was significant: It took an incident that would have been ignored and made it a celebrated news event. Several police officers were charged in state and then federal court, the Los Angeles Police Department was forced to investigate and reconsider its use-of-force policy, many other police departments across the country were forced to investigate police brutality accusations, and the city of Los Angeles and its citizens had to recover from two days of rioting following the acquittal of the officers of state charges.

This incident illustrates the challenges of policing in a television age. The public relies heavily on television for news and entertainment. Most national studies indicate that almost all households have at least one television set, and, on average, it is on for eight hours a day (Macionis 1997). Half of all Americans state that television is their primary source of news (Roper Center 1999). Since most people have only sporadic direct interactions with the police, what the public thinks about police officers is influenced by news and entertainment images. Television is a powerful vehicle through which a police department can communicate its goals, justify how it responds to crime, and request public involvement or assistance in solving open cases.

Although there are opportunities for police departments to capitalize on the power of television, there are great risks. Accusations of police misconduct, case investigation errors, and high-profile cases put incredible pressure on police departments to be prepared to respond via the media when such situations arise. This article first discusses the strategies police departments use to influence how they are presented in the news and then describes the images presented about policing on television.

The Relationship between Television and Police Organizations

Research indicates that crime is an important news topic and that media organizations tend to emphasize the beginning stages of the criminal justice system (Chermak 1995; Surette 1998). Crime incidents, police investigations, and arrests account for approximately half of all crime stories presented. Television news organizations will present, on average, between three and five crime stories in a newscast but also must be prepared for breaking disasters and celebrated crime events. News organizations have developed various strategies in order to produce crime stories efficiently. Perhaps the most significant strategy is a reliance on police departments for reports and information about crime incidents.

Police are available and can comment about an event immediately after it is discovered. These sources are publicly accepted as credible voices on crime, underscoring the media's authority and protecting their image as an objective conveyor of the important events of the day (Chibnall 1977; Ericson, Baranek, and Chan 1989). Existing research compares the frequency that police are cited as news sources to the citation of other criminal justice officials, government sources, victims, and defendants. For example,

Sherizen (1978, 220) reported that police sources accounted for more than 34% of the sources cited, and another study reported the police as the primary source of story information when compared to other criminal justice sources (Ericson, Baranek, and Chan 1991). A third study indicated that police are the dominant sources in all types of crime stories (incidents, policy stories, program stories, and statistical stories) and that when law enforcement sources are cited, individuals from the top levels of the police hierarchy provide more than one-fourth of the information (Chermak 1995).

Police departments invest considerable time and effort in order to be prepared to respond to reporters. Police departments usually provide space to reporters within headquarters so that reporters can easily access records, reports, and official sources. Most large-sized police departments have full-time, trained public information spokespersons to respond directly to questions from reporters (Chermak and Weiss 2003). Public information officers (PIOs) attempt to maximize the positive and minimize the negative images depicted about police organizations in the news. There have been a few studies examining the responsibilities of PIOs, providing general background on their role in the construction of a police department's image (Chermak and Weiss 2003; Lovall 2001; Skolnick and McCoy 1985; Surette and Richard 1995). Skolnick and McCoy (1985) illustrate how PIOs package information in a way that increases the likelihood that the media will cover the department in a positive way. Another study, by Surette and Richard (1995, 329), described the public information officers as "daily troubleshooters and first contact points" between the police and the media.

Police departments certainly respect the power of the media and have made significant organizational changes to take advantage of this resource to communicate their preferred meanings of events. Based on the scholarly understanding of the nature of the police–media relationship, one would expect that police departments are presented favorably on television. The next section addresses this question.

Television Images of Policing

The public is bombarded with images of crime and policing in news and entertainment programs on television. The long-running popularity of police dramas, such as *Dragnet, Hill Street Blues, Law and Order, NYPD Blue,* and the *CSI* shows, demonstrates the public's consistent fascination with police work. Research examining the representation of police on television dramas stresses that the police are depicted stereotypically (Maguire, Sandage, and Weatherby 1999): Police officers are shown as being effective (most cases are solved in the allotted time frame), intelligent, honest, and dedicated (Maguire 1988).

The presentation of policing in television dramas coexists with the constant bombardment of policing images in crime news stories. Most crime stories focus on specific crime incidents, with an emphasis on the circumstances of the crime and the characteristics of the victim and the defendant. Police departments are critical to the creation of these stories because they provide the incident and arrest reports to construct these stories. Although crime fighting is only a small part of the work police officers do, this part of their job is emphasized in the news. Police are thus presented as first responders to crime activity, conducting investigations to increase public safety.

Moreover, the police are able to use media interest in their activities to their advantage by attempting to accomplish investigation goals. For example, police departments request help from citizens to solve unsolved cases. In many jurisdictions, police departments have partnered directly with the media to fulfill crime fighting objectives in "Crimestoppers" programming. These media segments are collaborative efforts involving the public, the police, and the media (Rosenbaum, Lurigio, and Lavrakas 1987; Skolnick and McCoy 1985). Police departments have formalized the media's role in fighting crime by having them reenact unsolved crimes to generate additional leads and information. An evaluation of these programs indicates that (1) they were highly visible and well received by media executives, (2) they were successful (these segments resulted in 92,000 felony arrests, 20,000 convictions, and the recovery of stolen property valued at more than $500 million), and (3) they increased citizen awareness of anticrime efforts (Rosenbaum, Lurigio, and Lavrakas 1987, 54).

Maguire, Sandage, and Weatherby (1999) conclude that most television stories present the police in a positive way and that police are typically presented as crime fighters, although coverage varies by size of the media market examined. Television news stations are rarely critical of police departments and tend to emphasize accomplishments and ignore mistakes. Policing innovations, such as the implementation of a new program or a new strategy, are also frequently presented on television.

Conclusion

Although the general presentation of policing on television is positive, there are exceptions to this general pattern. Indeed, police departments are constantly under the microscope because of high-profile incidents such as the one discussed at the beginning of the article. When crimes go unsolved, when crime rates soar, and when officers are involved in a corruption scandal or deadly force incident, news media will relentlessly present the details, and police departments will be forced to

respond to the crisis by making personnel changes, adopting new policies, and changing tactics. The rare event tends to be sensationalized in the news. The end result is that the media presents and the public consumes conflicting images of policing on television.

STEVEN CHERMAK

See also **Accountability; Attitudes toward the Police: Overview; Community Attitudes toward the Police; Community Watch Programs; Crimestoppers; Media Images of Policing; Media Relations**

References and Further Reading

Alter, Jonathan. 1992. TV and the firebell. *Newsweek* 119: 43.

Chermak, Steven. 1995. *Victims in the news: Crime in American news media.* Boulder, CO: Westview Press.

Chermak, Steven, and Alexander Weiss. 2003. *Marketing community policing in the news: A missed opportunity?* Research in Brief, National Institute of Justice. Washington DC: U.S. Department of Justice.

Chibnall, Steven. 1977. *Law and order news.* London: Tavistock.

Ericson, Richard V., Patricia M. Baranek, and Janet B. L. Chan. 1991. *Representing order: Crime, law, and justice in the news media.* Toronto: University of Toronto Press.

———. 1989. *Negotiating control: A study of news sources.* Toronto: University of Toronto Press.

Lovall, Jarrett S. 2001. "Police performances": Media power and impression management in contemporary policing. Ph.D. diss. New Brunswick, NJ: Rutgers, The State University of New Jersey.

Macionis, John J. 1997. *Sociology.* Upper Saddle River, NJ: Prentice-Hall.

Maguire, Brendan. 1988. Image vs. reality: An analysis of prime-time television crime and police programs. *Journal of Crime and Justice* 11: 165–88.

Maguire, Brendan, Diane Sandage, and Georgie Ann Weatherby. 1999. Television news coverage of the police: An exploratory study from a small town locale. *Journal of Contemporary Criminal Justice* 15: 171–90.

Roper Center. 1999. *News interest index poll.* Storrs, CT: Princeton Survey Research Association.

Rosenbaum, Dennis P., Arthur J. Lurigio, and Paul Lavrakas. 1987. *Crimestoppers:*

A national evaluation of program operations and effects. Washington, DC: National Institute of Justice, U.S. Department of Justice.

Schlief, Stacy. 2005. Rodney King beating trial: Landmark for reform. In *Famous American crimes and trials,* ed. Bailey and Chermak, 143–64. Westport, CT: Praeger.

Sherizen, Sanford. 1978. Social creation of crime news: All the news fitted to print. In *Deviance and mass media,* ed. Winick, 203–24. Beverly Hills, CA: Sage.

Skolnick, Jerome H., and Candace McCoy. 1985. Police accountability and the media. *American Bar Foundation Journal* 3: 521–57.

Surette, Ray. 1998. *Media, crime, and criminal justice: Images and realities.* Belmont, CA: West /Wadsworth.

Surette, Ray, and Alfredo Richard. 1995. Public information officers: A descriptive study of crime news gatekeepers. *Journal of Criminal Justice* 23: 325–36.

TERRORISM: DEFINITIONAL PROBLEMS

The definitional problems associated with terrorism must first be addressed by looking at the etymology of the terms associated with terrorism—words such as terrorize, terrorist, freedom, guerilla, insurgent, and insurrection—and how often those terms are incorrectly interchanged in the media, causing confusion and misunderstanding. The *Oxford English Dictionary* (1933) offers the following definitions:

Freedom. Exemption or release from slavery or imprisonment; personal liberty. Exemption from arbitrary, despotic, or autocratic control; civil liberty. Independence: The state of being able to act without hindrance or restraint; liberty of action; the quality of being free from the control of fate or necessity; the power of self-determination attributed to the will.

Guerilla. 1. An irregular war carried on by small bodies of men acting independently. 2. One engaged in such warfare.

Insurgent. Rising in active revolt—One who rises in revolt against constituted authority; a rebel who is not recognized as a belligerent.

Insurrection. The action of rising in arms or open resistance against established authority or government restraint; with plural, an instance of this, an armed rising, a revolt: an incipient or limited rebellion.

Terrorist. 1. As a political term applied to the Jacobins and their agents and partisans in the French Revolution (1790–1795), especially to those connected with the Revolutionary tribunals during the 'Reign of Terror'. . . . 3. b. Anyone who attempts to further his views by a system of coercive intimidation; specifically applied to members of one of the extreme revolutionary societies in Russia.

Terrorize. To fill or inspire with terror, reduce to a state of terror; especially to coerce or deter by terror.

"Terrorism" has a pejorative connotation, and its meaning changes within social, political, religious, and historical contexts (White 2003, 4). The use of such words will also depend upon an individual's perception, whether that of victim or perpetrator. The difficulty of defining terrorism has been acknowledged by many (Poland 2005; Crank and Gregor 2005; White 2003; Combs 2003; Hoffman 1998).

A uniform definition of terrorism often will not exist across the various law enforcement agencies of a given country. This is the case in the United States, where a range of definitions is currently applied:

U.S. Department of Defense (2003): "The calculated use of unlawful violence to inculcate fear, intended to coerce or to intimidate governments or societies in the pursuit of goals that are generally political, religious, or ideological."

Federal Bureau of Investigation (1999): "[T]he unlawful use of force and violence against persons or property to intimidate or coerce a government, the civilian population, or any segment thereof, in furtherance of political or social objectives."

U.S. State Department (2003): "[P] remeditated, politically motivated violence perpetrated against noncombatant targets by sub-national groups or clandestine agents, usually intended to influence an audience." This document further states that "For purposes of this definition, the term 'noncombatant' is interpreted to include, in addition to civilians, military personnel who at the time of the incident are unarmed and/or not on duty."

These definitions identify three inter-related factors: first, the terrorist's identity, second, the methods employed, and third, motivation. (Other definitions also include the legitimacy of the action.) It is those factors that influence a workable definition and a construct that differentiates terrorism from everyday criminality.

In the global fight against terrorism there is talk of the "war" against terrorism. If war is "the continuation of political intercourse with the addition of other means" (Von Clausewitz 1989, 605), it may be argued that terrorism is also a continuation of political intercourse where violence is fueled not only by its practitioners' political motivations but also by ethnicity, cultural diversity, and religious parameters.

"Terrorism, in the most widely accepted contemporary usage of the term, is fundamentally and inherently political" (Hoffman 1998, 14). However, as with many definitional characteristics of terrorism, this view of it as always being political is not universally accepted. Nor is motivation always considered a factor in deciding what is and is not terrorism.

Eqbal Ahmad (2003, 46–53) argued that motivations "make no difference"; this position was acknowledged by Jessica Stern (1999), who further argued that any

definition of terrorism had to be unconstrained by either "perpetrator or purpose." This approach does not exclude or limit political goals as a terrorist aim but allows for other motivations, nationalistic, religious, or criminal. Stern identifies that the "deliberate evocation of dread is what sets terrorism apart from simple murder or assault" (Stern 1999, 11).

Political motivation is often identified as a prerequisite of terrorism, but criminal activity underpins many terrorist organizations. As Paul Pillar (2001, 13–14) states, "Terrorism is fundamentally different from these other forms of violence, however, in what gives rise to it and in how it must be countered, beyond simple physical security and police techniques. Terrorists' concerns are macro-concerns about changing a larger order; other violent criminals are focused on the micro-level of pecuniary gain and personal relationships. 'Political' in this regard encompasses not just traditional left–right politics but also what are frequently described as religious motivations or social issues."

While it may be argued that terrorism can be identified as political violence, all political violence cannot be regarded as terrorism. It is argued that war is a form of political violence, but one that is differentiated from terrorist action due to the rules of war contained within the Geneva Conventions (Kingshott 2003). This trend is partly connected to the tendency to label certain acts of political violence as terrorism on the basis of their perpetrators' identities. The connection between terrorism and political goals is related to the perceived illegitimacy of political violence. A Western-style democracy is considered to provide an alternative to violence as an agent of political change, with the state viewed as sole custodian of the monopoly of legitimate force. In this argument political violence *against* the state is more apt to be termed "terrorism" than is political violence *on the part of* the state.

However, this is not universally accepted to be the case. Totalitarian regimes such as those that once existed in Nazi Germany, Fascist Italy, and Stalinist Russia, as well as, more recently, the military dictatorships that previously ruled some South American countries and emerging African nations all used oppressive measures that can be described as state-sponsored terrorism. The literature identifies state sponsors of terrorism to include, but not limited to, Iran, Iraq, Libya, Syria, and North Korea.

Hoffman (1998, 25) contends that "such usages are generally termed 'terror' in order to distinguish that phenomenon from 'terrorism,' which is understood to be violence committed by non-state entities." Mark Burgess (2004) argues that "such a state-centric reading is Western in outlook, and would probably be questioned by those non-state actors who regard themselves as politically disenfranchised." The term "terrorism" may bestow illegitimacy on individuals or groups acting for a cause; it can also confer legitimacy on the governments combating it and their methods.

It should be acknowledged that culture, ethnicity, and religious upbringing may engender either sympathy or disapproval for a cause, for a regime, or for counterterrorism methods and strategies. The individual's perception can therefore lead to inconsistency in deciding what is and is not terrorism, epitomized in the oft used phrase "One man's terrorist is another man's freedom fighter." As a consequence of such reasoning, what might be viewed as terrorism by the Western democratic states may be regarded as legitimate protest when it happens in states found in less politically stable regions of the world and that do not embrace the philosophy of a liberal Western democracy.

Hoffman (1998, 42–43) argues that a debatable assertion is that "to qualify as terrorism, violence must be perpetrated by some organizational entity with at least some conspiratorial structure and identifiable chain of command beyond a single individual acting on his or her own."

That being so, then arguably an individual, if politically motivated and using the methods of terrorists, should also be called a terrorist. Pillar argues (2001, 43) that unless such an approach is adopted, the politically motivated acts of individuals such as Mir Aimal Kansi (who killed two CIA employees outside the organization's headquarters in 1993) and Sirhan Sirhan (who assassinated Senator Robert Kennedy in 1968) would be classed as criminal rather than terrorist (Hoffman 1998, 42). (The Sirhan case is representative of the difficulty in considering such instances of individuals carrying out such acts as "lone wolves," albeit that the actions are underpinned with political motivations.)

The academic consensus definition argued by Schmid (1983, 107–9) states

> Terrorism is an anxiety-inspiring method of repeated violent action, employed by (semi-) clandestine individual, group, or state actors, for idiosyncratic, criminal, or political reasons, whereby—in contrast to assassination—the direct targets of violence are not the main targets. The immediate human victims of violence are generally chosen randomly (targets of opportunity) or selectively (representative or symbolic targets) from a target population, and serve as message generators. Threat- and violence-based communication processes between terrorist (organization), (imperiled) victims, and main targets are used to manipulate the main target (audience(s)), turning it into a target of terror, a target of demands, or a target of attention, depending on whether intimidation, coercion, or propaganda is primarily sought.

Another definition from an Islamic perspective is that terrorism "is an act carried out to achieve an inhuman and corrupt ("mufsid") objective, and involving threat to security of any kind, and violation of rights acknowledged by religion and mankind" (Taskhiri 1987). Further explanation is given as to what is not considered acts of terrorism and that includes, but is not limited to, the following (Taskhiri 1987):

1. Acts of national resistance exercised against occupying forces, colonizers, and usurpers
2. Resistance of peoples against cliques imposed on them by the force of arms
3. Rejection of dictatorships and other forms of despotism and efforts to undermine their institutions
4. Resistance against racial discrimination and attacks on the latter's strongholds
5. Retaliation against any aggression if there is no other alternative

Terrorism, from an Islamic perspective, was defined as follows (Taskhiri 1987):

1. Acts of piracy on land, air, and sea
2. All colonialist operations, including wars and military expeditions
3. All dictatorial acts against peoples and all forms of protection of dictatorships, not to mention their imposition on nations
4. All military methods contrary to human practice, such as the use of chemical weapons, the shelling of civilian-populated areas, the blowing up of homes, the displacement of civilians, and so forth
5. All types of pollution of geographical, cultural, and informational environment; indeed, intellectual terrorism may be one of the most dangerous types of terrorism
6. All moves that undermine or adversely affect the condition of international or national economy, adversely affect the condition of the poor and the deprived, deepen up nations with the shackles of socioeconomic gaps, and chain up nations with the shackles of exorbitant debts
7. All conspiratorial acts aimed at crushing the determination of nations for liberation and independence and imposing disgraceful pacts on them

The difficulty of finding a definition that addresses issues of cultural, ethnic, and religious perceptions that is not couched in inflammatory rhetoric is problematic because "Even if there were an objective, value-free definition of terrorism, covering all its important aspects and features, it would still be rejected by some for ideological reasons . . ." (Laqueur 1987, 149–50).

It would appear that finding a definitive definition for terrorism acceptable to all is impossible due to differing cultures, religions, and global diversity. A definition is only sought for the purposes of international law, so that an individual may be correctly identified and tried for an act that is defined across cultures and criminal justice systems as a terrorist act.

BRIAN F. KINGSHOTT

See also **Terrorism: Domestic; Terrorism: International; Terrorism: Overview; Terrorism: Police Functions Associated with**

References and Further Reading

Ahmad, Eqbal. 2003. Terrorism: Theirs and ours. In *Terrorism and counterterrorism: Understanding the new security environment,* ed. Russell D. Howard and Reid L. Sawyer, 46–53. Guilford, CT: McGraw-Hill/ Dushkin.

Burgess, Mark. 2003. *Terrorism: The problems of definition.* Washington, DC: Center for Defense Information.

Combs, Cindy C. 2003. *Terrorism in the 21st century.* Upper Saddle River, NJ.: Prentice-Hall.

Crank, John P., and Patricia E. Gregor. 2005. *Counter terrorism after 9/11.* Cincinnati, OH: LexisNexis.

Evan, William M., ed. 2005. *War and peace in an age of terrorism.* Boston: Pearson/Allyn and Bacon.

Federal Bureau of Investigation, Counterterrorism Threat Assessment and Warning Unit, National Security Division. 1999. *Terrorism in the United States 1999: 30 years of terrorism—A special retrospective edition.* Washington, DC: U.S. Department of Justice. http://www.fbi.gov/publications/terror/terror99.pdf.

Hoffman, Bruce. 1998. *Inside terrorism.* New York: Columbia University Press.

Kingshott, Brian. 2003. Terrorism: The "new" religious war. *Criminal Justice Studies* 16 (1): 15–27.

Laqueur, Walter. 1987. *The age of terrorism.* Boston: Little, Brown and Company.

Oxford English Dictionary. 1933. Oxford: Clarendon Press.

Pillar, Paul R. 2001. *Terrorism and U.S. foreign policy.* Washington, DC: Brookings Institution Press.

Poland, James M. 2005. *Understanding terrorism.* Upper Saddle River, NJ: Pearson/Prentice-Hall.

Schmid, Alex. 1983. *Political terrorism.* Cincinnati, OH: Transaction Books Anderson Press.

Snowden, Lynne L., and Bradley C. Whitsel. 2005. *Terrorism—Research readings and realities.* Upper Saddle River, NJ: Pearson/Prentice-Hall.

Stern, Jessica. 1999. *The ultimate terrorists.* Cambridge, MA: Harvard University Press.

Taskhiri, Ayatullah Shaykh Muhammad Ali, Director of the International Relations Department, I.P.O. 1987. International Conference on Terrorism called by the Organization of the Islamic Conference, Geneva, June 22–26.

U.S. Department of Defense, Office of Joint Chiefs of Staff. 2003. *Joint Publication 1-02: Department of Defense Dictionary of Military and Associated Terms,* April 12, 2001, and amended through June 5, 2003, 531. Washington, DC: U.S. Department of Defense. http://www.dtic.mil/doctrine/jel/new_pubs/jp1_02.pdf.

U.S. State Department, Office of the Coordinator for Counterterrorism. 2003. *Patterns of global terrorism 2002.* U.S. Department of State Publication 11038, April, 13. Washington, DC: U. S. State Department. http://www.state.gov/documents/organization/20177.pdf.

Von Clausewitz, Carl. 1989. *On war,* ed. and trans. Michael Howard and Peter Paret, 605. Princeton, NJ: Princeton University Press.

White, Jonathan R. 2003. *Terrorism.* 4th ed, 4. Belmont, CA: Wadsworth/Thompson.

TERRORISM: DOMESTIC

Many Americans believe that domestic terrorism is a new crime. However, domestic terrorism has existed since humans first organized themselves into groups or tribes. Individuals and small groups within existing groups engaged in acts of violence against other members of the group with the limited purpose of overthrowing existing leaders, to scare away competing interests, or to frighten opposing groups from lands they wished to occupy.

Modern terrorism as we know it began around the 1960s. It is characterized by the use of technology to achieve its mission. Some controversy surrounds the definition of domestic terrorism. The United State Code of Federal Regulations defines it as ". . . the unlawful use of force and violence against persons or property to intimidate or coerce a government, the civilian population, or any segment thereof, in furtherance of political or social objectives" (28 CFR 85). The Federal Bureau of Investigation expands this definition by further classifying terrorism as either domestic or international. The FBI defines domestic terrorism as the unlawful use, or threatened use, of force or violence by a group or individual based and operating entirely within the United States or its territories without foreign direction committed against persons or property to intimidate or coerce a government, the civilian population, or any segment thereof, in furtherance of political or social objectives.

The FBI further divides domestic terrorism into three separate categories: terrorist incident, suspected terrorist incident, or terrorism prevention. A terrorist incident is a violent act that is dangerous to human life, in violation of the criminal codes in the United States that is used to intimate or coerce a government, the civilian population, or any segment thereof, in furtherance of political or social objectives. A suspected terrorist incident is a potential act of terrorism that cannot be traced to a known or suspected group. Terrorist prevention is a known instance where a violent act by a terrorist group or individual was successfully prevented by means of investigative activities.

Terrorist Groups or Organizations

Domestic terrorist groups generally fall within one of three orientations: right wing, left wing, or special interest. These groups focus on issues affecting American political or social activities. Their acts are directed at the U.S. government or its agents or the U.S. population or groups of that population.

Right-wing terrorist groups often believe in the principles of racial supremacy and denounce government and government regulations. Many right-wing groups engage in activity such as marches and assemblies that are protected by the First Amendment to the U.S. Constitution. It is when they cross the line between peaceful protests to violent acts that they become terrorist organizations. Formal right-wing hate groups such as the World Church of the Creator and the Aryan Nation represent examples of continuing domestic terrorist organizations.

During the late 1990s, patriotic and militia groups came to the nation's attention with their antigovernment, racial supremacy stance and conspiracy-oriented thinking. These groups reacted to gun control legislation and fears of a United Nations involvement in domestic affairs. These groups represent a serious threat to law enforcement since their members engage in paramilitary training, stockpile weapons, and espouse hatred of the federal government and law enforcement.

Right-wing terrorist groups also engage in what is known as paper terrorism. They file bogus legal actions against law enforcement officers, local governments, members of the judiciary, and other citizens. Local governments incur expense in defending these lawsuits, costing the taxpayers funds that could have been spent on other projects.

Left-wing terrorist groups embrace a revolutionary socialist philosophy and view themselves as protectors of the people. Their goal is to bring about drastic change in the United States, and they believe this change must occur by revolution rather than through the established political process. These groups were very popular and active in the 1960s through the 1980s, but their activities have declined since that time.

Special interest terrorist groups are different from either left- or right-wing terrorist groups. They seek to influence specific issues rather than bring about widespread political change. These groups engage in acts of violence to force segments of society to change their attitudes about specific issues such as the environment, abortion issues, animal rights, and other movements. Reporting of these incidents is sometimes lacking since some of their activities, such as incidents against doctors who perform abortions, may be reported as hate crimes rather than terrorism.

One of the most serious special interest domestic terrorist groups involves ecoterrorism. According to the FBI, these groups commit acts of violence, motivated by a concern for animals or the environment. It is estimated that these groups have committed more than a thousand criminal acts that have caused in excess of $110 million in damage since 1976.

Acts of Domestic Terrorism

Acts of domestic terrorism in America have caused death, destruction, and untold suffering. Some of the best known and most controversial incidents include Theodore Kaczynski, the "Unabomber"; Eric Rudolph, the Atlanta Olympics bomber; and Timothy McVeigh and Terry Nichols, the Oklahoma City bombers.

There is some controversy as to whether Kaczynski, the infamous Unabomber, was a domestic terrorist or simply a common criminal. Because many of his acts fit into the profile of domestic terrorism, it is appropriate to discuss the case.

Kaczynski graduated from Harvard University in 1962 and earned a master's degree and a Ph.D. in mathematics at the University of Michigan. His last involvement as an instructor was as an assistant professor in mathematics at the prestigious University of California at Berkley. In 1969, he resigned without giving any reason and moved to a remote shack outside Lincoln, Montana.

On May 25, 1978, the Unabomber began his reign of terror. Over the next eighteen years, he mailed or placed sixteen bombs that killed three people and injured twenty-nine others. He sent his first bomb to the University of Illinois Chicago Circle campus. He followed up with bombs at other universities and to business executives. He sent bombs to Northwestern University, Vanderbilt University, the University of California at Berkley, University of Michigan, and Yale University. He also sent bombs to airline executives, computer store owners, the president of the Forestry Association, and others.

In 1995, Kaczynski sent a demand that his 35,000-word paper entitled "Industrial Society and Its Future" be published by a major newspaper. He threatened to kill more victims unless his demands were met. On September 19, 1995, the *New York Times* and the *Washington Post* published his pamphlet. The article, commonly referred to as the "Unabomber Manifesto," argued that technological progress was undesirable and must be stopped. His brother recognized Kaczynski's writing style and alerted the authorities. Kaczynski was arrested on April 3, 1996.

On May 4, 1998, Kaczynski was sentenced to four life terms without the possibility of parole. He claimed that the government was trying to portray him as a common criminal when in fact, he stated, he was a principled technowarrior who was attempting to save society from technology. However, his personal diaries revealed that many of his acts were simply based on revenge.

Unlike Kaczynski, Eric Robert Rudolph's acts were those of a domestic terrorist. Rudolph was charged with the 1998 health center bombing, a 1997 bombing at an Atlanta health clinic, a bombing at a gay lifestyle nightclub, and the 1996 bombing at the Atlanta Centennial Olympic Park, where thousands of visitors had gathered during the 1996 Summer Olympics.

On July 27, 1996, a bomb was placed near a stage in the Atlanta Centennial Olympic Park, injuring more than a hundred people and killing one person. The second bombing occurred in January 1997, when two bombs went off at a family planning service. The bomb injured more than fifty persons. The third bomb occurred one month later at the Otherside Lounge, which Rudolph believed encouraged gay lifestyles. A fourth bombing occurred in January 1998 at another women's health clinic in Birmingham, Alabama.

On October 14, 1998, the federal government filed charges against Eric Rudolph for all four bombings. At the time of the filing of the criminal complaint and issuance of an arrest warrant, Rudolph's location was unknown. He was thought to be hiding in the hills of western North Carolina, where he eluded capture for more than five years despite a reward of $1 million being offered and despite his being on the FBI's Ten Most Wanted Fugitives list. He was finally arrested in May 2003, when he was seen looking for food near a grocery store trash bid in Murphy, North Carolina.

Rudolph was thought to believe in a white supremacist religion that was anti-abortion, antigay, and anti-Semitic. He pleaded guilty to all four bombings in order to avoid the death penalty and was sentenced to four concurrent life sentences without the possibility of parole.

Perhaps the most famous case of domestic terrorism involved Timothy McVeigh and his accomplish, Terry Nichols, who committed the Oklahoma City bombing. On April 19, 1995, a truck loaded with high explosives was detonated in front of the Alfred P. Murrah Federal Building.

The explosion occurred at 9:02 a.m., during the start of a regular business day, and killed 168 men, women, and children. Hundreds more were injured during this attack. Authorities believe that approximately five thousand pounds of improvised explosive arrived in the back of a rented Ryder truck. McVeigh walked away from the truck after igniting a time fuse in the front of the truck.

McVeigh was arrested approximately one hour after the explosion when an Oklahoma highway patrolman pulled him over for driving a car without a license plate. Prosecutors argued at McVeigh's trial that the attack was to avenge the deaths of the Branch Davidians who died during a siege near Waco, Texas. McVeigh believed that the Branch Davidians had been murdered by agents of the federal government. The attack occurred on the second anniversary of the Waco incident.

McVeigh was a Gulf War veteran and called the casualties in the bombing collateral damage. He served in the war and was awarded the Bronze Star. A copy of a white supremacist novel, *The Turner Diaries,* was found with McVeigh when he was arrested. *The Turner Diaries* was written by Dr. William Pierce, the founder of the white supremacist organization known as the National Alliance. Pierce used the pen name of Andrew Macdonald when he published the novel. McVeigh was convicted and sentenced to death for his acts. Nichols, his accomplice, was sentenced to life in prison.

While the above offenders are well-known terrorists, there are other not so well known but very serious domestic terrorists who have committed terrorist acts within the United States. These terrorists include William J. Krar and his possession of components that would have made a weapon of mass destruction and ecoterrorists in Utah and other states.

Starting in spring 2003, Krar began gathering large amounts of chemicals that could be used to produce cyanide gas, an extremely dangerous deadly gas. Krar was alleged to have ties with white supremacist groups in the United States. Krar was discovered when he sent a package to a fellow militia member in New Jersey. Fortunately, the package was delivered to the wrong address and when opened contained several phony documents, including U.N. and Pentagon ID cards. The recipient of the package turned it over to the authorities, and they traced it back to Krar. Upon searching Krar's house and storage facility, law enforcement officers discovered compounds necessary to make cyanide gas, illegal machine guns, boxes filled with approximately five hundred thousand rounds of ammunition, homemade bombs, bomb making instructions, and antidotes for nerve agents. The amount of chemicals that Krar possessed was sufficient to produce enough cyanide gas to kill everyone in a small town civic center or in a large retail store.

There were also mysterious papers that indicated plans for a cover operation. These papers included code words for meeting places in nine cities and instructions on how to throw law enforcement off the trail. There were also information on white supremacy and other antigovernment literature.

This was not the first run-in that Krar had with law enforcement. In 1985, Krar was arrested for impersonating a law enforcement officer. In 1989, he quit paying federal income taxes, and in the 1990s he was investigated by federal law enforcement officers for his ties to white supremacist and antigovernment militia groups. In June 2001, firefighters responding to a fire at a New Hampshire storage building found thousands of rounds of ammunition and four guns. Several of these weapons belonged to Krar.

As a result of Krar's arrest in November 2003, he pleaded guilty to one count of possessing a dangerous chemical weapon and faces a maximum sentence of life in prison. Krar continues to refuse to cooperate with the authorities regarding any targets he was considering.

Ecoterrorism has caused a tremendous amount of property damage. During 2004, in Utah, two men, Justus Ireland and Joshua Demmitt, pleaded guilty to acts of domestic terrorism. Ireland admitted to starting a fire at a lumber company that caused $1.5 million in damage and spraying "ELF" (Earth Liberation Front) at the site. The Earth Liberation Front has been connected to dozens of acts of property damage and vandalism in the United States since 1996. Demmitt pleaded guilty to starting a fire at a farm that was part of Brigham Young University. This farm was the site where animal experiments were conducted.

Responses to Domestic Terrorism

Responses to domestic terrorism include federal laws and plans to respond to acts of terrorism. In 1995, President Clinton issued an executive order that contained the U.S. Policy on Counterterrorism. This directive required interagency cooperation to combat both domestic and international terrorism. Congress enacted and President Clinton signed the 1996 Anti-Terrorist Act, which gave federal authorities $1 billion to combat terrorism. The act creates a federal death penalty for terrorist murders. Congress also has passed the Uniting and Strengthening America by Providing Appropriate Tools Required to Intercept and Obstruct Terrorism (USA PATRIOT) Act of 2001. This act was enacted forty-five days after the September 11, 2001, terrorist attack on the World Trade Center in New York and on the Pentagon. While the act was a reaction to international terrorism, many of its provisions also apply to domestic terrorism.

Conclusion

Domestic terrorism is not a new phenomenon. It has existed for centuries. What is new is its impact on American society. While there are differences regarding its definition, all authorities agree that it is a danger to the stability of our society. While most news stories focus on international terrorism, there have been several incidents of very serious domestic terrorism within the past several years. We must continue to monitor, intervene, and prevent further acts of domestic terrorism.

SHIHO YAMAMOTO and HARVEY WALLACE

See also **PATRIOT Acts I and II; Terrorism: Definitional Problems; Terrorism: Overview; Terrorism: Police Functions Associated with**

References and Further Reading

Bergesen, Albert J., and Yi Ham. 2005. New directions for terrorism research. *International Journal of Comparative Sociology* 133 (February–April): 46.

Federal Bureau of Investigation. 1999. *Terrorism in the United States 1999*. Washington, DC: U.S. Department of Justice.

Journal of Environmental Health. 2005. Department of Homeland Security's national response plan. 60 (April): 67.

Merari, Ariel. 2002. Deterring fear: Government responses to terrorist attacks. *Harvard International Review* 26 (Winter): 23.

Riley, Kevin Jack, and Bruce Hoffman. 1995. *Domestic terrorism: A national assessment of state and local preparedness*. Santa Monica, CA: RAND Corporation.

Schuster, Henry. 2005. *Domestic terror: Who's most dangerous?* http://www.cnn.com/2005 (August 24, 2005).

Vohryzek-Bolden, Miki, Gayle Olson-Raymer, and Jeffery O. Whamond. 2001. *Domestic terrorism and incident management: Issues and tactics*. Springfield, OH: Charles C Thomas.

TERRORISM: INTERNATIONAL

The term "terrorism" emerged in the aftermath of the French Revolution and was used to describe aggressive methods (arrests and executions) employed by the Jacobins against opponents and "enemies of state" in 1793–1794. Yet, the phenomena it is commonly meant to describe are centuries old. Politically motivated violence was not always regarded as negative or undesirable. Political offenders were initially considered as the "aristocrats of delinquency" by dint of their noble motives, altruism, and self-sacrifice. Tyrannicide (the killing of a tyrant) was not simply excused; it was a duty for classical Athenian citizens in order to protect their democracy, whereas in modern times, the doctrine of political offenders has been the reason for refusing requests for the extradition of wanted persons.

In recent years, the previous regime of lenience toward politically motivated offenders gave way to a regime of severity. International agreements and conventions increasingly included clauses doing away with the exception of political offense in matters of mutual legal assistance.

The term "terrorist" is neither scientific nor objective, but polemical. It is a contested label one seeks to attach to an adversary. Consequently, there is no universally accepted definition in law or academic circles. The winner in certain conflicts is a hero, while the loser is branded a terrorist. Definitions are ephemeral because the balance of power may shift. Algerian "terrorists" fighting French colonialism became legitimate governors. African National Congress leader Nelson Mandela spent decades behind bars before he became a remarkable head of state and Nobel Prize winner, guiding his country from apartheid to a process of reconciliation. In the Middle East, definitional battles between Palestinians and Israelis are ongoing, as they are between the United States and Cuba. The same occurs in areas of conflict in Asia, Africa, and the Americas.

Most controversies revolve around the legitimacy and identity of perpetrators (state and nonstate actors), the means employed (violence, threats, psychological, economic, military, or other), the victims (civilians, military, state representatives),

how direct or indirect the involvement is, the ultimate objective, and the wider context (war, civil war, foreign occupation, peacetime hostilities). It is often difficult to distinguish terrorism from related concepts, such as low-intensity warfare, genocide, banditry, subversion, insurgency, guerilla, paramilitarism, rebellion, aggression, war crimes, crimes against humanity, resistance, liberation war. Not coincidentally, adversaries occasionally use the metaphors of war and armies in support of claims to legitimacy: Irish Republican Army, Japanese Red Army, Red Army Faction, Islamic Army for the Liberation of Holy Places, Albanian National Army, Army of the Righteous and Pure (Lashkar-e-Tayyiba, Pakistan), People's Liberation Army (EPL, Peru), United Self-Defense Forces of Colombia (AUC), Sudan People's Liberation Army, and so forth. The following definitions illustrate the range of approaches at the U.S. and international legal levels as well as from scholarly perspectives. According to Title 22 of the United States Code, Section 2656f(d), "The term "terrorism" means premeditated, politically motivated violence perpetrated against noncombatant targets by subnational groups or clandestine agents, usually intended to influence an audience. The term 'international terrorism' means terrorism involving the territory or the citizens of more than one country." According to 18 USC 2331 (2000), the term "international terrorism" means activities that

1. Involve violent acts or acts dangerous to human life that are a violation of the criminal laws of the United States or of any state, or that would be a criminal violation if committed within the jurisdiction of the United States or of any state

2. Appear to be intended (i) to intimidate or coerce a civilian population; (ii) to influence the policy of a government by intimidation or coercion; or (iii) to affect the conduct of

a government by mass destruction, assassination, or kidnapping

3. Occur primarily outside the territorial jurisdiction of the United States, or transcend national boundaries in terms of the means by which they are accomplished, the persons they appear intended to intimidate or coerce, or the locale in which their perpetrators operate or seek asylum

The United Nations 1999 International Convention for the Suppression of the Financing of Terrorism covers financial support for any "act which constitutes an offence within the scope of and as defined in one of the treaties listed in the annex" (nine of the universal instruments against terrorism—see below) and any act "intended to cause death or serious bodily injury to a civilian, or to any other person not taking an active part in the hostilities in a situation of armed conflict, when the purpose of such act, by its nature or context, is to intimidate a population, or to compel a government or an international organization to do or to abstain from doing any act" (Article 2).

The RAND and MIPT terrorism knowledge chronology define terrorism by

... the nature of the act, not by the identity of the perpetrators or the nature of the cause. Terrorism is violence, or the threat of violence, calculated to create an atmosphere of fear and alarm. These acts are designed to coerce others into actions they would not otherwise undertake, or refrain from actions they desired to take. All terrorist acts are crimes. Many would also be violation of the rules of war if a state of war existed. This violence or threat of violence is generally directed against civilian targets. The motives of all terrorists are political, and terrorist actions are generally carried out in a way that will achieve maximum publicity.... Finally, terrorist acts are intended to produce effects beyond the immediate physical damage of the cause, having long-term psychological repercussions on a particular target audience. The fear created by terrorists may be intended to cause people to exaggerate the strengths of the terrorist and the importance of the cause, to provoke governmental overreaction, to discourage dissent, or simply to intimidate and thereby enforce compliance with their demands.

Whereas "domestic terrorism" is defined as "incidents perpetrated by local nationals against a purely domestic target," "international terrorism" refers to "incidents in which terrorists go abroad to strike their targets, select domestic targets associated with a foreign state, or create an international incident by attacking airline passengers, personnel or equipment."

None of the above definitions resolves all problems or satisfies all audiences. Some cases may be both domestic and international terrorism, for example, as in cases where a domestic group or government agency receives nonstate or state support from another jurisdiction.

International Actors and Causes

Mere listing of groups or organizations falling under the above definitions would require scores of pages, as shown by the long lists of designated terrorist individuals and groups maintained by U.S. agencies (for example, the Departments of State and Treasury), the United Nations, or the European Union.

Terrorism is usually associated with the activity of small groups, especially when state actors are not directly involved. Some groups enjoy more popularity or legitimacy than others, but the number of active participants is typically low (for example, Red Brigades in Italy or 17 of November in Greece), with the exception of widely supported insurgency, nationalist, and liberation types of movements (for example, PLO, IRA, Iraq insurgents). In general, the most radical and extreme groups can be expected to be more violent and least followed by the societal groups they may claim to represent. Sometimes, they are splinter groups of larger legitimate or illegal organizations.

In some instances, government agencies directly or indirectly support and sponsor terrorist groups (for example, the support of Hizbullah by Iran, the Pan Am plane bombing by Libya, Kashmir extremists by Pakistan, Islamic Jihad by Syria, or the Nicaraguan Contras by the United States). In other cases, governmental actors may engage in acts covered by some of the above definitions themselves (for example, French bombing of Greenpeace vessel or U.S. mining of Nicaraguan civilian ports— in the first case, the head of French intelligence was fired, while the World Court condemned the latter).

The varieties of international terrorist groups transcend the categories of left-wing, right-wing, and special interest causes of domestic terrorism. Even though the stigma of terrorist may also be meant to attribute irrationality and fanaticism to opponents, the causes and motives leading to extreme actions range from psychological to socioeconomic, political, ethnic, cultural, and religious.

Islamic extremism has received the lion's share of attention in the aftermath of the atrocities of September 11, 2001. Contrary to numerous writings in the West, the original meaning of "jihad" is not war or holy war (against the United States, the West, Jews, and Christians). Rather, it means struggle, exertion, or striving in a religious sense; doing one's best in the cause of Allah, which may include inner struggles as well as campaigning for justice and truth.

The Muslim community ("umma") contains many varieties, differing traditions, and currents even among conservative and political groups. Militant Islamists, often called "jihadists," are a small minority within such groups.

Research has demonstrated that terrorist actions have emerged from Christian, Islamic, Jewish, Sikh, and Buddhist communities. While some may be tempted to argue that this means all religions may give rise to militancy and violence, others may wonder whether this suggests that religion is actually not the main answer. If all religions can underlie militancy, perhaps sociopolitical, economic, and cultural explanations may offer better insights. It may be that religion is the means through which essentially secular grievances are articulated and propagated.

Issues such as freedom, self-determination, independence, poverty, justice, and equality have been at the core of both secular and religious militancy. Analysts note that even al-Qaeda and Osama bin Laden's variety of terror is due less to Islamic fundamentalism than to the pursuit of the strategic goal of noninterference in Muslim countries by the West.

Secular extremism has been the main concern during the past century, particularly during the Cold War and the proxy wars that accompanied it. Ironically, many see some roots of present-day religious extremism in the context of sponsorship of "mujahideen" (holy warriors) in Afghanistan against the Soviet-supported government in Kabul.

Some groups are hierarchically organized, others are simply a tiny team, while others are best described as loose networks. Some collaborate with each other, while others are mutually exclusive. There is no single theory on what drives ordinary people to do extraordinary things. Regardless of the particular perspective one employs to study international terrorism, the causes and effects of different groups can only be understood in their own historical, socioeconomic, and political context, taking into account grievances, available options, opportunities and resources, interactions among local and external political powers, and culture.

Globalization and easy communication have made terrorism to some extent contagious. Financial or intellectual support by sympathizers to a cause (confirmation of ethnic identity, for example) has been evident in virtually every conflict and ethnic group involved. Sometimes, terrorist groups get involved in purely criminal and profit-oriented misconduct or form ad hoc and temporary alliances with criminal entrepreneurs [for example, Abu Sayyaf, FARC (Fuerzas Armadas Revolucionarias de Colombia) and AUC (Autodefensas Unidas de Colombia), Tamil Tigers, the Kosovo Liberation Army, the Northern Alliance, the Islamic Movement of Uzbekistan or GIA (Armed Islamic Group)].

The resort to petty or organized crime for financial resources may have been aided by diminished state sponsorship of international terrorism after the end of the Cold War. State sponsorship remains a controversial issue to this day, since there is still material and military support of regimes with very poor human rights records.

Finally, states may be involved in terrorism directly or through proxies. The classification of the acts as terrorism will depend largely on whether they occur at war or other armed conflict and how necessary or justified they are regarded by the international community.

Acts of International Terrorism

Terrorism is most often intended as an act of communication. The terrorist message may be expressive, articulate, or inconsistent and unpersuasive. The audience is wider than the direct targets and victims, which points to the crucial role of the media, the Internet, and the battle for public perceptions. The 9/11 attacks illustrate the impact of spectacular, sensational, and widely seen attacks. This event became a landmark and brought about a dramatic shift in U.S. and international responses to terrorism—even though the total number of victims was much smaller than in other domestic and international crimes of organized violence. Genocidal events in Rwanda and other parts of Africa, which benefited of less or no television and global media coverage, generated a weaker response even though millions of people have been systematically massacred.

Acts of international terrorism may be effective but are seldom (if ever) successful in terms of achieving their ultimate or stated goals. Even if certain groups appear to succeed (Algerian, Palestinian, or Jewish groups fighting for independence or statehood), it is still questionable whether it was extreme actions or other factors that decided the final outcome. In other words, terrorism may produce serious consequences and attention, but it does not really work.

The most common means of attack are violence and information (use of cyberspace and the media for propaganda and public announcements), even though officials in many countries are concerned about the potential use of technology and weapons of mass destruction in the future. Typically, terrorist groups are too weak or small for open attacks, so their violence is in the form of assassinations, bombings, suicide attacks, targeted or random killings, sabotage, and hijackings.

The acts of state terrorism also cover a range of acts from bombings and mass killings of civilians to external support of local terrorist groups and militias. Colonial, occupational, and racist regimes have employed psychological terror, arbitrary arrests, summary trials and executions, torture, apartheid, disappearances, and other human right violations aimed at the elimination of opposition to their rule.

Measuring international terrorism is a difficult challenge. Statistical data and chronologies are available from the U.S. State Department, the CIA, the RAND Corporation, the Terrorism Knowledge Base, and many other sources. None of the above, however, includes state terrorism in its analyses. The State Department's *Patterns of Global Terrorism 2003* was discontinued after some controversy. The National Counterterrorism Center's methods are different and make analyses before and after 2005 harder.

Regardless of how one defines and counts nonstate international terrorism, the number of incidents and deaths has not been rising. Also contrary to popular perceptions, domestic terrorism (as defined above) is more significant than international terrorism and is concentrated mostly in the Middle East (including Iraq). Even jihadist groups target Muslims far more than the West.

Responses to International Terrorism

Such findings have serious policy implications, for they highlight the risk of overreacting. Self-proclaimed security experts, uncritical journalism, and single-cause agendas or biases have flooded the media with misleading analyses and misunderstandings.

As the United States deploys its full diplomatic, economic, law enforcement, financial, informational, intelligence, and military arsenal in the "war on terror," it is imperative to construct policy responses on the basis of good evidence and analysis.

At the domestic level, we have had the introduction of several acts in response to international terrorist threats, such as the Omnibus Diplomatic Security and Antiterrorism Act of 1986 and the Antiterrorism Acts of 1987, 1990, 1992, and 1996. More recently, Congress passed the Uniting and Strengthening America by Providing Appropriate Tools Required to Intercept and Obstruct Terrorism (USA PATRIOT) Act of 2001. Executive orders include one in 1995 by President Bill Clinton and a multitude by President George W. Bush. The U.S. war on terror came also with a higher defense budget, war in Afghanistan, a new strategy on preemption, a host of financial controls, and a drastic governmental reorganization.

At the international level, the lack of a definition of terrorism and the states' disagreements over the characterization of certain groups (for example, the Contras, IRA, Hamas) has led to instruments dealing with particular terrorist acts (such as hijackings and political assassinations) rather than terrorism in general.

Since 1963, twelve universal conventions and protocols against terrorism and the recent International Convention for the Suppression of Acts of Nuclear Terrorism are the core of the United Nations response to international terrorism. Typically, the instruments do the following:

- Define certain acts as offenses, such as seizure of an aircraft in flight by threat or violence
- Require state parties to criminalize the offenses in their domestic laws
- Identify bases for jurisdiction over the defined offenses
- Oblige parties where suspects are found to either prosecute or extradite them (principle of "no safe haven for terrorists")

Consequences

Some of the concrete measures involve the creation and regular update of a list of individuals and organizations suspected of terrorism, enhanced monitoring of international flows of funds, mandated reporting of suspicious transactions detected by financial institutions, outsourcing to private companies of many security functions, the closing of charitable organizations, and aggressive intelligence gathering processes in the United States and overseas.

Some of the measures were genuinely collaborative with other countries and consistent with international norms, but others have caused controversies at home and internationally. For example, as of the beginning of 2006, still unresolved and hotly debated are the status and treatment of "enemy combatants" in Guantanamo Bay, kidnapping and extraordinary rendition of suspects, torture, and the treatment of suspects, the criteria used to place suspects' names on the U.N. and other lists, monitoring of communications outside proper procedures applicable under emergency circumstances, the lack of due process, and actions based on executive orders rather than on evidence admissible in court.

The consequences of terrorism are sometimes as unpredictable or unintended as those of counterterrorism. There is consensus that democracy cannot be protected through its abolition. Many countries succeeded in maintaining law and order and in overcoming past experiences with terrorism—from the left, the right, nationalist, or separatist groups—with their democracies intact. How to balance the need to protect innocent victims now against the preservation of our fundamental legal principles and international norms is a challenge of leadership and moral authority.

Clear and undisputed is the need to construct and implement not only short-term and military or law enforcement responses but also medium- and longer-term strategies and approaches that bring the international community and various ethnic or religious groups together and address the grievances and deep sources of problems found to cause individuals and groups to think or do the unthinkable.

Conclusion

International terrorism of various kinds has existed for centuries. Americans' perceptions are shaped by the spectacular atrocities of 9/11 and the flood of reports in its aftermath. The threat may be sensationalized and exaggerated, leading to high costs, unnecessary measures, and limitations of freedoms and rights. Yet, it constitutes a serious challenge, especially in some regions outside the United States, which must be systematically monitored, studied, and analyzed. On this basis, we can expect an effective and just, preventive and reactive set of policies rendering this society and the international community more secure.

Nikos Passas

See also **International Police Cooperation; International Police Missions; INTERPOL and International Police Intelligence; PATRIOT Acts I and II; Terrorism: Definitional Problems; Terrorism: Domestic; Terrorism: Overview**

References and Further Reading

Bonney, Richard. 2004. *Jihad: From Qur'an to Bin Laden*. New York: Palgrave Macmillan.

Burke, Jason. 2003. *Al-Qaeda: Casting a shadow of terror*. New York: I. B. Tauris.

Chomsky, Noam. 1991. *Pirates and emperor: International terrorism in the real world*. Rev. ed. New York: Black Rose Books.

Cole, David. 2003. *Enemy aliens: Double standards and constitutional freedoms in the war on terrorism*. New York: New Press, W. W. Norton and Company.

Cooley, John K. 2000. *Unholy wars: Afghanistan, America, and international terrorism*. London: Pluto Press.

Crenshaw, Martha. 1995. *Terrorism in context*. University Park, PA: Pennsylvania State University Press.

Crenshaw, Martha, and John Pimlott. 1997. *Encyclopedia of world terrorism*. Armonk, NY: Sharpe Reference.

Esposito, John L. 2002. *Unholy war: Terror in the name of Islam*. New York: Oxford University Press.

Gareau, Frederick H. 2004. *State terrorism and the United States: From counterinsurgency to the war on terrorism*. Atlanta, GA: Clarity Press.

Heymann, Philip B. 2003. *Terrorism, freedom, and security: Winning without war*. Cambridge, MA: MIT Press.

Hoffman, Bruce. 1998. *Inside terrorism*. New York: Columbia University Press.

Jenkins, Brian. 1985. *Terrorism and beyond*. Santa Monica, CA: RAND Corporation.

Juergensmeyer, Mark. 2003. *Terror in the mind of God: The global rise of religious violence*. Berkeley, CA: University of California Press.

Laqueur, Walter, and Yonah Alexander. 1987. *The terrorism reader: A historical anthology*. New York: Penguin.

National Commission on Terrorist Attacks upon the United States. 2004. *The 9/11*

Commission report. Washington, DC: National Commission on Terrorist Attacks Upon the United States.

National Research Council. 2002. *Terrorism: Perspectives from the Behavioral and Social Sciences Center for Social and Economic Studies*. http://books.nap.edu/books/0309086124/html/1.html.

Naylor, R. T. 1993. The insurgent economy: Black market operations of guerilla organizations. *Crime, Law and Social Change* 20: 13–51.

Passas, N. 2003. *Informal value transfer systems, money laundering and terrorism*. Washington, DC: Report to the National Institute of Justice (NIJ) and Financial Crimes Enforcement Network (FINCEN).

RAND Corporation reports. http://www.rand.org/publications/electronic/terrorism.html.

Rashid, Ahmed. 2002. *Jihad: The rise of militant Islam in Central Asia*. New Haven, CT: Yale University Press.

Reich, Walter. 1998. *Origins of terrorism: Psychologies, ideologies, theologies, states of mind*. Baltimore, MD: Johns Hopkins University Press.

Schmid, Alex Peter, and A. J. Jongman. 1984. *Political terrorism: A research guide to concepts, theories, data bases, and literature*. New Brunswick, NJ: Transaction Books.

United Nations. 2001. *International instruments related to the prevention and suppression of international terrorism*. New York: United Nations.

————. Reports to the United Nations on progress made by member states and other documents. http://www.un.org/Docs/sc/committees/1373/.

U.S. Congressional Research Service. 2000. *International terrorism: A compilation of major laws, treaties, agreements, and executive documents*. Washington, DC: U.S. Government Printing Office.

Wilkinson, Paul. 1986. *Terrorism and the liberal state*. 2nd ed. New York: New York University Press.

TERRORISM: OVERVIEW

Terrorism is not a new phenomenon, though the understanding and categorization of it is relatively new. "Terrorism" is a controversial term with multiple definitions. A simple definition is that it is a premeditated threat of violence or an act of violence against an influential individual or a group in order to influence that group to initiate change. The U.S. State Department has defined terrorism as "premeditated, politically motivated violence perpetrated against noncombatant targets by subnational groups or clandestine agents, usually intended to influence an audience . . . ." (U.S. State Department 2002). The FBI has defined it as "the unlawful use of force or violence against persons or property to intimidate or coerce a government, the civilian population, or any segment thereof, in furtherance of political or social objectives" (Federal Bureau of Investigation, n.d.). The United Nations observed that the organization "[s]trongly condemns all acts, methods, and practices of terrorism as criminal and unjustifiable, wherever and by whomsoever committed" and "[r]eiterates that criminal acts intended or calculated to provoke a state of terror in the general public, a group of persons, or particular persons for political purposes are in any circumstance unjustifiable, whatever the considerations of a political, philosophical, ideological, racial, ethnic, religious, or other nature that may be invoked to justify them" (United Nations 1996). The terrorists' actions are orchestrated to challenge the status quo and to initiate change, and those actions will be underpinned by acts of violence that include bombings, hijackings, and assassination. Such acts are not random, spontaneous, or blind but are deliberately orchestrated for maximum effect (Kingshott 2003).

Historical Review

The origins of the word "terrorism" can be traced back to the French Revolution (1789–1799), a period in the history of France in which an absolute monarchy was overthrown and the Roman Catholic Church was forced to undergo radical restructuring. This was achieved through the "Constitution Civile du Clerge" (Civil Constitution of the Clergy, passed July 12,

1790), which subordinated the Roman Catholic Church in France to the French government. The clergy became employees of the state, requiring them to take an oath of loyalty to the nation.

September 1793 through July 1794 marked what was known as the Reign of Terror, a period characterized by brutal repression and violence in the pursuit of political aims. In this short time span a highly centralized political regime, led by Maximilien François Marie Isidore de Robespierre, suspended most of the democratic achievements gained by the revolution, and intended to pursue the revolution on social matters. Its stated aim was to destroy internal enemies and conspirators and to oust external enemies from French territory. Robespierre believed that terror was justified in order to root out those opposed to his rule. During the course of the reign, an estimated forty thousand people were executed using the guillotine.

Categorizing Violent Acts as "Terrorism"

Acts of violence that fit the modern construct parameters of terrorism can be traced back to early recorded history and include, but are not limited to, those committed by individuals or groups of individuals who intimidate others to change their behavior or aspects of their lives. For example, the first century Jewish group the Zealot-Sicarii (66–70 A.D.) was not only concerned with the members of their own religious culture but were also seeking an uprising against the Greek population in Judea and against the Romans who governed both. The revolt led to the destruction of the temple and mass suicide at Masada (Griset and Mahan 2003; Yadin 1997; Rapport 1984).

Other terrorist groups from past ages include the medieval Assassins, a group of fanatical Muslims who terrorized the Middle East in the eleventh and twelfth centuries, seeking political conquest for religious purposes and murdering leaders and others who deviated from the strict Muslim law (Lewis 1987). In India there were the Thuggees, an Indian cult thought responsible for more than a million deaths, which operated from the thirteenth to the nineteenth centuries. Their strategy was to kidnap travelers and offer them up as a sacrifice to Kali, a destructive and creative aspect of God as the Divine Mother in Hinduism. The method of killing was strangulation. However, this group seemed more intent on terrorizing their victims than trying to effect some change in society (Griset and Mahan 2003).

The beginnings of modern terrorism may go back to the mid nineteenth century when a German radical, Karl Heinzen, published Der Mord, in which he justified political murder in terms of its positive outcome on history. This work has been referred to as "the most important ideological statement of early terrorism" (Laqueur 1977, 47). In London, John Most, in the issue of his newspaper Freiheit published on September 13, 1884, advised would-be terrorists that "no one who considers the deed itself to be right can take offense at the manner in which the funds for it are acquired," thereby suggesting that criminal acts are allowed if they support and fund the terrorist action (Laqueur 1978, 101). In Italy, the anarchist Carlo Pisacane theorized that terrorism could deliver a message to an audience and draw attention to and support for a cause and is credited with developing the concept of "propaganda by the deed" (Hoffman 1998, 17).

During the nineteenth century, terrorism underwent a transformation, coming to be associated with nongovernmental groups. One such group—the Russian revolutionaries of "Narodnaya Volya" (The People's Will)—was active for a short period (1878–1881); they developed certain ideas and an ideology that were to become the hallmark of subsequent manifestations of terrorism in many countries. They believed in the targeted killing of political figures they identified as "leaders of oppression." The group embraced the developing technologies of the age, symbolized by bombs and bullets, which enabled them to strike directly and discriminately against a Tsarist hierarchy that they argued was corrupt. In their fight against the Tsar and the existing political system they propagated what has remained the common terrorist's belief that violent acts would ignite a revolution or civil war. Their efforts led to the assassination of Tsar Alexander II on March 13, 1881, but that event failed to achieve the revolutionary effects they hoped for (Gaucher 1968).

Terrorism continued for many decades to be associated primarily with the assassination of political leaders and heads of state, thereby reinforcing the view that it was primarily a political tool of expediency. Although there were many political assassinations during this period, including that of President William McKinley, assassinated by anarchist Leon Czolgosz in Buffalo, New York, in September 1901, it was the assassination of Archduke Ferdinand and his wife Sophie of the Austrian-Hungarian Empire by a nineteen-year-old Bosnian Serb student, Gavril Princip, in Sarajevo on June 28, 1914, that proved to be the catalyst for World War I. In general terms, historical analysis has identified that the practice of assassination in the nineteenth and twentieth centuries seldom had the particular effects for which terrorists had hoped.

The onset of the twentieth century saw terrorism appearing in global conflicts localized as revolution, an armed struggle for independence from foreign occupiers with a goal of independent statehood. What was not always understood was the means by which that goal was pursued. The violent struggles over supremacy of ideologies include but are not limited to anarchy, syndicalism, socialism, Marxism, Communism, Fascism, and capitalism.

Terrorism has a political dimension. Most definitions of terrorism identify four primary criteria, which are the objective, the motive, the target, and the legitimacy of the action. One definition may represent a shift from territorial, ideological, religious, or cultural disputes to the acts of violence against the public. Such an interpretation may be challenged as ideological and simplistic, ignoring environment, history, and ethnicity as well as social and economic factors that underpin political evolution in a state. It may be argued that "terrorism" is simply a demonizing term for an enemy's actions, as beneath any current state conflict may be found the same materialistic and ethnocentric reasons on which many past wars were based. The use of the terms "terrorism," "terrorist," "guerilla," and "freedom fighter" are politically weighted, and their use has a polarizing effect; terrorism sometimes seems to become a moral relativist term for violent actions from the point of view of the victim.

Terrorism's characteristics and trends are changing (Lesser et al. 2004) and one of the factors associated with that change relates to religious fundamentalism. Religious fundamentalism's violent struggle within the context of terrorism in the late twentieth century identified a grosser fanaticism to achieve the stated objective. The half-century since World War II has seen a change of group structures and the metamorphosis of terrorism (White 2003). The approach went beyond assassination of political leaders and heads of state. There was a global expectation after World War II of self-determination, acceptance of diversity, and religious freedom.

Much of the world had been under colonial masters (Britain, France, and Portugal). In many European colonies, terrorist movements developed, often with two distinct purposes. The first was to put pressure on the colonial powers to hasten their withdrawal. The second was to intimidate the indigenous population into supporting a particular group's claims to leadership. India's achievement of independence in 1947 and later that of Ceylon (now Sri Lanka) were mainly the result not of terrorism but of the movement of nonviolent civil disobedience led by Mahatma Gandhi (1869–1948). Conversely, in Malaya, communist terrorists launched a major campaign in 1948, but they failed due to two factors: British military opposition and a program of political reform leading to independence. Terrorist groups appeared in other colonial conflicts, including those in Palestine, Algeria, Kenya, Burma, and French Indochina.

The collapse of the main European overseas empires in the 1950s and 1960s did not see an end to terrorist activities. In Southeast Asia, the Middle East, and Latin America there were killings of politicians, industrialists, and policemen and terrorist actions included assassinations, hostage-takings, hijackings of aircraft, and bombings of buildings. In many actions the targeting of specific individuals was replaced by the targeting of civilians. The causes espoused by terrorists encompassed not just revolutionary socialism and nationalism but also a rise in religious fundamentalism. Religious fundamentalism allowed for the perpetrators to ignore the international law and the agreed rules of conflict (Geneva Conventions), justifying their actions as being moral because of the authority of a higher cause. Seeing how terrorism could have such an impact on a variety of issues, some governments became involved in supporting terrorism. This is known as state-sponsored terrorism.

Modern international terrorism as we know it today did not come into prominence until the 1960s. The colonial era had passed, and many postcolonial attempts at state formation had failed. It was the creation of the state of Israel that engendered a series of Marxist and anti-Western transformations and movements throughout Middle Eastern Arab states and the Islamic world. The growth of nationalist and revolutionary movements was not limited to the Middle East. It also included European groups, such as the Irish Republican Army (IRA) in Northern Ireland and Euzkadi Ta Azkatasuna (ETA) in the Basque region of Spain, along with their view that terrorism could be effective in reaching political goals, generating the first phase of modern international terrorism. There was an increased number of urban incidents using the strategies learned from guerrilla conflicts and the writing and ideologies of Carlos Marighella, Franz Fannon, Regis Debray, and Ernesto (Che) Guevara.

In the late 1960s, Palestinian secular movements such as Al Fatah and the Popular Front for the Liberation of Palestine (PFLP) began to target civilians outside the immediate arena of conflict. Following Israel's 1967 defeat of Arab forces, Palestinian leaders realized that the Arab world was unable to militarily confront Israel. At the same time, lessons drawn from revolutionary movements in Latin America, North Africa, and Southeast Asia as well the Jewish struggle against Britain in Palestine prompted the Palestinians to move away from classic guerrilla, typically rural-based, warfare toward urban terrorism. Radical Palestinians took advantage of modern communication, technology, and transportation systems to internationalize their struggle. The Palestine Liberation Organization (PLO), the Provisional Irish Republican Army (PIRA), and other terrorist groups used attacks against civilian populations in an attempt to effect change for religious, ideological, or political reasons. The failure of Arab nationalism in the 1967 war resulted in the strengthening of both progressive and extremist Islamic movements.

While secular Palestinians dominated the scene during the 1970s, Islamic movements increasingly came into opposition with secular nationalism. Islamic groups were supported by antinationalist conservative regimes, such as Saudi Arabia, to counter the expansion of nationalist ideology. Although political Islam was considered to be tolerant to progressive change, that change was seen as a threat to conservative Arab regimes. This threat provided the catalyst for the support as Islamic fundamentalist and other extremist groups evolved to combat both nationalist and political Islamist movements.

In Iran the move toward Shia Islam further eroded the power and legitimacy of the United States-backed authoritarian Pahlevi regime, which ended with the Shah being deposed. On February 1, 1979, exiled religious leader Ayatollah Ruhollah Khomeini returned from France to direct a revolution that resulted in a theocratic republic guided by Islamic principles. Iran's relations with many of its Arab neighbors have become strained due to the aggressive Iranian attempts to spread Islamic revolution throughout the region.

In 1979, there was a turning point in international terrorism, with the Iranian Islamic revolution sparking fears of a wave of revolutionary Shia Islam throughout the Arab world and the West. The Soviet invasion of Afghanistan and the subsequent anti-Soviet Mujahedeen War (1979–1989) initiated an expansion of terrorist groups. The end of the war provided a post-jihad cadre of trained militants whose skills would provide a key trend of enlisting mercenaries in contemporary international terrorism and insurgency-related violence. The Islamic mercenaries have supported local insurgencies in North Africa, Kashmir, Chechnya, China, Bosnia, and the Philippines.

State-Sponsored Terrorism

In 1979, the West's attention was focused on state-sponsored terrorism, and specifically on the Iranian-backed and Syrian-supported Hezbollah terrorist group, who trained secular Shia and Sunni Islamic movement members and who were the pioneers of suicide bombers in the Middle East. Iraq and Syria were involved in supporting various terrorist groups and state sponsors of terrorism who used various terrorist groups to attack Israel and Western interests in addition to domestic and regional opponents. The American policy of listing state sponsors of terrorism was heavily politicized and, prior to the September 11, 2001, attacks on the United States, did not include several countries, both allies and opponents of U.S foreign policy, that, under U.S. government definitions, were guilty of supporting or using terrorism. However, since the United States declared a "war on terrorism"—a global effort by governments (primarily the United States and its principal allies) to neutralize international groups and ensure that rogue nations no longer support terrorist activities—the United States has been consistent in naming and condemning such states.

The Globalization of Terror

The disintegration of post-Cold War states and the Cold War legacy provide both the conventional weapons and the technology that have assisted the proliferation of terrorism worldwide. Political instability created by conflict in areas such as the Balkans, Afghanistan, Colombia, and certain African countries and the abuse of human rights provides a fertile environment for terrorist recruitment, while smuggling and drug trafficking routes are often exploited by terrorists to support operations worldwide.

In addition, the trend toward and the rise in religious fundamentalism has identified a grosser fanaticism that is underpinned by the proliferation of suicide bombers as a cost-effective strategy against a stronger enemy. Since 1989, the increasing willingness of religious extremists to strike targets outside immediate country or regional areas underscores the global nature of contemporary terrorism. The

1993 bombing of the World Trade Center and the September 11, 2001, attacks on the World Trade Center and the Pentagon are representative of this trend.

No fully accepted definition of terrorism has been achieved, regardless of the government agencies or academic disciplines that have examined the phenomenon. It has been observed that "any explanation that attempts to account for all its many manifestations is bound to be exceedingly vague or altogether wrong" (Laqueur 1977, 133).

BRIAN F. KINGSHOTT

See also **Terrorism: Definitional Problems; Terrorism: Domestic; Terrorism, International**

References and Further Reading

Federal Bureau of Investigation. n.d. http://www.fbi.gov/publish/terror/terrusa.html (accessed April 13, 2004).

Gaucher, R. 1968. *The terrorists: From Tsarist Russia to the O.A.S.* London: Secker and Warburg.

Griset, P., and S. Mahan. 2003. *Terrorism in perspective*. London: Sage.

Hoffman, B. 1998. *Inside terrorism*. New York: Colombia University Press.

Hoge, J., and G. Rose, eds. 2005. *Understanding the war on terror*. New York: Council of Foreign Relations.

Howard, R., and R. Sawyer. 2003. *Terrorism and counter terrorism*. Guilford, CT: McGraw-Hill/Duskin.

Kingshott, B. 2003. The "new" religious war. *Criminal Justice Studies* 16 (1): 15–27.

Laqueur, W. 1977. *Terrorism*. Boston: Little, Brown and Company.

———. 1978. *The terrorist reader: A historical anthology*. Philadelphia: Temple University Press.

Laqueur, W., B. Lewis, Ajami, et al. 2003. *The war on terror*. New York: Council of Foreign Relations.

Lessor, I., B. Hoffman, J. Arquilla, D. Ronfeldt, and M. Zanini. 2004. *Countering the new terrorism*. Washington, DC: RAND Corporation.

Lewis, B. 1987. *The assassins*. Oxford: Oxford University Press.

Nyatepe-Coo, A., and D. Zeisler-Vralsted. 2004. *Understanding terrorism: Threats in an uncertain world*. Upper Saddle River, NJ: Pearson/Prentice-Hall.

Rapport, D. 1984. Fear and trembling: Terrorism in three religious traditions. *American Political Science Review* 78 (3): 658–77.

United Nations. 1996. *Measures to eliminate international terrorism,* G/A/Res/51/210, 88th Plenary Meeting, December 17 (accessed April 13, 2005). http://www.un.org/documents/ga/res/51/a51r210.htm.

U.S. State Department. 2001. *Patterns of global terrorism 2000*. Released by the Office of the Coordinator for Counterterrorism, April 30, 2001. Title 22 of the United States Code [Section 2656f(d)]. Washington, DC: U.S. Government Printing Office, 2002. http://www.state.gov/s/ct/rls/pgtrpt/2000/2419.htm (accessed April 13, 2005).

White, J. 2003. *Terrorism*. 4th ed. Belmont, CA: Thompson Wadsworth.

Yadin, Y. 1997. *Masada: Herod's fortress and the zealots' last stand*. London: Weidenfeld Nicolson.

TERRORISM: POLICE FUNCTIONS ASSOCIATED WITH

Terrorism has quickly emerged as a primary problem for law enforcement administrators and personnel working at both the federal and local levels. The frightening reality of homegrown terror became clear after the 1995 bombing of the Murrah Federal Building in Oklahoma City. The subsequent and stunningly successful attacks on the World Trade Center and the Pentagon on September 11, 2001, demonstrated that America had become a primary target of international terrorists as well. The law enforcement industry has attempted to quickly respond to these emerging threats by expanding the traditional roles of investigators and officers on the street and by using a broad range of strategies designed to mitigate both domestic and international terror threats. These antiterrorism strategies include (1) the expansion of federal law enforcement counterintelligence structures, (2) the targeting of terrorist funding sources, and (3) the development of antiterror and collaborative strategies at the state and local law enforcement levels (Swanson et al. 2005).

The existence of large-scale threats from terrorist groups has highlighted the importance of federal law enforcement counterintelligence structures, primarily involved in terrorism prevention and investigation, intelligence gathering, and foreign counterintelligence. Important federal law enforcement counterintelligence structures include the Department of Homeland Security, the National Infrastructure Protection Center, the Federal Bureau of Investigation's Counterterrorism Center, and the National Domestic Preparedness Office.

The Department of Homeland Security (DHS) was established by President George W. Bush as an immediate response to the 9/11 attacks on New York City and Washington, D.C. DHS has a significant role in intelligence gathering and analysis and has administered the development of Homeland Security Operations Centers across the United States. These centers are charged with gathering information and intelligence analysis, primarily as it relates to protecting the nation's critical infrastructure. Operating under the DHS banner, the U.S. Secret Service also continues to play a prominent role through its Threat Analysis Center. Beyond these strategies, the creation of DHS from numerous previously established federal law enforcement agencies is an attempt to implement a more comprehensive national strategy to prevent, respond to, and recover from terrorist acts occurring within the United States (Swanson et al. 2005).

The National Infrastructure Protection Center (NIPC) was founded in 1998, and the organization operates within the Federal Bureau of Investigation (FBI). NIPC was created on the recommendation of the President's Commission on Critical Infrastructure Protection (1998), which highlighted the role of federal agencies in protecting critical computer systems against terrorist activities. The federal government owns and operates many critical infrastructure systems, including transportation, energy, and government operations. Thus, federal agencies would be the primary responders in the event of a national crisis. NIPC's InfraGard, a pilot project designed to facilitate the exchange of information among academic institutions, the government, and the business community, serves as a prime example of the push toward interagency and business collaboration in the fight against terrorism (Taylor et al. 2005).

The FBI's Counterterrorism Center has also expanded since its inception in 1996 in order to respond to international terror operations emanating from both within the United States and abroad, as well as those threats that are purely domestic in character. The center uses personnel employed by eighteen federal agencies, including the Central Intelligence Agency (CIA), the Department of State, and the Secret Service. The Departments of Justice, Defense, Energy, and Health and Human Services, the Environmental Protection Agency, and the Federal Emergency Management Agency formed the National Domestic Preparedness Office (NDPO) in 1998 (Swanson et al. 2005). NDPO is responsible for assisting state and local authorities with the planning, training, and equipment necessary for responding to any terrorist attacks that may involve weapons of mass destruction (WMDs).

In addition to these initiatives aimed at revamping or improving traditional reactive strategies, the federal law enforcement community has increasingly recognized the need to become more proactive in the war against terror—to disrupt the support networks that enable terrorist organizations so that future terrorist acts can be prevented before they occur. One of these more proactive approaches involves the disruption of financial networks that support terrorist operations.

Terrorist organizations use a wide variety of funding sources to accomplish their objectives. The number of funding sources a given terrorist organization utilizes is necessarily dependent on the scope of the criminal organization. For example, smaller organizations such as some small-scale, domestic paramilitary right-wing groups may not have exorbitant financial needs; however, it is estimated that large-scale international terrorist activities such as the 9/11 attacks may cost upward of $500,000 to plan, coordinate, and carry out (National Commission on Terrorist Attacks upon the United States, n.d.). The law enforcement industry has implemented a range of strategies designed to cut off many of the most common revenue streams used by terrorist groups, including (1) fraudulent use of the international banking system, (2) drug smuggling, and (3) arms smuggling.

The international community has recently taken steps to halt the fraudulent use of banking systems. Terrorist groups use these systems primarily to "launder" illegally obtained funds so that the monies cannot be seized and/or detected by the police. In 2001, the USA PATRIOT Act was passed. Provisions of the law specifically strengthen measures used to prevent, detect, and prosecute terrorist financing and money laundering activities (Swanson et al. 2005). In addition, the Treasury Department, the FBI, and the CIA have collaborated on the creation of the Foreign Terrorist Asset Tracking Center (FTAT). FTAT is designed to identify terrorist financial infrastructures and eliminate the ability of terror groups to use the international monetary system as a means to protect their assets (Swanson et al. 2005). Finally, the United Nations created a Counter-Terrorism Committee to monitor and implement U.N. Resolution 1373. The resolution imposes binding measures on all member states to prevent the financing of international terrorism (United States Mission to the United Nations 2002).

Drug smuggling has traditionally provided terror groups a stable funding source. The term "narcoterrorism" has been used to describe the linkage between the illegal drug trade and terrorist organizations. It is estimated that profits derived from the sale of illegal narcotics fund terror

organizations in as many as thirty nations. The al Qaeda group responsible for the 9/11 attacks, for example, obtained much of its initial financing through the opium trade in Afghanistan (Swanson et al. 2005). The U.S. Drug Enforcement Administration identifies three critical elements to attacking narcoterrorism: law enforcement initiatives, intelligence operations, and global cooperation. These efforts have most recently focused on the activities of Middle Eastern terror groups. For instance, in 2002, Operation Mountain Express resulted in the arrest 136 people and the seizure of thirty-six tons of pseudophedrine, 179 pounds of methamphetamine, and $4.5 million (Swanson et al. 2005).

In addition to drug smuggling, terror groups commonly trade in weapons to generate funds. Often, weapons are traded for other commodities (such as drugs), which can then be converted into hard currency. Terrorist organizations have expanded their use of weapons smuggling since the collapse of the former Soviet Union and the resulting influx of dangerous arms into the global market (Bolz 2002). Law enforcement initiatives in this area demand a large degree of international cooperation, given the global scope of the arms trade. For example, the Peruvian government recently foiled an attempt by FARC (Columbia's oldest and best equipped insurgency group) to purchase ten thousand Russian-made AK-47 rifles through international cooperative law enforcement efforts (International Policy Institute for Counter-Terrorism 2000). So, too, U.S. law enforcement officials recently uncovered and were able to thwart a plot instigated by groups in Pakistan to purchase a variety of high-tech weapons, including two hundred U.S.-made Stinger missiles (Frieden 2001).

The role of local and state officers in combating terrorism has also greatly expanded since the 9/11 attacks. Knowledge gained by investigating terrorist groups since 9/11 has revealed that these groups often exhibit a pattern of activity or actions that typically precede major terror attacks (Swanson et al. 2005). These "pre-incident indicators" have quickly become the focus of local law enforcement antiterrorism training efforts. These indicators provide clues as to potential threats and future plans. This training often emphasizes the need for local officers to be aware of suspicious activities, use critical thinking skills, and update their knowledge base concerning potential terrorist threats in their local area (Swanson et al. 2005). The Bureau of Justice Assistance provides local and state agencies free intelligence-related training for street officers and detectives assigned to antiterrorism task forces through a program called SLATT (State and Local Anti-Terrorism Training).

Given that the planning, funding, and execution of terrorist activities invariably crosses multiple law enforcement jurisdictions, state and local agencies have greatly increased participation in Joint Terrorism Task Forces (JTTFs). JTTFs are responsible for gathering and acting on intelligence related to international and domestic terrorism and conducting investigations related to planned terrorist attacks. JTTFs are directly supervised by the FBI and consist of officers representing federal agencies and state and local organizations. Since the establishment of the first JTTF in New York City in 1980, twenty-seven JTTFs have been created nationwide (Federal Bureau of Investigation 1999).

JOHN LIEDERBACH and
ROBERT W. TAYLOR

See also **Terrorism: Definitional Problems; Terrorism: Domestic; Terrorism, International; Terrorism: Overview**

References and Further Reading

Bolz, F. 2002. *The counterterrorism handbook.* Boca Raton, FL: CRC Press.
Federal Bureau of Investigation. 1999. *Terrorism in the United States,* p. 44. Washington, DC: Federal Bureau of Investigation.
Frieden, T. 2001. *Federal agents charge four with arms smuggling.* http://archives.cnn.com/2001/LAW/06/15/arms.smuggling/ (June 15, 2001).
International Policy Institute for Counter-Terrorism. 2000. *Peru breaks up FARC arms smuggling ring.* August. Herzlia, Israel: Institute for Counterterrorism.
National Commission on Terrorist Attacks upon the United States. n.d. *Combating terrorist financing in the United States: The role of financial institutions,* 87–113. Staff Monograph.
Swanson, C. R., N. C. Chamelin, L. Territo, and R. W. Taylor. 2005. *Criminal investigation.* 9th ed. Boston: McGraw-Hill.
Taylor, R. W., T. J. Caeti, D. K. Loper, E. J. Fritsch, and J. Liederbach. 2005. *Digital crime and digital terrorism.* Upper Saddle River, NJ: Pearson/Prentice-Hall.
United States Mission to the United Nations. 2002. *Statement by James Shinn, Special Adviser to the U.S. Mission to the United Nations, on Agenda Item 160, Measures to Eliminate International Terrorism, in the Sixth Committee of the Fifty-Seventh Session of the United Nations General Assembly.* Press release #142-2 (02), October 3. http://www.un.int/usa/02_142-2.htm.

TEXAS RANGERS

In its duties, this unique law enforcement body operates somewhere between the military and local authorities. Historically, Texas Rangers have "ranged" over the state of Texas, assisting city and county officials with peacekeeping, investigations, and general cleanup of outlaws. As stated in Art. 4413 (11) of the Texas *Revised Civil Statutes*:

> They shall have authority to make arrests, and to execute process in criminal cases; and in civil cases when specially directed by the judge of a court of record; and in all cases shall be governed by the laws regulating and defining the powers and duties of sheriffs when in the discharge of similar duties; except that they shall have the power and shall be authorized to make arrests and to execute all process in criminal cases in any county in the state.

Since there are 254 counties in Texas stretching across 266,807 square miles, canvassing the state takes some doing.

Early History

In 1823, Stephen F. Austin, civil and military leader of the Anglo American colonists in Texas, employed ten men to serve as peace officers, naming them Rangers. Three years later, Austin added to their number in a written agreement with six militia districts to keep "twenty to thirty Rangers in service all the time." The force gained legal status in 1835 with the outbreak of the Texas Revolution. War with Mexico drained manpower from the western frontier, leaving settlers vulnerable to Indian attack, so a larger corps of Rangers was assembled to patrol the borderland. Then from 1836 to 1845, the period of the Republic, Texas, having won independence from Mexico, was fearful that the Mexicans no less than the Plains Indians would seek to recapture their land. How to handle the threat of encroachment was the burning question. Eminent Texas historian Walter Prescott Webb (1952, 756) tells what was decided by the leaders of the fledgling Republic:

> Experience proved that the most effective force was a squad of well-mounted men who would ride the great distances along the two frontiers and repel or destroy raiding parties. Legally these forces were given all sorts of titles, such as mounted gunmen, spies, mounted riflemen, etc., but it became the custom to refer to them in common parlance as Texas Rangers.

During this time men such as Ben McCulloch, Samuel H. Walker, W. A. A. "Big Foot" Wallace, and John Coffee Hays earned reputations as gutsy Rangers able to surmount whatever odds were against them. For instance, McCulloch and a group of Rangers rode alongside a volunteer army in pursuit of Comanches who had stolen from and murdered settlers in the Guadalupe Valley. They all met on August 12, 1840, in what was to be called the Plum Creek Fight. There the Rangers fought boldly, and the surviving Comanches retreated farther west out of Texas. Hays, equally a hero, also beat back Indians by using the newly developed Colt revolver.

Two Wars

In 1845, Texas entered the Union, and on the heels of that event a second war with Mexico commenced. John Coffee Hays, made a colonel, was ordered to raise a regiment of five hundred Texas Rangers to assist in the war effort. For the first time in their history the Rangers fought as a unit in the U.S. Army. It was to be something of a drawback, though, because they were not military per se but free spirits; they lacked spit-and-polish discipline and tended to despise the Mexicans to a degree beyond that generated by mere warfare.

Another development concomitant with entry into the Union was that Texans expected federal troops to take over defense of the borderlands. This relief never materialized; the federal troops remained stationary, not riding roughshod across the dusty miles meting out justice as did the Rangers. As a result, in the minds of many Texans, their Rangers were irreplaceable.

During the Civil War, the Rangers lost some of their luster, since they stayed at home to continue guarding the Indian frontier while other Texans trudged east to the real battle. After the Civil War, reconstruction governor E. J. Davis oversaw legislation to create the first state police for Texas, which would overshadow the Rangers. Davis's intention was to make sure that reconstruction policies would be adhered to, but what Texas got was three years of police corruption, culminating in Chief James Davidson's absconding to Belgium with $37,434.67 of the state's money. On April 22, 1873, the act authorizing the state police was repealed and the force abolished.

Rise to Greatness

Between 1874 and 1890, the Texas Rangers knew glory enough to fill a hundred legends. Lawlessness in the state had grown to alarming proportions before Governor Richard Coke charged the state legislature with enactment of a legal remedy. Out of its deliberation came the creation of two fighting forces. Major John B. Jones commanded the larger of the two, the Frontier Battalion, composed of six companies, each under the command of a captain. The battalion roamed the border to repulse any Indian uprising, although Major Jones and his Rangers spent more time correcting civil matters: riots, feuds, murders, and train robberies. Captain L. H. McNelly led the second contingent, called the Special Force, comprised of about thirty men. Its duty was to suppress cow theft and brigandage. One of McNelly's most famous actions was the Las Cuevas affair, in which sixteen bandits paid with their lives for driving stolen cattle into Mexico. The Texas Rangers were not to be trifled with, and almost any crime committed near the border was dealt with harshly—that was the widespread warning of Las Cuevas.

Men from these forces achieved even greater notoriety by hunting down and capturing such outlaw killers as John Wesley Hardin and Sam Bass when it appeared that no one else could stand up to them. The anecdote of the day was that in a small Texas town, an angry mob was about to destroy the place when, livid with fear, the mayor sent for the Texas Rangers. At noon a train arrived and off stepped a lone man armed with a Winchester rifle, his steely eyes fixed on the mob. The mayor asked, "Who are you?" "I'm a Texas Ranger," he replied. Hoots and laughter shook the town. "What, only one Ranger? When we've got a mob! Where are your men?" The Ranger answered in a calm, clear voice, "You've got only one mob, haven't you? Now what's the ruckus?"

A Well-Established Institution

Into the twentieth century, the Texas Rangers still maintained border patrol even though Indian raids had stopped and cattle rustling was on the decline. In 1911, Pancho Villa's bandits were smuggling guns from Texas into Mexico and had to be stopped. A few years later, in 1918, with the coming of Prohibition, the contraband reversed direction; this time illegal liquor flooded into Texas from Mexico. Both unlawful activities kept the Rangers more than busy.

Perhaps the single greatest search for a band of criminals on the loose occurred in 1934. Destiny ordained that the Barrow gang, led by Clyde Barrow and Bonnie Parker, was to meet head-on with Frank Hamer, the quintessential Texas Ranger. When Hamer got the assignment to go after them, the gang had already killed twelve people in cold blood. Hamer, a superlative looking man who was reported to have killed sixty-five outlaws in thirty years of law work, caught up with Bonnie and Clyde in Louisiana. He had stalked them for 102 days. From ambush he and other lawmen blasted the couple in their Ford, riddling metal and flesh with bullets, thus ending their spectacular crime spree. For bringing Bonnie and Clyde to justice, the State of Texas paid Hamer at the rate of $180 a month for the time he was on their trail.

But such heroics were not enough to sustain the life of the Texas Rangers, or so it seemed. In 1932, two years before Hamer's historic confrontation, during the gubernatorial race, the Rangers supported Ross Sterling in opposition to Miriam "Ma" Ferguson. When "Ma" won the election, she fired all forty-four Rangers in service and replaced them with her appointees. Her vendetta tarnished the good name of the force, built up over 110 years, as Texans witnessed one of her "Rangers" convicted of murder, several others declared guilty of using confiscated equipment to rig their own gambling hall, and a captain arrested for theft and embezzlement.

Understandably, after such misuse of authority, high-level talk centered around abolishing one of the best-known law enforcement bodies in the world. Only the election of a new governor, James V. Allred, saved the day. Governor Allred appointed Albert Sidney Johnson chairman of the new Public Safety Commission to resuscitate the Texas Rangers. Before Johnson was through, he had erected new quarters at Camp Mabry, placing the State Highway Patrol and the Rangers under one roof, had beefed up personnel, and had purchased every description of crime-solving equipment.

Today, the Texas Rangers operate as a part of the Texas Department of Public Safety and are still considered second to none in their role as free-agent lawmen. They carry on the tradition of their past brethren James B. Gillett, Ira Aten, Buck Barry, Captain John R. Hughes, Captain Bill McDonald, James Pike, and others who traversed Texas to make it a safe place to live. All of the Rangers mentioned in this brief history can be read about in colorful biographies that challenge any Western novel for genuine gallantry.

WILLIAM G. BAILEY

References and Further Reading

Douglas, Claude Leroy. 1934. *The gentlemen in the white hats: Dramatic episodes in the history of the Texas Rangers*. Dallas, TX: South West Press.

Mason, Herbert Molloy, Jr. 1967. *The Texas Rangers*. New York: Meredith Press.

Webb, Walter Prescott. 1935. *The Texas Rangers: A century of frontier defense*. Austin, TX: University of Texas Press.

———, ed. 1952. *The handbook of Texas*. 2 vols. Austin, TX: Texas State Historical Association.

———. 1957. *The story of the Texas Rangers*. Austin, TX: Encino Press.

THEORIES OF POLICING

Theories of policing, largely comparative in nature, seek to explain why policing systems differ widely in their organization, the powers and authority granted them, the roles and tasks they are entrusted with, the occupational cultures that characterize their work, their interactions with civic society and the state, the quality and effectiveness of their work, the extent of entanglements in the political life of their societies, and their capacity to shape the dominant ideologies of policing that, in turn, define for themselves and for society what constitutes good policing. In addition, as an underlying subtext, theories include a normative element by linking the basic purposes and historical developments of policing to hegemonic notions of social control and social order and ideologies of justice in a society. Do the police provide a service that seeks to benefit all or are the police a repressive force protecting the interests of the few at the expense of the many?

The police are crucial elements in systems of social control that protect the valued dominant distributions of material and symbolic goods in a society against challenges by crime, subversion, or riotous disorders through the threat or the exercise of coercive force and the collection and analysis of information. Since all social orders are divided by class, cultures, value systems, and gender and ethnic identities, the impacts of policing are never experienced equally by or imposed equally on all members of society. The work of policing is inherently political and conflict generating.

Developments in policing are seen as closely linked to and influenced by the same factors that drive developments in the societies in which they exist. The social ordering functions of policing are similar in any society, but the manner and ways in which these are carried out will reflect contextual societal changes, including fluctuations of criminal activity, disorder, and political instabilities. Some societies have developed patterns of policing that are extensive in their reach and activities and that reflect the original conception, at least in Western societies, that policing is the government of local communities, while other societies have over time arrived at quite restricted notions of what the police should be doing.

Answers to the question of why policing varies over time and place fall into three general theoretical perspectives. Each perspective links diverse forms of policing to specific histories, dynamics, and changes in societies but stresses particular causes and processes of change: political, cultural, and ideological modernization; the growth and decline of the nation-state; and the rise of a neoliberal domestic and international order exemplified in the emergence of risk-based calculations of security and threats and the multiple policing responses to the changing security conditions of the world that have emerged since the end of the Cold War and the collapse of the Soviet Union.

Modernization

The most commonly used framework links changes in policing to changes in societal contexts. The police change because the societies in which they operate change. For example, changes in the ideologies and practices of policing throughout American history (the political, progressive/professional, and community policing models) resulted from factors such as public and intellectual disillusionment with the performance of prior models, leading to the delegitimation of policing by large segments of society and the rise of reform advocacy in policing circles; the emergence of new politically influential civic society interest groups demanding change and greater accountability; changes in crime and disorder perceived as warranting a different formal and more effective control response; shifts in legal norms and conceptions of justice as these are applied to the police; and technological innovations in information processing and communication. Police cannot remain aloof from

the changing societal contexts within which they work if they wish to remain legitimate.

State Creation and Decline

Another framework links patterns of policing to the rise and decline of nation-states. As the emergent nation-state sought to entrench its power and rule, it was confronted by and had to overcome resistance to its expansion, which required an internal army (the first form of domestic policing, which continues to this day in Continental Europe in the form of constabulary and "gendarmerie" forces) and later a coercive force that could do its work without having to resort to outright repression.

As nation-states grew stronger and notions of democratic politics began to take hold, existing forms of informal control withered, were suppressed, and subsequently were replaced by formal systems of control centered in the state. The police became defined as the agency of the state that enjoys the monopoly of legitimate force within a territory in order to impose social control. To have that monopoly legitimated, the state and the police had to engage in work that was effective (protecting people and society) and needed to represent themselves symbolically as protecting a stable consensus of values and interests in society—that is, as apolitical experts in the provision of social control services.

This pattern of creating police systems was most visibly repeated in colonies. Colonizers routinely created and imposed policing systems based on the constabulary model in order to protect their economic interests and political authority against persistent and pervasive local resistance. As a result, the police forces of most former colonies, which most nations of the world are, originated as repressive functionaries of the colonial state and continue to suffer from that history, in terms of public image, effectiveness, and lack of community support.

A critical or neo-Marxist variant derives the explanation for what the police do in and for society from underlying conceptions of the nature of social formations and the state and notions of historical progress. As social formations progress through their historical stages, the tasks of policing will reflect the (increasingly declining) hegemony of dominating classes who use their control of the police to further their own interests and historical progress.

The Rise of a New Global Order

Since the prominence and capacity of the state to provide services to its populations has declined in recent years, the responsibility for policing has drifted away from the state toward subnational private, corporate, and communitarian forms of social control and has migrated to supranational levels. The decline of the state reflects domestic developments but more clearly the increasing permeability of international borders and the increasing connectedness of societies through technological improvements in communications, transportation, and industry.

The legitimate monopoly of coercive force by the state has given way to a field of action on which a multitude of policing actors pursue the goals of safety and security through resources and strategies that the state can no longer supply. At best, the state and formal policing maintain a market share of the provision of social control, with informal, non-state-based control mechanisms serving as fluctuating and contingent partners in the overall system of control.

The emergence of transnational security threats—mainly transnational terrorism—may have slowed the decline of the state and the state control of policing, since non-state security providers lack the necessary resources to effectively confront this old

and new threat. The disappearance of the state and the shrinking domain of state policing may have been overstated.

There are three strands of thinking on how globalization has changed policing: the notion of a risk society, the commodification of security, and the concept of a security sector and security sector reform.

The Rise of the "Risk Society"

The perceived ineffectiveness and inefficiencies of social control tactics used by the police have led to a rethinking of the nature of threats within societies in which social bonds and communal cohesion have broken down under the onslaught of economic, cultural, and technological factors. Threats have become conceptualized as risk factors associated with categories of people who threaten the security of a society and, ultimately, the global system. The goal of policing, hence, is to accumulate the information necessary to detect and control those categories of people who are seen as posing the greatest risks—that is, those deemed the marginal, dangerous, criminal, and deviant classes.

Risk-based security thinking leads to efforts at surveillance, detection, and prevention that will neutralize categories of threats even if no specific acts have been committed. The police, responding to demands to make society and the state be and feel safer, shift their working priorities toward policies that focus on the security of the state and on the collection, analysis, and organizational control of information. The police have become information specialists, a trend that is strengthened by the increasingly technologized form in which information flows within and between societies.

The Commodification of Security

Interpreting societal changes through a broader lens, some scholars have argued that postmodern society, characterized by a neocapitalist, neoliberal domestic and global system in which states, multinational corporations, nonstate political actors, private security agencies, and civic society groups share the policing field and compete for the authority to define the ideologies, control the resources, and legitimize the strategies that will best protect their interests and normative goals, necessarily alters the status, legitimacy, and power of the formal police.

The provision of security is offered by numerous actors and is sold and bought, as are other commodities, in the global and domestic markets on the basis of managerialist notions of effectiveness, efficiency, profits, and costs regarding how to best provide the needed security services. The monopoly of security is decentered from the state system, a development supported by ideological justifications for the market as an efficient allocator of valued resources within society.

The ongoing expansion of nonstate security providers is furthered by the dominance of the globalized production and market system by multinational corporations. Corporations have personnel and properties and conduct activities in numerous sovereign territories; their security needs are not met by the distribution of formal, sovereign state-based policing, and the cooperation of state police across national borders is not developed enough or sufficient to offer protection against domestic and transnational threats. Corporations—and one can add nongovernmental organizations and even tourists—turn to nonstate security providers or develop their own security methods.

The outcome is a system of policing in which nonstate security services and providers have gained an increasingly larger share, with state policing left to the roles of protecting those segments of their populations that cannot afford to buy their own security in the market and repressing risk-defined categories of threats, events, and people. It is the legitimacy of not only the

police that is undermined but that of the state itself as nonstate actors devise new models for the provision and governance of security that fit their needs, values, and resources.

Security Sector Reforms

A theoretical approach that seeks to tie many of the themes that have achieved salience in thinking about the police—why they do what they do and how progress can be institutionalized—is security sector reform (SSR). SSR arose within the international economic, political, and security advocacy and reform community and points to the fundamental political nature and importance of the policing systems, which include all state security providers as well as domestic and international nonstate security providers.

Security, provided effectively and with a view toward promoting human rights and democratic norms, is seen as an essential precondition for achieving and sustaining democracy, free markets, and progress—values one assumes are desired by all who live within the dominant neoliberal global order (with some reluctant but ultimately futile holdouts). SSR takes a holistic view of how security is achieved and the consequences of the methods whereby it is achieved. The activities and status of formal state police, and their organizational and policy linkages to other security agencies and civic society, can only be understood and theorized as part of ongoing responses by societies and states to changing global security threats and conditions that create domestic insecurities.

A Critical and Unresolved Issue

Theories of the police and policing continually reconceptualize and retheorize changing patterns of policing as the real world and work of policing and social ordering flow into different organizational channels. One issue on which theories differ dramatically is the role of the police themselves in processes of change—that is, whether the police are objects of historical changes or agents of change in their own right.

Following an old maxim that people create their destinies, albeit within the constraints imposed upon them by history, one needs to see the police as being both subjects and objects of history. They participate in their own creation but only within the limits constrained by societal and global contexts. Their capacity and desire to be agents of change within the social networks of other actors equally desirous to promote or delay societal changes means that theories of policing systems will remain as complex and fluid as they are. Policing actors shape their histories, and theories will follow once patterns of change and new forms of social ordering have become noticed and categorized.

OTWIN MARENIN

See also **Accountability; Crime Control Strategies; History of American Policing**

References and Further Reading

Bayley, David H. 1985. *Patterns of policing.* New Brunswick, NJ: Rutgers University Press.

Bayley, David H., and Clifford Shearing. 2001. *The new structure of policing: Description, conceptualization and research agenda.* Washington, DC: National Institute of Justice.

Ericson, R., and Haggerty, K. 1997. *Policing risk society.* Oxford: Oxford University Press.

Garland, David. 1996. The limits of the sovereign state: Strategies of crime control in contemporary society. *British Journal of Criminology* 36 (4): 445–71.

Harring, Sidney. 1983. *Policing a class society. The experience of American cities, 1865–1915.* New Brunswick: Rutgers University Press.

Hills, Alice. 2000. *Policing Africa: Internal security and the limits of liberalization.* Boulder, CO: Lynne Rienner.

Johnston, L., and Clifford Shearing. 2004. *Governing security: Explorations in security and justice.* London: Routledge.

Marenin, Otwin, ed. 1996. *Policing change, changing police: International perspectives.* New York: Garland Publishing.

Police Quarterly. 2005. Special Issue on International Policing. Vol. 8 (1).

Reiner, Robert. 1980. Fuzzy thoughts: The police and law and order politics. *Sociological Review* 28 (2): 377–413.

Stenning, Philip. 2000. Powers and accountability of private police. *European Journal of Criminal Policy and Research* 3: 325–52.

TRAFFIC SERVICES AND MANAGEMENT

Significance

One of the most dangerous places to find oneself in the United States is driving or walking on streets or highways. The staggering death toll averages approximately fifty thousand fatalities annually, and citizens would not be surprised to learn that highway accidents are one of the leading causes of death among young people and police officers. The ironic part of this American tragedy is that systematic vehicle traffic deaths are often preventable. Educators, researchers, engineers, and law enforcement personnel, working together, can reduce injuries and fatalities.

Research: Developing Countermeasures

Investigative research provides specific data related to the causes of vehicle and traffic-related injuries and fatalities. Professionals who develop and recommend prevention strategies and countermeasures carefully evaluate the data. The major investigative factors include location, age, sex, and mortality rates. Researchers gather the data, analyze results, and then suggest appropriate remedial responses. The data derived from these investigations provide accurate information for scientific evaluation and education.

The National Highway Traffic Safety Administration (NHTSA) is involved in considerable research to support their mission to save lives, prevent injuries, and reduce vehicle-related crashes. Their Research and Development (R&D) and National Center for Statistics and Analysis (NCSA) are involved in extensive data collection to increase highway safety. The Fatality Analysis Reporting System (FARS) focuses on motor vehicle standards, traffic safety programs, and highway safety initiatives.

Identifying the Problem

Traffic accidents are rarely random or chance occurrences. Accidents result because of identifiable sequences of behavioral activities or, less often, as a result of mechanical or environmental events. The concept of the "88–10–2 ratio" has been utilized to represent the quantitative involvement of (1) human failure, (2) mechanical failure, and (3) unusual circumstances. Drivers cause accidents, rarely the vehicle or road design. Statistics indicate that as much as 95% of motor vehicle accidents are driver related.

The primary cause of accidents is human error or inattention. Investigators apply the multiple cause concept and view results from a combination of closely interconnected factors. In other words, accidents result from a developing sequence of multiple events and should not simply be viewed in terms of the immediate emergency event, or the last factor. Causes and countermeasures can be identified from the data derived from three basic accident phases: (1) preevent, (2) event, and (3) postevent.

The Three "E's" of Traffic Management

The three "E's" of traffic management are (1) education, (2) engineering, and (3) enforcement. Most accidents are preventable through the modification of human behaviors. The following strategies influence the prevention of motor vehicle accidents and fatalities: (1) education, (2) proactive police patrol, and (3) legal sanctions. In addition, better highway engineering would result in improved road design and intersection traffic control, while better auto engineering would create safer cars. All of the above-mentioned strategies require synchronization, cooperation, and shared responsibility among the partners and stakeholders.

Traffic Education

The preferred mode of prevention is education, though high-risk drivers are the least receptive to this traffic management strategy. Law enforcement agencies offer a variety of public traffic safety programs taught by their officers through civic groups, schools, and community organizations around the country.

One of the best-known programs is the high school driver education elective offered by school districts. However, not all students participate in this excellent safety and lifesaving experience. High school driver education programs are particularly relevant to this high-risk student population. Police officers who participate in high school driver education programs provide a meaningful and important contribution to a lifesaving effort.

Traffic Engineering

The field of traffic engineering addresses highway safety hazards through the careful planning of streets and highways. The primary focus of traffic engineers is on the movement of traffic; they consider the safest, most convenient, and most effective transportation routes for citizens and road design services. Traffic engineering is dependent on public safety managers and police officers to identify problematic intersections that create hazardous conditions. Accurate information allows engineers to allocate resources for road excavation and the appropriate designation of traffic control signals. Traffic studies and traffic investigations serve as the basis for addressing successful highway engineering solutions.

Traffic Accident Investigation

The necessary reliance on engineering, education, and enforcement programs requires excellent traffic accident data. Therefore, these requirements place a significant emphasis on thorough and accurate traffic accident investigation. The police traffic manager encourages the proper collection of traffic and accident investigation data for prevention measures and remedial countermeasures. Electronic scan sheets and computer software have improved the collection, collation, and dissemination of timely traffic accident data.

Computer technology can assist in traffic management and accident reconstruction, saving time and personnel resources and producing accurate information for accident reconstruction and courtroom testimony. The computer-aided drafting (CAD) programs assist in traffic reconstruction. There are numerous versions that assist in accident reconstruction. Computer software can analyze and perform measurement calculations from a hand-held laser. In addition, the software has the capacity to provide velocity calculations and three-dimensional accident reconstruction sketches.

An officer at the scene using CAD has the ability to accurately diagram the traffic accident and avoid double-checking steel tape measurements. Moreover, the laser range finder is extremely accurate and convenient and automatically downloads the measurement and vehicle location data. The data derived from accident investigation serve as the foundation for traffic management and selective enforcement programs.

Traffic Services Management Data

Traffic services management can identify the location of statistically higher numbers of traffic fatalities and injuries related to vehicle accidents. This form of traffic analysis focuses on the what, where, when, and why of traffic accidents. In addition, it provides a snapshot of the intersection and driver. Ultimately, the data can provide a long-range strategic picture and planning strategies and answer questions concerning future highway safety remedial actions. The immediate tactical use of the data is to analyze the systemic causes of accidents and prevent property damage, injuries, and fatalities.

This analysis of information assists patrol officers, who can then concentrate their efforts on estimated times and location of probable traffic violations. The intersection information is extrapolated from police records. Selective enforcement identifies (1) the type of accident, (2) location, (3) time, (4) driver error or other type of error, and (5) type of violation.

Traffic accident location files and spot or computerized maps, together with record data concerning the type of moving violations that have caused accidents, is incorporated in the assignment of officers and patrol allocation. The selective enforcement program assists in identifying similar violations at problematic intersections. Enforcement officers then cite violators for the type of driving violations that are causing multiple accidents.

Selective Enforcement

Selective enforcement data do not make an absolute prediction but an assumption based on inferential statistics. The data may come from computer-based police records system. In addition, geographic information systems (GISs), more commonly referred to as crime mapping, serve as an excellent resource. Traffic mapping symbols are an excellent tool for visualizing the traffic accident problem at a particular intersection. Statistics alone seem rather abstract; however, the combination of a computer-illustrated intersection and related photographs graphically portray the need for remedial enforcement action.

In smaller departments, selective enforcement requires a manual study of accident records. The cumbersome process includes the use of an accident location file and wall spot map. Tabulated information allows traffic officers to project a possible traffic accident curve for the future. The target goal is to calculate how many accidents are expected to happen, when, and at what location.

Division of Motor Vehicles

State licensing authorities maintain a central file of all resident drivers. The Point System is an important part of traffic management; the service seeks to take high-risk drivers off the road. After conviction in a court of law, the operator's driving record will reflect the entries. A driver may get points on his or her license for traffic violations. Subsequent violations and convictions may result in suspension or revocation of the driver's license. While the Point System is an effective driver control system for many drivers, it is not perfect. Problem drivers continue to drive while on suspension or revocation, in spite of the severe penalties.

Present and Future Trends

In the future, traffic management will focus on improving traffic engineering and computer technology. Increasingly, computer and satellite communications specialists are making a valuable contribution to traffic management. Greater cooperation among law enforcement officers and technical experts will be necessary. Furthermore, the increased reliance on computer technology in traffic services and management will require additional funding and training for law enforcement officers.

The computer-aided dispatch (CAD) systems and global positioning system (GPS) will eventually be able to locate and cross-reference traffic locations by grid coordinates. Traffic control under the Advanced Transportation Management Systems (ATMS) will seek to avoid congestion and delays and detect traffic accidents. Finally, closed-circuit television (CCTV) will play an increasing role in regulating traffic and locating accidents. The goal will be real-time reporting of traffic problems and pinpointing exact locations of traffic accidents.

Conclusion

Traffic services represent a collaborative effort across many disciplines. While education, engineering, and law enforcement are important, there are many more factors at work. Creating safer roads, safer cars, and, most important, safer drivers will help prevent traffic-related fatalities. Traffic services and management will remain a vital part of these lifesaving efforts.

THOMAS E. BAKER

See also **Crime Analysis; Drunk Driving; Liability and High-Speed Chases; Police Pursuits; Technology and the Police**

References and Further Reading

Clark, Warren E. 1982. *Traffic management and collision investigation.* Upper Saddle River, NJ: Prentice-Hall.

Dix, Jay, Michael Graham, and Randy Hanzlick. 2000. *Investigation of road traffic fatalities: An atlas.* Boca Raton, FL: CRC Press.

National Law Enforcement and Corrections Technology. 2004. *Tech beat: At the scene of a crash.* Washington, DC: U.S. Government Printing Office.

TRANSNATIONAL ORGANIZED CRIME

Without doubt the most compelling development in organized crime at the end of the twentieth century is the trend toward the development of transnational organized crime groups and the suggestion that these groups are beginning to collaborate and cooperate in a systematic manner to facilitate the delivery of illicit goods and services on an international scale. While organized crime scholars have thus far been quite careful in their description of this phenomenon, a real danger of a re-constructed and rehabilitated "alien conspiracy theory" of organized crime as a replacement for the discredited "Mafia" model of years past, emanating from the news media and the state, lurks as an imminent danger.

The fact is, despite the internationalization of crime, little has changed in the organization of syndicates. They are still rather informal, loosely structured, open, flexible organizations highly reactive to changes in the political and economic environments. The internationalization of organized crime has not resulted from some master plan by arch-criminals. It is simply a reflection of that reactive, ephemeral, flexible characteristic of crime syndicates that has allowed them to respond to technological advancements in communications and transportation; to market adaptations resulting from the internationalization of investment capital, financial services, and banking; to the internationalization of manufacturing and increased segmentation and fragmentation of production across international borders; and to the increased emphasis on international and unrestricted trade across borders.

Organized crime syndicates are still rooted in local conditions, shielded by local politics, and limited by the need to control personnel at the local level. The European Union weakens borders and encourages the free flow of people and goods. Russian, Italian, Romanian, British, and Corsican syndicates simply respond to the new reality. It is neither the Malina nor the Mafia who created these opportunities; rather, it is the state and multinational corporations. Nigerian drug traffickers are not responsible for the enormous recent increase in international trade or heightened flow of people across borders. They merely take advantage of the situation. When they collaborate with Asian heroin producers, it does not signify the birth of a new international criminal order; it merely reflects the same types of arrangements that are occurring in the business community at large. Poppy growers can now market their products over a wider arena. Nigerian smugglers have a mechanism in place to efficiently take advantage of new technologies and opportunities. Collaboration is as natural as a compact between U.S. car manufacturers and parts producers in Brazil or Mexico. However, the fact remains that the Nigerian syndicates are firmly rooted in economic inequality and pervasive patterns of corruption that are distinctly Nigerian.

The major issue is not collaboration between and among organized crime groups but increased political corruption brought on by greater rewards from international commerce and weakened central governments whose powers have been surpassed and often usurped by multinational corporations. National sovereignty is not threatened by Colombian cartels, Southeast Asian warlords, Russian criminal entrepreneurs, or Zambian cattle poachers; it is threatened by pervasive and growing corruption and the increasing irrelevance of individual states in an international economy.

Organized crime has not changed very much from the system of patron–client relations described by Albini, the system that operates within the context of illicit entrepreneurship described by Smith, or that which is facilitated by the businessmen, law enforcement officials, and politicians of Chambliss's crime networks. Organized crime syndicates are still localized, fragmented, and highly ephemeral entities. The only difference is that the world has changed, and organized crime has adapted. An understanding of the nature of those world changes is vital for an understanding of transnational organized crime in the twenty-first century.

The International Political Economy and Organized Crime

As a complex social phenomenon, organized crime has always been highly sensitive to developments in the economy, the political environment, and the social world. Dramatic late twentieth and early twenty-first century changes in global politics and economics have impacted both the opportunities and constraints confronting organized crime and, as a result, have initiated a series of organic changes in the way criminal organizations do business. The contexts within which criminal organizations operate are undergoing fundamental change.

The emergence and development of the "global village" in the second half of the twentieth century has fundamentally changed the context in which both legitimate and illegitimate businesses operate (Williams 1994):

Increased interdependence between nations, the ease of international travel and communications, the permeability of national boundaries, and the globalization of international financial networks have facilitated the emergence of what is, in effect, a single global market for both licit and illicit commodities.

Certainly, recent years have seen a vast increase in transnational commerce, as information, money, physical goods, people, and other tangible commodities move freely across state boundaries. This globalization of trade and a growing international consumer demand for leisure products have created a natural impetus for a fundamental change in the character of many criminal organizations from essentially localized vice networks to transnational organized crime groups (Williams 1994). These opportunities have manifested themselves in five areas, all of which are outside the domain of organized crime groups, but each of which profoundly impacts criminal organizations: (1) the ease of international transport, (2) the growth of international trade, (3) new computer and communications technology, (4) the rapacious growth of global financial networks, and (5) the creation of and opening of new markets.

In the last half of the twentieth century, the ability of people to easily move across large distances increased dramatically, as did the ability of people to move materials across equally large distances. In 1999, some 395 million people entered the United States overland from Mexico and Canada, seventy-six million people arrived on more than 928,000 commercial airline and private flights, and nine million arrived by sea. In addition, 135 million vehicles—including automobiles and commercial trucks—crossed U.S. borders with Mexico and Canada, and more than two hundred thousand merchant and passenger ships and other maritime vessels docked at U.S. seaports or U.S. coastal harbors. U.S. seaports handled more than

4.4 million shipping containers and four hundred million tons of cargo in 1999. U.S. Customs is able to inspect only about 3% of the goods entering the United States, a figure that will drop to about 1% by the end of the first decade of the new century as the volume of trade continues to grow. The movement of vast numbers of people across international frontiers significantly increases the recruitment base for criminal organizations around the world (Godson and Olson 1995).

The growth of free trade and the gradual elimination of tariffs, restrictive covenants, and international barriers to commerce has resulted in an explosive growth in import and export markets. In the United States, the volume of trade doubled between 1994 and 2005. The same global trade network that facilitates legitimate import–export operations also serves criminal organizations well. Global trade networks enhance the mobility of criminal organizations and create new markets for both illicit and licit services provided by criminal organizations (Williams 1994). The shift of some cocaine cartels to heroin as a product line and the entry of other cocaine cartels into the European market are prime examples of market mobility enhanced by international trade (Godson and Olson 1995).

Recent innovations in computer and communications technology also have important implications for criminal organizations, particularly with regard to their overall flexibility and adaptability in hostile environments (Godson and Olson 1995). Electronic fund transfer systems move billions of dollars around the world with the click of a mouse, making money laundering and the concealment of financial assets much easier than in the past. Encryption technology for faxes and cellular telephones have rendered electronic monitoring and tracing problematic at best. Signal interceptors, now readily available on aircraft, make it much easier for drug couriers to plot radar and avoid monitoring (Elliott 1993). Conducting business across state borders enhances the ability of criminal organizations to keep law enforcement at bay. Problems of coordination, security, and corruption often become insurmountable for state agencies. In addition, diversifying illicit operations and locales greatly enhance the ability of criminal organizations to recover from losses resulting from social control activity or even the acts of competitors (Godson and Olson 1995).

Money is the most fungible of all commodities, since it can be transmitted instantaneously and at low cost. It is chameleon in character, changing its identity easily. In the newly expanded global financial networks, money can be traced only with the greatest of difficulty, if at all. Governments were already at extreme disadvantages in areas of taxation, regulation, and the control of economic activities. The present-day global financial network makes the transfer of profits from illegal transactions easy, fast, and virtually immune from discovery. Money laundering, already an art form, is now an art form conducted at warp speed. The internationalization of finance has rendered state law and state economic policy impotent (Williams 1994).

The expansion of international trade, the globalization of financial networks, and the revolution in communications technology have led to the development of new markets in industrial and postindustrial mass consumption societies. In addition, the heightened level of integration brought about by the creation of a global economy has resulted in a degree of global transparency that has accentuated inequalities between societies and that has led to the emulation by developing countries of patterns of consumption in economically advanced societies. This combined with the ease of travel and the expansion in international communications has led to a convergence of consumer tastes in many societies around the world. Entrepreneurs, both criminal and noncriminal, have recognized the opportunities this presents for global markets and have tried to exploit them (Williams 1994).

The Changing Character of Organized Crime in a Global Economy

The creation of mass consumer markets encourages the growth of organized crime in several ways. First, just as with multinational corporations, these new transnational markets are open to criminal organizations. Second, criminal organizations may be better suited to exploit these opportunities than legitimate corporations. Criminal organizations have expertise in operating outside the law, outside regulations, and outside norms of business practice, and they have few qualms about legal niceties in violating international borders. Criminal organizations operate outside the existing structures of authority and have developed strategies for circumventing law enforcement both in individual nations and across international boundaries (Williams 1994).

Increasingly, criminal organizations are becoming transnational in nature, conducting centrally directed operations in the territory of two or more nation-states, mobilizing resources and pursuing optimizing strategies across international borders. These organizations are still functionally specific in that they seek only to penetrate new markets, not to acquire new "turf." Unlike their multinational corporate counterparts, who seek to gain access to new territories and markets through negotiations with states, criminal organizations obtain access through circumventions, not consent. They engage in systematic activities to evade governmental controls, which is possible because the conditions that give rise to their emergence also make it very difficult for governments to contain and control them (Williams 1994).

Criminal organizations continue to be extremely diverse in their structure, outlook, and membership. But in the postmodern world what they have in common is that changes in technology, economy, and trade rules have made them highly mobile, even more adaptive than before, and have vested them with the ability to operate across national borders with ease. This is partly the result of the forces discussed above and partly because criminal organizations have always been constructed as informal social networks rather than formal organizations, immensely increasing their flexibility and adaptability.

It is a matter of more than passing interest that formal, legal organizations, including corporations and some agencies of the state, have been moving in the direction of more flexible, fluid, network structures in response to changes in the global economy. Not surprisingly, then, criminal organizations have a distinct advantage in that they have always operated covertly and have always deemphasized fixed structures as a rational response to their illegality (Williams 1994).

Strategic Alliances and Modern Organized Crime

As a result of their increasingly transnational character and following the lead of transnational corporations, criminal organizations have increasingly sought out strategic alliances with other criminal organizations. For multinational corporations, strategic alliances facilitate production where costs are low and allow corporations to take advantage of local knowledge and experience in marketing and distribution. Criminal organizations pursue strategic alliances for many of the same reasons (Williams 1994).

First of all, strategic alliances are simply rational responses to the emergence of global markets and in particular to what is called the global–local nexus. The concept of a global market may still sound foreboding to some, but in fact it is just a composite of local markets that have become increasingly homogenized. For any corporation, legal or illegal, there are two ways to increase profits in the marketplace: One is to gain entrance to new markets and the other to expand market share in existing markets. Multinational corporations and criminal organizations alike often find it easier to enter local markets that have been outside their purview or area of activity if they cooperate with organizations that are already entrenched in these markets, which have greater knowledge of local conditions and are more attuned to local problems, rather than trying to insert themselves as competitors in unfamiliar territory. Linking with host criminal groups to facilitate access to new markets is the major impetus behind transnational strategic alliances between criminal organizations (Williams 1994).

Strategic alliances are also quite useful as mechanisms to neutralize and/or co-opt potential competitors in a market. Cooperative strategies often offer a rational and effective response to a highly competitive situation. Cooperation with a strong competitor already enjoying high profitability in a market can lead to local market dominance. A strong local competitor can be offered various incentives for entering into a strategic alliance. For example, the local organization's market share could be increased through the introduction of more diverse products. The promise of an entirely new market might be contingent on a strategic alliance or the exchange of some other valuable goods or services (for example, political contacts, ancillary services, or specialized support). Whatever the reasons, the promise of mutual benefit is the foundation of transnational strategic alliances between criminal organizations (Williams 1995).

Third, strategic alliances are also very effective as a means of circumventing restrictions, regulations, and barriers to markets. Where state regulations make it difficult to enter a market, the formation of an alliance with an organization that already has access to the market is an attractive means of overcoming obstacles (Williams 1995).

Finally, the formation of a strategic alliance can be an indispensable means of minimizing or spreading risk. Multinational corporations know that expanding their activities and entering new markets requires new investments and capital cost outlays. Being able to reduce or spread risks enables both corporations and criminal organizations to take advantage of opportunities that might otherwise have appeared to be too risky. The synergy inherent in a strategic alliance means that the participants are able to do things that neither one could do alone, at least not with anything like the same effectiveness or confidence (Williams 1995).

Strategic alliances are usually configured in one of three ways, depending upon the objectives of the criminal organizations involved. The most common form is a franchise alliance that is anchored by a large, well-developed, and highly stable criminal organization that does business with several smaller, independent local criminal organizations. Another common form strategic alliances take is that of a compensatory alliance, in which two criminal organizations recognize that each one, acting alone, has several inherent weaknesses that are offset by an alliance. A third type of strategic alliance is the specialization alliance, in which one criminal organization seeks an alliance with another in order to fulfill needs for specialized tasks beyond the purview and abilities of the first organization. Specialization alliances are contractual relationships covering specific tasks and responsibilities. Countertrade alliances are simple exchange relationships between criminal organizations in which goods or services are exchanged for other goods or services. Finally, a supplier alliance involves regularized relationships between various suppliers of basic raw materials and organizations that transform these materials into consumer products. Such alliances are common in the drug trade (Williams 1995).

Future Trends Impacting Criminal Organizations

The character changes in organized crime initiated by rapidly expanding international travel and trade, developing communications technology, and the globalization of finance will likely continue to accelerate in the coming years. A number of factors point to this acceleration.

For poor farmers in many nations around the world, choosing to grow drug-related crops makes the greatest economic sense. Markets for other commodities such as coffee, rice, and gladiolus are far less profitable and very unstable. In most places, even where the necessary marketing infrastructure and expertise exist, government controls make entry into those legitimate markets almost impossible for peasants. At the same time, drug entrepreneurs are expanding into markets where drugs have not been a major consumer item in the past. Without dramatic and unlikely changes, raw materials for drug production will continue to be readily available (Godson and Olson 1995).

There is a global trend toward ungovernability—that is, the declining ability of governments to govern, to manage a modern state, and to provide adequate or effective services. In some cases criminal organizations have been able to capitalize on the fact that large areas, such as the Andes and Amazon regions in South America or much of the Golden Triangle in Southeast Asia, were never under effective government control. Criminal organizations have moved into these remote regions and have provided the major source of authority and social control in them. In other cases, criminal organizations have begun to contest local control of areas with the government. This situation provides favorable conditions for criminal groups to establish bases of operations and safe havens, particularly in areas key to drug trafficking and alien smuggling. Political geographers predict further continuing global fragmentation. Criminal organizations thrive where governments are weak (Godson and Olson 1995).

Local criminal organizations often expand following immigration patterns. As the new century unfolds, economic pressures and widespread ethnic turmoil are likely to generate refugees and immigrants from regions where international criminal groups are based. Criminal organizations tend to exploit immigrant communities in a variety of ways. Such communities may provide cover and concealment. Immigrants also provide a pool of recruits. In addition, new immigrants are also usually fearful of law enforcement. Their recent experiences in their countries of origin make them reluctant to cooperate with police in their new countries.

Technological and transportation advances will facilitate growth in transnational criminal operations. The ease of modern communications makes contact among criminal organizations easy, fast, and more secure. New digital technologies make it more difficult for law enforcement agencies to intercept communications. The movements of trillions of dollars in wire transfers each day make it possible for most actors to evade state monitoring (Godson and Olson 1995).

Preventing, disrupting, and prosecuting organized crime is difficult even under the best of conditions. The growth of transnational markets and the accompanying criminal organizations ready and willing to operate in those markets will make the task even more complex and immensely more difficult.

GARY W. POTTER

See also **Federal Police and Investigative Agencies; Intelligence Gathering and Analysis: Impacts on Terrorism; Organized Crime; Racketeer Influenced and Corrupt Organizations Act (RICO)**

References and Further Reading

Godson, R., and W. Olson. 1995. International organized crime. *Society* 32 (2): 18–29.

Reuter, P., and J. Haaga. 1989. *The organization of high-level drug markets: An exploratory study*. Santa Monica, CA: RAND Corporation.

Williams, P. 1994. Transnational criminal organizations and international security. *Survival* 36 (1): 96–113.

———. 1995. Transnational criminal organizations: Strategic alliances. *Washington Quarterly* 18 (1): 57–72.

TRIBAL POLICE

Tribal police are the primary law enforcement agencies on Native American Indian (hereafter, Indian) reservations. Historically, enforcement of tribal law has rested with the Tribal Council's appointee. Using the Southern Ute Indian Tribe, located in southwest Colorado, as one example, the War Sub-Chief was primarily responsible for enforcement of the laws of the tribe (Abril 2005). Treaties and public laws mandate that democratic governments and traditional American methods of tertiary social control follow the model of the European-based policing system found throughout the United States, according to the Wheeler-Howard Act of June 18, 1934, also known as the Indian Reorganization Act, or IRA.

All federally recognized Indian tribes that do not reside in states governed by Public Law 280 [67 Stat. 588 (1953)] are required to maintain a three-pronged (executive, legislative, and judicial) democratic government. Often this includes a law enforcement agency as part of its judicial arm. Many such tribes also maintain a tribal police department (Bureau of Justice Statistics 2003). Indian reservations located in states governed by Public Law 280 are usually policed by local city or county law enforcement agencies and are also required to have a democratic government in place. In addition to this,

Wakeling et al. (2001, 7) reported that the Indian Self-Determination and Education Assistance Act of 1975 (also known as Public Law 93-638), under which tribal police who hold contracts with the Bureau of Indian Affairs Division of Law Enforcement Services provide law enforcement on reservations, "establishes the department's organizational framework and performance standards and basic funding for the police function."

Powers of modern tribal police are also codified in two ways. First, tribal codes authorize the police to perform certain duties within the boundaries of the reservation. Such duties include responding to calls for service, enforcement of tribal laws and ordinances, and maintaining order on the reservation. Second, power is vested in the police by the members of the tribal community. When tribal members observe that the police act in a positive, unbiased manner, then the police earn the trust and confidence of the community. When this is accomplished, then the power the police exert is validated and will usually be accepted by the majority of the tribal membership. This is often evidenced by the tribal community's acquiescence to police directives. The implicit power of the tribal police is required to maintain order in times of crisis as well as during normal times (Abril, forthcoming).

The powers given to the tribal police exist only within the boundaries of the reservation unless they have been cross-deputized, a practice that is gradually becoming common. Cross-deputization occurs when the tribal police receive state-sanctioned training and are empowered to enforce local and state laws outside the boundaries of the reservation. Likewise, state or local police are expected to respond to issues occurring within the boundaries of a specific Indian reservation and are empowered by the local Tribal Council to enforce state laws on the reservation.

Cross-deputizing tribal police with local, county, or state law enforcement agencies is seen as a means to better facilitate apprehension of criminal offenders who travel from one jurisdiction to another in an attempt to elude capture. Having tribal police cross-deputized also allows officers to receive better training that is often more readily provided to nontribal police officers. Finally, cross-deputization of tribal and local police is necessary for Indian reservations whose territory includes both tribal and nontribal lands. These types of reservations are called "checkerboard" reservations and provide unique law enforcement challenges to tribal, local, and state law enforcement officers. For example, in one such Indian reservation, tribal, local, and county lands are located within a one-block area in a town situated within the boundaries of the reservation. When a crime is reported in this area, members of all relevant policing agencies often arrive at the scene to determine with whom investigative jurisdiction resides. Criminal jurisdiction is determined by the type of crime committed. Most tribal police have jurisdiction only over misdemeanors and ordinances found in the tribal code. Felonies fall under the jurisdiction of either the Bureau of Indian Affairs (BIA) Law Enforcement Services or the Federal Bureau of Investigation (FBI).

With some unique exceptions, the duties of tribal police are similar to those of the modern American police. Enforcement of traffic laws, preventing juvenile crime, protection of life and property, and criminal investigations are just a few of the responsibilities of the tribal police (Bureau of Justice Statistics 2003). Tribal police, however, are often called upon to respond to cultural and/or spiritual matters of the tribe by whom they are employed. Such cultural matters may include responding to spirit entities or trespassers into tribal ceremonies.

During a recent study of one tribal police department, tribal community members were asked why Indians might call for help from the police. One tribal member reported that she would call the tribal police "if something weird or evil was going on . . . Skin Walkers, they're all over the place . . . it's a shape shifter [an Indian spirit]." In this same study, it was found that only officers who are tribal members were believed to be able to respond to these types of calls for service (Abril 2004, 2005). In this particular tribe, a female officer who is also a member of the tribe is often called upon to respond to these cultural and spiritual incidents. The tribal members have given over powers to the police to respond to matters once under the jurisdiction of its tribal spiritual leaders. Tribal members have negotiated this exchange of tertiary power in order to free themselves of extraneous burdens for which they might lack the specialized skills and/or the desire to deal with (Abril, forthcoming).

Some of the challenges facing modern tribal police are similar to those faced by the American police in the early years of our country. Lack of adequate staffing levels, old equipment, and a poor reputation among the tribal community are just a few of the challenges facing some modern tribal police agencies (Abril 2004; Wakeling et al. 2001; Wood 2001). Other problems include a lack of jurisdictional maps and inadequate methods to record offenses and arrests for use in determining official crime rates. In one tribal police department, for example, it was found that arrests are currently hand-tallied on sheets of yellow legal paper. Moreover, it was found that only a few types of crimes are recorded. For example, arrests for drunkenness were not listed on the hand tally or in any other manner, yet public drunkenness is said to be one of the most common crimes on this reservation (Abril 2004).

Positive steps, however, are being taken to change these conditions. It is not uncommon for entire administrations to be replaced if they are perceived by the community to be corrupt or if there is evidence of corruption among the officers and/or the command staff. Such changes have often been welcomed by the tribal community, while the negative perception of the police (often the result of the behavior of officers of the previous administration) lingers on to shadow the new administration and officers for years to follow (Abril 2004).

Congress has allotted funds to help tribal police to fund capital improvements to their detention facilities, purchase state-of-the-art equipment, provide for advanced officer training, and generally improve tribal law enforcement on Indian reservations (Native American Law Enforcement Reform Act). Police dispatchers, too, are receiving aid for training.

Professionalization has become a priority among many tribal police agencies. Many send their officers to either a tribal police academy located in Albuquerque, New Mexico, or to a state-sponsored police academy. The National Native American Law Enforcement Association (NNALEA) is also experiencing a surge in membership as tribal police officers move toward the professionalization of both individual officers and entire departments (NNALEA 2001, 2002). Classes on cultural sensitivity, while a mainstay in large agencies located in major metropolitan areas where cultural diversity is the essence of the jurisdiction, are also being taken by tribal officers who are not Indian.

It is not uncommon for tribal police departments to employ officers who are either not members of the tribe, are members of other tribes, or are not Indian. These officers are learning the cultural idiosyncrasies of the tribal community in which they work. In the police study previously cited, it was found that tribal members do not, for the most part, feel that the officers of their police department must only be Indian. It was reported that tribal members respect non-Indian officers if such officers prove to be honest and fair.

Finally, most tribal police departments appear to be moving in the direction of modernization and into a form of professional assimilation with nontribal agencies. Modern tribal police departments are also growing in size and diversification. Their duties are varied, and the challenges they face are being overcome with congressional assistance and community support. It will, however, be some time before all tribal police departments are on the same level as local and state policing agencies.

JULIE C. ABRIL

See also **Accountability; Community Attitudes toward the Police**

References and Further Reading

Abril, J. C. 2004. *Final report to the Bureau of Justice Statistics from the Southern Ute Indian Community Safety Survey*. Washington, DC: U.S. Department of Justice/OJP/BJS. Award No. 2001-3277-CA-BJ.

———. 2005. The relevance of culture, ethnic identity, and collective: Efficacy to violent victimization in one Native American Indian tribal community. Ph.D. diss. University of California, Irvine. ProQuest/UMI 3167918.

———. Forthcoming. Negotiation of tertiary power in a Native American Indian tribal community.

Bureau of Justice Statistics. 2003. *Tribal law enforcement, 2000*. Washington, DC: U.S. Department of Justice /OJP/BJS.

Indian Self-Determination and Education Assistance Act of 1975, Public Law 93-638. 88 Stat. 2203 (1975).

National Native American Law Enforcement Association (NNALEA). 2001. *Indian tribes receive federal law enforcement grants*. http://www.nnalea.org/archives/fedlaenfgrants.htm.

———. 2002. *INNALEA 2002 accomplishments*. http://www.nnalea.org/archives/NNALEA2002Accomplishments.htm.

Native American Law Enforcement Reform Act. 25 USC 2801.

U.S. Public Law 280, 83rd Congress 67 Stat. 588 (1953).

Wakeling, S., M. Jorgensen, S. Michaelson, and M. Begay. 2001. *Policing on American Indian reservations: A report to the National Institute of Justice.* Washington, DC: U.S. Department of Justice/OJP/NIJ.

Wheeler-Howard Act of June 18, 1934 (also known as the Indian Reorganization Act (IRA). 48 Stat. 984 (1934).

Wood, D. 2001. *Police turnover in isolated communities: The Alaska experience.* Washington, DC: U.S. Department of Justice/OJP/NIJ.

U

UNDERCOVER INVESTIGATIONS

Undercover investigations involve covert means of discovering information based on the actions of a human agent. The agent may be a sworn police officer or an informer with unique access to criminal milieu. The informer may provide information and serve to introduce the police officer to the milieu, in return for leniency, financial benefits, or other benefits. The defining characteristic of such investigations is secrecy with respect to the true identity or purposes of the actor(s). Undercover means are often used in conjunction with other covert means such as hidden video and audio recorders and location tracking devices. But the presence of an active human agent who can influence the course of events sets the undercover investigation apart from more passive means of secretly gathering information.

The interaction may be impersonal. Consider the case of a police agent acting as a fence in a property theft sting, who pretends to be interested in purchasing stolen goods from whomever enters the storefront. Alternately, the interaction can be of a more intimate nature, involving friends (or one who pretends to be a friend) and even family members who covertly gather evidence against those with whom they have a personal relationship. The interaction can occur in places that are legally public and visible to the public, as on a street corner, or it may occur on private property and/or in places that are not visible. In such private settings an overt investigation requires a search warrant, but in the undercover context the search is deemed to be voluntary and hence there is no warrant requirement.

The police use of deception as a tool for gathering evidence can be viewed as a necessary evil in a context in which police face legal and logistical limitations when investigating crimes of a consensual nature that do not involve a direct victim as with vice or bribery; those in which victims may be unaware and thus not complain, as is frequently the case with white collar crimes such as consumer fraud; those where witnesses and victims are intimidated, rewarded, or indifferent and do not report crimes or cooperate with authorities; and those where there are well-organized and well-insulated criminal groups engaged in complex violations, against whom it is difficult to gather evidence. In such contexts the law is likely to be underenforced relative to more easily discoverable and prosecutable offenses. Undercover means offer a way of bringing some equity to that pattern.

The challenge is of course to prevent secret police means from becoming an unnecessary evil, serving private goals apart from the investigation of crime or by violating the spirit, if not the strict legality, of laws limiting police powers and protecting civil liberties and civil rights.

Undercover methods are a more common feature of conventional criminal investigations in the United States than in Europe. Police in the United States face very few restrictions in their use of deception before an arrest has been made. Even then, the use of jailhouse informers is not uncommon. Police can go very far in offering temptations and encouragement to those they suspect. Unlike police in much of Europe, police in the United States are generally exempt from criminal prosecution when their undercover role involves them in work-related violations of the criminal law.

However, in the American context, in contrast to many countries in Europe, those arrested can use the defense of entrapment. This was initially recognized by the Supreme Court in the 1932 *Sorrells* case. The government must carefully walk the line between laying a trap for the "unwary innocent" and the "unwary criminal" (a distinction noted in the 1958 *Sherman* case). But the entrapment defense is not commonly used. To successfully use this defense, arrested persons must convincingly argue that they were not otherwise predisposed to the violation that occurred. This permits the prosecution to introduce any relevant prior criminal record to prove the opposite. This subjective standard refers to the motivation of the person arrested rather than the objective behavior of police, who on occasion may go to extremes to induce, or contribute to, the violation. In principle, a constitutional standard of due process might be applied in support of the objective defense, but this is extremely rare.

Beyond the courts, covert police means are subject to varying degrees of control by legislatures. There are also internal means of control involving policy guidelines, review boards, personnel selection, training, and supervision.

Several types of undercover operation as defined by their basic objective can be noted: intelligence, preventive, and facilitative investigations. Intelligence undercover efforts may be postliminary or anticipatory. The former involves seeking information after the fact. Police know that a crime occurred and seek to learn the identity and location of those responsible. Anticipatory intelligence undercover efforts are more diffuse and open ended and involve an effort to learn about events that may be planned but have not yet occurred. Informers are central to such efforts.

Investigations with prevention as their main goal can involve strengthening a potential victim (sometimes called target hardening) or suspect weakening. Prevention is sought by making the victim less vulnerable, weakening the ability of suspects to act, and/or increasing the likelihood that they will be identified and apprehended. The latter is intended to deter. In place of formal arrest and prosecution in which actions taken are subject to court procedures and review, preventive undercover actions sometimes involve the legally and morally gray areas of disruption and subversion.

A form of prevention can also be seen when charges involving conspiracy are brought. These are difficult to prove and often controversial, since only the planning of the action, rather than its being carried out, is involved. The latter brings a presumption of guilt on someone's part after an event has occurred. In contrast, some planned actions stopped via conspiracy charges might not actually have been carried out even absent law enforcement attention. Those in law enforcement face difficult questions in deciding whether and when to take preventive actions.

Facilitative undercover operations are far more common than preventive ones. Perhaps ironically, their goal is to encourage the commission of a crime rather than to prevent it. This may be done to make arrests, remove contraband such as drugs or weapons from the street, recover stolen property, or generate leverage over an informer. In contrast to preventive efforts, we may see victim weakening and/or suspect strengthening.

Undercover operations can be very costly to other values and have the potential for unintended consequences and abuse, relative to overt means such as when those identified as police carry out interviews, do searches, and interrogate suspects. Civil liberties, privacy, and a general societal sense of trust may be undermined. The practice of making deals with criminals is troubling to some observers.

In addition, if not done cautiously and competently, the use of covert means can increase crime and cause events that would never have happened, absent police intervention. This could occur as a result of providing a motive or temptation for a crime, persuading or coercing an otherwise nonpredisposed person, providing a scarce skill or resource without which the crime could not be carried out, creating a market for the purchase or sale of illegal goods and services, and the indirect provision of resources used for other illegality. Resources can also be wasted in preventing actions that would never have occurred anyway. The tactic may also harm the undercover agent and innocent third parties.

With appropriate legal and departmental restrictions and supervision, problems can be reduced. Problems are more likely as we move from intelligence gathering to more active efforts aimed at deceptively shaping an event creating criminal milieu. Offering a target for victimization usually raises fewer problems than does carrying out preventive or coconspiratorial actions. Investigations based on prior intelligence or complaints that are close to real-world criminal environments are likely to raise fewer questions than those involving random integrity testing or the creation of an artificial criminal environment with unduly attractive temptations.

Even with the best of intentions, personnel, and policies, the use and control of covert tactics are more difficult than is the case with overt tactics. Undercover work is paradoxical and of necessity involves certain risks and tradeoffs.

Consider efforts to do good by doing bad (for example, lies, deceit, trickery), to try to reduce crime yet unintentionally increase it, to restrict police use of coercion associated with increased use of deception; consider seeing criminal informers act as police and police act as criminals. There are also conflicts between gathering intelligence and taking action that gives the intelligence away, between rigid bureaucratic efforts to eliminate or reduce discretion and the need for creativity and flexibility in ever-changing situations, between prevention and apprehension, and between the operational advantages offered by secrecy and the need for accountability.

The many contexts and types of undercover tactics and the different roles that informers and police agents may play prevent any sweeping conclusions. However, given the unique characteristics of undercover work such as secrecy, prevention, temptation, immersion in criminal worlds, and entrapment, the tactic should generally be one of last resort, used only for serious offenses and subjected to intense oversight at all stages. There must be proportionality between the seriousness of a problem and the risks associated with the means. Sometimes the risks or costs of taking action will be greater than not taking action.

GARY T. MARX

See also **Accountability; Attitudes toward the Police: Overview; Codes of Ethics;**

Criminal Informants; Criminal Investigation; Detectives; Entrapment; Ethics and Values in the Context of Community Policing; Informants, Use of; Intelligence Gathering and Analysis: Impacts on Terrorism; Organized Crime; Sting Tactics

References and Further Reading

Barefoot, J. K. 1995. *Undercover investigations.* Oxford: Butterworth Heinemann.

Bok, S. 1978. *Lying: Moral choice in public and private life.* New York: Pantheon Books.

Fijnaut, C., and G. T. Marx, eds. 1995. *Undercover: Police surveillance in comparative perspective.* The Hague: Kluwer International.

Marx, G. T. 1988. *Undercover: Police surveillance in America.* Berkeley: University of California Press.

Pistone, J. 1997. *Donnie Brasco: My undercover life in the Mafia.* New York: Signet.

Ross, J. 2005. Impediments to transnational cooperation in undercover policing: A comparative study of the United States and Italy. *American Journal of Comparative Law.*

Sherman v. United States, 356 U.S. 369, 372 (1958).

Skolnick, J., and R. Leo. 1992. The ethics of deceptive interrogation. *Criminal Justice Ethics* 11 (1): 3–12.

Sorrells v. United States, 287 U.S. 425 (1932).

UNIFORM CRIME REPORTS

Of all available statistical series on crime, criminality, victimization, and criminal justice processing of offenders, unquestionably the most widely used (and often misused) is the *Uniform Crime Reports* (UCR) maintained by the Federal Bureau of Investigation (FBI). The agency's well-known statistical report, *Crime in the United States,* published annually in print and online (http://www.fbi.gov/ucr/ucr. htm), presents summary and detailed tabulations of offenses known to the police and cleared by arrest, of persons arrested, and of counts of law enforcement personnel employed throughout the country.

Most attention is focused on Part I crimes—murder and nonnegligent manslaughter, forcible rape, robbery, aggravated assault, burglary, larceny/theft, motor vehicle theft, and arson. Crime counts, rates, and trends for these offenses are presented for the nation as a whole, for geographic divisions, population subgroups based on size, states, metropolitan areas, individual cities, counties, and college campuses. In addition, clearance rates—the percentages of offenses cleared by arrest or some other means—are provided in summary form for national and subnational aggregates.

Part II offenses include an array of violent, property, and status offenses, from simple assault to kidnapping, from drug violations to runaways. Because many of these criminal activities are not discrete countable offenses, the focus is only on the number of persons arrested. In addition, tabulations are generated by age, race, and sex of arrestees.

Thus, it is known offenses that are counted for Part I crimes but known offenders who are counted for Part II crimes.

History of the UCR Program

While federal initiatives to measure the nation's population, health, and economy are nearly as long-standing as the republic itself, federal involvement in efforts to measure crime dates only as far back as the 1920s. Partially out of concern for refuting media-constructed "crime waves" based on anecdotal evidence (Maltz 1977), the International Association of Chiefs of Police (IACP) recommended forcefully that the U.S. Department of Justice establish a report card on crime. On June 11, 1930, Congress passed legislation directing the Justice Department to undertake this venture, and the attorney general then assigned this responsibility to the FBI.

Initially, the UCR was published monthly but was converted to a quarterly publication in 1932. In 1942, the report was shifted to a semiannual timetable, and later, in 1958, it became the annual publication *(Crime in the United States)* that exists today (along with semiannual preliminary counts).

From its inception, participation in the UCR program by local police agencies has been strictly voluntary (except for congressional legislation in 1990 mandating that colleges and universities provide crime data). With much to do during the Depression and beyond, the level of participation was limited (initially only 879 cities participated) and grew slowly over the years. Not until the early 1960s did the level of compliance reach the point where 90% of the U.S. population was covered (Maltz 1999).

The first thirty years of crime reporting were not only spotty in terms of population coverage, but there was no attempt to produce a national crime figure. Not until 1958, following the recommendations of the Consultant Committee on Uniform Crime Reporting, chaired by criminologist Peter Lejins (see FBI 1958), did the FBI's Crime Index emerge.

The committee's report advanced a long list of recommendations, many of which were immediately adopted (see FBI 1958). For example, manslaughter by negligence was dropped from the Part I group of offenses, and statutory rape was eliminated from forcible rape counts. Larcenies of property valued less than $50, because of their relatively trivial nature, were removed from larceny tabulations, although fifteen years later, in 1973, they were reincorporated into the larceny/theft counts in recognition that a fixed threshold would have changing significance over time.

In 1979, by congressional mandate, arson was added to the list of Part I offenses. Even though arson was fundamentally different in terms of identification (by the fire marshal), the pressure from special interest groups led Congress to insist on this inclusion.

For the next half century, the Crime Index became a closely followed figure, on par with the cost of living index (CPI), the unemployment rate, and other national indicators. Unfortunately, its many limitations were not fully understood at first. But in 2004, after nearly fifty years of usage and recurrent criticism (see, for example, Wolfgang 1963), the Crime Index (specifically the reporting of the total volume and rate of all Part I crimes) was discontinued, even though violent and property aggregates were retained (and could easily be added to derive the previously used crime total). In suspending its use, the FBI hoped to discourage the notion that the crime total was in fact a real index (FBI 2004).

Measuring Crime Incidence

Unlike the efforts of the U.S. Bureau of the Census to conduct a complete enumeration of the population, the FBI's crime count is hardly considered complete as a picture of the level of crime nationally. Of course, only certain crimes are designated as Part I types and, therefore, included in the crime count. That is, the "Crime Known to Police" tallies are counts of criminal homicides, forcible rapes, robberies, aggravated assaults, burglaries, larcenies, and motor vehicle thefts and arsons, both completed and attempted, ignoring the large array of other criminal activity.

Although participation rates have improved over the years, certain law enforcement agencies do not contribute data to the FBI, either directly or through an intermediate state crime statistics agency. For this reason, the UCR section of the FBI has utilized a variety of imputation strategies for estimating crime levels for agencies that fail to report data for a partial or entire year (Maltz 1999).

No attempt is made, however, to adjust for the most critical and fundamental drawback in completeness stemming from crimes that go unreported to the police. The so-called dark figure of crime (see Biederman and Reiss 1967) varies considerably across offenses and over time, complicating the interpretation of crime measures. While some offenses, such as homicide and motor vehicle theft, have high rates of reporting by victims or other parties, crimes such as forcible rape and larceny are notoriously low in terms of reporting rates. This can be especially problematic when examining trends over time. For example, an increase in the number of rapes in a jurisdiction may reflect either a true rise in sexual assaults or greater willingness of victims to report to the police.

Aside from minor modifications (such as renaming auto theft as motor vehicle theft in 1974) and the temporary dollar threshold for larceny described above, the definition of what constitutes a Part I crime has remained fairly uniform since the designation was introduced in 1958. The application of these definitions is, however, hardly uniform in practice. For example, the number of aggravated assaults jumped in certain jurisdictions when the police started to recognize spousal assault as something much more than a private matter. Also, what constitutes an aggravated assault (designated as Part I) as opposed to other assault (designated as Part II) is far from clear-cut.

Despite all of these complications and caveats, the UCR remains the most widely used measure of crime, far more comprehensive in coverage than alternatives. As a barometer of crime, albeit an incomplete one, it is unmatched.

Combining Crime

For the fifty years it was used, the UCR Crime Index tallied the number of Part I offenses, without any adjustment for type or severity. Even following the recent abolition of the published Crime Index, the tally of violent crimes blends together all reported homicides, forcible rapes, robberies, and aggravated assaults (including attempts), and that of property crimes merges all reported burglaries, larceny/thefts, and motor vehicle thefts (including attempts). Unfortunately, the disparate

levels of these individual offenses make any summary count across offense categories highly suspect.

For example, for 2003 the estimated 1.38 million violent crimes in the United States included 16,503 homicides, 93,433 rapes, 413,402 robberies, and 857,921 aggravated assaults. For the most part, therefore, the tally of violent crime is largely an aggravated assaults indicator, their constituting more than 60% of the violent crime total. By contrast, if the number of homicides had jumped 20%, the violent crime tally would have increased by only one-quarter of 1%. The homicide and rape counts are dwarfed by the robbery and aggravated assault figures. The same problem exists with property crimes, where 70% of the property total is larcenies/thefts.

Another quirk in the counting of crime occurs with complex criminal events involving multiple acts or victims. According to the "hierarchy rule" (FBI 1980), only the most serious element (among the seven Part I crimes in rank order from homicide to motor vehicle theft) of a criminal act is counted. Thus, a carjacking in which the driver is raped is counted only as rape for the purposes of crime statistics, while the carjacking is ignored. Although this may make some intuitive sense, oddities can easily develop. For example, if an offender robs a group of three people on a street corner, it counts as three robberies (one for each victim), but if the robber shoots and kills one of the three victims, it becomes a single homicide (the other two robbery victims would not count by virtue of the crime hierarchy).

In addition to the matter of scale discussed earlier, crimes vary considerably by severity. Thus, crime can increase even when the total level of harm is declining. For example, if a city has four more robberies but two fewer homicides the violent crime count still increases.

In an attempt to address this problem, Sellin and Wolfgang (1964) developed a crime severity scale to weight crime and delinquency by their seriousness. By this protocol, a homicide would count far more than a robbery, and a robbery/murder would count more than just a homicide. Additionally, offenses would carry points according to the dollar value loss. Despite its theoretical appeal, practical limitations in implementing such an approach prevented it from ever being adopted systematically. In addition, Blumstein (1974) found the FBI index and the Sellin-Wolfgang index to be nearly perfectly linearly related, suggesting that the latter would contribute little new information.

Crime Rates

In recent years, Americans have become eager consumers of graphical displays of statistical information, some of which illuminate important facts while others are misleading. This may help to explain why a much criticized feature of the annual crime report—the "crime clock"—keeps on ticking, despite its significant limitations.

Since 1939, the FBI has offered this graphical presentation of the temporal frequency of crime. In 2003, for example, there was a homicide every 31.8 minutes and a rape every 5.6 minutes. It can be rather difficult to interpret or utilize these facts, however. Of course, a murder does not actually occur every 31.8 minutes in any particular town or neighborhood, so there is no cause for someone to breathe easy and feel spared every half hour. More important, since the length of an hour never changes, the acceleration in crime over time (for example, from one homicide every hour in 1961 to one every 31.8 minutes in 2003) confounds real changes in risk with increasing population. The rate of speed with which crime occurs is not really a rate reflecting anything about likelihood or risk.

Clearly, a rate should adjust for population. The UCR presents crime rates as the number of offenses per 100,000 population:

$$\text{Crime Rate} = \left(\frac{\text{Crime Volume}}{\text{Population}} \right) \times 100,000.$$

Using a 100,000 base, rather than per person or per capita, is simply for numerical convenience. For example, in 2004, there were an estimated 16,503 homicides nationally with a population of nearly 291 million. The per capita rate of homicide would be 0.000057, a rather awkward decimal. Scaling upward by the 100,000 multiplier yields a far more practical figure of 5.7 per 100,000 population.

While the problems outlined above pertaining to the crime volume are challenging, the pitfalls related to population counting are even more severe. Despite cautions printed in the UCR about comparing jurisdictions in terms of crime rates, the appeal in identifying the best and the worst places, and various rankings in between, may be just too great.

It is well known that urbanism can impact upon crime levels. One might expect higher crime rates in a densely populated urban center as compared to a small, rural community. But the effect extends even more in terms of the jurisdictional boundaries of an area. Some cities include within their jurisdictional boundaries large suburban fringe areas that have a moderating effect on the overall crime rate. By contrast, other places are essentially dense urban cores whose suburbs report crime statistics separately.

Jurisdictions differ not only in terms of their demographic makeup and socioeconomic conditions, which impact strongly on crime rates, but they differ in the extent to which the resident population reflects the number of people at risk. Simply put, crime incidents committed by or against nonresidents of a jurisdiction are counted in the numerator, but the nonresident offender or victim is not included in the denominator. As a consequence, cities that have substantial tourism tend to have inflated rates of crime. In a similar respect, part-year residents, including college students, may artificially distort crime rates. Finally, nonresident suburban commuters (and their property) are at risk during the workday, but they are not reflected in a city's population measure.

In truth, a rate should adjust for the number of eligibles, as is done in other statistical spheres. The birth rate, for example, is typically calculated based on only the count of women in child-bearing ages. Unemployment rates are based on only those who are considered to be part of the labor force. Moreover, mortality rates are typically age adjusted to reflect changing patterns in the risk of death. Unfortunately, crime measures are crude rates, unadjusted for demographic changes or the size of the at-risk population.

There have been persuasive proposals to recast rape rates in terms of the size of the female population and even to calculate auto theft rates in terms of the available stock of registered vehicles (Mosher, Miethe, and Phillips 2002). As compelling as these arguments may be, they have not gathered enough momentum to be implemented as alternative measures of risk.

Finally, like crime rates, clearance rates are also difficult to interpret and may be misleading. These rates are calculated annually by dividing the number of crimes solved (either through arrest or some other means) by the total number of crimes reported, for each type of crime. However, an offense is not always cleared in the same year it was committed (for example, an offense committed and reported in December of one year may not be cleared until January of the following year). In addition, five crimes may sometimes be cleared by a single arrest, while in other cases the arrest of five accomplices may clear only a single crime. And, as Maltz (1999) pointed out, clearance rates can also be misleading because a change in the crime reporting can significantly affect the rates by inflating or deflating the denominator.

Trends with Caution

Every year when the latest crime statistics are released, journalists and reporters tend to focus on the trends: "Is crime going up or down?" they typically ask. The answers are not always simple or easily interpreted. But the UCR does provide fodder for inquiring journalists, including one-year, five-year, and ten-year changes in crime counts.

One-year changes say little about crime swings. In other words, a one-year change does not a trend make. Unfortunately, civic leaders are often pressed for answers as to why a local crime figure has increased a few percentage points. An increase in crime from one year to the next (or any two points in time for that matter) may, however, reflect an unusually low count in the previous year, an unusually high count in the subsequent year, or part of a real trend. Determining which is the correct interpretation requires a longer, less myopic view of the trend.

To compound the problems related to the overemphasis on one-year changes, the greatest interest and attention is often given to homicide counts, which, because of their low numerical levels particularly in local areas, often fluctuate dramatically from year to year for no predictable reason. For a particular city, the number of murders can vary by some percentage just based on whether certain victims of assault die (thus constituting a homicide) or survive (thus remaining an aggravated assault).

Other Data Series

While "crimes known to police" is the best known and longest standing initiative, several other data series are collected and disseminated by the FBI's Uniform Crime Reporting Program. Like the *Crime in the*

United States report, these other data are available online or in printed forms.

In addition to the summary counts of offenses, clearances, and arrests collected from police agencies, detail on each homicide is gathered from the Supplementary Homicide Reports (SHR) form. On an incident-by-incident basis, the month and year, the age, race, and sex of victims and offenders (if known), the weapon, victim–offender relationship, and circumstances are obtained on approximately 92% of all killings in the United States. The SHR data are used to produce detailed tables in the preliminary pages of the *Crime in the United States* publication. The Bureau of Justice Statistics also maintains a website (http://www.ojp.usdoj.gov/bjs/homicide/homtrnd.htm) with a wide range of geographic and demographic breakdowns of trends and patterns in homicide, overall as well as for various subtypes of homicide (Fox and Zawitz 2005).

Responding to growing concern about hate-inspired crime, the U.S. Congress passed the Hate Crimes Statistics Act on April 23, 1990, directing the attorney general to collect data "about crimes that manifest evidence of prejudice based on race, religion, sexual orientation, or ethnicity." For each year since 1992, the FBI has published a separate compendium of national and local data on offenses, assailants, and victims of personal and property crimes (murder and nonnegligent manslaughter, forcible rape, aggravated assault, simple assault, intimidation, robbery, burglary, larceny/theft, motor vehicle theft, arson, and destruction/damage/vandalism and residual categories) where, as a result of investigation, hate is believed to be at least partially the motivation for the offense. Nearly a decade into the program, the reported incidence of hate crime still appears to be surprisingly low (fewer than eight thousand incidents in 2003) perhaps because of the significant difficulties in determining motivation, particularly for unsolved crimes.

Complementing the law enforcement employment data published in *Crime in the United States,* the FBI also produces an annual report on fatal and nonfatal assaults against police officers. Besides national and local tallies of such victimizations, the annual report also tabulates data on the use of body armor and the circumstances and weapons involved in the attacks upon officers.

By far the most fundamental and significant change in the history of the FBI's Uniform Crime Reporting Program was the launch of the National Incident-Based Reporting System (NIBRS) (Poggio et al. 1985). In addition to concerns over the lack of severity weighting and the effects of the hierarchy rule, important issues related to the lack of detail in the traditional UCR have been voiced over the years. Indeed, with the exception of homicide (through the SHR), the crime reports offer nothing in terms of the characteristics of victims and offenders and the incident itself. And because they are collected in summary form (specifically monthly tallies), it is not possible (again with the exception of homicide through the SHR) to examine subpatterns within the data.

NIBRS, on the other hand, is quite rich in detail, soliciting extensive information about the offense, the victim and his or her injuries, the property damaged or stolen, the offender, and subsequent arrest for each incident. Unlike the UCR, NIBRS does not use the hierarchy rule, so all crimes committed in a single incident are reported. And because NIBRS (like the SHR) is an incident-based reporting scheme, it allows an analyst to tabulate or correlate variables in almost any way desired.

The ambitiousness of the NIBRS planners is laudable, yet it has also resulted in slow implementation of the program. Although computerized data entry speeds the process of reporting, the level of detail required can be quite onerous, particularly if an agency experiences a large number of incidents. For this reason, NIBRS has been implemented more for small or rural agencies. However, despite not being representative of the entire nation, the ability of NIBRS to place criminal incidents in a richly detailed context makes it an extremely useful tool for criminologists.

Conclusion

Computerization and the Internet have altered the way that most public and private agencies do business. Technology has and will continue to have an impact on the UCR. More and more crime data will be available for online look-up and manipulation. More significant, as NIBRS continues to take hold across the nation and at some point becomes the standard model of crime data collection, crime reporting will take a very different form. With various software applications for user interface (some of which are already used at the Bureau of Justice Statistics), crime reports can be customized. While this will be a plus in enhancing our ability to understand crime, it remains to be seen whether new issues in data interpretation will surface—surely a worthy topic for future generations of criminologists.

JAMES ALAN FOX

See also **Accountability; Crime Analysis; Crime, Serious; Problem-Oriented Policing; Zero Tolerance Policing**

References and Further Reading

Biederman, Albert D., and Albert J. Reiss. 1967. On exploring the dark figure of crime. *Annals of the American Academy of Political and Social Science* 374: 1–15.
Blumstein, Alfred. 1974. Seriousness weights in an index of crime. *American Sociological Review* 39: 854–64.
Federal Bureau of Investigation. 1958. *Uniform crime reports for the United States*. Washington, DC: U.S. Department of Justice.
———. 1980. *Uniform crime reporting handbook*. Washington, DC: U.S. Department of Justice.
———. 2004. *Crime in the United States, 2003*. Washington, DC: U.S. Department of Justice.
Fox, James Alan, and Marianne Zawitz. 2005. *Homicide trends in the United States*. Washington, DC: U.S. Bureau of Justice Statistics. http://www.ojp.usdoj.gov/bjs/homicide/homtrnd.htm.
Maltz, Michael D. 1977. Crime statistics: A historical perspective. *Crime and Delinquency* 23: 30–40.
———. 1999. *Bridging gaps in police crime data*. BJS Report, NCJ 176365. Washington DC: U.S. Department of Justice.
Mosher, Clayton J., Terance D. Miethe, and Dretha M. Phillips. 2002. *The mismeasure of crime*. Thousand Oaks, CA: Sage.
Sellin, Thorsten, and Marvin E. Wolfgang. 1964. *The measurement of delinquency*. New York: Wiley and Sons.
Wolfgang, Marvin E. 1963. *Uniform Crime Reports*: A critical appraisal. *University of Pennsylvania Law Review* 3: 708–38.

UNIONIZATION, POLICE

Although unionization of police officers is not universal in the United States, all major agencies have either a formal labor organization or a professional association that functions as a labor organization. The right to collective bargaining varies state by state. Collective bargaining is authorized by almost all states in the Northeast, Mid-Atlantic, Midwest, and Far West. It is spotty in the South and Mountain states. Nevertheless, even in states without formal bargaining, police unions play a significant role in determining wages and working conditions for officers. Indeed, it is not unusual for a strong union or association to be more influential in a jurisdiction without bargaining than a weak union is in a jurisdiction with bargaining.

The Boston Police Strike in 1919 froze the development of police labor organizations until the 1960s. From 1960 to 1990, the police labor movement "matured." Since 1990, there has been a "settling in";

police unions now are part of the landscape of American law enforcement management. Police labor organizations are, however, highly fragmented. Most local organizations, although perhaps affiliated with various national associations, function independently.

Labor–Management Relations

Since the inception of organized labor, both management and union representatives have struggled to maintain a balance between advocacy and antagonism. Everyone recognizes there is a fine line between the two. We expect both management and labor to maintain a strong and healthy advocacy role. We recognize that when the line is crossed and management and labor become antagonistic, everyone suffers. But that line is crossed with regularity. Indeed, in some enterprises in America, extreme and unyielding antagonism has resulted in the ruin of the organization—the ultimate lose–lose outcome.

The problem is no easier to handle in law enforcement than in any other enterprise. Despite the facts that policing is a public sector occupation, that police unions are supposed to be quasi-professional associations, and that there is a prohibition against the ultimate job action—strike—nevertheless, relations frequently degenerate. Police managers often characterize relationships with the union as their most stressful role, even more stressful than with the American Civil Liberties Union or problematic city council members. Police union officials, on the other hand, frequently characterize the management of their organizations as "impossible to work with."

Employee associations must be an advocate for their membership. A reasonable reaction to such a statement might be "Well, yes, of course." But the issue goes beyond this simplistic observation. There is an expectation by membership that a union will be a strong, outspoken, vigorous advocate for membership. We expect cooperation and civility, but we also expect individuals who play a representation role to keep an arms length from advocates from the other side. When union leaders get "too cozy" with management, they are no longer trusted, and they are no longer reelected.

This has profound implications for the role of union leaders. Put simply, they must maintain some level of conflict if they expect to stay in office. This has profound implications for the implementation of innovative endeavors. A labor organization will not greet proposals for changes in philosophy or approach with unquestioning enthusiasm. Labor organizations are inherently mistrustful of change. The membership expects union leadership to challenge new ideas. Further, the first response is not likely to be "What's in this for our citizens?" but rather, "What's in this for our membership?" That reaction is not likely to sit well with managers just back from a conference about the need for innovation in law enforcement.

Police chiefs are often heard to say words to the effect that "no matter how good a job you do at cultivating positive relationships, they'll find an issue." Police chiefs are essentially correct. Although union leaders have no intention for their actions to be destructive or to undermine basically positive working relationships, they must maintain some level of strain. Put a little differently, they must at least occasionally fan the fires if they are to remain in office. Police managers who understand this are not as likely to personalize the conflict.

One must understand that this does not preclude cooperative, productive relationships. Management and labor can, and frequently do, work together for the greater good of the organization and the citizens served by the organization. But there are limits to joint, cooperative effort.

If everyone understands the limits, there will be less rancor. A police chief who takes office expecting that engagement and cooperation with the union will bring 100% support 100% of the time is in for a rude awakening. It will not happen. And, after all, it must be remembered that many innovations tried by management fail—as would be expected. The union probably should be skeptical. Some healthy skepticism by at least one element of the organization might be a good thing.

Police Unions and Politics

The vast majority of police unions in the United States have a distinct political advantage over nonelected police managers. What separates the police union from the police manager in the world of politics is that the police union has the ability to endorse a candidate and work in the candidate's political campaign. But the greatest advantage for the police union is its ability to contribute money to the candidate. In many parts of the United States, the police union's political action committee is the largest campaign contributor to a candidate. Despite protests from the editorial boards of newspapers about the perceived political power of many police unions, candidates for public office continue to seek the endorsement and resources of police unions.

While politics is an integral strength of police unions in the United States, it is also internally divisive. The endorsement of candidates for elected office, especially if the candidates are evenly matched, often causes stress within the union. Members and union leaders fear the consequences if they endorse a losing candidate. Political activity can also disrupt police labor–management relations when police management sees the union as having the ability to undermine or modify the changes or reforms desired by management.

Police Unions: Major Players

There are two major police associations in the United States independent of "organized labor." The Fraternal Order of Police (FOP) is the oldest, founded in 1915 in Pittsburgh. The national FOP reports a membership of three hundred thousand and has lodges in all fifty states. It also has several strong state lodges. Like the FOP, the National Association of Police Organizations (NAPO) is essentially an association of independent associations. NAPO provides a mechanism for otherwise independent local associations to work cooperatively on national legislation affecting their membership, as well as providing a forum for the exchange of ideas. NAPO reports a membership of 220,000 in four thousand local associations.

In addition to the FOP and NAPO organizations, there are a number of AFL-CIO affiliated unions with substantial police membership. The most prominent of these is the International Union of Police Associations (IUPA, AFL-CIO). IUPA is the only organization actually chartered by the AFL-CIO as a police union. It reports a membership of a hundred thousand. The International Brotherhood of Police Officers (IBPO, NAGE, SEIU, AFL-CIO) merged into the independent National Association of Government Employees (NAGE) in 1969. In 1982, NAGE affiliated as an autonomous division of the Service Employees International Union (SEIU, AFL-CIO). IBPO is a division of NAGE. SEIU has chartered police unions outside of IBPO/NAGE. NAGE reports a membership of fifty thousand, but no separate figures are available for IBPO membership. The best estimate for IBPO membership is about ten thousand. The National Coalition of Public Safety Officers (NCPSO, CWA, AFL-CIO) is a sector of Communications Workers of America (CWA, AFL-CIO). CWA reports a membership of seven hundred thousand, and NCPSO reports

Table 1 Summary of the police associations in the nation's ten largest cities

City	Police Union	Affiliation
New York	Patrolmen's Benevolent Association of New York	NAPO
Los Angeles	Los Angeles Police Protective League	IUPA/NAPO
Chicago	Fraternal Order of Police Lodge 7	FOP
Houston	Houston Police Officers Union	IUPA
Philadelphia	Fraternal Order of Police Lodge 5	FOP
Phoenix	Phoenix Law Enforcement Association	NAPO
San Diego	San Diego Police Officers Association	Independent
Dallas	Dallas Police Association	IUPA/NAPO
San Antonio	San Antonio Police Officers Association	NCPSO/NAPO
Detroit	Detroit Police Officers Association	NAPO

that twenty-six thousand of those members are in the police and corrections sector. The American Federation of State, County and Municipal Employees (AFSCME, AFL-CIO) includes police membership, but there are no membership figures available. Finally, the International Brotherhood of Teamsters (IBT) includes law enforcement officers as a part of the 140,000-member Public Employees Division, but no separate figures are reported.

Table 1 provides a summary of the police associations in the nation's ten largest cities. Note that most large city unions are independent associations, although some have multiple affiliations.

In addition, there are several strong state associations. In six states in particular—California, Florida, New Jersey, New York, Texas, and Wisconsin—independent state associations dominate the labor scene among all but the largest cities.

LARRY T. HOOVER and
RONALD G. DELORD

See also **Accountability; Administration of Police Agencies, Theories of; American Policing: Early Years; Autonomy and the Police; Boston Police Strike; Civilian Review Boards; History of American Policing; Police Chief Executive; Professionalism**

References and Further Reading

Bopp, William J. 1971. *The police rebellion.* Springfield, IL: Charles C Thomas.

Burpo, John H. 1971. *The police labor movement: Problems and perspectives.* Springfield, IL: Charles C Thomas.

DeLord, Ronald G., and Jerry Sanders. 2005. *Navigating dangerous waters: Survival in the real world of police labor—management relations.* Washington, DC: U.S. Government Printing Office.

Gammage, Allen Z., and Stanley L. Sachs. 1972. *Police unions.* Springfield, IL: Charles C Thomas.

Jurkanin, Thomas J., et al. 2001. *Enduring, surviving, and thriving as a law enforcement executive.* Springfield, IL: Charles C Thomas.

Levi, Margaret. 1977. *Bureaucratic insurgency: The case of police unions.* Lexington, MA: D. C. Heath.

Maddox, Charles. 1975. *Collective bargaining in law enforcement.* Springfield, IL: Charles C Thomas.

Sergevnin, Vladimir A., ed. 2005. Special Issue: Police unions. *Law Enforcement Executive Forum* 5 (2).

U.S. BORDER PATROL

The U.S. Border Patrol is a branch of the Department of Homeland Security. It represents a line of defense for America's borders. Its agents identify, capture, and sanction illegal immigrants entering the country. They also target "coyotes," people smuggling other people. The key sectors of the Border Patrol exist along the Mexican border in the states of Texas and California. However, since the terrorist attacks of September 11, 2001, the Border Patrol have started focusing on people with terrorist ties entering through states bordering Canada. Agents patrol more than six thousand miles of land. They also oversee nearly two thousand miles of coastal border surrounding the Florida peninsula and Puerto Rico. They apprehend around one million people attempting to illegally enter the country per year.

History of the Border Patrol

In the late 1800s, anti-Chinese attitudes were growing. Chinese immigrants, eager to work for very low wages, were taking jobs away from Americans. In 1882, the government passed the Chinese Exclusion Act outlawing Chinese immigration. Those still desiring to enter the United States started paying Mexican smugglers to carry them across the border. The government had mounted guards patrol for illegal immigrants. Their station was in El Paso, Texas. They never numbered more than seventy-five. By 1915, a separate group formed—the Mounted Inspectors. They would ride on horseback along the U.S. border and work at designated inspection stations.

Citizens started claiming that Chinese were not the only problem. Immigrants flooding in from European countries and Mexico were also considered problems. The Mounted Inspectors were not enough. On May 28, 1924, Congress signed the Labor Appropriation Act, turning the Mounted Inspectors into the U.S. Border Patrol. Placed under the Bureau of Immigration, the agency employed more than four hundred agents, recruiting from the Texas Rangers and border town sheriffs departments. They gave employees a badge, a revolver, and a $1,680 salary.

The agency hired people with maritime experience in 1925 when they started patrolling seacoasts. In the early 1930s, agent responsibilities widened. Due to Prohibition laws, tracking liquor smugglers became a priority. During this time, the agency located a majority of workers along the Canadian border. Following 1933, the U.S. Border Patrol was under control of the Bureau of Immigration and Naturalization Service. An academy opened in El Paso, Texas, in 1934.

In this part of the 1900s, due to labor shortages, the government temporarily allowed Mexican immigrants to freely cross the border. This policy was halted following the return of many Americans from war, but the immigrants kept coming. The responsibility for agents, especially those on the southern border, shifted to impeding the flow of illegal Mexican immigrants through the 1940s and 1950s. In the 1960s, focus shifted to Florida as Cuban defectors, especially during the missile crisis, attempted to make it to U.S. soil. However, illegal Mexican immigration remained a primary concern. In the 1970s through the 1990s, they continued to flood into America for legitimate economic reasons, but the underground market for drugs such as marijuana and cocaine exploded. Immigrants smuggling in drugs sharply increased. Agents were no longer just concerned with immigrants but also with the illegal substances they were bringing.

Following the terrorist attacks of September 11, 2001, the federal government reorganized several departments into one larger organization, the Department of Homeland Security. The reorganization placed the Border Patrol under its guidance. Due to the connection between foreign terrorists and illegal immigration, funding for the Border Patrol increased. The agency budget rose to more than $4 billion—a 200% increase from the previous decade. The number of agents doubled to seven thousand, with plans to add an additional thousand each year until 2008.

Training and Employment

Border Patrol training takes place at an academy in Charleston, South Carolina.

Classes concern foreign languages, firearms proficiency, police techniques, immigration law, criminal law, and statutory law. After graduating, a recruit then spends twenty-four weeks completing on-the-job training. In the field, an agent may carry out line watch operations, sign cut, or patrol.

With line watching, an agent remains stationary at a specific border point while looking for illegal immigrants. This involves the use of binoculars or the more complex night vision goggles or scopes. Sign cutting involves tracking illegal immigrants while looking for disruptions in the natural terrain. This includes the identification and interpretation of human footprints, broken branches, and automobile tracks. Patrols involve watching for illegal immigrants by automobile, boat, helicopter, or plane. Electronic sensors may call agents carrying out any of these activities to a specific location. New technology allows agents to place electronic surveillance sensors at high-traffic areas. If an illegal or a coyote leading a group of immigrants across the border trips one, a signal alerts agents.

Specialized arms of the Border Patrol exist. One is the Border Patrol Tactical Unit (BORTAC). This division is a national and international tactical division. They respond to special circumstances that arise within the U.S. borders. They also travel covertly around the world, working with other federal governments. Foreign governments use them to train their agents, to help in riot dissolution, and for drug cartel infiltration. Another division is the Border Patrol Search, Trauma, and Rescue group (BORSTAR). Agents in this group perform specialized rescues of agents and illegal immigrants caught in compromising situations in dangerous terrain.

Conclusion

The U.S. Border Patrol is receiving more attention than ever before. Funding multiplies as concerns about terrorism continue. In addition, agents have better education and a higher pay scale than at any point in history. However, the agency still faces a variety of problems. They include frequent military incursions, skilled drug traffickers, and a lack of personnel.

Research indicates that the Mexican military violates international law with armed incursions into the United States. More than one hundred incursions have been officially recognized. However, off the record, agents for the Border Patrol indicate that more than that have happened. Speculation exists that the Mexican military is involved with illegal drug trade on the border. The official position of the Mexican government is that their troops are helping in the war on drugs.

Aside from the Mexican military, agents constantly deal with skilled drug smugglers, also referred to as "mules." Smugglers, sometimes working for cartels, import drugs produced in Canada and Mexico. They also bring in drugs, such as cocaine, for distributors located in areas such as Brazil and Columbia. Apprehending them is problematic. Using the same technology as agents, they have the ability to easily evade agents before being spotted. Regardless, agents do have success against some smugglers. In 2001 alone, agents seized more than eighteen thousand pounds of cocaine and more than one million pounds of marijuana. These appear to be large numbers, but researchers speculate they are miniscule in comparison to what actually gets into the United States.

Critics believe we could catch more illegal immigrants if the border patrol had more agents. Though the size of the Border Patrol increased following September 11, 2001, they say it has not increased enough. Some citizens have taken matters into their own hands. Groups such as the Arizona Minutemen are designating themselves volunteer agents. The goal of these groups is to help stop not only traditional Mexican illegal immigrants but also new waves of illegal immigrants with possible terrorist ties from areas such as Asia, Syria, and Iran. The value of these groups and their ability to formally work with the Border Patrol remains in question.

JASON S. ULSPERGER

See also **Airport Safety and Security; Department of Homeland Security; Drug Enforcement Administration (DEA); Drug Markets; Texas Rangers**

References and Further Reading

Andreas, Peter. 2001. *Border games: Policing the U.S.–Mexico divide.* Ithaca, NY: Cornell University Press.

Colby, Caroll. 1974. *Border Patrol: How U.S. agents protect our borders from illegal entry.* New York: Coward, McCann and Geoghegan, Inc.

Krauss, Erich, and Alex Pacheco. 2004. *On the line: Inside the U.S. Border Patrol.* New York: Citadel Press Books.

Maril, Robert Lee. 2004. *Patrolling chaos: The U.S. Border Patrol in Deep South Texas.* Lubbock: Texas Tech University Press.

U.S. Customs and Border Patrol. 2003a. *U.S. Border Patrol history.* http://www.cbp.gov/xp/cgov/border_security/border_patrol/overview.xml (July 2003).

———. 2003b. *U.S. Border Patrol overview.* http://www.cbp.gov/xp/cgov/border_security/border_patrol/overview.xml (February 2003).

U.S. MARSHALS SERVICE

The offices of U.S. Marshal and Deputy U.S. Marshal were created by the Judiciary Act of 1789, the same law that erected the federal judicial system. The Judiciary Act provided for one U.S. marshal for each judicial district. Each marshal was empowered to hire as many deputy marshals as necessary, including the deputation of able-bodied citizens for special situations, such as posses. Originally, President George Washington nominated and the Senate confirmed thirteen U.S. marshals, one for each of the eleven states and one each for the districts of Kentucky (a territory in 1789) and Maine (a part of Massachusetts until 1820). As the nation expanded across the continent and acquired new territories, more judicial districts were added. As of 2005, there were ninety-four districts, each with its own presidentially appointed U.S. marshal, and more than 3,344 deputy marshals and criminal investigators.

As defined by the Judiciary Act of 1789, the marshals administered the federal courts, acting primarily as the disbursement officers. More important, the marshals were empowered to execute "all lawful precepts issued under the authority of the United States." These two duties, particularly the latter, have remained essentially unchanged for more than two hundred years, although the specific work of the marshals has changed considerably in response to changing circumstances and laws.

The marshals continue, as they have since 1789, to protect the operation of the federal court and its participants, to produce its prisoners and witnesses, and to enforce its orders. For most of this nation's history, the marshals, working in close cooperation with U.S. attorneys, provided the only nationwide law enforcement authority available to the federal government. Until well into the twentieth century, the marshals executed all arrest warrants, regardless of which agency conducted the initial investigation.

When new territories were established, marshals were appointed to provide a federal presence. In Indian Territory (present-day Oklahoma) and the territory of Alaska, marshals were essentially the only law enforcement authority. More than one hundred deputy marshals were killed enforcing the law in the Indian Territory between 1872 and 1896. It was during this period after the Civil War that the marshals earned their place in American folklore as lawmen.

Until 1853, U.S. marshals worked under the general supervision of the secretary of state, who established guidelines for the office, issued specific instructions, and coordinated the marshals' activities. Beginning in 1853, marshals increasingly came under the control of the attorney general, a process that was completed in 1861 by congressional statute. The marshals remained decentralized, with each marshal reporting directly to the attorney general.

In 1956, the Justice Department established the Executive Office of U.S. Marshals to centralize administrative responsibilities. In 1962, James J. P. McShane was appointed the first chief marshal, with limited supervision of the other marshals. The turmoil of the 1960s, particularly the problems the marshals confronted enforcing civil rights court decisions, pointed out the need for further centralized control. By 1969, the U.S. Marshals Service was created, with an office of director. Despite this move toward a nationally cohesive law enforcement agency, today's U.S. marshals retain considerable power within their districts, acting as local managers within a national organization to ensure that the duties assigned the Marshals Service are conducted efficiently and effectively.

As federal law enforcement officers, marshals retain the broadest authority and jurisdiction. Their congressionally defined duty to execute "all lawful precepts issued under the authority of the United States" allows them to respond to orders from the federal courts, the president and attorney general, and Congress. During the 1960s, deputy marshals effectively desegregated the nation's schools and colleges under numerous court orders. In 1973, acting under orders of the attorney general, the Marshals Service besieged members of the American Indian Movement who had occupied the small hamlet of Wounded Knee, South Dakota, during the longest civil disturbance since the Civil War. Congressional precepts issued to marshals have included such different activities as taking the national census from 1790 through 1870, controlling enemy aliens in times of war, and supervising congressional elections from 1879 to 1894.

Today's U.S. Marshals Service carries out a wide variety of responsibilities. U.S. marshals provide the physical security for federal courthouses. Whenever necessary, deputy marshals protect federal judges and attorneys who have been threatened with bodily harm. In fiscal year 2004, for example, the Marshals Service evaluated 674 inappropriate communications/threats made to federal judicial employees. The Marshals Service also operates the Witness Security Program to protect witnesses, even to the extent of giving them new identities, in exchange for their testimony against organized crime. Since 1970, more than 7,700 witnesses have entered the program.

As they have for more than two hundred years, U.S. marshals have custody of all federal prisoners from the time of arrest until the prisoner's acquittal or delivery to prison. These federal prisoners are housed under contract in local jails or facilities, escorted to and from court by marshals. During fiscal year 2004, more than 290,000 federal prisoner movements took place via the Justice Prisoner and Alien Transportation System (JPATS). The JPATS is a complex transportation network of aircraft, buses, and vans, further complicated by the need to provide tight security over the prisoners.

The Marshals Service also has responsibility for the arrest of federal fugitives, a traditional duty that was briefly transferred to the Federal Bureau of Investigation but was returned to the marshals in 1979. To combat this immense problem, the Marshals Service expends considerable daily effort to capture them, averaging 36,000 arrests nationwide each year, more than all other federal law enforcement agencies combined.

Periodically, the Marshals Service establishes fugitive task force operations, working in close cooperation with state and local law enforcement agencies. The specific purpose of these task forces is to provide intense fugitive hunts in specific locations for specific periods of time. An example is "Operation Falcon," conducted during a one-week period in April 2005.

The Marshals Service led this task force operation, working in conjunction with state, local, and other federal agencies, which arrested 10,340 fugitives in a nationwide sweep and cleared more than 13,800 felony warrants.

The marshals' traditional responsibility to seize property under court order was expanded under the Comprehensive Crime Control Act of 1984. This act gave the marshals responsibility to seize all assets accruing to criminals as a result of illegal, drug-related activities. These assets, which range from houses and businesses to racehorses and yachts, are managed by the Marshals Service until the courts decide their ultimate disposal. Currently, the Marshals Service manages assets valued at more than $964 million.

For more than two hundred years, the U.S. marshals have acted as the hub of the federal judicial system, administering its finances, handling its prisoners, serving its processes, protecting its functions and personnel, enforcing its orders, and working with other law enforcement agencies to ensure the supremacy of the law in this country. Marshals continue to play an essential role in the operation of justice. The marshals have, during the past two centuries, evolved into a centralized, cohesive law enforcement agency, populated with highly trained, professional personnel dedicated to law enforcement. In an age of specialization, U.S. marshals and their deputies remain the last of the generalists, fully capable of carrying out an incredibly complex array of duties.

BARBARA WEBSTER and ED CONNORS

See also **American Policing: Early Years; Federal Police and Investigative Agencies; History of American Policing**

References and Further Reading

Ball, Larry D. 1978. *The United States Marshals of New Mexico and Arizona Territories, 1846–1912.* Albuquerque: University of New Mexico Press.

Calhoun, Frederick S. 1990. *The Lawmen: United States Marshals and their deputies, 1789–1989.* Washington, DC: Smithsonian Institution Press.

U.S. SECRET SERVICE

In an irony of history, on April 14, 1865, President Abraham Lincoln signed legislation creating the U.S. Secret Service, the agency today that is best known for protecting America's president; that night, Lincoln was assassinated by John Wilkes Booth.

As the Civil War neared conclusion, counterfeit paper currency was rampant. The initial legislation authorized the newly created Secret Service to investigate crimes involving creation and distribution of counterfeit currency. The Secret Service was created as a bureau under the U.S. Treasury Department to combat this growing threat to the nation's economy. (The Treasury Police Force, established in 1789 to secure the Treasury's currency printing operations, was merged into the Secret Service in 1937.)

On March 1, 2003, the Secret Service moved from the Treasury Department to join twenty-two other agencies in the Department of Homeland Security, created by Congress in response to the attacks on the World Trade Center and the Pentagon on September 11, 2001 (P.L. 107–296).

The core missions of the Secret Service include (1) protecting the nation's president, top leaders, and visiting world leaders and (2) investigating and preventing crimes against the country's financial and critical infrastructure. The Secret Service employs about six thousand people—including more than twenty-four hundred special agents, twelve hundred uniformed division officers, as well as other professional, technical, and administrative staff.

Protection Responsibilities

The special agents and uniformed division personnel conduct the primary law enforcement responsibilities of the Secret Service. Historically, the uniformed division's roots date back to the beginning of the Civil War, with a few military members and Metropolitan Police Department officers protecting the White House grounds. In 1922, President Warren G. Harding created the White House Police Force. In 1930, after an unknown intruder entered the White House dining room, President Herbert Hoover convinced Congress to combine the Secret Service agents protecting him with the White House police. President Hoover wanted the Secret Service to control all facets of presidential protection.

Now, the Secret Service uniformed division, using a variety of special units such as countersniper teams, canine explosive detection teams, bicycle patrols, motorcycle units, and a magnetometer unit, protects the following:

- White House complex and other presidential offices
- President and immediate family
- Vice president and immediate family and residence in the District of Columbia
- Treasury building and annex
- Foreign diplomatic missions in the Washington, D.C., area and throughout the United States and its territories and possessions

However, the Secret Service is best known for its highest-profile assignment: protecting the president of the United States. After the assassination of President William McKinley in 1901 (the third U.S. president killed in thirty-six years), Congress informally requested that the Secret Service protect the new president, Theodore Roosevelt, who also carried his own firearm on occasion. In 1902, the Secret Service assumed full-time responsibility for protecting the president, with two agents, but it was not until 1906 that congressional legislation mandated presidential protection as a permanent responsibility for the Secret Service.

Today, the Secret Service is authorized by law to protect the following:

- President and vice president and their immediate families
- Former presidents and their spouses for ten years
- Children of former presidents until age sixteen
- Visiting heads of foreign governments and other distinguished foreign visitors to the United States
- Official representatives of the United States performing special missions abroad
- Major presidential and vice presidential candidates within 120 days of a general presidential election

"Protectees," a term used by the Secret Service to designate key protection responsibilities, such as the president and first lady, have details of special agents assigned to them. Advance teams survey sites that will be visited by protectees to determine resource needs, local support, emergency medical facilities, and evacuation routes for emergencies. They also coordinate with local law enforcement, fire/rescue, and emergency medical partnering agencies to implement protection plans and a wide range of protocols. Other assignments include establishing a command post with communications capabilities, reviewing intelligence information, establishing checkpoints, and limiting access to secured areas.

The Secret Service also investigates threats against the president and other high-level officials. The protective intelligence program is used to identify groups, individuals, and emerging technologies that may pose a threat to protectees, secure locations, or events. The Secret Service also provides training for local law enforcement in conducting threat assessments and investigating and preventing targeted violence.

In 1998, President Clinton issued Presidential Decision Directive 62 that established federal roles to provide security at newly designated National Special Security Events (NSSEs). At these major special events, the Secret Service becomes the lead agency for security design, planning, and implementation. The Secret Service, in conjunction with the Department of Homeland Security and other federal law enforcement agencies, such as the Federal Bureau of Investigation and state and local law enforcement, has developed strategies and plans to secure the NSSE facilities and protect the attending dignitaries and public. NSSEs in 2004 included both the Democratic and Republican national conventions and the G8 Summit held in Georgia. The NSSEs also include coordination with state and local law enforcement and advance security planning in areas such as motorcade routes, perimeter security, communications, credentialing, air space security, and training. Recently, the Secret Service has also invested resources in combating cyberthreats to major national event security.

Investigations Responsibilities

The Secret Service also has an extensive mission in investigating counterfeiting, financial crimes, computer crimes, and identity theft. The Secret Service has exclusive jurisdiction for investigating counterfeiting of U.S. obligations and securities—currency, Treasury checks, and food stamps (Title 18, United States Code, Section 3056). Counterfeiting currency was used as a "weapon of war" in the American Revolution, Civil War, and World Wars I and II (Bowen and Neal 1960). Enemies would dump counterfeit currency into the economy to ruin public faith in the currency and destroy morale.

The Secret Service also investigates crimes associated with financial institutions such as frauds related to banking transactions, electronic funds transfers (EFTs), telecommunications transactions, and credit cards. In 1998, Congress passed the Identity Theft and Assumption Deterrence Act (P.L. 105-318) that added identity theft investigations to the Secret Service's responsibilities. In recent years, identity theft has grown rapidly. The Secret Service also has an organized crime program that investigates money laundering.

ED CONNORS

See also **Federal Police and Investigative Agencies; Homeland Security and Law Enforcement; Money Laundering**

References and Further Reading

Bowen, Walter S., and Harry E. Neal. 1960. *The United States Secret Service*. Philadelphia: Chilton.

Columbia Pictures. 1993. *In the Line of Fire*. Movie starring Clint Eastwood as a Secret Service agent protecting the president from an assassin.

National Geographic. 2005. *Inside the U.S. Secret Service*. Television documentary. http://www.nationalgeographic.com.

Neal, Harry Edward. 1971. *The story of the Secret Service*. New York: Random House.

U.S. Secret Service. http://www.secretservice.gov.

VICTIM RIGHTS MOVEMENT IN THE UNITED STATES

The past forty years have been marked by a dramatic increase in awareness, education, specialized services, and system reform for crime victims, all of which promote healing and justice. The victim rights movement was informed and influenced by the Women's Rights and Civil Rights Movements of the 1960s, a confluence of issues and activism that sought to address oppression, dominance, power, control, and inequity.

Since then, victim rights and services have become institutionalized in laws and professional practice in the fields of law enforcement, medicine, social services, law, and victim advocacy. Although there have been notable advancements in the field of victim services over the decades, funding, research, and best practices continue to be areas of focus and advocacy on the state, national, and international levels.

Early History

In ancient cultures around the world and in pre-independence America, victims played a central role in the system of justice. With crimes being viewed as wrongs against individuals, the focus was largely on retribution and reparation to the victim. The victim played a primary role in decision making, and addressing the needs of the victim was paramount. The concepts of restitution and compensation were intended to make the victim whole again and to recognize the dramatic and traumatic impact of violent crimes and property crimes on the individual victims involved.

In post-independence America and after the signing of the Constitution, a more formal criminal justice system was established. No longer were victims the moving parties in a criminal action; crimes became recognized as violations against the public order and cases were thereafter brought and prosecuted by the government on behalf of "the people." The consequence of this historical change was that victims lost their central role; they were no longer empowered to make decisions, as the system was refocused on punishment and rehabilitation of the offender rather than reparation for the victim. For almost the next two centuries, victims were increasingly relegated to the role of a mere "witness" for the government in proving its case against the alleged offender. Victims rather quickly became invisible, neglected, and forgotten in the criminal justice system, compounding their sense of powerlessness and humiliation from the victimization itself.

Crime Rates, Victimization, and the Criminal Justice System

Early victimization studies in the late 1960s and early 1970s highlighted what survivors of crime already knew—that an astounding proportion of crimes were never reported to the police because victims feared becoming involved with law enforcement and the criminal justice system. When victims did report, however, they were so distressed by the police response and their court experience, and fearful of retaliation by the offender, that they refused to testify. At that time, the criminal justice system noted significant failures in its abilities to apprehend suspects and secure their convictions, the largest cause of these failures being the loss of cooperative victims and witnesses who were often surprised that their opinions mattered little and their needs were rarely considered.

Grassroots, Government, and Legislative Remedies

An enormous amount of credit is owed to those truly at the forefront of the victim rights movement—survivors of rape and domestic violence whose courage and powerful activism raised awareness and initiated a new societal response to victims. These individuals brought to light the harmful effects of the insensitive treatment of victims and witnesses by police, prosecutors, and judges. Through their efforts, survivors and their supporters highlighted the fact that victims were revictimized in the criminal justice system. Victims often turned to other victims for support and assistance, leading to the creation of the first rape crisis centers and battered women's shelters, and other survivor organizations such as Parents of Murdered Children (POMC) and Mothers Against Drunk Driving (MADD).

The noteworthy efforts of survivors, buoyed by the failures revealed through victimization studies, caused criminal justice and government officials to focus more intently on the concerns and experiences of victims and witnesses. Grassroots organizations began meeting with criminal justice personnel. With the leadership of the National Organization for Victim Assistance (NOVA), founded in 1975, the system began to develop strategies to address the needs of victims, including the creation of victim assistance programs within the criminal justice system.

The first law enforcement–based victim assistance programs were funded by the Law Enforcement Assistance Administration (LEAA) of the U.S. Department of Justice in the mid-1970s. Crime victim issues gained even greater national prominence with President Reagan's declaration of Crime Victim Rights Week in 1981 and the establishment of the President's Task Force on Victims of Crime in 1982. This task force, one of the most compelling milestones in the victim rights movement, reviewed research on criminal victimization and held hearings around the country to obtain testimony from crime victims, victim service providers, and other allied professionals of diverse disciplines regarding the experiences and needs of crime victims. The task force report outlined sixty-eight recommendations for the criminal justice system and other organizations (for example, hospitals, clergy, schools, mental health community, media) and has served as a blueprint for comprehensive change during the past two decades. In fact, almost all of the recommendations have resulted in significant changes in policy and practice at the federal, state, and local levels.

The task force's recommendations, coinciding with the elimination of federal LEAA funding for victim services, resulted in action by Congress and a majority of state legislatures. Among its recommendations was the need for victim witness units in prosecutors' offices to provide notification of rights and case status, information about the court process, and the right to be present and heard at various junctures in the system. Wisconsin was the first state to pass a Victim Bill of Rights in 1980 with other states following in the ensuing years. In addition, Congress passed the Victim and Witness Protection Act of 1982, which provided for victim restitution, victim impact statements at sentencing in federal courts, and redress for intimidation or retaliation against victims by their offenders. The Office for Victims of Crime (OVC) within the U.S. Department of Justice was established in 1983. The Victims of Crime Act of 1984 (VOCA), which funds victim services and victim compensation through fines levied against convicted federal offenders, was passed in 1984 and continues to be a notable part of the foundation for victim services on the federal and state level. A decade later, in 1995, the federal Violence Against Women Act (VAWA) was passed providing funding and enhanced services for survivors of family violence and for specialized training for criminal justice professionals.

Victim Rights in the New Millennium

Today, all fifty states and the District of Columbia have crime victim compensation programs and victim bills of rights, and thirty-three states have successfully passed victim rights amendments to their state constitutions. Although it was among the recommendations of the President's Task Force on Victims of Crime, a federal constitutional amendment has yet to come to fruition. However, the Justice for All Act, which was passed in 2004, enhances rights for victims of crime on the federal level and addresses the need for accountability and enforcement.

Victim rights have become institutionalized within the criminal justice system to a noteworthy degree. The changes that have come about from victim rights laws are best exemplified by survivors. A remarkable woman in Massachusetts, a survivor of her son's murder and a subsequent leader in the victim rights movement on the state and national levels, described the impact of victim rights best from her own experience. She and her family participated in the system twice after the murder, the first time before the passage of the state victim rights law, and the second time, several years after its enactment. Speaking at the 20th Anniversary of the Massachusetts Victim Bill of Rights Event at the Massachusetts State House in Boston in 2004, she describes:

> The conviction of my son's murderer was overturned and a victim advocate from the DA's Office contacted me to ensure that I did not hear the news on the radio or TV first. The prosecutor and victim advocate met with me and explained the process, sought my input, and answered my questions. . . . This time I would have a different experience. The Victim Bill of Rights said I was a victim and entitled to services. As horrible as it was, I felt that I was not alone; there was someone in the courtroom who cared about me, explained the court proceedings every step of the way and kept us informed. The best thing about this second trial was that I finally got a chance to speak to the court, to let them know what my son meant to me and the impact of his murder on my life. The cruel twist of fate in having to endure a second trial was that I, as

an early victim rights activist, was forced to experience the fruits of my labors.

During the past decade, new innovative programs and practices have been established and the breadth of victim issues has notably increased. The future of victim rights, however, requires constant vigilance, accountability and enforcement, and specialized training and education for many professionals and advocates, including law enforcement. It is through all of these efforts that law enforcement officers earn greater respect from victims and witnesses, and are more effective and efficient in their pursuit of justice.

JANET E. FINE

See also **Conflict Management; Crime, Serious Violent; Criminal Investigation; Domestic (or Intimate Partner) Violence and the Police; Drunk Driving; Fear of Crime; Hate Crime; Identity Theft; Mental Illness: Improved Law Enforcement Response; Victims' Attitudes toward the Police**

References and Further Reading

Davis, R. D., and M. Henley. 1990. Victim service programs. In *Victims of crime: Problems, policies and programs*, ed. Lurigio et al, 157–71. Beverly Hills, CA: Sage.

Esselman Tomz, J., and D. McGillis. 1997. *Serving crime victims and witnesses*. 2nd ed. February. Washington, DC: U.S. Department of Justice, Office of Justice Programs, National Institute of Justice.

Kelly, D. 1990. Victim participation in the criminal justice system. In *Victims of crime: Problems, policies and programs,* ed. Lurigio et al., 172–87. Beverly Hills, CA: Sage.

Kilpatrick, Dean G., D. Beatty, and S. S. Howley. 1998. *The rights of crime victims—Does legal protection make a difference?* NIJ Research in Brief. December. Washington, DC: U.S. Department of Justice, Office of Justice Programs.

Pepperdine Law Review Symposium Edition on Victims' Rights, Pepperdine University School of Law, August 1984, Vol. 11.

Young, Marlene, and J. Stein, eds. 1994. *2001: The next generation in victim assistance*. Dubuque: IA: Kendall/Hunt Publishing Company.

———. 2004. The history of the crime victims' movement in the United States. http://www.ojp.usdoj.gov/ovc/ncvrw/2005 (accessed December 2004).

VICTIMS' ATTITUDES TOWARD THE POLICE

When someone is assaulted by a family member, has his or her identity stolen, or arrives home to find the home burglarized, that person's first contact with the criminal justice system often begins with the police. The nature of this interaction is influenced by what the victim and the police officer each bring to the encounter, including contextual, experiential, and demographic factors. Any resulting attitudes the victim may come away with are likely impacted by these same factors. This article explores the elements that influence victims' attitudes toward the police. It also examines the development of surveys and other research methods used to assess victim attitudes and perceptions, and includes a discussion of the impact of the victim rights movement on raising the profile of crime victims.

Measuring Victim Attitudes toward the Police

Beginning in the 1970s in the United States and the United Kingdom, we began learning more about victimization in part as a result of the use of general citizen surveys to assess police–citizen interactions. Until this time, we knew little about the extent to which victims reported crime to the police or about their attitudes toward police. Now, surveying residents about their perceptions and experiences with police has become a regular endeavor around the world.

The National Crime Victimization Survey (NCVS) has measured the prevalence and nature of victimization in the

United States since 1973, although it does not include questions on victim satisfaction or attitudes. To supplement the NCVS, the Bureau of Justice Statistics (BJS) teamed up with the Office of Community Oriented Policing Services (COPS) and conducted a study of victimization and community perceptions in twelve American cities. The study found that of the crimes measured by the survey, roughly a third were reported to police. The British Crime Survey (BCS), which was first instituted in England in 1982, collects similar information on prevalence and on victim attitudes and satisfaction with police. According to the 2004 BCS, 42% of crimes were either known to or reported to the police. The International Crime Victim Survey is another source of information on victimization and victim attitudes toward police. Beginning in 1989, the survey has been conducted three times across fifty-six countries. In addition to these national and international surveys, research on citizen perceptions has been carried out by academics, practitioners, and government officials in cities across the United States and in other countries.

General opinion and perception surveys have consistently demonstrated that a majority of people are supportive of the police and satisfied with the way they perform their duties. This is true particularly during voluntary encounters when residents have called the police for help (see, for example, Homant, Kennedy, and Fleming 1984; O'Brien 1978; Skogan 2005). Most citizen surveys focus broadly on citizen perceptions and encounters with police and not specifically on victim experiences and attitudes, though researchers may be able to glean information on victims from select questions.

Generally, victimization surveys have shown that victims are less satisfied with the police than nonvictims. Victims were also more likely than nonvictims to rate the police poorly or believe that they were unfair. Research suggests that this is because of the way in which people envision the role of the police as protectors. When someone is victimized they may believe that the police have failed to uphold this pledge (Homant et al. 1984).

Nonetheless, overall surveys have shown that most victims (ranging from 50% to more than 75%) are satisfied with the police (Poister and McDavid 1978; Ringham and Salisbury 2004; Shapland 1984). As noted earlier, a series of factors influence victim attitudes: variables relating to the experience of dealing with the police, contextual variables relating to the situation itself—such as the type of crime, and finally demographic variables relating to victim characteristics.

Experiential Factors

The most important determinants of victim satisfaction and attitudes toward police are related to how the victim experiences the encounter with police. One of the most consistent findings is that response time is important to victims. Central to satisfaction is not whether the police arrive as fast as possible, but in an amount of time that is consistent with how long the victim expects it to take (Brandl and Horvath 1991; Percy 1980; Poister and McDavid 1978; and Shapland 1984). In some departments, dispatchers provide victims with an estimate of response time. There is some indication that if officers arrive sooner than expected, victims are likely to be more satisfied (Percy 1980).

Officer Behavior

In addition to response time, the way in which victims are treated by police during the encounter has a significant impact on victim satisfaction. Overall, the literature suggests that police professionalism—as measured by courtesy, concern, understanding, and competence—is a key factor influencing victim attitudes and satisfaction. Skogan (2005) found that the most important predictor of satisfaction among people who called the police for help was how they were treated. Qualities such as the officer's perceived level of concern, helpfulness, politeness, fairness, or interest in the victim's situation all greatly influence victim satisfaction.

Expectations: The Importance of Process

At a time when people may be feeling the most violated and vulnerable, the degree to which the responding police officers can treat them with dignity and respect greatly influences victim attitudes. Beginning with the earliest studies, researchers have identified that meeting victim expectations around the process and nature of the police response is more important than having favorable criminal justice outcomes. In fact, the fulfillment of expectations appears to be more important than victim characteristics such as age, race, and gender. Victims seem to care more about being given a voice in the process and treated with respect than whether an arrest was made or a sentence handed down. A few studies, which looked specifically at domestic violence victims, found that victims were most satisfied with police responses when expectations around being heard and given the opportunity to express their concerns were met (Robinson and Stroshine 2005). Studies by Tom Tyler (2005) in particular have shown that procedural justice has a greater impact on victim attitudes and satisfaction than outcomes or distributive justice.

Contextual Factors

Of the crimes reported to police, victims of violent crime are more likely to report than victims of property crime. Early victimization surveys suggest that along with differences in reporting, there are differences in attitudes and levels of satisfaction. Research has shown that victims of serious personal crimes are more satisfied overall with police performance than victims of property or less serious crimes (Poister and McDavid 1978). Scholars have hypothesized that this may be because victims of serious personal crimes are likely to be victimized by someone they know, and therefore are less likely to blame the police for any perceived lack of protection. In contrast, victims who finds their homes burglarized are likely to have been victimized by strangers and may feel the police could have done more to protect their belongings. For property crimes, because there is little relationship between police investigative activities and the likelihood of arrest, victims of property crime may find their expectations are unmet more often than other victims.

In England, results from the 2002/2003 British Crime Survey showed that victims of stranger violence were more satisfied with the way their case was handled than people who were victimized by an acquaintance (Ringham and Salisbury 2004).

Building on early victim satisfaction studies, Brandl and Horvath (1991) examined the determinants of satisfaction by type of victimization. For victims of personal crimes, response time and professionalism were the most important factors. For property crimes, victims were more satisfied when officers behaved professionally, but were more concerned with investigative effort rather than response time.

Demographic Factors

Citizen surveys have found that satisfaction with the police varies according to demographics. In contrast, evidence of a link between victim demographics and satisfaction is mixed. Some surveys have found that victims' socioeconomic status shaped how they viewed the police. An early study reported that victims with higher incomes were less satisfied with how police handled the incident (Poister and McDavid 1978), whereas a British study, which included an analysis of neighborhood characteristics, showed that poor residents or victims from lower income areas were less satisfied (Coupe and Griffiths 1999). Subsequent analysis illustrates that, in general, there is no consistent support that income affects victim attitudes or satisfaction with police.

Similarly, some studies have shown that older victims are more satisfied with the police; this is consistent with findings that demonstrate differences in attitudes toward police between older and younger people in the general population, with older people expressing more confidence in and greater satisfaction with the police (Coupe and Griffiths 1999; Percy 1980). Nonetheless, across-studies findings have been fairly consistent that characteristics such as age, race, and gender do not play a significant role in victim satisfaction.

General citizen surveys reaching back to the 1960s have found that African Americans evaluate the police more negatively than whites (for example, Brown and Benedict 2002; Scaglion and Condon 1980; Schafer, Huebner, and Bynum 2003). However, like income, the race of victims does not appear to be a strong determinant of satisfaction with police services. Though race appeared to influence attitudes on the surface, Skogan (2005) found that these characteristics mattered only in that they were linked to how police officers themselves treated victims during calls for service, which in turn, affected the victim's experience.

Though it seems that demographic characteristics such as age, race, and gender have limited impact on victim satisfaction with police services, we know little about immigrant victims. Studies that have examined immigrant victims suggest that immigrants confront a range of barriers when victimized. Different cultural expectations about what law enforcement can or should do may make it hard for immigrants to understand the reasons why police officers do or do not take particular actions (Laster and Taylor 1994; Shebanyi 1987).

Empirical evidence is mixed on how immigrants, compared to native-born citizens, view police. In Chicago, Skogan and his associates found that Spanish-speaking Latinos (a better proxy for immigrant status than simply Latino ethnicity) who called the police for help were the least satisfied. Of course, not all Latinos are immigrants, and even those who are do not represent the diverse cross section of immigrants in the country. On the other hand, a study that surveyed strictly immigrants found very positive perceptions of the police among immigrants. Davis, Erez, and Avitable (1998) reported that Latin American and Asian immigrants who became victims were as or more satisfied with how the police handled their case than native-born victims.

There is clear evidence that immigrants avoid contact with the police to a far greater degree than other Americans. Davis and his colleagues studied six ethnic communities in Queens, New York. Some were well established while others consisted overwhelmingly of foreign-born residents. Davis and Henderson (2003) found that members of longer established communities were more willing to report crimes to the police than members of largely immigrant communities. In a study of abused immigrant women in Canada, Wachholz and Miedema (2000) found that women would not seek police assistance if it meant interacting with law enforcement. Immigrants' reluctance to contact the police has been attributed to experiences with the police in their birth countries (Wachholz and Miedema 2000) and to fear of deportation (Menjívar and Bejarano 2004).

In a recent study of police public contacts in Seattle, Davis and Henderson (forthcoming) observed that immigrants rated officer handling of voluntary contacts more positively than nonimmigrants. Early studies of victimization did not include measures of citizenship or immigration status. There are reasons to believe that immigrants may hold lower opinions of the police, be less willing to use the police in instrumental ways, and be more likely to have unsatisfactory experiences with the police than other members of society. Future victimization research should include key demographic variables involving immigrant status.

Conclusion

During the last several decades, there has been a tremendous expansion in the rights of victims and a significant change in the way criminal justice officials treat victims. In addition to activists calling for greater involvement, national crime victimization surveys were instrumental in raising awareness among practitioners, policy makers, and the public that there were surprisingly high rates of crime, yet low levels of crime reporting by victims. Over time, we began to learn from citizen surveys that victims are generally satisfied with the way they are treated when they call for help, with some variation across crime types. We also know that victims care a great deal about how they are treated by police, particularly during the initial encounter or call for help. As Brandl and Horvath (1991, 118) conclude, "victim demographics explain less of the variation in satisfaction with police performance than does the nature of the criminal offense and the behavior and activities of police officers."

Given that the degree to which victims trust in the legitimacy of the criminal justice process influences whether they will or will not report crimes in the future, police officers play an important role as first responders. Victims are more likely to trust and demonstrate willingness to cooperate with the police when the police can respond within the parameters of what the victim expects in a respectful way, showing concern and willingness to listen. By fostering a relationship of trust, law enforcement can gain the cooperation of citizens to develop effective crime prevention strategies and to increase the availability of information needed to solve and prevent crimes.

NICOLE J. HENDERSON

See also **Attitudes toward the Police: Measurement Issues; Attitudes toward the Police: Overview; National Crime Victimization Survey (NCVS); Victim Rights Movement in the United States**

References and Further Reading

Brandl, S. G., and F. Horvath. 1991. Crime-victim evaluation of police investigative performance. *Journal of Criminal Justice* 19: 109–21.

Brown, B., and W. Benedict. 2002. Perceptions of the police: Past findings, methodological issues, conceptual issues, and policy implications. *Policing: An International Journal of Police Strategies and Management* 25: 543–80.

Bureau of Justice Statistics and Office of Community Oriented Policing Services. 1998. *Criminal victimization and perceptions of community safety in 12 cities, 1998.* Washington, DC: U.S. Department of Justice.

Coupe, T., and M. Griffiths. 1999. The influence of police actions on victim satisfaction in burglary investigations. *International Journal of the Sociology of Law* 27 (4): 413–31.

Davis, R. C., E. Erez, and N. E. Avitable. 1998. Immigrants and the criminal justice system: An exploratory study. *Violence and Victims* 13: 21–30.

Davis, R. C., and N. J. Henderson. Forthcoming. Immigrants and law enforcement: A comparison of native-born and foreign-born Americans' opinions of the police. *The International Review of Victimology.*

———. 2003. Willingness to report crimes: The role of ethnic group membership and community efficacy. *Crime and Delinquency* 49 (4): 564–80.

Homant, R. J., D. B. Kennedy, and R. M. Fleming. 1984. The effects of victimization and the police response on citizen attitudes toward police. *Journal of Police Science and Administration* 12: 323–32.

Laster, K., and V. L. Taylor. 1994. *Interpreters and the legal system*. Leichhardt, NSW, Australia: Federation Press.

Menjívar, C., and C. Bejarano. 2004. Latino immigrants' perceptions of crime and of police authorities: A case study from the Phoenix metropolitan area. *Ethnic and Racial Studies* 27 (1): 120–48.

Nicholas, S., D. Povey, A. Walker, and C. Kershaw. 2005. *Crime in England and Wales 2004/2005*. London: United Kingdom Home Office.

O'Brien, J. 1978. Public attitudes toward the police. *Journal of Police Science and Administration* 6: 303–10.

Percy, S. L. 1980. Response time and citizen evaluation of police. *Journal of Police Science and Administration* 8: 75–86.

Poister, T. H., and J. C. McDavid. 1978. Victims' evaluation of police performance. *Journal of Criminal Justice* 6 (2):133–49.

Ringham, L., and H. Salisbury. 2004. *Support for victims of crime: Findings from the 2002/2003 British Crime Survey*. London: United Kingdom Home Office.

Robinson, A. L., and M. S. Stroshine. 2005. The importance of expectation fulfillment on domestic violence victims' satisfaction with the police in the U.K. *Policing: An International Journal of Police Strategies and Management* 28 (2): 301–20.

Scaglion, R., and R. Condon. 1980. Determinants of attitudes toward city police. *Criminology* 17 (4): 485–94.

Schafer, J. A., B. M. Huebner, and T. S. Bynum. 2003. Citizen perceptions of police services: Race, neighborhood context, and community policing. *Police Quarterly* 6: 440–68.

Shapland, J. 1984. Victims, the criminal justice system, and compensation. *British Journal of Criminology* 24 (2): 131–49.

Shebanyi, M. 1987. Cultural defense: One person's culture is another's crime. *Loyola of Los Angeles International and Comparative Law Journal* 9: 751–83.

Skogan, W. G. 2005. Citizen satisfaction with police encounters. *Police Quarterly* 8 (3): 298–321.

Tuch, S. A., and R. Weitzer. 1997. Trends: Racial differences in attitudes toward the police. *Public Opinion Quarterly*.

Tyler, Tom R. 2005. Policing in black and white: Ethnic group differences in trust and confidence in the police. *Police Quarterly* (3): 322–42.

Wachholz, S., and B. Miedema. 2000. Fear, risk, harm: Immigrant women's perceptions of the "policing solution" to woman abuse. *Crime, Law and Social Change* 34: 301–17.

VIDEO TECHNOLOGY IN POLICING

Video emerged as an important technology for law enforcement in the 1980s with the development of the small, affordable, battery-powered camcorder (a single-unit camera and recorder). Among its early uses were in closed-circuit TV (CCTV) surveillance, crime scene documentation, drunk-driver testing, the taping of confessions, officer training, and public information. Technological advances have upgraded these applications and added new ones, such as in-car cameras, wireless street-to-car transmission, facial and behavioral recognition, video line-ups, and virtual reality training.

The expanded use of video technology has been encouraged by a changing political climate. Patterns of police misconduct and inadequate administrative controls created public pressure to video-monitor police practices. Yet with growing security concerns, citizens have also become more willing to turn the camera upon themselves.

The technical complexity of many video applications and their use in criminal proceedings have led to the development of an accredited specialization in forensic video analysis. Analog videotapes have long been accepted in court, but digital recordings may still meet with resistance because of their novelty and vulnerability to alteration.

Cameras in Patrol Cars

Introduced in the mid-1980s, mobile video systems (MVSs) in patrol cars are now the most widely used video technology in policing. Newer, digital MVSs have many advantages over their analog/videotape predecessors. They occupy little space in the patrol car, with a small camera pointing out of the front windshield and a compact computer hard drive secured in the trunk or beneath the seat. The units can record continuously, or can be activated by switching on the emergency/pursuit lights, retaining a few prior recorded minutes. The hard drive collects audio data via a wireless microphone worn by the officer, and at the end of the shift, the drive is removed and uploaded to a central repository. Alternatively, through wireless audio and visual transmission from the police car to a central location, an incident is monitored and recorded as it unfolds. Recordings are easily reviewed and analyzed, because there is no tape to rewind.

Car-mounted video cameras enhance officer safety, enrich written reports, and provide persuasive evidence in the courtroom. Yet the impetus for cameras in police cars also came from public concerns over racial profiling, high-speed pursuits, and other questionable police practices. In 2000, the U.S. Department of Justice offered an In-Car Camera Incentive Program. It funded MVS equipment in state police and highway patrol vehicles, to strengthen federal initiatives against profiling and drunk driving. Now more than 75% of eligible vehicles are camera equipped.

Police agencies find MVS to be of value in evaluating and improving officer performance, resolving citizen complaints, and reducing costly lawsuits. Officers report using their video recordings as a memory aid, as a self-training tool to correct dangerous tactical errors, and as a simple way to clear themselves when accused of wrongdoing.

Video Surveillance

Surveillance of criminal suspects became more effective with the use of camcorders.

Unlike movie film or still photography, they can operate unattended for hours, under low lighting, and easily capture sound. Detectives working undercover use wireless microphones that transmit directly to a recorder. Cameras situated within schools provide streaming real-time images to police agencies as they respond to a shooting or other crisis.

Improved, cheaper technology also has enlarged the appeal of surveillance equipment among homeowners and small businesses. Because private video surveillance cameras are now so common, they frequently provide important leads in criminal investigations. Sometimes these video recordings are featured on the "Wanted" page of police agency websites.

Government-sponsored video surveillance in public spaces, such as train stations and sidewalks, was not embraced as quickly. Advocates stressed its crime-fighting potential, but critics viewed it as a threat to Constitutional liberties. After the terrorist attacks of September 11, 2001, however, few protested the proliferation of video surveillance in areas where crowds of people could become targets. England served as a role model, having established a network of CCTV cameras in the 1960s in response to IRA terrorism. When, in 2005, Londoners themselves experienced subway and bus bombings at the hands of Islamist extremists, CCTV yielded vital information in tracking down those responsible.

Large enterprises, such as airline terminals and casinos, are now investing in "second-generation" CCTV. These computer-linked cameras can recognize faces and detect suspicious activity, then immediately alert security personnel. These systems avoid the drawbacks of human TV monitoring, such as image overload, voyeurism, bias, and boredom.

Most evaluations of CCTV conclude that it does reduce crime, though its effectiveness varies with offender perceptions, type of crime, attentiveness of the camera monitors, and other factors. CCTV in public areas may help revitalize neighborhoods by creating an enhanced sense of security. Judicial rulings and scholarly opinion suggest that the courts are unlikely to oppose such systems.

Traffic Enforcement and Analysis

Video cameras trained on major thoroughfares and traffic intersections are deployed in a number of ways. They document traffic offenses, capturing license plates on camera so that summonses can be issued to the owners of offending vehicles. They transmit images of car accidents and other vehicular delays to a base from which emergency and traffic personnel can be dispatched. They help traffic analysts find short- and long-term solutions to road congestion. Finally, they record data on motorist race and offense rate along thoroughfares where police profiling may be at issue.

Crime Scenes and Found Video Evidence

Investigators use video cameras as they walk through a crime scene and reconstruct what occurred. The recordings can capture and replay details that might otherwise be overlooked or forgotten. Presented in a courtroom, video recordings are an inclusive and compelling way to document the crime scene.

Investigators sometimes discover cameras, tapes, disks, or hard drives that contain incriminating video, such as child pornography or targets for a crime or terrorist attack. Sexual offenders have been known to record their own "trophy" videos as they commit their crimes. Recovery of such taped or digital evidence often requires expertise in video or computer forensics.

Interrogations

Video recordings of police interrogations at first were restricted to the most serious felonies and to the suspect's final, post-interrogation statement. Thus the persistent questions over *Miranda* procedures, coercive tactics, and the accurate recounting of statements were left for heated courtroom debate. Amid new recognition of the problem of false confessions, a growing number of prosecutors, state legislatures, and appellate courts are moving toward a requirement that police make complete recordings of custodial interrogations.

Of the jurisdictions that have been recording full custodial interviews for a number of years, most still limit the protocol to serious cases. Some states have eavesdropping laws that require the suspect's consent to be recorded. Others require suspect notification but not consent, while still other states allow covert recording. On the whole, video recording does not significantly affect suspects' willingness to talk, although individual reactions vary.

Experienced police interrogators praise the full-recording protocol for its ability to provide a complete, permanent, and uncontestable account. The recording enables them to interview suspects without the distraction of note-taking. It allows them to reexamine suspects' words and behavior for further clues. It reduces the number of suppression motions and hostile cross-examinations by the defense counsel. Most importantly, it increases the likelihood of conviction, despite initial fears that the interrogators' use of deceit, manipulation, and strong language would offend jurors.

Police administrators also find positive outcomes from the full recording of custodial interviews. The recordings can provide video training for investigators. They deter improper interrogation tactics and build public confidence in their agency. They also reduce court-related costs, by discrediting illegitimate claims of police coercion and expediting convictions.

Video Mug Books and Line-Ups

Video mug books and line-ups allow a witness to view video footage, rather than inanimate photos, of possible suspects. The video format can present dynamic cues such as voice, mannerisms, and gait. It can spare a victim the ordeal of being in proximity to the suspect. And, since the video portraits can be viewed with no investigator present, the witness's selection is essentially "double blind." Implementation of this promising technology must await further research on the role of dynamic traits in witness identification. It will also require police agencies to establish protocols for when and how the video format can be used.

Training and Public Information

Video recordings have long been an efficient way for police agencies to convey information to their officers and to the public. Police academies and in-service training centers present videos on such diverse topics as courtroom testimony, sexual harassment, and chemical weapons attacks. Actual video footage from car stops, surveillance cameras, and custodial interrogations provide vivid lessons. Interactive, virtual-reality video programs help officers prepare to make split-second decisions in vehicle pursuits and firearm use. For the public, videos on crime prevention, drug awareness, emergency preparedness, and other topics are either distributed or shown on police agency websites.

Police video applications are now firmly tied to advances in computer technology. Videos in cell phones and on personal websites may reflect a society that is less privacy conscious in general. Both of these developments suggest even more extensive use of police video in the future.

EDITH LINN

See also **Closed-Circuit Television Applications for Policing; Computer Technology; Criminal Investigation; Eyewitness Evidence; Interrogations, Criminal; Liability and High-Speed Chases; Liability and the Police; Liability and Use of Force; PATRIOT Acts I and II; Racial Profiling; Surveillance; Technology and the Police; Traffic Services and Management**

References and Further Reading

Bureau of Justice Statistics. *State and local law enforcement statistics.* http://www.ojp.usdoj.gov/bjs/sandlle.htm.

Daniels, Wayne, and Lynnette Spratley. 2003. Lawsuit defense. *Law and Order* 51 (6): 54–63.

Dees, Tim. 2003. Fifty years of police technology. *Law and Order* 51 (4): 107–10.

Fredericks, Grant. 2004. CCTV: A law enforcement tool. *Police Chief* 71 (8): 59–64.

Hickey, Thomas J., Christopher Capsambelis, and Anthony LaRose. 2003. Constitutional issues on the use of videos in public places. *Criminal Law Bulletin* 39 (5) (Sept./Oct.): 547–68.

Huntington, Roy. 2001. Streaming video—A cop's best friend. *Police Magazine* (Oct.): 30–32.

New England uses video of criminals in act to alert public to most wanted. 2004. *Crime Control Digest* 38 (38) (Sept. 24): 1.

Police car video a handy weapon. 2004. *Security* 41 (6): 10.

Sharpe, Arthur G. 2000. On the wrong side of the law—and the lens. *Law and Order* 48 (10): 97–103.

Sullivan, Thomas. 2005. Recording custodial interrogations. *Law and Order* 53 (3): 46–50.

Surette, Ray. 2005. The thinking eye: Pros and cons of second generation CCTV surveillance systems. *Policing: An International Journal of Police Strategies and Management* 28 (1): 152–73.

Westphal, Lonnie J. 2004. The in-car camera: Value and impact. *The Police Chief* 71 (8): 59–64.

VIGILANTISM

Introduction

Individuals who take the law into their own hands in search of justice are commonly referred to as *vigilantes*. The term *vigilantism* dates back to Roman times when *vigiles* (from the Latin root meaning "awake" or "observant") would be on the constant lookout for fires and other threats such as burglars and runaway slaves. While single individuals can resort to vigilante tactics, vigilantism can also include groups of people joined together by a common belief that existing systems and procedures can no longer provide justice. These groups want to reestablish public order through vengeance and they can sometimes develop into informal "secret police forces" (Zimring 2004).

On a philosophical level, vigilantism represents morally sanctimonious behavior aimed at rectifying or remedying a structural flaw in society (Brown 1975). As such, modern vigilantes are individuals who feel that violators of the social contract have avoided punishment and admonishment by the existing legal mechanisms. Complex legal procedures and court rulings perceived as being unfair to victims can fuel vigilante attitudes in their quest for retaliation.

Vigilantism is commonly defined by the use of flagrantly illegal methods and questionable practices in order to meet the ends of vengeance and justice. Numerous attempts have been made to define vigilantism formally, but the lack of congruence among these definitions reflects the biases of the different disciplines trying to define it. For example, political scientists normally classify vigilantism as a subtype of political violence (that is, establishment violence) (Rosenbaum and Sedberg 1976), whereas psychologists and some criminologists see a more noble motive in vigilante

actions, referring to them as acts of good citizenship that play a key role in establishing social order (Marx and Archer 1976; Culberson 1990). One of the more comprehensive definitions by Burrows (1976) highlights five key components of the vigilante phenomenon:

Vigilantes:

1. are members of an organized committee;
2. are established members of the community;
3. proceed for a finite time and with definite goals;
4. claim to act as a last resort because of a failure of the established law enforcement system; and
5. claim to work for the preservation and betterment of the existing system.

Contributing Factors

Vigilantism does not occur in a vacuum. Certain factors facilitate the development and growth of vigilante activities. For example, Good Samaritan laws, views on self-defense, attitudes toward firearms for self-protection, and the importance of property rights can create an atmosphere in which individuals feel they have the right to adopt unconventional means for protection. This is especially true when they believe that the state can no longer offer them the safety and sense of justice they desire. With vigilantes, protection becomes a matter of survival and self-responsibility. For example, in recent years, the computer world has seen the rise of "digilantism," which is a form of digital vigilantism (Zimring 2004). Individuals who engage in this type of behavior purposefully seek out transgressors in the digital arena and punish them with malicious computer codes and viruses. Digilantism is considered necessary to establish order in an arena without a formal monitoring system and to protect those wishing to utilize computers and the Internet without having to fear digital aggression.

Historical Background

In the last two hundred years, there have been three distinct type of vigilantism: classical vigilantism, neo-vigilantism, and pseudo-vigilantism (Hine 1998). Classical vigilantism dates back to frontier days of the Old West. During this time, volunteer associations called *vigilante committees* would aggressively pursue suspected thieves, alcoholics, and others deemed a threat to their families, communities, or privileges (Karmen 1968). Many of these groups often turned into violent lynch mobs that targeted immigrants and indiscriminately harassed or killed people they considered "undesirable." The Gold Rush of 1849 resulted in numerous vigilante groups that protected their property and other interests in the expanding Western frontier. The absence of a formal criminal justice system in those days compounded the problem, leaving many to rely on vigilante justice for order and the punishment of criminals. For example, vigilante groups in Montana savagely killed hundreds of suspected horse thieves in retaliation for past thefts. Lynching was the preferred method of vigilante groups as the fate of the transgressors became a public warning to would-be offenders.

The American frontier of the late 1800s saw many different ethnic groups—including Anglo-Americans, Mexicans, Chinese, Indians, freed blacks, Australians, and Scandinavians—compete for scarce resources, which led to violent fights between the settlers, many of which resulted in vengeful mob attacks. Economic conflicts were frequent between cattlemen and sheepherders, and these often led to major range wars. There was constant labor strife in the mines. The bitterness of the slavery issue remained, and many men

with firearms skills learned during the Civil War turned to outlawry after leaving the service. (Jesse James was one such person.)

Westerners did manage to establish peace by relying on a combination of four groups who assumed responsibility for law enforcement: private citizens, U.S. marshals (created by congressional legislation in 1789), businesspersons, and town police officers (Johnson 1981). Private citizens usually helped to enforce the law by joining a posse or through individual efforts. (A good example is the case of the infamous Dalton Gang in Coffeyville, Kansas, in 1892; the five gang members attempted to rob a bank there but, seeing what was occurring, private citizens armed themselves and killed four of the gang members.) Between 1849 and 1902, there were 210 vigilante movements in the United States, most of them in California (Johnson 1981). While it is true that these committees occasionally hung outlaws, they also performed valuable work by ridding their communities of dangerous criminals.

Neo-vigilantism can be traced back to San Francisco in the mid-1850s (Hine 1998). Unlike the classical vigilantes who targeted offenders, neo-vigilantes focused on less noble causes by persecuting ethnic and religious minorities. The lynchings of Mexicans and African Americans during the late 1800s demonstrate neo-vigilante tactics (O'Connor 2004).

Pseudo-vigilantism grew out of social unrest, social movements, and the increasing crime problems of the 1960s (Hine 1998). Modern neo-vigilantism and pseudo-vigilantism purport to defend social causes by targeting individuals or entities considered socially threatening or immoral. For example, the destruction of abortion clinics or the burning of laboratories that conduct animal research would be considered pseudo-vigilantism because violence and illegal means are used to bring public attention to a particular cause. Today, neo-vigilantes often seek violent retaliation against known offenders (such as child molesters) or other social groups they consider a threat (such as illegal immigrants or minorities).

Characteristics

Vigilantes are not defined by ethnic or geographic boundaries. Vigilantism is as common in America as it is in Africa, Asia, Latin America, or European settings. While all vigilantes consider their actions as necessary and justified, the manner in which vigilantes carry out their actions varies. For instance, the summary lynchings of the Wild West differ from the new generation of cyber-vigilantes or digilantes, who operate from the safe confines of their homes. In Africa, vigilantes do not shy away from public attention, as demonstrated by "necklacing" practices, which involve placing a gasoline-filled tire around a suspect's neck in public and lighting it on fire (Minnaar 2001).

Vigilantes are often middle-aged men seeking to redress a perceived wrong. What separates vigilantism from self-defense, however, is that vigilantes carefully plan their vengeance, stalking their victims, and premeditating their course of action (O'Connor 2004). The decision to plan a violent act is where many vigilantes run afoul of the law, making them legally culpable for their actions. It is important to remember, however, that the law does not expressly prohibit vigilantism. What becomes problematic for vigilantes are the criminal activities adopted in their pursuit of justice.

In an effort to avoid detection by authorities, most vigilantes not only plan their schemes, but they also seek help from individuals who share similar beliefs and who are willing to fight for the same cause. As Burrows (1976) states, most vigilantes do not carry out their actions for prolonged periods, choosing instead to act sporadically, responding to problems as they arise. This separates them from hate groups, religious fanatics, or militias, all of whom have long-term objectives that can only be met through constant action.

Vigilante groups are usually divided as to the nature of the cause they choose to defend. "Crime control" vigilantes are primarily concerned with the swift and severe punishment of an offender or transgressor. For these vigilantes, social order is dependent on offenders learning that criminal behavior is unacceptable and will not be tolerated. "Social control" vigilantes, however, are more concerned with more general threats to the social order. These can be people or events that are in conflict with established communal values and are perceived as threatening the quality of life. According to social control vigilantes, such conditions cannot be tolerated and they are quickly confronted (Johnston 1996). For example, social control vigilantes might harass a newcomer they do not consider as moral as the rest of the community, while the crime control group would be mobilized by actions they considered unacceptable. In short, the crime control vigilantes focus on retaliation, while the social control vigilantes are interested in maintaining the status quo.

Although vigilantes may feel justified in their actions and causes, vigilantism threatens the democratic notions of fairness, justice, and due process. According to one author, the vigilante mind-set is the opposite of the due process mind-set (Zimring 2004). Anger, fear, and the need for vengeance drive vigilantes to act, but their reactive and impulsive nature can have negative consequences. Lack of legal procedures or concerns for punishment proportionality can lead to unfairness, overly harsh sanctions, and the inability to prove one's innocence. In trying to dispense what they consider necessary justice, vigilantes often become victimizers themselves, entangled in a cycle of violence and justifications.

KENNETH J. PEAK and
EMMANUEL P. BARTHE

See also **Accountability**

References and Further Reading

Brown, R. 1975. *Strain of violence.* New York: Oxford University Press.

Burrows, W. 1976. *Vigilante!* New York: Harcourt Brace Jovanovich.

Culberson, W. 1990. *Vigilantism: Political history of private power in America.* Westport, CT: Greenwood.

Hine, D. K. 1998. Vigilantism revisited: An economic analysis of the law of extrajudicial self-help or why can't Dick shoot Henry for stealing Jane's truck? *The American University Law Review* 47: 1221.

Johnson, D. R. 1981. *American law enforcement: A history.* St. Louis, MO: Forum Press.

Johnston, L. 1996. What is vigilantism? *British Journal of Criminology* 36: 220–36.

Karmen, A. 1968. Vigilantism. In *International encyclopedia of the social sciences,* ed. D. Sills, 1645–49. New York: Macmillan.

Marx, G., and D. Archer. 1976. The urban vigilante. *Psychology Today,* January, 45–50.

Minnaar, Anthony. 2001. *The new vigilantism in post–April 1994 South Africa: Crime prevention or an expression of lawlessness?* Institute for Human Rights and Criminal Justice Studies. Paper presented at Technikon South Africa Conference. http://www.crimeinstitute.ac.za/reports/vigilantism.pdf (accessed May 2006).

O'Connor, T. R. 2004. *MegaLinks in criminal justice.* http://faculty.ncwc.edu/toconnor/300/300lect10.htm (accessed May 2006).

Rosenbaum, H., and P. Sedberg, eds. 1976. *Vigilante politics.* Philadelphia: University of Pennsylvania Press.

Zimring, F. 2004. In *MegaLinks in criminal justice,* ed. T. O'Connor. http://faculty.ncwc.edu/toconnor/300/300lect10.htm.

VOLLMER, AUGUST

August Vollmer (1876–1955), father of modern professional policing in the United States, was born in New Orleans, Louisiana. Orphaned as a child, he was educated in Germany before returning to the United States and settling in the San Francisco Bay area. After service in the Philippines during the Spanish-American War, which included two highly publicized acts of heroism, he was elected marshal of Berkeley, California, in 1905. From that point on his career never waned. In 1907 he was elected president of the California Police Chiefs Association; from 1909 to 1932 he served as chief of police for Berkeley; in 1922 he accepted the presidency of the International Association of Chiefs of Police; and from 1932 until his death he was an educator, a professor of police administration at the University of California. In between he reorganized the San Diego Police Department (1915), the Los Angeles Police Department (1923–1925), the Detroit Police Department (1925), the Havana (Cuba) Police (1926), the police agencies of Chicago and Kansas City (1929), the Minneapolis Police Department (1930), the Santa Barbara Police Department (1936), the police of Syracuse, New York (1943), of Dallas (1944), and of Portland, Oregon (1947). Moreover, in 1931 the Wickersham Commission retained him, and his *Report on Police* contributed in no small part to the successful campaign to repeal the Eighteenth Amendment (Prohibition) and the Volstead Act.

Vollmer was an innovator in an extremely conservative profession. He was an early advocate of college education for police officers and other unheard-of measures, such as probation for first offenders and the decriminalization of victimless crimes. He considered crime prevention a priority for police and opposed capital punishment. He instituted an in-service training program of such rigor and effectiveness that it was copied by numerous police agencies in the United States and other countries. In 1921 Vollmer introduced the first "lie detector" to be put to practical police use, and for many years was the sole police executive to endorse its use as an investigative tool. Polygraph pioneers Clarence D. Lee, John Larson, and Leonarde Keeler acknowledged their debt to him for employing and defending the new device. As early as 1922 he inaugurated a single fingerprint classification system and a simple but effective method of classifying handwriting specimens. He also initiated the modus operandi approach to criminal investigation. In the 1920s and early 1930s, the Berkeley police laboratory became the model and training ground for police laboratory technicians throughout the country.

Vollmer's dedication to stringent recruitment standards, high levels of integrity, and freedom from political interference were unpopular with his contemporaries. But the Berkeley Police Department soon became the darling of progressive journalists and academics. In succeeding decades Berkeley police officers such as O. W. Wilson, V. A. Leonard, John P. Kenney, and many others were recruited for high-ranking positions in other police agencies and were appointed to head up the many police science curricula that burgeoned on America's university campuses in the 1940s and 1950s. Second only to J. Edgar Hoover in public relations expertise, Vollmer insisted on complete cooperation with the news media. He seemed always to be promoting the police through contributions to both professional and popular journals, lectures to college classes and to a variety of business and professional clubs, and presentations describing Berkeley police initiatives and programs. He never tired of delineating the future of policing.

Unlike J. Edgar Hoover, Vollmer was at home with academic criminologists and he respected them. He conducted a voluminous correspondence with such leaders of American criminology as Edwin Sutherland, Sheldon Glueck, Paul Tappan, Thorsten Sellin, and Martin Neumeyer. As founder and president of the organization now known as the American Society of Criminology (which presents annually the August Vollmer Award to a distinguished criminologist), he extended his influence considerably. A faithful student of scientific management and public administration, he ceaselessly reeducated himself.

Vollmer authored or coauthored a number of books, all now out of print but many of which are still footnoted in the contemporary police literature. Clearly stated in his writings is his plea for centralization and consolidation of police units and services. To this day, his cherished wish for integrated policing is still elusive. On the national level centralization of criminal identification files and crime statistics has been realized, but the consolidation of many local police units into larger, more responsive law enforcement agencies has not come to pass. In 1955, weary and almost blind, Vollmer shot himself in the right temple to end his life.

The Bancroft Library of the University of California, Berkeley, is the repository of the Vollmer Collection and of the oral history *August Vollmer: Pioneer in Professionalism*. Included in the collection are Vollmer's private correspondence, his files from the Berkeley Police Department days, his unpublished manuscripts, and taped interviews with Vollmer colleagues and protégés, such as O. W. Wilson, John D. Holstrom, V. A. Leonard, Willard E. Schmidt, Thomas P. Hunter, William F. Dean, Gene B. Woods, Milton Chernin, Austin MacCormick, Spencer D. Parratt, and Donal E.J. MacNamara.

DONAL E. J. MACNAMARA

References and Further Reading

Carte, Gene E., and Elaine H. Carte. 1975. *Police reform in the United States: The era of August Vollmer*. Berkeley: University of California Press.

Deutsch, Albert. 1955. *The trouble with cops*. New York: Crown.

Kenney, John P. 1964. *The California police*. Springfield, IL: Charles C Thomas.

Leonard, V. A. 1968. *Police of the 20th century*. Brooklyn, NY: Foundation Press.

MacNamara, Donal E. J. 1977. August Vollmer: The vision of police professionalism. In *Pioneers in policing*, ed. P. J. Stead. Montclair, NJ: Patterson Smith.

Parker, Alfred E. 1961. *Crime fighter: August Vollmer*. New York: Macmillan.

———. 1972. *The Berkeley police story*. Springfield, IL: Charles C Thomas.

U.S. National Commission on Law Observance and Enforcement (Wickersham Commission). 1968. *Report no. 14: Police.*

Prepared under the direction of A. Vollmer, 1931. Reprint. Montclair, NJ: Patterson Smith.

Vollmer, August. 1936/1971. *The police and modern society*. Reprint. Montclair, NJ: Patterson Smith.

———. 1949. *The criminal*. Brooklyn, NY: Foundation Press.

Vollmer, August, and Alfred E. Parker. 1935. *Crime and the state police*. Berkeley: University of California Press.

———. 1937. *Crime, crooks and cops*. New York: Funk and Wagnall Press.

W. P. A. Writers Project. 1941. *Berkeley: The first 75 years*. Berkeley, CA: Gillick Press.

VOLUNTEERS IN POLICING

Policing and law enforcement organizations in the United States currently rely on a range of unpaid volunteers who assist with various tasks and operations. The use of volunteers by U.S. police agencies is a trend that appears to be increasing.

Police Volunteers Defined

Since the mid-1840s (in the United States), policing has predominantly been viewed as a vocation, best conducted by paid employees of police organizations (Klockars 1985). Police employees can be divided into two groups: sworn officers, who have arrest powers, and civilian employees who do not have arrest powers. Police volunteers represent a category of people who assist the police in performing police tasks but are not paid for their efforts and are thus not employees. Police volunteers take a variety of forms, so it helps to think in terms of how long the volunteer's relationship with the police agency lasts, and how organizationally involved the volunteer becomes. (For example, does the volunteer work in a police station, or is he or she located solely in the community while helping? Does the volunteer have contact with a number of police employees or only one or a few?) It is possible to array volunteers along a continuum representing the length and density of the voluntary relationship. This continuum represents the formality of the volunteer's relationship with the police agency and it is a useful device for thinking about police volunteers.

At one end of this formality continuum are people who briefly assist a police officer, for example, by helping chase a suspect or providing a little information to an officer. Such an individual's length of volunteering is short lived and they do not have contact with many officers. Further along the continuum are informants, who generally have more frequent contacts with the police, but do not frequent police facilities (such as police stations), their volunteer activities are not usually acknowledged by the agency, and they usually have contact with a limited number of employees. Still further along the continuum are citizens who become involved in longer term volunteer activities, such as neighborhood watch, citizen's patrols, or regularly scheduled police–community meetings associated with community policing. Finally, at the other end of the continuum are volunteers who regularly perform police-like tasks on a scheduled basis for the police agency (such as unpaid reserve police officers). In many instances the only difference between this last category of volunteer and regular police employees is that these volunteers are not paid.

This entry will concentrate on the more formal examples of police volunteers outlined above. The less formal examples of police volunteers such as serving as an informant or briefly assisting a police officer will not be covered here.

Police Volunteers Described

Perhaps the most widely known police volunteer program is Neighborhood Crime Watch, which is loosely organized by the National Crime Prevention Council. Crime watch programs are relatively ephemeral programs that involve community residents in watching out for crimes in their neighborhoods. If residents see a crime or suspicious activity, they are supposed to call the local police. Some versions of crime watch use citizens to patrol their neighborhoods, sometimes with radios or whistles. Crime watch participants are supposed to alert their local police and are forbidden from taking any actions on their own. There are no accurate estimates of the number of these watch programs although estimates run into the "tens of thousands" (Lab 2004, 62). Likewise, there are no accurate estimates on the number of participants, because many of these watch programs are relatively short-lived organizations with very fluid memberships. The number of watch programs appears to be increasing, however (Rosenbaum, Lurigio, and Davis 1998). See Lab (2004, chap. 4) for a full discussion of neighborhood crime prevention programs.

Some police agencies use volunteers to handle more formal police tasks. In some agencies volunteers serve as reserve police officers who are trained, wear uniforms, and patrol in marked police cars. Some states and agencies permit these volunteer reserves to carry a firearm and make arrests; other states and agencies do not (Hilal 2004). Other agencies, such as one in Santa Ana, California, use volunteers to patrol in marked cars, but they are distinguishable from regular patrol officers, usually by the type of uniform they wear and their title (for example, in Santa Ana they are called police service officers), and they do not respond to emergency calls (Skolnick and Bayley 1986). Older volunteers in Concord, California, and San Diego, California, patrol the community in marked cars while responding to non-emergency calls such as assisting disabled motorists, taking crime reports at the scene of cold calls, and conducting vacation checks of homes (King 2005).

Some police agencies (such as those in Detroit, Michigan; San Diego, California; and Lowell, Massachusetts) use volunteers as greeters or receptionists at police substations, where the volunteers assist citizen "walk-ins." Volunteers often recontact victims and witnesses, take statements, and generally assist police officers with clerical duties. Some agencies use volunteers for the special skills they bring to that agency. In many cases volunteers can bring a wealth of skills and experience that would be hard to find in a police officer or civilian employee. For example, in order to deal with its sizable Spanish-speaking population, the Colorado Springs (Colorado) Police Department uses bilingual volunteers to serve as interpreters. This arrangement is useful, because the agency can enlist the skills of bilingual individuals as needed, without hiring them. Concord, California, also staffs its chaplain's program with volunteers and relies on volunteers to produce the department's television show. Police agencies have also used volunteers to perform technical tasks, such as computer support, equipment maintenance, and data entry, and to assist crime victims.

An agency considering the use of volunteers should plan carefully. Some police agencies employ a paid volunteer coordinator. Agencies should also consider some type of training or orientation for their volunteers and should conduct a basic background check on possible volunteers, especially volunteers who will have more formal relationships with the agency and/or access to sensitive information (King 2005). Finally, agencies should monitor the relationships between paid employees (both sworn officers and civilian employees) and volunteers. There are significant differences between employees and volunteers in terms of status and power, and the agency should ensure that these differences do not become dysfunctional for the organization. For example, patrol officers may initially resent the use of volunteers for basic, nonemergency patrol duties and management should ensure that officers and volunteers cooperate.

WILLIAM R. KING

See also **Community Attitudes toward the Police; Community Watch Programs; Costs of Police Services; Neighborhood Watch**

References and Further Reading

Hilal, Susan M. 2004. *Volunteer police reserve officers: An identity theory perspective*. Ph.D. diss. South Dakota State University.

King, William R. 2005. Civilianization. In *Implementing community policing: Lessons from twelve agencies,* ed. Edward R. Maguire and William Wells, chap. 17. Washington, DC: Office of Community Oriented Policing Services.

Klockars, Carl. 1985. *The idea of police*. Beverly Hills, CA: Sage.

Lab, Steven P. 2004. *Crime prevention: Approaches, practices and evaluations.* 5th ed. Cincinnati, OH: Anderson Publishing Company.

Rosenbaum, Dennis, A. J. Lurigio, and R. C. Davis. 1998. *The prevention of crime: Social and situational strategies*. Belmont, CA: West/Wadsworth.

Skolnick, Jerome, and David Bayley. 1986. *The new blue line: Police innovation in six cities*. New York: The Free Press.

VORENBERG, JAMES

James Vorenberg (1928–2000), criminal justice and legal expert, was born in Cambridge, Massachusetts, on January 10, 1928, to Jewish parents F. Frank and Ida Vorenberg. Vorenberg graduated magna cum laude from Harvard College in 1948 with an A.B., and earned his LL.B. degree from Harvard Law School in 1951. During graduate school, he served as president of the *Harvard Law Review*. Upon graduation, he received the Sears Prize for his high grade point average.

Vorenberg's early career provided him with invaluable experience in the legal profession. Before clerking for U.S. Supreme Court Justice Felix Frankfurter between 1953 and 1954, Vorenberg was commissioned as a second lieutenant in the Air Force and spent two years working as a lawyer in the Air Force General Counsel's Office (*Harvard University Gazette* 2000). Between 1954 and 1962, Vorenberg worked for Ropes and Gray, a Boston law firm. He became a partner in the firm in 1960.

Vorenberg made several significant contributions to the field of criminal justice at both federal and state levels. Between 1964 and 1965, and at then Attorney General Robert F. Kennedy's request, Vorenberg served as director of the Office of Criminal Justice, an agency of the U.S. Department of Justice that later became the Office of Legal Counsel. Following this position, Vorenberg served as executive director of President Lyndon B. Johnson's Commission on Law Enforcement and Administration of Justice between 1965 and 1967. Established in 1965 to address concerns about violence and crime in the United States, this commission was charged with investigating the causes of delinquency and crime, producing reports detailing findings, and providing a set of recommendations to President Johnson. Of particular importance were the issues of crime prevention and "improving law enforcement and the administration of criminal justice" (President's Commission on Law Enforcement and Administration of Justice 1969, 685).

As executive director of the commission, Vorenberg's primary responsibilities included overseeing staff and ensuring the commission moved toward fulfilling the responsibilities with which it was charged. After an extensive two-year study of the major components of the criminal justice system, most notably the police, courts, and corrections, the commission produced a landmark ten-volume set of reports documenting research findings (President's Commission on Law Enforcement and Administration of Justice 1969).

Several positive advances in the efficiency and operation of the criminal justice system stemmed from the commission's work. Some of these included an increase in the quality of police education and training, enhanced police–community relations, increased professionalism in policing, and a better understanding of how criminal justice agencies operate from a systems perspective (U.S. Department of Justice 1997; President's Commission on Law Enforcement and Administration of Justice 1969). In addition to his work with the commission, Vorenberg was a key figure in the establishment of the Law Enforcement Assistance Administration (LEAA), a federal agency created in response to the commission's findings.

After completing his work with President Johnson's crime commission, Vorenberg served as Senator George S. McGovern's adviser on crime and drug policy during the 1972 presidential election. Between 1973 and 1975, he served as the associate special prosecutor to first Special Prosecutor Archibald Cox during the Watergate investigation. As Cox's right-hand man, Vorenberg was responsible for building the Watergate Special Prosecutor's Office, putting together the prosecution's legal team, hiring office personnel, and keeping a record of the decisions made by the legal team. After President Nixon dismissed Cox on October 21, 1973, Vorenberg, who left the legal team upon Cox's firing, returned at the request of second Special Prosecutor Leon Jaworski. Vorenberg engaged in much of the same work he had done while working under Cox.

Vorenberg also held several state government positions. He was the first chair of the Massachusetts State Ethics Commission between 1978 and 1983 and was charged with overseeing the commission and aiding in the enforcement of state conflict-of-interest laws. Other appointments included serving on the Massachusetts Supreme Judicial Court Advisory Committee between 1990 and 1993 and advising the Massachusetts State Senate Ethics Committee.

Aside from work in federal and Massachusetts State government, Vorenberg served Harvard Law School (HLS) in several capacities, most notably as a law professor, associate dean, and the ninth dean of the law school. Throughout his thirty-eight-year teaching career, which began in 1962, he taught courses on criminal law, legal ethics, and the legal profession.

Vorenberg's administrative career at Harvard began in 1977 with his appointment as associate dean. Vorenberg was appointed dean in 1981, and became Roscoe Pound Professor of Law. Under his eight-year deanship, several important advances in the HLS program were made. He approved the expansion of Harvard's Low Income Protection Plan, and aided in bolstering and/or founding the HLS Human Rights Program, Clinical Program, and the Program on the Legal Profession. The Program on the Legal Profession, designed to bring police officers to campus in an effort to increase educational interaction between these practitioners, faculty, and law students, was among the first of its kind in the country (Clark and Cox 2000). Vorenberg also spearheaded the planning strategy that formed the foundation for the Campaign for HLS, a fund-raiser that raised $183 million in donations. In 1987, Vorenberg was honored with the Harvard University Association of Black Faculty, Administrators, and Fellows C. Clyde Ferguson Award in recognition of his efforts in increasing the diversity of students and faculty (Clark and Cox 2000).

Vorenberg's research interests included addiction and crime (Vorenberg 1972), prostitution (Vorenberg and Vorenberg 1977), suspect interrogation and police detention, criminal law and procedure (Vorenberg 1981a), corporate law, and prosecutorial power (Vorenberg 1981b). Much of his scholarly work reflected his expressed interest in limiting the discretion of criminal justice officials, especially police and prosecutors. Recognizing that limiting excessive discretion in one stage of the criminal justice system will not successfully reform the entire system, Vorenberg advocated for controlling discretion at key stages in the criminal justice system. Some of his scholarly work discusses how discretion can be controlled at the charging, police investigation, sentencing, pretrial release, and correctional treatment decision points of the justice system (Vorenberg 1975). His concern over prosecutorial discretion centered on the lack of accountability that prosecutors might have when making decisions concerning whom to prosecute (Edelman 1973; Vorenberg 1981b).

Vorenberg was diagnosed with Parkinson's disease in 1986. He died of cardiac arrest on April 12, 2000, at Mount Auburn Hospital in Cambridge, Massachusetts, at the age of 72.

REBECCA J. BOYD

See also **Crime Commissions; Law Enforcement Assistance Administration**

References and Further Reading

Baron, Charles, Clyde Bergstressor, Dan Brock, Garrick Cole, Nancy Dorfman, Judith Johnson, Lowell Schnipper, James Vorenberg, and Sidney Wanzer. 1996. A model state act to authorize and regulate physician-assisted suicide. *Harvard Journal on Legislation* 33: 1–34.

Clark, Robert, and Archibald Cox. 2000. In memoriam: James Vorenberg. *Harvard Law Review* 114: 1–22.

Edelman, Richard. 1973. Vorenberg renews work on Watergate prosecution. *The Harvard Crimson,* December 14. http://www.thecrimson.harvard.edu/article.aspx?ref=110189.

Greenberg, Jack, and James Vorenberg. 1990. *Dean cuisine, or, the liberated man's guide to fine cooking.* New York: Sheep Meadow Press.

HLS in mourning: Three faculty remembered: Professors Gary Bellow, Abram Chayes, and James Vorenberg. 2000. *Harvard Law Bulletin* (Summer). http://www.law.harvard.edu/alumni/bulletin/backissues/sum2000/article1.html.

President's Commission on Law Enforcement and Administration of Justice. 1969. *The challenge of crime in a free society.* New York: E. P. Dutton.

———. 1971. *Task force report: The police.* New York: Arno Press.

U.S. Department of Justice. 1997. The challenge of crime in a free society: Looking back, looking forward. In *Symposium on the 30th anniversary of the President's Commission on Law Enforcement and Administration of Justice.* Washington, DC: U.S. Government Printing Office.

Vorenberg, Elizabeth, and James Vorenberg. 1973. Early diversion from the criminal justice system: Practice in search of a theory. In *Prisoners in America,* ed. Ohlin, 151–66. Englewood Cliffs, NJ: Prentice-Hall.

———. 1977. The biggest pimp of all. *Atlantic Monthly* 239: 27–39.

Vorenberg, James. 1972. The war on crime: The first five years. *Atlantic Monthly* 229: 63–69.

———. 1975. A.L.I. approves model code of pre-arraignment procedure. *American Bar Association Journal* 61: 1212–17.

———. 1976. Narrowing the discretion of criminal justice officials. *Duke Law Journal* 1976: 651–97.

———. 1981a. *Criminal law and procedure: Cases and materials.* Eagan, MN: West Group.

———. 1981b. Decent restraint of prosecutorial power. *Harvard Law Review* 94: 1521–73.

Vorenberg, ninth dean of law school, dies. 2000. *Harvard University Gazette,* April 20. http://www.news.harvard.edu/gazette/2000/04.20/vorenberg.html.

WEED AND SEED

History

Weed and Seed (W&S) was started in 1991 within the Executive Office of the President (EOP) as a discretionary federal grant program that provided funds for crime control and community revitalization to particularly troubled neighborhoods. U.S. attorney's offices (USAOs) were invited to partner with local agencies on funding requests. The USAO was given the responsibility of setting up a steering committee and formulating a local strategy. After federal review and approval, federal support flowed through the USAO to the local agencies and organizations that would implement the strategy.

There were three demonstration sites in 1991: Kansas City, Missouri; Trenton, New Jersey; and Omaha, Nebraska. By 1997, management of the program had moved from the EOP to the Executive Office for Weed and Seed in the Office of Justice Programs (OJP). In 2004, a new office—Community Capacity and Development

Office (CCDO), within the Bureau of Justice Assistance—took over W&S program management.

The number of funded sites has grown steadily, from twenty-one immediately after the demonstration to more than three hundred in 2005. Site funding levels have declined as a consequence of this growth because congressional appropriations have not changed in proportion to the increase in sites. In the early 1990s, roughly 36 sites were funded at $750,000 per year for four or five years. By 1997, about 120 sites were funded at $250,000 per year. In 2005, few sites got more than $150,000 annually, though funding is the same for all sites. Current sites range in size from a few blocks to several miles in area, with populations between three thousand and fifty thousand. While typically within a city, some sites are county based.

Operational Overview

A Weed and Seed Steering Committee identifies target neighborhoods and then seeks to establish local partnerships that will implement a specific strategy to reduce violence, drug trafficking, and crime, and provide a safe environment for residents.

The USAO that has jurisdiction over a candidate W&S site assembles the steering committee for that site. This committee is responsible for developing the strategic plan for the site; overseeing, monitoring, and implementing programs; distributing program funds; and evaluating the program. Committee participants may include the U.S. attorney, mayor, police, local non-profit leaders, federal agency representatives, private businesses, area corporations, residents, faith-based organizations, district prosecutors, and representatives of local agencies.

The first stage of W&S typically requires geographically targeted law enforcement by police and prosecutors (weeding). This is followed by enhanced social services and neighborhood improvements (seeding). Consequently, interagency cooperation and collaboration are required elements of most weed and seed strategies. Examples of such efforts include federal/local task forces involving the FBI, DEA, and some combination of city, county, and state police. Federal and local prosecutors also play a key role in identifying the optimal prosecution strategy when task force activities result in arrests. On the seeding side, increased communication and task sharing between social service agencies and community-based private sector organizations offer the potential for significant enhancement in the scope and quality of social service delivery. The usual pattern is to enhance a core of social services and organizations that are already collaborating.

Becoming a Weed and Seed Site

Before receiving funding, a community must attain official recognition as a W&S site from CCDO. To do this, the site must put together a steering committee and a strategic plan. Once official recognition is attained, the site may apply for funding from CCDO. Official recognition and funding are both temporary, with a five-year limit. A site that continues to implement its strategic plan and maintain its partnerships is considered to have graduated from W&S. Regardless, five years after official recognition, the site may not apply for W&S funding or official recognition status again.

Funds from CCDO depend on compliance with W&S Office of Justice Programs requirements. A site will only receive one award per fiscal year except when special emphasis funding is offered, usually on a competitive basis. Other outstanding OJP activities will be considered, as well as past awards and performance under them. Because federal W&S grants are not meant to completely fund all desired programs in a W&S site, the site will have to demonstrate the ability to obtain both financial and nonfinancial resources from other public and private sources. The site is expected to become self-sustaining during its W&S life, and a plan for accomplishing this goal must either be in the strategy or be developed shortly thereafter.

Weed and Seed in Action

A national evaluation of W&S was completed in 1999 (Dunworth and Mills 1999). Results of W&S programs varied: from wide reductions in Part I crimes (serious violent and drug-related offenses) and increased perceptions of public safety and police confidence, to small or no noticeable reductions in Part I crimes. Sites that concentrated federal resources on small geographic areas and leveraged additional funds in these areas experienced the most success in reducing crime.

Factors for Success

The initial state of a site has many implications for the success of a W&S program. The important factors include community social service infrastructure, crime levels, economic factors, and the rate of residential turnover within the community. With rapid turnover, the long-term community involvement and support for the seeding efforts of W&S are difficult to achieve and sustain. Once W&S funding is implemented, "early seeding, sustained weeding, high-level task forces combined with community policing, and an active prosecutorial role are critical elements of program design" (Dunworth and Mills 1999).

The national evaluation (Dunworth and Mills 1999) found that:

> The most effective implementation strategies were those that relied on bottom-up, participatory decision-making approaches, especially when combined with efforts to build capacity and partnership among local organizations. This required a long-term perspective about the program and its potential to bring about community change. Such sites, including some that achieved substantial crime reductions within the time period analyzed, have established a stronger foundation and more sustainable basis for further community-targeted initiatives.

Weeding

In most sites, law enforcement approaches have been tailored to fit the strategy. They typically involved multiagency/multijurisdictional task forces, stronger street patrols, and higher level police/prosecutor interagency cooperation. The law enforcement efforts developed increased local, state, and federal coordination in targeting offenders, halting drug trafficking, and in prosecution or probation/parole.

"Multi-agency task forces concentrated on the target area, although they pursued drug cases across jurisdictional lines" (Dunworth and Mills 1999). Increased police presence was funded through additional staffing and overtime, and a majority of sites assigned dedicated officers to the target area. These approaches helped build relationships with residents and aided enforcement through better local knowledge and intelligence, an increased ability to operate proactively, and enhanced communication between residents and police. "Weed and Seed provided a vehicle for mobilizing residents to participate in crime prevention. Responses ranged from increasing neighborhood watches, to community meetings, to a citizens' advisory committee that provided guidance on law enforcement priorities" (Dunworth and Mills 1999). Violent and drug-related crimes were especially targeted by these efforts.

Prosecution efforts were weaker than police efforts in W&S because of various institutional, political, and judicial concerns. "In general, district attorneys operate with limited resources and in politicized environments that act as barriers to the provision of the additional resources needed for local prosecution of W&S cases" (Dunworth and Mills 1999). Local police and prosecution operate through different political systems: Police departments are funded in a fairly well-defined process through cities, whereas prosecutors are funded through a competitive political process at the county level. In addition, police chiefs are usually appointed by mayors, whereas prosecutors are usually elected. Thus, though police were able to make concentrated arrests in the W&S areas, enhanced prosecution was often difficult to generate.

The majority of sites expanded or strengthened community policing efforts by dedicating officers to specific geographic areas. Though community residents would often protest weeding activities, fearing targeted harassment or discrimination by police, the community policing focus helped to improve relationships between communities and police, and led to increased public confidence in police in a number of locations. The result was a greater potential for making police–community partnerships sustainable after W&S funding was phased out. Little follow-on research has been done to see if this was in fact the result.

Seeding

The seeding process is much more political, problematic, and complicated than the weeding effort, and it is more difficult for most sites to implement. Engaging, coordinating, and mobilizing multiple public- and private-sector agencies that are not familiar with one another was daunting for many sites. Planning, relationship building, and gaining consensus and commitment from potential program participants generally took much more time and effort than weeding.

Typical seeding efforts fell into the following categories, in rough order of frequency: youth prevention and intervention programs, neighborhood restoration, community building and development, adult job training and employment programs, family support services, and community economic development activities.

Future

The future of Weed and Seed is uncertain. The program has low funding levels (around $60 million nationally per year), so it is not a very significant federal budget item. Therefore, it does not offer much savings potential during the annual appropriations process. However, for that very reason it would be a simple matter for it to be eliminated.

TERENCE DUNWORTH and
KEVIN ROLAND

See also **Community-Oriented Policing: Practices; Crime Prevention; Situational Crime Prevention; Social Disorganization, Theory of**

References and Further Reading

Community Capacity Development Office. 2005. *The Weed and Seed Data Center*. http://www.weedandseeddatacenter.org/ (accessed 2005).
———. 2005. *The Weed and Seed strategy*. http://www.jrsa.org/weedandseedinfo/strat egy.htm (accessed 2005).
Dunworth, Terry, and Gregory Mills. 1999. *National evaluation of Weed and Seed*. Washington, DC: U.S. Department of Justice, National Institute of Justice.
U.S. Office of Justice Programs. 2005. *Weed and Seed*. http://www.ojp.usdoj.gov/ccdo/ ws/welcome.html (accessed 2005).
———. 2005. *Weed and Seed—FAQS*. http:// www.ojp.usdoj.gov/ccdo/ws/official_recog. html (accessed 2005).
———. 2005. *Weed and Seed—Official recognition*. http://www.ojp.usdoj.gov/ccdo/ws/ official_recog.html (accessed 2005).

WESTERN PEACE OFFICER

The term *peace officer* refers to those people whose main job it is to preserve and maintain the public peace, and it encompasses a broad range of law enforcement officers including police officers, constables, mayors, sheriffs, wardens, marshals, corrections officers, and in earlier eras even judges (hence the term *justice of the peace*). While crime prevention is the focus of the peace officer, many conceptualize police officers and sheriffs, at least, as crime fighters as opposed to crime preventers. This impression is even more pronounced when the word *western* is added to the mix. The *western peace officer* brings forth images of dusty main streets, saloons, and gunslingers. These images have been shaped by folklore and the media, with a blurred distinction between the bandits and the peace officers themselves.

The connotation of the violent, rough-and-tumble American frontier is actually far from reality. There was violence and criminal activity in the frontier in the late 1800s, but much less so than compared to the urban areas of the time. In fact, the Western frontier was even safer than most of American cities today in terms of absolute numbers of homicides as well as characteristics of the crimes themselves, with modern crime often involving innocent victims, whereas frontier crime usually involved willing participants. This idea of a relatively safe western frontier is in contrast to most people's notions of the "Wild West" as being a place where shoot-outs were a common occurrence. It is true that many citizens had firearms to protect person and property; however, the overall notion of a gunslinging society with fast-drawing peace officers bringing justice to a crime-ridden American frontier is exaggerated. Stereotypes and folklore of the western peace officer (like stereotypes of other groups) do not capture the complexity and nuance of the people or their jobs.

- *Town officers*. Town officers often spent their time in common civic actions such as arresting drunks and looking for stray children and animals. They often secured their positions through friendships with mayors and judges. While the most glamorized of the western peace officers (for example, Wyatt and Virgil Earp) may have been periodically battling outlaws and dealing with vigilantism, many officers engaged in mundane policing activity and had reputations for being corrupt, lazy, and indifferent.
- *County sheriffs*. Compared to the town officers, county sheriffs enjoyed a great deal of police authority given their power over larger geographic areas that in some instances were larger than some states. Their responsibilities were thus diverse and included governmental duties (for example, collecting taxes, serving court orders), corrections (for example, running the county jail), and a wide range of other services (for example, inspecting livestock). They also had at their disposal deputies and local constables.
- *Private police agencies*. Private agencies provided detective services, centralized points of contact for other police organizations, and guard services. Specialized agencies like the railroad police had authority similar to that of their public counterparts, but focused their attention on preserving and securing safe delivery of their freight. Range inspectors similarly focused their law enforcement energies on minimizing cattle theft.
- *Rangers*. The rangers (of Texas Ranger fame) were small paramilitary units that were designed to scout Indian tribes in the western-most regions of development of East Texas.
- *Highway patrol officers*. The introduction of the automobile and expansion of networked roadways created the need for state police forces whose job was to focus completely on the problems, challenges, and criminal activities associated with the growing highways.
- *Native American police officers*. Tribes developed their own agencies to enforce order and tribal rules. Once recognized by Congress and federal authorities in 1878, these existing Native American officers gradually developed law enforcement systems that affected tribal lands across the United States, with independent forces upholding the law and maintaining the peace on reservations. The flip side is the specialized agents used as scouts by the U.S. military, and later, as investigators by the Bureau of Indian

Affairs, to focus specifically on crime associated with tribal lands.

- *U.S. marshals.* In terms of federal law enforcement, some segments of the military acted as law enforcement agencies; however, the U.S. marshals engaged in the most typical of police activity. With a national judicial system in place starting in 1789 came the need for a federal law enforcement system. These officers were typically businessmen appointed by the president. These federal officers carried out a wide range of police duties across their federal territories in the West. As the territories became states, their roles shrank to those we are familiar with today.

- *Other federal officers.* Customs officers and post office inspectors were needed in certain locations in the frontier. Although their duties were limited, they served an important function in those communities. Additionally, illegal immigration across the Mexican border led to the development of the Border Patrol. Other federal agencies active in the frontier were the Secret Service, FBI, and national park rangers.

The western peace officer remains an intriguing, nostalgic character for most people, an image that is buttressed by movies and novels that purport to portray gunslingers in a bygone age. The aura of rugged mystique and individualism that surrounds the western peace officer is hard to ignore—or dispel. The reality, though, does not burst the bubble, but rather highlights the complexities of these men, their jobs, and the social context that shaped them and the agencies they worked for. The western peace officer had fundamentally many of the same duties as today's law enforcement officers. They faced local, societal, and political challenges. Specialized agencies were developed and continued to evolve to accommodate unique societal circumstances. The peace officers of the frontier led the way for the protection of individual rights and freedom, a characteristic that is notoriously "western."

M. KIMBERLY MACLIN

See also **Arrest Powers of the Police; Constables; History of American Policing; Private Policing; Role of the Police; Sheriffs; Texas Rangers; Tribal Police**

References and Further Reading

Anderson, Terry L., and P. J. Hill. n.d. An American experiment in anarcho-capitalism: The not so wild, Wild West. *Journal of Libertarian Studies* 3 (1): 9–29.

Chaput, Don. 1994. *Virgil Earp: Western peace officer*. Encampment, WY: Affiliated Writers of America.

Eckhardt, Charles, F. 1973. Debunking the Wild West fantasy. *Guns and Ammo*, 36–37.

Hollon, W. Eugene. 1974. *Frontier violence: Another look*. New York: Oxford University Press.

Prassel, Frank. 1972. *The western peace officer: A legacy of law and order*. Norman, OK: University of Oklahoma Press.

WHITE COLLAR CRIME

The front pages of American newspapers during the months before the September 11, 2001, destruction of New York's World Trade Center by al-Qaeda terrorists often displayed pictures of corporate executives in very elegant business suits with handcuffs on their wrists and their arms pinioned behind their backs. They were being taken into custody or brought to a criminal court by government enforcement agents who often wore orange jackets with large black letters stenciled on the back that identified them as police and/or indicated their agency affiliation.

This development differed dramatically from earlier days when news that a business leader had been charged with a white collar crime was likely to be buried in the paper's business section, if it was attended to at all. The business offender in those bygone days was treated by the police in a gentle and respectable manner. Roscoe Pound, one of the major scholars of criminal law, noted that you never heard of an upper-class criminal who had committed an offense such as insider trading or an antitrust violation being subjected to third-degree interrogation sessions or being pushed around in the police station (Frank and Frank 1957, 161).

There is, of course, no sensible reason to handcuff business executives and to notify the media beforehand that they are going to be taken into custody. They are not escape risks and there is virtually no likelihood that they will attack those arresting them. But the performance, like all play-acting, is meant to convey a message. The message in these scenarios is that the police and the criminal justice system are equal opportunity enforcers and that they will treat the rich and the poor—the street criminals and the suite criminals—in the same manner.

Businessmen and businesswomen taken into custody by the police in the early years of the current century were involved in some of the most outrageous scandals since corporate enterprises came into being in the United States in the mid-eighteenth century. Billions of dollars were fraudulently manipulated so that executives could realize exorbitant personal financial gains. The offenses of companies such as Arthur Andersen, Enron, HealthSouth, Adelphia Communications, and WorldCom, among many others, challenged investigators for regulatory agencies and brought into question the dedication of those in power to protect the average citizen from the depredations of organizations whose campaign contributions helped significantly to put the politicians in power who control law enforcement and often have close ties to business.

The pace of enforcement of the laws to control business wrongdoing, however, declined dramatically after 9/11 when police agents were shifted from white collar crime assignments to counterterrorism activities.

In Los Angeles, following 9/11 the number of FBI agents assigned to white collar crimes, public corruption cases, and related work was reduced by nearly 60%, from 185 agents to 75. The former supervisor of the Los Angeles FBI antifraud unit noted: "The bureau can't get out of that business without losing market share, contacts, and expertise. Once it is lost you never get it back" (Reckard 2004, C5). Referrals of white collar crimes to the U. S. attorney's offices, where responsibility for prosecuting the cases is lodged, declined 6% from a total of 12,792 in the 2000 fiscal year to 12,507 two years later. In late 2004, the Securities and Exchange Commission reported that its total of enforcement actions had declined by 14.7% since the previous year. The agency thought that perhaps businesses had learned a lesson, though its head was quick to point out that "one swallow does not a summer make." Skeptics were inclined to believe that the reduction reflected changing enforcement strategies rather than changing business practices (Peterson 2004, C1). The lesson is that there always remains a "dark figure" of criminal activity—the offenses that are not discovered—and that the magnitude of this dark figure is strongly influenced by enforcement resources and the way in which they are deployed.

Background

The term *white collar crime* refers to a loosely defined category of illegal behavior that is differentiated from "street" or "traditional" forms of crime such as robbery, homicide, and burglary. Prototypical white collar crimes are insider trading in stocks (that is, trading on information that has not yet been made available to the public), antitrust agreements that undermine competitive bidding, the knowing maintenance of dangerous working conditions, and fraud by physicians against medical benefit programs. Beyond such areas of agreement, there are two competing definitions of white collar crime. The original conception, formulated by sociologist Edwin Sutherland (1949, 9), saw white collar crime as a "crime committed by a person of respectability and high social status in the course of his occupation." Use of the term had two purposes for Sutherland: first, to demonstrate that the then-current explanations of criminal behavior, such as Oedipus complexes and inferior intelligence, fell far short when applied to white collar criminals. Second, the goal was to call attention to lawbreaking with severe fiscal and physical consequences that tended to be ignored by students of crime.

More recently, and particularly in police circles, white collar crime has come to be defined as the violation of specified statutes. Yale Law School researchers identified eight offenses as white collar crimes that they would study: antitrust violations, bribery, securities fraud, tax fraud, false claims, credit fraud, mail fraud, and embezzlement (Weisburd et al. 1991). For them, the status of the criminal was irrelevant: Only 29% of their offenders met Sutherland's criteria and among the female white collar offenders in the Yale studies, almost a third were unemployed (Daly 1989).

Persons who advocate particularly strong law enforcement action against white collar crime maintain that regular crime has a tendency to unite a society. "Good" and "decent" people unite in condemning the common criminal. In doing so, they reinforce their own commitment to conformity, in part because they learn that such acts can lead to ill fame and to prison sentences. White collar crimes, on the other hand, threaten the integrity of the social order and undermine trust and a sense of justice. Besides, they visit much more harm and death upon their victims than street offenses. More money is embezzled by bank officers than is stolen by bank robbers; more persons are killed by

unnecessary surgery, sometimes prompted by mercenary goals, than are slain by more traditional forms of homicide.

The Police and White Collar Crime

Enforcement of the laws against white collar crime is largely the task of federal law enforcement agencies, such as the Food and Drug Administration, the Internal Revenue Service, the U.S. Postal Service, the Securities and Exchange Commission, the Federal Trade Commission, and, more generally, the Federal Bureau of Investigation (Friedrichs 2004). New concerns have led to a proliferation of additional federal agencies, including the Office of Surface Mining, the Environmental Protection Agency, the Occupational Safety and Health Administration, and a variety of federal bureaucracies that monitor nuclear plants.

In addition, fueled by a growing public cynicism about the honesty of those holding power that followed the Watergate scandal leading to President Richard Nixon's resignation, major federal agencies are now watched over by inspector generals whose job, in the words of former President Ronald Reagan, is to be "as mean as a junkyard watch dog."

A major structural difficulty with these arrangements lies in the uncertain and overlapping authority of many of the groups, a situation that can lead to internecine conflict, as one or another policing force seeks to control the investigation and prosecution of a major case. George Wilson (1981) emphasizes that collaborative work among enforcement agencies requires a great amount of diplomacy and that recognition must be carefully allocated in proportion to each agency's contribution. In the Archer Daniels Midland antitrust case, there was such a jumble of enforcement agencies vying for control of the case that, as Kurt Eichenwald (2000) has shown, mistakes, misunderstandings, and, most importantly, career considerations and turf wars seriously complicated the pursuit of the offenders.

Policing agencies live, and sometimes die, in terms of their performance record. They have to defend what they have accomplished before oversight committees that control their budget, and they are constantly concerned about whether to go after a large number of relatively insignificant offenders or to devote limited resources to tackle the much more demanding violations that are committed by wealthy corporations and their well-heeled executives who can employ notably intelligent and experienced attorneys to defend them.

State, Local, and Private Enforcement

Responses to fraudulent business, professional, and political practices have been less pronounced at levels below the federal government, primarily because of the absence of adequate resources to mount successful investigations and because of the federal preemption of much of the field.

Many states and counties have established economic crime units (ECUs) to deal with white collar offenses. These units tend to focus on quick-and-easy cases such as home improvement scams rather than on illegal acts of entrenched business interests. A handbook for economic crime investigators lists certain skills essential for this kind of work: (1) accounting, (2) computer sophistication, (3) advanced investigative ability, and (4) knowledge of the laws related to economic crimes (Somers 1984).

ECUs must prioritize the cases that they will handle. Typically, these are those in which conviction is likely to exert a strong deterrent force, those in which evidence can be gathered rather readily, cases in which the fraud appears likely to continue unless some intervention is made, and

cases in which there is a strong likelihood that victims can recover some of their losses. ECU officers routinely denounce what they regard as the lenient sentences that judges impose on the offenders they bring to court. "All things considered," insists Laurel Farcas, chief of the Montgomery County ECU in Pennsylvania, "for theses offenses, crime pays" (Fridrici 2000, 793).

On the local level, there is a need to get police officers to attend to white collar crime when possible. Some ECUs have generated reporting forms to be used whenever communication or squad car officers encounter what appear to be white collar offenses. What is wanted is a response such as that of an officer who observed an unusually large number of fights and arguments between the operators and customers at an auto repair shop and reported his suspicion that the owner was engaged in fraudulent activities. But one difficulty faced by police officers who concern themselves with white collar crime is that they may be disparaged by their fellows who see them as not dealing with "real crime" and by administrators who may not reward their work with salary increases and promotions (Alvesalo 2002). For their part, officers assigned to deal with white collar crime note disparagingly that most cops do not know a computer chip from a potato chip. The lone detective in Kalispell, Montana, assigned to handle white collar frauds finds the work stimulating. "It's a whole new breed of crime," Brian Fulford declares. "The guy who is most likely to get you is armed with a keyboard. He has a business card and he doesn't look anything like the guy your mother warned you about." Fulford notes that he had to learn how to paint the offenses he brings to the prosecutor in stark terms. "When the jury learns the charge is rape," he says, "the room falls silent. That doesn't happen when it's fraud or embezzlement. You need to find ways to engage the jury even though the evidence isn't spicy" (Jamison 2004).

Besides state and local police, a large number of private investigators are engaged in discovering white collar crimes committed against the companies that employ them. This has become one of the fastest growing professional fields and many sworn police officers, who tend to retire relatively early, make a second career in private security work. There also is a cadre of private enforcement specialists, known under a variety of names, such as fraud examiners, fraud auditors, and forensic accountants. The Association of Certified Fraud Examiners, founded in 1988 and headquartered in Austin, Texas, now has twenty-five thousand members and offers training courses nationwide on how to deal with offenses such as embezzlement, loan frauds, false claims, mail and wire fraud, money laundering, bribes and kickbacks, and contract and procurement frauds.

White Collar Crime Policing Styles

Clear differences are generally seen between the performance of regulatory agency investigators and the police who work street crime details. Regulatory inspectors, particularly if they have scientific training (and many former police officers take special courses when they enter regulatory work), come to think of themselves more as technical experts than as police officers. Their work pattern becomes much the same as a police officer who views his or her job as social service more than as crime control. Assumption of the "cooperative technical expert" role permits investigators to build mutually satisfying relationships with the businesses they oversee. These companies are believed to be more likely to inform the investigator of difficulties rather than to try to cover them up, thereby allowing rapid remedy and improving protection of the public. A tougher stance is taken toward violators who are seen to be "amoral calculators," those who are willing to violate the law and guidelines whenever they believe they can get away with it (Kagan and Scholz 1983, 67–68).

Rule-oriented inspectors, in contrast to those with a compliance orientation, issue citations for every violation they observe. They minimize negotiation strategies, such as consultation and bargaining. This crime enforcement style is faulted on the grounds that while it is likely to demonstrate short-term gains in compliance, it suffers in the long term because the businesses never develop an internal commitment to conformity. "A network of rules and regulations, backed by threats of litigation, breed distrust, destruction of documents, and an attitude that I won't do anything more than I am absolutely required to do," Stone (1975, 104) maintains.

White collar crime investigators typically keep a keen watch on the priorities of the prosecuting agency. Prosecutors tend to be reluctant to take on complicated white collar crimes because, among other things, they demand technical knowledge that may take a good deal of effort to master. They also are likely to be time consuming and to lack the glamour of big drug cases and dramatic crimes of violence.

George Wilson (1981, 173) emphasizes that for white collar crimes, compared to street crimes, "there is an absolute necessity for integrating the prosecutor in the investigative effort from the very beginning. This is probably the single most important aspect of investigating a complex economic crime." The prosecutor, Wilson points out, must continually analyze the facts, alter his or her anticipated courtroom strategy if necessary, and redirect the investigator's efforts.

GILBERT GEIS

See also **Computer Crimes; Environmental Crime; Federal Bureau of Investigation; Fraud Investigation; Politics and the Police; Styles of Policing**

References and Further Reading

Alvesalo, Anne. 2002. Downsized by law, ideology, and pragmatics—Policing white collar crime. In *Controversies in white collar crime,* ed. Gary W. Potter, 149–64. Cincinnati, OH: Anderson Publishing Company.

Daly, Kathleen. 1989. Gender and varieties of white collar crime. *Criminology* 27: 769–83.

Eichenwald, Kurt. 2000. *The informant: A true story.* New York: Broadway Books.

Frank, Jerome, and Barbara Frank. 1957. *Not guilty.* Garden City, NY: Doubleday.

Friedrichs, David O. 2004. *Trusted criminals: White collar crime in contemporary society.* 2nd ed. Belmont, CA: Wadsworth.

Fridrici, Peter. 2000. Does economic crime pay in Pennsylvania?: The perception of leniency in Pennsylvania's economic offender sentencing. *Villanova Law Review* 45: 793–825.

Jamison, Michael. 2004. *Fraud poses new police challenges.* Missoulian. http://www.missoulian.com/articles/2003/05/27/news/mtregional/news06.prt (December 2004).

Kagan, Robert, and John Scholz. 1983. The "criminology" of the corporations and regulatory enforcement strategies. In *Enforcing regulation,* ed. Keith Hawkins and John M. Thomas, 67–95. Boston: Kluwer-Nijhoff.

Peterson, Jonathan. 2004. Corporate fraud cases decline. *Los Angeles Times,* August 2, C1.

Reckard, E. Scott. 2004. FBI shift crimps white collar crime probes. *Los Angeles Times,* August 30, C1, C5.

Somers, Leigh E. 1984. *Economic crimes: Investigative principles and techniques.* New York: Clark Boardman.

Stone, Christopher D. 1975. *Where the law ends: The social control of corporate behavior.* New York: Harper Colophon.

Sutherland, Edwin H. 1949. *White collar crime.* New York: Dryden.

Weisburd, David, et al. 1991. *Crimes of the middle classes: White collar offenders in the federal courts.* New Haven, CT: Yale University Press.

Wilson, George E. 1981. *Economic crime.* Albany, NY: Bureau of Prosecution and Defense Services, Executive Office.

WICKERSHAM, GEORGE W.

George Woodward Wickersham (1858–1936), lawyer, public servant, attorney general of the United States, and chairman of the National Commission on Law Observance and Enforcement, was born in Pittsburgh, Pennsylvania, the only child of his father's second marriage. Sadly, his mother died while giving birth to him and shortly thereafter his father died. That left the rearing of the boy to his maternal grandparents. In partnership, his grandfather founded what was to become the Philadelphia Stock Exchange. His father had been a Union colonel in the Civil War and an inventor for the iron and steel industry. From 1873 to 1875 George studied civil engineering at Lehigh University. Next, he was private secretary to upcoming Senator Matthew S. Quay and a student of law in the office of a prominent attorney. The latter occupation led to his enrollment in the University of Pennsylvania Law School (1879). The following year he graduated and was admitted to the bar. For two years he practiced law in Philadelphia before going to New York to join the firm of Strong and Cadwalader. An industrious young man, he was made a partner within four years. Except for his tenure as attorney general of the United States, he continued to resolve legal matters for Cadwalader, Wickersham, and Taft until his death.

As President William Howard Taft's attorney general, Wickersham stringently enforced the Sherman Anti-Trust Law. From the start he commanded respect and engendered fear for his readiness to prosecute any corporation for attempting to monopolize an industry. Standard Oil, United States Steel, and International Harvester were some of the corporate giants he initiated suits against. With Taft's defeat in 1912, he returned to private practice but kept a keen eye on state, national, and international affairs. Between 1912 and 1929 he served on the commission for the reorganization of New York's state government, voiced enthusiasm for the Allied cause at the beginning of World War I when isolationism was the rule, and after the war pushed hard for ratification of the League of Nations, among other involvements.

At the age of seventy-one, a full career behind him, Wickersham, far from exhausted, accepted the chairmanship of the National Commission on Law Observance and Enforcement. President Herbert Hoover had assigned him to the post, and such was Wickersham's dominance over the proceedings that the investigative body soon bore the public name of the "Wickersham Commission." Its charge was to propose methods of enforcement of the Eighteenth Amendment (prohibition of intoxicating liquors) and to inquire into the entire federal system of jurisprudence and the administration of laws in relation to the amendment.

The results were published in fourteen book-length reports with an addendum, the Mooney-Billings report, submitted to the commission but not released by it. Of the reports, No. 11, *Report on Lawlessness in Law Enforcement,* and No. 14, *Report on Police,* were the most pertinent to everyday police activities. Report No. 11 warned against police use of "third degree" treatment, "the employment of methods which inflict suffering, physical or mental, upon a person, in order to obtain from that person information about a crime." The commission regarded third degree as usurping the fundamental rights of personal liberty, bail, protection from assault and battery, presumption of innocence until proven guilty, and access to legal counsel. A chapter each explored the general characteristics of third-degree harassment, arguments for and against it, and the types of unfairness experienced. Eleven recommendations followed, such as "the establishment of a statutory minimum time for the preparation of the defense" and "representation of the accused by counsel in all cases unless the penalty is very light or unless the accused has definitely refused counsel."

Report No. 14 addressed the "principal causes of the deficits in police administration that too generally leave the citizens helpless in the hands of the criminal class." August Vollmer, professor of police administration at the University of Chicago, directed the research and wrote two of the chapters. Vollmer and his staff identified the vexations faced by the police executive and called attention to the problems besetting proper selection and training of police personnel. Moreover, they reviewed communication system and equipment needs, expanded the definition of crime prevention, and reasserted that police power belonged to the state. Ten conclusions accrued, from removing the corrupting influence of politics to creating state bureaus of criminal investigation.

The other reports were equally imperative. Report No. 1, *Preliminary Report on Prohibition,* stated that there were major difficulties to enforcement of the law, but foreseeable solutions. Report No. 2, *Report on the Enforcement of the Prohibition Laws of the United States,* opposed repeal of the Eighteenth Amendment in the belief that enforcement of it was possible with revisions to the law. Wickersham wrote "The older generation very largely has forgotten and the younger never knew the evils of the saloon and the corroding influence upon politics, both local and national, of the organized liquor interests." Report No. 3, *Report on Criminal Statistics,* found a dearth of accurate data on crime; court-proceeding figures were all that was available. Report No. 4, *Report on Prosecution,* emphasized the "tremendous complexity" of ever learning the causes of crime and of administering criminal justice. Report No. 5, *Report on the Enforcement of the Deportation Laws of the United States,* sought to protect those unjustly deported while facilitating deportation of "aliens of the criminal classes" through revision of the laws.

Report No. 6, *Report on the Child Offender in the Federal System of Justice,* insisted that childhood deserves a status distinct from that of the adult. It recommended that persons under eighteen years of age should be tried in juvenile court, though for some child offenders transfer to adult court would be acceptable. Report No. 7, *Progress Report on the Study of the Federal Courts,* studied overcrowding in the federal courts, in particular the criminal caseloads in Connecticut. Report No. 8, *Report on Criminal Procedure,* focused on selection of judges and urged court reform to ease the burden on police. Report No. 9, *Report on Penal Institutions, Probation and Parole,* found that American penal institutions failed to rehabilitate inmates and, even worse, instituted a "deadening routine" that only aggravated the situation. Probation should be continued because it costs less than imprisonment, and parole, in the form of indeterminate sentencing, likewise should remain, given that every chance for successful adjustment of the inmate to society is available. Report No. 10, *Report on Crime and the Foreign Born,* showed no evidence that the foreign born commit any more crime than the native born. It held that placing blame on the foreign born for increased crime is an excuse for blindness to crime inducements in a complex society.

Report No. 12, *Report on the Cost of Crime,* suggested that cities reallocated their criminal justice expenditures to offset economic loss due to criminal acts. Expenditures, it said, should be at a level to ensure maximum safety to citizens and property. Report No. 13, *Reports on the Causes of Crime,* 2 vols., demonstrated that "crime fluctuates," not only in aggregate but for each type of offense. One remedy suggested was "security of employment." Verifiable, though, is that juveniles living in disorganized areas of a city often follow a natural process of development toward delinquency. The addendum, *Report on Mooney-Billings,* recounted the trial of Mooney and Billings, who were accused of planting a bomb in San Francisco at the site of the Preparedness Day Parade in 1916. The explosion killed nine people and injured at least forty others. At issue was the alleged railroading of the two defendants by police, the court, and public opinion.

After producing 4,023 pages totaling 1.6 million words, the Wickersham Commission (1929–1931) disbanded. For all of its consummate work, its findings went largely unheeded because of the Prohibition question. At first the rowdy debate staged by "wets" and "dries" prompted the commission to oppose repeal of the Eighteenth Amendment. Then, with hard evidence that enforcement of prohibition was futile, the commission reversed its opinion. Thus Reports No. 1 and 2 eclipsed the urgency of the remaining reports, those concerned with long-standing maladies. Nevertheless, the commission had done its job: to make known to the public that America's criminal justice system was flawed and in need of repair. It was not Wickersham's fault that the rage over booze subverted his clear message. Given hindsight, Herbert Hoover wrote about the Wickersham Commission in his memoirs: "Therefore, its investigations failed to prove of any great use so far as Prohibition was concerned, although it made recommendations for other legal reforms that were of lasting value." But police executives from across the country were not so kind; in the *New York Times* for August 2, 1931, a number of them rebutted the commission and a consensus of observers termed the whole investigation hasty. Too much obsolete data had been taken to heart. At the annual convention of the Religious Education Association held at Columbia University, May 3, 1932, Wickersham lamented the flagging interest in his reports. He closed by saying, "Lastly, we should remember that men will respect law only when law is respectable and that the method of administering justice is often more important than justice itself."

Wickersham was known for his "peppery treatment" and Spartan lifestyle. Multilingual, he read Dante in Italian and studied opera, collected French engravings, and excelled at photography.

His marriage to Mildred Wendell in 1883 produced four children. A heart attack claimed his life and he was buried in Rockside Cemetery, Englewood, New Jersey.

WILLIAM G. BAILEY

References and Further Reading

McManus, Robert C. 1930. Unhappy warrior: A portrait of George W. Wickersham. *Outlook and Independent* 156 (Sept. 17): 85–88.

Mowry, George E. 1958. George Woodward Wickersham. *Dictionary of American Biography* 11 (2): 713–15. New York: Charles Scribner and Sons.

New York Times. 1931/1932. August 2, 1931, 1: 3; August 3, 1931, 16: 2; August 4, 1931, 20: 6; August 24, 1931, 2: 1; September 18, 1931, 1: 5; May 4, 1932, 15: 1.

U.S. National Commission on Law Observance and Enforcement. 1931/1968. *Wickersham Commission Reports* and *Mooney-Billings Report*. 14 vols. Montclair, NJ: Patterson Smith.

WILSON, JAMES Q.

James Q. Wilson was born May 27, 1931. Wilson is considered a prominent figure in several disciplines, and his writings include public policy, economics, politics, and criminal justice topics.

Wilson was educated at the University of the Redlands and the University of Chicago, where he earned his Ph.D. in 1959. He also holds six honorary degrees, including one from Harvard University.

Wilson has taught at several prestigious universities, starting with his first teaching position at his alma mater, the University of Chicago (1959–1961). He left the University of Chicago in 1961 to accept a teaching position at Harvard University, where he stayed until 1987. He also taught at the University of California, Los Angeles, from 1985 to 1997; as of this writing, he is a Ronald Reagan Professor of Public Policy at Pepperdine University.

Dr. Wilson has held many distinguished offices and positions throughout his career, including serving as the chair of the National Advisory Commission on Drug Abuse (1972–1973). He has served on two separate presidential task forces, including serving as chairman of the White House Task Force on Crime in 1966, and as a member of the President's Foreign Intelligence Advisory Board from 1985 to 1991. Additionally, he was a member of the Attorney General's Task Force on Violent Crime in 1981. Wilson also served as a member of the board of directors of the Police Foundation (1971–1993), and was president of the American Political Science Association (APSA) from 1991 to 1992.

Throughout his career, Wilson has been acknowledged for his contributions and influence; most notably he received the Presidential Medal of Freedom on July 23, 2003. In addition, the APSA awarded Wilson the James Madison Award for distinguished scholarship in 1990, and in 2001 the APSA awarded him a Lifetime Achievement Award. Also, the Academy of Criminal Justice Sciences (ACJS) honored Wilson with the Bruce Smith Award for "Outstanding Contributions to Criminal Justice."

Wilson has written on a variety of topics, including policing, human nature, public policy, crime and race, drugs, rehabilitation, and morals. Some of his earlier works focused on policing, especially in urban environments. He was one of the first in the field to pragmatically look at the occupation of policing, and to describe police behavior in a rational and realistic way. His book *Varieties of Police Behavior* (1968) took some of the mysticism away from police work as he described different "styles" of policing that are still cited in the policing literature today (that is, watchman style, the legalistic style, and the service style).

In the 1970s, Wilson focused his research and writings on crime. In *Thinking About Crime* (1975, revised 1985) Wilson put together a group of his essays that discussed how public policies were in part responsible for rising crime rates in the 1970s. He also criticized other criminology scholars for being too idealistic in their writings and not basing their work on empirical fact. Other general themes from *Thinking About Crime* include Wilson's viewpoint that white collar crime does not negatively impact the "social contract" in the same way as conventional crimes do; therefore, it should not be treated equally. Additionally, Wilson considers crime to be a moral issue. This is a theme that Wilson has continued to write about throughout his career.

In 1982, Wilson published an article in the *Atlantic Monthly* with George Kelling titled "Broken Windows: The Police and Neighborhood Safety." In this piece, Wilson combines his interests in crime, policing, communities, and urban issues. "Broken Windows" is perhaps his most important contribution to the world of policing. The concept of broken windows has become an internationally known doctrine, and remains just as powerful and influential today as it was in the 1980s. In "Broken Windows" Wilson and Kelling discuss the concept of physical disorder, and how, if let untreated, that disorder can become a signal to criminals that the neighborhood will tolerate crime and other "nuisance" behaviors. The idea states that a neighborhood that leaves broken windows broken (or graffiti uncovered and so forth) is sending a message that it will also tolerate behaviors such as open-air drug sales and overt prostitution. This type of tolerance can lead to tolerance of more serious crime situations, and a community out of control and crawling with the criminal element. Therefore, Wilson and Kelling suggest that police should address the minor crimes and nuisance behaviors as well as the more serious criminal behaviors. This type of response has had great success in crime-ridden cities across the country, most notably in New York City in the 1990s. The New York City Police Department found that true to Wilson and Kelling's philosophy, criminals realized there were consequences to their actions, and that the police and community were not going to turn a blind eye to their antisocial behaviors anymore. Wilson and Kelling also discuss the role that citizens' fear of crime can play in the downfall of a neighborhood.

In the mid-1980s, Wilson cowrote another controversial book titled *Crime and Human Nature: The Definitive Study* (1985) with Richard Herrnstein. This volume looked at research conducted in a variety of disciplines in an attempt to answer the question "Why do people commit crimes?" This work challenges criminologists to look at crime from the level of the individual as opposed to the more commonly viewed societal level.

In the 1990s, Wilson coedited two prominent works, "Drugs and Crime" (1990) with Michael Tonry, and *Crime* (1995), an edited anthology on research with Joan Petersilia. The 1990s also saw Wilson focus his writings on morals. In 1991 he published "On Character," which was a series of essays that looked at character and responsibility. This theme continued through the 1990s and into the 2000s with books such as *The Moral Sense* (1993), *Moral Judgment: Does the Abuse Excuse Threaten Our Legal System?* (1997), and *The Marriage Problem* (2002), where he discusses the problems associated with the continuing dissolution of the institution of marriage and its effect on social problems, including crime.

ELIZABETH P. BIEBEL

See also **Broken-Windows Policing; Crime Control Strategies; Styles of Policing**

References and Further Reading

Cohn, E. G., and D. P. Farrington. 1994. Who are the most influential criminologists in the English-speaking world? *British Journal of Criminology* 22: 204–25.

Petersilia, J., A. Abrahamse, and J. Q. Wilson. 1990. The relationship between police practice, community characteristics, and case attrition. *Policing and Society* 1: 23–38.

Pruitt, C. R., and J. Q. Wilson. 1983. A longitudinal study of the effect of race on sentencing. *Law and Society Review* 17: 613–35.

Tonry, M., and J. Q. Wilson. 1990. Drugs and crime. *Crime and Justice: An Annual Review of Research* 13.

Wilson, J. Q. 1974. Crime and criminologists. *Commentary* 58: 47–53.

——. 1975. *Thinking about crime*. New York: Basic Books.

——. 1978. *The investigators: Managing FBI and narcotics agents*. New York: Basic Books.

——. 1985. *Thinking about crime*. Rev. ed. New York: Vintage.

——. 1989. *Bureaucracy: What government agencies do and why they do it*. New York: Basic Books.

——. 1991. *On character*. Washington, DC: American Enterprise Institute Press.

——. 1993. *The moral sense*. New York: The Free Press.

——. 1995. Crime and public policy. In *Crime*, ed. J. Q. Wilson and J. Petersilia. San Francisco: Institute for Contemporary Studies Press.

——. 1997. *Moral judgment: Does the abuse excuse threaten our legal system?* New York: Basic Books.

——. 2002. *The marriage problem: How our culture has weakened families*. New York: Harper Collins.

Wilson, J. Q., and A. Abrahamse. 1992. Does crime pay? *Justice Quarterly* 9: 357–77.

Wilson, J. Q., and B. Boland. 1978. The effect of police on crime. *Law and Society Review* 12: 367–90.

Wilson, J. Q., and R. J. Herrnstein. 1985. *Crime and human nature: The definitive study of the causes of crime*. New York: Simon and Schuster.

Wilson, J. Q., and G. L. Kelling. 1982. Broken windows: The police and neighborhood safety. *Atlantic Monthly* 249: 29–38.

Wilson, J. Q., and J. Petersilia, eds. 1995. *Crime*. San Francisco: Institute for Contemporary Studies Press.

WILSON, O. W.

Orlando Winfield Wilson (1900–1972), police chief, professor, Chicago police superintendent, and author, was born in Veblen, South Dakota, of Norwegian descent (Vraalson, his family name, was changed to Wilson when he was a boy). His father, a lawyer, took a keen interest in all of his children, expecting excellence from each of them. Therefore, studiousness and respect for learning permeated the family atmosphere. Orlando graduated from San Diego High School in California, where Ole Wilson had moved his family a few years before. Then he entered the University of California at Berkeley, obtaining his B.A. degree in 1924 with a major in criminology. While at the university he worked as a patrolman with the Berkeley Police Department from May 1921 to April 1925. His police chief was August Vollmer, considered by many authorities the top police mind of his day. In fact, it was Vollmer who influenced Wilson in his choice of criminology as a career. No young man interested in criminology could have had a better start in life, with the educational advantage of having studied at UC Berkeley, having Vollmer as mentor, and with police professionalism on the upswing.

Less than a year out of college, Wilson was appointed police chief of Fullerton, a small southern California community. But he lasted only a few months in the job, mainly because some of his academic notions did not sit well with the citizenry. Once in a public address he advocated birth control as a means of lessening crime, in keeping with the "concentric circle" theory of crime; that is, more population, more crime; less population, less crime, radiating outward from a congested center of lawbreaking. Even for California Wilson's ideas were a bit radical and after pressure from the police committee he resigned due to "lack of administrative experience." For the next two years he worked as an investigator for the Pacific Finance Corporation. It was dull employment from which he sought leave given the first opportunity. Soon he got his chance. Not forgetting his protégé, August Vollmer recommended Wilson as a replacement for the dismissed police chief of Wichita, Kansas. Times were bad there; scandal involving bootlegging operations gripped the puritanical city. Wilson hesitated, recalling his failure in Fullerton, but Vollmer reassured him that he could succeed in Wichita.

He heeded his former chief and in March 1928 accepted the position. What with crime to fight and organizational changes to make, he had few spare moments for theorizing, his Fullerton nemesis. Five years later he rejuvenated the department by introducing plainly marked police cars, lie detectors, and mobile crime laboratories; harking back to his recent youth, he hired college students as part-time policemen, among other innovations, and Wichita was on its way to stringent law and order.

Wilson compiled an enviable record during his years there, but his outstanding performance as chief eventually cost him his job. He enforced the vice laws too vigorously, thus cramping the style of Wichita racketeers, so he had to go. Two city commissioners, in league with the vice lords, rode him hard, conjuring up every possible charge against him. In a letter to August Vollmer, Wilson disclosed what the city commissioners planned to do to him if he stayed:

1. Have my salary slashed.
2. Have the commission order the discontinuance of certain police activities, such as the maintenance of records.
3. The appointment of a disloyal subordinate officer as assistant chief, with complete control over police personnel.
4. Appointment of the same men as director of public safety and over police and fire.
5. An investigation of the department with a view of raising sufficient stench to justify ordering my suspension and leaving me simmering on the pan without salary until I was tired out.

He acquiesced and on May 15, 1939, left Wichita on leave of absence, his formal resignation to follow later.

Wilson was not left to wander long. The Public Administration Service in Chicago hired him to survey municipal police departments and to write papers on police administration. To his dismay he discovered that in Peoria, Illinois; Hartford, Connecticut; Huntington, West Virginia; and San Antonio, Texas, the police bent to political will as much as in Wichita. While he was on the road with his surveys, plans were under way to attract him to teach at his alma mater, UC Berkeley. Once again August Vollmer was his guiding light, convincing the president of the university that O. W. Wilson knew more about police administration than anyone else available. On July 24, 1939, Wilson accepted a tenured position as full professor with a reduced teaching load, time for consultative work, and the freedom to reshape the academic program. Moreover, the university allowed him to continue his work for the Public Administration Service. In January 1943 World War II interrupted his busy schedule and tested his abilities all the more. He entered the U.S. Army as a lieutenant colonel in the corps of military police, serving as chief public safety officer in Italy and England. The war over, he was discharged in November 1946, having earned the rank of colonel, the Bronze Star, and the Legion of Merit. He did not return home right away but remained in Germany as the chief public safety officer in charge of denazification activities in the U.S. zone. Enforcing the regulations to the letter of the law was his trademark. He liked military life and leaned toward reenlisting, but by the next year he was back at Berkeley teaching police administration.

Wilson's second career at Berkeley had its ups and downs. From 1950 to 1960 he served as dean of the School of Criminology, during which time he successfully fought off efforts to relegate police studies to a minor academic status. Instead, he raised the program to an unprecedented level and made the school one of the foremost in the nation. He did this in spite of having to parry attacks from his fellow professors because he did not hold the Ph.D. degree, and from students because he was a poor lecturer. Always terse in his public and written comments, he was more a man of action than one of words. Wilson escaped the petty in-fighting at Berkeley whenever he visited various police departments to conduct reorganization surveys. Like August Vollmer before him, he crisscrossed the United States and beyond, sizing up local police conditions and recommending qualified colleagues to fill vacant positions. Known far and wide for his acuity as a police consultant, he was to put into practice every bit of his knowledge in the coming years.

In 1960 Chicago mayor Richard J. Daley named Wilson chairman of a five-man committee to choose a new police commissioner for the Windy City. The heat was on after city newspapers revealed that several policemen had aided and abetted a burglary ring. More than one hundred persons were considered for the office with the surprising result that O. W. Wilson, interrogator of the contenders, was finally selected. He took the job, but only after securing a promise that the police force would be free from political control. He then resigned his deanship at UC Berkeley, the university honoring him with the title of professor emeritus. The immediate changes he made in the Chicago Police Department were unpopular to say the least. He cut the number of police districts from thirty-eight to twenty-one, thus severing ties of favoritism between some police and criminal parties in certain neighborhoods. He established the Internal Investigation Division, whose main purpose was to uncover police corruption. He more than doubled the number of civilian employees to handle clerical duties, thereby releasing about one thousand regular policemen for patrol duty. He installed a $2 million modern police radio clock and doubled the size of the patrol car fleet. Other of his adjustments were equally hard to live with at first, but in the end greatly strengthened the department.

Wilson continued to do the unexpected. When the Reverend Martin Luther King, Jr., came to Chicago in 1966, having announced beforehand that he would lay bare housing discrimination in one of white America's mighty cities, he was invited to police headquarters to talk. Of all things, the two strong-willed men discussed police protection for King and his people, not police harassment. Later King acknowledged that Wilson had treated him more than fairly, unlike Southern police. Also in that year one of the worst crimes of the century occurred in Chicago. Eight student nurses were murdered at a residence maintained by the South Chicago Community Hospital. Wilson's police were swift off the mark and the next day arrested a twenty-four-year-old itinerant seaman named Richard Franklin Speck, whose left arm bore the tattoo "Born to Raise Hell." Wilson fingered the right man, but because he insisted that only Speck could have done the deed some legal authorities criticized him for "hanging the suspect" without a fair trial. Ironically, just a few months earlier in an article written for *Family Week,* he had said: "One of the problems that we, as police, face is when sympathy for the unfortunate merges into favoritism for the criminal. . . . In this country, tolerance for wrongdoers has turned into a fad. What we need is some intolerance toward criminal behavior."

On his sixty-seventh birthday he retired from the Chicago police force, stating in a letter to Mayor Daley, "It is my belief that the programs initiated slightly more than seven years ago for the reorganization of the police department are fully established." As befitted him, he was overly modest in assessing his accomplishments in Chicago, a city notorious for its haphazard law enforcement. But for all of his striking success he did display some faults. His biographer, William J. Bopp, explains:

> O. W. Wilson never questioned the idea that officers must be coerced, controlled, directed, and threatened before they would exert an effort to achieve the department's objectives. He instituted no job

enrichment programs, no participatory management techniques. . . . He ruled by fiat, instead of persuading his officers of the rightness of reform. . . . It may well be that policemen will not act democratically in the community until they are treated democratically in police headquarters. Wilson was not a democratic leader.

Wilson wrote a number of books, articles, and pamphlets during his checkered career, all of which added substantially to the police literature. He saw his best known book, *Police Administration* (McGraw-Hill 1950, 1963), through a third edition, with Roy C. McLaren as coauthor; it appeared the year of his death (1972). Married twice, he fathered three children. A stroke ended his life, his last years having been spent in Poway, California, an idyllic retreat far from the ingratitude of Wichita and the hustle of Chicago.

WILLIAM G. BAILEY

References and Further Reading

Bopp, William L. 1977. *O. W.: O. W. Wilson and the search for a police profession*. Port Washington, NY: Kennikat Press.
Current Biography. 1966. 452–54.
New York Times. 1960/1966/1972. March 3, 1960, 20: 4; June 15, 1966, 27: 2; October 19, 1972, 50: 5.

WOMEN IN LAW ENFORCEMENT

Women in law enforcement work in municipal agencies, state agencies, or federal agencies. Municipal agencies include city, county, and campus law enforcement. State agencies include state police, vehicle enforcement, highway patrol, and other state specialty organizations such as state bureaus of investigations or multipurpose organizations such as the Texas Rangers. Federal agencies include specialty organizations that serve the nation, such as the Drug Enforcement Administration and the Federal Bureau of Investigation. Currently more women are employed in municipal organizations than in any other type of law enforcement organization; however, women are more highly represented proportionally in federal organizations.

An accurate representation of the numbers of women in law enforcement is difficult at best primarily due to the inconsistency of data collection. Currently, women represent an average of 10.6% in local municipal organizations and 12.5% in sheriff's organizations, and they range from 1% to 14% in state law enforcement agencies and from 8.6% to 28% in federal agencies. In 1975, women represented only 2.2% of personnel in municipal organizations (Martin and Jurik 1996). Is an 8.4% increase over the course of thirty years notable? Perhaps so, but not in ways that support the strides women have made and barriers that have been overcome.

An examination of women in law enforcement is no different than any other examination of women in a nontraditional occupation, which is an occupation with less than 25% of the gender that is not stereotypically considered appropriate for the occupation. Hence, law enforcement is a nontraditional occupation for women. Stereotypical perceptions of gender role expectations dictate what is considered "appropriate behavior" for women in both their public and private lives. Women are to conform to traditional feminine activities to appease society and fit into proper occupations. Women in law enforcement have struggled since the early 1800s to survive in the world of law enforcement, and hopefully to succeed and be recognized as a valued part of the law enforcement organization, as are their male counterparts.

History and Legal Mandates

Schulz (1995) divides the history of women's participation in law enforcement into six eras: (1) Forerunners: The Matrons, 1820–1899; (2) The Early Policewomen,

1900–1928; (3) Depression Losses, 1929–1941; (4) World War II and the 1940s; (5) Paving the Way for Patrol, 1950–1967; and (6) Women Become Crime Fighters, 1968–Present. Women's presence in law enforcement, as is apparent in Schulz's work, has been significantly influenced by social movements of the times. As gender roles have developed over time, so have women's roles in policing. In the first historical phase of women in law enforcement, the "matron" era, women were performing tasks exclusively associated with their gender role expectations. For example, women primarily dealt with children and juvenile offenders, and female victims of crime. As time progressed, women's roles in law enforcement changed, as did their socially defined gender roles. Much of this change can be accounted for by the limited availability of male personnel due to the U.S. involvement in wars. While law enforcement was not the only occupation affected by the limited number of males available, the shortage of males did prompt administrators to hire more women to "fill in the gaps" left by the men, which also meant that women had to perform duties traditionally performed only by men.

After war efforts subsided and men were again more available for employment in law enforcement, some women were still kept in positions that were historically for men only. Leaving these women in place essentially paved the way for hiring more women for a greater variety of work in law enforcement. Simultaneously, significant social movements of the late 1960s and 1970s gave rise to the largest increases of women in law enforcement the United States has ever known.

Legal mandates such as the Equal Pay Act of 1963, Title VII of the Civil Rights Act of 1964, the Omnibus Crime Control and Safe Streets Act of 1968, the Equal Employment Opportunity Act of 1972, the Crime Control Act of 1973, and the Pregnancy Discrimination Act of 1978 have each affected women's equal opportunities in law enforcement. The Equal Pay Act of 1963 was one of the first pieces of legislation that provided a guarantee, albeit a limited one, of pay equity. Title VII of the Civil Rights Act of 1964, while primarily written to deal with race discrimination, affected other discriminatory practices, including discrimination based on religion, sex, and national origin. Additionally, Title VII made it illegal for private employers with twenty-five or more employees to discriminate in recruitment, hiring, working conditions, promotion, or other employment practices. It was not until 1972, however, that Title VII was extended to state and local governments, including law enforcement agencies, through the Equal Opportunity Employment Act. The Equal Employment Opportunity Commission (EEOC), which oversees the enforcement of Title VII, was also created in 1972.

The Omnibus Crime Control and Safe Streets Act of 1968 created the Law Enforcement Assistance Administration (LEAA), which provided numerous opportunities for education and training for law enforcement personnel. Women and men of color were significantly affected because this was the first time such opportunities had been made available to them. In 1973, the Crime Control Act prohibited discrimination against women in any agency that obtained LEAA funds.

The Pregnancy Discrimination Act of 1978 prohibited discrimination against women for pregnancy, childbirth, or related medical conditions. Employers were required to treat these conditions as any other type of temporary disability; therefore, women would not be improperly penalized for having children.

In addition to legislation, significant court cases have affected opportunities for women in law enforcement, including *Griggs v. Duke Power Company* (1971), *Meritor Savings Bank FSB v. Vinson* (1986), and *Harris v. Forklift Systems, Inc.* (1993). The *Griggs* case dealt primarily with bona fide occupational qualifications (BFOQs) and required that employer's must demonstrate BFOQs for jobs and use no other selection standard. What this meant for women in law enforcement was that previous exclusions often dealing with height and weight requirements were no longer valid.

Meritor Savings Bank FSB v. Vinson dealt primarily with issues of sexual harassment, reinforcing the legislation in Title VII. The Court in *Meritor* upheld the prohibition of both quid pro quo and hostile work environment as specified in Title VII. *Harris v. Forklift Systems, Inc.,* also dealt with a hostile work environment. In this case, the Court relaxed the standard for what constitutes a hostile work environment, indicating that a hostile work environment does not require extreme psychological damage to an individual, and may be considered as such with less damage instead.

Research

The importance of research cannot be understated. Occupational research is primarily used to describe the current status of workers in a profession, to identify challenges and barriers for workers, and to make policy recommendations. Ideally, academicians who typically conduct research collaborate with professionals in the field to identify important research questions or current issues.

Most of what we know about women in law enforcement comes from research looking at women in large municipal, or local, law enforcement organizations. Minimal research examining women in state, federal, or small municipal organizations exists. There are many more municipal law enforcement organizations than state and federal, but limited research and anecdotal evidence indicates that women in

all three types of law enforcement organizations have similar experiences in the workplace.

More specifically, the majority of research on women and law enforcement has examined issues of women's competency, attitudes toward and of women in law enforcement, stress, legal issues, and descriptions of the current population of women in the field. Multiple methods have been used to conduct the research including survey research, evaluation research, participant observation, and qualitative case studies. In more recent years, survey research using the Internet has become a popular method for gathering data.

Issues of women's competency in law enforcement were not significantly questioned until women were allowed to do patrol work in the late 1960s and early 1970s. Prior to this time period, women had been primarily used to perform tasks that were considered at the time reasonable for a woman to do, such as working with juvenile offenders or doing administrative tasks. After women's inclusion in patrol work, research increased significantly, in hopes of determining whether or not women could adequately meet the challenges of their male counterparts. During this time period (primarily 1970s) there were nine evaluations of women in different jurisdictions using various methods. The jurisdictions included Washington, D.C. (Bloch and Anderson 1974), St. Louis (Sherman 1975), New York City (Sichel et al. 1977), Denver (Bartlett and Rosenblum 1977), Newton, Massachusetts (Kizziah and Morris 1977), Philadelphia, Phases I and II (Bartell Associates 1978), California (California Highway Patrol 1976), and Pennsylvania (Pennsylvania State Police 1974). With the exception of the second phase of the Philadelphia study, all of these works found women to be as competent as their male counterparts. Most of these works were undertaken in large municipal organizations or large state organizations.Only one, in Newton, Massachusetts, was undertaken in a medium-sized organization.

Research on women in law enforcement has continued with various focuses since the early works examining competency. A number of attitudinal works followed the competency works of the 1970s, including examinations of women's attitudes toward their work (Bloch and Anderson 1974; Worden 1993; Zhao, Thurman, and He 1999), as well as attitudes of male officers and the public. Research examining women's attitudes toward their work has focused on variables such as job satisaction, perceptions of discrimination, and perceptions of utilization. Researchers have found that some male officers believe that women are ineffective and incompetent in their jobs (Bloch and Anderson 1974; Balkin 1988; Hindman 1975; Linden 1983; Vega and Silverman 1982; Martin 1980; Charles and Parson 1978). Finally, some researchers have examined public perceptions of women in law enforcement.

International Women in Law Enforcement

While descriptions of, and research in, women in law enforcement in the United States are somewhat lacking, information for international women in law enforcement is even more limited. Challenges to gathering this information include the paucity of source materials, lack of conceptual frameworks, and difficulties with cross-cultural comparisons. The European Network of Policewomen (ENP) has been instrumental in attempting to paint a picture of women in law enforcement abroad, with their biannual report, *Facts, Figures and General Information,* which began in 1989 with a total of six issues being completed. The reports began with a response rate of 18% in 1989 and had

risen to 50% for the last report, which was done in 2000. The report is one of the only comprehensive assessments of the status of women in policing internationally and provides a general overview of women in European police forces.

Cross-cultural research on women is limited, with Heidensohn (1992, 2000), Brown (1997), and Brown and Heidensohn (2000) being the most current and comprehensive works. Much of their work is comparisons on women in policing in the United Kingdom and the United States. However, in their most recent work, they surveyed women in thirty-five countries, with assistance from organizations and associations. They examined a variety of issues including discrimination, coping, support, and self-efficacy as related to the police culture. The authors proposed a taxonomy with which to examine police organizations, and in doing this they have provided a framework for future efforts, as well as insight into the current status of women internationally.

Organizations for Women in Law Enforcement

Useful strategies that facilitate success for women in policing include networking and mentoring. Key to networking and mentoring are professional associations for women in policing. Associations provide not only training opportunities, but also avenues for women to meet other women in similar places, and share their experiences, challenges, and lessons learned. Current professional associations for women in law enforcement include, but are not limited to, the International Association of Women in Police (IAWP), the European Network of Policewomen (ENP), the National Center for Women and Policing (NCWP), the National Association of Women Law Enforcement Executives (NAWLEE), the Australasian Council of

Women and Policing (ACWAP), and the Women in Federal Law Enforcement (WIFLE), as well as numerous local and regional affiliates.

Future Prospects

While women's opportunities and status have increased during the last three decades, much progress can still be gained. Women have moved out of the stereotypical positions of dealing with juveniles and other women, to positions of leadership in municipal organizations that serve major metropolitan cities. Women have also made strides in professional organizations, taking leadership roles in organizations in which they have historically been denied leadership.

With numerous changes in the landscape of contemporary law enforcement taking place on a daily basis, we may see women being utilized in even more areas and for a variety of tasks, as gender norms are further broken down, with primary consideration given to who the best candidate is for the job and to who can perform at the optimum levels at which societal expectations are set.

KATHRYN E. SCARBOROUGH

See also **National Association of Women Law Enforcement Executives (NAWLEE)**

References and Further Reading

Balkin, J. 1988. Why policemen don't like policewomen. *Journal of Police Science and Administration* 16 (1): 29–38.

Bartell Associates, Inc. 1978. *The study of police women competency in the performance of sector work in the City of Philadelphia*. State College, PA: Bartell Associates, Inc.

Bartlett, H. W., and A. Rosenblum. 1977. *Policewomen effectiveness*. Denver, CO: Civil Service Commission and Denver Police Department.

Bloch, Peter, and Deborah Anderson. 1974. *Policewomen on patrol: Final report*. Washington, DC: Urban Institute.

Brown, Jennifer. 1997. Women in policing: A comparative research perspective. *International Journal of the Sociology of the Law* 25: 1–19.

Brown, Jennifer, and Frances Heidensohn. 2000. *Gender and policing: Comparative perspectives*. New York: St. Martin's Press.

California Highway Patrol. 1976. *Women traffic officer report: Final report*. Sacramento, CA: California Highway Patrol.

Griggs v. Duke Power Company, 401 U.S. 424 (1971).

Harris v. Forklift Systems, Inc., 114 S. Ct. 367 (1993).

Heidensohn, Frances. 1992. *Women in control? The role of women in law enforcement*. New York: Oxford University Press.

Hindman, R. E. 1975. A survey related to the use of female law enforcement officers. *Police Chief* 42 (4): 58–60.

Kizziah, C., and M. Morris. 1977. *Evaluation of women in policing programs: Newton, Massachusetts*. Oakland, CA: Approach Associates.

Linden, R. 1983. Women in policing: A study of lower mainland Royal Canadian Mounted Police detachments. *Canadian Police College Journal* 7: 217–29.

Martin, Susan E. 1980. *Breaking and entering: Police women on patrol*. Berkeley: University of California Press.

———. 1990. *On the move: The status of women in policing*. Washington, DC: The Police Foundation.

Martin, Susan E., and Nancy C. Jurik. 1996. *Doing justice, doing gender: Women in law and criminal justice occupations*. Thousand Oaks, CA: Sage Publications.

Meritor Savings Bank FSB v. Vinson, 106 S. Ct. 2399, 2406 (1986).

Merlo, Alida V., and Joycelyn M. Pollock. 2005. *Women, law and social control*. 2nd ed. Boston, MA: Allyn and Bacon.

Miller, Susan L. 1999. *Gender and community policing*. Boston, MA: Northeastern University Press.

Pennsylvania State Police. 1974. *Pennsylvania State Police female trooper study*. Harrisburg: Pennsylvania State Police.

Scarborough, Kathryn E., and Pamela A. Collins. 2002. *Women in public and private law enforcement*. Boston, MA: Butterworth Heinemann.

Schulz, Dorothy M. 1995. *From social worker to crimefighter: Women in United States municipal policing*. London: Praeger.

Sherman, Larry J. 1975. An evaluation of policewomen on patrol in a suburban police department. *Journal of Police Science and Administration* 3 (4): 434–38.

Sichel, J. L., L. N. Friedman, J. C. Quint, and M. E. Smith. 1977. *Women on patrol: A pilot study of police performance in New York City*. Washington, DC: National Institute of Law Enforcement and Criminal Justice.

Vega, M., and I. J. Silverman. 1982. Female police officers as viewed by their male counterparts. *Police Studies* 5: 31–39.

Worden, A. P. 1993. The attitudes of women and men in policing: Testing conventional and contemporary wisdom. *Criminology* 31: 203–42.

Zhao, J., Q. Thurman, and N. He. 1999. Sources of job satisfaction among police officers: A test of demographic and work environment models. *Justice Quarterly* 16 (1): 153–73.

X-RAY TECHNOLOGY AND APPLICATIONS FOR POLICING

An X-ray is a form of electromagnetic radiation that is commonly known for its use in diagnostic medical imaging. However, this technology has applications for law enforcement that can safeguard life and property. Common uses for X-ray technology include object screening (such as packages, suspected bombs, or baggage) as well as the use of mobile X-ray applications to examine suspicious packages in the field and to look through walls, doors, and/or windows to acquire intelligence from a certain area. In this article, the history of the technology as well as law enforcement applications will be explored.

History of X-Ray Technology

Scholars claim that X-ray technology was invented by accident in 1895. At that time, German physicist Wilhelm Roentgen was experimenting with electron beams in a gas discharge tube. During this experiment, Roentgen discovered that a fluorescent screen in his laboratory began to glow when the electron beam was turned on. This reaction was unique because Roentgen's tube was encased with heavy black cardboard, which he assumed would block the radiation. Upon further experimentation, Roentgen placed various objects between the tube and the screen, and the same effect occurred—the screen still glowed. Finally, he put his hand in front of the tube and saw the silhouette of his bones projected onto the fluorescent screen (Harris 2006). This accidental discovery by Roentgen has impacted most human beings in the course of their lives. For law enforcement officers, this discovery has led to efficient operations in conducting screenings in various locations.

Object Screening

A primary use of X-ray technology for law enforcement personnel is the screening of objects (baggage, purses, and so on) prior to their entry into a controlled environment such as airport boarding areas and schools. At these locations, law enforcement is oftentimes responsible for safeguarding life and property.

Stringent airport regulations have led to the increased dependency on the use of X-ray technology by the Transportation Security Administration (TSA). The TSA utilizes X-ray machines of various sizes and from various vendors at public airports across the country. Enforcing federal laws, the TSA scans all baggage and personal possessions that are carried onto airplanes. One controversial use of X-ray technology in the airport is the use of an X-ray that will purportedly provide airport screeners with a clear picture of what is under passengers' clothes. This technology, called backscatter X-ray, is now under evaluation at several U.S. airports (Frank 2005).

Schools have become more security conscious since the occurrence of a number of highly publicized incidents of school violence. A common figure in the hallways of American schools is the school resource officer (SRO). The SRO, a sworn law enforcement officer, is assigned to one school or multiple schools depending on the jurisdiction. Additionally, one of the tools used to safeguard some schools is an X-ray scanner. For some high-risk schools, students enter the school building each day in the same manner as travelers at an airport. A National Institute of Justice report on school safety technologies states "given that all the available x-ray baggage scanners are priced similarly, operate easily, offer substantial training up front, and have good quality monitor images, schools will be most concerned about service. If a particular school district is planning on purchasing several units for multiple schools, the district may be able to negotiate an excellent price that will include one backup unit that will be stored by the vendor for use when needed. This backup unit may be a used product that is in good working order and easy to bring in quickly and set up during a crisis" (Green 1999, 101).

Mobile X-Ray Applications

In addition to permanent, stationary X-ray machines, the technology can also be mobilized to assist law enforcement officers in the field. One example is the investigation, and possible detonation, of suspicious packages. A portable machine developed by the U.S. Department of Energy uses reflected X-rays to determine the contents of the package. The detector is paired with a video camera and then placed on a mobile robotic platform that moves into potentially dangerous areas while the operator stays safely out of range, observing the progress through real-time video images. Even if the suspicious device explodes before transmitting a complete image, partial images that may be useful to law enforcement have already been transmitted back to the operator. The greatest benefit in that situation is that all that is lost is the video camera, X-ray machine, and cart, rather than lives (Singer 1999).

Next, the ability to look through walls, doors, and/or windows is a lesser known application of X-ray technology that is available for law enforcement use. Traditional X-ray technology can be combined with more sophisticated imaging technologies such as infrared and ultrasound to provide intelligence to officers who may be entering a volatile area. The Justice Department's Office of Science and Technology has stressed the development of long-range devices to detect weapons and criminals. Currently, funded projects seek to arm law enforcement personnel with handheld devices that can detect people hidden behind walls and briefcase-size devices designed to locate hostages.

Conclusions

Technological advances for law enforcement occur at a rapid rate in the United States. While traditional X-ray technology has been a proven method for law enforcement screening activities, advances will undoubtedly provide technologies that will continuously change the way that a community does business. Additionally, continuous debate surrounding privacy issues and imaging technologies may shape the development and utilization of these technologies. Until that occurs, the 1895 accidental discovery remains an effective tool for the law enforcement community.

RYAN BAGGETT

See also **Airport Safety and Security; Federal Police and Investigative Agencies; Responding to School Violence; School Resource Officers; Technology and the Police; Terrorism: Police Functions Associated with**

References and Further Reading

Frank, T. 2005. Air travelers stripped bare with X-ray machine. *USA Today,* May.

Green, M. 1999. *The appropriate and effective use of security technologies in U.S. schools.* Washington, DC: National Institute of Justice.

Harris, T. 2006. *X-ray technology.* http://www.Howstuffworks.com.

Singer, N. 1999. *Device to safely examine the insides of package bombs.* http://www.sandia.gov.

YOUTH GANGS: DEFINITIONS

During the past two decades, research and criminal justice practitioner communities have turned increasing attention toward youth gangs. This attention is exhibited by the increases in funding for gang research, the creation of research institutes focused on gang activity, the development of specialized gang units in the law enforcement agencies, and the enactment of legislation directed at controlling gang activity. With this increased interest has emerged a debate as to what qualifies as a gang. Although at first glance the matter of finding an adequate definition of youth gangs can appear trivial, it has important implications in a policy context. First, the definition utilized can determine whether a group in a given community will receive directed attention from law enforcement agencies. Second, falling within an official definition of a gang can increase the legal ramifications for the members of these groups, with such actions as sentencing enhancements for gang crimes or the enforcement of civil gang injunctions. Third, recognition as a gang can have an important implication for where social service agencies distribute their resources in order to reduce gang activity. Thus, developing an adequate definition of youth gangs is very important.

The point of contention over defining a group as a gang centers on what characteristics will form the checklist used to confer this title. The most common characteristic, and the most obvious, is that a gang must be composed of a group of individuals, which connotes the collective as opposed to the individual nature of gangs. Some definitions specify this characteristic by asserting a minimum number of individuals who must belong to the group, although there is no consensus as to what this number should be. Further, in the context of youth gangs, the focus is on groups composed of juveniles and young adults as opposed to exclusively adult criminal organizations. The characteristic of a group composed of young individuals alone, however, has little meaning since most acts of delinquency or crime committed by juveniles occur in a group context. Thus, other defining characteristics are required to distinguish gangs from other groups.

Another characteristic is the use of symbols by the members to identify the gang. This characteristic is often represented by the display of a name or insignia that is found on the attire of members (such as on their shirts or ball caps) or by tattoos. Some gangs will also adopt certain colors associated with their gang that are displayed in their clothing, or they will wear their clothing in a certain manner that is associated with the gang (such as the right pant leg pulled up to the knee). Further, graffiti is often used to display a gang's name or insignia in order to communicate their existence to others. In addition, some will display certain hand signs to identify their gang and members. The use of such symbols not only provides an observable indicator of the gang's existence, but also personal acknowledgment by the members of their association with one another.

The permanence of a gang's existence is another definitional characteristic. The intention of this characteristic is to avoid the inclusion of groups that form over a single time-bound issue and then disband a short period thereafter. One of the difficulties with this characteristic, however, is that the length of existence varies considerably across gangs. For example, large cities that have an extended history of gang activity, such as Los Angeles and Chicago, are comprised of some gangs that have existed for multiple generations. Whereas, other smaller cities that have only recently seen gangs emerge in their community may have groups that have existed for less than two years. There is no consistent measure found within the various definitions as to the required length of existence. In fact, to create such a fixed qualification of, say, five years could be a limitation in the efforts to understand and address gangs. The failure of law enforcement and social service providers to acknowledge groups that fall short of this criterion would hamper their ability to impact a gang before it becomes a fixed part of a community. Further, the exclusion of such groups in empirical research would limit our understanding of the early formation period for those groups that eventually progress past the five-year mark.

The claiming of turf or territory by a gang is also a characteristic commonly found in the various definitions. This geographic area usually includes the location where the gang began, where members currently reside, and/or where they currently hang out. This territory is usually marked with graffiti posted on various buildings, walls, and other fixed objects that carry the game name or insignia, which acts as a notice to community members and rivals of the gang's existence and perceived control over an area. There is some debate, however, about whether the claiming of turf should be a defining characteristic. There are a number of gangs who meet the four other characteristics listed here, yet they do not claim a specific territory as their own. For example, skinhead gangs often do not make such territorial claims.

A final characteristic often found in gang definitions is criminal activity. Some definitions simply state in a very general sense that the gang needs to be involved in "illegal activity." Alternatively, other definitions, particularly those related to antigang legislation, will specify the exact crimes that must be committed by the members to qualify a group as a gang. For example, California's antigang legislation specifies twenty-five specific crimes that include acts of serious violence, serious property crimes, and the sale of a controlled substance. Further, it is required within this legislation that the crimes must occur over a multiple-year period so as to show some level of persistence in the gang's criminal activity.

Although these five characteristics represent those most commonly found in the definitions of gangs utilized by the research and criminal justice practitioner communities, they are by no means the essential elements found in each. Currently, there is no nationally accepted definition of gangs on the part of law enforcement or corrections, a circumstance that does have some drawbacks. For example, there is likely little consistency as to what types of groups receive attention from law enforcement and social service agencies from one jurisdiction to the next. In addition, the lack of an accepted definition makes it difficult to accurately account for the prevalence of gangs and gang members nationwide or within given communities. Some researchers, however, have asserted that this definition dilemma does have a benefit. It is argued that adherence to a universal definition might cause researchers to ignore new variants of gangs that emerge in the future that do not fit such a definition or to ignore present-day groups that would fall short of inclusion but are nonetheless important to understand. An illustration of this latter concern would be tagger crews (a group of graffiti artists), which some gang definitions would include and others not. Although these groups do not resemble some of the more notorious and violent gangs found across the nation, they represent groups that are persistently involved in illegal activity that devalues or destroys public and private property, and as such they are of interest to the research and criminal justice communities.

JEFF ROJEK and SCOTT H. DECKER

See also **Age and Crime; Criminology; Juvenile Crime and Criminalization; Juvenile Delinquency; Youth Gangs: Dimensions; Youth Gangs: Interventions and Results**

References and Further Reading

Ball, Richard A., and G. David Curry. 1995. The logic of definition in criminology: Purposes and methods for defining "gangs." *Criminology* 33 (2): 225–45.

Burisk, Robert J., and Harold G. Grasmick. 1993. *Neighborhoods and crime: The dimensions of effective community control*. San Francisco: Lexington.

California Penal Code. 1995. Section 186.22.

Decker, Scott H. 2004. *From the street to the prison: Understanding and responding to gangs*. 2nd ed. Richmond, KY: National Major Gang Task Force, American Correctional Association.

Decker, Scott H., and Barrick Van Winkle. 1996. *Life in the gang: Family, friends, and violence*. New York: Cambridge University Press.

Hagedorn, John M. 1988. *People and folks: Gangs, crime, and the underclass in a rustbelt city*. Chicago: Lake View Press.

Horowitz, Ruth. 1990. Sociological perspectives on gangs: Conflicting definitions and concepts. In *Gangs in America,* ed. C. Ronald Huff, 37–54. Newbury Park, CA: Sage.

Howell, James C., Arlen Egley, Jr., and Debra K. Gleason. 2002. Modern-day youth gangs. Washington, DC: U.S. Department of Justice, Office of Justice Programs, Office of Juvenile Justice and Delinquency Prevention. http://www.ncjrs.org/pdffiles1/ojjdp/191524.pdf.

Huff, C. Ronald. 1990. *Gangs in America*. Newbury Park, CA: Sage.

Klein, Malcolm W. 1995. *The American street gang*. New York: Oxford University Press.

Maxson, Cheryl L., and Malcolm W. Klein. 1985. Differences between gang and non-gang homicides. *Criminology* 23: 209–22.

Moore, Joan W. 1978. *Homeboys: Gangs, drugs, and prison in the barrios of Los Angeles*. Philadelphia, PA: Temple University Press.

YOUTH GANGS: DIMENSIONS

Gangs and the response to gangs by other segments of society are two sides of the same coin. Frederic Thrasher (1927, 26, 46), who studied 1,313 gangs in Chicago in the early 1900s, wrote that gangs are "formed spontaneously" but become "integrated through conflict." For Thrasher, a pre-gang group does not "become a gang . . . until it begins to excite disapproval and opposition, and thus it acquires a more definite group-consciousness." The most important conflicts in the strengthening of gangs include other gangs, schools, and law enforcement.

Though gangs are organizations, what we know about them has come from studying individual gang members or community reactions to gang problems. Hence, studies of gangs have historically included both interviews and observational studies of limited samples of gang members from specific geographic areas, or analyses of official records compiled through the institutionalized processes of response. Although there has sometimes been antipathy between the two kinds of researchers, the findings of both are necessary for the widest possible understanding of gang phenomena.

Participant observation and interviews are more likely to capture the totality of behavior engaged in by some gang members on a day-to-day basis. Analysis of official records, while limited to the fraction of gang activity that is criminal in nature, makes it possible to make comparisons and study variations in gang crime and official reaction to it across different communities and points in time. The importance of such comparisons is substantiated by the conclusions of all researchers that gangs vary greatly over both space and time. Studies using both self-report and official records information on populations of at-risk juveniles have found substantial overlap and agreement between the two sources (Curry 2000; Curry, Decker, and Egley 2002).

What Are Gangs?

As in most social science research, individual researchers lay out their definition of what constitutes a *gang* in the context of their particular study. Differences in defining gangs occur among researchers as well as between researchers and criminal justice agencies. The kinds of analysis problems to which this process of multiple operational definitions can lead are reflected in a study by Maxson and Klein (1990), which showed that if the Chicago definition of a gang-related crime were applied to the gang-related homicides for Los Angeles, Los Angeles would have half as many gang-related homicides.

Another factor in defining gangs is that, for most people, gangs are associated with some preconceived images. This is the result of the degree to which news and the entertainment media have seized on the gang as a subject for eliciting interest and emotion. *West Side Story,* a relatively contemporary retelling of *Romeo and Juliet,* required gangs to be conflict-based, more or less close-knit, social entities so as to fit its central plot vehicle. More recent movies such as *Colors* portray gangs immersed in violence and other criminal behavior. Research has shown that neither of these images is completely accurate.

What Is the Magnitude of Gang Crime Problems?

Much of the activity in which gangs engage is neither violent nor criminal (Decker and Van Winkle 1996; Hagedorn 1998; Fleischer 1998; Spergel 1995). Instead of maturing out of gangs by getting married or finding a job, as was observed in the past, many young adults, unable to find jobs in a depressed inner-city economy, continue their gang affiliation into adulthood.

Prior to 1994, estimates of the size of national-level gang crime problems were made from nonsystematic samples of law enforcement agencies (Miller 1975; Curry, Ball, and Fox 1994). In 1994, the Office of Juvenile Justice and Delinquency prevention established the National Youth Gang Center (NYGC) in Tallahassee, Florida. In addition to serving as a clearinghouse for available gang information, the gang center has conducted annual systematic surveys of law enforcement agencies. From these surveys, trends in the distribution of gang problems have been observed. Particular measures of gang problems include the number of municipalities with gangs, the number of gangs, and the number of gang members. As can be seen in Table 1, these measures indicate that the magnitude of the U.S. gang problem has remained relatively stable across the NYGC surveys. There is no question,

Table 1 Magnitude of U.S. Gang Problem Estimated by National Youth Gang Survey

Year	Number of Municipalities	Number of Gangs	Number of Gang Members
1996	3,847	30,819	846,428
1997	3,783	30,553	815,896
1998	3,430	28,707	780,233
1999	3,192	26,175	840,613
2000	2,788	24,742	772,550

however, that the national gang problem is a large one, larger than at any previous period in American history.

At one time, there was a widespread belief that gangs were migrating to smaller cities and rural areas in order to expand criminal activity. In smaller cities and rural counties, however, the gang problem remains significantly smaller and less deadly than in larger cities (Egley and Major 2003). Gang problems remain a large-city urban phenomenon. Perceptions of gang migration as the source of gang proliferation in the early 1990s have been shown to be largely unfounded (Maxson 1998). Just like the rest of the U.S. population, gang members migrate for social reasons and not to extend gang crime.

How Are Females Involved in Gangs?

Female involvement in gangs has been differentiated from involvement by males (Miller 1998; Miller 2001). While male gang members are more violent than female members, gang-involved females engage in more violence than male delinquents not involved in gangs (Miller and Brunson 2000; Peterson, Miller, and Esbensen 2001). Female gang members create their own hierarchies that are independent of male hierarchies within the same gangs. Gender makeup of gangs

has been observed to have effects on levels of violence and other criminal activity.

What Are the Social Processes of Gang Involvement?

Research has continued to show that few gang members join gangs as a result of gang recruitment. Two factors that have been suggested to be associated with gangs across cities are the growth of isolated impoverished inner-city populations and the dissemination of gang culture in mass media (Klein 1995). At the individual level, gang involvement has been seen as a transitional process. Thornberry et al. (2002) show that for most gang members there is a distinct period of gang membership that is associated with more delinquent offending before and after the period of gang involvement. Egley (2003) emphasizes that between non–gang-involved youth and gang members is a large segment of youth in at-risk populations who are marginally involved in gangs.

These marginally involved youths are significantly more involved in delinquency than nongang youths, but significantly less involved in delinquency than youths who identify themselves as gang members. Decker and Van Winkle (1996) discuss a number of neighborhood dynamics that correspond with increased gang involvement. A major reason reported by gang members is that they join the gang for protection. Ironically violent victimization correlates highly with gang membership.

What Are Major Responses to Gangs?

Strategies of responding to gang-related crime problems have not changed much over the twentieth-century history of community reaction. Spergel and Curry (1990, 1993) group gang response strategies into five overarching categories: (1) suppression, (2) community organization, (3) opportunities provision, (4) social services, and (5) organizational change. The most common response for the heavily involved gang youth has almost always been suppression. Suppression includes all activities required to incarcerate gang members, which encompasses methods of member identification, agency coordination, and special processing of arrestees in terms of prosecution, trial, and sentencing. Community organization includes all efforts to promote the organization of legitimate forces within a community as a resistance to the organization of gangs. Opportunities provision is a strategy that operates under the long-standing assumption that gang involvement is not as appealing to individual youths as the alternative potential for employment and marriage. Social services provision operates under the assumption that gang members with counseling, role-modeling, attitude changes, and skills in conflict resolution will create their own opportunities to lead conventional lives. Organizational change incorporates increases in available resources or adjustments in institutional structures.

Based on an analysis of data gathered by the 1988 Office of Juvenile Justice and Delinquency Prevention/University of Chicago national survey of gang problems (Spergel and Curry 1990), suppression was most often the strategy identified as primary by respondents regardless of the perceived causes of gang crime problems. However, community organization and opportunities provision as primary strategies were the only ones statistically associated with perceived effectiveness of community-level gang response programs.

From the analyses of Spergel and his colleagues, a detailed model for implementing community programs in response to gangs has been created. During the last several years, the model (now called the "Spergel model") has been tested in a number of communities. A recent account of the outcomes of several of these pilot studies has shown successes and failures (Spergel et al. 2003). The next step is refining the model.

Policy Recommendations

Though limited in quantity, research on gang-related crime is rich in findings. From these findings a number of policy recommendations can be offered:

1. Additional research on both gang activity and community reactions to gang activity is required.
2. Strategies of response and research on gangs should not be based on narrow definitions of what constitutes a gang developed within the parameters of a single locale and time.
3. Strategies of response developed on the basis of research on one gender or ethnicity should not be frivolously applied to gang involvement of another gender or ethnicity.
4. On the basis of the third recommendation, strategies of gang response are best controlled by the people who reside in the communities concerned.
5. Strategies of community organization combined with strategies of opportunity provision offer the greatest potential for immediate improvements in the level of gang-related crime problems.

G. DAVID CURRY

See also **Gang Resistance Education and Training (G.R.E.A.T.); Juvenile Crime and Criminalization; Juvenile Delinquency; Youth Gangs: Definitions; Youth Gangs: Interventions and Results**

References and Further Reading

Curry, G. D. 2000. Self-reported gang involvement and officially recorded delinquency. *Criminology* 38: 1253–74.

Curry, G. D., R. A. Ball, and R. J. Fox. 1994. Criminal justice reaction to gang violence. In *Violence and law,* ed. M. Costanzo and S. Oskamp. Newbury Park, CA: Sage.

Curry, G. D., S. H. Decker, and A. Egley, Jr. 2002. Gang involvement and delinquency in a middle school population, *Justice Quarterly* 19: 275–92.

Egley, A. 2003. *Level of involvement: Gang member, gang-marginal, and non-gang youth.* Unpublished diss. University of Missouri–St. Louis.

Fleischer, Mark. 1998. *Dead end kids: Gang girls and the boys they know.* Madison: University of Wisconsin Press.

Hagedorn, J. M. 1998. *People and folks: Gangs, crime and the underclass in a rustbelt city.* 2nd ed. Chicago: Lake View Press.

Klein, M. W. 1995. *The American street gang.* New York: Oxford University Press.

Maxson, C. L., and M. W. Klein. 1990. Street gang violence: Twice as great or half as great? In *Gangs in America,* ed. C. Ronald Huff. Newbury Park, CA: Sage.

Miller, J. A. 1998. Gender and victimization risk among young women in gangs. *Journal of Research in Crime and Delinquency* 35: 429–53.

———. 2000. *One of the guys: Girls, gangs and gender.* New York: Oxford University Press.

Miller, W. B. 2001. *The growth of youth gang problems in the United States, 1970–1998.* Washington, DC: U.S. Department of Justice, Office of Juvenile Justice and Delinquency Prevention.

Peterson, D., J. A. Miller, and F. A. Esbensen. 2001. The impact of sex composition on gangs and gang member delinquency. *Criminology* 39: 411–39.

Spergel, I. A. 1995. *The youth gang problem: A community approach.* New York: Oxford University Press.

Spergel, I.A., and G. D. Curry. 1990. Strategies and perceived agency effectiveness in dealing with the youth gang problem. In *Gangs in America,* ed. C. Ronald Huff. Newbury Park, CA: Sage.

———. 1993. The National Youth Gang Survey: A research and development process. In *Gang intervention handbook,* ed. A. Goldstein and C. R. Huff. Champaign–Urbana, IL: Research Press.

Thornberry, T. P., M. D. Krohn, A. J. Lizotte, C. A. Smith, and K. Tobllin. 2002. *Gangs and delinquency in developmental perspective.* New York: Cambridge University Press.

Thrasher, F. M. 1927. *The gang.* Chicago: University of Chicago Press.

YOUTH GANGS: INTERVENTIONS AND RESULTS

In 1995, the National Youth Gang Center conducted its first assessment of the national gang problem. The numbers produced by that assessment were larger than those of any prior one-year survey, finding a total of 23,388 youth gangs. A total of 664,906 gang members were reported by 1,499 agencies. Gangs in the new millennium have greater access to automobiles and high-powered firearms than did their predecessors. There is also evidence that gangs are spreading beyond the boundaries of cities and gaining a foothold in suburban and rural communities (Klein 1995).

Responding to Gang-Related Crime and Delinquency

An effective response to gang problems is to address both institutional and community actions that affect the values that are the foundation of the gang. Spergel and Curry (1993) identified five basic gang intervention strategies, based on survey responses from 254 law enforcement and social service agencies. These strategies include suppression, social intervention, organizational change, community mobilization, and social opportunities provision.

1. *Suppression strategies* respond to the proximate causes of gangs. Suppression includes law enforcement and criminal justice interventions such as arrest, imprisonment, and surveillance. Forty-four percent of the responding agencies reported that suppression was their primary strategy in responding to gangs. To be effective, they must be part of a broader set of responses to the illegal actions of gang members. Cities that follow suppression policies exclusively are

likely to be frustrated in their efforts to reduce gang problems.

2. *Social intervention approaches* focus on emergency interventions, particularly in response to acts of violence or personal crisis. Nearly one-third of cities used social intervention strategies such as crisis intervention, treatment for youths and their families, and social service referrals. A number of studies support the use of crisis intervention and the provision of social services to gang members and their families. Such strategies are proximate, designed to address the needs of a more immediate nature. Gang members frequently are victims of violence or witnesses to a friend's victimization. The goals for these interventions should be the separation of gang members from at-risk individuals and the provision of mentoring and other social services that extend beyond emergency rooms. Interventions targeted at families are important because of their broad impact.

3. Strategies that concentrate on *organizational change* require the creation of a broad consensus about gang problems. Typically this occurs through the formation of task forces. Such an approach is targeted at the more immediate causes of gangs and by itself cannot solve gang problems. Organizational change was the next most frequent response. This method was used by 11% of the cities, and typically includes the development of task forces to address gang problems. In general, organizational change will either lead to an awareness of the gang problems in the community and mobilize efforts to address them, or produce a new set of relations among agencies and groups who respond to such problems.

4. *Community mobilization* is a strategy designed to address the fundamental causes of gangs and gang membership. This strategy coordinates and targets services so that the needs of gang members may be met more effectively. Only 9% of cities selected community mobilization as their modal response to gangs. This strategy was focused on cooperation across agencies and was designed to produce better coordination of existing services.

5. The expansion of job prospects and educational placements is the primary focus of the *social opportunities* approach. This approach stresses education and job-related interventions, and more than any other strategy responds to the fundamental causes of gang formation and gang membership. Despite this, the smallest number of cities, 5%, reported that the provision of social opportunities was their primary response. These gang intervention efforts incorporate job creation, training and residential placements designed to reshape values, peer commitments, and institutional participation by gang members and those at risk for membership.

Contemporary Responses to Gangs

Gang Legislation

By 1993, fourteen of the fifty states had enacted statutes specifically directed at criminal gang activity. A review conducted by the Institute for Law and Justice (1993) groups gang legislation into two major categories: (1) legislation that provides criminal sanctions for the justice system against offenders in gang-related crimes and (2) legislation that provides civil remedies for the victims of gang crime. Criminal sanction legislation most often enhances sentences for those found guilty of committing a gang-related crime or makes provisions for segregating incarcerated gang members. Civil remedy approaches have most often attempted to empower citizens to file civil suits against gang members collectively or individually. A major impediment to the effectiveness of gang legislation is court rulings that several specific legislative acts violate the First Amendment rights of gang members.

Maxson (1997) provides the only evaluation of the impact of the civil injunction in California. She notes that the long-term impact of this judicial act would be difficult to calculate, even under the best of circumstances.

Federal Policy and Gangs: DHHS's Youth Gang Drug Prevention Program

In 1988, the Youth Gang Drug Prevention Program was established in the Administration on Children, Youth, and Families (ACYF), part of the U.S. Department of Health and Human Services (DHHS). Applications for funding focused on single-purpose demonstration projects and innovative support programs for at-risk youths and their families. Sixteen consortium projects were funded for three years. In design, these programs constituted a federally initiated, coordinated, and monitored commitment to community organization of strategic responses to gang crime problems. This commitment was on a scale that was historically without precedent. Nine more consortium projects were funded in 1992 with a total of $5.9 million, each for a period of five years for up to $750,000 per year.

The ACYF program also included a number of projects employing social intervention strategies. During the five years of the program, projects provided peer counseling, family education, youth empowerment, mentoring, crisis intervention, community restitution, and recreation. Priority funding areas for the delivery of services also targeted intergenerational gang families, adolescent females, and new immigrant and refugee youth gangs. The national evaluation (Cohen et al. 1995) concluded that while local programs were generally effective in reducing delinquency and drug use among youth participants, *the programs were not successful at preventing or reducing gang involvement*. In 1995, the gang component of the program came to an end.

OJJDP's Comprehensive Response to America's Gang Problem: The Spergel Model

The Spergel model, a direct outgrowth of the earlier work of Spergel and Curry (1993), has become the driving force in the Office of Juvenile Justice and Delinquency Prevention (OJJDP) response to gangs. It is a flexible format for responding to gang problems at the community level. Separate required components focus on community mobilization and employment programs, with one agency acting as the lead or mobilizing agency. In addition, law enforcement plays a central role in this process. Key agencies that must be involved include the police, grassroots neighborhood organizations, and some form of jobs program. The flexibility of the Spergel model encourages local program planners to assess the special features of local gang problems and take advantage of local agency strengths. The guidelines for community mobilization are intended to facilitate interagency cooperation and minimize interagency conflict.

Five demonstration sites received funding from the OJJDP to implement and test the Spergel model in a variety of urban settings with coordinated technical assistance and a systematic evaluation led by Spergel. In the Chicago community of Little Village, Spergel (1994; Spergel and Grossman 1994) has been working with a network of police, outreach youth workers, probation officers, court service workers, and former gang members to reduce violence between two warring coalitions of Latino street gangs. Preliminary evaluation results of this project indicate a reduction in gang-related homicides, increased community organization and mobilization, and the channeling of gang-involved youths into educational programs and jobs.

Safe Futures

As the first few years of the 1990s brought record increases in levels of juvenile violence, the OJJDP became convinced that the problems of serious, violent, and chronic offending and gang-related crime were related. The policy result was the Safe Futures Program. With funding from the OJJDP, Safe Futures programs have been established in four urban sites (Boston; Seattle; Contra Costa County, California; and St. Louis), one rural site (Imperial Valley, California), and one Indian reservation (Fort Belknap, Montana). Funding for Safe Futures projects is larger ($1.4 million per year) and extended over a longer period of time (a five-year commitment) than funding for previous comparable efforts.

Safe Futures programs incorporate specific suppression, opportunities provision, and neighborhood-focused services. As such, they are consistent with the Spergel model and likely to provide a full test of the effectiveness of this model, a model that integrates suppression with community mobilization. It is often difficult to determine the impact of a program, owing to the fact that its implementation often changes substantially from the initial plan. A local evaluation was mandated for each site, and all sites participated in a national evaluation. No final results are available at this time, but it is clear that mounting large-scale interventions designed to change the delivery of services to youths is very difficult. A few sites have struggled with the Spergel model as well as local issues in

moving toward implementation. For example, in St. Louis, the Safe Futures site has had difficulty integrating law enforcement—a key component of the model—into service delivery and client identification.

Office of Community Oriented Policing Services: Antigang Initiative

Community-oriented policing represents an even broader federal effort to respond to crime in a way that integrates law enforcement into a cooperative community problem-solving framework. In 1996, the Community Oriented Policing Services (COPS) office in the Justice Department launched a fifteen city antigang initiative. Instead of being selected through a competitive application process, the fifteen cities were selected on the basis of their consistency in providing gang-related crime statistics to the Justice Department surveys described earlier. Eleven million dollars were provided to be spent on community policing efforts, to improve data collection, to integrate law enforcement agencies into community-wide responses to gangs, and to provide a safer setting in which less suppressive response programs can be given a chance to develop.

The program had three specific goals: (1) to develop strategies to reduce gang-related problems, (2) to develop strategies to reduce gang-related drug trafficking problems, and (3) to reduce the fear instilled by gang-related activities. Each jurisdiction was required to develop a formal written characterization of its local gang problem to include the number of gangs, members, age ranges, reasons for joining a gang, source and location of recruitment, location of activities, reasons for migration, and incidents of gang-related crime. It is clear from the sites that completed evaluations that areas of intervention that the police controlled themselves (that is, suppression) generally worked according to plan. However, partnership ventures were considerably more difficult to accomplish. Given the Spergel and Curry insistence on linking suppression and opportunities provision, the likely impact of these efforts is temporary or quite small.

Youth Firearms Violence Initiative

Another COPS response to increased levels of firearm violence among youth was the Youth Firearms Violence Initiative (YFVI). Ten cities were selected to each receive $1 million for a one-year period. The objective of this effort was to reduce violent firearms crime by youth. Departments were to develop innovative programs that enhanced proactive crime control efforts and prevention programs targeted at young persons. These programs were designed specifically to reduce the number of violent firearms crimes committed by youth and reduce the number of firearms-related gang offenses and the number of firearms-related drug offenses. Each participating department was required to develop new initiatives in three areas: (1) innovative strategies or tactics, (2) community policing orientation, and (3) new information systems.

The national evaluation demonstrated the plausibility of the hypothesis that the interventions in most cities were accompanied by reductions in gun offenses. A specific geographic area matched to the program area was chosen for comparison purposes and gun offenses were tracked by week for the two-year period prior to YFVI efforts and the one-year period after the program. In each of the five impact evaluation sites, the decline in gun offenses per week was greater than for the comparison area. In almost every case, YFVI was strictly a suppression program; only rarely did it effectively integrate the activities of social service or prevention activities.

The Boston Gun Suppression Project

Perhaps no single intervention in the 1990s has received as much public attention as the Boston Gun Suppression Project (Kennedy, Piehl, and Braga 1996; Boston Police Department and Partners 1997). Also known as Ceasefire, this project has been replicated in a number of cities across the country, including Minneapolis where it has been carefully evaluated (Kennedy and Braga 1998). At its heart, Ceasefire employs the SARA problem-solving model—scanning, analysis, response, and assessment—to assess youth violence. The apparent success of this intervention rests largely on two features: (1) the careful background work conducted to understand the nature of youth firearms markets and (2) partnerships among the participating groups.

The Boston Gun Suppression Project involves a large interagency working group that consists of representatives from the local police department, the Bureau of Alcohol, Tobacco, Firearms and Explosives (ATF), the U.S. attorney, the local prosecutor, the departments of probation and parole, city youth outreach workers, the school district, and Kennedy's research team. Two complementary strategies were developed, one that attempted to disrupt the illegal firearms market on the supply side, and the other targeted at the demand side. The initial evaluations of the Boston Gun Suppression Project have demonstrated that the program achieved its goals of reducing youth homicide in Boston. Youth gun crime, particularly homicide, recorded dramatic declines in Boston, even greater declines than throughout the rest of the nation.

The last decade has produced an unprecedented increase in gangs, gun assaults, and youth homicide. These increases have spurred federal and local governments to action. In the search for appropriate responses to these problems, suppression has been the strategy most likely to be adopted. This makes sense for a variety of political and pragmatic reasons; after all, the police are a visible and generally popular resource in the effort to combat crime. However, such responses are not likely to be successful on their own. When suppression occurs in a vacuum, when it is not accompanied by other more supportive actions, the chances of making lasting changes in gang crime are diminished.

Conclusion

A number of federal initiatives that emphasize suppression or social opportunities provision have been undertaken in the last decade. The COPS office's anti-gang initiative is a good example of programs that were based almost exclusively on suppression. This is counterbalanced by the effort of DHHS in its Youth Gang Drug Prevention program. This heavily funded federal effort focused exclusively on opportunities provision. Although the evaluation data do not enable a definitive conclusion about the effectiveness of these interventions, it is clear that they have not made substantial inroads into the gang problem in the communities where they were funded because of their failure to implement a balanced response. If there is a single message in this chapter, it is that law enforcement and social opportunities provision must work hand in hand if successful interventions are to be implemented.

Scott H. Decker

See also **Juvenile Crime and Criminalization; Juvenile Delinquency; Juvenile Diversion; Juvenile Justice System; Youth Gangs: Definitions; Youth Gangs: Dimensions**

References and Further Reading

Boston Police Department and Partners. 1997. *The Boston strategy to prevent youth violence*. Boston Police Department.

Cohen, M., K. Williams, A. Beckman, and S. Crosse. 1995. Evaluation of the National Youth Gang Drug Prevention Program. In *The modern gang reader,* ed. M. Klein, C. Maxson, and J. Miller, 266–75. Los Angeles: Roxbury.

Institute for Law and Justice. 1993. *Gang prosecution legislative review*. Report prepared for the National Institute of Justice, U.S. Department of Justice, Washington, DC.

Kennedy, D., and A. Braga. 1998. Homicide in Minneapolis. *Homicide Studies* 2: 263–90.

Kennedy, D., A. Piehl, and A. Braga. 1996. Youth violence in Boston: Gun markets, serious youth offenders, and a use-reduction strategy. *Law and Contemporary Problems* 59: 147–96.

Klein, M. 1995. *The American street gang*. New York: Oxford University Press.

Klein, M., and C. Maxson. 1994. Gangs and cocaine trafficking. In *Drugs and crime: Evaluating public–police initiatives,* ed. D. MacKenzie and C. Uchida. Thousand Oaks, CA: Sage.

Sheley, J., and J. Wright. 1993. *Drug activity and firearms possession and use by juveniles*. Report to the National Institute of Justice, Office of Juvenile Justice and Delinquency Prevention, U.S. Department of Justice, Washington, DC.

———. 1995. *In the line of fire*. New York: Aldine.

Spergel, I. 1994. *Gang suppression and intervention: Problem and response*. Washington, DC: Office of Juvenile Justice and Delinquency Prevention, U.S. Department of Justice.

Spergel, I., and G. D. Curry. 1993. The National Youth Gang Survey: A research and development process. In *Gang intervention handbook,* ed. A. P. Goldstein and C. R. Huff, 359–400. Champaign–Urbana, IL: Research Press.

Spergel, I., and S. Grossman. 1994. *Gang violence and crime theory: Gang violence reduction project*. Presentation at the American Society of Criminology Annual Meetings, Miami, FL.

ZERO TOLERANCE POLICING

Zero tolerance policing is the style of policing generally associated with the full and complete enforcement of all criminal violations, from minor infractions (such as disorderly conduct or public loitering) to major crimes (such as robbery and burglary). Many commentators trace zero tolerance policing to the style of policing implemented by New York City Mayor Rudolph Giuliani and his first police commissioner, William Bratton, in 1994. Their strategy was based on the broken-windows theory first articulated by James Q. Wilson and George L. Kelling in an *Atlantic Monthly* article in 1982—namely, the idea that minor physical and social disorder, if left unattended, would cause more serious crime in a neighborhood.

Elected in 1993 on a platform that focused largely on crime, disorder, and quality-of-life issues—especially on the notorious "squeegee men"—Giuliani appointed William Bratton police commissioner in December 1993, and, together, they soon began implementing a policing strategy called "the quality-of-life initiative," which was expressly premised on the broken-windows theory. Both Giuliani and Bratton cited the "Broken Windows" essay as the main source of their initiative. As soon as Bratton took over as police commissioner in early 1994, he began implementing a policy aimed at creating public order by aggressively enforcing laws against quality-of-life offenses, such as public drunkenness, loitering, vandalism, littering, public urination, panhandling, turnstile jumping, prostitution, and other minor misdemeanor offenses.

In *Police Strategy No. 5: Reclaiming the Public Spaces of New York*, Giuliani and Bratton explained the premises of the quality-of life initiative:

> More than ten years ago, James Q. Wilson and George L. Kelling, authors of the ground breaking article, "The Police and Neighborhood Safety" in the March 1982 issue of *The Atlantic Monthly*, postulated the "broken windows" thesis that unaddressed disorder is a sign that no one cares and invites both further disorder and more serious crime. By examining the Wilson-Kelling hypothesis in more than 40 cities, Wesley Skogan has found that disorder is indeed the first step in what he terms

"the downward spiral of urban decay."
(Giuliani and Bratton 1994, 6).

The quality-of-life initiative immediately resulted in a surge of misdemeanor
arrests in New York City that extended
well into the 1990s. According to the New
York State Division of Criminal Justice
Services, in 1993, the year before Giuliani
and Bratton began implementing broken-
windows policing, total adult misdemeanor arrests stood at 129,404. By the
year 2000, the number was up to 224,663—
an increase of almost 75%. What is particularly interesting is that the vast majority of
those arrests were for misdemeanor drug
charges, which increased almost 275%,
from 27,447 in 1993 to 102,712 in 2000. At
the same time, the NYPD implemented an
aggressive stop-and-frisk policy. Between
1997 and 1998, for instance, the Street
Crime Unit—with approximately 435 officers at the time—stopped and frisked about
45,000 people.

The quality-of-life initiative was one
of a number of policing strategies that
Bratton implemented during his two
years as police commissioner. Other strategies targeted gun possession, school violence, drug dealing, domestic violence, auto
theft, and police corruption. In addition,
Bratton also increased the power of precinct commanders and instituted biweekly
meetings, known as Crime Control Strategy
Meetings or COMPSTAT (for computer-
statistics meetings), where the top administrators would grill precinct commanders
on crime in their beat (Kelling and Coles
1996, 146). But, in the words of Bratton
himself, the quality-of-life initiative was
the "linchpin strategy" (Bratton 1998, 228).

The quality-of life initiative was soon
called by many *zero tolerance policing* because of the surge in arrests for minor
offenses, and the approach to policing
that focuses on enforcing minor violations
has been come to be known as *zero tolerance*. This is particularly true in Europe,
especially in the United Kingdom and
France, as well as in Australia and

New Zealand, where the broken-windows
approach is generally referred to as *zero
tolerance policing*. In France, for instance,
most criminologists and politicians refer
to zero tolerance as the approach initiated
in New York City and a number of books
have been authored under that very title.
Because of its close association to New
York City and the broken-windows
theory, this style of policing is more accurately called *broken-windows policing*.

The use of the rubric *zero tolerance
policing* to describe broken-windows policing is, however, a matter of some contention. George Kelling, the coauthor of
the original "Broken Windows" essay, ad-
amantly opposes the rubric *zero tolerance*,
arguing that the essence of the broken-
windows theory is the discretion afforded
police officers to decide when to enforce
minor infraction laws and when not to. As
a result, significant battle lines have been
drawn around these terms. Jeffrey Rosen
of the *New Republic,* for instance, has
suggested that the New York City's policing strategy fundamentally changed—in
his words, "morphed"—from a broken-
windows approach to a policy of zero
tolerance once the Giuliani administration
realized that aggressive misdemeanor
arrests resulted in the arrests of serious
criminals.

The truth is, however, that Bratton's
approach was, from its inception, a zero
tolerance approach. Bratton himself
describes his first experiment in the New
York subways as a "fare evasion mini-
sweep." "I put a sergeant and five, eight,
sometimes ten cops in plain clothes at
these problematic stations day and night,
and they arrested the people who were
streaming in for nothing. The cops nabbed
ten or twenty jumpers at a time. They
pulled these men and women in one by
one, cuffed them, lined them up on the
platform, and waited for the next wave"
(Bratton 1998, 153). This is not an exercise of police discretion. It is zero tolerance. Similarly, Bratton's strategy with
"squeegee people"—the first wave of the

quality-of-life strategy—was not about discretion. It was about sweeps—about constantly checking and rechecking the squeegee corners and arresting all violators (Bratton 1998, 213–14). Bratton and Giuliani understood, from the beginning, the close relationship between order-maintenance, sweeps, and catching criminals (Bratton 1998, 154).

Another semantic dispute has surrounded whether zero tolerance policing can be considered a form of community policing. *Community policing,* at its most general level, stands for the idea that police officers can prevent crimes by integrating themselves into the community and solving community problems, rather than by merely responding to emergency calls. Community policing is prevention oriented, in contrast to the earlier reform model—the model of professional crime fighting—which centered around the 911 strategy. It seeks to share with the public the tasks of problem identification, problem solving, and crime control—and it is a means of developing greater communication between the police and the community. In essence, community policing "consists of two complementary core components, community partnership and problem solving" (Community Policing Consortium 2000, 118). It rests on the idea that "effective crime-fighting is based upon a partnership between police and the residents of the immediate community they serve" (Spitzer 1999, 47).

The difficulty is that community policing comes in a wide variety, and, as George Kelling concedes, "has come to mean all things to all people" (Kelling and Coles 1996, 158). Some understand community policing to be a type of order maintenance, where police officers maintain neighborhood order by aggressively arresting low-level offenders. Kelling himself, for instance, has characterized New York City's quality-of-life initiative as community policing (Kelling and Coles 1996, 109, 145, 161–63). Others understand community policing as a style of community

integration where the beat cop specifically withholds enforcement as a way to build community contacts. For instance, in Chicago, some police officers on the beat reportedly tolerate disorder in order to ingratiate themselves with the community (Skogan 1997; Eig 1996).

The variations on the theme of community policing are numerous. This may explain why community policing has swept police departments in the United States and abroad during the past twenty years. In a recent National Institute of Justice survey of police departments, more than 80% of police chiefs polled stated that they were either implementing or intended to implement some aspect of community policing. The truth, however, is that the popularity and success of community policing is attributable, in large part, to the vagueness of the definition, to the recent seven-year national decline in crime, and to the fact that the term *community policing* is far better for public relations than terms such as *aggressive misdemeanor arrests, stop and frisk,* or *mass building searches.* It is important, then, to distinguish carefully between the specific types of community policing that are being discussed. Zero tolerance policing may, to some, qualify as a form of community policing, but is certainly different from other expressions of that policing approach.

BERNARD E. HARCOURT

See also **Broken-Windows Policing; Community-Oriented Policing: History; Problem-Oriented Policing: Rationale; Quality-of-Life Policing**

References and Further Reading

Bratton, William J. 1998. *Turnaround: How America's top cop reversed the crime epidemic,* with Peter Knobler. New York: Random House.
Community Policing Consortium. 2000. Understanding community policing: A framework for action. In *Community policing: Classical readings,* ed. Willard M. Oliver. Upper Saddle River, NJ: Prentice-Hall.

Eck, John E., and Edward R. Maguire. 2000. Have changes in policing reduced violent crime? an assessment of the evidence. In *The crime drop in America,* ed. Alfred Blumstein and Joel Wallman. New York: Cambridge University Press.

Eig, Jonathan. 1996. Eyes on the Street: Community Policing in Chicago. *American Prospect* 29 (Nov.–Dec.): 60–68.

Giuliani, Rudolph W., and William J. Bratton. 1994. *Police strategy no. 5: Reclaiming the public spaces of New York.* New York: City of New York Police Department.

Harcourt, Bernard E. 2001. *Illusion of order: The false promise of broken windows policing.* Cambridge, MA: Harvard University Press.

Harcourt, Bernard E., and Jens Ludwig. 2006. Broken windows: New evidence from New York City and a five-city social experiment. *University of Chicago Law Review* 73.

Kelling, George, and Catherine Coles. 1996. *Fixing broken windows: Restoring order and reducing crime in our communities.* New York: The Free Press.

Kelling, George L., and William H. Sousa, Jr. 2001. *Do police matter? An analysis of the impact of New York City's police reforms.* Civic Report No. 22. December. Manhattan, NY: Manhattan Institute Center for Civic Innovation.

Skogan, Wesley G. 1997. *Community policing, Chicago style.* New York: Oxford University Press.

Spitzer, Eliot. 1999. *The New York City Police Department's "Stop & frisk" practices: A report to the people of the state of New York from the Office of the Attorney General.* New York: Office of the Attorney General of the State of New York, Civil Rights Bureau. http://www.oag.state.ny.us/press/reports/stop_frisk/stop_frisk.html.

Wilson, James Q., and George L. Kelling. 1982. Broken windows: The police and neighborhood safety. *Atlantic Monthly* 127 (Mar.): 29–38.

INDEX

INDEX

INDEX